THE new London Property Guide '00/01

MITCHELL BEAZLEY

THE new London Property Guide '00/01

The **ONLY** guide you need to **buying**
and **selling, renting** and **letting**
homes in London

CARRIE SEGRAVE

The New London Property Guide '00/01

Published in 2000 by Mitchell Beazley,
an imprint of Octopus Publishing Group Ltd
2–4 Heron Quays, London, E14 4JP

ISBN 1 840 002 425

A CIP catalogue copy of this book is available from the British Library.

At Mitchell Beazley
Executive Editors   Vivien Antwi, Rachael Stock
Executive Art Editor   Kenny Grant
Project Editors   Chloë Garrow, Mary Loebig Giles
Editor   Katey Day
Designer   Christine Keilty
Production   Jessame Emms
Indexer   Ann Parry
Data Inputter   Gillian Towner

Advertising sales: Logie Bradshaw Media Ltd, Strathallan House, Fernville Lane,
Midland Road, Hemel Hempstead, Herts, HP2 4Ls. Tel. 01442 233331

Set in MetaPlus
Produced and printed by Bath Press, Bath

This book is for Christopher Foulkes; for Eleanor, a Londoner; and in memory of John Brennan

Carrie Segrave

Carrie Segrave began writing on London's residential property scene in the early 1980s. She was founder-editor of the capital's first property newspaper and from 1988 wrote and edited the annual editions of the *London Property Guide*. During the 1980s and early 1990s she wrote on property for *The Financial Times*, *The Sunday Times Magazine* and *The Illustrated London News* among others and was UK Property Editor for a Japanese investment magazine.

Specialist writers

David Spittles is Property and Personal Finance writer for *The London Evening Standard* and *The Observer*. Liz Lightfoot is Education Correspondent for *The Daily Telegraph*. Susan Ware is an architect with a special interest in London homes and is a partner in The Chartered Practice. She teaches Professional Practice at the Bartlett School of Architecture, University College, London.

Contributors

Sophie Allan, Elaine Allen, Amy Atkinson, Mike Baess, Lucy Baird, Beth Barling, Victoria Barlow, Eleanore Crompton, Carli Dhillon, Alex Dunbar, Chloe Garrow, Tabitha Garrow, Ben Gatty, Simon Gwynne, Isabel Kay, Matthew Lewin, Anna Macarthur, Robert Parker, Penny Ryder, Caroline Simpson (Boris), Nick Simpson, Alex Smith, Nigel Spalding, Michèle Stevens, Rachel Stock, Carina Trimingham, Heather Tyrrell, Helen Wilding, Frances Williams, Chris Wood, Ciara Woodley, Eljay Yildirim.

Acknowledgments and thanks . . .

This book would in no way be possible without the enormous contribution made by a small army of London fanatics, prepared to tramp the streets (literally) on its behalf, and cross-examine town halls and the like: their names are above. In the course of their, and our, research well over 300 estate agents and other property people also gave up their time to help; for their local and professional expertise we are, as ever, deeply grateful. Too many, alas, to thank individually; but among those whose assistance was invaluable are Simon Agace, Linda Beaney, Tom Dennes, Howard Elston, Simon Homes, Colin Lowman, Diana Rowell, Jonathan Rosenburg, Kevin Ryan, Jane Sandars, Sarah Shelley, Caroline Simpson (Boris), Jerry Sykes, Jonathan Vandermolen, John Vaughan, Hilary Wade, Peter Wetherall, Ann Wheat, Eljay Yildirim. It would not do to forget, either, the contributors to earlier editions of this Guide whose foot-slogging provided the foundations upon which this year's is built. Thanks, again, to the team at Mitchell Beazley: Mary Loebig Giles, Chloe Garrow and Kenny Grant, bearing up nobly under the whirling load of 600 closely-packed pages as they whizzed between us. As I have said teamwork is everything on this book and it doesn't stop when editors, designers and proofreaders have done their bit. At the very end is a fast and expert indexer, Ann Parry, and last of all a brilliant production team who have the worst job of the lot – getting it over the out-of-house hurdles of printing, binding and distributing in a timespan that makes other UK publishers blink.

CS

Contents

Introduction

This book is an annual report on the progress of London as a place to live. It is also, if you like, a shareholders' report on the biggest investment most Londoners will ever make: their homes, their stake in the city.

The heart of the book is an area-by-area description of London's residential districts, from 'A' for Acton to 'W' for Wimbledon. These pages describe the streets and the types of homes of each neighbourhood. Each chapter has details of prices, transport, journey times, schools, boroughs . . . the facts you need to know to decide where in London you'd like to live.

The first part of the book gives you the analysis and the background information on how the market is working, and why. Here you will find major sections on matters that affect people's choice of where to live – transport plans, London's schools. You'll also find information on renting a home, buying and selling, mortgages, choosing and instructing an estate agent, planning and building regulations, and more. Cross-London guide charts show average buying prices and average rent levels.

You will also find a brief run-down of what happened in the property market in 1999 – and what will affect it this year.

Property prices have been back on the public agenda with a bang. On one hand as a source of delicious gossip – our eyebrows flew when we saw a showbiz person spend £4 million on a tumbling-down Notting Hill/Holland Park mansion this spring. He could have bought the same house, in the same condition, for £2.5 million just last year – as detailed in this Guide. Could we say he'd been Robbed?

The other discussion point is whether rising house prices stoke up inflation, and are a Bad Thing, and/or make us all feel richer, which can be a Bad Thing too (we spend too much and save too little). The Bank of England cited property prices as a reason to nudge up interest rates. But then no-one seemed to take much notice. There are strong arguments for saying that house prices and general inflation are not linked the way they were. But one group did get the message: the buy-to-let investors, who began to melt away as lending rates started to rise last summer. For more on this, and on the hard figures behind becoming a property investor, see the *Renting and Investing* chapter on page 49.

One cause for real unease on the finance/politics interface is the way that everybody (government ministers included) looks to traditional indicators such as national-average homes prices related to national-average earnings, and comforts themselves that homes are still 'affordable'.

In London such rubrics seem to me to have lost what little point they ever had. The gap that separates the earnings of all those people who make life in the capital worth living (nurses, teachers, ambulance drivers – actually you could go right on to chefs, university professors, police sergeants) and those of City traders and e-commerce exponents is so great as to distort any 'average'. Anybody talking to estate agents, watching the market movements – not to mention reading the offers of mortgages of 90, 100 per cent or even more – knows that this comfortable theory that we are all being rational, sensible and have a good cushion against any possibility of negative equity is an illusion.

One factor that stops people being sensible, that forces them to buy in places and at prices they'd otherwise discount, is schools. Our chapter on schools lays bare some of the horrible pressures that parents face when trying to get their offspring educated. In every 'family' area, a good set of exam results at a school – and the Internet lays them all bare for us to pick over – can galvanize house prices in nearby streets. Head teachers are observing that selection by ability may be out of fashion, but selection by house price – or ability to pay those prices – is taking its place.

This will be the Year of the Mayor, an individual with a high profile but few actual powers (Whitehall saw to that). One thing he or she can and almost certainly will do is charge us to drive cars into Central London. It behoves house-hunters to look harder than ever at the public transport map. We offer some starting-points from page 21 onwards.

The Mayor will be lucky in his or her timing. London is regenerating. House prices aside, there's a wealth of good news to celebrate the Millennium. The city gleams with new monuments, bustles with confident, money-spending inhabitants, celebrates a dozen new or revived cultural centres. Soon a new footbridge will lead from the steps by St Paul's across to the South Bank, where the Tate Modern stands cheek by jowl with the rebuilding of Shakespeare's Globe Theatre. Just promenade here along the South Bank's Queen's Walk. Admire Somerset House across the river (also reopening to the public this year), the London Eye ferris wheel. For the first time since the confident mid-day of the Victorians, London is spending money on itself. High time too: there's a century of patching and making-do to catch up.

Best of all, in the unglamorous inner suburbs real cash is being poured into regeneration in another sense: tearing down uninhabitable council estates, building new homes that people actually want. Peckham's £8 million public library is as proud a statement as any opera house, and around it are £200 million's-worth of new homes where one of the worst, and largest, estates once stood.

CARRIE SEGRAVE
LONDON, FEBRUARY 2000

Note
Although this book carries advertising to help defray the enormous research costs, it should be noted that it remains entirely editorially independent.

How to use this book

The first part of the book contains the analysis and reference chapters: a guide to London's property market, how it works and the factors that will shape it in the coming year. Look here for information on the transport plans and their effects, the procedures of buying and selling property, the ins and outs of mortgages on offer today, the latest factors influencing the education system and the secondary schools performance tables . . . everything you need to know about moving house in London.

The core of this book is an alphabetical directory of London's main residential areas, from A for Acton to W for Wimbledon. Each area is profiled with descriptions of the neighbourhoods it is made up of.

To find out about an area look for it in the A–Z section, which starts on page 104. The initial letter of the area is printed in the margin of each page to help you find your way around. A list of the areas covered appears in the contents and on page 103.

There is also a full index of streets and neighbourhoods at the back of the book.

Maps

An overall area map of London is on page 12. Maps of individual areas are at the beginning of each area profile. A key to the symbols used in these is on page 102. See opposite for how to make best use of the maps and the information that accompanies them. These pages are for quick reference to the key facts about an area.

Prices

As it is an annual, this book is not intended to be used as a price guide. It does, however, gather together average prices for different sizes of property in each of the areas and provides a 'freeze-frame' picture taken at the start of the 2000 selling season. This gives you a basis for comparison throughout the year. For prices in a given area see the relevant area information section at the end of each chapter. See also the main price charts on pages 40–43, where you can search across London by price or by flat/house size.

Postal districts

These are listed on pages 14–17, each with a description of the areas it covers. Start with this list if you know only the postcode you are looking for. The postal districts are also listed in the information box alongside the maps at the start of each area profile.

Boroughs

Details about each of the Inner and Outer London boroughs are on pages 78–80. A map on page 79 shows where their boundaries fall, as does the area map on page 12.

Council tax

Detailed at the start of each area profile are the council tax rates of band D properties in the area. There can be a big difference from borough to borough. See pages 78–80 for a list of each borough's rate of council tax.

Future editions

This book is as accurate as the combined efforts of a large number of people could make it. We would be grateful to receive news from readers about changes to any areas and any other comments and (constructive!) criticism.

Area information

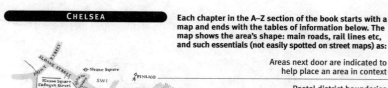

CHELSEA

Each chapter in the A–Z section of the book starts with a map and ends with the tables of information below. The map shows the area's shape: main roads, rail lines etc, and such essentials (not easily spotted on street maps) as:

Areas next door are indicated to help place an area in context

Postal district boundaries (can radically alter prices in some areas)

Map reference is to the standard edition of the *A–Z Street Atlas*

Borough council information and council tax rate for band D properties. Full details on pages 78–80

Borough boundaries (can make a big difference to council tax and education)

The maps also show the neighbourhoods we divide the area into. These correspond to the sub-headings in the text.

Map ref: p76 (4D)
Postal districts: SW3, SW10, SW1
Boroughs: Kensington & Chelsea (Con)
Council tax: Band D £534
Conservation areas: Most parts – check with town hall
Parking: Residents/meters. Clamping and towing away

Transport times: useful in comparing two areas. Zones refer to London Transport fare zones.

The main secondary schools, both Local Authority and private, are listed. See also neighbouring areas and *Schools in London* (pages 60–76).

Price averages give a 'freeze-frame' picture of the start of the 2000 selling season, researched in February. See also the price charts in the *Property Market in 2000*.

• Sales prices are in thousands: i.e. '100' means £100,000
• Rentals for this edition are shown weekly in £.

Summaries of home types to be found, and the market for them, encapsulate the chapter for quick reference. Search times can vary from days to months between boroughs – often the downfall of a sale.

Transport

Tubes: Sloane Sq (zone 1, District, Circle), South Kensington (zone 1, District, Circle, Piccadilly). From Sloane Sq: Oxford Circus 15 min (1 change), City 20 min, Heathrow 45 min (1 change).

Convenient for

West End, Knightsbridge, Victoria & Waterloo stations, Thames, M4 to West. Miles from centre: 2.

Schools

Local Authority: St Thomas More. Private: More House School. Many good prep schools. See also neighbouring areas.

SALES						
Flats	S	1B	2B	3B	4B	5B
AVERAGE PRICES	110–185	200–300+	300–500	500–800	700–1 M+	1 M'
Houses	2B	3B	4B	5B	6/7B	8B
AVERAGE PRICES	350–1 M	550–1.5 M	650–1.6 M	1.2–4 M	1.5–5 M	2–6 M+

RENTAL						
Flats	S	1B	2B	3B	4B	5B
AVERAGE PRICES	175–300	350–500	375–760	600–1300+	7500–3000	1000–6000
Houses	2B	3B	4B	5B	6/7B	8B
AVERAGE PRICES	500–950	750–1200	1000–1800	1500–2500	4000–6000	–

The properties

Lovely Georgian/early Victorian homes in garden squares, small streets of cottages and mews are the archetypal Chelsea properties. Also, N of King's Rd/Sloane Square, red-brick, Dutch-gabled mansion flats. Luxury flats schemes will soon replace King's College, part of the Duke of York's HQ and Barracks.

The market

Buyers are now mostly City-based and prosperous: the arty, up-market locals increasingly displaced by international bankers. Foreign buyers are Europeans and Americans rather than Far East. Chelsea's status and image ensure a lively market even in recessions, agents aver. Exceptional properties go well over the mainstream averages above. Local searches: 10 working days.

Map of areas covered

Key to areas

1	Acton	60	Knightsbridge
2	Acton Green	61	Lewisham
3	Balham	62	Leyton
4	Barnes	63	Maida Vale
5	Battersea	64	Marylebone
6	Bayswater	65	Mayfair
7	Bedford Park	66	Merton Park
8	Belgravia	67	Mill Hill
9	Bethnal Green	68	Mitcham
10	Blackheath	69	Morden
11	Bloomsbury	70	Mortlake
12	Bow	71	Muswell Hill
13	Brixton	72	Neasden
14	Camberwell	73	New Cross
15	Camden Town	74	Newham
16	Catford	75	Norbury
17	Chelsea	76	North Kensington
18	Chiswick	77	Notting Hill
19	City and Fringes	78	Palmers Green
20	Clapham	79	Peckham
21	Clerkenwell	80	Pimlico
22	Colliers Wood	81	Poplar
23	Covent Garden	82	Putney
24	Cricklewood	83	Queen's Park
25	Crouch End	84	Raynes Park
26	Crystal Palace	85	Regents Park
27	Deptford	86	Richmond
28	Docklands	87	Roehampton
29	Dollis Hill	88	Sheen
30	Dulwich	89	Shepherd's Bush
31	Ealing	90	Soho
32	Earls Court	91	The South Bank
33	Earlsfield	92	Southfields
34	Finchley	93	Southgate
35	Finsbury	94	South Kensington
36	Finsbury Park	95	St John's Wood
37	Fitzrovia	96	Stepney
38	Forest Hill	97	Stoke Newington
39	Fulham	98	Stockwell
40	Gipsy Hill	99	Streatham
41	Golders Green	100	Stroud Green
42	Greenwich	101	Teddington
43	Hackney	102	Tooting
44	Hammersmith	103	Tottenham
45	Hampstead	104	Totteridge
46	Hampstead Garden Suburb	105	Tufnell Park
47	Hendon	106	Tulse Hill
48	Herne Hill	107	Twickenham
49	Highbury	108	Vauxhall
50	Highgate	109	Walthamstow
51	Holland Park	110	Wandsworth
52	Islington	111	West Brompton
53	Kennington	112	West Hampstead
54	Kensal Rise	113	Westminster
55	Kensington	114	West Norwood
56	Kentish Town	115	Whetstone
57	Kew	116	Whitechapel
58	Kilburn	117	Willesden
59	King's Cross	118	Wimbledon

Map labels: 3, 109, 62, 43, 74, 96, 12, 81, 28, 73, 27, 42, 10, 61, 16, 38

E2 or not E2? Decoding the postcodes

London's postal districts are a matter first and foremost of Post Office convenience: they act as collection and delivery zones and are based around the location of sorting offices and the ease of routes. But those few letters and numbers also convey a powerful emotional and financial message. The difference between SW1 and SW2 is more than a digit: it is all of the gap between Belgravia and Brixton. Londoners absorb these subtleties with their mother's milk. But few natives appreciate quite how remote SE2 is, or that E4 is in Epping Forest while E14 is the upwardly mobile Isle of Dogs. And the borders can be arbitrary: some of Brixton is SW2, agreed – but so are the solidly respectable mansion blocks of Streatham Hill. Some postal districts are more logical than others. The Post Office says the whole system is quite clear: it's alphabetical. It is not, and it is not. Use this list to check which areas a zone includes, and to spot anomalies. Estate agents quite frequently quote just postal districts in advertisements and by using this list you can get an idea if the area is one you want to look at. Follow the area names into the main A–Z in this book for a map, which shows post boundaries, and a profile of the area.

E1 The East End heartland, from the City E through Whitechapel and Stepney to Mile End. Also includes the smart warehouse conversions of riverside Wapping (see Docklands) and City fringe areas like Spitalfields and Shoreditch.

E2 North from E1, Bethnal Green and council flat-dominated Haggerston. Also a chunk of City fringe in Shoreditch.

E3 Bow, either side of the Mile End Rd in the East End.

E4 The NE fringe of London on the edge of Essex beyond the North Circular, including the suburban streets of Chingford Green and Highams Hill.

E5 The N part of Hackney Borough, with Lower and Upper Clapton and a good chunk of the Hackney Marshes. Also fringes of Stoke Newington.

E6 London's eastern edge, on the way to Southend: East Ham and the Docklands suburb of Beckton.

E7 Forest Gate, the S part of Wanstead. East of Stratford East.

E8 The W side of Hackney, on the border with Islington, including the area around London Fields and the SE corner of Stoke Newington.

E9 The E part of Hackney, across the Lea Valley and the Hackney Marshes. Includes Victoria Park and Homerton.

E10 Most of Leyton, E of the Hackney Marshes from Hackney. Includes a corner of Walthamstow.

E11 Centres around Wanstead and Snaresbrook; residential suburbs where the M11 meets the North Circular.

E12 Manor Park and Little Ilford on the E fringe of the London postal district: E from here is Essex, Ilford in particular.

E13 West Ham and Plaistow on the Barking Rd E from the East End.

E14 Diverse area including the Isle of Dogs, heart of Docklands and site of Canary Wharf and other office and homes schemes, and housing in Limehouse and Poplar and the Limehouse riverside.

E15 Stratford, the metropolis of East London, and surrounding areas E of the Lea Valley.

E16 Contains the vast Royal Docks area, next on the hit-list for Docklands regeneration, as well as old-established industry and housing in riverside Silvertown and Canning Town.

E17 Walthamstow and Higham Hill in NE London.

E18 South Woodford on the suburban fringes of Epping Forest.

EC1 All four City postcodes are ECs. EC1 is the biggest, covering the relatively less prosperous tract from St Paul's N to the City Rd, and including large parts of Finsbury and all of Clerkenwell.

EC2 The money heart of the City, from the Bank of England N to Broad St. Includes the Barbican.

EC3 The E side of the City, including the Tower and the Lloyds building.

EC4 The riverside slice, including Fleet St, the Temple, Cannon St and Blackfriars.

N1 The classic Islington postcode, extending S from Highbury and Islington tube to the Angel. Includes Hoxton and De Beauvoir to the E, Barnsbury and King's Cross to the W.

N2 By contrast, the leafy streets and semis of East Finchley and Fortis Green in London's North West. Also the 'Millionaire's Row', Bishops Avenue, and the 'new' part of Hampstead Garden Suburb.

N3 Further out still, the next suburb NW covering most of Finchley.

N4 Crouch End, Stroud Green, Finsbury Park and Harringay, a widely contrasting chunk of North London.

N5 A small district covering Highbury, to the N of Islington. In Islington borough, so estate agents like to call it so.

N6 The centre of Highgate, Dartmouth Park to its S, some woods and a few streets of Fortis Green to the N.

N7 Where the Seven Sisters Rd crosses the Holloway Rd is the centre, with parts of Tufnell Park and a corner of Highbury.

N8 Hornsey, most of the 'ladder' district of Harringay, the N side of Crouch End.

N9 The N slice of Edmonton, especially Lower Edmonton.

N10 Most of Muswell Hill.

N11 Friern Barnet, New Southgate and Bounds Green: residential districts straddling the North Circular Rd.

N12 North Finchley and Woodside Park.

N13 Palmers Green, where the North Circular crosses Green Lanes due N of London.

N14 Southgate, on the northern edge of London on the Hertfordshire border.

N15 The southern part of Tottenham, at the NE end of the Seven Sisters Rd.

N16 Stoke Newington and the S part of Stamford Hill.

N17 Most of Tottenham.

N18 A slice along the North Circular N of Tottenham, including Edmonton and Upper Edmonton.

N19 Archway, from the fringes of Highgate and Crouch End in the N down to Tufnell Park.

N20 The semi-rural, prosperous and pony-infested Totteridge, Oakleigh Park and Whetstone, N of Finchley and S of Barnet.

N21 Winchmore Hill and Grange Park, suburbia plus a lot of golf courses on the fringe of North London.

N22 Wood Green, Alexandra Palace, the E side of Muswell Hill, Noel Park and the W edge of Tottenham.

NW1 One of London's most diverse districts, with the Nash villas of Regent's Park and the crowded streets of Camden Town sharing the same postcode. Starts in the S at the Marylebone Rd, takes in part of Lisson Grove in the W, the edge of Kentish Town in the NE, all of Camden Town and Primrose Hill.

NW2 One of the less helpful postcodes. Covers Cricklewood, Childs Hill, Dollis Hill, an arbitrary slice of Willesden and a bit of Brondesbury.

NW3 The Hampstead postcode, and one with hardly an undesirable corner. Includes Belsize Park, part of Primrose Hill, the Finchley Rd – but not West Hampstead, which is NW6.

NW4 Hendon, from Brent Cross up along the M1 to the edge of Mill Hill.

NW5 Kentish Town, Gospel Oak and Tufnell Park, on the SE fringes of Hampstead and Highgate.

NW6 Once thought of as the Kilburn postcode – which it still is – but now associated more with West Hampstead. Also spreads W to include Queen's Park and Brondesbury Park.

NW7 Mill Hill and assorted golf courses, detached houses and green belt countryside out along the M1.

NW8 Clearly defined as St John's Wood, with only a few acres of council housing around Lisson Grove to lower the tone.

NW9 West Hendon, Colindale and Kingsbury, suburban areas NW of the Welsh Harp reservoir.

NW10 A large area extending W from Kensal Rise to the North Circular, taking in Neasden, Harlesden and parts of Willesden.
NW11 Golders Green and the older, smarter side of Hampstead Garden Suburb.

SE1 A big tract in the bend of the river opposite the City and Westminster: The South Bank from Vauxhall in the W to the Old Kent Rd in the E. Very varied: many new homes schemes, plus the National Theatre, the new Tate, the Tower Bridge quarter.
SE2 In Kent, really, E of Woolwich and even Plumstead, it comprises Abbey Wood and part of Thamesmead.
SE3 Blackheath, Blackheath Park, East Greenwich and Kidbrooke.
SE4 A small district S of New Cross and W of Lewisham, centred around Brockley.
SE5 Essentially Camberwell, though the SW end of Coldharbour Lane is better described as Brixton, the NW corner is in Kennington and the NE in Walworth.
SE6 Catford, and Bellingham to the S.
SE7 Charlton, on the river E of the Blackwall Tunnel and W of Woolwich.
SE8 Deptford, extending along the riverside opposite the Isle of Dogs and S of the Surrey Docks. Not part of the Docklands area, though similar to it. A corner of SE8 sticks down towards Lewisham, taking in St John's.
SE9 Far, suburban SE London, including Eltham and Mottingham.
SE10 Greenwich, except for East Greenwhich which is SE3. SE10 also includes the Millenium Dome peninsula to the NE beneath which the Blackwall Tunnel motorway passes.
SE11 Most of Kennington, from the Oval N to the Elephant & Castle and W to the river at Vauxhall. More SW than SE.
SE12 Lee and Grove Park, SE of Catford.
SE13 Lewisham, plus Ladywell and Hither Green to the S.
SE14 New Cross and a slice of the inland side of Deptford.
SE15 Peckham, part of Peckham Rye (the rest is in SE22), and Nunhead.
SE16 Bermondsey and Rotherhithe, including the entire Surrey Docks district of Docklands. Away from the river. SE16 includes streets on the edge of North Peckham. The NW corner, along the river, has some big new riverside developments.
SE17 Walworth, from the Elephant & Castle southwards. Includes part of Kennington in the W.
SE18 Woolwich, Plumstead and Plumstead Common.
SE19 Centres around the Crystal Palace hilltop, including Norwood New Town and the fringes of Penge.
SE20 Penge and Anerley, to the SE of Crystal Palace.
SE21 Dulwich Village, and the fringes of Tulse Hill.
SE22 East Dulwich, part of Peckham Rye and a bit of Honor Oak.
SE23 Forest Hill, to the E of Dulwich. Also Honor Oak.
SE24 Herne Hill, also extending N towards Brixton's Loughborough Junction and NW to Brockwell Park and the Poets' Estate. Some streets in the SE corner are really in Dulwich.
SE25 South Norwood.
SE26 Sydenham, from Crystal Palace E to Bell Green and S to the edge of Penge.
SE27 West Norwood and the S half of Tulse Hill.
SE28 Thamesmead, the new town on the Plumstead Marshes E down the Thames.

SW1 Perhaps the smartest code of all, the postal address of Buckingham Palace and 10 Downing St, never mind the whole of Westminster, St James's, Belgravia, Victoria and part of Knightsbridge including Harrods, squeezed in by a dramatic jink in the frontier, forming an enclave in SW3. Pimlico is SW1 and now that has 'come up' there is hardly a cheap corner left. Sloane Square is SW1 too.
SW2 Part of Brixton, the southern slice, and also Streatham Hill, the edge of Clapham Park and part of Tulse Hill.
SW3 Chelsea, though the HQ of Chelseadom, Peter Jones, is in SW1. Also a good part of Knightsbridge and some of South Ken – see the area map for the quirks of the boundaries here. SW3 stops at Beaufort St in the W and large tracts of Chelsea are in SW10.

SW4 Clapham, plus a portion of Stockwell W of Clapham Rd and a corner of W Brixton.

SW5 A small zone, essentially Earl's Court.

SW6 By contrast, the entire island cut off by the river and the railway, which is Fulham. Only in the N, where the boundary runs along Lillie Rd, is there any doubt. Some streets N of here are really in Fulham though they have W6 and W14 codes.

SW7 South Kensington, Knightsbridge (though see also SW3) and the Museums.

SW8 A mixed area, much crossed by railways, between the river and Stockwell. Includes parts of Stockwell, the Oval, Vauxhall, the E part of Battersea's Queenstown neighbourhood, and the industrial zone of Nine Elms.

SW9 The northern half of Brixton, the E side of Stockwell and a corner in the N that is really the Oval.

SW10 The western end of Chelsea, plus a patch to the N which is really West Brompton and, by sheer good luck for the developers, the big Chelsea Harbour development which physical, if not postal, geography places across the creek in Fulham.

SW11 A big slice of smart and not-so-smart South London, from Battersea Park, through Central Battersea to Wandsworth Common.

SW12 Balham, including the streets in the 'Nightingale Triangle' where people say they're in Clapham South, and the lower tier of the 'Between the Commons' neighbourhood of Battersea.

SW13 Barnes, well-defined by common, river and White Hart Lane, which forms the boundary with SW14 and Mortlake.

SW14 Mortlake by the river and the suburban streets of East Sheen on the edge of Richmond Park.

SW15 Putney, plus Roehampton in the W and some streets that are virtually Wandsworth to the E.

SW16 Streatham, plus Streatham Vale and Norbury in the S.

SW17 Tooting.

SW18 Wandsworth, part of Wandsworth Common, Southfields and Earlsfield.

SW19 A large area including Wimbledon, Wimbledon Park, Merton and Colliers Wood.

SW20 The further reaches of Wimbledon towards the Kingston bypass, including Raynes Park.

W1 Grandeur and commerce, including Mayfair, Oxford St, Regent St . . . Essentially, the West End, plus homes in Soho and Marylebone.

W2 Bayswater and Paddington, plus Little Venice S of the canal.

W3 Acton, though not Acton Green in the S or the industry of North Acton.

W4 Chiswick, including Bedford Park and Acton Green.

W5 The centre of Ealing, including South Ealing. Ealing has three postcodes: see area map.

W6 Hammersmith and the northern fringes of Fulham.

W7 The western slice of Ealing Borough, including Hanwell and part of West Ealing.

W8 The heart of Kensington, around the High St and Church St.

W9 Maida Vale and Little Venice N of the canal, plus a sharply contrasting area to the W of Waterton Rd stretching up to Queen's Park.

W10 North Kensington N of the fly-over, plus Kensal as far N as Queen's Park.

W11 Notting Hill S of the fly-over and N of Notting Hill Gate. Includes the N part of Holland Park.

W12 Shepherd's Bush, plus East Acton and White City.

W13 The middle slice of Ealing, W of Ealing centre and E of Hanwell.

W14 A slice squeezed between Kensington and Hammersmith, including some of the smartest parts of Holland Park, Olympia, West Kensington and the NE quadrant of Hammersmith.

WC1 Bloomsbury, St Pancras and the W part of Finsbury.

WC2 Covent Garden, Theatreland, the Strand, part of Holborn.

London
in 2000

The property market in 2000

Well. What a year that was. The analysis on this page last year felt like positively unbridled optimism at time of writing – after the autumn of 1998 in which the homes market was dead in the water, and terms like 'global financial meltdown' were being bandied about. Now, after a year of runaway London property prices, it's plain – with hindsight – that its cautious note was plainly twelve months too soon. Instead of a world recession triggered (you may remember) by a complete financial crash in the Far East, the City boys got their bonuses, as 1999 opened mortgage rates were low and falling, and low returns from savings accounts persuaded ever more people to invest in a 'buy-to-let' property instead.

The speed of turnaround in sentiment from the gloom of late-'98 to the optimism of 1999 was extraordinary: a lesson that confidence can change as fast in the homes market as in the City – in either direction.

Now, in spring 2000, it is clear that the market is starting as brisk, if not even brisker, than last year's. Historically speaking, this is not good news; the longer homes prices go on outstripping the rest of the economy (and that sticky six months in '98 was only a hiccup in a long climb), the more vulnerable property becomes to any financial shocks in the wider world. Please do not believe those pundits who declare that there could not possibly be another crash like 1989's. Of course there could if things go on overheating.

Strategies for this year

'We must buy now or we'll miss the boat' is still a potent spur to panic-buying. But if you must buy now, you should reckon that this year is the top of this particular cycle; look, therefore, for no instant growth in value; buy a home which has such assets (proximity to good transport, say, or a popular school) that will ensure its saleability even in a stodgy market – and one that has a spare room that can be let if, to take the worst case, mortgage rates rise and prices once again fall.

All that being said, barring that destabilising shock to the world economy, the industry's consensus is that the upswing will continue through this year. A little heat has been taken off since buy-to-let yields no longer look so attractive; already interest rates have risen, and before this edition hits the streets the Chancellor will almost certainly attempt further control (and a nice slice of extra revenue) by raising the Stamp Duty levels.

But the best way – in fact the only way, short of an externally-caused slump or a sudden big blow to London's position as a world city – to bring the market back to some sort of balance is to encourage people to move. It is a rise in turnover, not prices, that's needed: it is an all-time low in the numbers of homes for sale across the capital that has driven, and is driving, prices up.

Nothing the government or the Bank of England has done is going to remedy that. Nor, indeed, will they greatly depress many eager buyers – bar those at the bottom of the heap who are just those who must not be discouraged, for the sake of a healthy city and a healthy property market. In case the Bank hasn't noticed, there are plenty of buyers in London who don't need mortgage money, or who are on fixed rates, or are financed, in the case of foreigners, from abroad. And increased Stamp Duty may well put a brake on price rises, but if it lowers turnover it will do more harm than good.

The government's other bright idea is to try to cut the time a home sale takes – the major deterrent to all but the most necessary of moves. But the proposed Seller's Pack, while it should certainly speed deals, looks even more likely to put people off bothering to move at all; and it could well herald the end of the small, independent local estate agent: for details see the Buying and Selling section, which starts on page 26.

However, if we are really lucky events may overtake the government's plan. The technology is catching up fast. On-line sites for everything from mortgages to the Land Registry are streamlining the system. Maybe we can speed up the process so much via the internet that we won't need that Seller's Pack . . . .

Reasons to be cheerful

Now (at last) for some reasons to be cheerful. This being 2000, it's a good moment to raise our eyes a little further than a twelvemonth, and in the medium-to-long term some enormous changes are at last under way.

First, and best, the serious sums being spent to renovate, or even demolish and rebuild, the worst of the grim council housing are showing real fruit (see Peckham, Hackney, Stepney). Allied to this is the move to replace councils with housing associations – who are developing all sorts of different tenures, from low-cost renting to shared ownership: we need much more of this, and quickly, to help with the truly appalling problem of getting housed on a low (or no) income in a city that American bankers find dear. We discuss this on page 36. And even the big builders are realising the potential of brownfield sites, and realising that a mixed community – a mix of uses and inhabitants, via mixed tenures – makes the most economic and social sense.

If this continues and speeds up, it is the best news for the well-being of London. I hope that I'm not being too optimistic in seeing the new approach as ultimately replacing ghettoes and rebuilding neighbourhoods. However cosy (and some are: look at Fulham) ghettoes are never healthy. It is devoutly to be hoped that the sealed-off modern gated development, just as much as the grim '60s council estate, will both become things of the past.

The Londonwide picture

London is gaining a Mayor and the Greater London Authority – the GLA. Watching how they settle down, and how they get on with each other, with the boroughs, and above all with the government, will be this year's most absorbing armchair sport. The capital's attention over the last year has been on personalities, not the boring bits like what the Mayor can or should do. We make no apology for reiterating our concerns.

The perception of a Mayor as an impotent if noisy figurehead will be uncomfortably short of the truth. Transport and planning are his or her headline tasks. Transport's knotty problems are discussed below, but there are concerns about planning. The Mayor will be able to intervene in any planning application for a major scheme or for a single building over 50 metres high – which means 80 per cent of new space in the City. The City fathers are uneasy: perhaps the first of many rows between the Mayor and the domain of the Lord Mayor. More optimistic observers hope that the Mayor will be able to take a Londonwide view, avoiding parochial planning decisions.

The Mayor and GLA will also have a role in planning London's long-term development by creating a Spatial Development Strategy (SDS). It's widely accepted that there is a vacuum here, but the last attempt was not promising. The GLC's Greater London Plan of 1969 was devised, observed London planning guru Professor Peter Hall, 'by a cast of thousands – and achieved almost nothing'. Its 1940s predecessor, the Abercrombie plan, which by contrast 'changed the face of London irreversibly for the better' had a staff of just 16. The blueprint for the GLA and Mayor speaks of a small staff. One hopes that their efforts will be closer to Abercrombie than the GLC.

Planning experts are worried that the GLA could prove to be a bottle-neck clogged up with planning applications. 'Major developments in the boroughs should fit in with the Mayor's overall scheme', says the government, which seems to presage some epic rows with the boroughs – just as in GLC days, when, commented Prof Hall, 'it seemed that most of [the GLC and borough planners'] energies were thus spent'.

One area where the Mayor will have a big effect is the road-charging issue. A detailed report by the ROCOL (Review of Charging Options for London) group came out in November. Given the remit to work out an overall transport strategy, and the problem of paying for it, one of the Mayor's key powers may be to raise money from road-use charges and/or a workplace parking levy. The Act which gives the Mayor his/her powers says that all revenue from such schemes must be spent on transport.

The ROCOL study sorted out what is technically feasible. It reckons electronic systems are still some way off, and the options envisaged see motorists either buying an 'area licence' which would be enforced by digital cameras reading number plates, or buying and displaying a paper licence. They plumped for the former, which they reckon could be operational by 2003. However mayoral candidate Ken Livingstone immediately opted for the paper-licence route and said that it could be started by August 2001.

The ROCOL experts suggest that the Inner Ring Road (did you know there was one?) defines Central London. The borders would be the Marylebone and Euston Rds, Pentonville Rd, Tower Bridge, Elephant & Castle, Vauxhall Bridge, Victoria and Hyde Park Corner. To drive within this area would cost £5 per day, though it would be free after 7 p.m. and at weekends. There are no proposals for exemptions for residents – inside or outside the central zone. Only buses (not private coaches) and emergency vehicles would be exempt.

If such a system is introduced, how would the people thus deterred get around? The tube and rail systems are at peak capacity already, so the only option would seem to be more buses. The rich, of course, would go on driving their cars.

The paper-licence system endorsed by Mr Livingstone would require an army of wardens, and special bays so drivers could be stopped and checked. Even so, the ROCOL report predicts that only one defaulter in five would be caught, and that large (and unpopular) fines would be needed to deter transgressors. A camera-based system would give a 70 per cent chance of catching non-payers.

The report admits there would be a 'significant' impact on traffic in the areas just outside the central area as drivers attempt to avoid the pay zone. It will obviously make busy roads, such as the Inner Ring, even busier, and there will be knock-on effects as drivers search for new routes.

Transport: getting the most out of London

To decide where to live in London these days, you need to be a bit of a trainspotter. The anorak is optional, but an informed interest in connections is not. The new public transport services detailed below, and a host of changes to existing ones, open up routes you may not have thought of. A new tube line (like the extended Jubilee) is not just a linear route, it connects with most of the others, and with 'overground' trains too. An hour or two with the London Connections map, and (if you can bear it) a timetable will make you think.

You have to think for yourself because – despite all the rhetoric about integrated transport – there's no-one else to do it for you. Ask Railtrack's web-site for the route from Richmond to Heathrow and it will suggest a tube to Earl's Court, another to Paddington and then the Heathrow Express train. Quite a tour of West London, with half the journey travelling in the wrong direction. Or – and the web site won't tell you this – there are trains direct from Richmond to Feltham, and then a shuttle bus out to the airport. Quicker, more direct, cheaper.

Another example: you live in Battersea and a job interview in north Fulham. The car's bust, you look at the tube map and shlep in by train from Clapham Junction to Victoria, and then trundle along the District Line for five stops to West Brompton. Or – if anyone has told you about it – you can use the West London train line from the Junction, travelling one stop to the new West Brompton station. Journey time: 5 minutes. The snag with this line is that there are only two trains an hour at present.

One idea that surfaced during the mayoral election was for a revised tube map, with the overground lines that run frequently added. Something of the sort would address the knowledge gap. The new connections affect nearby homes as surely as if they had physically moved.

But knowledge aside there are still glaring gaps in the actual infrastructure, and obvious failings in the way it is run. Tokyo has a well-organised loop rail line which connects all the main-line trains and metro lines with each other. We have the Circle Line, which came to a stop for two hours in February because it was raining (water got into the 50-year-old signal cables). We also have the bare bones of an outer circle in the combined North London, West London and East London lines. But they don't connect up – yet. Ninety eight per cent of Tokyo's metro trains arrive within a minute of their scheduled time. London claims 85 per cent within five minutes. Many stations on the overground network are unmanned, and many have had little or no repair and maintenance for years. Railtrack is spending millions on tackling the backlog, but few suburban stations are attractive places for old, young or female travellers – yet.

New trains, new connections

The good news is that London's new tube line, the extended **Jubilee**, is finished, and working – most of the time. The stations at Canada Water, Bermondsey, London Bridge and Southwark put these areas right between the West End and Docklands. Key interchanges are at London Bridge for the City (via Northern Line) and King's Cross (via Thameslink); Canary Wharf for the DLR to the rest of Docklands, and Green Park for the Victoria and Piccadilly Lines. Other areas that benefit are the Isle of Dogs, the Royal Docks/City Airport – and most of SE London via connections. Gainers too are Westminster with a direct link to Waterloo (and Eurostar) and Docklands; Mayfair with two Jubilee stations – Bond St and Green Park; and the St John's Wood/West Hampstead strip with links as above plus the proximity of Paddington. Belgravia and Mayfair rental agents have already seen an influx of young, affluent City-working tenants.

The Jubilee also opens up new links for rail commuters from the SW and NW. Developers have been touting the Jubilee Line as a plus as far out as Kingston. The Northern Line interchanges with the Jubilee at London Bridge, offering a Docklands link to the good City and West End connections that S London areas such as Clapham already enjoy. And as a property expert pointed out, the prosperous denizens of Canary Wharf can get to the Ritz in 16 minutes.

The also-new **Docklands Light Railway** (DLR) branch to Greenwich and Lewisham means that 500,000 more people are now within a sensible commute (ie, with connections, a journey-time of less than 45 minutes) from the Isle of Dogs. This links SE London – Lewisham, Deptford and Greenwich – to Canary Wharf and the City, and via interchanges, provides a range of new options which include links to Waterloo, Westminster and the West End by the Jubilee and (via the DLR) the City Airport. The new DLR extension has stations at the Cutty Sark, Greenwich railway station, Deptford Bridge, Elverson Rd and Lewisham. Lewisham is a busy shopping centre and also an interchange for rail and bus routes which between them serve much of SE London.

Deptford benefits too, with a DLR station at Deptford Creek: the waterfront is seeing much redevelopment as a consequence. Further S, Lee has good houses but a poor train service: a bus to Lewisham DLR expands its horizons. Brockley, Catford and Sydenham to the S, and Eltham to the E, all gain new travel options.

Other parts of SE London do well via interchanges. The **East London Line**, orphan of tube lines in its cut-off corner, now has an interchange with the Jubilee at the new Canada Water station. This gives New Cross, and points S on train and bus links, fast travel to the West End for the first time. What is more, there are at long last serious plans to extend the East London Line on southwards – see *Transport: the Future* below.

Getting to the airports

Most Londoners take the city's airports – all five of them – for granted. However, uniquely in Europe, they have direct flights to 80 per cent of the world's GDP. So an enormous property plus is swift public transport access to Heathrow, Europe's major airport, as well as to the centre of town. A nearby route to any of the other airports does no harm, either. Since mid-1998 the **Paddington–Heathrow Express** train has been running every 15 minutes, taking 15 minutes. It is a success, despite its £10 fare, with 6 million passengers in its first full year. A rank of airline-style desks is now in operation at Paddington, allowing travellers to check in before they board the train. Heathrow's other rail link is the Piccadilly Line, which takes 50 minutes, but is cheaper.

To get to **Gatwick**, look out for homes within reach of Thameslink trains, which call at London Bridge, Blackfriars, City Thameslink and Farringdon plus a range of N London stations. The airport is also served from Victoria (including the non-stop, 30-minute Gatwick Express) and Clapham Junction (close to Battersea, Clapham and Wandsworth). East Croydon takes on new importance as the hub where Gatwick trains intersect with the new Tramlink service, starting this spring, which connects with Wimbledon, Mitcham and Beckenham.

Stansted's rail link is from Liverpool St, with a stop at Tottenham Hale (Victoria Line connects here) and a 41-minute journey time. For **Luton**, use Thameslink (see Gatwick above) to the new Luton Airport Parkway station with a 30-minute, eight-trains-an-hour service from King's Cross. The **City Airport** in Docklands can be reached via DLR (Prince Regent station and 473 bus), Jubilee Line (Canning Town station then a shuttle bus) – it's 25 min from the West End this way – and Silverlink Metro (North London Line), which takes approximately 30 minutes from Highbury & Islington.

Future airport links

Thus all five London airports can now be reached by rail, but a lot more needs to be done before most London areas have sensible rail–air routes. The most important plan is for the **St Pancras–Heathrow Express**. This will benefit Mid-town, the West End and the City. It will have stops at Ealing Broadway and West Hampstead, with a journey time of 35 minutes and two trains an hour. This will do for West Hampstead and its environs what the Paddington link has done for Maida Vale.

However the timing has slipped back to 2005 at the earliest. The line has had to join a queue of big rail projects trying to cram into the St Pancras interchange, and it has been jostled aside by Thameslink 2000 and the Channel Tunnel link.

But so many travellers start their trek to the airport in the residential districts of SW London, an awkward tube journey from Paddington (or St Pancras). None of the Waterloo trains connect with the airport, though there is a line only a couple of miles away from the terminals. To remedy this, Feltham station is being promoted as **'Heathrow South Gateway'**. This links Waterloo and Clapham Junction trains to the airport via an upgraded station and a 20-minute coach service. It's working well – but passengers have been few in number, probably because no-one knows about it.

On the other (N) side of the airport Hayes & Harlington station, on the Paddington–Reading line, is **'Heathrow North Gateway'** or 'Hayes Hub'. Later this year a shuttle train will start from Hayes to the airport. This will allow Thames Trains passengers from Ealing, Acton and so on to get to Heathrow with one change. If this works out, the shuttle may be extended to Ealing.

Other plans depend on the Heathrow Terminal 5 inquiry, which has yet to report. BAA are talking about running Paris Eurostar trains into the terminals. Airtrack – a direct line into the terminals from the South West line around Staines – also depends on Terminal 5 going ahead. Trains from Richmond/Waterloo could use this link.

Cross-London, North–South

Thameslink 2000 is the decidedly optimistic name for a major revamp of the train service that runs N–S through Farringdon, City Thameslink and Blackfriars. Thameslink has been in operation for several years, and brings South London areas such as Elephant & Castle, Tulse Hill and Herne Hill within minutes of the City. Trains run deep into North London and beyond: West Hampstead, Kentish Town, on up to Cricklewood and Hendon. There are trains down to Gatwick, up to Luton.

But bottlenecks around London Bridge and at King's Cross restrict the number of trains Thameslink can run. The 2000 project will ease these pinch-points, allowing trains of 12 rather than eight carriages and extending the service to 169 stations in place of the existing 50. The £800 million plan aims to triple the number of trains through Central London from eight to 24 an hour. It will link into the burgeoning St Pancras interchange, and involve the virtual rebuilding of London Bridge station at a cost of £400 million. A public inquiry into the scheme, which would have a big impact on the Borough Market conservation area, is under way. It is now hoped that work will start in early 2002, with trains running from 2006.

Cross-London, East–West

Down in Croydon, the planned November 1999 opening of **Tramlink 2000** was held up by software snags – and the slowness of Croydon motorists in getting used to trams in the street (there was at least one nasty crash). It should be up and running this May. The network uses redundant rail lines but also runs through the streets of central Croydon. It links Wimbledon to Croydon and on to New Addington and Beckenham. The trams are made in Vienna and are just like their continental cousins, holding 200 people, travelling at 50 mph (though not through the streets) and running every 10 minutes. If it is a success the system could be replicated in other parts of London. A London Transport study has spotlighted several possible places, from Kingston to Thamesmead.

London to Europe

The **Channel Tunnel Rail Link**, or the lack of it, has been a recurrent theme of this Guide since 1987. Now, Eurostar trains struggle through South-East London, weave their way among the commuter trains of Kent and only really get up to speed when they reach the tunnel itself. A new railway – like those in France and Belgium – would cut half an hour off the Paris–London journey. But getting it built has proved a political and financial puzzle. The government say they've now solved it. Digging started in earnest in October 1998, with civil engineering work due to take 2–2¹/2 years.

In order to get it re-started the scheme was split into two: phase one is the line from the Channel through Kent, under the Thames Estuary and into the Essex Marshes. This should be finished by 2003, but the trains will divert from it onto the existing track into Waterloo – until (and if) phase two is finished. This is the expensive bit, mostly in tunnels under E and North London to Stratford and into a new station beneath St Pancras. Work is due to start in mid-2001 but there is quite a bit of financial and contractual horse-trading yet to do. The betting is on Paris–St Pancras trains by 2010.

Boats on the river – for now

Cinema-goers will have noted that in Shakespeare's time a Thames rowing boat was the equivalent of a taxi. For centuries the river was London's highway. Not in the 20th century, though, with attempt after attempt at a river-bus service ending up in failure. The Millennium Dome has prompted yet another try. £21 million has been spent on new or rebuilt piers at Westminster, Embankment, Waterloo – by the London Eye Wheel – Bankside, Blackfriars, Tower, Rotherhithe, Greenwich – and at the Dome. Further upgraded or new piers are proposed at Battersea Park, Cadogan Pier (Chelsea), Chelsea Harbour and other locations up-river – though nothing definite yet. Docklanders of 1980s vintage will recall that there are lots of piers on both banks, most paid for by public money and all unused, for regular services at least. No word on what will happen to these apart from Canary Wharf and Rotherhithe (Holiday Inn).

Boats will run to the Dome thoughout 2000, and on into 2001 if the Millennium Experience stays open. City Cruises is running the Millennium Express between the Wheel pier and the Dome. White Horse Ferries are providing a local service between Greenwich Pier, by the Cutty Sark, and the Dome. White Horse are also running the Central London River-Hopper which shuttles between four piers from Blackfriars to Canary Wharf. It runs at peak hours only, Monday to Friday. It was supposed to go as far west as Waterloo (by the Wheel), but shows no sign of doing so. The idea of linking nine piers at key attractions and transport interchanges along the river seems, like so many Thames dreams, to have sunk.

It is hoped that the River-Hopper will be among the 'legacy' services prompted by the Millennium investment. London Transport has set up a new subsidiary company, London River Services (LRS), which has taken over the piers owned by the Port of London Authority. As part of the new transport authority in the capital, LRS is responsible for overseeing fares and ticketing on river services. It is hoping to bring the scheduled boats into the Travelcard scheme.

However now that the public cash has been spent on the piers, no more is forthcoming to subsidize the boat services. LRS has to pay its way by charging boat operators, who in turn have to make their living without any subsidy. Not surprisingly, the boat operators are more keen on disco cruises and the traditional tourist boats than on scheduled services, which have higher overheads.

Past experience (1980s Docklands especially) has proved that no amount of new piers and ministerial exhortations will get commuters onto boats unless they (the boats, that is) are cheap, reliable and predictable. Those who bought homes close to the Docklands piers a decade ago are still smarting from the experience.

Who owns the tubes?

The big debate in London politics is proving to be who pays for the Underground, and how. Private money is going to have to come into London's tube system, the question is how it will be arranged. The government favour 'PPP' (Public-Private

Partnership) which, say the ministry, would bring £7 billion of private money to invest in the system. PPP may be dropped depending on who ends up as Mayor.

Whatever kind of part-privatized route emerges, much still comes down to how much public money is available, for the private 'leaseholders' would charge the tube operator (Transport for London, or TfL, the successor to London Transport) the costs of improving the network – plus their profit. TfL will need a subsidy or fares will rocket. How big a subsidy will be decided by central government – not by the Mayor, however much he or she may wish it were otherwise.

Transport: the future

From here on, it's promises. London is punch-drunk with transport 'schemes' and 'proposals'. The Guide's motto remains: don't believe in new tube lines until you see them digging. **Crossrail** is a plan for an E–W line joining the Heathrow and Reading to Paddington main-line train lines with the Essex to Liverpool Street ones: a deep-level Paris-style 'regional rail' across London. There's a clear need for this: it would add 70,000 seats in the rush hour and would help regenerate places like Stratford and the Lea Valley. Crossrail got a long way forward in the late 1980s, but was dropped in the early-'90s recession. The City Corporation is trying to start it up again using private finance, and has raised £200 million for land acquisition. The City reckons that Crossrail could pay a useful rate of return to investors. This spring they were hopeful of starting the legal procedures as soon as the GLA is in place, with a target opening date of 2006.

London Underground's list of new projects is currently headed by a northward extension of the **East London Line**, which would provide stations at Dalston and Hoxton – see the Hackney chapter. This is inching its way along the planning process, but was slowed up in 1999 and into 2000 by the uncertainty about the new London authority. On hold for elections, like so much else.

The southern extension of the East London was sprung on a sceptical South-East London last year in a smart brochure. However, as weary Peckhamites and Dulwichians know, similar plans have come (and gone) before. Some comfort came this March with the application for legal powers to build the necessary rail links. These will tie the East London Line into existing Railtrack lines and open up three new tube routes. One will run S from New Cross Gate to West Croydon (via Brockley, Honor Oak Park, Forest Hill, Sydenham, Penge West, Anerley, Norwood Junction). The second will branch off S of Surrey Quays and extend to Wimbledon (via a new station at Surrey Canal Road, Peckham Queens Rd, Peckham Rye, East Dulwich, North Dulwich, Tulse Hill, Streatham and Haydons Rd). The third line would reach Clapham Junction via Loughborough Junction, Brixton, Clapham High St and Wandsworth Rd.

London Underground say they want to develop all three – but they may not be the eventual operators. As Railtrack lines will be used for both N and S extensions, it's possible that a train operating company may get to develop and run the line. Decisions (and cash) rest with the new Mayor. An opening date of 2005 seems possible.

The **DLR**, flushed with the success of its Lewisham extension (on time and on budget, in contrast to the Jubilee Line, DLR points out) now plans a branch to the City Airport. The legal side of this is going through this spring as we go to press, and trains should be running by 2003. Next, DLR are planning a line along to North Woolwich. They might even tunnel under the river to Woolwich itself.

The new strategic rail authority is also trying to stitch together new London services. The first idea is Crosslink (as opposed to Crossrail) which will mean trains running from Hampshire, via Feltham (with its bus link to Heathrow), round the North London Line (with three tube interchanges) to Stratford (links with the DLR and Jubilee Line) and on to East Anglia. It will be run by Anglia Railways.

Buying and selling in London

The process of buying or selling has become as much of a discussion-point as the price paid for a home or the cost of the mortgage. Everyone – buyers, sellers, estate agents, even solicitors – has long agreed that the process is cumbersome and bursting with opportunities for it all to go wrong. What's different this year is that the government says it is going to sort it all out.

Pause here for cynical reflection that previous governments have made the same promise, only to fall foul of vested interests and the sheer complexity of the subject. This one, however, is testing a new system and proposes a new law. Vendors in Bristol have had the chance since October 1999 to sell their homes with the government's new-fangled Sellers' Pack. The trial involves 250 deals, and a dozen estate agents, a clutch of solicitors, two mortgage lenders and sundry surveyors have been roped in.

This year we can also report real progress on bringing information technology into home-buying. Suddenly, there's the prospect of paperless, on-line transactions, with everything from the mortgage to the searches done electronically.

Good news, too (though not enough of it) for those struggling to get onto the housing ladder: we look at the work of housing associations, fast taking up the reins from councils and providing a variety of ways not only to rent, but to buy, affordably.

Below we profile the pilot scheme, and set out the government's plan. But meanwhile – certainly for the currency of this edition of the Guide – we have to live with the old ways, so we offer advice on how to buy and sell under the steam-driven system.

Speeding up the process: enter the Seller's Pack

Buying or selling a home is usually slow and undoubtedly stressful. The present system allows too much time between the (non-binding) verbal agreement, the signing of the contract (still only committing the buyer to 10 per cent of the price) and (if you get there) completion. Plenty of room for sellers to accept a higher, later offer (gazumping), or for buyers in a slow market to try to force the price down for some trumped-up reason at the eleventh hour, hoping that the seller will be too committed to the move to stand firm (gazundering). Or for plain changes of heart or circumstances.

Labour promised in 1997 to stamp out both sins once in power, proposing that buyers or sellers who backed out of deals without good reason would have to pay the costs incurred by the other side. But the new minister was persuaded that this was just one symptom of a much bigger problem – the whole house-buying process had to be speeded up. Everyone involved wholeheartedly agreed – then promptly laid the blame at the door of one or more of the other participants. Estate agents blamed lenders and solicitors, lenders blamed borrowers and surveyors and so it went on.

The government then consulted with the property industry. A year-long study tracked 800 buyers and sellers though their negotiations. A working party of estate agents, lawyers and representatives of all the other bodies and professions involved in the process (and one human being from the Consumers' Association) came up with a set of proposals. All and sundry were next invited to comment direct to the ministry.

Then in October the government announced a plan which broadly followed the working party's suggestions. A trial run began in Bristol in December and runs until June 2000. The first home sale under the trial was completed this February in four and a half weeks – half the average time under the old system, the minister claimed.

The industry working party (still plus the Consumers' Association person) which thought up most of the ideas is now an advisory group, charged with helping the government see the plans through to legislation. It must be stressed that these proposals have yet to be put to the test of parliamentary debate and the eventual law could be very different from the present draft. The forecast date for it to start is 2003.

What the Pack will contain

The government's big new idea is that the 'seller's information pack' should be available immediately a home goes on the market. This will be a legal requirement: try to sell without it, and you could land in court, with a £5,000 fine in prospect. It will have a standard set of information and paperwork, giving would-be buyers most of what they need – deeds, any planning permissions, building regulations approvals and listed building consents, local authority searches, draft contract – to decide if they want to proceed, and get on with the purchase if they do. So far, so sensible.

More controversial (unless you are a surveyor) is the inclusion of a 'home condition report based upon a professional survey of the property'. This will cost sellers money, go out of date if the home fails to sell speedily – and, instead of saving time, will lose it, possibly crucially, by delaying the putting of the home onto the market. This goes, too, for another seller's-pack item, specifically for leasehold homes: service charge and management accounts, insurance details, and reams of legal bumpf about the management company. On top of all the rest, the seller will have to get his landlord or management to come up with these, and quickly, when he wants to sell.

To cope with the workload, the home condition report may be prepared by a new breed of expert who will be qualified to a lower level (some say different) from the fully-fledged chartered surveyor. There will be a new accreditation scheme, and people from non-surveying backgrounds will be able to qualify. It is already clear that lenders will take no notice of these home condition reports , but continue to use their own valuers. Then the vendor may well want his own full survey of anything except a fairly basic property. That means three surveyors tramping through the place.

Luckily, one idea has not survived into the draft legislation. This was the wheeze floated by the lawyers that perhaps it would be advisable (at an extra cost, of course, in both money and time) for them not only to provide a draft contract but also a summary 'in plain English' of the pack's contents . . . Strangely, there doesn't seem to be anything in the government's draft proposals on how we are to convince solicitors – frequently the worst culprits – to speed up *their* act.

So now we have lawyers (draft contract), surveyors, lenders (for the deeds), local authorities (searches and permissions) and then perhaps landlords (lease, service charge accounts, etc etc) who could all be required to do their stuff (and collect their fees). The pack will be prepared (says the government) by an estate agent and solicitor or licensed conveyancer at a cost estimated – conservatively, we feel – at £500. The industry is hopeful that this cost will be 'absorbed' in overall selling fees.

This all seems to take little account of the cyclical nature of the selling market: by the time you've filled your 'pack' – even if you don't pause for a furious row with the surveyor over his doleful findings – it will be quietening down for the summer hols.

True, there are exhortations from the government to various laggards and slow-coaches to try harder. Lenders are 'called upon' to make faster mortgage offers; local councils are likewise nagged to speed up searches, buyers 'encouraged' to get their finances sorted out before making an offer. But the actual work and expense falls to the would-be seller.

Should this come to pass, it will certainly mean that the decision to sell your home would have to be a serious one, not something sidled into on the 'let's put it on the market to see what happens' principle. It will cost you money, time and trouble. First conclusion: quite a lot of homes will simply not come to the market after all.

What the working party seems to have forgotten is that many deals are chivvied, jollied, worried along by estate agents. The vendor is a little half-hearted (and very often one half of a couple will be more enthusiastic than the other). A generous offer is extracted from a rather carried-away buyer, who has not been forced up against too much reality in the form of surveys, deeds and service charge accounts. The offer is accepted – and then the vendor is forced to rush about to get the paperwork together, something no amount of persuasion would have got him started on otherwise.

Some of this will indeed help speed things up and can easily be adopted by any keen seller (see Selling, below). But it has one other great flaw. All the onus seems to be on the seller, not the buyer. For every gazump-accepting seller, there is also a gazundering buyer. While the pack would undoubtedly help to bring him (or her) more swiftly up to the mark, there is no financial compulsion to prevent him stalling, keeping the seller (or several sellers, unbeknown to each other) dangling while he sees who he can tie down to the best deal. He, meanwhile, does not even have the cost of a survey to lose.

But why not a sum lodged by both sides at offer, forfeitable should the deal fall through, to cover the frustrated party for wasted legal and surveying fees? The government seem to have lost sight of this idea. The prospect of giving up, say, £1,000 would at least halt frivolous or cynical time-wasters.

Technology

That great panacea, the Internet, may do the government's job for it in speeding up deals. The Land Registry is now computerized and its response speed is not an issue. On-line conveyancing is now technically possible and the Land Registry is working with local authorities on the systems to provide it (the NLIS or National Land Information System Channel Implementation Project, would you believe). This should give a 'one-stop shop' for 'spacially-related data sets' –i.e., searches and checks on title. The system will include the National Land and Property Gazetteer, a marriage of computer mapping and property details, which is being compiled now, storing detailed maps of plots of land and the lines of garden fences, plus planning permission details and other search information for not just the property in question but for its neighbours. This has been trialed in Bristol, where it delivered dramatic savings in time, providing access to standard search material which takes about two weeks to collect by current methods.

Now you can know what your vendor paid

The energetic Land Registry has set the cat among the pigeons by restoring to its records – from April 1 2000 – the actual price paid for property deals. So if your neighbour sells, vulgar curiosity can be satisfied for a £4 fee. More to the point, if you are buying, any deal completed after April 1 will be open to inspection. You do this by downloading Form 109 from the Land Registry's web-site, or getting one from its offices.

Buying and selling on-line

Property buying and the Internet seem made for each other: lots of information needs to be gathered, comparisons made, terms compared. That goes for everything from searching for a property to finding a mortgage and booking the removal van. You can even find a virtual solicitor to sue the on-line surveyor who missed the (actual) subsidence. The speed of change of this whole area makes any survey of it here somewhat redundant. It's clear, though, that taken with (or overtaking) the government's plans, the Internet could radically change the way we go about property transactions.

Estate agents

Everyone knows that anyone can currently set up stall as an estate agent: there are no mandatory qualifications. There are three professional bodies and most good agents belong to one: the Royal Institution of Chartered Surveyors (RICS), the Incorporated Society of Valuers and Auctioneers (ISVA) and the National Association of Estate Agents (NAEA) – all useful sources of information. Members will have undergone courses and passed professional exams (the NAEA's members are not necessarily qualified; with the other two it's a condition). The bodies also guarantee deposits held by their members and can be approached if you have a dispute with a member agent. (See *Selling*, below, for the business of choosing and instructing an agent.)

If you have a problem with an agent, there is an ombudsman scheme. The trouble is that membership is voluntary and less than 3,000 of the 12,000 estate agents belong. The largest fine it has ever imposed is £3,000. The ombudsman can, though, award dissatisfied customers up to £50,000 compensation. Members are expected to subscribe to a code of practice, and must ensure all published material is accurate, that they do not discriminate against any prospective buyer or property, and keep buyers informed of any further offers on the property. Ask if the firm you instruct is a member.

The Estate Agents Act 1979 was tightened up in 1991 to clamp down on a number of nefarious practices, including failure to pass on all offers and omitting to tell sellers about potential conflicts of interest. The Director-General of Fair Trading has the power to ban agencies from practising, or to remove consumer credit licenses. Last autumn he warned agents that if they continued with two sins – trying to link mortgage sales to viewings (or even receiving details), and insisting on vendors signing restrictive agreements – they could and would be banned.

The Property Misdescriptions Act, implemented in 1993, outlaws the florid exaggeration which passed for marketing in the 1980s. Fear of being caught out under this Act may make estate agents' particulars duller reading, but at least they should be more accurate. So far 100 have been prosecuted. One problem, highlighted by reputable agencies is that since it is companies, not individuals, that are prosecuted, the usual result is that the employee concerned is sacked – only to resurface in another firm. Perhaps one day we will see more formal licensing requirements for entry into a profession that can, to say the least, have profound effects on the health, wealth and sanity of its clients, and equally some system for its practitioners to be 'struck off'.

The Misdescriptions Act is, by the way, supposed to cover developers' details too, though few seem to realize this: a big builder was fined in 1998 for omitting the trees between his flats and the river on billboards and in brochures. Note that, while the Act does not directly cover home-owners, they are bound to answer all enquiries truthfully – and not just on the concrete facts. One couple landed up being sued for omitting to inform their buyers about the state of open warfare with the neighbours.

Freehold and leasehold

Londoners have got used to the idea, which seems extraordinary to foreigners, that you can buy slices of houses for a chunk of years. Leasehold – which is what this is – is still the norm for flats. (In large measure this goes right back to the basic assumption, built deep into the nation's psyche, that property ownership equates to possessing a physical piece of land. When flats arrived, the Brits couldn't conceive of owning property suspended in mid-air.)

In many parts of London the houses are leasehold too, which is what really surprises out-of-town buyers. In strict legal terms, you pay what can easily be a freehold price for a house but you don't own what you buy. You're just a tenant who pays the landlord a large one-off premium to live in his property for as long as the lease lasts, plus a small (usually) annual ground rent for the land it stands on.

Behind this anomaly is another one: the surviving ownership of many areas of London by ancient estates. These are relics of the days when the fields around London were private property. When they were built on, the landlords kept the ownership of the land, granting long leases to developers who built and sold the houses – again on leases. This continuous ownership has by and large been beneficial, safeguarding the character and appearance of areas such as Belgravia. Some of these estates belong to aristocratic families, some to charities, some to schools, some to the Church of England. The leading landlord, in size as well as status, is the Crown.

The development of the fields around London began in earnest in the late 17th century and continued until the 19th. Landlords granted leases to developers in return for an annual ground rent. The developers laid out the streets and built the houses, and then sold slightly shorter leases on the houses to the public at slightly higher ground rents. If a building lease was for 100 years, for instance, and the houses took a year to build, they'd be sold on 99-year leases. And if the ground rent the developer paid to the landlord worked out at £5 a building plot, the developer would ask a ground rent of say £15 from the house-buyers to provide himself with an income as well as capital. Finally when the 99-year leases ran out, the houses reverted to the freehold landlord, who could sell a new lease to a developer or new leases to the public.

Only now is this basic leasehold/freehold pattern being seriously challenged by recent changes in legislation, giving leaseholders in flats, as well as houses, the right to buy the freehold of their block jointly – and new rules later this year should make this even easier (see below). The estates of many of the vast landlords are changing. The word 'freehold' is now to be found on sale details in Belgravia, for instance.

Leases can be for any length of time, and obviously the shorter they are, the lower the price. There are two exceptions to this. First, really short leases in good areas can be viewed as so many years' rent – paid, but therefore also fixed, in advance. This makes good sense to companies (who in any case don't have to worry about the difficulties of getting a mortgage for a short lease). Second, buying a short lease makes even more sense if you'll eventually qualify under the recent laws to buy the freehold from the landlord, or – a cheaper option – to extend your lease. Some great estates, including the Grosvenor and the Cadogan, have now started issuing leases of up to 99 years – in some cases up to 125. Most landlords sell new, or newly modernized, properties on 99-year leases, but the purchasers can sell the leases whenever they want to move elsewhere. Furthermore, as with freehold they can usually sell for a good profit, because although the lease will be several years shorter, the chances are that property values will have risen during those years. This explains why a long leasehold can be more or less as expensive as an equivalent freehold property.

If you are a leaseholder, your landlord will not necessarily be the freeholder. When a freeholder originally granted a lease to a developer, the lease the developer sold to the public was a sub-lease, making him the sub-leaseholders' landlord. But today the chain of leaseholds can be even longer. In some cases freeholders sold long head-leases to companies that specialized in getting vacant possession, and as houses fell empty, these companies sold sub-leases to development companies which converted them into flats. Once the flats were finished, they were sold to owner-occupiers on sub-sub-leases . . . But although being a sub-sub-leaseholder sounds horrendously complicated, all it really means in practice is that the ground rent will have been bumped up a bit at every stage.

There are rare cases when a freehold does exist 'up in the air'. An example of what is known as a 'flying freehold' might be a large house, long ago split into two – not vertically, but in such a way that a bedroom in one half extends over a downstairs room in the other. This partial flying freehold may work perfectly well in practice, but is legally murky. Take advice before buying.

A new Leasehold Reform Bill is promised for this session of Parliament, simplifying rules whereby flat-owners can collectively buy a block's freehold; giving all leaseholders the right to join in running blocks; strengthening leaseholders' rights to manage blocks; relaxing the qualifications needed to get a new, longer, lease; giving house leaseholders right of first refusal if the freehold is for sale; adding to the rights of those house leaseholders who extended leases under the 1967 Act.

Leasehold is the most complex subject in the London property world and very few people claim to fully understand all aspects. Take well-qualified advice before buying a leasehold property, and before attempting to extend the lease or buy the freehold.

Service charges, low and high

To ensure a building divided into flats is well-maintained, each leaseholder, as a condition of his lease, has to pay a bi-annual or annual service charge. This generally covers their share of any outgoings on structural repairs: having the exterior painted; heating (if the central heating is communal); paying for the cleaning and lighting of common areas such as the hall and stairs; and seeing that the building is fully insured. The service charge is usually made by a managing agent who arranges for work to be done when needed, and includes his fee – usually 10–15 per cent of the money spent.

Buying a flat over-stretches many people financially, so they're often tempted to choose one where the service charge is low; but unless the flat was recently converted, it's probably low because maintenance has been neglected. As a result, they get hit with an astronomical service charge once the neglect becomes too serious to ignore. Sudden demands for £40,000 apiece to fund new lifts and roof are apt to come as a shock . . . Note, too, that such neglect of capital expenditure may by no means be apparent in the general appearance of the building. It is essential to check, before buying, that your regular payments contribute to an adequate sinking fund to budget for major expenses.

Abuse by landlords, with problems of poor management, shoddy repairs and high service charges in flats forced changes in the law recently. These are still bedding down, and only last year did the first case get decided (the landlord lost).

The unscrupulous landlord uses a number of methods, usually beginning by issuing unsuspecting leaseholders with huge service-charge bills. Any repairs actually done are shoddy and carried out by cowboy builders – often working for companies linked to the landlord. Protests from leaseholders are countered with threats that they would forfeit their leases and lose their homes unless they paid. Existing laws including the Landlord and Tenant Acts of 1985 and 1987 (which in theory were meant to give leaseholders some protection against such abuses) were so poorly drafted that landlords flouted them with impunity, knowing that leaseholders would have to take them to court to stop them.

The latest attempt to curb these practices was the 1996 Housing Act. Leaseholders protesting about poor management and high service charges were given the right to take landlords and their agents to Leasehold Valuation Tribunals (LVTs) rather than to county courts. Taking a case to an LVT will cost leaseholders a maximum of £500 per block, and neither side will be forced to pay the costs of the other, thus removing the main obstacle for leaseholders trying to exercise their legal rights.

Leasehold Valuation Tribunals are the key to a number of important safeguards for leaseholders. Your landlord can no longer serve you with a notice forfeiting your lease because you refuse to pay high service charges, unless the charges have been accepted as 'reasonable' by an LVT. You can apply to the LVT for a new manager for your block if whoever is managing it (the landlord or his agent) is demonstrably incompetent, unscrupulous or both, and there's nothing to stop you and your neighbours forming yourselves into a company and applying to manage the block yourselves. But such an arrangement won't rid you of your landlord, who will still own the block unless you go the whole way and buy the freehold (see below).

Finally, the government is looking once more at a new form of tenure for flats – Commonhold – which enables individual owners in a block to own and manage the whole building collectively from the outset – as opposed to having to oust the developer as ground landlord. The Lord Chancellor's Department is working on this.

Extending the lease, buying the freehold

As things currently stand, if you *do* qualify to buy your freehold and want to do so, there's nothing your landlord can do to stop you (although he can make things difficult). Under the 1993 Act, flat-owners have the right to join with their neighbours and buy the freehold of their blocks even if the landlord doesn't want to sell. Owners of leasehold houses that met certain conditions won the right to buy in 1967. Buying qualifications for flats will be altered if the new Bill becomes law.

If you don't qualify you also have the right to extend your lease by up to 90 years, an important right because the shorter your lease gets, the less valuable your property and the trickier it is for any potential buyer to get a mortgage. Unlike buying the freehold, flat-owners can apply individually for a lease extension. Lease, the advisory service, offers free literature and advice on buying freeholds and extending leases. Leaflets are also available from the Department of the Environment (DETR).

The big landlords have reluctantly accepted changes in legislation and started selling off freeholds to qualifying residents – although they admit they don't go out of their way to encourage it. And some residents who have bought their freeholds on great estates have been outraged to discover that the erstwhile freeholder can still compel them to comply with estate management schemes set up to protect the appearance of some of the grandest neighbourhoods of London including Belgravia, Mayfair and parts of Kensington. The great estates argue that they have a duty to make sure people don't paint their houses purple or replace Georgian iron railings with chain fencing.

The big landlords are found in Central London, and in one or two suburbs:

Crown Estate: Regent's Park, plus homes in Pimlico, Kensington and Victoria Park, Hackney.
Duchy of Cornwall: now only directly controls around 50 homes in the Kennington lands that this royal estate has held since the Black Prince's days. The rest have been turned over to housing associations.
Church of England: Hyde Park Estate (see Bayswater), a scattering of houses and flats in Kensington, Chelsea, Belsize Park; three properties in Maida Vale (they used to own it all).
Grosvenor Estate: Belgravia and much of the northern half of Mayfair.
Cadogan Estate: 90 acres including a large slice of Chelsea around Sloane St.
Portman Estate: 110 acres north of Oxford St and east of Edgware Rd.
Howard de Walden: the 'medical district' around Harley St.
Duke of Bedford: 20 acres of Bloomsbury.
Wellcome Trust: now owns the former Henry Smith's Charity estate in South Kensington
Tonbridge School, Bedford School and **Rugby School** all own small pockets of WC1.
Eton College: 60 acres around Swiss Cottage.
Dulwich College: most of Dulwich.
Eyre Estate: Primrose Hill, Chalk Farm.

Buying

Buying your first home may seem an overwhelming step; in fact, once you have scraped up enough cash for a deposit and enough evidence of reliability to persuade a building society or equivalent to lend you three or three and a half times your salary, it will likely prove the most straightforward property deal you will ever make. You will find a wealth of advice, in print and in person, on this subject. Everyone smiles kindly on you and offers anything from free leaflets to better mortgage terms, special rates and money-off deals.

Estate agents in particular will be assiduous in their care, once you have convinced them that you have the money and the definite intention of buying. They'll escort you to view, ring afterwards to enquire politely as to your reactions, helpfully suggest alternatives. This is only partly tender solicitude on your behalf: you have, as a first-time buyer, one inestimable advantage: you are not encumbered with a home to sell before you can buy their client's. It is worth remembering this advantage that you have: it can clinch you a good deal if the seller is in a hurry to move. Remember too when looking for the first time that an estate agent is just that – an agent. Not yours, but the seller's (or vendor's, as they are known). It is the agent's job to present the goods in the best light. He is bound not to lie; he is not bound to point out that the tube line passes underneath, shakes the foundations and rattles the windows. Nevertheless a good agent with a reputation to maintain is concerned to have satisfied customers on both sides. His clients will then often come from people to whom he has sold.

General pointers: London is luckily a very well-mapped city. Many people – and not just first-time buyers – will need to keep an open mind about their choice of areas. If you are free to live anywhere within reasonable lines of communication, it's worth bearing in mind that some areas have been altering well ahead of their reputation; the road you remember as the scruffy place where a friend had a bedsit may have changed out of all recognition. But journeying to far-flung corners can be frustrating if you find the place backs onto the rail line that carries the Channel Tunnel trains. A good look at a decent map alongside this book can fill in the gaps in the property details. (Note that alongside our sketch maps are cross-references to the relevant page of the standard *A–Z London Street Atlas* (Geographers' A–Z Map Co) map book. Look too at the section on transport changes in the *The Property Market in 2000* chapter.)

That being said, one man's drawback is another soul's way in to an area above his means. If you are hell-bent on a certain area, there are likely to be cheaper corners; the essential thing to remember, though, is that anything inexpensive for an unalterable reason – views over graveyards, for instance, seem to be a minus-point – will likely not just stay relatively cheaper but also take longer to sell. *Always look at a home with a view to having, one day, to sell it to somebody else – fast.* For inside information on whether an area is likely to be on the way up – apart from that in this book – a good clue can be had from watching for any interest being shown by developers, or the sudden appearance of 'for sale' boards belonging to the classier Central London estate agents. At the first signs, move quickly – it's almost too late.

The more estate agents' details (which are at least free) and newspaper ads you can wade through, the better idea you will get of what is going on in the market in a given area at a given time. The one golden rule when looking at a procession of properties is always to make brief notes at the time or immediately on leaving; three flats further on and you won't be able to recall which was the one that smelt damp; which overlooked a noisy playground. If you seriously consider a place is a strong contender, don't be afraid to ask if you can wander round again on your own. When you think you've found the one, visit the locality at different times of day. Many people who only have weekends for home-hunting can find on moving in that the street is a solid traffic-jam on weekdays.

The anatomy of a purchase – until the government changes the rules – goes:

1. Budgeting for the move

Talk to a building society, bank or other lender as soon as you start looking, if not before. They will advise on how much you are likely to be able to borrow. (For further details, see the *Mortgages* chapter.) When looking, remember that you will need money for a deposit. You may be able to borrow up to 95 per cent of the property valuation over 25 years, but the more money you can put down as a deposit the better. For one thing, lenders will offer you better rates with a larger deposit. For another, you run a greater risk of being trapped in negative equity (your mortgage is higher than the value of your property) if you borrow a large proportion of the property's value, and the market then slumps. For a third, you might, with some lenders, still be forced to take out expensive insurance (to cover your lender, not you!) if you borrow over 90 per cent (sometimes as low as 75 per cent) of the value. Then, remember that all the attendant fees – searches, stamp duty, valuation, survey, solicitor – and the cost of moving will absorb another 2.5 per cent or more of the value. Stamp duty, in particular, has gone up a lot recently.

Price and value are not the same thing, as you may well discover when your mortgage-lender gets a valuer round. Try to get the lender to use the surveyor who you instruct for your own survey, especially if the house is not typical of the area. A surveyor not familiar with the area needs comparables to value the property. In a quiet market, with few if any recent sales, no such figures will exist, so the value will be lowered to be on the safe side. Some valuers are under pressure from lenders to do six surveys a day. How much can they discover in that amount of time?

2. Making an offer, and what happens next

Make an offer through the agency – who, by the way, must not insist you use their mortgage arm. If it's accepted, return to your lender with the details of the property and notify your solicitor who will start the searches and conveyancing process (see below). Remind yourself that although your offer has been accepted, neither side is legally committed. Even if a 'Sold' sign goes up, it will say, in small letters, *'subject to contract'*.

From that point, there are two definite stages to acquiring the property: the first, up to exchanging contracts and putting down a deposit and the second, up to completion and paying the balance of the price. Until you've exchanged contracts neither side is bound to the deal and there's nothing to stop your seller accepting a higher offer.

The longer this period, the more danger of such 'gazumping' – hence the government's attempt to short-cut it (see above). In the run-up to exchange of contracts, your solicitor and the seller's solicitor will be juggling a number of papers between them:

(a) **Title deeds:** The seller's solicitors will retrieve the title deeds to the house and the Land Registry certificate (nearly all London homes are registered) to confirm that the seller actually owns the property and has good title – ie, is free to sell it.

(b) **Drawing up the contract:** they will then draw up a contract containing information from the deeds and send it to your solicitor. At the same time, yours sends a list of pre-contract enquiries to the seller to get basic information about the property. This should answer such questions as who owns and is responsible for boundary fencing, whether the property is properly insured, who the managing agent or freeholder is (if the property is leasehold: see above) and whether service-charge bills are disputed or up-to-date. You should also find out if boilers have been serviced and get confirmation that the property is connected to all utilities (gas, electricity, water and telephone).

(c) **Local authority search:** Your solicitor will also arrange for a local search, which should tell you if there's a road planned at the back of your garden or a compulsory purchase order on the property. Search questions are set out on a standard printed form, but the answers will only relate to the area directly adjacent to your property so a road planned nearby, but not directly next to, you won't show up even though it could make your road a traffic nightmare. Check yourself with the town hall planning dept.

(d) **Surveys:** In the meantime, you're arranging your mortgage and getting a survey done. Lenders will insist on a valuation to make sure the property's worth the amount you want to borrow but this is to protect them, not you. Particularly if the house is old, you should arrange your own independent structural survey. This is expensive, but should highlight any major problems or areas of concern that need dealing with. The results may make you reconsider the deal as it stands: you might not have enough money left to renew the roof immediately (or even if you have, the cost of doing so, when added to the purchase price, may be too far above the house's value). You have not exchanged contracts; you are free to try to negotiate a lower price, or back out of buying altogether. (Note: surveys are hedged about with disclaimers and err on the pessimistic side, since you can sue if some glaring fault is missed; discuss the implications with someone experienced in reading them if this is your first.)

Surveyors who are members of the Royal Institution of Chartered Surveyors (RICS) have to accept a compulsory arbitration scheme to handle complaints from customers. For claims under £3,000 each side pays a £200 registration fee. If the claim is successful, the surveyor has to pay the registration fee. If the claim fails, the complainant will forfeit his/her fee but won't have to pay the surveyor's fee. The RICS will pay the costs of the actual arbitration. For claims between £3,000 and £50,000 each side pays a £200 registration fee with the surveyor paying the fee if the claim is successful. If the surveyor wins, the customer pays his fee but incurs no further cost.

3. Exchanging contracts

When all this is done, you exchange contracts and put down a 10 per cent deposit. If you back out now, you lose your money. You have bought a home; you must insure it immediately – even though you have not moved in, it is now your responsibility.

4. Completion

A month or so later (though it can be done in days if both sides are willing and able to move home fast) completion takes place, the balance of the purchase price is handed over and the deal is done. You are free to move in.

Buying a newly-built home

The basic process is the same whether the house is Georgian or brand new. The main difference is that with a new home you will probably be dealing with the developer, via a sales office on site, rather than a private individual.

New homes in London are nearly always either conversions – of everything from riverside warehouses, Victorian schools, factories, old depositories to long-despised 1960s office blocks – or on re-used land. Such sites tend to be former hospitals, water-works, power stations, sewage farms . . . . This raises the question of what level of decontamination has been done to the land. The new Environment Act has a lot to say about this: quiz the builder and the local authority.

Remember that fringe areas could be the first to suffer if there's a downturn. Be cautious about schemes aimed at investors. If you plan to live in such a block yourself, neighbouring flats may stand empty while investors try to let them. It can be hard to sell, too, in any new homes scheme, until all the units have been sold by the developer – he can offer inducements and deals that a private seller can't match.

Whatever you buy there are certain steps you should take to check out the development and its builder. Check out the terms of any special mortgage deal or discount carefully: any 'cheap' finance is almost certainly reflected in the price – there's no such thing as a free lunch.

For all new developments, a chat with existing dwellers as to the standards of after-care service can be informative. And ask the selling agents for names of schemes the developer has done before. Go and have a look to see how they are faring. Whoever you are buying from, check the specifications in the brochure. Do not assume you will get the standard of fittings in a show flat unless they are specifically listed. Do not assume room sizes are accurate: they have been known to be a good bit smaller than the show flat.

In any newly built home, there are certain simple checks like, for example, jumping up and down in the centre of the floor. See if the pictures fall off the show-flat walls. Send your partner to the next room and upstairs and see how loudly you hear footsteps or conversation. New homes should carry a 10-year warranty from the National House Building Council (NHBC). But this isn't a guarantee, regardless of what the developer might tell you. It's an insurance policy, mainly intended to cover the builder. The cover is fairly basic and may not include what you might think are pretty glaring defects. The NHBC was forced to revise its warranty in 1997 to clarify its cover and is also extending it to conversions for the first time.

Ask searching questions about the future of the development. The model and plans may show a lovely new leisure complex, but when will it be built, and is there anything in your contract with the developer to say it must be? What is going up next door? Check, and don't believe bland assurances from the (often part-time) staff in the sales office. Most town halls have helpful planning enquiry offices these days. They will tell you what else is planned for the neighbourhood and let you see local development plans. This will avoid buying under the impression that the land across the road is going to be (as the sales lady put it) 'local shops' when it has outline permission for a 50,000-sq ft superstore and a 'leisure complex'. Yes, it happened.

Onto the housing ladder: shared ownership, housing associations

Despite rises in interest rates over the winter of 1999–2000, mortgage rates are still relatively low. Fixed-rate deals and discounts for the first two to five years help ease the pain further, although coming to the end of the fixed-rate term can be a shock. Beware, too, of 'lock-in' clauses: see *Mortgages* chapter. But if you are struggling to put your first foot on the ladder, there are some schemes to help you.

The best news comes from housing associations, which are working to make housing affordable for Londoners – whether they want to rent, buy or even part-buy, part-rent a home. not only are they running property, they are building it too – often to a higher standard and more attractively than private developers manage. In many places they are taking over the erstwhile role of local councils; but while some schemes are restricted to council or housing association tenants, by no means all are. They are keen to help local people stay local, but you do not necessarily have to be a nurse or dustman. Some will even help you to buy on the open market.

• **Shared ownership** Many people want to own their own home, yet cannot afford open-market prices. This may be because they are young, in poorly-paid jobs, or both. Many Londoners working in areas like health, transport, the councils and the civil service fall into this group. The expansion – from a small base – of shared ownership is aimed at them.

You buy a share in a home, with the other share held by a RSL (Registered Social Landlord – a housing association, usually). You pay this shareholder rent on the portion of the home it owns. You can buy extra shares when you can afford it at the price set by the District Valuer. Many lenders will give you a mortgage, and you repay this in monthly installments in the normal way. When you come to sell, the profit on the share you own is yours. It is best to take at least a 50 per cent stake if you can; otherwise the rent, and the small proportion of the profit gained on resale, can make it uneconomic.

This year, over 700 homes are being built or converted for shared ownership, by 22 RSLs in 23 London boroughs. The homes are in schemes ranging from three units to 65, but the typical development is 12–20 homes. The RSLs usually work in specific localities, though some of the larger ones operate in several boroughs. Notting Hill Home Ownership, for example, has seven schemes for 2000/2001, across seven boroughs, totalling 138 homes. Peabody Trust, which works right across London, has one 39-home scheme in the programme for this year, and several more in the pipeline.

Peabody, like many RSLs, mixes tenures in its modern developments. This means that shared-ownership homes stand next to those for outright sale, for rent at market levels and for subsidised rent. The Peabody scheme in Stoke Newington, opened in December, mixes 24 shared-ownership homes with 20 for open-market sale which subsidize the development.

Northcote Housing Association, part of the Ealing Family Housing Association, sums it up by describing shared ownership as 'helping those who are committed to live and budget on their own incomes and who deserve access to good-quality homes which they can afford.'

The Homebuy scheme, under which you buy 75 per cent of the home and get a loan to cover the rest from the RSL, means higher outgoings (a bigger mortgage) but you own more of the property from the start. This is restricted to council tenants and those on a housing waiting list. There is even a DIY shared ownership scheme designed for people who want to buy on the open market, yet need help to finance the home: the RSL takes a stake in the normal shared-ownership way. There are also schemes whereby if you are a council tenant you can get grants to help you buy on the open market.

To find out about any of these options, the first stop is the local council. Many RSLs have web-sites, or a good starting point is Housingnet, which lists them by area.

• **Cost rent schemes**   These are built and run by RSLs and just what the name says: rents are more than the social-housing norm, yet less than the private-market level. An example is the Hackney Now scheme, where seven sites have been handed over by the council to an RSL which has built flats and is letting them to 'key workers' – nurses, for example. The rent can be lower than open-market levels as the sites come free and Government regeneration money helped fund building costs.

Selling

There is always limitless advice available for the guidance of first-time buyers, from free leaflets from the building society to whole books on the subject. Strangely, there is almost nothing to help the seller – first-time or otherwise. This is surprising: selling a home is an activity even more likely to be carried out in conditions of stress, since in most cases you will also be trying to buy your next one, co-ordinate it with the sale, and arrange for the move. Yet, even before the promised reforms, there is much that can be done in order to get off to a good, fast start – and speed is generally all-important to one party or the other in a London property deal.

For example, a problem peculiar to London is the length of time it takes to get the local authority searches carried out. Councils vary widely in the time they take to complete this bit of form-filling: the City of London, with only a few residents, has been known to reply in one day. Others drag their feet. With such councils, it's best if possible to do the searches in person: enquire at the town hall. You will find average search times listed in this book in each area's summary at the end of the chapter – the official target date is 10 working days, which is what the councils tend to say they achieve, but this is not always true. These searches, by the way, are a task generally undertaken by the prospective buyer, but there's no reason why the seller shouldn't get a search carried out: a small extra expense that can save weeks. The results are valid for three months.

Your solicitor can of course arrange this for you – which is a second point. Alert your solicitor to the fact that a move is impending: people often forget to do this, assuming that there will be time enough when a buyer is in view. That is a bad time at which to discover that your solicitor is on holiday or even – as has been known – has died, retired or sold his firm since you needed him last. Once notified, he can also draw up a draft contract in readiness, and can retrieve the deeds to your property from bank, building society or other mortgagor (you by this time have probably forgotten that whoever lent you the money holds the deeds – and that they, too, can take their time about getting them out of the system).

The role of solicitors, whose busy offices (to put the kindest light on it) can hold things up to the point of jeopardizing the sale, is, like everything else, under review: see the start of this chapter. Whether you use a solicitor or a licensed conveyancer, keep ringing to ensure they're getting on with things.

A top London estate agent added the interesting rider that not only can such preparation hasten the conclusion of a sale, it helps the agent to test the true worth of the would-be buyer. If the seller's side isn't ready to proceed, it can be weeks before you discover that the apparently eager buyer's own home isn't, after all, quite sold, or that they haven't, after all, got access to quite enough money.

A good agent will point all this out to you, and in London there is no shortage of agents to choose from. Like the little girl in the old rhyme, when they are good they are very, very good, and when they are bad . . . .

Choosing an agent

A lot hinges on the seller's ability to pick the right agent and then instruct them properly. You should see at least four. If you don't already have strong ideas on which are the most favoured locally, it can help to go window-shopping, checking for offices in a prominent position, with properties of the calibre of your own, well displayed, and run by welcoming staff. You can go in, describe your own place and ask for details of anything of that type on their books. This serves the dual purpose of finding what the competition is, and how much, and what their reception of your potential buyers is going to be like. You can get confirmation of your own feelings, and further recommendations, by asking people who come into contact with estate agents, such as building societies, banks, builders and solicitors – and local friends and neighbours.

Showing prospective agents your home is a good practice-run for showing potential buyers. Remember that agents are human too: they, like buyers, are seeing many different properties; they, too, can be put off by an untidy, uncleaned shambles smelling of last night's dinner. Light, warmth, flowers and furniture polish (the old-fashioned smelly sort) really can do wonders to underline a welcoming atmosphere. And tidy up – at least – outside: buyers can, and have, been put off before they've even got through the door. Clutter is a real turn-off.

Fixing a price

Having decided to sell and picked an agent, what do you need from them? First, of course, you want to know what price he (or she) suggests. A house is worth what someone is willing to pay: there is no absolute number. The agent needs to take into account not only what appears to be the going rate, but the state of the overall market and your personal circumstances, too. If you must sell by next week, both marketing and price will be different.

When you get your property valued, don't necessarily go for the agent predicting the highest price. They may be desperate to get instructions and inflate the price they say they can get just to impress you. (Their commission is also calculated on the price of the property.) It's no good putting your property on the market at an inflated price only to see it hang heavy for months. Ask the agent how he's arrived at that price and what evidence of other sales of similar properties there is to substantiate his view.

Conversely, there is the very low price that should in certain circumstances raise an eyebrow – perhaps suggested for the large, old, empty property you're selling on behalf of your dear departed aunty? Luckily it is, of course, illegal these days for agents to fail to disclose conflicts of interest – such as the developer who'd like him to look out for large, old, cheap properties . . .

Ask what the agent proposes to do to sell your home. Do they have a regular contract with national or local magazines or newspapers? This can be a benefit: contracts mean cheaper advertising rates and a saving to be passed on to you. It also indicates the level that the agency is working on. Maybe expensive brochures will be appropriate. Some firms have press offices who will send out a release to papers and magazines about interesting homes. Does the firm have its own magazine? Or an Internet site – and if so how often is it updated? Will your home be included – and if so, how quickly and for how long? Will it have a photograph? Look at existing advertisements by the firm. Are the photographs clear? Is the wording precise and proof-read?

Fees come last. Some agents make a point of a lower percentage, but take this on the 'you get what you pay for' principle. A skilled agent's negotiating acumen can easily save you the half of a per cent extra he charges. What *will* vary the rate charged is whether you appoint one firm sole agent or, as you are perfectly entitled to do, instruct several at once. Agencies charge less if they get sole agency, and they work harder, because all the effort they put in will be rewarded if they get a sale. Appoint more than one, and only one will get a fee from the transaction; all of them will know this and it will be reflected in the intensity of their efforts.

Don't listen if an agent says you are legally bound to sign his standard agreement. This is a negotiable contract, not a legal document. If you don't like the terms, haggle or go somewhere else. Buried in the small print may be 'sole selling rights' (as opposed to the more usual sole agency). Beware: this means you pay the agent's commission even if your brother buys your house after the agent has failed to sell it.

You'll find that agents come in all shapes and sizes, from one-partner, one-office, old-established concerns, through brash, keen newcomers to big independent practices and the local offices of large chains. Each has its advantages. Weigh local knowledge against marketing skill, the personal touch against chain-breaking clout. With big firms, ensure that the people you deal with know your area and have not just been transferred from Sidcup. All this said, choosing an agent is a personal business. Whatever the firm, it is only as good as the people in your local branch: choose those who impress you most.

However expert the agent, you know your home best. He should therefore look to you to check draft particulars. They should be set out clearly and logically, and remember that items mentioned in them are generally understood to be included in the price unless otherwise specified. If you are going to be showing people around, he should brief you, because he can provide an objective list of selling-points to mention. If you are not showing buyers round, who is? Can you meet them first, and are they both personable and intelligent (an elusive combination in junior staff in estate agents)? Who should you contact for progress reports – you should expect regular news, but remember that they have others places to sell too: don't ring them every day.

Selling tends to be fraught with excitements, and it's wise to keep cool. But what if you have appointed an agent and nothing seems to result? Give the agent a set number of weeks of sole agency, and if there is no action call him in for a progress report. There may be good reasons for the dearth of buyers. At this point decide whether to give him a longer period of sole agency, appoint a second agent as well, or even drop the first entirely. Good agents are loud in their encouragement of clients who are forthright: if there is a problem, let them hear about it.

Price charts: sales

The charts on the following pages consolidate the data in the Area Profiles in this book, showing broadly what certain kinds of homes cost in each of the areas covered. This gives you a freeze-frame picture across London at the start of the 2000 selling season: a basis for comparison thoughout the year.

The prices given are for typical examples of each type of home. Where a range of figures is shown, this reflects price variations within the area. Thus the range is also an indicator of the scope of the properties in the area: if the figures for, say, a 1-bed

FLATS — SALES		STARTING PRICES FOR 2000				
65–75: range in £1000s		— too few for price average		→ price carries over		
	STUDIO	1 BEDROOM	2 BEDROOM	3 BEDROOM	4 BEDROOM	5 + BEDROOM
Acton	80–100	95–155	110–200+	150–220	225+	—
Balham and Tooting	55–80	90–180	140–270	200–300+	—	—
Barnes, Mortlake and Sheen	90–120	120–190	150–250+	160–500+	—	—
Battersea	90–120	90–200	150–300	210–400	400+	—
Bayswater	95–150	135–225	160–350	220–500	350–850	450+
Bedford Park and Acton Green	90–160	115–250	170–300	210–350	340–400	—
Belgravia	160–300	350–600	450–1.3M	600+	800–2.5M	1.5M+
Bethnal Green	60–80	65–110	85–200	95–200	110+	—
Bloomsbury and King's Cross	90–110	135–200+	200–375	350–500	—	—
Bow	60–125	75–130	85–200	105–210	—	—
Brixton, Herne Hill and Tulse Hill	50–70	65–150	95–200	120–220	—	—
Camberwell	45–75	60–125	100–170	130–250	200+	—
Camden Town and Primrose Hill	80–160	100–210	200–500	350–600	500–1.5M	—
Chelsea	110–185	200–300+	300–500	500–800	700–1M+	1M+
Chiswick	80–110	120–180	170–300	250–300	—	—
City and Fringes	80–115	85–180+	200–400	250–500	300–600	—
Clapham	80–180	90–220	130–300	135–350	170–500	750+
Clerkenwell and Finsbury	90–115	170–230	240–285	325–400	—	—
Cricklewood	60–90	90–150	100–180	160–250	—	—
Crouch End and Stroud Green	60–120	85–135	120–250	135–375	—	—
Crystal Palace	40–50	55–80	75–170	95–180	—	—
Dollis Hill and Neasden	70–75	70–90	100–145	140–150	—	—
Dulwich	65–85	80–150	90–220	125–260	130–260	150+
Ealing	70–100	90–180	120–250	150–350	300+	—
Finchley	50–70	75–120	100–180	100–200	400+	—
Forest Hill	40–60	60–100	80–140	120–150	130+	—
Fulham	90–125	115–215+	135–265	250–320	260–300+	—
Golders Green	60–100	90–160	120–300+	145–350	185+	—
Greenwich and Blackheath	65–90	80–180	85–250	135–270+	—	—
Hackney	55–70	75–120	90–170	140–200	150–260	—
Hammersmith	80–100	140–180	150–250+	250–350	300+	—
Hampstead	80–150	150–295	200–550	250–900	300–1M+	500–3.5M
Hampstead Garden Suburb	50–80	100–150	120–350	160–450	240–500	—
Hendon and Mill Hill	50–70	70–110	120–180	150–350	—	—
Highgate	65–140	80–220	110–300	140–400	160–500	400–550
Holland Park	90–165	200–400	250–650	425–1M+	500–1.5M	750–2M+
Islington and Highbury	80–120	100–240	175–350	250+	500+	—
Kennington, Vauxhall and Stockwell	40–90	70–160	100–250	150–290	—	—

flat are 70–90, it is likely to be a fairly homogeneous area; £70–90,000 should give you a choice of such flats here. If 70–160, it is clear that that there are some neighbourhoods that warrant a good premium, or perhaps there is a supply of recently developed, more luxurious flats. In all brackets, you will be likely to find cheaper homes and exceptional ones at the other end of the scale: a plus sign is used where we have not included the prices for a small number of unusual examples which would distort the averages.

HOUSES — SALES   STARTING PRICES FOR 2000

65–75: range in £1000s   — too few for price average   → price carries over

	2 BEDROOM	3 BEDROOM	4 BEDROOM	5 BEDROOM	6–7 BEDROOM	8+ BEDROOM
Acton	85–250	150–300	200–425	250–450	325+	—
Balham and Tooting	120–300	150–350	230–400+	300–500+	600+	→
Barnes, Mortlake and Sheen	210–370	300–400	400–600+	500–1.2M+	900+	→
Battersea	200–300	300–500	350–500	450–1M	600+	—
Bayswater	230–700	400–1M	550–1.2M	650→	—	—
Bedford Park and Acton Green	260–400	290–425	395–850+	650–1M+	650–1.25M+	—
Belgravia	500+	750–1.5M	800–2M	1.5–5M	3–7M+	10M+
Bethnal Green	130–200	140–300	150–400	190+	—	—
Bloomsbury and King's Cross	300–600+	500–800	600–900+	650–1M+	800+	—
Bow	140–280	160–300	180–450	—	—	—
Brixton, Herne Hill and Tulse Hill	200–250	240–280	250–325	300–400	320–450	—
Camberwell	100–200	150–265	185–500+	260–500+	500+	—
Camden Town and Primrose Hill	150–310	210–450	375–1M+	500–2M	—	—
Chelsea	350–1M	550–1.5M	650–1.6M	1.2–4M	1.5–5M	2–6M+
Chiswick	260–330	330–480	350–500+	400–800	600–1.3M	→2.3M
City and Fringes	270–350	350–600	400–650+	—	—	—
Clapham	180–400	250–500	300–550	400–1M	600+	800–1M+
Clerkenwell and Finsbury	400+	500+	500–900+	—	—	—
Cricklewood	140–170	160–300	250–500	300–500	→	—
Crouch End and Stroud Green	180–220	200–360+	320–400+	350–750	—	—
Crystal Palace	110–140	155–200	180–290	250–400	300+	350
Dollis Hill and Neasden	140–155	140–260	250–350	300+	—	—
Dulwich	180–350	200–425	260–1M	300–1.3M+	325–2M+	750+
Ealing	150–260	160–360	250–450	300–650	400–1.5M	550–1.5M+
Finchley	180–220	195–300	270–400	400–900	650+	—
Forest Hill	115–140	130–200	150–300+	220–400	300–500	→450+
Fulham	250–350+	260–450+	350–600+	500–1M+	→800+	—
Golders Green	180–200	180–450	200–550+	350–950+	400–1M+	—
Greenwich and Blackheath	160–320	180–550	230–650	350–1.25M	650–1.5M	→1.75M+
Hackney	100–160	150–250	180–280	250–350	—	—
Hammersmith	265–350+	300–400	350–600	500+	700–1M+	—
Hampstead	250–650	325–800+	500–1M	750–3M	1.5–3.5M	2–10M+
Hampstead Garden Suburb	200–350	250–750	300–1.5M	500–3M	600–14M	1–14M
Hendon and Mill Hill	140–180	150–250	220–500+	350–600+	600–1.5M	1M+
Highgate	200–400	250–500	300–900	350–5M	420–6M	→7M+
Holland Park	500–700	600–1M+	800–2M	1–3M	2.8M→	12M+
Islington and Highbury	250–450	250–600	300–500+	500+	→2M	1M+
Kennington, Vauxhall and Stockwell	150–280	200–400	300–650	400–1M	→500	→700

FLATS — SALES

65–75: range in £1000s   — too few for price average   → price carries over

	STUDIO	1 BEDROOM	2 BEDROOM	3 BEDROOM	4 BEDROOM	5+ BEDROOM
Kensington	100–300	165–500	250–650	400–650+	600–1.5M	800–2M+
Kentish Town and Tufnell Park	80–120	85–200	125–300	200–400	220–400	—
Kilburn, Kensal Green and Queen's Park	80–100	100–200	140–250	190–300	300+	—
Knightsbridge	150–200	250–400	350–700	550–800	650–1.5M	1.2M+
Lewisham and Catford	40–55	65–80	70–120	80–150	110–150	110+
Leyton and Walthamstow	50–60	60–90	65–120	70–130	180–350	—
Maida Vale and Little Venice	80–200	125–300	170–400	220–800	350–950	—
Marylebone and Fitzrovia	100–150	150–300	225–500	300–1M+	500–1M+	800–1M
Mayfair and St James's	120–200	150–500+	275–1M	600–1.5M	800–2.5M+	1.5–3.5M+
Morden, Mitcham and Colliers Wood	50–60	60–80	70–90	80–100	120+	—
Muswell Hill	80–100	90–125	100–250	160–300	—	—
New Cross and Deptford	40–60	55–95	65–140	110–160	—	—
Newham	35–55	50–65	55–85	65–90	—	—
Notting Hill and North Kensington	100–150	130–300	175–500	220–700	250–900	—
Peckham	45–65	65–100	85–150	90–165	125+	—
Pimlico and Westminster	95–200	140–350	180–500	220–750	400–2M+	—
Poplar	55–70	65–80	75–90	85–100	—	—
Putney and Roehampton	80–120	110–190	150–230	170–350	300–500	350–500+
Regent's Park	125–300	175–400+	250–800	375+	500–1.2M	—
Richmond and Kew	100–140	130–250	150–350+	200–500+	—	—
Shepherd's Bush	90–110	130–160	175–220	190–270	230–300	—
Soho and Covent Garden	145+	190–425	185–500	400–650	600–1M	—
The South Bank	59–200	65–310	80–500	90–500+	100–500+	—
South Kensington, Earl's Court and West Brompton	90–180	150–400	200–500	240–750	400–1M+	500–2M+
Southfields and Earlsfield	65–95	100–160	125–220	150–300	—	—
Southgate and Palmers Green	60–80	75–95	100–150	175–275	—	—
St John's Wood	100–140	140–250+	250–450	350+	500+	→
Stepney and Whitechapel	60–115	80–150	90–180	100–200	—	—
Stoke Newington	60–80	75–150	110–220	150–250	180–250+	—
Streatham	40–55	65–85	80–120+	135+	—	—
Tottenham and Finsbury Park	50–90	65–130	75–180	90–220	—	—
Totteridge and Whetstone	65–70	80–115	95–350	130–350+	—	—
Twickenham and Teddington	60–110	90–160	120–250	140–450+	—	—
Wandsworth	80–140	135–180	160–300	175–375	—	—
West Hampstead	65–110	120–200	140–270	175–400	270–400	350–500
West Norwood, Norbury and Gipsy Hill	45–60	55–80	90–120	130–160	—	—
Willesden and Brondesbury Park	80–100	80–140	95–200	120–300	240–500	350+
Wimbledon, Raynes Park and Merton Park	70–110	120–200+	145–400+	200–500+	275–700	—

HOUSES — SALES

65–75: range in £1000s   — too few for price average   → price carries over

	2 BEDROOM	3 BEDROOM	4 BEDROOM	5 BEDROOM	6–7 BEDROOM	8+ BEDROOM
Kensington	400–650	450–1M	750–2M	1M–3M+	1.3M–5M+	4M+
Kentish Town and Tufnell Park	220–400	250–500	300–800	350–1M	400–2M	—
Kilburn, Kensal Green and Queen's Park	200–240	220–450	300–450+	500–700+	600+	→
Knightsbridge	500–800+	750–1.7M	1M+	1.5M+	2M+	—
Lewisham and Catford	80–120	95–170	115–200	170–280	200–300+	—
Leyton and Walthamstow	100–130	110–180	150–300	225+	—	—
Maida Vale and Little Venice	175–300	350–800	450–800	500–1M+	1M+	→
Marylebone and Fitzrovia	350–600	450–850	600–1.2M	800–1M+	1M+	2M+
Mayfair and St James's	600–750	750–1M+	950–2M+	1.3–2M+	2.5–5M	4.5M–12M+
Morden, Mitcham and Colliers Wood	95–115	100–180	175–200	200+	—	—
Muswell Hill	120–160	155–300+	300–500	350–700	700+	—
New Cross and Deptford	80–130	115–250	150–400	250–500	250–500+	—
Newham	70–95	85–140	110–250	180–250+	—	—
Notting Hill and North Kensington	200–400	280–500+	400–1M	600–1.5M+	1.5–3M	3M+
Peckham	125–175	150–260	180–300	200–400	275+	—
Pimlico and Westminster	300–625	400–800	500–950	600–1.5M	700–2M	—
Poplar	100–130	120–150	150–200+	175–250	—	—
Putney and Roehampton	220–300	260–450	350–550+	550–1M	700–1M	1.5M+
Regent's Park	450–750	700–1M	800–2M	1M+	2M+	→20M
Richmond and Kew	210–425	250–590+	300–750+	400–800+	690–1M+	—
Shepherd's Bush	240–280	260–330	350–450	400–600	500–700	—
Soho and Covent Garden	—	→1.4M	→	—	—	—
The South Bank	195–400+	200–500+	300–600+	—	—	—
South Kensington, Earl's Court and West Brompton	300–550	400–750+	500–2M+	600+	900+	1M+
Southfields and Earlsfield	175–240	240–300	300–400	350–500	—	—
Southgate and Palmers Green	150–200	180–350	225–450	325–500	500–600	—
St John's Wood	350–600	500–1M	750–2M	1M+	1.5M+	2.5M+
Stepney and Whitechapel	90–250	100–280	175–300	→	—	—
Stoke Newington	160–230	190–300	250–430	300–500	500–700	—
Streatham	120–160	130–220	150–350	250–600	—	—
Tottenham and Finsbury Park	100–250	130–350	200–375	—	—	—
Totteridge and Whetstone	150–160	130–350+	250–2M	375–2.5M	1–2M+	—
Twickenham and Teddington	150–250	160–350+	200–550+	300–800+	700–1.5M	850+
Wandsworth	300–350	300–500	300–700	420–850+	600–850+	600–950+
West Hampstead	200–350	280–450	350–550	450–700	550–1M	600–1M
West Norwood, Norbury and Gipsy Hill	110–130	130–190	210–300	250–400	280+	300+
Willesden and Brondesbury Park	120–140	125–260	250–350	350+	500+	550+
Wimbledon, Raynes Park and Merton Park	215–350	250–600+	300–800+	400–800+	700–2.5M	→2.5M+

Mortgages
by David Spittles

Mortgages have become synonymous with 'rip-off' Britain. Tens of thousands of borrowers have been duped, misled or pushed into taking out unsuitable loans by lenders who rake in billions of pounds in insurance commission, arrangement fees and redemption penalties on top of the interest they charge.

The good news is that the Government is finally getting to grips with the worst practices and attempting to clean up the Industry.

Meanwhile, lenders are responding with more consumer-friendly products; cut-throat competition is continuing to throw up enticing deals (like 'flexible' mortgages) and the Internet has spawned a new generation of easy-to-arrange on-line loans.

From April this year, lenders who want an official stamp of approval have had to apply new CAT standards (rules on 'Charges, Access and Terms' – see below).

By summer 2001, all the UK's mortgage lenders will be regulated by the Financial Services Authority (FSA), the new 'super watchdog', which will be given a range of powers to punish firms that break the rules. At the moment lenders are regulated by a voluntary code of practice regarded by many as pretty toothless.

The FSA will police mortgage advertising and insist that the information lenders give about their loans is clear, comprehensive and not misleading.

But, controversially, the Government has decided not to set rules to guarantee the quality of advice given to borrowers. In other words, the basic loan information you are given will probably be pretty sound but the quality of the advice you receive is not subject to scrutiny.

Surprisingly the FSA has not been given the power to take action against dodgy brokers. There are 43,000 intermediaries in the mortgage market and they account for more than half of all home loans sold in the UK. Of these, an estimated 9,000 conduct only mortgage business and so will remain entirely unregulated.

With about 5,000 loans to choose from, all with different bells and whistles, mortgages are an area where homebuyers rely heavily on decent advice. The CAT standards are voluntary – lenders don't have to comply with them, but they are required to tell you whether or not a particular loan meets the standards and if not, why not. Perhaps the biggest attraction of CAT mortgages is that they remove the sanctuary of the small print. In the past, too many lenders have enticed borrowers with headline-grabbing rates and then fleeced them with well-hidden caveats.

One of the best reasons for switching to a CAT mortgage is that the lender is required to calculate your interest on a daily rather than annual basis. However, one glaring weakness of the new system is that discounted variable rate mortgages and cashback deals are excluded.

Where to start looking

So where do you start if you are searching for your first mortgage or thinking of remortgaging in order to get a better deal? The obvious priority is to shop around.

For most of us, our mortgage is the biggest expense we have. It's a long-term commitment and choosing the right loan at the outset is something you could still be benefiting from 25 years later.

Most people have simple needs. All they require is a no-frills loan at a competitive rate of interest. It is usually a mistake to opt for something exotic like a foreign currency mortgage. The snag is that lenders have created 'classes' of borrower, giving preferential terms to certain homebuyers, particularly first-time buyers and people with a large deposit. Halifax, for example, sometimes has more than 40 deals on offer. So you need to be discerning.

A mortgage is two things: it is the interest rate and the repayment 'vehicle' (the latter is the means by which you repay the amount you have borrowed).

Don't pay a higher rate than you need to; avoid deals with tie-ins (like compulsory insurance or redemption penalties) and make sure the repayment vehicle is the right one for you.

Almost anyone paying the standard variable rate (currently 7.25 per cent) could save money by switching to a fixed rate or discounted deal. But don't choose one with a lock-in clause. Some discounted mortgages offer rates of less than three per cent. So even if you have to pay re-mortgage fees, switching will probably be worthwhile. Many high street names have been outflanked by the new breed of direct lenders, which are now the best starting point.

But check out mutual building societies. Some, like Nationwide, regularly undercut mortgage banks and offer loyalty bonuses to customers. Study the 'best buy' tables in the weekend newspapers. Don't just compare APRs, get figures for your particular loan.

If you need to borrow a high percentage loan (more than 75 per cent of the property's value) choose a lender that doesn't apply a 'mortgage indemnity' premium, which could cost anything up to £2,000.

Also consider a 'flexible' mortgage, offered by a growing number of lenders, which allows you to increase or reduce your monthly repayments or take payment holidays if you are short of money. Making extra payment can save staggering amounts in interest.

Many UK lenders still operate annual interest systems which result in borrowers paying interest on debt they no longer owe.

Get to know the pros and cons

It is worth spending time getting to know the various types of mortgage available and the pros and cons of each.

Discount loans are when the variable rate is reduced by a set amount for a specified time. The downside is that you may get a payment shock when the discount ends and you are locked into the variable rate.

Fixed rate loans are attractive because they provide certainty. You can fix the rate for as little as one year or as long as 10 years. Most experts advise against fixed rates of more than five years because of the prospects of lower rates if we join the single European currency.

Capped rates are popular when the interest rate trend is upwards. The amount you pay is guaranteed not to rise above the cap, but can drop if there is a reduction in interest rates. To an extent, this gives you the best of both worlds, provided the cap is not too high.

Tracker loans are linked to the Bank of England base rate – you pay a set margin over and above this rate. The appeal is that you know you will always be paying a reasonably competitive rate. But you may miss out on a better deal.

Cashbacks are useful for borrowers operating on a shoestring – say, first-time buyers who need money for a deposit or furniture. The drawback is that the interest rate is higher than average.

Paying it back

Endowments have attracted widespread criticism, but they continue to be pushed by many lenders and brokers who pocket a huge income in the form of commission paid by insurance companies. One policy can net up to £1,500 commission.

One in five mortgages is still backed by an endowment, which builds in life cover for a set period and provides a vehicle for your savings (the premiums you pay) to grow. As such they have a role to play in financial planning, particularly for younger people with no life insurance. But never feel obliged to take out an endowment. It is easy to arrange separate life cover to suit your needs.

High charges, poor investment returns and an inflexible 'exit' route are the main disadvantages. Charges are hidden (consolidated into the monthly premium you pay), while companies are scaling down projected maturity values. If you want to surrender the policy in the early years, you are unlikely to get more than you have paid in because of the charges involved.

Because of the consumer backlash, a number of big firms (Halifax, NatWest, Scottish Widows, Norwich Union) have withdrawn from the market. Other companies are trying to offer safeguards.

CGU, one of the biggest sellers of endowments, is promising policyholders that it will make up the shortfall if their plans fail to pay off their mortgage – as long as future investment earnings average six per cent a year. Other companies are expected to emulate this promise. If you do opt for an endowment, it makes sense to choose a company like CGU. But always check the charges and look at past performance.

The safest and usually the cheapest way to repay your loan is a traditional 'repayment' mortgage. You pay back interest and capital on a monthly basis and take out separate life insurance to cover the loan in the event of death.

You don't have to stick to a 25-year term if you can afford to pay more each month; it makes sense to opt for a shorter repayment schedule – perhaps 15 years. Ask your lender to quote you figures for different repayment periods. The arithmetic is compelling.

There is nothing to stop you repaying in a number of ways. If you have, say, a £100,000 loan, you could have £50,000 on a repayment basis and the other £50,000 on an interest-only basis backed by investments like an ISA or unit trust.

Financial advisers and mortgage brokers

Brokers can help if your circumstances are unusual or you don't have time to shop around. Most charge a fee of between 0.5 per cent and one per cent of the loan, though there may be a minimum of £250. Always ask for written confirmation of how fees are charged and when they are due.

It is amazing what some advisers will do to earn a living:
• Sell you the wrong product because it pays high commission. Apart from endowments, be wary when recommended complex health insurance, whole-of-life policies and long-term savings plans.
• Double up by selling two or more products that overlap. Many people, for example, don't need permanent health insurance (PHI) and critical illness cover.
• Fail to refund commissions. Always ask whether you qualify for a commission refund and not just when you are paying a fee for advice. Advisers may split their commission with you if you buy more than one policy from them.
• Sell policies with low premiums that rise after a few months.

How do you find a good adviser?
Talk to friends and relatives. Find out who they used. Were their advisers any good? Ring IFA Promotions Hotline (0117 971 117), which recommends three advisers in your area.
Visit them: find out how long they have been in business. How well equipped are they? Is their office well-organised? Do they treat you politely?
Check whether your IFA has passed his Financial Planning Certificate and whether he has had any problems with the regulators. You could ring the Personal Investment Authority (020 7538 8860).

Do's and don'ts of remortgaging

• Check what your existing lender is prepared to offer. This has the advantage of saving costs.

• Check whether there will be redemption penalties if you switch lenders.

• Find a good independent broker who will be able to recommend the most suitable deal for your circumstances.

• Remember, even if there is a penalty for moving, it may still pay you to remortgage. Get the broker to work it out for you.

• The penalty can be added to a new loan and can still produce a reduction in monthly outgoings.

• Remortgages of up to 95 per cent of the value of the property are available but sometimes the best deals are where you have more equity in your home.

• Remortgaging is usually the cheapest form of finance for everything from home improvements to consolidating debts and paying off credit card borrowings. If you have plenty of equity in your home, lenders are quite relaxed about what you use the money for.

• Always shop around - the best deal is never far away.

CAT standards - the model mortgage

• Interest calculated daily rather than annually.

• Lenders banned from charging mortgage indemnity guarantee premiums for borrowers with small deposits.

• Early repayments permitted at any time without penalty.

• Available to new and existing customers.

Variable rate loans

• No fees.

• No redemption penalties.

• Interest rate must not be more than two percentage points above the base rate.

Fixed and capped rate loans

• Booking or arrangement fee should not exceed £150.

• No redemption penalties after fixed or capped rate period.

• Ceiling on redemption penalties during fixed or capped rate period.

David Spittles is the Property and Personal Finance writer for the London Evening Standard.

Renting and investing in London

Why do people buy homes in London? To live in, stupid. Wrong. In each of the last five years the majority of buyers of new Central and West London homes have been investors. In the busiest year, 1997, investors made up 65 per cent. This is a specialized market: new flats, predominantly, with an average price of £367,000. Even in the 'second-hand' market, experts reckon that 30 per cent of Central and West London buyers are investors, not owner-occupiers.

Out, too, in the boondocks (which means Clapham and Acton and places like that) estate agents in the first months of last year were besieged by investment buyers. They may not call themselves that: they are buy-to-letters, or pension fund diversifiers, or just plain ordinary people scared of the stock market and eager for the extra yield and security they reckon a rented property will bring them.

One consequence has been a big increase in the choice and quality of homes to rent. Once polarised between mansions and bedsits, London's rental market now has something for most pockets.

This new aspect of the property market, and its effects on the wider picture, is discussed in *The Property Market in 2000* earlier in this book. Here, we look at the rental scene from the point of view of the tenant, then from the perspective of landlord/investor. For a guide to how much you have to pay for what where, see our London-wide rent charts on pages 56–59 and the tables at the end of each area chapter.

But first, the background. In most of the world's cities, renting is the normal form of tenancy. In London it is not. Why? Because in the years 1915–1974 a series of laws intended to protect tenants had the back-handed effect of making renting a home to anyone other than a company insecure and usually unprofitable. As with much else, things changed in the 1980s. The 1988 Housing Act made the rebirth of the private rented sector possible. For the first time, landlords could sign up tenants for just six months at a market rent, with no security of tenure after the initial period. Eviction of tenants for non-payment of rent or for abusing properties was made simpler and, providing the right contract was signed, landlords were in no danger of creating a 'sitting tenancy'. At last, homeseekers had a decent alternative to buying.

Renting

Landlords and tenants sign an assured shorthold tenancy agreement. This is for a minimum initial period of six months, after which the two sides can sign a further contract if everything is going well. To end the contract, the landlord or the tenant has to give notice (usually two months) in writing. The landlord has the right to raise the rent at the end of any six-month period. The tenant can refer his rent to a rent assessment panel if he thinks it's excessive, but only during the first six months of the tenancy.

Sharers should all sign the tenancy agreement so that they are jointly and severally responsible. The agreement should be drawn up by a solicitor or a reputable letting agency. The agency will also advise on matters such as deposits and references.

Before you are granted a tenancy the landlord or their agent typically asks for three references, one of which must be from your bank and another from your employer. A deposit of four to six weeks' rent is needed, to cover breakages and unpaid bills. This deposit is held by the landlord/agent and you should get a receipt for it. The landlord or agent should handle the transfer of utility and phone accounts into your name(s). Meters should be read on 'get-in'. Tenants are responsible for paying the council tax, and single occupiers can get a 25 per cent discount on applying to the local town hall. Tenants should insure their own possessions.

Rents are normally paid monthly, in advance. Note that most agents now quote rents in weekly amounts, and that as from this edition the tables in this book use weekly figures. There is no introductory fee payable by tenants, but there will be costs for leases and inventories. Lease costs will occur whenever a new lease is drawn up.

You should get, and check well, the inventory of contents and a schedule of condition, setting out the state the place is in. Once you have signed these, they form the basis for any deductions for breakages and 'dilapidations'. When the tenancy ends and you are about to leave, the inventory should be checked by the landlord, the agent or a specialist inventory clerk working for them. After allowance for wear and tear, any breakages or damage will come out of your deposit.

Letting

As a landlord, you enter into a legal agreement with your tenants in the terms outlined above. Landlords should insist that sharers all sign the agreement so that they are jointly and severally liable. If a sharer leaves and a new one comes in, a new agreement should be drawn up. A good lettings agent, or your solicitor, will give advice on this. It is important to get the paperwork right as errors can create problems and expense. The agreement really ought to be specific to the property, though many agents use a standard one. Ensure that it covers the particular needs of the property, such as looking after gardens, exclusion of pets if necessary (and in come cases children), security such as alarms and locks and the precise number of people who will live in the home.

Some landlords find tenants themselves, and handle the management of, and the paperwork for, their property (the latter should be with the help of a solicitor). Others use an agent. Agents will offer a range of services, from introducing tenants up to full management and rent collection. Landlords (not tenants) pay them a percentage of the rent, which varies according to the level of service.

Agents will, as their most basic service, find tenants, take up references, transfer utility accounts and arrange deposits. Be clear at the outset, before you sign anything, about how much you are contracted to pay to the agent. Consult your solicitor if in doubt.

Landlords need to insure the property, both structure and contents. You must also inform the insurer when it is let and check that cover continues if the property is vacant between lets. Insurance is also available to cover legal expenses and loss of rent due to damage such as a fire. If the property is mortgaged, the lender too will need to be informed of your intention to let.

As a landlord you have to comply with the safety legislation designed to protect tenants. You must have all gas appliances (boilers, cookers and so on) inspected every year by a CORGI-registered gas fitter. You must also make sure all your soft furnishings, such as beds, chairs and sofas, comply with fire regulations, which outlaw everything made before 1988 (antique furniture is OK: check the details of the regulations). If you fail to comply and your tenants are injured as a result, you could be sued by your tenants. If you're prosecuted you could face a prison term of up to six months or a fine of £5,000.

If you're a landlord, you should, in theory, find it possible under current legislation to repossess your property if the tenants are in arrears or are wrecking the place. In practice, it's not that simple. It takes months for the courts to handle repossession cases, even under the 'accelerated possessions procedure', and while the wheels of justice are grinding the tenants can stay on, leaving you powerless. You can use the accelerated procedure if the tenant is refusing to leave after the end of the agreement when you've served the correct notices. Otherwise there are two types of court proceedings for possession: discretionary and mandatory. Repossession for being at least two months in arrears with the rent is mandatory, while repossession for other reasons (eg having riotous parties or using the property as a business) are discretionary.

It should be stressed that existing 'fair rent' tenancies, established under the old law, continue without change. When a property falls vacant and is re-let it will then, however, be subject to the new rules.

Agents

There are now plenty of specialist lettings agents competing for landlords' custom, and established sales agencies have set up lettings departments. As a result, fees have dropped. Fees are based on a percentage of the rent for the whole term of the agreement. Do not be afraid to negotiate, especially if you have, or intend to acquire, several properties. Agents like to be paid their fee as soon as the agreement is signed – and in advance. This can cause cashflow problems on a new tenancy; also, problems may arise if the tenant leaves before the term of the agreement is complete. For these reasons try to negotiate payment of fees either monthly or six-monthly in arrears. Some rental firms offer this from the outset, others will swear it is never done. Reputable firms are quoting fees in the region of 10 per cent for finding a tenant and collecting rent, with about 15 per cent for full management. Other firms charge 10 per cent for merely finding the tenant.

Check potential agents with care: membership of ARLA (Association of Residential Lettings Agents) and/or one of the three main estate agents' bodies, the RICS (Royal Institution of Chartered Surveyors), the ISVA (Incorporated Society of Valuers and Auctioneers) or the NAEA (National Association of Estate Agents), are good signs. The trade body, ARLA, stipulates that its members have to have been in business for at least two years, hold professional indemnity insurance and run separate client accounts (as must RICS members). ARLA has an arbitration service to settle disputes.

From this April, ARLA has a bonding scheme which works on a 'first resort' basis that protects clients' money (rent or deposits) held by agents. This means that landlords are first in the queue to get their money back if things go wrong. An ARLA member-firm must have an ARLA-qualified person in each office. For ARLA members in a given area, phone 01494 431123. For a copy of their leaflet *Trouble-Free Letting* send a SAE to ARLA Admin, Maple House, 53–55 Woodside Road, Amersham, Bucks.

Other estate agents' bodies also supply useful information for both landlords and tenants. The RICS offers free leaflets to landlords and tenants: phone 020 7222 7000. The RICS also offers a £9.95 book entitled *Rent Only Residential Management Code*, which clarifies the law. The National Approved Lettings Scheme codifies the points outlined above and is subscribed to by all the above bodies.

Investing in property

The rush to invest into rental property by individuals during the first half of 1999 led to some estate agents reporting that half their buyers were investors. Then the hikes in interest rates, taken with the dramatic rises in property prices, made the equation unprofitable for many would-be investors and they fell out of the race. The suddenness of the turn-round surprised experts. In the space of two months, investors dropped back from a half or a third to ten per cent of buyers. By the autumn, with interest rates and property prices still rising, the small investor was a rare species.

The other side of the see-saw is rents. In early 1999, they were going down. There's some evidence that by the end of that year and the start of this they had stabilised, even started to creep up, but on the whole rent levels are at best static. This must be seen as inevitable with new properties coming onto the market, and a renewed trend towards owner-occupation by young buyers – former tenants.

The investor takes all these factors – finance costs, buying price and achievable rents – and puts them together to work out a yield equation. The gross yield is then reduced to a net figure by deducting costs (see below). The net figure can be half the gross, but this varies depending on the property. Looking ahead, the landlord takes a guess at rent trends and at property prices, a rise in which may give a capital gain. Tax matters are then considered by an expert accountant, and the whole equation is compared dispassionately to other investments available.

These hard-headed calculations ought to be done before every purchase, but there's good reason to suppose that few 'amateur' landlords face up to reality in this way. Many have other motives for buying a property: somewhere for the kids to live while at college, maybe letting out spare rooms to other students; or perhaps to keep a stake in London while working abroad. Some are not worried about yield (ie income) as long as costs are covered, looking instead to long-term capital growth in the property's value. They feel, perhaps, that unlike a paper share at least the property will still be standing there even if the market crashes. Many, though, just don't think the thing through. Agents report a trickle of disappointed landlords who find that they cannot get the rent they hoped for, or any rent at all (in many areas, and for some types of home, tenants can pick and choose), and are trying to sell.

Choosing the property

If you are professional investor, you will get lots of advice: the big agents have set up specialist units to help. But if you are an amateur, thinking along the lines of the paragraph above, what should you be looking for? If you are going to manage the property yourself, look close to home. An emergency at 3 a.m. is more easily coped with in walking distance, and you will probably know the tradesmen you need to keep the place running.

New developments can cause a glut of rental property in an area. If 40 flats in a new block are sold (especially pre-sold) to investors, on completion they will all be seeking tenants at the same time. Because of the recent rash of new developments, you are probably better off this year buying humbler properties aimed at sharers and sited close to hospitals, universities, etc – in other words close to a large and continuing cache of prospective tenants.

Buy with your head, not your heart: this is business, not nest-building. Look at a property through the eyes of potential tenants: is it very convenient or is the tube really close? Do your research: stick to areas you know, or can get to know. Read the relevant chapters in this Guide. Speak to several agents, asking specific advice on buying a rental property. Get hold of as many lists of homes for sale, and for rent, as you can, from agents' offices and the Internet. Once a likely prospect is found, pay for a survey and quiz the surveyor on the price compared to like properties: this is as important as dry rot in the basement.

Be sure about areas and neighbourhoods and postcodes: the information is all in this book. Ensure before buying that the common parts and block management of flats are of good quality, and if you do invest in it keep it looking smart.

The costs

To calculate net yield an investor must deduct agents' fees, service charges and ground rents (if any), insurance, repairs and maintenance. Some properties cost more to maintain: gardens, lavish common parts in blocks, lifts – all can run up bills. Make realistic provision for upgrading and refurbishing. And expect void periods (time when the property is un-let): even if replacement tenants are found straight away, it takes about 10 working days to take up references and process the paperwork. Finally, add in borrowing costs, or the cost in foregone interest of using your own capital. All these costs can soak up half your gross return. And don't forget the costs involved in buying the place: stamp duty, legal fees, etc.

The returns

The return from investment property takes two forms: rent and capital appreciation. It's the latter that most small landlords are most familiar with, having enjoyed it on their owner-occupied homes. It is the biggest slice of the yield in most cases. The trouble is, to realise your profit you have to sell. Professional investors know this and trade frequently. Small investors tend to get attached to their property, or react too slowly to the market. Novices also tend to forget that since this is not their home, an eventual sale can attract capital gains tax.

What worries some commentators is the possibility of a rapid change in sentiment towards property as an investment. In crude terms, if investors reckon that the boom has stopped, will they all try to sell – at once? For with rising prices, rising interest rates and static rents, net yields have been falling. FPDSavills reckoned in January that the net yield on Central London property was 4.3 per cent, compared to 5.3 per cent at the start of 1999. This is supported by Cluttons' figure of 4.6 per cent during 1998. In the suburbs, net yields around 6 per cent were being quoted at the start of this year. All yields are well down on the start of 1998, when gross figures of 17 per cent were being achieved in some areas and 12 per cent gross was normal.

Current single-figure yields can be contrasted with double-digit capital gains. Cluttons' cautious estimate is that rented properties appreciated between 10 and 12 per cent in 1998, followed on by FPDSavills' 17 per cent in 1999.

For a rosy period in 1998 and into mid-'99, loans to buy investment properties could be had at under 6 per cent, while net yields were a touch higher. Property looked a one-way bet, and so it has turned out – with the provisos that your yield is negative if you have no tenants and that your gain is a paper one until you sell. But this spring, with borrowing rates up to above 8 per cent, and cautious net yields half that, the picture is very different. Experts say that the market is still attractive – to those with a long-term perspective. When the agents start to list the safety of bricks and mortar as a bigger virtue than capital gain, perhaps it is time to look for alternative investments.

Who will be the gainers from property investment in 2000? Those who sell and realise the sometimes stunning gains of the last two or three years. Those who hang on for the long term and are fully let – with no voids. And those new investors who search out the less expensive areas, research their prospective tenants with great care, and look down-market.

There is good evidence that the smarter end of the market has reached a certain level of saturation. Two-bed, two-bath flats have formed more than half the new homes built in Central and West London over the past few years. Now, they are all looking for tenants. The market is also starting to differentiate: the older the block or house, the lower the rent: tenants are attracted to shiny, new homes and these command higher rents.

Rents are more stable for family homes in the leafy suburbs, and – paradoxically – at the cheaper end of the market. Sharers, a species regarded sniffily by many landlords, have become more loved as it's realised that three or four sharers can afford more than the single professional or couple that most landlords have preferred. Such tenants look for convenient locations first: the fare band of the local tube station is a key factor. Investors who aim at this market may find the competition for tenants less fierce, and the capital gains greater, in the more modest corners of Zone 2: start your search with the tube map, and see under Transport in the tables at the end of each area chapter.

Despite the evidence of the past year, quoted above, there is still a widespread assumption among investors that rents will at least stay the same if not rise. FPDSavills have researched figures back to 1985 and they reckon that rents rose steadily, in line with property prices, up to the end of 1998, though both fell ten years ago: prices fell from 1989 to 1992, and rents from 1990 to 1992, with a slight dip in 1994. Rents fell far less steeply than prices, however. A cautionary note is that London rents are quite a lot higher than in other European or American cities.

How big is the market?

Residential property as an investment remains virtually un-researched. It was moribund until around 1985, when individual investors began to reappear. After a lull they came back in strength in the mid-'90s, as City bonuses once again put flat-sized chunks of cash into bank accounts. The lack of institutional investment means that no-one in the financial world (with the honourable exception of the blue-chip London estate agents) takes much notice of it. However it is a growing sector: the total invested via the ARLA buy-to-let scheme (a loose grouping of ten lenders) up to the start of 2000 was £2.88 billion. To this figure add the (unknown) number of homes bought by institutions and companies and by individuals outside the ARLA scheme. There is little research yet on how many rental properties there are in total: the much-quoted national figure of 11 per cent probably includes tied properties, which are not in the open market. No-one knows exactly how many rented homes there are in London, though it naturally has a larger proportion than the country as a whole.

Last year, we reported rumours that a merchant bank was planning to enter the market in a big way. It has yet to do so, though one investment firm has built up a portfolio of more than 1,000 flats, and it's estimated that 500 are being built this year specifically as rental properties in 'branded blocks': places you know you may find flats to rent, with a greater or lesser level of extra services such as cleaning and catering.

The figures are hard to compute because a rented home can quickly become an owner-occupied home, and vice versa. After all, a tenant is a home-seeker who decides to rent not buy.

The foreign buyers return

London property has been rescued, many times, by the advent of foreign investment buyers. They were quiet through much of 1999, subdued by the high pound and hang-overs from 1998's near-crash in the Far East. Late last year and into this spring there were reports of their return. Knight Frank reports that buyers in new developments were 40 per cent foreign at the turn of the year, up from 34 per cent. Far East and Middle East buyers were active, the firm reports, with the latter's share of the market doubling to seven per cent. European buyers were also more in evidence. Foreign participation on the overall market (new and 'second-hand') is at a lower level, but still increasing. American purchasers are a declining sector.

Winkworth

Sales & Lettings Offices

LONDON CENTRAL

Clerkenwell & City	020 7253 1566
Kensington	020 7727 1500
Knightsbridge	020 7589 6616
Notting Hill	020 7727 3227
Paddington & Bayswater	020 7262 2900
Pimlico	020 7828 1786
St John's Wood	020 7586 7001
South Kensington	020 7373 5052
West End	020 7240 3322

LONDON WEST

Chiswick	020 8994 7096
Ealing & Acton	020 8896 0123
Fulham	020 7731 3388
Fulham Cross	020 7385 1115
Hammersmith	020 7371 4466
North Kensington	020 7792 5000
Shepherd's Bush	020 8749 3394
South Ealing	020 8567 4242

LONDON NORTH

Crouch End	020 8342 9999
Finchley	020 8349 3388
Golders Green	020 8458 8313
Hendon	020 8202 1031
Highgate	020 8341 1988
Islington	020 7354 2480
Kentish Town	020 7485 9210

LONDON SOUTH of the RIVER

Battersea	020 7228 9265
Blackheath & Greenwich	020 8852 0999
Clapham	020 7498 8600
Croydon	020 8686 6667
Dulwich	020 8299 2722
Kennington	020 7587 0600
New Cross	020 7277 7298
Putney	020 8788 9295
Streatham	020 8769 6699
Surrey Quays	020 7237 9119
Tooting	020 8767 5221

LONDON EAST

Bow	020 8981 6776
Hackney	020 8986 4216

SPECIALIST SERVICES

Auctions	020 8649 7255
Chartered Surveyors	020 7937 0959
Winkworth Mortgages Ltd	0800 1000 353
Winkworth Premium Client Management Ltd	020 7727 0563

EACH OFFICE IS INDEPENDENTLY OWNED AND OPERATED

FOR INFORMATION ON OUR WEBSITE - **www.winkworth.co.uk** - SEE BACK COVER

Price charts: rentals

The charts on the following pages consolidate the data in the Area Profiles, showing broadly what certain kinds of homes cost to rent per week in each of the areas covered. This gives you a freeze-frame picture across London at the start of 2000: a basis for comparison throughout the year.

The prices given are for typical examples of each type of home. Where a range of figures is shown, this reflects rent variations within the area. Thus the range is also

FLATS — RENTALS   STARTING PRICES FOR 2000

weekly rent in £s   — too few for price average   → price carries over

	STUDIO	1 BEDROOM	2 BEDROOM	3 BEDROOM	4 BEDROOM	5+ BEDROOM
Acton	100–130	150–270	175–375	250–450	350+	—
Balham and Tooting	90–105	125–220	140–300	180–350	360–440	—
Barnes, Mortlake and Sheen	90–200	140–270	200–370	250–400	—	—
Battersea	150–180	155–250	160–350	300–450+	400–500	—
Bayswater	150–200+	200–300+	260–400+	350–650	450–900	650–1400
Bedford Park and Acton Green	150–200	150–350	230–350	280–550	—	—
Belgravia	275–400	400–800	600–1300	800–2000	1200–2000	—
Bethnal Green	120–150	150–200	180–225	220–300	250–350	—
Bloomsbury and King's Cross	200+	250–300	325–400	450–550	600+	—
Bow	100–140	105–180	140–230	160–350	—	—
Brixton, Herne Hill and Tulse Hill	100–138	115–160	138–230	160–325	210–460	—
Camberwell	90–125	115–175	138–220	185–300	275+	300+
Camden Town and Primrose Hill	130–300+	170–450	220–650	300–750	400–750+	750+
Chelsea	175–500	350–500	375–760+	600–1300	750–3000	1000–6000
Chiswick	150–250	150–300	200–500+	330–600	695–1500	—
City and Fringes	150–235	175–350	220–500+	300–600+	—	—
Clapham	115–230	140–275	185–460	300–575	300+	400+
Clerkenwell and Finsbury	160–235	230–525	275–1200	345+→	—	—
Cricklewood	120–160	140–180	180–270	220–350	300–400	500+
Crouch End and Stroud Green	120–150	130–210	200–300	—	—	—
Crystal Palace	95–100	100–138	125–150	150–185	160–275	220+
Dollis Hill and Neasden	100–130	140–200	180–220	200–280	—	—
Dulwich	95–150	125–200	150–275	185–370	230+	—
Ealing	125–175	160–220	175–275	210–390	230–460	—
Finchley	130–135	150–170	180–320	270–350	—	—
Forest Hill	90–110	100–160	150–180	150–220	185–250	230–275
Fulham	160–200	180–250	260–450	300–550	400–700	—
Golders Green	100–160	150–250	200–450	220–500	300–550	330–430
Greenwich and Blackheath	110–138	115–265	160–275+	210–325+	—	—
Hackney	90–110	110–160	160–220	190–260	—	—
Hammersmith	120–150	200–300	240–400	400+	—	—
Hampstead	150–220	180–375	275–500	350–750	500–750+	700–1500+
Hampstead Garden Suburb	120–150	150–215	180–280	250–400	350–430	—
Hendon and Mill Hill	90–125	130–200	180–280	200–300	250–600	—
Highgate	120–200	150–250	200–400	275–500	300–500	—
Holland Park	150–300	200–400	350–700	600–2000	1000–3500	1200–5000+
Islington and Highbury	150–200	175–300	250–400	350–450+	—	—
Kennington, Vauxhall and Stockwell	100–200	150–250	200–375	270–500	300–600	300–600+

an indicator of the scope of the properties: a small range indicates a fairly homogeneous area; a wide one either that there are some neighbourhoods that warrant a premium, or perhaps there is a good supply of recently developed, more luxurious flats. In all brackets, you are likely to find cheaper homes and exceptional ones at the other end of the scale: a plus sign is used where we have not included the rents for a small number of unusual examples, which would distort the averages.

HOUSES — RENTALS   STARTING PRICES FOR 2000

weekly rent in £s   — too few for price average   → price carries over

	2 BEDROOM	3 BEDROOM	4 BEDROOM	5 BEDROOM	6–7 BEDROOM	8+ BEDROOM
Acton	250–300	275–450	325–550	400+	—	—
Balham and Tooting	170–300	200–350	250–375	300–450	500+	—
Barnes, Mortlake and Sheen	220–300	260–550	370–750	600–1300	—	—
Battersea	275–400	330–500	425–525+	550–1000	800–1300	—
Bayswater	250–400	400–750	580–900	600–1500	—	—
Bedford Park and Acton Green	160–400	250–500	500–1250	700–1500	—	—
Belgravia	650–1000	850–1500	1500–2500	2000–5000	3500–10,000	—
Bethnal Green	230–280	280–350	350–450	450–550	550–600	—
Bloomsbury and King's Cross	275–400	350–500+	500+	600+	→1100	—
Bow	160–275	175–370	205–460	460–690	600+	—
Brixton, Herne Hill and Tulse Hill	138–230	160–325	210–460	275–550	345+	—
Camberwell	138–230	185–300	250–325	325–460	395+	→485
Camden Town and Primrose Hill	250–400	330–550+	450–1200+	600–2000+	—	—
Chelsea	500–950	750–1200	1000–1800	1500–2500	4000–6000	—
Chiswick	240–500	330–600	460–1350	800–1600	—	—
City and Fringes	350+	450+	550+	—	—	—
Clapham	210–450	230–460	370–600	480–1000	650+	1200+
Clerkenwell and Finsbury	—	—	—	—	—	—
Cricklewood	200–250	260–370	325–400	650–800	—	—
Crouch End and Stroud Green	250–300	300–360	350–450	450–525	—	—
Crystal Palace	138–160	200–210	230–275	300–415	370–460	—
Dollis Hill and Neasden	200–250	220–300	250–350	350–400	—	—
Dulwich	175–300	230–390	275–460	345+	460–550+	—
Ealing	175–275	195–390	275–460	345–600	370–690	—
Finchley	200–225	220–360	400+	600+	800+	—
Forest Hill	150–175	160–210	230–370	230–500	325+	—
Fulham	300–500	400–600	550–750	600–800	850+	—
Golders Green	250–350	250–600	420–800	500–1000	600–1200	800–2000
Greenwich and Blackheath	155–275	275+	275–345	275–460	460+	—
Hackney	150–240	200–290	230–370	—	—	—
Hammersmith	300–350	300–450	400–600	500–750	900–1500	—
Hampstead	360–650	400–1000	450–1600	550–2000	750–3500	900–4000
Hampstead Garden Suburb	230–300	200–375+	350–900	550–1500	800–3000	1000–4000
Hendon and Mill Hill	160–230	210–320	250–500	300–1000	500–1000	—
Highgate	250–400	300–700	400–800+	475–2000	650–2500	700–2600+
Holland Park	500–650	700–1300	1000–2000	2500–4500	3500–5000	5000+
Islington and Highbury	350–450+	450–700+	500–750+	750+	—	—
Kennington, Vauxhall and Stockwell	220–500	250–600	300–600	350–700+	350+	→

FLATS — RENTALS

weekly rent in £s   — too few for price average   → price carries over

	STUDIO	1 BEDROOM	2 BEDROOM	3 BEDROOM	4 BEDROOM	5+ BEDROOM
Kensington	220–500	300–700	400–1000	500–1500	500–2500	1200+
Kentish Town and Tufnell Park	100–160	180–250	200–300	250–350+	350–600	400–700
Kilburn, Kensal Green and Queen's Park	120–140	140–200	180–260	200–320	—	—
Knightsbridge	225–300	275–800	350–1200	600–1600	850–2000	1000+
Lewisham and Catford	100–115	125–150	150–160	175–230	185–275	230–460
Leyton and Walthamstow	100–125	110–150	135–180	160–200	190–210	—
Maida Vale and Little Venice	150+	200–325	240–400	350+	700+	—
Marylebone and Fitzrovia	180–250	200–500	300–500	350–1000	600–2000	800–3500+
Mayfair and St James's	250–300	325–600	450–1400	550–2000	1000–3000+	2000+
Morden, Mitcham and Colliers Wood	80–100	115–125	138–160	175–185	210+	—
Muswell Hill	90–130	115–175	150–210	185–300	—	—
New Cross and Deptford	75–120	90–200	130–250	185–250	—	—
Newham	90–120	100–135	130–155	135–220	180–230	—
Notting Hill and North Kensington	200–275	200–350	280–500	350–500+	500–700+	—
Peckham	100–150	125–175	138–200	160–230	200–275	—
Pimlico and Westminster	150–300	200–400	250–700	300–850	350–1000	—
Poplar	95–180	100–180	145–250	160–300	—	—
Putney and Roehampton	100–170	180–250	200–500	300–600	400–870	—
Regent's Park	200–350	250–450	350–700	450–1500	600–2000	—
Richmond and Kew	140–190	150–300	200–350	250–400	—	—
Shepherd's Bush	130–180	180–220	220–300	260–350	350–500	450–550
Soho and Covent Garden	200–600	230–600	400–600	500–1000	—	—
The South Bank	120–170	150–300	170–450	350–450	400+	—
South Kensington, Earl's Court and West Brompton	200–300+	250–450+	300–600+	425–1M	550–1M+	600–1M+
Southfields and Earlsfield	125–150	150–250	185–550	275–575	370+	—
Southgate and Palmers Green	125–130	150–170	165–200	200–250	—	—
St John's Wood	200–250	250–350	300–600	400–1000	800+	—
Stepney and Whitechapel	140–240	210–300	240–350	—	—	—
Stoke Newington	100–130	130–170	160–240	250–350	—	—
Streatham	100–115	150+	200+	—	—	—
Tottenham and Finsbury Park	70–150	110–190	135–220	170–250	—	—
Totteridge and Whetstone	100–130	130–180	150–280	→325	—	—
Twickenham and Teddington	115–160	138–210	160–460	210–460+	275–800	325–925
Wandsworth	120–190	150–200	200–320	250–320	250–360	330–600
West Hampstead	120–250	175–350	210–550	280–600	425–750	550–900
West Norwood, Norbury and Gipsy Hill	95–122	115–150	138–230	175–250	275–575	—
Willesden and Brondesbury Park	100–120	150–210	180–250	225–330	300–400	350–450
Wimbledon, Raynes Park and Merton Park	105–170	150–230	175–450	210–550	530–700	—

HOUSES — RENTALS

weekly rent in £s   — too few for price average   → price carries over

	2 BEDROOM	3 BEDROOM	4 BEDROOM	5 BEDROOM	6–7 BEDROOM	8+ BEDROOM
Kensington	400–800	600–1000	700–2000+	1000–3000	2000–7000	3000–10,000
Kentish Town and Tufnell Park	220–300	280–500	380–600	500–700	600–1000	700–1500+
Kilburn, Kensal Green and Queen's Park	220–240	275–4500	320–450	400–500	—	—
Knightsbridge	600–1400	700–1500	1200–2000	3500+	5000+	5000+
Lewisham and Catford	155–185	175–230	220–345	230–345	345+	—
Leyton and Walthamstow	150–200	175–210	200–325	—	—	—
Maida Vale and Little Venice	350–650	400–800+	750+	1000+	—	—
Marylebone and Fitzrovia	375–500	600–800	750–1000	—	—	—
Mayfair and St James's	550–1200	575–1500+	1400–3000+	2000–13,000	—	—
Morden, Mitcham and Colliers Wood	150–160	175–250	200–275	230–275+	—	—
Muswell Hill	—	200–350	300–500	500–600	—	—
New Cross and Deptford	150–250	150–350	250–500	400–600	—	—
Newham	130–165	170–220	180–250	220–300	—	—
Notting Hill and North Kensington	400–900	450–1200	700–1600	1000+	2000+	—
Peckham	100–150	185–275	210–345	230–370	275+	—
Pimlico and Westminster	—	500–900	600–1000	700–2000	—	—
Poplar	150–300	190–450	250–450	—	—	—
Putney and Roehampton	250–380	300–600	500–800	600–1000	800–2000	—
Regent's Park	600–900	1100–2000	1500+	4000+	—	—
Richmond and Kew	260–390	300–400	310–600+	550–1500	900–2000	—
Shepherd's Bush	250–300	280–380	350–500	450–600	500–600	600–700
Soho and Covent Garden	400–1000	800–2500	→	—	—	—
The South Bank	250–350	300–400	—	—	—	—
South Kensington, Earl's Court and West Brompton	400–600	500–1000+	650–1800	860+	1M+	1M+
Southfields and Earlsfield	230–460	275–575	370–800	500+	—	—
Southgate and Palmers Green	200–230	250–350	300–450	450–550	—	—
St John's Wood	500+	600–1500	800+	1500+	—	—
Stepney and Whitechapel	70–150	80–150	120–250	180–380+	—	—
Stoke Newington	180–280	230–320	290–350	450–500	—	—
Streatham	200–250	250–500	250–600	400–600	—	—
Tottenham and Finsbury Park	200–300	225–350	250–450	375–500	—	—
Totteridge and Whetstone	160–200+	220–450	280–500+	400–500	—	—
Twickenham and Teddington	200–345	220–575	275–690	345–925	460+	→
Wandsworth	220–350	300–400	400–600	500–800	—	—
West Hampstead	275–330	325–650	400–1000	410–1100	820–1200	—
West Norwood, Norbury and Gipsy Hill	138–200	200–300	200–325	220–415	275–415	415+
Willesden and Brondesbury Park	180–260	300–360	350–370	500+	600+	1000+
Wimbledon, Raynes Park and Merton Park	200–375	210–600	370–1000	400–1200	—	—

Schools in London

by Liz Lightfoot

Anyone with children, or planning to have them, must include local schools as a factor when they decide where to live. Parents can't take a decent standard of state education for granted in the capital – which, despite having some of the finest, also holds more failing schools than any other part of the country.

There are some superb independent (fee-charging) day schools, but going private is not an easy option for people dragged down by high mortgages and living costs. Nor is leaving it to the state in Islington, Hackney and Southwark. So what do you do? Mix, match and move!

The school reforms put in train by successive Tory governments, and now being expanded by Tony Blair's government with its insistence on a return to traditional standards, are already bringing improvements.

But still, after three years of Labour's reforms, moving to inner London can be a lottery unless you know a lot about the schools that will be on offer. Parents in outer London are generally better served, but even Barnet and Richmond upon Thames, authorities which top league tables, have schools which could be doing better with the calibre of pupils they recruit. Kingston upon Thames has some excellent primary schools but a desperate shortage of secondary-school places, and admissions are so complicated in Barnet that a group of parents have set up their own school rather than have their children educated miles away at one they have not chosen.

The variety of schools on offer combined with a good public transport system should in theory offer more choice than in most areas of the country. In practice, the high number of mediocre and failing schools means the good ones are heavily over-subscribed, making a mockery of parental choice.

Parents in London find themselves forced to play cat and mouse with the state system. Either they move next to a good school – and pay for it through higher house prices – or they stay put and take their chances of either getting their children into a church school further afield or putting them in for competitive exams for one of the remaining 19 grammars and the sprinkling of partially-selective schools.

The vagaries of the admissions system, however, makes this a high-risk strategy, and parents sometimes find they have to move house when their children are coming to the end of their primary schooling because there is no local secondary acceptable to them. Or because they have no hope of getting a place in one that is.

There are some lovely parts of Hackney, for example, with elegant Georgian and Victorian terraces; but if you don't live in Victoria Park or De Beauvoir, two middle-class enclaves, your choice of primary school will be extremely limited in an authority which Ofsted said was so riven by political in-fighting and incompetence that it didn't even know how many pupils it educated. When it comes to secondary education, then, you have to attend church regularly and impress the priest or vicar to get into the Catholic or Church of England schools, or pay independent school fees. If you can't do either then the unhappy solution may be to leave your beautiful home and relocate to suburbia.

Mixing state and independent education is increasingly common. Parents with academically able children try to work the system by using fee-paying prep schools to give their children a head start in competitive exams for selective state schools. Others use local primaries and supplement them with tutors and weekend courses to prepare them for entry to independent secondary schools.

Rarely do you meet socially with other parents in London without an intense discussion about education. It's not just that some schools are appallingly bad – still wedded, even now, to failed mixed-ability teaching, discovery learning and muddling through the day. The difference is stark – in a city where parents in the same circles send their children to both – between the academic rigour of independent education and a state system which is only slowly being pulled back after two decades in which it largely abandoned the 3Rs, discipline and regular homework for fashionable progressive education.

So in London, more than anywhere else in the country, you have to plan your children's education like a military exercise. A mistake made early on can badly limit your choice later.

Who runs London's schools?

London has no uniform education system because the 32 boroughs and the City of London Corporation run the schools, each one acting as a separate education authority. The churches run and help fund a number of state schools in conjunction with the boroughs, and these are usually popular with parents on educational, as well as spiritual, grounds.

Though each borough council is legally responsible for providing education for any child of school age in its area, parents are not obliged to use wht's on offer and can apply to schools in other authorities. The school population is suprisingly mobile: 14 per cent of children travel outside their own boroughs: usually to schools that are close to them but over a boundary, but sometimes much further afield.

The boroughs don't like this cross-border drift and have to recoup the costs of educating pupils from one another, but they are hamstrung by a High Court judgement which has gone unchallenged. The court decided that it was unlawful, under the legislation regulating parental choice and school admissions, for Greenwich council to give a school place to a resident when a non-resident of the borough lived closer.

The 'Greenwich judgement' is good news for someone living, for example, on the borders of Lambeth who wants to use Wandsworth's more highly-rated schools, but bad news for those who live in good authorities who see 'outsiders' snapping up places in their borough's schools, funded by their council tax.

Most of the movement is from Inner to Outer London, which does not have the same level of socio-economic deprivation – and where the authorities have been running their own schools for longer and are thus generally better at it. The Inner authorities took over education when the Inner London Education Authority was abolished by the Thatcher government in 1990, and inherited a mass of problems which most of them have so far proved incapable of tackling. Because the ILEA ran all schools in the area, borough boundaries were obscured when catchments were drawn up, and the mobility is part of its legacy.

The biggest net importer of pupils is Bromley, where 23 per cent are from outside the borough – many lured by its two grammar schools, Newstead Wood girls and St Olave's and St Saviour's boys. In Inner London it is Camden which takes most out-of-borough pupils to its own well-run comprehensives, the ever-popular Camden School for Girls and several sought-after Roman Catholic schools which provide an escape-route for children from Brent, Haringey, Islington, Westminster and even further afield.

Sometimes parents trust their children to state primaries (some are outstanding) near home, but move them out of the area for secondary education. Nearly 40 per cent of the pupils in Islington's primary schools – a third of which are church schools – move to secondaries outside the borough.

Hackney, Lambeth, Southwark and Islington have all received damning reports and the Government has ordered them to appoint outside consultants and to hand over some of their services to private firms.

Hackney, the first to be inspected, was judged to be riven by political infighting and incompetence, and failing its pupils so badly that it didn't even know how many it educated. The running of its schools, and their improvement, has been contracted out to Nord Anglia, a private education company which is quoted on the stock exchange, but it seems to be having an uphill struggle. One of the problems for private firms is that employment regulations mean that unless a school is closed and re-opened under a new name, it is very difficult to get rid of weak staff. Council officials are also protected from dismissal under European regulations, so it's likely to be a while before residents see a significant improvement.

Another private education company, Cambridge Education Associates, has been appointed to sort out Islington, also judged by Ofsted last year to be incapable of running its own schools. The inspectors found the North London council was failing to provide its 25,000 pupils with a suitable and efficient education, and that a quarter of its 58 schools were failing, or in serious danger of being failed and put on 'special measures'.

Ofsted pointed to Islington as a vivid example of divided Britain. 'Some of the most expensive homes in London are to be found only a short distance away from very deprived areas with severe social problems, including drug abuse, high crime rates and vandalism' it said.

Southwark was likewise judged to be failing in its statutory duties to provide satisfactory education for its pupils, and some of its services, too, are to go to the private sector. Lambeth, one of the first to be accused of failing its pupils, is on the mend but still has a long way to go, according to the latest Ofsted inspection.

The two authorities with the best reputations are Barnet and Richmond upon Thames, but the success of their schools may be due mainly to the affluent, professional parents who choose to pay high mortgages rather than independent school fees. Certainly Richmond, which tops primary league tables, does less well at secondary level, where its comprehensives get only just above the national average.

Choosing a school: finding the information

One of the best things that the present Labour government has done for parents is to provide them with an internet site giving easy access to information about schools, their examination and test results, truancy rates and the number of pupils with special needs.

Though schools have been required to publish their test and exam results for some years, few made it easy for parents. House-hunters are understandably reluctant to approach hard-pressed head teachers and their secretaries before they can claim to be residents. Requesting exam or test results is always a tricky one. Head teachers have not sought to hide their dislike of league tables and there was always the danger that if prospective parents demanded to see them, they could be marked down as troublemakers who judged schools purely in terms of results.

The heads point out that raw results can be very misleading because they fail to take account of the pupils' abilities: is the standard of eduction higher in a school which is producing excellent improvements in the abilities of children who may be from deprived or non-English-speaking backgrounds, or one that gets higher grades but is going through the motions with already-bright, well-fed, well-supported pupils?

The Department for Education and Employment's new Parents site is an excellent resource for the house-hunter, who can access very valuable information to assess schools without having to approach them. The site – www.parents.dfee.gov.uk – allows you to search an area by postcode or to look up individual schools and local authorities. The site will tell you which primary or secondary schools are in the area and takes you to their exam and test results, their Ofsted inspection reports and any school web-sites that are available. It even gives you a comparison between the school's data and that for both the local education authority and England as a whole.

A word of caution, however. The site only works on postcodes, and does not include schools which are slightly further away but still used by parents in a particular street. Infant schools are not listed, since their test results are not published by local authorities or the Government, but if you know the name of the school you can access its Ofsted reports direct.

Nor does the site include a school's admission policy – or which primaries are regarded as 'feeders' for individual secondaries. If you keep these limitations in mind, however, the site is a very good starting-point for your research.

For those without access to the internet, secondary school results are published in the following pages, and primary school tables can be obtained from local authorities. Finding Ofsted reports is trickier. Either you have to visit the local library, or ask the school for a summary of its report, for which there may be a small charge.

However, the best way to find out about a school is to talk to the head teacher or the chairman of governors, and to try to obtain a copy of the governors' latest annual report to parents. This should include the school's test results, including the ones taken by seven-year-olds which are not published elsewhere, and a more useful breakdown of how many pupils achieved at the higher national curriculum levels. Above all, talk to local people in the area before you make any decision. A new head teacher or plans to expand the school can make all the difference.

Admissions: the tricks and the pit-falls

Children must start school in the term after their fifth birthday but generally they begin in reception classes when they are four. The Government promises nursery school places for all four-year-olds whose parents want them, either in pre-school playgroups, nursery schools or primary school reception classes.

It's against the spirit of the rules, but some schools persuade parents to send four-year-olds to their reception classes by warning that places might not be available later, once the children turn five. Such threats should be reported to the local authorities and to the Department for Education, which wants parents to have the choice of voluntary, private or school nursery classes.

Children transfer to state secondary schools at 11, at 11 or 13 in independent schools. Admissions are complicated by the three types of schools within the state sector:
• **Community**: run by local authorities, which also act as their admission authority.
• **Foundation**: funded by local authorities but with a measure of independence over admissions, and fewer local-authority nominees on the governing body.
• **Aided**: owned and partly funded by the churches.

Parents apply for places directly to Foundation and Aided schools, but through local authorities for the Community Schools.

It sounds easy until you want the same school as everyone else, and then the nightmare begins. If you are asked to express a preference, for example, and fail to get your choice, then the local authority may give your child a place at a school you don't want. For this reason parents sometimes plump for putting their second-best choice at the top of the list on the basis that they are more likely to be successful.

Almost all schools give preference to the brothers and sisters of existing pupils. Next comes proximity to the school premises, but catchment areas vary from year to year as families move in and out of the area. The Government's rule that no infant class can have more than 30 children means that some popular infant and primary schools are having to turn people away; many, however, are using Government grants to expand the number of places by adding more classes to meet the demand.

Moving to the same road as a school, however, will not guarantee a place if the school is run by one of the churches, which traditionally recruit more widely, valuing regular church attendance more than proximity to the school. Nor will it help if the school is one of the 19 remaining grammar schools in London which recruit on the basis of a competitive examination. There's also a sprinkling of partially-selective schools, such as three in Wandsworth, which allocate a proportion of places to those with the best scores in entrance tests, limiting the numbers taken from the local population.

If you choose the selective schools, then your ten- or eleven-year-old could face a term of exhausting examinations for different schools, ending up without a place at any of them. If that happens then you face a scrabble to get what's left in the state comprehensives, or spend the next seven years paying school fees.

There's another wild card which has been introduced to make finding a school even more complicated. London's grammars and partially-selective schools are under threat from Labour's recent legislation enabling local parents to challenge and abolish selection. So far, only anti-grammar campaigners in Barnet are seriously collecting signatures for a petition calling for a vote on its three grammars. All three have received glowing reports from Ofsted, however, and parents are not flooding to sign petitions to call their futures into doubt. The two Tiffin grammars in Kingston appear safe for the moment, but as they recruit half their pupils from outside the borough, they could face local agitation for a change to their selective status.

The Schools Adjudication Service has so far failed to abolish partial selection at the minority of London comprehensives which allocate a proportion of places on the grounds of ability. It has ordered some schools to reduce the proportion, however – notably in Wandsworth, the Tory authority which successfully challenged the decision in the High Court for this year. Despite its success on a legal technicality, the schools may be forced to amend their selection policies in future years.

Labour's alternative to selection is to urge comprehensives to introduce more streaming by ability, and to create many more specialist schools which can select pupils on the basis of aptitude for subjects such as music, information technology and sport. These schools get extra money and expect pupils and teachers to work longer hours, so they are worth investigating.

Admission policies are a minefield, however, and need very careful scrutiny because some secondaries have historic agreements with local primaries which they regard as 'feeder' or 'link' schools. So, despite all your careful research, you may find that even though you live nearer than another family, their child is given precedence because he or she went to the 'right' primary.

So watch out! You may be equidistant from two primaries and spend a lot of time deciding which gets the best test results or has the happiest children – only to discover that the one you rejected leads on to the secondary you would have chosen, and the other to a less palatable alternative.

Private schools

London is fortunate to have so many excellent independent prep and secondary schools. Most of the secondary schools are single-sex, at least until the sixth form, and they are almost exclusively day schools, though some have embraced weekly boarding with the children going home at weekends. There is fierce competition for places despite the high fees, with some parents registering their offspring while they are still in the womb. London's mobile population, however, means that places can become available at any stage, so it is always worth a phone call.

One tip is that head teachers tend to listen to others in the profession, so it is often worth getting your child's present school to contact them if you are moving to London. East London doesn't have many private schools, but there are plenty elsewhere, particularly in the south-west. It is generally easier to find places in Outer London.

The Government's performance tables give the exam results for private secondary schools, but no amount of pressure has yet persuaded prep schools to publish the scores their pupils achieve in Common Entrance, the exam they take for entry to independent secondary schools.

International schools

If you have come to London from abroad, you may wish to send your child to one of the international schools here. Some of the best known are listed below. Your embassy here will know of others.

American School in London
2/8 Loudoun Rd
NW8 0NP
Tel: 020 7449 1200

German School
Douglas House
Petersham Rd
Petersham, Richmond
Surrey
TW10 7AH
Tel: 020 8948 3410

Japanese School in London
87 Creffield Rd,
W3 9PU
Tel: 020 8993 7145

King Fahad Academy
Bromyard Avenue
W3 7HD
Tel: 020 8743 0131

Lycée Français
35 Cromwell Rd
SW7 2DG
Tel: 020 7584 6322

Norwegian School in London
28 Arteberry Rd
SW20 8AH
Tel: 020 8946 2058

Swedish School
Lonsdale Rd
SW13 9JS
Tel: 020 8741 1751

Liz Lightfoot is the Education Correspondent of The Daily Telegraph.

Secondary school performance tables

The following tables illustrate the performance of secondary schools throughout London, borough by borough. Published in November 1999, these are the third to be produced by the Blair government and the eighth overall. Although their introduction was clogged by controversy, they are now relied upon by parents choosing secondary schools.

Complete tables, containing previous results and the proportion of pupils with special educational needs, can be obtained from the Department of Education. They will be supplied free of charge on request (tel: 0800 242322) or by writing to School and College Performance Tables, Department of Education and Employment, FREEPOST (LON 102450), London SW1P 3YS.

Key

SCHOOL TYPE:	CY: County (ie state), GM: grant maintained, VC: voluntary controlled, VA: voluntary aided, SA: special agreement, CTC: city technology college, IND: independent school
ENTRY POLICY:	COMP: comprehensive, SEL: selective, NONSEL: non-selective (independent school)
GCSE SUCCESS RATE:	per cent of 15-year-olds who achieved five or more GCSEs grades A*–C
AVE. 'A' LEVEL SCORE:	Average score per A-level /AS Exam

BARNET

	SCHOOL TYPE	ENTRY POLICY	GCSE SUCCESS RATE	AVE. 'A' LEVEL SCORE
The Henrietta Barnett School	VA	Sel	100%	24.8
Pardes House Grammar School	IND	Nonsel	100%	-
St Michael's Catholic Grammar School	VA	Sel	98%	22.5
Queen Elizabeth's School	FD	Sel	95%	27.5
Menorah Grammar School	IND	Sel	93%	19.1
King Alfred School	IND	Nonsel	92%	18.9
St Martha's Senior School	IND	Sel	91%	20.4
Hasmonean High School	VA	Comp	86%	22.3
Woodside Park School	IND	Sel	83%	-
The Mount School	IND	Sel	80%	14.1
Mill Hill School Foundation	IND	Sel	76%	18.6
Beth Jacob Grammar School for Girls	IND	Nonsel	75%	12.9
Copthall School	CY	Comp	71%	19/-
Mill Hill High School	FD	Comp	68%	19.9
Queen Elizabeth's Girls' School	CY	Comp	68%	16.6
Ashmole School	FD	Comp	66%	17.8
The Compton School	CY	Comp	59%	-
St James' Catholic High School	VA	Comp	59%	12.0
Christ's College	CY	Comp	56%	15.2
East Barnet School	CY	Comp	55%	15.2
Bishop Douglass RC High School	VA	Comp	54%	14.7
Hendon School	FD	Comp	54%	15.6
Finchley RC High School	VA	Comp	49%	-
The Albany College	IND	Sel	46%	16.3
Christ Church CofE VA School	VA	Comp	46%	-
St Marty's CofE High School	VA	Comp	45%	13.9
Tuition Centre	IND	Sel	40%	20.2
Friern Barnet School	CY	Comp	32%	-
The Edgware School	CY	Comp	26%	11.0
Whitefield School	CY	Comp	15%	4.0
Wentworth Tutorial College	IND	Sel	14%	14.3
The Ravenscroft School	CY	Comp	13%	12.1
LEA average			**56.9%**	

BRENT

	SCHOOL TYPE	ENTRY POLICY	GCSE SUCCESS RATE	AVE. 'A' LEVEL SCORE
Al-Sadiq and Al-Zahra Schools	IND	Nonsel	91%	-
The Swaminarayan School	IND	Sel	88%	15.2
Islamia Girls' High School	IND	Sel	86%	-
Convent of Jesus and Mary Language College	VA	Comp	61%	14.6
St Gregory RC High School	VA	Comp	57%	14.8
Claremont High School	FD	Comp	54%	17.6
Kingsbury High School	FD	Comp	54%	17.1
Preston Manor High School	FD	Comp	46%	17.5
Copeland Community School and Technology Centre	FD	Comp	41%	15.3
Wembley High School	CY	Comp	41%	13.3
Alperton Community School	FD	Comp	38%	13.1
John Kelly Girls' Technology College	FD	Comp	33%	12.1
John Kelly Boys' Technology College	FD	Comp	31%	7.7
Queen's Park Community School	FD	Comp	31%	11.1
Cardinal Hinsley High School	VA	Comp	30%	10.8
Willesden High School	CY	Comp	13%	6.3
LEA average			**43.0%**	

CAMDEN

	SCHOOL TYPE	ENTRY POLICY	GCSE SUCCESS RATE	AVE. 'A' LEVEL SCORE
North Bridge House School	IND	Sel	100%	-
South Hampstead High School	IND	Sel	97%	28.5
University College School	IND	Sel	97%	25.8
St Margaret's School	IND	Sel	93%	-
JFS	VA	Comp	76%	18.8
La Sainte Union Convent School	VA	Comp	71%	15.5
Royal School Hampstead	IND	Sel	67%	22.0
Camden School for Girls	VA	Comp	59%	19.4
Hampstead School	CY	Comp	47%	14.3
Parliament Hill School	CY	Comp	45%	16.9
William Ellis School	VA	Comp	45%	14.5
Acland Burghley School	CY	Comp	40%	19.4
Maria Fidelis Convent School (Upper School)	VA	Comp	40%	13.3
Haverstock School	CY	Comp	24%	14.1
South Camden Community School	CY	Comp	19%	7.8
Fine Arts College	IND	Nonsel	0%	17.2
LEA average			**47.1%**	

EALING

	SCHOOL TYPE	ENTRY POLICY	GCSE SUCCESS RATE	AVE. 'A' LEVEL SCORE
Notting Hill and Ealing High School	IND	Sel	100%	25.6
Harvington School	IND	Sel	92%	-
St Augustine's Priory	IND	Sel	91%	23.0
St Benedict's School	IND	Sel	85%	19.8
King Fahad Academy	IND	Nonsel	72%	17.3
Ealing College Upper School	IND	Nonsel	68%	15.2
Twyford CofE High School	VA	Comp	67%	15.0
The Ellen Wilkinson School for Girls	FD	Comp	63%	14.6
Cardinal Wiseman RC High School	VA	Comp	62%	12.3
Greenford High School	FD	Comp	62%	16.0
Drayton Manor High School	FD	Comp	58%	16.6
Villiers High School	CY	Comp	47%	9.4
Featherstone High School	CY	Comp	41%	-
Barbara Speake Stage School	IND	Sel	38%	-
Brentside High School	FD	Comp	34%	11.7
Acton High School	CY	Comp	32%	-
Dormers Wells High School	CY	Comp	30%	-
Northolt High School	FD	Comp	27%	13.5
Walford High School	CY	Comp	21%	9.4
Greek School of London	IND	Nonsel	0%	-
Elthorne Park High School	CY	Comp		-
The Japanese School	IND	Sel	-	-
LEA average			**45.6%**	

ENFIELD

	SCHOOL TYPE	ENTRY POLICY	GCSE SUCCESS RATE	AVE. 'A' LEVEL SCORE
St John's Preparatory and Senior School	IND	Sel	100%	22.3
The Latymer School	VA	Sel	98%	24.8
Palmers Green High School	IND	Sel	95%	-
Enfield County School	CY	Comp	81%	13.8
Broomfield School	FD	Comp	63%	12.1
Southgate School	CY	Comp	61%	15.6
St Anne's Catholic High School for Girls	VA	Comp	60%	-
St Ignatius College	VA	Comp	59%	17.3
Enfield Grammar School	FD	Comp	57%	15.6
Bishop Stopford's School	VA	Comp	45%	12.6
Edmonton County School	CY	Comp	45%	15.6
Winchmore School	CY	Comp	45%	11.9
Chace Community School	CY	Comp	40%	10.0
Kingsmead School	CY	Comp	29%	7.2
Albany School	FD	Comp	24%	10.8
Aylward School	CY	Comp	22%	8.8
Lea Valley High School	CY	Comp	22%	6.8
Salisbury School	CY	Comp	16%	8.7
LEA average			**46.8%**	

GREENWICH

	SCHOOL TYPE	ENTRY POLICY	GCSE SUCCESS RATE	AVE. 'A' LEVEL SCORE
Blackheath High School	IND	Sel	93%	19.0
Colfes School	IND	Sel	93%	25.3
St Ursula's Convent School	VA	Comp	72%	-
St Thomas More RC Comprehensive School	VA	Comp	68%	-
Riverston School	IND	Nonsel	61%	-
St Paul's RC Comprehensive School	VA	Comp	47%	-
Eltham Hill Technology College for Girls	CY	Comp	44%	15.2
Thomas Tallis School	CY	Comp	42%	8.3
Crown Woods School	CY	Comp	36%	14.8
Plumstead Manor School	CY	Comp	33%	11.9
Woolwich Polytechnic Boys' School	CY	Comp	27%	10.7
Blackheath Bluecoat CofE School	VA	Comp	22%	7.8
Abbey Wood School	CY	Comp	21%	-
The John Roan School	VC	Comp	21%	8.7
Kidbrooke School	CY	Comp	18%	8.3
Eaglesfield School	CY	Comp	16%	10.1
Eltham Green School	CY	Comp	13%	-
BLA Theatre School	IND	Sel	0%	-
LEA average			**31.7%**	

HACKNEY

	SCHOOL TYPE	ENTRY POLICY	GCSE SUCCESS RATE	AVE. 'A' LEVEL SCORE
Tayyibah Girls' School	IND	Nonsel	80%	-
Yesodey Hatorah School	IND	Nonsel	67%	-
Our Lady's Convent High School	VA	Comp	63%	13.1
Lubavitch House Senior School	IND	Nonsel	62%	-
Stoke Newington School	CY	Comp	40%	-
Beis Malka Girls' School	IND	Nonsel	39%	-
Cardinal Pole RC School	VA	Comp	35%	12.5
Haggerston School	CY	Comp	32%	-
The Skinners' Company's School for Girls	VA	Comp	24%	9.0
Clapton Girls' Technology College	CY	Comp	23%	-
Homerton College of Technology	CY	Comp	22%	-
Kingsland School	CY	Comp	21%	-
Hackney Free and Parochial CofE Secondary School	VA	Comp	12%	10.4
Beis Chinuch Lebonos Girls School	IND	Nonsel	0%	-
Beis Rochel d'Satmar Girls' School	IND	Sel	0%	-
Home School of Stoke Newington	IND	Nonsel	0%	-
LEA average			**27.8%**	

HAMMERSMITH AND FULHAM

	SCHOOL TYPE	ENTRY POLICY	GCSE SUCCESS RATE	AVE. 'A' LEVEL SCORE
The Godolphin and Latymer School	IND	Sel	100%	27.6
Latymer Upper School	IND	Sel	99%	23.0
St Paul's Girls' School	IND	SEL	99%	30.5
Lady Margaret School	VA	Comp	93%	18.2
The London Oratory School	VA	Comp	93%	22.2
Sacred Heart High School	VA	Comp	80%	·
Burlington Danes CofE School	VA	Comp	35%	10.8
Fulham Cross Secondary School	CY	Comp	30%	13.4
Hurlingham and Chelsea School	CY	Comp	17%	14.2
Henry Compton School	CY	Comp	15%	20.0
Ravenscourt Theatre School	IND	Sel	8%	·
Phoenix High School	CY	Comp	4%	16.0
Holborn College	IND	Sel	0%	·
Twynholm School	IND	Nonsel	·	·
LEA average			**48.9%**	

HARINGEY

Channing School	IND	Sel	96%	25.1
Highgate School	IND	Sel	95%	23.5
Fortismere School	CY	Comp	74%	16.7
Hornsey School for Girls	CY	Comp	45%	14.1
Highgate Wood School	CY	Comp	40%	11.1
St Thomas More RC School	VA	Comp	26%	14.2
Gladesmore Community School	CY	Comp	22%	5.7
Northumberland Park Community School	CY	Comp	21%	5.1
St David and St Katharine School	VA	Comp	15%	5.9
White Hart Lane School	CY	Comp	13%	8.3
The John Loughborough School	VA	Comp	12%	·
Alexandra Park School	CY	Comp	n/a	·
Hillside School	IND	Sel	·	·
Park View Academy	CY	Comp	n/a	·
LEA average			**30.3%**	

HOUNSLOW

	SCHOOL TYPE	ENTRY POLICY	GCSE SUCCESS RATE	AVE. 'A' LEVEL SCORE
The Arts Educational School	IND	Sel	95%	·
St Mark's Catholic School	VA	Comp	72%	17.3
Gumley House Convent School	VA	Comp	70%	16.0
The Green School for Girls	VA	Comp	69%	15.2
Heston Community School	CY	Comp	58%	17.9
The Heathland School	CY	Comp	56%	15.5
Gunnersbury Catholic School	VA	Comp	55%	15.1
International School of London	Ind	Nonsel	52%	·
Isleworth and Syon Boys' School	VC	Comp	49%	11.3
Lampton School	CY	Comp	48%	14.4
Chiswick Community School	CY	Comp	43%	15.9
Brentford School for Girls	CY	Comp	36%	13.4

	SCHOOL TYPE	ENTRY POLICY	GCSE SUCCESS RATE	AVE. 'A' LEVEL SCORE
Cranford Community College	CY	Comp	36%	12.2
Feltham Community College	CY	Comp	28%	12.3
Longford Community School	CY	Comp	28%	8.8
Hounslow Manor School	CY	Comp	17%	7.3
St Thomas More School	IND	Nonsel	-	-
LEA average			**49.0%**	

ISLINGTON

	SCHOOL TYPE	ENTRY POLICY	GCSE SUCCESS RATE	AVE. 'A' LEVEL SCORE
Italia Conti Academy of Theatre Arts	IND	Sel	67%	18.0
Highbury Fields School	CY	Comp	47%	9.4
Mount Carmel RC Girls' School	VA	Comp	39%	-
Islington Green School	CY	Comp	30%	-
Central Foundation for Boys' School	VA	Comp	28%	9.0
St Aloysius College	VA	Comp	28%	9.4
Highbury Grove School	CY	Comp	25%	6.6
Elizabeth Garrett Anderson School	CY	Comp	23%	-
Holloway School	CY	Comp	17%	-
The Islington Arts and Media School	CY	Comp	n/a	-
LEA average			**27.4%**	

KENSINGTON AND CHELSEA

	SCHOOL TYPE	ENTRY POLICY	GCSE SUCCESS RATE	AVE. 'A' LEVEL SCORE
Collingham	IND	Sel	100%	16.1
More House School	IND	Sel	100%	18.1
Cardinal Vaughan Memorial School	VA	Comp	87%	20.8
Queen's Gate School	IND	Sel	86%	23.6
Lycee Francais Charles de Gaulle (British Section)	IND	Sel	82%	23.3
Hellenic College of London	IND	Sel	80%	11.6
Mander Portman Woodward School	IND	Sel	76%	17.3
Davies Laing and Dick College	IND	Sel	67%	15.6
St James Independent School for Girls	IND	Nonsel	65%	22.9
Landsdowne College	IND	Nonsel	60%	15.6
Sion-Manning School	VA	Comp	44%	-
Ashbourne Independent School	IND	Nonsel	43%	16.4
St Thomas More's RC School	VA	Comp	41%	-
Holland Park School	CY	Comp	32%	16.9
Duff Miller College	IND	Sel	11%	17.3
David Game College	IND	Sel	0%	12.6
Parayhouse School	IND	Sel	0%	-
Colegio Espanol Vicente Canada Blanch	IND	Nonsel	-	-
Lycee Francias Charles de Gaulle	IND	Sel	-	-
Southbank International School	IND	Sel	-	-
LEA average			**44.5%**	

LAMBETH

Streatham Hill and Clapham High School	IND	Sel	95%	20.4
La Retraite RC Girls' School	VA	Comp	55%	15.3
The London Nautical School	FD	Comp	47%	8.6
St Martin in the Fields High School for Girls	VA	Comp	43%	-
Bishop Thomas Grant RC School	VA	Comp	42%	-
Dunraven School	FD	Comp	36%	-
Charles Edward Brooke School	VC	Comp	30%	8.9
Archbishop Tenison's School	VA	Comp	22%	12.8
Norwood School	CY	Comp	17%	-
Stockwell Park School	CY	Comp	16%	-
Lilian Baylis School	CY	Comp	12%	-
LEA average			**31.9%**	

LEWISHAM

	SCHOOL TYPE	ENTRY POLICY	GCSE SUCCESS RATE	AVE. 'A' LEVEL SCORE
St Dunstan's College	IND	Sel	98%	19.6
Sydenham High School GDST	IND	Sel	95%	21.8
Haberdasher's Aske's Hatcham College	CTC	Comp	69%	17.0
Prendergast School	VA	Comp	67%	15.9
Bonus Pastor RC School	VA	Comp	47%	-
Sydenham School	CY	Comp	41%	14.3
Addey and Stanhope School	VA	Comp	35%	11.8
Forest Hill School	CY	Comp	34%	12.6
Catford Girls' School	CY	Comp	26%	-
Northbrook CofE School	VA	Comp	26%	-
Deptford Green School	CY	Comp	25%	11.2
Sedgehill School	CY	Comp	25%	12.7
St Joseph's Academy	VA	Comp	22%	-
Crofton School	CY	Comp	20%	9.5
Malory School	CY	Comp	10%	-
Telegraph Hill School	CY	Comp	n/a	-
LEA average			**32.3%**	

MERTON

	SCHOOL TYPE	ENTRY POLICY	GCSE SUCCESS RATE	AVE. 'A' LEVEL SCORE
King's College School	IND	Sel	100%	27.9
Wimbledon High School	IND	Sel	100%	27.4
Hazelhurst School for Girls	IND	Sel	91%	-
Ursuline Convent High School	VA	Comp	64%	19.6
Ricards Lodge High School	CY	Comp	58%	-
Wimbledon College	VA	Comp	52%	18.6
Rowan High School	CY	Comp	36%	-
Raynes Park High School (Mixed)	CY	Comp	35%	-
Rutlish School	VC	Comp	33%	11.0
Tamworth Manor High School	CY	Comp	27%	-
Eastfields High School (Boys)	CY	Comp	17%	-
Bishopsford Community School	CY	Comp	n/a	-
The Norwegian School in London	IND	Nonsel	-	-
LEA average			**38.8%**	

NEWHAM

	SCHOOL TYPE	ENTRY POLICY	GCSE SUCCESS RATE	AVE. 'A' LEVEL SCORE
St Bonaventure's RC School	VA	Comp	63%	14.0
St Angela's Ursuline Convent School	VA	Comp	61%	15.2
Plashet School	CY	Comp	56%	-
Sarah Bonnell School	CY	Comp	51%	-
Langdon School	CY	Comp	43%	-
Stratford School	FD	Comp	28%	-
Lister Community School	CY	Comp	26%	-
Brampton Manor School	CY	Comp	25%	-
Little Ilford School	CY	Comp	22%	-
Forest Gate Community School	CY	Comp	21%	-
Rokeby School	CY	Comp	20%	-
Eastlea Community School	CY	Comp	18%	-
Cumberland School	CY	Comp	13%	-
Jamia Ramania Islamic Institute	IND	Sel	-	-
The Royal Docks Community School	CY	Comp	n/a	-
LEA average			**34.6%**	

RICHMOND UPON THAMES

	SCHOOL TYPE	ENTRY POLICY	GCSE SUCCESS RATE	AVE. 'A' LEVEL SCORE
Hampton School	IND	Sel	100%	33.3
The Lady Eleanor Holles School	IND	Sel	100%	34.6
St Paul's School	IND	Sel	99%	32.2
St Catherine's School	IND	Sel	90%	-
The Royal Ballet School	IND	Sel	85%	7.9
St James Independent School for Boys	IND	Sel	84%	24.2
Waldegrave School for Girls	CY	Comp	77%	-
Teddington School	CY	Comp	62%	-
Grey Court School	CY	Comp	57%	-
Orleans Park School	CY	Comp	56%	-
Hampton Community College	CY	Comp	49%	-
Shene School	CY	Comp	41%	-
Christ's School	VA	Comp	35%	-
Whitton School	CY	Comp	33%	-
The German School	IND	Sel	-	-
The Harrodian School	IND	Sel	-	-
The Swedish School	IND	Nonsel	-	-
LEA average			**51.9%**	

SOUTHWARK

	SCHOOL TYPE	ENTRY POLICY	GCSE SUCCESS RATE	AVE. 'A' LEVEL SCORE
James Allen's Girls' School	IND	Sel	100%	27.0
Alleyn's School	IND	Sel	98%	25.1
Dulwich College	IND	Sel	98%	26.0
Notre Dame School	VA	Comp	62%	-
Bacon's College	CTC	Comp	54%	13.5
St Saviour's and St Olave's School	VA	Comp	54%	27.0
Sacred Heart RC School	VA	Comp	44%	-
St Michael's RC School	VA	Comp	44%	-
The St Thomas the Apostle College	VA	Comp	43%	-
Aylwin Girls' School	CY	Comp	27%	-
Waverley School	CY	Comp	20%	-
Geoffrey Chaucer School	CY	Comp	19%	-
Warwick Park School	CY	Comp	18%	-
Archbishop Michael Ramsey Technology College	VA	Comp	16%	4.0
Walworth School	CY	Comp	16%	-
Kingsdale school	CY	Comp	14%	-
LEA average			**29.5%**	

TOWER HAMLETS

	SCHOOL TYPE	ENTRY POLICY	GCSE SUCCESS RATE	AVE. 'A' LEVEL SCORE
Mulberry School for Girls	CY	Comp	48%	12.8
Raine's Foundation School	VA	Comp	45%	10.9
Central Foundation Girls' School	VC	Comp	42%	9.1
Bishop Challoner RC School	VA	Comp	40%	7.6
Bethnal Green Technology College	CY	Comp	38%	-
Oaklands School	CY	Comp	37%	-
Morpeth School	CY	Comp	32%	-
Stepney Green School	CY	Comp	31%	-
Swanlea Mixed County Secondary School	CY	Comp	31%	-
St Paul's Way Community School	CY	Comp	29%	-
Madni Girls' School (London)	IND	Sel	27%	-
George Green's School	VC	Comp	24%	11.9
Sir John Cass Redcoat School	VA	Comp	22%	-
The Blessed John Roche Catholic School	VA	Comp	17%	12.6
Langdon Park School	CY	Comp	17%	-
Bow School	CY	Comp	14%	-
LEA average			**31.1%**	

WALTHAM FOREST

	SCHOOL TYPE	ENTRY POLICY	GCSE SUCCESS RATE	AVE. 'A' LEVEL SCORE
Forest School	IND	Sel	95%	26.7
Normanhurst School	IND	Nonsel	70%	-
Connaught School for Girls	CY	Comp	60%	-
Walthamstow School for Girls	CY	Comp	58%	-
Highams Park School	VA	Comp	56%	15.9
Chingford School	FD	Comp	47%	8.5
Willowfield School	CY	Comp	42%	-
Leytonstone School	CY	Comp	39%	-
Norlington School for Boys	CY	Comp	38%	-
The Holy Family College	VA	Comp	36%	7.8
George Mitchell School	CY	Comp	32%	-
Tom Hood School	CY	Comp	27%	-
Heathcoate School	CY	Comp	24%	-
Kelmscott School	CY	Comp	24%	-
Rush Croft School	CY	Comp	24%	-
Aveling Park School	CY	Comp	23%	-
Warwick School for Boys	CY	Comp	22%	-
McEntee School	CY	Comp	17%	-
LEA average			**36.6%**	

WANDSWORTH

	SCHOOL TYPE	ENTRY POLICY	GCSE SUCCESS RATE	AVE. 'A' LEVEL SCORE
Putney High School	IND	Sel	99%	23.4
Ibstock Place	IND	Sel	97%	-
Emanuel School	IND	Sel	95%	17.9
Putney Park School	IND	Sel	86%	-
ADT College	CTC	Comp	62%	14.9
Graveney School	FD	Comp	55%	16.5
Burntwood School	FD	Comp	54%	16.5
Elliott School	FD	Comp	37%	18.5
John Paul II School	VA	Comp	33%	-
Chestnut Grove School	CY	Comp	28%	9.3
Salesian College	VA	Comp	26%	-
Southfields Community College	FD	Comp	26%	11.4
Ernest Bevin College	CY	Comp	18%	12.3
Battersea Technology College	CY	Comp	4%	-
Balham Preparatory School	IND	Nonsel	-	-
Hall School Wimbledon	IND	Sel	-	-
LEA average			**35.6%**	

WESTMINSTER, CITY OF

	SCHOOL TYPE	ENTRY POLICY	GCSE SUCCESS RATE	AVE. 'A' LEVEL SCORE
Westminster School	IND	Sel	97%	32.2
Francis Holland School	IND	Sel	95%	21.5
Queen's College London	IND	Sel	92%	21.7
Francis Holland School	IND	Sel	91%	24.2
The St Marylebone School	VA	Comp	77%	12.8
The Grey Coat Hospital	VA	Comp	74%	19.5
Portland Place School	IND	Sel	68%	15.5
Sylvia Young Theatre School	IND	Sel	65%	-
The Urdang Academy of Ballet	IND	Sel	44%	8.0
Westminster City School	VA	Comp	38%	10.5
Centre Academy	IND	Sel	33%	-
Pimlico School	CY	Comp	31%	17.0
Bales College	IND	Nonsel	25%	10.4
St George's School Westminster	VA	Comp	21%	-
North Westminster School	CY	Comp	20%	14.5
St Augustine's CofE School	VA	Comp	20%	10.1
Quintin Kynaston School	CY	Comp	16%	16.8
International Community School	IND	Nonsel	0%	-
The American School in London	IND	Sel	-	-
LEA average			35.0%	

First Class accommodation for as long as you like

Visiting London for an extended period? It makes sense to choose an Oakwood apartment.

Stay in the capital's finest residential areas. Be close to major centres of entertainment and leisure. Enjoy a high standard of meticulous living matched by a quality service tailored to your individual needs.

As the world leader in corporate accommodation we know how to make you feel truly at home.

Your stay* in London will seem all too short – no matter how long you're here.

Come Home to Oakwood

Tel: +44 (0)171 408 1992
Fax: +44 (0)171 495 4572

Oakwood.

Depending on location, the minimum stay in some of our apartments is 90 days.

The Most Trusted Name in Corporate Housing Worldwide℠

The Boroughs

Does it matter which of the 32 London boroughs you live in or move to? Under the unlamented poll tax, it certainly did: crossing the street from Wandsworth to Lambeth could cost a couple well over a thousand a year. Under the council tax, with its charge per dwelling, things have evened out – but not entirely. The list that follows gives the 'band D' council tax for each borough as an 'at-a-glance' comparison to show how charges differ. (Band D is the 'anchor' band: the other bands will differ in proportion.) The amounts change this spring.

Who governs London? No-one in particular until the Mayor gets elected, though lots of people tinker with bits of it. The most powerful is the Government Office for London, which is supposed to coordinate the actions of the various ministries. The boroughs work together to deal with things like Thames bridges, which mostly have different boroughs at each end. Each borough runs the schools in its area, and in this respect they differ greatly. Boroughs also have most planning powers, but the government will deal with any big development. The much-discussed Mayor of London, and the 25-member Greater London Authority (GLA) will be elected this year (2000). The Authority will have powers, so far rather ill-defined, over transport, planning and many other matters. The Mayor will be a figurehead – or more – for all of London. Together, he or she and the GLA will certainly be more powerful than the old GLC – but will only have a 'small staff'. The borders betwen the powers of the GLA and the boroughs are bound to be contentious – especially over planning matters.

Barnet
Controlling party: Lib Dem/Labour Coal.
Make-up: 28 Con, 26 Lab, 6 Lib Dem
Town Hall tel: 020 8359 2000
Search: 5 working days
Council tax, band D: £760

Brent
Controlling party: Labour
Make-up: 43 Lab, 19 Con, 4 Lib Dem
Town Hall tel: 020 8937 1234
Search: 5–10 working days
Council tax, band D: £678

Bromley
Controlling party: Lib Dem/Labour Coal.
Make-up: 27 Con, 25 Lib Dem, 7 Lab
Town Hall tel: 020 84643333
Search: 2 working days
Council tax, band D: £669

Camden
Controlling party: Labour
Make-up: 42 Lab, 11 Con, 6 Lib Dem
Town Hall tel: 020 7278 4444
Search: 7–10 working days
Council tax, band D: £897

Corporation of London
Controlling party: Apolitical
Town Hall tel: 020 76063030
Search: 7 working days
Council tax, band D: £556

Croydon
Controlling party: Labour
Make-up: 38 Lab, 31 Con, 1 Lib Dem
Town Hall tel: 020 86864433
Search: 27 working days
Council tax, band D: £758

Ealing
Controlling party: Labour
Make-up: 53 Lab, 15 Con, 3 Lib Dem
Town Hall tel: 020 8579 2424
Search: 5 working days
Council tax, band D: £703

Enfield
Controlling party: Labour
Make-up: 43 Lab, 23 Con
Town Hall tel: 020 8854 8888
Search: 10 days
Council tax, band D: £732

Greenwich
Controlling party: Labour
Make-up: 51 Lab, 7 Con, 2 Lib Dem
Town Hall tel: 020 8854 8888
Search: 10 working days
Council tax, band D: £883

Hackney
Controlling party: Labour
Make-up: 29 Lab, 17 Lib Dem, 11 Con, 2 Green, 1 Ind
Town Hall tel: 020 8356 5000

HAVERING

BARKING

REDBRIDGE

BEXLEY

WALTHAM FOREST

NEWHAM

GREENWICH

BROMLEY

HACKNEY

TOWER HAMLETS

LEWISHAM

ENFIELD

ISLINGTON

CITY

SOUTHWARK

CROYDON

HARINGEY

WESTMINSTER

LAMBETH

CAMDEN

KENSINGTON AND CHELSEA

BARNET

HAMMERSMITH AND FULHAM

WANDSWORTH

SUTTON

MERTON

BRENT

KINGSTON

HARROW

EALING

HOUNSLOW

RICHMOND UPON THAMES

HILLINGDON

Boroughs in **bold** are covered in this book

Search: 10 working days
Council tax, band D: £789

Hammersmith & Fulham
Controlling party: Labour
Make-up: 35 Lab, 14 Con, 1 Ind Labour
Town Hall tel: 020 8748 3020
Search: 10 working days
Council tax, band D: £827

Haringey
Controlling party: Labour
Make-up: 54 Lab, 3 Lib Dem, 2 Con
Town Hall tel: 020 8489 0000
Search: 10 working days
Council tax, band D: £898

Hounslow
Controlling party: Labour
Make-up: 44 Lab, 11 Con, 4 Lib Dem, 1 Ind
Town Hall tel: 020 8583 2000
Search: 1 day
Council tax, band D: £860

Islington
Controlling party: Joint Control
Make-up: 25 Lab, 27 Lib Dem
Town Hall tel: 020 7226 1234
Search: 10 working days
Council tax, band D: £912

Kensington & Chelsea
Controlling party: Conservative
Make-up: 39 Con, 15 Lab
Town Hall tel: 020 7937 5464
Search: 10 working days
Council tax, band D: £534

Lambeth
Controlling party: Labour
Make-up: 41 Lab, 18 Lib Dem, 5 Con
Town Hall tel: 020 7926 1000
Search: 10 working days
Council tax, band D: £750

Lewisham
Controlling party: Labour
Make-up: 60 Lab, 3 Lib Dem, 2 Con,
1 Socialist Lab
Town Hall tel: 020 8314 6000
Search: 3 weeks
Council tax, band D: £727

Merton
Controlling party: Labour
Make-up: 39 Lab, 12 Con, 3 Lib Dem, 3 Ind
Town Hall tel: 020 8543 2222

Search: 10 working days
Council tax, band D: £866

Newham
Controlling party: Labour
Make-up: 60 Lab
Town Hall tel: 020 8472 1430
Search: 10 days
Council tax, band D: £768

Richmond
Controlling party: Liberal Democrat
Make-up: 34 Lib Dem, 14 Con, 4 Lab
Town Hall tel: 020 8891 1411
Search: 7 working days
Council tax, band D: £908

Southwark
Controlling party: Labour
Make-up: 32 Lab, 27 Lib Dem, 4 Con, 1 Ind
Town Hall tel: 020 7525 5000
Search: 15 working days
Council tax, band D: £809

Tower Hamlets
Controlling party: Labour
Make-up: 43 Lab, 6 Lib Dem, Ind 1
Town Hall tel: 020 7364 5000
Search: 2–4 weeks
Council tax, band D: £674

Waltham Forest
Controlling party: Labour
Make-up: 30 Lab, 14 Con, 12 Lib Dem,
1 Ind
Town Hall tel: 020 8527 5544
Search: 4–5 working days
Council tax, band D: £840

Wandsworth
Controlling party: Conservative
Make-up: 50 Con, 11 Lab
Town Hall tel: 020 8871 6000
Search: 3–4 weeks
Council tax, band D: £370

City of Westminster
Controlling party: Conservative
Make-up: 47 Con, 13 Lab
Town Hall tel: 020 7641 6000
Search: 10 working days
Council tax, band D: £350

Planning and building regulations
by Soo Ware

When buying a home, it is advisable to know something of the law that affects the development of residential property. There are, broadly, three building legislation acts that apply to domestic property: the Town and Country Planning Acts, the Building Regulations, and the Party Wall Act.

If you are buying a property that has been modernized or converted – possibly over the course of a number of years – you will wish to reassure yourself and your building society or other lender that the conversion has been done with the full approval of the planning authorities, to the standards required by the Building Regulations and with the agreement of the adjoining owners.

The searches for conveyancing purposes should reveal whether or not applications for planning permission and building regulation approval have been made. If not, you can visit the council offices and make your own enquiries, but finding out about Party Wall agreements with adjoining owners may be more difficult: the vendor should disclose this information if you ask.

However, once purchased, no matter how ideal the property appears to be, some alteration or extension to your new home may be necessary to adapt someone else's ideas to your own. This again brings you into contact with building law.

Planning permission
The Town and Country Planning Acts are complex and it may be necessary to obtain expert advice early on from architects, planning consultants or chartered surveyors. This chapter deals with controls on dwelling houses in terraces, semi-detached or detached houses. Blocks of flats are more complex and demand expert advice.

The Planning Acts are there to regulate development and protect the public interest in the development of land. Each application is looked at in context against the background of the development plan prepared by each London borough. Copies of the development plans can be obtained from town halls. Some areas within boroughs are designated conservation areas and usually the borough produces a separate, stricter policy document for such areas. Buildings that are listed (i.e. buildings of historic or architectural interest) are even more tightly controlled and you may need to obtain permission from English Heritage through the borough's Conservation Officer in the planning department.

What might seem to you a very minor extension or alteration to a house can nevertheless have a far-reaching impact on the adjoining owners, the amenity and the appearance of a whole area. For example, motley roof conversions or new dormer windows on front elevations of terraces can change the appearance of a whole street. A planning application may be necessary for any of the following:

1. Extensions, alterations, garage, conservatories, roof gardens, balconies and loft conversions.
2. Garden fences, walls and the removal of trees (which are either the subject of preservation orders or in conservation areas). However, some garden sheds, greenhouses, swimming pools, sauna baths and summer houses may not require planning permission provided certain conditions are met.
3. Alterations to road access, drives and off-street parking. Additional consent from the highway authority (in London, the Department of Transport) may also be required.
4. Alterations to a previous planning consent or a change of use – for example, dividing a house into flats or flats back into a house.
5. The building is in a conservation area or covered by an Article 4 direction (an order placed on a whole street to maintain the integrity of its appearance). This can include

changing doors, windows and roofs, painting brickwork, pebbledashing, sandblasting brickwork, etc.

6. If the building is listed a separate listed building consent will also be required. Make initial enquiries to the planning department of the appropriate borough council. A specialist Conservation Officer or Historic Buildings Officer will deal with your application and advise you as to whether or not you need to contact English Heritage. It is a criminal offence to make alterations (or even undertake some forms of maintenance) to a listed building without prior approval from English Heritage.

However, not all building work requires planning permission, and some quite modest extensions and alterations fall into the category of permitted development. Planning permission may not be required if you wish to extend your home by less than a certain volume, providing you can comply with certain conditions to do with height and location and (usually) make no changes to the front elevation.

The way in which the volume of a house is assessed is quite simple and relates to the 'original' house, that is as it was when first built or as it was on July 1, 1948 (if any extensions have taken place since then, the allowance may have been exceeded). The volume is based on the external dimensions of the house including the roof and the cellar. At present, the allowance for extensions to a terraced house is 1,765 cubic feet or 10 per cent of the original volume of the house up to 4,061 cubic feet; for a semi-detached or detached house, it is 2,472 cubic feet, or 15 per cent of the original volume of the house up to 4,061 cubic feet. However, there are no permitted development rights for flats. Planning permission for extensions or alterations will be necessary as will consent from the freeholder.

Even if the proposals fall within the volume for permitted development, it is advisable to consult the planning officer who deals with your area to confirm that no permission is necessary.

Planning permission is also often necessary for demolitions, even for such things as garden walls or fences or for changes to railings and gates: check with the local authority before proceeding.

Planning permission may not be necessary but Building Regulation approval for the work will probably be required and a separate application should be made to the Building Control department. A Party Wall agreement or, at least, formal agreement by your neighbours may also be necessary. This is obtained through negotiation, and it is advisable to seek expert help.

How to apply

All boroughs have a planning enquiry office and most produce leaflets explaining their requirements for different types of development. Whenever possible, it is a good idea to have preliminary talks with the borough before making an application. It is, in theory, possible to contact the planning office to discuss your proposals before lodging a planning application. You should also talk to the Conservation Officer if appropriate. In some cases you may be able to arrange to meet an officer on site. However, the huge volume of planning applications and appeals made in London means that many boroughs are no longer able to offer these services until a formal application has been lodged.

Four sets of forms and a scale of fees can be obtained from the planning office. For the submission, you will need to provide four sets of drawings. It is also useful to include photographs of both the property concerned and the surrounding buildings as well as a description of the proposed work. The drawings are very important and must be done well. A location plan showing the street and surrounding area on the Ordnance Survey map at a scale of 1:1250 is required together with the drawings of plans, elevations and sections differentiating between the proposed new work and existing buildings. For work to be carried out in conservation areas and on listed buildings additional detailed, large-scale drawings will also be required. There is a statutory fee payable on application, which varies according to the type of alterations.

How long should it take?

In theory, planning applications should be processed within eight weeks; this is a statutory requirement. It is possible to check up on the progress of your application after four weeks from receipt of acknowledgement.

Your application will normally be considered by a planning committee, though minor issues can be determined by the planning officer. The borough is obliged to consult with the immediate neighbours and, in certain circumstances, with more distant neighbours as well. Letters may be sent to adjacent properties and notice may be posted on the boundary of the property (a town hall euphemism for the front gate-post or fence) so that local people are informed and can comment if they want to. Usually the council also puts notices in local newspapers about planning applications received. The procedures for public consultation vary from council to council.

Once responses to consultations have been received it is possible to get some idea of the council's view of your application. Many London boroughs are taking considerably longer than the eight weeks to process (technically called 'determine') applications – in some cases up to six months – before permission is granted or refused. The first hint of a possible delay over the eight weeks may come in the form of a letter from the council requesting a time extension. The eight weeks is counted from the time the authority acknowledges receipt of your application and many boroughs are taking a considerable number of weeks just to do this.

On receipt of the letter asking for a time extension, you can either accept the delay or appeal to the Secretary of State at the Department of the Environment, Transport and the Regions (DETR) on the basis that the authority has effectively refused the application because it has not issued a decision in time.

If you are thinking of an appeal, it is certainly advisable to seek the assistance of a planning consultant, architect or surveyor with special planning expertise. There are three types of appeal: a written representation (which is called a written appeal), a hearing, where an inspector listens to the case presented by the parties involved, and an inquiry, which is like a court case and involves the appointment of a planning QC to act on your behalf.

Planning appeals are a lengthy and expensive business. It is usually quicker to negotiate with the borough to determine your application rather than appeal to the Secretary of State. However, if you are reasonably certain the borough is going to refuse your application and you feel you have a good case, you can refuse a time extension and appeal after the statutory eight weeks period. Once you have set the appeal in motion, the borough will not process the application any further.

Where to get help and advice

Councils produce free leaflets available from their enquiry offices which explain the borough's own planning policies: these cover the Development plan, Conservation Area Policy documents, Borough Design Guides, and often a handbook explaining the procedures.

There are two useful Department of the Environment, Transport and the Regions booklets: *Planning Permission – A Guide to the Householder* and *Planning Appeals – A Guide to Procedure*. These are often available from council offices or, if not, from the DETR, Tolgate House, Houltorn Street, Bristol BS2 9DJ.

The Royal Institute of British Architects provides leaflets describing services that architects offer in respect of planning applications and leaflets describing how drawings are prepared. These are available from the Clients Advisory Service, Royal Institute of British Architects, 66 Portland Place, London W1N 4AD. Tel: 020 7580 5533.

The Royal Town Planning Institute has leaflets about planning application procedure and appeals, lists of sources of planning advice in London, and can put people in touch with 'Planning Aid for Londoners' which is a free advice service manned by chartered town planners, 26 Portland Place, London W1N 4BE. Tel: 020 7636 9107.

Lists of architects can be obtained from the Clients Advisory Service (CAS) at the Royal Institute of British Architects (address above) who can give lists of local architects with special planning expertise. Further information is also available by e-mail (cas@inst.riba.org) or phone 020 7307 3700.

The Royal Town Planning Institute (address above) can give lists of planning consultants who will help with applications.

The Royal Institution of Chartered Surveyors (12 Great George St, London SW1, Tel: 020 7222 7000) also produce lists of chartered surveyors and estate agents with expertise in planning matters.

Building regulations

To some extent, making an application for building regulation approval is more straightforward than making a planning application. There are two clearly defined procedures for obtaining approval: a building notice and full plans submission. It is also worth knowing a little about the background to the legislation and the kinds of work which need approval.

Background

The 1985 Building Regulations Acts introduced new regulations that now apply to both Inner and Outer London boroughs and are run by each borough council's Building Control Department. The new regulations have re-organized and superseded all previous legislation relating to those building works that were covered by the old building regulations and many separate local bylaws for Inner and Outer London.

The 1985 regulations have been regularly updated with amendments and new regulations have been introduced covering matters such as sound and thermal insulation, control of condensation and energy, heat-producing appliances and provisions for the disabled.

What do you need building regulation approval for?

The procedures for obtaining building regulation approval are now the same whether you are building in a London borough or elsewhere in the country, and are administered through each borough Building Control Department. The kind of work for which approval is necessary includes:

1. The erection of a building.
2. The extension of a building (conversion into flats, loft conversions, some forms of conservatory).
3. 'Material' alterations to a building – alterations to structural walls (for example, knocking two rooms together, taking down a chimney breast), means of escape and fire resistance, particularly in relation to conversions into flats and loft extensions for individual houses.
4. Provision, extension or 'material' alteration to sanitary equipment (putting in a new bathroom or shower or extra WC), drainage, unvented water systems and putting in a stove, boiler or fire which runs on solid fuel, oil or gas.
5. Provision, extension or 'material' alteration of energy conservation, insulation (including cavity wall systems) and ventilation in dwellings (particularly when installing an internal bathroom, WC or internal kitchen), ventilation of heating appliances.

The Party Wall Act 1997

Since the Great Fire of 1666, there has always been special legislation for the Inner London boroughs relating to the rights of adjoining owners and covering joint concerns such as party walls which provide support between dwellings and the prevention of the spread of fire between dwellings. Formal procedures were in place which worked very successfully in the prevention of neighbourly disputes. In 1997 a Party Wall Act was passed by Parliament to extend the procedures for party walls throughout the country.

The procedures set out in the Act formalize agreements between owners when one building owner is undertaking building work to a party wall or fence or within certain distances of adjoining owners' foundations. The Act sets out the process for agreeing the condition of the buildings involved, the nature of the work proposed and the apportionment of costs. This involves serving notices on the adjoining owner and agreeing the appointment of architects or surveyors to act on behalf of the building owner and adjoining owner to ensure that the latter's property does not suffer as a result of the work. It is specialized and if you are considering any work which involves a Party Wall Award (meaning an agreement) you will need an architect or surveyor with the appropriate expertise.

Examples of work which would require a Party Wall Award include loft extensions, underpinning, extensions along the boundary or within certain distances of the boundary depending on the type of foundations proposed, works to the boundary walls, taking down chimney breasts, opening up between rooms where new beams are required bearing on the party wall and cellar/basement conversions.

How to set about it

Using forms obtained from your local authority you need to submit an application with a fee. Except in the case of very simple work, the services of an architect or chartered surveyor will be essential because detailed drawings are often required giving calculations and technical information on materials, insulation values, drainage and fire protection.

You'll also need, in the case of any structural work, technical drawings and calculations. It is possible to make an appointment with the building control officer, before putting in an application, to discuss the proposals and to find out if any particular information should be included (for example, specific calculations). Sometimes the officer (still called District Surveyors in some boroughs) will be happy to meet you on site if this is easier.

Building Notice route

Eighty per cent of building control applications involve a Building Notice. For buildings where it is not necessary to obtain a fire certificate before occupation – that is most homes – it is possible to serve a Building Notice. You should submit a completed application form (available from the Building Control Department), two sets of drawings and calculations, the appropriate fee and notice that you will commence work 48hrs later without waiting for approval. You should arrange a meeting immediately afterwards to establish whether or not there are any difficulties. As work progresses, the building control officer will pay regular visits to the site to ensure everything is done to his or her satisfaction.

A certain amount of confidence is needed to take this course, for if the regulations are not complied with, the local authority can enforce them up to a year after the work is completed, and this can prove to be extremely expensive for you. Less information needs to be shown on the drawings than on the Full Plan route, but the building control officer, during inspections, can (and does) insist on additional works being incorporated to ensure that the regulations are complied with as the work goes along. These people have very wide powers, and they use them.

There are other types of building work that may require additional applications. For example, some structures require a licence (a boundary wall more than 6ft high or a steel balcony or external fire escape). These are regarded as temporary and special buildings. In the case of flats or maisonettes over shops, applications have also to be made to the fire brigade, but your building control officer will give you details of these.

Full Plan route

This is best used if you wish to have very tight control over the cost of the job and wish to have all details sewn up before the work starts to minimize the possibility of extra expenses. It's also necessary to have a reasonably long lead-in – at least five to eight weeks for the application to be processed.

Building regulation approval for the Full Plan route is in two stages: firstly, the drawings must be approved. A fee is payable and it should take between five and eight weeks. However, for complex submissions where a relaxation of the regulations is required, or where inadequate information is provided, building regulation approval can take considerably longer. Secondly, when work begins a Notice of Commencement should be submitted to the building control officer together with a further fee to cover the building control officer's inspection. The officer may need to be informed when certain work is taking place (for example, building foundations, damp-proof courses, laying new drains or covering up structural work), in which case further notices (but no fee) need to be served with one full working day's notice.

For the first stage, two sets of drawings and information should be submitted together with a letter or, in some boroughs, a form requesting that the proposals are considered for building regulation approval together with the appropriate fee. You can get details of the fees from the Building Control Department. During the five to eight week period before the Full Plan approval is given, a building control officer may ask for additional information or explanations and it is possible to have discussions with the officer about the best way to meet requirements.

Whichever route you select, when the works are completed, you or sometimes the solicitors doing searches will need to write to the Building Control Department requesting confirmation that the work was constructed in accordance with the regulations and a letter of confirmation will usually be sent to you.

What happens if you decide to go without Building Control approval? You could find it difficult to sell your property, as solicitors' searches may reveal that the work was done without the proper approval, licences, or Party Wall Awards. Or, you may be caught red-handed doing work for which approval has not been obtained, as building control officers take an eagle-eyed interest in the contents of skips. This may lead to the council taking legal action.

Soo Ware is an architect with a special interest in London property and is a partner in The Chartered Practice. She teaches Professional Practice at the Bartlett School of Architecture, University College, London.

Architectural styles

by Soo Ware

Foreigners coming to London have been known to express surprise that so many homes here are 'second-hand'. It is true that the majority of the city's houses are pre-1919. The only chance to buy a totally new house in Inner London comes with comparatively rare developments in odd corners.

The nearest most London buyers get to a 'new' home is a newly converted flat or a heavily modernized house. Even then, the façade will usually be carefully restored 'old' and many of the original features inside redesigned.

New homes have been built recently on a large scale along the riverside. From Greenwich to Richmond the riverside is being developed by the private sector to provide up-market flats and houses on previously industrial 'brown sites'. Away from the river, developers have been building on small infill sites and converting warehouses and offices to flats and 'loft' shells. At the very top of the market, there are also modern houses and new blocks of flats around Hampstead and near Regent's Park. Pockets of 'mews' type developments are taking place on infill sites in other areas. Some new estates of conventional family homes are being squeezed into surplus land beside railways in parts of South London. The architectural style of these new developers ranges from the high-tech avant-garde, through Post-modernism to Classical pastiche and bijou traditional.

A glance at London's skyline, with its many tower blocks of flats, shows that many homes have been built since the war. These homes have been built by London's local authorities, and until very recently were effectively outside the mainstream housing market as they were rented. Now, however, the 'Right to Buy' laws are bringing these flats, and the many council houses down at ground level, onto the market. This adds a new dimension to the choice of homes: modern properties (some simply convenient, some in fact excellent in both style and soundness) in central locations.

Most buyers, now and in the future, will be buying 'period' homes. This is a phrase widely used by estate agents who have no idea how old a house really is. It is often useful to know the vintage of a property, not just for interest but because different kinds of homes were built at different periods. Some are spacious, some cramped. Some were usually well-built, others a hurried response to fashion. Some kinds of architecture throw up more maintenance problems than others.

It should be said that there is some cause for sympathy with the agents' 'period' tag. First, some styles – eg 'Georgian' – were built, with little discernible evolution, for decades. Some were derived from earlier periods than when they were built – take the turn-of-the-century 'Queen Anne'. And this is still going on, with new London 'mews' popping up where none was there before. So the illustrations here are a starting point, a framework for reference. It can literally be impossible even for experts to date a London house by appearance only.

18th-century Georgian

These very elegant and much sought-after houses are found in small pockets. There are some in Mayfair, many of which were used as offices and are now being converted back into homes. Others are found in Islington, Hackney, Greenwich, Kennington, Kew, Clapham, Battersea, Richmond, Highgate and Hampstead. Detached or in terraces, each house is different. Flat-fronted, of Classical proportions, 2- or 3-storey with a slate mansard attic storey, usually three or five sash windows on each floor, often simple in appearance, soft yellow or red bricks, weathered in appearance. Often a fine front door with a carved wood door case with Classical details – pediments, columns and fan lights. Principal rooms on the first floor are reached by an elegant staircase. These buildings are invariably listed.

Georgian, late-18th and early 19th centuries

Built from the 1780s to the 1840s: often hard to date accurately without local knowledge. Found in Islington and Camden Town, Chelsea and Kensington, Bloomsbury, Kennington, Stockwell and parts of the West End. Usually in terraces, sometimes in squares and crescents, always in groups arranged as a whole. Three- or 4-storeys; sometimes an attic behind a parapet and a basement behind railings. Ground floor often stucco in an ashlar pattern. Other features: fanlight above front doors and ironwork balcony. Two sash windows per floor, brickwork usually soft London stocks, sometimes rendered with stucco and painted. Rooms are often modest-sized, main ones on first floor.

Regency villas and cottages

Built in the early 19th century, these pretty villas and terraces were intended to reflect a rural idyll in urban or suburban surroundings. Normally 2-storey, terraced or semi-detached, with ironwork canopies and wooden or cast-iron conservatories, trellises, sash windows and decorative railings. The front doors and porches often have delicate canopies. Slate roof, shallow-pitched with wide eaves. Rooms pretty but small. Found in pockets (Putney, Richmond, Kew or Twickenham), though a few survive in Chelsea, Mayfair and Regent's Park. A style much sought-after.

Regency terraces

In contrast to the picturesque Regency villas and cottages, there are also the more formal and magnificent terraces around Regent's Park and elsewhere in London and the river front at Richmond. These are buildings of Classical proportions, with 3, 4 or 5 storeys in sweeping crescents, terraces or lodges and substantial villas. Terraces are formed by a number of identical houses joined together, with the end of the terraces being defined separately like full stops. They are generally part of large estates, and are stucco – faced with identical decorations. Some are still single homes of truly magnificent proportions, others are converted into smart flats. Many are now used as offices or as company/diplomatic accommodation. Some have been rebuilt behind the original façade. Sometimes hard to distinguish from the early Victorian equivalent (see next page).

Early Victorian

Vast areas of London were built at this period, forming a ring stretching from Kensington and Chelsea through Camden and Islington, down through Hackney and to a lesser degree in South London: Blackheath, Camberwell, Kennington. They form part of the great estates of the time: Grosvenor, Gunter, Pimlico. Three-, 4- or 5-storey flat-fronted terraces or squares, usually with Classical leanings: porticoes, Doric or Ionic columns, pediments and brackets. Almost always with a stucco, symbolic ashlar ground-floor storey, and sometimes painted above. Frequently whole areas are painted with the same colours. Now mostly flats, but planned as family homes for the burgeoning middle classes. Rooms often very large and well-proportioned, with attractive plasterwork, fireplaces and staircases.

Mews

Surviving mews date mostly from the 1830s to the 1890s. They were built to provide stabling and servants' housing, behind the terraces and squares in Belgravia, Knightsbridge, Mayfair, Marylebone and other parts. Today, they are converted to cottages in a hotchpotch of styles, with the coach house or stable used for garaging and the upper floor(s) forming 1 or 2 bedrooms. Some have been virtually rebuilt as larger houses. Usually brick, maybe painted or rendered or with a stucco finish. During conversion, they often gain features such as bay windows, shutters, ironwork, window boxes, hanging baskets. Some mews are still cobbled streets entered through an archway which once defined the estate.

Mid-Victorian

These large villas were typically built in pairs with the front door to the side, usually approached up some steps. They have a pitched roof with elaborate overhang or eaves. Detailing is 'Classical' stucco around windows and on the ground floor, with some being clad in stucco all over. Vestigal balconies, with ironwork, are found below sash windows. These are found in Chelsea, Kensington and other areas. Terraced houses in the same style, with similar Classical details, are widely seen. They are the result of a building boom in the 1850s and '60s and are found all round Inner London. Some, in less fashionable areas, fell into disrepair but many are now being restored. They are frequently turned into flats.

Late-Victorian

Houses of this period fall into three kinds: small, medium and large. Together, they are by far the most common type of house found in Inner London and many outer suburbs. It is difficult to imagine what London must have been like towards the end of the 19th century, with thousands of these houses being built all within 20 years. While the middle of the 19th century saw the construction of houses decorated with Classical 18th-century architectural details, the houses of this later period follow the Gothic fashion, with columns decorated with foliage, stained-glass windows, pointed arches and generally fussy detailing. They are usually built of yellow London stock brick or with stucco or red-brick dressing, mostly with slate roofs. Their front doors are set back in decorated porches. However, despite the Gothic detailing, most have sash windows. They are found particularly in a ring round London within the North and South Circular Rds.

The smallest houses (pictured on page 92) were working-class terraces, 2-storeys high, usually with white stucco bay windows on the ground floor to the front parlour with columns carrying foliage capitals, a narrow frontage and with rooms usually 2-up, 2-down.

The medium-sized house are the most common (pictured below), usually 2-storeys, sometimes with an extra room in the roof with dormer windows. These houses are found either in terraces or semi-detached. They often have stucco bay windows on both ground and first floors, with a small pointed hip roof to the gable. These houses have wider frontages, extend far back and usually have 3 or 4 bedrooms. The main rooms have high, moulded ceilings and iron fireplaces with marble surrounds. Generally the small and middle-sized houses have small front gardens and modest back gardens or yards.

The large detached, semi-detached or terraced versions (pictured below) can be very grand, like the red-brick lion houses of Peterborough Estate, Fulham and the similar ones around Barnes Pond, Tooting Common, Highgate, Dulwich, Sydenham and Crystal Palace. They have 5 or 6 bedrooms, are usually 3 storeys high with very attractive decorative mouldings both inside and out. Double-fronted or asymmetrical they are set back from the road with medium-to-large back gardens, square bay windows with gables, large rooms with high ceilings and attractive proportions. About half of all these three sizes of houses are still family homes, but many have been converted into flats – the large houses making excellent conversions into three flats.

Late-19th-century Dutch style

These tall, usually narrow-fronted soft terracotta-coloured brick houses, with elaborate moulded brick or faience decorations, are found in Knightsbridge and tucked away in Holland Park, South Kensington and Chelsea. Now softened with weathering, they were built at the end of the 19th century in a very free and eclectic style, usually in terraces (although sometimes semi-detached), but each house having varied features. Normally 4- or 5-storeys, with enormous chimneys and wiggly 2-storey gables (decorated with everything but the kitchen sink), and an elaborate porch up a few steps. The main rooms are on the first floor, very much following the plan of the mid-19th-century stucco estates. The windows have a different design on each floor, often with fiddly glazing patterns. The first floor sometimes has decorative ironwork, and rather fine railings separate the semi-basement from the street. Although some are still private houses, most are now flats or offices.

Mansion flats

These very large blocks of flats, usually 4, 5 or 6 storeys high, were built around the end of the 19th century and the beginning of this (1880–1910). Usually built of red bricks, with a horizontal stripy appearance formed by white stone banding and rows of windows picked out in white with white reveals. Façades are broken up with elaborate gable ends, bay windows, balconies and other features, giving an overall exuberant effect. They often have 'interesting' window designs, with glazing bars forming attractive patterns for both sash and casement windows. Arranged with two or four flats off a central staircase, often with well-proportioned rooms on the street frontage and secondary rooms facing rather dreary light wells. Mansion blocks range from very scruffy and poorly maintained to the extremely luxurious. Found all over London, examples include Prince of Wales Drive facing Battersea Park, around Baker St and behind the Royal Albert Hall in Kensington.

Early 20th century

These large detached and semi-detached houses were built for the wealthy middle classes who commuted from the healthy suburbs by train or tube. Many are found in such areas as Wimbledon, Putney, Hampstead, Dulwich, Greenwich and Streatham. They display the individuality of their original owners and a wide range of features were often used in one house.

Usually 2- or 3-storeys with 5 or 6 bedrooms, large reception rooms and entrance halls and generous staircases. Often double-fronted, built of brick or brick with render. Features include bay windows, steep gabled pitched tiled roofs, a variety of different types of casement window. Fewer Gothic touches than the late-Victorian buildings. More modest versions have a similar approach.

Nondescript 'Georgian'

Much loved by estate agents who call them 'period', which means they are unable to date them accurately or to define precisely the architectural style. Built early this century, in the '20s and '30s, and still being built. Very large, 2-storey, double-fronted houses, detached, with attic rooms in the steep pitched roof. Set back from the road,

with a sweeping drive, a full flight of steps and an imposing Classical front door. Many 'Georgian' features are incorporated: pediments, the Palladian window. Several large reception rooms, bedrooms with ensuite bathrooms as standard, staff quarters, large gardens. Found in Bishops Avenue in Hampstead, St John's Wood, Wimbledon Common, Bromley and Finchley.

Mock-Tudor

Built in large quantities around the perimeter of London mainly during the 1930s. More interesting examples occur nearer the centre of London and were built early in the century. And even now, still a popular style with the speculative developer. 1930s examples are found in ribbon development along arterial roads and on large estates. Detached, semi-detached or terraced, many with garages, and almost all family houses with 3 or 4 bedrooms and often substantial back gardens and smaller front gardens with off-street parking. Features: leaded lights in casement windows, steep pitched tiled gabled roofs, black and white timber decoration on white rendered walls, usually red brick on the ground floor and often with fussy brick decoration. Many now heavily altered with new windows etc.

1930s blocks of flats

These very large and rather anonymous blocks of flats, 5 to 7 storeys high, were widely built during the 1930s. Some were private developments (for example, those around Baker St, Maida Vale, Dolphin Square, Streatham). Others were built by the LCC or charitable trusts and are now coming on the market as individual flats. Built from yellow or red bricks with horizontal and vertical bands of render giving a stripy effect. Often they have balconies or bay windows. Windows sometimes are Georgian-type sash, but steel casement windows with very thin glazing bars also common. Blocks are set back a little from the street, with a landscaped area for parking or an entrance drive, and are often U-shaped or courtyard buildings with a central landscaped or paved area. Flats vary from 1- to 4-bedrooms.

Loft apartments

This is the new inner-city domestic building form of the 1990s. Whether it goes on being fashionable will depend on how easy it is to resell these flats when the original buyers move on. The location of these conversions, often on the riverside or in up-and-coming city locations, should ensure continuous interest. Converted from redundant industrial buildings, offices and schools, these highly individual flats were often sold as 'shells' to be fitted out by the purchaser with idiosyncratic results. Frequently these shells are double-height, allowing open plan, modern interiors. The structure, eg bare brickwork, roof construction and columns, is exposed to indicate the building's original use.

Modern private estates

Security and pastiche sum up the appearance of these modern developments. Prime sites in good locations, these estates are enclosed by a discrete security envelope and make no reference to any characteristic London vernacular. The developments, which include flats, maisonettes and houses, feature electronic gates, security personnel, private roads with garages and parking, all in well-landscaped surroundings offering an anonymous secure environment. These new estates are located on land purchased from the Health Authorities, public utilities and educational bodies, freed up by privatization legislation. Many of the sites are located in prestigious areas including areas along the riverbank.

Glossary of architectural terms

Beetle infestation: timber in buildings can become infested with insect life. The most common is woodworm, which is often found in floor joists and roof timbers. The infected timber has numerous small holes, a little smaller than a pinhead in size. Depending on the amount of damage, the timber can be chemically treated or may need replacement. There are other wood boring beetles found in houses and causing damage usually identified by the size and shape of the flight holes in the timber left by the hatching insects.

Bricks: London stock bricks are the most common, made from yellowish clay in Kent. They weather down to greyish black but are often cleaned up and have a soft appearance. Red bricks are also widely used, often with London stocks as a decorative feature.

Casement window: a window with the opening part hinged on one side. Traditionally wood, but in the '20s they were made of steel and now also of aluminium or plastic.

Columns and capitals: vertical pillars with decorative tops. Can be either in Doric, a simple geometric style, or Ionic, a more elaborate style with curled motifs. Occasionally the third order, Corinthian, is seen and are elaborate designs decorated with leaves.

Doorcase: a wooden surround to a door opening, often very elaborate with carving or mouldings and Classical decorative features — eg, pediments or columns.

Dormer window: a vertical window (sash or casement) with upright sides coming through a sloping roof, having its own pitched or flat roof.

Dry rot: a fungus affecting timber in older houses. This is serious as all infected timber usually needs to be removed and destroyed and associated areas of brickwork chemically treated. Dry rot is often invisible and not detected until alterations reveal its existence, although the sensitive nose may detect a smell. The fungus spreads in hairline strands behind plasterwork and in brickwork courses. Timber becomes dry and powdery and loses its strength.

Faience: decorative moulded bricks, usually terracotta-coloured or yellowish, sometimes glazed; used in late-Victorian times for picking out features.

Frieze: a band of mouldings around a building usually at high level.

Gabled end or gable: a triangular end wall of a pitched roof, often becoming a decorative feature in its own right, for example, Dutch gables.

Glazing bars: the narrow strips of moulded timber or metal which hold the panes of glass together.

Leaded lights: small panes of diamond-shaped glass held together with narrow strips of lead.

Mansard roof: first rises steeply, almost vertically, with windows in it, and then has a flat top.

Moulding: continuous grove or ridge which forms a decorative feature with an original functional purpose, to throw water away from the face of a building. Can be in any material — brick, timber, stone, stucco. Internally, the term applies to decorative plasterwork or joinery, externally to many design features.

Palladian window: a composite window, designed to look like one big window but made up of three, of which the middle section has a semi-circular fanlight over.

Parapet: a small wall guarding the edge of a roof or, alternatively, the wall of the building extended above the roof line to conceal the gutters.

Pediment: triangular decorative motif usually found over doors and windows.

Render: a thick finish, usually sand and cement or pebbledash, which covers all the brickwork and can be painted as well. Popular on Edwardian or mock-Tudor houses with areas of brickwork or tile hanging.

Sash window: a window in which the opening parts slide up and down. They are usually balanced with ropes and weights concealed inside the frame. Traditionally wood, but replacement windows are now aluminium or plastic.

Slates: thin sheets of grey rock, once used extensively for roofing in London.

Stucco: similar to render, but popular in the 18th and 19th centuries as a smooth finish covering large areas of a building (often the whole wall), sometimes with Classical mouldings or details. Normally painted cream or white.

Tiles: made of clay, traditionally plain tiles, small rectangular rusty red and flat in shape, have been used in some areas for hundreds of years, and are seen on all periods of houses. They are used on roofs or can be hung vertically on walls as a decorative feature. In modern times, a wide variety of much larger profiled clay tiles have been used for replacement of old slate or tile roofs.

Velux window: a manufacturer's name for a window inserted into the sloping part of a roof, frequently used in loft conversions.

Wet rot: another fungus affecting timber in buildings. Usually more obvious than dry rot and found in areas where timber becomes wet, eg windowsills, the bottom of doors, the ends of joists in external walls, skirting boards on outside walls, in bathrooms and kitchens where there is condensation. The timber becomes wet and spongy and loses its strength. When the timber is painted the surface looks crazed if wet rot is present. Infected timber can be cut out and new pieces inserted. Generally not as serious as dry rot.

Soo Ware is an architect with a special interest in London property and is a partner in The Chartered Practice. She teaches at the Bartlett, University College, London.

A NOTICE

PLEASE DO NOT BUY OR RENT
A LONDON PROPERTY BEFORE READING THIS:

Your alternative to calling hundreds of agents
is to make just one call to **020 7491 8977**
the **FREE PROPERTY LOCATOR SERVICE**

offered by RUMC Ltd, 21 Grafton Street, Mayfair, W1X 3LD.
E-mail: rumc@btinternet.com
Website: www.property-locator.com

How it works

- ☐ A Property Locator Service Consultant will take the details of precisely what you want.
- ☐ An extensive search of Estate Agent Databases, private vendors and landlords is done.
- ☐ An initial short-list is compiled
- ☐ Together with you, from that short list are selected the properties that most closely match your requirements.
- ☐ Arrangements are made for you to view this shortlist at your convenience.
- ☐ Once you have made an offer on a property, you are guided and helped through all stages of renting or buying your property.

This unique service saves you hours of wasted time
and is **ENTIRELY FREE** to you

At the time of going to print
THIS SERVICE COVERS MAINLY:

MAYFAIR	KNIGHTSBRIDGE	KENSINGTON
CHELSEA	BELGRAVIA	FITZROVIA
HOLLAND PARK	ST JOHN'S WOOD	HAMPSTEAD
REGENT'S PARK	MAIDA VALE	CONVENT GARDEN
NOTTING HILL GATE	SOHO	WESTMINSTER

Each month the service is being expanded until it covers the whole of London

A
B
C
D
E
F
G
H
I
K
L
M
N
P
R
S
T
W

London's Areas A–Z

How to use the A–Z section

This central section of the Guide is an alphabetically-organized guide to London's areas. The system is a two-tier one: each chapter covers an area of London, and each chapter is subdivided into the various neighbourhoods within the area. Parson's Green can thus be found under 'F' for Fulham, of which it is a part. This division, although less clear-cut than using the hard-and-fast boundaries of postal districts or boroughs, makes for more sense since, on the ground, areas refuse to stop at bureaucratic boundaries.

On page 103 is an *Index to Areas,* which lists the areas covered in this book for quick reference. All streets, areas and neighbourhoods are also listed in the *Main Index* at the end of the book.

If you only know the postal district of the place you are looking for, check the list that starts on page 14.

Maps

An outline map of London appears on pages 12–13. This shows the areas covered in the guide. The first page of each area chapter has a location map and a table of information. The map is designed to be a guide to the shape of the area, its main roads, railways and stations, the neighbourhoods it divides into, and which areas lie next door. Borough and postal district boundaries are also shown. These are rarely shown on street maps but can be important when house-hunting.

The maps are not designed to be street maps: to locate a particular street we refer you to the relevant page of the standard-sized *A–Z London Street Atlas* published by the Geographers' A–Z Map Company Ltd. The first line of information in the box beside each map in the book is a reference to the page and grid square of the *A–Z* that covers a central point of the area concerned. For example, the first page of the Acton section has 'Map ref p73 (1J)' indicating the page and grid square of Acton High Street. There is a key to these maps on page 102.

Boxed information

The map reference is to the standard-sized *A–Z London Street Atlas*. The postal district(s) of the area is given, and so is the borough(s) and controlling political party. Further details on both postcode and borough can be found on pages 14–17 and 78–80 respectively.

Conservation areas are indicated where relevant. These are zones subject to special planning protection and where new building is generally not allowed unless it is in harmony with the existing architecture. Check with the local town hall (see *Boroughs*, page 78, for phone numbers) for exact boundaries.

Car parking restrictions are listed where information is available. The note on parking refers to residential, not commercial, streets. In most areas, there are restrictions on parking in shopping areas and on main through-routes.

Area profiles

The text on each area consists of an area profile and sub-sections on neighbourhoods. These are the areas that people who live in the area divide it up into. Some have 'proper' names, others are defined as, for example, west or east of a certain point. See the area map for an indication of next-door areas. And note that the neighbourhoods are marked on the maps.

At the end of each area chapter there is a list of some of the main estate agents active in the area. This is neither an endorsement of the agents mentioned nor does it (or could it) mention all those you might encounter.

Each chapter ends with a summary of further useful information:

Transport

At the end of each area profile, you will find transport details giving the area's tube stations and local rail stations, and the fare zone the stations are in. The London Transport network is split into Zones 1, 2, 3, 4, 5 and 6 with 1 at the centre. Times are given from a central station in the area to three key points: the City (Bank station), Oxford Circus and Heathrow Airport. Where local rail lines are available, their main central destinations are given. Note that official journey times assume no hold-ups! Use the times given as a point of comparison with other areas. See the *Transport* section of the *Property Market in 2000* (pages 20–25) for the latest news on new routes and improvements to existing ones.

The 'miles from centre' note under 'Convenient for' is the distance from the centre of the area to Charing Cross. The purpose of this figure is to give an immediate picture of an area's relationship to the centre of London, and as a quick point of comparison between areas.

Schools

At the end of each area profile we also list the main secondary schools and private secondary schools in the area. For more information see *Schools in London* (page 60) with the borough performance tables and *Boroughs* (pages 78–80) to find out who to contact.

Prices

Average prices are given for both sales and rentals of flats and houses of all sizes in the area. These prices give a 'freeze-frame' picture of where prices stood at the start of the 2000 selling season and are based on data collated in February. They indicate the price range into which each size of home mainly falls, not the price of the meanest

A

B

C

D

E

F

G

H

I

K

L

M

N

P

R

S

T

W

slum or the grandest palace. Thus a narrow or a wide range for, say, a 2-bed flat is in itself an indication of the range of homes to be found in the area, and of the different neighbourhoods within the area. See also *How to Use this Book* (page 10).

Below the price bands is a note on the kinds of homes to be found in the area and on the state of the property market there, and how long the local council takes over searches. This varies widely across London.

Finding a street

To find a particular street, refer to the *Main Index*, which lists all the streets, areas and neighbourhoods mentioned in this book.

How to use the maps

Maps are not to scale and are intended for orientation and general reference. Check north point for orientation. Only main roads are shown. The neighbourhoods are those discussed in the accompanying text.

To locate a map, see arrows for surrounding areas and see the key map at the start of the A–Z section. For full details refer to the *A–Z London Street Atlas:* each map has a cross-reference to the A–Z page and map square covering the centre of the mapped neighbourhood.

N10 Postal district	**East Dulwich** Neighbourhood	**N** North point
Postal district boundary	Road	Dockland light railway station
EALING Borough	Railway	Rail station
Borough boundary	Open space	Underground station

Index to areas

These are the areas and neighbourhoods covered in the following pages. For streets, see the main index at the back of the book.

ACTON

A

Map ref: p73 (1J)
Postal districts: W3
Boroughs: Ealing (Lab)
Council tax: Band D £703
Conservation areas:
  Gunnersbury Park,
  Mill Hill Rd
Parking: Free off main
  roads, though residents'
  schemes soon, incl round
  E Acton Station

The W3 postcode never carries the cachet of its neighbours W4, Chiswick, or W5, Ealing. This means that those who need a home more than they need status will do well here. In Acton, they get more for their money. They also get the benefits of Acton's many rail lines: fast communications. The rail lines, however, conspire with the main roads to carve the area into small, badly-linked pieces, eroding any sense of community the place might have. Again, contrast Ealing and Chiswick. But when you are struggling with a mortgage, a fast train to work and a few pounds less to pay each month compensate for a lot. The focus on value led to a good few of Acton's drabber corners being spruced up as old houses were converted into flats under the impetus of the BBC's move to their new White City headquarters.

Much of the northern half of the area dates from the 1920s or later, and even the Victorian southern corner has been extensively re-built in parts. Of the hamlets and farms of pre-industrial Acton only the skeleton of the old High Street remains. Several grandiose schemes were shelved as the last recession hit – sometimes to residents' relief. A long-discussed widening of the A40 was scrapped. The workaday **High St** did, however, gain a small shopping centre, The Oaks, and **King St** was pedestrianized. The High St runs from the railway (and Acton Central station) in the E along past the Town Hall, public baths and court to a 1990s Safeway at the W end. St Mary's Church marks the heart of the old village. A new flats block by St George, Cooper's Court, offers 2-bed flats with underground parking from £157–180,000.

If the young buyers and renters who visit Acton's good ethnic restaurants are not Islington or Battersea high-flyers, at the top end of the family homes market there's a different picture. Schools are the draw (Japanese School and King Fahad Academy, plus some good comprehensives) and have pushed the houses to very un-Acton prices. However some of the large, old houses are rented, and often brim-full of young (and sometimes noisy) Australians, South Africans and other transients.

Acton Central

Acton Central, the neighbourhood to the NW of the High St between **Horn Lane, Hanger Lane, Uxbridge Rd** and the railway line, is nowhere near the train station so-named: a common problem around here. The neighbourhood has some large family houses, although many fell to the Acton speciality – flat conversions. The people buying or renting the family homes in central Acton – particularly the 5-bed Victorian houses in leafy **Rosemont Rd** – may well be Japanese. Attracted by the school that moved here a few years ago from Camden Town, Japanese families moved into West London, served by their own estate agencies. Recent bad economic news has led to some families returning to Japan, but a nucleus remains. The area is also popular with families who want their daughters to go to Ealing Borough's only girls' comprehensive, Ellen Wilkinson in **Queens Drive**.

The general rule in central Acton, that prices rise the nearer you get to Ealing, means that flats in **Creffield Rd** and **Inglis Rd** are popular. Those in **Inglis** and some in **Creffield Rd** come with that dream of an Acton home-buyer . . . a W5 postcode. Further E, **Horn Lane** is a dirty, noisy main road; but **Pierrepoint Rd** and **Rosemont Rd** could be in another world – secluded, green and quiet. **Lynton Rd** is a mixture – a busy road with some '30s and '40s houses, some Edwardian, with an equal mix of flat conversions and houses. A 1920s 4-bed semi was on the market here last winter for £345,000. Check which side of the street it's on: the railway line lies to the N. Parking is slightly easier in this long, wide road than in most of Acton's jam-packed streets. Central Acton does suffer from being a long way from tube stations, and proximity to one of them adds to the price.

Acton Town/South Acton

The triangle S of **Acton High St**, E of **Gunnersbury Lane** and W of the railway line is dominated both physically and in reputation by the South Acton Estate (some call it the Authors Estate). The council estate's ugly concrete towers loom above the pleasant Edwardian terraces around Acton Town tube station.

The main attraction for buyers of the terraced Edwardian houses and flat conversions in pleasant streets like **Avenue Rd** and **Mill Hill Rd** is the nearby tube station. These streets date from around 1877 and are collectively called Mill Hill Park. The terraced houses are smart, the roads are tree-lined, and **Mill Hill Rd** is particularly pretty in the summer, with flowery front gardens and a new garden and playground in Mill Hill park. Three-bed houses in this conservation area cost around £220–300,000. Off Avenue Rd lies **Heathfield Rd**, a hidden cresecent with a mix of purpose-built flats, imposing 5-storey houses and 3-bed family homes with spacious gardens.

Poets' Corner

Estate agents wax lyrical about Poets' Corner – it is central, pleasant, full of converted flats and intensely gentrified. The area stretches N of the **High St**, between **Horn Lane** and **East Acton Lane**. The streets grouped (appropriately) around **Shakespeare Rd** give you a cultural choice which includes **Chaucer, Spencer, Milton** and **Cowper**. (Who, though, was **Myrtle**?) Home-buyers are mostly looking at pretty, small-scale terraces in tree-lined streets (2-bed houses range between £225–275,000). The houses in streets like **Cumberland Rd** and **Maldon Rd** were once grand family homes but are now almost all 2- or 3-bed flats (c. £170,000 for 2-bed garden flat).

Goldsmith Rd turns, northwards, into **Goldsmith Avenue** and an even more favoured corner: the Goldsmith estate's Victorian and Edwardian homes, some of which have been converted into large flats: £175,000 for 2-beds. Some of the houses in surrounding streets are later, built about 1950. Across the railway to the E, **Shaa Rd** and around, N from Acton Park, is popular with Arab families, because of the road's exclusive school for Arab children – and there's the Barbara Speake Stage School nearby in **East Acton Lane**. The 4- and 5-bed houses in **Shaa Rd** go for £375-650,000. Around **Beech Avenue**, across **East Acton Lane**, there are some modern developments, including one very popular estate by Barratt which includes a stylish block of retirement flats. **Beech Avenue** itself has a mix of council and private homes. The spacious grounds of the Acton Sports Association, with cricket, tennis and football, also house a very smart Hogarth health club.

Back across in Poets' Corner, **Cowper Rd** and **Milton Rd** have small 2-bed terraced houses that were once the homes of Victorian workers. They are too small to be turned into flats, and have tiny gardens, but a delightfully cottage feel. They sell for around £175,000. **Shakespeare Rd** is a better bet for conversions, and some have big rooms and elegant façades. The huge 3-storey Victorian terraces in **Alfred Rd**, **Burlington Gardens** and **Birbeck Rd** look imposing, but many have been run down for years. Some have been bought up by housing associations, while others have been done up for sale. You get space for your money here: a 4-storey, 6-bed house in Birbeck Rd with its own coach house went recently for £475,000, while a 4-bed house was on the market last winter for £425,000. A 2-bed flat around here may cost £110,000 – but these streets link into the **High St** one-way system, so traffic is heavy.

West Acton

West Acton was the scene of a property buyer's dream in the early '80s – 3-bed semis were sold off for a fraction of the market prices, fetching just a few thousand pounds. These were the 'railway cottages': homes in and around **Saxon Drive**, built in the 1930s for rail employees to rent, and sold to the tenants years later. Today these are very popular (and close to West Acton tube), and fetch around £185,000.

West Acton, which lies in the angle between **Horn Lane** and **Western Avenue**, is dominated by rail lines – the Piccadilly line to the N, the main line to the S, and the Central line which crosses it diagonally for good measure. But it is popular for more than its good access to public transport. It is greener than the rest of Acton, with a liberal scattering of sports grounds and playing-fields. And, to the W of West Acton station, is the Hanger Hill garden estate – impeccable 1930s mock-Tudor and different from anything else in either Ealing or Acton, with black and white half-timbered houses and flats and plenty of green space. Japanese and other families love this estate, with its 3-bed, up to £300,000 houses in roads such as **Queens Drive**, **Monks Drive** and **Princes Gardens**. Acton stops here. Across the tracks the desirable curving roads that climb **Hanger Hill** to the **North Circular** mark the start of W5 and Ealing.

North Acton

North Acton might be called Leamington Park by some estate agents, but don't let the up-market name blind you to the area's drawbacks. It has none of the Ealingesque atmosphere to which many in Acton are drawn, not least because it is ringed by three industrial estates. Much of the property in the triangle between **Old Oak Lane**, **Victoria Rd** and the **Western Avenue** is run-down, with a few unappealing blocks of flats. £100,000 may buy you a 2-bed flat in **Leamington Park**, but this road is on the one-way system onto the A40, and there is no parking in the street. But between Acton main line station and the North Acton tube, an area which straddles the A40 **Western Avenue** has seen some new developments. Westcott Park in **Cotton Avenue**, built in the late '80s, is a source of studios and 1- and 2-bed flats at reasonable prices.

Watch out for further transformation in this corner: there were plans for several hundreds of homes in the bullish '80s, variously dropped or delayed as recession struck and uncertainty over the road-widening scheme for the A40 **Western Avenue** reigned. The depressingly boarded-up houses that were blighted by this came back on the market at bargain prices, but the traffic pollution and noise would put off most.

Tucked into the corner between **Western Avenue** and the **North Circular** is the Park Royal neighbourhood, where a few streets of homes struggle on amid a vast industrial estate. Guinness, whose brewery is here, continue to push for a major business and leisure development. This would include new housing, restaurants and even a new tube station. However, existing residents are unhappy about the impact on their homes. You would never consider this area for peace, quiet and clean air, but get to understand the scale of the development if you're thinking of living here.

The Park Royal scheme will have an impact on the wider area, of course, bring amenities where few exist and provide many new homes, but its effects on the already clogged Hanger Lane road junction can only be guessed at.

East Acton

East Acton is a small area in the midst of railway lines and bordered to the S by the busy A40 **Western Avenue**. The neighbourhood lies on the Hammersmith borough boundary close to Wormwood Scrubs Prison and the common to the E. Nevertheless East Acton, a collection of two dozen or so roads, has a pleasant villagey feel – a mixture of council-built and private homes. The area may soon have a residents' parking scheme – the streets in Hammersmith borough have one, which has displaced parkers into Ealing's patch.

Running N from the **Western Avenue**, **St Andrews Rd** has 1930s red-brick terraces with square bays extending from the ground to first floor. Council-built properties dominate **The Fairway** running W-E between the main line and **Old Oak Common Lane**. The majority are stone-clad semis and terraces – but some are of a warmer brown brick. Nearby on the pleasant green the homes – 1930s once again – are privately owned and arranged in both terraces and semis. Moving N through **The Bye** to **Long Drive**, clusters of 12 semis (prices around £150,000) are grouped around small greens in closes – creating a friendly atmosphere. Further down **Long Drive** towards the **Western Avenue** are one or two larger detached houses, some with gables, some with bays. However, these types are rare in East Acton.

Turning left into the heart of the neighbourhood once more, **Brassie Avenue** offers a mixture of council-built and private semi-detached homes. The main shopping area is in nearby **Old Oak Common Lane** to the E near the A40 intersection. All the essentials are there for a quiet, pleasant corner.

Borders: Gunnersbury

A no-man's-land between Ealing and Acton, trapped in the triangle of **Gunnersbury Lane, Uxbridge Rd** and **Gunnersbury Avenue**, Gunnersbury is a pleasant area, with some roads of detached family homes that fetch high prices. **Lillian Avenue, Gunnersbury Gardens** and **Gunnersbury Crescent** are good for family homes, with large gardens. And the area is very convenient for the huge Gunnersbury Park, with its stately home-turned-museum. The 4-bed mock-Tudor homes of **Carbery Avenue** are especially popular. For Acton Green – the neighbourhood SE of South Acton station – see the Bedford Park chapter.

Transport	Tubes: Acton Town (zone 3, Piccadilly, District), North Acton (zone 2/3, Central), others see map. From Acton Town: Oxford Circus 30 min (1 change), City 45 min, Heathrow 20 min. Trains: Acton main line (Paddington 15 min), Acton Central and South Acton on N London Line, Silverlink. Miles from centre: 6.5.
Convenient for	Heathrow, routes to Oxford and the West, BBC in Shepherd's Bush.
Schools	Ealing Education Authority: Acton School, Ellen Wilkinson (g), Twyford C of E. Private: Japanese School, King Fahad Academy, Greek School. See also Ealing.

SALES

Flats	S	1B	2B	3B	4B	5B
Average prices	80–100	95–155	110–200+	150–220	225+	—
Houses	2B	3B	4B	5B	6/7B	8B
Average prices	85–250	150–300	200–425	250–450	325+	—

RENTAL

Flats	S	1B	2B	3B	4B	5B
Average prices	100–130	150–270	175–375	250–450	350+	—
Houses	2B	3B	4B	5B	6/7B	8B
Average prices	250–300	275–450	325–550	400+	—	—

The properties	Mix of late-Victorian and Edwardian terraces and inter-war suburbia. Fewer large houses. Ample 1- and 2-bed flat conversions. Recently some new-build including several big schemes. Best streets include those of Poets' Corner.
The market	First-time buyers' stepping-stone, and family homes. Best parts of Acton can approach Ealing prices. These are bought by BBC types, or rented to families who move here for the Japanese School or King Fahad Academy. Local searches: 5 working days.

Among those estate agents active in this area are:

- Bushells
- Rolfe East
- Churchill
- Barnard Marcus
- Haart
- Landsdowne
- Winkworth *
- Northfields *
- Robertson Smith & Kempson *

further details: see advertisers index on p671

BALHAM AND TOOTING

Map ref: p108 (2E)
Postal districts: SW12, SW17
Boroughs: Wandsworth (Con), Lambeth (Lab)
Council tax: Band D Wandsworth £370, Lambeth £750
Conservation areas: Include Heaver, Totterdown Fields, Trinity Rd
Parking: Residents' zones around stations etc.

These days bits of Balham are deeply desirable, while the solid family homes of Tooting's Heaver Estate heave with bankers and lawyers. Like a lot of South London, Balham and Tooting spent much of the 20th century asleep in seedy respectability; it was only in the '80s that they began to be of interest to any but strictly local buyers. In some parts, the market is very local still, and there is a thriving Asian community. In the late-19th century Balham and Tooting were merely small hamlets on the main road into London. Their popularity grew with the advent of the railway, and the extension of the Northern line underground in 1926 was the final stage of metamorphosis from genteel settlement to inner city.

'Balham, Gateway to the South', as it was immortalized by the late Peter Sellers, was favoured as the ideal area for a country residence by the professional classes of the 19th century, and this accounts for the impressive houses near to the commons still standing today. The later terraces crowd around the spine of the area, running S-E from the bottom tip of Clapham Common and called, successively, **Balham Hill/ Balham High Rd/Upper Tooting Rd/Tooting High St** (A24). 'Gateway' is right, in the sense of constriction. But the area is fringed with greenery: Tooting Bec, Tooting Graveney, Wandsworth and Clapham Commons, plus a golf course – and a couple of large cemeteries. There is also a major teaching hospital, St George's, which moved here from Hyde Park Corner in the 1980s. Today's incomers are attracted by easy transport by tube and train into and out of town, and the good supply of period properties still at a discount on Clapham and Battersea prices. There are relatively cheap buys around – particularly in Tooting Broadway and areas further from tubes: note that a car is not an alternative for commuters who want to arrive on time.

Most homes in Balham are Victorian, whereas Tooting ranges from the 1800s to the present day – the bulk, though, are mainly Victorian, Edwardian and '30s. The 1980s contributed, first, widespread flats conversions and then small pockets of new homes – mainly in Balham – and the late '90s saw further development. It is Tooting Bec that is seeing the area's first really large-scale new housing: the site of the old Tooting Bec Hospital is adding a tract of more than 600 new flats and houses to the area. Homes are springing up here – see below – but a planning row held up the latest stage during 1999. The Minister has given Wandsworth Council power to approve the plans and the Town Hall are negotiating with the developer to get some cash for extra school places.

Conversions of houses into small flats fell rapidly from favour during the 1990s as pressure on parking spaces and family-sized homes mounted. Wandsworth's planning policies are strict; anything less than 120 sq m is deemed too small to convert (excludes many 2-storey terraces) – and there are now 'house conversion restraint areas' across the borough where the minimum is 150 sq m. Split-ups *must* include a flat big enough for a family of four, unless you can show very good reason why not. Planning permission is also unlikely in areas with parking problems: no off-street parking, no conversions.

Parking is a problem across both areas, especially close to tube and rail stations, and hospitals. Both councils are bringing in residents' zones: Tooting Broadway's zone had to be extended last winter only six months after it was set up: commuters just parked further away.

Shopping provision improves steadily as the big retailers discover quite how many affluent families there are in the area. Sainsbury's are building a new store in Tooting Bec. At Clapham South, right on the edge of the area, a fiercely-contested plan to add a Tesco Metro across from the tube, on the site of the old Women's Hospital, is the subject of a planning inquiry. At least Tesco's latest plans keep the façade, and there will also be new homes on the site.

Balham has seen several new pubs and wine bars open in the last couple of years catering for a typically up-market, young professional crowd, mainly around the bustling **High Rd** which, though small, provides a real focus to town life in the area. A smart new pub in **Chestnut Grove** is another pointer to change. Civic services are restricted to Central Balham Library, adjacent to Safeway on **Ramsden Rd**. However, neighbouring areas supply the cinemas (Clapham, Streatham), theatres and pub theatres (Wimbledon, Battersea), and villagy **Bellevue Rd**, at the foot of Wandsworth Common, has the fashionably smart shops, pubs and restaurants. Indeed

Wandsworth Council's policy is now to try to restrict the increasing number of new bars and cafés in several 'hot spots' across the borough – **Bellevue** and **Balham High Rd** among them.

Traffic flow is always congested along the A24, and the many railway lines – with few road bridges – make car journeys tortuous and bus travel erratic at best (at least there is a large car park behind the smart, revamped Sainsbury's). Homes prices are thus, with reason, higher near tube and train stations, and also opposite commons; lower on main roads and (say local agents) near the graveyards . . . The further S you go, the less you pay – Balham and Tooting Bec are more desirable than Tooting Broadway.

Balham

Some time around 1985 a local estate agent confided 'it's all right to talk about Balham now'. The combined efforts of Peter Sellers and Nikolaus Pevsner ('nothing of interest on **Balham Hill** except the Odeon') had damned the place into a sort of property limbo. Half-hearted attempts were made to shift it into 'south South Wandsworth'. Clapham South tube station gave its name to a swathe of what is really Balham. The quiet and pleasant streets between **Nightingale Lane** and **Balham High Rd** migrated upwards to become the Nightingale Triangle and, again, honorary Clapham, but are covered here – despite a recent concerted attempt to rename the area Clapham South.

Balham has all the attributes of a real place: a **High Rd**, a station (main line and Northern Line tube), a parish church (St Mary's, 1805) and a library. The rail line to Croydon, running W-E on its embankment, divides Balham in half and contributes largely to traffic congestion: there are only three bridges beneath it.

Nightingale Triangle

This is the most exclusive area in Balham: quiet, attractive and convenient for transport, and bordering Clapham and Battersea. It is bounded by **Nightingale Lane**, **Balham High Rd** and the railway. Roads running between **Ravenslea Rd** and **Chestnut Grove** contain neat Victorian terraced 3/4-bed houses, popular but smaller than some properties in the triangle: prices here start at around £260,000. There are larger gardens in **Calbourne Rd** and **Mayford Rd**. **Nightingale Lane** starts on the brow of the Wandsworth Common railway bridge and contains very large and distinctive semi-detached 5/6/7-bed houses including some by T E Collcutt (1879) opposite **Endlesham Rd**. Some are flats: £340,000 was being asked last autumn for a duplex 3-bed here. Then come '30s 4-bed houses leading to mansion flats near Clapham South tube, including Clapham Mansions (2/3/4-bed flats, mix of owner-occupied and tenants) and Hightrees House (Art Deco) overlooking the cricket ground. Service charges are quite high – but this includes insurance, porterage and use of gym and pool. **Western Lane**, leading S from the popular Nightingale pub, is a leafy alley with mid-19th-century cottages, newly and attractively paved, with Victorian-style lamp-posts. Through to **Linnet Mews** – built 1983 – with smart 1/2-bed red-brick houses and flats. South is the picturesque **Nightingale Square** – coveted large Victorian houses (around £700,000) that surround a garden for residents. Despite the bustle of two schools and a church at the far end, the square remains a popular corner. Nearby in **Oldridge Rd**, eight loft-style houses are planned. **Endlesham Rd** has some double-fronted Victorian houses which offer 6/7-beds for around £625,000 when done up.

Chestnut Grove, running on to the S, has pleasant cottagey terraces and a large school on the W side. It gets less popular as it nears busy **Balham High Rd** and the tube. **Ramsden Rd**, cutting through the middle of the triangle, has a variety of red-brick and flat-fronted Victorian houses and terraces, some large (£650,000 for a 5-bed) and some small. The houses are generally larger at the two ends of the road, but

Even the most ordinary corners provide quirky details for those who look. This unusual window, above the front door of a Balham home, shows its late-Victorian date with Gothic-style carving and decoration and the pattern of the glazing bars in the sash windows. Attractive as they may be, such bays need careful maintenance if damp is not to be a problem.

the **High Rd** end does get congested with Safeway's car park entrance on the E side. Twenty new homes are planned for the old Unigate Dairy site.

Two-bed cottages (once workmen's quarters) feature in **Bellamy St, Pickets St, Balham Grove** and **Temperley Rd**. Stretched to provide 3-bed, 2-bath they go for £300,000-plus. **Bracken Avenue** is leafy and pleasant. **Badminton Rd** has period red-brick homes on the E side, early 20th-century unusual double-fronted maisonettes on the W. Front gardens on the E side are smaller (Nos 1–54). **Balham Grove** has a Safeway supermarket's goods entrance at the southern end but then a couple of lovely Georgian houses – one now apartments.

Large Victorian houses follow with a small recent estate in **Ainslie Walk**. The Lochinvar Estate ('60s, concrete, low-rise) is an affordable, if uninspiring, first-time buy. **Liberty Mews**, built in the '80s, is off **Malwood St** at the apex of the triangle and just around the corner from the tube Malwood St's Victorian 3-storey, 4-bed houses sell for around £500,000. At 18–20 **Balham Hill** a 1990 mews has cottages and flats opening out around a courtyard, behind some small office units developed in the late 1990s.

Hyde Farm Estate

A rectangle bounded by **Hydethorpe Rd, Emmanuel Rd** and **Radbourne Rd** in the eastern part of Balham and in Lambeth, not Wandsworth, borough. Building of the Hyde Farm estate was begun in 1901 by speculative developers led by Ernest Hayes-Dashwood on land leased from Cambridge's Emmanuel College. Today, parts of **Radbourne Rd** and **Telferscot Rd** are set aside as rent-free accommodation for retired servicemen. This network of streets consists of red-brick Victorian 3/4-bed terraces and maisonettes, with only slight variations in style from road to road (more 'bell-fronted' in **Haverhill Rd** than in **Scholars Rd**, for example). **Emmanuel Rd** is increasingly popular – it overlooks Tooting Bec Common, the railway line beyond being screened by trees. A 5-bed house here was on the market for £700,000 last autumn. Two schools – Henry Cavendish and Telferscot (both mixed, Junior and Infants). Laing are busy in **Telferscot Rd** with a courtyard scheme of five 4-bed houses priced from £320,000. In **Radbourne Rd**, Sapcote have loft-style houses developed from an Edwardian school, fully fitted, from £295,000.

The area N of Hyde Farm is more mixed, with an industrial estate in **Zennor Rd**. **Weir Rd** is industrial on the W side (lots of vacant space) but soon calms down to Victorian terraces on the right and **Molly Huggins Close** on the left, and a recent development of 40 flats and houses for rent on an old hospital site. **Belthorn Crescent** has the smart Weir Estate. **Atkins Rd** has pleasant 20th-century semi-detached and terraced houses on the right – mainly in good repair, some mock-Tudor. Also St Bernadette Catholic Primary School (girls) and the La Retraite 6th-form college.

The roads running E from the **High Rd** to **Cavendish Rd**, between **Englewood Rd** to the N (really in Clapham) and **Rossiter Rd** (S), are almost entirely period terraces of 3/4/5-bed houses. Exceptions include gated, cobbled **Anchor Mews** off **Hazelbourne Rd** (around corner from Clapham South tube and Clapham Common), with loft-style flats with garages. There are also recent flats in **Hanson Close**, but it's back to period in **Ravenswood Rd. Old Devonshire Rd** has a mosque and some industrial buildings giving way to a mix of period and recent properties. **Laitwood Rd, Ormeley Rd** and **Ranmere St** form a quiet, pretty enclave. On either side of the railway line, **Fernlea Rd** and **Byrne Rd** have attractive, flat-fronted upper façades, early Victorian in style, leading to Victorian terraces.

B

Byrne Rd, to the S of the railway, and E of **Bedford Hill**, curves into the leafy **Culverden Rd** with its impressive 6/7-bed period semi-detached houses – some converted to flats, some still single homes. Those on the E side overlook Tooting Bec Common. Neat terraces in **Dornton Rd** (some purpose-built flats with balconies) and **Fontenoy Rd**. There are plenty of homes to let in these roads. Smart new maisonettes on the E of **Brierley Rd** are opposite period terraces. The Ryde Vale Estate (entrance **Ryde Vale Rd**) has a mix of styles – small blocks of terraced flats, low-rise concrete blocks and bungalows.

Bedford Hill's once notorious 'red-light' reputation is now largely unmerited, kerb-crawlers having been discouraged by CCTV and by blocking off the E end of **Elmfield Rd** and making **Carminia Rd, Childebert Rd** and **Cloudesdale Rd** one-way. The hill has large period properties – some very grand with ornamental brickwork. Many are flats: £200,000 buys a 3-bed. Recent schemes include 14 new 1- and 2-bed flats on the corner of **Culverden Rd**, and 12 flats in the shadow of the railway bridge for the Wandle Housing Association. The Priory, on the edge of Tooting Bec Common, dates from 1822 and is now flats.

Marius Rd, W of the **High Rd**, has attractive period houses and Marius Mansions – impressive Victorian flats, recently renovated – at the far end. More mansion flats are at the S ends of **Nevis Rd** (Cecil Mansions) and **Wontner Rd** (Stanley Mansions). There are many period terraces and some recent developments – notably the pleasant brick houses in **Ashdown Way** and the not-so-pretty yellow Flowersmead council estate (1940s) opposite where many homes are in private ownership.

The N end of **St James's Drive** boasts large covetable homes overlooking Wandsworth Common – popular because they are close to the train station, the good local schools (private and state) and the amenities of **Bellevue Rd. St James's Close** is an attractive new development of houses and flats around a central garden. **Old Hospital Close** is similar but larger. **Balham Park Rd**, leading E from **St James's Drive** back to the **High Rd**, has half-million pound houses by the common, Victorian terraces, and towards the E end more modern flats and houses. Ducane Court on the main road – once the largest block in Europe – is a '30s block of 650 studio and 1/3-bed flats.

Balham Borders

West of **St James's Rd**, at the foot of the common in the triangle between it, deeply fashionable **Bellevue Rd** and **Trinity Rd**, are tucked some neat, prosperous, pricey, grey-brick terraced cottages. In SW17 rather than SW12, and emotionally Wandsworth Common (see Wandsworth chapter) rather than Balham.

The roads N of **Nightingale Lane** and S of **Thurleigh Rd**, while still in SW12, have been annexed into the area known these days as 'Between the Commons' in Battersea – see Battersea chapter.

The area E of Hyde Farm, and S of the **South Circular** with the wide **Kings Avenue** running N-S, has generally large, pleasant inter-wars and post-war housing with some flats scattered around. **Thornton Rd** is semi-detached mock-Tudor; **Thornton Gardens** is a small estate. There is also a late-'80s development off **Thornton Rd**: **St Stephens Mews** is 1- and 2-bed flats. The flats at the S of **Kings Avenue** give way to large modern houses with garages. More 20th-century houses in **Copthorne Avenue** and **Parkthorne Rd**. This area has aspirations to be Clapham Park, or perhaps Streatham Hill.

On the Tooting borders, the roads directly N of the Heaver Estate, from **Ritherdon Rd** up to **Elmfield Rd**, are neat period terraces apart from some '60s flats at the N ends of **Carminia Rd** and **Childebert Rd**. At the W end of **Elmfield Rd** there are mansion flats of impressive red-brick, currently being smartened up. Ravenstone School (primary) opposite and Balham Leisure Centre (pool, gym, solarium, etc) are the other features of the road. **Cheriton Square** is opposite the leisure complex: its curving terraces always enjoy top billing in estate agents' ads.

Tooting

The name Tooting excites a certain amusement, but the place has more history than nearby Balham and can boast a past back to Domesday. Little remains of the villages of upper Tooting (Tooting Bec) and lower Tooting (Tooting Graveney). The place stayed small and rural well into the 19th century, and the big development of houses happened relatively late. The result is a district of orderly grids of late-19th-century homes, some spacious, some small, all well served by the Northern line tube.

Tooting's two commons, Bec and Graveney, boast lido, sports and tennis facilities but are sadly cut up by rail and roads. They do, however, give Tooting a clear boundary to the E. To the N is Balham; W, beyond the sprawl of Springfield University Hospital and the (perhaps unfortunately placed) Streatham Cemetery, is Earlsfield. To the S, the rail line between Wimbledon and Streatham forms the boundary. Beyond is Colliers Wood. Tooting rail station is right on the (SE) edge of the district it is named after.

Tooting Broadway more closely resembles a typical South London inner-city neighbourhood, albeit with better shopping than say nearby Streatham, which was more superior (and up-market) 20 years ago. The shopping and commercial hub of the area is centred on **Upper Tooting Rd/Tooting High St**, particularly concentrated around the junction with **Mitcham Lane**, around Tooting Broadway tube station. The two Northern line stations at either end of **Upper Tooting Rd**, the A24, provide useful access to the City and West End. Now, with the redevelopment of the Tooting Bec Hospital site, located on the south-western edge of Tooting Bec Common – see below – Tooting's main public landmark has become the enormous, sprawling complex of St George's Hospital, sitting quietly behind the bustling Tooting Broadway streets, on the edge of the Wandsworth/Merton border. Wandsworth Council has also introduced a scheme offering refurbishment grants for commercial property in a bid to revitalize the shopping area and secure its prosperity, especially around the **High Rd** in Tooting.

Heaver

By far the grandest and priciest neighbourhood in Tooting and Balham. The main conservation area lies between **Balham High Rd**, **Tooting Bec Rd**, the Common and **Ritherdon Rd**; with the neat terraces between **Ritherdon** and **Elmfield Rds** claimed by agents as outliers. This turn-of-the-century estate was built by the Heaver brothers, and consists of distinguished double- and single-fronted 3-storey houses and some maisonettes, all in red-brick with white detail. Approximately half have been split into flats, and these make for frequently very generous-sized homes. The unconverted houses are enormous – typical interior for an intact property would have 6 to 8 beds, two baths, kitchen plus three reception rooms and a huge garden. Many original features remain inside and out – note the ornate front doors with stained-glass insets. Largely untouched by modern developments, the main exceptions being infill maisonettes in **Manville Gardens** and **Carnie Hall**, and smart flats at N end of **Hillbury**

Rd, which also boasts some modern 3-bed town-houses and some 4/5-bed 'mock-Heaver' houses, built in 1989. Families wishing to escape cramped modern housing find havens in these popular, individually distinctive streets – for example, **Elmbourne Rd** (ornate brickwork framing door arches and windows) overlooking Tooting Graveney Common, and the wide, tree-lined **Streathbourne Rd** (each house name inlaid in decorative plaques). Average prices for intact houses are high: a 6-bed in a good road might be £500,000-plus, with £430,000 being asked on the edges of the estate.

B

Tooting Bec

The stretch enclosed by **Tooting Bec Rd** (N) to **Mitcham Rd** (S), **Upper Tooting Rd** (E) and **Rectory Lane** (W), this includes the area's main talking-point, the ex-Tooting Bec Hospital site. The largest development site by far, Fairview has re-christened this swathe between **Tooting Bec Rd, Franciscan Rd, Mantilla Rd** and **Church Lane** 'Heritage Park': now nearly complete, it contains a mix of everything from studio flatlets to 4/5-bed houses, beginning with a handsome crescent. Last winter, 4/5-bed, 3 bath/shower town-houses were from £257,000; 1-bed flats £112,000; 2-bed 2-bath flats from £143,000. Wandsworth Council are negotiating with Fairview over plans for the second phase, at the N end. In general, this smart development has been a great success, with prices soaring. Houses in the crescent now change hands for £360,000, up from £235,000 18 months ago.

This corner also holds an earlier, innovative, development – the delightfully named Totterdown Fields (streets between **Derinton Rd** and **Cowick Rd**), which has the distinction of being the first cottage council estate in the world – started in 1903. A pity, some say, councils didn't stick to this style: now a conservation area, the houses are an 'olde-worlde' mixture of red-brick and grey stucco. Above this, close to Tooting Bec tube, the roads N of **Foulser Rd** are lined with charming Victorian terraces in red-brick, Edwardian and '30s in **Lynwood Rd**; more cottage-council in **Topsham Rd**. An ex-army building in **Brudenell Rd** was converted into 10 2-bed flats.

South of the Totterdown Fields comes more Victoriana. **Vant Rd** has modern maisonettes at the S end. **Franciscan Rd**, running S through the entire neighbourhood from **Tooting Bec Rd** to **Mitcham Rd**, is mainly period with a few modern 'pockets' – the latest at the Common end. **Barringer Square** is yellow 7-storey flats surrounded by smaller, pleasant, brown-brick blocks, with a communal garden for residents. **Bruce Hall Mews** is a small, smart development of 20 houses and flats based around a courtyard and **Groomfield Close** is '80s maisonettes opposite the church.

St Benedict's, in the triangle between **Mitcham Rd, Rectory Lane** and **Church Lane**, is a pleasant and popular estate; built mainly by Laing in 1984, it's made particularly nice by trees and landscaping, and has off-street parking. It has 1-, 2- and 3-bed houses and flats, with big lounges and relatively modest service charges.

Furzedown

Running between **Links Rd** to the S, **Rectory Lane, Thrale Rd** and **Mitcham Lane**, Furzedown is filled with Edwardian/Victorian properties popular with families, plus some students' halls of residence for the London Institute. No tube line nearby, so prices tend to be lower than elsewhere in Tooting. The feel is generally a bit down-market compared to Tooting Bec. Approximately half is counted as Tooting – the area S of **Southcroft Rd** plus **Crowborough Rd, Idlecombe Rd, Salterford Rd** and **Freshwater Rd**. The remainder is thought of as Streatham. The borough boundary runs E-W between **Southcroft Rd** and **Seely Rd**. **Seely Rd** and **Links Rd** running parallel have identical terraces of solid, deep-porched turn-of-the-century houses. East of the junction with **Eastbourne Rd**, however, **Seely Rd** changes to less appealing, and often badly modernized, 20th-century terraces and then to bay-windowed, gabled homes.

B

Signs of activity here as buyers refurbish the houses. Crossing between **Seely Rd** and **Links Rd** are orderly rows of uniform terraces. Their regimentation is reflected in the road names, which run alphabetically from 'A' to 'J'. The only breaks in the regularity are the striking Links Primary School and the modern orange-brick flats of St Andrews Hall at S end of **Hailsham Rd** – horribly inappropriate amongst such general order. **Vectis Gardens** surrounds a small rectangle of fenced-off grass. The whole section has an air of well-cared-for, quiet suburbia. The side of **Links Rd** backs onto the railway.

Southcroft Rd has at its E end older terraces, giving way as you go W to post-war rows on the right and a series of pleasant 2-storey ex-council red-brick flats on the left. On the corner of **Nimrod Rd** is a low-rise block of modern flats. Both sides of **Southcroft Rd** are now brick flats. Ditto **Freshwater Rd** and roads off; these are similar buildings, but in less attractive orange-brick with stucco top halves. We regain Victorian terraces at the western end of **Southcroft Rd** and adjoining roads running to the N, parallel with **Mitcham Rd**.

Tooting Graveney

West of Furzedown is Tooting Graveney, named after the Graveney family who owned the manor in the 12th and 13th centuries. The area, which is bounded by the Wimbledon–Streatham railway line to the S, **Tooting High St** to the W and **Mitcham Rd** to the N, is the cheaper end of Tooting. First-time buyers head for this area. At the E end of **Longley Rd** there is a small block of red-brick flats/houses on the right – Kilmarnock Court – with a play-area for the kids. Opposite is Tooting Baptist Church and the intriguingly ugly Jubilee Villa (1887) – a pale yellow house with white trim and mosaic work insets. Handsome Victorian terraces continue left and right. Some later houses on the right. The railway runs behind S side of **Longley Rd**. Area to N of **Longley Rd** is a maze of period terraces and maisonettes with modern infills. **Bickersteth Rd**, leading N from **Longley Rd**, contains a veritable cocktail of architecture in places, and thus looks a little ragged. Prices for 3-bed terraces can be between £180-200,000, more in the best roads. **Otterburn St** (off **Byton Rd**) has well-cared-for large mock-Tudor houses opposite Edwardian maisonettes. The school in **Selincourt Rd** (Infants and Junior) stands among terraced houses each divided into two maisonettes (generally 2/3-bed). These provide a popular source of often rented homes; also found in **Trevelyan Rd**. On **London Rd** the old police station is now 1- and 2-bed flats.

Across the A24, (here **Tooting High St**) **Garratt Lane** leading W from Tooting Broadway tube is lined with large, flat-fronted period semi-detached houses (first few with front gardens) and smaller terraces. Parking is a problem on this main road and larger properties have the usual uneasy mixture of garden and parking space. Smaller terraces without gardens on the left side have garages behind in **Garratt Terrace**. Opposite these garages is a long row of Victorian 2-storey houses, curving round to **Tooting High St** (resembling a pale imitation of the Royal Crescent, Bath). These include some conversions and are good first-time buys. A few smart modern houses stand at the top on the left. Roads to the S of **Garratt Terrace** have similar rows of period housing, but modern maisonettes appear in **Recovery St** and smart-looking '30s flats in **Tooting Grove**. Quaint cottage terraces line **Aldis St** and **Carwell St**. There is a recent development to be found in **Aldis Mews**.

Blackshaw Rd, SW of St George's Hospital, has smart 2/3-bed Edwardian terraces – these tend to be cheap as they're next to Lambeth Cemetery. Anderson House (1931) on the corner of **Fountain Rd** is a handsome-looking 3-storey block of red- and cream-brick flats with, as they say, scope for improvement inside. An archway in the block leads through to a public recreation ground. More Victorian terraces left and right in **Fountain Rd**, undone-up as yet – which also goes for some earlier flat-fronted 2-storey stucco houses. **Cranmer Terrace**, off **Fountain Rd**, leads down to Tooting Gardens – a small park with swings, etc – not quite Regent's Park, but quite a surprise among such intensive housing. Period terraces lie W of **Fountain Rd**, some quite quaint: for instance the cottage rows of **Bertal Rd**. **Alston Rd**'s Edwardian terraces seem in better repair on left. At the junction with **Hazelhurst Rd** on the opposite corner is a school (Smallwood Junior and Infants) and on the left is the imposing grey concrete of the Hazelhurst council estate. **Greaves Place**, E of **Fountain Rd**, holds the striking 'geometrics' of Tooting Leisure Centre (swimming, gym, etc).

The Bell Estate

The Bell Estate, to the W of **Upper Tooting Rd**, belonged to an old family trust which was developed during the 1930s and '40s by the Bell in question. Comprising **Fishponds Rd, Ansell Rd, Hebdon Rd** and **Lingwell Rd**, its neat purpose-built 3/4-bed terraced houses are now very popular with families and convenient for Tooting Bec tube station. It is a stable community with a low turnover of properties. Houses in **Ansell Rd** have small roof extensions. **Lingwell Rd** and **Hebdon Rd** tend to be slightly cheaper as they back onto Springfield Hospital (built as Surrey County Lunatic Asylum, 1840s) and Streatham Cemetery respectively. Off **Hebdon Rd**, at the E end, is **Herlwyn Gardens** – a few pleasant brick bungalows and maisonettes. Parking here is a mystery as the road stops short of the buildings. **Holmbury Court**, at the N end of **Fishponds Rd**, has uninspiring maisonettes. **Fishponds Rd** itself has the occasional Edwardian property alongside.

The roads between **Broadwater Rd** and **Garratt Lane** have Victorian terraces, most of which have been painted, giving a multi-coloured effect to the streets. Endearing cottage terraces at E end of **Graveney Rd** and modern maisonettes opposite the junction with **Selkirk Rd**. Ungainly semi-detached maisonettes line **Rogers Rd** and the top of **Broadwater Rd** as it turns E to the A24. On the corner of **Rogers Rd** and **Garratt Lane** stands Bellamy House: council flats, stylish in red-brick and white detail.

Glenburnie Rd on the other (N) side of the Bell Estate has mainly smart Edwardian properties, but on S side of **Beechcroft Rd** there are some attractive large mock-Tudor detached houses. These are now joined, in the angle of the two roads, by Barratt's gated 'Trinity Square': handsome, pedimented Georgian-style 3-bed/3-bath town-houses and 4-bed/3-bath houses around a garden complete with fountain. The final 4-bed, 3-bath ex-show house was marketed last winter at £425,000. **Beeches Rd** has pleasant red-brick terraces (Victorian), both sides giving way to less attractive small beige-brick maisonettes on the right (c. '83). To the left is **Parkhill Court** – an impressive '30s block of large 2/3-bed flats, although not much to look at from behind.

The roads between **Trinity Rd** and **Beechcroft Rd**, to the N of the Bell Estate, are part of a conservation area filled with large, appealing Victorian properties lining leafy streets. Red-brick dominates, although **Brodrick Rd** has some lovely Georgian-style 3-storey stucco houses. **Crockerton Rd** and **Dalebury Rd** have stately red-brick courtesy of the Heaver brothers. Modern flats at S end of **Crockerton Rd**. Ernest Bevan School is opposite in **Beechcroft Rd**. To the N of the school is the College Gardens Estate, built 1983, an attractive development of 1/2-bedroom houses and flats similar to Balham's **Ashdown Way** but slightly cheaper as further from the Northern line tube.

At the N end of **Trinity Rd**, where it crosses into Wandsworth, are shops and restaurants facing a playing-field. Then, going S, come impressive mid-19th-century flat-fronted stucco terraces and houses. Note No 172 – once home of Thomas Hardy. Victorian red-brick continues. Tooting Bec fire station and police station are close to the junction with **Trinity Crescent**, one of the most expensive roads in the area with magnificent mid-19th-century stucco houses of 7/8-bedrooms and large gardens.

Impressive mansion flats on the right-hand side (St Nicholas). **Holderness Rd** has mock-Tudor houses, terraced and semi-detached, and the faithful Victorian terrace reappears in **Chetwode Rd.**

B

Transport	Tubes: Balham, Tooting Bec, Tooting Broadway (zone 3, Northern) direct to City, Charing Cross, Waterloo. From Tooting Bec: Oxford Circus 30 min (1 change), City 30 min, Heathrow 1 hr 30 min (1 change). Trains: Balham to Victoria 15 min; Tooting to London Bridge, Blackfriars.
Convenient for	South Coast routes and transport into town. Miles from centre: 5.
Schools	Local Authority: Graveney, Ernest Bevin (b), Burntwood (g). Private: Upper Tooting High.

SALES

Flats	S	1B	2B	3B	4B	5B
Average prices	55–80	90–180	140–270	200–300+	—	—
Houses	2B	3B	4B	5B	6/7B	8B
Average prices	120–300	150–350	230–400+	300–500+	→600+	—

RENTAL

Flats	S	1B	2B	3B	4B	5B
Average prices	90–105	125–220	140–300	180–350	360–440	—
Houses	2B	3B	4B	5B	6/7B	8B
Average prices	170–300	200–350	250–375	300–450	500+	—

The properties	Balham is Victorian, Tooting Edwardian/'30s, with a (very) few older homes in both. Terraced houses of all sizes (including very large), plus conversions and some p/b flats. Inter-war suburban homes, too — and, of course, areas of '80s and '90s housing.
The market	Buyers have traditionally been first-timers plus families seeking big, more affordable homes. Balham (especially the N end, which is now called 'Clapham South' and 'The Nightingale Triangle') and Tooting Bec (especially the Heaver Estate, and now a swathe of new homes) are popular as overspill from posher neighbouring areas. Tooting Broadway is cheaper, more cosmopolitan: a much more local market. Local searches: Wandsworth 3–4 weeks, Lambeth 10 working days.

Among those estate agents active in this area are:

- Douglas & Gordon
- Barnard Marcus
- Hooper & Jackson
- Heaver
- Winkworth *

- Woolwich
- Halifax Property
- Bells
- Haart
- Nightingales

- John Hollingsworth
- Vanstons
- Courtenay *
- Foxtons *

further details: see advertisers' index on p671

BARNES, MORTLAKE AND SHEEN

Map ref: p90 (2B)
Postal districts: SW13, SW14
Boroughs: Richmond upon Thames
   (Lib Dem)
Council tax: Band D £908
Conservation areas: Include Barnes Pond,
   Green and Common; Mortlake Green
Parking: Mostly still free, controlled zone
   in North Barnes, meters on High St

The meandering Thames on one side, parks and commons on two others:
were it not for the road congestion and lack of a tube, this would be the ideal London
location. Barnes occupies a peninsula bounded by the River Thames to east, north
and west. Much of the land is open, including playing-fields and the enormous
wetlands nature reserve that once used to be Barn Elms Reservoirs. Mortlake, to the
W of Barnes, is more built-up, an ex-village lining the river bank. Sheen is away from
the river to the S, bordering Richmond Park and its adjoining enormous commons,
the great green tract that defines the whole area to the south.

Barnes

The outside world is impinging upon the Barnes idyll: Hammersmith Bridge has just
been re-opened after three years of closure. Many locals welcomed the closure as it
cut traffic. Perhaps coincidentally, house prices in **Castelnau** rocketed while the
bridge was closed. What now? No-one is sure. And plans to put a mammoth sports
centre on the Barn Elms playing fields would, fear locals, mean yet more traffic:
access would be onto the junction of **Castelnau/Rocks Lane and Church Rd**. Indeed,
ecologists worry that the proposed £12 million sports centre, which would have 20
pitches plus sports hall, would upset the bird-life on the nature reserve.

Despite these uncertainties, here – a stone's throw or two across the bridge from grubby, noisy Hammersmith – we are in a bourgeois heaven: river, green spaces, pretty houses (from cottage to mansion), interesting shops and atmospheric pubs . . . Barnes, some feel, goes just a little over the top, even for this idyll, with its village duck pond.

Barnes thrived on market gardening throughout the 18th century. London merchants and nobility built their weekend retreats here. Some survive – **The Terrace** – others are remembered in local street names, such as **St Anne's, Elm Grove** and **Ranelagh**. Only 5½ miles from Hyde Park Corner, Barnes still has a rural atmosphere: locals say this is because it has no tube station (Barnes and Barnes Bridge rail stations – the latter with a limited service – make up for it). Once S of Hammersmith Bridge, urban grime gives way to Surrey village charm, with a village green, duck pond and the Sun Inn (crux of **Church Rd** and **Station Rd**).

Leafy riverside walks, more than 100 acres of pretty common, Leg of Mutton Reservoir (NW) where swans breed, Barn Elms Wetland Reserve, opening this May for all kinds of aquatic wildlife, make Barnes a family favourite. Good local schools include St Paul's (boys) in Lonsdale Rd; Godolphin & Latymer (girls), Latymer Upper (boys) and St Paul's (girls) are in nearby Hammersmith. The Swedish School (in Lonsdale Rd) draws in expatriate and diplomatic families. The Harrodian School (independent, 4–16 years) is just along the same road. Richmond borough's schools achieve good ratings in the league tables, especially at primary level.

There are a few black spots. One penalty of living 30 minutes' drive from Heathrow is some aircraft noise. An effective pressure group, supported by a local MP, monitors problems. Alternative use of the north and south runways at Heathrow ensures occasional noise relief, but inhabitants pray for an east wind which removes the planes entirely. The planned Terminal 5 expansion of Heathrow is raising the temperature of this debate. Locals predict yet more planes.

There is a sprinkling of council property throughout Barnes; all spruce and no graffiti and many now in private hands. These offer good buys at the lower end of the price range, with 2-bed cottages starting at around £165,000.

Barnes has a good range of 5- to 8-bed houses but coveted locations near the river or common mean prices can reach well over £1 million. The best houses sell very fast, often without involving agents or appearing on the open market. Smaller family houses form the bulk of the market. Expect to pay from £270,000 upwards. There is a limited supply of 2-bed converted flats. Larger flats can be found in purpose-built blocks and those with prime locations like Riverview Gardens and Elm Bank Mansions and those close to Hammersmith Bridge like Arundel Mansions.

The predominant home in Barnes is a Victorian or Edwardian terraced house. Houses greatly outnumber flats or maisonettes – though new developments are increasing supply. Great difficulty is experienced in finding flats and detached 3- or 4-bedroomed houses. Conversion into flats is rare as most houses have been well-maintained and are in demand as family homes.

The most sought-after streets are **Castelnau, Lonsdale Rd, Woodlands, The Crescent, Vine Rd** and **Station Rd**. Values fall where properties are near the railway line. The most expensive homes in Barnes are in the £1.5 million bracket, and there are whole streets with 'nothing under a million'. To the frustration of local estate agents these houses only change hands every 10–20 years. The Waterside development on the old filter beds site (see below) has added several dozen detached villas to the top end of the market, plus town-houses and apartments, and the Harrods Village scheme (also detailed below) is boosting the supply of flats.

The whole area benefits from an abnormally active and well-supported community association, which monitors schemes like that for the sports centre at Barn Elms.

Actors and writers of the more successful sort find Barnes congenial, and the new developments in the N of the area attract an international clientele. Newcomers join long-serving locals in defending Barnes' 'village' status. The typical newcomer starts in a mansion flat or Little Chelsea cottage and trades up to a family home. Schools tend to lock families into the area. Many homes are sold to locals, though City money makes its presence felt. Once the bonuses stack up there are million-plus early Victorian houses in **Castelnau** to aspire to.

North Barnes

Castelnau – a boulevard named after the French lands of the Boilieu family – forms the spine of Barnes, leading S from Hammersmith Bridge via **Rocks Lane** down to the **Upper Richmond Rd**. The residents of this prime location were the main beneficiares of the long closure of the bridge: for three years they had the uncanny experience of blissfully-reduced traffic levels, and blissfully rising property values. In any case, even with the bridge now re-opened, the large 1840s semi-detached villas of **Castelnau are** set well back; driveways and trees mask them from the road. Early Victorian styles near the bridge lead to later double-fronted houses towards the Red Lion pub (junction of **Rocks Lane/Church Rd**). Prices are £1.5 million-plus for good examples, with about £850,000 being asked for smaller (5-bed) houses and £650,000 for 3/4-bed ones.

Lonsdale Rd peels off W from **Castelnau** at the N end. Another area for Victorian villas, some with stunning white exteriors and Italianate towers (next to St Paul's playing-fields). Some are still rather seedy looking flats. Close to St Paul's School **St Hilda's Rd** leads to a few streets of terraced cottages. As **Lonsdale Rd** follows the river's curve, there is open land on the riverside and a range of property on the left (some flats, '30s and Edwardian houses) down to the Bull's Head pub and **The Terrace**.

Lonsdale Rd and **Castelnau** are linked by a lattice of streets – **Suffolk Rd, Nassau Rd, Lowther Rd, Westmoreland Rd** and **Baronsmead Rd** – with buyers hunting hard for a range of 3- to 5-bed family houses; a mix of Edwardian/'30s/Victorian. Around **Verdun Rd/Barnes Avenue/Stillingfleet Rd** there is a council-built estate. The 2- to 4-bed houses are selling at up to £200,000 and are much sought-after, bearing in mind that the adjacent Victorian mini-mansions can go for over £1 million. But agents say these homes are hardest to sell when the market is quiet.

The Barnes Waterside estate is a new complex of 320 homes on a 34-acre site E of **Castelnau: Wyatt Drive** and **Merthyr Terrace** are the entrances. The southern part of the site is a 105-acre nature reserve formed from the old waterworks filter beds. There are terraces, a crescent (Regency in style, as far as the ironwork goes) and enviably large sub-Palladian villas which sell for around £1.4 million. The water lies to the S, jutting into the site as reed-lined ponds. The last phase of the Waterside, two blocks of flats overlooking the Thames, was sold in 1998. Adjoining is 'Harrods Village', a 250-homes scheme involving new flats and houses and the conversion of the giant, looming, faience-decorated warehouse that recalls the parent store, only marooned amid trees. About 25 were left unsold by Christmas, priced from £485,000.

South Barnes

South of **Church Rd** (with shops, art galleries and restaurants) are more 3- to 5-bed houses. Roads off **Glebe Rd** are popular; their solid red-brick 'Lion' houses (like those found in Fulham's Peterborough Estate) are among the most requested local homes – at up to £1.2 million. **Ranelagh Avenue** (some double-fronted Victorian property) faces the common. **Bellevue Rd, Rectory Rd** and **Elm Grove Rd** spill onto the common and have a touch of Little Venice as Beverley Brook passes beneath them. To the W **Laurel Rd** and **The Crescent** branch onto the green.

Opposite Barnes Green is **Station Rd**, off **Barnes High St** leading to Barnes station; houses include 17th-century Milbourne House where Henry Fielding lived, a mix of small bow-windowed Victorian terraces; workers' flat-fronted cottages; pretty 18th-century cottages leading to the inevitable large Victorian houses close to the common. The former postal sorting office in **Station Rd** is now shops, offices and 12 flats, several available to let at the start of the year. **Beverley Rd** has 2-bed flats and houses.

Behind **Station Rd** and Barnes Bridge railway line is an area worth exploring. It was traditionally the 'wrong' side of the village but is now firmly OK, due (say locals) to an influx of 'new money' squeezing out the humbler inhabitants. Architecturally it is confused – small 2-bed cottages give way to flat-fronted 3-storey houses in **Cleveland Rd** with an outcrop of eight 'Lion' houses marooned at the corner of **Cleveland Gardens**.

North of **Station Rd** is **Barnes High St** (with a good range of family-run shops and restaurants) which runs down to the river. Turn left into the riverside **Terrace** and a sweep of pastel coloured 18th-century houses – wisteria wrapped around wrought-iron balconies – gives a whiff of Brighton. These rarely change hands. Those closer to the bridge go for lower sums. A new block near the bridge is named River House. Past Barnes Bridge (said by the unkind to be the ugliest to span the Thames) and the rail station are **Elm Bank Gardens** (large 5-bed houses), Elm Bank Mansions (red-brick blocks of flats) and more ivy-clad Georgian houses. **The Terrace** ends at the White Hart pub; **White Hart Lane** cuts S, marking the boundary between Mortlake and Barnes. Barnes continues beyond the railway crossing down to the **Upper Richmond Rd**.

Little Chelsea

East of **White Hart Lane** and W of the railway lie **Charles St, Thorne St, Archway St** and **Westfields Avenue**. The vogue for renovating these 2-bed cottages (some have three) was apparently started by a Polish builder in the '60s. His wife saw the potential of the area, comparing the brewery workers' home with their mews counterparts in Chelsea. An irregular style – they were added to as the Victorian workforce grew – makes them less stately then their namesakes but prettier. Extensive renovation means some have an extra bedroom or conservatory and can fetch up to £380,000. Skirting the area are **Thorne Passage** and **Beverley Path** (reached on foot); cottages here are smaller or have the Hounslow loop rail line running behind their garden, factors which may give a discount. The same drawback applies to the **Railwayside** cottages, though their line is the busier.

Mortlake

Best known as the end of the Oxford and Cambridge Boat Race (rowed upstream from Putney), Mortlake is historically more important than Barnes. In medieval times the Archbishop of Canterbury built his palace here (long gone); brewing has been a local industry since the 15th century and the large modern brewery dominates the river bank towards Chiswick Bridge. There is an active community association. The boundary with Barnes to the E is the postal district, with Barnes in SW13 and Mortlake in SW14. **White Hart Lane** marks the border. The railway line hems Mortlake in to the S: some of its prettier homes are unfortunately closest to the busy line.

The most popular type of home in Mortlake is the 2-bed flat or maisonette. Large detached houses are scarce, but there are plenty of houses in terraces and some pretty cottages. The more expensive streets are considered to be **Cowley** and **Ashleigh Rds**, with **First Avenue** and **Victoria Rd** also popular. Riverside houses when available rate the highest prices. Prices generally fall away with proximity to the railway line and the brewery.

Two riverside sites on the **High St** have been developed to add to the stock of new homes. The strangely named 'Capatus' has 'wharf-style' flats, some with river views: prices last autumn were £140–240,000. More riverside homes, big flats with underground parking, were on sale at £315–335,000 last winter.

Property is cheaper than in Barnes, though an influx of younger buyers and renters – often groups sharing – has pushed prices up after a quiet 1998. There are some gems for those who care to look; **Victoria Rd** and **Wrights Walk** have large cottages with unusually large gardens. **Rosemary Cottages** (a row of pretty almshouses) is sandwiched between recently tidied-up blocks of flats and overlooks Mortlake station. **Cowley, Ashleigh** and **Avondale Rds** are mostly Edwardian terraces with 2-bed flats. It's worth noting that property along **North Worple Way** overlooks the railway. Two-bed cottages in well-regarded roads command £300,000,

The green and the area to E and W surrounding it are a conservation area. **Tideway Yard**, near the White Hart, is a refurbished refuse depot and power station. There is a busy wine bar (with fittings from Aintree race course) which has stunning riverside views. The site was extended to include 18 riverside flats, built in Victorian warehouse style to blend in with existing buildings. Prices for these sybaritic apartments are around £300,000 for 3-bed.

Parliament Mews, off **Thames Bank**, is a quiet gated enclave with smart houses and flats with lovely river views. They rarely come up for sale, but last winter a 4-bed house was £515,000.

Cowley Mansions has a range of flats from 1- to 3-bed. Overlooking Mortlake Green, some Victorian shops have been refurbished into a small development of flats. On the W side, a large Victorian building looks out across the green and holds flats.

Sheen

East Sheen lies either side of the **Upper Richmond Rd West**, (the local name for the ever-busy, now Red Route, South Circular). To the E are Mortlake and Barnes; to the W Richmond. Its S boundaries are Sheen and Palewell Commons. In the W, the streets around **Clifford Avenue** and **Derby Rd** blend into Richmond.

B

Richmond was once called Shene until Henry VII built a palace there and named it after his Yorkshire estates. East Sheen – a hamlet until the turn of the century – hangs on to the name. There is nothing rural about the **Upper Richmond Rd West**. It comprises a sprawl of '30s shops, with excellent supermarkets and plenty of restaurants attracting people from both Richmond and Barnes. **Sheen Lane** has developed recently into a useful street of specialist shops. However, there are stunning houses to the S on the fringes of Richmond Park (with prices to match) and bargain surprises on the N, Mortlake, side. Sheen may not be as fashionable an address as Barnes or Richmond, but it attracts young families and first-time buyers who enjoy much the same facilities and at much lower prices. The 1990s saw a further shift in the area's character as older people have moved away to be replaced by professional families. Once dug in, schools and other ties mean they stay.

Between **South Worple Way** and **Upper Richmond Rd West** lie **Trehern Rd, Lewin Rd, Kings Rd, Princes Rd** and **Queens Rd** (sometimes referred to as The Royals). These are 2-bed cottages which mirror those found in Little Chelsea, Barnes. They are slightly cheaper (2-beds £230,000) and some seem a little larger – though the bigger 3-bed, ones command up to £350,000. A pretty 2-bed cottage along **South Worple Way** may cost less, but all the houses face a main railway line which runs along the N side. Further W, where **Vernon Rd** joins **Portman Avenue** and **Thornton Rd**, is an area of 3/4-bed Edwardian property. Across **Sheen Lane** (small shops) is **St Leonard's Rd** which parallels the **Upper Richmond Rd West** and finally swings into a curve before meeting **Clifford Avenue** (another pseudonym for the South Circular). At the **Sheen Lane** end there are some lovely 3-storey, flat-fronted houses painted in pastel shades.

Behind **St Leonard's Rd** and **Elm Rd** there is a pathway called **Model Cottages**. These semi-detached cottages were built for poor labourers in the 1850s and have pretty front gardens with fruit trees and lavender bushes. Many have been extended to provide garages or extra rooms. A surfaced road provides car access which makes them more desirable still. The western curve of **St Leonard's Rd** is tree-lined and has large semi-detached Edwardian houses. Despite the railway it is surprisingly quiet.

In the angle formed by the South Circular and **St Leonard's Rd** is a grid of interesting Edwardian homes. **Graemsdyke Avenue** has quite plain terraced houses made pretty by tiny bay windows. **Holmesdale Avenue** has unusual cottages, with Dutch-style gables, and facing doorways slightly at a slant. **Ormonde Rd** and **Carlton Rd** have grey houses with white wooden fences. Converted flats are scattered throughout this area but particularly along **Elm Rd** and **St Leonard's Rd**. There are some 1930s blocks on the main road, where 2-bed flats cost around £130,000, but on the whole flats are scarce.

Parkside

South of the **Upper Richmond Rd**, between **Stanley Rd** (with pretty cottages at the bottom and the common end) and **Hertford Avenue**, a number of roads snake up to the common. **Stanley Rd** and **Derby Rd** begin with terraced cottages, '30s blocks and terraces. These cottages are popular with young buyers despite being further from the station than those N of the main road. **Deanhill Rd** has Edwardian semis with good-sized gardens; **Coval Rd** has more of the same, plus some terraced houses. Coval Passage has an old warehouse now converted into live/work units. Prices range from £390,000 in lower Parkside for 3/4-bed houses with a garden, but climb as the houses grow in size towards the common. The roads are wide and curving and houses are semi-detached or detached with driveways. Around **Vicarage Rd, Stonehill Rd** and **Hood Avenue** large post-war family houses enjoy the kind of space associated with the Surrey suburbs and yet East Sheen is less than 7 miles from London. A 7-bed Edwardian semi-detached house in **Parkside** was on the market for £700,000 in November. The most prestigious houses are found along **Fife Rd** (from £1 million to £2.5 million) and **Christ Church Rd**. There's a mix of Victorian/'30s/post-war mansions in the kind of individual architecture that money can buy.

B

Transport	Trains: From Barnes, Barnes Bridge, Mortlake to Waterloo 16–20 min. Tube at Hammersmith.
Convenient for	Richmond Park, River Thames, Kew Gardens. Richmond shopping. Miles from centre: 6.
Schools	Richmond Education Authority: Shene School, Richmond C of E High School. Private: Swedish School, St Paul's School (b), Harrodian School. See also Hammersmith and Richmond.

SALES

Flats	S	1B	2B	3B	4B	5B
Average prices	90–120	120–190	150–250+	160–500+	—	—

Houses	2B	3B	4B	5B	6/7B	8B
Average prices	210–370	300–400+	400–600+	500–1.2 M+	900+	—

RENTAL

Flats	S	1B	2B	3B	4B	5B
Average prices	90–200	140–270	200–370	250–400	—	—

Houses	2B	3B	4B	5B	6/7B	8B
Average prices	220–300	260–550	370–750	600–1300	—	—

The properties	Charming cottages and 3/4-bed terraces; some large early Victoriana in Barnes, also splendid 18th-century and modern riverside homes. Mortlake is more Victorian; some excellent flat conversions here. Sheen has Edwardian and other 20th-century; cottages to mini-mansions.
The market	Barnes is the more expensive area, but none is cheap. Ex-council property can offer bargains. The media, sporting and political people living here are diluted by European (especially Scandinavians) and US businessmen/diplomats, who find the area conforms to their idea of Englishness. Sheen is seeing an influx of professional families. Local searches: 7 working days.

Among those estate agents active in this area are:
- Barnard Marcus
- Friend & Falcke *
- Gascoigne Pees
- Boileau Braxton
- Allen Briegel
- Michael Gregory
- James Anderson
- Geoffrey Jardine
- FPDSavills
- Priory Management *

further details: see advertisers' index on p671

BATTERSEA

B

Map ref: p92 (1D)
Postal districts: SW11, SW8
Boroughs: Wandsworth (Con)
Council tax: Band D £370
Conservation areas:
   Numerous – check with
   town hall
Parking: Residents/meters
   in much of area. Red Route
   on Battersea Park Rd

The steady rise of Montevetro, the Richard Rogers-designed tower slab of expensive flats inexorably dwarfing the riverside St Mary's Church, is a sure sign of the times. Battersea has joined fashionable London with a vengeance. Now it has a 'statement' building from Lord Rogers, who has done the same for the City and Paris. A mountain of glass it certainly is: a wedge-shaped finger looming over the Thames in reply to Chelsea Harbour's tower.

Battersea has come a long way from the seedy Sixties days of Up the Junction. Redundant Victorian schools now offer seven-figure 'loft' apartments (office-block conversions providing the poor(er) man's version), and the bemused original Batterseans – who watched the '80s property market crash just as they exercised their 'Right to Buy' in one of the council tower blocks – are hoping that someday their often spacious homes will also become desirable to the chattering classes . . . .

Today City types park their families in the grid of Victorian streets between Wandsworth and Clapham Commons; their staff rent flats above shops around the Junction. **Northcote Rd**, a mere dozen years ago a cheery South London street market, now has bars, bars and more bars, wine merchants, bespoke tailors and wall-to-wall estate agents. Masters of Wine muster round villagey **Battersea Square**; there's haute cuisine in **Queenstown Rd**. Refugees from Chelsea prices bagged the roomy mansion flats around leafy Battersea Park decades ago; the '80s economic migrants found the streets off **Lavender Hill** and, misled by the name of the common and the railway station, believed they had moved to Clapham (this includes estate agents).

No matter; Battersea is now so trendy, they'll be glad they joined. The sons of royalty, the daughters of celebrities roost in Battersea's latest lofts or smartest

Thames-side schemes, along with all the City's baby bankers and their sisters with plum PR jobs in the West End. Mummy lives in Fulham; Dad has a pad in Chelsea Harbour . . . . 'Minutes King's Rd' is a phrase that still crops up in property details.

Just so: at four in the morning. The rest of the time, driving through or from the area is bad for the blood pressure – and there is no tube, though if you are within reach of it the mainline Clapham Junction more than compensates. Battersea's traffic tangle, hemmed in by river and (largely bridgeless) rail lines, is further enhanced by the South Circular, otherwise known as **Battersea Rise/Clapham Common North Side**. If the old Power Station *ever* gets redeveloped, gridlock could be total. **Battersea Park Rd** is now a Red Route, though traffic has been made even busier by traffic calming on parallel **Prince of Wales Drive**. Locals use buses: Vauxhall (Victoria Line) and Clapham Common (Northern line) tubes are (in theory) 15 and 10 minutes by bus respectively.

However, Battersea intends to mark the new Millennium by getting tough with the traffic: lorry bans, 20-mph limits and commuter-parking curbs are appearing in the worst-hit corners.

Central Battersea and the river

From Clapham Junction shopping centre **Falcon Rd** leads N into the heartland of Battersea. En route for the original village, across the **York Way/Battersea Park Rd** junction, this convenient corner holds the enclave of 'Little India', 3-bed Victorian terraces with road names straight from the Raj – **Cabul Rd**, **Afghan Rd**, **Khyber Rd** and **Candahar Rd**. Houses on the N side of **Rowena Crescent** are nearest the tracks.

Off **Falcon Rd** itself, with a fine view of Clapham Junction railway station, is The Falcons, a '60s council estate bought from Wandsworth Council by Regalian in the '80s and tidied up for sale. The flats are quite spacious and facilities include a swimming pool, sauna and gym (included in the service charge).

Frere St, off **Battersea Park Rd**, has some pleasant 2-bed 3-storey semi-basement houses and a small terrace of town-houses (with garages). **Abercrombie St** – small late-Victorian terraces – is another Battersea road embraced by a railway. A development of town-houses here, **Ambrose Mews**, includes four 4-bed, 4-bath homes in close proximity to the Channel Tunnel freight line.

To the N of traffic-plagued, restaurant-ridden, Red-Routed **Battersea Park Rd** lies the oldest part of Battersea, a sometimes uneasy mixture of high-rise council estates and conservation areas. At the heart of the 'village' is **Battersea Square** – the charming if traffic-ridden junction of **Battersea High St** (almost entirely residential at this point), **Vicarage Crescent** and **Westbridge Rd**. The confluence of these three streets make for a Triangle, rather than a Square: cobbled and café-tabled. The little brick flat-fronted 3- and 4-bedroom houses may look early Victorian, but looks are misleading: virtually all were reconstructed by a sympathetic developer. The dutch-gabled pub is extremely old, though. The space above some High St shops has been converted back to homes: 1- and 2-bed flats (the latter c. £175,000). Happily, plans to cram a 76-bed hotel on the sites of nos. 1-3 **Battersea Square** have been withdrawn.

Nearby, Restoration Square on **Battersea High St** is the latest cache of homes: as the name suggests, behind the varied Victorian high-street frontages the houses have been remodelled; through the archways are communal gardens, parking and three new mews houses, while bracketing the site are a restored warehouse plus a new-built replica which hold 16 flats. Houses from £285-385,000 on release.

Across the **High St**, off **Shuttleworth Rd**, is a grid of five streets running S from **Orbel St** – among the most popular locations in Battersea but hidden in an impenetrable road system. Agents dub these roads 'The Sisters': if you don't fancy **Edna**, take your pick from **Octavia** or **Ursula**. They offer 3- and 4-bedroom late-Victorian semi-detached houses with creamy gold brickwork. In **Shuttleworth Rd** are smaller, terraced houses.

Round on **Bridge Lane**, one of the area's Victorian school conversions, 'The Lanterns', offers huge, million-plus flats: 4,000 sq ft and 18-ft ceiling heights can be had.

B

Overlooking the Thames and Chelsea Harbour, Valiant House on **Vicarage Crescent** is a popular block of early '70s brick-built flats; around £265-325,000 for the 2-beds here, depending on floor and view. On the other side of **Vicarage Crescent**, still overlooking the river, are some of Battersea's oldest buildings – including the early 18th-century Devonshire House, and Old Battersea House which dates from 1699.

'Battersea Village', at the junction of **Vicarage Crescent** and **Lombard Rd**, is a pre-war estate of brick-built flats, set around courtyards, that was sold in the 1980s by Wandsworth Council to Regalian. Across the road, Groveside Court is an '80s block of 1-, 2- and 3-bed flats and maisonettes. Riverside, yes. Good-sized flats, yes – but buy at the end away from the adjacent Channel Tunnel freight line. Inland, Windsor Court is a charming conversion of an old school, with gated parking behind. The Fred Wells Garden is an asset to this corner with a children's playground and tennis court.

Westbridge Rd, another conservation area, has some attractive early Victorian villas and the pretty, late-18th-century Battersea Laundry (close to the junction with **Battersea High St**): now flats with a (small) outdoor swimming pool. It fronts the high-rise Surrey Lane Estate, whose towers gave planners the excuse to allow the building of Montevetro (see below) on the riverbank behind.

And so back to the river. Either side of the existing flats described above in the **Vicarage Crescent** area, the entire Battersea riverside from Wandsworth Bridge to Albert Bridge is alive with homes developments, replacing the old industrial wasteland. These run the gamut: the imaginative, the sadly pedestrian, the gross – in terms of design, bulk and relationship to the river. One of the first and nicest was Plantation Wharf, built in the late '80s halfway between Wandsworth Bridge and the heliport: a large and attractive scheme mixing business and residential to create, in effect, an entire new village with Thames-side flats and 4-bed 'atelier' work-homes. Further S, Riverside Plaza has 74 flats, with maybe more to come. To the E, the Price's Candles factory, reprieved by the recession, has finally succumbed to redevelopment by Fairview: at the river end are 118 flats and penthouses, from £225-550,000. So far, Price's intend to keep their warehouses and factory shop on the inland, **York Rd**, end, but there are plans, too, to convert and extend some of the original factory buildings: 80 flats, offices and shops are proposed. Shops would certainly be welcome in this stretch, sandwiched between river and roaring **York Rd**.

Past the heliport and railway bridge, and the existing homes of Groveside Court and Valiant House, **Battersea Church St** swings down to the river and one of the gems of the area, the Grade I listed parish church of St Mary's, built in 1777 but dating back to Domesday. Its fate is now to be flanked by modern slabs: Old Swan Wharf to the W (3-bed, 2-terrace penthouse, £995,000) – and to the E, where once the great manor house stood, Lord Rogers' new 'statement' glass tower, Montevetro, rears its wedge-shaped head, stepping down to the church from its 18-storey high point. Prices here start at £430,000 for a 975 sq ft balconied flat at the bottom to £1,780,000 for 2,016 sq ft of the 15th floor. The penthouses (with roof terrace and winter garden) are in the £3 million region. The early talk of a jetty and a resurgence of river buses has gone very quiet.

A return to a more family, domestic scale can be found in earlier schemes like the 1970s flats and houses of Morgan's Walk next to Battersea Bridge. (Street names in this gated estate include riverside **Thorney Crescent** and **Whistler's Avenue**.) Stanton Gate on **Battersea Church Rd** added 5-bedroomed modern houses to the area.

Across **Battersea Bridge Rd** to the E, Thames Walk is a plate-glass office block with flats alongside the river. The Battersea Bus Garage site next door, also known as Albion Wharf, will sprout a major development this year – possibly: this site, along with Gargoyle Wharf and Point Pleasant further along the river in neighbouring Wandsworth,

B

marked the high-water point of the Department of the Environment's patience with Thames-side gigantism last year. The 16-storey tower planned for Albion was duly thrown out by John Prescott after local planners had approved it. Now flats, offices, shops, restaurants and, naturally, a leisure centre are under consideration at time of writing. Next door, Majestic Wine's riverside site is also under siege. A hideous block appeared beside it at the head of **Ransome's Dock**: designed (unbelievably) by Norman Foster, prices for flats in this plate-glass palace are only topped by those of Montevetro. Sir Norman wanted to add two more floors on too: the planners disagree. Across the dock, Waterside Point runs up to the bridge with houses inland; flats including vast penthouses (£4 million; own pools) on the river. Another block better to look out of than at. And finally, Albert Bridge House added another 30 luxury flats and penthouses to the tally last year. Note that the public will be allowed to trot along a Thames-side path in front of all these gleaming ramparts of stratospheric homes; impossible, though, not to mourn the lost opportunity for the area to regain a proper relationship to its riverside, at least in part, after the long age of industrial sequestration.

Battersea Park

Between Albert and Chelsea bridges, the oasis of Battersea Park is at least inalienable. Difficult to guess, now, looking at the leafy riverside expanse ringed by staid, respectable mansion blocks, that here was the favourite haunt of Regency London's low-life. The park swept away the notorious dens and taverns in 1853, and peace reigned – at least, until the 1890s, when the scandalous sight of lady bicyclists, banned from Hyde Park, shocked residents. The favoured **Prince of Wales Drive** late-Victorian mansion flats run the entire length of Battersea Park. Service charges can be high, and there have been problems in the past with maintenance charges, so leaseholders got together as the law changed, and bought out their landlords. Today, virtually all flats are sold with a share in the freehold of the block. The best is York Mansions (the only one with a lift), followed by Overstrand. Behind are more such blocks in **Lurline Gardens** and **Warriner Gardens**. Roads leading off, like **Soudan** and **Kassala**, feature 3-storey, 4- and 5-bedroomed, red-brick houses.

The **Prince of Wales Drive** area is not just popular for being close to the 200 acres of Battersea Park, complete with art gallery, children's zoo, lake (the café has been smartened up), running track, tennis courts and the splendid Peace Pagoda, gift of Japanese Buddhists. Even given Battersea's notorious traffic, Sloane Square and Knightsbridge are not far away. The flats often have balconies from which to enjoy the leafy park views; best of all are those with sweeping windows in the corner turrets.

On the other side of traffic-plagued **Battersea Park Rd** lie the high-rise Doddington and Rollo council-built estates. The '80s saw energetic work by

B

the council to eradicate the notorious reputation of this corner. The hated exterior walkways were removed; one tower block was sold off to developers and renamed Park South and another, Park Court, was comprehensively refitted by the council, who sold the flats as starter homes: 500 buyers chased the 96 flats. Turpin House, on the corner of **Queenstown Rd**, has been smartened up, and further work continues.

The mansion flats which run most of the length of **Albert Bridge Rd** face E, thus benefiting from more light than **Prince of Wales Drive**, and also overlook Battersea Park. Best blocks are probably Albert and Albany, but all are popular. The mansion blocks are interspersed with some fine, large, mid-Victorian semi- and detached houses. Council-built blocks lie just to the rear. **Parkgate Rd** runs between **Albert** and **Battersea Bridge Rds**, with large plain 3-storey houses, mainly converted to flats. On the corner of **Anhalt Rd** and **Albert Bridge Rd**, Prince Regent House is five recent flats.

Back to the unreality of the riverside now, across the park. Since the mid-'80s the well-named Marco Polo building was a lone outpost of gleaming, smart offices, just S of Chelsea Bridge, confidently expecting to be imminently surrounded with a brave new world on the cleared ex-industrial land behind, stretching to the landmark Battersea Power Station. The uncertainty over the long-drawn-out power station saga left it that way. Now Berkeley Homes have plans in for Battersea Wharf, the site immediately next to the bridge: 450 homes (100 of them affordable housing), hotel, offices, cinemas, shops, restaurants and yes, a health club. Mindful of the DoE, the highest building is a mere 11 storeys. Some real life here would be fun, though it is to be hoped the council will ignore the cheeky suggestion that this should be re-named *Chelsea* Wharf.

A more modest scheme for new flats will begin this summer on the site of the old Davies Turner office block near the Marco Polo centre on **Queenstown Rd**.

The grand plan to transform Battersea Power Station into a massive fantasy-land leisure centre turned out itself to be a fantasy. It's hard not to believe this site is jinxed. Serious money problems hit the first owners to try, and the landmark remains sadly open to the elements more than a decade after they backed away. Confusion – and much recrimination – abounded. The current owners, Hong Kong-based Parkview International, have outline permission for a comprehensive scheme to include two hotels, 500–750 flats, a multiplex cinema plus one or two theatres, a post-production film studio, smart shops. But this January – just as last, and the one before that – there is no firm news. The past year has seen: Parkview holding out for a new train link to Victoria; National Grid holding out for large sums for a 3-acre 'ransom strip' they still own; Regalian reported as wanting to re-house the Coldstream Guards here from Chelsea Barracks; and finally, Parkview rumoured to be selling the whole shooting-match to a housing consortium for some £90 million . . . . Watch this space.

Queenstown

Leaving aside the river end, busy **Queenstown Rd** leads on up from Chelsea Bridge, past Battersea Park and Queenstown train stations, to **Lavender Hill**. Much changed from its grimy past, these days it boasts a good parade of shops and smart restaurants from **St Philip Square** to **Lavender Hill**. The mainly flat-fronted Victorian houses and flats along the road have been steadily renovated and improved for sale: they are popular with young buyers, who now pay £170,000-plus for a 2-bed flat – £35,000 up in the past year. Between busy **Silverthorne Rd** and **Queenstown Rd** is the Park Town Estate, now a conservation area, much of which is still owned by the Peabody Trust. At the **Silverthorne Rd** end of **Tennyson St** the houses are 3-storey flat-fronted. Most of the Estate has Victorian cottage-style houses; some are purpose-built flats with roof terraces for the first-floor-flats. In parallel **Montefiore St**, Laing has inserted a new mews development on the site of an old school: £290-300,000 on release last summer.

The larger houses with ornate carved balconies overlooking **St Philip Square** and the church have been modernized and converted. The flat-fronted cottages with their distinctive high chimneys in **St Philip St** are very rarely available.

On the other side of **Queenstown Rd** lie the perfect Gothic cottages of the Shaftesbury Estate (built in the 1870s by the Artisans, Labourers and General Dwellings Co), which runs across to the traffic-snarled **Latchmere Rd**. The Peabody Trust were also the main landlords in the area: they sold off many of the 2- and 3-bedroom terraced cottages, previously let, as they became vacant. Popular with buyers seeking small, manageable houses – so small as to be better described as vertical flats – they now fetch some £265,000. A traffic scheme stops rat-running in **Eversleigh Rd**, which has the railway line on its northern side. **Eland Rd**, leading down into the Shaftesbury Estate from **Lavender Hill**, has some of the larger houses in the area, up to 4-bed and upwards of £400,000.

Separated from the Shaftesbury Estate by the railway line behind **Eversleigh Rd** lies a triangle made up of **Poyntz Rd, Knowsley Rd** and **Shellwood Rd**. Approached from **Latchmere Rd** and cut off by railway sidings on three sides are small 2- and occasionally 3-bedroom mainly flat-fronted cottages. The area is useful for access to the excellent (council-owned) Latchmere Leisure Centre off **Sheepcote Lane**. Prices are lower than in the Shaftesbury Estate, thanks to the train lines.

Busy **Latchmere Rd** features flats (3-storey blocks) at the upper (**Lavender Hill**) end, Victorian one side, modern on the W, and the usual flat-fronted cottages, normally comparatively reasonably priced because of traffic noise.

However, the roar of the road and the constant trains proved no bar to the success of two schemes featuring that hottest of trends, the loft apartment. Victorian school buildings have proved fertile ground for Sapcote Real Lofts, who created The Village (in **Amies St**) and Southside Quarter here. The Village is considered seriously posh, with security, parking convenience for the Junction and above all large, light-flooded spaces: one such – 2-bed, 2-bath, 32x22-ft galleried living-room – was £775,000 last summer. The Southside Quarter, near the leisure centre in **Burns Rd**, added some purpose-built 'loft houses' to the school conversion: conventional from the front, galleried and with floor-to-rafters glass at the back. Recent prices here in the £395-440,000 range.

This handsome Gothic tower stands somewhat incongruously above a shop on the Shaftesbury Estate. One of a pair, it marks the entrance to the estate of little cottages built a century ago as low-rent housing for the working classes. Today, the neat little homes are fashionable with young buyers. Pointed gables and other cottagey details set these terraces apart from the norm.

Clapham Common North Side

South of **Lavender Hill** and bordered by **Cedars Rd, Lavender Sweep** and **Clapham Common North Side** is the grid of late-Victorian terraced houses known by local estate agents as the North Side Square. **Lavender Hill** has sprouted shops, wine bars and restaurants, with a good parade close to the junction with **Cedars Rd/Queenstown Rd** (this junction, by the way, is smartening up:

demolition work on two corners at time of writing, with a further site a few doors on into **Wandsworth Rd**). Between Battersea Arts Centre and the library, estate agencies are almost wall-to-wall: easier to buy a house than a loaf of bread here.

B

Virtually the entire area consists of terraced 2- and 3-storey houses – although a fair number were converted into flats. The exception is **Wix's Lane** (where both the SW4 and the borough boundaries run) which offers spacious purpose-built Victorian flats (backing onto a school playground) and some new mews houses (c. £320,000 plus). **Nansen Rd** and **Gowrie Rd**, running parallel to the common, offer 3-storey, 4-bed houses, as does **Garfield Rd**, where there is a thriving community centre. The E side of this area is within reach of Clapham Common tube.

Roads running between Clapham Common and **Lavender Hill** such as **Stormont Rd**, **Sugden Rd** and **Taybridge Rd** suffer slightly from rat-running, but **Elspeth Rd** is a through-route for traffic from the South Circular heading for Battersea Bridge. **Sugden Rd** is unusual for its semi-detached houses. **Parma Crescent** and **Eccles Rd** – more early Edwardian terraces – are also popular for their easy access to Clapham Junction station. Residents' parking schemes are almost universal in the streets off North Side.

Larger houses, mainly converted into flats, are found in wide **Sisters Avenue**, **Mysore Rd**, **Lavender Gardens** and **Altenburg Gardens**. Homes in **Lavender Gardens** near the junction with **Lavender Hill** could experience late-night excitement from Jongleurs, the fringe cabaret venue. This does not prevent prices of £900,000 or more for a 6-bed house. On **Lavender Hill**, the old Battersea Town Hall is now the home of the Battersea Arts Centre. The flats in Avenue Mansions, **Sisters Avenue** are unusually spacious, and the top flats offer good (N-facing) views across London. At the top of **Lavender Gardens** is The Shrubbery, a stunning late-Georgian mansion, complete with ballroom, converted to 16 flats under the watchful eye of conservationists.

The Junction

Clapham Junction's busy station and shops form a local centre: Railtrack seems to be making slow running with its plans to rebuild the station at enormous expense, with the inevitable shopping and office development to pay for it. Leading off **Lavender Sweep**, roads like **Barnard Rd** and **Eckstein Rd** offer spacious purpose-built early Edwardian 2- and 3-storey red-brick flats and maisonettes, the upper-floor flats with large roof terraces. **Ilminster Gardens** and **Beauchamp Rd** feature plain 3-storey Victorian houses, virtually all converted to flats. Both suffer somewhat from their proximity to Arding & Hobbs, the area's very own department store, which has been expensively re-vamped to keep up with the Junction's new image. The triangle between **Boutflower Rd**, **St John's Hill** and **St John's Rd**, once a cheaper corner, now sees close proximity to the Junction as a benefit: c. £150,000 for a 1-bed conversion flat here now. Just across Battersea Rise, in the corner between it and **Northcote Rd**, **Cairns Rd** might prove a quieter location: it borders the cemetery. Here Laing have tucked in a gated development of 2- and 3-bed mews cottages which nevertheless have sold well at £265,000 for the former and £390-450,000 for the latter.

Back across **St John's Hill**, past **Plough Rd**, are **Louvaine Rd**, **Cologne Rd** and **Oberstein Rd**, which feature some imposing early Edwardian and late-Victorian terraced houses – some, notably in **Louvaine**, ornate 3-storey-plus basement with porticoes. Virtually all of these are flat conversions. Houses in the northern leg of **Harbut Rd** (smaller 3- and 4-bed Edwardian – and mostly still family homes) will hear the passing trains. The prettiest – and most popular – road in the area is tree-lined **St John's Hill Grove** with some charming Regency and early Victorian cottages, some semi-detached. It is a conservation area and the older houses command a premium.

Strathblaine Rd, **Vardens Rd** and **Sangora Rd**, running between **St John's Hill** and the railway line, are quite smart now and still improving. There are more large 3-storey

Victorian houses here. Some, notably in **Vardens Rd**, are exceptionally large semi-detached 3-storey semi-basement houses, some of which have converted into very pleasant flats. This road gains from having been cut off from the traffic at the S end. Houses to the S side of **Strathblaine Rd** back onto the railway.

At the top of **St John's Hill** and running down alongside **Trinity Rd** is the East Hill Estate. The low-rise flats and houses were built by Wandsworth Council in the late 1970s. When the Conservatives took power in 1978, the estate was designated for a low-cost home ownership initiative, and it is entirely owner-occupied.

Between the Commons

Northcote Rd is the spine of the area properly called Northcote but now known as 'Between the Commons', which runs from **Battersea Rise** to **Thurleigh Rd** and is flanked to E and W by Clapham and Wandsworth Commons. These protect the area from through traffic, and the leafy, peaceful streets are filled with prosperous families who send their children to the rash of prep schools that have moved into Clapham Common, after the local nurseries with names like The Mouse House. Most of this tract is in SW11, though the southernmost roads tip into SW12.

The mainly late-Victorian/early Edwardian terraced houses sweep down from the Commons to **Northcote Rd** which, from **Battersea Rise** to **Salcott Rd**, features a fruit and vegetable market twice a week. The once humdrum shops are now cafés, delis, restaurants, excellent butchers, a serious cheese shop . . . The S end is the smarter.

The majority of houses are 2-storey, 3- or 4-bed Edwardian homes – some of considerable charm inside, and remain in single-family occupation. Prices for these are between £360-460,000. There are pockets of larger, 3-storey mainly flat-fronted houses (some with semi-basement) notably in **Mallinson Rd, Bennerly Rd** and **Salcott Rd**. Many of the houses in these three roads have been converted to flats. **Broomwood Rd** (some 5-bed houses here: pushing £600,000) and **Thurleigh Rd** are the through roads between Clapham and Wandsworth Commons, and **Webbs Rd**, where there are local shops, has traffic running N-S between **Battersea Rise** and **Broomwood Rd**.

Chatham Rd boasts a row of attractive Victoriana: Hyde's Cottages, 1863 (facing a small, low-rise council estate) and one of the oldest pubs in the area, The Eagle. The private **Stonell's Rd**, (cul-de-sac off **Chatham Rd**) offers tiny flat-fronted early Victorian cottages facing a school playground. **Hillier Rd, Devereux Rd** and **Montholme St** are popular because of easy access to Clapham South tube (direct if not always speedy Northern line), as are **Kyrle Rd, Broxash Rd** and **Manchuria Rd**.

On **Clapham Common West Side**, and running back to form a continuation of **Roseneath Rd**, Rialto's latest scheme is 30 new houses on the old Walsingham School site. All have parking and garages, and the grandest face out over the common.

There are virtually no private purpose-built flats in the area with the exception of Broomwood Chambers off **Broomwood Rd**, but former council flats are increasingly available. Ex-council property in the area tends to be flats and small houses: for example, a £200,000, 3-bed terrace in a quiet cul-de sac off **Bolingbroke Grove**. **Broomwood** and **Northcote Rds**, the through-routes, get new traffic-calming this year.

The largest houses in the area are on and just off **Bolingbroke Grove** which runs along the length of Wandsworth Common. Most are late-Victorian semi-detached and terraced. Those on **Bolingbroke Grove** itself balance road noise with open views over the common. Here Bolingbroke House has become seven flats (£200,000- plus for 2-bed). The large 3-storey red-brick terraced or semi-detached Victorian houses of **Gorst Rd** and **Dents Rd** are quieter – and more expensive. Smaller mid-Victorian houses on **Bolingbroke Grove** are close to the junction with **Battersea Rise**. Separated from the road by a stretch of grassland, the mid-Victorian cottages overlook a cemetery. Off **Chivalry Rd**, which forms an L-shape between **Battersea Rise** and **Bolingbroke**

B

Grove, is Commonside, a small estate of houses and flats. A number of the homes back directly onto the railway. A traffic scheme has eased rat-running in **Chivalry Rd**, which has attractive late-Victorian houses. South of **Thurleigh Rd** is SW12, but the streets between **Thurleigh** and **Nightingale Lane** belong to 'Between the Commons'. These have the shops of Balham to call on, and nearby Clapham South tube.

Transport	No tubes; nearest are Clapham Common, Clapham South. Trains: Clapham Junction to Victoria 9 min, Waterloo 7 min; Queenstown Rd to Waterloo 7 min; Battersea Park to Victoria 5 min.
Convenient for	Victoria and Waterloo, Gatwick Airport (28 min), Sloane Square, Thames, Clapham Common, Battersea Park. Miles from centre: 3.
Schools	Local Authority: Battersea Technical, Salesian College RC (b). Private: Emanuel School, St Francis Xavier RC.

SALES

Flats	S	1B	2B	3B	4B	5B
Average prices	90–120	90–200	150–300	210–400	400+	—

Houses	2B	3B	4B	5B	6/7B	8B
Average prices	200–300	300–500	350–500	450–1 M	600+	—

RENTAL

Flats	S	1B	2B	3B	4B	5B
Average prices	150–180	155–250	160–350	300–450+	400–500	—

Houses	2B	3B	4B	5B	6/7B	8B
Average prices	275–400	330–500	425–525+	550–1000	800–1300	—

The properties	Terraced late-Victorian houses, flat conversions and smart new town-house/flat developments. Five-bed-plus houses and larger flats are scarce (try round the park for bigger mansion flats). Smartest new homes are the new riverside developments and loft-style conversions of old Victorian schools.
The market	Ultra-luxury developments attract 'buy-to-rent' investors as much as well-heeled owner-occupiers, so the range and numbers of homes to rent (from ex-council to sub-Manhattan) increasing here. Clapham Junction (despite the name) is in Battersea: this draws City types who compete with Fulham's children for the smarter homes. Good, cheap ex-council to be had. Local searches: 3-4 weeks.

Among those estate agents active in this area are:

- Foxtons *
- John Hollingsworth
- Bairstow Eves
- Winkworth *
- Barnard Marcus
- John D Wood
- John Thorogood
- Edwin Evans
- Bishop Beamish
- Douglas & Gordon
- Thresher Owen
- Andrew Kent & Ptnrs
- Haart
- Wellingtons
- FPDSavills
- Chestertons
- Courtenay *
- Andrew Kent

further details: see advertisers' index on p671

BAYSWATER

B

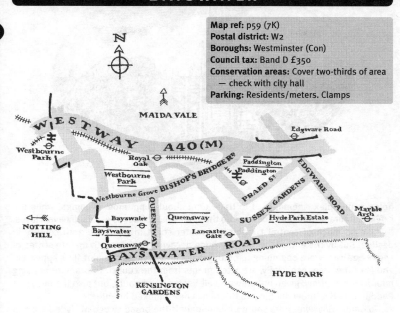

Map ref: p59 (7K)
Postal district: W2
Boroughs: Westminster (Con)
Council tax: Band D £350
Conservation areas: Cover two-thirds of area
— check with city hall
Parking: Residents/meters. Clamps

Bayswater probably has the fastest population turnover of any London district. It has long been a quarter of hotels of all descriptions, of short-stay flats, of rooming-houses and bedsits. But hidden among these are several close-knit, long-established neighbourhoods, several more fast-changing ones and some of London's grandest properties. Bayswater offers just about every kind and status of home, all with two things in common: you can't get much more central, and they're all in W2.

Bayswater's building boom took place in the mid-19th century, when the grand squares and terraces were laid out and acres of cream stucco was applied to endless pompous facades. The grandeur always had a slightly down-rent air: Bayswater was stigmatized as 'the wrong side of the park' by the upper-crust inhabitants of Knightsbridge and Belgravia.

The wider area takes in fascinating neighbourhoods such as Westbourne Grove, riding high on Notting Hill's trendy coat-tails, and Paddington, scene of one of London's biggest redevelopment schemes. It has deprived corners and (some would claim) depraved corners – mainline rail stations attract cheap hotels and all that goes with them. It is home to more nationalities than you can count.

Some of the West End's most luxurious homes are here, fronting Hyde Park and hidden behind in the area's best-kept secret, the Hyde Park Estate. But this select triangle ends at **Sussex Gardens**: N of the estate is fast-changing Paddington, with its cheap hotels and the hidden acres of water and quayside around the canal basin, about to be redeveloped at last. Westwards from **Lancaster Gate** to the borders of now-so-fashionable Notting Hill, there spreads, away from the park, a lively and very mixed web of streets (including, amid the bustle, prettier corners and occasional quiet, tucked-away mews). This has at its heart **Queensway**, a cosmopolitan shopping and restaurant street. Shops in the Whiteley's shopping mall, which also holds a multiplex cinema, tend to trade until about 10pm most evenings, while the cafés, restaurants and bars operate into the small hours. Queensway itself never closes.

Like so much of central London, Bayswater spent most of the 20th century in decline. But by the end of the '80s the huge decaying houses, split up into scores of seedy bed-sits, were beginning to be tidied up, and pockets of smart flats appeared. The N of the area, especially, attracted grants from the council to promote housing improvements. Now, given not only its well-heeled neighbours, but also the new, fast Paddington–Heathrow rail link, its future has never looked brighter.

To define Bayswater: its southern boundary is the broad sweep of Hyde Park and Kensington Gardens. To the E the **Edgware Rd** is the frontier with the Marylebone area. To the N, beyond the elevated M40, the railway and the canal, is Maida Vale. To the W Bayswater blends into Notting Hill. The entire area is within Westminster City Council's jurisdiction, and the W2 postcode boundary also neatly encompasses it.

Its residents are as varied as its homes. The area, being close to the railway station and to the West End, has always catered for London's transient population and for low-income workers and students. At the same time it is surprisingly parochial: the established home for many long-term residents – in council-built homes, as well as those who can afford the Monopoly-money prices commanded by the better properties. There are many tiny – but vociferous – residents' associations, covering single streets. They care passionately about every road hump here.

Renting is the other dimension to the Bayswater scene: thanks to the changes in the letting laws of the '80s, and its splendidly central position, there has been an explosion of homes to rent. For those buying – particularly flats – this is an area where it pays to check the age and quality of the conversion. Standards have risen considerably over the years, as developers realized the need for more spacious and higher-standard flats. Because there is such a huge variety of properties and such a variation in the quality of the conversions, prices, taken in isolation, can often be misleading.

Traffic and parking are contentious issues here, as the number of flats and hotels put intolerable pressure on the available road space. However, much has been achieved by no-through-roads and one-way streets, as any outsider trying to navigate through by car discovers. The best advice is to go by public transport – or take a taxi.

Bayswater is set to get its own mini-Docklands. The Paddington area holds not only the railway station but a large if well-hidden canal basin, too. Between them, the Paddington Goods Yards site, N of the station, and the Paddington Basin area to the E, behind St Mary's Hospital, add up to 40 acres, ripe for redevelopment. It has been poised to become 'the alternative West End', with offices dominating, and smart homes on the waterfront sites, since the '80s. Things stopped dead in 1990 as the last recession bit, but the scheme got going again during 1999. Westminster council is working with the Paddington Regeneration Partnership, which includes Railtrack (which has spent £50m on the station), British Waterways, which owns the canal, and the developers which own the various sites. New bridges, a footpath to Little Venice, boat moorings, cafés and restaurants – all are promised.

There are big names involved. Paddington Basin Developments, a combination of Elliot Bernerd's Chelsfield and Godfrey Bradman's European Land, has brought in Terry Farrell as master planners, and Richard Rodgers as architects for the key building. Their scheme has a big office complex (due to start this year) and 450 flats by Rialto – these have yet to begin. The big Hilton Metropole hotel on the **Edgware Rd** will be upgraded at a cost of £100m (it will be Europe's largest convention hotel) and a new Hilton will emerge from the chrysalis of the 1850s Great Western Royal at the rail station end. The Bishopsbridge site N of the station will have 240 flats plus offices and shops.

There's a lot of future tense in the above, and plans for these big schemes do go awry, but as of last winter the basin was being drained and work was about to begin, with a 3-5-year timescale. A complicating factor is the need to enhance road access to Paddington Station now the Heathrow train is running: this could mean the closure and rebuilding of Bishop's Bridge, which also gives access to the Basin scheme.

Bayswater – Westbourne Grove

Bounded by **Westbourne Grove** (N), **Queensway** (E), the borough boundary (W) and **Bayswater Rd**, this neighbourhood, with its once-gracious 5-storey stucco terraces, was the heart of Bayswater's traditional bed-sit land. As the London market boomed in the 1980s the larger houses were split and sold off as flats, especially in the S close to Hyde Park and convenient for the West End. Now those that are still single homes can command very high prices – in the right street: **Orme Square** opens onto the busy **Bayswater Rd**, thus gaining views over Kensington Gardens. One of its large Regency houses, in less than immaculate condition, still commands around a million.

As you head N into the district from Bayswater Rd and the Park, the noise level drops dramatically. Quiet, leafy streets and mews meander up to **Moscow Rd**, which has Bayswater tube at its Queensway end, and the Orthodox Cathedral that serves the large Greek community. Alexandra Court here is a smart 1989 development. Larger mansion flats in this road: 4-beds in Burnham Court command around £550,000. Some of the mansion blocks are distinctly Manhattan-smart and attract star names. **St Petersburg Place**, running S, contains an attractive terrace of period maisonettes, plus Georgian houses and mansion blocks. It's also home to the imposing New West End Synagogue and St Matthew's Church. A 2-bed flat opposite the church was £395,000 last winter. Further W is **Hereford Rd**, which contains a mixture of properties. There are smaller, less ornate, brick houses with wrought-iron balconies; the road is serviced by a few small shops and restaurants. Evesham House is a development of 26 1/3-bed flats, with car park; **Hereford Mews** also has new homes.

Three very much larger squares dominate the N part of the neighbourhood – **Leinster Square, Princes Square** and **Kensington Gardens Square**. For many years very down-at-heel, with improvement slow and patchy. Now, though **Kensington Gardens Square** still holds some busy hotels, most of the tall houses are split into smart flats. Each square has a large communal garden to which neighbouring residents have access – an oasis of peace in a noisy area (much of it emitting from foreign students at the area's many language schools). Nearby, in **Redan Place** behind Whiteley's, Barratt's grandly-named Kensington Gardens Lodge is fully sold: recent resales include a 3-bed at £315,000 (same as 1998 when new). There is also basement parking.

B

Westbourne Grove itself has become positively chi-chi in parts. New bars and restaurants join those supplying Chinese, Malaysian, Indian, Greek or Lebanese food. Dotted about this gastronomic mecca are specialist shops for cooks or collectors of Oriental furnishings, an Arabic bookshop and more. The western end of the Grove becomes part of the smart Notting Hill antiques district. With Queensway, this is an ideal part of town for the nocturnal, rivalling Earl's Court in its ability to stay up late.

Where W2 runs into W11, in **Chepstow Place** and **Hereford Rd**, Regalian have carved 80 'open-plan' flats out of a Victorian department store plus some modern additions: prices start at £270,000 for 1-bed – and a shower. Each flat has a parking space. Nearly all the flats were sold off-plan late in 1999. Completion is due in April 2000. Westbourne Grove Terrace is a 16-flat scheme behind the facades of four stucco-fronted building: 1- to 3-bed flats £170-370,000.

Queensway – Lancaster Gate

The neighbourhood bounded by **Queensway** in the W, **Bayswater Rd** to the S, **Gloucester Terrace** (E) and **Bishop's Bridge Rd** (N) reflects the tremendous social mix that is characteristic of this part of town. In the N is the council-built Hallfield Estate, bordered by **Inverness Terrace** and **Gloucester Terrace** – blocks of flats angled away from the roads in a classic 1950s garden layout, very daring for its time. The estate has a strong community feeling, its own health centre and school. Flats in the 6- and 10-storey blocks come onto the open market at around £160,000 for a 2-bed. By contrast, in the S, **Lancaster Gate** sports some of the neighbourhood's most luxurious developments, facing Kensington Gardens. Here you can pay £950,000 for a 2-bed flat, though £600,000 for a 2-bed in a stucco terrace is more typical.

Gloucester Terrace is a wide, sweeping road which brings much traffic off the M40 motorway and into Central London. S from the Hallfield Estate the road features large, well-kept stucco houses, most divided up into luxury flats (around £240,000 for a 2-bed one). These are broken by terraced brick houses. Where the road meets **Craven Rd**, another small 'village' begins. Going W along **Craven Rd**, there is a cluster of shops providing local services. And on either side are two sets of mews with steeply sloped entrances (**Gloucester Mews, Smallbrook Mews, Upbrook Mews** and **Craven Hill Mews**, whose little houses, once stables, are now capable of leaving scant change out of half a million). **Brook Mews North** will have 34 new flats in a Berkeley scheme this year. In **Westbourne Terrace** some of the enormous houses, long hotels, are reverting to homes. Expect to pay £270,000 for a ground-floor 2-bed. A luxury block appeared in the '80s on the site of Holy Trinity Church in **Bishop's Bridge Rd**. In the same road distinctive Bishop's Court, handsomely clad in stock brick above stucco, is 49 flats on seven floors: a duplex with roof terrace was marketed at £325,000 last winter.

B

Around the corner off **Leinster Gardens, Craven Hill Gardens** and **Queens Gardens** contain more large, 5-storey multi-occupieds; plus some opulent flats carved from the grand old houses, such as the lateral 3-bed affair going for £750,000 last autumn. Also in **Queen's Gardens** a couple of the big houses have been split into six flats, with two mews houses tucked in behind: £465-700,000 when launched last autumn. **Cleveland Square** and **Devonshire Terrace** generally have smaller 3-storey houses, fast emerging from their B&B/holiday-lets image. Some bigger houses have been split into smart flats. Expect to pay £165,000 for a 1-bed; 2-beds go for £275,000.

The most desirable homes in Bayswater, beside those on the Hyde Park Estate, are to be found in the **Lancaster Gate** and **Porchester Terrace** areas. **Porchester Terrace**, which runs N from the park, contains an intriguing mixture of period town-houses with well-maintained gardens, interspersed with the occasional modern one with off-street parking. Many of the cars along this road bear diplomatic plates, and anti-burglar bars are evident on many a ground floor window. Dotted among the detached houses are some flat-fronted brick apartment blocks. The modern Hyde Park Towers apartment block has wide views across Kensington Gardens. In **Inverness Terrace** is Park Gate, a major recent development of 37 flats. No 1 **Porchester Gate** is a block of 27 flats completed in 1988.

Lancaster Gate is a street of surprises. Here the large hotels have solid, respectable frontages. The square itself surrounds an eye-catching development of luxury flats created from a former church. On the corner, another luxury-level development produced 24 flats carved out of several 5-storey, colonnaded terraced houses. This sort of scheme allowed for Tardis-like lateral conversions – one boasted 4/5-bedrooms and a 43-ft living room.

In contrast to the atmosphere and scale of **Lancaster Gate**, neighbouring **Lancaster Mews** is like a small country village. Its sloping entrance is topped by the Mitre pub. Cottages here are beautifully maintained and colour-washed in attractive pastels. Mediterranean blue paintwork and abundant window boxes complete the picture of the busy light industrial/residential 'village'. The twin mews across **Craven Terrace** is smaller but equally well-maintained. There are rarely signs of sales.

Back on **Queensway** itself, at the W end of the neighbourhood, the traditional night life continues with restaurants pulling in tourists and visitors, and small shops catering for local residents. Thirties brick apartments, served by walkways, top the shopping arcades at the lower end of **Queensway** (£85–90,000 will buy you a studio flat here; c. £165,000 for a 2-bed). The famous Whiteley's department store – London's first, opened in 1863 – was reborn in 1989 as a shopping complex, harbouring a Marks & Spencer food hall as well as dozens of smaller shops, plus a multiplex cinema. This modern combination of shopping, eating and entertainment under one roof, open late and with parking, provided a much-needed and popular focus for this side of town.

Westbourne Park

Porchester Rd takes you N from the **Queensway** neighbourhood and up towards the motorway and **Harrow Rd**. Leaving **Bishop's Bridge Rd**, go N into **Porchester Rd** and you are heading towards Royal Oak tube station. Pass by the local landmark of Porchester Hall, council-owned (you can hire this splendid venue) and always busy. Behind this is the Porchester Baths (public and private), with a luxurious health club.

To the E this end of **Gloucester Terrace** is the motorway access route: large 4-storey 1850s houses form what was once an elegant terrace; now the **Westway** overshadows them. The buildings, which have attractive wrought-iron balconies, were restored and split into flats by the old GLC back in the 1960s and '70s. **Porchester Sq** and **Porchester Place** are tucked into a corner N of **Bishop's Bridge Rd**: worth a look with 2-bed flats in a 16-storey block at around £285,000. The GLC was active here too (see Gloucester Terrace above). Porchester Square has a busy communal gardens with playground. In **Orsett Terrace** 90 flats were converted from the houses in the late '80s. The Colonnades is a 1980-ish development opposite the Hallfield Estate: mews cottages, some restored Victoriana, 2-bed maisonettes for £310,000.

B

To the W of **Porchester Rd**, **Westbourne Park Rd** has a curious mixture of properties ranging from the flat-fronted brick apartment blocks to detached villas with ornate, oriental-inspired decorations and colonnaded entrances. Eight new mews houses and some offices were built in **Celbridge Mews** off **Porchester Rd** in the '80s.

West of the triangle bounding the church, **St Stephens Crescent** has an attractive terrace of stucco 5-storey properties with steps up to front entrances guarded by columns. Major work on a pair of houses here will result in an opulent private home. Around the corner, just off **Talbot Rd**, and E of **Chepstow Rd**, lies **Bridstow Place**, a tiny row of colour-washed Victorian cottages. Climbing roses and trailing plants splash colour over the pastel brickwork from their little gardens. Small-scale homes again in **Shrewsbury Mews**, where the tiny, modern cottages have garages. But turn the corner, and you're back with **Chepstow Rd**'s tall, 5-storey houses, scene of many a conversion scheme. **Talbot Rd** itself has seen homes expensively renovated in recent years. This corner, in fact, has been a hotbed of improvement and is now distinctly fashionable, numbering musicians and the odd pop star among its residents. Running between Talbot and tree-lined **Artesian Rd**, **Courtnell St** has more attractive colour-washed, brick-fronted homes, overlooked by copper beeches. W of here is the boundary of the W2 district and of Westminster borough: across it lies Notting Hill.

Paddington

Paddington station is the hub of the neighbourhood bounded by **Eastbourne Terrace**, **Harrow Rd**, **Edgware Rd** and **Sussex Gardens**. Like the surroundings of most major stations, there is a mixture of expensive homes, services and run-down property catering to transients. Soon, though, this corner will be transformed: see introduction.

South of bustling **Praed St**, in **Sale Place**, **St Michael St** and **Star St** are little Victorian cottages, most once owned by St Mary's Hospital or by the railway companies for their workers. Some cottages date back before the railway to the canal boom of the early 19th century. Over time these homes fell into disrepair; housing associations acquired some, but many benefited from the declaration 20 years ago of a Housing Action Area, which helped owners to improve their homes. Now their charm and location can command high prices.

Five new houses in **Praed Mews** added to the air of revival. More new homes appeared around a courtyard off **Star St**. But **Praed St**, next to the station, reflects the dominant trend of the area: exchange bureaux, instant photos, heel bars and dealers in gold, silver and second-hand goods abound. **Norfolk Square** lies S of **Praed St** and contains mostly small hotels surrounding a communal garden. Westminster Council took over and renovated the neglected square gardens. South again, **Sussex Gardens** is a major road connecting **Lancaster Gate** and the **Edgware Rd**, its once-grand 4-storey terraces now flats (2-bed, £250,000; 3-bed £425,000) and bed-and-breakfast hotels. Three-bed flats rise to half a million or so in a private apartment block, Sussex Lodge, around the corner in **Sussex Place**. Across **Sussex Gardens**, in the triangle it makes between the park and the **Edgware Rd**, lies the exclusive Hyde Park Estate.

Hyde Park Estate

From Marble Arch (originally built as an entrance to Buckingham Palace, but today standing at the western end of Oxford St as an entrance to nowhere), walk up busy **Edgware Rd**, turn left into cheap-hotel-lined **Sussex Gardens**, left again at the towering Royal Lancaster Hotel onto **Bayswater Rd**, and back along the Park to Marble

Arch. You have thus circumnavigated the Hyde Park Estate. Better, branch to your left and penetrate the Estate's peace and quiet. It is like an island: hard to believe, once inside, how close is Oxford St. Leaving Edgware Rd is like going from a weekday to an old-fashioned Sunday.

B

The Estate owes its character to its long-time landlords, the Church Commissioners. Once, the Bishop of London owned nearly all of Paddington. At the start of the 19th century the Bishop's architect built an elegant estate of squares and crescents – and called it, rather inauspiciously, Tyburnia. The Church Commissioners, heirs of the bishops, sold off all their Paddington land except this Hyde Park triangle in the 1950s. Much of ecclesiastical Paddington had sunk into a slum, populated largely by prostitutes (one corner, W of the station, was known as 'Sin Triangle'). Concentrating on the Hyde Park Estate, the Commissioners started widespread rebuilding. The result is a neighbourhood mixing lovely Regency stucco terraces, quiet little mews, handsome (some, anyway) modern houses and flats and – most notably forming a protective rampart along **Edgware Rd** – tower block apartments. The key is the Regency street-plan, which has survived the redevelopment. The Estate's lack of through-routes, and its clearly defined borders, keep it quiet and pleasant. It is a tribute to the Commissioners, or more especially to their agents and architects, that the Estate is still a desirable place to live.

Prices on the Estate are governed by whether they are for a (still less common than elsewhere) freehold – or, if leasehold, the length of the remaining lease. Also by period: the modern homes amid the stucco may be less attractive to the Brits, but more so to the international set; they often have a key advantage in this crowded corner: a garage. Thanks to the rebuilding and later conversions, there are flats, flats, flats of every size, period and lease length, at a commensurately wide span of prices: generalizations are difficult here. Note that, although the Leasehold Reform Acts have seen some at least of the residents able to buy their freeholds, the Church Commissioners still hold sway here: even freehold houses are liable to come under an estate management scheme.

The centre of life on the Estate is the Connaught 'village', with its mix of small shops, offices and homes; **Connaught St** is the 'high street'. It's a varied corner: for example **Connaught Place**, a mix of hi-tech offices and homes reconstructed behind the original stucco façade which faces out over Marble Arch and Hyde Park, houses the headquarters of a large multinational. And quietly camouflaged into the white stucco front of **Hyde Park Gardens** is the Sri Lankan embassy. The corner of **Sussex Place** and **Hyde Park Gardens Mews** is another picturesque hive of activity for eating, meeting and drinking, where on warm summer evenings people sit out at tables on the pavement – in (almost) Parisian style.

The centrepiece of the Hyde Park Estate is **Hyde Park Crescent**, and the lovely old church of St John's, which can be seen as a long-distance vista from as far as **Sussex Square**. The Crescent adds space and dignity to the church. Mirroring it to the E is **Norfolk Crescent**. The two form an elongated circle embracing the church, two squares (**Oxford** and **Cambridge**) and two high-rise blocks. **Norfolk Crescent**, a post-war rebuild of tall thin family houses, feels slightly crammed in contrast to **Hyde Park Crescent**.

Garden squares are a feature of the Estate, each with a character and atmosphere of its own. **Oxford Square** and **Cambridge Square**, for example, are bordered by '60s town-houses (a 4-bed one might be £675,000 – but watch length of lease) and tall blocks of flats (2-bed upwards of £250,000) with underground garages. **Hyde Park Square** on the other hand is larger and has a range of styles surrounding it, from grandiose 5-storey stucco houses yielding conversions to spacious modern family homes to blocks of flats. **Sussex Square** has an even more spacious feel about it, with a circular green at the centre. One of the handsomest is **Connaught Square**, enclosed by classic Regency terraces. While being just a stone's throw from the Marble Arch

B

madness, it manages to retain its dignity and leafy peacefulness. Its houses are large; most are now flats, but not all. But the jewel in the crown is probably **Gloucester Square**. One can walk around the perimeter and not always be aware that it *is* a square: some of the (highly priced: £1.5m is typical for a freehold) houses have the luxury of backing directly onto the central green, concealing the communal central garden from the untutored eye. A recent block of de luxe flats added onto the end of a cream stucco terrace were all eagerly snapped up. Some large 5-storey homes to be found here, too.

Many of the Estate's big town-houses, once occupied by the wealthy families from the pages of history books and by the merchant classes and empire builders, have now been converted into ultra-luxurious flats. Some of the most exclusive are the stucco-fronted Regency buildings in **Hyde Park Gardens**, having their own huge communal garden opposite Hyde Park. Grand apartments here (some vast), with their high ceilings, huge windows and Park views come up both for buying and renting.

In contrast to this quiet elegance and opulence, there is a variety of purpose-built modern blocks on the Estate, ranging from the workaday Park West in **Kendal St** on the E fringe, to the fountain-laden Water Gardens and the Quadrangle, both bordering on **Sussex Gardens**. The Water Gardens estate is a complex of towers and smaller blocks, with a '60s split-level feel and a profusion of pools and fountains.

Mews houses are ever more popular, here as elsewhere in London. They were originally built behind the big houses of the gentry as accommodation for horses, coaches and coachmen. It is only since the last war that they have been converted into homes, providing compact, easily manageable houses in villagey cobbled streets, retaining their period frontage and last-century atmosphere – helped, in most cases, by being cul-de-sacs. Some of the most charming and coveted mews on the Hyde Park Estate are **Hyde Park Gardens Mews**, off **Hyde Park Square**, and two smaller mews off **Albion St**: **Albion Mews** and **Albion Close**. The Estate is lucky to have a mews that is still used for its original purpose: **Bathurst Mews** houses a riding school, where you can hire horses and go riding in Hyde Park. Apart from the charm, mews houses often have their own garages, thus solving the main drawback to such central living. Nearly all the post-war flats and houses also have underground garages. But parking meters and parking permits put considerable pressure on movement, space and life in general.

The atmosphere on the Estate, once intimate, slow-moving and village-like, has become rather more cosmopolitan and anonymous with the years. The variety of languages that you can hear within a few paces ranges from Filipino to Swahili: many diplomats live here. Wealthy Arabs, many of whom only come for the summer months, also have their London bases here. The estate agents, banks, clothes shops, cinemas and restaurants at the top end of **Edgware Rd** all reflect this diversity. Nevertheless, the estate remains a prized oasis.

The Hyde Park Estate stops at **Sussex Gardens**, lined on either side by hotels and bed-and-breakfast houses filled with young travellers – as somewhere cheap and central to stay, you can't beat it. (**Sussex Gardens'** other claim to fame was traditionally that of being a red-light district – obviously encouraged by its proximity to both Paddington and Marylebone stations.) The Hyde Park Estate, however, feels genteel and safe, with **Sussex Gardens** acting like a divide. On the other side of the road, you're no longer on the Estate – there is a different atmosphere, the pace is faster and more commercial and the streets dingier as you near Paddington station. However, from there it is now a mere 15 min by express train to Heathrow airport, and the massive redevelopment long planned for the Paddington area will one day transform that corner, too.

B

Transport　　Tubes, zone 1: Bayswater (District, Circle); Lancaster Gate, Queensway (Central); Paddington (District, Circle, Bakerloo, Hammersmith & City). From Lancaster Gate: Oxford Circus 6 min, Bank 20 min, Heathrow 55 min (2 changes).
Trains: Paddington–Heathrow Express 17 min.

Convenient for　　Hyde Park, West End, City, M40 to West, Heathrow. Miles from centre: 2.5.

Schools　　Local Authority: North Westminster Community School. Private: Pembridge Hall School (g).

SALES

Flats	S	1B	2B	3B	4B	5B
Average prices	95–150	135–225	160–350	220–500	350–850	450+

Houses	2B	3B	4B	5B	6/7B	8B
Average prices	230–700	400–1 M	550–1.2 M	650+	—	—

RENTAL

Flats	S	1B	2B	3B	4B	5B
Average prices	150–200+	200–300+	260–400+	350–650	450–900	650–1400

Houses	2B	3B	4B	5B	6/7B	8B
Average prices	250–400	400–750	580–900	600–1500	—	—

The properties　　Bayswater's traditional image of seediness (fast altering) means its prettier, well-hidden corners and occasional quiet mews come as a shock to many. White terraces were once all grand; currently a total mix: everything from pristine millionaires' squares (Hyde Park Estate) to hostels. Ramparts of flats along Edgware Rd. Flats most common. Houses either small or very expensive: the rest were converted to flats.

The market　　The 17 min rail link to Heathrow has set the seal on this fast-changing area. Its excellence as a London base attracts the international set. Grand plans to regenerate Paddington will complete the transformation – one day. Local searches: 10 working days.

Among those estate agents active in this area are:
- Chestertons
- Lurot Brand
- The London Mews Co
- FPDSavills
- Marsh & Parsons
- Kinleigh, Folkard & Hayward
- Winkworth *
- Foxtons *
- Plaza Estates
- John D Wood
- Cluttons Daniel Smith
- Keith Cardale Groves
- Jackson-Stops & Staff
- Harrods Estates
- Sterling
- Anscombe & Ringland *
- Beaney Pearce *
- Grangeview Estates
- Capital Agencies
- Brian Lack & Co

further details: see advertisers' index on p671

BEDFORD PARK AND ACTON GREEN

B

Map ref: p73 (3K)
Postal districts: W4
Boroughs: Ealing (Lab),
   Hounslow (Lab)
Council tax: Band D
   Ealing £703, Hounslow
   £860
Conservation areas:
   Bedford Park
Parking: Controlled
   Parking Zone likely to
   expand to take in rest
   of area this year

It is, of course, quite possible to live in Bedford Park without being keen on architecture, but it would be rather a waste. For this was London's first purpose-built suburb – laid out, and the houses designed, in the 1870s to high artistic standards for those of aesthetic (*the* in-word of the day) tendencies. It has survived virtually intact, an island in the less creative sprawl of West London. And a good number of the inhabitants spend a good part of their time protecting their neighbourhood against philistine encroachment.

Convenient position (it lies just N of Chiswick – under which title you will almost certainly find it listed in estate agents' ads), a distinctive charm and family-sized – some outsized – houses are the solid attractions of this corner. Corner it is: Bedford Park is not very big, and its cachet leads to an extension of the name into Acton Green. 'Bedford Park borders' or 'West Bedford Park' are terms to beware of if you have set your heart on the homes of the conservation area. Some roads outside the original estate belong in spirit, but to the true Park residents, the world immediately outside their conserved streets is, and will remain, forever Acton.

True Bedford Park consists of a mere dozen streets, contained by **Esmond**, **Blenheim** and **Abinger Rds**. Acton Green, the L-shaped area to the N and W of the conservation area, may hold more everyday homes, but these bordering streets are themselves a well-defined enclave: only a single road, **Acton Lane**, crosses the rail-tracks to Acton proper, (and only **Bath Rd** connects through from Bedford Park to Hammersmith). You would think the W4 postcode was a solid wall. Popular and peaceful (apart from the odd train rumble) family homes here – ever more so, as Chiswick prices escalate – particularly the corner to the W, which has the tube.

B

Confusion is to a certain extent understandable: the tube station that serves Acton Green is called Chiswick Park, so agents naturally tend to adopt this name for the surrounding streets. Then, the open space of Acton Green Common itself lies S of **South Parade**, leading up to Bedford Park's tube – which is called Turnham Green. In its turn, the once-thriving hamlet of Turnham Green seems to have been subsumed entirely into Chiswick (which chapter see), its name only commemorated, sadly, by the tube station, a Civil War battle, its green (which lies away to the S of **Chiswick High Rd**) and **Turnham Green Terrace** – a busy street of shops, restaurants and estate agencies which leads across the tracks to **The Avenue**, the spine of Bedford Park.

Bedford Park

Founded in 1875 by Jonathan Carr, a cloth merchant with a taste for speculation and art, Bedford Park was the prototype garden suburb. Carr employed such well-known architects as (principally) Norman Shaw, plus E J May, E W Godwin and Maurice B Adams to design houses in the Queen Anne Revival style – all red-brick, dormer windows, Dutch gables, hanging tiles, balconies and pretty porches. Some 400 buildings, mostly Grade II listed, now make up the conservation area. Despite the odd bit of war damage and modern infilling, the estate remains remarkably homogeneous; the most obtrusive new building is St Catherine's Court, a 1930s block built on the site of Carr's own magnificent home, the Tower House.

There is great variety in homes, from little 2-storey 3-bedroom cottages to 6/7-bedroom detached houses, semis and terraces of up to 4 storeys. There are a couple of large mansion blocks, but apart from that very few flats: those of the larger houses that *were* split into flats in the '80s are wherever possible being reunited. Homes here are owner-occupied: only a few are rented. Despite its sobriquet of garden suburb many of the gardens are disappointingly small ('though not for Central London, which for practical purposes we are!' objected one resident), and prices reflect garden as much as house size and position. Garden flats also fetch proportionately more. Houses on street corners, often set at an angle to the road, have enviable extra garden space and beautiful detailing: perhaps a conservatory or pleasing gables or balconies. Because there is such a good size mix, residents often move within the area and many properties are sold through the grapevine – which is why some people move to Bedford Park's borders before working their way in. The other lack can be parking space: Streets E of **The Avenue** (the premier roads) became a controlled parking zone a year back, and it is planned to extend this to the whole Bedford Park/Acton Green area over the next. The

Just about every house in Bedford Park is listed, and the whole place is a conservation area. So splendid details like this assemblage of gable, balcony and bay will survive. The wooden railings, close-set glazing bars in the square bay, heavy gable and tiled roof are typical. The houses are late-Victorian, but they hark back to Queen Anne.

Aesthetic types for whom the estate was planned were plainly proto-Greens (or just plain poor): they were not expected to set up their carriages . . . . The average **Priory Avenue** house, for example, is a semi-detached that boasts 4/6 beds, 2 receptions, 2 bathrooms – but no garage or off-street parking.

The whole estate with its irregular layout (designed by Norman Shaw to preserve existing trees) was modelled on the ideal of a village complete with shops, pub – the Tabard, which today boasts excellent pub theatre – church of St Michael and All Angels, church hall and club. The village atmosphere remains, which means lots of social and cultural activities plus a friendly atmosphere where everyone seems to know everyone else's business. The community spirit is fostered by the Bedford Park Society, which protects the area's architectural heritage.

Originally built, then, as homes at modest rents for the aesthetic middle classes, Bedford Park from the first attracted many artists (the occasional purpose-built artist's studio can be seen) and personalities of the day. Nowadays it is more likely to house media folk, professionals such as architects, and others who can afford the considerably less-than-modest buying prices.

Carr chose the spot because of its proximity to the newly opened Turnham Green station; these excellent links to the West End and City remain, with the added advantage of being 20 minutes' drive (on a good day) from Heathrow down the M4. The area is, too, within walking distance of the shops and restaurants on **Chiswick High Rd**, as well as other W4 facilities. Acton Green Common, abutting the tube line, is the nearest open space, but the river, Kew Gardens and Richmond Park are only a short drive away. **Bath Rd, The Avenue** and **South Parade** are the main routes, with buses, while the latter, along with **Flanders Rd**, lie close to the tube line. **Abinger Rd, Blenheim Rd, Bedford Rd** and streets off **South Parade** are busy; it follows that roads in the heart of the conservation area, such as **Queen Anne's Gardens**, are quiet – but all roads have covetable houses.

Prices vary considerably with the desirability of the roads and the purity of the architecture, but you can count on spending well over half a million for an 'ordinary' family house in the conservation area. It goes up from there (say £700-900,000 for 5-bed semis), with classic Norman Shaw houses rarely for sale and priced accordingly. One of the earliest E J May-designed houses has a coveted corner plot in Newton Grove: the 6-bed, 3-reception, 3-bath mansion, with gardens fore and aft – and parking – cost £1.5 million last winter. Another such monster with artist's studio on **Priory Avenue**, £1,850,000 (by contrast, a 6-bed, 2-reception, 2-bath, 27ft-kitchen semi just outside the conservation area was £850,000). A curiosity was a £190,000 1-bed garden flat on **The Avenue** which pre-dates the suburb: it is part of the stables of the original Bedford House, in the grounds of which Bedford Park was built.

Bedford Park Borders; Acton Green

Non-listed houses, such as those in streets off **Flanders Rd** to the SE, along with mansion blocks and houses just outside the conservation area in **Blandford Rd, Fielding Rd** and **Vanbrugh Rd** to the N, and **Esmond Rd, Ramilles Rd, Rusthall Avenue** and **St Albans Avenue** – 'West Bedford Park' in estate-agentese – were built later than Bedford Park proper, with some inter-war additions (though note that the E side of **Esmond Rd** is still in the conservation area, and has some substantial houses – in size and price – at its S end). Homes here are cheaper in design and price, but still above the more everyday homes of the surrounding 'borders' streets further N and W, which form the lower brackets of our price chart.

West of **St Albans Avenue** are the first streets of Acton Green, a neighbourhood still considered Chiswick for estate agents' purposes: since this corner is still in the W4 postcode and uses Chiswick Park tube, perhaps they have a point. The homes are more ordinary than Bedford Park's, but some are of much the same date, with a good sprinkling of Edwardian and some mid-20th-century. It is here, and to the N of the area, that any new homes can be found, and there is also activity from developers splitting terraced homes into flats. These streets run off **Acton Lane**, but are kept distinct from Acton proper by the railway line that curls protectingly round to the NW. There is a difference between the streets to the W, which are wider and have some good-sized houses amid the terraces, and those just E of Acton Lane, which tend to be narrower with smaller homes.

To the W of **Acton Lane, Church Path** winds through the area; at one point **Cleveland Rd** joins it to run parallel behind a paved and treed strip: a pleasant villagey spot. At the head of this is a pretty corner house at the end of opulent-sounding and certainly pleasant **Rothschild Rd**. **Kingswood Rd** and **Cunnington St** cut through: wide roads with better architecture than average. **Bridgeman** and **Weston Rds** running beside the (not very busy) railway are popular. **Antrobus Rd** is also well-regarded. **Ivy Crescent**, which backs onto the railway, is a fertile field for flat conversions. Across the tracks, the old Gunnersbury London Transport depot is at last to become Chiswick Business Park. Courtesy of major developers Stanhope low-level offices plus leisure facilities are planned, and a link road to **Bollo Lane**. Locals are hoping that when it's complete the Piccadilly line will stop at Chiswick Park station, as well as the District.

Acton Green gained its first fashionable warehouse conversion last year: 18 1-, 2- and 3-bed flats on the corner of **Acton Lane/Fletcher Rd**, close to the rail line in the N of the area. Now an old transformer station has been transformed into 'Chiswick View', classy flats that include a 1-bed triplex, the glass-roofed top floor reached via spiral staircase (£240,000). Off **Steele Rd**, a refurbished/rebuilt mews is tucked in behind smart and firmly shut gates. Round the corner off **Church Path, Chapter Close** is a modern mews development; Laing have added another: behind the gates of Amblemede Court there are eight 3-bed houses (c. £300-320,000) and a 2-bed bungalow. Converted flats, too, are a staple around here.

In **Rothschild Rd**, 2- and 3-bed terraces could be had for around £260-400,000 last winter; busy **Acton Lane** had a 3-bed terrace 'with potential' for £280,000. Tucked behind the Acton Green Common/**South Parade** end of **Acton Lane**, first-time buyers can get a foot in the area in the ex-council maisonettes of **Clement Close** from c. £85,000 for a 1-bed.

The northern borderlands centre around **Southfield Rd**, a continuation of **The Avenue**, which leads on round to **Acton Lane**, past a large recreation ground with tennis courts, which again cuts this corner off from Acton proper to the N. **Southfield Rd** has standard square-bayed 1914 terraces (some are purpose-built 3-bed maisonettes; c. £220-260,000), **Fielding Rd** similar; while **Speldhurst Rd** and the N end of **St Alban's Avenue** have homes from a slightly earlier period. There is a recreation ground and Southfields Infants and Junior school on **Southfield Rd**, as well as some 1980s houses and flats, and a 1990 cache of 3-bed, 2-bath mews houses.

A final point: unlike neighbouring Chiswick, Bedford Park is far enough from the flight paths to escape aircraft noise being a nuisance.

B

Transport	Tube stations: Turnham Green, Stamford Brook, Chiswick Park (zone 2, District). From Turnham Green: Oxford Circus 25 min (1 change), City 40 min, Heathrow 25 min (1 change). Trains: South Acton on N London line/Silverlink.
Convenient for	Heathrow and M4. Miles from centre: 4.
Schools	Ealing and Hounslow Education Authorities: Chiswick School, Acton School. Private: Latymer (b), Godolphin & Latymer (g), St Paul's (g), Arts Educational School.

SALES

Flats

	S	1B	2B	3B	4B	5B
Average prices	90–160	150–250	170–300	210–350	340–400	—

Houses

	2B	3B	4B	5B	6/7B	8B
Average prices	260–400	290–425	395–850+	650–1 M+ →650–1.25 M+		—

RENTAL

Flats

	S	1B	2B	3B	4B	5B
Average prices	150–200	150–350	230–350	280–550	—	—

Houses

	2B	3B	4B	5B	6/7B	8B
Average prices	160–400	250–500	500–1250	700–1500	—	—

The properties	Distinctive enclave of late-19th-century Queen Anne-style houses, from 3-bed cottages up to large houses. Bordering streets are more everyday Victorian/Edwardian, plus mansion blocks and pockets of new houses and flats.
The market	Always fierce competition for the small number of genuine, conservation-area homes. Surrounding streets are also popular family homes — increasingly so, as Chiswick prices rise. These are at cheaper end of above prices. Local searches: Ealing 5 working days, Hounslow 1 day.

Among those estate agents active in this area are:

- Barnard Marcus
- Knight Frank
- Foxtons *
- Winkworth *
- Bellenger Locke
- Lauristons
- Quintons
- Bushells
- Whitman & Co
- Fletcher Estates
- Chestertons
- Haart

further details: see advertisers' index on p671

BELGRAVIA

Map ref: p145 (6H)
Postal districts: SW1
Boroughs: Westminster
   (Con)
Council tax: Band D
   £350
Conservation areas:
   Whole estate
Parking:
   Residents/meters.
   Clamps

To live in Belgravia is to be seriously rich – or at least to have someone else (like your company or embassy) paying the rent. For your money you get unrivalled ambience, discreetly excellent management of the overall estate, plus a position mid-way between Harrods and Buckingham Palace – and a short taxi ride from everywhere you would ever want to be. The key to Belgravia's charm is its changes of scale, from minute and charming mews homes in their cobbled cul-de-sacs, through low-storeyed terraces to the gleaming grandeur of the set-pieces of **Eaton Square**, **Belgrave Square** and **Chester Square**.

This pristine part of London, which fills the angle between Hyde Park, Green Park and **Sloane St**, must rank among the best property investments of all time. The sole proprietor of the whole of this patch of enviable real estate since its building, the enjoyer of its rents and revenues, has been the Grosvenor Estate, personified by the sixth Duke of Westminster. His family has owned the land for generations and in Regency times developed it with the help of builder and architect Thomas Cubitt. Much of London was built up at this time or a little later, but no other district has kept its character in quite the same way. The credit goes partly to Cubitt, whose building standards were, if not exactly high, then better than those of Nash. But the main upholder of the Belgravian character has been the Grosvenor Estate, and the snowy sweep of stuccoed terraces and squares stand seemingly unchanged. That said, the Duke's inheritance has been nibbled at of late by tenants exercising their rights under the Leasehold Reform Acts. The Estate contested the buy-outs and took the case to the European Court of Human Rights under the complaint that the Acts infringed the

Duke's right to freely enjoy his property. But the Estate now accepts the inevitability of people's right to buy and, while it doesn't go out of its way to offer freeholds, it negotiates with those leaseholders who approach it on this – or on extending their leases by up to 90 years. The Estate also changed its leasing policy in 1998, and will now offer new leases of 99 years or more – up to 125 years – outside **Eaton Square** (previously, the maximum was 75).

So, for the first time in two centuries, the word 'freehold' appears increasingly in Belgravia. The Estate office is still very much in charge, however: controlling tenancies, developing its own properties and stipulating just how the inhabitants – even the new freeholders – behave (try drinking on the pavement outside one of the Belgravia pubs). The control of the Estate office may be discreet but it is firm. Whatever their personal tastes, householders must paint their façades cream – and not just any old cream but the precise British Standard shade of magnolia that is the official Estate colour. Whether or not the Estate still owns the property, goes the thinking, safeguarding the integrity of the area protects everybody's investment.

Central Belgravia is almost wholly residential. The Estate's policy is to use the fringes for offices and shops and hotels, but to keep the heartland free of commerce – unless you count embassies. Shops are to be found in a few streets: **Elizabeth St** and **Motcomb St** have the majority – and of course you can commission your furniture from Viscount Linley's shop among the galleries and antique shops on Belgravia's southern borders, around 'Pimlico Green' down on the **Pimlico Rd**. There are a few discreetly hidden pubs in mews. But the rest is houses and flats.

The properties vary considerably in size. The grandest homes, those in **Belgrave Square**, have virtually all become embassies or institutes. Nearly all of the only slightly more modest **Eaton Square** mansions are now flats. Smaller-scale houses often survive as single homes, as do many of the mews cottages – which were originally the stables for the grand streets and squares.

There are more freeholds available now, particularly of houses – though this should change faster now under the provisions of the next stage of the leasehold reform legislation: a bill is due this autumn. But for the time being the standard commodity on sale here is the lease, either direct from the Estate or a sub-lease. Some leases can be very short, but those expecting a 15-year lease to be one-fifth the cost of a 75-year one are doomed to disappointment. For one thing, a short lease may qualify you to buy the freehold in due course. Then there are those buyers of short leases, usually companies, who view the price as so many years' rent paid upfront, rather than as a purchase. (Companies, though, do not have the right to enfranchise.) On the third hand, private foreign buyers hate leasehold, so prices for the still fairly rare freehold houses have rocketed. Understandably, all these considerations make price comparisons a tricky sport in Belgravia. Leasehold means paying ground rent, which can be noticeable: £3,000 a year on an Eaton Square flat, to add to a service charge of £6–12,000 – much more in a year when the Estate decides the façade needs painting.

The area is very popular with foreign diplomats and business people. Due to the positive ghetto of embassies in and around Belgrave Square there is a plethora of police, including the always-armed Diplomatic Protection Group. This reassures foreigners, say estate agents. There was a time, not more than a couple of decades ago, when Belgravia's grand houses were considered too big to inhabit. They have been brought back into use by the great improvement in the art of conversion. The splendid old buildings are sometimes just façades, concealing flats which are in some cases vast and equally grand. Sometimes the conversions are lateral, running behind two or even three house façades to give house-sized apartments on one floor.

Southern Belgravia

Once, the Grosvenor family also owned the whole tract S from Victoria station down to the Thames: Pimlico was developed at the same time, and was once considered part of Belgravia. The railway cut Pimlico off, and it never achieved the same status as its senior neighbour. The Estate sold Pimlico, known as the 'southern estate', 50 years ago to cover death duties and to fund other, international investments – partly in Canada.

Belgravia thus starts at **Buckingham Palace Rd**, an anonymous, workaday through-route which runs alongside Victoria Station. The strip between this road and **Ebury St**, another busy traffic route, contains little of the Belgravia character. The occasional mews, and some flats in **Ebury Square**, compete for space with the Victoria Coach Station. In this southern corner, off **Pimlico Rd**, are also the Peabody Buildings.

Ebury St has small (for Belgravia) early terraced houses, many of which are hotels. Until recently it was quite run-down, but now it is improving – and these homes have some of the area's largest gardens. The houses are mostly brick, not stucco. To the W **Bunhouse Place**, tucked behind **Bourne St**, has 1970s neo-Georgian town-houses: quiet and popular.

However, between **Ebury St** and **Eaton Square** comes the first slice of Belgravia proper. And how proper it is, with quiet, pretty **Chester Square** as its showpiece. These houses were built as 'second rank' homes (second, that is, to the monster ones of **Belgrave** and **Eaton Squares**) but are today considered to be some of the best in the area. Nearly all are still single houses: £5 million plus. A smaller one was on the market for £3.1 million this spring. **Chester Row** is similar, but the houses are on a much smaller scale, and vary in size and price: expect to pay £1.5–3 million.

Eccleston St, which bisects **Chester Square**, is a busy one-way road taking traffic up to **Hyde Park Corner**. This is where the mews begin: the Belgravia 'back streets' where the little cottages, built to house the gentry's horses, now house the gentry. These, often cul-de-sacs boasting arched entrances and cobbles, can have enormous charm. **Ebury Mews**, running through from **Eccleston St** to **Elizabeth St**, is typical, although not a cul-de-sac. It has a mix of converted mews cottages of greater and lesser degrees of opulence, plus some new-build homes in mews style. Quite a few have garages where the stable once was. Mews houses may be smaller, but that does not mean they are cheap: one in **Eaton Mews South** was £880,000 for a 60-year lease last autumn.

Lower Belgrave St is another busy road, southbound this time, with plain but handsome brick houses. **Elizabeth St** has very up-market shops (including some serving quite everyday needs) and, increasingly, some good restaurants. Its homes include a very beautiful, low-built house – its style more reminiscent of the Nash villas of Regent's Park than of the usual lofty Belgravia terraces.

To the W, houses in **Eaton Terrace** range from 4 to 7 beds and you can expect to pay between £1.8–3 million depending on lease. A 5-bed went on the market for £2.95 million late last year; another came up for sale this spring at £2.4 million for the freehold. **Caroline Terrace** has more handsome houses – most still single homes: typically 3- to 4-bed, with gardens and a few with garages, which sell at around £1–1.5 million. **South Eaton Place** has one or two freehold houses, one of which reached £2.5 million in late 1999. The far SW corner of the area has some smaller homes. **Bourne St**'s 2-storey and semi-basement houses have 2 or 3 beds. **Graham Terrace**, too, has more modest sizes. **Belgrave Place** is off here: a new development – a rarity in this area – on an old school site of 28 town-houses, 3-,4-, 5- and 6-beds (some with pools) and 13 1-, 2-, 3- and 4-bed flats. Flats from £350,000; houses from £1.2–3.8 million. Almost all were sold as we went to press. **Grosvenor Cottages** is tucked away off **Eaton Terrace**: a gated mews with a row of sweet 2-bed cottages, some double-fronted, and at the far end an elaborate, discreetly hidden 3-bed house.

Eaton Square is the centrepiece on which this area turns. It has, to say the least, considerable presence. The buildings, in long, dignified terraces entered from large and pillared porches, are enormous. It could more properly be called 'Eaton Squares': it is on so large a scale that inhabitants hardly seem to notice the slight disadvantage of the main **King's Rd** running down the middle. And two smaller roads cross at right angles, thus dividing the central garden into six – all of good size. Only a handful of houses (literally: there are five, to be exact, allowing for the reversion of another last year to a single house: £10 million for a 99-year lease) are still single homes; the rest of these towering terraces have yielded some 350 flats. Penthouses top most of them, and prices for these too are in the 'if you have to ask . . .' bracket. The Grosvenor Estate has itself recently developed Nos 1–4 **Eaton Square**, which has added a further 13 2- to 5-bed flats. **Eaton Place**, on the way northwards towards the centre of the Estate, runs parallel to **Eaton Square**, its large houses, divided into grand flats, second only in scale to those of the Square. A first-floor lateral conversion sold at Christmas 1999 for £1.7 million with, unusually, a share of the freehold. **Eaton Gate** three new duplex flats of 3 beds each, priced at £1–1.6 million.

B

Central Belgravia

Belgrave Square was planned as homes but is now mostly embassies and institutions. This is principally due to an earlier restrictive planning policy, which decreed that the buildings could only be used for diplomatic or charitable purposes. However, in the last couple of years a few of the institutional buildings have, now that that policy has been relaxed, reverted to homes or offices. The three enormous corner mansions, set slant-wise across the Square's corners, are as big as any in London and are home to the likes of the Portuguese and Spanish Ambassadors.

Nevertheless, **Belgrave Square** is unlikely to figure on your shortlist unless you are the envoy of a new and fairly rich country. It is such embassies which saved the square from decline: since the Second World War, several dozen 'new' countries have set up shop in London – and all, to the relief of the Grosvenor Estate at the time, needed rather imposing buildings.

North of **Belgrave Square** are more mews – on a grander scale this time – with the stucco continuing behind the scenes. The arched entrances cut the mews off from the busy main streets. **Wilton Crescent** is the queen of this corner, its Regency sweep re-faced with stone at the turn of the century. A house was over £8 million in 1999. The N end of **Wilton Place** has some rare early, pre-Cubitt brick houses: freehold, these fetch around £2.5 million. Little, villagey **Kinnerton St**, leading off, has concealed surprises: it is the entrance to an unusual warren of old and new cottages in mews and courtyards. To the S are some big blocks of purpose-built flats with car parking, then **Motcomb St** with more shops. The succession of mews and terraces continues on past **West Halkin St** back to **Eaton Square**.

The E corner of Belgravia has a cut-off collection of mews and little streets with a villagey feel, a couple of good pubs and even a general store. Streets like **Groom Place** and **Wilton Mews** have all the Belgravia assets plus a little more atmosphere. Chester St, by contrast, which runs through the middle has double-fronted Chandos House, 5/6 beds for £3.75 million freehold. The NE corner is dominated by the Lanesborough Hotel, on **Hyde Park Corner**. A nest of little mews cottages behind it offers more charming and very desirable homes: these, in **Grosvenor Crescent Mews**, are deceptive – the Estate created 17 new homes behind the original façades three years ago, with more sybaritically sized rooms: a large house here sold for £4 million recently. Some really small 1-bed £500,000-plus cottages can be found in charming **Old Barrack Yard**, a pathway through to **Knightsbridge** from **Wilton Row**. To the

W, the borough boundary running down **Lowndes St** and **Chesham St** marks, more or less, the end of the Duke's remit. **Lowndes Square**, often referred to as Belgravia, is more properly Knightsbridge. The end of the Estate's control is marked.

B

Transport	Tubes, all zone 1: Knightsbridge (Piccadilly), Sloane Sq (District, Circle), Victoria (District, Circle, Victoria). From Sloane Square to Oxford Circus 15 min (1 change), City 20 min, Heathrow 55 min.
Convenient for	West End, Hyde Park, Gatwick Airport. Miles from centre: 1.5.
Schools	Local Authority: Pimlico School, Greycoat Hospital C of E (g). Private: Francis Holland (g), The American International School, Westminster School (b), More House School (g).

SALES

Flats	S	1B	2B	3B	4B	5B
Average prices	160–300	350–600	450–1.3M	600+	800–2.5M	1.5M→
Houses	2B	3B	4B	5B	6/7B	8B
Average prices	500+	750–1.5M	800–2M	1.5–5M	3–7M	10M+

RENTAL

Flats	S	1B	2B	3B	4B	5B
Average prices	275–400	400–800	600–1300	800–2000	1200–2000	–
Houses	2B	3B	4B	5B	6/7B	8B
Average prices	650–1000	850–1500	1500–2500	2000–5000+	3500–10,000	–

The properties	Mainly owned by the Grosvenor Estate; longer leases and freeholds now, thanks to Leasehold Reform Acts. Grand Regency homes provide equally grand converted apartments. Also houses of all sizes from mews cottage to embassy.
The market	'Average' prices here are a very general guide: all depends on length of lease and location. Discounting embassy-sized houses, Eaton Square commands highest prices and kudos. Short leases, c. 9–20 years, equate to rental, rather than sale, prices: those above are for reasonable leases. Small proportion of freeholds of (relatively) smaller houses. Local searches: 10 working days.

Among those estate agents active in this area are:

- Best Gapp & Cassells
- DTZ Debenham Thorpe
- De Groot Collis
- Chesterfields
- Knight Frank
- Friend & Falcke*
- FPDSavills
- W A Ellis *

- George Trollope
- Aylesford
- Hamptons
- Cluttons
- Beaney Pearce *
- Strutt & Parker *
- Beauchamp Estates
- Lane Fox

- Douglas Lyons & Lyons
- John D Wood
- Lord Francis Russell & Co
- Foxtons *
- Ayrton Wylie
- Anscombe & Ringland *

further details: see advertisers' index on p671

BETHNAL GREEN

Map ref: p143 (4J)
Postal districts: E2
Boroughs: Tower Hamlets (Lab), Hackney (Labour)
Council tax: Band D Hackney £789, Tower Hamlets £674
Conservation areas: include Victoria Park, Jesus Hospital Estate, Bethnal Green Gardens
Parking: Permits and meters

The boom in inner-city living has made Clerkenwell a residential area once again, has brought loft-dwellers to Hoxton and Shoreditch and is now having its effects on Bethnal Green.

Bethnal Green is the spiritual heart of the East End, with a vivid past of gangsters, boxing and poverty. It is still poor, but its proximity to the wealth of the City and the new developments of Docklands, and the comparative cheapness of the property, is leading to its upwards ascent. Indeed, it takes in the Shoreditch neighbourhood where both nightlife and home life have been transformed in the past five years.

Economic refugees from Clerkenwell will still have to travel for their nightlife and café culture: Bethnal Green's latest venue is a lap-dancing club ('American-style gentlemen's entertainment') – not a cool bar.

The City is just one stop away; some City souls even cycle to work. Docklands, with its mushrooming developments, is a mere mile or so to the SE but Bethnal Green's rows of 2-storey 1840–60s terraces, interspersed with the Model Dwellings of the Victorian philanthropists and later council-build, remain down to earth in character and price. The late '80s, in the wake of Docklands developments, spawned new flats and dual-purpose work-homes. Now, we are seeing a new rash of studios/work spaces and flats, some created by joint ventures between the area's traditional landlords, the local councils and the philanthropic trusts.

Recently there has been an influx of buyers from places like Clerkenwell, Shoreditch and Islington as flat-dwellers trade up to houses and those unable to

B

afford the smarter areas look here for flats. Evidence for this is the opening of local offices by Clerkenwell-based agents. Agents reported brisk business last winter with prices climbing. The new inhabitants are mainly couples without children: Tower Hamlets' schools have a poor reputation and an improvement here would boost house prices, say local estate agents.

Locals say that Bethnal Green is now, in many respects, an established place to live. The population has changed, as many inhabitants sold their ex-council homes and retired to Essex, to be replaced by a younger generation. But you don't need to be an avant-garde artist or a self-concious inner-city pioneer to move here now.

Bethnal Green lies alongside the City: Hackney is to the N, Bow to the E, and Stepney to the S. **Cambridge Heath Rd**, **Hackney Rd** and **Bethnal Green Rd** are the three main thoroughfares. Busy **Cambridge Heath Rd** runs from Stepney through to Hackney and includes Bethnal Green Gardens, one of four conservation areas, and the Bethnal Green Museum of Childhood. The green is the centre of the old village.

Shoreditch, to the W of Bethnal Green, forms the boundary with the City. An indication for Bethnal Green is that this area was mainly commercial, but is seeing an influx of loft developments and is becoming positively fashionable: see City chapter. There are council-built flats in the Boundary Estate conservation area to the E of **Shoreditch High St**, which includes **Arnold Circus** with its bandstand. The imposing landmark of Shoreditch Church, which houses the impressive St Leonard's Gardens in its grounds, stands on the corner of **Shoreditch High St** which runs S to **Bishopsgate** and Liverpool St station. Sunday morning markets are a treat: try the wonderful **Columbia Rd** for flowers, or **Brick Lane** for Europe's biggest flea-market. The E end of **Bethnal Green Road** offers the traditional High Street shops.

Bethnal Green

The Victoria Park conservation area forms part of Bethnal Green's NE boundary; it is edged, on the Bethnal Green side, by the Grand Union Canal: homes in the conservation area with views over canal and park command a premium. **Sewardstone Rd** and **Approach Rd**, where 3- and 4-storey Victorian houses have been converted into flats, are popular but **Cyprus St** is more sought-after. Some of these neat 2-bed terraced houses, built before World War I, are Grade II listed, with original shuttered windows adding to their tidy appearance. The well-kept Victorian terraces have immense character and a plaque, dedicated to the memory of the men of **Cyprus St** who died in two world wars, hangs between Nos 76–78. The terrace is continued by the Duke of Wellington pub and further S is the Cranbrook Estate of council homes, largely 2- and 3-bed flats.

Roman Rd, a busy thoroughfare which runs E into Bow, has more council homes to the S and Meath Gardens, a welcome relief from the blocks of flats. Before the canal bridge in the corner of the Cranbrook Estate is the new Twig Folly development of 40 2-bed canalside flats. These proved a success and a second tranche is now complete and sold. Next to this is Bow Brook, a converted school with interesting loft-style flats. The area W to Bethnal Green tube is known as Globe Town: with the London Buddhist Centre, a Thai restaurant on **Burnham St** and art and photography galleries on the **Roman Rd** itself, it has a very different atmosphere. Off **Globe Rd** to the S of **Roman Rd** is a new development, Sceptre Court, with 16 1-, 2- and 3-bed flats.

At the junction of **Roman Rd** with **Cambridge Heath Rd**, the tube station is situated in the splendour of Bethnal Green Gardens, another conservation area. **Victoria Park Square**, behind Bethnal Green Museum, leads to **Sugar Loaf Walk** and then a cluster of close-knit red-brick terrace houses in **Moravian St**, **Gawber St**, **Welwyn St** and **Globe Rd**. On **Sceptre Rd** is a new development of 1- to 3-bed flats called Park View. Opposite York Hall Baths in **Old Ford Rd** is an imposing Georgian house, called The

B

Terraces, part of which has been converted into flats. Terraced houses, many refurbished, are on either side. Further E down **Old Ford Rd** is **Bonner Rd**, with a row of impressive council-built houses. N of the railway on **Hadleigh St** are new Peabody Trust flats for rent, and some very Victorian, and still-functioning, stables.

North along **Cambridge Heath Rd** is Millennium Place, a new flats block, and more council-built homes in **Patriot Square**, opposite the town hall. These command good prices and quick sales when they come onto the market. At the junction with **Hackney Rd** is Cambridge Heath station (trains to Liverpool St) and to the NW is a large refurbished council estate which takes in **Pritchard's Rd**, **Coate St**, **Teale St** and **Emma St**. Close by, **Wharf Place** has a canalside warehouse conversion of 2-bed flats, London Wharf. Next door, Regent's Wharf is an '80s apartment block. Both are very popular. On the corner of **Bishop's Way** and **Cambridge Heath Rd**, behind the Metroplis 'gentlemen's club', is a new block of a dozen new flats for rent.

To the W, the Jesus Hospital Estate is on the S side of **Hackney Rd** and includes **Columbia Rd**, **Baxendale St**, **Quilter St**, **Elwin St**, **Durant St**, **Ezra St**, **Wimbolt St** and **Wellington Row**. These pretty, flat-fronted, two-up, two-down Victorian terraced houses are very popular and sell fast: £200,000-plus is a typical price. Many have hanging baskets of flowers outside in summer, in keeping with the area which has the famous flower market in **Columbia Rd** on Sunday mornings. **Columbia Rd** has seen some new and much sought-after developments: it is becoming positively desirable.

Off **Hackney Rd** are a number of small developments, two by Peabody and a clutch of new studio/workshops. **Cheshire St** has some tidied-up flats above shops. Here, too, Furlong Homes have built (and sold off-plan) the live/work units of Portrait Place.

Bustling **Bethnal Green Rd** has a street market, a fantastic Italian café and a Tesco Metro, but a short stroll to the S is another contrast in **Derbyshire St** where delightful 2- and 3-storey Victorian terraced houses fringe the green space of Weavers Fields. In **Wilmot St**, opposite Hague Primary School, is the Waterlow estate, a 1980s Barratt conversion of a large Victorian terrace to studio, 1- and 2-bed flats. This has around 400 homes including some sheltered homes. At the bottom of **Wilmot St**, in **Three Colts Lane**, is Bethnal Green station. Across from the station, in **Dunbridge St**, the old public baths are being converted into 1- and 2-bed flats.

East along **Bethnal Green Rd**, at the junction with **Punderson's Gardens** and almost opposite the old Bethnal Green police station, is the City View block. This converted bakery now holds 110 flats, while the old police station is now 2- and 3-bed flats. **Paradise Row**, where **Bethnal Green Rd** meets **Cambridge Heath Rd**, lives up to its name, with 3- and 4-storey Georgian terraced houses. At the end of **Birkbeck St** off **Cambridge Heath Rd**, a converted factory, Sunlight Square, has 1-, 2- and 3-bed flats.

Shoreditch

Across the busy **Kingsland Rd**, the old Roman road due N out of the City, Shoreditch has reinvented itself, replete with trendy bars, the Lux cinema and new-media companies. Most of the action takes place W of **Shoreditch High St** and the **Kingsland Rd**: see City chapter. On the E side of Shoreditch, most of the homes are council-owned: the Boundary Estate conservation area is the oldest council-built housing in London. It includes **Palissy St**, **Rochelle St**, **Navarre St**, **Calvert Avenue** and **Montclare St**. These streets, containing mostly flats, ring **Arnold Circus** with its bandstand. **Calvert Avenue** leads W to **Shoreditch High St** and Shoreditch Church, with the picturesque St Leonard's Gardens. North of the Circus is the Mildmay Mission Hospital while **Sclater St**, which has an animal market every Sunday morning, is to the S.

North of **Hackney Rd**, on the E side of **Kingsland Rd**, the area is mostly light-industrial, though Peabody and Hackney Council have a joint scheme with 69 flats for sale in **Crewer St**, behind the recently revamped Geffrye Museum.

B

Shoreditch is bordered to the E by the Bethnal Green part of **Brick Lane**, now billed as 'the Portobello of the East': the Truman brewery conversion into artists' and designers' workspaces, together with the rebranding of this Asian community area as 'Bangla Town', is changing the character of the district. The erstwhile run-down tenement flats are being improved steadily. This area is the heart of the Asian garment industry. **Brick Lane** has been home to successive waves of immigrants: a chapel built for protestant Huguenots in the 1740s has been used in succession by Methodists, Jews and now Muslims. Some houses in the street date back to the first decade of the 18th century. Today, it has a thriving restaurant scene attracting City lunchers. Much renovation of council property has taken place recently. The Spitalfields scheme (see City chapter) will clearly have an impact on the neighbourhood.

Transport   Tubes: Bethnal Green (zone 2, Central), Shoreditch (zone 2, East London line). From Bethnal Green: Oxford Circus 15 min, City 5 min, Heathrow 1 hr 20 min (1 change). Trains: Cambridge Heath, Bethnal Green – trains to Liverpool St, Essex and Herts.

Convenient for   The City, Docklands. Miles from centre: 3.

Schools   Local Authority: Daneford School C of E, Morpeth Secondary School C of E, St Bernards Secondary School RC.

SALES

Flats	S	1B	2B	3B	4B	5B
Average prices	60–80	65–110	85–200	95–200	110+	–
Houses	2B	3B	4B	5B	6/7B	8B
Average prices	130–200	140–300	150–400	190+	–	–

RENTAL

Flats	S	1B	2B	3B	4B	5B
Average prices	120–150	150–200	180–225	220–300	250–350	–
Houses	2B	3B	4B	5B	6/7B	8B
Average prices	230–280	280–350	350–450	450—550	550–600	–

The properties   Two- and 3-bed terraced houses increasingly available, plus new and ex-council flats. Large houses rare. Increasing: smaller flats and smart, Docklands-style warehouse conversions.

The market   Buy the best as you'll have plenty of competition when selling from all the new developments here and in Docklands. Lack of good schools deters families. Local searches: Tower Hamlets 2-4 weeks, Hackney 10 working days.

Among those estate agents active in this area are:

- Land & Co
- Meade
- Alex Neil
- Mitchelson McCarthy
- Winkworth *
- Hamilton Fox
- Keatons *
- Bridge Estates
- Mark James
- Spicer McColl

* further details: see advertisers' index on p671

BLOOMSBURY AND KING'S CROSS

Map ref: p142 (3C) or use p61 (4G)
Postal districts: WC1, N1
Boroughs: Camden (Lab), Islington
  (Lab/Lib Dem)
Council tax: Band D Camden £897,
  Islington £912
Conservation areas: Most of area
Parking: Residents/meters. Clamps

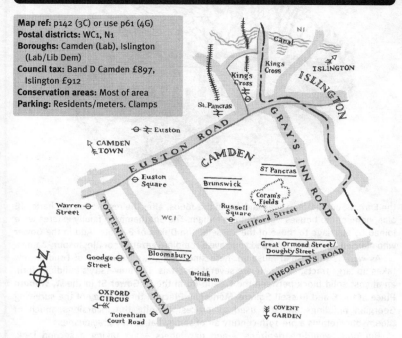

In the very heart of London, and once renowned as the home of the literary *beau monde* of the early 20th century, Bloomsbury is the capital's forgotten quarter. The City lies to the E, the West End and theatreland to the SW, all the big rail stations are within a walk or a cab ride, and the British Musuem, London University, British Library and dozens of academic institutions lie scattered around an area with Georgian bone structure and, for so central a location, green and peaceful corners.

But this mixture of academia and offices heavily dilutes the residential component, which is why the area is not well-known as an OK London address. One of Bloomsbury's most striking groups of houses – **Bedford Square,** built in the late-18th century and combining creamy classical stucco façades, Coade stone keystones and other delightful Georgian detailing – is now almost solely used for commercial purposes. If, that is, 'commercial' is the correct term for the polite trades like publishing, lawyering and running think-tanks.

Bloomsbury does not appeal to those international home-buyers who have been programmed only to look at W1, SW1 or SW3 because everywhere else in London is nowhere. (Indeed, such buyers will find the absence of designer dress shops and glossy restaurants unsettling.) For anyone not so concerned with fashionable addresses, and lucky enough to find a home here, it is a great place to live. One big boon is transport links. Bloomsbury is already central; with the St Pancras-Heathrow rail link (see St Pancras, below) it will become still better.

As a glance at its street names shows, Bloomsbury owes its existence to the nobility: the Southampton and Bedford families, to be exact, who developed the area as one of London's first planned suburbs. **Bloomsbury Square**, originally named after the Earl of Southampton, was laid out in the 1660s, after the restoration of Charles II: alas, none of the houses from that era remain. The Southampton family estates were joined by marriage to those of the Russells, the Dukes of Bedford. Add in the Gower who married the fourth Duke and you have a complete gazetteer of Bloomsbury names.

As well as the British Museum, here since 1755, the University of London now takes up large tracts, and there are several hospitals. The university's buildings form an almost solid block between the **Euston Rd** in the N, **Gower St** in the W, **Woburn Place** in the E and **Russell Square/Montague Place** in the S. Many of the surviving Georgian buildings are still used as offices. Despite the incursions, much of Bloomsbury retains a pre-19th-century air of somewhat dowdy graciousness.

But now, would-be denizens – and developers – are taking a second look. Bloomsbury has received a boost from the revival of Clerkenwell, to the E, and from the inexorable price rises in Mayfair and other Central London residential neighbourhoods. Another boost has been a change of policy by the Bedford Estate, still Bloomsbury's largest landowner. They are starting to return buildings to use as homes after decades as offices. The other big landlord here is Camden council, which steadily built up its stock of homes, both new-built and existing, during the years when parts of Bloomsbury were declining in status and a few corners were virtual slums – one whole row of neglected Georgian houses actually collapsed in the 1970s.

King's Cross, Bloomsbury's northern neighbour, could be the site of London's biggest single redevelopment scheme, or it could be left to moulder on. Meanwhile, it has some enviable houses in rather edgy surroundings.

The most common dwelling in Bloomsbury is the flat, with whole houses an almost impossible luxury. Studios, 1- and 2-bed are obtainable either in purpose-built blocks (mostly from the 1930s) or as new conversions. New homes of any sort are scarce: a survey in late 1999 found that the number under construction was precisely zero.

The area, for our purposes, is bounded by **Tottenham Court Rd** in the W, the **Farringdon Rd** in the E, **Theobalds Rd** and **New Oxford St** in the S and the **Euston Rd** to the N. This is a larger area than 'traditional' Bloomsbury, taking in streets which are allied to, but not quite part of, the old estate.

Bloomsbury can be divided into four distinct neighbourhoods: St Pancras in the NE, Great Ormond St/Doughty St to the SE, and Brunswick and Bloomsbury to the W. These four neighbourhoods radiate out from Brunswick Square and Russell Square, which lie together in the middle of the area. The SW quadrant, towards Bedford Square, is the most expensive, with the NE, towards King's Cross, the cheapest.

Great Ormond St/Doughty St

Sheltering between the busy main routes of **Southampton Row**, **Guilford St**, **Theobalds Rd** and the **Gray's Inn Rd** is a lovely quiet part of London with wide pedestrian-only streets and an abundance of patisseries, cafés and small shops. **Guilford St** is only partly Georgian: 1960s hospital and college buildings replace some of the originals, with an abundance of small hotels at the E end. The Rugby School Estate owns several streets, Camden Council is also a big landlord. Much of the surviving Georgian in **Guilford St** has belonged for years to Great Ormond Street Hospital: they are now selling, and the run-down, beautiful but fundamentally intact 1790s houses should revert to homes. Some, on the corner of **Grenville St**, have already been entirely replaced by impeccable fake-Georgian homes.

Take a footpath S from **Guilford St** to delightful, little-known **Queen Square**. Most of it is lined by offices, hospitals (and a good pub) but on the N side some handsome 1930s flats have excellent views across the square's gardens. One or two of the early Georgian houses on the W side have flats, as does little **Cosmo Place**, which leads through to **Southampton Row**, busy and hotel-lined – but with 1900 and 1930s mansion flats too.

Millman St runs S from **Guilford St**, and has a row of modern council-built maisonettes opposite some converted flats in Victorian 3-storey houses. This runs into **Rugby St** which combines shops and offices with very ornate, terraced 4-storey Victorian houses converted into flats. **Lamb's Conduit St**, which is partly pedestrianized, is the centrepiece of the area with some good pubs and restaurants. There is a new block of flats above the shops at the N end. This links with a conversion of several houses on the corner into flats. In 1997 14 new flats were marketed here, adding to a stock which includes some 1930s flats. The remaining property is shops with often spacious flats above. **Dombey St** leads W off **Lamb's Conduit St** with houses built in 1884 and quiet courtyards at the back, and some Georgian houses split into flats. An early Georgian house in **Great James St**, long used as offices and in a sad state, sold for £710,000 last autumn for conversion back to a home. **New North St** has some big blocks of 1950s council-built flats, now often for sale and reasonably priced.

Orde Hall St, running N from **Dombey St**, again has 19th-century 3/4-storey sand-coloured houses decorated with red-brick. These have now been converted into flats. **Orde Hall** runs into **Great Ormond St**, which splits the area roughly in half. The W part of this has the hospital, but there are still some 18th-century houses (some un-restored still) scattered either side, with flats at the E end.

Doughty St, which runs S from **Guilford St**, is most famous for once housing Dickens at No 48. But now the street has few private residents – although the lucky ones have 3- and 4-storey Georgian buildings with attics and grand pillared porches. A done-up family house with a garden sold last autumn for £800,000, and higher prices are rumoured. **John St** is a continuation of **Doughty St** to the S with similar but slightly older houses, though many are offices. One house, however, sold recently for £1.5 million – it is 5,000 sq ft.

Also running S, to the W of **Doughty St**, is cobbled **Doughty Mews**, which has some small houses with roof gardens above garages (and a good pub). Two smart 1980s ones were done up (to even smarter 1999 levels) and sold last autumn for £450,000 and £700,000. There is also a '30s block of flats at the junction with **Roger St** called Mytre Court, which is in very good condition and overlooking a primary school. There are a number of other mews in the neighbourhood, but they are mostly commercial.

Gray's Inn Rd is a busy mix of modern offices, small shops and surviving period homes. Flats in plenty, from late-19th-century mansion blocks at the S end to conversions above shops: a 2-bed in a Georgian house £205,000. **North Mews**, off to the W, has six 1980s town houses; **Northington St** some flats in Georgian conversions.

Holborn

South of **Theobalds Rd** and E of **Kingsway**, the Holborn district has a few homes dotted among the shops, offices and lawyers' chambers. Holborn was once a borough in its own right, London's smallest. **Red Lion Square** has some surviving 17th-century houses. They were built when the square was laid out in 1684, despite the violent opposition of the Gray's Inn lawyers, who resented the loss of their view. After a pitched battle, won by the builders, work went ahead. A careful look S and E from here, towards **High Holborn**, will reveal some superbly central homes, mostly flats above shops. The beautiful Georgian houses of **Bedford Row** are nearly all offices – though there are some flats at the N end. There are signs of life in this neighbourhood, with a dozen new flats in a white, modern block in **Red Lion St** to add to the 1930s mansion blocks, and a 16-flat Berkeley Homes refurbishment in **Red Lion Square**.

St Pancras/Coram's Fields

Like Holborn, St Pancras was once a borough, and its town hall stands in **Judd St**. The area is best known for its station, and for the new British Library building next door to it. The astonishing architecture of the hotel attached to the station could come into its own again if Manhattan Lofts proceed with their plans to convert the upper floors to homes. These could be some of the best-placed flats in Central London if (another if) the fast rail link to Heathrow opens: maybe in 2002? The new service could in the future be extended to link up with Thameslink 2000 (see Transport chapter).

Judd St forms the border of St Pancras in the W, and **Guilford St** in the S. A lot of the N part, around **Cromer St** and **Argyle Walk**, has council-built housing, but with wide open courtyards often decorated with small trees, plants and bright wall paintings. These homes date from the very early 20th century and from the big building programme which followed bombing in World War II. **Argyle Square** and other streets round it are mid-19th century, and most of the houses are small hotels. Potentially these could revert to homes, but King's Cross and St Pancras stations are so close that the inevitable seediness is hard to expunge. Going S, **Regent Square** is not as its name implies: much is 1950s council-built flats. **Judd St** runs S from **Euston Rd**, and has some flats above shops and three large blocks of private flats. Continuing S into **Hunter St** there is another large block of 63 apartments (1930s).

The best homes in this corner are in the S and W: there are some lovely 3-storey houses on quiet, tree-lined **Mecklenburgh Square**. A Georgian house in the square was on the market for £825,000 in 1998, and a big lateral-conversion 2-bed flat sold last winter for £375,000. Some of the big houses have been converted into flats (including a 10-flat scheme in late 1997) and there is a purpose-built block, also on the square, facing the open space of Coram's Fields. Coram was a philanthropist who left the land to charity: the Fields are now a playground with animals, including sheep, for the delight of local children. Just to the N of **Mecklenburgh Square** in **Heathcote St** there are also some pleasant neo-Georgian flats.

Crossing the **Gray's Inn Rd** E into **Calthorpe St,** there are flats in large 4-storey Georgian houses. The street was almost entirely scruffy a few years back but the number of derelict and poorly kept properties is now much smaller. Flats in some newly revived buildings were marketed in winter 1998. The adjacent **Wren St** has a number of smaller 2-storey houses with white façades and basements. To the S **Gough St** has some new flats; and in **Green Yard Mews** some smartly designed new flats in that very 1999 colour turquoise.

Brunswick

The Brunswick neighbourhood, to the W of St Pancras, is arranged around the busy crossroads at **Tavistock Place** and **Marchmont St**, which run W-E and N-S respectively.

There are a number of small bookshops, an art gallery, grocers, barbers and so on at this junction and on down **Marchmont St**, with flats above the shops: a characterful corner with a community feel.

Leigh St runs W-E out of **Marchmont St** and again has a number of converted flats in 3-storey buildings above bookshops, hardware stores and restaurants, with a modern development of flats and shops on the corner. **Thanet St** and **Sandwich St**, which run N from **Leigh St**, have some small early 19th century houses, and there is a large block of flats on the corner of **Hastings St** and **Thanet St**. **Leigh St** leads into the elegant Regency crescent of **Cartwright Gardens** which features tennis courts surrounded by (mostly rented) flats, hotels and student hostels. Tucked behind the crescent is **Burton Place**, with a little enclave of modern, somewhat suburban, homes ('Woolf Mews') built by Camden Council. **Burton St** has Tiger House, a recent flats block with underground car park, hidden behind the original terrace façade. **Duke's Rd** and **Woburn Walk** have some delightful surviving Regency shops and houses. N is some council-built housing and the roaring **Euston Rd**. Soon for sale, rumour has it, will be a complex of five new houses and some flats on a site tucked behind the junction of **Tavistock Place** and **Marchmont St**.

In the S the **Brunswick Centre** dominates; built around 1970 in a striking stepped pattern around a square, this enterprise encompasses flats, shops (including supermarket), offices, a cinema and pubs. It is being refurbished at the moment. There are flats to rent and to buy here, though the majority are still council-owned.

The hotel district is centred here around **Bernard St** and Russell Square tube station, which is served by lifts and gets incredibly busy in the tourist season. There is very little private housing from here S, except occasional flats above shops. However, **Russell Square** itself has seen a series of developments along the southern side – for example, a 1989 refurbishment of Nos 54–56 as a mix of offices and flats. Recently the square has gained further homes with the conversion of an office building at Nos 13–16 into Bloomsbury Mansions: 58 1- to 3-bed flats plus nine low-cost homes. Most were sold to ex-pats and Asian investors. Russell Court is a 1930s blocks with ingenious if tiny studio flats which sell for £85-100,000. The big mansion flats around the Square command £375,000 for a 3-bed.

Bloomsbury

Bloomsbury proper is reckoned to cover the area from **Russell Square** and **Woburn Place** W to **Tottenham Court Rd**. The regular grid of streets betrays its 18th-century origins, but London University's buildings have replaced many of the terraces and squares. Many of the homes in Bloomsbury today are purpose-built blocks consisting of studios, 1-, 2- and 3-bedroom flats. Typical of these blocks, which normally charge service fees ranging from £500–1,000 per annum, are Endsleigh Court on **Woburn Place** (60 per cent studios, 30 per cent 1-bed and 10 per cent 2-bed flats) and Russell Court (95 per cent studios, 5 per cent 1-bed). Endsleigh Court, owned by Freshwater, is undergoing a £1 million makeover. Popular blocks are Bedford Court Mansions (a 3-bed, 2-bath needing updating went for £410,000 recently), Bloomsbury Mansions (£350-875,000, the latter for a penthouse) and blocks in **Southampton Row**.

Apart from the mansion flats there are a number of flats in converted houses in many of the area's quiet backstreets. Running N off **Store St** is **Ridgmount St**, which has a number of recent flats above garages. These are a development of the Bedford Estate, which is still the ground landlord in this area. Further N, the entire block between **Ridgmount St** and **Huntley St** is a vast mansion block. N again, several of the mansion blocks are council-owned: Gordon Mansions to the E and W of **Huntley St** for example. **Chenies St** also has Camden Council-owned mansion flats. **Store St** has flats over shops. **Chenies Mews** is part residential with a mansion block and the back gardens of **Gower St**. Eight houses built here in 1991/92 were the first in Bloomsbury for a century. The N end of the mews is industrial, hospital and college premises. At the N end of **Huntley St** a row of flat-fronted 3-storey houses are split into flats.

B

For a real Bloomsbury feel look for one of the rare surviving houses, like the 6-storey, 5-bed ones in **Gordon Square**. One of these, owned by the University of London, was to let last year.

Chenies St runs E into **Gower St**. The buildings in this busy road are mostly early 19th-century and are now used as hotels or for commercial or university purposes, with a few rather run-down flats. One of the quieter streets in the neighbourhood is **Gower Mews**, with Gower Mews Mansions, small '30s flats above garages. And to the S of here is **Bedford Square**, which is nearly all commercial – though 19 new flats were created behind an original façade in 1987. **Adeline Place** and **Bedford Avenue**, which run directly off it, have Bedford Court: blocks of well-appointed 1900-vintage flats. Penthouses have been added to these in recent years.

At the S end of the neighbourhood, between the British Museum and High Holborn, a small area includes some interesting old houses as well as flats above shops. In **Coptic St**, just S of the Museum, a 5-bed, 5-storey freehold house was suprisingly slow to sell last spring priced at around £700,000. A 3-floor, 3-bed chunk of another cream-stucco period house (all but the attic, in fact) in **Little Russell Street** was £500,000 last autumn. In contrast, the same street has some smart 1990 homes.

King's Cross

The vast area of under-used and partly derelict land to the N of King's Cross and St Pancras stations is one of London's great lost opportunities. With the great new British Library open at last, and prosperity on every side, it is waiting in its weed-overgrown siding to join modern London. Instead, the astonishing and ongoing saga of the Channel Tunnel rail link has blighted these 200 acres for a dozen years.

In early 1998, another about-turn stopped work on the Channel Tunnel rail link, a line to join London to the European high-speed rail network, and which was to terminate at St Pancras. During that year, the government lashed together a deal whereby the line will be built – but in two stages. Stage One is under way, across Kent. Stage Two involves the section into London – and there's no start date for this. So yet again the King's Cross area is in limbo: see Transport chapter for more details.

The rail scheme will unlock the whole area for development – if it happens. This tract includes a canal, several very fine surviving Victorian railway buildings, and acre upon acre of space. A major scheme was planned in 1987 but that fell through without progressing beyond the wish-list-and-model stage. Chunnel Link prevarication has been the story ever since. For now, we must wait to see what will happen to a tract of land that reaches in the N right up to Camden Town. Don't hold your breath, or trust your searches.

King's Cross, as it stands at the moment, is a blend of commercial and small business premises, with a scattering of residential property to the E of **York Way**. The borough boundary runs through the area, down **York Way**. This may be part of the area's problems: it's no-one's baby.

Despite the potential, King's Cross is not a home for the faint-hearted. Leaving aside the deep uncertainty about the rail plans, there's all the colourful (if you are selling) and threatening (if buying) life that revolves around rail stations: cheap hotels and all-night traffic are but the start of it. A new police station and video surveillance have had a positive impact, but Chelsea it is not.

The area's greatest advantage is of course its extraordinary convenience. Apart from King's Cross, St Pancras is next door, Euston station down the road. You can stroll to the City. King's Cross also runs Oxford Circus a close second as the single most useful tube station on the entire network: the Northern, the splendid Victoria, the Circle, the Piccadilly (direct to Heathrow) and even the Hammersmith & City lines pass through here. The new King's Cross Thameslink station provides further options: S to the City and Gatwick, N to Luton and Bedford.

Across the Grand Union Canal, which acts as the northern boundary, lie the select realms of Barnsbury and Islington. The other boundaries are formed by **St Pancras Rd** to the W and **Calshot St** to the E. The southernmost part infringes the borough of Camden ending at **Argyle St** and **Swinton St**.

Beware of the rail plans, which have on several occasions since 1987 blighted whole streets in this district, with homes bought up by the developers, only for the plans to be abandoned and the homes resold. Both the Channel Tunnel link and Thameslink 2000 converge here, so careful searches are vital if planning a purchase.

Because Islington council was in the past reluctant to stop developers from splitting up houses into 2-bed units, anything like a 3-bed flat or 4-bed house is now extremely rare and hard to find. But 2-bed houses and small flats predominate with new conversions constantly under way. To spot them in time, though, requires a careful watching brief. Not many estate agents at any given time have properties on their books in King's Cross because of the shortage of private houses and flats. However, ex-council homes are sold at significant discounts to comparable 'private' prices.

The best houses tend to be in small, secluded groups and can surprise with the quality of their architecture. The closest thing to a residential neighbourhood in King's Cross is SE of the **Caledonian Rd**. It includes quiet backwaters like **Keystone Crescent** and **Balfe St**. The southern part of **Northdown Rd** runs S from the Caledonian Rd and features a major development of mostly 1-bed flats with original façade intact. The northern part over the **Caledonian Rd** has 2-bed houses dating from 1845. This is probably one of the nicest streets in the area. **Balfe St** runs S from **Wharfdale Rd** and is similar to **Northdown Rd** with modernized flats and some small houses. Some of its 3-storey houses have been well converted into 1-bed flats behind the early Victorian façade. This street also has some modern homes. **Keystone Crescent**'s curve is echoed in the rounded windows of its pretty 2-storey, £500,000 houses. **Caledonian Rd** has a number of converted flats and flats above shops – almost exclusively studios and 1-beds – with many in a poor state of repair.

Other areas of small 2-bed houses include those of **Southern St**. There is a recent 14-flat conversion on the **King's Cross Rd** by Tilbury and a number of 3-storey Victorian houses clustered at the bottom end of **Wicklow St**, which look to be in good condition. Nearby **Swinton St** has some 5-bed houses: these go for about £375,000. **Leeke St** in this corner has some new bars. These streets apart, most of the King's Cross station hinterland combines flats above shops, commercial property and council flats like the Derby Lodge estate on **Britannia St**.

There is also a new mixed commercial and residential development across the canal at **Thornhill Bridge Wharf** (see also Islington chapter) which epitomizes the new breed moving into the area – young couples without children. **New Wharf Rd** is dominated by the recently-built Ice Wharf, which has nearly 100 1- to 4-bed flats with re-sale prices of £250,000 for a 2-bed. Look along **All Saints Rd** for other similar schemes. Other schemes are under way or planned along the canal, including the re-use of some canal buildings such as a pumping station. The northern part of the **Gray's Inn Rd** is mostly commercial with a few flats above offices. But the area bounded by **Argyle St**, **Gray's Inn Rd** and **Euston Rd** is dominated by the Birkenhead Estate which is a complex of seven 1960s blocks. The remaining property is a mixture of private 3-storey Victorian houses (some split into flats), B & B establishments and private hotels. This is the place for lower prices. In **Penton Rise**, on the E edge of the area, there are plans to convert some old college buildings into homes and a hotel.

York Way is seeing the conversion of a Victorian school N of the canal into 21 loft-style flats. Four new family houses and 19 flats are being built in the grounds. The lofts are for sale, the new-build to rent, in an innovative scheme by the North British Housing Association. Completion summer 2000.

Transport
Tubes, all zone 1: King's Cross (Victoria, Piccadilly, Northern, Hammersmith & City, Circle), Russell Square (Piccadilly), others see map. From King's Cross: Oxford Circus 8 min, City 15 min, Heathrow 1 hr 10 min. Rail: King's Cross, St Pancras, Euston. To come: a fast link from St Pancras to Heathrow, due 2002.

Convenient for
Everywhere: British Museum, British Library, City, West End. Miles from centre: 1.5.

Schools
Camden School for Girls, Jewish Free School, University College School.

SALES

Flats	S	1B	2B	3B	4B	5B
Average prices	90–110	135–200+	200–375	350–500	—	—
Houses	2B	3B	4B	5B	6/7B	8B
Average prices	300–600+	500–800+	600–900+	650–1 M+	800+	—

RENTAL

Flats	S	1B	2B	3B	4B	5B
Average prices	200+	250–300	325–400	450–550	600+	—
Houses	2B	3B	4B	5B	6/7B	8B
Average prices	275–400	350–500+	500+	600+	1100	—

The properties
Many of Bloomsbury's Georgian and early Victorian houses have been converted into offices. Flats, however, abound in mansion, '30s or more recent blocks. King's Cross has some surprising corners of handsome Victoriana. King's Cross/St Pancras redevelopment will boost the area as a whole if it happens, but can blight nearest streets.

The market   Young, single people, couples without children and business-men find homes here to buy or rent from student-poor to quiet luxury. King's Cross is the cheaper end of the scale, and scene of much development. Local searches: Islington 10 working days, Camden 7-10 working days.

B

Among those estate agents active in this area are:

- Copping Joyce
- Winkworth *
- Barnard Marcus
- Property Bureau

- Banbury & Ball
- Frank Harris & Co *
- Hurford Salvi Carr

* further details: see advertisers' index on p671

BOW

HACKNEY

Victoria
Park

A 102 (M)

Canal

Old
Ford

OLD FORD ROAD

BLACKWALL

Bromley
by
Bow

TUNNEL APPROACH

STRATFORD

BOW ROAD

Tredegar

Bow
Road

Bow
Church

MILE END ROAD

Mile
End

BURDETT ROAD

Ropery
Street

Docklands Light Railway

Bromley
By-Bow

Devons
Road

RIVER LEA

STEPNEY

LIMEHOUSE CUT

LIMEHOUSE

N

Map ref: p64 (2B)
Postal districts: E3
Boroughs: Tower
    Hamlets (Lab)
Council tax: Band D £674
Conservation areas: Five
    Including Victoria Park,
    Tredegar Square,
    Ropery St
Parking: Restrictions
    around Roman Rd market

After the Tate Bankside and the new British Museum, Mile End in Bow is
home to the third biggest lottery-funded Millennium project in London. Victoria Park,
on the Hackney borders, and Tredegar Square to the south, are already well-known
caches of fine period houses (cheap only by comparison with very much more
'established' areas); and now the £33.5 million Mile End Park project will consolidate
the renaissance of this East End heartland. This linear park runs southwards from
Victoria Park, making a green corridor along the Grand Union Canal; now a 'green
bridge' will span the Mile End Road to join the two main segments, and the new
attractions include a children's park, a play arena, leafy cycle-ways and even an
electric go-kart track. The streets bordering the southern, Burdett Rd, end of the park
are likely to benefit especially.

To add to the remaining Georgiana and the Victorian rows, the last dozen years
have seen a veritable boom in the provision of new homes, cementing this area's
status as a residential area, attracting locals to owner-occupation as well as
'refugees' from other, pricier, areas of London. The first, and the biggest, was the
triumphant conversion of the giant, Victorian Bryant & May match factory, re-named
the Bow Quarter: this added 700 homes to the local stock. Recent developments have
included homes with workspace attached, and a sprinkling of loft apartments. At the
same time, the renovation programme for hundreds of existing council homes is in
full swing, with many having been transferred to housing associations, with a joint
Bow and Poplar housing action plan co-ordinating the larger projects. Thus the choice
of 2-bed flats in Bow can cost anywhere between £60–220,000.

The demolition of slums (artist Rachel Whiteread's award-winning 'house'
sculpture was the cast of an old terraced house, the last in its row to be pulled down)
is a good symbol of the modern East End. The artistic/professional classes are

B

infiltrating previously working-class space. The Chisenhale Gallery and the Bow Wharf development, including bars and a comedy club, are symptomatic. The attitude to living here has changed from feeling proud and different to its being a sensible investment option. Bow has moved onto the conventional property ladder.

Bow has always been the tidier end of the East End, but is still a widely varying mixture of gaunt council towers, ostentatious Victorian terraces, industry, railway tracks and street markets. Residential property in Bow is not grouped in neat neighbourhoods, it is scattered in pockets between all the other things jostling for space in this crowded corner. Typical inner London, in fact. Transport is fairly good, with Central, District and Hammersmith & City Line tubes and the DLR for the rapidly growing north-south traffic: Bow, like much of the rest of Tower Hamlets, is benefiting from its new role as hinterland to Docklands.

Bow, as described here, is essentially the E3 postal district, but the name is used rather sporadically. People who live in the Tredegar conservation area are proud to say so, others nearby talk of living in Mile End. Victoria Park is a prestigious name attached to streets in the N of the area – it adds a premium to house prices – while in the S, along Limehouse Cut, new canalside developments annexe the name Limehouse, made smart by Docklands. Of the old village of Bow, a crossing place over the River Lea, virtually nothing survives except the name. Just to confuse, there is a corner called Bromley-by-Bow, complete with tube station and high street.

The Lea Valley, to the E of Bow, is a sprawling flood-plain covered by industry, derelict, but still extant; gasworks ditto; railways and sundry waterways. This 650-acre tract features in sporadic plans as a place for big new developments . . . one day. Unlike so many areas, the land, and the opportunity, is here. But at present the development corridor is running east from Canary Wharf, rather than north.

Mile End & Tredegar Square

Tredegar Square, N of the busy **Bow Rd** and within a stone's throw of Mile End tube station, is the pride of the East London property market. This delightful Georgian garden square is a conservation area and boasts the area's most impressive – and expensive – houses, some of which have 5 or 6 bedrooms. These rose sharply in value last year, and can now reach over £400,000. It also boasts seven modern houses; but these, tucked on the corner, don't disrupt the unbroken Georgiana overlooking the central gardens.

The square is the centrepiece of a conservation area which includes **Lichfield Rd, Alloway Rd, Aberavon Rd, Rhondda Grove, Tredegar Terrace, College Terrace** and **Coburn Rd**. Sometimes referred to by estate agents as Mile End village, the area is made even more distinctive by its blue lamp-posts in keeping with the period. A three-storey, 3-bed Georgian house on **Aberavon Rd** was £295,000 last winter.

B

In **Coborn St** Tredegar Villas, a recent development of 2-bed terraced houses and flats built around a central courtyard, were carefully built in a similar style to neighbouring houses. **Morgan St**, too, has new homes: particularly **Pembroke Mews**, a neo-Georgian development built around a cobbled courtyard with 2- and 3-bed houses. On **Bow Rd** and within the conservation area is Tredegar House, a fine 19th-century brick building that was first a shipbuilder's mansion, then a college and last year became 20 flats: two 1-bed, 17 2-beds and a penthouse.

At the S end of **Aberavon Rd**, almost opposite the tube, is **Eaton Terrace**, a row of 1980s luxury 4-storey houses with ornamental pillars at each entrance. **Ropery St**, another conservation area, lies S of **Bow Rd** and E of **Burdett Rd**, and has Victorian terraced houses, as do **Mossford St, Maritime St** and Lockhart St. **Bow Common Lane** leads on down to the Limehouse canal and Poplar. Between the Lane and **Ropery St** a development of terraced houses has been completed by Furlong Homes.

South of Victoria Park

Over the railway line, N of the **Tredegar Square** conservation area, are the popular 2-storey bay-fronted Victorian houses of **Antill Rd, Strahan Rd, Lyal Rd** and **Medway Rd**. In nearby **Arbery Rd** is the award-winning 1980s development of **School Bell Mews**, a converted school that provides a perfect setting for new flats with galleries and houses. Three-storey Victorian properties, some of which have been converted into flats, in **Old Ford Rd** and **Chisenhale Rd** are made more appealing by backing onto the canal. Nightingale Mews is a recent development of 12 3- and 4-bed houses in **Kenilworth Rd**. In nearby **Haverfield Rd** is one section of Mile End Park, running beside the canal.

Victoria Park, which divides Bow and Hackney, is the East End's jewel; it is indeed one of the largest parks in London. It was laid out in the 1840s and has several lakes and a fountain as well as the Hertford Union Canal, which runs along the S side. It has a very good lakeside café, and is used for concerts, etc, in the summer.

On the S side of the canal is a 4-acre site, extending from **Parnell Rd** in the E to **Gunmakers Lane** in the W. The redevelopment here involved the refurbishing of close on 400 existing council tower block and low-build homes, and the building of nearly 500 new housing association ones. More affordable homes, in the shape of new flats to rent, have been completed on **Old Ford Rd; Royal Victor Place** is a 1990 development in the same road.

Bow Wharf is the canalside development which holds not only homes but both a bar and a branch of Jongleurs comedy club – proof of the changing nature of the area. Off **Parnell Rd** is the optimistically named **Hampstead Walk**, with 3-bed 1994-vintage terraced houses. Empire Wharf is another recent block of flats, which boasts both park and canal views.

The canal runs along Victoria Park's S border to **Cadogan Terrace**, where 3-storey Victorian properties, overlooking the park, command a premium although parking can be a problem, and the busy A102M motorway is just behind. **Morville St**, off **Tredegar Rd**, is the site for 69 new flats for rent, developed by Wimpey and the Tower Hamlets Action Trust. The Hermitage, a 1989 development of flats and houses in **Wrexham Rd**, is appealing despite being near the motorway, which leads to the Blackwall Tunnel to the S and out to the M11 on the new relief road through Leyton. **Brymay Close**, one of the Hermitage streets, is named after the old Bryant & May match factory nearby.

The factory itself, now known as the Bow Quarter, has been cleverly converted and extended into 730 flats around landscaped, fountain-filled squares. It boasts swimming pools and a sports complex, The Powerhouse, and has a bar, shop, video library and a laundry. This extraordinary old factory is vast, stretching back over six acres from **Fairfield Rd**. It has created its own environment and given a considerable boost to the area. About half the homes are rented, often through the on-site agency owned by the leaseholders. Sale prices vary with size and position: a ground-floor studio was £105,000 last winter, and a 2-bed, third-floor galleried flat was £219,000. Also in **Fairfield Rd** is a 1980s development of a dozen 2-, 3- and 4-bedroom houses. Red-brick bay-fronted houses in **Baldock St**, **Ridgdale St** and **Jebb St** lead to Grove Hall Park with its children's playground and football pitch. Alongside the park, a new development of flats has appeared in **Baldock St**.

Along **Bow Rd**, which is part of the main route E to Stratford, there are some handsome early Victorian and Georgian houses. A conversion of an existing building has produced 200 flats close to the town hall – and opposite the Bow Bells pub.

Bow Church

Bow police station, which has stables for horses, is on the opposite side of **Bow Rd** to the **Tomlin's Grove** conservation area where steps lead up to the 2-storey Victorian houses, some with attic rooms. The DLR station of Bow Church stands on the corner of **Campbell Rd**, part of which falls within the conservation area.

S of the railway line is the Lincoln Estate, which includes council-built flats and houses in **Rounton Rd**, part of **Campbell Rd**, **Devons Rd**, **Blackthorne St**, **Whitethorn St**, **Tidey St**, **Bow Common Lane**, **Fern St** and **Swaton**, **Spanby**, **Fairfoot** and **Knapp Rds**. These are some of Bow's less desirable properties, as well as the Coventry Cross council estate. This estate includes **Devas St**, **Brickfield Rd**, **Empson St** and **St Leonard's St**. However, housing action plans are afoot. A large tract of land beside the DLR between the Limehouse Cut and **Devons Rd** is designated for Housing Association homes. There have been some good conversions of Victorian homes in **Devons Rd** among others. The canal is the focus for several work-home schemes, including Enterprise Works, in **Hawgood St**, a scheme where houses and flats include their own workspaces. Off **Hawgood St** is **Alphabet Square**, a development of industrially-styled flats.

Between the Blackwall Tunnel approach road and River Lea is Bow's fifth conservation area, situated in **Three Mills Lane** behind the Tesco's supermarket. Here, too, there are facilities for weight training, floodlight football and for the more tranquil sport of fishing on the River Lea towpaths.

Transport	Tubes: Mile End (zone 2, Central, Hammersmith & City, District); Bow Rd, Bromley-by-Bow (zone 3, Hammersmith & City, District). From Mile End: Oxford Circus 20 min, City 10 min, Heathrow 75 min (1 change). DLR: links to Stratford, Tower, Isle of Dogs, Bank – and now Greenwich & Lewisham.
Convenient for	City, Docklands, City Airport & Stanstead, East Cross Route and Blackwall Tunnel. Miles from centre: 4.5.
Schools	Local Authority: Central Foundation Girls, St Paul's Way, Bow Boys.

B

SALES

Flats	S	1B	2B	3B	4B	5B
Average prices	60–125	75–130	85–200	105–210	—	—

Houses	2B	3B	4B	5B	6/7B	8B
Average prices	140–280	160–300	180–450	—	—	—

RENTAL

Flats	S	1B	2B	3B	4B	5B
Average prices	100–140	105–180	140–230	160–350	—	—

Houses	2B	3B	4B	5B	6/7B	8B
Average prices	160–275	175–370	205–460	460–690	600+	—

The properties

Bow's Georgian glories, among the myriad 2/3-bed terraced houses, have long since been rediscovered. Old housing stock is now much improved; untouched property harder to find. Real action to renovate/rebuild council housing is restoring whole areas. Several new and recent developments; the 700-home Bow Quarter is an example of conversion at its best.

The market

Owner-occupation is higher than other parts of Tower Hamlets, and rising in this increasingly popular East End heartland. Best properties are mainly N of Bow Rd, especially the Roman Rd to Victoria Park stretch, and new-build. Local searches: 2–4 weeks.

Among those estate agents active in this area are:

- Alex Neil
- Land & Co
- Mitchelson McCarthy
- Winkworth *
- W J Meade
- LMD
- Look Property Services
- Keatons*
- Strutt and Parker *

further details: see advertisers' index on p671

BRIXTON, HERNE HILL AND TULSE HILL

B

Map ref: p94 (A4)
Postal districts: SW2, SW9, SE24
Boroughs: Lambeth (Lab), Southwark (Lab)
Council tax: Band D Lambeth £750, Southwark £809
Conservation areas: Several and increasing (some rather unlikely)
Parking: Residents/meters increasingly common

Brixton is shaping up to be the nearest thing London has to the downtown districts of an American city – with all that implies. Fast-changing, a crucible of new ideas and a magnet for the young and unconventional, its social mix strikes the staid as explosive. But for others it works: for a lot of people, Brixton is liberated London.

At some unnoticed point in the late 1990s the media began thinking first of Brixton's vibrant social scene and good-value homes and only second of its erstwhile bad character. Brixton spent the 1980s as one of London's most notorious, and misunderstood, neighbourhoods. Everyone had heard of it, usually for the same reason: trouble. Few who judged it had been there. And you do need to visit Brixton, to spend time there, get to know it, before you buy or rent. Fascinating it may be, but – some fringe neighbourhoods apart – polite it ain't. Not everyone is a Brixton person.

Brixton today is on the upswing, with a new generation of young home-buyers adding to the cosmopolitan mix, and a born-again local council which is making a real difference. It remains wholly urban, sometimes abrasive, in places grimy, in a few places threatening – currently, some overt on-street drug dealing. It offers an endlessly imaginative street scene, which even during its current nightlife renaissance still manages to be busier at midday than midnight (no mean feat in Brixton), the integration of several strong, self-contained communities at street level, and the feeling that, even after the last 20 years of rapid change, it remains an oasis of essential difference in a grey, sprawling, patchily gentrified South London.

B

Brixton has always led a melodramatic, larger-than-life existence. Not content to be a workaday South London suburb, like its neighbours Clapham and Camberwell, it has undergone a series of booms and busts, a succession of rags-to-riches-and-rags-again swings of fortune. It is restless, transient, yet a real community. Indeed a truly urban place, Brixton. Here, no-one pretends they are living in the country.

At the start of the 20th century Brixton was a fashionable place to live and to shop. Its department stores and markets drew people from all over South London. Many large houses had been built in the 19th century, though few survived the pincer attacks of the German bombers and the 1960s council planners. Between the wars Brixton began to decline, becoming an area of seedy flats and lodging houses. It had, and still has, its streets of little Victorian terraces as well as the grander – some are Georgian – homes. But the big houses suffered as the City commuters, who had once favoured Brixton for its transport links, moved out to the green new suburbs. Their place was taken by a transient population; the latest and most permanent (and noticeable) wave being the West Indian immigrants of the '50s and '60s. Melodrama reasserted itself in Brixton once more as street life, local politics and rhetoric took on a distinctly Caribbean tone. Many of the West Indian families settled down in Brixton, and the third generation of black Londoners is now raising the fourth.

Things got pretty low in the early '80s, with well-publicized riots, a theatrically entertaining but inept and sometimes corrupt council and heated words (and deeds) between locals and the police. Lambeth Town Hall has seen more rows over the last 20 years than Brixton's inhabitants could muster, singularly or collectively. All too often, the council showed the kind of inefficiency and leadership which has caused its citizens varying degrees of hardship. In such unhappy times, not even the lure of the Victoria line tube, which had once more made Brixton a good commute from the centre, did much to help.

If the story of the '80s was of bristling confrontation, then in the '90s the typical Brixton renaissance followed closely behind. While the council urged that more money must be spent, with a typical twist of irony it was the movement of young people into the area, not Whitehall mega-bucks, that really made the difference. The government-led £187 million Brixton Challenge ran from 1993 to 1998. All too soon the grand plans faltered. Delays both inside and outside Lambeth Council got the project off to a late start, and while some of the flagship schemes were eventually completed, albeit late, many quietly dropped off the end of the schedule never to be heard of again; as deadlines were missed, part of the money was forfeited and had to be returned.

Meanwhile, clubs and bars were opening, young and clever people were remaking Brixton the way they wanted it. The area is now a key point on the London music and fashion circuits.

Brixton's most prosperous period was the mid-Victorian, when houses of all sizes were built, many with interesting detailing such as this elaborate porch and balcony. The carved leaves are typical. Stone or brick in contrasting colours was used for details, with stock brick and/or stucco for the walls themselves, the whole under a slate roof behind, in this street, a large gable.

Successes include the new, improved 5-screen Ritzy cinema and venues like The Fridge bar and nightclub, the Brixton Academy and the Loughborough Hotel. At last, a council-funded scheme to redevelop a key site on the High St should bring some new shops late this year. Decent restaurants are joining the rash of new cafés and bars.

B

The current council administration is a big change for the better, showing great zeal in pursuing those who dodge paying rent or council tax, ignore their parking fines, defraud the council or drop crisp packets. It is determined to improve life in Lambeth, and could bring the first effective leadership Brixton has had in a generation.

But a crucial component in the Brixton revival is its steady discovery by home-buyers. The 1970s saw a wave of young, radical squatters. Many stayed – some even bought their squats. In the 1980s, Brixton was found to be one of the last areas of relatively cheap, unconverted housing in Inner London. The seductive charms of a proper house, with room to move, are not lost on cramped flat-dwellers in more fashionable but less convenient areas. The 1990s saw a new wave of incomers, attracted by lifestyle and the lure of a young, lively population. School and factory conversions added lofts to the local choice. The new Brixtonians find Clapham and Battersea too expensive. They dither between Brixton and Hoxton, and aspire to Notting Hill Gate or a Clerkenwell loft.

Brixton retains the atmosphere of a town. It has a proper centre – not, as with so much of South London, a shapeless grey sprawl. The imposing town hall looks out from the corner of **Acre Lane** and **Brixton Hill** over a wide green triangle, with St Matthew's (church turned arts centre/nightclub/restaurant) as its focal point. A new park has been laid out here, linking the centre to the green strip of Rush Common, which runs beside **Brixton Hill**. The triangle's apex points N, to the high street shops of **Brixton Rd** and the famous market. By the station is the leisure centre; there are lots of good sports facilities in the area. And there's the pleasant expanse of Brockwell Park with its outdoor swimming pool, tennis courts and a walled garden.

While plenty of people live in Brixton by choice, it's worth remembering that plenty more do so by necessity, stuck in grim council flats. True, it is a lively and entertaining place: some say that it has become the Left Bank of London. Others fear it is doomed to be forever peripheral, a place for people who can't afford to escape elsewhere.

The image of Brixton as the centre of London's Afro-Caribbean life is true enough, but that is only one side of Brixton's personality. Black people make up less than a third of the residents. Whites are the biggest single group, and there is a growing gay community, but these broad figures conceal a place where everyone is a minority, where there are communities of Chileans and Chinese, City workers and anarchist squatters, artists and – well, every other kind of -ist and -ian.

The Post Office confuses the geography of Brixton. It is often thought that Brixton equals SW2, but a glance at the map shows that Brixton station, and most of the town centre, lies in SW9, while SW2 takes in the positively suburban streets of Streatham Hill as well as grimy **Acre Lane**. Much of **Railton Rd**, the melodramatically named 'Front Line' street where police/black tension was highest in the 1980s, is in SE24 – a district known more for the solid respectability of Herne Hill, rubbing shoulders with desirable Dulwich. And chunks of West Brixton stray into SW4, home of the Claphamites.

There are several conservation areas in Brixton protecting districts of outstanding architectural quality, and the number is growing. Properties in these corners command a premium. Examples are Angell Town, Loughborough Park and **Trinity Gardens**. Lambeth is putting great stress on tidying up the town centre, with some success.

One Lambeth policy has helped boost the residential side of the area, residents' parking: many of Brixton streets have long attracted commuter parking. However, residents claim that these schemes have only partly alleviated parking problems, and local estate agents observe that the parking schemes are a mixed blessing.

The property market became brisk in 1996–97, with a new emphasis on the Clapham side of the area, and is still brisk at the start of 2000. People move from Clapham, or look here as an alternative, for bigger and better buys. Two-bed flats and 2-, 3- and 4-bed houses, preferably with period features, are popular. The most desirable homes lie just off either side of **Brixton Hill**, handy for the frequent bus services to the town centre, the tube and Central London. There are, however, pockets of interesting houses all over Brixton, though their surroundings can sometimes be on the grim side.

Acre Lane

Acre Lane is a broad, busy street linking the centre of Brixton with Clapham. The neighbourhood to the N, bounded by **Bedford Rd** to the W, **Ferndale Rd** to the N and **Brixton Rd** to the E consists of small 3- and 4-bed houses and larger 3- and 4-storey Victorian ones, many converted into flats. The W side of the neighbourhood, including the W half of **Ferndale Rd**, is in SW4 and used to harbour aspirations to be Clapham until Brixton got more trendy. Indeed, many of these streets are closer to Clapham North tube than they are to Brixton. **Ferndale Rd** is wide and busy; to the N it backs onto a railway line taking the Dover trains into Victoria (and the Eurostar ones to Waterloo) and carrying a lot of freight traffic. Good-sized 3-storey Victorian terraces predominate, getting bigger at the W end, as they do on the parallel **Sandmere Rd**. Prices in **Sandmere Rd** in November last year were around £300,000 for a 5-bed house. Two-bed flats in a newly refurbished building go for £170,000. The old college building on **Ferndale Rd** was split by developer Charles Church into 22 1/3-bed flats, with three new blocks adding more (1-beds £150–220,000). **Tintern St** is small 3-bed flat-fronted Victorian terraces, as are **Ducie St**, **Medwin St** and **Allardyce St**. Ducie St has Gothic-style houses with pointed-arched doorways and decorative brickwork. The names of **Plato Rd** and **Solon Rd** (not the architecture . . .) have gained this area the tag of Philosophers' Corner. Many houses have been split into two or more flats. A delapidated 4-bed house in Plato Rd was on the market for £225,000 last winter.

Off **Acre Lane**, the old Victorian Santley Primary School in **Santley St** has been split into lofts: queues formed when they were launched last year and the whole lot sold instantly. Rialto has converted a large late-Georgian house on **Acre Lane** into flats, built a facsimile next door, and then used the deep plot of land behind them, behind existing homes on Concannon Rd, for two more blocks. There are 66 flats in total, priced from £120-225,000. Just next door is the showpiece of the neighbourhood, **Trinity Gardens**, a Regency square of 3-bed cottages tucked away behind **Acre Lane** and close to Brixton centre. These sell for up to £330,000. At the Clapham end of **Acre Lane** well-placed former council offices have now been refurbished into smart flats. It's a short step from here to Clapham's answer to Fulham, the well-heeled Abbeville Village . . .

South West Brixton

South of **Acre Lane**, across to **Lyham Rd** in the W, **Brixton Hill** in E and Windmill Gardens to the S lies a mixed area of large Victorian houses, Edwardian maisonettes and inter-war semis. The land rises towards the S, where a preserved windmill stands in a park. Beyond again is Brixton Prison. All this is SW2. It is one of the quietest parts of Brixton. To its W is Clapham Park, and some estate agents have taken to using this name for the **Lyham Rd** corner. **Lyham Rd** branches off **Kings Avenue**. Streets of small Victorian terraces – **Kildoran Rd**, **Margate Rd**, **Mauleverer Rd** – run off to E. Clapham agents have been boosting this area recently. Going S, **Lyham Rd** has council homes on both sides, with the spreading low-rise **Ramilles Close** estate running up to the windmill. **Lyham Rd** then has some pretty, flat-fronted brick cottages, followed by the back wall of Brixton Prison, which is less overwhelming than some prisons one could mention. Two-bed cottages here fetch £150,000. Sapcate are planing to convert a school in **Lyham Rd** into loft apartments.

South of the prison, **Dumbarton Rd** has 1914-ish purpose-built flats, 2-storey terraces with gables and fancy porches. Some of those in the N side of the road back onto the prison. **Doverfield Rd** has similar flats, while **Felsberg Rd** has more – this time with an arts-and-crafts air. Dumbarton Court, a big block of inter-war flats, runs round onto **Brixton Hill**. This district is quite high up, and some homes in these peaceful, hilly streets have good views across London to the N and W. It is convenient for the buses that run down **Brixton Hill** to the tube station, and for Streatham's shops.

East of **Kings Avenue** in the furthest SW corner of the neighbourhood lie more streets of small 3-bed Victorian terraced houses. **Rosebery Rd**, **Thornbury Rd**, **Wingford Rd** and **Kingswood Rd** are typical of this area of clean, narrow streets full of family housing. There are relatively few flat conversions here. Nearby Windmill Gardens and the sportsground provide a welcome bit of greenery.

Back down the hill to the N, in the angle between **Brixton Hill** and **Acre Lane**, another grid of streets is almost cut off from those of **Lyham Rd** described above. **Hayter Rd** is typical, with large 3-storey double-fronted Victorian houses, many converted to flats, and eight very large 6-bed-plus 4-storey detached Victorian houses. **Bonham Rd**, **Lambert Rd** and the tree-lined **Haycroft Rd** follow a similar pattern. **Sudbourne Rd** has as its focus one of London's most successful primary schools. This has brought families to the area. One of the big houses was split into flats last year: 2-beds from £160-185,000. **Baytree Rd** in the N is a good example of suburban-type inter-war semi-detached housing, a quiet leafy street yet close to Brixton centre. The Tesco store on **Acre Lane** backs onto some of these houses.

Brixton Hill

The biggest concentration of desirable properties in Brixton lies to the E of **Brixton Hill** around the **Brixton Water Lane** conservation area. In **Josephine Avenue** and **Helix Gardens** (new conservation area), some of the large, handsome, 3-storey Victorian terraced houses have 75-ft of garden frontage. These grandly curving, leafy streets were spaciously planned by the Victorian builders, and about 10 years ago were the subject of a highly successful community architecture scheme. The long front gardens were reclaimed from the dumped-car-dotted wastelands they had become. New reproduction railings, improved street lighting, car parking spaces – it's all been done and has made a dramatic difference. The houses are 3-storey and quite wide. They make spacious family homes but many are flats. The 4-bed houses command £280-300,000 or so, while a 6-bed was on the market, unmodernized, for £335,000 last autumn. Two-bed flats are around £155,000. **Josephine Avenue** is known world-wide for No 7, a gay and lesbian guest house.

The nearby loop of **Appach Rd** is made up of small 3-bed Victorian terraces, which sell for around £250,000, with some charming 2-storey double-fronted houses on one side. Many houses in this area have retained their original period features such as marble fireplaces and ornate ceilings and picture rails.

Brixton Water Lane itself is busy, but has some of the area's most charming homes. They include a Georgian farmhouse, a few similar-period cottages – and all with Brockwell Park close by. The enclave of **Brailsford** and **Arlingford Rd**s has big Victorian houses, some converted to flats. A quiet corner, and the homes on the E of **Brailsford Rd** back onto the Park.

The area further S, between **Brixton Hill** to the W and **Tulse Hill** to the E, is disputed between the neighbourhoods named for both those roads. **Holmewood Rd**, which runs E from **Brixton Hill**, is a wide road of rather ordinary Victorian terraced

B

brick and stucco houses (4-beds sell for about £250,000). But it leads into surprising **Holmewood Gardens**, where the same terraces suddenly open out to surround an irregular green. The road is wide, the effect spacious and cut off. **Maplestead Rd**, to the E, has similar houses. East of here is covered under Tulse Hill on the next page.

Upper Tulse Hill winds across these slopes, with its E end in Tulse Hill, while to the W are a mixture of big mid-Victorian detached houses (mostly flats), 1920s terraced homes and council blocks. A Victorian semi was £225,000 last winter. Tree-lined **Athlone Rd**, which runs off to the E, has '20s terraced homes, square-bayed. The neat, cared for atmosphere is maintained in **Elm Park** where topiary features in one front garden. **Claverdale Rd** is more Edwardian. Further down **Elm Park** is a mix of Victorian homes of varying sizes, some flat-fronted ones being quite attractive. **Elm Park** meets **Brixton Hill** opposite the prison entrance. On the Hill here is Tudor Close, a large block of '30s flats. Some inter-war houses, such as those in **Mackie Rd**, punctuate the Victoriana.

There are several mansion blocks along the length of **Brixton Hill**, varying in price and status. Christchurch House, a 1930s block, is a landmark, with 2-bed flats around £85,000. It, and similar Effra Court and Brixton Hill Court, have relatively high service charges – and watch for length of lease.

Somers Rd leads, somewhat unpromisingly, into the unexpected, hidden corner of **Archbishop's Place** with its pretty little early Victorian semi-detached 2-bed cottages. The Place is a cul-de-sac, with a few of the cottages tucked down paths at the end. They sell – when they come on the market, which is rarely, with sales often by word of mouth – for around £175,000, £200,000 if 3-bed. **Brading Rd** has more ordinary Victorian houses. **Upper Tulse Hill** nearby, at the junction with **Ostade Rd**, has pairs of pretty early Victorian villas facing mock-Tudor inter-war terraced homes.

Central Brixton

Central Brixton is mostly shops, offices, railways and council-built flats. There are pockets of private housing, though. South of **Coldharbour Lane** to **Morval Rd** and between **Effra Rd** W and **Railton Rd** E are streets of 2- and 3-storey Victorian housing. North of the railway that divides Brixton in two are some streets of 3- to 4-storey Victorian housing between **Dalyell Rd** and busy **Stockwell Rd**. Between **Stockwell Rd** and **Brixton Rd** is a triangle of council homes, with Stockwell to the N. **Brixton Rd** was once lined with solid early Victorian houses, and some still survive, though many are in commercial use. Converted flats in the old houses go for £100,000 upwards for 1-bed. If you want an exciting life, flats in **Electric Avenue**, right in the middle of the market, can be yours for £100,000.

East Brixton

East of the centre are neighbourhoods that have been changed most by Brixton's unruly past. Railways, the Blitz and the council between them have destroyed what were once two smart Victorian suburbs, Loughborough Park and Angell Town. **Loughborough Park**, the road, survives in part, wide and leafy, with pairs of Victorian villas of varying sizes. There is a small park, then a modern low-rise council estate off **Moorland Rd**. Here, too, there are some cream stucco Victorian villas that would be worth a couple of million each in St John's Wood. The giant reversed ziggurat council slab of **Clarewood Walk**, S of **Coldharbour Lane**, makes sense when you realize it was designed to turn its back on an eight-lane highway, planned but never built.

North of the railway, the street pattern is that of the mid-19th-century Angell Town Estate, but most of the buildings are '60s council flats. An exception is the rather grand 1880s complex on **Barrington Rd** that is now the loft apartments of College Green, though it was built as the Brixton Orphanage for Fatherless Girls. Being a

Brixton loft development, there is a shared bicycle store. A few Victorian homes survive in **Villa Rd**: a tall, rather run-down terrace. Lambeth Council has restored some more original Angell Town detached double-fronted houses in **St John's Crescent**. **Vassall Rd** in the extreme N of the area has some handsome and expensive early Victorian terraced homes: see Kennington chapter.

Many houses in this part of Brixton are owned by, even if not built by, the council. Lambeth used to hang onto these tenaciously, 'Right to Buy' laws notwithstanding, but recently they have become keen sellers, with vacant homes selling by auction.

Brixton/Herne Hill Borders

Railton Rd had one of the worst reputations in Brixton. This is changing as empty shops have been compulsorily purchased by the council and smartened up. Last autumn a 3-bed house commanded £165,000.

At the N end, where it runs into **Atlantic Rd**, **Railton Rd** to a large extent deserved its reputation. But further S there is a grid of pleasant streets between **Railton** and **Dulwich Rd**s. With the inevitability of estate agents, these roads, each named after a literary giant, have been dubbed the Poets' estate (London has several others such). Despite its position, Poets' Corner, as the area is alternatively known, is highly desirable. Indeed one could be miles away from trouble of any sort in these tree-lined, well-cared for streets. It is a short walk from the town centre and borders on to Brockwell Park in the S. The Victorian houses were built on spec for letting. They are much sought-after for each one is largely unique – they were purpose-built and architecturally designed – most are detached 3-, 4- and 5-bed houses. A 3-bed one will cost you around £250,000, with 4-bed going for £275,000-plus. **Mayall Rd** is 'coming up' according to local agents, but bear in mind that houses on the E side of the latter back onto the railway.

Most of the streets are short and homogeneous, but **Shakespeare** runs on E beyond **Railton Rd** and the railway. This eastern section is scruffier than the traditional 'poet' area but, interestingly, a new series of council-built cul-de-sacs have appeared named after contemporary writers such as **Derek Walcott Close**, **James Joyce Walk** and **Alice Walker Close**.

To the W of Railton Rd, **Rattray Rd** forms the spine of a small grid of Victorian terraces. The 4- and 5-bed houses here go for £275,000 with 1-bed flats £104,000.

Herne Hill and Tulse Hill

South of Brixton are two more areas with subtly different personalities. Their boundaries with Brixton are hard to define, but once in the centres of either Herne Hill or Tulse Hill you will know you are in another place. The bustle of Brixton is lacking, and some streets, especially in Herne Hill, have a solidly suburban feel. Another difference is the lack of a tube. Both places have rail stations on the Thameslink line, with trains to Blackfriars, City Thameslink, Farringdon and King's Cross, and to Victoria. As family areas, they benefit from the clutch of schools, in nearby Dulwich.

House prices are similar to those in Brixton, though Tulse Hill is less desirable than Herne Hill because of the latter's border with expensive and fashionable Dulwich, and because it is on the South Circular. Both districts are convenient for Brockwell Park. Large 3-storey Victorian houses are very common, though most have been converted into flats. They are popular because they are spacious and full of character. Two-bed flats find ready first-time buyers, while the young couples who inhabit the smaller 2- and 3-bed houses move on to the roomy 4- and 5-bed houses when the children come along.

The smaller 2- and 3-bed Victorian houses and Edwardian maisonettes are largely concentrated in Tulse Hill, while the larger family housing of 4- and 5-bed-plus is more characteristic of Herne Hill – particularly along **Norwood Rd** facing Brockwell Park and in the streets running directly off **Herne Hill** and **Half Moon Lane**.

B

Tulse Hill

Along **Tulse Hill**, S from **Brixton Water Lane**, council-built housing gives way to private properties on the E side at **Craignair Rd** and the W side at **Trinity Rise**. Homes are a mixture of inter-war semis, some with mock-Tudor fronts, and smaller 3-bed Victorian houses. The site of Dick Shepherd girls' school – it was closed down by Lambeth – has become 'Brockwell Gate', a Fairclough development of 65 4-bed houses from £300,000 and 158 flats from £130,000. The site backs onto Brockwell Park.

Inter-war semis, selling for £160–170,000, line **Craignair Rd** and **Claverdale Rd**, giving way to small 3-bed Victorian houses at the W end. **Trinity Rise** comprises 4-bed Edwardian houses and inter-war semis, leading to the very desirable **Brockwell Park Gardens**, 3-bed Victorian terraces overlooking the park. **Deronda Rd, Deerbrook Rd** and **Romola Rd** contain semi-detached Victorian houses with 4-, 5- and 6-beds. Many of these have been converted into flats. Going W, **Upper Tulse Hill** is mostly council-built housing – some of the more attractive in this part of London. Some of these homes, and some on nearby **Tulse Hill**, are on the open market as former tenants sell. Downhill to the S is Tulse Hill station, with a collection of small shops. Opposite runs **Perran Rd** with small 3-bed Victorian terraces; to the W lies West Norwood. The A205/South Circular runs around this southern boundary.

Tulse Hill provides properties with better-sized gardens and a far more suburban feel than further N. It is a good place to look for the distinctive Art Deco-style houses that are seeing an up-turn in their desirability.

Looking ahead five years, Tulse Hill *may* get a tube connection, if the East London line is extended south. See Transport chapter.

Herne Hill

Brockwell Park, a wide sweep of grassy hill surrounding a Victorian mansion, edges Herne Hill to the W. To the NW is the 'poets' district on the borders with Brixton (see Dulwich chapter). A railway line from Herne Hill station N to Loughborough Junction forms a barrier against Brixton. The ground rises to the E of this line, forming a pleasant, hilly quarter of solid red-brick houses between **Herne Hill** and **Milkwood Rd** and the railway. The area consists of predominantly Victorian and Edwardian 3- and 4-bed houses as in **Kestrel Avenue, Gubyon Avenue, Shardcroft Avenue** and **Woodquest Avenue** and larger double-fronted Victorian and Edwardian houses as in **Rollscourt Avenue** and **Fawnbrake Avenue**. Some are handsome examples of their period, some – thanks to the quite steep hill slopes – have sweeping views, and all are well-placed for the station and shops.

There is a mixture of homes strung along **Herne Hill**, from very large Victorian or Edwardian detached and semi-detached houses, plus some inter-war housing, to mansion blocks. To the N, the area between **Herne Hill Rd** and **Milkwood Rd** has smaller Victorian houses, and merges into Brixton around the multiple railway bridges of Loughborough Junction.

To the E of Herne Hill's central parades of shops around the station, the atmosphere becomes strongly suburban. Off **Half Moon Lane,** on the Dulwich borders and much sought-after, lie **Stradella Rd, Winterbrook Rd** and **Burbage Rd**. They are wide, tree-lined and quiet, predominantly late-Victorian/Edwardian terraced and semi-detached houses with small front gardens and 60-ft back gardens. **Burbage Rd** holds many surprises, with several large period-style detached houses with large gardens and driveways. It is a very popular road because it forms a direct link through to Dulwich Village.

There is a determined attempt on the part of estate agents to disinvent Herne Hill: the area bounded by **Half Moon Lane** to the S, **Herne Hill** to the N and **Red Post Hill** to the E has now been dubbed the 'North Dulwich Triangle', and those searching for a home here should look out for the term in property details. It contains many delightful streets of family housing – a mixture of Victorian, Edwardian and more modern terraced, detached and semi-detached homes. **Holmdene** is a good example, with its wide roadway, trees and hedges and 3-storey Victorian houses, with some modern semi-detacheds at the **Herne Hill** end. The solid Edwardian 3-bed terraced houses in streets like **Elfindale Rd** are popular. Dulwich Mead, off **Half Moon Lane**, is a development of smart 1-, 2- and 3-bed retirement homes.

Beckwith Rd, Ardbeg Rd and **Elmwood Rd** are more exclusive and expensive. These streets are even quieter, and stand on the Dulwich border. They have very popular 3-bed Edwardian terraced houses with small front gardens. They are close to a charming, well-kept public park, Sunray Gardens, with its duck pond, tennis courts and children's play-area.

Back N of **Herne Hill,** on the slopes which lead to the Ruskin Park neighbourhood of Dulwich, **Brantwood Rd** and **Dorchester Drive** are quiet and could be anywhere in suburban London with their '30s-built semis and rose gardens. Becoming increasingly popular are the '20s purpose-built architecturally designed blocks in Dorchester Court. **Milkwood Rd**'s southern end is convenient for the station and has small 3-bed Victorian terraces.

To the S of the station, **Norwood Rd** runs down towards Tulse Hill, with Brockwell Park on the W side. Just off **Norwood Rd**, but still well placed for Herne Hill station, lie **Guernsey Grove** and **Harwarden Grove**, next to a small estate of Peabody Trust housing. Mainly small houses and flats on **Guernsey**, 4- to 5-bed houses on **Harwarden**. Both back onto the railway which can be noisy. Facing Brockwell Park along **Norwood Rd** lie large 3-storey double-fronted Victorian houses, some detached, some semis, turning into smaller 3- and 2-storey houses nearer to Herne Hill.

Tulse Hill Borders

The area bounded by, but cut off from, **Christchurch Rd** – the busy South Circular – to the N, and **Palace Rd** and its side streets to the S, is very pleasant. The roads stand on the Streatham/Norwood borders and are spacious, tidy and tree-lined. **Palace Rd** is by far the most expensive road in the area, with conversions becoming more widely available in these huge Victorian and Edwardian properties. As single homes, these have 5 or 6 beds: £425,000 is a typical price. **Christchurch Rd** is mainly lined with large 3-storey and 5-storey Victorian houses of 5-bed-plus, most split into flats, though there are some double-fronted 2-storey, 5-bed houses available, and a large council estate in **Coburg Crescent**. The shorter roads between, like **Probyn Rd** and **Perran Rd**, are predominantly smallish 3-bed Victorian terraces. **Lanercost Rd** is the exception to this, having larger 5-bed Victorian houses, many that retain their original internal features.

Transport	Tubes: Brixton (zone 2, Victoria), to Oxford Circus 15 min, City 15 min (1 change), Heathrow 1 hr 10 min (1 change). Trains: Brixton to Victoria 10 min; Herne Hill to Victoria, Blackfriars, Tulse Hill to London Bridge, Blackfriars. Both on Thameslink.
Convenient for	Victoria and West End, City, South Circular, A23/M23 for Gatwick Airport and Brighton. Miles from centre: 3.5.

B

| **Schools** | Local Authority: St Martins-in-the-Fields (g). Private: Streatham Hill & Clapham High School (g). See also Dulwich chapter. |

SALES

Flats	S	1B	2B	3B	4B	5B
Average prices	50–70	65–150	95–200	120–220	—	—
Houses	2B	3B	4B	5B	6/7B	8B
Average prices	200–250	240–280	250–325	300–400	320–450	—

RENTAL

Flats	S	1B	2B	3B	4B	5B
Average prices	100–140	115–160	140–230	160–325	210–460	—
Houses	2B	3B	4B	5B	6/7B	8B
Average prices	140–230	160–325	210–460	275–550	345+	—

| **The properties** | Wide range in Brixton: rows of Victorian houses, some of real quality. Also lots of council-build – ditto. Flats are mostly conversions; some '30s blocks. Tulse and Herne Hills have Victorian/'30s family homes, often in quiet streets. Three-bed flats converted from roomy Edwardian houses can have larger rooms than p/b 3-bed houses. Lots of council-owned homes have been sold recently. |

| **The market** | Fashion and good transport links drive a market in which younger buyers predominate. They also move here to swap flats in pricier areas for roomy houses. Brixton prices are cheaper; gap widens as size increases. Herne/Tulse Hill houses range higher, especially for big houses and near stations, but Clapham overspill has driven Brixton prices up. Local searches: Lambeth 10 working days, Southwark 15 working days. |

Among those estate agents active in this area are:

- Burnet Ware & Graves
- Galloways
- Halifax Property
- Winkworth *
- Morgan Berry
- Martin Barry
- Creary's
- Charles Sinclair
- Barnard Marcus
- Haart
- Gordon & Keenes

further details: see advertisers' index on p671

CAMBERWELL

KENNINGTON

CAMBERWELL RD.

CAMBERWELL NEW RD.

North Camberwell

SOUTHWARK

LAMBETH

PECKHAM

PECKHAM ROAD

Central Camberwell

East Camberwell

Peckham Rye

Denmark Hill

Camberwell Grove

Loughborough Junction

COLD HARBOUR LANE

Park

GROVE LANE

DENMARK HILL

Ruskin Park

BRIXTON

East Dulwich

DULWICH

Map ref: p94 (2D)
Postal districts: SE5
Boroughs: Lambeth (Lab),
  Southwark (Lab)
Council tax: Band D Lambeth
  £750, Southwark £809
Conservation areas:
  Addington Square, Myatt's
  Fields, Camberwell Grove
Parking: Red Route rumoured

In a rather crowded corner of South East London you suddenly come across Camberwell Green, clearly a former village centre but now rather more of a traffic island, surrounded by shops. It takes time to get one's bearings around here as every street seems to be called 'Camberwell Something-or-other' or 'Grove This-or-that', but persistence is rewarded with the discovery of some fine and interesting residential corners – some with splendid Georgian houses – tucked amongst the drab streets and dire council buildings. Camberwell is very much a place of enclaves.

Camberwell is where the streets start to slope up from the flat ground of Walworth and Bermondsey towards the southern heights of Dulwich. This means homes with unexpected views of London. What Camberwell still lacks is a tube – and the latest plans (still at least five years off) speak of Peckham, not Camberwell . . . . Still, once you've struggled out of the immediate area, via traffic jams, copious buses and Loughborough Junction and Denmark Hill rail stations, the opening up of SE London transport links (Jubilee line, re-opened East London line, Docklands Light Railway) come into play. Indefinably, Camberwell no longer feels quite as cut-off as it did.

The main shopping area is **Denmark Hill** (with **Walworth Rd** not far away). There is a large Safeway supermarket with car park and a Sainsbury's on **Dog Kennel Hill**. A number of lively and colourful bars have appeared in the area; restaurants are few but varied. Parking in Camberwell is restricted to side streets off the main roads – there are plans for an eventual Red Route – and is especially difficult around **Denmark Hill**: a lot of the spaces are taken up by people visiting the local hospitals, King's College and the Maudsley. Because of the teaching hospitals and Camberwell Art School the area is rich in student-rented property.

The contrast between **Camberwell Grove** and **Champion Hill** half a mile to the S of the Green, and the streets to the N, is marked. **Camberwell Grove** has a good number of some of the handsomest Georgian houses S of the Thames. There are leafy, quiet streets of villas of every period from Regency to '30s. And there are some of the nastiest of ex-GLC flats interspersed with some very ordinary late-Victorian terraces of the ubiquitous South London sort.

Camberwell Green, the centre of the area, sits at the junction of **Camberwell Church St**, **Camberwell Rd**, **Denmark Hill** and **Camberwell New Rd**. These busy roads define the various neighbourhoods of Camberwell, which is further divided by two railway lines. The boundary with Brixton to the W is ill-defined, and Camberwell fades into Walworth to the N. On the whole, the SE5 postcode equals Camberwell.

The area's price range is wide. Ex-council flats in walk-up blocks can be £55,000, while a conversion of a Victorian home can yield 2-bed flats around £100,000. A Victorian terraced house in a decent corner will be £185,000-plus, with the Georgian gems rising above half a million. Prices rise when within reach of Oval tube.

Camberwell Grove

The area S and E of the Green, on the gentle slopes up towards Herne Hill and Dulwich, was the first to be developed as Camberwell began its expansion from village to suburb. **Camberwell Grove** survives virtually intact as a street of late-Georgian houses. Some, at the N end, date from the 1770s; others further up the street, such as **Grove Crescent**, are early 19th century. Sixteen houses in two stucco terraces at the S end were beautifully restored by Shorham Properties in 1997. Those on the E side, dating from 1845, were split into 35 flats, while the 1830 terrace on the W side became 10 houses which were offered as shell finish from £250,000, complete from £350,000: last autumn a 4-bedroomed one was on the market for £495,000. The flats surface as resales at around £175,000 for a 2-bed. **Letsome St** runs E off the Grove with 1970s council-built flats.

The Georgian atmosphere continues on E into **Grove Park** (a few original homes, but largely lined with particularly peaceful Edwardian houses) and **Grove Lane**. Grove Lane is not as grand as Camberwell Grove, but it does have some lovely early 19th-century houses mixed with just about every 20th-century period. Railway land in the angle of **Camberwell Grove** and **Grove Park** yielded two new caches of homes in the late '80s: **Grovelands Close**, off the Grove, has modern mews-style houses including some 1-bed ones which now sell for some £86,500, while the 137 homes of **Linwood Close**, off **Grove**

Park, fetch c. £58,000 for the studios, £90,000 for 1-beds, £100,000 upwards for 2-beds.

West of **Grove Lane**, **Champion Hill** and surrounding streets were developed in the 1840s. Some of these elegant villas still survive. The style continues N of the railway and the Maudsley Hospital in **De Crespigny Park**. Back to the S, **Langford Green** is a 1968 enclave built in Regency style, and has large town-houses in pleasant stock brick: highly desirable. Also off **Champion Hill** is Ruskin Park House, a pair of large blocks of '20s mansion flats where 3-bed flats can range between £115-140,000.

Ruskin Park

West across **Denmark Hill**, the bulk of King's College Hospital and the E-W railway line form a frontier cutting off the Ruskin Park corner in South Camberwell. The park is the centre of an enclave of 20th-century streets with a strongly, but pleasingly, suburban feel. A 2-bed flat in good condition above a shop can now cost £85–90,000. **Denmark Hill** itself is a busy but pleasant road. To the E are large brick council-built blocks, and further on the **Sunray Avenue** estate of 1920s homes on the borders of Herne Hill, built by the government as part of the post-First World War 'homes fit for heroes' campaign. West of **Denmark Hill**, roads like **Deepdene** and **Sunset**, with their '30s semis – not to mention a green-roofed, Spanish-style bungalow – slope peacefully down to Ruskin Park. **Ferndene Rd** lines the E side of the park, its 1920s gabled and bay-windowed villas having fine views across it and the rooftops towards Central London.

West of the park, **Finsen Rd** has handsome (c. 1914) terraces looking out over the green park from particularly pretty square-bayed windows. To the N, **Kemerton Rd** and surrounding streets have neat little Victorian cottages.

East Camberwell

Between **Peckham Rd** and the railway line to the S, there are several streets of late-19th-century terraces such as **Bushey Hill Rd**, **Vestry Rd**, **Crofton Rd** and **Shenley Rd**. The 4-bed Victorian houses in this sought-after corner command about £285,000, while some 1990s 4-bed houses in Crofton Rd are around £255,000. **Vestry Mews** has gained some new homes and a number of old houses have been converted into flats. These flats are popular but rarely on the market: when they do come up a 2-bed flat can reach £235,000.

Central Camberwell

You could drive through the area's traffic-filled heart every day without discovering Camberwell's most surprising corner. Off **Denmark Hill**, a tiny turning called **Love Walk** is, indeed, a no-through road for cars. At this end traffic can only penetrate, alongside a short terrace, as far as the entrance to a tucked-away group of 3- and 4-storey brick blocks of flats, owned by the Orbit Housing Association. Walk on, and **Love Walk** reveals its surprise. Surprising prices, too: a small 2-storey building reached £460,000 in 1998. On the left is Selbourne Village, a 1982 Wates estate of small cottagey houses built – with great attention to materials and detailing – in the highest flight of village vernacular. It is undoubtedly pleasant, peaceful and a successfully human-scale, well-hidden corner – but an extraordinary stylistic jolt in so urban an environment. Cars can enter from the E end: garages are hidden in groups between the houses. On the other side of **Love Walk** are older, but equally unlikely homes. First comes a little row of earlier versions of the country cottage, tile-hung, gabled and hidden behind an older wall, reached only through two arched gateways. And further on are splendid, double-fronted small Regency detached houses with garages, which lead out onto **Grove Lane** where some dignified larger Georgian terraces still stand. These are very popular with those who aspire to – but just can't afford – their counterparts in **Camberwell Grove**. A 4-bed one sold here for £265,000 last winter; expect to pay £390,000 and upwards for the grander, 5-bed ones.

North Camberwell

Most of the area E of **Camberwell Rd** is taken up by large council developments, but a few older streets survive, notably W of the road, around **Addington Square**. The square itself, which runs up to Burgess Park, is early 19th-century; its irregular houses of the classic, tall, late-Georgian style plus a pair of low, Regency villas. It is, of course, a conservation area. To the S is **Rust Square**, a pleasant Victorian corner.

Where once omnibuses and horses were stabled, Hopewell Yard in **Hopewell St** harbours a distinctive, late-'80s homes development: an enclosed corner of flats, maisonettes and offices around a central courtyard, with basement parking. **Vicarage Grove** has some large Victorian houses. Other streets where private housing remains include **Havil St** and **Ada Rd** with its little flat-fronted cottages; the tower belonging to an old workhouse in Ada Rd was converted into flats in the 1980s. The old Victorian St Giles Hospital off **St Giles Rd** and **Peckham Rd** has re-emerged as Peacock House: flats, mostly 2-beds, courtesy of Londonwide Properties. Completing at time of writing but all already sold at prices from £95,000 for a 1-bed.

Georgian houses – some intact, recently restored and used as single homes, while others are nowadays flats – line long stretches of both **Camberwell Rd** and **Camberwell New Rd**. The latter leads directly to Vauxhall Bridge, passing the Oval and Vauxhall tubes: Camberwell is very close to Central London. Both roads are busy, however: **Camberwell New Rd** is the route E to Peckham and the A2/Dover Rd. Tucked in the angle of **Vassall Rd**, **Langton Rd** and **Camberwell New Rd** is Salisbury Place, a mewsy 1989 development: a pleasant and popular enclave within striking distance of Oval tube.

South of **Camberwell New Rd**, Camberwell merges with Brixton. There are big council estates but also the conservation area around Myatt's Fields, where the houses of the 1890s Minet Estate, in roads such as **Knatchbull Rd**, always attract interest. A splendid one-off coach house went for £600,000 in 1998, but £500,000 is a more normal price for one of these often 5- (and sometimes 6-) bedded houses. St Gabriel's Manor, off **Calais St**, is a conversion of an 1899 college into 50 homes: a first-floor mezzanine example was £189,000 last autumn. Towards **Coldharbour Lane** there are cheaper homes in streets such as **Lilford Rd**: a 4-bed Victorian house would now fetch in the region of £245,000.

Transport	Trains: Loughborough Junction to City Thameslink 12 min; East Dulwich/Denmark Hill to Blackfriars, London Bridge, Charing Cross and Victoria. Nearest tube Oval.
Convenient for	City, Westminster, Dulwich. Miles from centre: 3.
Schools	Local Authority: Archbishop Michael Ramsey C of E, Sacred Heart RC. See also Dulwich chapter.

SALES

Flats	S	1B	2B	3B	4B	5B
Average prices	45–75	60–125	100–170	130–250	1200+	—

Houses	2B	3B	4B	5B	6/7B	8B
Average prices	100–200	150–265	185–500+	260–500+	500+	—

RENTAL

Flats	S	1B	2B	3B	4B	5B
Average prices	90–125	115–175	140–220	185–300	275+	300+

Houses	2B	3B	4B	5B	6/7B	8B
Average prices	140–230	185–300	250–325	325–460	395+	485

The properties   Scruffy main roads conceal pockets of fine Georgiana. Also ordinary terraces and converted flats. New developments appearing, adding town-houses and flats to an area which mixes some of the best and some of the worst of London homes.

The market   Not as well-known as it ought to be, the area has less bustle and street-cred than Brixton, but nicer houses: unconverted Georgian coveted. Price range dependent on location and architecture as much as size. Local searches: Lambeth 10 working days, Southwark 15 working days.

Among those estate agents active in this area are:
- Andrews & Robertson
- Roy Brooks
- Hindwoods & White Dent
- First Property Sales
- Kinleigh Folkard & Hayward
- Winkworth*

further details: see advertisers' index on p671

CAMDEN TOWN AND PRIMROSE HILL

Map ref: p61 (1G)
Postal districts: NW1, NW5
Boroughs: Camden (Lab)
Council tax: Band D £897
Conservation areas: Include Camden
  Square, Jeffreys St, Camden Town,
  Primrose Hill
Parking: Residents/meters

Camden Town is probably a smarter place to live today than at any time since Earl Camden started to build in 1791. His attempts to create a sort of North London Belgravia were frustrated within a few years: the estate was successively crossed and split up by the Grand Union Canal and the main railways from the N. These, and linked industry, lowered the tone. In the mid-19th century, though it had some claim to be a professional persons' suburb, it was never a smart one. With the 20th, the ill-maintained homes went down-hill and the denizens of cheap boarding-houses and tacky flat conversions outnumbered owner-occupiers.

A few enclaves apart, Camden Town remained cheap and cheerful, a haven for broke artists and struggling newcomers, until the start of the 1990s. Then bohemian London got rich. Writers became, or were replaced by, media stars. Warrens of bed-sits became carefully restored Victorian houses. People in Camden Town still don't wear ties to work. It's just that their shirts cost a small fortune.

The last few years have seen unremitting pressure on the housing stock here. New developments are rare: there's no spare land, until the King's Cross scheme gets going (see below). Prices went up by 30% in 1999, according to local agents, who report that would-be Camdenites want to move here whatever the cost. The problem is that people already here tend to stay put.

Primrose Hill, an enclave of quiet streets beside the 110-acre open space of the Hill to the W, has a less eventful past. It has been known for handsome houses and spacious flats for several decades. Despite the property prices, Primrose Hill is still intellectual-smart rather than mere money-smart.

Camden Town is still bracketed by railway lines – but this means that it will eventually border not a desolate hinterland of derelict goods yards but the brave new world of the King's Cross development, set to create a virtual new town – eventually. The rail lines also mean excellent transport links, though Camden Town station is in a sad state and needs £65 million spending on it, cash the council is trying to extract from the government. Next-door St Pancras, when the Heathrow link opens (2002) and the Paris line reaches it (2007?) will be the hottest transport hub in London.

In the mid-20th century Greek, Irish and Italian communities took advantage of the area's cheap housing. Most are now gone, displaced by designers, architects, writers – and, increasingly, media stars. Nevertheless, Camden retains its cosmopolitan atmosphere, with lots of excellent restaurants and specialist food shops. Clubs, pubs and other venues serve young people: the area's a tourist destination as well as a place to live. The canalside markets at Camden Lock have been tidied up, as has the **High St**. Long-established locals complain that all the pubs are being smartened up beyond belief, and that traditional 'caffs' are being replaced by coffee houses.

Living here often means having to put up with noisy main roads or the sound of tube or trains; as a result, each street commands a different price. Homes are nearly all Victorian houses and conversions of these into flats – new flats and maisonettes sell less well here. The narrow-fronted Victorian houses give no more than 1-, possibly 2-bed flats; larger flats tend, therefore, to be maisonettes. The largest and smartest homes are in Primrose Hill (which is among London's top residential districts), around **Gloucester Crescent** and in the Camden Square neighbourhood.

The satellite areas, grouped around central Camden Town, are Chalk Farm, Mornington Crescent, Primrose Hill and, to the S, what little housing there is in Euston. Note that Camden the borough covers a much larger area than Camden Town.

Camden Town

The heart of Camden Town is a busy road junction with the tube station on its busiest corner. **Camden High St**, running N from **Mornington Crescent**, is Camden's main shopping street, lively and always busy. The best residential area of Camden Town is – perhaps suprisingly – in the narrow strip W of the **High St**. On the map it looks hemmed in by roads and railways, but the houses are good-period early Victorian and the streets both handsome and interesting.

On **Camden High St** there are flats and maisonettes above the shops in flat-fronted Victorian terraced buildings at the S end, and red-brick mansion blocks near the tube station. **Delancey St**, also busy and wide, is one-way going W towards Regent's Park, and has youthful cafés and shops at the **High St** end, with flats above; thereafter terraces on either side. The narrow, flat-fronted Victorian buildings provide flats, maisonettes and houses, some with gardens. The W end overlooks the main railway line into Euston – which is being extensively and noisily modernised.

Parkway is a colourful, crowded street going W towards Regent's Park; a good range of shops and restaurants on either side, the redeveloped Camden Odeon cinema and some terrific bookshops; 1- and 2-bed flats and studios above. The decayed bingo hall site is at last due for redevelopment: offices and shops (Gap, Virgin Megastore).

Albert St, one of Camden's most attractive and expensive roads, is wide and has elegant and beautifully maintained terraces on both sides, providing large 4-, 5- and 6-bed family houses. In some, basements have been sold off separately. A house here would command around £850,000 (1971: £14,000; 1998: £625,000). Berkeley are offering 14 new flats in 'The Atlantic Building'. **Arlington Rd**, parallel, has a similar middle section with terraced houses (smaller than in Albert) along either side, though prices are lower in this slightly less attractive street. Busy **Jamestown Rd** has a recent development of period-style properties and older terraces opposite commercial buildings, providing flats and maisonettes. On the corner with Arlington Rd, 16 new flats to a Piers Gough design sold fast in late 1998. As part of the same development a new canal-side hotel, accessed from **Jamestown Rd**, is about to open. The Glass Building ('dazzling' – Sunday Times) has one penthouse left at £675,000, the other 31 flats having sold in 1999. These developments should raise the tone of a street best known for its down-and-outs hostel and council refuse depot. Gilbey House, a conversion of an 1890s canalside bottling plant to 76 flats, has proved popular: 1-bed flats around £335,000.

At the N end of **Arlington Rd**, after the **Delancey St** junction, council housing is on the E side, more large terraced Victorian homes opposite. An office development in **Carlow St** is crowned with 14 penthouse flats, ultra-smart, ultra-modern, with roof terraces. Twelve new houses appeared in **Beatty St** early in the 1990s.

Inverness St leads W off **Arlington St** to **Gloucester Crescent**, today reckoned the best address in Camden Town (unless, like some agents, you maintain it's part of Primrose Hill). Some of these big 1840s semi-detached houses are flats, some are enviable whole houses, and there is some later infill. Like the rest of Camden Town, the Crescent failed to cling to the status intended for it, and by the 1960s many of the big villas were split into seedy lodging houses. Writer Alan Bennett has amusingly described how he and other young people, the first wave of 'gentrifiers', began to buy these houses in the '60s and return them to single homes. You need to be a lot more prosperous than the average young playwright to live there today. Prices are now comparable to those of Primrose Hill: £900,000-plus for a 4-bed house.

Mornington Terrace is council in the S part; the N part has housing in Victorian terraces on E side only; the W side overlooks the main railway line into Euston. Most are still single houses, both modernized and unmodernized. **Mornington Place** ditto.

In the triangle formed by **Camden High St**, **Hawley Crescent** and **Kentish Town Rd**, small new developments of town-houses and purpose-built flats rub shoulders with the vast GMTV complex and large, ugly commercial and office buildings. In the triangle on the other side of **Kentish Town Rd**, bounded by **Camden St**, is a large Sainsbury's supermarket. On the canal edge of the Sainsbury's site is a real surprise: 10 high-tech houses by architect Nicholas Grimshaw, metal-clad pods with lofty galleried rooms behind vast, electrically operated windows. These award-winning (naturally) homes sold for £260,000 in 1989, and now are offered at c. £350,000.

Camden St, the main southbound highway into the West End, has period terracing at the N end providing converted flats and maisonettes, plus a mix of old and new council housing. The Greek Orthodox church is on the E side. **Bayham St** is similar, with heavy traffic southbound, and has small light industrial factories and council housing on E side; shops with flats above in period terracing opposite, and Victorian terraces.

East of **Bayham St** is a relatively quiet, conveniently placed group of streets which form the best place to live in central Camden (Gloucester Crescent/Albert St excepted). **Greenland Rd** is a quiet tree-lined street with yellowish-grey brick flat-fronted Victorian terraced houses; these are 3-storeyed, with gardens both front and back, providing 3-bed houses. Some are privately owned, some housing association and some council-assisted, resulting in varying conditions of housing and a good mix of residents. **Carol St**, **St Martin's Close** and **Georgiana St** ditto. **Lyme St** has a pleasant row of early Victorian terraces on the E side overlooking the canal: the S part is best. Both **Lyme** and **Georgiana St**s are blocked off to traffic which pushes prices up slightly. **Pratt St** only has private housing between **Bayham St** and the **High St**, in flats and maisonettes over shops, and some individual houses. **Plender St**, with a small fruit-and-veg market at its W end is similar, though it also has housing in some purpose-built blocks of flats.

The roads S of **Pratt St** to **Crowndale Rd** are mainly council with the exception of **College Place**, which has large Victorian terraced houses in the N section only. **Royal College St** (main through road, northbound only) has council housing at its S end; then terraces on both sides, some still single properties, some converted into flats.

On **Baynes St** a 1985 development of mews houses and flats, Reachview, occupies the S side overlooking the canal. **Rossendale Way** has conversions in period terrace to right, new mews houses beyond; it overlooks the canal at the rear. At the bottom of **Rossendale Way** is Elm Village, a development of town-houses, flats and maisonettes

built by Camden Council in the mid-'80s, where some of the cheaper homes in Camden are to be found. **Rousden St**, a narrow street running up to Camden Rd station (the tracks run on the S side), has a run-down aspect but also some terraces of new town-houses, purpose-built flats, maisonettes and conversions in period houses. **St Pancras Way**, which runs S from **Camden Rd**, is a through road with industrial and commercial buildings.

Tall Victorian terraced houses then reappear on the northern part of **St Pancras Way** and **Royal College St**. **Jeffreys St**, through to **St Pancras Way**, has 3- and 4-storey Victorian terraces on either side with basements, black railings in front and small balconies on first floor. **Prowse Place**, closer to the railway line, has four brick-fronted cottages to the right, and is cobbled. **Ivor St** is a quiet, tree-lined street with brightly painted 2- and 3-storey houses, most in single occupancy, and many recently done up or being renovated. **Bonny St** is very mixed; some period houses offer conversions. A

Camden Town has many houses of mid-Victorian date, which feature sash windows such as this, often with vestigial 'balconies' in wrought iron. The window surrounds, of classically detailed stucco, form a pleasing contrast to the earlier Georgian small ones, which staged a reappearance late in the century.

development of town-houses has recently been built, and there is railway-owned housing next to the bridge. In **Jeffreys Place** there are a dozen substantial new town-houses with garages.

To the NE of **St Pancras Way** lie 'the Rochesters', a group of streets tucked in beneath the borders of NW5 and Kentish Town, which rank next in desirability and price to **Gloucester Crescent/Albert St** and **Camden Square**. **Rochester Rd** is part of an environmental area and a no-through road. It overlooks a small playground area, which lies between **Rochester Rd** and **Rochester Terrace**. Here prices are slightly higher, thanks to S-facing gardens and larger, grander houses: £750,000 last autumn for a 4-bed. **Rochester Place** is a very narrow street in which are council blocks, small workshops and a school. To the W, **Reed's Place** is a tiny, hidden-away street, blocked off to traffic at both ends. Square, stucco-fronted Victorian houses, most still in single occupation, set the tone; most have pretty front gardens. **Wilmot Place** has substantial pairs of brick and stucco-fronted houses and terraces. **Rochester Mews** has several little, white-painted mews houses in its E section. **Whitcher Place** is low brick-built halls of residence for London University.

Camden Square

The area on the Kentish borders, bounded by **York Way** to the E, **Camden Rd** to the W and **Agar Grove** to the S, has some good houses in spacious streets and squares, and has become popular as a consequence. The bigger 4-storey houses here now command around £650,000 (1998: £450,000), while a 1-bed garden flat might be £150,000.

On the Kentish Town side of **Camden Rd** is the 1,500-pupil Jews Free School (JFS), which has a good record. It is soon to move out to a spacious new home in Brent, and there are plans to redevelop its Camden site with 150 homes.

Camden Square, where substantial 1850s houses, good-sized flats and maisonettes are to be had in a quiet attractive garden-square setting, establishes the tone. **Camden Rd** is a main road, but the Victorian houses on the E side, almost all converted into flats, are well-shaded by trees and set well back. Some garden flats available. **Camden Park Rd**, **Cliff Rd** and **Cliff Villas** are a mix of council blocks, Victorian terraces mostly converted into flats, and mid-Victorian semi-detached cottages.

North Villas and **South Villas** run N from **Camden Square** and have huge grey-brick villas on both sides. Garden flats are available in deep basements. All these villas are now conversions, providing 1-, 2- and 3-bedroomed flats and maisonettes, **Camden Terrace** likewise. **St Augustine's Rd** – pleasant, wide, tree-lined and quiet – has large pairs of villas to either side in varying conditions of repair. Unmodernized examples are still sometimes available; conversions yield garden flats, flats and maisonettes. **Marquis Rd**, **Cantelowes Rd** and **St Paul's Crescent** ditto. **Camden Mews** runs parallel to the square on the NW side: a group of seven new mews houses were added in 1998 to an eclectic mix of styles and sizes (and thus prices). 'It's had every architect you could name playing with them,' observes a local estate agent. The same can be said of **Murray Mews**. Indeed Cherry & Pevsner's *Buildings of England: London 4* comments 'architects' offices and homes . . . are thicker on the ground [in Camden Town] than anywhere else in England, squeezed, often with great ingenuity, into inexpensive plots along mews and back lanes behind the larger houses.'

Camden Square itself – an elegant, leafy, subdued (and recently tidied-up) square – provides large family houses, especially on the S side, and flats and maisonettes in conversions. A whole house sold last year for £750,000. **Murray St** has a period terrace at its N end, modern parade of shops on W side with flats above. The narrow 6-ft wide entrance to **Agar Grove** restricts heavy traffic. **Stratford Villas**, council at S end, thereafter has tall grey-brick and stucco-fronted terraces, up to five storeys high, on both sides.

Rochester Square has private homes on two sides; some in pairs of Edwardian-style villas, 2-storey villas with raised ground floors plus semi-basements below, some in Victorian terraces, many also in the process of renovation. **Agar Grove** is a thoroughfare and prices here are 20–25 per cent cheaper than in **Camden Square**: noise from the road is augmented by noise from the railway lines. There is a mix of old and new council blocks on the S side particularly, interspersed with modern town-houses and tall Victorian terraces, which yield lots of converted flats and maisonettes. **St Paul's Crescent**, a crescent no longer, leads to a low-level white-painted council estate. On either side are terraces of grey-brick houses, 2-storeys with basements. **St Paul's Mews**, 25 town-houses, dates from 1990. Council housing continues S and E around **Maiden Lane**. S towards Kings's Cross is at present a wasteland of car parks and folorn Victorian warehouses, sidings and canals.

Chalk Farm

Going N, **Camden High St** holds a lively fruit-and-veg market from Monday to Saturday in **Inverness St** to the left and Saturday market stalls to the right. This one-way street becomes **Chalk Farm Rd** as it reaches the canal and Camden Lock – across which the famous (but rather touristy) weekend market takes place. To the W is The Roundhouse, a remarkable building used as a music/theatre venue. Beyond, on former railway land, is a Safeway food store and housing association flats. Land off Chalk Farm Rd at Stables Market, known to older residents as Stanley Sidings, is earmarked for a new scheme of restaurants, offices and a 7-day market.

Hartland Rd's 2-storey brick and stucco-fronted brightly painted late-Georgian terraces provided 3-bed houses on three floors, with small gardens. The railway line runs overhead at the end of the street. No private housing beyond the junction with **Clarence Way**. Similar terraces are found in the N part of **Clarence Way**.

Hadley Street, to the E of the railway line, runs up to the borders of NW5 and Kentish Town. The street is divided in two by road block; the end is a peaceful cul-de-sac of narrow-fronted terraced houses, some Victorian, some built in the 1980s in original style. The railway line passes overhead on N side; council housing surrounds. The N section of street is pretty, tree-lined and not used by traffic; rows of brick and stucco-fronted 2-storey houses on both sides. Trains using Kentish Town West station pass behind; the street has a prosperous air. **Healing St** likewise, though houses here are slightly grander and taller.

Grafton Crescent, tucked in behind the main road, has large grey-brick and stucco-fronted terraced houses on both sides. Homes here are mostly 3-bed, some with gardens. The E end of **Prince of Wales Rd** is busy and noisy, but grey-brick and stucco houses, mostly conversions, are set well back. Homes in flats over the shops on **Kentish Town Rd** going N. **Hawley Rd** is a mix of old properties restored into spacious houses and new purpose-built flats, with more being built. Prices are lower here because of extremely heavy traffic.

Chalk Farm 'proper' lies W of **Harmood St**, taking in the area around the tube station. It is a small and highly convenient corner with a good deal of council housing intermingled with homes which borrow some of the aura of Belsize Park and some of the trendiness of Kentish Town.

Most of the homes here are in the huge blocks of mansion flats in **Eton College Rd**, or in small Edwardian villa-type houses in roads off the **Chalk Farm Rd**. The area has seen some modern redevelopment, with new blocks on the **Chalk Farm Rd** and on the corner of **Adelaide Rd**.

The S part of **Queen's Crescent** is worth a look, with pleasant little streets of cottages (3-bed c. £450,000) on the W side, but E of **Malden Rd** the Crescent goes down-hill as a place to live. This part is in NW5 and is debated with Kentish Town. **Prince of Wales Rd**: the N side has large blocks of red-brick council flats; on the S side are terraces of period houses, some in good condition, others run-down. Best terrace of the three is Nos 131–151. A converted school offers loft-style flats at loft-style prices. **Crogsland Rd**, likewise, is council on one side; on the W side, a short terrace of 4-storey houses have been laterally converted into flats. Further along **Prince of Wales Rd** going E there are terraces of period properties on both sides of the street; some single houses, some maisonettes, some flats. **Harmood St**: rows of low 2-storey Edwardian terraced houses here, very mixed; some done up, some run-down. Chalk Farm bus garage and more council housing towards S part of street. **Clarence Way**, a pretty street, has rows of brick terraced houses similar to Harmood St, though the railway bridge for the North London line passes over the middle of the street. **Chalk Farm Rd**, the busy main road, has new developments of purpose-built flats and offices; flats over shops on E side.

Just to the W of the Chalk Farm tube station is **Eton College Rd**, a very pleasant, quiet road which has three huge mansion blocks known as The Etons. Flats in these blocks change hands regularly. A major refurbishment programme went on through the 1990s and is still under way, so service charges are high – but prices, correspondingly, lower than normal. Two-bed flats are selling for around £200,000, 1-bed £130,000-plus. A service charge figure of around £2,000 is normal. Some of these flats have had problems with short leases and lease extensions.

This end of **Adelaide Rd** is also regarded as part of Chalk Farm. The houses here are large, stucco-fronted terraces, converted into flats. **Adelaide Rd** is busy, and these houses overlook the railway. Flats in modern blocks such as King's College Court command prices around £200,000 for 2-bed.

Primrose Hill

Tucked away between St John's Wood, Regent's Park, Camden Town and Chalk Farm lies a small public park with soaring hilltop views over London. On its eastern slopes is a picturesque and prosperous enclave whose residents – many of whom are writers, photographers, actors and musicians – take great pride in the area. This is more of a family, settled area than the rest of Camden Town.

The 'village' of Primrose Hill is tucked in between the main line railway to the E and the hill to the W. Quiet and secluded (due mainly to traffic controls on through roads), it commands high prices. This is the most coveted part of the neighbourhood, being composed mainly of wide, tree-lined streets and elegant stucco-fronted houses. It boasts a quaint shopping street with a good selection of increasingly smart shops. There are very few small houses to be had: the majority of Primrose Hill housing is 1-and 2-bed flats in converted period houses, and surviving 3/4-bed houses. There is strong demand for property here.

Regent's Park Rd, curving round past the Hill and back to Chalk Farm, forms the W boundary of the 'village' and at its bottom end is a busy thoroughfare for cars and infrequent buses, though its substantial semi-detached stucco homes, some with views over Primrose Hill, many still family houses, are still highly popular. A garden flat with 3 bedrooms might go for £475,000.

Gloucester Avenue forms an eastern boundary to the area: a wide, tree-lined street with the main line railway (Euston-bound) behind the homes on the E side – this can lower prices on some houses by as much as 40 per cent, though the W side of the avenue is as smart as anywhere in the neighbourhood. Most of the period terraces on both sides have been converted into flats. There are also some modern blocks of flats. Unlike many Primrose Hill homes, these come on the market fairly frequently as young couples move on to bigger and better things. Expect to pay up to £450,000 for good 3-bed flats in a modern block, around £225,000 for a more modest modern 2-bed and between £320,000 and £375,000 for a 2-bed garden flat in a period conversion.

The 'village' to the W is a maze of quiet streets, secluded and sleepy. **Rothwell St**, **Chalcot Crescent** and **St Mark's Crescent** are among the most prestigious addresses: 4-storey stucco-fronted houses. Even bigger and better are the enviable mid-1850s houses of **Chalcot Square**. House prices in **Chalcot Square** and **Crescent** range up to £1.2 million, though an extra-large one is reputed to have sold for £1.7 million. A 1-bed flat (a big one, presumably) went for £450,000 recently. **Chalcot Rd**, **Fitzroy Rd** and **Princess Rd** have rows of tall period terraces, now mostly flats. The canal, running between **St Mark's Crescent** and **Princess Rd**, makes for attractive back gardens.

Off the N end of **Regent's Park Rd**, where prices are (slightly) lower, **Ainger Rd**, **Oppidans Rd** and **Meadowbank** form a quiet triangle. **Oppidans Rd** and **Ainger Rd** have large grey-brick terraces and semis divided into flats; in addition, **Meadowbank** has Primrose Hill Court (council), a well-maintained block, and some large modern town-houses. **Primrose Hill Rd** has two big modern blocks overlooking the hill, and the highly desirable period **St George's Terrace** at the bottom.

The E end of **King Henry's Rd** has strong links with Eton College and much of the land is still owned by the college: leasehold only here. Most of the elegant, tall grey-brick houses have been split into flats with well-proportioned rooms; garden flats available here. On the N side, and in the roads leading up to **Adelaide Rd**, are groups of small, modern, 2-storey, white-painted houses.

Mornington Crescent and Euston

To the S of Camden Town lies another area centred on a convenient tube station. Mornington Crescent (the tube stop) is actually on the junction of busy **Hampstead Rd** and **Eversholt St**. **Mornington Crescent** (the street), once a grand, semi-circular terrace of tall stucco-fronted Victorian houses, is gradually being renovated and converted into flats. The Crescent's garden was sold off in the 1930s and is now a giant office block. Prices here are lower than in central Camden.

Crowndale Rd, E of **Eversholt St**, has tall brick and cream stucco terraces on either side, mostly conversions: thereafter there is council housing and a small parade of shops. The N end of **Eversholt St** also has 4-storey terraces.

Oakley Square's S side is council; the N side is a pleasant terrace of Victorian houses, brick and stucco-fronted with elaborate detail on doors and window frames, black railings in front, and deep basements. In keeping with the rest of the area, this is gradually being restored and renovated. One 5-storey house was £795,000 last autumn. At the N end a block of luxury flats, St Matthew's Lodge, has apartments of all sizes including studios. A 3-bed flat here might fetch

£275,000. Both flats and houses face onto the leafy, green, small public garden. **Harrington Square** has a terrace of Victorian houses, most flat conversions, on section running N-S only; in front runs a busy one-way street carrying traffic into the West End. Hurdwick Place, off **Hampstead Rd**, has flats in period terraces, and garden flats in some basements.

The Euston area, bounded by **Euston Rd** to the S, **St Pancras Way** to the E, **Hampstead Rd** to the W and **Oakley Square** to the N, was (until Right to Buy) virtually all council-owned or chartitable housing, except for some flats and maisonettes over shops on **Churchway** and **Chalton St**, which have the benefit of this very central location. Many of the council homes are handsomely restored period houses. Similar housing, too, on the S part of **Eversholt St**, in **Starcross St**, **North Gower St** and **Drummond St** to the W, where there is privately owned housing in Victorian terraces, well-sheltered from the main road and centrally located. **Drummond St**'s exotic restaurants are well-known. This S part of Camden will one day benefit from all the amenities – and disruption – of the vast King's Cross/St Pancras redevelopment. For the moment, this remains a tightly-knit and rather traditional community.

Transport	Tubes: Camden Town, Chalk Farm, Mornington Crescent, Euston (zone 1/2, Northern). From Camden Town: Oxford Circus 15 min (1 change), City 15 min, Heathrow 1 hr (1 change). Trains: Camden Rd to Liverpool St 20 min, Kentish Town West (Silverlink Metro).
Convienient for	City & West End, Euston & King's Cross stations, Euston Rd to M40, M11 to Cambridge, Regent's Park. Miles from centre: 2.5.
Schools	Local Authority: Haverstock School, South Camden Community School, William Ellis (b), Camden School for Girls. Private: Jews Free School (soon to move to Brent). See also Hampstead.

SALES

Flats	S	1B	2B	3B	4B	5B
Average prices	80–160	100–210	200–500	350–600	500–1.5 M	–
Houses	2B	3B	4B	5B	6/7B	8B
Average prices	150–310	210–450+	375–1 M+	500–2 M	–	–

RENTAL

Flats	S	1B	2B	3B	4B	5B
Average prices	130–300	170–450	220–650	300–750	400–750	750+
Houses	2B	3B	4B	5B	6/7B	8B
Average prices	250–600	330–550+	450–1200+	600–2000+	–	–

The properties	Victorian housing of all shapes and sizes, with wide variations in status and condition. Lots of converted flats. Quite a few modern homes and more on the way: flats and mews-style houses. Lots of council-built homes – some quite desirable.
The market	Influx of prosperous, bohemian new buyers 'discovering' good period homes. General flats market, centres on conversions. The few family homes are in demand: once here, people stay. Primrose Hill and Gloucester Crescent are the smartest neighbourhoods. Local searches: 7–10 working days.

Among those estate agents active in this area are:

- Bairstow Eves
- Stickley & Kent
- Camden Bus
- Hotblack Desiato
- Keith Cardale Groves
- Winkworth *
- Anscombe & Ringland *
- Benham & Reeves

- Regents Park Property Services
- John D Wood
- Tatlers
- Dennis & Hayes
- Hetheringtons
- Goldschmidt & Howland
- Compton Reeback

further details: see advertisers' index on p671

CHELSEA

Map ref: p76 (4D)
Postal districts: SW3,
  SW10, SW1
Boroughs: Kensington &
  Chelsea (Con)
Council tax: Band D £534
Conservation areas: Most
  parts – check with town hall
Parking: Residents/meters.
  Clamping and towing away

Chelsea is more than a place, it is a byword, a symbol for a rather special kind of urban living: smart yet artistic, prosperous yet individual, expensive yet free-wheeling. In recent years the stress has moved to the corporate and away from the arty and individual. Bohemian Chelsea, home of artists and their models, site of studio parties, has not survived successive property booms. The painters and sculptors have moved out, and their studios are owned by the usual mix of international residents found in any rich London area. Now, a buyer of a £2 million-plus studio house will find the neighbours are merchant bankers not Royal Academicians.

All this said, the special Chelsea flavour lives on in the little pastel-painted streets, the elaborate mansion blocks, the occasional superb Georgian house. There is nowhere else in London quite like it.

It is easy to forget that until around 1980 quite a few of Chelsea's people were very ordinary, even poor, living in tenanted homes. Gentrification has done its work here too, with West Chelsea, spurred on by Chelsea Harbour and adjacent developments, the last enclave to be 'improved'. Housing association and charitable trust flats still take up large areas, mostly in the Chelsea Green neighbourhood.

Chelsea, strung along the **King's Rd** and the river, has a self-contained air. It has its own department store (Peter Jones in **Sloane Square**), a shop which is a way of life as much as a source of supply. You need not leave the area to be fed or entertained:

C

restaurants abound, it has its own theatre, the Royal Court (just re-opened after a £28 million rebuilding). Shops sell most things, especially if they are ephemeral or expensive. The **King's Rd** fortunes wax and wane with fashion: it is still a key destination for every visitor to London, especially the young and well-heeled. The arrival of big supermarkets and Marks & Spencer added to its attractions. You will search in vain, though, for the butcher, the baker or the other 'village' shops. The last of these went in the early '80s.

The **King's Rd** may be busy, even tawdry at times, but a street away all is quiet: you are in a Georgian village, or a Victorian square. Chelsea keeps the villagey ambience that Fulham and such places aspire to yet somehow never quite attain.

The area was first made popular by Sir Thomas More, who went to live there in the 16th century. The aristocracy followed, building large country houses. They stayed and, over the years, their rural retreats have been replaced by their town-houses. To reach his country estate, Sir Thomas travelled by boat: the all-important road, genuinely as royal as its name implies, came later when King Charles II had a farm track cleared so he could journey via Putney to Hampton Court and, presumably, visit Nell Gwynn en route in Fulham.

The track became, literally, the **King's Rd**, later famous throughout the world as a symbol of the Swinging Sixties. **King's Rd** remains the main thoroughfare. It runs the entire length of Chelsea, W–E, 'playing every note in the social scale', as one of the area's most famous former inhabitants, writer/wit Quentin Crisp, observed. As it wends its way from fashionable **Sloane Square** in the E to World's End in the W, the restaurants, pubs, bars, boutiques, galleries and smart shops make way for handsome squares of traditional terraced houses.

The local council have the robust aim of 'restoring the King's Rd's pavements to their pre-war condition' by re-paving the street with York stone slabs, just like those Christopher Robin (and countless Chelsea children since) dodged the bears along.

Some may moan that Chelsea lacks a tube station apart from Sloane Square, and (off the map to the N) South Kensington. But there is the No 11 bus, used by everyone (knightly actors and ancient peers jostle on the stairs with German punk tourists and American bankers in Burberries) and the almost equally useful 19 and 22. And we have the testimony from 1834 of Thomas Carlyle that it took 'thirty-two minutes of my walking to Buckingham Gate' (just beside the palace). Carlyle lived in a house in **Cheyne Row**, for which he paid rent of £35 a year.

Chelsea's added bonus is the River Thames, which flows along its southern border.

Once an inspiration for the likes of Turner, Whistler and the Greaves brothers, it now excites estate agents, who are well aware that anything with a view of the river commands a premium. The Thames was a highway in Thomas More's time, and was used by a riverbus to Westminster and the City for a brief period in the 1980s. There are hopes that this may be revived soon, with boats from Chelsea Harbour and Cadogan Pier, next to Albert Bridge.

C   Large parts of Chelsea, including a big chunk of the eastern, **Sloane St**, side, are owned by the Cadogan Estate. The Cadogan, Sloane and Stanley families, all linked by marriage, gave their names to many streets and squares, and the estate is still a big factor in the property scene in Chelsea.

Sloane Square, Cadogans and Pont St

This is the neighbourhood bounded by **Pont St** and **Walton St** in the N, **King's Rd** and **Sloane Square** to the S, **Sloane Avenue** to the W, and the borough border in the E.

Unlike the rest of Chelsea's squares, **Sloane Square** is a busy shopping area and traffic junction with traffic converging from Knightsbridge, the King's Rd and Pimlico. The paved square has plane trees and a fountain.

Lining the square are hotels, pubs, Peter Jones department store, the Royal Court Theatre and Sloane Square tube station. Both store and theatre are undergoing expensive refits. Peter Jones is soaking up £50 million: it should be quite a shop. The Royal Court has been virtually rebuilt at a cost of £28 million and has gained an underground restaurant. Many of the commercial uses occupy lower floors of the 19th-century residential blocks overlooking the square. These flats are convenient, if noisy. **Lower Sloane St** and **Sloane Gardens** to the S are dominated by the tall red-brick and stone-gabled mansion blocks found in most of the E chunk of the neighbourhood. They tend to be on leases of 40–50 years. Prices for such leases start at over £250,000 for a 2-bed flat.

Heading N, **Sloane St** is the main thoroughfare to **Knightsbridge**. It is lined by a jumble of modern and period buildings, mainly flats, with concentrations of fashion shops and some embassies. This is the heart of what was once called Hans Town, a complete estate built in the 1780s–90s. The developer was the architect Henry Holland. The name Hans Town has died out and most of the area dates from after 1880, though some of Holland's houses survive in **Sloane St** and **Cadogan Place**. The name refers to Sir Hans Sloane, Lord of the Manor of Chelsea in the 18th century: his heiress granddaughter married Lord Cadogan.

The private square gardens of **Cadogan Place** (car parking beneath), spread along most of the E side of **Sloane St**, are overlooked by terraces of mixed-style period houses. An exclusive and opulent late-'80s development, Royal Court House, takes up the S side of the square (24 flats and maisonettes, from 1-bed to house-sized).

Tucked away behind **Cadogan Place** on the borders with Belgravia is quiet **Cadogan Lane** with its appealing mix of mews-type cottages and small houses.

West of **Sloane St**, in **Pont St**, are classic examples of the late-19th-century red-brick style which Osbert Lancaster dubbed 'Pont St Dutch'. These tall houses with stone detailing and splendid gables were derived from 17th-century Flemish and Dutch architecture. They form the predominant style in most of the area from **Cadogan Square** (a select address overlooking leafy gardens) W to Lennox Gardens, which curves round central gardens. Most of the houses have been split into flats and many are on short leases.

Some leaseholders are exercising their right to extend their leases but many are not able to do so as the flats are not their main home. When the Cadogan Estate grants new leases these can be for 125 years, but 20–25 years is more usual. Prices reflect leases: a 2-bed flat on a 105-year lease in **Pont St** was £450,000 last winter. There has been a lot of renovating of 2- and 3-bed flats in **Cadogan Place** in the last few years. Houses are still eagerly sought: a big house in **Cadogan Sq**, with attached mews cottage, was being returned to a single home from flats this spring. Hidden behind these tall buildings are occasional quiet mews (**Shafto Mews, Clabon Mews**).

West of **Lennox Gardens** between **Walton St** and **Cadogan St** lies an enclave of much sought-after smaller houses – some freehold, some leasehold. **Ovington St, Hasker St, First St** – the most popular group – and **Moore St, Halsey St** and **Rawlings St** all have similar terraces of attractive 2/3-storey plus basement period brick and stucco houses. A small house in First St was £750,000 last winter. Running between the two groups is **Milner St** with its ornate 5-storey stucco terraces.

Walton St, a narrow, busy little thoroughfare between South Kensington and Knightsbridge, is a mix of up-market shops/restaurants and stretches of pretty terraced houses. West of the cottage terraces are the Marlborough Buildings flats, the tall backs of which create a cul-de-sac in **Donne Place**, which has charming little mews-type houses at big prices. A London Underground line runs beneath some homes here which lowers prices. To the S, **Cadogan St** is a mix of late-Georgian terraced properties on the N side, with St Mary's Church, St Thomas More Secondary School, St Joseph's Catholic Primary School and the Guinness Trust Estate to the S. A smart 3-bed house in this street might be £950,000, against £800,000 in 1998.

More red-bricks and a pocket of 2/3-storey terraced Victoriana (**Coulson St, Lincoln St, Anderson St**) lie between **Cadogan St, King's Rd** and **Sloane Avenue**.

Royal Hospital

This area stretches between the **King's Rd** and the river, W of **Lower Sloane St/Chelsea Bridge Rd** and E of **Smith St/Tedworth Square/Tite St**.

The most coveted address in this neighbourhood is **St Leonard's Terrace**, which boasts some of the oldest houses in Chelsea (18th and early 19th century), which fetch £2–5 million (up from under £1 million in 1993). Most are listed, with leafy front gardens. But their main attraction, along with the grand mansions in **Durham Place**, is their view over Burton's Court (sports ground) and Wren's famous Royal Hospital. This imposing home for old soldiers forms the centrepiece of the area, with its extensive grounds (public tennis courts, handicapped children's adventure playground) and the neighbouring Ranelagh Gardens, stretching towards the river. Residents of **Embankment Gardens** have the best of both worlds with views of both the Royal Hospital and the Thames – the latter over the embankment traffic.

Dividing the neighbourhood in two is **Royal Hospital Rd**, lined at its W end by a mix of period and modern houses, flats, restaurants and shops. At its W end stands the National Army Museum and the drab modern concrete St Wilfrid's Convent. **Tite St**, running down to the river, boasts studio houses (ie homes with artists' studios, not today's 1-room flats) which recall Chelsea's bohemian past. Now their 2-storey windows stare glumly at the side of the convent. Nearer the river there are plans to replace two houses with a single vast house. Some of these big studio houses change hands at sobering prices. Across **Royal Hospital Rd**, the 1930s mock-Tudor houses in **Ormonde Gate** give way to tall red mansion blocks. The 1980s redevelopment of Cheyne House at the river end of **Royal Hospital Rd** resulted in 11 smart flats, most with splendid views along the river.

In **Tedworth Square** the new, ungainly brick development (1981) on the N side contrasts sharply with the handsome, traditional 4/5-storey terraces of brick and stucco/red-brick houses on the other three sides of the central gardens. These go for £1–2 million.

Head back along **St Leonard's Terrace** to reach **Royal Avenue**. This tree-lined, gravelled parade is flanked on both sides by gracious terraces of 19th-century houses, except for a post-war development at the **King's Rd** end. Its peace is guarded by the sensible barring of this end to traffic.

Just a few steps from the hustle and bustle of **King's Rd** stands **Wellington Square**, a fine group of 4-storey ornamental stucco Victorian houses. Despite its position, the terraces are set back from the road and the tall trees in the central garden give an air of seclusion and privacy. Beyond the brick and stucco terraces in **Walpole St** is the huge Whitelands House flats complex in **Cheltenham Terrace**, which dominates the terraces further along the W side of the street. Facing **Cheltenham Terrace** is the Duke of York's Headquarters, S of which lie blocks of flats and modern town-houses. The mansion flats in **Sloane Court** E and W share expanses of communal gardens: ground floor flats have direct access from graceful living-rooms. Negotiations are under way with the Ministry of Defence to sell off part of the Duke of York's Headquarters for development. A consortium involving the Cadogan Estate and a group of well-connected City-type territorial officers has outline permission for a plan which involves 30 flats, 34 shops and offices. Completion is due in 2002.

Just round the corner in **Chelsea Bridge Rd**, the sprawling Chelsea Barracks is up for sale. There are a number of listed buildings on the site, and local conservationists are keeping a beady eye on plans. Several developers have expressed interest but no details yet.

Old Chelsea

As its name suggests, this area takes in the oldest parts of Chelsea and contains the most expensive properties. It is bounded on the N by **King's Rd**, by **Cheyne Walk/Chelsea Embankment** in the S, **Beaufort St** to the W, and **Smith St/Tedworth Square/Tite St** to the E.

Beaufort St is a main road N–S leading to Battersea Bridge. Most of the W side is lined with the red-brick and stone-gabled blocks of Beaufort Mansions. More than 60 of the 242 tenants on the council's Thomas More Estate opposite bought their flats: resales do come up. More mansion block with shops beneath front the **King's Rd**.

Neighbouring **Paultons Square** is one of the best-preserved of its type in the borough. Here handsome terraces of the 1840s with decorative black iron balconies and railings are arranged on three sides of an elongated central garden square. Terraces of a later date continue down **Danvers St**.

Crosby Hall, on the corner of **Danvers St** and **Cheyne Walk**, is a Chelsea curiosity. It is a late-medieval building, which once stood in the City and was moved, stone by stone, to Chelsea in 1910. It became a student hall of residence, but is now the centrepiece of a vast neo-Tudor mansion, built by businessman Christopher Moran after years of planning battles.

Turn E along riverside **Cheyne Walk**, which is one of the most sought-after addresses in London with its fine 18th-century town-houses. Some are older still: a genuine 1686-built, but totally modernized, gem was £1.6 million in late 1998. Another 4-bed house was £1.9 million last winter. **Cheyne Walk** continues past Chelsea Old Church (much of which is new: it was badly bombed in 1941) into **Old Church St**, the oldest in Chelsea. It now contains a hotchpotch of residential and commercial buildings in period and modern styles. It also holds the Old Rectory (1725) with its 2¼-acre garden which sold in 1997 for £6 million. A builders' merchants' warehouse survived until 1997, but has now been replaced by Painters Yard: 19 flats and four houses.

Cut through the alleyway into **Justice Walk**, a delightful lane leading to the traditional heart and most exclusive part of Old Chelsea, **Lawrence St** and the **Cheynes**: quiet little streets with picturesque groups of houses and cottages, and fine brick and stucco terraces. Many houses here are dotted with blue plaques commemorating famous residents, from Rossetti and Isambard Kingdom Brunel to Thomas Carlyle.

Rossetti left many memorials: one is the clause in local Cadogan Estate laws, which bans the keeping of peacocks. These noisy fowl were among a domestic zoo assembled by the artist at Tudor House, where to quote a local 'he kept a lot of poets and other wild beasts'. Today's **Cheyne Walk** houses are among Chelsea's most expensive, and house few poets and no peacocks. The district has a real mix of houses of all sizes from cottages to splendid Cheyne Walk houses with studio and garden cottage.

The crossroads of **Cheyne Row/Upper Cheyne Row** and **Glebe Place** form one of the prettiest spots in the area. From here, **Glebe Place** follows a dog-leg course through to **King's Rd**. On the W side of the first leg is West House, a Queen Anne Revival studio house and one of the landmarks in the history of 19th-century British architecture. The W–E leg of the street has a mix of highly individual studio houses and the main N–S leg has purpose-built artists' studios (late 19th and early 20th century) facing a long terrace of 3-storey plus basement 19th-century terraced houses to the W (large rear gardens). One of the studios, smartened up to award-winning standards, was on the market last winter for £2 million despite having only 2 bedrooms. Between **Lawrence St** and **Oakley St** lie more red-brick mansion blocks.

Oakley St is another major through-route N–S, leading to elegant Albert Bridge, Cadogan Pier and Battersea Park, Chelsea's adopted open space. On the W corner of the bridge stands Pier House, a vast 1970s red-brick development stretching well up **Oakley St** to merge with older red-brick blocks. The E side of the street is lined with tall formal terraces of stucco, or stucco and brick houses (£1.15 million, typically). Behind **Oakley St** lie smaller homes in **Margaretta Terrace**. Car parking is the main problem and a garage can sell for between £60–80,000, while a garage can add more than £100,000 to the value of a house. This street leads to **Phene St** and horseshoe-shaped **Oakley Gardens**. Here 3-storey brick and stucco terraces in leafy streets with pretty gardens convey a village character.

At the top of **Chelsea Manor St** stands the Old Chelsea Town Hall, housing the library and sports centre. Behind the town hall is the prestigious Swan Court apartment block, stretching through to **Flood St**: nine storeys built around a central courtyard. In **Flood St**, 3-storey brick houses with tall hedges and established front gardens lead to more brick and stone mansion blocks near the river and a striking top-of-the-market town-house development in similar traditional style on the corner of **Alpha Place** (1986), which won a borough environmental award.

The scene changes again E of **Flood St** with a network of roads of smaller houses and cottages. Prettiest is **Christchurch St** with its 1830–50s artisan cottages, some with front gardens, which sell for up to £1.2 million. Christ Church stands at the W end of the street near the infants' school. Between the gaily painted cottages in **Smith Terrace** and the **King's Rd**, 50 3/4-bed freehold houses are set around a cobbled courtyard: award-winning **Charles II Place** was finished in the early '90s. The homes sell for £600–900,000 (1990: £545–750,000).

The SE corner of the neighbourhood is covered by the famous Chelsea Physic Garden, founded 1673. **Swan Walk** with its glorious, and rare, detached Georgian houses (£1.85–12 million on the rare occasions they change hands), and **Dilke St** with its rows of mews and studio houses, lead to **Paradise Walk**. The W side is lined by a terrace of brick 2-storey town-houses (Wates 1986). Phase II of the development is **Physic Place**, a mews of £625,000 cottages behind the completed houses, through an arch off **Royal Hospital Rd**, next to Ramsey's Restaurant.

West Chelsea

West Chelsea, until recently the area's poor relation, and beset by busy roads, has now come up in the world. It is bounded by **Fulham Rd** to the N, the Thames to the S, the West London railway line to the W, and **Edith Grove/Beaufort St** to the E.

The Chelsea Harbour development (see Fulham chapter) has helped push up prices in a previously neglected part of Chelsea. But its timing could hardly have been worse – no sooner was it finished than the recession of the early 1990s set in. Some of the buildings, particularly the ones near the **Lots Rd** power station, are looking a bit tired. The inhabitants also lost their battle to have the borough boundary line moved so that they were within the coveted Royal Borough of Kensington and Chelsea. They still pay their council tax to Hammersmith and Fulham.

The power station, which supplies power to London Underground, is due to close in 2001. Or not – it has survived several previous deadlines since 1990. The council has released a planning brief stating what it would like to see there – houses, offices, shops and a museum – but so far no developer has come forward to work with London Transport.

The old gasworks to the W (in Fulham) has just been bought by

Berkeley and work is imminent on 1,660 homes (see Fulham chapter). The scheme includes a new station on the West London line (Clapham Junction – Olympia). Without a tube link, the **Lots Rd** area is poorly served by public transport. Minibuses run from Chelsea Harbour to Earl's Court and Kensington.

L-shaped **Lots Rd** comprises mainly light industrial/commercial uses ranging from Bonhams auction rooms to a scrap metal yard in the W leg. The exception is a modern town-house development, **Poole's Lane**, walled off from the street on the E side.

Turning the corner, the S leg is dominated by the power station, with its tall chimneys and vast wall of arched glass windows. Next to it stands a refuse transfer station, water-pumping station and Chelsea Wharf – a complex of small businesses and light industrial studios. The residential part lies along the extreme E end of the leg. Most of the brick and painted houses overlook the public Cremorne Gardens fronting the Thames. This corner is well-known for its villagey feel.

Lying inside the L-shape is a network of small streets lined with terraces of predominantly brick and stucco houses in varying styles and conditions. Many have been converted into flats/maisonettes. **Burnaby St** is typical: a 3/4-bed Victorian terraced house might cost £450–600,000. Many homes are owned by the council and Notting Hill Housing Trust. A park, West Field, cuts across the northern corner of the neighbourhood behind the World's End Health Centre in **King's Rd**. South of the park in **Uverdale Rd** is the Ashburnham Community Centre, which also houses the Heatherley School of Fine Art. A handful of red-brick/stone mansion blocks are found in **Ashburnham Rd**. The N end of the street merges with **Cremorne Rd** to form the S end of the West London one-way traffic system, a constantly busy road. The heavy traffic runs N up **Gunter Grove**, S down **Edith Grove**. A mixed commercial and residential development stands on the old Chelsea College site between **Gunter Grove** and **Hortensia Rd**. There is planning permission to develop the 20-acre main college site, between **King's Rd** and **Fulham Rd**, as flats. The site, which includes the early-Georgian Stanley House, will have 291 homes, plus a one-acre public open space.

The one-way system creates a dividing line between the **Lots Rd** area and World's End, dominated by the dramatic World's End council estate with its handsome, angular red-brick towers. More than 100 tenants out of the 700-plus on the estate have bought their homes. World's End Place, a landscaped piazza facing **King's Rd**, leads into the estate. Standing within the piazza are the Chelsea Centre, a purpose-built community centre for the area (adult education classes), and Ashburnham Primary School. St John's Church is part of the flats complex. East of the estate, behind the 1950s Cremorne parade of shops, lie modern low-rise council flats, some now coming up for sale by former tenants who bought their homes.

Across **Milman's St** on the S-bend in **King's Rd** stands 355 King's Rd, an ex-council block which has been rehabilitated and converted into 50 luxury apartments. Nearby on the corner of **Milman's St** is Berkeley's 'the Quant Building' with a dozen 1-, 2- and 3-bed flats. Only the latter were left in December at £645,000-plus.

At the S end of the street, the houseboat colony moored on the river at **Cheyne Walk** comes into view. Houseboats offer a cheaper way of securing a smart Chelsea address, and are used as homes and business premises.

Elm Park/North Stanley

This prime residential neighbourhood between the **Fulham Rd** and **King's Rd** to the W of **Sydney St** includes some of the choicest streets and best squares in Chelsea. It also boasts some of the world's top specialist hospitals, such as the Brompton and the Royal Marsden, as well as Chelsea's general hospital – the new Chelsea and Westminster. Part of the Brompton, on the N side of **Fulham Rd** at the corner of **Foulis Terrace**, is being converted into luxury flats (see South Kensington).

Sydney St, the broad N–S link between South Kensington and **King's Rd**, has dignified terraces, some listed, at its N end. Opposite St Luke's Church is the National Heart and Chest Hospital. South of **Britten St** sits the Chelsea Gardener gardening centre and Chelsea Farmers' Market – an off-street colony of smart food, arts and crafts shops and outdoor cafés.

Through the back of the market, fronting **King's Rd**, is **Dovehouse Green**. It backs on to the council's Thamesbrook home for the elderly, adjoining the Heart and Chest Hospital. The Brompton Hospital and Royal Marsden cancer hospital stand each side of **Dovehouse St**, stretching through to **Fulham Rd** (main entrances).

Tucked in behind the Marsden is **Chelsea Square**, one of the area's most prestigious addresses, with 3-storey 1930s brick houses overlooking a tree-lined garden square. A new, detached and very large 7-bed house here was on the market last winter for £5.75 million. The E leg of the square becomes **Manresa Rd**, where houses have price tags £900,000 up to £1.2 million. The buildings on the corner of **Manresa Rd** and **King's Rd** are to be redeveloped as flats. The SW leg leads into **Carlyle Square**, the jewel in the neighbourhood's crown. The beautiful mid-19th-century brick and creamy stucco houses overlooking the square gardens change hands for £1.5–2 million. The square is unique in that it is blocked off from the traffic in the **King's Rd** by a barrier of railings, trees and shrubs.

Turn W into **Old Church St**, a main through-route between **Fulham Rd** and the **King's Rd**, and head N to **Queen's Elm Square**, where a group of mock-Tudor houses sit in a semi-circle off the street. The famous Queen's Elm pub, on the corner with **Fulham Rd**, haunt of writers and artists, is no more. Their surviving watering hole, the Chelsea Arts Club, is a short walk S along **Old Church St**.

Between here and **Beaufort St** many of the big houses have been converted into flats. **Beaufort St** and **Elm Park Rd** are the main areas of conversions. The more desirable **Vale**, **Mulberry Walk** and **Mallord St** form a uniform colony of houses and purpose-built flats, developed in the early part of the 20th century for artists, architects, musicians and writers of modest means.

At the S end of **Beaufort St** are the two parts of **Chelsea Park Gardens**, a development of 1920/30s 3-storey brick suburban villas. These much sought-after houses stand well back from the road on the E side behind a screen of trees and gardens. West side ones have leafy front gardens and the central section backs on to a communal garden. Some were once artists' studios: blue commemorative plaques dot the brick walls. The houses are worth as much as their owners' paintings: £1.75 million was asked for Sir Alfred Munnings' former home in early 1999.

Park Walk is dominated by the huge **Elm Park Mansions**, unique in the area in that the freehold is owned by the residents. The mansions have undergone major repairs and renovation in the last few years: current prices are around £250,000 for a 1-bed and £350,000 for a 2-bed. At the bottom of **Park Walk** is Park Walk Primary School, opposite the Man in the Moon pub on the **King's Rd** S-bend.

Between **Park Walk** and **Edith Grove** can be found a popular residential area of big mid-Victorian family houses with gardens (**Limerston St**, **Gertrude St**, **Hobury St**, **Shalcomb St** and **Langton St**). Surprisingly uniform terraces of mostly 4-storey brick and stucco houses.

Distance from the underground used to be thought a disadvantage of this quarter, but today estate agents say this does not matter. Presumably residents drive everywhere. And taxis are thick along both King's and Fulham Roads.

Chelsea Green/St Luke's

From **Sydney St** eastwards to **Sloane Avenue**, this largely residential neighbourhood N of **King's Rd** is characterized by big 1890s flats blocks to the N and a mix of bijou 'dolls house' pastel-painted cottages and 1930s brick houses S of **Cale St/Elystan Place**.

Sloane Avenue, a main N–S through-route between Chelsea and South Kensington, is lined by sprawling flats blocks like Nell Gwynn House (E), Cranmer Court and Chelsea Cloisters (W). A 'bed-sit' in the former was £148,000 last winter. The latter has been refurbished and converted into luxury pied-à-terre apartments with back-up business services. **Draycott Avenue**, which runs parallel to **Sloane Avenue**, is similar. The buildings are smaller and the street somewhat quieter. Many conversions are under way. A studio on **Draycott Place** was £135,000 last year.

Around the corner in **Lucan Place** (across the road from Chelsea police station) stands a 1989 Regalian development, Crown Lodge, set in an acre of landscaped gardens with fountains, waterfalls and pergolas. The building was once housing for policemen: now penthouses top a million. Covering the whole block, bounded on the other three sides by **Petyward**, **Elystan St** (the entrance) and **Ixworth Place**, it contains 130 1/3-bed flats with a Romanesque-style swimming pool and gymnasium in the basement. A further block of 24 flats in **Petyward** is called Bryon Court. Across **Elystan St**, the NW corner of the neighbourhood is dominated by rented flats: the Sutton Dwellings and Samuel Lewis Trust Buildings, with the exception of narrow lanes of houses in **Pond Place** and **Bury Walk**.

At the S end of **Elystan St** at its junction with **Elystan Place** and **Cale St** lies **Chelsea Green**, with a pleasant village green atmosphere. An Elystan Place 2-bed cottage was £845,000 last winter. The tiny green is encircled by up-market food shops, restaurants, art galleries and a general store, among others. On the edge of the green between **Whiteheads Grove** and **Sprimont Place** is the ivy-clad **Gateways** – 1930s brick houses, laid out cloister-style around fountain courtyards. They have covetable garages: a 4-bed house with one was on the market last winter for £1.4 million.

South of the green lies a series of much-favoured small-scale streets – **Bywater St**, **Markham St** and **Godfrey St** in particular – with their colourfully painted 19th-century 3-storey houses, and around the corner **Burnsall St** is extremely striking with its painted, gabled houses.

Caught up between them is **Markham Square**, one of the six formal squares facing the **King's Rd**. It is laid out in terraces of 3-storey plus basement brick and stucco houses with black iron railings. The Square gardens have won awards.

In contrast are the 1930s brick houses in **Astell St** and **Jubilee Place** with their leafy front gardens. Different again is **St Luke's St**, lined with tidy terraces of 2-storey plus basement brick and stucco houses.

The terraces on the W side back on to the public **St Luke's Gardens**, the leafy 'lungs' of the area. They were once a graveyard for St Luke's Church, a 19th-century Grade I listed building fronting **Sydney St**. North of the church lies St Luke's public playground.

Transport — Tubes: Sloane Sq (zone 1, District, Circle), South Kensington (zone 1, District, Circle, Piccadilly). From Sloane Sq: Oxford Circus 15 min (1 change), City 20 min, Heathrow 45 min (1 change).

Convenient for — West End, Knightsbridge, Victoria & Waterloo stations, Thames, M4 to West. Miles from centre: 2.

Schools — Local Authority: St Thomas More. Private: More House School. Many good prep schools. See also neighbouring areas.

SALES

Flats	S	1B	2B	3B	4B	5B
Average prices	110–185	200–300+	300–500	500–800	700–1 M+	1 M→

Houses	2B	3B	4B	5B	6/7B	8B
Average prices	350–1 M	550–1.5 M	650–1.6 M	1.2–4 M	1.5–5 M	2–6 M+

RENTAL

Flats	S	1B	2B	3B	4B	5B
Average prices	175–300	350–500	375–760	600–1300+	7500–3000	1000–6000

Houses	2B	3B	4B	5B	6/7B	8B
Average prices	500–950	750–1200	1000–1800	1500–2500	4000–6000	—

The properties — Lovely Georgian/early Victorian homes in garden squares, small streets of cottages and mews are the archetypal Chelsea properties. Also, N of King's Rd/Sloane Square, red-brick, Dutch-gabled mansion flats. Luxury flats schemes will soon replace King's College, part of the Duke of York's HQ and Barracks.

The market — Buyers are now mostly City-based and prosperous: the arty, up-market locals increasingly displaced by international bankers. Foreign buyers are Europeans and Americans rather than Far East. Chelsea's status and image ensure a lively market even in recessions, agents aver. Exceptional properties go well over the mainstream averages above. Local searches: 10 working days.

Among those estate agents active in this area are:
- Jackson-Stops & Staff
- Aylesfords
- John D Wood & Co
- Knight Frank
- Marsh & Parsons
- Farley & Co*
- Farrar & Co
- Foxtons*
- FPDSavills
- Friend & Falcke *
- Winkworth *
- Hamptons
- Lane Fox
- Strutt & Parker*
- De Groot Collis
- Egerton
- Russell Simpson
- Hobart Slater
- Beaney Pearce *
- Humberts
- Douglas & Gordon
- W A Ellis *
- Gascoigne Pees
- Cluttons Daniel Smith
- Read Cunningham

* further details: see advertisers' index on p671

CHISWICK

Map ref: p73 (5K)
Postal districts: W4
Boroughs: Hounslow (Lab)
Council tax: Band D £860
Conservation areas: Include
  Grove Park, Chiswick Mall,
  Strand-on-the-Green
Parking: Controlled along
  High Rd and streets
  towards Hammersmith

Leafy Chiswick, sitting snugly (and smugly) above its green open spaces in a protecting loop of the Thames, is nevertheless a community divided by the A4 **Great West Rd**. Although the twain meet frequently there is a slight difference of orientation between those who live between the A4 and the river and those who dwell on the other, northern, side. The riverside community uses South West Trains and looks as much towards Richmond and Sheen for its shopping, while the other half has easier access to District line tubes and to **Chiswick High Rd** – as its name suggests, the area's high street.

But the A4 is boon as much as bane. Lying on the most direct route out of London saves Chiswick from being a mere suburban backwater: dwellers here can live in its leafy, sleepy streets and yet get to Heathrow Airport in – theoretically – as little as 20 minutes.

Old Chiswick began as a riverside village whose traces can still be seen in **Church St**, where St Nicolas Parish Church has parts dating back to the 15th century. Glorious Georgian (some, behind rebuilt facades, are considerably earlier) homes front the Thames here, and at Strand-on-the-Green – the corresponding hamlet at the Kew end of the river loop. Today's Chiswick covers everything between the two, subsuming another old village site, Turnham Green, which lay along **Chiswick High Rd**. This name is less and less heard, though there is a tiny pocket-handkerchief green still, and a tube station on the District line. Across the underground's tracks lie Acton Green and, alongside it, a different world: the splendid

C

select little enclave of London's first garden suburb, Bedford Park (which chapter see).

An immediate attraction is the greenery; apart from the river and wide, open spaces of Dukes Meadows, many parts of Chiswick have their own little green, while the deer-filled acres of Richmond Park, and Kew's famous botanical gardens, are an easy drive away. Note, too, Ravenscourt Park on the Hammersmith borders: prized by mothers (1 o'clock club, adventure playground, etc). The resultant atmosphere is a combination of busy city and green suburb – even the **High Rd** is tree-lined and runs by Turnham Green. This is the main shopping street – although there are many little local parades of shops scattered all round the area – with a large Sainsbury's (enormous car park; open all hours) and token-sized multiples including a mainly food-purveying Marks & Spencer. **Turnham Green Terrace** and **Devonshire Rd** have a range of up-market specialist shops, with many late hours to suit working customers. There's an ever-growing number of bars and cafés, and restaurants from the everyday to the starry. Good transport to the City or West End with Heathrow just down the M4 complete the list of pluses; the E side uses Stamford Brook and Turnham Green tube stations while the W has Chiswick Park and Gunnersbury, the latter being both tube and rail station. Those S of the A4 use Chiswick rail station.

Although a few earlier houses survive, Chiswick really began growing in the mid-19th century, the bulk of development happening between then and World War II. The result is a variety of choice from tiny early-Victorian cottages to huge Edwardian properties, from inter-war semis and vast mansion blocks to the odd infill of modern town-houses. Generally, the more recent the property the tinier it is likely to be – even 1960s town-houses are positively roomy compared with the toy boxes of the '80s. Where this rule does not hold good (eg luxurious riverside developments), expect to pay dearly for the space.

Some of the larger houses, especially in the western half and to the N of the **High Rd**, have been converted to flats. Established locals prefer the spaciousness of older houses and mansion flats, for which they are prepared to put up with lack of garage and consequent parking problems – not helped by 'overspill' parking thanks to the controlled parking zone (E from the Hammersmith border to **Turnham Green Terrace** and **Chiswick Lane North**, down to the A4), in addition to the pay-and-display zones around **Chiswick High Rd**. (The futuristic 26-storey office tower, 'The Pinnacle', planned for the Chiswick Roundabout at the Strand-on-the-Green end of Chiswick, will mean another controlled zone to cover all streets within 15 minutes' walk.)

Chiswick prices (which for the best homes can be high even by London standards) reflect the wide range of homes as well as their location. The biggest and most expensive houses are riverside ones – foremost among them those on **Chiswick Mall** (see p 213), but Grove Park conservation area, streets surrounding the Chiswick House conservation area, and roads between the **High Rd** and A4, all contain good-sized houses with generous gardens. Despite locals' preference for period homes, the most recent Thames-side developments are of a level of style and quality to command premium prices – very likely paid by 'outsiders'.

Higher density housing – lots of flats, more conversions and rentals – are clustered round Turnham Green and Gunnersbury stations, along with the area by the Hogarth Roundabout and flyover. Council-built estates are small, scattered and low-rise, with a high percentage of owner-occupiers – and thus, nowadays, sales. The main industrial area is a small estate by Gunnersbury, but this is separated from the bulk of the residential sector by the railway and **High Rd**. Office development is confined to the **High Rd** environs, but controversial plans to turn the old Chiswick bus depot into a 1.5 million sq ft business park are going ahead after several years on the back burner during the early '90s recession. In general terms, any home too close to the railway, A4 or **Great Chertsey Rd** loses a little value because of noise and dirt from traffic. Certain parts of Chiswick are also prone to aircraft noise (the local paper even lists flight-path schedules).

Chiswick has attracted artists of all types ever since Hogarth bought a house (delightful, still standing and open to the public) in 1749, along with leading businessmen. The current mixture remains much the same; it is popular with media people, City types, well-heeled executives, actors and professionals, especially architects. Young people try to gain a foothold near the tubes, marry and move southwards into a flat or small house then progress to a larger house with a garden. They contribute to various cultural and social activities and patronize the Riverside Studios and Lyric Theatre in Hammersmith, the Watermans Arts Centre, Brentford, local pub theatres such as the Tabard, or the almost professional Questors Theatre in Ealing. They play hard at the Hogarth Health Club or Riverside Club – both private – or Fountains Leisure Centre, Brentford, and are furious that there is doubt over the future of the local swimming pool. It is a predominantly middle-class family district, where it still feels safe on the streets at night. Once people have found Chiswick, they tend to stay.

To begin, then, in the heart of Chiswick: just S of the **High Rd** lies the Glebe Estate (between **Duke** and **Devonshire Rds**), tiny 2- and 3-bed workmen's cottages now trendified into fashionable residences: prices start c. £190–195,000; double that for the largest. Best to have a tiny car to match your tiny home here. There are other pockets of bijou homes, such as those round Chiswick Common, N of the High Rd, and many solid houses built just before and after World War I in neighbourhoods such as Stamford Brook on the Hammersmith borders – this corner is set to see new homes when Queen Charlotte's Hospital, just across that border, moves sites (see Hammersmith chapter). One of the top purpose-built flats blocks is the 1930s Watchfield Court, a complex at the Turnham Green end of **Sutton Court Rd** that is large enough to show up on maps. Running S from the High Rd, **Netheravon Rd N**, **Airedale Avenue** and **Homefield Rd** are desirable streets with larger houses, close to transport and Hammersmith: look here for 4-, 5- and 6-bed homes at prices that can range from £445–770,000. Right on the Chiswick/Hammersmith borders, **British Grove** sprouted a clutch of 'executive homes' in 1997. Westwards, down towards the Gunnersbury station end of the area, mansion blocks and houses of varying sizes, styles and periods are to be found.

Adding to the mix are conversions of industrial or commercial sites and buildings (a trend that caught on quite early here, where developers gaze in frustration at the rolling – and protected – green acres between A4 and river). Bovis Homes fashioned 'Devonhurst Place' from a splendid Victorian warehouse in the 1980s, and 51 flats surround a spectacular central atrium in what was the Army and Navy depot in **Heathfield Terrace**, S of Turnham Green. Another six penthouses perch above offices on the site. Porterage, secure parking and communal roof terrace; 2-beds fetch c. £300–350,000. On the Chiswick/Acton Green borders, near Chiswick Park tube, Chiswick Green Studios is another example of industrial space turned into homes – this time that most trendy of styles, loft apartments. These have proved popular, both to buy or rent; apart from high ceilings and galleries, you're buying basement parking, porter and a 'gym facility'. Resales of penthouses under the curving roofline were topping £1 million last winter, and flats here are commanding high rents.

Barratt are adding rather more modest flats on **Chiswick High Rd** itself: around 100 2- and 3-beds (underground parking; two penthouses), and another 100 flats behind Sainsbury's. Prices from £200,000.

Grove Park

Grove Park is quintessentially Chiswick, with its wide, tree-lined roads (some specimens dating back to the original Grove House gardens) and range of properties. It takes its name from Grove House, in whose grounds the Duke of Devonshire built Chiswick's first large housing estate as a high-class area for wealthy merchants. The original estate was roughly bounded by the river, the **Great Chertsey Rd**, which leads up from Chiswick Bridge, the N London rail line, Silverlink, which marks the start of **Strand-on-the-Green**, and the Waterloo line. Estate agents today are insistent that Grove Park extends north of its railway and up to the A4. In terms of house style and price this is not unreasonable.

Some of the earliest houses are in **Grove Park Rd**; Grove House itself stood, until the 1920s, on the site of **Kinnaird Avenue**. Over the years further tracts were developed – and redeveloped in some cases, as war damage and demolition of bigger houses and gardens followed. Grove Park's leafy streets are particularly rich in Victorian architecture, from mid-19th-century terraces to Gothic, and from red-brick with hanging tiles to later brick and creamy stucco terraces. A 4-bed, double-fronted Edwardian example with river views at the foot of **Grove Park Rd** was £450,000 this spring. The last big chunk of the estate was developed between the wars with roomy semis, detached houses and the odd bungalow, while since the war there have been various small estates of town-houses and even the occasional striking example of modern brick and glass architecture. Flat-hunters can choose between prestigious, 1930s balconied Hartington Court, right on the river, or modern small-scale blocks. There are virtually no conversions of bigger houses into smaller units.

Some of the best houses are in **Hartington Rd**, despite its busy rush

Grove Park has long been popular for its solid, Gothic-looking late-Victorian villas. As this detail shows, they were designed as a piece, with even the front gate in style with the rest of the house. Note, too, the stone window surrounds, the stone detailing on the corners and the ecclesiastical tone conveyed by the perforation in the balcony over the bay window.

hour traffic, with a few having huge gardens which sweep down to the river. Between **Hartington Rd** and the river, too, are three earlier examples of the modern Thames-side developments:

Chiswick Quay: this a 1970s development of 3- to 6-bedroom town-houses round a marina, was designed to appeal to boat owners, although tidal variations do not allow for spur-of-the-moment sailings. A wide spread of prices, depending on size and whether it includes a river view. Despite their size these homes are unsuited to younger children since lack of garden and the sheer sides of the marina make playing near the water highly dangerous.

Chiswick Staithe: the word 'staithe' meant embankment, an appropriate name for these 69 3- and 4-bedroom houses, built in 1964 around a landscaped, traffic-free centre facing the Thames. These come with stringent regulations concerning activities and development. The estate attracts couples (often both working), with older children, or retired couples. A spacious 4-bed example with 29ft living-room was £465,000 last winter.

Thames Village: the peace of this low-density estate is much appreciated by its mainly retired residents. Built in 1955, the 2-bed maisonettes (a riverside example, £272,500; inland, £205,000) are set amid immaculate lawns and flower beds. The residents' association holds the freehold, and strict covenants apply here.

Grove Park commuters use Chiswick station to reach Waterloo and the City; they may walk to Chiswick Park or Turnham Green tubes (District); some even commute outwards to satellite towns in the Thames Valley. Whatever their choice they need a car, or at least the local hoppa buses, to cross the A4 divide for school runs and shopping.

Streets around Chiswick House, once the home of the Dukes of Devonshire, are spacious turn-of-the-century dwellings, often with gardens to match. **Park Rd** is generally considered one of the best addresses in Chiswick, while **Staveley Rd** is famous for its avenue of flowering cherries. The site of a former school between **Staveley Rd** and **Burlington Lane** now holds flats and houses (all with parking space or garages) built around courts and crescents named, rather tenuously, after former famous Chiswickites: **Fitzroy Crescent, Huntingdon Gardens, Crofton Avenue**. The Duke began selling off this part of his estate in 1884, but the charming little neo-Palladian Chiswick House remains in its 66-acre garden, open to the public now and a haven for urban wildlife such as foxes, squirrels and 20 different types of bird. Extra green space in the form of school grounds, allotments and playing-fields makes it a particularly low-density neighbourhood.

Much to the satisfaction of its predominantly owner-occupier residents, this whole district N of the Waterloo line between **Sutton Court Rd**, the A4 and the **Great Chertsey Rd/Burlington Lane**, was declared a conservation area in 1977. In **Wolseley Gardens** and **Elmwood Rd**, the streets closest to the A4, 5-bed houses were £450,000 and £510,000 respectively at the turn of the year, while another, just round the corner in **Sutton Lane South** (which leads into **Fauconberg Rd**, with the local shops) merited £595,000. This area also includes a little corner between the Chiswick House grounds and the Hogarth Roundabout – **Paxton Rd, Sutherland Rd** and **Short Rd** – of early Victorian cottage terraces once inhabited by the Chiswick House gardeners and Reckitt & Coleman employees: a 2-bed example, £225,000.

Chiswick Mall/Old Chiswick

This riverside corner, where Chiswick began, is a paradox: it has remained a hidden time capsule, cut off and somehow protected by the **Great West Rd**. Winding **Church St**, with its pretty houses and parish church, spans the centuries: the Hogarth Roundabout is at one end, the glorious Georgiana of **Chiswick Mall** looks tranquilly out over the Thames at the other.

There is still very much a village feel to this tiny strip. Houses range from little add-on cottages to magnificent brick or stuccoed residences in a charming jumble of periods and styles facing on to the river. The façades indicate every century from the 17th to the 20th: some, however, are even older than they look, having been modernized 200 years or so ago.

Despite the apparent dangers of water – not to mention the greedy eyes of developers – this remains a predominantly family area where neighbours know each other and children play together. Several houses have vast gardens behind, while others have a garden patch across the road bordering the river; virtually none have been converted into flats. Usually owned by big families and passed, if possible, down to the next generation, if these plum properties do appear on the market they are priced in the millions (a smaller, 3-bedroomed Regency example, which has one of the riverside strips, plus more private rear garden and garage, at £950,000).

The list of residents, past and present, is a roll-call of aristocratic, artistic and big-business names. Their community spirit is fostered by the shared fear of flooding: the river comes right over the road and there is a neighbourhood warning system so that cars are not marooned. Despite invasions from summer visitors strolling down the historic Mall, residents still love their pretty riverside pubs – not to mention the river life which passes their windows.

There have been three smallish modern developments, with houses of up to four bedrooms: **Eyot Green**, built in 1960 round a green just off the Mall; **Millers Court**, a 1970s square leading directly to it; and **Chiswick Wharf**, 1980s brick town-houses facing the river on the W side of **Church St**.

Southwards from here, Chiswick's most concentrated (and smartest) clutch of 1990s developments have transformed the once industrial stretch of riverside along **Pumping Station Rd**. A peaceful corner: the road stops short of **Church St**, allowing access to the ancient village, but only by foot – and behind the inland side lies the church's cemetery.

Electric gates (albeit handsome ones) guard the landward privacy of Regency Quay, where McAlpine has confused its monarchs and named one road **Gwynne Close**. The riverside path is open to all, however. The long sweep of the Corney Reach scheme, by contrast, invites the public in, via its attractive central piazza, to a splendid bit of planning gain: a partnership with the developers, Persimmon, has resulted in a new pier that anyone is welcome to use. The Chiswick Pier Trust runs the pier from its offices here. Corney Reach also boasts a bar/restaurant, which has good views over the river.

Even smarter homes (sweeping crescents, distinctive gables, decorative ironwork) at Barratt's Royal Thames Crescent, mark the southern end of **Pumping Station Rd**.

A pleasing aspect of these Thames-side schemes is their mix of homes – from small flats to young mansions – and prices: 2-bed flats, £210–260,000; with garden £287,000; 6-bed, 4-bath balconied town-house with garage and on river, £780,000.

Strand-on-the-Green

At the other, Kew, end of Chiswick is **Strand-on-the Green**, another ancient riverside village mirroring **Chiswick Mall** in the E. Where fishermen once caught eels and boatyards and breweries plied their trade, now tourists throng the popular towpath pubs. A working riverside village up to a generation ago, though light industry has all but disappeared this is still a deliberately unpretentious community. Here, too, many houses are older than they look; the village dates back to the 15th century. The medley of styles ranges from quite grand to a row of Arts and Crafts cottages, while little passages between the houses down to the towpath add to the informality. Artists (the most famous was Zoffany) were often attracted to the area and some houses have studios at the back. Many desirable residences have humble origins, having once been shops, pubs, a post office or tea house. Gardens tend to be small. It is a conservation area, with many listed buildings along the river frontage. Flats are rare; the main inhabitants are families who stay for years, watching their children grow up messing around with boats on the river, which is the area's main hobby and focus. A riverside address with charming, but slightly less large and grand homes than **Chiswick Mall**. That being said, Georgian gems come in the million-pound bracket. Cheapest way to enjoy the river: a houseboat. A 1920s barge, 92ft long and complete with 4 cabins and conservatory, near Kew Bridge was £190,000 last winter.

Residents use Kew Bridge Waterloo line or take a 10 min walk under the **Great West Rd** for **Chiswick High Rd** buses, or Gunnersbury on the District line tube and the N London line, Silverlink. Like other inhabitants on this side of Chiswick most find a car a necessity, though happily the bus service is good. Most riverside houses have garaging at the back since, unlike the Mall, which has a proper road running alongside the river, they only have a towpath. Flooding is, however, not often a problem here since the advent of the Thames Barrier. Parking is difficult at the beginning and end of the school day as mothers sweep up in the car to collect their offspring from school (Strand-on-the-Green Primary has a reputation which extends beyond the immediate district), while **Thames Rd** is a dangerously busy rat-run. Unlike most of Chiswick they are free of aircraft noise (the threatened Terminal 5 might change this . . .), although Kew Bridge produces a background drone. The only other drawbacks seem to be bums and beermugs on their window sills during the summer.

Since homes still often pass to the next generation (anyone with less than 10 years' residence is considered a newcomer), any new developments that can be sneaked in are popular; Barratts have a couple of schemes here: they are converting an office block, Kew Bridge House on the bridge approach, into apartments with floor-to-ceiling windows, completing July this year: 2-beds, £200–330,000; higher floors get river views – including the penthouses which range from £625–875,000. In contrast, Duke's Place is a small-scale scheme of a dozen £200,000-plus 2-bed flats with parking due this year in **Chiswick Village**, tucked away in the backwater of little streets just N of the rail-line. 'Quiet' might be too strong a word, given the tracks and the A4/M4 close by, but peaceful this cut-off corner is, and Gunnersbury tube/trains are handy. In the same corner, St James's Court, 3- and 4-bed town-houses, appeared last year in **Brooks Rd**. Nearer the river, six more mews-style town-houses will complete this summer on the site of the old Worth perfume factory in busy **Thames Rd**. Other caches of modern homes were squeezed in in the late-'80s: 61 studio, 1- and 2-bedroom flats in **Wellesley Rd**, the tiny houses and flats of **Oliver Close**, off Thames Rd, and the half-million pound houses of **Magnolia Wharf**. The roads behind were developed in late-Victorian red-brick; 3-bed working-class homes that now find buyers in young middle-class families.

C

Transport Tubes: Turnham Green (zone 2, District, restricted service Piccadilly); Stamford Brook (zone 2, District); Chiswick Park, Gunnersbury (zone 3, District). From Turnham Green: Oxford Circus 30 min (1 change), City 30 min, Heathrow 25 min (1 change). Trains: Chiswick station to Waterloo 20 min; Gunnersbury station for Silverlink/North London line.

Convenient for Heathrow and M4. Kew Gardens. Miles from centre: 6.

Schools Hounslow Education Authority: Chiswick Community School. Private: St Paul's (g), Godolphin & Latymer (g), Latymer (b), Arts Educational School.

SALES

Flats	S	1B	2B	3B	4B	5B
Average prices	80–110	120–180	170–300	250–300	—	—
Houses	2B	3B	4B	5B	6/7B	8B
Average prices	260–330	330–480	350–500+	400–800	600–1.3 M+	2.3 M

RENTAL

Flats	S	1B	2B	3B	4B	5B
Average prices	150–250	150–300	200–500+	330–600	695–1500	—
Houses	2B	3B	4B	5B	6/7B	8B
Average prices	240–500	330–600	460–1350	800–1600	—	—

The properties Solid family homes, mainly Victorian/Edwardian (though larger ones scarce); some smaller terraces; also popular '30s mansion blocks. Riverside has superb Georgian buildings, plus cottages and new developments, some enviable.

The market Riverside and Grove Park are smart, with high prices for family homes; best period riverside ones rarely for sale (and in the million-pound bracket). New developments too are pricey. The peaceful streets inland popular with families. Younger people moving in: they cluster near underground. Local searches: 1 day.

Among those estate agents active in this area are:
- Barnard Marcus
- Foxtons *
- Winkworth *
- Haart
- John Spencer
- Whitman & Co
- Quintons
- Chestertons
- Northfields *
- Bushells
- Faron Sutaria
- Townsend Tyser Greenwood
- Finlay Brewer *
- Lauristons
- Fletcher Estates
- Priory Management *
- Harrison Management

further details: see advertisers' index on p671

CITY AND FRINGES

Map ref: p144 (6D) or p62 (5D)
Postal districts: EC1, EC2, EC3, EC4
Boroughs: City of London, Tower
   Hamlets (Lab), Hackney (Lab)
Council tax: Band D Hackney: £789,
   Tower Hamlets: £674
Conservation areas: Several – check
   with corporation/council
Parking: Residents/meters/clamps

More homes were being built or converted in the City last winter than in neighbouring Clerkenwell. This turnaround is mostly due to Clerkenwell's available space being used up. But the City's revival as a place to live, not just work, is still remarkable. This year you can buy a home in **Monument St**, in **Fleet St**, in **Queen St** – or you could if an Irish investor hadn't bought the whole block.

Extend your search across all four EC postcodes and many more opportunities appear within the Clerkenwell area (which has its own chapter) and the area up round **Old St** now dubbed the 'Shoreditch Triangle'. (You know that an area has happened once the agents start inventing names for it.) Go East into E1 and E2 – the City's fringe – and there are yet more, with a further cluster of homes in hitherto unpromising Hoxton, just across in N1.

Once again, after a century, it is possible to live in the City. Most homes are in fringe areas such as Spitalfields and Smithfield, but quite a few are in the heart of the financial district. Despite the jostling presence of 500 foreign banks and myriad other companies and institutions, the urge to fill every corner with offices and dealing floors has gone. Docklands has taken some of the pressure, some sectors have moved out wholesale – the press, for instance, has deserted **Fleet St** – and there is space for homes as well as jobs.

The City's sleeping population reached a low in 1970 of about 4,500 people, compared to 30,000 at the start of the century. Around 1995 the numbers began to seriously increase. This was in part due to a boundary change which brought the Golden Lane council estate into the City. It was also due to the building of new homes and the conversion of existing buildings. It is estimated that the figure is now close

C

to 7,000, compared to a workforce of about 270,000. There could be 3,000 more homes in the City by 2006: most resulting from conversion of offices or industrial buildings, some new, and a few (as has already happened) old houses reverting after a century as offices. The only thing to slow this trend is the rise in office rents, which during 1999 started to choke off the supply of buildings for conversion to homes.

Between 1995 and the end of 1999, 1,500 homes were completed in the City. Last winter, some 600 more were under construction, with permission for several hundred more. Just over half the City's homes are owner-occupied – and a surprising nine per cent is 'tied' to specific jobs – caretakers and the like.

The 'Square Mile' of the City of London is enclosed by **Commercial St** in the E, **Old St** in the N, **Chancery Lane** in the W and the River Thames. Here we deal with the Square Mile and its fringe areas to E, N and W. The City retains its place as one of the top three global finance centres, and the banks' towers loom over the narrow streets, unchanged in their alignment since medieval days. Despite its image, the City contains scruffy streets as well as rich ones. Until the 1980s, industries – printing and graphics, leather, metal-working, textiles – dominated tracts on the edge. These fringe areas still also house poorer, sometimes deprived, groups.

Living in the City is now possible. But is it pleasant? Go and see. If you have not visited the Square Mile for a few years it could surprise you. The 'ring of steel' street closures designed to ward off terrorists have cut traffic by 30 per cent (and air pollution by 15 per cent). Such was the popularity of this scheme that the 1997 extension to take in St Paul's, parts of Barbican, Smithfield and the Old Bailey has been made permanent. Shops, restaurants and bars have opened – even multiples like Tesco Metro and Marks & Spencer, which now has three City stores. Lion Plaza, in **Old Broad St**, is a new scheme with shops and offices. Demand for retail space in the City doubled between 1995 and 1998. And these days, amenities open at weekends – they used to close at 5pm on Friday.

Transport is excellent during the week, and all other parts of London are within easy reach. Close by is the world-renowned Barbican Arts Centre, and the 'village' atmosphere of the City is prized by all its residents. The City is unique in that its local council, the City of London Corporation, is entirely independent and non-political – which contributes greatly to the area's feeling of detachment from the rest of London. There are a few downsides to living here: noise from traffic, lack of open space, few local services such as doctors and schools, cramped and overlooked homes, lack of daylight in some, and extremely limited parking space.

The swing back to City living began in the 1980s, but was hard to discern above the din of office building. It started when top firms insisted that key staff be close to their work places, with the change to virtual 24-hour working as markets became global. One luxury block, Norfolk House, appeared on the riverside in **Trig Lane**, near the steps to St Paul's in 1988, with prices of up to £1.5 million. Then came 140 new flats in **Little Britain** by St George. Their parent Berkeley Homes knew a good idea when they saw it, and have followed up with schemes at **Ludgate Hill**, in various fringe locations (see below) and in the heart of the City at Monument. Now, it's possible to look in the City proper, in the Fleet St/Holborn area to the W, and in Barbican and its neighbours to the N. Then there is Smithfield just within the City boundary to the NW, and Shoreditch and Spitalfields outside the City walls to the NE.

The City Proper

Berkeley Homes' **Monument St** scheme has 37 flats with three left last winter from £200–395,000. Lambert House in Ludgate Hill has flats from 1-bed to penthouses with views of St Paul's: prices yet to be revealed. At **Trinity Square**, 16 flats offer views across to the Tower of London: prices range from £210–430,000. Berkeley have also just built 93 flats in **Queen St** – but have sold the whole lot to an Irish investor. The area around the Monument also has nine small flats and an enviable duplex in **Monument St** by developer Marldon priced from £180,000. Nearby, **Botolph Alley** has Berkeley at work yet again with eight 1-bed flats: two left last Christmas at £185,000.

Dotted around the heart of the City are smaller schemes: in a lovely corner near St Paul's, five flats have been created from a period building in **St Andrew's Hill**. **Ludgate Hill** has a block of flats intended to be let. On the river, **Queens Quay** has 1-bed flats. There is even a new conversion behind a listed façade in **Cornhill**: studios a biscuit-toss from the Bank. And there are homes including a 2-floor, 4-bed penthouse in what must be the best street address in the City, **Crutched Friars**. Barratt has built 88 homes in **Aldersgate St** and **Pemberton Row**, and have just finished 136 at 'Globe View', Brooks Wharf, **Upper Thames St**. Not all the flats have river, or Globe Theatre, views. A 2-bed 'atrium apartment' was £290,000 last autumn. Goldcrest Homes has City Wall Apartments in **Wormwood St**. And there are more, for the first time in a hundred years.

Barbican and its Neighbours

For 20 years after the estate's completion in 1976, City living meant the Barbican. It had no competitors. With its 2,014 homes, it is still the largest residential district. The Barbican complex is bordered by **London Wall**, **Aldersgate St**, **Moorgate** and **Chiswell St**. It's described by the City Corporation, which controls it, as a 'city within a City' – and so it is. The fortress image is even more accurate: the whole thing turns inwards, looking down on the open space in front of the magnificent Barbican Arts Centre. Worryingly, there is no street level: walkways, stairs and lifts form a maze so cunning that yellow stripes had to be painted on the paving to guide bemused visitors to the arts centre. The three main towers – just some of the 21 residential blocks – dominate much of the Square Mile's skyline. To those expecting a world of penthouse flats and luxurious living, first impressions can disappoint. The complex looks rather drab, grey, concrete and uniform, and greenery on the balconies struggles to compete.

But the inside of many Barbican flats tells a different story – they belie their outward appearance and provide some of the most exciting homes in Central London. Biggest prices are paid for the luxury penthouses of Lauderdale, Cromwell and Shakespeare Towers. The latter is Britain's tallest residential building. The view from it reaches the hills surrounding London.

Only 260 of the Barbican's homes are now rented from the City Corporation, the rest are leasehold. Leasehold is definitely the growing trend (it was 60 per cent in 1990, nearly 90 per cent now) and the estate's managers are keen to sell as many homes as possible. The turnover of properties has increased and local agents usually have a selection on their books. Homes range from studios right through to a small number of town-houses. The majority are 1- and 2-bed flats. As would be expected, services such as estate cleaning and security are given a high priority and are of an excellent standard. The downsides are the under-floor heating, which is inflexible and expensive, and the service charges. A renewal programme has meant high charges over the last few years, but local agents reckon that when these stabilise selling prices will go up. At the moment, a 1-bed flat which might attract £5,000 a year in charges would sell for £150,000. Two-beds are around £210,000, while the tower-block flats start at around £300,000. An unmodernised 37th-floor one went for £400,000 last summer. These prices reflect increases of 20 per cent on average in 1999.

The Barbican has a very strong and active residents' association which presents a powerful voice at local council meetings. It has a strong community feel and many residents stay put for many years. Good security means low crime.

North of the Barbican is the well-regarded council-built **Golden Lane** estate, with about half the 550 homes now privately owned. Two-bed flats go for £145,000-plus and are very much in demand. Since 1994 this has actually been in the City, though it has always been run by it. In adjacent **Fann St** 38 sheltered homes have been built. On the E side of **Golden Lane** is a big Peabody estate, with further council housing away E along **Banner St**. Just N of the Barbican **Bridgewater Sq** has newly converted 2-bed flats. Also in this neighbourhood, Berkeley have just sold 10 flats in **Carthusian St**. To the N, The Apex (formerly City Point) is another Berkeley conversion in **Bunhill Row**, on the fringes of the Old St area (see Clerkenwell). **Dufferin Avenue** has warehouse conversions, while **Dufferin St** offers 1,000 sq ft galleried lofts in another ex-commercial building at around £295,000. **Finsbury Square** has 10 1998 2-bed flats and a penthouse. One-bed flats in older blocks here sell for around £170,000. In **Tabernacle St**, an old factory was split into 23 lofts in 1999, some live/work units, others penthouses, priced from £160–445,000.

Spitalfields

Spitalfields is where the City merges with the East End. **Commercial St, Middlesex St** and **Bishopsgate** form the boundaries of this unique part of London, which is mostly in Tower Hamlets borough. The big wholesale fruit and vegetable market between **Lamb St** and **Brushfield St** has now gone. Part of its site was intended for an enormous new complex for the LIFFE futures exchange, but things move fast in finance and it's no longer needed. Less ambitious office schemes will replace it, according to current plans. For the moment, ad hoc markets use the old halls. The market site will also include homes, some for Tower Hamlets Council. St George have a few flats left unsold at **Bishops Court** opposite the market site: 2-beds at £225,000. Just to the W, the multi-million pound Broadgate office development now dominates the whole neighbourhood. There are, however, older buildings in Spitalfields: some beautiful early Georgian houses, built by Huguenot silk merchants, with interiors to make a Classicist swoon. Some have been lovingly restored, and will of course be retained in the area's redevelopment. These are found in **Fournier St, Folgate St, Elder St** and **Princelet St**. They command prices of around £450,000.

Conversions of old buildings provide nearly all the other homes. An early example was Pennybank Chambers, **Great Eastern St**, which has 65 small flats. The Cloisters, **Commercial St**, a purpose-built portered block, has 1-bed flats. Opposite, a new conversion called The Xchange offers smart lofts: all now sold. Next to it, and part of the same scheme, some quirky, round-cornered flats are from £195-325,000. Just behind in **Calvin St**, Laing's 'Blue House' offers nine 1- and 2-bed workspace flats and 13 ordinary ones at £170-220,000. In what they reckon is called 'The Silk Quarter', St George built 16 1- and 2-bed flats in **Lamb St** behind a Georgian-style façade overlooking Elder Gardens: all sold in 1999. **Middlesex St** has a few developments: The Wexner Building is a 1901 cigar warehouse, now fitted (as opposed to shell-finish) flats. Rialto's Grade II listed Victorian pub opposite Broadgate is now 10 flats. Just off **Middlesex St**, in **Strype St**, are 1999 1-bed flats and penthouses. A small row of new homes in Georgian style in **Wilkes St** provides 2-bed houses at around £365,000. The odd warehouse conversion: a £500,000, 2,500 sq ft live/work space in **Phipp St** was on the market late last year. Other live/work homes can be had nearby for around £300,000.

Further S, the **Leman St** area on the W edge of Whitechapel has a few homes. Leybourne House is a modern block with swimming pool and that ever more vital City amenity, an underground car park. **Leman St** aquired a block of seven new flats last autumn. The Rialto scheme in **Prescot St** of fully-fitted 'loft-style' flats is now sold, though Berkeley's 84-flat Prospect Tower in the same street had eight homes unsold in December. There is Guinness Trust housing in **Mansell St**. Developer Willow Acre's Prospero House in **The Minories**, once a bank, has 14 flats above a restaurant. For more developments see the Stepney and Whitechapel chapter.

Smithfield

Smithfield, at the NW edge of the City, is dominated by the splendid Victorian wholesale meat market. It is rather under the influence of Clerkenwell (see chapter) as that successful neighbourhood expands its borders. The meat market, however, is prospering and has been expensively modernized: the City Corporation is keen for it to stay. And, to the delight of the whole of London, Bart's Hospital has been at least in part reprieved. Smithfield is a good place for restaurants, and of course the well-known pubs which serve carnivorous breakfasts from 4am. Contained by **Charterhouse St, Aldersgate St** and **Newgate St**, Smithfield has an increasing, if still small, clutch of homes amid the commercial buildings. This is definitely one of the City's up-and-coming areas, a trend strongly backed by the Corporation. Its policy is 'to encourage an increase of residential accommodation in suitable locations within Smithfield' – though they reckon flats overlooking the market itself might be a bad idea. One popular development is Florin Court in **Charterhouse Square**: 2-bed flats and studios, the latter go for £80-90,000. Regalian refurbished the 9-storey 1936 building to provide over 100 luxury flats. A smart hotel is also planned for the square, which also has Georgian houses dating from 1700–1775, used as offices at present. In **Long Lane**, nine new flats have just appeared and there are two schemes in **Carthusian St** on the Barbican borders. A parade of 10 mews-style homes in the side street of **Cloth Fair** dates from the late '80s, as do 10 flats in **Charterhouse St**. See also Barbican.

Fleet St and Holborn

It seems an age, not just a decade, since **Fleet St** meant national newspapers. They have all gone, leaving the Street of Shame for the shiny new world of Docklands. It has, though, taken the best part of a decade for the area to find a new identity, as a place to work (but on a modest scale, no big blocks of offices) and to live. It is very popular with lawyers and City firms wanting company flats – Goldman Sachs recently rented an entire block. Big developers Barratt and Berkeley have been active. The latter were responsible for the sought-after Gallery in nearby **Ludgate Hill**, and a six-flats refurbishment in **Fleet St** itself. Sovereign House, in **Poppin's Court**, off the street, has 14 flats. Barratt's Pemberton House, just off **Fleet St**, has 39 flats. The

Whitefriars Estate, **Carmelite St**, is to gain 52 homes in an offices/flats plan: St George again. Just to the S the Temples, Inner and Middle, house lawyers and a few favoured others in a very select live/work estate: London's oldest. **Wine Office Court** off **Fleet St** – an enviable address, and a charming paved courtyard – has six flats converted from a Victorian newspaper building. One re-sale was £265,000 last autumn. In **Furnival St**, close to Chancery Lane tube, a six-floor 1995 block has 16 1- and 2-bed flats priced at £150-200,000.

The Holborn area to the N has surprisingly few homes. **Red Lion Square** has some handsome houses, and there are a few small modern blocks. There is plenty of semi-redundant commercial space here so, like Smithfield, it could be an area to watch. (See also Bloomsbury chapter.) However the rise in office rents has made homes a less attractive bet for developers, and two or three planned flats conversions have reverted to office use.

Such is the pressure of all this development that agents have yet to invent a name for the riverside strip between **The Strand** and **The Embankment**. There are homes here: Berkeley sold Blythe House, 4- bed, 4-bath: at £895,000 in late 1998. There are others – and where is more central?

Hoxton and Shoreditch

Those who have not been following the City Fringe closely may blink at eulogies about 'the many bars and restaurants of **Rivington St** and **Charlotte Rd**' – these streets are in EC2, not W11 or N1. But here we are in the 'Shoreditch Triangle', no less, between **Old St**, **Great Eastern St** and **Curtain Rd**. An influx of computer and new media firms is taking advantage of the cheap office space. More customers for the new bars come from the loft apartments such as those in **New Inn Yard** and **Curtain Rd**. The London College of Fashion in **Bateman's Row** brings yet another group of potential residents.

New schemes this year include 91-113 **Curtain Rd**: 28 flats in a six-floor block, a dozen with work/home permission, at £215-300,000. Over in Whitechapel on the **Commercial Rd**, 'The Aldgate Triangle' is a big development: see Stepney chapter.

Another newly fashionable loft-living area is Hoxton, lying due N of the City and W of the **Kingsland Rd**. Blighted by well-intentioned post-war council monstrosities (would you believe a block of flats called Caliban Tower?), it yet manages to cling to the remnants of its vigorous past: the music hall in **Hoxton St** still stands as a thriving theatre/community centre. It has been joined by a highly fashionable cinema, The Lux. **Hoxton Square**, once a very dangerous place to enter without an entrée, now has a name as an artists' hangout. Lots of action here: St George are building in the N of the Square, Durkin Homes have a scheme and a site on the S side will soon be live/work spaces.

The canal which runs W to Islington is the focus of several factory conversions: Manhattan Lofts have completed The Factory in **Shepherdess Walk**, with resales of 1,600 sq ft flats at around £365,000. In the same street is Millennium Lofts' Canal Building: 74 lofts and live/work units in shell finish from £207,000 to £405,000. Close by on Wenlock Basin an old print works called the Royle Building has 82 fitted loft-style flats which sold during 1999 from £150,000 for 2-bed, with just one penthouse left last Christmas at £295,000. See Hackney chapter for more such in Kingsland Rd.

Transport   Tubes and main line, all zone 1, in profusion: see map. From Bank: Oxford Circus 10 min, Heathrow 1 hr 15 min (1 change).

Convenient for   West End, Docklands & City Airport. Miles from centre: 1.5.

Schools   Local Authority: no secondary schools in City, see neighbouring areas. Private: City of London School (b) (g).

SALES

Flats	S	1B	2B	3B	4B	5B
Average prices	80–115	85–180+	200–400+	250–500	300–600	–

Houses	2B	3B	4B	5B	6/7B	8B
Average prices	270–350	350–650	400–650+	–	–	–

RENTAL

Flats	S	1B	2B	3B	4B	5B
Average prices	150–235	175–350	220–500+	300–600	–	–

Houses	2B	3B	4B	5B	6/7B	8B
Average prices	350+	450+	550+	–	–	–

The properties   Homes at last re-appearing both on fringes, including Fleet St and Holborn, and among the offices. Barbican has modern flats and houses. A very few period homes in fringe areas like Spitalfields and Smithfield, plus company flats, a few ex-council homes – and a clutch of new flats and loft conversions.

The market   Barbican homes, originally rented, are now bought and sold. Prices can be good value compared with West End — but watch service charges. Rare period homes joined by a rash of new developments and conversions. Local searches: City of London 1–2 weeks, Hackney 10 working days, Tower Hamlets 2–4 weeks.

Among those estate agents active in this area are:

- Hurford Salvi Carr
- Frank Harris *
- Hamptons
- Stirling Ackroyd

- Barbican Estate Office
- Jarvis Keller
- Daniel Watney
- Phillips Residential *

further details: see advertisers' index on p671

CLAPHAM

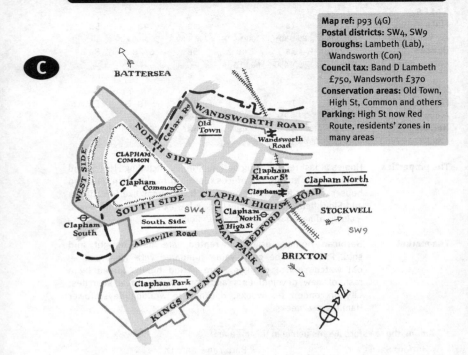

Map ref: p93 (4G)
Postal districts: SW4, SW9
Boroughs: Lambeth (Lab),
    Wandsworth (Con)
Council tax: Band D Lambeth
    £750, Wandsworth £370
Conservation areas: Old Town,
    High St, Common and others
Parking: High St now Red
    Route, residents' zones in
    many areas

'Clapham,' observed a fashionable young thing just setting up home in Brixton, 'is *mumsy*'. By which she meant that the tract around **Abbeville Rd** and South Side is so blessed with offspring that the nursery schools can be counted in dozens, and that the domesticity was a trifle stifling. Clapham is indeed now a solid, family area – with home prices to suit. Its key assets are tube, common and plenty of 3- and 4-bed houses. The hyper-modern, designer-Sainsbury's in the **High St**, the fashionable cinema, bars and restaurants – Clapham at last has a night-life – set the seal on an area that had been 'up-and-coming' for 15 years. Rocketing prices confirmed that it had 'up-and-come' – not to mention the arrival, due mid-2001, of a Holmes Place health club.

Clapham was once a little hamlet surrounded by big houses, where prosperous Londoners kept country retreats. Pepys, for instance, lived and died here. In early Victorian times more grand houses appeared as the ubiquitous Thomas Cubitt of Belgravia and Pimlico fame built a whole suburb of them and called it Clapham Park. But as the century went on, and trams and later tubes made Clapham cheap and easy to get to, the houses got smaller and smaller. By the turn of the century, Clapham was a byword for ordinariness. 'The man on the Clapham omnibus' became a judicial simile for all that was everyday and reasonable.

The tube, the arrival of which abetted the demolition (begun with the railways) of so many grand houses and their replacement with modest terraces, has more recently been Clapham's salvation. For thanks to the Northern line, Clapham, unlike most parts of South London, has a direct link to the West End and the City. In the '80s, house-buyers began to discover that Clapham is as close to Sloane Square as Fulham is, and that the journey to Oxford Circus or the City is a whole lot quicker. Clapham was re-established, after spending most of the 20th century in genteel, steady decline.

Clapham began as a village at the NE corner of the wide common. The old village is still there, with a pleasant mix of buildings that includes a row of fine Queen Anne houses. From here the houses spread out S and W, beginning with a handsome 1820s row and going on to Cubitt's 250 acres of 'capacious detached villas' in Clapham Park. Later Victorian times saw the growth of **Clapham High St** and a shift in Clapham's commercial centre of gravity from the **Old Town** eastwards: for once the postcode is a fairly accurate delineation: with a few bordering streets, Clapham is SW4.

Clapham divides into several distinct neighbourhoods radiating out from the **Old Town** – both a street name and the heart of the old village. The area W of the common is Battersea (see Battersea chapter), or now 'Between the Commons'. The flat, low-lying streets N of **Wandsworth Rd** are Battersea too: Clapham is proud of being on a low but distinct hill. South of the foot of the Common, the roads around Clapham South tube are now called 'Clapham South' but were Balham (see Balham and Tooting chapter): it would have been less confusing if the tube people had stuck to their original name for the station, Nightingale Lane. East, beyond Clapham Park, is a zone debated with Brixton. Clapham Junction, by the way, is in Battersea: a source of confusion for over a century.

The Common survived the Victorians, and is now a valuable green lung and backdrop – and the source of some fine, open views from the handsome houses, flats and prep schools that gaze out over it.

Old Town

Strictly speaking, **Old Town** is a street, but the core of old Clapham has annexed the name. As with all such desirable tags, estate agents try to stretch it as far as possible: it is usually reckoned to run N as far as **Wandsworth Rd** and W to **Cedars Rd** and the borough boundary. **Old Town** proper has Clapham's oldest and handsomest houses, a row of three rare Queen Anne survivals, dating from 1705, looking out over the little triangle that marks the original village heart (now a bus halt). To the E is Clapham's only garden square: peaceful **Grafton Square** is surrounded on three sides by tall, handsome white-stucco 1850s houses – shades of Cubitt's Pimlico, though one Captain Ross was responsible – that often have attractive semi-basement flats. There are also three pretty 2-storey stucco houses; the humdrum block on the fourth side hardly detracts. The site

SW of the square is owned by the Home Office; plans for a new police headquarters (an earlier one, for 60 holding cells, was dropped after vociferous outcry) have gone quiet.

North of **Grafton Square** are several streets of solid, 3/4-storey Victorian houses: **Offerton Rd** (particularly nice), **Liston Rd** and **Fitzwilliam Rd**. An original 5-bed house here can now fetch c.£750,000, but these are being joined by new-build: **Fitzwilliam Rd** runs across **Rectory Grove** to **North St**, making a triangular site where building is beginning to transform it from redundant factory to the 'Fitzwilliam Quarter', a cache of 1- and 2-bed flats, 2/3-bed maisonettes and 2/3- or 4-bed houses by Persimmon. The 16 homes will be in a gated courtyard – and next door will be the new Holmes Place gym.

Rectory Grove runs N from the **Old Town** to link with **Larkhall Rise**. This is normally a busy traffic route, but the closure for two years of the railway bridge at its E end has reduced the flow. The Rise has some lovely houses from Georgian days onwards. **Rectory Gardens** is a row of tiny mews cottages. **Turret Grove**, named after a feature of the Elizabethan manor which once stood here, has some pretty 1840s cottages as well as the Victorian terraces (c. £400,000) it shares with **Rozel Rd** and **Iveley Rd**, the latter tucked away by the church. This is Clapham's most charming corner.

West of **Old Town** and its continuation **North St** is a quiet network of streets. **Macaulay Rd** was built in late-Victorian times with very large gabled detached and semi-detached houses, many of which survive. Most are flats, but there are still a few vast, single, million-plus when done up, homes. **Macaulay Square** is a small council-built estate. Macaulay Court is a block of '30s flats, nicely positioned in the angle of **Macauley Rd** and **Lillieshall Rd** (2-bed flat, £195,000 last winter): there's a five-year refurbishment going on here. **Lillieshall Rd** has some substantial Victorian terraces plus some pretty, very small cottages at the E end. Parallel **Broadhinton Rd** has some attractive early Victorian cottages; **Orlando Rd** large 3-storey Victorian houses, many flats. Recent additions include **Redwood Mews**, off **Hannington Rd**: nine 1- and 2-bed houses around a courtyard, and **Sycamore Mews**, on the site of the old royal laundry between **North St** and **Orlando Rd** – now a smart mews scheme of flats and houses.

Across **Macaulay Rd** to the E, **The Chase**, a parallel grand avenue, has similarly vast Victorian homes: where possible, the large houses of this corner of Clapham are being re-converted back to single homes. Some of the enormous double-fronted houses boast 6 or 7 bedrooms, and 120-ft gardens – and prices that have reached over £2 million. A third avenue, **Victoria Rise**, has gaunter and less kempt, but still huge, grey-brick and stucco houses: often now flats that share the equally huge gardens,

The **North Side** of Clapham Common has a succession of terraces of various eras, from 1695 through early Georgian, mid-Victorian and 1930s flats. It is also (sign of the times) now prep-school alley. The two commanding blocks on either side of **Cedars Rd** are splendid examples of 1860s grandiose. Enviable flats come up for sale occasionally in the E block. Several of the enormous houses are also now flats, which have fine views across London to the N and the common to the S. If you fancy a whole house, a Georgian 5-bed will cost £1.2 million or so now. **Cedars Rd**, once lined with villas, is now a main bus and traffic artery, and mostly set-back, council-built housing: resales are common. Tiny **Wix's Lane**, to the W of **Cedars Rd**, marks the border both of Lambeth borough and SW4 (for the SW11 streets that run down from **North Side** to **Lavender Hill**, see the Battersea chapter). The Lane now houses the latest private school, the Lycée Charles de Gaulle.

Back now towards the Old Town where, next to the library at the E end of **Clapham Common North Side**, a big computer company has done up an old factory as offices for its 300 staff. **North Side**, **Old Town** and **The Pavement** meet to form a triangle that, though paved, irresistibly betrays its village-green origins; a curve of increasingly tidy shops face Holy Trinity Church on the common. There are some flats above shops (with three smart 3-bed ones coming soon), and two popular inter-war blocks of flats.

Clapham Manor St

The Old Town area is bounded to the E by a tract of council-built housing around **Cubitt Terrace**. These are nicely designed, brick-built, mainly 2-storey, and arranged in pleasant closes and green squares. Some are appearing on the resale market, a cheaper alternative to the original 2-bed early Victorian cottages, which are now c. £330,000. To the N of **Larkhall Rise** are some sloping streets of terraced houses: **Brayburne Avenue**, with 4-bedroom houses, has become quieter since access to **Wandsworth Rd** was cut off at the northern end. **Hesewall Close**, completed in 1995, is a street of 12 3-bed family houses on land which was once allotments. **Netherford Rd** and, E of the railway, **Killyon Rd** are Victorian terraces. The little Wandsworth Rd station runs to Victoria and London Bridge. The line is used by Channel Tunnel trains.

Clapham Manor St, especially at its N end, is handsome with 2- and 3-storey Cubitt terraces, much in demand as family homes. The S end, towards the **High St**, is more mixed. The little roads off to the E like **Navy St** and **Voltaire Rd** have later Victorian terraces, and **Edgeley Rd** has rather looming 3-storey Victorian ones, most flats. The E side backs onto the railway. Twelve new mews houses have been inserted behind a Victorian façade. Elmhurst Mansions is a purpose-built block. A 2-bed flat around here might go for £170–200,000. The corner between **Old Town** and **Clapham Manor St** has some 3-storey purpose-built Victorian flats in **Bromells Rd** and some flats in smaller terraces in **Venn St**, 2 min from Clapham Common tube station.

High St

Clapham High St has been transformed by the advent of the modernistic Sainsbury's, with its sloping front wall of video screens. It has a large and fairly cheap (2hr max) car park. Another important plus is the Clapham Picture House, in **Venn St**. Its bar has added to a rash of new drinking holes: seedy shops are being replaced by tapas bars, an Egyptian pizza joint patronized by supermodels, and smart cafés. The biggest undeveloped site on the **High St** is a row of seedy shops between **Venn St** and **Stonehouse St** once owned by the Church Commissioners, but now sold on. At last plans are in for three new shops and 22 1/3-bed flats. Rumours abound about which chain will take the shops. Note that the **High St** and **South Side** are now a Red Route, and that the ever-growing controlled parking zone, while popular with residents, hampers shoppers.

South of the **High St** is a mixed area of Victorian terraces and council housing. It is very close to tubes (Claphams North and Common), shops and common, and offers better value than the more 'tidy' areas of Clapham. **Nelson's Row** with its dozen flat-fronted Victorian cottages leads on down to smart new flats, replacing some old offices, then a much-tidied-up '30s red-brick council estate, then the attractive modern council-built houses of **Haselrigge Rd**. **St Luke's Avenue** and the roads to the E (**Tremadoc Rd, Kenwyn Rd, Cato Rd**) are mostly 3-storey Victorian, many now flats, which are cheaper here than in other Clapham neighbourhoods: 1-bed flats start from c. £140,000. On the corner of **Aristotle Rd** and **Bedford Rd** is **Aristotle Mews**: 17 houses by Fairview (a 4-bed last winter, £295,000). **Lion Yard** is a development of business units, built in mews style, in **Tremadoc Rd**.

The streets off the south side of **Clapham Park Rd**, down as far as the corner with **Abbeville Rd**, are largely council-built homes. There is a large and smart new mews of 'business units' near the junction of the two. **St Alphonsus Rd** has some Victorian terraces and 14 new flats. **Northbourne Rd** has some well-preserved detached and semi-detached mid-Victorian houses on a handsome scale. These are some of the nicest houses in Clapham, if tucked away in rather drab surroundings – nevertheless substantial, 5-bed houses here can be £950,000. A once-derelict 19th-century building has recently been restored as four flats, while a rather sad office block on **Clapham Park Rd** gained a new floor and façade and became St Paul's View ('wiv a ladder and some glasses'. . .). These 1- to 3-bed flats help to tidy up what was a scruffy corner. **Park Hill** runs off down to Clapham Park: it contains some '20s gabled terraces, some modern flats and a few large early 19th-century detached houses – a pair has been split into eight flats: 'The White House'.

Clapham North

East of the tube station and N of the railway (used by Channel Tunnel trains), and in the SW9 postcode, is a rather cut-off corner of Victorian terraces and council housing. The Southwestern Hospital forms the border with Brixton. Homes in this district were until recently cheaper than in other Clapham corners: it is further from the common and some streets were distinctly down-at-heel. However, the little network of roads N of **Landor Rd** – **Atherfold Rd**, **Hemberton Rd** and **Prideaux Rd** – is becoming a popular area now that neighbouring Brixton is downright fashionable. Little Clapham North houses, which were £80,000 in 1994/5, now reach £200–250,000; bigger ones £300,000. **Landor Rd** itself is busy and unreconstructed. Along **Clapham Rd** towards Stockwell are some fine Georgian houses, most used as offices, but some reverting to homes.

West of **Clapham Rd**, **Gauden Rd**, **Bromfelde Rd**, **Sibella Rd** and **Chelsham Rd** have some big Victorian houses. Good flat conversions can be found, including one in **Gauden Rd** where several houses have been split into flats: all share the large communal garden and a swimming pool. Some houses are still single dwellings: these are large, £600,000-plus homes; including the occasional spectacular 6-bedded, large-gardened example.

Clapham Park

Cubitt's elegant suburb of detached mansions has vanished, leaving as its legacy large trees and the occasional surviving square early 19th-century house, now flats. This area, centred on **King's Avenue**, is furthest from tubes or trains – though the South Circular marks the southern borders with Balham. **King's Avenue** has several blocks of flats – Queenswood Court includes one of the Victorian houses – Robins, Oakfield and Thorncliffe Courts are '30s blocks; Peters Court is '60s. Prices for a 2-bed in these blocks are c. £175–200,000. Inter-war suburban-style detached houses punctuate the flats. **King's Mews** is a modern group of houses that is tucked behind an old house. East of **King's Avenue** is in SW2 and is a border zone between Brixton and Clapham Park. There are several quiet streets of Victorian terraces. Brixton Prison dominates the eastern end of **Thornbury Rd**. **Kingswood Rd** has some larger, 3-storey houses. These streets are fairly evenly split between single houses and flat conversions. A typical price is £150,000 for a 2-bedroom garden flat. The S end of **King's Avenue** and west to **Clarence Avenue** is all council-built housing, houses and low blocks set in a pleasant green space. Some resales: a pleasant 3-bed semi was £150,000 last November. The northern end of **Clarence Avenue** has some 1930s semi-detached houses.

Continuing N, the streets leading E off **Lyham Rd** are SW2, and have received a boost from the renaissance of Brixton (see Brixton, Herne Hill and Tulse Hill chapter).

South Side/Abbeville

This is the largest residential neighbourhood in Clapham and the most uniform, consisting almost entirely of Victorian terraced housing. The grid of streets runs down a gentle slope from **Clapham Common South Side** to **Abbeville Rd** then on up again towards Clapham Park. The parade of shops at the junction of **Abbeville Rd** and **Narbonne Avenue** was dignified in the '80s by estate agents with the name 'Abbeville Village'. Here life has followed art, and what was a humdrum little suburban parade is now truly a neighbourhood, with its own night life, designer shops – and even a village fair. It is a family area undergoing a positive baby boom: nursery schools abound, with an Anglo-Spanish one the latest to open.

There is no way through from **Clarence Avenue** in Clapham Park to the next road W, **Rodenhurst Rd**, which belongs to the Abbeville neighbourhood. This divide is architectural as well as physical: much of **Rodenhurst Rd** (except the S end) is large, popular Edwardian semi-detached double-fronted houses set well back from the wide road; these now command prices of £600–700,000, though really big and/or good ones can go up to £800,000. New homes appearing here, too: five 4-bed mews houses at nos. 129–137. **Poynders Rd** forms the S boundary of Clapham – and is also the **South Circular Rd**. It has some rather depressed-looking inter-war flats, some modern town-houses and some Edwardian ones. Its equally busy continuation, **Cavendish Rd**, has big turn-of-the-century houses.

West from **Rodenhurst Rd** is **Elms Crescent**, which is lined with late-19th-century bay-windowed terraced houses. It and the roads off it to the W are very uniform: exceptions to the 2-storey terraced rule include **Elms Rd**, which has some handsome tall-gabled, wider than average houses on the N side. A 6-bed semi can command £800–900,000. The W end of **Elms Rd** runs up towards the common and has some large 1880s houses, some detached and double-fronted. Five vast, square Victorian houses at the W end are flats. The parallel streets such as **Leppoc Rd** and **Narbonne Avenue** have mostly 4-bed family houses. The number of trees, width of the road (and thus ease of parking) and distance from the tube and shops are the variables around here. The 4-bed houses, typical of the area, go for c. £400–450,000. **Hambalt** and **Mandalay Rds** are mostly terraced housing with quite a few purpose-built flats, which can be spotted by their pairs of front doors under a single arch. These are popular, and go for £210–250,000. The streets S of **Narbonne Avenue** are mostly Victorian terraces, but with some post-war 3-storey flats.

Abbeville Rd, with its villagey shops and wine bar, has some bigger than usual houses, many divided into flats. It carries a fair amount of through traffic (and now is speed-humped). There are also flats above the shops in the parade and a few nice (very) big purpose-built flats to rent in Edwardian mansion blocks.

The common, at the junction with **Elms Rd**, is lined with big mid-Victorian terraces set back behind a strip of grass. These are South Kensington-like houses with pillared porches, all flats. A splendid low-built detached villa, now offices, is on the market if you want a truly grand Clapham home. **St Gerards Close** is a little estate of 4-storey flats built within the last 10 years. On **Clapham Common South Side**, next to **Elms Rd**, is Brook House, a development of 11 luxury apartments. Also on **South Side**, former halls of residence have become a new-build scheme of flats and houses for a housing association. Opposite, on the common, is the popular Windmill pub with a few tall houses behind it in **Windmill Drive**. Most are splendid flats, their turret roofs partially glazed to form big rooms with wide views. Some smart, recently converted flats can fetch up to £400,000.

South Side continues with the hideous Notre Dame estate. But past **Crescent Lane**, which meanders through to **Abbeville Rd** and on to **King's Avenue**, lies Clapham's premier street, **Crescent Grove**. This is a fine Regency crescent facing a row of grand semi-detached villas of the same period, the whole forming a private road entered through a gateway. These enviable houses command prices from £750,000 upwards to a million or more. The coach-houses which link the big villas have themselves become sought-after small homes attracting c. £425,000.

The old women's hospital at the S end of **South Side**, across from Clapham South tube, is under seige from Tesco who plan a Metro store: after a planning appeal. This has now been referred to the DOE for a final decision.

From here, running up the remaining, W, side of the common, **Clapham Common West Side** scrapes into the SW4 postcode though its hinterland is SW11 (see Battersea chapter). The tall popular houses stand in their quiet road facing out over the common: traffic is deflected down **The Avenue,** part of the South Circular.

C

Transport	Tubes: Clapham South, Clapham Common, Clapham North (zones 2/3, Northern); Oxford Circus 20 min (1 change), City 25 min, Heathrow 1 hr 10 min (2 changes). Trains: Wandsworth Rd, Clapham High St, to Victoria and London Bridge.
Convenient for	City, West End, Sloane Square. Miles from centre: 3.
Schools	Local Authority: No local authority secondary schools in area. See Battersea, Dulwich and Streatham chapters.

SALES

Flats	S	1B	2B	3B	4B	5B
Average prices	80–180	90–220	130–300	135–350	170–500	750+
Houses	2B	3B	4B	5B	6/7B	8B
Average prices	180–400	250–500	300–550	400–1 M	600+	800–1 M+

RENTAL

Flats	S	1B	2B	3B	4B	5B
Average prices	115–230	140–275	185–460	300–575	300+	400+
Houses	2B	3B	4B	5B	6/7B	8B
Average prices	210–450	230–460	370–600	480–1000	650+	1200+

The properties	Many Victorian terraces; some splendid Queen Anne, Georgian and Regency around the Clapham Common, Old Town and Crescent Grove, lots of converted flats (including good large ones) and some 20th-century flats blocks. Large houses in The Chase, Macaulay Rd, Rodenhurst Avenue; typical house is 3/4-bed terraced, 4/5-bed around Abbeville.
The market	South Side, Abbeville 'village' and Old Town are well 'discovered'; former pair attract families wanting space, latter has older, properties with more character. High St improving fast. Prices drop in N and E, but catching up due to 'Brixton effect'. Local searches: Lambeth:10 working days, Wandsworth 3–4 weeks.

Among those estate agents active in this area are:

- Barnard Marcus
- Bells
- Winkworth *
- Hamptons
- Price & Co
- Kinleigh Folkard & Hayward
- Bushells
- Hugh Henry
- Friend & Falcke *
- Haart
- Richard Oakey
- John Hollingsworth
- Foxtons *

further details: see advertisers' index on p671

CLERKENWELL AND FINSBURY

Map ref: p62 (4A)
Postal districts: N1, EC1
Boroughs: Islington
   (Lab/Lib Dem),
   Camden (Lab)
Council tax: Band D
   Islington £912, Camden
   £897
Conservation areas:
   Several – check Town Halls
Parking: Residents/meters

Clerkenwell is full. The supply of redundant factories ripe to be loft apartments
has dried up. With the rise in office rents, buildings are worth more kept in
commercial use, and – for now – a six-year boom in loft conversions has come to a
halt. There are still homes to buy, but they are either re-sales of earlier conversions,
or new flats which make only a passing stylistic reference to the loft aesthetic.

The Clerkenwell loft has become a byword for smart urban living, the successor to
the mews houses (redundant stables) and church conversions of earlier generations
of achievers. 'Loft living' is an established London sub-culture, and it is apparently
blossoming as far away as Leeds and Glasgow (wherever they may be).

The 1990s saw Clerkenwell establish itself as a good place to live, work and relax.
A London neighbourhood has been re-born. Back in 1988 this book commented
'Clerkenwell and Finsbury have at first sight enormous potential as a residential area:
ideally situated, with a high proportion of Georgian buildings . . .' Any homes that did
appear in those days were snapped up; the problem was, very few did.

How things have changed: there are now around 1,300 more homes than a decade
ago, and 1,200 more are in the pipeline. The catalyst was a switch in planning policy.
Islington Council finally acknowledged that the commercial space in the area was
largely redundant. The light industries and crafts that had grown up over the previous
two centuries – printing, metalwork, wines and spirits – departed suddenly as
technology changed. The City offices expanded eastwards, into Docklands, not north
as had been expected. Only the media business stayed put.

The planners at last relaxed the usage conditions early in the 1990s; pioneer
developers bought empty warehouses, offices and factories and started to convert

them to homes around 1994. The precedent was the Docklands warehouse boom of a decade before; but since the Docks had caught a bad cold when the market crashed before the infrastructure was well in place, these new conversions looked to Manhattan for a new gloss, and the term 'loft apartments' became the '90s buzzword.

Today, Clerkenwell has risen in status and price to overtake the Finsbury neighbourhoods to the N, which have always maintained a somewhat fragile respectability. As a result Clerkenwell 'proper' is extremely expensive so would-be loft-dwellers are now looking E to the area between **Old St**, **Goswell Rd** and the **City Rd**. The live/work concept, so slow to mature elsewhere in London, has caught on here. Photographers, designers, artists all find it an attractive way of life. But they have to be successful ones. The majority of homes are 1- to 2-bed flats (lofts or otherwise); large houses and studios are rare. Such 2-, 3- and 4-bed houses that exist are mostly in the N of the area: finding them is like pulling plums out of the pudding.

Streets are a rich mixture of architectural styles and periods, and residential and commercial uses: this is what gives the area its distinctive flavour. The property here is also a mixture: there's Georgian, converted commercial, modern. The Victorian housing – the staple for so much of London – was either bombed or has been demolished since the war and replaced by council homes. For four decades after 1945, it was the council that provided almost the only opportunity for living in this historic corner of London: most tenants lived there all their lives, often working in the printing trade; this led to a continuity in the population which has now, sadly, all but gone.

The first wave of lofts, essentially ex-industrial space, were airy, galleried affairs, sold as shells; these have been joined by smaller, much more cramped versions and by new-build blocks. The 'real' lofts are much in demand as existing residents trade up within the area and newcomers arrive. Renting is on the rise as City people discover the area, joining and to an extent replacing the artistic pioneers (the academic, publishing, design, media, computer and fashion worlds are well-represented, both in workplaces and inhabitants).

The residential wave may have peaked: there are few sites left in Clerkenwell proper, and some are seeing redevelopment for offices as commercial rents rise: they have doubled since 1997, though they are still less than half City and West End levels.

To define the area: it lies N of the City and **Fleet St**, E of the **Gray's Inn Rd**, St Pancras and Bloomsbury, S of **City Rd** and the Angel – close to the West and East Ends, 5–10 min from the City, and close to major stations, it's convenient for just about everywhere. Despite a large number of squares and parks, it remains essentially urban. This is the place for restaurants, bars and general buzz . . . the people who work here tend to party rather than go home to the family, and the loft-dwellers join them.

It divides into four neighbourhoods. In the middle is Clerkenwell (which includes Farringdon and Charterhouse). Over to the E is Lower Islington, better known now as City Rd/Old St. In the W, towards Holborn, is Hatton Garden. Finally, to the N is the Finsbury district centred around the Lloyd Baker estate. These are all approximations; there are no definitive boundaries, and no clear consensus among either inhabitants or estate agents as to what to call neighbourhoods. Finsbury, once the accepted local name, is easily confused with Finsbury Park, a couple of miles to the N. Finsbury was a separate borough from 1900 to 1965, when Islington took over. (There is, too, a confusing tendency among agents and developers to use the name 'Islington' for everything in the borough.) The EC1 postcode covers the area quite neatly.

The real point about Clerkenwell is its history. It has been urban since the Middle Ages. Monasteries, mansions, churches, almshouses, sober Georgian homes, Victorian slums and distilleries succeeded one another. Some roads retain their medieval flavour still, twisting and turning like snakes and ladders on a board. Clerkenwell and its sub-zones Farringdon and Charterhouse are districts of narrow, dense streets, with concealed alleys and arches and mixtures of architectural styles and residential and commercial uses. There is a high percentage of Georgian; many other buildings have been given post-modern spruce-ups – some homes have had two renovations in a dozen years.

Clerkenwell has shot in a decade from cheapest to priciest neighbourhood, overtaking the Smithfield and Barbican borders and Finsbury's Lloyd Baker estate. In the last-named, prices are still below those in Islington. If you want to buy more cheaply try the King's Cross (see chapter) borders – especially in the streets with dense traffic such as **King's Cross Rd** or those near railway lines – for example **Britannia St**. Or near densely populated housing estates such as **Wynyatt St** or **Exmouth Market**. Shoreditch (see City chapter) is another area to try.

Lower Islington, between the **City Rd** and **Goswell Rd**, is almost exclusively council-built housing, with a large number of tall '60s-style tower blocks with 20-plus floors. Some lower-rise housing occurs towards the Clerkenwell border and in the N towards the Angel, and there is a lot of commercial property, some of which is being converted to residential. **Goswell Rd** is currently scene of much new building as developers deprived of Clerkenwell proper move in.

On the N edge of the area lies the late-Georgian Lloyd Baker estate, the similar New River Estate and a swathe to the E of **Rosebery Avenue** and W of Lower Islington which has no accepted name, but is sometimes referred to as North Clerkenwell. The architecture is mainly Georgian mixed with some modern high-rises, a little commercial and a high proportion of council housing. Still not as select as Islington proper, but getting there. This is the place to look for a family home. The cultured find it to be conveniently close to Sadler's Wells Theatre (open again after a massive lottery-financed rebuild).

Hatton Garden is traditionally the centre of London's jewellery trade, especially diamonds. It's next door to Holborn, and so has a distinctly up-market, big-business feel; streets are wider and less medieval in appearance. The surviving Georgian houses are being joined by a rash of new-build and converted apartments.

Clerkenwell and Charterhouse

This is the epicentre of the residential boom. There are reckoned to be 6,000 homes – conversions of industrial space plus burgeoning new-build – and hundreds of new businesses to replace the crafts and light industry of a generation ago. Most of the existing homes are conversions, with new-build predominating among the planned schemes: the supply of suitable buildings for conversion has dried up. Small, smart offices and studios are starting to appear alongside flats as components of new developments. Computing and Internet businesses are starting to migrate from Soho and the West End. Restaurants blossom, as do bars and cafés.

Clerkenwell centres around **Clerkenwell Green** and the surrounding small streets. The very busy **Clerkenwell Rd** cuts through the neighbourhood from W-E, and **Farringdon Rd** runs N-S. To begin from the N, from the crossroads of **Rosebery Avenue** and **Farringdon Rd**, the area W up to **Calthorpe St** is on the NW boundary of central Clerkenwell and houses a variety of commercial buildings, including the old Times newspaper building in **Coley St** and **Gough St**, and the vast Mount Pleasant Post Office, which dominates **Farringdon Rd** and the top of **Mount Pleasant**. Continuing S down **Rosebery Avenue** there are a number of Victorian commercial buildings and some mansion flats with shops beneath, followed by Rosebery Square Buildings, a large refurbished Victorian workmen's flats development that dominates both sides of the street as it goes to join the **Clerkenwell Rd**.

Clerkenwell Rd runs W-E, with **Rosebery Avenue** forking off to form a triangle. The area between the two is typical Clerkenwell, with a warren of narrow, densely packed streets running higgledy piggledy, their names betraying their medieval origins: **Herbal Hill, Vine Hill, Baker's Row**. The architecture is mainly Georgian or early Victorian, and uses have traditionally been mainly commercial – though now four modern blocks in **Topham St** and **Warner St** provide some flats as well as shops and offices. The Herbal Hill apartments, 1–10 **Summers St** and the Warner Building were among the early conversions and provide some of the most expensive flats in the district. The Ziggurat Building in **Saffron Hill** has sought-after 'true' lofts. This part of Clerkenwell ends at **Farringdon Rd**, which completes the triangle in the E. On the corner with **Clerkenwell Rd** is a 1994 flats block which was planned as offices but which switched uses during construction.

Just E of the **Farringdon Rd** and the railway in its deep cutting is **Clerkenwell Green**. This is the centre of old Clerkenwell, gathering place for the Peasants' Revolt and now home to the Karl Marx Library. The heart of the area is a jumble of Victorian, Georgian and modern architecture, with its bars, up-market restaurants, pubs and posh design studios . . . a decidedly prosperous atmosphere. Some homes too: distinctive no 8 has flats, with a 1,000 sq ft one on the market last winter for £400,000, while next door is a 6-storey, 3-bed, 1-garage house round a light-well: much swooned over by archirects, it can be yours for £1.5 million.

The two main streets of central Clerkenwell are **Clerkenwell Close**, running NW from the Green, and **Sekforde St** running NE. **Clerkenwell Close** retains a number of small Georgian terraced houses. To the left is a new commercial and residential development by Islington Council, with shops below and 28 flats above. To the right is the imposing, Georgian St James's Church, with its spire and surrounding small garden. At the end of the Close are the distinctive yellow-and-white-brick Peabody flats, which go on round into **Pear Tree Court**. No 1 Pear Tree Court is a new scheme of 18 flats, some with work-spaces, starting at £185,000. To the E, **Clerkenwell Close** twists round to meet **Bowling Green Lane** (10 new flats in 1999 at no 18/19, £215,000-plus) and **Corporation Row**, both mainly commercial of mixed periods; after this Clerkenwell Close becomes **Rosoman St**. Past **Northampton Row** is an adventure playground, followed by the gardens of **Rosoman Place** on the left; opposite is a high tower block. Along **Rosoman St**, the turning to the left is **Exmouth Market**, a pedestrian street smartening up with restaurants and cafés – even a designer jewellers.

Sekforde St, one of Clerkenwell's finest streets, runs NE from **Clerkenwell Green**. It is made up of 2- and 3-storey Regency terraces, the middle portion of which have balconies. Residential and commercial uses mingle, with a former bank now stylishly changed into a single, 7,000 sq ft house, on the market in late 1998 for £1.85 million. Towards **St John St**, **Woodbridge St** to the N has 3-storey Georgian terraces overlooking a school. Between **Sekforde St** and **St John St** is Bellway's St Paul's Square: a big complex of flats behind a listed façade (of an old debtors' prison, actually). Forking to the N from **Sekforde St** is **St James's Walk**: on one side a mixture of Georgian homes and Victorian commercial buildings; on the other a children's playground and the garden surrounding St James's Church. The originally fine network of medieval streets that made up the middle of this area has now been obliterated, and the area is bordered by **Sans Walk** in the N and **Clerkenwell Close** in the W. An old 1890s college in **Sans Walk** (with the remains of an older prison in the basement . . .) will have 46 flats and commercial space in a conversion by Persimmon. Due 2000.

East of **St John St** across to the **Goswell Rd**, bounded on the S by **Clerkenwell Rd**, is an 8-acre block of property called the Clerkenwell Estate. This was owned by the Governors of Sutton Hospital for 350 years until 1995, when they sold to Bee Bee Developments. The new landlords, working closely with Islington Council, have drawn up a long-term plan to improve and develop the estate: 100 homes have so far resulted. Three developments were completed in 1999: 14 clever modern-style flats next to the smart Gee St Studios, from £150,000; 17 flats in **Goswell Rd**; and 21 in **Great Sutton St**. Goswell Rd will have 300 further homes during 2000, with prices in the various schemes starting at £170,000 for 1-beds (nearer £200,000 is the norm in Clerkenwell central). Three-bed flats start at £300,000.

Charterhouse & Farringdon

The area S of **Clerkenwell Rd** down to **Charterhouse St** and W to **Farringdon St** is also Clerkenwell, although the streets to the E of **St John St** up to **Aldersgate** are more commonly termed Charterhouse. Anything in this area or along the Smithfield border is at a premium because of its proximity to the City. There are virtually no houses here, what homes there are being predominantly small flats used as pieds-à-terre and commercial conversions. The Charterhouse, which gives this corner its name, was a medieval Carthusian monastery. The site is located on the corner of **St John St** and **Charterhouse St**, and stretches back to the **Clerkenwell Rd**. Used since the war by St Bart's Medical School, it is still a special corner which mixes the Elizabethan with the utilitarian around a central park with plane trees, with tall commercial property in the W and down **Charterhouse Mews**.

In **Charterhouse Square** – one of London's last private, gated squares – are peaceful Georgian homes, plus a '30s Art Deco block refurbished a decade ago to provide nine floors of very small pieds-à-terre for City folk, complete with pool, gym and roof garden. To the E, Charterhouse Square becomes **Carthusian St**, with the occasional small flats block. Roads to the N off **Aldersgate** are solidly commercial.

To the W, off **St John St**, roads continue in a familiar Clerkenwell pattern, though a little more orderly. This is the site of the medieval Priory of St John, of which only the gatehouse survives. The lower end of **St John St** used to be largely commercial with many tall Victorian and Georgian buildings, some adapted in a post-modern style to provide posh office space close to the City, some concealing flats. Large chunks of the street have been or are being converted into homes, and quite a few of the ground floors have become restaurants. The site of the old gin distillery, derelict for years, has planning consent for new shops – rumours vary, with Tesco reported to be very keen last winter – offices and flats, and there's talk of a cinema. Parallel to **St John St** is **St John's Lane**, which terminates in the N at St John's Gate, a stone arch dating from 1504 and the original entrance to the Grand Priory of St John of Jerusalem.

Britton St to the W runs parallel to **St John's Lane**, with mainly 4-storey Georgian and Victorian commercial. No 1 Britton St was mostly sold off-plan in late 1997 at prices up to £800,000 for the penthouse. Next door is Persimmon's Clerkenwell Central: 20 warehouse apartments, five houses and 28 new-build flats on the **Turnmill St** frontage (facing the railway cutting). Six 1-bed flats were still on the market just before completion in December at £195-210,000. Continuing down **Britton St** to the junction with **Brisset St**, there is a modern 5-storey office/home with intriguing post-modern exterior, built for a well-known showbiz client. Also in Brisset St is The Red House, converted into large, £325,000, workspace flats. 'City Piazza' by Fairbriar will have 1- and 2-bed flats around a courtyard priced at £195-395,000, some of the highest prices per sq ft seen in Clerkenwell.

Between **Benjamin St** and **Cowcross St** Exchange Place, a hotel/offices/100 flats scheme now complete, has short-let apartments in Zinc House. Further down, at the corner of **Benjamin St** is tiny **St John's Garden**; to the S is **Eagle Court** which joins **Britton St** to **St John's Lane**. It is mainly modern commercial, but has one 3-storey Georgian mews house. Down **Benjamin St** and left into **Turnmill St** is Farringdon station, the tube and train link for the area. It has been expanded, being on the north-south Thameslink rail line. **Cowcross St**, where the tube is, has been tidied up and that sign of residential neighbourhood success, a Pizza Express, has just opened. Flats above the Post Office ('The Montgomery Building') are all sold bar two. **Charterhouse St** runs E-W, forming the southernmost boundary of the area, passing behind Smithfield Market and across the **Farringdon Rd** divide on its way to Holborn Circus.

Hatton Garden

The area to the N of **Holborn** and W of **Farringdon Rd** is Hatton Garden, traditionally and still the home of the diamond business. Its streets are wider, less densely packed and more logical in layout than Clerkenwell's. **Hatton Garden** itself leads N from **Holborn Circus**, and is a mixture of modern office blocks, including the sumptuous New Garden House, and smaller Georgian and Victorian terraces. It houses the best and most expensive jewellers of the area. The district to the E has some smart new flats, such as the Ziggurat and Da Vinci buildings in **Saffron Hill**. **Viaduct Buildings**, a cul-de-sac (entrance at the corner of **Charterhouse St** and **Saffron Hill**), has a 4-storey flats block refurbished in a post-modern style. Camden Council, whose patch this is, resists further change of use to homes. Despite this, over 150 homes have emerged since 1996. Local prices (with late 1998 in brackets) typically are: £100,000 for studios (£80,000), £160,000 for 1-bed (£140,000), £240,000 for 2-bed (£200,000).

To the W of **Leather Lane, Dorrington** and **Beauchamp St**s form a quiet square with plane trees: mainly commercial with a row of modern maisonettes at the end. **Leather Lane** itself is the site of the famous market, which runs down the length of the street between Georgian terraces with shops below. In **Baldwins Gardens** the Beeching Building is now lofts. Further W, off the **Gray's Inn Rd**, is **Brookes Court**, a 1980s 3-storey maisonette development in dark brown-brick, facing gardens.

The streets between **Verulam St** and **Clerkenwell Rd** surround the council's Bourne Estate – quiet, '30s-style 5-storey flats entered by arches from the surrounding roads. Many of these solid Victorian homes are now privately-owned.

Old Street/Lower Islington

The **Old St** roundabout is the most easterly point of this area; from it **City Rd** runs NW and **Old St** SW. The area between the fork is sometimes dubbed 'Lower Islington': almost exclusively modern council-built housing, mixed with some commercial property. Following a decade of low demand, there's renewed interest in commercial space here, with offices now competing with homes schemes as developers move E from Clerkenwell.

Bath St runs N-S: at the Old St end, modern low-rise maisonettes extend W towards **Lizard St**. Continuing N, you enter the council-built St Luke's Estate, a mix of tower blocks of between 16 and 20 storeys and low-rise, including roads to the E and W: **Peerless St, Galway St, Radnor St, Mora St** and the lower portion of **Lever St**. Some homes (especially in the later, 4-storey brick blocks) are now privately-owned, with 2- and 3-bed flats on the market for £120-160,000. At the **City Rd/Bath St** junction, City Approach is a new flats scheme. Ten years ago the Old St fire station was turned into studios and 1-bed flats. It also houses a restaurant. Turning W along **Lever St**, roads to the N are mainly commercial. To the E of **Macclesfield Rd**, a successful development of derelict land has brought a business centre and several conversions, including the £280,000-plus loft apartments of No 1 Dingley Place carved out of a former coffee warehouse. Next door are some rare shell-finish lofts in an old print works: £125-190,000 last winter. The new Barbican Hotel is off **Dingley Rd**. Further W, **King Square** has 4- and 6-storey blocks, with a shopping precinct and a large rose garden.

To the S of **Lever St** is commercial property in **Ironmonger Row**, followed by the Turkish baths and swimming pools and more offices in **Europa Place**, at the back of which is a 5-storey tenement building. Further S past **Norman St** is a park and the

Finsbury Leisure Centre; this is bordered by **Mitchell St** which, together with **Bartholomew Square**, runs W-E. Both are commercial, although the streets at right angles to them off to **Old St** are residential, including the refurbished tenement block in **Anchor Yard** and the 3-storey Georgian terraces in **Helmet Row** (partly, including the old vicarage, offices). St Luke's View in **Bartholomew Square** has seven new flats.

Goswell Rd, to the W, has seen little action so far but this is about to change. Several schemes started in 1999, including Dallington Lofts (corner **Dallington St**), 32 loft-style flats by Berkeley; a new-build block from Weston Homes ('Silverdale': £260,000-plus for a 2-bed) and 14 modern-style flats at 93–99 **Goswell Rd** ('The Design Works'). Existing homes include the Triangle development, 5-storeys on the corner of **Percival St**; local authority-built homes now selling at £90,000-plus. The rest of the housing is mainly scruffy Victorian and Georgian terraces with a multitude of small shops beneath.

To the E of **Goswell Rd**, running like the rungs of a ladder, are **Seward St, Pear Tree Court, Bastwick St, Ludlow St** and **Gee St**, all of which have commercial developments of between 3 and 5 storeys: homes are planned for several buildings here. Barratt's 'City View' in Seward St has 1-bed flats from £169,000, 2-beds from £225,000. **Gee St** also has a 12-floor tower block, Parmoor Court, and a large City University hall of residence. A 3-bed house, façade Victorian but with the inevitable 1990s glass bricks, was on the market here for £500,000 last autumn.

To the W of **Goswell Rd**, street patterns are a little more diverse. **Compton St** has a row of low Georgian terraces to the S, and an 8-storey tower block to the N. Running at a diagonal to **Compton St** is **Cyrus St**, which has low '30s-style tenement blocks at the **Compton St** end. The Percival Estate continues on the other side of **Percival St** with Harold Laski House, and tower blocks continue on both sides ending at College Heights on the corner of **St John St**.

The end of **Goswell Rd** forms an acute angle with **City Rd**. Several big commercial users have left this corner, to be slowly replaced by homes and small office schemes. Grove Manor Homes are just starting work on a site at the N end of Goswell Rd opposite the Angel. **Gard St** and **Masons Place** to the S, and **Pickard St** to the N, have large '60s tower blocks to flamboyant heights. Continuing N, **Hall St** has the 25-storey Peregrine House. The area to the W up to the Angel is mostly commercial. **City Rd** is mainly 3- and 4-storey Georgian terraces, set back from the road on both sides with shops and offices down to **Nelsons Terrace**; from here the height drops dramatically, the standard becomes more uneven, and begins to include modern developments. One such is a dozen flats on the N side at the junction with **Haverstock St**. Some of the **City Rd** terraces are reverting to homes: houses command £500,000-plus.

Finsbury, the Lloyd Baker estate and North Clerkenwell

South across the **Pentonville Rd** from Islington, this neighbourhood is bounded by **St John St** and **Rosebery Avenue** to the E and S, and **King's Cross Rd** and **Penton Rise** in the W. It includes two distinctive enclaves of early 19th-century houses, the Lloyd Baker and New River estates. From the Angel tube, **St John St** runs N-S along the E edge of the neighbourhood. Modern and Victorian commercial buildings soon give way to flat-fronted Georgian terraces on both sides. Past the **Chadwell St** junction is a row of little shops, early gentrified. More Georgiana in tiny **Owens Row**, where gracious houses have been painstakingly restored. **Rosebery Avenue** has the newly rebuilt Sadler's Wells Theatre on the N side and some fine Georgian terraces on the S, which also command good prices when they come up for sale. Further down, past the theatre, is the imposing New River Head Building. This important (indeed, historic) building has now become flats. The splendid boardroom makes a superb dining room – available to all the flats. St James's Homes have sold all the first phase and 'the Lab

Building', an Art Deco block converted to 35 1- and 2-bed flats. Phase three, a modern block, has just started. New River re-sales include a 2-floor penthouse, on the market last winter at £1.2 million. **Rosebery Avenue** continues in a mixture of predominantly industrial Victorian buildings and Victorian workmen's flats; at the intersection with **Rosoman St** is the old Finsbury Town Hall with its distinctive stained-glass and wrought-iron porch. Near the **Farringdon Rd** junction, a large mixed development known as Rosebery Court has light industrial workshop space, offices and a new block of 27 flats at the corner of **Rosebery Avenue** and **Coldbath Square**.

Chadwell St runs from **St John St** into the centre of the New River Estate, built in the 1820s. The street has a modern Georgian-style mews development through an arch on the right; the rest is Georgian terraces which open out into the vast **Myddleton Square** with its central garden and church, surrounded on all sides by tall Georgian homes – one of the finest squares in the area. The roads running off to the W – **River St**, **Inglebert St** and **Mylne St** – have fine, wide streets and terraces of large houses. **Claremont Square**, which completes a right-angle with **Amwell St**, is particularly imposing. It runs N-S to join **St John St**, and has Georgian terraces of varying sizes and states of repair, and a number of small shops.

Amwell St marks the boundary between the New River and Lloyd Baker estates. The Lloyd Baker estate was originally built by the eponymous family in 1819, and was partly sold to Islington Council on the death of Miss Lloyd Baker in 1975. Islington still owns a lot of property. It consists mainly of Georgian flat-fronted brick terraced houses, retaining its charm with its fine squares with central gardens. Streets are wider here and houses larger, generally 3/4-bed houses and 2-bed flats. Three roads parallel each other W from **Amwell St**. First is **Great Percy St**: tall Georgian terraces, 4 storeys with first-floor balconies. The road is steep and drops sharply just before **Percy Circus**, giving a superb view to the W over London. **Percy Circus** is a fine square with a park in the centre, two-thirds encircled by a long crescent of terraces. But it is sadly marred by the last third, which is a low-level flats block and car park. Parallel to **Great Percy St**, **Wharton St** and **Lloyd Baker St** converge at **Lloyd Square**. This is the heart of the estate, with a railed garden in the centre, a fine view across to the Post Office Tower and spacious double-fronted Georgian houses. The style continues down **Wharton St** (both sides) and **Lloyd Baker St**; NW of **Rosebery Avenue** is composed of large Victorian and Edwardian tenements and modern commercial and residential blocks, until **Wilmington Square** and **Tysoe St** which border on **Rosebery Avenue** and mark the limit of the area. **Wilmington** is the last fine period square, with tall Georgian terraces and a large central garden. **Tysoe St** has smaller and slightly scruffier terraces but is now up-and-coming. A new block in **Margery St** offers 2-bed flats, selling last winter from £200,000.

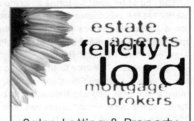

The area E of **Rosebery Avenue** up to **Goswell Rd** and N of **Skinner St** and **Percival St** is not part of the Lloyd Baker estate but has some similar features. West of **St John St** is predominantly council tower blocks: **Gloucester Way** has the 23-storey Michael Cliffe House on stilts. **Myddleton St** is the only period street, with neat Georgian houses and a handful of tidy shops at the bottom. **Lloyd's Row** has another large tower block. The point where it joins **St John St** also marks the end of the Georgian terraces there, which are replaced to the S by more modern commercial and academic buildings. An airline office building here is now 14 flats called St John's Point.

The last part of North Clerkenwell is enclosed by **St John St** and **Goswell Rd** as they diverge away from the Angel, making a triangle bounded by **Percival St** in the S. The whole of this area is very mixed. In the S, on the corner of **St John St** and **Percival St**, is the 4-storey College Heights development. Originally an old warehouse, it was stylishly refurbished in the late '80s into a 24-flat complex with gym and car park. More recent schemes include Pattern House, which is known as the Ingersoll Building.

To the N, forming a circle with roads radiating off it, is **Northampton Square** and the central core of the City University. The quiet square, with a garden and folly in the centre, is bounded on the N by the 7-storey university complex and on the other side by a crescent of 4-storey Georgian terraces with first-floor balconies. One of these, restored to English Heritage standards, was on the market last winter for £550,000. The streets leading off to the E, **Ashby St** and **Sebastian St**, are also mainly Georgian terraces. Where **Sebastian St** meets **Northampton Square**, an ex-factory/warehouse has been converted into four 2-bed, 2-bath flats. They go for around £240,000. **Spencer St** to the N has anonymous university buildings on one side and **Earlstoke St** council estate on the other. Among the best ways of buying into the area cheaply are either to pick up ex-council property or to find property which overlooks modern council estates. This is possible in North Cleveland since there are many small clusters of Georgian houses dotted about. **Rawstorne St** up to **Friend St** is a mixture of low modern mews developments, ex-council homes and small period terraces. The last remaining streets up to the Angel are mostly commercial.

Transport	Tubes: Angel (zone 1, Northern), Farringdon (zone 1, Circle, Metropolitan). From Angel: Oxford Circus 10 min (1 change), City 6 min, Heathrow 1 hr 10 min (1 change). Trains: Farringdon (Moorgate 10 min and Thameslink to Gatwick and Luton).
Convenient for	The City and West End, stations. Miles from centre: 1.5.
Schools	Local Authority: Central Foundation (b).

SALES

Flats	S	1B	2B	3B	4B	5B
Average price	90–115	170–230	240–285	325–400	—	—
Houses	2B	3B	4B	5B	6/7B	8B
Average prices	400+	500+	500–900+	—	—	—

RENTAL

Flats	S	1B	2B	3B	4B	5B
Average prices	160–235	230–525	275–1200	345+	—	—
Houses	2B	3B	4B	5B	6/7B	8B
Average prices	—	—	—	—	—	—

The properties   In Finsbury, handsome Regency and Victorian houses; everywhere, loft conversions of offices/factories/warehouses, new flats blocks (many apeing the lofts), a few mews houses and council- and housing trust-built flats.

The market   Waiting lists for the biggest (earliest) lofts, and for new-build schemes. Newer developments have less space for the money. The market has been rising since 1993 with a blip in late '98. Those priced out of the heart of Clerkenwell look E and N. Finsbury looks best value now. Local searches: Islington 10 working days, Camden 7–10 working days.

Among those estate agents active in this area are:

- Hurford Salvi Carr
- Urban Spaces
- Hamptons
- Kerr Gilchrist
- Stirling Ackroyd
- Jarvis Keller
- Daniel Watney
- Winkworth *
- Felicity J Lord *

* further details: see advertisers' index on p671

CRICKLEWOOD

Map ref: p43 (4G)
Postal districts: NW2
Boroughs: Barnet (Lib
Dem/Lab coalition),
Brent (Lab)
Council tax: Band D
Barnet £760, Brent £678
Conservation areas:
Hermitage Terrace
Parking: Free off main roads

It's good news/bad news time for Cricklewood. Plans loom large in the area until now unkindly dismissed as 'rather a no-man's-land' by estate agents, who like to upgrade it (and its property prices) to 'Hampstead borders', 'West Heath estate', even solidly respectable Golders Green or Willesden Green. And yet . . . might the railway, whose spread began the blurring of London's original hamlets, yet reinstate the name of Cricklewood?

Outline planning permission has now been given for a multi-million pound Railtrack scheme to create a new complex of homes, plus leisure, entertainment and shopping, out of the vast swathe of disused railway sidings along **Claremont Rd**. Also planned are new roads, pedestrian and cycle access routes, and a footbridge across the railway. Once the plans have been fine-tuned and passed by the council, this major scheme to reinvent the heart of the area will take five years to complete.

Less likely is the great hope that Cricklewood Station will become a major staging-post on the planned St Pancras/Heathrow express rail link – but the alternative, West Hampstead, is only one stop away in any case. Both the land redevelopment and the (eventual) airport link will certainly provide a splendid boost to an area whose main claim to fame is the ease at which you can get out of it to almost anywhere else.

The bad news is that these are not the only plans for the vast stretch of old railway land. BNFL intend to use the siding to store (wait for it) spent nuclear fuel for 'a few hours' each week – *if* they are not stopped by existing residents who, it hardly needs saying, are up in (non-nuclear) arms. The fight over this continues.

Meanwhile, harbingers of a new mood by outsiders to take Cricklewood seriously include that most '90s of status symbols, an up-market private gym: Holmes Place opened a branch, plus shops, hairdressers', beauticians', in **Cricklewood Lane** last year. Big developers are eyeing Cricklewood: Fairview added Somerton Gardens, 1- and 2-bed flats (c. £110,000 and £145,000 respectively) off **Claremont Rd** near the station. And one man, at least, firmly believes Cricklewood to be the next boom town. He bought its biggest and oldest pub, the run-down Crown, which he is transforming into a magnificent 4-star hotel, creating 250 new jobs into the bargain: the Crown – the name will remain – is to open this summer. It is difficult to attribute last year's sharp upturn in Cricklewood prices to all these pointers, given the general London property boom, but they certainly underpinned it.

Road access in and out of town is good: as well as the North Circular, Junction 1 of the M1 is a couple of streets away. But once again the railway, thanks to Thameslink, is the key. Nowadays you can wheel your suitcase up to the platform and, when your train arrives, get to King's Cross, or Moorgate for the City, in 15–16 min. You can even travel direct, unimpeded by road traffic, N to Luton Airport or S to South London, Gatwick Airport, Brighton and the whole of the South East Network. Cricklewood does, though, lack one form of transport: the Underground. Nearest stations are Golders Green or Willesden Green, both a brisk walk or bus-ride away.

As a general rule, prices sag in the centre of Cricklewood, rise expectantly towards its borders with West Hampstead on the SE, Gladstone Park on the W and Golders Green to the N. Child's Hill, now part of the same postal district, is on the Hampstead side. Both are ancient places compared to the *nouveau* London boroughs in which they lie.

The grip of the past lingers in the main roads, such as **Cricklewood Lane**, (formerly Child's Hill Lane) and **Cricklewood Broadway**, part of Roman Watling St. Ancient rights of way are still here, but are now secluded footpaths between the houses. People have lived, and worked here (often catering for their more prosperous neighbours in Hampstead or Central London) for centuries: traditionally running laundries, storing furniture, driving carriages and repairing cars. There's still a good amount of open space, not only in gardens but in local parks, playing-fields, sports grounds and municipal playgrounds, offering breathing-space for relaxation and exercise.

Development of the area has come in recognizable spurts. The opening of Cricklewood station in 1868 resulted in a rash of Victorian brick villas in **Claremont Rd** and **Cricklewood Lane** alongside, also in streets opposite called misleadingly after the trees of the forest (to fit into the Wood of the Crickles?): **Oak, Ash, Elm** and **Yew Groves**. Roads named respectively **Olive, Larch, Pine, Cedar, Ivy,** etc, are further to the W on the other side of **Cricklewood Broadway**.

Hendon Way to the E followed in the years between the wars; a bypass, precursor to the roads leading northwards, now the M1. Ribbon development spread alongside: semi-detached houses with garages for the new mobile motor age. Council housing from those years, and post-1945, began to appear on the market as tenants cashed in on their 'Right to Buy' in the late '80s, broadening the spread of homes available. (Some are now downright desirable, others well-nigh unmortgageable.)

Child's Hill and more particularly Cricklewood are mixed areas: predominantly, though not exclusively, residential. Infilling in such a long-established area has produced some apparently unselfconscious mixes of homes cheek-by-jowl with industrial property. There is a great deal of shopping – and some historic pubs – available, including antique shops, pine furniture emporiums and restaurants. But local shops along the main road arteries are mostly specialist and mini-markets: Brent Cross, conveniently a mile or so up the road, throws a large (and due to get larger) shadow. A new shopping centre opened in **Cricklewood Lane** in 1991, which added a little more convenience, and a little more employment beyond the shops, factories and workshops, which already enable many local residents to walk to work. This retention of neighbourhood facilities also enables elderly and relatively immobile residents to find many of their requirements locally.

Churches of various denominations include St Agnes' Catholic Church and Primary School in **Cricklewood Lane**, and a Mosque and Islamic Centre stretching from **Chichele Rd** to **Howard Rd**. There are two local libraries, half a dozen primary schools, and Hampstead (comprehensive) School in **Westbere Rd**. The disadvantages include lack of access to London's tube network, to local hospitals and fee-paying schools – all outside the area. When the various schemes for the ex-railway land take place, however, an area within 3.5 miles of Marble Arch with homes available at so many levels is going to be increasingly worth looking at – especially if access to the City is important.

Child's Hill

On the electoral map, Child's Hill is a Barnet ward extending well into NW11. Not so in estate agents' descriptions, where it's usually defined as the NW2 area of Hampstead.

Semantics apart, the select Hocroft estate certainly includes some very prestigious and expensive houses, and residents to match. Hocroft houses are one-off brick-built neo-Georgian: detached in **Ranulf Rd** (which leads down towards Fortune Green), detached and semis in **Hocroft Rd, Hocroft Avenue, Farm Avenue, Harman Drive**. Even the semis here are 5-bed, usually 2-bath plus car port for the second car. **Harman Close** is a surprise: it has some half-dozen architect-designed 1970s houses, all individual, young and smart.

Most of the area's blocks of flats are in Child's Hill; Vernon Court at the corner of **Finchley Rd** and **Hendon Way**, Wendover and Moreland Courts about 30 yards further on at the top of **Lyndale Avenue**. All three were built in the 1930s: mock-Tudor red-brick with 1/2/3-bed flats. Ground-floor flats have access to the garden. As original tenants slowly gave up the ghost (and their protected tenancies), flats have been modernized and come on the market with regularity. They're popular with the newly retired (some of whom may always have lived nearby, or have children living there), and with young professionals whose pockets don't run to West Hampstead prices. **Finchley Rd** dwellers also have the option of a longer bus-ride down to Finchley Rd tube. It's further away than Golders Green, but reckoned worth it for Jubilee line (half the stops to Charing Cross) and the large Waitrose for shopping on the way home.

Further along the **Finchley Rd**, Orchard Mead, a former police barracks, was spruced up in the late '80s with porters, sauna, small garden to sit out in, parking . . . though the gym was reported to have been replaced by a snooker room. Owners have a share of the freehold; it is at least partly let for investment. Heathway, at the corner with **West Heath Rd**, has 54 flats. At the top of the 1980s boom, in 1989, the 20 luxury 1-, 2- and 3-bedroom flats of Portman Heights opposite appeared at £200–340,000 for a 125-year lease. Popular at least partly because of their NW3 postcode, we reported a year ago that, by the start of 1999, they had now regained their pre-slump values. Recent examples include a 2-bed at £245,000, a 3-bed at £395,000.

Those buying to let in the area need to pick with care: the large number of flats, both purpose-built and conversions, led to less-good properties chasing tenants last year.

The former Child's Hill House, near the junction of **Hermitage Lane** and **Pattison Rd**, is still in single occupation, but most of the Victorian 3-floor houses in the latter street were converted into flats and/or maisonettes in the '80s. There's an intermingling of older houses with others built pre-1914, between the wars, and since, in these sought-after roads which lead up to Hampstead Heath. Often, as in **Hermitage Lane**, there has been a deliberate attempt to adapt to existing spacious pre-war houses with latticed windows and mock-antique touches, but there are also two terraces of newer, more frankly functional, houses for people who prefer equipping their homes to looking after them full-time. More enthusiastic gardeners live in the bungalows of **Hermitage Terrace**, a secluded place where children and/or grandchildren can play in safety; last year it became a conservation area.

C

Back across the **Finchley Rd,** there's concrete-jungle Sunnyside House above shops and motor car showrooms. Opposite, **Crewys Rd** – sometimes known as Little Sicily – has small turn-of-the-century houses, mostly terraced with gardens and lovingly spruced up by owners, apparently oblivious of industrial premises nearby. More light industry, and less space for housing, in **Granville Rd** though this includes Granville Nurseries at its junction with **The Vale.** Nurseries are useful in areas with so many individual gardens, and locals with space and taste for keeping their gardens looking better than the Jones's next door.

There are also ex-council properties on the market here. In the '80s Barnet encouraged tenants to exercise their enterprise this way, and sold off close to a third of its housing stock. The range of these homes is, to say the least, wide: buyers have difficulties getting a mortgage on some ex-authority homes. But others are very popular: look for 2/3-bed houses, terraced, in **Garth** and **Cloister Rds** off **Hendon Way,** 2/3-bedroom flats in **Longberrys, Cricklewood Lane** and 2-bed flats in Hermitage Court.

Cricklewood Central

This area covers a broad band each side of **Cricklewood Lane,** starting from **Hendon Way** to the NE, the **Farm Avenue** sportsground on its S side, and with its other two sides bordered by **Cricklewood Broadway** and the **North Circular Rd.** The railway runs right through the middle. It includes large areas of council-built housing in the **Claremont Rd** area, also the Westcroft Estate in **Lichfield Rd** which is Camden Council housing on land leased from Barnet. Main kinds of property to look for: pre-1914 housing near the railway station (as already mentioned) and the semis built between the wars the time the **Hendon Way** was being developed.

Often the two mix and mingle, 1930s 3-bedroom semis alongside and opposite Victorian villas in **Cricklewood Lane,** solid residential semis with gabled entrance lobbies and steep-sided roofs, sometimes joined up in terraces of four and six as in **Somerton** and **Gillingham Rds.** Then there are stretches of widely spaced semis in **Greenfield Gardens, Purley** and **Sanderstead Avenues,** roads which are incongruously wider than the main thoroughfares. Most of the semis are owner-occupied, although there's also a certain amount of letting. Some former bungalows in **The Vale** and nearby have had their roofs opened up and extended and indeed, much individual attention, money and ingenuity has gone into changing and adapting these houses and gardens.

But building land is scarce here now. Developers manage to find patches of land to build on, though: sandwiched in the angle between **Brent Terrace** and **Claremont Rd, Romney Row** – a smart terrace of 2-bed houses – was completed in the early '90s next to 32 new flats at **Dover Close** and **Rye Close.**

Behind the other side of **Brent Terrace,** however, is the aforementioned vast wasteland of redundant railway sidings and depots. One day, the terrace should back onto the bright new landscape of housing, offices, shops – even parks – that figure in the ambitious regeneration plan. But will BNFL get their way? (See Introduction.) Whatever, 3-bed semis here cost the gambling man, or woman, some £130,000 at present . . .

An expensive, inward-looking 1990s Shakespearean fantasy development lies between **The Vale** and **Somerton Rd.** Boasting over 150 flats and houses, **Elsinore Gardens, Hamlet Square** and **Ophelia Gardens** attract prices above the average for the area (these can be £225,000 for 3-bed houses). Next door, on the corner of **The Vale** and **Claremont Rd,** Wimpey's Compton Place, 21 3-storey, 3-bed town-houses, c. £300,000, appeared in 1998. Further S on **Claremont Rd,** on the site of Express Dairies, Fairview Homes squeezed in Somerton Gardens, a development of 99 studio, 1- and 2-bed flats; prices c. £110,000 for 1-bed, £145,000 for 2-bed flats (again good for this area), location definitely convenient: views over Cricklewood station. Quite a lot of industry remains in these residential streets, but rubs shoulders fairly unobtrusively with placid suburban semis in **Somerton Rd** and **The Vale**, less so in **Dersingham Rd**.

Most of the houses in these streets are well-maintained, often on a do-it-yourself basis. Many of the older houses in the **Cricklewood Lane** end of **Claremont Rd** are subdivided for letting, but when they come up for sale are attracting 'Hampstead overspill' young professionals.

It's a different, more crowded world on the other side of the railway bridge. It is more cosmopolitan: shops near and in **Cricklewood Broadway** include Halal butchers, sari shops, jewellery and Oriental greengrocers, grocers and bakers.

'The Groves' – **Yew Grove, Ash Grove, Elm Grove, Oak Grove** – are all Edwardian 2-storey houses which seem to have been rebuilt, converted, improved and adapted as if to show just how many variations on the original could be achieved: dormer windows, balconies, teak and glass doors, cladding. They must be among the most economically priced 2-bed conversions within 3 miles of Marble Arch.

But there's simply not enough pavement and kerbside space for residents, shoppers and railway users to park their cars. They try, which helps to explain why the council sweepers don't seem to be able to keep these streets litter-free. There's not much they can do to sweep behind and under parked cars.

So far, so predictable. But the former railway cottages (know locally as just 'the Cottages') some 300 yards up **Cricklewood Broadway** on the E, Barnet, side are a surprise. Sold off to the then residents some 30 years ago, these are five parallel terraces of 2- and 3-bedroom houses, some boasting pretty gardens, sometimes with one large communal lawn on one side and individual private patches on the other. Access by car is limited, but it's a cosy spot (if close to the tracks, it's also close to the station) where residents have shrugged off the original railway grime and coal dust. In the '90s it attracted an artistic if impecunious bunch (including actors and magicians); many got to love it and stuck, even starting families in accommodation where it might not be easy to swing a cat or a baby. Then these houses became viewed as collectors' pieces: prices here have shot up. A 2-bed cottage in **Johnson Terrace** that would have fetched around £80,000 in 1996 was on the market in 1997 for £129,950. Prices for these rows rose by another £10,000 over 1998; one was listed at £160,000. By the end of 1999 asking prices were anything up to £225,000. Four-beds (also tiny), which a year back could be found at £175,000, now aspire, say agents, towards the £300,000 mark.

West Cricklewood

Streets named after trees to the E of **Cricklewood Broadway** are 'the Groves'; here, on the W (Brent) side, are 'the Roads'. Most of them contain 2-storey houses built at the turn of the century, so there has been plenty of time for **Pine, Larch, Cedar, Olive, Ivy, Oaklands** etc, **Rds** to have developed leafy mature trees (not of appropriate species) and for conversions into flats, maisonettes and garden flats.

Multi-occupation usually means parking problems, especially in streets built before cars – or indeed bathrooms – were considered necessary, so it's worth considering the width of any road before deciding to live in it (there have been arguments at the kerbside in streets like **Ashford Rd** between residents and 'outside' parkers). Ashford Court is the only really large blocks of flats, with 180 1/2/3-bedroom flats at quite moderate prices. An active Lessees' Association operates here.

Between **Sheldon Rd** and **Cricklewood Broadway**, **Sylvan Grove**, a clutch of 33 flats and 21 houses, appeared in 1992 on the site of an old aircraft factory. The whole development has now been taken over by a housing association.

Purpose-built flats, two to each house, were built pre-1914 in **Wotton, Temple** and **Langton Rds**. Note the double front doors: one leads to the staircase for upstairs.

There are also late-'80s Laing flats and houses in and off **Langton Rd**, not far from either the station or the park: again now mainly housing association.

More conventionally up-market are the wide leafy roads near **Gladstone Park** with comfortable 4/5-bed houses, some of them detached in **Anson Rd**, **Oman Avenue** and many of the roads running into the former. Some, ie **Oman Avenue**, also have blocks of flats where elderly parents of local residents can live near, but not with, their children.

These are sights for the eyes for anyone who thinks that civilization stops at the boundary with Brent (which includes at least one Child's Hill estate agent). It's true that this area contains a larger percentage of industrial buildings, also garages, workshops and even itinerant sellers of produce and textiles. **Hassop Rd** is totally industrial. What happens is that the better roads are dubbed Willesden Green. (See also Willesden and Dollis Hill chapters.) No wonder Cricklewood is said to be shrinking.

Transport Trains: Cricklewood, direct to King's Cross/Moorgate (16 min).

Convenient for Gatwick and Luton Airports by train. Routes both into and out of town: M1 (Junction 1), Golders Green, Willesden Green, Kilburn tubes and roads to the West End. Ikea and Tesco superstores. Hampstead Heath. Miles from centre: 4.5.

Schools Barnet and Brent Education Authorities: Hampstead School. See also Hampstead.

SALES

Flats	S	1B	2B	3B	4B	5B
Average prices	60–90	90–150	100–180	160–250	–	–
Houses	2B	3B	4B	5B	6/7B	8B
Average prices	140–170	160–300	250–500	300–800+	400+	1.5 M

RENTAL

Flats	S	1B	2B	3B	4B	5B
Average prices	120–160	140–180	180–270	220–350	300–400	500+
Houses	2B	3B	4B	5B	6/7B	8B
Average prices	200–250	260–370	325–400	650–800	–	–

The properties Wide range, from prestigious Hampstead-fringe detached houses and mansion flats, via '30s semis, to Victorian and Edwardian terraces, semis, cottages and converted flats. Prices for individual houses can rise over a million towards Hampstead. Pockets of new-build; more to come.

The market Good prospects for area with good links to everywhere else. The smarter corners gained as a knock-on from Hampstead as prices rose. Large supply of flats held rents firmly down last year. Local searches: Barnet 5 working days, Brent 5–10 working days.

Among those estate agents active in this area are:
- Albert & Co
- Kaye & Co
- Homeview Estates *
- Callaway & Co
- Carltons
- Nelhams William
- Kinleigh, Folkard & Hayward
- Winkworth *
- Ellis & Co
- Gladstones
- Bairstow Eves

* *further details: see advertisers' index on p671*

CROUCH END AND STROUD GREEN

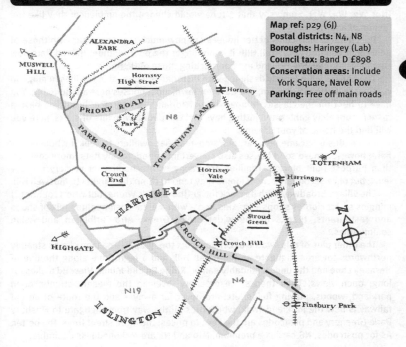

Map ref: p29 (6J)
Postal districts: N4, N8
Boroughs: Haringey (Lab)
Council tax: Band D £898
Conservation areas: Include York Square, Navel Row
Parking: Free off main roads

Crouch End prices got into a spiral in 1999 due to impatient buyers chasing a strictly limited supply of homes. So much, so normal in much of London last year, but the frothy market cemented Crouch End's claim to be the downright fashionable – at last. Price rises were boosted by an influx of outsiders willing to pay what some local agents reckoned over-the-top prices in an area with no tube. On the plus side, they found spacious family homes for under £400,000: compare neighbouring Highgate and Kentish Town.

The districts of Crouch End, Stroud Green and Hornsey, like so many others, began to change rapidly in the heady days of the '80s as landlords of neglected old houses sold out to developers – both companies and owner-occupiers – and those priced out of its neighbours began to search the streets. You can still find un-done-up houses here, complete with wheezing Ascot heaters and roll-top baths from the first time they were fashionable. In the little parades of shops, chic health clubs and cafés have sprung up, a testament to – well, gentrification is perhaps the wrong word, but certainly modish bohemianization: newcomers are more media than City.

The area is indeed strategically placed: to the N it is bounded by lovely, hilly Alexandra Park, to the W by up-market, Georgian Highgate, to the S by the residential streets of Finsbury Park and to the E by the Great Northern railway line. It became a respectable suburb in the second half of the 19th century, but spent most of the 20th in unassuming obscurity. It is now a solid 15 years into a revival, and is lively both by night and day.

The inward flow of young professionals renting or buying here highlights this area's convenience for both City and West End – although it lacks a tube station.

There are, however, four within a 1-mile radius (Finsbury Park, Highgate, Archway and Turnpike Lane), and three buses to get you to Finsbury Park tube and train station (Nos W2, W3, W7). Some say that a tube would change the ambience: they like the feeling of apartness.

Prices for Crouch End's better houses are now much more on a par with those of genteel, prosperous Muswell Hill: it is no longer the poor relation. Indeed flats now cost more than up the Hill and are approaching those of Highgate.

The houses were largely designed with Victorian or Edwardian families in mind. In contrast to districts further in, like Camden Town, most houses here are quite big. You have to hunt for the classic, compact late-Victorian 3-bed terrace, but if you have a taste for ungainly gables and jutting bays and can put up with lots of stairs, here you will find the home of your dreams.

In the '80s it became popular for Hampstead flat-dwellers to seek a whole house here; however, these solid houses also convert into good, roomy flats (more common than purpose-built blocks). Families are happy with schooling at nursery/primary level, but once secondary school looms they tend to climb the heights to Muswell Hill.

The village Broadway, with its clock tower (the clock is wrong, but who's counting?) mingles smart clothes shops – for kids, too – with a great cosmopolitan mix of shops and restaurants, thanks to the wider area's Greek, Afro-Caribbean and Asian communities.

The other plus of this swathe of London is its topography. The land climbs steadily northwards towards Highgate and Muswell Hill, and a high ridge along the line of **Hornsey Lane** and the understandably named **Ridge Rd** and **Mount View Rd** makes for long, open views. Then there's the greenery: even in the meaner streets, open parkland, woods, playing fields, etc, are never far away – and the route of an old railway is now the Parkland Walk, which runs all the way from Highgate to Finsbury Park. Greenery and postcodes are the keys to prices: the more street trees, the better. As for postcodes, N8 carries a premium. N19 and N4 are reckoned less desirable.

Crouch End

The Broadway, at the heart of this part of the old borough of Hornsey, eventually eclipsed Hornsey's **High St**, away to the N at the end of **Middle Lane**, as the area's centre. The many tree-lined streets and green spaces away from the main roads lend Crouch End an almost rural feel, but there has been a sea change in the population. The first wave of young singles and the dual-income-no-kids-yet brigade are being joined by more and more families.

As in Muswell Hill, this is arts-and-media land – but more rock than opera here. Indeed, Crouch Hill boasts a recording studio in an old church, and everyone hangs out at the World Café opposite. Lots of new shops (arty, funky furniture – that sort of thing), and loads more cafés, bars, nice coffee houses, eclectic eateries from Thai to West Indian, have appeared for the largely kid-free and carefree to chill out in. Now there's 'yet another health club' (as an observer put it) in **Topsfield Parade**. Alas, the old-fashioned corset shop has closed.

Flats above shops and a few purpose-built blocks offer homes to those who want to be close to the Crouch End action. Expect to pay £150,000-plus for a 2- to 3-bed flat on two floors.

Highgate Borders

The most expensive homes in Crouch End are found to the W of **Park Rd**, **The Broadway** and **Crouch End Hill** because of their proximity to Highgate. Roads such as **Glasslyn Rd**, **Wolseley Rd**, **Coolhurst Rd** and **Clifton Rd** going down to **Coleridge Rd** and **Crescent Rd**, are tree-lined and mainly contain large Victorian Gothic and

Edwardian 3-storey terraces or semi-detached houses. Many of these have been converted into roomy flats: whole houses command prices up to £750,000.

The 1980s contributed smart modern flats and maisonettes to **Crescent Rd** and **Coolhurst Rd**, and more new homes off **Wolsely Rd** and **Stanhope Rd**. Some of the best streets have gardens bordering the Parkland Walk nature reserve along the former railway line – though this patch considers itself Highgate. This area is particularly well off for open spaces, which include Crouch End playing-fields off **Park Rd**. There's an up-market tennis club, too.

Similar Victorian/Edwardian houses occur in the streets between **Crouch End Hill** and **Crouch Hill**, in for example **Christchurch Rd** and **Haslemere Rd**. They sometimes belie their staid exteriors, though: one quietly unassuming house in **Haslemere Rd** has a Moorish-inspired interior, designed for an eccentric Russian banker in 1911.

Further S, in the N19 district, roads between **Crouch Hill** and **Hornsey Rise** such as **Warltersville Rd**, **Heathville Rd**, **Ashley Rd** (the best) and **Shaftesbury Rd** have some mansion flats, council-built blocks and 3-storey Victorian houses, mostly reborn as flats: the postcode lowers the prices here, though these streets are closer to tubes. There are a few roads W of **Hornsey Rise** and S of **Hornsey Lane**, such as **Sunnyside Rd** and **Beaumont Rise**, which are on the borders of Crouch End and Archway. This corner also holds the Whitehall Park conservation area. (See also the Highgate and Kentish Town chapters.)

Middle Lane

The triangle of roads N of **Tottenham Lane** and **Park Rd**, which is bisected by **Middle Lane**, is a less expensive hotchpotch of different types of houses, which reflect the different stages of growth and function of Crouch End. There are the large Victorian and Edwardian houses, which yield many flats, such as in **Hillfield Avenue**, **Harold Rd** and some in **Middle Lane**, and the more modern ones like those found in **Rokesly Avenue** and **Elmfield Avenue**, which are more likely to remain intact. There are also some original cottage houses to be found in **New Rd**. This is one of the few corners of Crouch End where smaller, 3-bed houses predominate: only 10–15 per cent of local houses are of this size. Scarcity has meant even higher price rises in proportion.

Houses get grander, sprouting gables and spires, as you go north: £400,000-plus near Priory Park. The bus route to Finsbury Park tube goes down **Middle Lane** from **Priory Rd** and then turns up **Rokesly Avenue**, where a 3-bed house costs £290–300,000. This is also the home of the high-scoring Rokesly Primary School.

Hornsey

The Hornsey High St neighbourhood lies N of **Priory Rd** and **High St Hornsey**, and S of Alexandra Park. **Nightingale Lane** divides the district in two: to the E are mainly council-built properties and to the W mainly private. **Linzee Rd** is popular, **Redston Rd** ditto with its good, bigger villas at £500,000 or so. **North View Rd** has a good number of purpose-built Edwardian maisonettes.

Some homes here have beautiful views of Alexandra Park, where 'Ally Pally' limped back to life after fire almost destroyed it. Exhibitions and concerts are held there once more, and there's an ice rink and the famous Palm Court: the best place in North London on November 5th!

High St Hornsey is looking up as a shopping centre: the ubiquitous interior shops are moving in, and the old waterworks site between Alexandra Park and the High St is set to become a vast Sainsbury's superstore plus 129 new houses. Agents opine that this will boost the area – but there has been strong local opposition to the superstore. This neighbourhood could be one to look at: whatever the existing inhabitants think, a superstore seems to boost house prices.

Hornsey Vale

Agents are trying to rename this neighbourhood, S of **Tottenham Lane** and E of **The Broadway** and **Crouch Hill**, 'Crouch End Heights' – a sure sign of rising fashionability. There are two distinct areas, shown by prices: N of **Ridge Rd**, down to **Tottenham Lane**, and E of **Ferme Park Rd** is the cheaper part – 'but getting there' according to local agents. West of **Ferme Park Rd** streets like **Weston Park** and **Cecile Park** command higher prices.

From **Weston Park** there is a steep hill up to **Mount View Rd**, which forms the border with Stroud Green. Several streets climb the hill, including **Mayfield Rd** with the little Stationers Park and a splendidly Gothic Victorian church that is now split into flats. Look in **Nelson Rd**, and some of its neighbours, for 6- and 7-bed homes, big even by Crouch End standards. **Mount View Rd** has huge, double-fronted houses. The roads either side of Weston Park contain mainly 2- (but some 3-) storey terraced houses, often converted into flats. **Ferme Park Rd** is on the bus route to Finsbury Park tube. Good family houses can be had around here in the £325–475,000 bracket.

The streets between **Ferme Park Rd** and **Crouch Hill** hold a mixture of good-quality homes of varying sizes, mostly now smart or being improved. Look out for those with spacious, convertible basements. Good roads here include spring blossom-lined **Cecile Park**, **Tregaron Avenue** and **Weston Park** – this is the better end of this long road. Crouch Hill has some Victorian mansion blocks offering good-sized flats.

Stroud Green

This neighbourhood forms a triangle which lies to the S of **Mount View Rd** and is bordered by **Stroud Green Rd** to the W and the railway line to the E. It used to have large areas of sub-standard housing but this area is slowly improving. Hopeful talk about 'Stroud Green Village', however, has yet to bring about mass gentrification. Residents think the volume of traffic in the area may be to blame for this. In some roads, prices are close to Crouch End's, and prices have risen at the same rate over the last year, but other parts are both scruffier and cheaper. At the N end of Stroud Green **Mount View Rd** has some expensive houses which overlook a green space atop a covered reservoir and – as they are at the top of Crouch Hill – the rest of Stroud Green too. The streets coming down off **Mount View Rd** are wide and tree-lined: roads like **Mount Pleasant Villas**, **Granville Rd** and **Oakfield Rd** contain large 3-storey terraced houses which are almost all converted into flats. Again, those at the top get splendid views.

At the bottom, towards the tracks, **Mount Pleasant Villas** contains pretty little early Victorian villas. In 1999 this corner saw the highest percentage rises in the whole Crouch End/Stroud Green area, say agents. A good harbinger for this corner is the transformation of the old dairy (once a car repair shop) into a smart wine bar/restaurant, one of a clutch of new arrivals. **Stapleton Hall Rd,** which snakes across both the railway and the Parkland Walk, is a long street of substantial Victoriana. Crouch Hill railway station, with trains into St Pancras, serves this area.

The roads to the E of **Lancaster Rd,** like **Cornwall Rd** and **Connaught Rd,** contain 3-storey houses decorated with white stucco – again, good flat-hunting territory. Intact houses command £325,000–370,000. Moving down towards Finsbury Park tube, the roads and the houses in them are not in such good order, with noisier, more crowded streets and more of an inner-city feel: lots of local shops, clothing manufacturers, ironmongers, launderettes and garages intersperse the houses. Look for cheap, convenient homes here. **Upper Tollington Place** has big houses in a busy road; **Florence Rd** and **Victoria Rd** have nice early Victorian homes; **Osbourne Rd** and **Marquis Rd** are mostly council blocks.

Borders

East of Hornsey, across the railway line, is the Harringey 'ladder' – so-called because its streets march parallel to each other like rungs between the busy through-routes of **Wightman Rd** and **Green Lanes/Grand Parade.** The houses here are cheaper than those further W: nice suburban terraces of 3/4-bed houses, but a little too close to Wood Green for high prices. You can pay around £210,000 for a 3-bed house here. The area is popular with young couples, who enjoy the local shops in **Green Lanes** which are open all hours (Greek and Turkish food in abundance) and the inexpensive eateries here. The northern 'ladder' roads have the coveted N8 postcode. The W ends of the roads, away from crowded **Green Lanes,** are most popular. The Park Ridings streets N of **Turnpike Lane** may offer a 3-bed Victorian house for under £200,000.

West of **Stroud Green Rd** Stroud Green merges with Finsbury Park. In streets such as **Evershot Rd** and **Marriot Rd** you'll find 2- and 3-storey terraced houses, many of which have been converted into flats. The N4 postal boundary runs along the **Hornsey Rd.** N and W of here is in the N19 zone.

Between **Hornsey Rd** and **Holloway Rd,** there is a tract which does not really belong to Crouch End but is not quite Tufnell Park either. Once it was Holloway, but this is a name that today seems less used, perhaps because of the prison (though Brixton survives a similar stigma). Perhaps the name is due for a renaissance: agents are tipping this area for bargain-hunters looking for a corner that should improve. The houses are spacious and away from the **Holloway Rd** the streets are fairly quiet. North of the railway there are flat-fronted Victorian houses in **Fairbridge Rd.** The rather mixed area round about is said to be coming up. South of the railway the houses are smaller. Housing associations are active here.

The streets with **Tollington** in their names form a fairly distinct district: wide roads with big churches and solid houses. In **Tollington Way,** Bellway are building on a fairly large scale: 2- and 3-bed flats and 3-bed town-houses round a quad. The town houses were priced from £230,000 last autumn. Off **Sussex Way,** 23 flats and houses have been carved out of a mews: some are converted stables, some new-build; in the same street an old mission hall is now eight £250,000 2-bed flats.

Transport	Tubes: Finsbury Park (zone 2, Victoria, Piccadilly); to Oxford Circus 11 min, City 30 min (1 change), Heathrow 1 hr. Trains: Hornsey, Haringey, Finsbury Park (Moorgate 13 min, Kings Cross 8 min). Crouch Hill (Silverlink/North London line).
Convenient for	Wood Green Shopping City, Alexandra Park. Miles from centre: 5.

Schools   Haringey Education Authority: Hornsey School, St David
& St Katherine. Private: Highgate Boys School.

SALES

Flats	S	1B	2B	3B	4B	5B
Average prices	60–120	85–135	120–250	135–375	—	—
Houses	2B	3B	4B	5B	6/7B	8B
Average prices	180–220	200–360+	320–400+	350–750	—	—

RENTAL

Flats	S	1B	2B	3B	4B	5B
Average prices	120–150	130–210	200–300	–	—	—
Houses	2B	3B	4B	5B	6/7B	8B
Average prices	250–300	300–360	350–450	450–525	—	—

The properties   19th-century suburban houses, many now converted to flats.
Largest and smartest close to Highgate, smaller ones elsewhere,
though the typical house is on the big side. Some p/b flats. Also
ex-council bargains.

The market   Crouch End's status has risen: now very popular with young
professionals commuting to City or West End – though
pressure on school places has lessened its appeal to families.
More impecunious home-hunters head away from the pleasant
(and pricey) hilly streets of Crouch End and parts of Hornsey;
meaner, cheaper streets, though even more convenient, towards
Finsbury Park. Local searches: 10 working days.

Among those estate agents active in this area are:

- Dennells
- Martyn Gerrard
- Paul Simon
- Prickett & Ellis
- Tatlers
- Davies & Davies
- Winkworth*

further details: see advertisers' index on p671

CRYSTAL PALACE

Map ref: p111 (7G)
Postal districts: SE26, SE19, SE20
Boroughs: Bromley (Lib/Lab Coalition), Croydon (Lab), Lambeth (Lab), Lewisham (Lab), Southwark (Lab)
Council tax: Band D Bromley £669, Croydon £758, Lambeth £750, Lewisham £727, Southwark £808
Conservation areas: Check with town hall
Parking: Free

The wooded heights of South London offer long prospects, cleanish air and solace for those who get claustrophobia in the former marshlands closer to the heart of town. Sydenham Hill rises greenly and abruptly from Dulwich and forms a distinct boundary between inner London to the NW and the essentially suburban borough of Bromley which meanders off SE into Kent. Indeed, the London postal districts stop on the hill's SE slopes and the inhabitants of Beckenham put 'Kent' on their notepaper.

Crystal Palace – which took its name from Paxton's vast glasshouse, moved to the hilltop from Hyde Park after the Great Exhibition of 1851 – is the name of a park and a landmark (the soaring TV masts), rather than a place. Anerley and Penge slope away to the SE, Sydenham is to the E, Upper Sydenham to the N, Gipsy Hill to the W and Upper Norwood along the ridge to the SW. Five boroughs meet at the hilltop, so it's more than usually necessary to enquire who gets, and spends, your council tax.

The hills and valley of this interesting landscape give character to the area, define the neighbourhoods and influence the type of property. Large houses and mansions (the popularity of the Palace persuaded wealthy Victorians to build here) occupy lofty vantage points with compelling views; modest terraces cluster the lower reaches.

With dramatic irony, a century and a half later the major talking-point – or rather, bitter row – is *still* the Crystal Palace. The building itself is long gone: burnt down spectacularly in 1936. The site has remained empty, but the 1960s construction of the National Sports Centre and Bromley Council's current £3 million plans to modernize it, restore the park and regenerate the area contributed to an upturn in fortunes.

The late lamented Palace was a famous venue for concerts. Optimists hoped that it might rise again. However, the sight of the drawings of the proposed 'leisure complex', with its 18-screen multiplex cinema, its nine restaurants 'carefully selected to avoid conflict with existing outlets' and its 'cultural space' for local groups to use, sparked a major protest campaign. The 1990 Crystal Palace Act says that any new building on the site should reflect the style of the original. Bromley Council says it does. Campaigners disagreed. So did eco-warriors, camped out in the trees until ejected by bailiffs. The plans went to the Ministry and were eventually given the go-ahead. A by-product of the new complex is the investment of £5.5 million in local transport: a new bus depot has already appeared, and the future will bring more bus measures and (perhaps) a link to the Croydon Tramlink.

There's also the Crystal Palace Partnership, one of the government's schemes to cheer up areas through injection of some cash and a lot of exhortation. Watch this space. A move to get businesses into the area, and to persuade landlords to rent out empty properties, has already had some succees.

At the summit of the Crystal Palace Hill is the area known locally as the 'Triangle', bordered by **Westow Hill** to the N, **Westow St** to the W and **Church Rd** to the E. It's part of Croydon but abutted by Lambeth, Southwark and Bromley Boroughs. **Fox Hill** and **Belvedere Rd** make an elegant descent from **Church Rd** parallel to the busy **Anerley Hill** and houses here are much sought-after. North of **Anerley Hill**, beyond Crystal Palace railway station, Crystal Palace Park acts as a barrier with Penge.

Sydenham, to the N of Penge, is an elegant suburb which enjoys a good community spirit – the Sydenham Society is very active. Upper Sydenham historically had more lavish properties – surviving examples on **Westwood Hill** and **Sydenham Hill**. Other hill-climbers here are **Wells Park Rd** and **Longton Avenue**. Historic **Jews Walk** enjoys repute. Sydenham today still has the atmosphere, which it shares with the other slopes of the hill, of having strayed from an Edwardian novel. A character from H. G. Wells, perhaps, or even Sherlock Holmes himself, seems likely to emerge from the pillared drives lined with laurels. Houses of that period were lavishly spacious, and even flats made from them are as big as any in London.

Lower Sydenham has the sought-after, turn-of-the-century Thorpe Estate but ends modestly round **Bell Green**. To the S of **Westwood Hill**, the roads starting with the name **Lawrie Park** are popular.

The even spread of rail stations across the area makes for convenient commuting. Gipsy Hill station between **Westow Hill** and **Crystal Palace Parade** to the N has a quarter-hourly service into Victoria station and is in zone 3, which is popular with commuters – the other rail stations are in zone 4. There are also good bus routes, many ending at **Crystal Palace Parade**. The new Tramlink links Beckenham with Croydon. There are hopes that the tram can be extended up the hill to Crystal Palace itself. Once you get to Croydon, there are fast trains to Gatwick Airport. By car, the M25 is not far away.

Westow Hill

Westow Hill, Victorian and villagy in character, has a good selection of shops and many new better-than-average restaurants – some quite chic. To the N, the bay-fronted Victorian semis of **Farquhar Rd** are bed-sit and flat-land: one of these solid old houses is being split into 10 flats this winter. Further down are large detached Tudor-timber-style houses in **Dulwich Wood Avenue**. **Jasper Rd** has large Victorian terraces, not all as tidy as they could be: the pair of new 4-bed £225,000 semis stands out. **Westow St** to the S has small shops, a supermarket and community centre complex. There are luxury 1- and 2-bed retirement apartments here; also a rather pedestrian new development of flats squeezed in behind the shops between **Westow Hill** and **Church Rd**. Up-and-coming **Church Rd** (which runs S towards Croydon) has Nesbitt Square, an award-winning small development of eight 5-bed homes; also Nightingale Court, luxury sheltered retirement apartments. In the 'Triangle' between **Westow Hill** and **Church Rd**, **St Aubyn's Rd** has recent bay-window-style houses and modern terraced houses in **Brunel Close**. A deconsecrated church tower re-emerged as a £1.2 million 5-bed des' res' in 1997 – on the rental market for £1,000 a week last summer.

Fox Hill

This leafy district slopes down from the hilltop between **Church Rd** and **Anerley Hill**. **Fox Hill Rd** starts with small cottages and a modern development. It's steep (20 per cent gradient) and offers a truly panoramic view. It has large Victorian houses, semis and detached, plus '60s town-houses. Many homes are being done up. A low terrace of stuccoed watermen's cottages, which used to back on to the canal, starts **Belvedere Rd**. Composition of the road is similar to **Fox Hill** – No 73, Tower House, is a striking property. At the corner of **Anerley Rd**, a large house is becoming flats. Many of **Hamlet Rd's** large Victorian homes have been split into flats. Modern town-houses (3-bed, with garage) off **Stambourne Way** in **Fitzroy Gardens** now command £140,000-plus. This tree-lined neighbourhood is further enhanced by small greens. Trees shield the large houses, some split into flats, in **Auckland Rd**, which has traffic-calming width curbs. There is a modern development here of a coach house, plus six new 5-bed houses by Sunley Estates. The road continues with private flats, Victorian detached and semis, and travels down past playing-fields to South Norwood. **Sylvan Rd** has modern terraces as well as Victorian. It also has Harris City Technology College and Sports Centre.

Anerley

Busy **Anerley Hill** starts loftily at the roundabout with **Westow Hill** – commanding views of South London and beyond. Victorian detached and terraced properties – many converted into flats – and '60s town-houses make the descent. Midway, there are a number of council estates. New homes for shared ownership are going up on two sites here. Shops near Anerley station provide for basic needs. **Thicket Rd's** large detached houses follow the S edge of Crystal Palace Park. Here, Orchard Park is a 'village-style' scheme on a 5-acre former goods yard. Its studios, 1- and 2-bed flats fetch from around £40–70,000. **Anerley Park's** large Victorian semis yield many a flat. Terraced, cottage homes are found in **Trenholme Rd**.

Penge

Modern shopping facilities in **Penge High St** contrast with the quiet dignity of the King William IV Naval Asylum and the almshouses of **Watermen's Square**. The focal point of the four low-built rows is the chapel, now the area's most unusual home, twin-towered and standing loftily above its neighbours. More almshouses are found in **King William IV Gardens** – sadly fronted by a council block. **Wordsworth Rd** has bay-fronted Victorian terraces, while **Parish Lane** is cottage terraces, popular with first-time buyers who paid around £75,000 in 1997/8 and are now sitting in homes worth £110–120,000. Swallows Court is a recent development of 2-bed flats in **Morland Rd**, a cul-de-sac. Larger houses in **Lennard Rd** (Victorian and mock-Tudor semis), **Cator Rd** (Vict detached) and **Woodbastwick Rd** ('30s semis) with its view up to the TV mast.

Running parallel to the A213 **Croydon Rd**, **Maple Rd** has a street market at the **High St** end. To the E, **Kenilworth Rd's** bay-fronted 1930s terraces have wooden porches. **Clevedon Rd** is similar. Quiet and popular roads are **Chesham Crescent** and **Chesham Rd** – '30s semis. **Ravenscroft Rd** and **Birkbeck Rd** have more Victoriana.

Sydenham

The N–S railway line divides Sydenham Park from Lower Sydenham to the E. In the triangle between the railway and **Kirkdale**, quiet leafy **Sydenham Park Road** starts with Victorian, then at the E some council blocks, and a new flats development. **Sydenham Park** crosses it, mixing '30s bay-fronted and large Victorian terraces with some cottages and large semis. **Wells Park Rd** runs W from **Kirkdale**, starting modestly with Victorian terraces and small shops. A rather run-down 3-bed house was £145,000 last winter. Off on the right, narrow **Halifax St** comes as a surprise – bright-painted terraced cottages with white wooden fences. Council-built homes occupy the lower part of the hill. Further up on the left is the hilly **Sydenham Wells Park** (Sydenham was a minor 19th-century spa). Halfway up the hill, modern private flats start to appear – they have balconies and raised gardens protected by fences and hedges. **Canonbury Mews** is a modern estate with neatly tended lawns. Right at the top is the large, modern St Clement's Heights estate with its white picket fences.

Sydenham Hill skirts the NW edge of the neighbourhood. From **Kirkdale**, the wide, busy road continues SW with flats and detached houses. Here some woodland appears; there is a walled-off, modern Corporation of the City of London estate. Lammas Green council estate has some stuccoed terraces. Seven smart 4-bed town houses round a private square have just been built: all sold. Council estates appear – including high-rise blocks. Victoriana mingles with '30s detached, modern terraces and town-houses; also the occasional, almost enchanted, wooded cul-de-sac. Impressive, sweeping views of London are a major plus. Near the roundabout with **Westwood Hill**, back on the hilltop, there's the recent **Wavel Place** development and a large flats block being smartened up. The TV mast soars into view.

Westwood Hill descends to the E towards central Sydenham with modern town-houses on the left and mansions on the right. Torrington Court is a '30s mansion block. Sydenham High School is here; next to it an imaginative flats scheme uses a tower motif. Off **Westwood Hill** is popular **Jews Walk** where a 2-bed conversion flat can cost £130,000. Some modern town-houses are followed by retirement flats on the corner with **Kirkdale**. Sheltered from main traffic is **Beaulieu Avenue** – '60s town-houses with neat handkerchief-size front lawns around two greens. Wide **Longton Avenue**, beside the Wells Park, has large 19th-century bay-fronted semis and modern terrace house infills. Further up are '30s semis with sloping front gardens; higher still these become larger, with the occasional detached. Delightful views of the park.

South of **Westwood Hill**, **Lawrie Park Rd**, wide, tree-lined and gently undulating, is a variety of Victoriana: mansions, detached, semis and bay-fronted terraces. Many flat conversions and also modern terraces and flats. A new H-shaped clutch of flats and houses shelters behind security gates, while **Lyric Mews** is a new cul-de-sac with 36 flats. Off **Sydenham Avenue** Bewley have built eight 3-bed, 3-bath town-houses. **Lawrie Park Rd** ends by **Crystal Palace Park Rd** with mansion blocks – '30s Park Court and the more modern Ashley Court.

On **Crystal Palace Park Rd,** now a conservation area, large Victorian red-brick mansions overlook the park – many are now flats. Also large detached '30s infills. **Sydenham Avenue** (mock-Georgian and big Victorian semis) has a bucolic air – there's a bench beneath the protective branches of a tree on the green, and it looks towards St Bartholomew Church in **Westwood Hill**. It continues as **Lawrie Park Avenue** – Victorian mansions and 1930s detached, while **Lawrie Park Gardens** adds some modern flats to the mixture.

Sydenham Rd leads past the station into Lower Sydenham. This Victorian red-brick street has a useful range of shops in the upper part. Behind lies the popular Thorpe Estate (every street name ends in '-thorpe') of turn-of-the-century terraces. A warehouse in **Silverdale Rd**, near the station, is an imaginative conversion of 24 flats.

Transport	Trains: Crystal Palace to Victoria; Penge West, Sydenham to London Bridge and Charing Cross; Sydenham Hill, fast line to Victoria.
Convenient for	Crystal Palace Park. Miles from centre: 7.
Schools	Local Authority: Westwood Secondary School (g), Harris City Technology College.

SALES

Flats	S	1B	2B	3B	4B	5B
Average prices	40–50	55–80	75–170	95–180	–	–
Houses	2B	3B	4B	5B	6/7B	8B
Average prices	110–140	155–200	180–290	250–400	300+	350+

RENTAL

Flats	S	1B	2B	3B	4B	5B
Average prices	95–100	100–140	125–150	150–185	160–275	220+
Houses	2B	3B	4B	5B	6/7B	8B
Average prices	140–160	200–210	230–275	300–415	370–460	–

The properties	Grand Victorian villas, many now flats; smaller terraced Victorian, flats blocks and inter-war homes. Quite a few modern houses and flats. Gardens and long, long views.
The market	Substantial growth in rental market. Larger houses popular with families particularly in the conservation area of Fox Hill, Belvedere Rd. Few very large houses left: most now flats. 1- and 2-bed flats are plentiful. Agents have high hopes for 'up-and-coming' Sydenham & Crystal Palace. Local searches: Lewisham 10 working days, Bromley 2 working days, Lambeth 10 working days, Southwark 15 working days, Croydon 27 working days.

Among those estate agents active in this area are:
- Kinleigh Folkard & Hayward
- Halifax Property
- Park Regent
- Bradford & Bingley
- Wates
- Conrad Fox
- Cooper Giles

DOCKLANDS

Today you can stroll out of the Ritz to Green Park tube, hop on a gleaming Jubilee line train and just have time for the FT before you slide into Canary Wharf station. Hotel lobby to office desk in about 25 minutes. At least, on the days when the Jubilee line is working properly.

Most Docklands workers start their journey from Lewisham, Stratford or Surbiton, not Piccadilly. Thanks to the new tube and the Docklands Light Railway extention to Lewisham – and the connections these make possible – commuters can get to the Isle of Dogs in more comfort than their City- or West End-based colleagues can reach their desks. Transport has at last stitched Docklands into London, making it a viable place to travel to – or from.

About time too. Docklands is 20, in its post-modern, non-functional, ex-seaport reincarnation. It has grown up. The rest of London accepts its new neighbour: no-one now predicts the demise of Docklands. In property terms, there are two sides to this maturity: the market for homes, both owning and letting, is now not that different from other leading London areas. And the workplaces – offices, in large part – are built and full of busy and well-paid people.

When you have 27,000 working in Canary Wharf alone, buildings going up now for 15,000 more, and plans for a workforce of 100,000 by 2006, then Docklands has something solid to it. This is now a business district on a world scale. The early '90s recession prompted talk (though not from this Guide) of Docklands staying forever a depressed, half-empty, third-best location. Now, blue-chip companies are taking Canary Wharf space at rents higher than on the fringes of the City, and international banks are building their own towers alongside the pioneer skyscraper.

The droves of people in smart suits (it's very much that sort of place) are attracting shops, restaurants and other amenities which benefit residents as well as workers. Interestingly, these two groups often overlap, with proximity to the office towers a big selling point in residential schemes. This in part reflects the transport picture up until now. It also raises a question: will Isle of Dogs homes be seen as paradoxically less attractive now it is easier to commute to the Wharf by tube? Or will people buy into Docklands because they can more speedily get to their work/leisure in the West End?

Compare Docklands prices with other areas with plenty of flats for sale, and the Docks homes will seem good value. Look more closely, and you will find a very wide range of styles and standards, from the 5-star international gloss of Canary Riverside through every species of flat to the new-build suburbia of Beckton. This is a mature market, the only difference compared to other parts of town being that an 'old' home is 15 years old, not 150.

Twenty years ago there was no homes market here at all. . . First, an explanation of those 20 years. Then, we survey Docklands area by area, development by gleaming development: this starts on page 265.

The what, where and when of Docklands

I once stood in a warehouse flat in Wapping with a Japanese visitor and gazed out across the deserted Thames. He was puzzled: where were the ships? Why was the river not used? Why was the warehouse no longer a warehouse? What had happened? It was hard to explain to him; indeed it is hard to convey to anyone how sudden the change, how total the death of London's docks. Ships still unload way down the river at Tilbury, but the six miles from the Tower eastwards is no longer a trading port. It is Docklands. From being the busiest port in the world in the 1950s it is now . . . read on, and you will see.

So what is Docklands, and how did it get this way? A map helps a lot, first to make the point that Docklands is big. If a home in Docklands appeals, the first thing to know is that some bits of it are a stroll from the City, while others are more or less in Essex. It is 6 miles long – it's as far from the Hogarth roundabout on the A4 in Chiswick to London Bridge, as from London Bridge to the eastern edge of Docklands.

Match Docklands against some other world cities: from our City it is 6.3 miles in a straight line to the far end of the Royal Docks. Drive the same distance in New York, and you cover most of Manhattan from Battery Park to somewhere in the middle of Central Park. In Paris, you cross the whole city inside the ring of the *Périphérique*.

Second, Docklands is not one place but a confederation of areas: Wapping, Limehouse, Shad Thames – about a dozen definable districts. Some, like Rotherhithe, are ancient villages; others, like the Surrey Quays and most of the Isle of Dogs, did not exist as residential neighbourhoods before about 1982. Now, Docklands is the biggest single source of new homes in London, perhaps the UK. From 660 new homes built in 1984 the annual crop has fluctuated, yielding in total some 30,000 homes.

No ships on the river: the sudden death of London's docks

The history would be a book in itself, beginning on the Roman quays of Londinium. The legacies of that history are the great sheets of water, the surviving warehouses, the beleaguered communities of little houses built for dockworkers. Another legacy is a virtually empty river. Up to the late 1960s all these docks were lined with ocean-going ships. The river was packed with lighters, barges and tugs. The tideway from the Tower to the sea was a highway for vessels of all sizes. Then, from 1967 to 1981, the docks closed one by one; the ships vanished. Suddenly, the London docks were out-of-date. New methods of cargo handling had made them unworkable: a freighter took up to a fortnight to unload using traditional methods, but a container ship could be turned round in 24hrs. Equally important was the change from rail to road for transport to and from the docks. Much of the cargo transferred to truck ferries.

The Docklands dilemma

London was faced with a problem on an epic scale: what to do with 700 acres of water, 5,000 acres of land, 20 miles of river bank and hundreds of buildings that suddenly had no function. The response was indecision, wrangling and piecemeal demolition as the docks closed, one by one. The Port of London Authority (PLA) had, and still has, the job of running the port. The rest of the area was split between four boroughs and a myriad of private owners, each with different powers and priorities. The City fathers looked on the docks as potential opposition, not opportunity. London has never been a place for grand strategic plans, but the docks certainly needed one.

Various wacky schemes were mooted: one that sticks in the mind was a plan for a linear park from the Tower to the sea – in effect, grassing Docklands over.

After much talking and several abortive attempts at co-operation, in 1981 Mrs Thatcher's government imposed a new kind of body, a development corporation, on a great swathe of riverside London. Fierce rows arose, with the established communities, and more especially their politicians, opposing the centralized, undemocratic London Docklands Development Corporation (LDDC). The Greater London Council (GLC), in particular, was a sworn enemy.

Lest we forget, let's recall the words of George Nicholson, Chairman of the GLC's Planning Committee in 1985: 'Anyone who regards as a success story the systematic attacks by the LDDC on local and strategic planning, and on local accountability . . . the madcap schemes for an airport, luxury housing and huge office developments, cannot be said to have the interests of the residents of Docklands at heart. The truth is that Docklands is for sale to the highest bidder.'

Mr Nicholson was, happily, wrong about much of this, as this chapter shows; but he was right on his last point, right to bemoan the fate of the residents. Despite much well-intentioned effort by the LDDC and others, the traditional communities of Millwall and Poplar were late and reluctant converts to the Docklands dream. There is still an uneasy air of two cultures, with the gleaming office towers rising above some pretty mean streets.

The LDDC has now been wound up. While it ruled, it wielded great power. It decided planning applications, compulsorily bought and then sold derelict sites and also planned the infrastructure. While it could not force private firms to build what they did not see as profitable, it was able to steer and direct in ways no local council has ever managed. One key achievement by the LDDC was to get the rest of London to think of 'Docklands' as an entity. This is valid: it is a new place overlaying a clutch of old ones, and newness and the attitudes it engenders are common to places well apart, in geography as well as character. But from the Docklands collective the local neighbourhoods are happily re-emerging.

The first dock to re-emerge from decline was St Katharine's, next door to Tower Bridge. In 1828 it cost £1,700,000 to build; in 1969 the PLA sold it to Taylor Woodrow on a 125-year lease for £200,000 less. By the mid-'70s a large new hotel had been built (opening to a noisy 'homes before hotels' protest) and the marina, shops and homes complex now in being had taken its basic shape. Most of the London Docks, a little to the E, were filled in as if they had never existed. Shadwell Basin is all the water that survived, though some homes face ornamental canals: sort of watery memorials.

The Surrey Docks closed in 1969 and by 1974 their deserted, overgrown acres were the home of 90 species of birds. Within 10 years several thousand new homes in park-like surroundings had arisen. The West India and Millwall Docks on the Isle of Dogs survived until 1980, and the last ship to unload in the the Royals, the great down-river complex, steamed away in October 1981. The same year, the LDDC took over.

The transformation begins

The 1980s were the most remarkable decade in the docks' long history. No-one at the LDDC in 1981 knew they were starting a new business city; they thought they might with luck achieve a business park and some new homes. In 1982, land in Wapping sold for £60,000 an acre and by 1987 the going rate was £4 million. In early 1988 this Guide described the completion of the Docklands Light Railway (DLR), listed literally thousands of new and converted homes and reported on the first stages of Canary Wharf. The 1988 Guide also recorded that the warehouse buildings constructed only six or seven years beforehand, in the first days of the Enterprize Zone (EZ), were being torn down and replaced as they no longer earned their keep on the rapidly appreciating sites.

The real, untold story of 1980s Docklands was the rapid rise in the area's expectations. After decades in which many hopeful plans dissolved on contact with reality, this time the problem was due to the plans being far too timid. The growing pains – awful traffic congestion, lack of services – were the product of totally unpredicted success. The Docklands Light Railway was only five years old when Canary Wharf came along: the DLR had to be virtually rebuilt to allow more people to use it than had ever been foreseen. Even the much-derided City Airport has survived and is now a big success with flights to many useful European destinations.

Then came the 1990 recession. Wiseacres across London bored innumerable dinner parties with how they knew Docklands would never work. For quite a few people, the disaster was real. Developers went bust, owners of smart new flats found their blocks filled up with council tenants as despairing landlords struck discount deals at Tower Hamlets Town Hall. Even Canary Wharf went bust. It would have taken a brave speculator to buy into Docklands around 1992. But they would have been wise: Shad Thames and Bermondsey came second to Kensington on a survey of property price growth from December 1992 to March 1997. Investment buying reappeared and became one component of a very various property market.

The Docklands property market

The years 1997 and 1998 saw the Docklands market return to a steady state: price increases were seen, but no frenzied queues of buyers before a new block was 'released'. Last year – 1999 – got going with a bang: the queues were back, and developers reported half a new block sold on the first morning. People were putting down deposits on homes that were a year or more from completion.

As spring 2000 began, agents were reporting a real shortage of good property to sell, and consequent distortions of the market through gazumping and 'silly prices' for the best. A positive strand to the story, and contrary to perception, is that buyers are overwhelmingly owner-occupiers, and from the UK. Better still, of the investment buyers, many are existing Docklands residents. People who know the area see the point of it and buy another flat to rent out. There is still 'outside' investment buying: 1999 saw an influx of Irish buyers capitalising on rocketing house prices in Dublin. However, the high pound deterred quite a few foreigners. Agents confide that only New Yorkers study London prices without wincing.

Docklands prices rose during 1999 at about the same pace as the rest of London: 25% was reported for some homes, with river views and car parking the factors that push prices up. Of the Docklands area, Bermondsey/Shad Thames achieves perhaps the highest prices, with Wapping very close behind. The place for value is still the Surrey Docks, though it shot up (from a low base) thanks to its Jubilee line station, with some of the more remote Isle of Dogs developments also attractive in price terms. Compare the attractions of a 2-bed, 2-bath, marina-view secure-parking Surrey Docks flat at £200,000 with what the same money will buy elsewhere: a 1-bed flat in Clerkenwell, a 2-bed Victorian conversion in Shepherd's Bush, a modern flat with the same features in Clapham – but on a main road.

A river-view flat will always cost you more: agents reckon a budget of between £150–250,000 is needed for a 1-bed pied-à-terre.

Amid all the euphoria it's worth remembering that if you bought in Docklands in 1988-89 in one or two over-hyped developments, your home would have only just climbed out of negative equity. Factor in inflation and interest costs, and you are well out of pocket. However, investors who bought between 1991 and 1993 will have seen some dramatic returns – in some cases over 200 per cent and on average over 100 per cent. This has been possible because Docklands, caught out as the market crashed without transport and services infrastructures in place, fell more than probably anywhere else in London.

The difference between today and 1989 is that, while some property may be nominally a similar price, the place has grown up: the transport is there and real communities are emerging from the building dust. It is a different world, and so it should be – more public money has been spent here than anywhere else in the UK in the same period. Something like £11 billion of public and private cash has been sunk into Docklands. Price growth has – until now – been built on solid foundations. Buyers should think hard whether these foundations will support further price jumps.

The maturity of at least some of the neighbourhoods can surprise outsiders. Wapping and Limehouse riversides have settled down into being largely middle-class districts. The English have the ability to create a village idyll in the most unlikely surroundings. People who used to have a little place in SW7 now live in Wapping and talk about 'going down to the Village'. There – in Wapping Lane – they will visit the excellent butcher (who sells foie gras), the post office and the pharmacy. Over in Bermondsey they will patronise the top-flight restaurants, on the Isle of Dogs they have a multi-cinema to stroll to as well as about 20 places to eat and drink – and that's just in Canary Wharf.

The homes

Mention Docklands in Hampstead or Hammersmith and people will think of smart riverside flats. Perhaps warehouse conversions come to mind. Once, that was about all you could find. Today, the choice is much wider. There are whole districts of modern 3- and 4-bed houses with gardens, some of just above council standard and others as good as anything you'll find in London. There are fairly ordinary 'inland' flats, there are indeed riverside ones, and dockside ones. Some blocks are serviced and have every luxury, and compete in style with the grand apartment buildings of Regent's Park or Mayfair. Others are very ordinary indeed.

There are warehouse conversions, and these range from vast airy spaces full of river-reflected light to cramped little dens looking out on stagnant, sunless docks or back streets. Even the bigger warehouse flats can have a lot of floor space relative to the window area. Check you get some sun. And, of course, there are new, shiny, straight-from-the developer properties and others that go back 15 or 20 years. If you look really hard, you might find a flat or (even rarer) a house that pre-dates the Docklands boom of the 1980s. People have been living round here since Shakespeare was a lad.

Progress report

In many respects progress in Docklands can be judged by the number of cranes active around Canary Wharf. For those with a long-term vision, the success of the Wharf was never in doubt – but that didn't stop some of those visionaries going bust on a scale to match the project.

The tower was completed in November 1990; Olympia & York, the developers, went into receivership in May 1992 and re-emerged (owned by the banks) in October 1993; in December 1995 it was sold to a consortium led by Paul Reichman (other investors include Saudi and US/Canadian interests). Mr Reichman was one of the three Canadian brothers who, as Olympia & York, rescued the scheme the first time round after the original backers got cold feet. Last year saw a proportion of the shares floated on the London Stock Exchange.

Canary Wharf now has 4.5 million sq ft of extremely high quality offices (the 36 ft lobby of the Tower has 90,000 sq ft of Italian and Guatemalan marble) and retail space in 10 buildings. The working population has grown to 27,000 and Canary Wharf is over 99 per cent let. There are now firm plans to complete the complex as planned in the '80s. Speculative building has re-started with a 200,000 sq ft Terry Farrell-designed block. A further 2.3 million sq ft of space is under construction.

Big banks continue to dominate the occupiers' lists: HSBC's Norman Foster tower will rise almost as high as the existing one, with 1.1 million sq ft of space and room for 8,000 staff. Citigroup's 42-storey tower (one more floor than HSBC's) joins its subsidiary Citibank's existing building. Both towers are on schedule for 2002, and the complex shakes with the piles being driven for yet more office space at Heron Quays, to the S. Newspapers also cluster at Canary Wharf, which has led to quite a few 'as I gaze out of my window at the shining Thames below' features (and to a sharp decline in articles knocking Docklands). On current predictions, the workforce will rise to 43,000 by 2002, and by 2006 there will be 100,000. It is a good thing that the Jubilee line station is designed to cope with 16,000 passengers an hour.

We have been here before: commercial property is a boom-to-bust business, just like the homes market but on a grander scale, so it's reasonable to expect downturns, cancelled plans and empty office blocks. But short of a seismic shift in the world of finance, Canary Wharf looks like a permanent part of the global business jigsaw.

There are over 60 shops and restaurants in Canary Wharf including the crucial Tesco Metro that provides a community focus for the whole N side of the Docklands. More High Street names are due this spring. There are also more than 20 bars, cafés, pubs and restaurants, including very smart ones in the Riverside complex – and now they stay open in the evenings. Back in 1992 the few bars used to shut at 8pm.

Phase one of Canary Riverside is nearly ready. This is a 750,000 sq ft development to the W of the main complex, beside Westferry Circus. The four residential blocks have 322 flats and there's a luxury Four Seasons hotel, which opened in December, a health and leisure club (swimming pool and two tennis courts) and restaurants; all due to open this spring. Singapore investors, with Canary Wharf Ltd in a minority role, own the Riverside complex. There are plans for Riverside phases 2 and 3.

The Jubilee line tube station at Canary Wharf connects Docklands to the West End in 15 minutes – and, perhaps more crucially, it links the area to London Bridge, Waterloo and their commuter trains. The Limehouse Link, a 4-lane underground highway, links Tower Hill to Canary Wharf; it and a big network of fast (most of the time) roads now provide access to City, West End, City Airport and the M25.

A new riverbus service from Central London started last June, primarily to serve the Millennium Dome but with stops at Canary Wharf and other Docklands piers. However, riverbus services have come and gone before and it would be a fool who bets his property investment on river connections until the service has survived at least one recession. The Docklands Light Railway is now running through to Greenwich and Lewisham, adding yet another swathe of London to Docklands' hinterland. Those other elements of an infrastructure, entertainment and shopping, are now coming. Surrey Quays has a big shopping development around a Tesco hypermarket, opened in 1988 and a major success. An 8-screen UCI cinema is next to the shopping centre. On the Isle of Dogs, Virgin's 10-screen cinema, opening this spring, forms part of the West India Quay complex.

The shape of Docklands

First-time visitors start here for a whistle-stop tour. The most central areas are N and S of the Thames within view of Tower Bridge. Downstream on the N bank is Wapping, with the restored St Katharine's Dock, a mature, successful business/tourist/homes centre. The waterfront has the best warehouse conversions, with sunny river views and a large choice of new-build flats. Inland are new streets of small, well-placed houses and flats. The S bank, around Shad Thames and Butler's Wharf, has new and converted flats in a classy new neighbourhood with shops, restaurants and a museum.

Further E on the N bank comes Limehouse: a riverside strip between Wapping and Canary Wharf with more converted warehouses, new flats and the large-scale Limehouse Basin development. And here begins the great bend of the river that wraps around the Isle of Dogs, Docklands' heart. This is now a vibrant mix of giant office schemes – including Canary Wharf – and homes. Look here for riverside homes of varying views and quality, inland houses and apartments at good prices.

Across the river, the Isle's mirror image is the Surrey Docks peninsula. Riverside homes are backed by many new-build schemes of family homes and the giant Surrey Quays shopping complex. The SE corner of the area has the dock- and marina-side homes. Surrey Quays and Rotherhithe already has an established community feel.

East from the Isle of Dogs, the Docklands is future not present. The Leamouth sites have been cleared for development which is now beginning. East again, the vast Royal Docks has the thriving City Airport, plenty of new roads, an exhibition centre, a new university and an increasing supply of new homes.

Wapping

Wapping is the oldest-established of the Dockland neighbourhoods – perhaps because it is the closest N of the river to the City. The W parts are a pleasant walk from city offices, further E people use the DLR at Shadwell. The DLR and the Limehouse road tunnel provide the links to Canary Wharf. Now, too, the East London line's new Canada Water station makes the Jubilee line two stops from Wapping. Shopping has improved with the Safeway on **St Thomas More St**, but most people shop at Canary Wharf or in the City (which these days has shops as well as offices). The useful small shops in **Wapping Lane** are fiercely championed by locals.

There are several sides to Wapping. St Katharine's Dock is a neighbourhood on its own. Then along the river to the E come the smart flats, in old warehouses or newbuild, of **Wapping High St** and **Wapping Wall**. Inland, to the N, the tract once taken up by London Docks has 200 well-planned acres of mostly council-built housing, some 1,500 homes, plus some industry. At the E end is Shadwell, with the sole surviving dock basin (St K's apart) and some attractive waterside homes.

Wapping starts, in the shadow of the Tower, with **St Katharine's Dock**. This is only just Docklands; more City-with-scenery: the two dock basins shelter yachts and provide an attractive outlook for homes and a hotel just a step from the City. Development of this quarter has been underway since 1971, and most of the buildings are 20th-century with just one 19th-century warehouse left intact. There are 300 local authority homes around the E and N sides of the dock – some bought by tenants. **Mews St** has 10 small cottages; **Marble Quay** has four flats in an office development. **The Ivory House**, a fine old converted warehouse, has 2-bed apartments to let from £600-plus a week. Spread over two sides of St Katharine's Dock, Taylor Woodrows' **City Quay** is an impressive block which offers 209 1-, 2- and 3-bed flats and 3- and 4-bed penthouses; prices from £460,000. Towards the entrance to the dock is **Tower Walk**, a crescent of seven 4/5-bed 'Nash' style stucco £1 million houses amid a large commercial scheme. Barratt have been active in the area with **Hermitage Waterside** around the little Hermitage Basin E of the dock, all that survives of the W end of the old London Docks complex. This features 1/2-bed flats and 3-bed houses. A detached Georgian house on the edge of the dock is now reckoned to be worth over £2 million.

Back on the river, **President's Quay** is a particularly stylish development; the twin glass-roofed pyramids of its penthouses a riverside landmark: 1-bed flats: £195,000. Quality is high. Next door, **Miller's Wharf** has 22 homes in a handsome Terry Farrell-designed warehouse conversion. **Tower Bridge Wharf** is a 64-home new-build (1990) development. One end is semi-circular, with a courtyard, which gives the opportunity for some unusual shapes and two differing, but enviable, penthouses at either end of the crescent. On **St Katharine's Way** and next to the **Hermitage Wharf** block is **Riviera Court** which has a dozen new-build riverside 2- and 3-bed flats.

Berkeley Homes' **Capital Wharf** has 85 riverside flats which sold in 1998–9 from £330,000 to £695,000. **Hermitage Wharf** is a big (2+ acre) Berkeley scheme, half sold within three hours of launch last winter. There are 95 flats in three stylish blocks and a new public park. Prices from £200–700,000 for 1- to 3-beds.

On the inland side of **Wapping High St** is **Hermitage Court**: 97 homes. Next comes the glorious **Wapping Pierhead**: the area's one remaining enclave of Georgian houses. Some are split into flats, others remain as 3-bed, 3-recep houses. All share a half-acre garden. Extending inland, new local authority houses match the Pierhead style exactly. **Pierhead Wharf** has a cheerful, typical brick and red paint look.

Back on the riverside, **Oliver's Wharf** has some of the most coveted flats in Docklands: it was converted in 1973 by a group of architects and artists, some of whom still live there. This is the one that started the whole conversion fever off. The group each paid some £14,000 for their industrial space. Today they remain some of the largest of Docklands (or, indeed, London) flats – a typical one has a 54 x 38 ft galleried living room. Expect to pay over £600,000 for a riverside one, over £400,000 on the inland side.

Orient Wharf is let by a housing association. The Town of Ramsgate pub sits on a sliver of riverside real estate. On the inland side of the High St, **Dundee Court** has 48 1- to 3-bed flats in a 19th-century warehouse converted in 1986. **The Sanctuary** is inland, but with some good river views. It boasts rooftop pool and gym and basement parking. Also inland on **Brewhouse Lane** is warehouse-style **Chimney Court**, with 41 studios plus 1- and 2-bed flats. 78 **Wapping High St** was once a wine warehouse; now 16 homes. The spectacular white and cream stucco **Aberdeen Wharf** is probably the last warehouse conversions on the Wapping riverside. It dates from the 1840s and was split into 17 flats in 1998; a few were left last winter from £335–550,000. Those with river views gain from the wharf's location on the southern tip of the Wapping bend. No crime fears here: the River Police HQ is next-door. The '60s apparition nearby covered with abstract glass-fibre heiroglyphs and bound to be listed one day is the police's boathouse.

St John's Wharf was turned into 22 large flats in 1984. Resales are sought-after. **King Henry's Wharves** are next, then another warehouse conversion.

Barratt's **Gun Wharf** conversion provided 68 flats in 1985. Prices last winter around £500,000 for a 3-bed. The adjoining **Gun House**, by the same developer, eight flats plus a penthouse, is new-build. **Gun Place** is on the inland side of the High St and has 73 flats in a conversion. Alongside, **Bridewell Place** is also Barratt: this one is a mews-style scheme with 52 homes completed in 1988. Also on the inland side – and close to Wapping tube station – is **The Carronade**, 42 flats, some double-height and galleried, by Broadwell. **Towerside**, by Wates, straddles **Wapping High St**; the waterside part is new; the rest – **Prusom's Island** – award-winning refurbished warehouses. A total of 97 flats and new-build houses were built. Although not the most sophisticated of Wapping schemes, it does provide among the least expensive riverside flats: a 1-bed riverside flat might be £160,000, a 2-bed: £250,000. **St Hilda's Wharf** is a late-1980s riverside scheme of 39 large, especially for new-build, flats.

New Crane Wharf is a warehouse conversion with a courtyard, around which are grouped 143 homes plus some offices, shops and also restaurants. This is a very popular development and of good quality, too; 1-bed non-river view flats go for around £150,000. River-front penthouses reach £600–800,000.

Great Jubilee Wharf, refurbished and extended in 1996 by Galliard, created 30 flats. Further along, in a development that straddles **Wapping High St**, Persimmon's **Thorpe's Yard**, a group of three buildings – riverside warehouse conversion and new-build – dates from 1998. The riverside chunk is called **Merchant Court** and is all sold. The final phase, on the market last winter, is **Spinnaker Mews**, six 4-storey, 3-bed houses on **Wapping Wall** from £300,000.

Pelican Wharf, next door to the Prospect of Whitby, has 13 large 2,000 sq ft apartments – each bigger than a normal family house. Walkways round an atrium and a whole floor penthouse with three roof gardens are among its attractions. The painstaking Roger Malcolm had problems with this tricky site (taking due care of the historic pub not least among them).

On the other side of the pub **Prospect Wharf** is in a rather ungainly, gabled-roof 1980s warehouse style, built by Trafalgar House in an enviable position between the river and Shadwell Basin. Great views, therefore, on both sides, though some eccentrically-shaped rooms. Another plus is the open courtyard between the river and the curve of the buildings: a rare commodity in crowded Wapping. The flats are 1- and 2-bed. **Prospect Place**, N of **Wapping Wall**, has 70 houses and flats in a successful layout next to a Regalian refurb of a block of council flats, **Riverside Mansions**, **Milk Yard**, which were sold to waiting-list locals at a discount. These are 750 sq ft 2-bed maisonettes, many with views over Shadwell Basin. **Monza Street**, which runs down to the river, has the new **Monza Building**: Furlong Homes' 20-flat, modern-looking block. Some homes have Basin views; prices from £255,000 for 2-beds.

Shadwell Basin has 172 flats and houses, some with 5 beds, grouped round three sides of the dock, which is home to a youth watersports club. The gabled brick buildings with their distinctive semi-circular windows and red detailing are popular: not surprising, given their attractive dockside position. **Peartree Lane** has 4-bed dockside houses; **Newlands Quay** has 3-bed duplex flats at around £150,000. Heading W, Tobacco Dock, a listed warehouse, started out as a shopping centre around 1990 but has never really taken off: rumours persist that part of it may be becoming an hotel. The conversion is glorious, though.

Wapping's inland quarter is mostly built on the site of the old London Docks, but only Shadwell Basin and a shallow, ornamental tree-lined canal remains to remind us. The canal provides an attractive environment for some good-value homes in developments now mature after 10–15 years. Industry such as News International's giant printworks come rather close to some homes, though. Among several 'inland' schemes, award-winning **East Quay** and **Waterman Quay** have 170 houses and flats grouped around the canal. **Portland Square** is a 1986 Barratt development with some (rare) large 3-storey houses grouped around a private square with fountain, and a range of other homes. Also on the old site of the London Docks are **South Quay** – 182 low-cost (originally) homes by Broseley (some houses are shared-ownership through a housing association) and **Quay 430**, a 300-home Regalian scheme. Sample prices: in **Waterman Way**, a 2-bed canalside flat might be £120,000; another such in **Welland Mews** £150,000. Also 'inland' are some ex-council homes which sell at lower prices.

On **The Highway**, Wapping's main road, **Telford's Yard** has 68 particularly spacious flats in a warehouse conversion. The largest, some 3,000 sq ft, go for £450,000. Next door **Breezers Court** was divided, in 1985, into 30 flats. Further along **The Highway**, Barratt's **Pennington Court** is a 1987 scheme.

Limehouse

Limehouse is a hugely popular area, being between the City and Canary Wharf, and is more domestic in scale than its neighbours Limehouse and the Isle of Dogs. Villagey **Narrow St** has shaken off the dust of development and is now most attractive. Limehouse Basin, also badly affected by the road tunnel beneath it, which finally opened in 1993, is at last emerging as another marina-style development.

A number of major developers built landmark riverside developments in the late 1990s, although the area still retains a sense of history. The launch (against the trend of the times) by Galliard Homes of the **Papermill Wharf** development in 1992, which sold out within hours, is credited with having kick-started the entire Docklands property market in the last recession.

Working along the river from the Wapping, or W end, the (non-functional) mouth of Shadwell Basin is followed by the riverside King Edward Memorial Park. N of the park is **The Highway**, which lives up to its name. This runs N of most of the big riverside blocks and its noise and dirt must be borne in mind. Regalian's orange ziggurat landmark **Free Trade Wharf** stands sentinel at the beginning of Limehouse. This is a large scheme of 171 new, and six luxurious converted warehouse apartments. The scheme includes its own gym and swimming pool, but the shops never found tenants and they are to be converted into flats. Part of the Wharf dates from 1795 – an old gunpowder store. These form the chunk marketed in 1999 under the name **The Listed Building**: 37 river-view 1- and 2-bed flats from £160–395,000. Regalian's rather gaunt riverside **Atlantic Wharf**, which has 213 1-, 2- and 3-bed flats – most with river views – continues the riverside line of flats. Two-beds here go for around £245,000.

Keepier Wharf, a re-clad warehouse with 24 spacious flats completed in 1987, stands at the beginning of Limehouse's best-known address, **Narrow St**. This runs the length of the waterfront and is famous for its short surviving row of riverside Georgian houses as well as for the venerable Grapes pub.

A number of riverside developments were built on Narrow St in the 1990s: **Papermill Wharf** where the foresight of the 1992 buyers has been rewarded with 1-bed flats priced today at £215,000; Barratt's **Victoria Wharf**, 67 2-bed flats completed in 1998; **Chinnocks Wharf** by St George's (2- and 3-bed flats); **Old Sun Wharf**, a joint venture by Galliard Homes and Frogmore Estates of 36 2- and 3-bed duplex apartments all with river views (£247,500 for a 2-bed, 2-bath). Opposite **Victoria Wharf** is Fairclough's **Victoria Lock** – a mix of 1-, 2- and 3-bed flats and 3- and 4-bed houses. The latest Narrow St riverside scheme is Angel Property's **Phoenix Wharf**, right at the W end. There are 11 large flats: three were left last winter at £320–475,000.

On the inland side, between **Narrow St** and **The Highway**, is **St George's Square**, a remarkable mixture of architectural styles from neo-Docklands vernacular to mock-Tudor, executed in red-brick. Forty-one houses and flats surround a small courtyard. **The Mosaic** is a St James development on the N side of **Narrow St** running through to **Horsleydown Rd**: some of the 195 flats (presumably on the top floors) will have river views. These launched this spring at prices from £150,000 to £450,000.

Along the riverside are several smaller new buildings and conversions: **Ratcliffe Wharf**, which is new, and **London** and **Commercial Wharves**, both conversions. Both **Ratcliffe** and **Commercial** are by the hand of the unquenchable Mrs Rae Hoffenburg, a Docklands pioneer who started converting warehouses (and living in them) in the early 1970s when Tower Hamlets Council wanted them kept in industrial use.

D

Sun Wharf is just one 11,000 sq ft home: it changed hands in the mid-'90s for nearly £3 million; it used to belong to the film director David Lean. It is unique in Docklands in having a complete waterside garden – lawns, trees and all – with a 124-ft frontage to the river. The whole place was carved out of four old warehouses in 1985.

Across the road from **Victoria Wharf** sits the Limehouse Basin, a 25-acre site and the entrance to the country's canal system. The Basin's development was held up not just by the 1990 recession but by the digging of the giant road tunnel which runs beneath it. Now, several developers are busy. St George has produced **Quayside** – a modern but classical-looking development of 1-, 2- and 3-bed apartments and duplexes around a courtyard. **Commercial Wharf** (yes, another one) is Barratt's scheme of low, brick terraces just back from the E side of the Basin.

Bellway are busy on the W side of the Basin with **Limehouse Basin**: six rather dramatic blocks and a smart steel tower: 280 homes in the first phase priced at £130–370,000. By last winter 170 of these had sold and work had started on phase 2: 200 flats on the N side of the dock. The Basin houses a thriving marina and the HQ of the Cruising Club.

Back on the river, **Blyth's Wharf** is a terrace of 16 2,000 sq ft-plus 4-bed houses, all with river views. It boasts an extensive pier, giving a promenade now open to the public. Opposite Blyth's Wharf inland is **The Watergardens**, a stylish refurbishment of former council property by Ballymore with 1- and 2-bed flats. Past these two are the real thing: the Georgian waterside homes and the Grapes pub. **Duke Shore Wharf** is next, a successful new-build development in a horseshoe shape.

Inland, opposite the Grapes pub on Ropemaker Fields, is a terrace of large modern 4-bed houses attached to a pub on the end of the terrace called 'The House They Left Behind' (which refers to a former terrace of Victorian houses that were demolished). Between this and the Watergardens is **Sovereign Place**, by Persimmon: 51 homes ranging from 1- and 2-bed flats to 3-bed town-houses.

Narrow St curves on round the N side of Limekiln Dock, an inlet off the main river which survived the Limehouse Link tunnelling – at one time it was going to be filled in, but it was reprieved. At 98–100 **Narrow St**, Fairbriar have built eight flats which sold at £195–335,000. The N side of the dock is lined by Fairbriar's **Dunbar Wharf**, which has been converted into 109 flats, including a split-level penthouse. The existing old warehouse was converted last year and three new buildings added (Block A has eight 2-bed flats, Block B has 31 1- and 2-bed flats, and Block C 61 with nine in the old warehouse). All are now sold. **Limehouse Wharf** is a small 1840 warehouse, an early conversion into flats/working studios: large with unusually high ceilings. **Limekiln Wharf** at the head of the inlet has six flats in a renovated building, and 23 new ones in an L-shaped block.

Just inland on **Three Colts St** is **Dundee Wharf**, a 10-storey block variously described as 'futuristic' and 'imposing', with spidery balconies and a tower that looks like a post-functional crane. There are 112 flats, 21 penthouses and five houses. Most have splendid views up river to the City or across to Canary Wharf. The 2-bed flats go from £250,000, with penthouses at £750–900,000. A footbridge across Limekiln Dock w give access to the Canary Wharf complex when work on the Riverside bit (see Isle of Dogs) is finished.

London Bridge

The westernmost tongue of Docklands intrudes right into the heart of London, facing the City, between London and Tower Bridges. **London Bridge City** has a million sq ft of offices, plus shops and restaurants in the handsome Hays Galleria with its soaring atrium, flats to rent, health club and a private hospital. A riverside walkway continues the promenade which now runs W as far as Vauxhall. The 13-acre vacant site to the E, stretching to Tower Bridge, was planned as London Bridge City Phases II and III. It went quiet in the early '90s but was bought by CIT in 1998, and they appointed Stanhope (the people behind Broadgate) to develop it. They named it 'More London Bridge' and plan 1.5 million sq ft of offices including the futuristic 'pod' for the Mayor of London. Leisure space will be involved but no homes are envisaged.

Now the Jubilee line tube is running through London Bridge this area has good links with Waterloo, the West End and Canary Wharf.

The area S of London Bridge, discussed in the South Bank chapter, is a good hunting-ground for warehouse conversions and new-build homes. There is a lot of activity, including the £9 million conversion of a former factory on **Tanner St** into an hotel and a Travel Lodge hotel, completed in early 1999, on **Tower Bridge Rd.**

Shad Thames/Tower Bridge and Bermondsey

Not so long ago, Shad Thames was of interest only to TV companies looking for seedy, derelict locations. The dripping brickwork of the abandoned warehouses, the sinister iron walkways spanning the narrow streets, the weed-grown cobbles . . . it's a bit different now. This is the most successful, established and expensive Docklands neighbourhood, known both for its flats (few houses here) and its restaurants. It could be said to have moved out of Docklands and into Central London, except for its concentration on warehouse conversions and modern copies of them. In price terms it has now overtaken longer-established Wapping.

Shad Thames is the name of the atmospheric, narrow street which runs behind the riverside wall of warehouses, curves behind the Design Museum and runs parallel to St Saviour's Dock to **Jamaica Rd.** It has given its name to the neighbourhood, though some prefer the classier-sounding Tower Bridge, and Butler's Wharf, the biggest single warehouse complex, also lends its name to the district.

This area, which stretches on the southside downstream from Tower Bridge, starts with one of the river's most splendid buildings. Not another warehouse, but an old Courage brewery. The **Anchor Brewhouse** is a 10-storey edifice rising sheer from the river right next to the bridge. The interior has been totally rebuilt: the shell of the old Boilerhouse, with its towering landmark chimney, has 35 flats including the spectacular triple-decker penthouse. This changed hands in 1997 for around £1.5 million. Its opening price (1988) was £2 million – though it's unclear if this was ever reached. Certainly the flat saw more use as a film-set than a home: Docklands-addicts spotted it again and again whenever a flash pad was called for. It was on the market again last autumn – for £1.5m.

The Malt Mill, nearest the bridge, has more large flats, all with river views. Here too, is an amazing penthouse: this time on four floors, and boasting the original cupola and belvedere galley. Where the first was glass-walled modern, its main room like the deck of a '30s liner, this one will be more like owning a Georgian house – set high in the air. It even has a garden: a double-height conservatory. It was for sale in late 1998, and again on the market last winter – both times for £3.95 million, if you can take the silly name 'High Command'. On a more mundane level, there are 1-bed and 2-bed flats. From here you see the Tower of London framed within Tower Bridge.

Directly behind the brewery lies **Horsleydown Square**, where unlovely 1950/60s buildings were cleared to be replaced by shops, offices, workshops et al, around an open landscaped square. 178 homes, some conversion, some new-build, have been built. Names to look out for in this corner are **Eagle Wharf, The Cooperage, Crown Court** and **Horsleydown Court. Tower Bridge Square**, on **Gainsford St**, was built for sale by the Nationwide Housing Trust: 1- and 2-bed flats and town-houses. **The Cardomom Building** is a smart warehouse conversion fronting Shad Thames. Behind the Cardamom Building, moving away from the River, is Galliard's **Cayenne Court** building. At the moment this is just open land that used to be a car park for Butler's Wharf and Cardomom residents, but there are plans to build more luxury flats ready for occupation in early 2001. Residents' parking has now moved to underneath Fairview's Butlers Court.

Next comes **Butler's Wharf**, a very large and long converted riverside warehouse comprising five blocks of apartments which until recently was owned by a Danish pension fund which rented out all of the homes. It now belongs to Prestbury Group. They are refurbishing the flat to a very high specification, creating in all around 80 2-, and 3- bed flats, duplexes and penthouses (from 1,600 sq ft). Prices start from £220,000 and go to £3 million in phase one which has 30 units. On the ground floor three out of the four local Terence Conran restaurants are housed: The Chop House, Pont de la Tour and Cantina del Ponto; it is to the long-term vision of Conran that the Shad Thames area owes a lot of its fortunes. This 'gastrodome' complex revived Conran's own fortunes after Butlers Wharf Development Company (in which he had a large interest) went into receivership in the early '90s.

Also beside the river is **Spice Quay**, a new block just completed by Galliard Homes, with 92 1- and 2-bed flats and penthouses: two left in November priced at £475,000 and £560,000. Two-bed flats were re-selling last winter for £550,000, up from a 'new' price of £435,000. The ground floor has shops, bars and a restaurant. Next to this is the Design Museum, in which is the Blue Print Café (the fourth local Conran restaurant – but first to open). Fairview's **Butlers Court**, comprising Vanilla and Sesame Courts, is just behind Spice Quay and now nearing completion. There are 124 1-, 2- and 3-bed flats over seven floors with 1 beds £190–£250,000 and from £280,000 for a 2-bed. They will be ready from May 2000. On the ground floor, there are commercial units for let. Next to Butlers Court and also behind Spice Quay is **Wheat Wharf** (developed by R Maskell Ltd) – a recently-refurbished 18th century grain store now 25 flats. Prices started at £235,000 for a 2-bed. They have now all sold.

East of the Design Museum is the still-derelict original Butler's Wharf Building no 15. This is owned by Galliard, who plan to develop it – but timing is unknown. It has a superb site on the corner of **St Saviour's Dock**, a river inlet, now bridged. Many warehouse conversions and new-build schemes crowd together along the narrow waterway. It is north-facing, so lack of light can be a drawback especially on lower floors. On the W side of St Saviour's Dock is **Cinnamon Wharf** – a stylish late-'80s conversion of a former 1950s block into 66 flats. **Saffron Wharf** followed – an '80s office converted into 13 units by Berkeley Homes.

(All these spicy names refer to the uses to which many of the warehouses were put. The area specialised in foodstuffs: spices were ground in odd little workshops as late as 1995. This led to excited flat-buyers claiming that the very walls of their new homes were scented by the long-gone spice trade. Had they gone round the corner, they could have met the dusty, blue-overalled grinders in person.)

Christian's Warehouse is a 1989 conversion and new-build scheme, with 87 flats

overlooking St Saviour's Dock. Next door is **Java Wharf**. Behind Spice Quay and stretching to **Gainsford St** is **Tamarind Court** – a warehouse carved into 62 flats by Galliard. On the other side of **Gainsford St** on the corner with **Shad Thames**, Nicholson Estates has created a complex of homes located around a gated courtyard. The splendidly-named Butler's Grinders & Operators buildings ('spice and gum grinders' in the old days) are being reborn as **Butlers and Colonial Wharf** (why wharf?), with some new town-houses and flats – and, the last to be released late in 1999, some live/work units at £315,000-plus – completing the quadrangle. Across the road from Tamarind on the corner of Gainsford Street, and opposite Butlers and Colonial Wharf on **Maguire Street** are the **Anise** and **Coriander** buildings (that's enough spices, lads), a conversion of two Victorian warehouses by R Maskell Ltd into 25 1- and 2-bed flats from £190–£425,000.

D

Straddling **Queen Elizabeth St** is **The Circle**, with its fluid lines and blue-brick fascias. Further along on the same side of the street and at 16–19 **Lafone St** is **Raven Wharf** – 21 new-build 2- and 3-bed flats and two live/work units by Gleeson Homes. **Boss House** on **Boss St** is a conversion of a 20th century warehouse where spacious 2-bed flats command £250–270,000 for 2-beds; £300,000 for 3-bed.

The beautiful footbridge at the mouth of St Saviour's Dock links the Shad Thames quarter to the Bermondsey riverside. On the E side of the creek is **Scott's Sufferance Wharf**: a courtyard of shops, offices and 93 flats of various sizes. **Lloyd's Wharf** has 24 flats sold as shells in 1985 for £30–60,000. **Unity Wharf** has four gloriously large work/live flats.

Vogan's Mill sits on a big, deep site: it is the conversion of an old flour mill; providing 64 2/4-bed flats and a penthouse in six buildings, some old others new. Thanks to the existence of the mill's tall silo, the developer got the chance to replace the structure with a new 18-storey high-tech tower – prices in this quality development range from £230,000 to £1,500,000-plus for the penthouse in the tower.

St Saviour's Wharf, back on the Dock, is a refurbishment which provided 47 flats and offices. And downstream, at the creek's mouth, is the award-winning **New Concordia Wharf**, discovered on the point of demolition by young developer Andrew Wadsworth; his 1981–85 conversion sparked the revival of the entire Bermondsey bank. The development is still the benchmark for Bermondsey quality, and is much requested by home-seekers. Next to New Concordia Wharf is the 1986 **China Wharf**: smaller rooms, glorious views, architecture (by CZWG; more awards) loved by some, not by others. **Reeds Wharf**, adjoining, has flats and offices. Next to Reeds Wharf a single 5-storey house is being built on a riverside plot.

Jacob's Island – a new-build scheme by Berkeley Homes – has eight contemporary blocks of 1- and 2-bed flats and penthouses on the E side of **Mill St**: river-view 2-bed flats re-sell for around £270,000. **Springalls Wharf** is a handsome new flats block just after Berkeley's **Providence Tower**. Next to Jacob Island is **River View Heights** (formerly **Tower View Wharf**) – 62 1-, 2- and 3-bed flats on eight floors, nearly all sold: there are only a couple of penthouses left here priced at £1.5 million each.

The smart conversions and new-builds contrast with the Dickens estate, 1930s council flats. East again, the future of the large, empty **Chambers Wharf** site is still unclear. Next comes **Cherry Garden Pier**, with 64 riverside council-built houses (new and rehab) and five terraces of flats and town-houses built in the 1980s. **Corbetts Wharf** was converted to flats back in 1984; **Angel Wharf** on the other side of the road in 1995. The semi-rural cottages around **Marigold St** are 1920s. Next to Corbetts Wharf and on the river is **National Terrace**, 10 4-storey, 4-bed houses with garages.

Rotherhithe

The surviving waterside hamlet of Rotherhithe boasts a glorious 1715 parish church,

St Mary's, whose internal pillars are not stone but old ships' masts, plastered over. Surrounding the church, the old school, rectory and some of the warehouses – not to mention the Mayflower pub – also date from at least Georgian days. As a plaque on the 16th-century inn (formerly named the Spread Eagle) states, this is where the Pilgrim Fathers set off from in 1620 on their way to America. On the W edge of the village **Elephant Lane/Mayflower Court** has 76 houses and flats, plus offices, built in 1984 in an avenue running away from the river to the Rotherhithe Tunnel roundabout. Around the old village are several blocks of pre-war council flats.

At the very beginning of **Rotherhithe St** at King's Stairs Close stands an imposing 1930s-inspired white block of apartments known as **Princes Tower**. This has 1-, 2- and 3-bed flats which sell for £190–600,000. The historic, award-winning **Thames Tunnel Mills** is a riverside warehouse converted into fair-rent flats, while **Ronald Buckingham Court** is sheltered housing. The conversion of two warehouses and also the building of a new block at **Hope Wharf** between the river, Rotherhithe St and Mary Church St has created 32 homes: flats and stylish 2-bed glasshouses (10 houses left unsold in January). **Isambard Place**, whose name recalls the tunnel's builder, has 94 2- to 4-bed flats plus 44 for a housing association. Across the road, the **Atlas Reach** scheme adds a further 100 flats.

Surrey Quays

The river bends like the shape of an upside down horseshoe as we travel downstream from Rotherhithe to Surrey Quays. This area is uninterrupted by the traffic and general mayhem that one would normally expect so close to the City; there are no main roads so there is no through traffic. It is quiet beyond belief.

From Rotherhithe on E, round the great bend of the river, is the frontage of the old Surrey Docks. Nearly all the docks were filled in, and over the last 15 years large areas of new housing have been built. These houses differ markedly in character, if not in style, from the river-front schemes: houses with gardens predominate, rather than warehouse flats. Prices are also lower here. The Surrey Quays shopping centre has been joined by Surrey Quays Phase II and includes an 8-screen cinema, bingo and bowling and restaurants/cafés.

To the N of the Centre, on **Surrey Quays Rd**, the splendid new Canada Water tube station is where the new Jubilee line and the re-furbished East London line intersect. The Jubilee line has been the spur for a new leap in development: the long river frontage has changed beyond recognition since the dead days after the docks' closure, and now derelict and vacant tranches of river front land have now been bought up and built on; old empty warehouses have been refurbished. Take a good look at the tube map: the East London offers a one-stop hop to Wapping, then another stop to Shadwell which intersects with the DLR which runs into Bank in the heart of the City. The Jubilee is one stop to Canary Wharf, and minutes in the other direction from Waterloo and the West End. There are plans (see Transport chapter) to extend the East London both N and S.

Right next to the new tube station is a century-old hydraulic pumping station, being converted this year into 31 large loft flats, with a further 23 new-build flats and houses in a courtyard. About half have been sold off-plan, and prices for the remainder start at £230,000.

Rotherhithe St runs right round the peninsula. On from Isambard Place and to the E of **Brunel Rd**, Bellway Homes have built **Brunel Point**: 2- and 3-bed flats, some with river views, and town-houses on the other side of **Rotherhithe St**. Two-beds here go for upwards of £220,000. The pier on the river was refurbished by Bellway and is now open to the public. This part of **Rotherhithe St** has been permanently closed off to traffic. An inlet leads through a disused lock to Surrey Water, an ornamental lake surrounded by homes. From Surrey Water a canal (again, just to look at) called Albion Channel winds through various housing developments to Canada Water, the site of the new Jubilee/East London tube interchange station. Along the canal are various pleasant developments which vary from social housing flats, to **Wolfe Crescent** built by Lovell (includes 1-, 2- and 3-bed flats and 4-bed houses, the latter selling now for about £230,000) in a red-brick semi-circle curled around four pale-coloured strikingly designed octagonal blocks. **Hithe Point** was built by Barratt (includes 1-, 2- and 3-bed flats and 2- and 3-bed houses). Opposite **Wolfe Crescent** and bordering **Surrey Quays Rd** is Persimmon's 1999 **Canada Waters** (2- and 3-bed flats and 3- and 4-bed houses). These homes are very close to the new tube station.

At Island Yard, by the lock, a large pub called Spice Island has been built by one of the major breweries. Adjacent to Island Yard and on the corner of **Rotherhithe St** and the YMCA a new block of 18 flats known as **Tradewinds** has 1-bed flats from £125,000, 2-beds from £180,000. Next to this on **Rotherhithe St**, and before **King & Queen Wharf**, is **Prince's Riverside** – a large development (184 units) of 1- and 2-bed river view flats and 2/3-bed houses completed at the end of 1997. Three-bed houses sell now for £250,000. **King & Queen Wharf** is nicely detailed new-build by Fairclough, first marketed in 1990: 140 flats with porterage and swimming pool/leisure complex.

Next to **King & Queen Wharf** is Berkeley's **Globe Wharf**, a sensitive restoration of this former flour warehouse. **Sovereign View** – a large neo-Georgian development (including the refurbishment of the old fire station on Rotherhithe St) – was built by Barratt between 1991–93; units vary from 1- and 2-bed flats (700–900 sq ft) to 2- and 3-bed houses with garages built round six squares, most with river views. Also facing the river is **Pageant Steps**, built by Barratt in 1996. This consists of three blocks of 1, 2- and 3-bed flats, some with river views and 3- and 4- bed houses (from £300,000) with conservatories and gardens and direct river views. Opposite **Pageant Steps**, and inland, is the 141-home **Lavender Dock**.

Canada Wharf is the glitzy refurbishment of a former flour mill by Metropolis Developments. Homes are 1- to 3-bed flats (from 500–1,600 sq ft), several with high ceilings and bed decks. Next on the riverside is the Holiday Inn Hotel (622-bed) – formerly the Crown Scandic Hotel. The original warehouse Columbia Wharf, and Nelson Dock and Lawrence Wharf were all part of Port Nelson, a scheme developed by Islef. Columbia Wharf and Nelson Dock now form part of the hotel while the original Lawrence Wharf apartments were turned into timeshare apartments, and have now been sold to Brookhouse which is refurbishing them for sale. Lawrence Wharf has 114 1-,2- and 3-bed flats with river views in three main blocks together with 30 3-bed garden flats and 1-bed ground floor flats built in a terrace on Rotherhithe Street. There is a large selection which (expect the developers) will take about three years to sell. Prices range from £125,000 to £250,000. Opposite, on the inland side, the **Amos Estate** has 131 housing association flats. Next comes **Lavender Dock North**, 51 1985 Wimpey houses, inland. Alongside is Lavender Pond nature park. **Lavender Green**, inland across **Salter Rd**, is 1981 low-cost housing by Lovell.

Opposite **Lawrence Wharf** is Silver Walk, a local authority refurbishment of flats and 21 stylish 3- and 4-bed houses (selling for £230–260,000) and some new-build units (Patina Walk). Patina Walk was sold to the LSE for student housing in the early '90s. In the midst of the scheme Nelson House is a rare and charming Georgian survival.

A tiny, peaceful park (**Durands Wharf**) gives access to the riverside plus views to the Isle of Dogs and the Canary Wharf towers. Next to the park is **Trinity Wharf**, where Bellway have sold the first phase of 42 homes and released the next batch: 1-, 2- and 3-bed flats from £200–400,000. Further flats on the inland side may result from conversion of office space. **Barnard's Wharf** and **Commercial Pier Wharf**, next to the splendid Surrey Docks Farm, have 139 homes built by housing associations. This is

Downtown, for years a very depressed corner of council flats, now a thriving area after a £55 million rehabilitation of the flats blocks by a group of housing associations. Further down is the riverside **New Caledonian Wharf**, which is 104 luxurious flats and includes swimming pool and sports centre, extensively sold off-plan in 1987; prices last winter were £220,000 for 2-beds, £250,000 for 3-beds. Next door is **Custom House Reach**, a 1970s 9-storey block of undistinguished flats.

Greenland Dock in the SE corner of the Surrey Docks area is the only surviving, unfilled-in dock. It, plus adjoining South Dock, has provided sites for a variety of builders (British and European) since 1982, and there are 1,500 homes. It is also a thriving marina. **Greenland Passage** at the dock's mouth has 152 homes, many of family size. These flats and houses, originally built by the Danish firm Islef in 1986, are some of the most expensive in the Surrey Docks and fulfill the early Docklands ideal of living in generous airy spaces with ashwood flooring, white walls and marbled bathrooms and kitchens. (4-bed houses from £350,000, 2-bed river view flats from £280,000.) Next inland is **Rainbow Quay**, just built with 144 1-, 2- and 3-bed flats, most having dock views.

Back on Greenland Dock, **Finland Quay** has 1- 2- and 3-bed flats and duplexes (Lovell). **Russia Court East** juts into the dock, with a circular 7-storey tower of flats on the point; the scheme includes further homes, shops, offices and a pub.

Finland Yard was new last year: 1- to 3-bed flats priced. **Greenland Quay** uses open courtyard layouts to give everyone water views. **Swedish Quays** sits between **Greenland** and **South Docks**: 96 flats and houses (some very large) completed in 1990. Two-bed flats here sell for £250,000. **Brunswick Quay** and **Russia Court West** are close to Surrey Quays shopping centre and the new cinema complex. In **Rope St**, just N of South Dock, a new flats block is due this year.

Just N of Greenland Dock is **The Lakes**, built on **Plover Way** on the site of Norway Dock (177 houses and flats around a shallow lake, with the largest villas actually on pontoons, by Ideal Homes). It was completed in 1995 after a long pause during the recession. This is a very popular development with flats and large 4-bed semi-detached villa-style houses which sell for around £350,000.

Baltic Quay, in **Sweden Gate**, is on the S side of South Dock. A 13-storey tower has 24 flats and a 5-storey block another 133, currently the market for £165–265,000 for 2-bed. The scheme dates back to the '80s and was blue and yellow (Swedish national colours) but current owners Pathfinder toned it down to white and grey. The flats were let for a decade and Pathfinder are doing them up for sale. Ask, though, and they'll quote you on an un-done one 'as seen'.

The Surrey Quays Marina, London's biggest working marina, opened in South Dock in 1989. On the S side of the dock, Fairview completed a range of flats and houses in 1996. These flats have fantastic views of the marina and

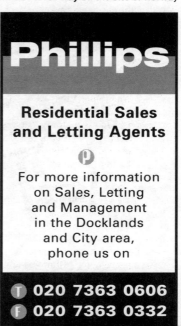

Canary Wharf. The marina has prompted a marine workshops building, and there are offices overlooking the water. At the mouth of the dock stands **Dock Master's Quay**, a stylish terrace of 3-bed houses overlooking the dock and the river. Houses tend to go for £240–270,000. At the tip of Greenland Dock on a corner of the dock near the shopping centre and **Lower Rd** two blocks of flats sit next to each other – **Howland Quay** (Fairclough, 1996) and **Lock Keepers Gate** (Redrow, 1997).

The interior of the Surrey Docks has large areas of 'normal' housing: put up by large builders, the wide open expanse giving them more familiar greenfield sites, and the result has a strong flavour of Milton Keynes. No new town, however, has the dramatic view of the City towers offered by Stave Hill, the artificial hill at the centre of the area. A tree-lined walk, flanked by new houses, leads from the hill to Surrey Water, an artificial lake with a tall fountain. The walkway is cleverly aligned to point straight at the City skyscape across the river: a view which contains more of London's landmarks than almost any other. This is the affordable side of Docklands, with 4-bed houses still available for the sort of money which would barely buy you a studio in some of the top-flight Docklands developments. There's further choice in re-sales of the Southwark Council-built family homes along and off **Salter Rd** that date from the 1970s, before yuppie flats were thought of. If the close-packed terraced streets of South and West London give you and your family claustrophobia, Surrey Docks is the place to look. And note that now the Canada Water tube station will take you to Waterloo and Westminster – or one stop under the river to Canary Wharf.

The Isle of Dogs

The Isle of Dogs is indeed an island, cut off by a great bend of the Thames and with its isthmus all but severed by the West India Docks. Unlike the Surrey Docks it has kept its water, providing vast lengths of quayside. The Isle is special in two other

GREENWICH

ways: it has the most cut-off indigenous community, for decades hardly part of London at all and only tenuously involved in the rest of Docklands, and it has Canary Wharf, described in detail under Progress Report on page 263.

By the end of the 1970s the Isle of Dogs had lost all its working docks and most of its other employers. Many sites and buildings werte derelict. The housing, such as it was, was council-owned: these homes are still there, all on 'inland' sites away from river and docks. Now, two decades after the start in 1981, the Isle renaissance is old enough to have a history. The hesitant days of light industry, timidly built on land almost given away by the LDDC with no rates to pay thanks to the Enterprize Zone (the EZ, 1982–92), were succeeded by homes and taller, smarter, more self-confident commercial buildings. By the time the DLR arrived, early-1980s buildings were being torn down: they no longer earned their keep on the rapidly appreciating sites. Then the 1990 recession came and everything halted. Now the property world is eyeing the low-rise office buildings in the S half of the Isle and wondering if it is worth replacing them with proper towers. The Isle of Dogs is now a city-centre location, not a business park, say the experts.

Not all the building sites are office blocks: homes are appearing at a pace. The Isle's riverside has a wide and varying range of residential developments, from modern social housing to glitzy apartment blocks with state of the art features. Watch for the date of the development, since nobody could at first believe quite how smart the Isle would become and things built after 1985 tend to be a lot better quality.

Most Isle housing is new-build: there were no old riverside warehouses to convert. The exception to this are the listed buildings of **Burrell's Wharf** and the flats in the West India Quay scheme. The second point is that the homes are around the 'coast' of the Isle: the centre, much of which was in the EZ, is nearly all commercial – and is becoming more so as Canary Wharf restarts building.

Coming onto the Isle from the NW, **Canary Wharf** dominates. This enormous 'city within a city' spreads from the river across the Isle between two of the surviving West India Docks – one dock, the old middle section, has been built over. The Canary Wharf complex is now expanding across the E part of the **Heron Quays** site just to the S, and two enormous towers will soon rival the original pyramid-topped skyscraper.

West India Quay, to the N of Canary Wharf, has some of the finest warehouses to survive the last war as well as the developers. They date from 1802 and are Grade I listed, so the builders working on them have had to number every one of the 6,000 paving slabs from the York stone floors – and put them back in the right order. Flats in the warehouse conversions offer plenty of bare brick, sturdy iron columns and oak beams. New oak and slate floors complement the old materials. Developers are Manhattan Lofts/Marylebone Warwick Balfour; prices range up to to £650,000 for a 3-bed penthouse. On sale at the time of going to press were 2-bed flats at around £300,000 in the 'Port East' quarter. There are also shops, restaurants, a 10-screen Virgin cinema and the Museum of Docklands – and, sometime soon, a hotel in a futuristic 34-storey tower. Also on West India Quay, St George has **The Horizon Building**, a new-build 12-storey block with 2-bed duplex flats from £360,000. Ninety per cent sold last winter.

In **Garford St**, in the shadow of Canary Wharf and close to Westferry DLR stop, is Regalians' **Premier Place**, a development of 1-, 2- and 3-bed flats. On **Westferry Rd** close to the station is a CZWG-designed building with 27 live-work units built by the Peabody Trust. The name 'Westferry' in 9-metre letters in the brickwork has become a landmark.

On the river front is **Canary Riverside**, an enormous complex with a 5-star Four Seasons hotel designed by Philippe Starck, a health club, several restaurants, 322 1-, 2-, 3- and 4-bed flats and double-height penthouses (ranging from 625 sq ft to

2,400 sq ft) and gardens. Prices for the homes range from £267,000 to £2.6 million, with health club membership thrown in. Two-thirds were sold or reserved in January. The first residents moved in in February.

Cascades, completed in 1988, is also close-by: a landmark, a stepped, 21-storey riverside tower of 171 flats. Equally well placed is **The Anchorage**, on **Sufference Wharf**, which is next door, beside the river pier on **Cuba St**. Built out of light-coloured brick it is understated chic and expensive; there are 123 homes in this block ranging from 1- to 3-bed flats to eight houses. Typical 2-bed flats sell for from £250,000.

Next to the Anchorage on **Westferry Rd** is Ballymore's **Millennium Harbour** with **D** 276 flats in a 10-storey tower new in 1999, ranging from 1- to 3-bed, plus four penthouses marketed last year for £1 million each. Seacon seems likely to keep their riverside site industrial, as they have throughout the Isle's booms and busts. To the S, **Hutchings Wharf** and **Ocean Wharf** (flats by Furlong Homes, £190–350,000) are riverside flats, being built now. A welcome open riverside space, Sir John McDougal Gardens, will remain a park. Opposite, **Glengall Place** is an early inland estate by Barratt with 79 houses. **Arnhem Wharf** is 62 1989/90 1- and 2-bed flats and 2-bed penthouses. Next to this and opposite the Docklands Sailing Club is **Old Bell Gate** by Galliard Homes – 61 1- and 2-bed flats; prices for 2-bed from £170,000.

Back on the river, and S of the park, soon to come is Persimmon's **Icon Building**, (formerly Atlas Wharf); 151 high-spec flats from £170–550,000.

Cyclops Wharf is a new-build late-'80s development with 176 waterfront flats and 24 houses on the inland side, grouped around a square. Inland along **Spindrift Avenue** Fairview Homes completed 390 homes at **Mill Quay** in 1999.

Other inland sites are **Island Square, Cahir St**, which has 31 homes – 1-bed flats to 3-bed town-houses – built by Laing. **Cahir St** also has a few Edwardian terraced cottages. **Clipper's Quay** is 256 homes around an old dock. **Quay West** comprises 127 homes, including some 4-bed town-houses by Wimpey, in a surprisingly undistinguished style.

Riverside land at **Crews St** provides the site for Redrow's forthcoming **Merchant's Point** scheme which will have 460 flats in blocks up to 18 storeys high. At **Napier Avenue**, N of Burrells Wharf, is **Maritime Quay** by Redrow Homes; 60 2-, 3- and 4-bed houses; prices from £120,000–200,000 (700 sq ft to 2,000 sq ft) currently under way (a third sold off plan). There are plans to build a further 99 2-bed flats. One of the few remaining historic sites in the Isle is **Burrell's Wharf**. Here the Great Eastern, the largest ship of its time, was built in the 1850s. The piles of its launching slipway can be seen, and remain on public view. The development combines old with new-build: 2-bed flats go from £190,000. Next is Fairview Homes' **Westferry Quay**; there are plans for 180 1- and 2-bed flats with prices from £140,000 (1-bed non-river view) to over £230,000 (2-bed river view).

Machonochie's Wharf is the site of a self-build project, where local people have created their own houses. **Clyde Wharf** and **Langbourne Wharf** (the British Steel site) are superbly placed at the very tip of the Island. Fairview Homes have 1- and 2-bed flats and penthouses. On the southernmost site on the Isle, 7-acre **Lockes Wharf**, St George are building 464 homes (including 3- and 4-storey houses, some with top floor studio room onto roof terrace) and a leisure centre. Prices are from £90,000 to £600,000. **Felstead Wharf**, a 1984 Wates scheme of 28 homes in an open square onto the river, has great views across to Greenwich. Next to it is the 14-house **De Bruin Court**. **Horseshoe Court** has 80 homes, mostly flats, on an inland site very close to the Island Gardens DLR station. Inland are terraces of pre-war cottage council houses, with large gardens. Some occasionally come up for sale. Back on the river, Barratt's **Luralda Gardens** scheme of 48 flats, their first Docklands venture, also shares views of the Cutty Sark and Greenwich.

Cumberland Mills is architecturally one of the most pleasing new-build developments anywhere in Docklands. Its tiers of roof gardens step courteously down to the riverside from the high point of its four quarters without looming over its surroundings, which include a fine church. Flats change hands for around £240,000 for 2-beds, £280,000 for 3-beds. It is sobering to recall that the 3-bed show flat was £350,000 when the block was new in 1989.

It is worth noting that riverside homes past Cumberland Mills on eastwards have views of the Millennium Dome site at East Greenwich. The award-winning **Caledonian Wharf** comes next; an earlier 104-home scheme by the same developer as Cumberland Mills, Bates. Inland is Tower Hamlets' **Cubitt Town Estate**; on the riverside is **Plymouth Wharf**, a 2-acre site with 62 homes around a square. Going N from **Mariners Mews**, Redrow Homes are building **Millennium Wharf** – a selection of 160 1- and 2-bedroom flats including some warehouse conversions, which are spread over 10 blocks (prices start at £200,000).

Compass Point, one of the best 1980s developments, has 134 houses and some flats, stretching inland across the road. Unusually, the riverside has 5-bed town-houses rather than flats. Two rows of houses reminiscent of early Victorian brick villas run inland, facing each other across a central garden; across the road the square is completed by a white-rendered crescent of flats. **London Yard**, one of the earlier schemes on the eastern bank, consists of very large orangey brick buildings grouped around ornamental water. Inland from this is **Friars Mead**, 72 houses built in 1986. The attractive 'pagoda' blocks of four houses are also unusual in having gardens.

From **London Yard** north for a long stretch is council-built housing. Barratt's **Pierhead Lock** at **Stewart St** is one of the more ambitious current schemes marketed to capitalize on the Isle of Dogs views of the Millennium site. This white high-tech development includes a crescent and a 14-storey tower. There is a total of 91, 2- and 3-bed flats; only the (2-bed) penthouse remains, despite extensive marketing, at a price of £900,000. Nearby on **Preston's Rd**, Wates' **Vantage 2000** on either side of the Blackwall Lock has 132 1- and 2-bed apartments, duplexes and town-houses: 2-beds go for around £200,000.

There are a few 19th-century riverside houses along **Coldharbour**: the Isle's only answer to Limehouse. Rarely do they come up for sale. **Crown Wharf** is 1970s houses, and the old river police station has been split into homes.

On the dock waterfront at **Marsh Wall** is Cor-Dor Group's **Meridian Place**, a development of 32 1-bed and 80 2-bed flats; prices from £120,000 and £160,000. On the same street is Galliard's Antilles Bay: 46 2-bed flats, all with river views, all now sold. On the waterfront in the E side of Millwall Dock, Epsom Homes' 6-storey glass and brick **City Harbour** has 2-bed with balconies and dock views in a complex which also includes offices. Crossharbour DLR station is close by.

At the entrance to and around Blackwall Basin is **Jamestown Harbour**, developed since 1982 by Wates; its latest phase, known as **Cotton's Landing**, has 101 homes. A picturesque site, making good use of the water – which offers private mooring as well as watersports. It gets fine views of the towers of **Canary Wharf**. So does Bellway's **The Boardwalk** between the W side of **Poplar Dock** and the N side of **Blackwall Basin** over 300 homes including houses in this stylish development: current release has 2- and 3-bed flats from £250–375,000. The W side is next to the Trafalgar Way road into Canary Wharf. There will be a marina on one quay, say the developers.

By now we are at the top NE corner of the Isle of Dogs. This corner is one to watch, with enormous empty sites and potentially good communications. Going on round to Blackwall, one of those enormous sites, once a power station, lay empty for a decade after the 1990 crash. But its fallow years are over: Barratt are building 700 homes at what is re-named **Virginia Quay**. The site borders the old East India Dock, now a nature reserve, with the Thames to the S and a big S-facing piazza with views down both sides of the river bend, and of the Dome. The Greenwich Meridian runs through the site: it will be marked by an avenue. A terrace of 4-bed, £320,000 houses looks out over the piazza and the river, and there will be a variety of flats. Some 200 homes have been sold so far, and this year's crop ranges from 1-bed flats (from £145,000) to 3-bed penthouses (from £350,000).

The Royals and Beckton

Get as far E as the Greenwich Meridian, longitude of the Millennium Dome, and you are only half-way in your journey from the Tower to the far frontier of Docklands at Gallions Reach. The Royal Docks, graveyard of grand plans in the 1980s, are still to come. Very slowly, plans are becoming reality – as the chapter on Newham reveals.

Among those estate agents active in this area are:

• Carleton Smith & Prt.	• FPDSavills	• Roger Lewis
• Knight Frank	• Alex Neil	• John D Wood
• Lincoln Radley	• Oliver Jaques	• Burnet Ware & Graves
• Michael Kalmar & Co	• Tower Property Services	• Phillips Residential *
• Kinleigh Folkard & Hayward	• Winkworth *	• Alan Selby
	• Chestertons	• L Spring
• Duncan Allen	• Hamptons	• Property Liaisons
• Burwood Marsh	• Chandlers	• Felicity J Lord *
• McDowells	• Phoenix	• Seagers
• Cluttons Daniel Smith	• Cityscope	• Keatons *

further details: see advertisers' index on p671

DOLLIS HILL AND NEASDEN

D

Map ref: p42 (3D)
Postal districts:
NW2, NW10
Boroughs: Brent (Lab)
Council tax: Band D £678
Conservation areas:
Neasden village
Parking: Free off main roads

You might be forgiven for thinking that North West London road planners intended to prevent people from going to either Dollis Hill or Neasden. The **North Circular** and the **Edgware Rd** will carry you along past these suburban enclaves, leaving you blissfully unaware of their existence. But people do live here. Very happily. According to one estate agent, every community of the globe has a representative somewhere among the local population . . .

The conversion bug that saw so many London houses split into flats in the '80s never really bit here; property is largely in the form of 3-bed semis, with flats in purpose-built blocks, and there is a strong family feel to the area. That said, here groups of sharers find whole houses to rent affordably, and the impact of riotous housefuls of, say, youthful Antipodeans on neighbouring homes has been the subject of not a little discussion this year.

Schools, churches and little parades of shops proliferate to serve the local inhabitants. Unfortunately, the tube stations of Dollis Hill and Neasden lie away towards the S of the area – but the line that both are on is the Jubilee: direct access, therefore, to the West End and, since the extension opened, to Westminster (for MPs/London Mayoral hopefuls), Waterloo, London Bridge . . . then on, should you so wish, to Canary Wharf, even the Dome.

There are also good bus services and the **North Circular** and **Edgware Rd** (A5) are nearby, providing links into the centre of town. When at home, there are numerous local pleasures: the Brent Reservoir – known as the Welsh Harp (see also Hendon) – where you can indulge in all kinds of watery pursuits; Gladstone Park in Dollis Hill for weekend walks, the tiny Stables Art Gallery on **Dollis Hill Lane** for a touch of culture, and the Grange Museum, marooned on its island at the junction of **Neasden Lane/Dollis Hill Lane/Dudden Hill Lane** – although there's talk of moving it to somewhere more accessible.

Dollis Hill

Charmingly named Dolly's Hill after an ancient local resident, Dollis Hill lies on two sides of Gladstone Park, partly in NW2 and partly in NW10. Like so much of London's inner suburbia, Dollis Hill joined the 'up-and-coming' brigade with a vengeance last year as those priced out of Willesden to the S overflowed across the tracks onto the Hill. "A crazy year", say agents.

D

'Hill' is right: from this high spot you get fine views over Harrow and Ealing. The view to the S is almost as good as that from Hampstead; on a clear day the North Downs are visible. The NW10 neighbourhood – streets such as **Fleetwood Rd**, **Ellesmere Rd**, **Dewsbury Rd** and **Burnley Rd** – has been dubbed the 'Dollis Hill estate' by estate agents. While most of Dollis Hill is inter-war, this enclave of older, Edwardian houses S of the park and close to the tube commands a premium; typically 3-bed, they sell for some £190–220,000. (Don't confuse the agents' 'estate' with the Dollis Hill Estate on **Brook Rd**, which is council-owned and on the other side of the park.)

Flat-hunters crossing the tube line from pricier areas find more for their money in Dollis Hill: first-time buyers can still find 1-bed flats in the £70–80,000 bracket. **Cornmow Drive**, off **Aberdeen Rd**, is one source of recent flats in this corner, but is tucked away by the railway line. For renters, more Dollis Hill homes lie within reach of the tube, and are thus pricier than Neasden rents.

Dollis Hill Avenue and **Gladstone Park Gardens** (small neat semis, c. £160–195,000; a detached 3-bed with garage in cul-de-sac off, £260,000 last winter) lead away from the busy **Edgware Rd** towards the park where Prime Minister Gladstone often stayed with Lord and Lady Aberdeen in the late 19th century. Sadly their Regency mansion, Dollis Hill House, by then owned by the council, suffered a great fire in 1995. In the same year, residents were startled to learn that accommodation for 200, hitherto unsuspected, lay in the grounds beneath the park's putting green. The 'Paddock' bunker would, if the last war had gone differently, have been the secret headquarters for Churchill and the War Cabinet. Might the last action of World War II have been fought on these green suburban slopes?

Last year the mansion's future seemed assured, courtesy of some lottery money and a housing association. The intention was to preserve the design of the existing building, to keep those underground bunkers open for visitors and to provide flats and houses for rent, sale and/or shared ownership. Alas, the lottery cash was lost as the council couldn't match the amount, and Dollis Hill House remains the subject of council rows, with a strong lobby of locals wanting it preserved as a historic monument, others its redevelopment, and some councillors, seemingly, its demolition. Gladstone Park itself also won lottery funding for restoration work and sports facilities.

Dollis Hill Lane, the busy thoroughfare linking Dollis Hill and Neasden, skirts the top of Gladstone Park. As well as houses and bungalows, this is the place to look for purpose-built blocks of flats. In particular, look at Dollis Heights and Neville's Court where some flats will have views overlooking the park and, in Neville's Court, command prices of £125,000 – a 3-bed, £165,000. Off **Parkside**, the E side of the park, the site of William Gladstone School was converted into **Campbell Gordon Way** in 1995 – a Wimpey development of 1- and 2-bed flats.

Neasden

'Everyone makes fun of Neasden,' complain residents and local estate agents – which is rather unfair. Neasden boasts one of Tesco's largest superstores (24 hours, six days a week) at Brent Park, the Ikea home furnishings warehouse on the **North Circular**, while N across the rail sidings the streets around **Neasden Lane North** get the Welsh Harp Reservoir and the drive-in McDonalds on **Blackbird Hill**. What more could you possibly want? More spectacularly, the largest Hindu temple outside India, hand-carved from white marble, now rises above the rooftops of the semis on **Brentfield Rd**. Neasden too benefited, if modestly, from last year's booming homes market, but local businesses still find it hard to compete with the lure of the big guns around the North Circular; Holmes Place has yet to find Neasden. However, convenient it is, if you need access to the motorway network: it lies just S, across the **North Circular/Edgware Rd** junction, from the foot of the M1.

D

The first homes in Neasden were 2-bed cottages built for workers on the Metropolitan Railway in 1876, and there was further development in the late 1920s and '30s when the **North Circular Rd**, which bisects the area, arrived.

The majority of homes in Neasden are 3-bed terraced and semi-detached houses in roads such as **Tanfield Avenue** and **Cairnfield Avenue**, though there are also some purpose-built blocks. In the heady days of the late '80s eager developers somewhat over-estimated the need for 1-bed flats in this family-semi land – and it has taken this last year to mop up the final pockets of negative equity. **Hawarden Hill** off **Brook Rd**, right down on the Neasden/Dollis Hill border, was one such. Built by Barratt, it is a red-brick block of 1- and 2-bed flats very near to Gladstone Park, but also to the large Dollis Hill council estate. A 1-bed here now costs around £70,000, compared to £67,000 in 1990; 2-bed flats, at £80–90,000, have done better. At nearby **Shepherds Walk** (1- and 2-bed flats, 2- and 3-bed houses) homes start from £80-90,000 – at last having risen well past the £65,000 at which they started a decade ago. However, in keeping with the latest trends **Brook Rd**'s old 1900s telephone exchange has now been redeveloped as smart 1- and 2-bed flats – and these are £155–175,000. By Copthorne Homes, they are due to be completed this spring, but most were already sold last winter.

A development by Beverley Homes on **Dog Lane** (called, would you believe, Baskerville Court) has contributed a cache of 2-bed flats (no 1-beds here) and 2-, 3- and 4-bedroom houses over the past few years, handy for the **North Circular** and also the Jubilee line tube. These replaced – another sign of the times – the 200-year-old Spotted Dog pub. As 2000 dawns we still await the building of a replacement Spotted Dog, for which they have permission . . .

Across **Neasden Lane** (which leads to Neasden tube), lies **Prout Grove**, whose 4-bed Victorian houses are accounted Neasden's top homes. Agents also talk about the Brent Water estate to the N of Neasden, which includes roads such as **Review Rd**, **Dawpool Rd** and **Warren Rds** – but transport here is not as good as other parts of the area: rental prices, in particular, are thus cheaper. Shopping, however, is not a problem. What Neasden lacks in charm it makes up for with shops. Not only is there Ikea and the Tesco superstore (markers along the **Edgware Rd** tell motorists how far they are from the store) but also the huge stores at Staples Corner, the **North Circular/Edgware Rd** junction. Staples' bed shop has long gone and in its place are all manner of furniture superstores, electrical, computer and office suppliers; also a huge multiplex cinema. To the E, over the junction, lies Brent Cross shopping centre.

More new homes are found (to navigate by superstores) across the **North Circular** from Ikea, in the southernmost reaches of Neasden. Here **Brentfield Rd** leads towards Harlesden, and the old Neasden Hospital site gave way in the late '80s to developments such as the flats and studios of Mitchell Brook Gardens.

Coles Green Rd runs all the way from the stores at Staples Corner to **Dollis Hill Lane**. Here there are purpose-built blocks such as Coles Green Court and, to the E, smaller terraced houses scattered amid the little industrial pockets: 3-bed houses can reach around the £160,000 mark. Along what was a country lane is the Ox and Gate pub by **Oxgate Lane**, and a delightful surprise: a little ivy-covered cottage called Oxgate Farm, last remnant of a more rural, Tudor Neasden.

Transport		Tubes: Dollis Hill, Neasden (zone 3, Jubilee). From Dollis Hill: Oxford Circus 25 min, City 30 min, Heathrow 1 hr 15 min.
Convenient for		North Circular Rd, Brent Cross shopping centre, Ikea, Edgware Rd. Miles from centre: 6.
Schools		Brent Education Authority: John Kelly Technical College (b), John Kelly Technical College (g).

D

SALES

Flats	S	1B	2B	3B	4B	5B
Average prices	70–75	70–90	100–145	140–150	–	–
Houses	2B	3B	4B	5B	6/7B	8B
Average prices	140–155	140–260	250–350	300+	–	–

RENTAL

Flats	S	1B	2B	3B	4B	5B
Average prices	100–130	140–200	180–220	200–280	–	–
Houses	2B	3B	4B	5B	6/7B	8B
Average prices	200–250	220–300	250–350	350–400	–	–

The properties	Thirties semis dominate in Neasden, plus smaller blocks of flats – private, council and housing association; first sighting of fashionable conversions of unlikely buildings – in this case the old fire-station. Dollis Hill is more spacious: similar to Neasden plus some older, turn-of-the-century properties to the south. Some early 20th-century terraces. Some expensive new-build and larger period houses.
The market	Families and DIY enthusiasts dominate this self-contained area: families on restricted budgets buy here for gardens and open space; flat-buyers are looking to Dollis Hill if they can't find what they want in Willesden Green. 1999 finally mopped up the last pockets of negative equity in Neasden, legacy of the early '90s crash. Local searches: 5–10 working days.

Among those estate agents active in this area are:
- Hoopers
- Homeview Estates*
- Rainbow Reid
- Gladstones
- McGowan Estates
- Carltons
- Haart
- Chattin Estates

further details: see advertisers' index on p671

DULWICH

D

Map ref: p94 (7E)
Postal districts: SE21, SE22, SE24
Boroughs: Southwark (Lab)
Council tax: Band D £809
Conservation areas: Most of the area
Parking: Free off main roads

Dulwich – as befits a village – is alive with rumours. The tiny glimmer that we reported last year over the long-hoped-for tube line has become a gleam. London Underground has now been granted legal powers to extend the East London Line down from Surrey Quays. Will this prove any more substantial than the tales of Nicole Kidman/Tom Cruise buying into Dulwich Village for £2.3 million, or Madonna's reported puchase of a £4.5 million mansion (of which nobody has ever heard)? All depends on imponderables such as the new London Mayor, and of course funding. Even if all goes well, 2005 is the earliest projected date for you to catch a tube from East or North Dulwich. . . (See the Transport chapter for full details.)

With its mill pond and cottages, finger-post road signs, its tollgate and its wide sweep of green space, Dulwich is a true village, as opposed to an estate agent's fabrication. An island in the South London sprawl, 'the Village' gains its character, and its history, from the charitable foundation set up by Edward Alleyn, an actor-contemporary of Shakespeare who prospered in the reign of James I. Alleyn was a successful businessman, a partner in the Rose Theatre, where Shakespeare also acted, around the corner from the Globe. He spent his money on the manor of Dulwich, leaving the 1,500-acre estate as an endowment for a school. Dulwich College still exists, and its playing-fields are among several extensive green expanses which surround the Village. The College (in the person of the estate governors) is a major landowner still: many Dulwich homes are on long estate leases.

There is more to Dulwich than the Village. East Dulwich – where the fabled tube will call, and really NE of the old centre – is straightforward 1880s suburbia. There are fringe areas to the W and S too; as with any reputable area, bits of surrounding

D

neighbourhoods try to edge into Dulwich. All of Dulwich proper is in SE21, with East Dulwich over in SE22 – and what is rapidly becoming known as the 'North Dulwich Triangle' spilling into SE24.

But between **Croxted Rd** in the W and **Lordship Lane** in the E, the heights of Crystal Palace to the S and Denmark Hill to the N, you are in Dulwich estate country. Owning a home here means playing by its rules – but you get to live in one of the tidiest, and most charming, corners of London. Everything within the boundary has a certain leafy unity, though the ages of the houses vary. Despite the Village's ancient air, there are not many truly old houses: it was not a very big place, Dulwich, until the railways came. The estate has sold off various of its green acres for development over the last century, and in consequence Dulwich has houses from the Victorian, Edwardian, inter-war and modern periods. Even the College is 19th-century, the foundation having fallen into positively Trollopian corruption and disrepute until it was reformed. The whole area relies on trains for commuting, with stations all around, but not in, the Village (the estate governors were reluctant to let the railways near the place at all; when forced to concede, they stipulated that all railway bridges should be to their own architect's design).

The estate today maintains a strong interest in its 1,500 acres, be they built-on or open space. Leaseholders have to adhere to strict conditions. About half of the 6,000 houses on estate land have been bought by leaseholders under the Leasehold Reform Acts – but even then the estate keeps control: it has retained powers over the appearance of houses and (a major concern, this) the trees in their gardens. Touch a tree in Dulwich and the estate governors will have something to say about it.

Led by the College, the area is well served by good private schools: 95 per cent of buyers are families and/or professional people, say agents. First-time buyers and singles may look at fringe areas – which have better rail links – but the Village is family country. Clapham, Battersea and Wandsworth families migrate here for more greenery and more space, but above all for the schools. For those that haven't yet, the (private) schools in Dulwich extend their catchment areas with a (private) school bus service, which brings in pupils from as far away as Clapham to the four prep schools that emerged in the 1990s to serve the three big independent schools (see end of chapter).

On the local authority front, The Charter School opens in September 2000. On the site of Dulwich High (formerly William Penn), which catered for boys up to 16, this new secondary will be coeducational and take children up to 19. It starts with high hopes, a £4 million design with the sort of glass-roofed atrium usually reserved for big business – and a head who also means business: Pam Bowmaker, OBE, ex-head of Brighton's outstanding Varndean School. Local primaries like Dulwich Hamlet Junior School in the Village and St Anthony's RC in East Dulwich do well in SATS tests. Look out for code in estate agents' lists: 'in the parish of St Barnabas' translates as 'a sporting chance of a place at Dulwich Village C of E Infants, which feeds Dulwich Hamlet Junior, which sent 16 boys to Dulwich College last year . . .'

Dulwich Village

First, outsiders should note that the main street in Dulwich Village is called. . . **Dulwich Village**, and that **Dulwich Common** is not an open space but a stretch of the South Circular. The Village (the neighbourhood) starts abruptly; a busy W–E suburban road, starting in Herne Hill as **Half Moon Lane**, becomes **Village Way**, then **East Dulwich Grove**, and skirts the village centre. Turn S into **Dulwich Village** (the road) and you are instantly in the old village. Houses are Georgian (or well-built 20th-century Georgian pastiche) and highly desirable. A glorious detached example of grand, 6-bedroomed, spacious Georgiana, set in its large garden in the angle of **Village Way** and **Red Post Hill**, was for sale last winter at a mere £1.45 million. If it had been in the golden triangle 'between pub and Park' – the core of the Village – that sum would certainly double.

Noteworthy roads in Dulwich are **Dulwich Village** (possibly the most coveted street) and **College Rd**. Pickwick Rd and **Aysgarth Rd** have about the only smaller terraces in the area (popular, pretty Edwardiana here, 2- to 3-bed terraced and semis, around £300,000); **Roseway** features picturesque 1920s semi-detached overlooking the sports ground. Some new mansions called Dulwich Oaks were added to **College Rd** in the '80s; a further clutch of 3- and 4- bed houses, Chapel Walk, appeared 18 months back. **Mitchell's Place**, off **Aysgarth Rd**, has 10 smart new houses by Osborn ranging up to £425,000. **Turney Rd** has open ground to the rear of the houses on both sides, a fairly common feature in Dulwich. Desirability continues S and W past the Picture Gallery (currently renovating; reopens next year) and the College. **Alleyn Park** runs close to the College and on down into West Dulwich near the station. **College Rd** runs S across the **South Circular** (a regrettable intrusion) with the modern 5/6-bedroom homes of **Frank Dixon Way** in the angle.

South, on the slopes of Sydenham Hill, you find a mixture of a few older properties and big inter-war modern detached homes. Hereabouts, views across much of London can be an extra bonus. The '60s Wates townhouses (£150,000-plus) of **Peckarman's Wood**, for example, are built on the S edge of the golf course.

To the E of the Village, roads of large, smart inter-war semis and detached houses run as far as **Lordship Lane**. On the W side of **Court Lane** (£325,000 for a 3-bed end-of-terrace) they overlook Dulwich Park. There is so much green space in Dulwich that many houses back onto parks, sports grounds or golf courses. This includes **Hambledon Place**: had Mrs Thatcher kept the detached house she bought in the mid-'80s Barratt's development here, it would now be worth some £700,000 . . .

East Dulwich

To the E and NE of the old centre, there is **Lordship Lane** and East Dulwich. **Lordship Lane** is the main shopping area; it has most shops necessary for everyday existence, an ever-expanding variety of restaurants and a small pub/comedy theatre. The Lane itself meets, at its S end, the A205 – which is of course the **South Circular**.

East Dulwich really describes the area that flanks **Lordship Lane**. Properties are mainly early Victorian terraced or semi-detached houses. At the N end they are smaller 2- or 3-bedroom terraces; to the S and E (in for example **Friern Rd** and **Upland Rd**) the houses are larger, 4-bedroom family style: many of these have been converted to flats. High up in **Overhill Rd** are some late-'80s flats: expect £150–160,000 for a 2-bed with 'City view'. At its junction with **Lordship Lane**, Berkeley Homes' new terrace of six 3-bed houses were £210–249,000 last winter. With the exception of the Lane itself, the above streets have unrestricted parking; many have speed bumps.

Many new homes have been appearing near East Dulwich station: Wimpey built 185 2- and 3-bed houses in **Abbots Wood Rd, Burrow Rd, Shaw Rd**, and **Talbot Rd**. Access is from **Dog Kennel Hill**; the 3-beds fetch around £145,000. Sainsbury's superstore is next door. Behind this, and accessed from **Dulwich Grove**, St Barnabas Gate is a recent (1998) development of 3- and 4-bed houses. Now Fairclough plan 111 flats and houses – 25 per cent of them affordable housing – opposite the station in **Vale End**.

Goose Green, a small wedge-shaped park, forms the N border of East Dulwich. The neighbourhood stretches a good way E towards Peckham Rye Common. North of **Goose Green** and **East Dulwich Rd** are streets of turn-of-the-century terraces. These streets are considered Peckham Rye, not Dulwich, but prices on the fringes of Dulwich have soared: large Victorian houses in **The Gardens**, off **Peckham Rye,** passed the half-million mark some years back.

West Dulwich

West Dulwich is the SW tip of the area, running down to Sydenham. There are fewer homes here: the land is largely taken up by the golf course, allotments and the sports ground belonging to the College. **Alleyn Park** and **College Rd** lead from the Village southwards off **Dulwich Common**, the South Circular; there are some popular Edwardian houses and '60s flats at the top end of **College Rd**. Choice **Alleyn Park** is joined by **Alleyn Rd** as it crosses the tracks below West Dulwich station; between **Alleyn Park** and the rail line, Rialto contributed five new detached houses 'in linear style', priced in 1998 from £220,000. As Dulwich meets Sydenham there are blocks of purpose-built maisonettes and flats on the borders: these can command superb views.

Dulwich Borders

The allure of Dulwich leads to a slow spread of the name into neighbouring areas. One border district that has a good claim to the revered name is the neighbourhood W of **Croxted Rd** and centering around **Rosendale Rd** (last winter, a 3/4-bed house in the former was £265,000; 2-bed conversions at the N end of the latter, £210,000). This road runs down from Brockwell Park and Herne Hill, and the railway bridge which crosses it perhaps marks the true Dulwich frontier. There is a street of local shops with a growing number of trendy (and good) stores and cafés, a sports ground with tennis courts and attractive streets of mixed terraced houses. The neighbourhood is equidistant from West Dulwich and Herne Hill stations. Recent homes here include a cobbled mews of 14 traditional-style houses with garages in the angle of **Croxted Rd** and **Thurlow Park Rd** (AKA the South Circular). Also in **Thurlow Park Rd** is Thurlow Mews, again in period style, but with a mix of new flats, maisonettes and bungalows, plus a conversion of the original Victorian house.

In the N of the area, the two railway stations of North and East Dulwich confuse geography: they lie a mere few hundred yards apart – and East Dulwich station is N of North Dulwich station. Many now call the streets off **Half Moon Lane** North Dulwich. Those E of **Beckwith Rd** perhaps qualify, but the other pleasant streets further W, such as **Stradella Rd, Winterbrook Rd** and **Burbage Rd** with their spacious family homes, are Herne Hill borders, and are dealt with under that neighbourhood (see Brixton chapter). **Burbage Rd,** after crossing S of the railway, does indeed run down to Dulwich. The houses have sports grounds (and Herne Hill stadium) behind them.

There is a determined effort to disinvent Herne Hill; the tract bounded by **Half Moon Lane, Herne Hill** and **Red Post Hill** has been branded, in estate-agent-speak, the 'North Dulwich Triangle'; whether the people who live here think of their homes as Dulwich or Herne Hill (see Brixton chapter) probably depends on which station they use: Herne Hill for Victoria, North Dulwich for London Bridge. The latest move is to lay claim to the area across **Herne Hill** (the road) as far as **Milkwood Rd**: this is definitively Herne Hill; beyond **Milkwood Rd** is Brixton.

Transport

Trains: East Dulwich, North Dulwich (to London Bridge); West Dulwich, Sydenham Hill (to Victoria, some to Blackfriars), Herne Hill (Thameslink to Kings Cross, Blackfriars, Cannon St). Average times to London terminals: 15–20 min.

D

Convenient for

Parks and golf courses, Dulwich schools, South Circular. Miles from centre: 5.

Schools

Local Authority: The Charter School (new co-ed: opens Sept 2000 on site of Dulwich High/formerly William Penn), Kingsdale School. Private: Dulwich College (b), Alleyn's School, James Allen's Girls School.

SALES

Flats	S	1B	2B	3B	4B	5B
Average prices	65–85	80–150	90–220	125–260	130–260	150+
Houses	2B	3B	4B	5B	6/7B	8B
Average prices	180–350	200–425	260–1 M	300–1.3 M+	325–2 M+	750+

RENTAL

Flats	S	1B	2B	3B	4B	5B
Average prices	95–150	125–200	150–275	185–370	230+	—
Houses	2B	3B	4B	5B	6/7B	8B
Average prices	175–300	230–390	275–460	345+	460–550+	—

The properties

Centuries-old Dulwich Village has carefully tended family homes from 18th to 20th centuries; some 'country' cottages; few flats. Fringe areas were developed later and have late-Victorian terraces, converted flats and increasing pockets of new homes.

The market

Family homes within Dulwich College Estate extremely popular: large gardens, lots of open space, schools, schools, schools. East Dulwich attracts flat-dwellers and buyers of Victorian terraces. The lower prices above are East Dulwich and fringes, but there are also very large, very expensive houses which range from modern mansions to glorious Georgiana priced in millions. Local searches: 15 working days.

Among those estate agents active in this area are:

- Burnet Ware & Graves
- Winkworth*
- Harvey & Wheeler
- Wates
- Acorn
- Ludlow Thompson
- Spencer Kennedy

further details: see advertisers' index on p671

EALING

E

Map ref: p56 (7D)
Postal districts: W5,
  W13, W7
Boroughs: Ealing (Lab)
Council tax: Band D £703
Conservation areas: Several –
  check with town hall
Parking: Residents/meters
  for central area

Ealing – pretty, leafy, genteel Ealing, the 'Queen of Suburbs'. The ghost of this soubriquet, earned in the 1880s when a determined local authority only allowed the building of solid, middle-class homes, hangs over Ealing still. 'In short,' explained a local agent, 'the sort of place you'd expect Agatha Christie's grandmother to live in – as, of course, she did.'

The post-war years brought a whiff of greasepaint: Ealing Film Studios in Ealing Green, famous for a string of 1940s and 1950s comedies, is still making films under the name of the National Film & TV School. It's up for sale – but it's said that any new owner will go on making films here.

Today the borough as a whole – it takes in Acton and places outside the Guide's scope such as Greenford and Southall – is prospering, with house prices up 25 per cent in 1999, the third-biggest rise in borough terms in London. Ealing's old guard of middle-class inhabitants are still holding strong – particularly in the Castlebar/ Montpelier area. They are joined by an increasingly young population – couples and singles who cannot afford to be closer into town, or who like Ealing's pretty streets and good facilities. They are 'lecturers and advertising executives', according to estate agents, and workers from Heathrow Airport and the vast BBC complex at White City. Two tube lines – Central and Piccadilly – serve the area, and there are hopes of a fast train to Heathrow from Ealing Broadway.

Ealing has a rich cultural mix, which includes Irish and Asian families, Japanese and Arabs – and it is also the centre of London's large Polish community.

The town centre has an attractive 'mall', a large M&S and a Bentalls department store. However, Ealing fears competition from other centres and to boost the town centre there are plans to build another shopping mall, which would double the size of the present one. This could mean the demolition of homes S of **The Broadway**. Plans could become more definite during 2000. The existing stores and mall are complemented by interesting and individual chocolatiers, interiors shops and designer hair salons. Central Ealing now also has many good restaurants, pubs and wine bars.

Traffic and parking are hot issues. The North Circular, and in particular its junction with the A40 at Hangar Lane, star frequently in radio traffic bulletins. Residents' parking zones, underway in Northfields and St Mary's, are planned for all areas.

Ealing Common

A room with a view comes at a price on the common. Ealing Common's outlook is so popular with house-buyers that they are prepared to pay through the nose for it. The common is convenient – for the shopping centre, for the North Circular and the A40 and for the Ealing Common tube station which is on the District and Piccadilly lines, and the station at Ealing Broadway (District, Central tubes and trains to Paddington).

Properties around the common are predominantly large family homes, like those on **Creffield Rd** which snakes off E towards Acton, where 3-storey, 7-bed homes can reach £550,000. **Fordhook Avenue** and **Byron Rd**, opposite Ealing Common tube station, are popular for family homes including 2-storey 4-beds around £400,000 and 3-storey 5-beds at £450,000. To the SE lies **Tring Avenue**, with some very large 7-bed Victorian houses, which can fetch £750,000, and 1920s and '30s detached and semi-detached houses. The **Delamere Rd** estate has an enclave of smaller 3- and 4-bed Art Deco semis which command £350-450,000. **Warwick Dene** is in a different league: the big Victorian houses look across the Common and can command £1.3 million. A short distance away, to the smart Grange pub, tiny, 1-bed 19th-century farm workers' cottages in **St Mark's Rd** and **St Matthew's Rd** command £180,000.

Greystoke/Brentham

Popular schools are a draw on this estate of semis in the N of the area, which is home for many young families. Homes on the Art Deco Greystoke estate, S of the **Western Avenue** and just W of **Hanger Lane** junction, are snapped up by parents who want their children to go to Montpelier Primary School. The '30s 3/4-bed semis are not as imposing as the older homes further S. But they are spacious, with large gardens and easy access to major roads, Ealing Golf Club, Helena Park and the pretty Hanger Hill park. The atmosphere is rather 'villagey' and very family orientated. You can spend £300,000 on a 3-bed house in **Brunswick Rd** – the road closest to Western Avenue – but quieter roads such as **Kingfield Rd**, **Ainsdale Rd** or **Brookfield Avenue** command 10% more. Going up the scale, **Lynwood Rd**'s 4-bed homes go for £400–450,000 while the 4- to 5-bed double-fonted **Birkdale Rd** houses, near to the Montpelier neighbourhood, fetch £600–700,000.

The Brentham Garden Estate around **Brentham Way** is for anyone who yearns for a romantic rose-covered cottage. They date from Edwardian times, when 60 acres were developed according to the garden suburb ethos in the manner of Hampstead Garden Suburb. Prices are high for these little houses, with young professional couples ready to spend £210–220,000 on the small, 2-bed cottages of **Ludlow Rd**, **Fowler's Walk**, **Denison Rd** and **Neville Rd** and £275–300,000 on the 3-bed ones in **Brentham Way**. They know they will have little problem reselling, as the estate, which is a conservation area, is one of the most coveted corners in Ealing.

Hanwell

Canalside walks and the cutely nicknamed 'Bunny Park' give a real village atmosphere (if you ignore the run-down Broadway) to Hanwell, the district which borders the River

Brent in the W of the borough. It has its up-market enclaves, but is the cheaper compromise for those who cannot quite afford Ealing proper – yet.

To the S the area around Boston Manor Piccadilly line station is popular with commuters. There are '30s semis in the roads off **Clitherow Avenue**, which boast that prized commodity to Londoners – a garage. Three-bed houses there are around £240–260,000. Properties in **Haslemere Avenue** may be older – turn-of-the-century, but the road is a locals' cut-through from Boston Manor to **Northfield Avenue** and is therefore less popular.

Further N along **Boston Rd** is 'Old Hanwell', a series of streets leading off SW down to the Grand Union Canal. The name is a bit of estate agents' jargon, but this corner has no through traffic, a charming (and successful) small primary school in St Mark's and a country-style pub, The Fox, whose garden is a magnet for families in the summer. Century-old cottages, in **Green Lane, St Dunstan's Rd** and **Rosebank Rd** in particular, are popular: 2-beds £140–175,000 and 3-beds £170–200,000. A small estate of red-brick houses and flats, built by in 1996 Laing beside the canal, has raised the general popularity of the area say agents. Three-bedroom houses there may fetch £195,000 with 2-bed flats at around £145,000.

Heading N you come to the run-down **Hanwell Broadway**, a hotch-potch of junk shops, take-aways and off-licences – and, unexpectedly, a Rolls Royce dealership. Even the comedy club has decamped to the brighter lights of Ealing.

N of the Broadway are some streets of Edwardian houses – **Laurel Gardens, Myrtle Gardens, Connolly Rd** and **Lawn Gardens** – where 3-bed houses fetch £200–210,000. The 2-bed terraces of **Halfacre Rd** have long gardens sloping down to the River Brent, and are priced around £180,000. These homes are close to one of Ealing's most popular beauty spots – the popular, if slightly neglected, Brent Lodge Park bunny park, full of frolicking pets, adored by children and parents.

Backing onto the park, NW of Hanwell railway station (direct line to Paddington), is the aptly named Golden Manor estate – the jewel in Hanwell's crown. The gardens are beautiful and the houses large and well-maintained. Among the most desirable streets is **Manor Court Rd** by virtue of its location and the individual architectural styles. A 4-bed Victorian house may sell for £400,000, but prices for the larger, double-fronted homes can nudge up to £600,000, prices comparable to some of the more select parts of Ealing. In the less popular **Campbell Rd**, which has the railway station, you may find a 5-bedroom house for £300,000. The side nearer the railway line tends to fetch cheaper prices.

Church Rd is the centre of the old village of Hanwell, complete with church, a few old houses and even a thatched cottage.

To the NE of Hanwell station, across the busy **Greenford Avenue,** is a 'Poets' Corner' – **Shakespeare, Milton, Cowper, Tennyson** and **Drydon Rds,** where 3- and 4-bed semis are sought-after (not to be confused with the similarly named enclave in Acton). A 4-bed house here might command £250,000.

As you progress further N towards the Council-built Cuckoo and Copley Close estates, prices drop steadily. In **Framfield Rd** a 2-bed house might cost £150,000. On the Cuckoo estate, mostly private now, the 3-bed 1930s 'suntrap'-style homes sell for £120,000. A 3- or 4-bed house on the nearby Copley Close estate – one of Ealing's least desirable areas – can be had for £60,000.

West Ealing

The run-down streets of parts of this poor-relation neighbourhood of Ealing are hunting grounds for a bargain, though prices and respectability rise as you go E.

North of the **Uxbridge Rd** the area is dominated by the Green Man council estate, an area lacking in facilities. There are a few streets of owner-occupied homes, backing onto West Ealing Broadway – **Ecclestone Rd, Endsleigh Rd** and **Felix Rd,** where flats are the norm. A 1-bed garden flat can be yours for £115,000.

South of the **Broadway,** West Ealing is more up-and-coming – particularly in the streets nearest **Northfield Avenue** in the E. The terraced houses that line the parallel streets E of **Grosvenor Rd** have a more suburban feel. The pebbledashers have done their worst here and in many cases the Victorian and Edwardian character has been smothered by faddish renovation. Here a 2-bed house may cost you £160,000-plus. The whole scene changes as you venture N away from the busy **Uxbridge Rd.** By the time you hit the **Waldeck Rd** area you will be expecting to pay £600,000 for a double-fronted Victorian home with 6 bedrooms, while 1- and 2-bed converted flats go for £120–150,000.

West Ealing **Broadway** is not too exciting as a shopping area. Marks & Spencer, British Homes Stores and Sainsbury's are the main attractions; the rest is cheap and (not very) cheerful. An up-market Waitrose supermarket was, however, built on **Alexandria Rd,** near West Ealing station – despite controversy with neighbours about traffic problems. A new development of 14 flats in an old warehouse opposite Waitrose is selling at £190–200,000 for 2-beds and £240,000 for 3-beds.

Northfields

Northfields boasts a popular shopping street, **Northfield Avenue,** bustling with interesting and useful independent shops. It is an area very popular with families, attracted by road upon road of solid, 1900 houses, the successful Fielding Primary School in **Wyndham Rd,** the spacious Lammas Park – and the Piccadilly line tube. A new residents' parking scheme has abated one problem – commuter parking. To the W of **Northfield Avenue,** a 3-bed house in a typical road such as such as **Midhurst Rd** might cost £250,000, while a 2-bed house in **Altenburg Avenue,** closer to the station, would be £230–240,000. To the E of Northfield Avenue, houses get bigger and pricier as you get closer to Lammas Park, and then on E towards Walpole Park and central Ealing. **Elers Rd** is a cut-through from Northfield Avenue to central Ealing, but its imposing 4- and 5-bed houses are at a premium: £400,000 for a 4-bed, £560,000 for 5-bed. Add another £70,000 for a home on the S side, backing onto the park. Moving E towards Walpole Park are substantial houses, many split into flats which command £160–220,000 for a 2-bed. An intact house might well be £500,000-plus.

Haven Green/Castlebar/Montpelier

Some would call this Ealing's best area – it is certainly the home of the 'old guard' of middle-class Ealing residents, whose families have often lived in the borough for generations. Haven Green is a pretty parkland patch just N of the **Broadway,** and the Castlebar/Montpelier area lies N of the green, leading up the hill to Hanger Hill Park. Haven Green is the heart of Ealing's transport network, with the Broadway mainline station and tube, taxi rank and bus terminals. Homes overlooking the green are mostly in luxury purpose-built blocks or, to the E along **Madeley Rd,** in large red-brick detached houses – mostly split into flats. One-bed conversion flats here fetch £120–170,000, and 2-beds £150–250,000. **Haven Lane,** leading N from the green, is a charming street of terraced cottage-style homes, each with pretty gardens. The lane is tight for parking, but also has a nice pub: it is one of Ealing's most popular roads.

In the **Montpelier Rd** area, the houses are large, Edwardian and detached, with some flat conversions and a some 1920s/30s mansion blocks. Modern town houses are found in pockets. Prices are high, as befits the most popular area in Ealing. A 2-bed mansion flat might be £160–200,000, up to £250,000 for a 3-bed. A grand Victorian 7-bed house in **Corfton Rd** was on the market last year for £1.5m. Modern town houses, such as those in **Goldcrest Mews,** may fetch £350,000. A short distance W is **Castlebar Park,** a wide attractive road that winds down from **Castlebar Hill** into Pitshangar Village. At the top of the hill is Queen's Place, a new development of nine 4-bed houses with garages, priced at £415–450,000. Don't confuse Castlebar Park with the branch-line rail station of Castle Bar Park – at least half a mile separates them and in terms of status they're worlds apart: the station serves the unfortunate Copley Close council estate (see under Hanwell above).

The area is particularly popular with the parents of young children, thanks to the excellent reputation of the Montpelier primary school in **Helena Rd.** The Greystoke estate of '30s semis to the N of the Montpelier area, and the cottage-style Brentham estate are also in the school catchment zone.

St Mary's

St Mary's is real village Ealing, the oldest part of the area. The roads around the parish church on **St Mary's Rd** are Victorian terraces and detached homes. The area is close to the **Broadway,** and to all the facilities of central Ealing. The Grange schools are popular. The homes nearest Lammas Park top the bill, but all the streets are pretty, tree-lined and very expensive. This favoured little spot offers a mish-mash of styles from Victorian to Art Deco. Two small new developments have just appeared, which blend well. 2- and 3-bed houses at the junction of **Ealing Green** and **Webster Gardens** are selling at £395,000, and Laing's 3- and 4-bed town houses in Primrose Mews, off **St Mary's Rd,** are priced around £400,000. Period 3-bed houses in nearby **Conigsby Rd** fetch £220–260,000, despite being small and having downstairs bathrooms. **Clovelly Rd** runs beside Lammas Park and its Victorian/Edwardian homes are popular, with 4-beds (thanks to loft conversions) selling for £450–500,000.

Further S, around the Piccadilly line station of South Ealing, the streets are less rarified but still popular: 3-bed homes fetch £300–330,000. A Residents' zone has curbed commuter parking around here.

Pitshanger and Scotch Common

The northernmost area of Ealing, S of the A40, is a lively neighbourhood with a village atmosphere – indeed, you'll find estate agents have dubbed it 'Pitshanger Village'. Centred on the bustling **Pitshanger Lane,** the streets leading down to Pitshanger Park are nearly all Edwardian 3-bed terraced homes in the £250,000 range – £50,000 more with loft/rear extensions. Pitshanger is good for access to the A40, though the nearest station is the one at Castle Bar Park half a mile away. It is close to Ealing Golf Course and Brentham Lawn Tennis and Country Club and is in the catchment area for the popular North Ealing Primary School, which adds £30,000-plus to house prices.

Pitshanger residents are fiercely protective of their 'village' and are vociferous foes of any 'intrusive' developments. Their latest 'scalp' is Laing, with work on their six new £325,000 semis in **Pitshanger Lane** halted by planners when homes were spotted to be too close to the road. A revised plan has been submitted for four homes.

To the western end of the area is Scotch Common, where a large modern development built in the early 1970s provides a variety of homes from small studios through to 4/5-bed town-houses. Among the purpose-built blocks in this part of town, called the Cleveland Estate, some are decidedly better built than others. Check surveys. Two-bed flats here cost £150–160,000; 4-bed houses £290–300,000. West of the common, there are '30s-style houses in the £240–250,000 bracket for 3-beds.

St Stephens and Drayton Green

South from Scotch Common, this is a large area forming the bulk of middle-class Ealing. In the centre is St Stephen's Church, a landmark converted into plush and expensive flats, which caused quite a stir when they appeared on the property market in 1987. Take with you £440,000 and you can buy a lovely 5-bed detached Victorian house in leafy **St Stephen's Avenue**. To the SW are The Draytons, terraced houses built for railway workers at the nearby West Ealing station with its direct line to Paddington. They vary in size and status, with both increasing as you move further from the tracks: **Manor Rd** has the smallest (3-beds £175,000) with bigger and better homes (4-beds £280,000) in **Drayton Avenue**, **Drayton Gardens**, **Drayton Grove** and **Drayton Road**. The Green at the W end of the neighbourhood is attractive, but the council-built housing to the NW around Copley Close casts a shadow.

Hanger Hill

For those who live on Hanger Hill estate it is '*the* Estate of Ealing' – large 1930s houses, with spacious gardens and garages. It has recently been made a conservation area. Park Royal and North Ealing tubes bracket this corner. This select enclave lies just E of **Hanger Lane**, and its concentric rings of roads include **Corringway**, **Audley Rd**, **Beaufort Rd**, **Chatsworth Rd**, **The Ridings** and **Ashbourne Rd**. For those who do not live on the estate, Hanger Hill is sneered at slightly for a certain ostentation: a place of stone lions roaring on pillars. The homes, built by builders Haymills in the late '30s, are quite varied in their styles and generally fetch £360–500,000 for 3- to 5-beds. **Corringway** and **Ashbourne Rds** are a bit of a rat-run, but recent traffic-calming has improved matters. **Beaufort** and **Audley Rds** are quieter, and 5-bed houses can reach £570,000. A 7-bed, 4-bath house in **Chatsworth Rd** went last year for £800,000.

Borders: Brentford

Although strictly speaking Hounslow, Brentford just lies to the S of Ealing. It is divided in two, some may say blighted, by the M4 motorway: New Brentford, the part N of the motorway, has areas of suburban housing. S of the motorway is Brentford's run-down centre, the football stadium, and the confluence of the Rivers Brent and Thames and the Grand Union Canal. The corner people get excited about is **The Butts**, a square in the old town, of which little else remains. It has several late-17th- and early 18th-century houses: look here for genuine Queen Anne, with 4/5-bedrooms and huge gardens. Posh Central London agents solemnly make the journey to Brentford for these: when they come on the market, they sell for £500,000–£1 million.

The other bit of Brentford that matters is the waterside. Brentford Dock – a 21-acre complex of flats and houses – is one of W London's best-kept secrets. Reached via **Augustus Close**, its equally classically named blocks of typical 1970s-vintage architecture have worn well, and the trees and gardens have filled out. Here is a very active community: all owners share the freehold of the estate, which is grouped around a marina and forms a triangular island. On one side is the Thames, another is the Brent and the mouth of the Grand Union Canal – and the third is the boundary wall of Syon Park. You pay £310,000 for a 4-bed maisonette (£350,000 if on the Thames) and £550,000 for a 5-bed house. Flats start at £110,000 for a 1-bed, rising to £180,000-plus for a 3-bed.

Brentford is bracing itself for regeneration on a major scale: the riverside offers one of the last Thames-bank opportunities in West London, and there are plans for 800 homes, two hotels and a transformation of the town centre. Watch this space.

E

Transport Tubes: Ealing Broadway (zone 3, Central, District), Ealing Common (zone 3, District, Piccadilly). Others see map. From Ealing Common: Oxford Circus 40 min (1 change), City 1 hr 10 min (1 change), Heathrow 25 min. Trains: Ealing Broadway to Paddington 10 min.

Convenient for Heathrow, M4/M40, North Circular Rd. Miles from centre: 8.

Schools Ealing Education Authority: Brentside High, Drayton Manor High, Ellen Wilkinson (g) Elthorne Park High. Private: Ealing College Upper, King Fahd Academy, St Benedict's School (b), St Augustines Priory (g), Notting & Ealing High School (g).

SALES

Flats	S	1B	2B	3B	4B	5B
Average prices	70–100	90–180	120–250	150–350	300+	–

Houses	2B	3B	4B	5B	6/7B	8B
Average prices	150–260	160–360	250–450	300–650	400–1.5 M	550–1.5 M+

RENTAL

Flats	S	1B	2B	3B	4B	5B
Average prices	125–175	160–220	175–275	210–390	230–460	–

Houses	2B	3B	4B	5B	6/7B	8B
Average prices	175–275	195–390	275–460	345–600	370–690	–

The properties Late-Victorian and turn-of-the-century red-brick houses and terraces. Some '30s semis and modern blocks. Lots of conversions, a few mansion blocks. Hanger Hill, Castlebar and Montpelier are the most favoured areas.

The market People with young children move here thanks to family houses and good schools, and stay for the green environs, local services and good communications. Local searches: 5 working days.

Among those estate agents active in this area are:

- Sinton Andrews
- Rolfe East
- Bairstow Eves
- Barnard Marcus

- Grimshaw & Co
- Brendons
- Winkworth *
- Northfields *

- Robertson Smith & Kempson *

further details: see advertisers' index on p671

FINCHLEY

Map ref: p27 (1J)
Postal districts: N2,
N3, N12
Boroughs: Barnet (Lib
Dem/Lab Coalitionl)
Council tax: Band D £760
Conservation areas:
Church End, Finchley
Garden Estate
Parking: Free

Londoners once headed for Finchley Common to escape the Great Plague. Three hundred and forty years later the exodus starts at 5.30pm as commuters leave the City concrete and make their way north-westwards to the quiet, dignified, leafy suburb of Finchley.

Originally part of the forest of Middlesex, the woods that are echoed in names like Woodside Park and Finchley ('a wood frequented by finches') slowly disappeared when the manor belonged to the Bishop of London, who found sheep-raising more profitable. Finchley was once a busy coaching stop, placed as it is on the old main road to the North, and a favourite haunt of highwaymen – but these days vehicular travellers are more likely to be held up in streets crammed with parked cars, a result of the '80s spate of flat conversions. Finchley, originally defined as East End, Church End and North End, grew naturally as hamlets sprang up along the main **Great North Rd** (which still doubles as the area's **High Rd**) from London. But today the roaring dual-carriageways of the **North Circular Rd** effectively cut off East Finchley to the south.

With the 19th-century train whistle that heralded the arrival of the Great Northern Railway, the suburb began to blossom; soon most of the large houses, estates and meadow land gave way to mainly middle-class housing. The first big villas of the 1860s are still in evidence to the E of the **High Rd** in North Finchley. Later, the Northern line tube opened up further tracts for development.

But developers were careful to retain the green open spaces, and residents can enjoy the untethered Dollis Brook, which cuts N–S and separates Finchley from Hendon, as well as the cultivated Victoria Park in Finchley Central, Friary Park on the Friern Barnet borders of North Finchley, and Cherry Tree Wood in East Finchley. (This latter was called Dirt House Woods in a less sensitive era.) There is even, in the midst of suburban splendour, a working farm overlooking **Regents Park Rd**.

The last real vestiges of the original woods of Finchley, Coppetts Wood, forms part of a green area sandwiched between the **High Rd, Summers Lane, Colney Hatch Lane** and the **North Circular**. The wood (which also masks the 24hr Tesco superstore at the North Circular/Colney Hatch Lane junction) adjoins allotments and a nature reserve that run almost as far as the sports fields on Summers Lane and the Finchley Lido sports complex, at the High Rd end, which includes an open-air swimming pool. The mixed civic and private facilities here have been extensively developed in recent years: bowling alley, tennis, multi-screen cinema and an increasing number of cafés and restaurants; at the Summers Lane end of this stretch is a David Lloyd sports centre. On the S side of the North Circular, more green 'lungs' are provided by the two large cemeteries serving Central London parishes (St Marylebone, St Pancras & Islington), a golf course and numerous playing-fields.

Finchley boasts some fine surviving Georgiana – including the original manor house off **East End Rd**, a listed building dating back to 1793. Renamed the Sternberg Centre, it is now used as a private Jewish teaching centre, museum and school. Further along **East End Rd** stands Avenue House, once the home of 'Inky' Stephens, the philanthropist MP and pioneering ink manufacturer. Almost opposite, its remaining grounds – now public – hold a collection of rare trees.

There is an abundance of 3-bedroomed semi-detached property throughout Finchley. Houses are larger and more spacious in Woodside Park; terraced and more cosy in the 'county' roads of East Finchley. Otherwise the area is bursting with flats. Many of the old suburban villas were converted in the '80s, and more and more luxurious (and expensive) blocks have sprung up wherever developers can get planning permission. There are still examples of 1930s blocks between Finchley Central and Tally Ho Corner shopping areas, and beyond North Finchley along the **High Rd** to Whetstone. Plenty of homes, but still plenty of demand too – especially for flats, either for occupation or to be rented out as an investment: this 'buy-to-let' activity has been a considerable slice of the action for the past year or two.

Local shopping is concentrated along Finchley's spine, the **High Rd**, and on **Ballards Lane**, which meet at Tally Ho Corner; this, though, has been affected by the huge, and growing, Brent Cross shopping centre, just 10 min away by car or by the regular bus services. The area has a large and powerful watchdog in the guise of the Finchley Society.

Finchley suburban style makes constant references to rural models in its streets and buildings and, thanks to generous gardens and plentiful trees, goes a good way towards achieving the idyll. Mock-Tudor touches such as half-timbering, leaded light windows and tile hanging add to the charm. Such houses are more appreciated today than they were and purists deplore the excesses of DIY improvers.

East Finchley

Row upon row of terraced houses give a distinct flavour to what was traditionally called East End (and changed by sensitive residents lest they be confused with the Cockneys). Today the area is wider than the site of the original hamlet, with its weekly hog market, within the triangle made by **East End Rd**, the **North Circular** and **East Finchley High Rd**, and is fertile hunting-ground for flats, too. Barnet Council has erected a sign welcoming you to 'East Finchley Village' – not entirely without justification: it does indeed have that feel, with local shops that still include a butcher, baker, fishmonger and greengrocer, and a cinema that's old, atmospheric and single-screened. (Not so villagey, though, is the High Rd's congestion.)

This is home to those who balk at Highgate prices, and (unlike Muswell Hill to the E) it has the tube. It also has its own red-brick 'university' by the tube station – the hamburger training centre which forms part of McDonald's British HQ. Behind this academy, and a common sight elsewhere to the W of the **High Rd**, are purpose-built maisonettes and blocks of flats, some exclusively for retired people.

On the E side of the **High Rd**, **Fortis Green** is busy but picturesque: here large houses accompanied by their attached cottages (originally staff quarters), lie along a tree-lined route to Muswell Hill (see chapter). Last year's rocketing prices were underpinned in this corner by the draw of good schools. There are firemen's cottages and Grade II listed farmworkers' cottages from the early part of the 20th century, an '80s mews and modern flats. South of **Fortis Green**, homes in the roads that run down to pleasant Cherry Tree Wood, one of East Finchley's few open spaces, have the benefit of being close to the tube as well. Here **Summerlee Avenue's** terraces of 3-bed white-painted 1930s homes can now fetch as much as £300,000 for the best examples. Neighbouring streets such as **Park Hall Rd** have older and more varied terraces. Nearby, at the end of **Southern Rd**, a clutch of new houses appeared by the archery club in 1996, in their own private, gated road.

North of **Fortis Green** are the so-called 'county' roads – **Hertford**, **Bedford**, **Huntingdon**, **Leicester**, **Lincoln** and **Durham Rds** – ever popular with 30-something professionals and minor soap celebrities who can afford the premium attracted for the best of these terraces of cottagey little 2- and 3-bed Victorian/Edwardian homes: these were not built to accommodate cars, as evidenced by the heavily parked streets. The 'county' roads are fairly quiet, although they are used as a shortcut around the traffic lights at the Bald Faced Stag junction.

The further away from the High Rd, and the nearer to Muswell Hill, the larger and more detached the houses in roads like **Creighton Avenue**, just N of the 'county' roads, with the luxury of their own drives and garages – and prices to match.

Across to the W of the **High Rd**, popular streets include pleasant **Leslie Rd**, which has a cache of 2-bed maisonettes; round the corner, **Church Lane** runs the gamut of property styles from imposing Victorian residences to 1990s red-brick modern town-houses.

South of **East End Rd**, and W of the tube station, is a different ball game: this is the Hampstead Garden Suburb and Highgate borders (see chapters), with prices as large as the houses in **Abbots Gardens**, the top end of **Deans Way**, **Bancroft Avenue** and the northern stretch of 'Millionaire's Row', the **Bishop's Avenue**.

Returning northwards, the North Circular end of the **High Rd** is flanked by two strongly contrasting council-built estates: Barnet's own Grange Estate, an older-style, modest complex, runs well back from the High Rd in small tree-surrounded blocks. Almost opposite is the Strawberry Vale Estate, a Camden Council-controlled estate on Barnet land, sandwiched between the **North Circular Rd** and the St Pancras & Islington cemetery. Outside, this estate looks like a prison with its semi-circular wall shielding the noise of the North Circular traffic from the '70s mix of flats and houses inside.

North Finchley

Beyond the complex fly-over system of the **North Circular**, the terraces begin to disappear and the suburban 3-bedroom semis spring up in roads like **Squires Lane** and

Queens Avenue. This is far more family homes territory (hence, no doubt, Sainsbury's decision to open a Homebase on the **High Rd** near Tally Ho Corner). New flats appear where there's space, and **Bow Lane** is home to a housing association development built on the site of the old school kitchens. Across on the E side of the High Rd, **Summers Lane** skirts Finchley's green heart (see introduction), with playing fields, sport facilities both private and public including the Lido; the nature reserve, allotments and the wonderful leafy oasis of Coppetts Wood. Barnet's refuse disposal and recycling facilities, happily, moved away some time ago; the site is still empty.

North from Tally Ho Corner, **Friern Park** and **Torrington Park** are typical of the roads to the E of the High Rd: at this end a mixed bag of late-Victorian terraces, purpose-built flats and conversions. For families, house numbers are everything: the school catchment areas are different at each end of **Torrington Park**.

As you continue northwards the mood changes, with the E-side streets becoming blissful suburbia: grass verges appear in roads such as **Ravensdale Avenue** (it may start by Sainsbury's superstore, but it ends down the road from the golf course), and quiet, tree-lined streets such as **Mayfield Avenue**, where uniform rows of white-fronted, 3-bedded homes have gardens fore and aft and, as the millennium dawned, price tickets averaging £200–220,000. These streets have benefited from the recent traffic-calming measures. On eastwards, towards Friern Barnet, in the tract bordered by **Woodhouse Rd** to the S and **Friern Barnet Lane** to the E the '30s suburbia is in full blossom, with many mock-Tudor and modern town-houses overlooking Friary Park.

To the W of the **High Rd** the picture is a mix of large villas, converted into attractive and spacious flats, and rows of 1920s terraces, many converted to maisonettes. **Lodge Lane** is particularly pretty (although busy – thanks in the main to lorries from the bakery and the Post Office sorting office) with rows of tiny cottages all beautifully modernized and spruced up. **Coleridge Rd** saw the completion of a new mews development at the end of 1999: five 3-bedroomed houses, prices upwards of £200,000. Pleasant streets between the **High Rd** and the tube line lead across to Woodside Park – many have 'Woodside' in their names.

Woodside Park

These 'Woodside' streets, near the Woodside Park underground, reflect the popularity of this side of Finchley as a place to settle into a comfortable and convenient flat – perhaps after the children have left home. Here large houses mingle with modern schemes both basic and (the more recent developments) sybaritic. But above all, flats spring up wherever sufficient square footage can be found. The architectural mix is thus eclectic: alongside a 1998 block of luxury flats in **Woodside Lane** stands a magnificent late-Victorian mansion, all intricate plasterwork and turreted roofline.

Across on the W side of the tube tracks, there is an air of affluence to Woodside Park proper. Houses are larger, the cars are BMWs and Mercedes, the roads are wider. **Holden Rd** itself has changed its character in the last 30 years: what was once an avenue of enormous houses with gardens tumbling down the banks to Dollis Brook has been transformed. A section of the road is devoted to a mid-'70s development of square town-houses facing late-'80s flats and the remaining original houses. One such, a 7-bedroomed mansion was recently for sale for £365,000. This is developers' paradise – Goldsmith's Court is the latest luxurious development to be completed: the 28 2-bedroomed flats from £220,000; the four 1-beds some £160,000.

Next door is another outbreak of rows of early '70s houses – entirely council-built, but nicely developed on the corner of **Holden Rd** and **Laurel View** – which was held up by an illustrious resident who refused to sell until almost the last bricks were laid all around his house and garden. There have been problems with a few of the units built too near the brook, but otherwise they are pleasant.

Across Dollis Brook, in the angle between it and the delightfully named Folly Brook, **Southover** and **Northiam** (*just* Southover and Northiam, note: nothing so common as 'Road' or 'Street' added) are leafy boulevards of posh detacheds or semis, with driveways, columns and roof extensions. Below Folly Brook, the streets with South Downs names – **Lullington Garth, Walmington Fold, Chanctonbury Way, Cissbury Ring North** and **South**, etc – are ideal for families whose purse strings are a little more tied. The prices can dip further away from the tube stations and the shops – but not far, thanks to the green, open aspect and the peace and quiet. A 3-bed semi here costs upwards of £250,000: a 3-bed example on **Lullington Garth** was £270,000 last winter; a 4-bed on **Sussex Ring**, £360,000.

Church End

The home of Finchley's largest houses, most picturesque avenues and most historic buildings: the Christ's College building, St Mary's school house and, on **East End Rd**, Avenue House and the original manor house. This is the area most often depicted in paintings and sketches representing old Finchley.

East End Rd, linking the High Rd of East Finchley with Regents Park Road and Church End, has some interesting residents: opposite the huge cemetery where it passes over the North Circular is a convent, the home of the Good Shepherd Sisters and Carmelite Friars. The surrounding streets such as **Thomas More Way** and **Hamilton Rd** have attractive, 2- and 3-storey yellow-brick flats and houses with low walls and cottage gardens that cluster in such a way as to give them a neighbourhood feel.

Church End itself surrounds St Mary's Church in **Hendon Lane**; this is the heart of the old village, and the site of the turnpike on the old road from Marylebone. At the apex of **Hendon Lane** and **Regents Park Rd**, it is Finchley's most visible and congested conservation area, lying close to the shops and Finchley Central tube.

To the W down prestigious (million-plus) **Hendon Avenue** is a more peaceful idyll, and another conservation area. **Village Rd** is the core of Finchley Garden Village, 54 semi-detached houses built around a rectangular green in the early 1900s. It was the brainwave of architect Frank Stratton who lived there himself. Equally attractive, and with its own 'village green', is the wonderfully-named **Crooked Usage**.

But the immediate triangle of Old England at Church End, around the cottages of **College Terrace**, has become a virtual island – surrounded by tasteful, luxury flat developments down **Hendon Lane** (the latest, at no. 101, will be completed late this year) and a vast outbreak of red-brick flats and office blocks in **Regents Park Rd**. More flats across the road, including the 1980s Embassy Lodge for retired people (c. £200,000 for a 2-bed apartment).

The luxury developments continue down this road, punctuated by the fields of the picturesque College Farm, once the Express Dairies show-place farm, to the **North Circular Rd**, the famous Naked Lady statue and Henly's Corner. The homes of **Allandale Avenue** and **Fitzalan Rd** have the amazing bonus of overlooking what is still a working farm, with an emphasis on rare breeds. Cars flock to the regular Sunday open days, but they are reckoned a small price to pay for this slice of the country.

Around the side-streets like **Tillingbourne Gardens** the houses are impressive, detached and dear. The **Kinloss Gardens** Synagogue is at the corner of the ambitious but popular Chessington Estate.

Road experts at Barnet Council have turned the streets to the east of **Regents Park Rd – Mountfield Rd, Stanhope Avenue, Cavendish Avenue, Holly Park** and **Holly Park Gardens** – into a maze of one-ways and no-through roads to stop rat-running. The older houses here have gradually been converted into flats. St Luke's Court, a 1980s development in **Mountfield Rd**, however, went for exclusivity with a private courtyard behind remote-control gates. It has as its star the refurbished, 6-bed old vicarage (the developers built the vicar a new one), sold in 1988 for half a million. Two new houses, flats and penthouses with 'cathedral-proportion living rooms' completed the scheme.

Finchley Central

What's in a name? Finchley Central is really just the name of the tube and belt of shops along **Ballards Lane**, but estate agents seized on it in the '80s to describe the area N of the railway line on either side of **Ballards Lane** before you come to the postal district of N12 and Woodside Park. Now Barnet Council have attempted to reverse this trend with a sign near the tube station firmly labelling this end of Ballards Lane as 'Church End Town Centre'. If many of the streets have neither the leafy charm of Woodside Park or the cosy trendiness of East Finchley, there are good local shops, pubs and restaurants, and the Finchley hallmark of homes of all shapes, ages, sizes and convenience (for which you pay: a small 1-bed top-floor conversion in **Station Rd**, £100,000). Further N is the equally nebulous West Finchley which, again, covers the few streets around the tube station of the same name.

The overwhelming appearance in the residential streets on either side of **Ballards Lane** is of overcrowding – largely due to commuters' cars. Again there are lots of flats converted from houses in the '80s, although the further away from **Ballards Lane** you go, the more the 3-bedroomed semi dominates.

Victoria Park is the outstanding feature of Finchley Central – a small but pretty park with tennis courts and bowling green, it is an oasis in suburbia's sprawl of large detached houses and purpose-built flats such as those of **Etchingham Park Rd** (a 2-bed example in Etchingham Court, £150,000). The park is also home to the annual Finchley Carnival. Houses here have large gardens – but no garages. Almost opposite the park are the flats of Finchley Court. A spacious, well-maintained '30s development – complete with stunningly blue roof – this is still one of Finchley's most attractive.

West of **Ballards Lane**, **Alexandra Grove** covers the whole spectrum of property styles – from larger, detached mock-Tudor homes through medium-sized semis and a few '70s town-houses, to purpose-built flats of all ages: dull, everyday but sturdy '30s blocks to far more appealing recent luxury schemes. It ends with a curious yellow purpose-built block at the junction with **Nether St**. **Moss Hall Crescent**, just off **Ballards Lane**, is a parade of attractive mansions reclaimed from the ravages of post-war use as bed-sits.

Nether St joins Finchley Central to North Finchley and runs beside West Finchley tube station. In the past it has been used as a parallel short-cut to the **High Rd** and road planners have tried to stop this with a complicated junction at **Dollis Rd/Crescent Rd**. Traffic has always been a problem here, particularly on weekdays, by Moss Hall Junior and Infants Schools (junction with **Moss Hall Grove**) and by the West Finchley tube station which has no car park. Now the very N end, at Tally Ho Corner, is pedestrianized.

Transport	Tubes: East Finchley (zone 3, Northern); Finchley Central, West Finchley, Woodside Park (zone 4, Northern). From Finchley Central: Oxford Circus 32 min (1 change), City 40 min, Heathrow 1 hr 30 min (1 change).
Convenient for	Brent Cross shopping centre, Wembley Stadium. M1 to the North, M25, North Circular Rd. Miles from centre: 7.
Schools	Barnet Education Authority: Christchurch C of E, Woodhouse 6th-form College, Christ's College (b), Compton School, Finchley Catholic High School, St Michael's Catholic Grammar (g).

SALES

Flats	S	1B	2B	3B	4B	5B
Average prices	50–70	75–120	100–180	100–200	400+	—
Houses	2B	3B	4B	5B	6/7B	8B
Average prices	180–220	195–300	270–400	400–900	650+	—

RENTAL

Flats	S	1B	2B	3B	4B	5B
Average prices	130–135	150–170	180–320	270–350	—	—
Houses	2B	3B	4B	5B	6/7B	8B
Average prices	200–225	220–360	400+	600+	800+	—

The properties Quintessential suburbia: typical home is the 3-bed inter-war semi. Also Victorian/Edwardian terraced and larger homes, and modern flats in smart blocks, plus large houses in select streets. Higher flat prices in recent luxury blocks. £1 million mansions in best streets.

The market A settled family community, strong but changing as newcomers move in. Popular with young singles and professional couples who rent or buy; older couples swap family-sized homes for luxury flats here after the kids move out. Strong Jewish and Asian communities. Local searches: 5 working days.

(F)

Among those estate agents active in this area are:
- Anscombe & Ringland *
- Arthur Benabo
- Ellis & Co
- Jeremy Leaf & Co
- Copping Joyce
- Stevens & Son
- Addisons
- Winkworth *
- Bernard Tomkins
- Martyn Gerrard
- Bairstow Eves
- Capital Estates
- JAC Strattons
- Spicer McColl
- Barnard Marcus

further details: see advertisers' index on p671

FOREST HILL

Map ref: p111 (2K)
Postal districts: SE23
Boroughs: Lewisham (Lab)
Council tax: Band D £727
Conservation areas: Check
  with town hall
Parking: Free off main
  roads

This South London eminence rises to the east of Dulwich, north of Sydenham, and west of Catford and Lewisham. The 'forest on the hill' of ages past is long gone, but wooded areas and quiet, tree-lined roads continue to give the name meaning. Like Sydenham, the area owes its development to the railway, which reached here in 1836. Some impressive 19th-century villas have survived the depredations of developers.

This could be a canny moment to consider the Hill, with transport once again the key: London Bridge is under 15 minutes via the umbilical cord of the railway – and from there the super-fast, super-smart Jubilee line extension now reaches the West End or Canary Wharf in about another 10. Neighbouring Lewisham, the area's main shopping centre, is now on the Docklands Light Railway. There are even plans drawn to extend the tube here from New Cross Gate – eventually.

The hilly land gives Forest Hill its character, but (if you discount tenuous royal connections with Elizabeth I, in whose honour Honor Oak is said to have been named) its hero is a tea merchant, who gave it a 21-acre park and a museum. F. J. Horniman amassed an extensive anthropological and natural history collection from his world travels. This he made a gift to the people, along with the museum he had built (1897–1901). This splendid local asset is currently undergoing redevelopment and expansion, thanks to a £10 million lottery grant. By 2004 there will be additional exhibition space and a new café, while the delightful gardens with their interesting views are also to be revamped. Forest Hill's best homes are in this corner.

The area, which is essentially the SE23 postal district, divides roughly into two parts – the hilly ground in the W (between **Honor Oak Park** to N, the railway line to the E, **Thorpewood Avenue** to S, **Wood Vale/Sydenham Hill** to W), and the lower-lying ground to the E of the railway line. The centre and principal area for shops, restaurants, etc, **London Rd/Dartmouth Rd** meets basic needs but lacks the attractive character of, say, Blackheath Village – witness the tatty state of the (listed) bingo hall. It is, however, being tidied up; Sainsbury's is expanding, ex-commercial buildings have become bistros and even new pubs. Some of the modern council-build in this corner would not look out of place in a private development. A plot on **Devonshire Rd**, near the bingo hall and behind existing shopfronts, is earmarked for a residential/commercial redevelopment.

The **South Circular** runs through Forest Hill in the guise of **London Rd, Waldram Park Rd** and **Stanstead Rd**, and is now a Red Route, with road closures and sleeping policemen to deter those trying to skirt the congested centre.

In terms of homes, the most sought-after neighbourhood and most elevated – in price and geography – is Hornimans, the estate agent shorthand for the roads N of the Horniman Museum and Gardens. The south-eastern quarter, across the tracks and between **Waldram Park Rd**, **Stanstead Rd** and **Perry Vale/Perry Rise**, is generally flatter and has a mix of property – detached and semis, terraced, Victorian/turn-of-the-century and '30s/modern as well as council blocks. Streets off **Honor Oak Park** near Honor Oak rail station have modest terraces.

The largest properties are usually found on the high ground, but few roads are homogeneous – you'll find Victorian houses next to bay-fronted '30s semis. Victorian properties predominate, though, and top the popularity list. Although many larger properties were split into flats in the '80s, in the '90s the tide swung back the other way and this is still a hunting-ground for a bigger home at a (relatively) affordable level.

Forest Hill's leafiness and quiet tend to belie its inner-suburban location. It has a good share of gardens and parks, and Dulwich and Sydenham Hill golf course is nearby. There are no real pockets of deprivation. The steepness of the hills demands fitness (some have 18 per cent gradients) and in heavy snow, leaves cars immobilized.

Hornimans

One approach to Hornimans is up popular **Honor Oak Rd** at the **London Rd** entrance. **Honor Oak Rd** has surviving Italianate villas, which have largely become roomy flats. The road is a mixture, but not jarringly so – modern box developments, a council estate, '30s semis, Victorian homes (a top-floor conversion studio flat reached £65,000 last year). A block of flats, Angela Court, has been twinned; next to Katherine Court, a new, white, 3-storey family house roosts behind its gated entrance. Dainty Ashberry Cottage speaks of the rural past: the Regency cottage, built 1809, was once home to William Duke of Clarence, later King William IV, and his actress-mistress Mrs Jordan.

Trailing hillward off **Honor Oak Rd** are **Westwood Park** and **Horniman Drive**. Desirable **Horniman Drive** has '30s detached homes with pretty front gardens, a primary school, some recent low, 3-storey flats, and ends, by an entrance (currently closed during the renovations) to Hornimans Gardens, with modern town-house cul-de-sacs. It also has enviable views over London – which gazes back at a towering, unsightly mobile phone transmitter recently added to the top of the hill. Large, detached '30s also in demand in **Ringmore Rise**. The Drive and the Rise meet at a quaint, triangular communal garden, with **Liphook Crescent** and **Rocombe Crescent** curving round the other sides. Baxter House, a modern development, sits comfortably in the area, but is next to that transmitter. (At the top of **Ringmore Rise**, a '40s-style house, unexpected and out of keeping, adds a sense of light relief to this very proper corner.)

Westwood Park starts with some large Victorian semis and later follows round the hillside with '30s bay-fronted detacheds and semis. Smaller '30s in **Tewkesbury Avenue**. For spectacular views of the City and a mixture of Victorian, turn-of-the-century, '30s semis there's **Canonbie Rd**. Canary Wharf, the Houses of Parliament, St Paul's, Battersea Power Station, the Telecom Tower . . . all the capital's landmarks are there – even if the steep slope is hard for the elderly and impossible in snow. **Netherby Rd** (bay-fronted semis; occasional large Victorian ones) looks to wooded One Tree Hill.

Wood Vale, with its road humps, marks the area's W boundary. It has seen some conversions, with names like Beech Court and Woodlands Court; also some new-build, but in traditional brick-and-white-stucco style. A redundant pub, too, has been turned into flats (closing-time never comes. . .). Nearby, however, other large and hitherto neglected Victorian houses have been lovingly restored and sold as grand, £350,000-plus family homes, with views out over the Hornimans nature trail. In other parts of this long road a 2-bed flat can be had for c. £85,000. **Langton Rise**, which crosses Wood Vale (and the borough boundary), has a recent development of flats and four modern houses.

Worth investigation is **Devonshire Rd**, running parallel to the railway line – and thus with a station at either end; Victorian semis, detacheds, Edwardiana, 1930s. Plenty of renovation has gone on here, and speed humps slow those rushing for a train; untidier, though, at the Honor Oak end, where the Boveney Rd Estate is in need of refubishment. A small nature reserve comes as a pleasant surprise; in short, a very central corner. Several small blocks of flats replaced rambling Victorian piles here. These are not always harmonious: Leyton Court's garish yellow brick, for instance; but then the '30s Postmens' Office (red-brick, sculptures on roof) is not exactly retiring, either . . .

Busy **London Rd** in its western stages near the museum has council blocks, but also brightly painted terraces – now flats – further down. On the N side is Horniman Grange, a 1988 redevelopment of some wrecked Victoriana: now studios, 1- and 2-bed flats. South lies **Sydenham Rise**, with small, leafy private closes of colourful 3-storey houses sheltered from the South Circular. Off **Dartmouth Rd** are some more tucked-away homes, in little unmade-up roads. **Thorpewood Avenue** – here '30s semis outnumber the occasional Victorian houses – marks the southern boundary of this side of Forest Hill, and holds the renovated and expanded Holy Trinity School.

Forest Hill East

East of Honor Oak Park station the more illustrious properties are left behind. Shops line both sides – a small gallery, a good music shop. Small roads such as **Ballina St** and **Gabriel St** have stolid, uniform Edwardian terraces – also some '60s town-houses in **Grierson Rd** (the streets in the right angle between **Honor Oak Park** and **Brockley Rise** have a fiendishly confusing traffic system). In Blythe Hill Place, **Brockley Park**, a development of 2-bed 'cottages', sold fast in 1998 (then £80,000 upwards).

Tucked behind the **Waldram Park Rd**/**Stanstead Rd** stretch of the South Circular, **Rockbourne Rd** has a smart new scheme of 2- and 3-bed flats, with video entryphones: ready this spring; five new 2-storey houses have also appeared nearby. Large Victorian houses on **Waldram Park Rd** make for excellent flat conversions, close to Forest Hill station and buses into town. **Stanstead Rd** has big Victorian semis (a 4-bed house, £150,000 here last winter) and cottage-style dwellings. The streets leading off both sides of **Vancouver Rd** are quieter, period terraces; also some 1930s and modern infills.

Perry Vale, which runs SE from Forest Hill rail station, starts with Christchurch C of E Primary School, and a concentration of unattractive council estates. Older-type constructions with walkways, their impact is lessened by the surrounding trees. Large Edwardian semis follow, with a parade of shops in the curve. Running S from Perry Vale, a council-built estate, Forest Hill School and a town-house development make up **Dacres Rd** until the right turn. Then come detached Victorian houses – a 5-bed house sold here for £325,000 last winter – leaf-obscured modern town-houses and a modern mansion building. Off **Mayow Rd**, which leads back up to Perry Vale, **Acorn Way** is a small cul-de-sac of 2-storey homes, built three or four years ago, where children play in the street. There's a real mixture of house styles in this corner: **Wynell Rd**, for example, contains council-built estates and 3-storey red-brick houses; but by the time it joins Perry Vale these have given way to larger, brick-and-stucco houses, with fittingly large gardens, that would not look out of place in Notting Hill.

Across on the N side of Perry Vale, **Sunderland Rd** has large Victorian, turn-of-the-century detacheds, and '30s semis. Some of the big Victorian mansions remain as single homes (one vast, 8-bedded one); some are flats (a 2-bed, £125,000). **Woolstone Rd** starts with bay-fronted terraces and neat 1930s semis; tree-lined, the leaves brush together in the middle of the road. Some large Victorian detacheds towards St George's Church. One in **Hurstbourne Rd** is becoming smart flats.

Off **Perry Rise, Allenby Rd** is quiet and leafy: large detached Victoriana. **Garlies Rd** is less uniform – it mixes in some 1930s semis. **Paxton Rd** boasts one of the area's biggest redevelopments: more than 150 flats made pretty by balconies and gardens, in 3-storey blocks. More, 4-storey and in the same red-brick, behind. **Queenswood Rd** is terraced – Victorian, turn-of-the-century and '30s semis; a small development of 3-bed houses. **Perry Rise** itself offers bay-fronted Victorian semis before giving way to small terraced houses near **Bell Green**, on the Lower Sydenham borders, with its hypermarket.

F

Transport	Train: Forest Hill to London Bridge (for Jubilee line) 14 min, Victoria 30 min. Also to Croydon (for Gatwick). Buses to West End.
Convenient for	Dulwich golf course, Crystal Palace Park and National Sports Centre, Lewisham shops and DLR. Miles from centre: 6.
Schools	Local Authority: Forest Hill School (b), Sydenham School (g). Private: Sydenham High (see Dulwich, Catford).

SALES

Flats	S	1B	2B	3B	4B	5B
Average prices	40–60	60–100	80–140	120–150	130+	–
Houses	2B	3B	4B	5B	6/7B	8B
Average prices	115–140	130–200	150–300+	220–400	300–500	450+

RENTAL

Flats	S	1B	2B	3B	4B	5B
Average prices	90–110	100–160	150–180	150–220	185–250	230–275
Houses	2B	3B	4B	5B	6/7B	8B
Average prices	150–175	160–210	230–370	230–500	325+	–

The properties	Respectable Victoriana, larger homes in the W of the area, smaller terraces to the E. 3-bed houses most common; larger houses have often become flats; some now converting back. Little 2-bed houses a popular alternative to flats.
The market	First-time buyers after 1/2-bed flats join families seeking space and greenery. They, and agents, reckon area is still good value. Local searches: 3 weeks.

Among those estate agents active in this area are:
- Woolwich Property Services
- Robert Stanford
- Halifax Property
- Scotchbrooks
- Acorn
- Oak Estates*

further details: see advertisers' index on p671

FULHAM

Map ref: p91 (1G)
Postal districts: SW6, W6
Boroughs: Hammersmith
  & Fulham (Lab)
Council tax: Band D £827
Conservation areas: Check
  with town hall
Parking: Residents' zones
  and relatively few meters

At last, a renaissance is planned for Walham Green – or Fulham Broadway, as
this village is known today. Despite being the nearest thing the modern Fulham has
to a centre, the Broadway has always remained cheerfully dowdy and down-at-heel
while the surrounding mean streets rocketed in status and value, becoming the
heartland of middle-class London. Now Fulham Broadway tube station is to get a
gleaming new building as part of a multi-million pound shops scheme, with the usual
multi-screen cinema, health and leisure components.

Even better news is that of another new station – where none has existed before.
Plans for a vast cache of new homes (half of them to be affordable housing) on the
old Sands End gasworks site on **Imperial Rd** are conditional on a train station between
it and Chelsea Harbour, on the main West London rail line: this carves N–S through the
area – but does not stop. This will mean direct links to Clapham Junction and, via a
second new halt at West Brompton, an interchange onto the tube at the existing
District line station there. The Imperial Wharf development is large enough to have
attracted government attention, though, and a public inquiry may well be needed
before all comes to pass – watch this space.

A glance at a map shows why the thought of a new train station sets hearts a-flutter
in Sands End and Chelsea Harbour: it's a very long way, via very congested roads, to any
of the three tube stops that struggle inadequately to serve the densely-packed,
desirable steets of Fulham. Until 1880 almost all of this deep, cut-off pocket of the
Thames was market gardens. With the completion of the District line tube an enormous
development took place – the bulk between 1880 and 1900, but extending up to World
War I in various small areas. These houses – almost entirely terraced, with only a few

detached and semi-detached in areas such as Hurlingham and Bishop's Park – cover most of Fulham. There still exist a very few 18th-century buildings, mainly associated with the original villages of Walham Green (now **Fulham Broadway**) and Fulham (down by what is now Putney Bridge) and extending along the **New King's Rd**.

After the pre-1914 building boom, Fulham relapsed into a condition of quiet respectability. Much of the housing was let unfurnished: as late as 1971, more than 40 per cent of the homes in most of Fulham were privately let. In that year over 20 per cent of Fulham homes still lacked an inside WC. It was a stable community, with strong local loyalties and a tendency to stay put: three generations of the same family would live in the same group of streets. This pattern was shattered by the closure of the many industrial firms which provided employment for the locals, and by the property boom of the early '70s. Demand from would-be owner-occupiers spilt over from Chelsea and Kensington, and the first quiet streets of Fulham were 'discovered'. Landlords, beset by the Rent Acts then in force, hastened to sell their tenanted homes as soon as the residents could be persuaded to leave. The early '80s cemented the trend, which spread across the whole area. In came the young, middle-class professionals, out went the skilled workers and their families to new estates on the fringes of London. In a few frantic years, the face of Fulham changed . . .

Fulham has a fair sprinkling of council estates, though they have been gradually changing as residents exercised their 'Right to Buy', and as modernization has taken place. The biggest is Clem Attlee Court in the N of the area, off **Lillie Rd**. These large blocks, named after Socialist luminaries of the 1940s, form a community of their own and provide a source of good-value housing. Two have been demolished to make room for low-rise housing association homes. Sand's End has more council blocks in a fast-changing area. Smaller clusters of council-built and housing-association homes occur across the borough; some, such as those by the river off **Stevenage Rd**, are very attractive.

The old Fulham turned its back on the river, which curves around it on three sides. Or to be more precise, it used the river rather than looked at it. The banks were lined with wharves and with industry, and barges delivered materials to many a riverside works. Almost none remain, with many of the industrial sites replaced, or being replaced, by housing. A by-product is the opening up of the riverside: public paths now follow much of the western bank.

The wide sweep of the Thames forms Fulham's southern and western boundaries. The river is crossed at two points to the S, by Putney (the oldest and lowest fording point on the River Thames, and used by the Romans) and Wandsworth Bridges. The eastern boundary is the main N–S railway line, running down from Kensington Olympia to cross the river alongside Chelsea Harbour: only three roads cross this line. Closing off the northern approaches is the barrier of the A4/Hammersmith Flyover and **Cromwell Rd Extension/Talgarth Rd**, leading westwards to the M4 motorway. Three roads cross this. There are thus only eight roads into or out of Fulham – something which often becomes painfully obvious.

The E–W roads define neighbourhoods. Going northwards, they are **New King's Rd**, **Fulham Rd**, **Dawes Rd** and **Lillie Rd**. There are two main N–S routes: **Fulham Palace Rd**, leading to Putney Bridge; and **North End Rd/Wandsworth Bridge Rd**, leading to Wandsworth Bridge. Again these routes are neighbourhood demarcation lines.

New King's Rd and **Fulham Rd** have changed a lot in the last 20 years, acquiring fashionable shops selling antique furniture, clothing and specialist delicatessen, plus restaurants and bars. **Lillie Rd** and **Dawes Rd** still maintain many of the old-style small local shops, selling a wide range of goods, but they are changing fast: one sign of the times: the old municipal swimming pools on Lillie Rd are being demolished (the roof is unsafe); they will be replaced with a new leisure complex via a public/private partnership with upmarket Holmes Place health clubs. To the amazement of those who knew it a few years back, **Munster Rd** boasts street cafés, bars and restaurants. **Fulham Palace Rd**, especially S of **Lillie Rd**, is predominantly residential. **North End Rd** has a colourful street fruit-and-veg market operating side by side with a Safeway supermarket, while **Wandsworth Bridge Rd** is a mix of homes and trendy shopping – it has been the stripped-pine capital of West London for years. The Sainsbury's on **Townmead Rd** is a hub of life for the southern end of the area.

Fulham has a number of open spaces and parks. In the S is Hurlingham Park with its sports ground. The Hurlingham Club, which adjoins it and has all the river frontage, is (very) private. It has a swimming pool and tennis courts and is centred around the 18th-century Hurlingham House. South Park, also in the S, has children's play-areas, a cricket pitch and tennis courts. Parson's Green and Eel Brook Common are tree-lined open spaces overlooked by many attractive homes. To the W, Bishop's Park borders the river above Putney Bridge: this was originally the gardens of the 16th-century Bishop's Palace. To the N is the Queens Club private tennis club and Normand Park, which houses a modern swimming pool complex. Assiduous tree-planting along the streets has also helped to mitigate the main difference between Fulham and neighbouring Chelsea: the lack of the general leafy impression provided by Chelsea's square gardens. Fulham, built later, has dense rows of streets, not squares.

Fulham also boasts two football grounds. To the W is Fulham's riverside ground, while on the Kensington/Chelsea borders is Stamford Bridge, home of Chelsea FC. Both grounds have for years been the focus of plans, rows and more plans. Chelsea's ground, now called 'Chelsea Village', has seen the biggest changes. It has acquired a hotel, a 9-storey block of flats, three restaurants and more. The stadium has grown from a capacity of 28,000 to 43,000, and gone are the days when it was used only twice a week in winter. Both this and Craven Cottage, Fulham's ground, had further planning applications in at the start of the year. Fulham wants a new 26,000-seat stadium, among other things. Both grounds attract much traffic, which looks set to grow.

The three District line tube stations are augmented by two Piccadilly line stops just N of the area, at Baron's Court and West Kensington: these give direct links to Heathrow. However, large tracts are quite a distance from a tube station. Roads are strategically placed to take you out of London to the W along the M4 to Heathrow and the M25, to the S over Putney or Wandsworth Bridges to join the South Circular or A3, and to the N through Shepherd's Bush. However, the traffic saturation on these routes means incalculable journey times (particularly if Chelsea are playing at home). At least the long closure of Hammersmith Bridge, which resulted in virtual gridlock at certain times of day, is now behind us. Parking in the residential streets is an ever more desperate problem, as many owners of the narrow-fronted terraced houses have two cars (at least); overnight double parking is common. Most of the residential roads are now in controlled parking zones. A parking space is the first asset an estate agent will mention.

As far as most estate agents and inhabitants are concerned, Fulham tends to end at **Lillie Rd**, the SW6 border. The W14 area to the N between **Lillie Rd** and **Talgarth Rd** has a very different character, centred around Barons Court and West Kensington tube stations. It is largely composed of big, late-Victorian houses and mansion blocks, and until recently rental property was dominant. As of last year, one major agent is now dubbing this tract 'Fulham Cross'; however, it has more in common with Hammersmith (see Hammersmith chapter).

The neighbourhoods of Fulham can be divided into the expensive, the established and the up-and-coming, and are dealt with here in that order:

Peterborough Estate

Perhaps the best-known neighbourhood in Fulham is the ever-popular but ever-so-pricey Peterborough Estate, a conservation area between **New King's Rd** and South Park bounded by **Peterborough Rd** to the W and **Bagleys Lane** to the E. Incoming owner-occupiers started buying these houses in the early 1970s (and called the neighbourhood Hurlingham: no-one in Chelsea had heard of Fulham as an address in those days). By the end of the decade these houses, smartened up, were the first in Fulham to break the £100,000 barrier. Now the Peterborough Estate is a top-rank name.

The most sought-after roads are those to the W of **Wandsworth Bridge Rd**, a series of N–S streets off the Parson's Green stretch of **New King's Rd**: **Perrymead St, Chipstead St, Quarrendon St, Chiddingstone St, Bradbourne St** and **Coniger St**. These are matching rows of substantial terraced houses: red-brick, gabled, flat-fronted late Victoriana (c. 1895), of 3-, 4- or 5-bedrooms, many with additional space from loft and cellar conversions, extensions and conservatories. They have small back gardens. They are very distinctive houses, with attractive mullioned windows and terracotta lions (the trademark of J Nicholls, the builder) decorating the party walls at roof level. The majority are still single-family houses. A variety of internal layouts can be found as many have been virtually rebuilt. Average price, c. £695,000. By contrast, a 4-bed house built in 1853, but on the main **New King's Rd**, was £450,000 last winter.

F

Hurlingham/High St

Hurlingham, also S of **New King's Rd**, is a much smaller conservation area, consisting of **Napier Avenue, Ranelagh Avenue, Ranelagh Gardens, Edenhurst Avenue** and **Hurlingham Gardens**, bounded to the N by **Hurlingham Rd**, which skirts Hurlingham Park. This, and the grounds of the Hurlingham Club, which continues the greenery right down to the river, are what remain of the grounds of Hurlingham House: the Georgian mansion is still there, and serves as the clubhouse. Hurlingham Lodge, 'a country house in London', sold this spring for a vast but undisclosed (thought to be eight-figure) sum.

Fulham, at first sight a district of uniform terraces, has some unusual domestic buildings such as this splendidly ornate turret house near Hurlingham. The slate-capped turret, the Romanesque detailing around its eaves, the handsome sash windows and the iron railings make up an attractive whole.

Predominantly, though, this enclave has imposing late-19th-century detached and semi-detached 5- or 6-bed houses set back from tree-lined streets, each with its own character and architectural style, with drives and off-street parking. The appeal of this corner is this leafiness, (there's also the larger Bishop's Park within reach), and the convenience of nearby Putney Bridge tube.

In **Ranelagh Gardens**, there are two, much sought-after, '60s apartment blocks and a late-'80s riverside development, **Carrara Wharf**, a private enclave of 20 houses (a 2-bed, £300,000-plus) and 69 flats. Along the river on **Hurlingham Gardens** is a large inter-war luxury apartment block. On **Hurlingham Rd**, **Melbray Mews** is a group of live/work units, unusual for this part of town. This corner is also due to gain Connaught Mews, an enclave of five new mews houses, this spring.

On the far (E) side of Hurlingham Park, Barratt added a new square to the area in the late '80s. **Hurlingham Square**, in the angle of **Peterborough** and **Sulivan Rds**, has 50 4/5-bed homes in an enclave reached via electric gates. A 4-bed house can sell for around £600,000. Further N off **Peterborough Rd** the neat, pleasant Sulivan Court estate of council-built homes runs through to **Broomhouse Lane**, which bounds Hurlingham Park. These can come up for sale at around £170,000 for a 3-bed flat. Skirting South Park, **Clancarty Rd**'s N side can provide larger than usual Fulham gardens between it and the Peterborough Estate's Studdridge St. With loft-conversion 4th bedroom suite and 16ft back extension, a house here still has a 40-ft garden (£450,000). The riverside **Carnwath Rd** has seen big changes as industry and commerce are replaced by homes. Here a 1950s office block, the former British Gas research HQ, was sold as 'The Piper Building' (artist John Piper was commissioned by the Gas people to adorn the outside with a large abstract mural), which was transformed into fashionable shell-finish 'loft' apartments (the largest on a par with house, rather than flat, prices) in 1997/98.

On the other (W) side of the Hurlingham enclave **Fulham High St**, down by Putney Bridge, marks the site of the original village of Fulham, but today is a bit of a misnomer. It has a few shops, but is mostly tall blocks of mansion flats on the W side and a mix of uses on the E. Parkview Court is one such mansion block: 124 flats backing onto the grounds of Fulham Palace. A 2-bed flat might be £200–250,000, while a balconied, 3-bed/2-bath penthouse, one of the dozen recently added to the top of the block, was £390,000 this spring. **Steeple Close**, too, backs onto the park and is enviably tucked away off **Church Gate**: 4-bed modern town-houses with (gold-dust in Fulham) garages – and thus attracts prices between c. £450–950,000.

Bishop's Park

Another small conservation area, Bishop's Park takes in the pleasant tree-lined streets which are the first few of a ladder of alphabetically-named roads running between **Fulham Palace Rd** and **Stevenage Rd**, which here borders Bishop's Park: **Bishop's Park Rd, Cloncurry St, Doneraile St, Ellerby St** and **Finlay St**. Here the style changes, and you'll find terraced or semi-detached houses which were built at the end of the 19th century or later, and have 4/5 bedrooms. Many have been extended upwards (not always sympathetically), with loft conversions, and to the rear with back extensions and conservatories. Most (untypically for Fulham) have substantial gardens; a good one can go for £675–700,000 plus. The later date of these houses reflects the stubborn hold-out of the last major market gardener in what was once known as 'London's kitchen garden'.

This orderly grid of roads marches on, past Fulham FC at the W end of **Finlay St**, up to **Niton St** (though the alphabet gets jumbled after **Inglethorpe**). Here you will find more flat conversions, and more modest houses. The small, 3-bed (c. £400,000) houses are now more typically extended to give four bedrooms. Along the river-bank are a string of apartment blocks built in the '70s, with fine views across the river to the old Barnes water meadows, now a wildlife sanctuary and (the N part) the expensive Barnes Waterside housing. River Gardens, which has pool and sauna, has 2/3-bed flats with spectacular terracing and balconies; Rosebank is a conventional high-rise block with 2/3-bed flats. Service charges must be considered in these blocks.

At **Crabtree Lane**, SW6 gives way to W6. The grid of streets running N between the lane, **Fulham Palace Rd** and the river is the 1911 Crabtree estate, an up-and-coming corner; across the road is Baron's Court, with its Piccadilly line tube.

Chelsea Harbour

The area's biggest clutch of modern apartments and houses can be found on the Fulham/Chelsea borders. Many more will be added near here when the Imperial Wharf scheme gets the go-ahead (see Sand's End). Chelsea Harbour is a parable of our times: only in the 1980s could a developer take a triangular site bounded by a railway and a muddy creek and present these as advantages – even if the third side, as here, is river frontage. But this inconvenient and cut-off corner could offer that goal of every really top-flight development: complete security. Chelsea Harbour was the W side of town's answer to Docklands: a gated community of 310 homes in blocks, terraces, crescents and the landmark tower, plus starry health club, hotel, restaurants, shops, offices – and alongside (if not part of) Chelsea, not the Isle of Dogs.

The centrepiece is the reopened harbour. This marina provides the neighbourhood with a much-needed tranquil spot to relax by the bobbing boats (a public walkway runs along the Thames) – not, of course, possible along the Chelsea embankment, nor yet the Sand's End stretch. The flats and houses vary widely in size and price. Check position, condition and sound insulation: some back onto the increasingly busy rail line.

What will make Chelsea Harbour is better public transport – far from any station, a hoppa bus supplies the missing link to Earl's Court tube, High St Kensington and Putney – but the neighbouring Imperial Wharf scheme is conditional on the long-hoped-for rail station (see introduction).

And that's not the only scheme planned for this corner: the **Lots Rd** power station, which is owned by London Transport, was due to close in 1990. Then last year. Then this. To the disgust of Chelsea Harbourites it has stayed open, although Kensington and Chelsea Council, whose writ runs here, has drawn up a planning brief for 150 flats, offices, art gallery and a museum (of Delayed Developments perhaps?). No developer has yet taken the bait.

Moore Park Rd

A pocket of large mid-Victorian stucco terraced houses and later Victorian detached and semi-detached houses on the Fulham/Chelsea borders, between **Fulham Rd** and **King's Rd**. Some houses have been converted into flats. This was the first bit of Fulham to become respectable – almost Chelsea actually – and it is a stable, established corner. The proximity to busy Chelsea football ground is mitigated because the streets (**Moore Park Rd, Waterford Rd, Britannia Rd, Maxwell Rd, Holmead Rd, Rumbold Rd**) are barricaded off to through traffic. However as 'Chelsea Village' grows, so does the pressure on these roads, where the shops already close on football Saturdays. A house in **Blake Gardens**, which runs across to Eel Brook Common ('would benefit from updating . . . can be extended') was nevertheless £585,000 this spring.

Parson's Green

In estate agents' terms, this covers an ever-larger area, bounded by streets either side of **Fulham Rd** to the N (up as far as **Bishop's Rd**) and either side of **New King's Rd** to the S, extending as far as Eel Brook Common to the E and **Munster Road** to the W. This neighbourhood is regarded as being that which is within easy walking distance of pretty, triangular Parson's Green (another ancient hamlet) and its tube station. The big 3-storey houses overlooking the actual, rather charming, green are coveted and priced accordingly: uncomfortably close to a million. There are a very few Georgian houses, but mostly the streets are lined with 1890s bay-windowed terraces, many of which have been extended upwards with loft conversions to provide a fourth bedroom. Popular streets include **Delvino Rd** (a 4-bed example, £635,000), **Linver Rd, Guion Rd, Crondace Rd, Felden St**. There are more substantial houses of a different architectural style of 5/6 bedrooms in **Whittingstall Rd, St Maur Rd, Winchendon Rd, Lillyville Rd, Clonmel Rd**. In this latter area many of the houses have been converted into 1- or 2-bed flats, or 2- to 3-bed maisonettes; but the trend now is to convert them back into family homes. Prices of well over half a million are routine for these 4/5-bed houses; more like three-quarters for the biggest. **Mustow Place**, homes in attractive mews style, has been squeezed in between the railway and **Munster Rd**. Another new mews, Claridge Court, has 10 town-houses and two flats. And 35 homes appeared on the Courtaulds site, also in **Munster Rd**: the Coda Centre.

On the fringes of Parson's Green are two small neighbourhoods. To the E is Eel Brook Common, with the large, late-19th-century terraced houses overlooking a pretty park with tennis courts in flanking **Musgrave Crescent** and **Favart Rd** being particularly popular. Five new 2- and 3-bed houses have been squeezed in on a corner site: the secure parking is a big plus. To the W, **Fulham Park Gardens** is a small conservation area of very distinctive substantial red-brick houses of 5/6 bedrooms and considerable character. The tube line from Parson's Green into town is one of most crowded on the network, according to London Transport.

Fulham Broadway

This old but now submerged village was known as Walham Green until London Transport renamed the station **Fulham Broadway** in 1948. Conservation areas include **Walham Grove**, which is a street of 1860s semi-detached villas, and **Barclay Rd**, mid-Victorian terraced houses. The Broadway which, with its tube and town hall, should be the hub of modern Fulham, has stayed resolutely down-at-heel as the area climbed socially around it – a situation not unconnected with the close proximity of Chelsea's Stamford Bridge football ground. It has been subject to a major redevelopment plan – the 'Fulham Centre Plan' – for many years, but progress has been limited to the paving of part of the shopping area to form 'Fulham Piazza', intended to be a mini Covent Garden.

Five plans for transforming the **Broadway** foundered in the last 10 years; now at last one has the go-ahead. Under this, Fulham Broadway tube station is to get a gleaming new building as part of a multi-million pound shops scheme, plus multi-screen cinema, health and leisure.

Homes exist in the gaps between roads and shops. Pleasantly named **Farm Lane** curves round behind the big Samuel Lewis Trust housing estate N of the Broadway. **North End Rd** is the scene of a thriving street market. East of it, a fairly cut-off corner of streets runs through to **Seagrave Rd**, off which is 'Brompton Park': flats and houses, complete with pool and health club. This otherwise peaceful area is affected by the growth of 'Chelsea Village' – the Stamford Bridge stadium, where far more than football goes on these days (900-person raves until 6am caused one row). To the S of the Broadway, Harwood Mews is a cache of town-houses (c. £415,000) in **Harwood Rd**.

Central Fulham

To the N of **Bishop's Rd**, the street pattern changes; the N–S roads running off Fulham Rd give way to later, tight-packed E–W rows running up to Lillie Rd. These hold similar 3/4-bedroom terraced houses, all built between 1890 and 1910; many were converted into flats in the '80s. There are several pockets of pretty roads (**Marville St, Brookville St, Rosaville St, Parkville St**) with occasional streets of unusual mansion blocks in yellow London brick (**St Olafs Rd, Orbain Rd**). This area is attracting more interest as it offers better value than the southern neighbourhoods of Fulham (a 4-bed house in **Delaford St** was £345,000 last winter). Even **Dawes Rd**, once a byword for dowdiness, is cheering up. Shops and restaurants are joining the immemorial dirty-windowed bike shop, the pet shop and the gents' barbers. An attempt to boost the area is the use of the term 'Dawes Village' – though whoever thought that up must have quite an imagination. There are some big, older-style flats, though many of the flats around here are above shops.

To the E, across **Fulham Palace Rd**, a number of interesting streets lead down towards the river: **Kenyon St, Lysia St, Niton St**. These continue on from the 'alphabet' streets of the Bishop's Park neighbourhood, but are more modest.

Sand's End/Riverside

Sandy End, Addison called it, when he stayed here in 1708. The house survives as Sandford Manor, but its surroundings went downhill from then on, attracting a monster gasworks in 1824 and gaining a name for slums and later for dodgy council estates. Meanwhile, the riverside was lined with factories, warehouses and (in 1936) a coal-fired power station. Sand's End became a pretty grim place.

Its revival began when it was declared a Housing Action Area in the '70s. Owner-occupiers dipped tentative toes into the little terraces in the '80s, reasoning that the Peterborough Estate was not that far away. The Chelsea Harbour development and a large Sainsbury's in **Townmead Rd** put the seal on Sand's End's rehabilitation.

The big news here is the future of the land along **Imperial Rd** down to the river. For a decade British Gas has been trying, on and off, to develop this site, which it inherited from the Imperial Gas Company. Now the council has approved a vast scheme which would provide 1600–1800 new homes, half of them to be affordable housing, plus other goodies like a 20-acre riverside park and – best of all – a station on the West London line. But this is a scheme large enough to require ministerial approval, so the final outcome may yet be some way off . . . Tucked behind the still-standing (but for how long?) gasometer are the delightful, restored Victorian cottages of **Imperial Square**. Sandford Manor is in there somewhere, used as the gasworks manager's house for decades.

Along the S river frontage, on the site of the former Fulham power station, is a modern complex of 250 flats all with a river view. They range from 1-bed to 4-bed penthouses, and the name changed from Sand's Wharf to 'Regent on the River' and 'Sailmakers Court'. Two-bed examples, £300–375,000 last winter; a 3-bed 3-bath penthouse in the former was £540,000. Another part is called Ferrymans Quay. A leisure centre (the Harbour Club) has been built in the power station's old turbine rooms with squash, tennis and a swimming pool. Residents get a free minibus ride to the tube at peak hours. Barratt have built two developments off **Harwood Terrace** in the N corner of Sand's End. Chelsea Walk and Chelsea Lodge – named to stress proximity to the borough border – have a total of 20 4-bed houses.

There are small pockets of council housing and a large area of typical Fulham-style late-Victorian terraces not yet completely smartened up: **Stephendale Rd, Broughton Rd, Lindrop St, Glenrosa St, Byam St**. The exception is a small area of **Wandsworth Bridge Rd**, where **Rosebury Rd, Oakbury Rd, Cranbury Rd, Haslebury Rd** are smaller Peterborough Estate-type houses, many of which have been converted to flats and maisonettes and have 'come up' to make a very attractive corner. They even have an estate agent name: 'the Bury Triangle' (as in 'don't bury me in Fulham'?). You pay £400,000-plus for a 4-bed house here, a 3-bed in **Glenrosa** was £365,000 last winter.

Borders

North of Lillie Road Fulham gives way to Barons Court and West Kensington (see Hammersmith chapter), despite the current attempt to re-brand this corner 'Fulham Cross'.

Transport	Tubes: Parsons Green, Fulham Broadway, Putney Bridge (zone 2, District). From Fulham Broadway: Oxford Circus 30 min (1 change), City 45 min (1 change), Heathrow 45 min (1 change).
Convenient for	A4, M4, Sloane Square and King's Rd shops. Miles from centre: 4.
Schools	Local Authority: Fulham Cross (g), Hurlingham & Chelsea, London Oratory RC (b), St Edmunds RC, St Marks C of E, Lady Margaret C of E (g).

SALES

Flats	S	1B	2B	3B	4B	5B
Average prices	90–125	115–215	135–265	250–320	260–300+	—
Houses	2B	3B	4B	5B	6/7B	8B
Average prices	250–350+	260–450+	350–600+	500–1M+	800+	—

RENTAL

Flats	S	1B	2B	3B	4B	5B
Average prices	160–200	180–250	260–450	300–550	400–700	—
Houses	2B	3B	4B	5B	6/7B	8B
Average prices	300–500	400–600	550–750	600–800	850+	—

The properties Row after row of solid, late-19th-century family houses. Also some Victorian/Edwardian/'30s p/b flats and many flats conversions. After two decades of energetic renovation, many houses boast top-flight interiors. Much new-build and conversions on infill and river sites, including Chelsea Harbour.

The market Fulham, with its overgeared, school-fee'd families, was hit hard by the last recession. But aided by City bonuses (lots of bankers live here) it was one of the first areas to bounce back to well above last-boom prices. Local searches: 10 working days.

Among those estate agents active in this area are:
- Hamptons
- Douglas & Gordon
- Winkworth *
- John D Wood
- Friend & Falcke *
- Lawson & Daughters
- Chesterfields
- FPDSavills
- Sebastian Estates
- Foxtons *
- Faron Sutaria
- Wellingtons

further details: see advertisers' index on p671

GOLDERS GREEN

Map ref: p27 (7H)
Postal districts: NW11
Boroughs: Barnet (Lib
  Dem/Lab Coalition)
Council tax: Band D £760
Conservation areas: Check
  with town hall
Parking: Free off main roads

Until not so long ago there were still people living in North-West London who could remember the crossroads at Golders Green as being in the middle of open farmland, with a signpost pointing south 'To London'.

This rural seclusion gave way as the tube bored its way through from beneath Hampstead Heath in 1907, sparking a fury of development here and in neighbouring fields: 'next door', Hampstead Garden Suburb was built by that idealistic philanthropist, Dame Henrietta Barnett.

Many were seduced by 'Sanctuary', the famous 1908 Underground poster, exhorting them to hear the roar of the 'great Babel' at a safe distance – from a bright new, turn-of-the-century, stockbroker-Tudory, Arts-and-Craftsery, Golders Green home. The Green's advent was also nicely timed to attract some first- and second-generation immigrants, notably the Jewish community, which was then ready to move on from the East End to more congenial surroundings. And few places could be more congenial than Golders Green.

Although the shortage of good housing coming onto the market has pushed prices up here as it has all over North-West London, it is still, as one estate agent put it, 'the first affordable suburb you get to when you drive north from the West End'. Nowadays, the immigrants are just as likely to be from the gold-paved streets of Hampstead or St John's Wood – trading in their now-stratospheric 2- and 3-bedroomed flats in NW3 and NW8 for houses here, particularly in the area off **North End Rd**, close to Golders Hill Park.

G

Unlike other areas which have merged into an amorphous suburban sprawl, Golders Green's boundaries are well-defined. Its limits are the **Finchley Rd** to the E, the **North Circular Rd** to the N, the **Hendon Way** to the W as far as **The Vale**, and S to the NW11 border, which runs along **Dunstan Rd, Hodford Rd** and **Golders Hill Park**. Property-wise, Golders Green is, still, primarily an area of family houses: 3-, 4- or 5-bedroomed homes, which are large if not grand, and speak of comfortable, semi-detached family life. These are Edwardian villas, the area having been developed too late for the usual tide of Victorian terraces – though there are some patches of '20s and '30s ones. There are also many purpose-built blocks (along **Golders Green** and **Finchley Rds** and in the area around **Woodlands**) and the '80s saw a lot of flats conversions around Temple Fortune. Here, too, is a fair amount of rented accommodation, so there are lots of young single people: Golders Green is very convenient for several of the London University colleges.

The bustling **Golders Green Rd**, which runs through the centre from the tube up to the **North Circular Rd** and Hendon, boasts some of North London's best shops. Today these are staying open later, and a bit of a café society is developing. People swear by Carmelli's Bakery, get fit at the new gym, head for Blooms, an off-shoot of the famous East End restaurant. Still home for many of London's Jews, Golders Green is awash with delicatessens, kosher bakeries and take-aways. At festival times you'll see people in their holiday clothes strolling the streets, and during Chanukah (December's festival of lights) the tube station houses a huge candelabrum which is lit every evening. There are also Asian and Far Eastern communities, and these too are reflected in the area's shops and restaurants.

Golders Green is blessed with churches of every denomination, and synagogues, official and unofficial, of every shade of orthodoxy. Estate agents know the synagogues in detail, since purchasers will often only consider properties in roads near to a particular one. There's plenty of open space too, if you'd rather commune with the Almighty in less formal surroundings; and the Hampstead Heath extension is nearby.

If godliness is its first name, convenience in the form of transport is its second. The Northern line provides great links to West End and City; direct to Tottenham Court Rd, Leicester Square and Bank. Buses are very good, too.

After several years of heated argument, the issue of the proposed North London 'eruv' is still not settled. The eruv is an area within which Sabbath laws would be relaxed for Orthodox Jews. The largely notional boundary would be defined by existing features (for example, the M1), but gaps or 'gateways' would be bridged by wires strung between poles. Permission for the controversial scheme was finally given planning approval as long ago as October 1998, but Barnet Council is still working through a huge document outlining detailed licencing conditions for each street pole . . . the final go-ahead is expected 'soon'. When it comes, will interest from Orthodox families, for whom the eruv will make a profound difference, mean that the desirability (and the prices) of the homes within it will rise? (See also the Hendon and Hampstead Garden Suburb chapters.)

The Ridgeway

Some of the best houses in Golders Green are found in the area to the W of the **Golders Green Rd**, off **The Ridgeway**. In roads such as **Ridge Hill**, **Gresham Gardens**, **Armitage Rd**, **Basing Hill**, **Hodford Rd** and **Dunstan Rd** you'll find 4- and 5-bedroom houses, detached and semi-detached, with large gardens: two recent examples in **Gresham Gardens**, both 5-bed detacheds, attracted price tags of £450,000 ('needing work') and £625,000. Little Basing Hill Park, the nearby tube station, cinema and shops are all attractions, though parking can be a problem in **Rodborough Rd** and **Helenslea Avenue**. Jewish residents have often chosen to live here because of the proximity to synagogues in **Dunstan Rd** and **The Riding**. The busy **Hendon Way** runs past the bottom of **Wessex Gardens** and **Ridge Hill**, so prices may be lower at that end. Cheaper, too, S towards Cricklewood.

A former school building in **Hodford Rd** is one of the last potential development sites in Golders Green, but no plans have yet been disclosed by its (private) owners.

Brent Cross

Brent Cross does not really constitute a neighbourhood by itself, though it houses the famous shopping centre and has a tube station (the two aren't as near to each other as you might think). Smaller, 3-bed terraces can be found for around £200,000, and 4-bed semis c. £260,000: **Highfield Avenue**, with the tube station, is one of the nicest roads in Golders Green and **Highfield Gardens** is where you'll find one of Golders Green's most popular purpose-built blocks, Windsor Court. In **Hamilton Rd** prices may be more modest since the street runs parallel to the **Hendon Way**; houses on the **Sandringham Rd** side won't suffer from noise as much as those right by the main road, but will still be relatively inexpensive for the area. Also look out among the 3-bed terraces and semis in **Woodville Rd** and **Elmcroft Crescent** for homes at the lower end of the price scale.

Golders Green Rd

This runs northwards like a main artery through the area from the station and the Hippodrome – first a music hall, then a theatre, now a BBC studio. Shopping, much of it seven days a week, causes parking problems; triple-parking in Golders Green is legendary. Busy residents can buy a suit on Sunday and toiletries until midnight every day, but the local shopping centre has suffered from the competition from Brent Cross. Heading towards Hendon, the flats above the shops give way to large family houses around **Ravenscroft Avenue**; some towards the **North Circular** are run-down.

Golders Green isn't usually noted for exceptionally pretty houses, but there are some surprises in **Brookside Rd**. You'll find conversions and family houses in streets off **Golders Green Rd**, **Gainsborough** and **Powis Gardens** to the W, **Beechcroft** and **Elmcroft Avenues** to the E, where there are also a couple of blocks of flats and small hotels. There are larger purpose-built blocks along the main road – Gloucester Court and Eagle Lodge, for example (c. £230–250,000 for a 2-bed flat). The 1930s block in **Golders Green Rd**, Riverside Drive, holds its value well (the large 3-bed flats here can cost £400,000).

Princes Park Avenue

As with the streets around **The Ridgeway**, there are some very large houses to be found in the vicinity of Princes Park, to the N of **Brookside Rd** between the **Finchley** and **Golders Green Rds**. Look for them in the **Princes Park Avenue/Leeside Crescent/Bridge Lane** triangle. Princes Park in the centre makes houses here particularly desirable; on Saturday afternoons the little park is full of children. Again, agents mention the synagogue factor; Jewish people who live here have often chosen the neighbourhood specifically. Coveted bungalows, some with extra rooms in the roof, are to be found in **Decoy Avenue** across **Bridge Lane**. Popular purpose-built blocks in the neighbourhood include Dolphin Court in **Woodlands** and the luxurious Riverside Drive on **Golders Green Rd**. Not as convenient as the Ridgeway area, though buses to Golders Green are numerous and frequent on the main road.

Temple Fortune

This area brackets the **Finchley Rd** northwards from **Hoop Lane/Wentworth Rd** up to Henly's Corner, the junction with the **North Circular**. The neighbourhood takes its name from the **Temple Fortune Parade** of shops (among them the police station), which is slightly less frantic than the chic **Golders Green Rd**. There's also a tennis club for sporty types, and a major Marks & Spencer food hall. Roads between **Hoop Lane** and **Temple Fortune Lane** have small houses and some conversions, cheaper even though nearer the prestigious Hampstead Garden Suburb because they back onto a cemetery. Further up on that side of the **Finchley Rd** you find purpose-built blocks like Belmont Court. Roads on the other (W) side of the **Finchley Rd** – **Templars Avenue, St Johns Rd, Portsdown Avenue, St George's Rd** and further up, **Hallswelle Rd** and **Monkville Avenue** – have smaller family houses and some conversions. To the S, homes in **Corringham, Middleton** and **Rotherwick Rds** are now well in excess of the half-million mark.

North End Rd

The neighbourhood to the S of the tube station, nestling in the angle between **North End Rd** and the **Finchley Rd**, sports Golders Hill Park (look out for the flamingos and wallabies in the zoo). Enviable roads like **West Heath Avenue** and **The Park** triangle have lovely views of the park, which merges into West Heath; a home 'needing updating' but with direct access to the park was £595,000 last winter; you can pay nearer £800,000. Flat conversions and blocks are gathered along **North End Rd** itself.

Land for new homes is decidedly scarce – however, smart developers Octagon Homes have bought the site of the former Manor House Hospital in **North End Rd**: watch this space . . .

Transport	Tubes: Golders Green, Brent Cross (zone 3, Northern). From Golders Green: Oxford Circus 20 min (1 change), City 30 min, Heathrow 1 hr 25 min (1 change).
Convenient for	Brent Cross shopping centre, Hampstead Heath, North Circular Rd. Miles from centre: 6.
Schools	Barnet Education Authority: Hendon School, Whitefield School. Private: Henrietta Barnett (g), King Alfred, Menorah GS (b).

SALES

Flats	S	1B	2B	3B	4B	5B
Average prices	60–100	90–160	120–300+	145–350	185+	—
Houses	2B	3B	4B	5B	6/7B	8B
Average prices	180–200	180–450	200–550+	350–950+	400–1 M+	—

RENTAL

Flats	S	1B	2B	3B	4B	5B
Average prices	100–160	150–250	200–450	220–450	300–550	330–430
Houses	2B	3B	4B	5B	6/7B	8B
Average prices	250–350	250–600	420–800	500–1000	600–1200	800–2000

The properties   Mock-Tudor suburban homes, large and comfortable, mix with prosperous blocks of flats and some conversions. These now supplemented by some luxury flats schemes. Less pricy suburbia, and some good value ex-local authority (the lower end of our price guide) towards Hendon Way and Brent Cross.

The market   Primarily family; long-established community (largely Jewish; also Japanese) now joined by househunters from Hampstead, St Johns Wood. Good transport links and solid, peaceful family homes ensure its position. Local searches: 5 working days.

Among those estate agents active in this area are:

- Winkworth *
- Ellis & Co
- Alexander Ross
- Glentree Estates
- Kinleight Folkard & Hayward
- Kingsleys

* further details: see advertisers' index on p671

G

GREENWICH AND BLACKHEATH

Map ref: p80 (7E)
Postal districts: SE10, SE3
Boroughs: Greenwich (Lab),
   Lewisham (Lab)
Council tax: Band D
   Greenwich £883,
   Lewisham £727
Conservation areas: Several,
   check with town hall
Parking: Residents/meters

Greenwich has gained new notoriety as the home of the The Dome. In truth the controversial structure is way out on a literal limb, the North Greenwich Pensinsula. You can forgive people who live in SE10 and SE3 their ignorance of this neighbourhood: it's long been an industrial wasteland, and the only time anyone went near it was to dive under it via the Blackwall Tunnel. Now the 200-plus acres of British Gas land has been cleaned up, and the Millennium has at least jolted London's transport planners into connecting Greenwich to the rest of London.

Riverside Greenwich has long suffered as well as gained from its position. Unrivalled views of the majestic Thames have to be traded against grossly overloaded roads, and rail lines stuck in the 1940s. Greenwich grew up as a royal favourite at a time when monarchs – and everyone else – used the Thames to get places. Now the only river users are tourists. There are no bridges closer than Tower Bridge one way and Dartford the other. The tunnels are notorious choke-points. Greenwich is cut off from vibrant Docklands by the river, and from the West End by traffic-ridden Deptford and Peckham.

The solutions are two new rail lines – the Jubilee line tube and the extended Docklands Light Railway (DLR) – both now running. The Jubilee line is a little frustrating for Greenwich as it only actually calls at North Greenwich, AKA The Dome. The DLR is a lot more useful. Its stations at the Cutty Sark, Greenwich rail station, Deptford Creek and Lewisham offer direct travel to Canary Wharf and the City.

What the Jubilee does offer Greenwich is connection possibilities. The DLR interchange at Canary Wharf, and that with the East London line at Canada Water, open up routes to many parts of London hirtherto hard to reach, if you started from here. For instance, Waterloo is about 12 minutes from Canary Wharf, the West End a few minutes further on. Until now, the only way to get to the West End from Greenwich was by train and then tube, or bus.

G

The real bad news is the amount of traffic trying to get through the area. It is on the route from most of London to the roads to Dover and Folkestone. Giant continental lorries rumble through streets designed for horses. Pollution levels are well above official limits. Lorry bans are forever mooted and modified, but the outcome cannot please both Greenwich *and* Blackheath. Meanwhile, the Millennium brings yet more tourists: the idea is that they get to the Dome by boat or by tube, but coach traffic has rocketed and quiet streets are finding themselves on signposted coach routes.

One response is the Millenium Transit, a hi-tech bus service from Greenwich and Charlton to the Dome. The idea is that this will survive the Millenium year and extend right round the Greenwich peninsula.

In one respect, the most impressive way to approach the area is to drive (or try to) across South London through the congested tide of Victorian expansionism. Suddenly you reach the hills and high heathland where Greenwich and Blackheath speak of an earlier, more gracious time. One must dispose of the history quickly: the whole place reeks of it, and any local will fill you in at length, beginning with Romans, Saxons and marauding Danes, via half the Kings and Queens of England (all the best died at/were born in/rebuilt the country palace beside the Thames) to romantic 18th-century highwaymen. As far as the streetscape goes, however, the period that has stuck is the Georgian/Regency one: glorious examples encouraged some of the better exponents of Victorian building in their wake.

Greenwich, gathered around the royal park by the Thames, has the bustle and air of a seaside, more than riverside, town. Trippers flock to the Cutty Sark, the Maritime Museum, the Observatory. It is a happily mixed area: here the property market can, and does, embrace everything from tiny 2-up, 2-down terraces to a wing of a red-brick, battlemented castle, built by Sir John Vanbrugh for himself in 1719. On the high plateau at the top of Shooter's Hill, Blackheath – at heart a country hamlet – considers itself a cut above. Those with money can choose Georgian restrained elegance or even, tucked away, Marbella-level opulence.

Greenwich divides neatly into two, the boundary being the superb sweep of park from hill to river. East Greenwich still retains a working identity through its riverside industry. Its cottages have been snapped up recently by young professional couples. Westcombe Park, sloping up the hill S of the railway, is grander though still affordable.

West Greenwich is steeped in history and boasts 17th-century masterpieces such as the former Royal Naval College (originally Greenwich Hospital for retired sailors, now Greenwich University), the re-vamped National Maritime Museum and Royal Observatory. It also has street after street of superb 18th-century houses.

Blackheath, over the hill to the S, has long been regarded as a more sought-after area than Greenwich. Native SE Londoners cruelly regard it as a home for snobs; but Blackheathens say it attracts those who love elegance and culture.

Westcombe Park

This is the name for the rectangle of residential streets E of **Maze Hill**, S of the railway and W of the A102 motorway. Around Westcombe Park station is a cluster of tree-lined streets of small terraced family houses, which are more reasonably priced than their near neighbours in East Greenwich. **Maze Hill**, with its large Victorian and turn-of-the-century houses, runs along the side of Greenwich Park. Climbing up the slopes away from the river are the larger 3- and 4-bed houses of peaceful **Mycenae Rd** and **Beaconsfield Rd** (Victorian Gothic and '30s, all with large gardens). One of the Victorian Gothic houses – a 5-bedder in half an acre – sold for £900,000 last winter, while a 1930s 4-bed Mycenae Rd house fetched £485,000. These streets adjoin **Westcombe Park Rd** with its delightful, ornate 2- and 3-storey Victorian mansions. **Vanbrugh Hill** has Victorian houses and flats: a 2-bed may be £140–160,000. **Westcombe Hill** is a busier road with smaller terraced houses at £170–180,000. A truly unique collection of homes can be found in the converted flats of Vanbrugh's Castle.

East Greenwich

North of the railway (and thus in SE10, not Westcombe Park's SE3) and E of the Royal Naval College is East Greenwich. The riverside has some enviable homes: a dozen new houses by Berkeley on **Highbridge Wharf** (from £400,000) have splendid views, as do the Georgian houses on charming **Ballast Quay**. Expect to pay £550,000-plus for one of these. To the S and N of **Trafalgar Rd** and around Greenwich District Hospital, typical East Greenwich homes – terraced workmen's cottages – quickly reassert themselves. Land to the N of the hospital is largely filled by well-kept, low-rise council homes. But to the S and W 3-bed terraces abound. The little houses lacked inside toilets and bathrooms until the 1980s, but have been converted by waves of young buyers. Today they go for around £200,000, less for 20th-century ex-council. Parking is the bugbear here.

Prices are highest to the W: a 3-bed terraced house on **Old Woolwich Rd**, in the shadow of the (disused) power station, was £280,000 in December. In contrast, the old Plaza cinema on **Trafalgar Rd** is now 37 1- and 2-bed modern flats, most sold by last winter. Those left at the start of 2000 were 2-beds from £160-190,000.

Heading E along **Trafalgar Rd** the picture is largely the same, although there is some low-rise council housing. Most cottages are 2-bedroom, with tiled roofs and signs of recent renovation. Many were formerly rented from the Morden College estate, but owner-occupying young City types are increasingly common.

The extension of the riverside path N to the Millennium site has generated excitement as developers bid for the derelict industrial sites. There will be homes here soon: watch this space.

West Greenwich

Heading W, Wren's Royal Hospital, until recently the Royal Naval College, is to become the home of Greenwich University. Past its grandeur, **Romney Rd** leads into the heart of West Greenwich with its generous mix of Georgian and Regency style. **Croom's Hill**, with its huge high-ceilinged Georgian and Victorian houses overlooking the park, is the most enviable address in Greenwich. Near the bottom of the hill lies one of the prettiest streets in South London – **Crooms Hill Grove**. Thousands pass by its tiny entrance, not realizing that a beautiful row of 2- and 3-storey terraced homes lies yards from the park's entrance.

Also off **Croom's Hill** and near to Greenwich Theatre lies the late-18th-century crescent of **Gloucester Circus**, with its 2-storey houses and fenced garden to the front. The perfect proportion of the Circus is, however, spoiled by the block of brick-built council flats which stands opposite. Nearby **Burney St** has handsome 1840 terraced houses, complete with wrought-iron balconies. They go for up to £600,000. **Luton Place** has early Victorian brick-faced semis which command £400–430,000. A 3-bed house in **Royal Place** was £365,000 last winter.

From the Circus you can cross over **Royal Hill** and **Circus St** (£575,000 for a Georgian 4-bed house) to the **Brand St** area, where the grander mansions give way to 3-storey Victorian terraces. The Royal Hill council estate stands at the base of **Royal Hill**, but is medium-rise and not too intrusive. Travel up the hill and pass the marvellous **Hamilton Terrace**, 3-storey with garden flats. Six 1930s semis near the top of the hill make a sudden appearance. **Hyde Vale** has some neo-Georgian 20th-century houses to compete with the real thing: £550,000 for a 4-bed. Going back down **Royal Hill** you arrive in **Greenwich South St**, a busy thoroughfare but with some lovely late-Georgian, early Victorian houses and a charming terrace of almshouses. Between **South St** and **Greenwich High Rd** is the Ashburnham Triangle conservation area: roads lined with 2/3-storey flat-fronted, early Victorian homes.

Some houses in this area can be quite small, but no-one seems to mind if the style is right. Style comes in all shapes and sizes. Heading W towards Deptford, the listed former West Greenwich Boys' School has undergone the loft treatment by Sapcote. More typical are the handsome 3-bed early Victorian semis of **Egerton Drive**. Off **Guildford Rd** is Admiral's Gate, a new close of a dozen neo-Georgian houses by Buxton Homes.

To be at the heart of traditional, naval, Greenwich, what could beat a house in **King William Walk**, an 1830 terrace with the Cutty Sark's masts looming at the end of the street? Some are in less than pristine condition. Expect to pay £450,000 for a bay-fronted 3-bed house here – though one went for £230,000 early in 1998.

Blackheath

Most of Blackheath is in the borough of Lewisham, not Greenwich. The busy A2, **Shooters Hill**, forms the boundary. It also carries the traffic from Central London to Dover, as it has done for two millennia. Blackheath grew up in Georgian times as a smart suburb and the heart of the neighbourhood so remains. Elegant terraces line the wind-blown heath, and the Village is a good facsimile of a rural one, only the shops are smarter. The wider area is defined to the N by the heath; by **Lewisham Rd** in the W; by **Lee High Rd** to the S; and by an upwardly curving arc which excludes the Ferrier council estate before joining with **Kidbrooke Park Rd** in the E.

The best way to approach Blackheath must be from the W up the steep **Blackheath Hill**. Taking a right turn into **Dartmouth Hill**, you are rewarded with a breathtaking view of the heath and the Village. In **Dartmouth Row**, many of the 18th-century houses are now smart flats: a 2-bed one would be £200,000 recently, while those in Dartmouth House itself are £230,000. Crossing the heath into **Hare and Billet Rd**, you first pass a small '60s development of box-shaped houses with flat roofs, and then some typical terraced 2- and 3-storey houses in a dip in the ground which appear from a distance to stand just a few feet tall. **Aberdeen Terrace** has grand mid-Victorian houses, one, a former student residence, carved last year into four flats and a coach house, plus nine more homes in its 1960s extension. Other splendidly confident terraces and mansions – in roads like **The Pagoda, Eliot Hill, The Paragon, South Row** – gaze across the heath all the way to the Village and beyond. Many have been split into flats. Tucked behind the Georgiana in **Fulthorpe Rd** is one of the poshest council-built estates in Britain, dating from the 1950s. N of the heath the streets round **Vanbrugh Park** and **St John's Park** are Victorian and blend into Westcombe Park. Prices are lower here than in Blackheath proper and some modern flats add to the choice available.

Blackheath Park

Go down **Pond Rd** and into Blackheath's surprise package – the exclusive Blackheath Park or Cator Estate. This incredible array of private housing was first built by a developer called John Cator at the start of the 19th century, and now has every conceivable architectural style. The estate spreads E from **Lee Rd** and S to **Manor Way**. Gates at the five entrances are closed during rush hours, though the lodge keepers have long gone. There are Victorian and Edwardian mansions, mock-Tudor 1930s detached houses and a sprinkling of 14 small 1960s Span estates, highly praised by architects: one estate is listed. Many homes here have swimming pools. Some are very opulent. In contrast, the SE corner has the ugly Ferriers Estate of brutal GLC public housing.

The Span houses seem good value: the larger houses realise £220,000. Some smart modern houses have been squeezed in, such as the 4-bedder which went for £500,000 recently, and there are others of older vintage: a 4-bed detached house, in need of work but on a good-sized plot, sold for £425,000 last autumn.

SW of Blackheath Village, **Lee Terrace** marks the N edge of a district of pleasant streets such as **Belmont Park** and **Dacre Park**, where a 4-storey Georgian house might be worth £325,000 or so, and larger family houses fit the £370–400,000 bracket. There have been no great gains here since the start of 1999, and houses with small gardens struggle to sell. The W edge of Blackheath, towards Lewisham, has excellent transport links now the DLR is open: Canary Wharf 15 minutes. **Belmont Hill** has a dozen smart flats newly converted from The Cedars, a fine 1860s mansion.

Borders

Along **Lee High Rd**, properties are a jumble of council-built and terraced homes with the quality generally declining as you leave the heath behind. On the steep slopes just to the N there is a fair sprinkling of 1- and 2-bed conversion flats, where incomers are replacing fireplaces ripped out by over-zealous workmen in the 1970s. Properties here are cheaper than those with a heath view. For a cheaper alternative with Victorian charm, try Charlton Village, a mile to the E of Blackheath, or Brockley conservation area to the W (see Lewisham). Charlton saw a brisk market last year.

Beware of estate agents selling Kidbrooke (or indeed places halfway to Dover) as Blackheath. The only thing they have in common is the SE3 postal address.

Woolwich to the E is cheaper, but too industrial for most people's liking. However, this corner, and Plumstead and the 'new town' of Thamesmead beyond, offer some relative bargains. Hundreds of homes at Thamesmead are now under control of a private company, having been sold off after the demise of the GLC. New waterside homes at affordable prices get more numerous the closer you get to Thamesmead.

North Greenwich

Here on a windy riverside tract you have a tube station, beautiful; a Sainsbury's, ditto, and a Dome, future uses unclear. You should have a Millenium Village of 1,377 homes. They may have scrambled the Millenium Experience into being by January 1, but the Village – supposed to be ready, or at least in evidence, at the same time, lagged behind. The idea is that big builders – Barratt, Fairview etc – build homes in a 'template for urban living' with lots of ecological awareness, public transport, hi-tech cabling, bike routes and so on. The scheme has however followed another template with bitter rows between architects and developers, developers and planners, builders and suppliers. After you visit the Dome take a look: there may be show houses by the summer. In the future, good transport and waterside locations should mean a future for the peninsula, but it's a 10-year project.

Transport   Trains: Greenwich to London Bridge 15 min, Charing Cross 20 min; Blackheath to London Bridge 12 min. DLR extension from Cutty Sark and Greenwich station to Docklands and City; Jubilee line links North Greenwich to West End. See also map.

Convenient for   Docklands, A2 to Dover/Channel Tunnel, Millennium Dome. Miles from centre: 5.5.

Schools   Local Authority: St Ursulas' Convent RC (g), The John Roan School, Blackheath Bluecoat C of E, St Joseph's Academy RC (b), St Theresa's RC (g), Hatcham CTC. Private: Blackheath High School (g), Thomas Tallis, Haberdashers Askes.

G

SALES

Flats	S	1B	2B	3B	4B	5B
Average prices	65–90	80–180	85–250	135–270+	—	—
Houses	2B	3B	4B	5B	6/7B	8B
Average prices	160–320	180–550	230–650	350–1.25 M	650–1.5 M	1.75 M+

RENTAL

Flats	S	1B	2B	3B	4B	5B
Average prices	110–138	115–265	160–275+	210–325+	—	—
Houses	2B	3B	4B	5B	6/7B	8B
Average prices	155–275	275+	275–345	275–460	460+	—

The properties   Superb Georgian in Greenwich and Blackheath, mid-Victorian in Blackheath Park and Westcombe Park, plus more ordinary period and modern homes in E Greenwich and other fringe areas.

The market   Prices vary dramatically from East Greenwich (still cheaper) to heath views and period homes in top roads, eg Croom's Hill. These are the nearest established residential areas to Docklands and are now linked by tube from the Greenwich Peninsula and the DLR extension. Local searches: Greenwich 10 working days, Lewisham 3 weeks.

Among those estate agents active in this area are:
- Halifax
- John Payne
- Winkworth *
- Haart
- Humphreys Skitt & Co
- GA Property Services
- Harrison Ingram
- Comber & Co

* further details: see advertisers' index on p671

HACKNEY

Map ref: p47 (5H)
Postal districts: E5, E8, E9
Boroughs: Hackney (Labour)
Council tax: Band D £789
Conservation areas: Include Victoria
  Park, Albion Square, Sutton Place,
  Clapton Square
Parking: Pay and display, residents',
  some meters

Hackney was the fastest-rising borough in London on some house price charts in 1999. This was because it had a good deal of catching up to do: like many of the non-blue chip areas, home prices dipped deep into negative-equity land in the 1990s.

Behind the borough-wide averages in 1999 were some remarkable local leaps in both status and price. Neighbourhoods like Victoria Park and Dalston led the way, with the big Victorian homes in the former pushing half a million. Other parts, like Clapton, lagged behind while Homerton and Hackney Wick remain the cheapest corners.

Just as in the last boom in the 1980s, the buyers are young City and media types, the sellers (in many cases) long-term residents who are selling up and moving out. So despite strenuous and successful efforts to revive Hackney's wide areas of public housing, the gap between the prosperous and the poor is growing.

There is good news at last about transport. Hackney needs help: it has not a single underground station. The Chelsea–Hackney tube line plan is again gathering dust at LT headquarters, after a brief airing to celebrate its 50th birthday: it was first mooted in 1949. But a northward extension of the East London line to Dalston seems to be on the cards at last.

The new line would transform the accessibility of the W side of the area, bringing a direct link with Docklands and the City. Stations would be at Bishopsgate, Hoxton (Geffrye St), Haggerston (Stonebridge Park) and Dalston Junction. There are hopes of a further extension W to Highbury Corner. London Transport was given the go-ahead to plan the line back in 1997, but all still depends on money and that will depend at least in part on the new London Mayor and Assembly. LT hope to start work in 2001, with an opening date of 2004.

The borough of Hackney takes in Clapton, Homerton, Dalston, Stoke Newington and half a dozen other former hamlets. Stoke Newington has its own chapter, and the southern edge of the borough is described in the City chapter. Hackney abuts the City to the S, Islington to the W and ends in the E with the Hackney Marshes in the Lea Valley.

Like most of North London, all was sylvan peace here once, interspersed with country seats and pleasure gardens. The late-Georgian era saw houses spread along the main roads – look above the shops and you'll see them still. Hackney became smart for a while, as its few surviving Georgian squares show. Then came the railways and the Victorian housing boom. The underground missed Hackney, but the many thousands of City clerks and respectable working men who rented the terraced homes found their way to work by foot, by horse, bus or train into Liverpool St, and they formed the heart of Hackney. Outright slums and filthy factories intruded into the SE corner, around Hackney Wick, but the bulk of the place was a commuter suburb for the great army of London's ordinary people. And so it remains today.

Hackney has moved on from the days when rich and poor where polarized. Today it contains homes for thousands of London's less well-paid young couples and families – though the last 12 months have seen homes here grow less affordable than they were. Most newcomers find the place a happy mixture of inner-city scruffiness and enlivening bustle. That is because, perhaps, the typical incomer is a computer programmer, a social worker, a secretary or a teacher rather than a stockbroker – a millennial Blairite rather than yesterday's yuppy. And the council estates are being redeemed by enlightened town hall and housing association activity – those that have not been dynamited and replaced by better-planned homes.

H

The newcomers are rediscovering Hackney's proximity to the City and discovering some of the community spirit in a new form. They find that Hackney has surprisingly usable communications (buses and trains, not tubes – yet) and that local amenities are improving, especially on the cultural side.

Hackney's town square at the north end of **Mare St** is being spruced up: the council see it as a cultural centre. Landscaping of the Square will include digital screens, light sculptures, illuminated water slides and metallic paving. The Hackney Empire music hall will be redeveloped at a cost of £12 million, due for completion in 2001. Also set for next year are the new Technology and Learning Centre with high-tech library, museum, gym and shops, and the Ocean Music Venue with its large auditorium, training and rehearsal rooms, bars and cafés. Next door will be a Weatherspoons pub.

Hackney's young population, and ample (if no longer very cheap) warehouse/living space, lends credence to the borough's claim to be home to the biggest concentration of working artists in Europe. They concentrate in the S of the area, in Hoxton and the City fringes (see City chapter). Agents in Hackney routinely list live/work units as well as flats and houses.

Hackney has a high percentage of parkland for inner London. Some areas stand out as attractive for home-buyers, usually because they are close to these parks but primarily because they have some surviving 19th-century homes. Properties around London Fields and Victoria Park are popular and, among the regulation terraces, some grander Victoriana and even some Georgian corners survive. The De Beauvoir area, W of the busy **Kingsland Rd**, carries a premium as it is near the border with fashionable Islington (see Islington and Highbury chapter) and has an N1 postal address.

Victoria Park, a conservation area, is divided between Hackney and the neighbouring borough of Tower Hamlets. The wide park forms part of Hackney's boundary while the

River Lea provides the border with Waltham Forest to the E. Hackney Marshes is marshland no longer, but is another large area of welcoming greenery – its flat expanse makes for excellent football pitches. Look in this direction for cheaper homes. The Marshes are in the SE part of Clapton; further N is picturesque Springfield Park, a much more attractive hilly area with Springfield Marina and City Orient Rowing Club on the River Lea. The **Ridley Rd** market area of Dalston, leading to busy **Kingsland High St**, is less enticing, but does have a new multi-screen cinema opening in spring 2000.

Hackney's house prices rose by 28 per cent in 1999 following a 17 per cent rise in 1998, according to Land Registry figures. Ex-council homes offer a lot of space for a little money: plenty of 3-bed homes for 5-figure prices. Some estates remain unhappy places, but others have been transformed and are pleasant communities.

Hackney Central

The central spine of Hackney is the N–S road variously named **Mare St** and **Lower Clapton Rd**. Here are the town hall, the famous Russian baths, now refurbished as the King's Hall Leisure Centre, and Hackney Central station. Hackney Downs station, with trains to **Liverpool St**, is close by. Off **Lower Clapton Rd** is **Clapton Square**, a conservation area and one of several garden squares in Hackney. It is surrounded by Georgian listed terraced houses, some 5-storeys. The square leads on to **Clarence Place** and **Clapton Passage**, which both have a charming villagey feel and coveted homes: large impressive 3-storey terraced Georgian houses graced with entrance steps, railings and tiny wrought-iron balconies. This whole network of streets forms a green oasis in the midst of Hackney. A 2-bed flat just off the Square changed hands last winter for £135,000, while one of the **Clapton Square** houses might cost £400,000.

On **Lower Clapton Rd**, an Art Deco factory has become The Strand Building: 1- and 2-bed flats. West of the Duke of Clarence pub, at the junction with **Clarence Rd**, is the Pembury council estate, which includes **Hindrey Rd, Shellness Rd, Bodney Rd, Pembury Rd, Dalston Lane** and **Downs Park Rd**.

From the southern edge of the estate **Amhurst Rd**, a busy bus route, leads back SE to the **Mare St** shopping centre. The Aspland council estate lies along part of **Amhurst Rd**. On the junction of **Dalston Lane** and **Amhurst Rd** is Eastside, the 1998 conversion of an Edwardian college, now 57 flats. One-bed loft flats here sell for £140–160,000.

To the S of the railway serving Hackney Central, **Graham Rd**, another busy main road, is a source of good business for estate agents with numerous decent 3-storey terraced houses, some with basements, on both sides. A good number of these houses have been converted into flats. On the E side of **Lower Clapton Rd**, opposite **Clapton Passage**, more 2- and 3-storey Victorian houses can be found in **Powerscroft Rd** and **Glenarm Rd**, close to Hackney police station.

Another notable street in central Hackney is **Sutton Place,** backing onto the grounds of St John's Church, S of **Lower Clapton Rd.** Sutton House in **Homerton High St** here is the oldest brick-built house in East London. Owned by the National Trust, it can be used for receptions, concerts and even weddings. This is another conservation area, with big listed Georgian terraced houses with steps, railings and basements. Several were bought from 1990 by intrepid DIY converters and turned into superb homes. Now, people pay £450,000. The land behind these houses, once the old Metal Box factory, has been developed as **Sutton Square,** an up-market development built around central gardens, with a courtyard and illuminated fountains. Other attractive streets S of **Sutton Place** include **Mehetabel Rd** and **Isabella Rd.** The former has well-preserved flat-fronted cottages, while the houses in the latter are grander in scale.

Other changes in this busy area include a Tesco superstore on previously derelict land in **Morning Lane,** close to **Mare Street** and S of **Sutton Place**; and a school conversion in **Chelmer Rd,** next to Homerton Hospital: 30 flats launched in 1999.

Victoria Park

The park, laid out in 1845 conveniently in time for the Chartist rallies of 1848, is one of London's largest. It gives its name to a neighbourhood containing some of the biggest and most expensive houses in Hackney. Much of the housing is on land owned by the Crown Estate, so residents can claim to have Crown leases just like their grander counterparts in Regent's Park. There are homes of all kinds, both Victorian and modern. These houses tend to change hands privately. Purpose-built flats in roads such as **Pennethorne Close,** near the park, offer good value. Conversions of the big old houses provide flats with far more space than in higher-priced areas, and quite a number have lovely views of the park and its several lakes. Another green space, Well Street Common, adjoins the park and provides open views for the Victorian and 1930s mock-Tudor houses of **Meynell Rd** and **Meynell Crescent.** Some of the priciest homes in Hackney are here: a 5-bed house overlooking the Common goes for £450–500,000 (only two years back in 1998 the benchmark was £250,000, but £275,000 was reached in 1989). In **Victoria Park Rd,** Ideal Homes refurbished six Victorian houses as 6-bed homes rather than flats, and tucked in the 'Sovereign Mews': 2- and 3-bed town-houses and 1-bed flats. Expect to pay £165–170,000 for a 2-bed flat in this road.

On **Cassland Rd,** St George have built 'Victoria Park Crescent', a terrace of flats and a single 3-storey house. **Cassland Crescent** is the real thing, a beautiful Georgian terrace with walled gardens. Some of its early Victorian neighbours are almost as fine. A Victorian school building on the corner of **Cassland Rd** and **Bradshaw Rd** has just become loft apartments at the hands of Sapcote.

The disadvantage around here is lack of communications. Bethnal Green tube is a mile or so to the S and Cambridge Heath and London Fields stations give access to Liverpool St.

Gore Rd, overlooking the N side of Victoria Park, has some of Hackney's most desirable properties. Imposing 3- and 4-storey terraced houses with steps to their front doors present a dignified front to the large and pleasant park. **Gore Rd** leads W into **Victoria Park Rd** and, at the junction with **Mare St,** boasts a new development in **Earlston Grove** and **Northam St.** Flats and houses here are blessed with private garages – an important plus in such a busy area. A little to the N, the conservation area of **Fremont St** and **Warneford St** provides fine 2- and 3-storey mid-19th-century terraced houses with basements. By contrast, nearby **Sharon Gardens** (said to have been built by Jewish immigrants) offers some of the few 1930s semis in the area. **Beck Rd** is also popular. In nearby **King Edward Rd** is a new development of live/work units in a converted 1930s industrial building: a typical price is £115,000 for 600 sq ft.

London Fields

The 26 acres of London Fields, successively sheep pasture and cricket pitch, are the centre of a neighbourhood W of **Mare St** and N of the canal which shadows De Beauvoir to the W in popularity. Here are streets of solid, readily modernized houses that are popular with young couples. Impressive 4-storey Victorian terraced houses, some converted into flats, are found in **Lansdowne Drive**, W of London Fields. On the corner of **Lansdowne Drive** and **Gayhurst Rd** is a converted pub, now 1/3-bed flats. You might pay £135,000 for a 2-bed flat here. **Mapledene Rd** and **Lavender Grove** have smaller but attractive homes.

To the N, **Navarino Grove** has neat flat-fronted terraced cottages. The Old Vicarage, a conversion of a Victorian Gothic parsonage beside the Fields, has added lavish flats with period features. Yet another school conversion is in train where **Walton Way** meets **Lansdowne Rd,** and just across the road a warehouse is going the same way.

The E side of London Fields is less attractive with industrial units and London Fields rail station. Even here, new homes are being built: 2-bed flats from £140,000. **Middleton Rd**, **Albion Drive** and **Shrubland Rd** border the Fields council estate. The council-built homes are in a good location and they are popular buys. These roads, too, have pleasant 2/3-storey flat-fronted Victorian houses, some with 120-ft gardens. To the W, **Albion Square** is one of the finest garden squares in Hackney. Early 19th-century semi-detached and detached houses with pretty gardens lie away from the main traffic route: expect to pay up to £475,000 for a 4-bed detached. To the N of London Fields a 3-bed house in **St Phillip's Rd** might cost £165,000. Goldcrest Homes plan to build on a site in **Bocking St**.

Clapton

Clapton is an area to the N and E of Hackney on ground rising up from the Lea Valley. This is still one of the cheapest parts of the borough in which to buy a home: it holds more streets of Victorian and Edwardian housing, modern council estates and, in the far N of the area, attractive Springfield Park. Agents report a price divide between Lower and Upper Clapton, which is to the N. The latter is still more expensive, but the former has seen a large jump in prices in the last two years. A 3-bed terraced house typically costs £155,000 in Lower Clapton, £20,000 more in Upper Clapton.

Near the junction of **Lea Bridge Rd** and **Lower Clapton Rd**, two of the area's busiest thoroughfares, are **Thistlewaite Rd**, **Thornby Rd**, **Newick Rd** and **Fletching Rd**: a cache of large 2- and 3-storey Victorian terraced houses in tree-lined streets. **Hillstowe Rd** has a Victorian building being split into homes by Lovell. Among other corners worth noting is attractive **Ashenden Rd** in the SE of the district. This street includes Tower Mews, a warehouse conversion of flats that have kept some of the original features. Parking space is provided in a tidy courtyard. On **Charnock Rd** there's an ongoing conversion of a brush factory into flats. A large 'warehouse-style' flat was £210,000 in December, with 1-beds £75,000.

Homes in the hilly Springfield Park area of Upper Clapton, E of the Clapton Common conservation area, have the added attraction of the nearby River Lea and the open spaces of the Walthamstow Marshes. North of the park is **Watermint Quay**, on the river and reached via **Craven Walk**. This is a facing pair of 1980s terraces set end-on to the river towpath, with 77 houses and 18 flats at the river end. The houses have 33-ft basements running the full length of the house, which can be used as play-areas, storage or cellarage. Three-bed houses sell for £130–140,000 – about the same as in 1990. Just to the S, rows of 2-storey Victorian terraced houses in **Spring Hill** lead down directly to the Lea with its Springfield Marina and City Orient Rowing Club. Similar homes are in **Lingwood Rd** and **Overlea Rd**. In **Theydon Rd**, a 1930s factory is now 'The de Havilland Building' with loft apartments.

Overlooking Clapton Common is **Clapton Terrace,** where large Georgian terraced houses with basements and gardens give respite from the prevailing 19th-century rows. By contrast, some of Clapton's cheaper (and smaller) properties are found to the S beside Hackney Marshes which also border the River Lea. **Riverside Walk,** a recent development by Wimpey in **Mount Pleasant Hill,** has 1- and 2-bed flats. Close by is the massive Kingsmead council estate, encircled by **Kingsmead Way.** This has seen a remarkable turn-round, with tenants now in charge of the estate, the worst system-built homes razed and replaced and crime plummeting. The final phase involves 277 homes built on the sites of four unloved and now demolished tower blocks. There are 74 homes are for open-market sale and 176 for low-cost/shared ownership.

The big builders have found sites in Hackney Wick for low-priced schemes. The trouble is, they have stayed low-priced. **Victoria Mews,** off **Swinnerton St,** is a 1980s scheme with 1- and 2-bed flats and 3- and 4-bed houses. A riverside factory site off **Berkshire Rd** has been redeveloped as **Leabank Square:** flats and houses. Its developer went bankrupt in 1989 due to over-exposure to Docklands, and the estate went through a rough patch. Prices, however, recovered here during 1999, as they did in the wider neighbourhood. A 3-bed house in **Swinneton St** might now cost you £150,000. The at-last-complete road to the M11 makes this corner more accessible.

Dalston

Dalston is N of the London Fields neighbourhood, W of Hackney central and on the borders with Stoke Newington and Islington. Despite its position, it remains the least promising Hackney neighbourhood. Stoke Newington police station is in **Kingsland Rd. Ridley Rd** market, where anything and everything can be bought, is one of Hackney's best-known landmarks. The bustling market leads to more shops in busy **Kingsland High St** and the surrounding streets reflect the area's cosmopolitan image. Dalston Kingsland rail station is also in **Kingsland High St.** Dalston Cross shopping centre, off **Dalston Lane** and **Kingsland Rd,** opened in 1989. Plans for a multi-screen at the junction of **Kingsland High St** and **Dalston Lane,** next to the site for the proposed tube station (see introduction) seem to have fallen through.

Downs Park Rd, Cecilia Rd, Ferncliff Rd and **Sandringham Rd** are part of the Mountford council estate. Large 3- and 4-storey Victorian terraced houses with steps can be found in sought-after **Sandringham Rd** and **Montague Rd. Colvestone Crescent,** another of the streets around St Mark's Church, has more massive 4-storey Victorian houses. Chester Gate, a new development off **Ridley Rd,** provides some relief. Impressive 2- and 3-bed 3-storey houses are sited away from through traffic. Off **Wilton Way,** new homes have been built in **Walkers Court.** Independent Place is a work/homes development off **Shacklewell Lane** and opposite is **Gateway Mews** – a complex of flats in a converted warehouse and listed buildings.

Centenary Place is a Laing development off **Queensbridge Rd** and next to **Holly St** council estate: the first 28 sold very fast, and the next phase has 1-bed flats from £118,000 and 4-bed 'Georgian style' town houses at £325,000. Nearby, the Queensbridge Rd sport and community centre has been done up.

Look to the SW corner of Dalston for canal-side developments overlooking the Kingsland Basin: two such are Quebec Wharf and Waterside Lofts.

| **Transport** | Trains: Hackney Central, Hackney Wick, Homerton (N London line/Silverlink); London Fields, Hackney Downs (Liverpool St). Future tube plans for Dalston etc: see introduction. |

Convenient for   Victoria Park, the City, Docklands, Blackwall Tunnel.
Miles from centre: 4.

Schools   Local Authority: Cardinal Pole School, Homerton House School,
Hackney Free & Parochial School.

SALES

Flats	S	1B	2B	3B	4B	5B
Average prices	55–70	75–120	90–170	140–200	150–260	–

Houses	2B	3B	4B	5B	6/7B	8B
Average prices	100–160	150–250	180–280	250–350	–	–

RENTAL

Flats	S	1B	2B	3B	4B	5B
Average prices	90–110	110–160	160–220	190–260	–	–

Houses	2B	3B	4B	5B	6/7B	8B
Average prices	150–240	200–290	230–370	–	–	–

The properties   Many Victorian houses, some early and desirable, a few
Georgian. De Beauvoir and Victoria Park now established
residential zones, other parts more mixed with widespread
council housing and 'gentrified' pockets. Agents prefer to keep
quiet about Hackney's schools, with a few exceptions like
Lauriston Primary near Victoria Park.

The market   Owner-occupation rising: people who cannot afford Islington
take advantage of Hackney's lower prices. Smart new
developments and converted schools/factories among the
Victorian rows. Local searches: 10 working days.

Among those estate agents active in this area are:

- Winkworth *
- Strettons
- Shaw & Co
- Douglas Allen Spiro
- Spicer McColl
- Sovereign

- Bunch & Duke
- Castles
- Bennett-Walden *
- Foxtons *
- Keatons *

further details: see advertisers' index on p671

HAMMERSMITH

Map ref: p74 (4E)
Postal districts: W6
Boroughs: Hammersmith &
  Fulham (Lab)
Council tax: Band D £827
Conservation areas: Several
Parking: Mainly
  residents/meters

H

Hammersmith would be a large square on the map if it were not for the curving Thames, which bites off the south-western corner. As it is, the boundaries are the protective arm of the **Goldhawk Rd** to the W and N, the river and **Lillie Rd** to the S, and to the E the borough boundary — reinforced by the much more physical barrier of the railway, which runs N–S. Within this square lies Hammersmith proper (essentially the W6 postal district), Baron's Court and West Kensington – which, with Kensington's name but in Hammersmith's borough, is always good for confusing outsiders.

At first sight, Hammersmith is an everyday sort of corner. There are some prestigious arts outposts here that give the West End a run for its money: the Lyric Theatre, the vast Labbats Apollo and the Riverside Studios, whose stage productions and art-house and European film screenings receive a lot of national media attention. But the **Great West Road** charges through, cutting off the river end, and **King Street**, which is Hammersmith's high street, has never quite taken off in the way that Chiswick's has. And the effect of the gleaming redevelopment of **Hammersmith Broadway** (shops, restaurants, new tube and bus stations, Coca-Cola's European HQ offices) immured on its roundabout, does not seem to have spilled out into the area as a whole.

However, if the luxury properties (with a few well-recognized exceptions) are not that luxurious, the down-market bits are very far from slums. Leading the enclaves of family homes is some glorious Georgiana (and even earlier) by the riverside; then there are the unexpected delights of the pretty, tucked-away villas and rows off Brook Green and the leafy, well-established and popular terraces of corners such as Ravenscourt Park and Brackenbury 'village'. For the rest, by and large, the streets are a little too narrow, the houses rather too tall (the most common homes in the Hammersmith area are small 1- and 2-bed flats) and the ways through too confined. A built-up borough – but, largely thanks to the river, not that claustrophobic.

Hammersmith's main asset is its position: in West London, on the way to Heathrow – and close to the BBC's vast White City HQ in next-door Shepherd's Bush. The area attracts media workers: apart from the BBC, there's EMI in Brook Green and Disney in Hammersmith. The direct route to the airport reinforces the area's attractions for such people. It also, of course, means heavy traffic, but public transport is good. (Just as well: the area has 24 controlled parking zones, reserving 20,000 parking spaces for residents.)

Now, just over its borders, comes the plans for the vast, 40-acre, £50 million, futuristic White City shopping and leisure centre (see Shepherd's Bush chapter). Will this be an asset? Or will it presage the final clogging of routes in and out of Hammersmith, despite the new railway station to be opened on the West London line?

Office developments are dotted over the entire borough: neighbourhoods with the fewest are most in demand. But it is a general (very general) rule that those who want access to Central London will opt for the east side of Hammersmith, while those who focus on the airport opt for the area W of **Fulham Palace/Shepherd's Bush Rds**.

Hammersmith has a low-key cosmopolitan character; all social classes and most races are represented here, with small, well-established Irish, Polish and Afro-Caribbean communities; but there are no high concentrations of individual groups. Hammersmith divides fairly neatly into districts.

Barons Court/West Kensington

Fulham Palace Rd is the boundary to the W; **Hammersmith Rd** to the N; **Lillie Rd** to the S; the railway line to the E. The whole district is bisected by the A4 **Talgarth Rd**.

Most properties in this neatly defined square are those tall Victorian houses that convert well to flats – and flat-land it is: it's estimated that they outnumber houses by 10:1. These streets are truly a hotchpotch: on almost every road there's one building that won't please the aesthetically inclined, though council-build is not sprawling. Greenery, apart from little Normand Park, is supplied by the quiet, well-kept gardens of Hammersmith Cemetery. With little room for new developments, it's not an area prone to change. Convenience is its watchword; a middle-market, middle-of-the-road, middle-of-everywhere neighbourhood: within a taxi-ride of West End or airport; on both District and Piccadilly (direct to Heathrow) tube lines.

So flats prevail. But floorspace is limited and little 2-bed apartments are the norm: usually one large bedroom and a much smaller one – fine if you only need a spare room; less so for sharing renters (and thus investors). Three-bedroomed flats are rare, but occasionally they can be constructed out of the top two floors since, in these tall, thin houses (pity the Victorian servants), one floor more often than not simply won't accommodate more than one or two rooms. North of **Talgarth Rd**/A4, in streets such as **Gunterstone Rd**, lined with roomier mid/late-19th century houses, the 2-bed flats get more spacious, but 3-bedroomed places are still scarce.

A particularly popular segment of Barons Court/West Kensington is the grid bordered by **Gledstanes Rd, North End Rd, Barons Court Rd** and **Star Rd**. This corner is close to both Barons Court (District and Piccadilly) and West Kensington tube stations. The Barons Court station area is now a residents' parking zone, which has alleviated problems caused by commuter parking. Young, as yet childless, couples in their 20s and 30s discovered the Gledstanes grid in a big way a decade ago – along with investors looking for buy-to-let opportunities, and developers on the lookout for yet more properties to convert . . . . But note, as you drive westwards along the **Talgarth Rd** highway past this corner, the splendid, soaring, idiosyncratic windows of a row of High Victorian artists' studios: it's a sad irony that such windows should have inherited such a view.

The most sought-after properties in Barons Court are the red-brick Victorian houses in **Queen's Club Gardens**, just south of the famous tennis club itself. **Queen's**

Club Gardens, a conservation area, has a small central park; this, and its aura of affluence and gentility, makes it something of an oasis. **Fitzgeorge** and **Fitzjames Avenues** and **Queen's Club Gardens** contain examples of the few mansion blocks available in this district, built around 1910. Prices in these vary widely to reflect their differing ages and conditions: some still lack central heating and rejoice in original kitchen and bathroom fittings. They can, though, be large: last winter a 3-bed flat (in good order) was £310,000; a 4-bed one, £385,000.

The pastel-coloured 1930s villas on and around **Palliser Rd** are in great demand. The triangle enclosed by **Palliser, Barons Court** and **Barton Rds** consists of about three-quarters of an acre of communal greenery. These villas are rarely sold – well, they have something rarer than hens' teeth: their own garages.

There are a lot of council properties – on **North End Rd** itself as well as in the less popular part of this neighbourhood, the roads leading E off **Fulham Palace Rd** such as **Greyhound Rd**. This mixed street has cheaper flats above shops as well as conversions (1-beds, c. £90–145,000; rents from £180–200 a week). **Greyhound Rd** is close to the big Charing Cross Hospital, with sports facilities including gym and pool.

Riverside

The thin strip of river bank bounded – and protected – by the roaring traffic of the **Great West Rd/A4** to the N, **Hammersmith Bridge Rd** to the E and the borough boundary to the W is an eastward continuation of **Chiswick Mall**. The river, here suddenly smaller-looking and more rural (despite the traffic once more crossing the now-reopened bridge) than in Central London, runs to the S. In summer, the small patches of grass and trees fill with locals enjoying the rowing on the river. Their wants are supplied by a couple of pubs, among them one of the nicest, oldest riverside pubs in London: The Dove, originally a Georgian coffee-house.

This slice of Hammersmith is the exception that proves the rule: as with next-door **Chiswick Mall**, some of London's rarer surviving Georgian homes are here, strung along **Hammersmith Terrace** (which dates from the 1750s) and **Upper** and **Lower Malls**. The homes on **Hammersmith Terrace** have no road separating them from the river, but the two Malls are a little more public than the corresponding Chiswick stretch. Still, this most affluent and desirable corner of Hammersmith has estate agents reaching for words such as 'ambassadorial'. When the riverside houses do come onto the market (which is hardly ever), expect to pay in the millions: for instance, a 4-bedroomed **Hammersmith Terrace** example with sunken garden and direct river access, £1.4 million. Some modern homes here, too: King Henry's Reach, a 1996 block of 70 flats, yields a wide range of sizes and prices, (a recent 2-bed example was £269,000, but larger flats go for nearer half a million; more for penthouses). **Lord Napier Place** is a peaceful enclave of town-houses just off **Upper Mall**. Recent prices included a 3-bed one, with garage, for £335,000; a 4-bed with riverside garden, £750,000. A new home, or homes, will appear here atop a Victorian boathouse on **Upper Mall**: the Sons of the Thames rowing club are below, but the council, who own the site, have now won a seven-year battle to convert the upper storey.

North from the riverside and **Great West Rd/A4**, just S of **King St** (Hammersmith's high street, with stores and small shopping mall), is **St Peter's Square**, a conservation area full of unusually large (for Hammersmith), handsome, 5/6-bedroomed stucco-fronted houses. These were built around 1825–30 in sub-Belgravia mode, around one of Hammersmith's rare garden squares. A 5-bed house for sale here recently was £850,000. The surrounding streets of more modest houses and 2-bed cottages are plainly of the same date. In this area there are also several red-brick, Art Deco blocks of mansion flats (recent examples: a 1-bed flat in Digby Mansions, £150,000; a 2-bed in Bridge Avenue Mansions, £250,000).

Brackenbury Village

North of Hammersmith's shopping centre, this neighbourhood is bounded by **Paddenswick Rd, Hammersmith Grove, Glenthorne Rd** and **Goldhawk Rd**. Over the past 10 years it has moved from newly discovered, through up-and-coming, to firmly established. It still has a delightful villagey atmosphere: little shops, pretty, unspoilt Victorian street-corner pubs with hanging baskets, pavement seating or gardens. Buyers who moved in from Notting Hill and Kensington in search of affordable family homes have spent money on their houses and tidied the neighbourhood up. To serve them, smart restaurants have joined (sometimes replaced) the pubs. There is very little through traffic, but a 24-hr parking problem in these streets – commuters by day, residents by night – is being solved by the growing residential parking zones. Generally the homes are small 2- and 3-bed early Victorian terraced cottages and small villas, especially on the W side of the area (for example **Carthew Rd, Cardross St** and **Dalling Rd**), while larger houses, sometimes split into flats, can be found towards the E in the streets leading to **Hammersmith Grove** (for example **Benbow Rd**, where a 2-bed garden flat was £240,00 last winter, while a 5-bedroomed, just-done-up **Agate Rd** house was £760,000 and another, less tarted, £650,000). **Brackenbury Rd**'s 3-storey houses fetch c. £450,000 for 4/5 bed examples.

In the NW, **Wingate Rd, Wellesley Avenue** and **Dorville Crescent** fringe the Ravenscourt Park conservation area and are seen by their residents as being part of Ravenscourt Park: these very pretty streets contain early Victorian terraced houses (4/5-beds, c. £525,000) or villas with many a desirable feature. And buyers, especially young couples, are still willing to pay a premium for 2-bedroom cottagey homes, with larger houses and those in the conservation area going for considerably more. Demand from the BBC in Shepherd's Bush – more prosperous BBC people have moved out from Central London – underscores the popularity of this area.

Ravenscourt Park

To the west of Brackenbury, on the Chiswick border, this neighbourhood is bounded by **Goldhawk Rd, King St** and **Paddenswick Rd**. Ravenscourt Park has a laid-back, suburban feel to it, more reminiscent of Chiswick's wide open spaces across the borough border than of densely-packed Hammersmith. This area and Brook Green (see below) are neck and neck in the desirability stakes, but Ravenscourt Park has a definite edge thanks to houses that include some that are not only more substantial in size, but detached.

Most of it falls within a conservation area centred around Ravenscourt Park itself, formerly the grounds of a fine 18th-century house, which was bombed during the war. All that is left now are delightful gardens and formal lake, a pretty coach house (used as tea-rooms) and rather splendid gates. There are also a number of leisure facilities (including tennis courts) available for the locals to use. The park itself is geared to children, which is not surprising: until now it has had Queen Charlotte's, one of London's foremost maternity hospitals, alongside.

There are not that many homes in this area – but this is likely to change, since much land is taken up for the Queen Charlotte's complex. The hospital is, however, scheduled to move in the near future to a new site in Du Cane Rd in Shepherd's Bush, and outline planning permission has been given for a mix of homes, including affordable housing, to replace it: detailed plans will go before the council later this year. The vast Royal Masonic Hospital site, which stands between the park and Queen Charlotte's, has already re-emerged as a clutch of 870 sq ft, 2-bed, 2-bath flats, completed in 1998.

For the moment, however, look for pockets of charming 18th- and 19th-century villas and terraces (**Ravenscourt Park, Ravenscourt Gardens, Hamlet Gardens**) in this leafy corner, and a rather pretty square (**Ravenscourt Park Square**) which has some lovely houses on three sides – the fourth side opens to the park. There are also homes backing onto the park – for example along **Goldhawk Rd** and **Ravenscourt Rd** – with prices that can sail over £800,000 for 4-bed detached houses. In the latter road, a row of half a dozen houses opposite Queen Charlotte's, await redevelopment.

On the fringes of Ravenscourt Park, it is worth looking at **Wingate Rd, Dorvill Crescent** (where a 5-bed home can fetch £525,000) and **Wellesley Avenue**; and to the N, on the other side of the **Goldhawk Rd** (but still in the conservation area), **Ashchurch Park Villas**, **Rylett Rd** and **Ashchurch Grove, Minden Rd** and **Ashchurch Terrace** (see also Shepherd's Bush chapter). Further towards Chiswick, St Mary's Court is a converted church, where original stonework meets parking-space-and-entryphone: £182,500 for a 1-bed abode, last winter.

Brook Green

Strictly speaking 'Brook Green' consists only of pretty **Brook Green** itself (a conservation area), plus the small network of roads leading immediately off either side of it – **Blythe Rd** is the obvious divide to the E. But the term is often used to describe an entire area that stretches as far N as **Minford Gardens/Sinclair Gardens** and as far E as **Sinclair Rd**, which runs alongside the railway line down to Olympia. It is one of the biggest residential parking zones in the borough, covering the streets to the N of **Hammersmith Rd** to Shepherd's Bush Green, from the Hammersmith & City line to the W and the railway line to the E.

Brook Green proper, despite its rather smaller houses and location just off the less than inspiring **Shepherd's Bush Rd**, is every bit as popular with house- and apartment-hunters as Ravenscourt Park. The scattered family houses in **Brook Green** (the road) overlooking the green itself are splendid, often leafily secluded and highly prized (and priced: a 5-bed house, c. £800,000). They also get access to the green's tennis courts. There's also a mansion block, Queen's Mansions, in which a 2-bed top floor flat with the attraction of an original artists' studio recently came on the market at £305,000. Two smart modern developments are tucked in off the **Hammersmith Rd** end of **Brook Green** (the road): **Windsor Way** is a group of 200 top-of-the-market houses and flats; Oxford Gate has 3-storey town-houses behind electric gates: a 4-bed/3-bath/garage/garden/balcony example, £650,000.

Look next at the peaceful network of little streets to the S, tucked into the triangle between the green, **Shepherd's Bush Rd** and **Hammersmith Rd**. A closer inspection of the homes in streets like **Rowan Rd** and **Bute Gardens** can prove them to be deceptively big, wider than average and particularly pleasant. **Rowan Terrace** is a tiny close of cottages. A one-way system protects this enclave from through traffic.

Back across the green, the streets running off to the N have tall redbrick and stucco terraces – a good hunting-ground for flats – interspersed with some smaller Victoriana. **Blythe Rd**, which curls through from **Shepherd's Bush Rd** to **Hammersmith Rd** to enclose the Brook Green enclave, has a mix of Victorian and later houses (a 1980s terrace of 4-bed houses boast 3 baths plus garages, but also gables in a graceful nod to 19th-century neighbours). Other, older homes have been refurbished or extended; houses here can thus cost c.£400–750,000 or so. At the **Hammersmith Rd** end of **Blythe Rd** stands Kensington West, an 8-storey, luxury 1989 apartment block with its own sports complex. Lots of flats to rent in the 1- to 4-bed homes of the big 1930s Latymer Court mansion block (complete with porter and ornate cage lift) on **Hammersmith Rd**: rents c. £200–400 pw includes heating and hot water.

The Brook Green borders area between **Blythe** and **Sinclair Rds** (I seem to remember 'Blythe village' being touted as a name for it in the '80s) is a great hunting-ground for BBC workers: it too contains many larger terraced houses, frequently converted into 1- and 2-bed flats. They often have semi-basement or garden-level flats, which have the advantage of Victorian-sized back gardens, often with mature trees. In some cases, semi-basement and ground floors combine to make good maisonettes. High-ceilinged rooms with ornate plasterwork on the ground floors are attractive features. Look out for property in **Addison Gardens**, **Bolingbroke Rd**, **Lakeside Rd**, **Irving Rd**, **Hofland Rd** and **Milson Rd** (prices for a whole 3-bed house in **Bolingbroke**, £395,000, and a 5-bed £650,000, last winter; a grand 2-bed, split-level, patio'd flat, £270,000). **Ceylon Rd** has some modern town-houses: 4-bed, 2-bath, garage (and well over half a million pounds). Needless to say, homes on the E side of **Sinclair Rd**, which back onto the tracks, are not so popular with insomniac buyers. But, apart from properties which are bang next to the railway, the Olympia corner is in no less demand than is any other part of Hammersmith.

Crabtree

This neighbourhood takes its name from the 1911 Crabtree Estate, a small grid of streets running N from **Crabtree Lane** on the Fulham borders between the river and **Fulham Palace Rd**, up to **Hammersmith Bridge Rd**. Apart from the Estate, this corner – particularly the riverside itself – used to be predominantly industrial, but more and more homes (some in exceedingly smart new developments) have appeared as the industry receded. Leading the new-build is the Richard Rogers-designed Thames Reach complex, whose living rooms have floor-to-ceiling glass on the riverside, giving them wide, uninterrupted views across to Barnes Waterside (the nature reserve and up-market housing estate), and the picturesque Harrods Depository building, now also flats. The River Café is next door ... Along the Thames path modern maisonettes in purpose-built blocks on **Wingate Rd** can be had for around £250,000 for 2-beds plus garden; but the best balconied Thames Reach flats can fetch up to double the price (around £350,000) of one of the 3-bed Crabtree houses.

As well as the famous River Café, this corner also holds the splendid Riverside Studios arts and performance centre. Another Thames-side scheme lies next door: Chancellor's Wharf is a £10 million 1990 vintage development of eight 5-storey town-houses and 32 flats in **Crisp Rd**, just downstream from the bridge. These, in the words of the developers, boast 'dramatic brick-clad elevations, slightly nautical in appearance, with large porthole windows'.

Transport	Tubes: Hammersmith (zone 2, Piccadilly, Hammersmith & City, District), West Kensington (zone 2, District), Barons Court (zone 2, Piccadilly, District). See also map. From Hammersmith: Oxford Circus 25 min (1 change), City 35 min (1 change), Heathrow 40 min.
Convenient for	Heathrow via M4, roads to the West. Miles from centre: 4.
Schools	Local Authority: Phoenix High, St Edmund's, Sacred Heart (g). Private: St Paul's (g), Godolphin & Latymer (g), Latymer (b).

SALES

Flats	S	1B	2B	3B	4B	5B
Average prices	80–100	140–180	150–250+	250–350	300+	—

Houses	2B	3B	4B	5B	6/7B	8B
Average prices	265–350+	300–400	350–600	500+	700–1 M+	—

RENTAL

Flats	S	1B	2B	3B	4B	5B
Average prices	120–150	200–300	240–400	400+	—	—

Houses	2B	3B	4B	5B	6/7B	8B
Average prices	300–350	300–450	400–600	500–750	900–1500	—

H

The properties	Close-packed Victorian terraces predominate – but also pockets of beautiful earlier riverside homes, handsome houses in leafy corners, mansion blocks, some smart new flats and houses. Many converted flats. Thames-side industrial swept away by luxury new developments towards Fulham border.
The market	BBC workforce and City commuters look for homes here. Riverside houses scarce and expensive. Good location (tubes, M4 to airport) and BBC HQ in nearby Shepherd's Bush make this a hunting-ground for both flats and family houses. Local searches: 10 working days.

Among those estate agents active in this area are:

- Barnard Marcus
- Marsh & Parsons
- Bushells
- Lawsons
- FPDSavills
- Knight Frank
- Wilmotts
- Foxtons *

- Winkworth *
- Finlay Brewer *
- Northfields *
- Austin d'Arcy
- Sturgis
- Quintons
- Latymers

further details: see advertisers' index on p671

HAMPSTEAD

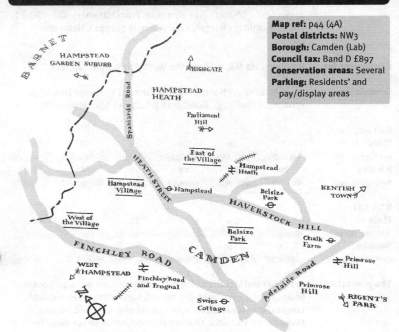

Map ref: p44 (4A)
Postal districts: NW3
Borough: Camden (Lab)
Council tax: Band D £897
Conservation areas: Several
Parking: Residents' and
pay/display areas

'Buyers now' said a Hampstead agent last winter 'have proper money'. By
this he means not over-burdened with mortgage needs, and in command of ample
ready cash. They will need plenty of money, proper or not, and it will need to be at
their fingertips, for sellers are scarce here and would-be buyers are legion.

Since around 1985 Hampstead has gained more than its fair share of London's
lavish new flats and security-conscious, multi-bathroomed houses. Their inhabitants
add to a community that deserves its reputation for prosperous intellectualism.
Hardly a writer of note is published who does not live here, or on its shores – though
the pressure on the intelligentsia's pockets has become intense as the merely
wealthy have come after a share of the Hampstead charm.

There is, nevertheless, still a strong community feeling about the way Hampstead
looks. Residents fought the advent of a McDonalds by means of a heavily supported
campaign, although the burger chain finally won – after a 12-year battle. And any
attempt to touch as much as a sapling on Hampstead Heath is fiercely resisted.
Equally, any planning issue, from a conservatory to a block of flats, faces scrutiny
from an informed and vocal public. Once roused, the Hampstead intellectuals are a
force to be reckoned with.

Hampstead dates back a thousand years to 986 AD, when King Ethelred the
Unready gave the old Saxon 'homestead' to the monks of Westminster. Later, the
village was to become a fashionable spa resort in the 17th and 18th centuries, a
popular retreat in the 19th century, and today a prime residential area, the main
attractions of this essentially Georgian village being its elevation above the smog of
the city, and its proximity to the famous 800 acres of Hampstead Heath.

If Hampstead has a drawback it is traffic congestion and parking. Nearly every corner of Camden borough has or soon will have residents' parking schemes, and the council is keen to discourage school-run traffic and other car movements it deems unnecessary. Two-car families (probably the majority) face the threat of being denied street parking permits if their home has off-road parking.

Hampstead today is up in the top handful of London residential areas: as an agent put it, quizzed on where was best, 'Hampstead is good roads surrounded by better roads.' Recent years have seen Hampstead very much a sellers' market with demand far outstripping supply, resulting in property price rises probably not matched in any but the most exclusive areas of Central London. Prices went up 20% in 1999 – and that's a percentage of some very hefty sums. Mortgage rate increases had no discernible effect.

Hampstead has everything the modern affluent want: the Heath, smart shops, good restaurants, reasonable transport – Northern Line to City and West End – excellent schools and smart, characterful, high-specification homes.

It is a popular area to rent in, with 70 per cent of the tenants – and quite a few of the landlords – foreign. The American School down the hill in St John's Wood generates a regular flow of families – there are never enough family homes to let, say agents – and international business people fill up the 2-bed flats.

Hampstead Village

Few visit Hampstead Village without wanting to live there, the only constraint being the failure of the lottery numbers to come up. The choice ranges from wide, leafy avenues with imposing detached mansions to picturesque, almost medieval lanes, squares and cul-de-sacs. The place is packed with a fascinating variety of homes dating back 300 years and more – many with historical and literary connections.

The population still contains a remarkably high proportion of artists, writers, actors, musicians, diplomats and professionals, and the shopping centre reflects the cosmopolitan flavour of the area with many fashion boutiques, specialist food shops, bookshops, restaurants of all descriptions and some celebrated pubs, like the Flask and the Hollybush. Difficult to buy a needle and thread here, though.

From **Hampstead High St**, streets like **Gayton Rd** and **Flask Walk** lead to the old spa area where roads named **Well Rd** and **Well Walk** reflect the history. Here, too, is Burgh House, the Grade I listed mansion built in 1702, now a community centre, art gallery and local history museum. The Everyman cinema in **Holly Bush Vale** went bust after an expensive re-fit last year, but is being rescued. Houses in this area are mainly

Georgian, Edwardian and Victorian terraces, the majority of which have been converted into flats. But there are still the occasional large and medium-sized detached and semi-detached houses in secluded streets like **New End, Cannon Place** and **Christchurch Hill**, where you'll find the New End Theatre. All the prices, however, reflect the area's proximity (across **East Heath Rd**) to Hampstead Heath. You will be asked £700,000 for a 3-bed cottage, and £900,000 for a 4-bed house. Particularly attractive is the **Gainsborough Gardens** private estate, off **Well Walk**, a ring of houses on its own circular access road. Mansion block flats in The Pryors and Bell Moor, literally overlooking the heath, are also reckoned an excellent investment. Look out, too, for terraced houses and flats in the **Vale of Health**, an exclusive enclave on the heath itself. Once known as Hatche's Bottom, the land was drained in 1777 and a few houses are Georgian. A new traffic scheme in this area has dramatically reduced rat-running and infuriated car-borne commuters.

The other main road through the village is **Heath St** leading, on the N side, to the upper part of the old town, with beautiful houses in tightly packed squares such as **Golden Yard** and **The Mount Square**, and delightful secluded streets including **Windmill Hill**, **Hampstead Grove** and **Admiral's Walk**, with its unusually shaped houses with naval names.

The potential for new homes schemes of any size is limited by the extreme scarcity of available land, with nearly all the new homes of the last decade resulting from the conversion or replacement of redundant public buildings like hospitals and colleges. The old New End Hospital in **Heath St** became flats in 1998; last year saw the marketing of 60 flats and penthouses converted from the old Mount Vernon Hospital in **Frognal Rise**, in the heart of the Village. Prices started at £200,000 for a studio, rising to £2.5 million for a penthouse. All were sold by the start of 2000.

Heath St leads, on the S side, to the splendid terraces (some Queen Anne) in **Church Row**, past the ancient St John's Parish Church and **Frognal Gardens**, to **Frognal** – one of the oldest roads in Hampstead, and the site of University College School. A 2-bed flat in Frognall Gardens was £450,000 last autumn. There are some magnificent hidden properties in this area: a 2-bed Queen Anne house was sold for £1 million last winter. Further S are the very large houses in **Fitzjohns Avenue**, many of which have been converted into schools, hotels and clinics. A penthouse in one of the surviving domestic buildings commanded £1 million last winter. **Maresfield Gardens** also has large houses, the Freud Museum in the house where Sigmund Freud died in 1939, and UCS's sister school South Hampstead High. Some of these homes are now luxury flats. **Thurlow Rd** will gain 10 flats through the demolition of an old peoples' home.

West of the Village

These are the quiet, tree-lined avenues, bounded by **West Heath Rd, Platts Lane**, **Finchley Rd** and **Arkwright Rd**, which have attracted so much attention from developers as it becomes more and more difficult for individual families to maintain large Victorian mansions. Luxury flat conversions have been flowing in a steady stream in this area since the mid-'80s, and quite a few new homes – houses and flats – have either replaced, or been squeezed in between, the surviving mansions.

At the top of the heath on **North End Way**, the enormous Inverforth House, built as a single mansion, is now homes once more after a career as a hospital. Three of the nine vast homes into which it's been split – flats is the wrong word – were on the market last winter at prices between £2.25 million and £2.75 million.

Up on Hampstead's northern edge, close to the Spaniards Inn, is **Spaniards Rd**, where £15 million will buy you a 15,000 sq ft house.

Examples of the upper-tier apartment blocks include Heath Park Gardens, 13 flats overlooking the heath on the corner of **Templewood Avenue** and **West Heath Rd**.

Living rooms resemble football pitches, averaging around 45 x 30 ft, and all the flats share a private swimming pool – except for the 6,000 sq ft duplex apartment which has its own. Similarly luxurious is Summit Lodge in **Upper Terrace** next to Whitestone Pond which, at 440 ft above sea level, is the highest point in London. There are 12 large flats (some around 2,800 sq ft), also sharing a swimming pool complex. The top flats have unbeatable 360-degree views of the capital from the roof.

The best bet for someone looking for a new home in Hampstead this year could be the big new Westfield College scheme in 4 acres of land on **Kidderpore Avenue** where 145 flats are being released in phases until March 2001. About half were sold by January 2000, but others remain at from £240,000 for a 1-bed flat up to £1.4 million. If you prefer period, a 3-bed coach house in the same road was £600,000 last winter.

The biggest Hampstead houses – some positively ambassadorial – are in **West Heath Rd**, opposite the West Heath, all with price tags around £2 million. Most remarkable, near the junction with **Platts Lane**, is 'Sarum Chase', which Pevsner described as 'unashamed Hollywood Tudor'. These were joined in 1999 by eight new houses in **Eden Terrace**, just off **West Heath Rd**, which sold from £2.75 million to £2.9 million.

But there are also houses of all sizes and in all conditions in roads such as **Redington Gardens, Heath Drive, Hollycroft Avenue, Ferncroft Avenue, Templewood Avenue** and **Greenaway Gardens**, some with very large gardens. **Chesterford Gardens** has a particularly fine terrace of houses, as does **Redington Rd**, an extremely graceful curving street which links **West Heath Rd** with **Frognal**. You can pay £900,000 for a 3-bed garden flat in **Redington Rd**, though half that will buy the less opulent ones. The award-winning Firecrest development, between **West Heath Rd** and **Templewood Avenue**, has exciting modern houses and flats on a beautiful, wooded site. The two largest houses have their own basement pools.

These roads have easy access to **Finchley Rd** which runs N to connect with the M1 and A1, and S through St John's Wood and Regent's Park to the West End. Bus services along the **Finchley Rd** are good and it's a short hop to Golders Green or Finchley Rd tubes – and to the new O2 shopping/cinema complex on the **Finchley Rd**.

East of the Village

South of **Willow Rd** is a district of pleasant Victorian terraced roads, now almost exclusively converted into flats and maisonettes, though the odd entire house does come onto the market. Down the hill is what is sometimes known as the Downshire Hill triangle, comprising **Downshire Hill**, **Keats Grove** and **South End Rd**. This is one of the most elegant (and sought-after) areas in Hampstead. **Downshire Hill** has a pleasing number of stuccoed brick houses dating from the early 19th century, the majority of which have remained as single-family houses. They are nearly all listed, and as a group they are listed Grade II as being of 'considerable merit'. One was on the market for £1.4 million last autumn. **Keats Grove** contains lovely Keats House, now a public library and museum.

Further down the hill is villagey **South End Green**, with its shops and cafés, Hampstead Heath rail station (N London line, Silverlink) and a three-screen cinema. Here, too, is **Pond St** and the giant, modern, Royal Free Hospital.

Also off **South End Green** is the attractive enclave of streets, reached only via **South Hill Park**, which juts out into the heath at the foot of Parliament Hill. It holds a mixture of family houses and flat conversions, as well as a few post-war blocks of flats in **Parliament Hill** (the road). Two 4-bed houses in **Tanza Rd** were new in 1999. The great attraction here is the lack of through traffic and the instant access to the heath and hill. Most popular are the houses on the N side of **South Hill Park** which overlook the Hampstead Ponds.

There is a very attractive group of streets bounded by **Fleet Rd, Constantine Rd**

Savernake Rd, and Mansfield Rd, known as the Mansfield Road Conservation Area. It is surrounded by busy roads but is virtually free of traffic – and it has direct access to Hampstead Heath across a footbridge. This used to be thought of as the cheaper end of Hampstead, as it borders Gospel Oak and Kentish Town, but in the last year price rises have been greater in percentage terms than up the hill. These streets still have the coveted NW3 postcode. Many of the houses have been split into flats, but a few 4-storey houses remain intact: one in Courthorpe Rd which was £250,000 in the mid-'80s was under offer at £700,000 in December. Family houses in Rona Rd, Estelle Rd and Shirlock Rd go for £500–600,000.

Also interesting are Parkhill Rd, Upper Park Rd and Lawn Rd, which have a mixture of flat conversions, family houses and some modern council estates. The architecturally famous 1930s Isokon Flats block is in Lawn Rd; built in the Bauhaus style, it was originally designed for artists and musicians and is now owned by Camden Council.

Belsize Park

Originally from the French 'Bel Assis' ('beautifully situated'), Belsize Park was once regarded as the less desirable end of Hampstead, but now has a character and atmosphere all its own. It has two shopping centres, around the Belsize Park underground station in Haverstock Hill, and in what has become known as 'Belsize Village' in Belsize Lane which has some attractive mews. The population density is high, and the streets are very congested, but the architecture is charming and the typical Belsize Park flat will have generous-sized rooms and gloriously high ceilings. But like everywhere in Hampstead, family-sized houses are now very scarce indeed.

The dominant road is Belsize Avenue, which runs from Haverstock Hill across to the Swiss Cottage end of the suburb. On the N side are the roads that lead up to the graceful, tree-lined Lyndhurst Gardens and Wedderburn Rd. On the S side are Belsize Park, Belsize Park Gardens and Belsize Square. A 5-bed Victorian house in Belsize Crescent, off Belsize Lane, was on the market for £1.8 million last autumn. Also interesting are 'The Glens' – Glenloch Rd, Glenilla Rd and Glenmore Rd, only a minute or two's walk from the tube.

Englands Lane has a very useful shopping centre, convenient to the large houses in Steeles Rd (home of several film stars), where homes regularly sell for well over £1 million. There are interesting terraces in secluded Primrose Gardens, and some new town-houses in Antrim Rd. Haverstock Hill itself has a good selection of purpose-built blocks of flats, some of which are quite modern.

Swiss Cottage

Long-standing Central European residents wistfully remember the days when Swiss Cottage was known as Schweizerhof, and they whiled away the hours drinking coffee and eating pastries in Viennese cafés like Louis. But the street market disappeared, they built a business complex, and the area lost most of its student party atmosphere and became a sharply contrasting area divided between those who use the community centre and City/estate agent types. Conservation area status has enhanced the appeal.

Swiss Cottage took its name from the original Regency chalet-style tavern: this architectural oddity has been perpetuated by a more recent pub and restaurant complex opposite the tube station (Jubilee line). It also has one of the best libraries in the country, a hotel, a six-screen cinema and close proximity to the thriving **Finchley Rd** shopping centre – and the new O2 complex (see West Hampstead chapter).

After about 30 years of dithering, something is to be done with the Swiss Cottage civic centre site, which at present takes in the library and the 1960s swimming pool/sports centre. The latter is to go, and a new one will be built, financed by a big development of some hundreds of flats. The new sports centre will be between **Adelaide Rd** and **Winchester Rd**. The idea is that a £10 million theatre for the Hampstead Theatre Club will complete the scheme – if Lottery money can be obtained. Four developers are competing to build the flats and more details are expected during 2000.

Much of the area – some 243 acres – was once owned by Eton College which was also responsible for a great deal of the housing development. The estate still owns a great deal of property in the area, particularly in roads like **Eton Avenue, Fellows Rd, Provost Rd** and **King Henry's Rd**. There are still large detached Victorian houses here, but most are subdivided into flats. The area gained over 100 modern flats and townhouses in the Quadrangles development, between **Adelaide** and **Fellows Rds**. Typical prices are £650,000 for a 4-bed garden flat, £400,000 for a 3-bed flat.

The district is also characterized by a number of council estates and tower block developments, as well as a number of large privately owned mansion blocks, including Regency Lodge in **Avenue Rd**, and Northways in **College Crescent**. There are some beautiful houses in the broad sweep of **Elsworthy Rd**, but the street does suffer a little from being an unofficial traffic through-route from Primrose Hill to St John's Wood. Some of the houses on the N side share a magnificent common garden with houses in **Wadham Gardens**.

Transport	Tubes: Hampstead (zone 2/3), Belsize Park (zone 2), both Northern line. From Hampstead: Oxford Circus 20 min (1 change), Bank 25 min, Heathrow 1 hr 10 min (1 change). Trains: Hampstead Heath, Primrose Hill, both North London line/Silverlink. To Liverpool St: 20 min.
Convenient for	Hampstead Heath; M1, A1 to North. Miles from centre: 4.
Schools	Local Authority: Hampstead School, Haverstock School. Private: University College School (b), South Hampstead High School (g), The Hall School (b).

SALES

Flats	S	1B	2B	3B	4B	5B
Average prices	80–150	150–295	200–550	250–900	300–1 M+	500–3.5 M

Houses	2B	3B	4B	5B	6/7B	8B
Average prices	250–650	325–800+	500–1 M+	750–3 M+	1.5–3.5 M+	2–10 M

RENTAL

Flats	S	1B	2B	3B	4B	5B
Average prices	150–220	180–375	275–500	350–750	500–750+	700–1500
Houses	2B	3B	4B	5B	6/7B	8B
Average prices	360–650	400–1000	450–1600	550–2000	750–3500	900–4000

The properties   Georgian gems in heart of Village and scattered among the surrounding gracious streets. New developments, generally towards the heath, are luxury-level: some innovative, some merely opulent. Victoriana reasserts itself down the hill towards Belsize Park.

The market   Everyone wants to live here. Prices rise, with the hill, to ultra-luxury level homes around the heath: figures above reflect the wide spread of quality. Houses (and even flats) inclined to sprout swimming pools etc. Local searches: 7–10 working days.

Among those estate agents active in this area are:

- Anscombe & Ringland *
- Knight Frank
- Foxtons *
- Behr & Butchoff *
- Day Morris
- Glentree

- Goldschmidt Howland
- Benham & Reeves
- Talisman Wayne
- Faron Sutaria
- Chestertons
- Naylius McKenzie

- FPDSavills
- Hamptons
- Parkheath
- Alan Charles
- Heywoods
- Keith Cardale

* further details: see advertisers' index on 671

HAMPSTEAD GARDEN SUBURB

Map ref: p27 (6K)
Postal districts: NW11, N2
Boroughs: Barnet – (Lib
  Dem/Lab Coalition)
Council tax: Band D £760
Conservation areas:
  Whole area
Parking: Free

At the birth of the 20th century, a woman had a philanthropic dream. The result was a model village — known across North West London simply as 'The Suburb' — gathered at the head of its own extension of Hampstead Heath.

Leafy Hampstead Garden Suburb is still a place apart, though the farmland which once surrounded it has long since vanished under a sea of brick. It remains that way in large part thanks to the ministrations of the HGS Trust, which keeps a strong regulatory eye on things. It lies just to the north of the Hampstead golf course and the Hampstead Heath extension, across the **Finchley Rd** from Golders Green. The Trust provides a map with the boundaries of the area clearly marked, though less punctilious estate agents claim swathes of Golders Green and East Finchley as 'HGS borders'.

Hampstead Garden Suburb was built at the beginning of the 20th century; it was carefully designed by architects Parker, Unwin and Lutyens, but the inspiration was Dame Henrietta Barnett's. Her dream was for it to be an area where people of all classes, conditions and ages would co-exist happily in beautiful tree-lined streets, with woods and open spaces available to all.

Consequently you find a great variety of type and style of housing in the area, from the terraced cottages around **Erskine Hill** and **Hampstead Way** (where 'artisans' were to live) to the double-fronted mansions of **Winnington Rd**, built later for those who didn't need to work quite so hard. Baillie Scott's purpose-built block, Waterlow Court in **Heath Close**, was originally intended for that then strange phenomenon, the working woman.

Alas, Dame Henrietta would find that few indeed of the deserving poor dwell here today, though the fabric of her model suburb remains virtually unchanged.

H

Few corners of London have seen a more frenetic housing market in the past year than The Suburb: agents report they have 10 home-seekers for every property on their books, and price records have been broken only to be smashed within the month. European buyers are to the fore at the upper end of the market. One house in **Meadway** was sold three times in the space of 10 months, the price rising 20% in that time. Even the 'artisan cottages' are nudging half a million. Local agents describe these as 'ideal for first-time buyers' and observe that many of these buyers are the children of local families who stay within the area.

The Suburb was once viewed as being inhabited largely by eccentrics – 'crazy, freakish people', observed *The Times*, not mincing matters. It is very different from Hampstead across the heath, and it was designed to be. When a careless journalist accorded government Minister Peter Mandelson a Hampstead childhood, his old teacher from Hampstead Garden Suburb Infants' School was careful to set the record straight in a letter to the *Telegraph*. Today the Suburb's residents are much like those in the rest of North West London – though probably rather richer. There are many Jewish inhabitants, and also Americans and South Africans who love the feeling of space here. In the last few years the inhabitants have changed, with most of the old founding families now gone and a younger age-group moving in.

Despite several years of heated argument, the issue of the North London 'eruv' is still not settled. The eruv is a notional boundary within which Sabbath laws will be relaxed for Orthodox Jews. The largely notional boundaries would be defined by existing features such as gardenwalls and the M1 motorway, etc, but gaps or 'gateways' would be spanned by wires strung between poles. It will cover much of the Suburb as well as Golders Green and parts of Hendon. Planning permission was given by Barnet in 1988, but the council is still working through a huge document outling detailed conditions for each and every one of the 80 poles. Go-ahead is expected this year. Estate agents at one time predicted an influx of Orthodox property buyers, but some now feel it will make no difference.

Market Place, along the **Falloden Way**, provides some (expensive) shopping and a welter of estate agents, but you have to go down to Golders Green/Temple Fortune or up to East Finchley for most things. There's a well-concealed post office along **Lyttelton Rd**, a library, schools, churches, a synagogue and – the Suburb's pride and joy – the Institute on **Central Square**, which is as old as the Suburb itself. Founded in the spirit of self-improvement, it's where you can take courses in everything from photography to pottery and where your au pair (this is very much au pair country) can learn English.

Suburb residents tend to stay once they've lived in the area for a while, and there are always people looking to move in. It's an estate agent's dream. The houses, particularly those in the Old Suburb or NW11 area, really are 'full of character'. The major roads are wide and tree-lined, and hedges rather than fences divide the plots. Little secluded closes suit those who prefer more privacy. Living in the Suburb means you're close to Kenwood House and the heath for summer walks and concerts, yet you are just five miles from the centre of London, combining the advantages of both town and country.

When it comes to disadvantages the major one, apart from the price of property, is transport. Neither Golders Green nor East Finchley stations are close by and those who don't drive or have access to a car are apt to feel stranded. There are no amenities for teenagers in the Suburb itself, though the area is great for small children. The Suburb mini-buses, the H2 and H3 'Hopper', run a circular tour from Golders Green station – prospective buyers might invest 50p on a round trip to see the area. Ask the driver to stop when you see a house you like the look of; he'll halt anywhere along his route.

Parking in the Old Suburb, which is full of closes and cul-de-sacs, can be problematic – particularly as few of the houses were built with garages. Residents in **Willifield Way** often have to resort to parking on the pavement, much to the fury of Barnet Council officials. Residents were not intended to have carriages or cars – especially the 'contented artisans' the founders hoped would populate the Suburb alongside the middle classes. A number of traffic calming measures have recently been introduced in busy **Meadway** among other roads.

Depending on which way you look at it, another possible disadvantage of the area is that it is a conservation area and you have to apply to the Trust (862 Finchley Rd, NW11 6AB) as well as to Barnet borough before making any alterations to your property down to painting the front door – even if you own the freehold. Wily residents in need of extra living space have been known to develop very luxurious 'garages'.

On the other hand, you can be sure that the character of the area and the price of property in it won't be massacred by unscrupulous types or those with a penchant for modern, incongruous architecture. Indeed, many of the houses are listed Grade II as being of significant architectural and historical importance – and many of them are 'starred' listings. In 1997 there was a mass listing of a further batch of more than 500 houses in the Suburb that had not been listed before, and many already listed were given a star. This was the result of years of pressure by the Hampstead Garden Suburb Trust on English Heritage and the Government. Most residents were delighted by the decision.

NW11, the Old Suburb

The area around Big and Little Woods and around **Central Square** and **Meadway** is known as the Old Suburb, although it is actually not that much older than the New. Generally, it covers the NW11 part of the Suburb, where the houses – built between 1907 and 1914 – are full of character and are more expensive.

Central Square, designed by Lutyens, is the heart of the suburb; a very green and peaceful centre, where you'll find neo-Georgian terraced houses and flats at prices guaranteed to give you sleepless nights. Here, too, you'll find the parish church of St Jude, the Free Church for Non-Conformist worshippers and the Institute which also accommodates the Henrietta Barnett School for Girls. In the corner of **North Square** is a Meeting House for the Society of Friends and in **South Square**, opposite St Jude's Church, is a purpose-built block of flats. There's a memorial to Dame Henrietta on the fourth side of the square, and one of the Suburb's many passageways (the aim was to keep pedestrian and motor traffic separate) leads down to **Willifield Way**. This is possibly the most charming road in the area, with a village green which is overlooked by Fellowship House where the over-60s meet. Many of the Suburb's younger residents attend the Garden Suburb School which is also in **Willifield Way**.

If your taste is for a cottage with roses round the door, then the roads around **Willifield Way** are where you should look. The first cottages to be built in the Suburb were at Nos 140 and 142 **Hampstead Way** in 1907. They were designed by Parker and Unwin who were strongly influenced by the Arts and Crafts movement, hence the traditional East Anglian cottages with medieval German vernacular gable, dormers and wood window frames. Particularly charming are **Erskine Hill** and **Asmuns Hill** where you'll find 2- and 3-bed cottages with pretty gardens.

The cottages are favourites with the more affluent sort of young couple (local agents still reckon them suitable for first-time buyers . . .) and with older people. **The Orchard**, nearby, is still inhabited by elderly residents, just as Dame Henrietta intended – though the original homes have been rebuilt. **Addison Way**, where the cottages and purpose-built maisonettes have slightly less character, leads into **Falloden Way**, the busy A1, where prices are lower because of the noise. Still, if you're immune to traffic or want to save money, these houses have lovely views over **Northway Gardens** where there are tennis courts. **Market Place** has flats above the shops and some purpose-built maisonettes tucked away on the **Ossulton Way** side, but these can be noisy, too.

Cross over the **Falloden Way** and you're on the 'wrong' side of the Suburb, although the roads are just as pretty and cottages in **Westholm**, **Midholm** and **Eastholm** (the names indicate how carefully planned the Suburb was) and in **Brookland Rise** are decidedly desirable. **Hill Top**, **Maurice Walk** and **Midholm Close** all have purpose-built maisonettes, usually with their own gardens.

Back in the main part of the Suburb, **Oakwood Rd** links **Addison Way** with **Northway** and the New Suburb. The road used to be something of a rat-run until speed bumps were built to dissuade motorists from using it as a short-cut.

South of **Central Square** is **Meadway**, the Suburb's main thoroughfare which leads from **Hoop Lane** and Golders Green. Meadway Court, a mansion block, lies on the N side of the road, and leading off on the S side are the prestigious Closes, some of them private roads, where the 6- and 7-bed houses are the largest in this part of the Suburb. A 6-bed house went for £900,000 last autumn. Unless you knew they were there, you'd never come across **Linnell, Turner** or **Meadway Closes**. The same applies to **Linnell** and **Turner Drives** which both have terrific views over the Hampstead Heath extension. For splendid views – and splendid 6-bedroomed houses – look in **Wildwood Rd**, where an outlook over the heath and Hampstead Golf Course commands high prices: £2.3 million for a 6-bed house last winter. **Heathgate,** just S of Central Square, has some 6-bed houses. On the other side of the heath extension runs **Hampstead Way** where you'll find Heathcroft, a popular block not far from Golders Green station, and some splendid 5-bed, close-to-a-million houses that share coveted access to the HGS Trust-run tennis courts.

N2, the New Suburb

Suburb snobs are rather patronizing about the 'New Suburb', the N2 area, which lies E of **Ossulton** and **Kingsley Ways,** plus **Northway, Southway** and **Middleway** back in NW11. It's true that the architecture is less interesting and the area is more densely constructed, but the houses are large (and expensive), with grand gardens and plenty of space. Parking – which is difficult in the Old Suburb – is not such a problem here. Cars were considered a normal adjunct to life when the New Suburb was laid out in the 1920s and 1930s and were catered for (if not necessarily approved of) by the architects.

Holne Chase is the continuation of **Meadway** and off it run the elegant **Spencer Close** and **Neville Drive**. Houses on the 'right' side of **Neville Drive** have a splendid view of the golf course: prices between £1 million and £1.7 million. **Linden Lea** and **Norrice Lea** (where you find the Suburb synagogue) both have large family houses, often detached, and are very much in demand.

North of the noisy **Lyttelton Rd** – where popular purpose-built blocks include Widecombe Court, set back from the road – are roads like **Gurney Drive, Widecombe Way** and **Edmund's Walk**: all quiet, pretty and with the advantage of being nearer East Finchley station. Westwards, at the top of **Ossulton Way, Neale Close** is a favourite with first-time buyers and has purpose-built 2-bedroomed maisonettes kept private by hedges. Across the road, **Denison Close** has a popular block set around a pretty garden square. This northern district is reckoned better for schools than the Surburb's heart.

Fanning out from **Central Square** and counted as the New Suburb despite their NW11 postcodes, are **Northway, Middleway** and **Southway,** which are joined by **Thornton** and **Litchfield Ways**. Here you'll find large family houses with gardens to match in spacious hedge-lined roads. A house in **Bigwood Rd** was sold for £600,000 last autumn.

The most expensive roads in the Suburb are **Ingram Avenue** and **Winnington Rd**, where prices resemble telephone numbers and the detached houses are huge and (particularly in **Winnington Rd**) rather ostentatious. Agents in the area also claim the famous **The Bishops Avenue,** known with reason as 'Millionaires' Row'. It is favoured by the ultra-rich international set as much for the privacy and security that the vast (for London) 2- and 3-acre plots afford as for the houses themselves, which are imposing but undistinguished 1950s mansions. There are more Middle Eastern royals here than in Marbella. 'In the Middle East,' observes a knowledgeable estate agent, 'the Bishop's Avenue is probably the best-known road in London.' In 1991 King Fahd bought five more homes opposite his family's existing mansion – to house his guests. Lana Turner's old home went for £5.95 million last year.

Such are the Avenue's prices that developers often find it worthwhile buying one of the (relatively) modest homes in order to knock it down and build a really palatial one. This can lead to houses standing empty while planners and residents debate the details.

Transport No trains or tube, but Golders Green and East Finchley tubes are nearby. H2 and H3 buses do circular routes via Golders Green.

Convenient for Brent Cross shopping centre, Hampstead Heath, North Circular Rd. Miles from centre: 7.

Schools Barnet Education Authority: Henrietta Barnett (g), Whitefield School.

SALES

Flats	S	1B	2B	3B	4B	5B
Average prices	50–80	100–150	120–350	160–450	240–500	–

Houses	2B	3B	4B	5B	6/7B	8B
Average prices	200–350	250–750	300–1.5 M	500–3 M	600–14 M	1–14 M

RENTAL

Flats	S	1B	2B	3B	4B	5B
Average prices	120–150	150–215	180–280	250–400	350–430	–

Houses	2B	3B	4B	5B	6/7B	8B
Average prices	230–300	200–375+	350–900	550–1500	800–3000	1000–4000

H

The market Inhabitants include international and Jewish families. Radical, doctrinaire past is now a memory. Million-pound properties found on fringes of area – principally in The Bishops Avenue. These attract princes, showbiz stars and tycoons.

The properties Purpose-built turn-of-the-century suburb mixing picturesque cottages with houses of all sizes including mansion scale. A few flats. 'Old Suburb' is smaller-scale, distinguished English-picturesque. 'New' (most in N2) has less distinguished, more ostentatious larger, later houses. Local searches: 5 days.

Among those estate agents active in this area are:
- Glentree Estates
- Hotblack Dixon
- Godfrey & Barr
- Goldschmidt & Howland
- Benham & Reeves
- Foxtons *
- Chestertons
- Ellis & Co
- Kinleigh, Folkard & Hayward
- Litchfields
- Anscombe & Ringland *
- FPDSavills
- Knight Frank
- Felicity J Lord *

further details: see advertisers' index on p671

HENDON AND MILL HILL

Map ref: p26 (5D)
Postal districts: NW4,
   NW7, NW9
Borough: Barnet
   (Lib Dem/Lab Coalition)
Council tax: Band D £760
Conservation areas:
   The Burroughs, Church
   End, Mill Hill Village
Parking: Pay and display

H

Somehow Hendon seems to be the crossroads for all roads that lead somewhere else. The area is dissected by the **Hendon/Watford Way**, the **Edgware Rd**, the **A1 Great North Way** and the M1 motorway – not to mention the **North Circular Rd**, which forms an eastern boundary. Consequently, the North West London suburb of Hendon still divides into several old-style hamlets, each with their own identity. There is no real centre.

When Hendon Central tube station opened in 1923 it was surrounded by open fields – as witnessed by the 17th-century Church Farm House, still standing and today a museum. Hendon Hall in **Ashley Lane**, too, still stands – complete with the famous, but incongruous, brick columns which the renowned actor David Garrick reputedly won in a card game. He became Lord of the Manor in 1796 and rebuilt the Hall, today a select hotel. Garrick Park is the remnant of his estate.

Such rural tranquillity is hard to imagine in the busy and congested suburb today; the '30s saw a rash of speculative development – one of the biggest architects of this suburban sprawl being John Laing, whose headquarters were, and are, in Mill Hill's **Pursley Rd**. (One of Laing's award-winning designs was first used to build the Sunnyfield site, off **Lawrence St** in **Mill Hill**). Nevertheless, the area today has a wide range of amenities to offer – among them the Brent Cross shopping centre, the Copthall sports stadium, the RAF Museum and all the water-sport activities associated with the Welsh Harp.

However, the mills of God, and planners, grind slow, and after a year there is no firm resolution on plans that went to public inquiries which concern the first two of these: the final outcomes will affect neighbouring homes. First, the Copthall sports complex on **Pursley Rd** is appealing against the Secretary of State's refusal to allow it a new 10,000-seater stadium. Barnet Football Club chairman Tony Kleanthous has reapplied for a 9,999-seater one, and is saying that the club will have to leave the borough if this is refused. Second, the Brent Cross shopping centre is looking to develop new shops, more parking and continental-style cafés and bars out along the River Brent; the result of the inquiry had not been announced at time of writing, but if this goes ahead it will also mean improved transport links for the surrounding areas. A third public inquiry turned down plans for a new equestrian centre on **The Ridgeway**, Mill Hill.

Another reminder of a more spacious past has been the amount of land devoted to the forces; these days, though, it pays to remember that Ministry of Defence land may well not stay that way: more and more sites are being sold off wholly or in part for housing. The famous Hendon aerodrome (actually one of two in Hendon; the other was in **Stag Lane**) is now in part the site of the council's Grahame Park Estate. The rest of the land is now a large and ongoing development site for new homes, and the same goes for the Inglis Barracks in Mill Hill. Only some street names and the RAF Museum commemorate the aerodrome that Claude Grahame White established in 1910: it saw the first British loop-the-loop, the first parachute descent and also the first British air mail delivery, a flight from Hendon to Windsor. The law likes this corner, too: residents sleep safely in their beds since the Metropolitan Police training school is here, just off **Aerodrome Rd** – and the North West London Police HQ is up the road in Colindale.

A focal point in the area is the Victorian town hall in **The Burroughs**. Hendon is the oldest part of the Borough of Barnet, and it is fitting that it should be the political centre of the borough. Next door is a fine public library, which also lends records, tapes, videos and CDs – convenient for students at nearby Middlesex University (Hendon campus of a very split site).

The area's major talking-point of recent years, the proposed introduction of a Jewish 'eruv', was finally given planning permission in October 1998. But as the Millennium dawned Barnet council was still working through a huge document outlining detailed licencing conditions for each of the requisite poles which, joined by wires, will span the gaps, or 'gateways', in this notional boundary line. Within this boundary – which encompasses much of Hendon, Golders Green and Hampstead Garden Suburb – the strict Jewish Sabbath laws will be relaxed. Controversial even among Jewish communities, it has nevertheless attracted many Orthodox families to buy or rent here, in anticipation of the freedom to push wheelchairs and carry their children on the Sabbath.

Mill Hill – contrastingly green and pleasant, with an abundance of wide open spaces – lies to the N of Hendon. Psychologically, too, Mill Hill is further out of town, and prices can be slightly cheaper. The original village stands on a hill, and close by is Mill Hill School, built in 1807 with a splendid Classical frontage. It was here that James Murray, a master at the school, edited much of the *Oxford English Dictionary*. Established for the sons of Protestant Dissenters, the school was originally known as 'an island of nonconformity in a sea of Roman Catholicism' – there are still several notable Roman Catholic institutions here, led by St Joseph's College in **Lawrence St**. Mill Hill is also home to the Medical Research Laboratory.

Cut off from the rest of Mill Hill by the roaring **Watford Way** is **The Broadway**, a busy shopping parade with bars, boutiques, health food shops and a Marks & Spencer. The train station, Mill Hill Broadway (26 min to Moorgate, 20 min to King's Cross), is located here too, and there are also buses both to local destinations and to Central London.

Hendon

If you take a detour from the speeding roads, Hendon has homes to suit every taste, from large detached houses in **Brampton Grove**, **The Downage** and **Cedars Close** (expect to pay £600–700,000 here), to luxury retirement flats in **Church Rd**, rows of suburban terraces round **Montague Rd**, West Hendon, and quaint cottages which border the picturesque **The Burroughs**.

Turning into **The Burroughs** from the **Watford Way** is a surprise. Immediately the grey commercial buildings, which match the busy road, make way for cottages and larger old houses converted into luxurious modern flats. The old bus garage has now become a luxury office block, changing the appearance of the street. **Brampton Grove**, the first on the right, is probably Hendon's most exclusive road; a pair of new houses here fell effortlessly into the million-pound-plus bracket. Just along the road from the imposing town hall, flanked by a modern library and fire station, is the beautiful corner of Church End, which has the Norman St Mary's Church in **Greyhound Hill** as a focal point. Next door, the old Church Farm House (dating back in parts to the 17th century) is home to the borough's museum. It twice escaped the post-war bulldozers.

Between the museum and church stands the Greyhound Inn, originally the Church House and used for parish meetings. Opposite the museum, the back of the Middlesex University campus includes a fitness centre, which is open to residents. Further down **Greyhound Hill** the suburban semis are neat and tidy, just as the planners of the '30s imagined them: many with lovely green views, though the road is used as a cut-through from the **Watford Way** to **The Burroughs/Church Rd** and isn't as tranquil as it once was. A cache of new homes – flats and small houses – appeared behind **The Burroughs** on a large site, originally the back of school playing-fields, in the late '80s.

Heading down **Church Rd** (permanently congested) towards **The Quadrant**, **Sunningfields Rd** and **Sunningfields Crescent** are to your left: both pretty, both with plenty of conversions (a roomy 3-bed example, with shared garden, £185,000 last winter). Smart new flats developments grace **Sunningfields Rd**; opening prices at Cala's pleasant 1998-built King's Mount were from £180,000 for 2-bed apartments (considered on the steep side at the time, this is now fairly average for new schemes). This corner leads up to Sunny Hill Park, and also houses a private hospital. **Florence St**, just off **The Quadrant**, is a real find: not as cut off as the Sunningfields roads, it has charming little houses set along a narrow street. The corner of **The Quadrant**, once the local cinema, is now sheltered housing (the area is well supplied with homes and housing for the elderly.)

Turning left down **Parson St** brings you to some of the premier streets in Hendon: **Downage**, **Ashley Lane** and **Cedars Close** with its mock-Tudor houses set in a circle around little private gardens. **Tenterden Grove**, **Tenterden Close** and **Tenterden Gardens** are also nice, but homes at either end of **Tenterden Drive** may suffer a little from noise from the **Great North Way** (a 4-bed house here, £280,000 last winter). **Westchester Drive**, at the junction of **Parson St** and the **Great North Way**, is surprisingly unaffected by its proximity to the main roads, and has small houses and the Westchester Court flats.

Parson St itself has seen several new schemes: Bishop's Manor is this year's development, by Laing: it has 16 2-bed, 2-bath flats and four houses. At time of writing the remaining five flats were £255–295,000, the houses expected to be released at around the £600,000 mark. Glebe Court is another luxury flats development, by Berkeley Homes, which began life 18 months back at £275–450,000 (now c. £300–485,000). Across the A1 divide, more have sprouted in leafy **Holders Hill Rd**, which is the route that links Hendon with Mill Hill (see page 360).

If Hendon could be said to have a high street, then **Brent St** is probably it. Here you'll find the mini-shopping centre at **Sentinel Square**, with its revamped Tesco's and pay-and-display parking. Fashionable ciabatta-bread sandwiches have made it to Hendon in one of several new sandwich shops. (There are also many kosher eateries – including one of only two kosher Chinese restaurants in the UK.)

Bell Lane leads down towards the **North Circular**; to the left, roads like **Alexandra Rd** and **Albert Rd** have smaller semis and terraced houses. **Albert Rd** is the site of Jew's College with its fine library. To the right, **Green Lane** and the roads around have large family houses and a number of synagogues. The **Brent St** shops give way to a number of attractive '30s semis. South of **Brent St** lies the Shirehall Estate, where many of the detached and semi-detached 4/5-bed houses have delightful views over Hendon Park. **Shirehall Lane**, which runs through the middle, is however used as a shortcut by Hendon's shoppers on the Brent Cross trail. At the Golders Green end of **Brent St**, a recent block dubbed The Carltons by its developers has prices that rise, with the storeys, to half-million-plus penthouses.

Queen's Rd runs alongside the park down to Hendon Central tube station – not to mention that new health club. **Queen's Gardens** has the benefit of the park without the commuter-traffic drawback. **Queen's Rd** is very much the target for developers, both for new-build (two new flat blocks have been added in recent years) and for luxurious conversions: look in this street for spacious, bathroom-per-bedroom apartments, and expect to pay a quarter-million plus.

To the N of **Queen's Rd** lie more of Hendon's best streets. **Brampton Grove**, **Wykeham Rd** and **Raleigh Close** have large family houses. They are particularly popular with Jewish residents due to the proximity of synagogues in **Egerton Gardens** (the Yakar centre) and in **Raleigh Close** itself.

Station Rd, where you'll find the popular Highmount block, runs down from **The Burroughs** to Hendon rail station and provides a link between the **Watford Way** and the **Edgware Rd**. The grid of roads off **Vivian Avenue** have 4-bed semis, which get less expensive as you near the M1 motorway. To the S of them lies the Brent Cross shopping centre, which plans to expand yet further.

West Hendon, on the other side of the motorway, is the cheaper end of Hendon. Shopping facilities are not very good (the locals use Brent Cross) and the area, with its terraces and small semis, has a slightly run-down air. However, it is convenient for the **Edgware Rd,** leading all the way to Marble Arch, for the facilities of the Welsh Harp and for Wembley Stadium. Welsh Harp Village, in **Goldsmith Avenue** at the northern tip of the Welsh Harp Reservoir, is one of this area's most popular developments (you'll have seen it, if you remember the 'dancing milk bottles' TV ad). Its wide range of homes and prices – from studios (c. £50,000) to 3-bed (around £135,000) – attract first-time buyers.

Mill Hill

A trip to Mill Hill is in order for London house-hunters who would prefer to be in the country. It lies to the N of Hendon, from which it is cut off by the **Great North Way** (the A1) and a swathe of green open space that holds golf course, cemetery and playing-fields. The link between the two is **Holders Hill Rd**, a major hunting-ground for luxurious new homes – mainly flats, to take advantage of the views of the golf course. It sprouted four or five new blocks in the '80s, and several more in the last couple of years: look not only in the **Rd**, but also in the **Crescent**, **Gardens** and **Drive**. You can pay as much and more for the more luxurious of these as for the modest 3-bed semis that this stretch holds ,which go for c. £200–250,000. Indeed, the key to Mill Hill is the range (in size, in price, in vintage) of homes here, from humdrum flats to luxury, Surrey-style new-build, and from everyday semis to large detached double-fronted period residences that sit behind drives in leafy locations.

The road leads up towards Mill Hill East. Mill Hill has a rail station, but the tube line ends here (Mill Hill East; Northern Line) at the bottom of **Bittacy Hill** – definitely the cheaper end of Mill Hill: it doesn't venture up to the dizzy heights (in terms of both altitude and price) of **Uphill Rd**. But the E edge of Mill Hill has a popular riding school at the N end of **Frith Lane**, which seems to take in every little North London girl.

Mill Hill East is an attractive belt of suburbia with a carefully planned grid of roads. Here the semis each have their own identity with a variety of modern windows and extensions. The main avenue, **Devonshire Rd/Sanders Lane**, radiates out from **Holders Hill Circus** and overlooks Hendon golf course and Copthall playing-fields – where a planning battle over the proposal to build a new 9,999-seater stadium is awaiting the outcome of a public inquiry.

At the bottom end of **Devonshire Rd**, formerly overshadowed by huge gasometers behind **Bittacy Hill**, residents' prayers have been answered: the gasometers have gone at last, leaving another area that will see major redevelopment. The former Inglis barracks is another tranche of MoD land that has been sold off to be replaced by new homes – beginning with mainly 2-bed flats.

Moving W, you come to **Pursley Rd**, **Page St** and **Wyse Lane**. The houses here are fairly ordinary semis but, surrounded by green open spaces, they are very pleasant (John Laing added new 2- and 3-bed houses, from around £160,000, in 1998 on the site of its former headquarters). From there, climb **Milespit Hill** to **The Ridgeway**. Here, Mill Hill Village stands quiet and glorious, still with its village pond, overlooking the green fields. Not all the houses are old: a handful are 'modern architect-designed', as the estate agents say, but all are very des' res'. The **High St** belies its name: the nearest main shops are in **Mill Hill Broadway**. At **The Ridgeway** end, **Wills Grove**, which branches off to the left just before Mill Hill School, is charming, with larger houses and plenty of trees. Across **The Ridgeway**, the Belmont Farm Riding School has been refused permission for an Equestrian Centre which, locals feared, would affect traffic, and views on footpaths along Totteridge Common and Folly Brook.

In the angle of **Daws Lane** and **Hammers Lane** lies Mill Hill's 'poets' corner'. This one is a surprise, with pleasant 4- and 5-bedroom houses in roads named after literary greats such as **Tennyson, Milton** and **Shakespeare**: a 4-bed semi here was £255,000 last winter. Further along **The Ridgeway** at **Holcombe Hill**, where the Old Forge stands, lies **Lawrence St**, off which is Mill Hill's premier road, **Uphill Rd**. Home-owners in neighbouring **Sunnyfield, The Reddings, Uphill Grove** and the **Tretawn** roads have extended their houses in all directions. With spacious gardens and views over the grounds of St Joseph's College, they stand on gently undulating ground, which enhances the feeling of space that they enjoy.

Highwood Hill has larger-than-average old cottages along just one side – which therefore also have splendid views; off it, the very exclusive (and reputedly haunted) **Nan Clarke's Lane**: a home here can cost £2 million. Roads to the N of the picturesque **Marsh Lane** (which takes motorists down to the busy A1), such as **Hankins Lane** and **Glenwood Rd**, are equally pleasant up-market residential turnings. A large, recent 5-bed, 4-bath, double garage and own drive detached, built in Tudor-mansion style off **Marsh Lane** by Cala Homes was on the market for £855,000 last winter.

Back across **Watford Way** lies the area's high street: the shops and restaurants of **The Broadway**. A convenient corner, flanked by fast roads (A1, M1) and rail routes: **Flower Lane** has an estate of Georgian-style houses, and a new one, of 4-bed houses, completed in 1998 (prices were from £375,000.) **Russell Grove** and **Weymouth Avenue** are both good roads with detached houses. **Newcombe Park** is popular, too.

Transport	Tubes: Mill Hill East, Hendon Central (zone 3, Northern). From Hendon Central: Oxford Circus 30 min (1 change), City 30 min, Heathrow 1 hr 30 min (1 change). Trains: Mill Hill Broadway (King's Cross 20 min, Moorgate 26 min).
Convenient for	Brent Cross shopping centre, Yoahan Plaza Japanese shopping centre, 24-hr superstores, Copthall Sports/Swimming Centre, Welsh Harp/Brent Reservoir. A1, M1, North Circular Rd. Miles from centre: 7.
Schools	Barnet Education Authority: Copthall (g), Hasmonean (Jewish) Schools (b) & (g), Mill Hill County High, St James' High RC, St Mary's C of E. Grant Maintained: Hendon. Private: Mill Hill (b), The Mount (g).

SALES

Flats	S	1B	2B	3B	4B	5B
Average prices	50–70	70–110	120–180	150–350	–	–
Houses	2B	3B	4B	5B	6/7B	8B
Average prices	140–180	150–250	220–500+	350–600+	600–1.5 M	1 M+

RENTAL

Flats	S	1B	2B	3B	4B	5B
Average prices	90–125	130–200	180–280	200–300	250–600	–
Houses	2B	3B	4B	5B	6/7B	8B
Average prices	160–230	210–320+	250–500	300–1000	500–1000	–

The properties	The 3-bed semi of inter-war vintage is most common. An increasing number of flat conversions, plus smaller houses, including some ex-council. Some larger prestige homes and new flats.
The market	Popular for family homes: sizeable Jewish and Indian communities. Also commuting flat-dwellers, students renting and first-time buyers. Homes backing on to the main routes are cheapest. Local searches: 5 working days.

Among those estate agents active in this area are:

- Alexander Jay
- Martyn Gerrard
- Warren Bradley
- Philip Phillips
- Ellis & Co
- Bairstow Eves
- Douglas Martin
- Barnard Marcus
- Shaw & Reeves
- Seymours
- Cosway
- Culwick Lerner
- Gerald Linke & Co
- Talbots
- Winkworth *
- Karina Associates

further details: see advertisers' index on p671

HIGHGATE

Map ref: p29 (6F)
Postal districts: N6
Boroughs: Haringey (Lab),
Camden (Lab)
Council tax: Band D Camden
£897, Haringey £898
Conservation areas:
Highgate Village
Parking: Free, but residents'
parking planned for
Highgate Hill. Congested
in village

Highgate's residents claim that their village is just as nice as Hampstead – but without the noise, congestion and over-inflated property prices. Those prices, however, have been steadily catching up with NW3. Indeed, mansions with grounds and security gates are becoming as much part of Highgate as gentlemanly Georgian gems. Taking the wider area, Victorian and Edwardian homes are more common than Georgian, which are found only in the heart of the village. The 20th century added blocks of flats and suburban houses of every level from modest to opulent.

One of the old villages that command the 'northern heights' around London, Highgate has plenty of history, and considerable charm. It was on Highgate Hill that the disillusioned young Dick Whittington heard the sound of Bow Bells and was persuaded to 'turn again' to resume his progress towards becoming 'thrice Mayor of London'. The alleged spot is marked with a stone and a statue of his famous cat.

Highgate is certainly not cheap. The overflow from Hampstead continued through the '80s and '90s as the neighbouring 'village' became more and more expensive. Furthermore, the increasing buying pressure in Highgate created its own overflow areas in the rest of N6 – especially the section E of **Archway Rd** – Muswell Hill and Crouch End that, until the '80s, were fairly sleepy enclaves with relatively stable property prices.

The population is well-heeled (there are more millionaires in N6 than in NW3) and traditional, with musicians and media folk among the area's best-known residents. It is not quite as cosmopolitan as Hampstead but there are pockets of wealthy Middle

Eastern residents: the splendid Beechwood stately home in Hampstead Lane is owned by the Sultan of Oman. The vast Witanhurst mansion at the top of **Highgate West Hill** (the largest house in London – if you exclude the royal palaces) is set to become an international conference centre.

H

As well as the international set Highgate has its own, settled, population: 'a huge base of local moneyed people who move within the area,' says one agent. The recent boom has seen a new influx of buyers from down the hill in Islington, chasing safer streets, bigger houses, gardens and (perhaps most of all) excellent schools. Demand has been so great that one agent reckoned that 20 per cent of the homes in Highgate could have been sold in 1999 – if, that is, anyone wanted to sell.

Highgate shares with Hampstead the 800 acres of fields, woods and ponds of the Heath – owned and managed by the City of London Corporation – plus the grounds of Kenwood where open-air concerts are held during the summer. Kenwood, a beautiful Adam mansion, houses the Iveagh Bequest, a notable collection of old masters.

Transport is less than ideal: Highgate tube is N of the village off **Archway Rd**. Its escalators periodically break down – a daunting problem given that it is one of the deepest stations in London. There were fears that it would be closed, but funds have been found to keep it limping along.

Highgate Village

This is what residents reckon is Highgate proper: the old village, still recognizable as such, with its accretion of lovely homes that have offered fresh air and sylvan views to prosperous Londoners from the time of Elizabeth I onwards. It is bisected by **Highgate High St**, with its smart (though still useful) shops and restaurants. The **High St** is the boundary between Camden borough in the S and Haringey in the N. The main residential section of the village is on the Camden side, including the marvellous **Pond Square** with its 18th-century houses, late-Victorian mansion flats and the headquarters of the Highgate Society and the Highgate Literary and Scientific Institution, side by side in **South Grove** at one end of the square. South Grove House, opposite Witanhurst and the internationally famous Flask pub, is still one of the most desirable blocks in the village. A listed house in **Highgate West Hill**, once a popular youth hostel, sold in December for £3.3 million.

The premier address in the village is, however, **The Grove**; a row of houses, some of which date back to the 1680s, set back from the road behind an avenue of trees. Distinguished residents include pop icons such as Sting and Annie Lennox (it's noticeable that later, brasher stars like sundry Spice Girls choose Hampstead, Highgateians sniff). Houses in **The Grove** command £2–4.5 million. **North Grove**, just across **Hampstead Lane**, has some modern neo-Georgian houses.

Off **The Grove** is **Fitzroy Park**, an exclusive private road leading to a number of sumptuous and secluded homes – two new ones in 1999 – as well as to the 24 luxury houses in **Highfields Grove** on the lower slopes of the grounds of Witanhurst. The 10-year-old gated estate is very popular, and when they come onto the market the houses command £1.6 million or so. Near the bottom of **Fitzroy Park** is a splendid 15th-century house called Fitzroy Farm, set in well over an acre of land adjoining Hampstead Heath, and with its own private access road.

Back at the village, the terraced houses in **Bisham Gardens** are almost all converted into flats which, on the S side, have stunning views towards the City over Waterlow Park (one of London's most delightful parks), Lauderdale House (one-time home of Nell Gwynn) and the extraordinary Highgate Cemetery which, apart from being the last resting place of Karl Marx, is a major tourist attraction – guided tours are given.

Swain's Lane with its Victorian homes – 3-bed flats around £350,000 – leads down from the village to enclose, with **Highgate West Hill**, the celebrated cemetery and the Holly Lodge estate. This enormously popular residential area on the site of philanthropist Baroness Burdett-Coutts' estate comprises a mixture of houses and blocks of flats (the flats now council-owned) built between the wars in a mainly mock-Tudor style which is either smashing or vulgar, depending on your point of view. A house in Holly Lodge Gardens was on the market in December at £1.2 million – with three prospective buyers chasing it. Next door is **Holly Village**, a group of 1865 Gothic houses around a 'village green', built for the estate servants. Also popular is **West Hill Park**, an award-winning private estate of flats and houses built in the 1970s in **Merton Lane**, overlooking the Highgate Ponds. Houses here start at £700,000 and go up to £1.8 million. South of **Swain's Lane** is NW5, and the popular streets of Dartmouth Park (see Kentish Town chapter).

H

The Haringey side of the village, N of the **High St**, is slightly less dramatic, but attractive nevertheless, with some lovely leafy and secluded streets well-supplied with a mixture of semi-detached houses and conversions, and even a few large post-war purpose-built blocks of flats, such as Southwood Hall, Cholmeley Lodge and Northwood Hall. Particularly popular are **Southwood Lawn Rd**, **Cholmeley Park**, **Cholmeley Crescent** and **Cromwell Avenue**, with a fascinating development of flats in a converted church. The spacious Victorian houses in these streets are popular: a Grade II-listed house was £725,000 in late 1999.

Kenwood

Hampstead Lane leads from the village around the N end of Hampstead Heath to the grounds of Kenwood House. Directly opposite Kenwood are expensive roads like **Courtenay Avenue**, **Compton Avenue**, **Sheldon Avenue** (£1.7 million for 6 beds and a pool) and **Stormont Rd**, all a stone's throw from **The Bishops Avenue** (better known as Millionaires' Row) in the neighbouring borough of Barnet. These streets, almost exclusively with large detached houses, lead to Highgate Golf Club in **Denewood Rd**. Prices of £4–5 million are normal and sums regularly top well over £10 million. For more on **The Bishops Avenue** see the Hampstead Garden Suburb chapter.

Other roads in the area encircle the large grounds of Highgate School (which also owns a lot of property in the vicinity), such as **Bishopswood Rd**, **Broadlands Rd** and **View Rd**. Mostly traditional large houses, but a sprinkling of new properties as well.

North Rd and **North Hill** have some Georgian houses and a number of large mansion blocks, including the architecturally renowned 1938 Highpoint block, which has the distinction of having the highest rooftop in the whole of London. Also worth scrutiny are the well-mixed properties in **Talbot Rd**, **Bishops Rd**, **Bloomfield Rd** and **The Park**. An un-modernised 7-bed house in Talbot Rd sold in December for £750,000: smarten them up and these homes top £1 million. Unfortunately, the **Archway Rd** ends of these streets suffer noise and vibration from the heavy traffic.

Stanhope

East of **Archway Rd** is a clearly defined area of Highgate bounded in the N by **Shepherds Hill** and **Priory Gardens** (a sought-after cul-de-sac leading to Highgate tube station), in the E by **Coolhurst Rd**, and in the S by **Hornsey Lane**.

Shepherds Hill, with an increasing number of modern blocks of flats replacing the semis, has unparalleled views to the N over Muswell Hill and Alexandra Palace and Park for those properties whose outlook is not obscured, and dramatic views to the S for others. Blocks like Panorama Court and Highgate Heights are well-named.

The area is bisected N–S by **Stanhope Rd** which carries most of the traffic, leaving other streets relatively free. The prime road is **Hurst Avenue** which has very large £1.5 million houses overlooking the playing-fields of nearby St Aloysius Catholic Boys' High School. There is occasionally talk of the playing-fields being developed at some stage – which could bring prices down a little. **Avenue Rd**, at the bottom of the dip, now has a row of fairly new blocks of flats on the south side – much to the disgust of the house- and flat-owners across the road. The main drawback of this area is its distance from public transport – it's a stiff walk in either direction to Archway or Highgate tube stations, although there are buses along **Archway Rd** to the City and West End.

An important feature of this area is the Parkland Walk, formerly the route of the old railway, which ran from Finsbury Park to Alexandra Palace, now turned by Haringey Council into a nature trail and wildlife reserve very popular with ramblers, walkers and joggers. Houses adjacent to or with access to the Parkland Walk are much in demand (despite the slightly increased security risk). Streets in this vicinity are **Avenue Rd**, **Stanhope Rd**, **Hornsey Lane**, **Milton Park**, **Orchard Rd** and **Claremont Rd**, all of which have increased in popularity in recent years. Parkgate Mews, a development of 16 flats and four houses in **Stanhope Rd**, was snapped up quickly in 1997. 'The Miltons': **Milton Park Avenue** and **Milton Park Rd** are popular with a good selection of smaller flats and houses which get less expensive the closer they are to **Archway Rd**. Lots of purpose-built flats in **Avenue Rd** and **Hornsey Lane**, including the huge Northwood Hall block.

Borders

South of Hornsey Lane is an attractive group of streets called the Whitehall Park Conservation Area (in Islington borough) with beautifully preserved Victorian terraces in **Whitehall Park**, **Gladsmuir Rd** and **Harbetton Rd**. These have increased in value dramatically in the last decade. The district is sometimes called 'Highgate borders' and even 'Highgate slopes', but is really Archway (see Kentish Town chapter).

On the E side there are some pleasant streets more correctly called Crouch End, including **Crouch Hall Rd, Coleridge Rd** and **Birchington Rd.**

The boundary with Muswell Hill has some very interesting streets, including **Lanchester Rd** with its 5-bed houses and **Woodside Avenue** behind Highgate Wood, and the group of streets surrounding Haringey's Queen's Wood, including **Onslow Gardens, Connaught Gardens, Summersby Rd** and **Wood Lane.**

Transport   Tubes: Highgate, Archway (zones 2/3, Northern).
From Highgate: Oxford Circus 25 min (1 change),
City 18 min, Heathrow 1 hr (1 change).

Convenient for   Hampstead Heath, Kenwood. A1/M1 to North, City.
Miles from centre: 5.

Schools   Local authority: William Ellis (b), Acland Burghley, Parliament
Hill (g), Highgate Wood. Private: Highgate (b), Highfield,
Channing (g), St Aloysius (b).

SALES

Flats	S	1B	2B	3B	4B	5B
Average prices	65–140	80–220	110–300	140–400	160–500	400–550
Houses	2B	3B	4B	5B	6/7B	8B
Average prices	200–400	250–500	300–900+	350–5 M	420–6 M	7 M+

RENTAL

Flats	S	1B	2B	3B	4B	5B
Average prices	120–200	150–250	200–400	275–500	300–500	—
Houses	2B	3B	4B	5B	6/7B	8B
Average prices	250–400	300–700	400–800+	475–2000	650–2500	700–2600+

The properties   The roads around this ancient hill village hold not only
18th-century houses, but some 1680s ones. Victorian terraces
and converted and purpose-built flats have been added,
plus large and ever-more-opulent mansions, town-houses and
coveted private estates, from 1930s to present-day.

The market   The thinking star's Hampstead, say locals: musicians, media folk
and the professions buy here, joined by exalted foreign
potentates for the large mansions in vast grounds. Flat-buyers
get glorious views. Prices and range of homes vary widely. Local
searches: Haringey 10 working days, Camden 7–10 working days.

Among those estate agents active in this area are:
- Anscombe & Ringland *
- Prickett & Ellis Underhill
- Winkworth *
- Sturt & Tivendale
- Stonebridge
- Keith Cardale Groves
- Benham & Reeves
- Godfrey & Barr
- Taylor Gibbs
- Fitzroys
- Knight Frank
- Goldschmidt Howland
- Hamptons
- Heathgate
- FPDSavills
- Foxtons*

further details: see advertisers' index on p671

HOLLAND PARK

Map ref: p75(1G)
Postal districts: W11, W14
Borough: Kensington & Chelsea (Con)
Council tax: Band D £534
Conservation areas: Holland Park
Parking: Red Routes (see text), residents/meters. Clamps

H

The serene streets of Holland Park slope gently away from Kensington, down the western flanks of Campden Hill. Green and spacious, the area known as Holland Park boasts the biggest concentration of large houses in the Royal Borough. 'The area known as' is said with care, since there's Holland Park (the park) and also **Holland Park** (the road – which isn't: it's more a sort of square, in the middle of which is sandwiched **Holland Park Mews**). The grandest, largest, ambassadorial residences – some *are* embassies – are here. On the S side is the park, on the N side, the busy **Holland Park Avenue**, which runs westwards to even busier Shepherd's Bush roundabout. 'The area known as' fans leafily out on either side of the broad, tree-lined avenue: southwards it runs between the park and **Holland Rd**, down towards the W end of **Kensington High St**. Here there is further confusion in the shape of **Holland Park Rd**, which is right at the S of the area. Northwards the area has, over the years, pushed upwards into Notting Hill and Notting Dale to take in the pleasant corners between **Portland Rd**, **St James's Gardens** and **Royal Crescent**.

Holland Park, wherever its frontiers, is one of the luckier parts of London. Lucky to have been in the right place at the wrong time.

Perhaps because Notting Hill, with its then raffish connotations, was a little close, the area escaped the knock-down-and-build-flats boom of the 1960s and '70s. Its early Victorian elegance remained intact, if seedy. Now the grand old houses are once again solidly fashionable, either as single homes or converted into unusually roomy flats.

Add to these a number of modern flats/town-house developments, usually set in their own landscaped grounds, and also the small mews cottages with their garages that are the legacy of the horse-drawn age in which the area grew up, and you have a neighbourhood with a very good range of home sizes and styles – though not of prices. Nothing is cheap. This has attracted families (schools, the park, communal square and crescent gardens), City people (the Central line goes straight there) and Hampstead-style politicians, actors and media people (the BBC mega-HQ is down the road at Shepherd's Bush). And now ambassadorial-level personages and international millionaires have completed the circle and re-inhabited the ambassadorial-sized homes, reclaimed after years as rented flats.

Today, the pleasant, community feel is added to by small, villagey shops and good restaurants. Thanks to the neighbouring areas' amenities, there's been no incentive to clutter up the place with sprawling supermarkets and the like. Most streets are within easy walking distance of either of the two main shopping/entertainment centres of **Kensington High St** and **Notting Hill Gate**. Between them these boast three cinemas, numerous clubs, pubs, restaurants and a wide range of shops. Several leading stores line **Kensington High St**. If, as seems likely, the White City development goes ahead (see Shepherd's Bush chapter) Holland Park will be a stroll away from a monster-Marks & Spencer.

Another of the area's attractions is the vast amount of public open space in the shape of Holland Park itself and in nearby Kensington Gardens. Holland Park covers 55 acres of woodlands and formal gardens, many sports, an adventure play park and an open-air theatre. Note though that **Holland Rd, Addison Crescent** and the southern part of **Addison Rd** now form a Red Route. Residents fear it will increase traffic flow – the council believes it will reduce congestion. Locals lost the battle and must now live with the curbs on parking.

Because much of the property reached a good international standard of finish some time back, and because of the embassies in the area, this has long been a favoured area for renting. The big blocks of flats in Holland Park South, and the converted mansions in the heart of the area, offer flats of varying sizes and characters. There is usually a choice of family houses with gardens and parking: plenty of these, too are being revamped and the quality on offer is rising.

Holland Park South

Tree-lined **Holland Park Avenue** sets the tone for this choice neighbourhood made up of large houses and leafy gardens. Vast stucco, or brick and stucco, mansions set back from the road behind sloping front gardens spread along the southern side of the busy avenue. Some have been converted into hotels. Pairs of large brick and stucco houses, split into flats, lie to the W, beyond the increasingly up-market shops and restaurants clustered around newly refurbished Holland Park underground station. Values vary as there is quite a mix of property on this long road: recent examples are a 1-bed flat for £240,000; a 2-bed for £485,000.

The most coveted of imposing Victorian mansions are found in **Holland Park** (the road). Many of these double-fronted, detached, creamy stucco houses still have their decorative, highly ornate cast-iron and glass entrance canopies. (This delightfully idiosyncratic feature sits strangely, to be honest, on the dignified, pillared entrances: they look for all the world as if they were drawn in as an afterthought by Ronald Searle.) Many have been divided into flats, particularly popular with the diplomatic community. Security video cameras are a regular feature of the area. Some are indeed used as embassies, but the council's Unitary Development Plan states that planning permission to convert houses into embassies will be given less readily in the future. Whole houses, backing onto the park, can fetch eight-figure prices: one was on the market last year for £15 million, for which you get a swimming pool, gym and solarium. A whole-floor, and thus spacious, flat in one of the big houses pushes up towards a million. Cheaper (unmodernized) ones do exist. Size, individuality, condition and proximity to the park all affect the price.

Lying between the N and S arms of the street through a stone arch is **Holland Park Mews**, lined by 2-storey cottages with ground-floor garages. Note that **Holland Park** (the road) and its mews takes the W11 postcode together with the streets N of **Holland Park Avenue**.

H

Holland Park merges with **Abbotsbury Rd**, which runs southwards along the W side of the park itself: the postcode changes to W14. The road has road humps in a bid to slow traffic down but it is still a popular route from **Holland Park** to **Kensington High St**. Most of the homes on the W side of the street are from the second half of the 20th century, from the 10-storey flats block, Abbotsbury House, at the NW end to the series of select private cul-de-sacs, some with garages, which make up **Abbotsbury Close**. A two-bed flat overlooking the park in Abbotsbury House was £335,000 last winter. Immaculate 2/3-storey terraced brick houses stand in neatly landscaped enclaves set well back from **Abbotsbury Rd**. This is the deepest, most secluded part of Holland Park, select even for Kensington. Urban grime seems a world away.

The scene changes dramatically with the appearance of **Oakwood Court**, a complex of 7-storey red-brick Victorian mansion blocks, which form the street of the same name. A strip of lawn, trees and shrubs divides the blocks on each side of the street. The mansions have recently been refurbished. On the corner is a new development of 3-storey red-brick homes and some mock-Tudor flats called Manderley. **Ilchester Place** opposite is leafy and salubrious. The big low-built houses, some with gardens backing on to Holland Park, command top prices.

Melbury Rd to the S is noted for its artist's-studio houses designed by the likes of Norman Shaw and Halsey Ricardo. An outstanding example is the eccentric red-brick Tower House, a copy of the Welsh Castell Coch. Built in the 1870s, it was renovated in the 1960s by actor Richard Harris. The houses are a legacy of the days when **Melbury Rd** and **Holland Park Rd** to the S formed a 19th-century artist's quarter. There are several more big red-brick detached studio houses, including Leighton House, once the home of painter Lord Leighton, now an art gallery and museum. The size of these Victorian mansions, built on the scale of country houses, makes for spectacular flats in those that are converted. These include the erstwhile home of pre-Raphaelite artist Holman ('Light of the World') Hunt, and a pair designed by architect Halsey Ricardo for his father-in-law and his patron respectively. They are now six huge apartments of which the smallest is a mere 1,723 sq ft (3-bed, 3-bath, 3-recep) and the most impressive the vast 4-bed/4-bath/3-reception room one of 3,036 sq ft – excluding its two terraces, conservatory and 76-ft private garden. Another spectacular conversion, of sculptor Sir Hamo Thorneycroft's 1870s studio, produced three flats. To the S of **Melbury Rd**, near the **Kensington High St** end, grand houses are punctuated by exclusive modern flats. Woodsford is a 5-storey red-brick development, Stavordale Lodge a 5-storey slate-coloured block with private parking and Park Close a 9-storey flat development overlooking the park and Commonwealth Institute grounds.

The S side of the street forms **St Mary Abbots Terrace**, a modern development of neo-Georgian town-houses. The 3-storey houses are set around a series of three cul-de-sacs. Some are turned sideways on to the street, their rear gardens adding to its leafy look. At the end of this terrace facing **Addison Rd** lies a 9-storey block of flats. Opposite this is the private road **Strangeway Terrace** with its water sculpture and attractive flats. It is closed to through traffic from **Holland Park** to **Melbury Rd**.

Addison Rd S of **Addison Crescent** forms part of the southbound one-way traffic system, which detracts from the character of this otherwise exclusive road. Detached and semi-detached stucco and brick/stucco villas, and a terrace of Gothic-style houses, sit on the W side. Opposite them are two large modern flats blocks, 10-storey Monckton Court and 6-storey Farley Court. Both are set in landscaped grounds off the road. On **Addison Rd** is one of London's grandest homes, built in 1905 for millionaire draper Ernest Debenham and designed by Ricardo (see Melbury Rd above). It is now listed Grade I and yours – coloured tiles and all – for £20 million. More down-to-earth prices for flats along here: £250,000 for a 1-bed.

The S curve of **Addison Crescent** forms the link in the Red Route one-way system between **Addison Rd** and **Holland Rd**. This short stretch of detached and paired villas consequently suffers from the heavy traffic and noise. The N curve with its big 2/3-storey detached brick and stucco villas and walled front gardens is noticeably quieter and more desirable. Traffic or not, these enormous villas make enviable homes.

Grander white stucco-fronted detached villas line the W side of the N stretch of **Addison Rd**. They are set back behind walled gardens and small sweeping driveways. Security cameras are another feature of the street scene here. On the opposite side of the road is a group of detached and semi-detached houses, including the intriguing glazed brick and tile Richmond House, headquarters of the Richmond Fellowship. Selby Court, a 9-storey block of flats, lies between **Somerset Square**, a modern development of red-brick town-houses and flats, and **Woodsford Square**, a 1970s development of large town-houses. Both are set in landscaped grounds walled off from the road behind a shield of trees. An unusual home for the area, a 2-bed cottage in **Addison Rd** with garden and parking, was on the market for £550,000 last winter.

Homes at the N end of **Woodsford Square** overlook the Holland Park tennis club, tucked in behind **Holland Park Gardens**. Holland Park Mansions, a 4-storey red and white block on the E side of **Holland Park Gardens**, also overlooks the courts. There's always a choice of rental flats here.

At the N end of **Addison Rd** next to Cardinal Vaughan School stands Addisland Court, an 8-storey brick and stone 1930s block, which stretches around the corner into exclusive **Holland Villas Rd**. A 2-bed flat here might be around £335,000. Opposite this stands the 4-storey modern Parkland flats. The large brick and stucco detached villas in this quiet, leafy street fetch eye-watering prices: an 8-bed house was £6.5 million late last year. Developers still find the occasional one in a tatty state: one was being worked on last winter. Off the NW end of **Holland Villas Rd** are **Upper** and **Lower Addison Gardens**, both tree-lined streets of 3-storey terraced houses. At the top end, near **Holland Park Rd**, a new development of 27 flats is called Fitzclarence House.

Holland Park North

On the N side of **Holland Park Avenue** stands **Royal Crescent**. Two curving terraces of white-painted, 5-storey homes sweep around a tree-lined semicircular garden with ornate iron railings, which were recently reintroduced after residents and the council raised the money. Each of the end houses has graceful circular pavilions to finish the row, and the whole crescent appears to have been transported from Regency Brighton. Alas, it gazes out on the unfortunate 1970s Kensington Hilton rather than the English Channel. One-bed flats in the Crescent go for around £200–220,000. Tucked in behind the W side is the curve of **Royal Crescent Mews**, a 1980s terrace of 2-storey brick and stucco cottages with their own garages.

   St Ann's Villas, which leads off **Royal Crescent**, is a relatively busy local road, much improved by residents' parking. It has a mix of houses and flats – notably a group of Victorian Gothic detached brown-brick gabled houses. Cutting W–E through this street is **Queensdale Rd**, a pleasant and very popular street of Victorian terraced houses. Boundary changes have brought **Queensdale Crescent, Norland Rd** and **Kingsdale Gardens** into the Royal borough rather than Hammersmith. At the end of **Norland Rd** stands a splendid Sikh temple with a roof adorned with gold. **Norland Rd** is made up of pink stucco and brick houses with railings and is closed to traffic: on foot, it leads to Holland Park roundabout. Opposite these homes a large Victorian stucco house has been converted into social housing and next to this is another new development of affordable housing. Norland House, set behind these homes, is a 22-storey council block. This still belongs to Hammersmith and Fulham Council, which has just finished modernizing the flats. The best stretch of **Queensdale Rd**, E of **St Ann's Villas**, has 3/4-storey and basement brick and pastel-painted stucco houses. Two 5-bed houses were on the market last winter at just under £1.5 million each. Off it, **Queensdale Place** is a pleasant little cul-de-sac of 2-storey stock-brick and stucco terraces (3-bed house: £825,000), to which has been added a spectacular trio of homes, one of which has an indoor pool. **St Ann's Rd**, the northern continuation of **St Ann's Villas**, has some pleasant 4-storey houses.

   Addison Place, off the opposite side of **Queensdale Rd**, is lined by a variety of period and modern 2-storey mews cottages (a small one in need of work was £400,000 last autumn) and ends in cobbles. It curves around behind the E parade of **Royal Crescent**, debouching into **Addison Avenue**, the showpiece of the area with handsome 2-storey houses (one for sale last autumn for £1.65 million – needing restoration) and a few incongruous stockbroker-tudor ones. The best stretch of this wide tree-lined avenue with its splendid vista of St James Norlands Church lies N of **Queensdale Rd**: here homes can fetch more than £1 million. Elegant paired stucco houses painted in pastel shades line both sides. The smaller paired stucco houses S of **Queensdale Rd** give way to an attractive parade of shops, offices and the Norland Arms pub. Green Victorian street lamps add to the avenue's period character. Opposite is **Taverners Close** with five red-brick detached houses.

   St James Church sits in the central garden of **St James's Gardens**, another of the neighbourhood's choicest addresses. Pairs of attractive semi-detached houses linked by paired entrances are set around the communal gardens. The lower floors of these handsome 3-storey plus basement brick and stucco houses are painted in pastel shades, adding to the distinctive character of this Victorian square.

   Return down **Addison Avenue** to **Queensdale Rd** and turn S into **Queensdale Walk**, a tranquil cul-de-sac of 2-storey painted cottages, E, facing a long garden wall with overhanging trees. North into **Princess Place** are three 2-storey homes. One street away is **Norland Square** where three terraces of 4-storey with basement stucco-fronted houses stand around a large tree-filled private central garden with a tennis court. Off the square runs **Norland Place**, a cobbled mews of 2-storey painted cottages, which stretches through to **Princedale Rd**. **Princedale Rd** has mainly Victorian terraces, a mix of houses (£650,000 for a 3-bed) and flats, plus speciality shops near the junction with **Penzance Place**. Here the homes are individually coloured. More brick and stucco terraces are found here, next to St Clements and St James Primary School.

Penzance Place with its flat-fronted Victorian terraced houses leads into **Portland Rd**, another popular street of Victorian terraced houses. Many of the 3-storey plus basement houses here have now been converted into flats. Properties on the E side are more expensive, being wider with larger gardens. The road is sealed off to traffic at Clarendon Cross, a smart villagey enclave of posh shops, galleries, antique shops and restaurants/wine bars.

Lying behind the NW side of **Portland Rd**, across the road from Avondale Park, is award-winning **Hippodrome Mews**. Two terraces of 3-storey brown-brick town-houses face each other across a narrow cobbled mews in this private cul-de-sac (1970s). The pleasingly bulbous shape of an old kiln, as high as the houses, is preserved among them, and no doubt accounts for the name of **Pottery Lane**, which, running S from here, has an attractive group of 3-storey painted brick and stucco terraced houses at its junction with **Penzance Place**. **Clarendon Rd**, which parallels **Portland Rd** to the E, marks the start of the climb up Notting Hill (see Notting Hill chapter), where graceful crescents still echo the shape of the racecourse they replaced.

Many of the big detached and semi-detached Victorian houses are split into flats. Not all, though: one, complete with cottage/garage, was £2.5 million unmodernized in January 1999. Might this be the house that sold for £4 million to a showbiz client a year later, still unmodernized? Now there's inflation. Slightly lesser mortals pay £750,000 for a 3-bed maisonette in the same road.

Close to the tube station, between **Holland Park Avenue** and **Lansdowne Mews**, 12 new houses were built in 1989.

Borders

Holland Rd (N–S), the area's western boundary, is a major traffic artery running down to **Kensington High St** from the M41, which ends at Shepherd's Bush roundabout. Its S end is one-way: the traffic flows northwards, while the southbound stream dives down the bottom half of **Addison Crescent** into **Addison Rd**. The Red Route affects these streets.

A series of small hotels cluster around the S end of **Holland Rd**. The rest is lined by mainly 4-storey and basement stucco, or brick and stucco, terraced houses of varying quality. In common with most properties in the neighbourhood, they are split into flats. Double glazing is cited in sales details: you'll need it. This is where you look if prices in Holland Park Proper make you go as white as the stucco: 2-bed flats around £225,000.

More bed-and-breakfast hotels are found in **Russell Rd** to the W. They are mixed in with further flats in the 3-storey and basement brick and stucco terraces overlooking the increasingly busy West London railway line (which carries Channel Tunnel freight trains) and the glass façade of the Olympia Exhibition Centre.

A thin strip of land along the railway, which for years was home to a variety of small firms – and which was forever under threat from various road schemes – has become 'Kensington Park', an ongoing development of new homes by Barratt. All now sold: prices were from £240,000. A footbridge over the tracks links **Russell Rd** with the Kensington Olympia station, just across the borough boundary with Hammersmith. This has increasingly useful services on what has become known as the West London line.

Russell Gardens is a short parade of small local shops and restaurants, plus a pub. **Russell Gardens Mews** has several working garages at its S entrance, giving way to 2-storey brick/painted cottages towards the rear. Properties at the NW end of tree-lined **Elsham Rd** also back on to the railway. Here a 2-bed flat might cost £215,000.

Transport	Tubes: Holland Park, Shepherd's Bush (zone 2, Central); Kensington Olympia. To Oxford Circus 12 min, City 22 min, Heathrow 50 min (2 changes). Trains: Kensington Olympia, trains to Clapham Junction, Willesden Junction and some long-distance services.
Convenient for	BBC TV Centre at Shepherd's Bush, M4/M40 to Heathrow and the West. Direct tube line to West End, City. Miles from centre: 3.5.
Schools	Local Authority/Foundation: Holland Park School, Cardinal 6th-form College, Cardinal Vaughan School (b). Private: Norland Place School, Notting Hill & Ealing High (g).

SALES

Flats	S	1B	2B	3B	4B	5B
Average prices	90–165	200–400	250–650	425–1 M +	500–1.5 M	750–2 M+

Houses	2B	3B	4B	5B	6/7B	8B
Average prices	500–700	600–1 M+	800–2 M	1–3 M+	2.8 M+	12 M+

RENTAL

Flats	S	1B	2B	3B	4B	5B
Average prices	150–300	200–400	350–700	600–2000	1000–3500	1200–5000+

Houses	2B	3B	4B	5B	6/7B	8B
Average prices	500–650	700–1300	1000–2000	2500–4500	3500–5000	5000+

The properties	Vast, snowy-white villas and terraces, imposing Victorian red brick, smaller-scale squares, modern town-houses, all gather round Holland Park and Avenue. Rich source of family homes, flats converted and mansion, ambassador-level grandeur, in leafy streets. Some new conversions and mews houses to be found.
The market	Firmly in the top bracket: prices reflect that it is N of Kensington rather than next door to North Kensington. The embassy-sized houses have reverted to multi-million pound single occupancy after years as tatty flats. Local searches: 10 working days.

Among those estate agents active in this area are:

- John Wilcox
- Aylesfords
- Marsh & Parsons
- Addison Properties
- John D Wood
- Berkeley International
- Beauchamp Estates
- Winkworth *
- Faron Sutaria
- FPDSavills
- Hamptons
- Anscombe & Ringland *
- Foxtons*
- Jackson-Stops & Staff
- De Groot Collis
- Scotts *
- Beaney Pearce *
- Finlay Brewer *

further details: see advertisers' index on p671

ISLINGTON AND HIGHBURY

Map ref: p46 (7B)
Postal districts: N1, N5
Boroughs: Islington
  (Lab/Lib Dem)
Council tax: Band D £912
Conservation areas:
  Numerous — check with
  town hall
Parking: Residents/meters

Islington, perched high above the City, has come of age. It never quite made it in the '80s, the area as a whole staying cheerfully scruffy – though decidedly 'up-and-coming' throughout – while individually its Georgian terraces were fought over. Then came the last few years of City bonuses (plus the Blair factor: New Labour, new Islington), which saw the '90s complete what the '80s had begun.

Fundamentally, Islington's axis swung: it stopped lifting its eyes northwards unto to the hills, and saw itself no longer as sub-Hampstead, but rather as super-City. Fast transport to Docklands via the DLR from Bank, as well as easy access to City and West End, brought a new breed of well-heeled buyers.

Now **Upper St** (standing today for Upwardly-Mobile instead of On-its-Uppers) is one of London's smarter locations, with designer chic and coffee shops from the Angel up to Highbury Corner. This was led by the success of The Business Design Centre (home, this year, of the BAFTA Awards) and the smart Angel Square office complex.

New apartments, with security systems and state-of-the-art fittings, duly began to appear in any corner available, to meet the behests of the New Islingtonians – selling, as well, off-plan as investments rather than homes. It follows that there is also an increase in smart homes to rent.

However the original period homes are perennially popular – as conversions or as whole houses. Very British pleasures, these; and their inhabitants (wherever they may have hailed from originally) are somehow very British folk. The international jet-set do not appreciate, as do we, the inconvenience of the tucked-away, charming – but often narrow-gutted, many-staired – houses, however Georgian the terraces. ('The madness of King George is explained,' claimed one.)

But for all its inhabitants, old or new, city-slickers or middle-class radicals in 'the

Arts', Islington, with Highbury to the N, is a most satisfactory place. Due N from the City, the Highbury and Islington territory lies E of **Caledonian Rd** and King's Cross, W of **Green Lanes** and thus Hackney and Stoke Newington, and S of Finsbury Park (**Gillespie Rd**). It has a definite shape, which starts from the southern base-line of **Pentonville Rd**/**City Rd**, unfurls on either side of the central spine of **Upper St**, and is neatly capped by Highbury with its green, open fields. Then, too, it is set on pleasantly hilly ground for variety; it boasts a village green to offset the commercialism of the S end; also theatres (the internationally-renowned Almeida, for one), clubs, galleries, a canal – and real gems of residential corners which are made all the more pleasing by the fact that through-traffic can dash along the main routes without suspecting their existence.

The area divides into four neighbourhoods: the Angel, Canonbury and Barnsbury in Islington, plus, to the N, Highbury around the green open spaces of its Fields.

Follow **Essex Rd** as it forks off along the E side of Islington Green to reach Canonbury, Islington's heartland. A popular spot since the days of Elizabeth I, it thrived under the Georges and still has some fine terraces from that period set in its leafy roads. It commands a premium over comparably-sized homes in the other neighbourhoods. Mainly family terraces here, but flats and some larger houses, too.

Barnsbury is a little later: a stock-brick-and-stucco land laid out by Cubitt (see Belgravia) in the 1820s. This is almost exclusively family housing, quieter (thanks to a fiendishly maze-like traffic scheme) and more completely residential in character, arranged in pretty streets around half a dozen garden squares.

The Angel corner, aside from the commercial area, has some glorious flat-fronted Georgian and early Victorian terraces tucked away to the E of **Islington High St**. Front gardens are rare, but some streets have central greenery – or water: the Grand Union Canal runs here. Roads tend to be narrower, broadening towards the N, where the streets in the angle of **New North Rd** and **Essex Rd** have larger property and more flats.

By contrast, Highbury is virtually all Victorian, aside from roads bordering Highbury Fields. Generally you'll find ornate late-Victorian houses with broader avenues and gardens, split between flats and family homes. Some large properties in **Highbury New Park** and **Highbury Hill** – if you can find one that has not been transformed into flats.

In short, the area around the Angel and the southern end of **Upper St** is definitely a young singles corner, barring the Georgian terraces; the real family stamping-grounds remain Barnsbury, Highbury and Canonbury. Traditional buyers (from the media, the law) still look for period properties, while the incomers go for the new developments, one step away from the fashionable 'lofts' of Clerkenwell. These continue to come on-stream – the latest are mushrooming around the Wenlock Canal Basin (see below) to the E of Essex Rd.

Once here, people tend to stay. This last year has seen prices rise as those moving within the area and the incoming City types have been joined in the hunt for homes by price refugees from overheated places like Fulham and Notting Hill. Families, though, have to consider schooling. Even Tony Blair balked at sending his kids to the local state schools; now the running of Islington's entire education department has been handed over to a private consultant – see *Schools in London* chapter.

The Angel

The Angel is the gateway to Islington, spreading northwards from the baseline of **Pentonville Rd/City Rd** at the junction with **Islington High St**, where Angel Square, a big office complex over the tube, provided a new entrance to the underground with the longest escalators in London. **Islington High St, Upper St** and adjacent roads are Islington's main shopping streets. From the **High St** westwards to **Penton Rd** is mainly commercial property and offices. This has become an important office centre, though a flats scheme appeared a couple of years back, running N from **Pentonville Rd** to **White Lion St**. Running W–E is **Chapel Market**, which indeed has a large, well-known fruit-and-veg market – supplemented by a big Sainsbury's and Marks & Spencer in **Liverpool Rd**.

Now, however, an 'exciting' £25 million shopping mall, with all the big names and the inevitable multiplex cinema, is to appear in the angle of **Liverpool Rd** and **Parkfield St**, curving around an open square – and, in the process, engulfing two shops apiece in Liverpool Rd and Upper St, the Angel drugs project, Le Montmartre French restaurant, Barstow & Barr's cheese shop and an entire street: **Layton Rd**.

On the E side of **Upper St**, just before the green, is the distinctive Mall antiques arcade; behind this, and running parallel, are **Islington High St** (a surprise: it is more of a charming lane) and **Camden Passage** (an equally confusing name), a great centre for antiques. Antiques and small, old-fashioned shops continue down **Essex Rd**.

The area to the E of **Upper St** and **Essex Rd** is quiet and residential, and almost exclusively glorious flat-fronted Georgian terraces. Streets are narrow and parking is restricted. When the graceful rows of **Duncan Terrace** and **Colebrooke Row** first faced each other in 1768, what separated them was not a strip of greenery but the New River, the first attempt to supply London with clean water. Off **Colebrooke Row**'s later, N end, **Bridel Mews** is a rare new one: the 3-storey homes, all contemporary curves in designer-industrial style, range from 870-1590 sq ft in size, £380–610,000 in price.

Back to the S end, off which runs **Vincent Terrace**: fine Georgian houses with lovely views onto the Grand Union Canal; across it, **Noel Rd**'s houses turn their back on the water, and thus have raised gardens that stop at – or rather, above – the towpath: the Hanging Gardens of Islington (a **Noel Rd** house was £735,000 last winter). S of **Vincent Terrace** and W of the City Rd Canal Basin, houses tend to be smaller, streets narrower and more mixed towards the **City Rd**: **Elia St** has low Georgian terraces on one side, low council-built blocks on the other. There's now a new cache of 80 flats to rent (£165–450 per week): thus the fate of the old St Marks Hospital in **City Rd**.

Wharf Rd, between the two canal basins, marks the borough boundary: Wenlock Basin, on the Hackney side (see City chapter), is the current building hot-spot: here Lemon Land have already developed the 90 flats of the Royle Building, and are now adding 49 flats and loft-style, galleried live/work units in the Wenlock Building, **Wenlock Rd**: £199,000 (1-beds) to £265,000.

North of the canal, at the corner of **Packington St** and **Prebend St**, is the Packington Square Estate – modern '70s low-rise blocks (still one of the less-popular parts of Islington, despite a council clear-up scheme). E from here, across to the **Southgate Rd** and the borough boundary, are some fine period terraces (mainly family houses). Streets are wider, squares and trees more common, parking easier and prices higher. **Arlington Avenue** and **Square**, with the tucked-away Clock Tower Mews development (one of the pioneers of the modern mews re-creations), are typical. A 3-bed house in the Mews was £325,000 last winter. **Wilton Square** is also particularly quiet and fine.

Essex Rd

The streets that lie N of the **New North Rd**, between **Essex Rd** and the borough boundary at **Southgate Rd**, are more mixed, with different periods appearing in the same road (witness the 8-storey tower block in **Elizabeth Avenue**). Streets are wider and parking a little less of a problem, despite the large houses and many flat conversions. The roads in this neighbourhood have predominantly flat-fronted, substantial terraces, and some houses are double-fronted. Other streets are later in period, such as **Elmore St** and **Northchurch Rd**. Dover Court council estate is just beneath the **Essex Rd** and **Balls Pond Rd** junction. This corner is attracting developers, too: The Pinnacle's 19 1- and 2-bed flats, complete with rooftop terrace and Japanese garden, appeared here last year. Nearby, off **Ockendon Rd**, Ockendon Mews is a cobbled courtyard redevelopment of ex-industrial buildings: flats (some galleried), one house and a large live/work unit. A 4-bed house in the same street was £495,000 last winter; a 3-bed, flat-fronted period one in **Southgate Rd** £475,000.

Islington Green and Canonbury

Upper St is the main artery of Islington, running N into its heart. At **Islington Green** the road forks: **Upper St** continues N and **Essex Rd** NE. The key site on the N side of the green, in the sharp angle between the two roads through to **Gaskin St**, now holds 'The Angel on the Green' by award-winning Grove Manor Homes (see below): 1- to 3-bed flats and penthouses, grouped round a central courtyard with angel sculpture, completed a year ago. (Release prices ranged from £147,500 for 1-bed flats to million-pound penthouses.) Also on the Green itself, London Town had added seven roomy 1- and 2-bed flats plus 3-bed penthouse next door to the Slug & Lettuce pub by the end of last year, when a 2-bed, 2-bath flat was on the market for £295,000, and the house-sized penthouse was 'price on application only'. More new flats on the adjoining site, too.

Little passageways and courtyards continue N up to the period terraces of **Florence St** and **Cross St**. Beyond these are the red-brick mansion flats of **Halton Rd** and **Canonbury Villas**. Running NW and intersecting with the **Essex Rd** is **Canonbury Rd**: the heartland of Canonbury lies in the triangle between these two with **St Paul's Rd** at the top. At the **Essex Rd**/**Canonbury Rd** junction is Essex Rd station, which has a service into Moorgate on weekdays; City Heights' 66 flats (Grove Manor Homes again) are just opposite: Georgian flat-fronted terraces on either side of **Canonbury Rd** give way to modern council blocks just before **Canonbury Square**, a superb Regency square with tall, thin terraced houses round the central garden. One of Canonbury's most prized corners – but not as peaceful as you'd expect, since busy **Canonbury Rd** cuts across it.

Round the corner we rejoin the main **Upper St** where **Compton Terrace**, a fine, lofty Regency row, is set back from the street behind a sheltering line of trees and a garden. New homes appeared in 1990 behind the S end of the terrace in **Compton Avenue**: 11 3- and 4-bed houses called The Cloisters. Just to the N, **Upper St** and **Canonbury Rd** meet at Highbury Corner, the vast roundabout beyond which Highbury begins. Eastwards from **Canonbury Square**, **Compton Rd** has tall Georgian terraces which give way to double-fronted period houses where it joins **Alwyne Villas'** broader-fronted rows. On the corner with the Georgian **Canonbury Place** you'll find Canonbury Tower, a romantic 16th-century relic: the remains of the area's monastic manor house. The famed Tower Theatre amateur company, which mounts ambitious rep seasons, is based here.

To the N along **St Marys Grove** are a whole series of neo-Georgian developments, low flat-fronted terraces culminating in **John Spencer Square**. At the end of **Canonbury Place**, the road splits into **Grange Grove** and **Canonbury Park North** and **South**. The area is very mixed: modern semis nestle with mock-Georgian ones which rub shoulders with the real thing. Grove Manor Homes squeezed nine houses and 25 flats into **Canonbury Park South** to such good effect that they received a 1998 Civic Trust award. At the corner of **Canonbury Park South** and **Willow Bridge Rd** is an imposing red-brick Victorian mansion which sets the tone for the rest of the street – quiet, spacious, covetable Victorian semis. This, along with **Canonbury Park North** and **Alwyne Place**, **Villas** and **Rd**, holds Canonbury's Victoriana: particularly large and grand in **Alwyne Rd** (a 4-bed example here, £1.55 million). Between its back gardens and those of **Canonbury Grove** to the S, runs the New River: built in the 17th century as London's first proper water supply, this used to flow through Canonbury. It now ends in Stoke Newington, but a replica channel runs through a small, linear park from **St Paul's Rd** down to **Canonbury Rd** – the charming New River Walk. **Willow Bridge Rd** (as the name suggests) crosses this, leading to **Canonbury St**, where 'Royal Canonbury Tower' is 35 flats, with communal gym and rooftop terrace, and four houses; next door, the same firm built City View, where the 25 flats share a roof terrace with fine views to the S (2-bed, c. £265,000).

Across the New River, in the angle of **Essex Rd** and **St Paul's Rd**, are the quiet, low-rise council houses, maisonettes and interconnected walkways of the Marquess Estate, which is centred around **Clephane Rd**. Unmanageably large, it is now being carved up and re-modelled, and part has been sold off to private developers. You'll have to cross the **St Paul's Rd** highway to find Canonbury's little station, which links with the N London Line, Silverlink, and has a handful of shops. **Wallace Rd**, which leads to it, has fine, tall flat-fronted terraces on the right, and on the left later ones with good front gardens. To the E are the fine terraces of **St Paul's Place** and **Northampton Park**. Much of the area towards Highbury to the W is large period houses, (comparatively) realistically priced near the tracks or along busy **St Paul's Rd.**

Barnsbury

Liverpool Rd, running N from the Angel, is the main avenue of the Barnsbury side, and is typically composed of flat-fronted brick terraces (half a million these days, while a semi-detached was £625,000 recently). The streets to the E of it, across to **Upper St**, are not strictly Barnsbury but may well be referred to as such by estate agents. **Barford St** marks the site of the newly restored Business Design Centre, with its glass arches. North is **Old Royal Free Square**: early-90s flats and houses converted from the eponymous ex-hospital. Next, the fine **Gibson Square**, and above this **Milner Square**, an 1840s creation completely restored by the council in the 1970s. A modern private development around the corner mimics its rather eccentric, vertical style. East lies **Almeida St**, home of the Almeida Theatre, and small period terraces continue up to **Islington Park St**.

Barnsbury *proper*, a tract of homogeneous residential groves laid out – by Cubitt, among others – in the 1820–40s, stretches westwards from **Liverpool Rd** across to the **Caledonian Rd**. In the best Islington traditions, it's a secretive corner. Its peace is unassailable, courtesy of an outsider-proof one-way system: maps are issued to friends. To the S **Ritchie St** and **Bachelor St**, with their neat terraces and first-floor balconies, border on the Angel and end in Culpeper community garden. Continue W along **Tolpuddle (Culpeper) St**, which intersects with **Barnsbury Rd** and **Penton St** running S–N. To the W **Copenhagen St** crosses **Barnsbury Rd** and curves round to meet the **Caledonian Rd**; S of here are Pentonville council estates.

Cloudesley Rd runs N from **Culpeper Gardens**, and to the W is Barnard Park – a rare open space for the Islington area, it boasts tennis courts. To the E is **Cloudesley St** with its wide avenues and dignified double-fronted houses, leading into the superb **Cloudesley Square** (1820s Regency with the Celestial Church of Christ in the centre). **Richmond Avenue** runs W from **Liverpool Rd**, and connects with the **Caledonian Rd**. To the N is the secluded **Lonsdale Square**, substantial terraces of – a sudden shock – heavily Gothic styling: the only high-Victorian square in the area.

North of this is the ivy-clad **Morland Mews**, one of the few modern developments; this corner, taking in **Lonsdale Place**, **Barnsbury St**, and **Gissing Walk**, saw some rebuilding around 1970. Then we regain 1820's terraces in **Brooksby St** and **Bewdley St**, which lead into **Barnsbury Square**: sadly this has not survived intact, but is the site of the original monastic moated farmhouse and grange. The square boasts some large homes – a 7-bed house was on the market for £1.67 million last winter. Returning S, there is the delightful, hilly **Ripplevale Grove** – small, tidy cottage terraces and gardens – and, to the W, **Thornhill Square**, a fine Regency square with substantial properties. Its curved end mirrors **Thornhill Crescent**. Off **Matilda St**, which runs S from Thornhill Square, is the 1995-built **Bramwell Mews**.

Barnsbury ends with the **Caledonian Rd**: predominantly small, old shops, cheerfully and irredeemably scruffy, though tidying. The junction with **Offord Rd** in the N marks the top limit of Barnsbury. **Offord Rd**, close to the tracks but also the station, is full of rather dishevelled Georgian houses – many, however, now being done up; it travels E to join the **Liverpool Rd** at a junction marked by the 1910 Samuel Lewis red-brick flats.

Highbury

Highbury & Islington station (train/Victoria Line tube) is at Highbury Corner, at the start of the **Holloway Rd**. **Highbury Grove/Park** runs N from **St Paul's Rd**, bisecting the area. To the W of **Highbury Grove**, **Corsica Rd** and **Baalbec Rd** describe an area of late-(1889)

Victorian terraces with elaborate façades. Parallel with this is **Highbury Place,** which marks the beginning of the green acres of Highbury Fields. Flat-fronted Georgian terraces gaze out over them: the poshest part of Highbury. The lovely open expanse of the Fields lives up to its name, a breath-of-fresh-air common with the civilized addition of a swimming pool at the S end, tennis courts in the N, and an award-winning adventure playground (staffed at times – but check). They are bounded on the W side by **Highbury Crescent** and **Terrace** (respectively vast detached mansions and tall period terrace, many now flats), which are Highbury's only Georgian streets. Just off Highbury Fields is **Ronalds Rd,** where the old central hall has been split into 10 flats.

Otherwise homes are exclusively Victorian rows with bay windows, wide streets – though **Highbury Terrace Mews** is an exception. Tucked behind **Highbury Terrace,** this is a modern development of the 3-bed houses. To the N of the Fields is **Highbury Hill,** a pretty corner with St John's Church to the E and a clock tower at the centre. Another coveted location, this: houses are large Victorian double-fronted, decreasing in size and becoming terraced towards Arsenal. A new mews, **De Barowe Mews,** appeared a few years back in **Leigh Rd.**

Roads to the N of **Highbury Hill** and W of **Highbury Park** are later Victorian terraces, again reducing in size and quality towards **Gillespie Rd** – and Arsenal football ground. Some still-unrenovated properties towards the bottom, and prices around the football stadium are naturally cheaper – but not much: units in a converted chapel on **Gillespie Rd,** £325,000. Plans to expand the Arsenal ground were shelved, and some matches are now played at Wembley; the area is still best avoided on match days, though. Despite this, 100 **Drayton Park,** a vast office-block (or rather a whole square, around courtyard with 'water feature'), has become Art Deco-inspired flats, adding 84 new homes plus 'the largest roof garden in Islington' to the road to the footie ground. At time of writing, two 2/3-bed flats remained, at £235,000.

Victoriana continues NE off Highbury Park and **Riversdale Rd** to **Mountgrove Rd.** Off **Mountgrove Rd** is a development of 1- and 2-bed flats, 'Old Stable Mews', which is built round a cobbled courtyard. At the corner of **Highbury New Park** overlooking Clissold Park is the noted White Horse pub. The Highbury Quadrant estate covers the area from here down to **Green Lanes:** housing is low-level tower blocks. South from **Sotheby Rd** to **Highbury New Park** in the SE is late Victoriana: large terraces with ornate exteriors and quiet tree-lined streets. The exceptions are **Kelross Rd,** off Highbury Park, which has some modest 1930s semis, and **Fountain Mews** which opens onto **Highbury Grange,** an extensive development of post-modernist and tower blocks.

Across the road are a series of large mansion flats, **Taverner Square** and **Peckett Square,** with interconnecting courtyards. **Aberdeen Rd** runs S to **Aberdeen Park,** the most secluded corner in the district: prices are high and styles range from 1930s semis to spacious Victorian mansions. **Highbury New Park** skirts the area to the E, broad and long, with newer property on the right-hand side, Quadrant estate in the N and Spring Gardens estate in the S. On one side vast period mansions have mainly been converted into flats such as the sophisticated Belmont Court, on the corner of **Balfour Rd.** To the E, **Petherton Rd** runs N to **Green Lanes** with 4-storey Victorian terraces in a wide avenue with a grassy shoulder down the middle. A grid of roads crosses W–E to **Newington Green Rd,** made up of Victorian terraces decreasing in size from **Poets Rd** to **Green Lanes.**

Borders

Highbury and Islington have three main border areas. To the E of Islington lie 'the De Beauvoirs'. Still in the N1 postal district but just across the borough boundary (it runs along **Southgate St**), the pleasant cache of wide streets around **De Beauvoir Square/Rd** came up rapidly in the '80s, and its denizens look to Islington rather than Hackney. Another sign of evolution is the way the place has changed its name: you'll find it labelled 'Kingsland' on maps, but that word seems to have dropped out of use. (The part to the S of **Downham Rd** labelled 'De Beauvoir Town' is now largely occupied by the high- and medium-rise tower blocks of the De Beauvoir council estate. To the N of **Downham Rd**, the terraces resume.)

De Beauvoir lies to the N of **Downham Rd**, W of the **Kingsland Rd** and S of the **Balls Pond Rd**. Its modest-sized, unfussy villas come in ones, twos and threes as well as the more usual rows, offering a rare chance to buy half a house rather than a slice of terrace. Even rarer is the size of garden these 2/3-bed homes enjoy: 75–100 ft or more is not uncommon – and some get garages. A fourth bedroom often betokens roof or back extensions. **De Beauvoir Square** is an 1840s Gothic square of smart pairs of 4-storey villas with bay windows and ornate gables, around a central garden. The square is the hub of a network of streets – similar homes can be found in streets like **Mortimer Rd, De Beauvoir Rd** (a busy thoroughfare), **Hertford Rd** and **Englefield Rd**. Those closest to **De Beauvoir Square** tend to be best; quality frays a little towards the edges, eg **Southgate Grove**. In **Culford Rd** a recent development, Eagle Court, added 30 flats and houses to the area, while **Orchard Mews**, off **Southgate Grove**, is an individualistic 1980s addition complete with corner towers by Kentish Homes. On **Kingsland Rd**, the E edge of the neighbourhood, 'De Beauvoir Place' is a conversion of listed Georgian terraces into 1- and 2-bed flats and 2- and 3-bed duplexes. Apart from being across the border in Hackney, two other factors hold De Beauvoir prices back: many houses are leasehold rather than freehold, and there is no tube.

Lower Holloway, to the N of Barnsbury, lies N of the railway line and W of the **Holloway Rd**. Property is almost totally council-built (modern) radiating off **Paradise Passage**. The exceptions include **Arundel Place** and **Arundel Square**: spacious flat-fronted terraces surrounding a central garden and playground, and **Ellington St**, which has lower-level Georgian terraces, rising to the substantial. Look, too, at **Furlong Rd** which, with **Orleston Rd**, runs E from **Liverpool Rd**: both have large semi-detached period houses. North along **Liverpool Rd** are a few small Victorian terraces, **Morgan Rd, Ringcroft St** and **Sheringham Rd**, quality uneven. **Liverpool Rd** itself has some handsome, flat-fronted early 19th-century houses.

Over on the **Caledonian Rd**, there's a Piccadilly Line tube station. There are some recent developments around here, for example in Stock Orchard Crescent and Frederica St, and the old police station opposite the tube.

The area towards King's Cross, on the W of Islington between the **Caledonian Rd** and **York Way**, N of **Wharfdale Rd**, is also mainly low-level council homes, of various periods. The main interest here is Thornhill Bridge Wharf, a recent development, post-modern in style, coral pink in colour, overlooking the canalside walk. Lots more schemes appearing in this corner: see the Bloomsbury and Kings Cross chapter.

Transport Tubes: Highbury & Islington (zone 2, Victoria), Angel (zone 1, Northern). From Highbury & Islington: Oxford Circus 8 min, City 18 min (1 change), Heathrow 1 hr 10 min (1 change). Trains: Highbury & Islington (Liverpool St 10 min and N London line/Silverlink); Drayton Park, Essex Road, Caledonian Rd, Canonbury.

Convenient for City, Docklands and West End; King's Cross, St Pancras and Euston. Miles from centre: 2.5.

Schools Local Authority: Islington Green School, Highbury Fields (g), Highbury Grove (b), Elizabeth Garrett Anderson School (g), St Aloysius College. Arts & Media School.

SALES

Flats	S	1B	2B	3B	4B	5B
Average prices	80–120	100–240	175–350	250+	500+	–

Houses	2B	3B	4B	5B	6/7B	8B
Average prices	250–450	250–600	300–500+	500+	→2M	1M+–

RENTAL

Flats	S	1B	2B	3B	4B	5B
Average prices	150–200	175–300	250–400	350–450+	–	–

Houses	2B	3B	4B	5B	6/7B	8B
Average prices	350–450+	450–700+	500–750+	750+	–	–

The properties Good choice of early and mid-Victorian houses in attractive areas such as Barnsbury and Canonbury (latter also some stunning Georgian). Highbury has more small houses. Two-bed converted flats in good supply. New developments appear where space allows: particularly round the canal basin.

The market Character period homes in interesting area attract City workers, media types, lawyers. Influx last year of those priced out of West London, and/or looking to invest in Highbury homes (cheaper than Islington) for student offspring to share rather than pay rent. Local searches: 10 working days.

Among those estate agents active in this area are:
- Bairstow Eves
- Holden Matthews
- Evans Baker
- Hotblack & Co
- Brooks & Co
- Hugh Grover Associates*
- Healey, Graham & Co
- The Property Bureau
- Kinleigh, Folkard & Hayward
- Stickley & Kent
- Hamptons
- Winkworth *
- Copping Joyce
- Thompson Currie
- Foxtons *
- Michael Naik & Co*

further details: see advertisers' index on p671

KENNINGTON, VAUXHALL AND STOCKWELL

Map ref: p77 (6K)
Postal districts: SE11, SE17, SW8, SW4, SW9
Boroughs: Lambeth (Lab), Southwark (Lab)
Council tax: Band D Lambeth £750, Southwark £809
Conservation areas: Many – check with town halls
Parking: Residents/meters

Kennington is – at last – becoming a great place to live. It has plenty going for it: a position on the apex of a compact triangle whose other corners are the West End and the City, quite large areas of Georgian and early Victorian housing, the river and all its South Bank excitement, and plenty of tubes and buses. Yet until now Kennington has stubbornly failed to gell as a vibrant London area. Partly this is due to busy roads, partly to the blighting legacies of industry and wartime bombing, partly to a lack of homes to buy. All this is changing. Lambeth Council is determined to improve its patch, proactive in developing long-empty sites, stern in combating fraud and mayhem on its housing estates, proud of the area's many architectural gems. Most important of all, it has drawn a firm line under the looniness and corruption of the past and decided to be a modern, helpful organisation. It does not always succeed, but it is certainly trying. That makes a difference to the whole area.

Lambeth is certainly diverse: 110 languages are spoken here, and this diversity is clear on the streets. Kennington shelters a strong Portuguese community, a clutch of judges and MPs, and people who hail from everywhere from Azerbaijan to Vietnam.

The area lacks a 'high street', though several centres provide focal points for neighbourhoods. Kennington's heart is at the crossroads where **Kennington Lane** intersects with **Kennington Rd**. The tube station is on **Kennington Park Rd** to the E. Vauxhall, until 1859 the site of a famous pleasure gardens, has shrunk to be little more than a giant traffic intersection – and the Victoria line tube station. However,

Vauxhall is now seeing action as several schemes – including a modern pleasure (we now call it leisure) centre – and big homes complexes get under way. The Oval, to the E, centres round its tube station at a busy crossroads and the world-famous cricket stadium. Stockwell, to the S, is a mix of lovely houses and grim council-built estates, and lacks a focus apart from its tube station and a rather down-rent parade of shops on busy **Clapham Road**. Stockwell received a boost 25 years ago when the Victoria line brought it within minutes of the West End; it has some enclaves of real character, but does not seem to have kept up the momentum of improvement begun in the 1970s. Over to the E, a few pockets of interesting housing are to be found on the borders with Walworth and Camberwell. There are no tubes here, so distance from Kennington station becomes an important factor. To the N, Waterloo and the Lambeth area (the site of the old village, not the sprawling borough) have moved into the residential frame (see the South Bank chapter). This renaissance may spill over into North Kennington; there's even talk of major investment (state and private) in the Elephant & Castle, at present perhaps the direst corner.

The whole area is very mixed, with quiet squares that could hold their own in Chelsea only yards away from roaring, dirty throughroads; with mews tucked into corners behind gasworks and with council tower blocks looming over the Georgian terraces. If you look hard and don't mind being part of the patchwork, a Georgian house can be had in a handsome square at a handsome discount to north-of-the-river prices.

People looking to buy here are mostly young, always busy and usually childless. Government ministers may base their families in Kennington's Georgian houses (though they try to keep their teenagers out of the pubs), but couples with kids tend to look at Clapham and points southwest. Much of Vauxhall and Kennington are in the Division Bell zone, and MPs favour the area as being about the closest place to Westminster where one can find a family house. (Partly because of the MPs, judges and other notables who live here, the area is considered part of Inner London by cabbies.)

Young families who want to find a house but stay in the area, or who cannot afford the move to Clapham or Wandsworth, look at the southern and eastern fringes, towards Clapham and Brixton. The neighbourhood served by Clapham North tube is 'moving from funky to family' to quote a local agent. Price rises around there suggest the move has happened.

These areas are 'discovered' every time the London market gets busy. There was a veritable boom in Stockwell in the early '70s, following the first discovery of Kennington in the late '60s. The 1980s saw big increases in prices, but as the boom collapsed, buyers looked to safer areas such as Clapham and Battersea – or to more daring, and cheaper, ones like Brixton and the South Bank. Both 1998 and 1999 saw brisk rises – the real bargains were back in 1996 or so – but the area can still offer more for your money (and a quicker commute) than Clapham or Battersea. Of the three areas in this chapter, Kennington is the most sought-after. Bargain-hunting pioneers should head south and east, to the Clapham North/Brixton fringes and over towards Camberwell New Rd.

As the young flat-buyers of the 1980s enter middle age, the market for houses is growing larger and more broadly based: hitherto only the Georgian gems excited much interest; the action was in flats. The rental market is busy, with landlords trawling the area for investments – even dipping toes into council-built estates like Stockwell Gardens, which though grim is but a step from a Victoria line tube. Rents rose in 1998 but seem to have been stable through 1999.

More than in most places this area demands careful use of the map when considering a move. There are two railway lines running through the area at high level. The W one, leading to Waterloo, takes Channel Tunnel trains. The main roads are choked with traffic more often than not. Red Routes and bus lanes affect main roads (some of which are also residential) and there's been work to restrict rat-runs through residential areas. The E–W route past the Oval to Vauxhall Bridge is signposted as an 'inner ring road' and therefore attracts much heavy through traffic. There is also quite a bit of industry scattered around, though the premises of Sarson's Vinegar are now homes and several other factories (and old Victorian schools) have become 'lofts'.

Transport is good, with Northern and Victoria line tubes and Waterloo (Eurostar and the Jubilee tube to Docklands) just up the road. There is a big Sainsbury's at Vauxhall, and a Tesco in **Kennington Lane** should be open this spring. The area falls into no less than three boroughs – Wandsworth illogically sticks a finger into the W corner. Their council tax, education and other policies differ, so look hard at the map. There are also four postcodes, plus a bit of SW4. None carries much of a premium.

Kennington

The heart of the area, Kennington, gains much of its character from its historical association with the Duchy of Cornwall Estate. The Princes of Wales have owned land here since the Black Prince had his palace in Kennington. In the last decade, however, that influence has waned as most of the Duchy's homes have been passed on to housing associations or sold.

The road names around here are very confusing: it is hard to recall which is **Kennington Park Rd**, which is **Kennington Rd** and which is **Kennington Lane**. The first-named is the main road, following the line of the old Roman Stane Street and linking the Elephant & Castle in the N with the Oval and Stockwell, passing Kennington and Oval tubes. **Kennington Rd** runs due N from near the Oval to the Imperial War Museum at Waterloo. The area called 'Kennington Cross', at the junction of **Kennington Rd** and **Kennington Lane**, is the nearest thing to a villagey bit, boasting tapas bars, deli, etc – not to mention a plethora of estate agents. A Pizza Express and a French restaurant have just opened in **Windmill Row**.

To the W of **Kennington Rd** is the old heart of the neighbourhood, the 45-acre Duchy of Cornwall Estate. A chunk stands NW of **Kennington Lane**, S of the site of the Black Prince's palace, which lay between **Black Prince Rd** and **Sandcroft St**. **Courtney Square**, **Cardigan St** and **Courtney St** are Duchy-built homes in neo-Georgian style: however authentic they look, they were built in 1913. Ex-Duchy cottages here cost around £275–350,000. **Woodstock Court** is an attractive enclosed square of homes, which the Duchy rents to elderly tenants.

Kennington Rd owes its existence to the building of Westminster Bridge (1750) and its regular rows of Georgian terraced houses are still largely in place. Many are flats, some offices – but some remain as large, potentially grand, houses. Some have had their potential realized: agents, though, report them as being slow to shift (traffic may be the snag). Expect to pay £450–500,000 – in 1998 prices started around £375,000. To the E of the road, in the angle formed by its intersection with **Kennington Lane**, is another part of the Duchy Estate. Pretty **Denny Crescent**, **Denny St** and **Chester Way** are all 20th-century Georgian. These, like other Duchy homes, have come onto the open market and are considered a good buy, although they may well be in need of total modernization. Unmodernized ones go for upwards of £225,000; done up, a 2/3-bed cottage can command prices of over £300,000. There are also some ex-Duchy flats blocks in these streets: expect to pay £210,000 for a 3-bed.

Kennington Rd has at its N end the park which surrounds the Imperial War Museum. Just S of the museum, between it and the Lambeth Hospital, is very early Victorian **Walcot Square**, which dates from the 1830s. The charitable Walcot Estate occasionally sells unmodernized houses: prices start at £300,000; £375,000 for a modernized one. **West Square**, which is in truth to the E, has houses from three decades earlier, as does **St George's Rd** on the N edge of the area – but this road carries heavy traffic from the Elephant. **West Square** and the surrounding streets are by contrast peaceful. These Georgian houses overlook a garden square and sell for £500,000-plus. Those with smaller budgets look in streets such as nearby **Hayles St**, with its 2-bed, flat-fronted cottages. **Brook Drive** offers plenty of flats, and some houses, all late-Victorian 3-storey. A 2-bed flat might be £150–160,000. Nearby **Oswin St** has solid 4-storey Victorian houses. Lovely Georgian houses in **Walnut Tree Walk** were offered unmodernized in 1989, and those who bought did well.

Much of the rest of the district E of **Kennington Rd** and W of **Kennington Park Rd** is council-built housing. One mid-'70s flats development is private, however: Vanbrugh Court on **Wincott St**. This popular complex has communal gardens and an underground garage. S of the hospital, a 1980s mews development has been slotted into the angle between **Gilbert Rd** and **Renfrew Rd: Heralds Place** has underground parking for its compact 3-bed houses. **Renfrew Rd** itself has some ex-council houses: 3-storey 3-beds around £200,000. Round the corner is 'Parliament Terrace', off **Gilbert Rd**, 1997 houses in neo-Georgian style, now reselling from £275,000.

To the E of the **Kennington Lane/Kennington Rd** junction is **Cleaver Square**, one of the best places to live in the area and the first to be 'discovered' – allegedly by a '60s barrister trying to find his way back to civilization from a court hearing at Newington Causeway. This urban-feeling square has a mixture of houses, but all are extremely attractive. Those '60s barristers were scandalized when houses in the square reached £20,000 in 1971. Today, their sons and daughters might have to find £550,000-plus for the biggest ones, perhaps £350,000 for a 3-bed cottage. Going S from here, in the angle of **Kennington Rd** and **Kennington Park Rd**, is a neighbourhood of smaller terraced Victorian houses of an unusual design, with spacious semi-basements.

Kennington is best known for its Georgian terraces, but the area also has some interesting survivals from other periods including these almshouses with their Gothic porches and windows. Other interesting architecture can be found on the Duchy of Cornwall Estate, where small houses in Georgian style were built before World War I.

Stannary St's name makes clear the connection with Cornwall and thus the Duchy. **Ravensdon St**, **Methley St** and **Radcot St** are similar. **Kennington Green**, a small widening of **Kennington Rd**, has a few pleasant old houses. **Montford Place** adjoins the site of the new Tesco. Flat-fronted Georgian 3-bed houses here go for around £275–300,000.

To the W, along **Black Prince Rd**, Lambeth Council have big plans for the 30-acre 1960s ex-GLC housing estate up to Lambeth Walk. Under the name 'Project Vauxhall' Lambeth, working with housing associations, plans demolition of bad council housing and relocation of the Lilian Baylis School to **Kennington Lane** as a flagship technology college. There will be homes to buy and rent, plus some for shared ownership. The project is taking its time, but will still happen: expect work to start in 2001.

The loft boom has had its effects on Kennington. The old college situated on **Kennington Rd**, close to **Stannary St**, is now 'The Lycée' loft apartments. Over towards the river in **Vauxhall Walk**, Spring Gardens Court has 1- to 3-bed flats. On **Albert Embankment**, the riverside office block long graced by Lord Archer's penthouse is now flats, and soon no 9 will be 97 flats. At the N end, across from Lambeth Palace, 'Parliament View' is a well-named new block: £390,000 for a 2-bed with river view. In **Kennington Lane** Imperial Court, with its fine 1836 portico, has become flats: £300,000 for a 2-bed.

The Oval

Partly because of heavy traffic, and also owing to the depressing influence of some pre-war council estates, the Oval neighbourhood has less charm than Kennington. Cricket fanatics might consider the period houses on the S side of the **Oval** itself, although the new stands will restrict their view of the pitch. The other sides of the Oval are lined with council blocks. South of the Oval, and sealed off from the traffic, **Ashmole St** and **Claylands Rd** have small terraced houses, rather overwhelmed by the huge amounts of council developments. **Meadow Rd** has flat-fronted terraces.

The prime street here is **Fentiman Rd**, a terrace of dignified mid-Victorian houses. Most lack Kennington's Georgian charm, but are big and conveniently between Oval and Vauxhall tubes. Periods vary between Regency and mid-Victorian. Higher odd numbers overlook the park. One of the larger houses might go for up to £600,000. Off neighbouring **Rita Rd**, with its smaller terraced houses, is the gated entrance to **Regent's Bridge Gardens** – often called 'the Vinegar Works'. This is an expensive 1986 conversion of the Regency/early-Victorian Sarson's works, the manager's house and his splendid ballroom. There are lofts, and flats and town-houses, too; some are conversions, some are skillfully matched new-build. All have access to a private swimming pool complex. Between **Fentiman Rd** and **Richbourne Terrace** is 1980s **Usborne Mews**. **Richbourne Terrace** has early Victorian houses in a area once scruffy, now smartening up. **Palfrey Place** runs behind the W side of **Clapham Rd**. Here, seven new 2-bed, 2-bath town-houses (from £365,000) were on the market last winter.

Close to the Oval tube, **Hanover Gardens** is a very popular pocket of early Victorian houses and cottages in a pretty cul-de-sac. A few streets such as **Handforth Rd** have 3-storey Victorian houses, which convert into pleasant flats that sell for £120,000 if unmodernized; £180,000-plus for a smart one. A few survive as single homes. Round the corner, **Offley Rd** is well-placed for the tube and park – but also close to the big road junction. Plenty of converted flats: 1-bed about £115,000, 2-bed c. £150,000.

To the E again, in **Langton Rd** off the **Camberwell New Rd**, is 1980s **Salisbury Place**: 100 homes from studio flats to 4-bed houses. **Vassall Rd** has big Georgian houses that can command the area's top prices – £675,000 for a 5-bed detached. Further S in **Lothian Rd**, close to **Camberwell New Rd**, Buxton Homes have a development of 2-bed flats (from £140,000) and 2- and 3-bed houses.

Vauxhall

Roads, railways and the New Covent Garden Market take up much of the floorspace in Vauxhall, and council-built homes dominate the rest. The shadow of the vast (still as yet only planned) Battersea Power Station scheme falls over the S of the area. Another shadow is now cast by the giant St George's Wharf towers which are filling the horizon between the traffic and the river. When complete in 2004, this scheme will have 650,000 sq ft of offices and 206 flats in three towers. Phase one is well under way, and will be ready this summer. Prices for 13th-floor, 3-bed 3-bath flats nudge £1 million. On the opposite corner of the bridge approach is the Hollywood-Babylonian biscuit-coloured lair of spymasters MI6, forced out of Mayfair by rising rents.

Inland, Lambeth Council has big plans for its housing N of **Kennington Lane**: under Project Vauxhall, some homes will be knocked down, others refurbished. Residents were being consulted over the winter, with the hope that work will begin in 2001.

Spring Gardens, a little park on the site of the old pleasure gardens, may be halved in area under another major scheme, for a leisure centre/hotel/cinema. As yet, this is merely at the planning stage. Indeed, a year after its announcement little progress had been made – as of last winter a planning application was still anticipated.

Back at Vauxhall Cross, **Vauxhall Grove** looks promising on the map: a square tucked in off the Vauxhall Cross junction. The Grove has long been partly squatted and wholly scruffy: 3-storey Victoriana looms over the narrow streets. Now, however, Lambeth is regaining control and the Grove is smartening up. Round in **Bonnington Square**, a housing association has improved some similar 3-storey flats buildings. Much of the square seems to be inhabited by young people in a sort of post-hippie timewarp; there's a community garden, a café, an annual street parade . . . At the junction of **Langley Lane** and **South Lambeth Rd** is a turn-of-the-century mansion block, Park Mansions, which has a steady turnover of flats for sale. At the end of **Lawn Lane** is a council estate around **Ebbisham Drive**: 2-storey houses and two tower blocks. To the S – in what used to be called 'South Lambeth', but is now a fringe area between Vauxhall and Lambeth – roads such as **Tradescant Rd** have a lot of flats carved out of 3-storey Victorian terraces. **Meadow Place**, nearby, has some 3- and 4-bed Victorian houses still intact for around £240,000. Some recent mews houses in **Dorset Rd**. From here S is considered Stockwell.

A tract to the W of **Wandsworth Rd**, towards Battersea, is attached to Vauxhall – mostly because railway lines shut it off from anywhere else. Most is the Patmore Estate, council-built homes of varying sizes. You can still buy a 2-bed flat here for £75,000. North of the railway, off **Stewart's Rd**, is a 1980s development of studio and 2-bed flats with a fine view of the Eurostar trains on their roof-level viaduct. Back up **Wandsworth Rd**, a complex entered from **Cowthorpe Rd** including **Crimsworth Rd** has rather scruffy late-Victorian cottages and some purpose-built flats. Round the corner in **Thorpatch Rd**, a development of town-houses and flats dates from 1988. Along the river towards Battersea Power Station are some new blocks of flats with good views of Pimlico (better views, in fact, than the other way round). The enormous riverside Regalian development of 'Elm Quay' in **Nine Elms Lane** includes a sports and leisure complex complete with heated swimming pool, gymnasium, sauna and whirlpool spa for the health-conscious. It comprises 1-, 2- and 3-bedroomed flats and penthouses.

Stockwell

Stockwell struck lucky in the early 19th century, with an expansive estate of Regency villas. Just enough survives to provide some gracious streets and architecturally interesting homes, but not enough to make Stockwell a fully-fledged gentrified suburb. The select streets have an air of being marooned in an ordinary patch of South London. Indeed, Lambeth Council reckon Stockwell ward is the 12th most deprived ward in England – due to the big council-built estates.

West of Clapham Rd is **Albert Square** and its associated streets. The giant mid-Victorian houses in the square loom over the central gardens, and are in turn dominated by the nearby tower blocks of the Mursell Estate. Houses in the Square sell at prices between £600,000 and £900,000. **Wilkinson St** and **Aldebert Terrace** have a more human scale. The former is the smarter. **St Stephen's Terrace** has pretty early-Victorian houses priced at around £330,000. Just off **South Lambeth Rd** is 'Sadlers Mews', recent 2-bed houses. Down the street, Wingfield House, a former masonic banqueting hall, is now flats. West of South Lambeth Rd is a mixed neighbourhood of pleasant new council houses and surviving Regency villas. Most of the period homes are clustered around **Landsdowne Gardens**, which opens up in the middle into a perfect circus. The 1840 houses are double-fronted, detached, with big pillared porches: expect to pay £650,000. **Guildford Rd** and linking roads are similar.

Landsdowne Way is a busy E–W road with a mix of properties, some Georgian. A church hall has been carved into five smart 3-bed houses, ultra-modern in style, priced from £380,000 depending on finish. **Thorne Rd**'s handsome 1840s houses offer 4-beds starting at £400,000. West of **Hartington Rd** is a big council-built estate.

East of **Clapham Rd** comes Stockwell Park, the surviving Regency suburb and now a conservation area. Over the last few years it has become – to quote a local agent – 'dead posh'. Many of the houses are good-sized family homes, often inhabited by parents with young children. This encourages more sense of community, with the sharing of school runs etc. Beware, though, confusion with the Stockwell Park Estate, a concrete jungle as yet unredeemed by Lambeth's efforts. **Stockwell Terrace** overlooks the roundabout and tube station: tall early 19th-century houses. There are similar homes – many split into flats – in adjoining **South Lambeth Rd** and **Clapham Rd**. **Stockwell Park Rd** runs E with a mix of homes from small Regency to '20s gabled villas. Again, plenty of flats conversions amid surviving 4-bed Victorian semis which command £350–380,000. At the junction with **Groveway** and **Stockwell Park Crescent**, the road opens out. All these streets have a mix of 1830s villas and terraces, with lots of trees and gardens.

Durand Gardens, hidden away to the N, is a surprise: a pear-shaped square with big Victorian houses, mostly semi- and detached. One 5-bed house topped £1 million last autumn. A little Gothic villa and an enormous detached house add variety. A few arts-and-craftsy 1898 gabled terraces stand on the way out to **Clapham Rd**.

West of **Stockwell Park Crescent**, **St Michael's Rd** and **St Martin's Rd** have 3-storey mid-Victorian brick terraces. Flats converted from these start at c. £130,000 for 1-bed. A little to the E, **Hackford Rd** has some handsome flat-fronted early Victorian houses, some split into spacious flats (a 3-bed was £165,000 last winter). New (1994) 3-storey houses here are around £220,000. S of Stockwell tube is a mixed district of council

blocks and routine Victorian terraces. **Landor Rd** marks the border with Clapham North and Brixton. Agents point out that this side of Stockwell is close to Brixton. This used to be kept quiet, but Brixton is now buzzing – and Stockwellites frequent its bars, cinemas and night life. Thus little houses off **Landor Rd** that were £80,000 in 1994–95 are selling for £200–250,000, and 2-bed converted flats are £130,000.

Larkhall Lane becomes **Larkhall Rise** as it runs through to Clapham, carrying a lot of morning and evening traffic – though work on the railway bridge has kept it closed for the last two years – and will for the forseeable future. The housing off it is mostly council, though there are a few good corners. The Lane itself has some early Victorian houses, much interrupted by car sales yards and council blocks. West of the Lane, **Priory Grove**, overlooking the recently created Larkhall Park, has some pretty, small houses. From **Larkhall Lane** E to Stockwell tube is council. To the S of the area lies a grid of wide streets on the Clapham borders (see Clapham chapter): **Chelsham Rd** and **Bromfelde Rd** have big houses, some with generous Victorian Gothic gables, and mostly now flats. One or two are large (up to 6-bed) family homes. **Gauden Rd** is similar, with some extensive flat conversions and family houses.

Walworth Borders

East from Kennington tube is mostly council housing. Some, indeed, is council-owned but no-one knew (or was saying): a whole stretch of **St Agnes Place** was discovered last autumn to be squatted, as it had been for 20 years. Lambeth asked for it back, saying the previous administration had forgotten it owned it. The Town Hall also asked locals to inform them about any more council-owned homes they'd lost track of.

Firmly in the private sector, **Sutherland Square** has some handsome 4-bed, 4-storey early Victorian houses: these are popular despite the proximity of the railway line just beyond the E side of the square. Nearby streets such as **Fielding St** and (to the N) **Berryfield Rd** have Victorian terraced houses around £200,000. **Lorrimore Square** has a mix of Victorian terraces and new houses. All the streets S of here are part of, or are dominated by, a vast council estate. The mostly post-war flats and houses are interspersed with restored Victorian terraces. A few handsome early Victorian houses survive to the W in **St Agnes Place**, by Kennington Park. This area also has several streets of rather run-down purpose-built Edwardian flats. **Surrey Square**, over towards the **Old Kent Rd**, has some Georgian houses.

This is a good hunting-ground for really cheap, mostly ex-council homes. A 2-bed flat in a tower block can be around £65,000 – but ask about the service charges.

Transport	Tubes: Kennington, Elephant & Castle, Oval, Clapham North (zones 1/2, Northern), Stockwell (zone 2, Victoria, Northern), Vauxhall (zones 1/2, Victoria). From Stockwell: Oxford Circus 10 min, City 20 min, Heathrow 1 hr 15 min (2 changes). Trains: Elephant & Castle (Thameslink), Vauxhall (to Waterloo), Clapham High St, Wandsworth Rd (both to Victoria & London Bridge).
Convenient for	City and Westminster. Miles from centre: 2.
Schools	Local Authority: Lilian Baylis, Stockwell Park, Archbishop Tenison's C of E (b).

SALES

Flats	S	1B	2B	3B	4B	5B
Average prices	40–90	70–160	100–250	150–290	–	–
Houses	2B	3B	4B	5B	6/7B	8B
Average prices	150–280	200–400	300–650	400–1 M	500+	700+

RENTAL

Flats	S	1B	2B	3B	4B	5B
Average prices	100–200	150–250	200–375	270–500	300–600	300–600+
Houses	2B	3B	4B	5B	6/7B	8B
Average prices	220–500	250–600	300–600	350–700+	350+	–

K

The properties	Enclaves of handsome Georgian amid Victorian houses and flats; some modern mews and flats, pretty repro-Georgian on Duchy of Cornwall Estate. Widespread council-built housing. Old schools and factories fast becoming loft apartments.
The market	Good communications attract professionals, City people, MPs, lawyers and doctors. Location matters a lot: select enclaves are close to run-down inner-city. Local searches: Lambeth 10 working days, Southwark 15 working days.

Among those estate agents active in this area are:

- Ludlow Thomson
- Barnard Marcus
- Murray Estates
- Daniel Cobb *
- Alan Fraser
- Halifax
- Winkworth *
- Kinleigh Folkard & Hayward
- Foxtons*

further details: see advertisers' index on p671

KENSINGTON

Map ref: p75 (3J)
Postal districts: W8, SW7
Boroughs: Kensington & Chelsea (Con)
Council tax: Band D £534
Conservation areas: Kensington, Kensington Palace, Edwardes Square, Scarsdale and Abingdon, Kensington Square, Kensington Court, De Vere, Cornwall Gardens, Queens Gate
Parking: Residents' permits, parking meters and clamping. Red Route along Warwick Rd/ Earl's Court Rd

Kensington deserves its 'Royal Borough' title. It owed its origin as a fashionable suburb to the presence of Kensington Palace, and the royal connection continues. It is not many years since the nonagenarian Princess Alice, last surviving granddaughter of Queen Victoria, used to potter around from the Palace to morning service at St Mary Abbots. The Prince and Princess of Wales lived in the Palace during their marriage and Princess Diana continued to live there after their divorce. Following her death, part of Kensington Gardens is to become a memorial to her, though plans have been scaled down following opposition from residents who feared being overwhelmed by 'pilgrims'.

The favoured streets of this corner, closely thronged with some of London's most enviable homes, seldom yield space for new ones. Perhaps the last large site was that of the old St Mary Abbots Hospital in **Marloes Rd**. This is now the gated 'Kensington Green' complex. In **Wrights Lane** is 'Royal Gate Kensington': yet more flats and penthouses completed in 1999. But the star is **Earls Terrace**, an entire row of Grade II listed Regency – 23 houses, from £3 million, or £4 million depending on who you ask – with choice of swimming pool or cinema in the basements.

Kensington began as a roadside hamlet, but real development began after 1689 when King William III moved his court to Kensington Palace, drawing people of rank to the area. However, the main building boom came during the second half of the 19th century, immediately after the Great Exhibition. The result is a rich mix of Georgian and Victorian terraces, grand stucco villas, attractive cobbled mews, tall red-brick mansion blocks and eccentric studio houses. It is very much a desirable place to live: estate agents estimate that house prices went up by 50 per cent between 1990 and 1997, though buyers became a lot more cautious during 1998.

Most streets are within easy walking distance of either of the two main shopping/entertainment centres of **Kensington High St** and **Notting Hill Gate**. Between them they boast cinemas, clubs, pubs, high street stores and designer shops, and **Kensington High St** has a supermarket. The shopping area has attracted big high street names and has become more popular than ever with tourists, but it retains its character and the tiny lanes and roads off the **High St** and **Kensington Church St** are still quiet. A £3 million investment should this year smarten up the High Street. However the Kensington market, haunt of fashion-loving teenage tourists for three decades, is to close this year.

Restaurants dot the affluent streets, and every service is on offer for those with money but no time. Another of the area's attractions is the vast amount of public open space in the shape of Kensington Gardens and Holland Park.

This chapter deals with Kensington proper: Holland Park has its own chapter, as do North and South Kensington.

Campden Hill

Campden Hill Rd climbs sedately uphill from **Kensington High St** and down again to **Notting Hill Gate**. A through-route between the two main shopping streets, it is lined by a wide range of period and modern homes, merging with pubs, shops and restaurants at its N end. Off it are some of the most charming, private and unexpectedly peaceful places to live in inner London.

King's College's Kensington campus lies hidden away behind a tall brick wall and trees on the corner with **Duchess of Bedford's Walk**. Opposite stands Campden Hill Court, a red-brick and stone gabled mansion block with elaborate towers, turrets and domes. The Uruguayan Embassy and the securely walled South African ambassador's residence lie just beyond here, down the hill on the W side. A short distance away in **Airlie Gardens** is Holland Park Comprehensive School. A series of large modern flat blocks extend between **Airlie Gardens** and **Notting Hill Gate**. Many have superb views E across London.

Turn W into **Aubrey Walk**, a surprisingly quiet leafy backwater sitting on the hilltop. Brick and stucco terraces, 20th-century Dutch-gabled houses and some highly individual studio houses line the S side facing the waterworks opposite. Campden Hill Tennis Courts are in **Aubrey Walk** and are above an underground reservoir. This site to be redeveloped with 13 new covered and open courts and homes: 48 2- and 3-bed flats and 19 4-bed houses with gardens. There will also be 17 flats at affordable rents.

The large houses around the corner in **Aubrey Rd** slope downhill to **Holland Park Avenue**. Halfway down **Aubrey Rd** is the entrance to select **Campden Hill Square**. The main terrace of this three-sided Regency square perches near the brow of the hill above the private, tree-lined central gardens. The remaining two terraces are stepped down on either side. Street trees add to the summer canopy of greenery. The houses also have leafy front gardens.

The houses and painted cottages in **Hillsleigh Rd**, E of the square, slope down to **Holland Park Avenue**. This corner also hides two enormous mansions, which crown the Hill. One, Hill Lodge, a virtual country mansion, boasts 60 ft of reception rooms and has a separate cottage within its walled grounds. Another, Aubrey House, in **Aubrey Walk**, sold in 1999 for around £20 million.

The Royal Borough of Kens
and Chelsea

WWW.FOXTON
.COM

Location, location, location?

Buy, sell, rent - Find what you're looking for
on-line at London's leading property website,
or call us on 0800 083 2454

 Foxtons

East across **Campden Hill Rd** is Hillgate Village, an extremely popular enclave of pretty painted little 1850s cottages. The village is bounded by **Notting Hill Gate** (N), **Campden St** (S), **Campden Hill Rd** (W) and **Kensington Church St** (E). Best examples of the gaily coloured all-cottage lanes are **Jameson St, Calcott St, Farmer St, Hillgate Place** and tree-lined **Farm Place**.

Kensington Place has terraces of attractive 2-storey and basement stucco/brick cottages on the N side. Opposite are Fox Primary School and a 1970s red-brick development of 3-storey town-houses lying between two tall blocks of flats set back from the road. **Peel St** and **Campden St** are more mixed. The latter has terraces of 2/3-storey period/modern cottages and houses – and also Byam Shaw House, once the studio and art school of the famous Pre-Raphelite artist. More painted/brick and stucco cottages are found in **Peel St,** where half of the N side is taken up by the tall red- and grey-brick blocks of Campden Houses. **Bedford Gardens** to the S is a leafy street with mainly 4-storey houses including one with a 2-bed cottage in the garden.

Terraces of mainly 3-storey white stucco houses and some big villas stand on the N side of **Sheffield Terrace.** (Poet and novelist G. K. Chesterton lived at No 32.) By contrast, most of the S side is lined by a long row of matching tall red-brick gabled buildings with white stucco and striped entrances. Another 6-storey red-brick and stone block, Campden House, lies at the corner of **Hornton St.** Hidden away behind the S side of **Sheffield Terrace** is a 2½-acre private communal garden. Residents of properties in **Hornton St** and **Gloucester Walk** also have access. **Gloucester Walk** has a mix of modern flats and red-brick gabled mansions as well as 3/4-storey brick and stucco houses. **Campden Grove** has 5-bed houses and some 3-bed houses: one was £1.5 million last winter.

Tucked away off the NW end of **Hornton St** opposite **Gloucester Walk** is **Campden House Close.** A narrow lane leads to a group of 2-storey cottages set around a pleasant spacious courtyard. Varying styles of houses and flats stretch down **Hornton St,** including some large semi-detached stucco properties. An eye-catching terrace of brown-brick and white striped Victorian buildings with elaborate stucco decoration is stepped down the W side as far as **Holland St.** The style continues into **Observatory Gardens** with its red-brick and stone striped 3-storey houses. An attractive terrace of 20th-century Dutch-gabled houses extends down **Hornton St** opposite the town hall.

Cutting across **Horton St** is **Holland St,** a popular narrow road where detached stucco houses and Georgian-style terraces are interspersed with a handful of speciality shops and restaurants. An undistinguished terrace of 20th-century houses lies on the S side. Halfway along **Holland St** is **Gordon Place,** where a 3-bed house was £950,000 last winter. The S end forms a pretty, overgrown walkway, set back from the road and looking like a country lane. Hidden behind the trees and mature front gardens are two terraces of Georgian-style houses turned sideways on to **Holland St.** Just N of the E end of **Holland St,** through a gateway off **Kensington Church St,** is Bullingham Mansions. This yellow- and red-brick and stone Dutch-style block is built around a landscape fountain courtyard guarded by some impressive stone lions.

Dominating the SE corner of the neighbourhood is Kensington's parish church, St Mary Abbots, with its dramatic 250-ft spire, the tallest in London.

Kensington Palace

The focal point of the neighbourhood is the Renaissance palace, rebuilt in the late 17th century by Sir Christopher Wren, and set in beautiful Kensington Gardens.

The next most exclusive address in the neighbourhood is a long tree-lined avenue running N–S past the palace and gardens. The N end is called **Kensington Palace Gardens,** the S end (it's the same road) **Palace Green.** Stately mansions with sweeping driveways and landscaped grounds line this prestigious private road.

Although known as 'Millionaires' Row', most of the once private residences have now been taken over by embassies. The road is guarded by gates and gatekeepers at both ends and the police Diplomatic Protection Corps takes an interest, which reassures the more nervous among the incoming rich. One complete house, once leased by the Soviet government, was on the market last winter for £35 million for a long Crown lease. At the SW end, overlooking Kensington Palace is 3A Palace Green. These flats were marketed in 1990 – just as the market crashed – at up to £10 million. Last winter one of the three penthouses was priced at £4.95 million.

Alongside 3A Palace Green in **York House Place**, a narrow passageway leads to York House, a prestigious Victorian mansion block. The 7-storey red-brick and stone block with red-and-white striped gables stands in a relatively quiet cul-de-sac with an ornamental water garden in the middle, creating a courtyard.

The passageway continues into **Kensington Church St**. From here the streets wend their way gradually uphill to **Notting Hill Gate**. **Church Close**, opposite the Carmelite Church in **Kensington Church St,** is a 3-storey red-brick and stone Tudor-style complex, set around an inner garden courtyard.

The scale suddenly changes where **Vicarage Gate** branches off **Kensington Church St**. Two 8-storey 1930s flat blocks, Winchester Court (W) and Vicarage Court (E), spread along each side of the street. The side of the latter block also occupies most of the S side of the E arm of **Vicarage Gate**. A Victorian brick and stucco terrace with polished marble porch columns stands on the N side.

St Marys Abbot's modern vicarage is set in a private courtyard at the end of the street, forming a cul-de-sac. **Vicarage Gate** N contains a jumble of tall houses in varying styles. It leads to **Vicarage Gardens**, lined terraces of white stucco properties at the N end and brick and stuccos. A barrier of trees and shrubs separates **Vicarage Gate** from **Inverness Gardens**, a semi-circular sweep of 3-storey white stucco houses. More terraces of white stucco houses, some split into flats, are found in **Brunswick** **Gardens** and **Berkeley Gardens**.

The white paint continues in tree-lined **Palace Gardens Terrace** – 3-storey basement terraces on the E side and 4-storey basement houses with elaborate Greek-style columned porches on the W. **Strathmore Gardens**, lying off the W side of the street, is a short cul-de-sac of 4-storey and basement stucco terraces. A 4-bed house in **Kensington Church St** was £1.5 million last winter. Just beyond here, **Palace Gardens Terrace** becomes part of a district one-way traffic system linking **Notting Hill Gate** with **Kensington Church St**. **Church St**, a residential/shopping street lined by pubs, antique shops, galleries and jewellers among others, is a main N–S traffic route running between **Notting Hill Gate** and **Kensington High St**.

Queen's Gate

Queen's Gate is a busy boulevard lined by the grand stucco terraces which are a feature of this neighbourhood. The majority were built between 1850 and 1870 and have now been converted into vast, grand flats, hotels, embassies and ambassadorial homes. East of here is considered Knightsbridge.

More long stretches of 4/5-storey Victorian terraces, with columned porches, stand on both sides of **Queen's Gate Terrace** (white and cream stucco) and **Elvaston Place** (brick and stucco). Both are wide streets with extra parking space in the middle, as in **Queen's Gate**. Prices for newly-renovated 1- to 3-bed flats in Queen's Gate Terrace were £350–750,000 last autumn. A penthouse in Queen's Gate was £850,000. In **Queens's Gate Gardens**, the imposing 5/6-storey stucco terraces are set around three sides of a large leafy central garden screened by trees. A 1960s flats block, Campbell Court, which fronts **Gloucester Rd**, backs on to the W side of the garden with its extensive lawns.

Dotted around this network of streets is a series of small-scale mews, which once served as stables and staff quarters for the large houses behind which they lie. Most have mixtures of groups of 2-storey brick/painted cottages and working garages and car showrooms. **Queen's Gate Mews**, lying just off **Queen's Gate Terrace**, has the added attraction of its own pub, the Queen's Arms. Impressive Classical-style stone arches lead into **Elvaston Mews** and **Queen's Gate Place Mews**. The latter sits behind more 5-storey brick and stucco terraces in **Queen's Gate Place**. It is wider that the other mews, leaving room for cobbled forecourts in front of the varied modern and period 2-storey cottages.

The tall brick and stucco terraces reappear in **Gloucester Rd**, a busy district road and shopping centre. They have been turned into hotels, offices or flats, usually with shops on the ground floor. **Gloucester Rd** merges into **Palace Gate**, which is lined mainly by highly individual stone, or red-brick and stone, period buildings, occupied by offices, flats and embassies.

It may look 18th century – but it is modern. A clever pastiche of the Kensington town-house style, with 'Georgian' fanlight, panelled door with windows either side – even the ivy is authentic. For the real thing in Kensington, visit Kensington Square, which grew up as homes for Palace courtiers and has some beautiful Queen Anne and early Georgian houses.

Exclusive **Kensington Gate** lies to the E at the point where **Palace Gate** and **Gloucester Rd** meet. Two grand terraces of richly ornamented 3/4-storey white stucco Victorian houses stretch along a narrow strip of garden with tall trees and well-kept flower beds. At each end of the terraces stand paired 'tower' houses, looking like iced wedding cakes. **Kensington Gate** and **Hyde Park Gate** to the N still have high proportions of single-family houses.

The E leg of **Hyde Park Gate** contains a mix of period/modern houses and flats, plus some large 'one-off' houses such as No 28, where Sir Winston Churchill lived and died. Tall red-brick and stone mansions and 11-storey 1960s red-brick flats block, Broadwalk House, stand on either side of the entrance to the more exclusive W leg of the street. Beyond here, the street opens out into a circle with a central garden. A handful of elegant detached villas with their own large gardens sit around the circle. Halfway along the street off to the W is **Reston Place**, a charming little enclave of 2-storey white-painted cottages set around a secluded courtyard.

The **Kensington Rd** frontage of the neighbourhood is dominated by the huge modern 11-storey red-brick Thorney Court flats block, and Broadwalk House, which overlook Kensington Gardens. In common with the other period/modern properties lining the N boundary (flats, embassies and offices), they are set back from the road behind driveways and screens of trees.

De Vere/Cornwall

West of **Gloucester Rd** is a neighbourhood that in many ways is the heart of Kensington. The area runs southwards from the centuries-old **Kensington Square** with a series of quiet, leafy streets. On the E side of the neighbourhood **Gloucester Rd** is a busy road lined by a mix of residential and commercial properties and shops. It also has a tube station. The main residential grouping is the 4/5-storey Edwardian red-brick and stone mansion block of St George's Court, which has a row of shops on the ground floor.

Behind St Stephen's Church at the SW end of **Gloucester Rd** is **Emperor's Gate**. This almost triangular-shaped street has a tiny triangle of green in the middle and a central block of painted stucco terraced properties sitting on a similarly shaped site. A terrace of late-Victorian red-brick and stucco buildings with ornate columned porches stand on the W side and a terrace of 5-storey and basement buildings on the E. Most are split into flats. Concealed behind a red-brick and stone arch in the NE corner of the street is **Osten Mews**, a looped cobbled mews of 2-storey painted cottages.

The view here is dominated by the towering shape of Point West – an apartment block converted from the former West London Air Terminal fronting **Cromwell Rd**. This huge development was on hold for a decade after the former owners ran out of money in 1987, but in 1997 a consortium restarted the scheme. It is now complete, with over 300 flats priced (for 2- and 3-beds) at £350–680,000, £800,000-plus for a penthouse. Also in the block are offices, a David Lloyd health club and shops.

On either side of **Grenville Place** (brick and stucco terraces) lies pretty **Cornwall Mews South** with a mix of 2-storey period/modern brick painted cottages. Just up the road, the scale changes dramatically in **Cornwall Gardens** with its tall cliffs of white stucco. Terraces of mid-19th-century Italianate houses with columned porches stretch along both sides of three large private gardens. The trees match the height of the 5-storey and basement houses, long ago divided into flats of various sizes and conditions.

Launceston Place to the N signals the beginning of an enclave of highly desirable, quiet streets lying in the heart of the neighbourhood. The group is bounded by **Launceston Place** itself and **Victoria Grove** E, **Stanford Rd** W, **Albert Place** N and **Kynance Mews** S. **Canning Place** is in the same style: the whole enclave dates from around 1840.

Picturesque **Kynance Mews** must rate as the most attractive mews in the whole of the Kensington and Chelsea area. Divided in two by **Launceston Place**, the shorter E section is lined by 2/3-storey white/cream painted cottages and has a splendid view of Queen's Tower. The W and most delightful selection is full of charming vine-covered 2-storey cottages of different styles. A profusion of flowers and shrubs spread along the mews in tubs and urns. Part of the N side backs on to the walled gardens of houses in **Eldon Rd** and the prize-winning gardens of Christ Church in **Victoria Rd**, giving the mews a particularly leafy look at this point.

Halfway along the mews, a set of steps leads to **Victoria Rd**. Many a household name has been attracted to the elegant homes in this 1840s street known in former days as 'Love Walk'. Small groups of semi-detached stucco or brick-and-stucco villas with leafy front gardens line the most desirable stretch of the street S of **Cambridge Place**, where homes range from £1.75–3 million. North of here, the road is flanked by the backs of hotels fronting adjoining streets. **Victoria Rd** continues N to meet **Kensington Rd** and Kensington Gardens.

More 2-storey semi-detached early-Victorian villas are found in **Launceston Place**, running parallel. The black and white colour scheme is accentuated by the black window canopies remaining on the houses on the W side of the street. **Eldon Rd** is a particularly attractive street with terraces of pastel-painted 3-storey stucco houses adjoining Christ Church on the corner of **Victoria Rd**. Groups of highly individual brick/stucco houses stand on the N side. Tree-lined **Cottesmore Gardens** to the N has paired 3-storey stucco villas and more big individual houses.

The W end of the street runs into **Stanford Rd**, lined by detached brick and stucco villas, with some paired houses and simple brick and stucco terraces. Standing in their midst is Cottesmore Court, a tall 1930s brown-brick flats block, which spreads around into **Kelso Place**. The S arm of this T-shaped street has rows of 2/3-storey brick terraced houses backing onto the Kensington Green development on the W side (see below). The modern brown-brick town-house development lies in a private cul-de-sac at the end of the W arm of **Kelso Place**, which flanks the underground line (running above ground at this point).

Running across the N end of **Stanford Rd** is **St Alban's Grove**. More brick and stucco detached and paired houses can be found on the S side opposite Richmond College, the American international college of London. Next to it is the red-brick and stucco block of St Alban's Mansions. The W end of the street culminates in a small local shopping centre, a feature of which is the famous Leith School of Food and Wine. A bunch of grapes and a knife and fork have been wittily worked into the brickwork of the gabled building. Just around the corner to the S, hidden from the street, are the vine-covered St Alban's Studios, set around a neo-Tudor courtyard.

The E end of the street also forms a pleasant villagey centre at its junction with **Victoria Grove**. A terrace of 1840s stucco houses with a continuous black first-floor canopy and unusual decorative ironwork columns stretches along the N side. It joins up with more shops spilling around the corner from **Gloucester Rd**.

Canning Place just to the N is a pleasant, leafy street with pairs of linked stucco villas and a terrace of 2/3-storey and basement stucco houses. On the N side are the entrances to two converted mews developments, **De Vere Cottages** and **De Vere Mews**. **De Vere Gardens** off to the N is lined mainly by tall brick and stucco terraces converted into flats with hotels at its N end.

Canning Passage, a pedestrian walkway, runs through to **Victoria Rd**. Off this road is a series of three leafy cul-de-sacs – **Albert Place**, **Cambridge Place** and **Douro Place**. The first two have early Victorian stucco villas. Much of **Douro Place** was completely rebuilt following war damage, resulting in modern and period houses standing side by side. The cul-de-sac here is created by the rear of the flats in Kensington Court.

Kensington Court is both the name of the street and the red-brick Dutch-style development which dominates this 7-acre triangular site S of **Kensington High St**. A series of mansion blocks and terraces of gabled houses of differing heights and degrees of ornamentation make up the complex. Built 1880–1900, Kensington Court was the first group of buildings in London to be lighted by electricity. At the S end of **Kensington Court** is **Kensington Court Mews**, an unusual late-Victorian multi-storey stable block, which now has two tiers of flats above ground-floor garages.

Another 5/6-storey red-brick block, Kensington Court Gardens, stands on the E side of **Kensington Court Place**, dwarfing the terrace of early 19th-century cottages opposite.

Beyond **Thackeray St** with its parade of shops is **Kensington Square**. This is one of London's oldest squares, dating back to 1685, when it was built to house Palace courtiers. Blue plaques dotted around the square with its large central gardens give a clue to its former distinguished residents, including Edward Burne-Jones, Mrs Patrick Campbell and John Stuart Mill. Some of the buildings, which range from Jacobean and Georgian to 1905, remain as houses. Others have been converted into offices.

Scarsdale/Abingdon

The Circle line in its deep cutting and the Kensington Green development divide this neighbourhood from **Kensington Square** to the E. **Wrights Lane** is the entry point from **Kensington High St**. A short way down **Wrights Lane** the Royal Gate development of 119 1-, 2- and 3-bed apartments and penthouses is now complete with its underground parking and fitness centre. **Wrights Lane** leads on to the big London Copthorne Tara and Kensington Close Hotels. On the W side of the street, not far from its junction with the **Kensington High St**, stand two of the late-Victorian mansions blocks which make up Iverna Court, a set-piece complex of 5/7/8-storey and basement red-brick and stone mansion blocks with elaborate entrances and black cast-iron balconies. The blocks spread around the corner into **Iverna Gardens**, stretching almost to its junction with **Abingdon Villas**. Flats in the square at the N end of the street overlook the unusual white marble St Sarkis Armenian Church, which sits in the middle, behind a strip of trees and shrubs.

More tall brick and stone mansion blocks, including the popular Zetland House, line the E side of busy **Marloes Rd**. A 4-bed flat in Zetland House was £800,000 last winter. Off Marloes Rd, on the site which was successively the local workhouse and then the hospital, is 'Kensington Green', a 1991 complex of 1- to 4-bed houses and flats. Access is via **St Mary's Gate**, with the main street called **St Mary's Place**. The rest of **Marloes Rd** has terraces of 3/4-storey and basement brick and stucco properties, some with shops and offices on the ground floors. The large grey concrete and blue glass building at the S junction with **Cromwell Rd** is the private Cromwell Hospital. **Pennant Mews** runs behind the hospital.

Lexham Gardens stretches across the neighbourhood, changing in character as it goes. The S crescent, which curves N from **Cromwell Rd**, contains mainly hotels, presumably remnants from the days when the West London Air Terminal stood behind the street. The rest of the brick and stucco terraced properties here have been converted into flats: you might be asked £485,000 for a 2-bed garden flat. Leading off the N end of the crescent is **Lexham Walk**, a pleasant passageway lined by white 2-storey cottages. It crosses into the De Vere/Cornwall neighbourhood to the E. **Lexham Gardens** E of **Marloes Rd** is made up of 4/5-storey and basement brick and stucco terraced houses of varying quality set around narrow central gardens. The houses in the W arm across **Marloes Rd** are built in the same style but generally of better quality. As in the E arm, most have been split into flats.

Tucked away behind the W end of **Lexham Gardens** are **Lexham Mews** and **Radley Mews**, which join together at the S end of **Allen St**. The long cobbled mews has mostly 2-storey period/rebuilt brick/painted cottages with some garages and other light industrial uses. A tiny Victorian mews house, 2 beds and a garage, was £650,000 freehold last winter; another re-built in 1985, £495,000. Emerge from the mews into **Stratford Rd** with its up-market 'village' shops and terraces of 3-storey and basement brick and stucco houses, some with small front gardens and forecourt parking.

Lying off the N side of **Stratford Rd** around the corner from the parade of shops is **Blithfield St**, an appealing tree-lined cul-de-sac of colourfully painted 3-storey terraced houses dating back to the 1860s. **Sunningdale Gardens** stands on the S side of **Stratford Rd** at the junction with **Abingdon Rd**. Here the terraces turn sideways on to form an attractive enclave of 3-storey and basement brick and stucco houses on two sides of a small central garden with trees in the middle.

Well-hidden behind the houses in the N side of **Stratford Rd** near its junction with **Earls Court Rd** is **Shaftesbury Mews**, a development of modern 4-storey brown-brick houses with garages. **Scarsdale Studios**, off **Stratford Rd**, is an enclave of nine artists' studios built in the 1890s around a private courtyard.

Tree-lined **Scarsdale Villas** has Victorian terraces of 3-storey and basement stucco, or brick and stucco houses up to **Allen St**. Going E they become paired 3-storey and basement stucco-fronted villas on the N side, and similar style in groups of four on the S. In tree-lined **Abingdon Villas**, a mix of 3-storey Victorian terraces stand next to tall red-brick and stone mansion blocks. **Abingdon Court** N, which stretches from **Iverna Gardens** to **Allen St**, is a late-Victorian block, and **Abingdon Gardens** S is Edwardian.

Allen St and **Abingdon Rd**, which runs N–S from **Kensington High St** to **Stratford Rd**, combine a mix of homes and commercial uses. Shops and restaurants spill around the corner from the **High St** into both. A short distance S of the **High St** in **Allen St** is **Wynnstay Gardens**, a development of 4/5-storey red-brick and stucco flats blocks. One group fronts **Allen St** while further blocks are tucked away behind, lining a private road. Allen House, a red-brick gabled block of timeshare flats, stands on the opposite side of the street near the listed Kensington Chapel, built in 1855 and noted for its classical façade. More mansion flats and 3-storey brick and stucco terraces lie to the S. Flats hereabouts go for around £600,000 for a 2-bed, 2-bath, share of freehold.

Beside the chapel is one of two entrances to **Adam and Eve Mews**. (The other is in **Kensington High St**.) The mews contain 2/3-storey modern/period houses, some

K

garages and offices. Houses command prices up to and beyond £1 million. **Eden Close** at the NW end is a new red-brick development, where a mews has been created within a mews.

Abingdon Rd is lined with 2/3-storey terraced houses of varying styles. The brown- and red-brick late-Victorian flats in **Pater St** to the W spread around the corner into the N end of the street, merging with the shops and restaurants which lead to the **High St**.

Earls Court Rd on the W boundary of the neighbourhood is a two-way street as far as **Stratford Rd** where it joins the notorious West London one-way traffic system, now a Red Route. The most attractive residential section – a terrace of 4-storey and basement stucco-fronted houses – lies between **Stratford Rd** and **Scarsdale Villas**. The unusual new cream- and brown-stone, brick and glass development at the junction of **Earls Court Rd** and **Kensington High St** is a flats and offices block, topped by a penthouse overlooking Holland Park. Monarch House has luxury flats to let, aimed at businessmen and expatriates, with hotel-style amenities.

Pembrokes/Edwardes Square

Although bounded by some of the busiest and noisiest roads in the borough this desirable neighbourhood contains some of the earliest and choicest properties in Kensington. The first surprise lies at the end of an unpromising lane off the N end of bustling **Earls Court Rd**, behind the Odeon Cinema. Turn the corner to find **Pembroke Place**, an oasis of pretty painted 3-storey Victorian houses set around a courtyard with trees in the middle. The 3-storey brick and stucco terrace on the E side is a modern rebuild.

Tucked away behind Kensington police station immediately to the S is **Pembroke Mews**. The mostly 2-storey brick/painted brick and stucco cottages vary widely in quality and condition but rebuilding and renovation is under way.

Within yards of **Earls Court Rd** with its mix of residential/commercial properties is **Pembroke Square**. This Georgian square is neatly shielded from the main road by Rassells garden centre and the flower-bedecked Hansom Cab pub. Two terraces of 4-storey mellow brick terraced houses with stucco-faced ground floors line a long private central garden. The garden has its own tennis court and even a daily weather chart posted on the gate. The W end of **Pembroke Square** becomes **Pembroke Villas** to the S, an attractive colony of 3-storey paired stucco or brick and stucco villas set in gardens with tall trees overhanging the street.

Pembroke Walk, an easily missed cul-de-sac tucked away off the E side of the street, is a narrow lane with unusual, nay eccentric, 2/3-storey period and modern houses/studios. North of **Pembroke Square**, past the pretty Scarsdale pub with its profusion of hanging baskets, stands **Edwardes Square**, the gem of the neighbourhood.

This fine late-Georgian square was built 1811–20. Immaculate terraces of beautiful 3-storey and basement brick houses with stucco ground floor stretch along the W and E sides of mature central gardens. Front gardens, wisteria-covered houses, hedges and overhanging trees contribute to the leafy look of the spacious square, only a short walk from the shops and restaurants which line **Kensington High St**. Green Victorian street lamps, original cast-iron fanlights and black cast-iron railings with unusual pineapple kingheads add to the period character of the area.

The N side of the square is bounded by a long brick wall and a mass of trees in the rear gardens of **Earls Terrace**, which fronts **Kensington High St**. Here a long uniform Regency terrace, set back from the main road behind a private carriageway, with iron gates and trees, is the talking-point of Kensington – its high-security, 6-bedroomed, £3–6 million houses have been renovated to superstar status. The real gossip is that despite high-profile marketing and many sightings of superstars none have as yet moved in (or have admitted to it). Eventually, reckon the developers, the need for security will overcome the prejudice against living in a terrace (and being a long way from Harvey Nicks).

The S arm of **Edwardes Square** feels like a separate street, being a complete contrast to the Georgian terraces. It has mostly studio houses (Annigoni lived here) alongside 1930s Pembroke Court, a 5-storey brick and stone flats block. These buildings face the white 'Temple', a listed gardener's cottage in the square garden designed to look like a Grecian temple. Lying just to the S of the square at its W end is **Pembroke Gardens Close**, a private landscaped cul-de-sac of very desirable 2-storey brick houses. This exceptional enclave has the peaceful air of a village green.

Pembroke Gardens (the name derives from the Welsh estates of Lord Kensington's family) is split into two arms. A feature of the N arm is **Pembroke Studios**, 2-storey red-and brown-brick Victorian houses looking like a group of 19th-century almshouses. The studios are set around a central courtyard and the complex itself is separated from the street by a garden and cast-iron gates. The rest of the street has a mix of brick and stucco paired houses, 1920s Dutch-gabled houses, modern brick terraces and Victorian brick and stucco terraces.

Pembroke Rd is cut in two by the heavily trafficked Earls Court one-way system, which runs southbound along the E stretch to join **Earls Court Rd**. Two large flats blocks – Chatsworth and Marlborough Courts – dominate the S side of the E arm. A long lease on a 1-bed flat might be £200,000. Painted brick, or stucco and brick, paired/detached stucco houses line the rest of the S and N sides.

A new red-brick block, Huntsmore House (formerly Pembroke Heights), stands at the junction of **Pembroke Rd** and **Cromwell Crescent**. The block of 79 1- to 3-bed flats stretches to the council's central works depot on the corner with **Warwick Rd** W. It encloses a large garden and boasts a swimming pool and gym.

Although **Warwick Gardens** forms the S-bound section of the Earls Court one-way system, it is a relatively pleasant tree-lined street. Pairs of large Victorian stucco houses with columned porches and terraces of 3-storey and basement brick and stucco houses predominate. St Mary Abbots Court is a group of three large 7-storey brick flats blocks, which congregate at the NW end of **Warwick Gardens**.

Warwick Rd is a major route on the N-bound section of the one-way system. The council's central works depot with a modern housing estate perched on top dominates the E side of the road. On the W side, public car and lorry parks, a petrol station, a Sainsbury's Homebase DIY centre, a smart new Tesco superstore and the West Kensington telephone exchange lie between the road and railway line. St George's 'Kensington Westside' is here: nearly 300 flats including 60 affordable homes, prices (for the un-affordable ones) start at £375,000.

Phillimore Estate

Substantial Victorian houses and villas predominate in this leafy, salubrious neighbourhood. The streets climb gently uphill and are remarkable peaceful considering their proximity to busy **Kensington High St**, just to the S. Most of the big white stucco detached villas and 4/5-storey stucco or brick-and-stucco terraced houses on the W side of **Phillimore Gardens** have the added advantage of rear gardens backing on to Holland Park. Leases are short at under 20 years. More large detached mansions are on the E side, alongside 4-storey semi-detached houses. Some have front gardens, others patios with flower-filled tubs.

A pedestrian passageway leads into Holland Park from the N side of the street where it joins **Duchess of Bedford's Walk** at the top of the hill. Plane Tree House, an award-winning 7-storey 1960s flats development, stands in the N corner overlooking the park. Two-bed flats here command prices around £500,000. A series of Edwardian flats blocks, including the prestigious Duchess of Bedford House, spread along the rest of this tree-lined street, adjoining the campus of King's College on the E corner. The 7-storey brown-brick and stone blocks stand in beautifully kept landscaped grounds, set back behind neatly clipped hedges.

They overlook the walled back gardens of houses in **Upper Phillimore Gardens**. This street is lined by large white stucco linked houses and smaller brick and stucco terraced homes, all front gardens, hedges and doorstep urns full of roses and shrubs and bushes. Tall trees add to the street's charm. **Phillimore Place**, a one-way street, and **Essex Villas** have mainly 3-storey and basement brick and stucco terraced houses. The exception is a group of Tudor Gothic houses in the former. Taller, more ornate, brick and stucco terraces are found in **Stafford Terrace**.

The scene changes completely in **Phillimore Walk**, which is overshadowed by the back of Stafford Court, a big early 20th-century brown-brick and stone flats block. It fronts **Kensington High St** and takes up the whole block between **Phillimore Gardens** and **Argyll Rd**. More large semi-detached houses and white stucco terraces with front gardens line **Argyll Rd**.

The S end of **Campden Hill Rd**, which forms the neighbourhood's E boundary, also has big white houses and brick and stucco terraces. They look across to the modern red-brick Kensington Town Hall in the E side of the street.

Transport   Tubes: Notting Hill Gate (zone 1/2, District, Circle, Central), Queensway (zone 1, Central), High St Kensington (zone 1, District, Circle), Gloucester Rd (zone 1, Piccadilly, District, Circle). From High St Kensington: Oxford Circus 15 min (1 change), City 25 min (1 change), Heathrow 40 min (1 change).

Convenient for Hyde Park, West End, Heathrow and West. Miles from centre: 3.
Schools Local Authority: Holland Park, Cardinal Manning RC (b), Cardinal
Vaughan RC (b), St Thomas More RC, Sion Manning RC (g).
Private: St James', Falkner House (g), Queens' Gate School (g).

SALES

Flats	S	1B	2B	3B	4B	5B
Average prices	100–300	165–500	250–650	400–650+	600–1.5 M	800–2 M+
Houses	2B	3B	4B	5B	6/7B	8B
Average prices	400–650	450–1 M	750–2 M	1–3 M+	1.3–5 M+	→4 M+

RENTAL

Flats	S	1B	2B	3B	4B	5B
Average prices	220–500	300–700	400–1000	500–1500	500–2500	1200+
Houses	2B	3B	4B	5B	6/7B	8B
Average prices	400–800	600–1000	700–2000+	1000–3000	2000–7000	3000–10,000

The properties Heart of desirable, residential London: Victorian houses, some
earlier; large numbers of flats, both mansion and converted; plus
mews cottages and some new-build flats and houses in smart
gated developments. Hardly a bad street in the place.

The market Kensington has never been unfashionable. Today, the settled,
prosperous population is joined by international buyers/renters.
More domestic than Knightsbridge, smarter than South Ken,
more respectable than Notting Hill. Some glorious multi-million
homes. Local searches: 10 working days.

K

Among those estate agents active in this area are:
- W A Ellis *
- Knight Frank
- Chesterfield
- Marsh & Parsons*
- Aylesfords*
- Friend & Falcke*
- Jackson-Stops & Staff
- FPDSavills
- John D Wood
- Douglas & Gordon *
- Century 21
- Daniel Cobb *
- Foxtons *
- Winkworth *
- Lane Fox
- Strutt & Parker *
- Hamptons
- Beaney Pearce *
- Scotts *
- Berkeley International
- Chestertons
- Finlay Brewer *
- Farley & Co *

further details: see advertisers' index on p671

KENTISH TOWN AND TUFNELL PARK

Map ref: p45 (5G)
Postal districts: NW5, N7
Boroughs: Camden (Lab),
  Islington (Lib Dem/Lab
  Coalition)
Council tax: Band D
  Camden £897,
  Islington £912
Conservation areas: Kelly
  St, Torriano Cottages,
  Dartmouth Park
Parking: Residents' zones
  spreading from Camden
  Town end

Kentish Town basks in the reflected glow from Hampstead and Highgate,
and its image continues to improve. Indeed, the grander, larger houses of Dartmouth
Park are cheap only in comparison to these lofty neighbours. For the rest, the
handsome early Victorian terraces that survive in a somewhat mixed area are now
'riddled with trendy property' according to local agents, who pray that, given its
neighbours and its convenience, it's only a matter of time before it catches up with
Camden. We draw your attention to the N London line, Silverlink, which goes direct to
the City Airport – thus making Gospel Oak rail station a mere 2 hours 10 minutes from
Paris. No need to wait, then, for the Eurostar to arrive at St Pancras . . .

Transport is much in residents' minds just now – or rather parking. Those areas that
haven't got residents' parking now will certainly have them within a year or three.
Clampers are rampant, and the council is threatening not to give permits to inhabitants
of any new developments in the borough with their own parking spaces.

The first mentions of 'Kentystown', 'Kentisshton' and 'Kentissetone' appear in
documents dating from as early as the 13th century, when it probably started life as a
cluster of houses around an inn – a welcome refuge on what was one of the few roads
leading northwards from the City through the forbidding Forest of Middlesex. The
village grew as the area around became important farm land, but the real population
explosion came in the 1840s, when large-scale development began – catering for
middle-class families with servants, but not able to compete with its illustrious
northern neighbours, Hampstead and Highgate, for really wealthy inhabitants.

The area passed through ups and downs, becoming at first a rather pretty and fashionable place, but then (as the railways carved the area up) falling into a long and steady decline, which lasted until the 1960s when two important things happened. The first was the dramatic acceleration of large council housing development schemes started by St Pancras Council and continued, with more vigour, by the newly formed larger borough of Camden, which changed the face of Kentish Town, particularly the W.

The second was that Kentish Town – in particular, leafy Dartmouth Park – began to benefit as an overflow area into which trickled those who just couldn't quite afford to buy homes in Hampstead or Highgate. This factor is still the dominant feature of the property market in the area – only now people moving in are those who just can't quite afford Belsize Park or Camden . . . Here they find pockets of substantial family houses, a good supply of small- and medium-sized homes, and a good number of converted flats, particularly 1- and 2-bed ones – though the conversion frenzy of the '80s assumed nothing like the proportions here that it did in, for example, West Hampstead.

Dartmouth Park

This is the area where people first realized that Kentish Town had streets to offer that were every bit as nice as in Hampstead, *and* just as close to Hampstead Heath *and* with all the same advantages of good transport links *and* close to the West End, but where prices were, and still are comparatively lower.

Formerly owned by the Earl of Dartmouth and developed in the 1870s, the area lies between **Dartmouth Park Hill** in the E to **Highgate Rd** in the W, and from Highgate's Holly Lodge Estate and the famous cemetery down to busy **Chetwynd Rd**. Particularly popular (prices can approach a million) are **Dartmouth Park Rd** and **Dartmouth Park Avenue** with their grand terraced houses in blocks of three, many of which have been converted; as well as **Boscastle Rd**, which is literally a stone's throw from the heath across **Highgate Rd.**

Camden Council has brought in a number of measures to stop rush hour through-traffic from using the area, but these streets can still get a bit choked in the morning rush hour as motorists desperately search for alternative ways through the Kentish Town bottleneck. However, myriad attractions (including four excellent state secondary schools virtually on the doorstep – William Ellis, Parliament Hill and Acland Burghley, as well as La Sainte Union convent school) heavily outweigh the disadvantages.

There are also hidden delights, such as the sports ground, tennis courts and bowling club tucked away off **Croftdown Rd**, and the sudden views W and S from some of the houses in the higher streets. This is not the corner to look for glitzy new developments, though a cache of 11 houses appeared in 1989 in **St Albans Rd**.

Perhaps the most elegant (and pricey) homes in Kentish Town are the splendid row of deceptively large houses in **Grove Terrace** off **Highgate Rd** which significantly pre-date the rest of the area, having been built in the late 18th century.

West Kentish Town

This is the area of Kentish Town (W of the busy **Kentish Town Rd** shopping centre) dominated by huge council estates which have swallowed up dozens of Victorian streets. They range from some of the worst of municipal mistakes to shining showpieces of successful modern urban development. But, in among the large estates and tower blocks, there are still pleasant streets where bargain-hunters search for unmodernized homes in some handsome, early Victorian terraces (c. £300–350,000). There is also, of course, ex-council. There are interesting terraces in Maitland Park, on the W edge of the neighbourhood, in **St Leonard's Square**, and also at the SW end of **Queen's Crescent** (the NE end becomes a bustling street market on some days), with its set of little cul-de-sacs running off: **St Thomas's Gardens, Baptist Gardens, St Ann's Gardens** and **Modbury Gardens**. In the angle of **Gordon House Rd** and **Highgate Rd** little **Mortimer Terrace** has a dozen 3-bed houses, built in 1989. Watch for change in West Kentish Town as tenants' associations take control on council estates.

Pockets of good properties can also be found in the S, towards Chalk Farm, in streets around **Castle Rd** in the area S of **Prince of Wales Rd**. There is a positively delightful group of streets including **Healey St, Grafton Crescent** and the northern end of **Hadley St** containing cheerful and exquisitely preserved 2-storey terraces, which are part of the Kelly St conservation area – the only one to be found in Kentish Town proper.

The former North London Polytechnic building at 1 **Prince of Wales Rd** was transformed by Dorrington into 65 mainly 2-bed galleried loft apartments, some with terraces – the last of which were snapped up quickly last year. From an off-plan start in 1997, the release prices ranged from c. £180,000 to £299,000. The resale price of a 1-bed flat was £210,000 last December.

East Kentish Town

The triangle bounded by **Kentish Town Rd, Camden Rd** and **Brecknock Rd** contains the heartland of Kentish Town and is largely unvandalized by the council, with the exception of some crumbling pre-war estates in the **Islip St** area. Otherwise the area is awash with improving and improvable streets, with a good supply of (smaller) family houses and conversions. Residents are cheered by more and better shopping; a Pizza Express has arrived, other well-known names are eyeing the area and even Woolworths has gone in for a million-pound refit.

There is also a great deal of charm and elegance, particularly in roads like **Patshull Rd, Bartholomew Rd, Lawford Rd** and **Bartholomew Villas** (which contains the well-known Kentish Town Community Health Centre), most of which have attractive 3-storey terraces, with pleasing architectural features such as cast-iron balconies. A 5-bed, end-of-terrace example was on the market recently at £665,000. Closer to the tube lie **Gaisford St** and **Caversham, Holmes** and **Inkerman Rds**.

North of the narrow and busy **Leighton Rd** there are more rewards and surprises. The main surprise is **Lady Margaret Rd**, built in the early 1860s, which is almost twice as wide and gracious as any other street in the area. Leading off it are the rewards, traditionally narrow streets that are among the most intensively gentrified in London, including **Falkland Rd, Ascham St, Dunollie Rd, Leverton St, Ravely St, Countess Rd** and **Montpelier Grove**, all with 2- and 3-storey terraces and semi-detached rows.

With small scope for new developments in this crowded corner, what new homes appear come from imaginative conversions: this year's is a redundant church in Junction Rd, re-emerging as St Christopher's Court: 18 interesting flats plus two 2,000-sq-ft penthouses. Prices for the latter were yet to be announced at time of writing; those for the more ordinary-sized flats were from £135,000.

Tufnell Park

Mainly in the borough of Islington, this area, bounded by **Camden Rd, Brecknock Rd** and **Holloway Rd**, was almost completely ignored by buyers and even estate agents until the last couple of decades, and it is still more blighted by its rather down-market reputation – and association with the Holloway area – than it deserves. In reality it contains a nest of extremely pleasant streets which, although bordered by some polluted and juggernaut-dominated trunk roads, are themselves quiet, charming and relatively free of through traffic. Flat conversions proliferated throughout the area.

This is a friendly area, with a real community spirit – for example, new parents who move in find that local families have set up a support group to help with everything from advice to holiday playgroups. There are some large council estates in the southern part (as well as the famous Holloway Prison for women), but closer to the tube station in the W there are popular streets: **Hugo Rd** and **Corinne Rd** with attractive 2-storey terraces; **Lady Somerset** and **Burghley Rds** on the Kentish Town side (a 1-bed flat conversion here, £175,000 recently); **St Georges Avenue**, S of **Tufnell Park Rd**, where 2- and 3-bed flats can make up to £250,000, houses c. £400,000.

North of **Tufnell Park Rd** itself there is the very pleasant **Huddleston Rd** cul-de-sac, and the group of roads around **Tytherton Rd,** which include **Mercers Rd** (convenient for open playing-fields), **Yerbury Rd, Beversbrook Rd** (a 3-storey, 5-bed house here was on the market last winter at £385,000), **Campdale Rd** and **Foxham Rd** with its unusually pleasing development of modern council houses together with communal gardens and children's playground.

In Tufnell Park, the rule of thumb is: avoid **Holloway Rd**. But at the same time it is interesting to see just how close one can get to that road before it starts impinging on the neighbouring properties. Watch out also for rail lines – some may one day carry Eurostar trains if the St Pancras terminal gets built (see below).

King's Cross Borders

The southernmost part of Kentish Town is destined to benefit dramatically from plans to develop – eventually – the giant King's Cross railway lands site. This is linked to the Channel Tunnel Eurostar terminal, which will – one day – be at St Pancras. This vast scheme has been on/off since the early 1980s, and the whole Channel rail link, and thus the King's Cross scheme, has yet to get the final green light. Locals, remembering past false dawns, will believe it when they see it. Or, more likely, when they feel the vibration from the enormous Eurostar trains. Streets closest to the vast site will no doubt suffer the inconvenience of being near what will be the largest single development in Europe, but eventually proximity to it, with its envisaged housing, new park and huge commercial centre, can only have a beneficial effect on prices. Values in the immediate area of the site began to rise sharply in the late 1980s, and will doubtless be good long-term investments. (See also Bloomsbury & King's Cross chapter.)

K

Camden Road Borders

Strictly speaking part of Camden Town (see Camden Town and Primrose Hill chapter) and in the NW1 postal district, the Camden Square conservation area is in essence part of the eastern section of Kentish Town. The houses are larger here, though, and more splendid, particularly the terraced and semi-detached examples in **Camden Square**, with its children's playground, itself, **Cantelowes Rd**, **St Augustine's Rd** (where an unmodernized house fetched £725,000 in December), **North Villas**, **South Villas** and **Murray St**. There are also attractive houses in **Camden Mews** and smaller terraces in **Marquis Rd**. These roads are protected from traffic by a series of road closures.

Across **York Way** and NE of a large council estate, there are roads off **Hillmarton Rd** which have grand houses, now mostly flats. These streets, too, are well-blocked off to through traffic and are convenient for Caledonian Rd tube on the Piccadilly line. On the Islington borders, on old railway sidings off **Stock Orchard St**, **Heddington Grove** is a street of 134 flats and town-houses that appeared in the late '80s.

Archway Borders

On the Camden (W) side, this area is sometimes known as Highgate New Town because of its proximity to the superior examples of council housing built by Camden at the N end. But between **Junction Rd** and **Dartmouth Park Hill** roads like **Bickerton Rd** and **Tremlett Grove** adjoin a quiet unnamed park around a covered reservoir.

On the Islington side, and E of **Archway Rd**, which is virtually a motorway at this point, there is a surprisingly secluded set of roads, which have become very popular in recent years. North of the huge GLC-built council estate blocks in **St John's Way**, these streets include the Whitehall Park conservation area, comprising **Whitehall Park, Gladsmuir Rd** and **Harberton Rd**, a relatively well-preserved Victorian estate ranging from grand semis to modest 2-storey terraces, but all with attractive architectural features. The land slopes quite steeply giving splendid views, up to a ridge along which runs **Hornsey Lane**, the N19 postcode boundary and the northern frontier of Islington borough. Beyond are N6 and Haringey. Other streets here well worth a long second look include **Gresley Rd, Dresden Rd, Cheverton Rd, Parolles Rd** and **Prospero Rd**.

Transport	Tubes: Kentish Town, Tufnell Park (zone 2, Northern). From Tufnell Park: Oxford Circus 20 min (1 change), City 15 min, Heathrow 55 min (1 change). Trains: Kentish Town (to St Pancras); Gospel Oak, Kentish Town West, Camden Rd (North London line/Silverlink).
Convenient for	Hampstead Heath, Islington, road links to North. Miles from centre: 3.
Schools	Local Authority: Acland Burghley, Parliament Hill, Jewish Free School, Camden School for Girls, William Ellis (b), La Sainte Union Convent (g).

SALES

Flats	S	1B	2B	3B	4B	5B
Average prices	80–120	85–200	125–300	200–400	220–400	—
Houses	2B	3B	4B	5B	6/7B	8B
Average prices	220–400	250–500	300–800	350–1 M	400–2 M	—

RENTAL

Flats	S	1B	2B	3B	4B	5B
Average prices	100–160	180–250	200–300	250–350+	350–600	400–700
Houses	2B	3B	4B	5B	6/7B	8B
Average prices	220–300	280–500	390–600	500–700	600–1000	700–1500+

The properties	Victorian terraces appeared early – 1840s onwards – so those remaining can be handsome; many houses now flats. Some streets of Hampstead quality, other parts disrupted by council building good and bad. Grander in Dartmouth Park and on Camden borders.
The market	The rental investment market has its eyes on this convenient area, where many homes have been spruced up or turned into flats. The closer to tubes and the further from main through-routes, the higher the price. An area growing in status. Local searches: Camden 7–10 working days, Islington 10 working days.

Among those estate agents active in this area are:

- Winkworth *
- Captital Sales
- Barnard Marcus
- Dennis & Hayes
- Salter Rex
- Day Morris
- Benham & Reeves
- Hotblack Desiato

further details: see advertisers' index on p671

KILBURN, KENSAL GREEN AND QUEEN'S PARK

Map ref: p59 (2J)
Postal districts: NW6, W10, W9
Boroughs: Brent (Lab), Westminster (Con)
Council tax: Band D Brent £678, Westminster £350
Conservation areas: Queen's Park, Kilburn, N Kilburn, S Kilburn, Queen's Park Estate
Parking: Increasingly restricted/residents

Caught between creeping West Hampstead to the E, expansionist Maida Vale to the S and a swollen Queen's Park to the W, Kilburn seems in danger of extinction. Confusion over tube station names and postal districts further erodes Kilburn as a residential area.

Whatever this tract is called, it has several things in its favour, first being location. It is just up Ladbroke Grove from ever-so-trendy Notting Hill, and just as close to the centre of London as North Kensington – closer than Hammersmith, let alone Shepherd's Bush. The Bakerloo and Jubilee lines, which serve it, have useful connections, not least with Paddington and its Heathrow link. In addition, there is a good choice of (mostly converted) flats of a decent size, and a range of family houses from artisan's cottage to spacious Edwardian. Even those sensitive to postcode subtleties need not miss out: Kilburn and Kensal share NW6 with West Hampstead and W10 with North Kensington, the Kensal Rise bit is in NW10 and there's even a corner with Maida Vale's postcode, W9.

All kinds of home can be had here at prices a good bit lower than in nearby areas, but that does not mean they've stood still: a flood of would-be buyers hit the area last spring, with one agent reporting glumly that he had 600 eager applicants on his books and not a lot to sell. Price rises were hard to keep up with: bijou 2-bed Queen's Park Estate cottages started 1999 around £145,000, added £20,000 between January and March, gained another £15,000 by July and began 2000 at £205,000.

Much of the present-day Kilburn and Kensal Green was built between 1860 and 1890, as what was a vaguely-defined village on the **Edgware Rd** became organized urban sprawl. The railway lines that cross the area became punctuated with stations to meet the needs of the new inhabitants, and **Kilburn High Rd** grew into a flourishing shopping centre. Another wave of building spread up from Paddington along the canal, to add Kensal Town and Kensal Green to the area's neighbourhoods.

Today, good transport, and solid Victorian terraces, underpin Kilburn's growing popularity. It is no longer a down-market area (once you look beyond the modern council-built estates to the S), but the respectable and increasingly fashionable neighbour of West Hampstead, North Kensington and Maida Vale.

Up to 1890, most of the housing (and perhaps many of the residents) finished at Kensal Rise Cemetery. Next (1895–1905) and to the N came the larger houses and wider avenues of Queen's Park.

There is much confusion over the name 'Queen's Park', because there are two of them: parks (or green spaces) as well as suburbs (streets around said spaces). The name was first used for the estate of terraced cottages which are to be found to the S of the railway line in W10 (hereafter referred to more properly as Queen's Park Estate). These were built for renting to respectable artisans in the 1870s and '80s.

However, the 33-acre park N of **Harvist Rd**, laid out in 1886, was given the same name, and Queen's Park as a neighbourhood now signifies the rather grander NW6 streets around the park itself.

Kensal Green, west from Queen's Park across **Chamberlayne Rd** and in NW10, is less assuming. Built up in 1880–1900 and run-down by 1920, it is now reasserting itself on the market, increasingly popular because of its proximity to the Sainsbury's superstore and the top end of terribly fash **Ladbroke Grove** (without that area's prices). Its high-density terraces, now mixed in with some dull council houses, are arranged (by means of barriers and no-entry signs) into curious little groups of roads that the casual house-hunting motorist may never happen across.

Another neighbourhood that must be treated separately is West Kilburn, S of **Kilburn Lane** – not least because it is in Westminster rather than in Brent, and in W9 not NW6. Apart from the unspoilt Queen's Park Estate (which is in W10 . . .), it is an area undergoing much change, with new flats fitted snugly in Victorian terraces.

Rail and tube station names seem designed to confuse the local geography. Kilburn tube (Jubilee line) is on **Shoot Up Hill** in the far N of the area, just in NW6 but outside Kilburn by most definitions. It serves the Mapesbury Estate neighbourhood, between Willesden Green and Brondesbury Park. Local zealots want the station name changed to Mapesbury. Kilburn Park tube (Bakerloo), to the S, is closer to the **High Rd**. Queen's Park and Kensal Green stations (also Bakerloo) are sensibly placed, as is Kensal Rise (N London/Silverlink) though Brondesbury station is on **Kilburn High Rd** – as is Kilburn High Rd station (trains to Euston). Confused? Blame the Victorians.

Kilburn has the rebuilt Tricycle Theatre for street cred, and some well-regarded bars on the **Harrow Rd**. The first organic cafe and health club have been spotted in hithertoo down-at-heel **Salusbury Rd**. Estate agents assert that schools are not an issue, as it is largely first-time buyers and young couples who are moving in, though this is certainly changing around Queen's Park: just count the kids in the park's playground. Professional people with families continue to buy into leafy Queen's Park and are looking hard at the streets W of **Kilburn High Rd** and on the borders with Maida Vale. Prices have risen briskly since the mid-1990s, but are still attractive compared to neighbouring areas.

Kilburn

The **High Rd**, with its shops, chain stores, pubs and stations (from N to S Kilburn tube and Brondesbury and Kilburn High Rd rail stations), is the main artery rather than the heart of Kilburn. At its southernmost end, the Regents Plaza hotel was finished in

1995, complete with restaurants and health club – and, as well as the hotel rooms, serviced 1-, 2- and 3-bed flats. See Maida Vale chapter for details.

The junction of **Kilburn High Rd** and **Kilburn Priory** marks the centre of the old village, virtually nothing of which survives. A baroque 4-storey terrace on **Kilburn Priory** and four Georgian town-houses on **Springfield Lane** stand out from their surroundings. Less distinguished corners include the Abbey Estate – council-built on the NW8 border towards **Abbey Rd** – and Kilburn Vale Estate S of **Quex Rd**. The latter includes 1980s mews-type homes over garages on **Mutrix Rd** and **Bransdale Close**.

Kilburn High Rd forms the border between Westminster and Camden. The latter, to the E, has stern views about car parking and residents' permits here may become expensive and scarce. Just about every residential street to the E of the **High Rd** is claimed by West Hampstead. **West End Lane** here has some purpose-built flats blocks, both private and council; **Birchington Rd** has 4-storey terraces with imposing porches. Off **Quex Rd**, in **Quex Mews**, 10 1- and 2-bed flats have been added to the existing five mews houses. North of here near the enormous Catholic church are the ornate terraces of **Mazenod Avenue**, while **Kingsgate Rd** has a mixture of terraces with basement flats, council blocks and flats over shops. The terraces of **Messina Avenue** stand opposite a school and little Kilburn Grange park, N of which is more council-built housing up to the railway line.

Across the **High Rd** to the W, and N of **Willesden Lane**, **Dyne Rd** has some large square-fronted houses, not all converted into flats, that look at a first glance like semis but which are linked at the back. Note that the N side of the road backs onto the railway. **Torbay Rd** has smaller terraces while **Plympton Rd** and **Buckley Rd** have 3-storey ones – all bright and cheerful houses on quiet streets. These roads are a conservation area. Houses in **Buckley Rd** command prices around £400,000 unmodernized, with £500,000 more typical for done-up ones with 5 bedrooms (both figures up £100,000 on last year).

Willesden Lane, with its small shops, mansion blocks and junior school, is the N border of a tract of more modest rows running S to **Glengall Rd**. Mansion flats on **Willesden Lane** might cost £160,000 for 2-bed, while a 3-bed conversion from a Victorian house might reach £200,000-plus. In the grid of streets to the S **Tennyson Rd**, for example, has an unbroken terrace along the W side incorporating a dozen minor variations on, and later amendments to, its Victorian artisan theme. These back onto Willesden Lane Cemetery, as do homes on the N side of **Lonsdale Rd**. The houses on **Donaldson Rd**, **Victoria Rd** and **Hartland Rd**, many of which have been converted into flats, display a touching homogeneity: nearly all highlight the decorative panels on the 2-storey bays. Buyers look here for 2-bed converted flats at £200,000 and 3-bed houses at £350–400,000.

Brondesbury Rd runs the gamut from council tower blocks at **Kilburn Square** in the E, through large red-brick 3-storey terraces – some ornate, some Italianate, but nearly all flats – to some very suburban semis near Queen's Park station in the W. Homes range from 1-bed flats, which can be spacious if in the enormous Victorian houses, through normal-sized 2-bed conversions to some large, elegant 2-bed, 2-recep garden flats. The latter can command £250,000-plus prices. **Brondesbury Villas**, which runs parallel to the S, echoes its namesake for much of its length, but has some particularly ornate houses, now mostly flats. The fact that it backs onto the railway line does little to lower prices; a sought-after address. Both roads, as well as **Honiton** and **Lynton Rds**, are a conservation area.

South of the railway is largely sprawling council estates on either side of **Carlton Vale** and surrounding the 1860s James Bailey villas of **Cambridge Avenue**, **Chichester Rd**, **Cambridge Rd** and **Oxford Rd** near Kilburn Park (tube) station. These villas have been restored in a £12 million scheme by freeholder Paddington Churches Housing

Association. Some are now coming onto the market. Expect to pay £245,000 for a 4-bed maisonette in **Princess Rd**, which gains from its proximity to both Kilburn Park and Maida Vale tubes. **Malvern Rd** has some flats above shops: just off this street is Malvern Mews, a mixed residential (mostly) and commercial corner.

The modest terraces of the **Fernhead Rd/Saltram Crescent** area are a less expensive corner in a mixed council/private area (see Maida Vale chapter). Visible just to the S of **Kilburn Park Rd**, across Paddington recreation ground, are the mansion blocks of Maida Vale.

West Kilburn

West Kilburn is between **Harrow Rd** on the S and **Kilburn Lane** on the N. The E boundary with Maida Vale runs along **Fernhead Rd, Shirland Rd** and **Walterton Rds**, and former Westminster council tenants in these 1860s–1880s terraced streets – after epic battles with the authority and developers – banded together to form a housing association, take over their own homes and carry out a major programme of repairs. Their successful initiative is widely praised but, sadly, has been rarely emulated.

The late '80s added several new flats developments to this corner. A modern estate separates these streets from the terraces of **Bravington Rd, Portnall Rd** and **Ashmore Rd**: there are many rented flats here. Next is the Mozart council estate, a jumble of red-brick blocks, which boasts a sports centre on **Caird St**. Despite much work, the Mozart estate still has a poor reputation. **Beethoven St** has a few private houses, some light industry and schools.

The Queen's Park Estate

Just follow Ladbroke Grove northwards, dears; you'll still be in W10 . . . . And here, just across the canal and the Harrow Rd, you will find the placid Queen's Park Estate,

happily sheltering all the actors and writers who can't possibly afford W11 and who prefer a cottage of one's own to a grotty North Ken flat. There are 2,000 charming terraced brick cottages, many with Gothic porches suggesting benign ecclesiastical origins, despite the rationalism of the **First Avenue** to **Sixth Avenue** names – the E–W streets work down the alphabet from **Alperton St** to **Peach St**.

The estate was built in the 1870s and '80s by the Artisans, Labourers and General Dwelling Co, which ran an orderly grid of streets across farmland at the Kensal Green/West Kilburn borders and built homes for rent. The aim of the 'five per cent philanthropists', as these landlords were called, was to 'provide the labouring man with an increase of the comforts and convenience of life', with – a true Victorian touch, this – 'full compensation for the capitalist'.

Now a conservation area, the estate passed through council hands but today most of the houses are privately owned.

They are a popular buy: a W10 post code, neat, cut-off streets without through traffic, plenty of charm. Buyers of these bijou two-storey houses – more vertical flats – should note that the conservation area rules are very strict (and the main boulevard, **Fifth Avenue**, is listed). Roofs must be of Welsh slate; double-glazing, even of a sympathetic nature, is banned – and the supply of improvement grants has dried up.

The tree-lined streets are uncluttered and pleasingly domestic in scale: road closures mean children can still play ball in the streets at the weekends, and you can park your car. Inhabitants are a good mixture: locals whose families have been there for years, and media-but-broke types who found the place before the prices rose. Today's refugees from pricier areas include younger, still-single professionals, often women, who like the small-scale homes. They can expect to pay £205–225,000 for a 2-bed, the cheaper ones still have downstairs bathrooms. **Oliphant** and **Peach** are indeed peachy streets, while the A, B, C corner is less favoured, being close to the hard-red-brick 1970s Mozart council estate.

From the E, busy **Harrow Rd** has shops and pubs near its junction with **Great Western Rd**, then has modern council housing below Queen's Park Estate opposite the canal, up to the junction with **Ladbroke Grove**. W of the Queens Park Estate, flats and houses in a triangle of Kensal Green streets – **Wakeman, Raynham, Buller Rds**, etc – are hot property right now. The deeply trendy William IV on the **Harrow Rd** and the Paradise Bar have put the spotlight on this corner.

Housing associations are very active in this area, offering shared ownership deals and putting up new developments. Between the **Harrow Rd** and the canal, Paddington Churches Housing Association has built 80 2-bed flats on **Woodfield Rd**. Some shared ownership. The PCHA also owns the modern canalside homes of **John Collins Close.**

Kensal Green

The small triangle bounded by **Chamberlayne Rd, Harrow Rd** and the North London rail line, is Kensal Green. **Harrow Rd** here has cemeteries to the S, offices etc on the N, behind which are 3-storey terraces giving way to smaller ones in the quiet area of **Wakemen Rd, Pember Rd** and **Rainham Rd. College Rd** passes Kensal Green station (rail station and tube), and divides larger terraces of **Ashburnam Rd** and **Mortimer Rd** from smaller homes (including some council) S of **Purves Rd**. The similar terraces of **Napier Rd** and **Victor Rds** are tucked away behind, and very easy to miss from **Harrow Rd**, which here has shops and some flats above; note terraced cottages next to **Alma Place. Purves Rd**, running back E, leads to the shops of **Station Terrace** below Kensal Rise station, and a mansion block. Here are the shops of busy and steep **Chamberlayne Rd.** The pleasant name 'Kensal Rise' seems to have been eclipsed (save for the station) by that of Queen's Park.

Queen's Park

Across **Chamberlayne Rd** are the putative beginnings of desirable Queen's Park, marked by the monkey puzzle trees of **Chevening Rd**; this runs E with its huge semis, some flats (a 2-bed is c. £200,000), and large terraces – those above **Dunmore Rd** having garages at rear. But Queen's Park proper, the conservation area with its rich mixture of late-Victorian and Edwardian styles, begins only at **Peploe Rd** (and continues between the railway lines as far as **Salusbury Rd**). On roads that cross this W border, such as **Kempe Rd** and **Keslake Rd,** both house prices and flights of architectural fancy can soar as one nears the park: £400–450,000 buys a 3-bed house. The most desirable road is reckoned to be **Kingswood Avenue**. The smaller houses of **Milman Rd** directly across the park are also sought-after.

The smaller terraces of the streets behind **Kingswood Avenue** are popular but **Montrose Avenue** and **Hopefield Avenue** are marred by some drab modern houses, which detract from the essentially gracious tone of Queen's Park. **Harvist Rd** has a variety of 3-storey terraces (note the Dutch touches of Nos 10–16) running up parallel to the rail line to **Salisbury Rd**. This runs between Brondesbury Park and Queen's Park stations, and furnishes the locals with schools, shops, churches, constabulary and a library – and, as of last year, an organic cafe and a wine bar. On **Salisbury Rd**, Vicarage Place, a 30-flat development by Laing, went up in 1995. St Anne's Court, in the same street, is a 1998 development of 1- and 2-bed flats – and a new church completed next door – that has been built on the site of St Anne's church.

Transport   Tubes: Kilburn (zone 2, Jubilee); Queen's Park, Kensal Green, Kilburn Park (zone 2, Bakerloo). From Kilburn: Oxford Circus 20 min (1 change), City 25 min (1 change), Heathrow 50 min (1 change). Trains: Brondesbury 35 min to Liverpool St; Kilburn High Rd 8 min to Euston, 30 min to Liverpool St. Others see map.

Convenient for   West End, M1, Notting Hill. A40. Miles from centre: 4.

Schools   Local Authority: Queen's Park Community School, St Augustine's C of E, St George's RC.

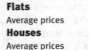

SALES

Flats	S	1B	2B	3B	4B	5B
Average prices	80–100	100–200	140–250	190–300	300+	—
Houses	2B	3B	4B	5B	6/7B	8B
Average prices	200–240	220–450	300–450+	500–700+	600+	—

RENTAL

Flats	S	1B	2B	3B	4B	5B
Average prices	120–140	140–200	180–260	200–320	—	—
Houses	2B	3B	4B	5B	6/7B	8B
Average prices	220–240	275–450	320–450	400–500	—	—

The properties   Terraces of small Victorian homes give way, round Queen's Park, to large Edwardian ones in broader streets.

The market   Continues to grow in popularity thanks to good transport links and this area's position next door to West Hampstead, Maida Vale and Ladbroke Grove. Good hunting-ground for first-time and investment buyers of flats and small houses; Queen's Park area's family homes command a premium. Local searches: Brent 5–10 working days, Westminster 10 working days.

KNIGHTSBRIDGE

Map ref: p144 (5E)
Postal districts: SW1, SW3, SW7
Boroughs: Kensington &
    Chelsea (Con), Westminster
    (Con)
Council tax: Band D:
    Kensington & Chelsea £534,
    Westminster £350
Conservation areas: Most of
    the area
Parking: Residents' permit
    parking/meters and clamps.
    Red Route on Brompton Rd

Knightsbridge is beyond doubt one of the most prestigious and traditional addresses in London. Here the wealthy in their grand apartment buildings, elegant terraced houses and pretty mews cottages cluster around one of the world's most famous shopping centres.

The area lies S of Hyde Park, which is fringed by the busy road variously named **Kensington Gore/Kensington Rd/Knightsbridge**. To the S the boundary is **Walton St/Pont St**. In the W, the museums and colleges cut Knightsbridge off from Kensington, while Belgravia is on the E. The old hamlet of Knightsbridge was originally part of a large forest around London, of which Hyde Park and Kensington Gardens are surviving open remnants. The parks are the area's biggest asset, providing a 600-acre playground and some fine views.

The other big draw is the cluster of shops and department stores, which may grow further if plans for a new store come to fruition. Harrods, century-old department store in **Brompton Rd**, with its distinctive green and gold canopies and royal warrants, sets the tone for the high-class shops in the area, where the 'by appointment' sign is a familiar sight. Gold-braided commissionaires, chauffeur-driven limousines and security cameras over the doorways are also essentials of the Knightsbridge streetscape. In recent years, Harvey Nichols and the stores in **Sloane St** have added a fashion dimension to Knightsbridge shopping.

The 4½-acre Knightsbridge Green development plans a new department store, on the **Brompton Rd** just across from Harrods, with 220 flats and a hotel facing the park, and a 19-storey office tower. There is another scheme for the same site: ownership is extremely tangled. There's a big hole in the ground but no planning permission yet.

Like Harrods, the Royal Albert Hall and the other establishments within it, Knightsbridge is itself an institution. As one estate agent put it: 'you have the confidence that the market is never really going to collapse because there is too much to go down with it'. This is, of course, to take the long view: what's the odd stock market dive to the Old Money of Knightsbridge? This was borne out in the 1989–90 economic crash as Knightsbridge was one of the few areas in London where asking prices for properties were routinely achieved. As the new century dawns, things are busier now than they have ever been and investment buying is strong: this is seen by foreigners as the best London area in which to invest for the long term.

The area is favoured by bankers, both British and international, businesses and diplomats. Several embassies and foreign cultural centres are located here. Buyers from the Far East see this area as the shopping capital of Europe.

Every urban taste in homes is catered for, from the tall late-Victorian red-brick gabled apartment buildings in the **Hans Gardens/Egerton Gardens** neighbourhoods to the grand Portland stone blocks in **Ennismore Gardens**. Bijou mews cottages and 19th-century terraced houses, large and small, are spread throughout the area in some particularly pretty streets and cobbled mews.

Most homes are flats, and leases are often short, though some longer leases are coming onto the market. Strict maintenance conditions are contained in many leases to keep up the tone of the area by preventing properties slipping into disrepair. Service charges can vary widely but you usually get what you pay for, according to local estate agents. Leasehold reform has changed the game in some streets, finally allowing leaseholders to buy the freeholds. Both the Cadogan and Wellcome Estates have property in this area – and both enforce estate management agreements even on homes they do not own.

A peculiarity of the area is that it falls within two boroughs. All of the area N of **Brompton Rd** (with the exception of **Brompton Square, Cottage Place**, the Oratory, Holy Trinity Church, **Cheval Place, Rutland St, Fairholt St** and **Rutland Mews South**) is in the City of Westminster. The rest is in Kensington. The confusion of the two boroughs within Knightsbridge leads to chaos with residents' parking. Where the boundaries run through the middle of the streets (as in **Lowndes St**) or squares (as in **Rutland Gate**) neighbourly co-existence can be strained.

Brompton Rd is the main shopping street, lined by a jumble of period and modern flats, blocks and offices with shops beneath. These range from fashion and shoe shops to jewellers, antique shops, galleries, banks, restaurants and bars.

Knightsbridge and its continuation **Kensington Rd** is a busy main through-route running alongside the tracts of park in the W to Kensington and in the E to the West End. It is flanked by a combination of tall apartment buildings and various embassies and institutions – and by the enormous bulk of the Albert Hall.

Lowndes

Lowndes Square forms the heart of the neighbourhood, which is bounded to the W by **Sloane St**. It differs from other garden squares in Kensington and Chelsea in that it is dominated by huge 1900s flat blocks. The 6/7-storey brown-brick buildings spread along whole blocks of the square and loom over its narrow central garden. Some earlier properties remain, mostly 5-storey and basement stucco-fronted terraced houses, many split into flats. But overall, the atmosphere is of a square of hotels. This impression is heightened by the appearance at the N end of the Sheraton Park Tower Hotel, which fronts **Knightsbridge**. **Lowndes Square** is very popular, especially with foreign buyers. Lowndes Court is an ultra-luxurious 25-flat development dating from 1989 including two 6/7-bed penthouses which have gone for well over £2 million recently.

   Lowndes St, a continuation of the square's E leg, contains more flats, shops, galleries and banks. Terraces of 4-storey stucco-fronted houses stand on both sides of the S end of the street. Another 1900s flat block, Chelsea House, provides visual interest as it curves around the corner of **Lowndes St** into **Cadogan Place**. A collection of period and modern houses and flats at the N end of **Cadogan Place** overlook its large tree-lined gardens. The prettily named **Harriet Walk** has gained seven 1990 mews houses and two studios. **Sloane St** on the neighbourhood's W boundary serves as both the main road to Chelsea and an increasingly smart shopping street.

Hans/Harrods

This neighbourhood is dominated by Harrods: the store covers 4½ acres. It is surrounded by tall red-brick and stone gabled blocks of flats in **Hans Crescent**, **Hans Rd** and **Basil St**. In Hans Rd, nos 18–20 have become 1-, 2- and 3-bed flats from £650,000 to £1 million. The most ornate blocks are in **Basil St** alongside a mix of hotels, restaurants, shops and Knightsbridge fire station. A big block on the corner of **Basil St** and **Hans Crescent** spent many years doing duty as one of London's crown courts, but is now flats and offices with underground parking. **Hans Crescent** is another shopping street. It links up with **Herbert Crescent**, where a group of large mock-Tudor houses stand out among the prevailing ornate red-brick mansions. The site of Harrods' warehouse in **Hans Crescent** will be 37 £400,000-plus flats, 1-, 2- and 3 beds, by the end of 2000 – with a waiting list of 250 people in February.

   The crescent leads into **Hans Place**, a very popular garden square where largely red-brick Dutch-gabled buildings, converted into flats, encircle the private central gardens. Hill House prep school stands in the SE corner of this relatively quiet square. Just beyond the NW entrance to the square, the red-bricks are replaced by terraces of mid-19th-century (around £2 million freehold) white stucco houses in **Walton Place**. At the S end of this attractive street is the brick Gothic-style St Saviour's Church, providing a striking contrast to the white stucco. The church is due to be redeveloped: the E half will remain a church, the rest will become a 6-bed house complete with leisure complex, due to be ready in summer 2000. It is expected to sell for around £8 million.

A drawback here is the amount of traffic taking short-cuts through the street. To the E of **Walton Place** through a pointed red-brick arch and an automatic barrier lies **Pont St Mews**, a collection of 2-bed gabled cottages.

Beaufort Gardens used to be lined by small hotels, but many of the tall brick and stucco Victorian terraced buildings have been converted into luxury flats. An unusual feature of this wide street is the line of trees down the middle with car parking on each side. The street is closed off at its S end by a stucco balustrade and the backs of the houses in **Walton St**. **Beauchamp Place** at the W edge of the neighbourhood is a high-class shopping street, containing some of the area's top shops and restaurants. A building being developed fell down in 1998 and the gap is still there.

Egertons/Ovingtons

This corner, enclosed by **Brompton Rd** to the N and W, contains several streets and squares of handsome houses. **Ovington Square** contains good examples of the 'Kensington Italianate' style – tall narrow white stucco terraced houses with rich detailing. The 4-storey and basement houses, built in the 1840/50s, are set around narrow private gardens. The **Square** and **Ovington Gardens** to the N are both relatively busy roads because they are used as a short-cut by through traffic from **Brompton Rd** and **Walton St**. **Ovington Gardens** has 3/4-storey stucco-fronted or brick and stucco terraced houses. Tucked away at right angles to the eastern side of the street is **Ovington Mews**. Pretty 2-storey painted cottages line this pleasant little backwater. Tubs of flowers and window boxes add extra colour. **Yeoman's Row**, situated just one street away, is different again. A short terrace of 2-storey Georgian cottages remain on the eastern side of this small-scale street: expect to pay £1.5–2 million for these, depending on the size of the garden. Further along the same side is an attractive group of paired brick houses with stucco entrances and leafy front gardens. Another handful of cottages is to be found in **Egerton Garden Mews** through a red-brick arch.

Rows of late-Victorian red-brick gabled buildings congregate around rear

Knightsbridge has several enticing corners of mews cottages, which have evolved a long way from their earthy origins to become a style of home all their own. Many are in cul-de-sacs, tucked away from the busy streets. Mansard roof extensions are popular, as are shutters and flower tubs beside the doors. The most prized are those with a surviving garage: parking around here is impossible.

communal gardens in **Egerton Gardens** and the northern end of **Egerton Terrace**. The blocks, built during the 1880s/90s, form the main concentration of flats. Leases are often short: 18 years on average. However, recently the Wellcome Trust has been granting 105-year leases. Cross the road to the two most exclusive streets in Knightsbridge − **Egerton Crescent** and the S end of **Egerton Terrace**. A curved terrace of elegant early Victorian white stucco houses sweeps around **Egerton Crescent**. Described as the grandest location in Knightsbridge. The 3/4-storey houses are screened from the road by a semi-circular private garden. One house has two enormous gardens tucked behind the crescent. Victorian lamps line the crescent and tubs of trees and shrubs on the first-floor balconies emphasize the green and white colour scheme. In **Egerton Terrace**, pairs of mid-19th-century white stucco houses have large leafy front gardens. The street is closed off at its S end by a balustrade and trees.

No 1A Walton St, the old court house opposite the police station, is rumoured to be redeveloped as 4 flats. However work has yet to start: access problems affect the site.

Brompton Square

Brompton Square, to the N of **Brompton Rd**, is a very distinct neighbourhood in itself. Terraces of 3/4-storey early 19th-century houses stretch along narrow central gardens. Virtually all the houses in the square, built 1824–39, are Grade II listed buildings. Houses here are very popular: one is on the market for £1.5 million, the standard-sized ones top £2 million, and a large one (twice the normal size) at the end of the Square was on the market for £3.5 million. A few have been converted into flats. The gardens are also listed as being of architectural or historic interest.

To the W is one of Knightsbridge's most important landmarks, the Oratory Catholic Church. This Renaissance-style church with its impressive white stone façade and dome is the focal point of this end of **Brompton Rd**. Behind the Oratory sits Holy Trinity Church. Its large tree-lined churchyard provides welcome fresh air and a leafy open space and outlook for adjoining properties in the Ennismores and a playground for inner-city squirrels. To the W the Victoria & Albert decorative arts museum ('V&A') forms the boundary with Kensington.

Ennismore/Rutlands

North of **Brompton Square** as far as Hyde Park stretches a quiet, cut-off neighbourhood of mews and squares. L-shaped **Ennismore Gardens Mews** is a delightful long cobbled mews lined by gaily coloured 2-storey cottages. Tubs of flowers and window boxes add a picturesque touch. The cottages in the S leg of the mews overlook the peaceful tree-lined graveyard of Holy Trinity Church. An imposing stone arch of Greek-style columns at the entrance to the mews is a hint of things to come in **Ennismore Gardens**. Here grand 5-storey Portland stone terraces with double-columned porches and ornate black iron balconies are set around a large private garden (much sought-after). The majority of properties are now divided into flats with only two houses remaining complete. Three sides of Ennismore Gardens are on short lease, but the white stucco side is on longer leases. Most of the sales are for short leases: though a second-floor 2-bed flat was for sale at £650,000 on a long lease in February. Longer leases are sometimes available. The more traditional stucco-fronted terraces reappear in the eastern arm of the square, and further stucco terraces can be found in **Princess Gardens**.

Spreading along the W−E section of **Ennismore Gardens** is the highly rated Kingston House flats complex, which stretches right back to **Kensington Rd**. The apartments are very popular with foreign buyers including Americans, Italians and Spanish. Around the corner, on the western side of the N leg of **Ennismore Gardens**, is **Bolney Gate**, a development of modern 5-storey brick and stone town-houses.

When they come on the market these are priced at more than £1.8 million. On the E side of the road stand, in quirky juxtaposition, the Russian Orthodox Church and the Omani Embassy. S of the church is **Ennismore Mews**, an exceptional example of its type with often large 2-storey painted/brick houses. Window boxes, flower tubs and Victorian street lamps abound. Another attractive feature is the Ennismore Arms pub at the corner with **Ennismore St**. **Ennismore St** leads into **Rutland Gate**, which is made up of two separate garden squares. Terraces of brick and stucco houses line the N square, just off **Knightsbridge**, and cream and white stucco-fronted houses are set around the more desirable southern square. The homes have mostly been converted into flats or house foreign cultural institutes and other organizations. A large brick mansion block – Eresby House – stands at the point where the two squares meet.

Rutland Gardens and its tiny mews contain a mix of interesting houses, cottages and flats of very different sizes and styles, but the dominant view here is of the tower of Knightsbridge Barracks, consistently voted one of London's biggest eyesores in public opinion polls. S of **Rutland Gate** lie more small mews, including **Rutland Mews W**, no more than a tiny group of white stucco cottages clustered around a cobbled courtyard. A freehold 3-bed cottage here was £850,000 last winter. **Rutland St** and **Fairholt St** are two more small-scale streets. They have mainly 2-storey stucco/brick and stucco/painted houses.

Knightsbridge Village

Exclusive **Montpelier Square** is the centrepiece of this neighbourhood of predominantly single family houses. The 19th-century brick and stucco/painted stucco houses in the square face on to mature private gardens.

Narrow **Montpelier Walk** is a mix of painted brick/stucco houses. It leads to **Cheval Place**, where the 2/3-storey painted cottages stand alongside modern flat blocks, smart shops, restaurants and the Aston Martin salesroom. Prices for these cottages start at around £850,000. **Montpelier Place** is a pleasant street of 3-storey brick and stucco/stucco-fronted houses with two flower-bedecked pubs, one right next to the German Evangelist Church. Houses range from £800,000–1,100,000 depending on size and condition. One in poor condition went for £825,000 last winter. **Montpelier St** to the E is the main street of the village, lined with 3/4-storey brick and stucco terraced houses, pubs, restaurants, shops and galleries. There is no route for traffic W from the village to the adjoining **Rutland Gate**. A footpath through a gap in an old brick wall, allows you to walk through to **Rutland Mews** and on, under a grand archway, along **Ennismore Gardens Mews** to **Prince's Gate Mews** and the museum/university quarter of South Kensington; one of the most charming walks in London.

The Trevors

East of Knightsbridge Village come the streets around **Trevor Square**, which are dominated by 3/4-storey 19th-century terraced houses. In **Trevor Square**, they are set on two sides of a long narrow private garden. A stretch of modern flats can be found at the NW end of **Trevor Place**, a quite busy road taking traffic to Harrods despatch depot S of **Trevor Square** and through to **Brompton Rd**. Harrods have permission to convert their depot into a 5-star hotel, but work has yet to start. In **Lancelot Place**, a row of 2-storey brick cottages stands opposite the post office.

Turn E into **Raphael St**, which links up with **Knightsbridge Green**, a pedestrian passageway lined with small shops, cafés and restaurants. Standing alongside the passageway is Park Mansions, a large red-brick block fronting **Knightsbridge** and stretching to Scotch Corner. The Knight's Arcade of shops runs beneath the mansions at ground-floor and basement level through to **Brompton Rd**. This whole quarter could be transformed if the Knightbridge Green scheme (see Introduction) goes ahead.

Transport

Tubes, both zone 1: Knightsbridge (Piccadilly), South Kensington (Piccadilly, Circle, District). From Knightsbridge: Oxford Circus 10 min (1 change), City 22 min (1 change), Heathrow 42 min.

Convenient for

Hyde Park, fashionable shopping, West End, Heathrow (via taxi, tube or Paddington). Miles from centre: 1.5.

Schools

Local Authority: Holland Park, Cardinal Manning RC (b), Cardinal Vaughan RC (b), St Thomas More RC, Sion Manning RC (g). Private: St James' Independent (b) (g), Falkner House (g), Queen's Gate (g), St Charles 6th-form College.

SALES

Flats	S	1B	2B	3B	4B	5B
Average prices	150–200	250–400	350–700	550–800	650–1.5 M	1.2 M+
Houses	2B	3B	4B	5B	6/7B	8B
Average prices	500–800+	750–1.75 M	1 M+	1.5 M+	2 M+	—

RENTAL

Flats	S	1B	2B	3B	4B	5B
Average prices	225–300	275–800	350–1200	600–1600	850–2000	1000+
Houses	2B	3B	4B	5B	6/7B	8B
Average prices	600–1400	700–1500	1200–2000	3500+	5000+	6000+

The properties

The scale ranges from tiny mews via elegant 18th/19th-century squares and terraces, to lofty apartment blocks in stone or the red-brick, gabled style widely known as 'Pont St Dutch'.

The market

The wealthy market for these coveted homes, whether true-blue British or international jet-set, are as one in considering this the hub of London. Large homes are scarce and at a premium. Flats reign, with companies buying the short-lease ones as London bases. Prices vary widely according to degree of luxury/lease length/views: a quiet square is more desirable than a park view, as this can mean traffic noise. Rental market strong as families live here: half renters under 40 years old. International renters and buyers still 80 per cent of the market. Local searches: Kensington & Chelsea 10 working days, Westminster 10 working days.

Among those estate agents active in this area are:

- De Groot Collis
- Knight Frank
- Allsop & Co *
- Winkworth *
- FPDSavills
- Foxtons *
- Keith Cardale Groves

- Hobart Slater
- Harrods Estates
- Druce
- Hamptons
- W A Ellis *
- Beaney Pearce *
- Douglas & Gordon

- Lane Fox
- Aylesfords
- Anscombe & Ringland *
- Strutt & Parker *
- Cluttons

further details: see advertisers' index on p671

LEWISHAM AND CATFORD

Map ref: p96 (3D)
Postal districts: SE4, SE13,
    SE6, SE8
Boroughs: Lewisham (Lab)
Council tax: Band D £727
Conservation areas: Brockley,
    St John's
Parking: Residents/meters in
    High St and shopping centre

Lewisham, lying to the south-west of historic Greenwich, also has its roots in the past: a large village was already established there in Domesday times, but the area hardly grew until the 1840s, when the railway arrived and turned it into a new centre for commuting. By the start of the 20th century much of the available land had been built over. The area is ringed with convenient little stations (and therefore criss-crossed with less-than-convenient rail-lines, which carry fast through trains as well as local traffic).

Now the prospects for Lewisham and surrounding areas are once again bound up with transport – first, the Docklands Light Railway (DLR) extension, which opened early, in November. A mere 4.2km of track, this link across to Canary Wharf is a major boost to the area. Next, the tantalising possibility of a tube link at last: see Brockley, page 411.

The DLR, with its futuristic design, boosts the image of a borough which, although a major shopping centre for the area, can still look tatty and run-down in parts. More good news, though: the introduction of a Red Route down the main Lewisham–Bromley through-route has eased the congestion which plagues the town centre.

Already a new breed of resident – with disposable income – is settling in. Families and young professionals are finding more for their money here: along with little terraces and '30s infill, the area has patches of large-scale (with large gardens) Victoriana: 6/7-bed houses, split into flats in the '80s, are now being reunited by enterprising incomers. Away from the rail-tracks and the busy main roads (speed humps are appearing to protect residential streets), the area has a surprising number of parks and open spaces. Some, like Ladywell, have tennis courts and running-track. Fitness enthusiasts find health clubs in most neighbourhoods. Best known for its shopping, Lewisham lacks good restaurants and theatres. A multi-screen cinema is planned for Lewisham, however.

Central Lewisham

The best bits of Lewisham are those closest to the southern tip of Blackheath. From Blackheath Village turn W into **Lee Terrace** and explore the roads to your left bearing the SE13 postcode. Some of Lewisham's best buildings were destroyed by the heavy bombing from which the borough suffered during World War II, but happily roads such as **Quentin Rd, Dacre Park, Eton Grove** and surrounding streets escaped untouched. These 4-storey mansions with their grand sash windows and huge back gardens are extremely well-kept and would not be out of place in Kensington. Most were converted into flats, but some remain as superb family homes. The nearby parish church of St Margarets, and little backstreet pubs all add to the quiet, country feel – until the atmosphere is broken by modern low-rise council housing off busy **Lee High Rd.**

Belmont Hill, the continuation of **Lee Terrace**, has seen the biggest development in the area: The Cedars involved the restoration of a Grade II listed mansion to create 10 apartments. The site, in front of Our Lady of Lourdes School, also has new flats, courtesy of a separate company: all were reserved before completion. Nearby, 4-storey flats also appeared on the corner of **Brandram** and **Blessington Rds**. More new flats, too, N of the tracks in William Close off **Granville Park**, which curves from **Lewisham Rd** back up to Blackheath. Some homes in this area – on **Morden Hill**, for example – boast views right across London.

Lee High Rd joins **Lewisham High St**, with its massive indoor shopping complex and most well-known, big-name stores. 'Lewisham 2000', a regeneration programme that ended last year, helped to improve the High Street by turning it into a well-managed shopping area with pedestrianization (buses are allowed). Traffic was re-routed around the back of the Riverdale shopping centre down **Molesworth St**, and a new road bridge was added over the river Ravensbourne. The pedestrianization has encouraged the wonderful (daily) market and shopping is an altogether more pleasant experience. The clock tower has been moved back to where it stood in Victorian times, and the town centre now also boasts a variety of pubs, a night club and a large new modern library.

Roads to the E mostly contain Victorian town houses, many of which have undergone conversion work after years of neglect. **Limes Grove** with its 3-storey pitched roofs and sash windows is a prime example of this process, as are **Clarendon Rise** and **Gilmore Rd**, which sport terraces with steps to the front door and black wrought-iron balustrades. On the corner of **Morley Rd** three new flats are being inserted in a site that looks like a tight squeeze.

Back across **Clarendon Rise** stands a 20-year-old development of red-brick terraces. Each home has its own garden and there's a small park at the centre. These were council-built, but not suprisingly tenants exercized their Right to Buy and these homes now appear on the open market. A good area for children: the streets are paved over and can be played in without fear of traffic; however, inside, the houses are tight for space compared with their Victorian counterparts opposite.

In **Crosslet Vale** and **Armoury Rd** – two streets which overlook the DLR line and **Connington Rd** – Fairview have completed a development of studios, 1- and 2-bed flats. In this area, with its light industrial units, Brockmill Park, Ravensbourne River and close proximity to the DLR, you will find most of Lewisham's new homes. Another corner to watch out for is the area around **Connington Rd**. The two-storey homes in this basically light-industrial corner may look unloved now, but may well soon be popular with commuters.

St John's

Next, explore St John's – which you'll find by following road signs for Deptford. Little St John's Village is bordered by **St John's Vale, Albyn Rd, Lewisham Way** and **Tanner's Hill**. Some streets are sealed to traffic by ornamental bollards, and the rows of neat yellow-brick terraces and 'Coronation Street' style shops and pubs remain quiet. The area has its own station, and rail commuters are relieved to find that the erstwhile patchy service has become eight trains an hour. The SE8 postal address is usually associated with Deptford, but this corner is well worth a look.

There's a variety of housing here. **Tanner's Hill** has red-brick council blocks (currently undergoing refurbishment) along its entirety, with small shops, pubs and a restaurant at the top end – and on a good day you can see the top of the Millennium Dome. **St John's Vale** starts with 2-storey, 3-bed terraces, gains basements halfway up and ends with 3-storey, semi-detached and basemented houses past the station. (Lewisham College is also nearby, so parking is at a premium.) The homes in **Lucas St** have a park area for the kids to play in. The top end of **Friendly St** is made up of neatly kept, pretty little close-packed 2-bed workmen's cottages, many of which are listed. **Ashmead Rd**, by contrast, has 2/3-storey Victorian houses, some enormous, some still whole family homes (the coach house to one of these was £215,000 recently).

Leaving St John's, travel back along **Lewisham Way** uphill to **Loampit Vale** (MFI, Allied Carpets and other DIY sheds, here). The small 2-up/2-downs are replaced by grander 4-storey homes, now converted into flats, but still neatly kept with window boxes and many with new roofs. From here turn right into **Shell Rd**, which winds its way towards Hilly Fields and Brockley. **Shell Rd** and surrounding streets are dominated by 2- and 3-storey houses with exuberant Gothic-style turrets, ornate porches and high-pitched roofs. Cognoscenti of this period will find fine examples of decorative plaster mouldings – often a shell motif echoes the street name. **Algernon Rd**, however, boasts a modern development of 3-storey houses called Highland Terrace.

Brockley

On reaching the Hilly Fields park area, where '30s-style semis (c. £130–150,000 for a 3-bed) are dotted among the Victorian conversions, turn back towards New Cross and the still improving – and charming – Brockley conservation area. By the end of the '80s these quiet tree-lined avenues had already been discovered by young, upwardly mobile commuters. Four-bed homes can be c. £250,000, but many houses here can boast 5–7 bedrooms, and price tags of £350–400,000; conversions thus make large, spacious, sought-after flats (they can be the size, and price, of '30s semis in nearby streets).

Note, though, that Brockley's charms are contained almost exclusively within its conservation area: land to the W of **Brockley Rd** is still seen as the wrong side of the tracks, though the '90s Crofton Gate Way has tried to break away from this stigma. Its private road of 38 flats and homes – some with glass balconies and modern designs – are a breath of fresh air.

So, first check out the conservation area boundary: **Tyrwhitt Rd** to the E, **Lewisham Way** to the N, **Upper Brockley Rd** and **Brockley Rd** to the W, down to the **Adelaide Avenue** junction. These streets are largely filled with 3- and 4-storey houses, mostly – but not entirely – converted into flats. Some have huge 150-ft gardens and there are panoramic views across to St Paul's for people with attic bedrooms. Inside the grand yellow-brick mansions the rooms are large, with high ceilings. Flats in **Manor Avenue**, **Breakspears Rd** and **Tressillian Rd** are particularly popular. The **Wickham Rd/Breakspears Rd** part of the conservation area have a cache of recent homes: **Breakspears Mews** is a development of 3- and 4-bed houses (£120–139,000 at launch in 1997/8) and 2-bed flats (launched £80–82,000). Look out, too, for some original mews and coach houses in this corner: for example the unreconstructed, un-tarmaced **Wickham Mews**. Off **Wickham Rd** is **Wickham Gardens**, a delightful crescent with a small woodland area in the centre and a mixture of gothicy 2-storey homes at one end, '70s-style council blocks at the other.

One harbinger for the future is the possibility (at least five years away) of the tube coming to Brockley: this would be two stops from Canada Water and the Jubilee line.

Ladywell

From Brockley travel on to the nearby Hilly Fields playing-area, mostly surrounded by post-war 2-storey family homes, some with balconies. From **Vicars Hill** look out for **Adelaide Avenue's** ornate terrace fronting the park. Next, head down the hill into Ladywell Village, perhaps more of an invention of local estate agents than a real village, but getting smarter. There is a good selection of shops in the 'Village' centre on **Ladywell Rd** – and yet another station within a few minutes' walk (the best option: cars block up trying to turn into **Lewisham High St**). The impressive and huge Ladywell Leisure Centre is also just round the corner. 'Village' properties are largely Victorian conversions of 2- and 3-storeys – some with huge gardens – although there are some '30s semis to provide a contrast, notably in **Veda Rd** and **Ermine Rd**.

Catford and the Corbett Estate

Catford will never be quaint. The centre has indeed recently begun to look a little run-down – particularly in and around **Plassy Rd**, despite the Catford Island shops/leisure complex: many homes have been boarded up and shopfronts remain unoccupied). However, now the DLR has arrived at Lewisham and the wider area is on the move, Catford (despite being Zone 3) may well prove estate agents' assertions that the long-sighted may find they've bought a bargain . . .

Like the rest of the area, Catford was rapidly developed towards the end of the 19th century, but unlike Lewisham owes much of its housing character to a single man – Archibald Corbett. This canny Scot bought nearly 300 acres of then virgin land and proceeded to build thousands of houses, laying out the roads in a strict grid pattern. Catford today has its own shopping centre, two rail stations and even its own dog track; but it is best known for the massive Corbett Estate and its distinct lack of pubs – Archibald Corbett was tea-total. Many of the street names have a Scottish flavour – **Arngask** and **Glenfarg Rds**, for example. The boundary roads are **Wellmeadow** to the E, **Hazelbank** to the S, **Brownhill** to the N and **Muirkirk** to the W.

Homes here range from 3- to 6-bedroomed houses, all solidly built, with spacious rooms. Many of the bigger properties were split into flats (a trend now reversing), but the estate still retains its prim-and-proper identity. All the houses have their own front garden, and most have 80-ft rear ones; prices are around the £185–300,000 bracket. The smaller, single-fronted Corbett houses are almost exactly half the size of the double-fronted ones, which are slightly more ornate. The area remains very quiet, very respectable – very desirable. Doctors, solicitors and the like head for these large family homes. Be warned though: visitors will need a map; every road really does look the same!

Another popular estate lies close by, this time made up of '30s-style semis and bounded by **Bellingham Rd** to the S, **Thornsbeach** to the E, **Bromley Rd** to the W and **Culverley Rd** to the N. Extremely wide roads here: 3- and 4-bed homes boast large gardens – one or two even have swimming pools . . . . Look to **Culverley Rd** for flats: eight or nine big houses here were converted in the late '80s (a 2-bed maisonette can cost £83,000), and there's a recent red-brick, 4-storey block. At the Catford end of **Bromley Rd** a large new Sainsbury's, plus a Currys Superstore and PC World, are appearing.

After years of running to seed, the shopping centre is now being redeveloped: 'Catford Island' is a retail/leisure complex in **Plassy Rd**, part of the one-way system in the town centre. New shops are appearing in **Bromley Rd**, and a huge Halfords nearby. Flats in **Bromley Rd** can be found at around £50,000 for 1-bed, up to c. £70,000 for 3-bed; housing associations and other developers are also busy in the road.

Some down-market streets surround the stations, but popular St Dunstan's College lies on **Stanstead Rd** backed by the open space of Blythe Hill Fields and attractive 3-storey Victorian family homes in roads such as **Ravensbourne Rd** and **Montem Rd**.

Even here, the offices-to-homes trend is seen: one block has already become flats.

Bordering Areas

Hither Green is a fertile hunting-ground for first-time buyers seeking inexpensive flat conversions or terraced cottages. The area is bordered by Lewisham, Lee Green and Blackheath; it has its own well-served station. To the W leafy Forest Hill (see Forest Hill chapter) has a mixture of Victoriana and '30s semis in peaceful roads, but also many flat conversions and a good cache of properties for first-time buyers. Crofton Park, sandwiched between Brockley and Catford, consists mainly of terraced streets that some will probably find too drab. Some new-build near Crofton Park station, however.

Transport	Trains: St John's, Lewisham (London Bridge 14 min, Charing Cross 18 min), Ladywell, Brockley, Catford, Catford Bridge. Docklands Light Railway extension to Canary Wharf.
Convenient for	Docklands, West End, City, Greenwich, Kent. Miles from centre: 6.
Schools	Local Authority: Crofton, Prendergast (g), Addey & Stanhope. Private: Blackheath High School (g), St Dunstan's College (b).

SALES

Flats	S	1B	2B	3B	4B	5B
Average prices	40–55	65–80	70–120	80–150	110–150	110+
Houses	2B	3B	4B	5B	6/7B	8B
Average prices	80–120	95–170	115–200	170–280	200–300+	—

RENTAL

Flats	S	1B	2B	3B	4B	5B
Average prices	100–115	125–150	150–160	175–230	185–275	230–460
Houses	2B	3B	4B	5B	6/7B	8B
Average prices	155–185	175–230	220–345	230–345	345+	—

L

The properties	Mainly Victorian, from tiny workers' homes through larger terraces to grand villas with conservatories. '20s/'30s suburbia intersperses, and increasing new-build. Catford has a well-preserved and popular estate of 3/6-bed 1880s houses, many now flats, plus '30s semis in large gardens.
The market	The Lewisham area, once hardly considered London, is now on the Central London workers' list of possibles, and large (up to 7-bed) houses are being turned back from flats to family homes. Prices can be modest considering City/Docklands proximity — though this is changing with the DLR now up and running. Fertile first-home hunting-ground. Local searches: 3 weeks.

Among those estate agents active in this area are:

- Mann & Co
- Oak Estates *
- Winkworth *
- Kinleigh Folkard & Hayward
- Charles Gordon
- Acorn
- Rocodells
- Saxtons
- Quest

* further details: see advertisers' index on p671

LEYTON AND WALTHAMSTOW

Map ref: p48 (3E)
Postal districts: E10, E11, E17
Boroughs: Waltham
   Forest (Lab)
Council tax: Band D £840
Conservation areas:
   Include Hollow Pond,
   Walthamstow Village
Parking: Residents' zones

Waltham Forest – the borough which covers these two areas – has for a long time been seen as the place for first-time buyers to get a foothold on the London housing ladder. In Leyton and parts of Leytonstone especially, cheap rents and sales have lured many a first-timer over to East London. In fact these areas are still the second-cheapest place to buy in London after Newham.

But things are slowly beginning to change, with long-promised improvements to road and transport connections finally taking shape. Estate agents now find middle-class first-time buyers moving into the area after being priced out of N London's more salubrious spots by 1999's property boom. Price increases have been noticeable in the last year; while Leyton is still cheap it is not quite the bargain basement it was a year or two ago.

Buyers whose first choice might have been Stoke Newington or the better parts of Hackney are now coming out further E to find that the price matches their pockets better. And one thing is for sure, not very many parts of London can boast such affordable homes and offer such varied and fast transport connections to the City and West End. Estate agents say the most common questions from buyers – apart from about the property itself – are about transport, and the answers can clinch a deal. Even though they are separated from Tottenham and Hackney by reservoirs and marshland, Walthamstow and Leyton are not cut off. For instance, Walthamstow in the centre of the borough has a bus terminal, a tube station on the fast and mostly reliable Victoria line and an overland rail station. Using the Victoria line you can be at King's Cross inside a quarter of an hour and at Oxford Circus in 25 minutes. There are also good bus connections and should all else fail there is the WAGN Chingford to Liverpool Street train which takes about 15 minutes to get you into the heart of the City. One day – 2007 is the latest guess – nearby Stratford may get a station on the Eurostar line to the Channel Tunnel. It has already got the tube, and now the Jubilee line greatly speeds up journeys to Docklands, the South Bank, Waterloo, Westminster.

It's not only public transport that's an asset here: roads are good (for London). The upgraded North Circular Road passes through the borough. The M11 is now connected to the Blackwall Tunnels, Docklands and the City via a newly-opened road with connections at Leytonstone. This link drives right through Leyton, Leytonstone and Wanstead – its planning and construction entailed years of sometimes bitter wrangling with locals. One positive benefit is an end to the appalling congestion of **Leytonstone High Rd**. It also means the M25 is about 15 minutes away. Traffic permitting you can be at Heathrow, Gatwick or Luton airports in around an hour; at Stansted in 35 minutes and London City Airport in about 20 minutes.

A planned town-centre redevelopment for Walthamstow, which will include a multiplex cinema/shops complex and more parking and leisure facilities, has now got government funding. The council is currently listening to ideas from developers. The aim is to turn Walthamstow into one of the biggest leisure centres in London, with clubs, pubs, cinema and music venues. This will doubtless win approval from some, if not all, of the incoming home-buyers.

To the N, the top slice of the Borough of Waltham Forest is Chingford. Here we are in the suburbs, with most homes 20th century. What this corner lacks in convenience – it lies across the North Circular, with trains to Liverpool St but no tube – it makes up for by its position on the edge of Epping Forest.

Walthamstow

This may not be one of London's most elegant corners, but it is probably one of its liveliest – and will be livelier if the council gets its way (see above). The **High St** boasts a mile-long, six-day street market – and as a sign of the times, a cybercafe now stands amid the stalls. The town centre enjoys excellent transport links: it has a tube/overland rail link, good bus connections, and close proximity to the M11 and North Circular. Most of the homes are terraced houses (or flats converted from them) built in late-Victorian and Edwardian times, but there are also purpose-built blocks of flats; small cottages behind the Vestry Museum in Walthamstow Village and large detached houses in the area to the E known as Upper Walthamstow.

Walthamstow is very popular with first-time buyers, and prices are still relatively cheap when compared with other London areas. The Village/Walthamstow Central neighbourhood is steadily the most popular corner for home-hunters, but agents comment on the growth of the rentals market in the Lloyd Park area. The Village, which is E of the stations, is a conservation area with quaint streets, good pubs and a popular summer street festival. Among the best roads here are **Church Hall Rd, Church Lane** and **Byron Lane**. Besides the bohemian atmosphere the major attraction is the closeness to Walthamstow Central tube/rail station, good buses and excellent shopping facilities. This attracts City and West End workers into the area, drawn by the Chingford to Liverpool St train and Victoria line tube. Being a ten-minute walk from tube or train means prices are relatively high: from £90,000 for a 2-bed flat up to £165,000 for a 3-bed house with a decent garden. The brisk market in 1999 saw homes here selling inside a day. Some of the biggest and most expensive homes are in the **Cedars Avenue** corner S of Central: a 5-bed house here sold for £225,000 last autumn.

The Higham Hill neighbourhood, lying N of **Forest Rd** and W of the **Chingford Rd**, has small homes – a mixture of 2- and 3-bed houses and purpose-built flats – ideal for first-time buyers. These flats go for £65–70,000. This is a quiet corner, with the pleasant, green Lloyd Park, and there's a tube/train station nearby at **Blackhorse Rd**. Homes described as 'Warner' houses were built by local landowners of that name: their standards were high, and some homes still sport a proud 'W' on their facades. Nearby, **William Morris Close** recalls Walthamstow's most famous resident, who lived in Water House on **Forest Rd**. There's a museum which is dedicated to his work. Prices round here start from £55,000 for a 1-bed maisonette or £70,000 for a 1- to 2-bed maisonette (both figures up by £10,000 on 1998 prices). S of the High St prices are rather cheaper.

More terraced houses are to be found to the S in the **St James St** corner of Walthamstow, and property here is still cheaper than elsewhere; it has, though, its own railway station (trains into Liverpool St) and it too is convenient for the tube and rail station at **Blackhorse Rd**. Places to look include the St James's Park estate and the Markhouse Road estate. A Warner-built 2-bed flat in one of these quiet streets might go for £85,000. There's a 1980s development of flats in **Markhouse St**. Heading E, there are also many reasonably priced 2- and 3-bed houses in the area off **Hoe St**, S of Walthamstow Central stations.

New homes are being built in odd pockets: the latest additions have been near the **High St** and off **Hale End Rd**. In **Willow Walk**, just off the **High St**, The Willows is a recent Rialto scheme of 1- and 2-bed flats, now changing hands for £60–70,000; another recent housing development appeared in **Westbury Rd**, also close to the market and behind the tube car park. But most developments are by housing associations who are building low-rise homes for residents moving out of grim '60s tower blocks that are being demolished.

Travelling eastwards again brings you to **Wood St** – a road with its own station. Upper Walthamstow leaves the tiny terraces behind. The tree-lined roads of big 1930s properties boast many large detached houses, often with five or more bedrooms.

Leyton and Leytonstone

Leyton and Leytonstone lie between the green open expanses of Hackney Marsh and Wanstead Flats, their postcodes being (broadly) E10 and E11. Well situated, the area is on a direct tube – the Central line – to the City and West End and, equally, is near Epping Forest heading out to Essex. Despite the rises of the last couple of years, here is still some of the cheapest property this close to Central London. Leytonstone in particular is an area of continual improvement. The new M11 Link Rd is at last open, relieving both neighbourhoods of much intrusive traffic.

The area features a good mix of high-quality century-old houses in wide streets. Most of the homes here are in terraces built in the early 1900s, though some date back to the 1880s. Three-bed terraced houses are the most common though there are a few with 4, possibly 5, beds. Many converted flats are available, and these can still be bought quite cheaply – though the council tightened up on the rash of new conversions in an attempt to avert parking problems. Developers have been quietly adding to the stock (small, so far) of purpose-built flats. There is also still scope to buy cheaper and unrepaired property. Look, too, for the terraces of little houses built as two flats. Sometimes these provide an interesting phenomenon: first-floor flats with external steps down to their own gardens. The most sought-after areas in Leytonstone includes the leafy Bushwood estate, while in Leyton the Barclay estate is very popular. Flats close to the stations are naturally in big demand.

Prices in the area, which rose by an average of 10–15 per cent in 1997, went right on climbing through the first half of '98 – another 12–13 per cent – before levelling off. The 1999 season saw further sharp increases. Thus 3-bed houses in Leyton, which could be found for as little as £63,000 at the start of 1988, began 1999 at nearer the £70,000 mark and ended the year at around £95,000. The smarter roads attract prices of around £125,000 for 3-bed houses.

Upper Leytonstone, though sadly split by the new M11 link road, contains some of the largest and most desirable properties, and has the advantage of being close to public transport. **Forest Drive East**, **Forest Drive West** and the surrounding areas have big, double-fronted houses in tree-lined streets. A new Tesco superstore is scheduled to open this year alongside the re-shaped Green Man roundabout. New homes are planned for an adjacent site.

On the borders of Upper Leytonstone is the area known as the Barclay estate, which contains some of the best houses in Leyton, both Victorian and 1930s. These lie behind Leyton Midland Rd station: the roads here are quieter and pleasanter in appearance, with more trees than is common in the area. A good 3-bed house might be £150,000, though smaller ones start around £100,000. Nearby, a cache of good-value, and equally convenient, terraces include roads like **Colchester**, **Nottingham**, **Canterbury**, **Ely**, **Epsom**, **Cromer**, **Essex** and **Sandringham**. **Grove Green Rd** stretches from Leytonstone to Leyton, and the streets which lie off it are plentifully supplied with terraced houses and flat conversions, though there are also many run-down properties. The roads surrounding Leyton Orient football club also hold an abundance of terraced houses at reasonable prices, and are close to Leyton tube station.

There are few blocks of flats in the area, save for some council-build, and the majority of flats are conversions. However, there is a large purpose-built block on the corner of **Francis Rd**. This, and the homes near the station and football ground, are well served by the shops in **High Rd Leyton**. A 6-acre site in **Church Rd** has been developed partly as light industrial, partly as homes/workspaces.

The area along **High Rd Leyton** is residential, and purpose-built flats are a feature here; Leytonstone Court – 1- and 2-bedroom flats – is towards the Stratford end of the **High Rd**. **Buckland Rd**, which runs parallel, has some 1990 1-bed flats; **Ruckholt Rd** too has sprouted smart 1- and 2-bed apartments.

South of **Leytonstone High Rd**, almost in Wanstead, lies the popular Bushwood estate. Here are some of the largest properties in the area. **Bushwood**, overlooking the open ground of Wanstead Flats, is sought-after for its grand late-Victorian 4-bed terraced houses. **Browning Rd** is a pretty conservation area of tiny early-Victorian cottages, refurbished in the '70s. **Barclay**, **Leybourne** and **Leyspring Rds** contain solidly-built 3-bed terraced houses. A well-planned one-way system leaves this estate free from all but residential traffic.

Chingford

The salubrious northern end of the borough holds the spacious streets of Chingford, its origins as a cluster of rural hamlets showing in the old village names like Chingford Green and Chingford Hatch. Airier streets and larger, roomier houses – though 5-beds are quite hard to find – characterize this area, with the occasional older building still to be found amid the Victoriana.

Select North Chingford, based around the Ridgeway area, holds the premier streets. At Chingford Green the streets peter out on the edge of Epping Forest – all homes bordering the forest are much prized. **Connaught Avenue** is a typical plum location: its 3-bedroomed Victorian homes now go for up to £200,000 – though all will depend on the rate of survival of original features. No garages here, though.

Among the less expensive but equally spacious streets of South Chingford, the Palace View estate is considered to be one of the most desirable corners. Turn-of-the-century 3-bed semis average about £130,000 in this leafy enclave, which lies close to beautiful Larkswood. Some of the best Victorian/Edwardian and 1930s houses are in the Highams Park neighbourhood, which boasts its own park with boating lake. Some homes display the W of the Warner family estate: these are coveted due to the high building standards.

Borders: Redbridge

At the old Green Man roundabout at the top of **Leytonstone High Rd**, you cross the borough boundary and enter Wanstead. Prices rise in this leafy corner, and larger homes can be found in roads running off **Overton Drive** near the golf course. Local first-time buyers look here for flats: it's cheaper than next-door Redbridge, but just as well placed for travel into town. Redbridge itself is a solidly middle-class area, with tidy blocks of flats and family houses of good appearance. Well served by its Central Line tube. Running alongside Wanstead are Snaresbrook and South Woodford. Here, too, are smart areas with a lot of quiet, tree-lined streets: all sizes of houses, some smart purpose-built flats and some of the best roads in that part of Redbridge Borough.

Transport	Tubes: Leyton, Leytonstone (zone 3, Central); Walthamstow Central, Blackhorse Rd (zone 3, Victoria). From Walthamstow Central: Oxford Circus 25 min, City 40 min (1 change), Heathrow 1 hr 20 min (1 change). Trains: Walthamstow Central to Liverpool St 15 min.
Convenient for	Transport to City, West End, Epping Forest, Lea Valley, M11 to Cambridge, M25, City Airport, Stanstead Airport; tubes/trains into town. Miles to centre: 6–7.
Schools	Waltham Forest Education Authority: Leytonstone School, Aveling Park School, McEntee Secondary School, Walthamstow Girls. Private: Forest School.

SALES

Flats	S	1B	2B	3B	4B	5B
Average prices	50–60	60–90	65–120	70–130	180–350	–
Houses	2B	3B	4B	5B	6/7B	8B
Average prices	100–130	110–180	150–300	225+	–	–

RENTAL

Flats	S	1B	2B	3B	4B	5B
Average prices	100–125	110–150	135–180	160–200	190–210	–
Houses	2B	3B	4B	5B	6/7B	8B
Average prices	150–200	175–210	200–325	–	–	–

The properties	Largely 1900s terraces of 2/3-bed homes and p/b flats. Upper Walthamstow boasts some large detached houses; bigger ones, too, in Leyton's Barclay estate. Flats, converted and p/b, abound.
The market	Good transport links and cheap first homes provide a stepping-stone for buyers from a lot further afield than the East End. Local searches: 4–5 working days.

Among those estate agents active in this area are:

- A Kennedy
- Central Estates
- Clarke Hillyer
- Douglas Allen Spiro
- Bairstow Eves
- Haart
- Spicer McColl
- Churchill
- W J Meade
- Trading Places

MAIDA VALE AND LITTLE VENICE

Map ref: p59 (4K)
Postal districts: W9, W2
Boroughs:
    Westminster (Con)
Council tax: £350
Conservation areas:
    Most of area, check
    with town hall
Parking: Residents/meters

Maida Vale is a wholly residential district, spacious, well-placed and decidedly popular. The area is N of the **Harrow Rd** and W of the **Edgware Rd** and its continuation to the N, **Maida Vale** (the road). Strategically placed for the main routes out of town to the W and N, its position was confirmed in 1998 by the long-awaited Paddington–Heathrow 15-min rail link: you can now check in for most major airlines at the station. Next-door neighbour to St John's Wood, replete with the sort of creamy, dignified terraces that typify Belgravia, its slower rise to full-throttle desirability despite this excellent location was only because, until some 15 years back, hardly any of its homes were for sale.

Maida Vale's character was largely determined by the district's long-time ownership by the Church Commissioners, who planned, built, maintained, laid down the rules for, and also let the property. This meant very little buying and selling: nearly all homes were rented. Only in the 1980s did this begin to change. Those tenants who could afford to bought their homes at preferential rates (20 per cent discount), some making large sums by reselling (often in 'back-to-back' deals). Developers moved in wholesale; the snowy terraces were converted, the hitherto run-down – and, it must be said, decidedly seedy – area was transformed; prices soared.

Renting remains a staple (a lot of buy-to-let sales here): flats, rather than houses, are the norm in this corner of wide streets and large-scale terraces, and their accessibility makes them favourites with multinational companies, embassies and the like.

It is now quite common for flats to appear for sale with a share of the freehold. Many leaseholders jointly bought the freehold to their homes after 1993, when the law changed to make this easier. This accelerated in the mid-'90s when some faced five-figure bills for major refurbishments to their mansion blocks. Take good advice, if buying, about whether the (frequently high) service charges contribute to an adequate sinking fund to guard against enormous extra outlay when the roof needs replacing.

Warwick Avenue, running N from the **Harrow Rd** across the Regent's Canal, set the tone for this extremely pleasant corner in the 1840s and '50s. The large cream stucco houses here and fronting the canal are still the area's biggest single homes, and the smartest. This leafy waterside neighbourhood, alongside the canal and the pretty triangular pool where it meets the Paddington Canal, is known as Little Venice.

Later building confirmed the spacious feel: wide avenues of tall white terraces and red-brick mansion blocks, behind whose ramparts are often concealed large (some vast) shared gardens – a secret unsuspected by passers-by. These delightful 'inverted square' gardens are the area's hidden bonus: they can include tennis courts, and ground floor flats often have direct access through gates at the bottom of their own back gardens: a delight for those with kids.

Overall, Maida Vale is a rich mine of particularly nice flats, big and small, old and new. What you won't find here are the usual London rows of small terraced houses, although there is a scattering of new and refurbished mews houses. In this area the garden-level maisonette replaces the house – and can be bigger and nicer than other areas' narrow Victorian rows. The spacious layout of Maida Vale makes for exceptionally light and pleasant flats with leafy outlooks.

The most coveted homes, however, are those nearest to or overlooking the canal: truly a 'Little Venice' – though estate agents now use this more picturesque name for all Maida Vale's most desirable white stucco streets (which leads to Kilburn homes being described as 'borders Little Venice'). These snowy rows form the heart of the area, and are succeeded further N and W by streets of red-brick mansion flats: these can provide a lot of space for your money. The Church land ends in the W at **Shirland Rd**: next come smaller-scale Victorian terraces, fast improving.

One question mark hangs over the area: the rare peace of Little Venice could be disturbed by the impending Paddington Basin development scheme, the northernmost tip of which crosses the Westway barrier. Certainly the new towers of this vast sub-Docklands swathe will be visible from the multi-million pound **Blomfield Rd** villas; agents, however, reckon that this will lead to further price rises as this hitherto cut-off corner is 'discovered'.

Little Venice

Blomfield Rd and **Maida Avenue** residents have homes made magic (and even more expensive) by the presence of water. The canal runs between the two, widening by the **Warwick Rd** bridge – where it branches – into a young lake with willow-pattern islet and waterside public gardens and walk. The canal-ends of adjoining roads also get called Little Venice; non-natives can be startled by narrowboats apparently gliding across the top of the street. A charming, prized corner of London.

Starting from **Paddington Green** to the S of the canal (today marooned between the **Westway** and '60s college blocks and council towers) **St Mary's Terrace** runs up towards the canal: No 1, in classic double-fronted stucco, sets the tone for the left side. On the other side is Fleming Court (council-built), then the stately red-brick mansion blocks of Osborne House and **St Mary's Mansions,** which comprises several blocks around its own courtyard (unmodernized flats are very occasionally available). **Porteus Rd** opposite leads to **Hogan Mews,** an early '80s mews development close to the **Westway.** The opposite side has council-built flats. **St Mary's Terrace** becomes **Park Place Villas,** which runs to the canal – and Little Venice proper. On the corner with **Maida Avenue,** an enormous Italianate villa has a prime position (this 9-bed, 9-bath, indoor swimming pool mansion came up for sale for £4.5 million in 1997 – and went for more). Both **Maida Avenue** and **Blomfield Rd** have large and covetable white stucco villas – strictly for multi-millionaires – facing over the water. These give way to later Victoriana towards the **Edgware Rd** end; mansion blocks can provide flats the size of young houses, and as various: 3-bed examples might merit £310,000, £685,000 or anywhere in between, depending on the block.

From the Harrow Rd Bridge westwards, the S bank of the canal is Westminster City's Warwick Estate; pleasant '60s low-rise, now increasingly in private hands. Prices are low for their neighbourhood: a 3-bed flat overlooking the canal might be £165,000. The canal then dips below the **Harrow Rd,** and between the two on the site of St Mary's Hospital is Maida Vale's biggest new-build area: on **Admiral Walk,** Carlton Gate and neighbouring Swift and Swallow Courts were completed in 1995. These blocks of 1- and 2-bed flats (recent examples, £169,000 and £218,000 respectively) are strategically placed to serve as a London base for country-hopping executives and the like – but note that those who opt for canalside flats here also get fine views of the elevated section of the Westway and the tower blocks of North Kensington.

Behind **Blomfield Rd,** to the W of **Warwick Avenue** lies villagey **Warwick Place,** with the pleasant Warwick Castle pub, which overlooks Clifton Nurseries (entrance in **Clifton Villas**), one of London's first and best garden centres. More little shops in **Bristol Gardens,** off which **Bristol Mews** was reborn in 1995 as 15 smart new homes. Across **Formosa St,** the same year finally saw the complete refurbishment of the 44 mews homes of **Elnathan Mews** (a process which had been rudely halted by the 1990 slump). These mews corners add a cache of small houses – otherwise a rarity in both Little Venice and Maida Vale – to the area. Even rarer, they have garages. A whole house in **Bristol Gardens** went for £925,000 last winter. East of **Warwick Way,** the streets that lie between the canal and **Clifton Gardens** also enjoy the Little Venice premium.

Maida Vale Central

The name really applies to the old Church estate, from Little Venice northwards, with **Maida Vale** (the road) forming the E boundary. **Warwick Avenue,** which is the Vale's boulevard, runs NW from Little Venice into the heart of the district with the clean, striking lines of the modern St Saviour's Church (junction with **Clifton Gardens**) as its focal point. The church has matching flats, Manor House Court, behind. The Avenue is a delight – lined with classical white early 1850s mansions, many of which escaped being sub-divided and are still single homes, particularly on the E side.

Clifton Gardens, a wide and desirable street of 1860s stucco terraces, runs NE from St Saviour's (and the tube station) to **Maida Vale.** Top-class conversions into luxury flats back, on the N side, onto vast communal gardens. Cumberland House, on the junction with **Warwick Avenue,** is new (1987) despite its handsome 'period' appearance: top-of-the-market apartments. Another such is Europa House in **Randolph Avenue**: this has underground parking. Many flats here are rented out rather than sold. **Randolph Avenue** saw several more luxurious developments in 1988. **Clifton Gardens** becomes, at the E end, **Clifton Rd** – the Vale's 'high street'. Enviable **Warrington Crescent** curves N from **Clifton Gardens** to **Sutherland Avenue**, and is mostly more flats with communal gardens both sides, reckoned to be some of the area's best. Flats in **Warrington Crescent** can rise from modest 2-beds for c. £225,000, to quadruple that for a big, 4-bed, garden level one. Ditto for style and price in **Randolph Crescent**, running parallel, though the 3-acre triangular gardens the E side shares with stretches of **Clifton Gardens** and **Randolph Avenue** are even more highly rated.

Castellain Rd, parallel to (and converging with) **Warwick Avenue** on the E, is a long road which crosses **Sutherland Avenue** to reach **Elgin Avenue**. Between these two avenues is Castellain Mansions, a large block of red- and grey-brick mansion flats. A 2-bed flat here on a long lease might be £230,000. Behind, to the E, are communal gardens; to the W, Paddington Bowling and Sports Club offering 'bowls, tennis, squash, social'. In the angle behind **Castellain** and **Sutherland**, the communal gardens boast tennis courts. An old garage site in **Castellain Rd** has become Katherine Court, whose style handsomely acknowledges its neighbours'. Across the road in **Warrington Gardens** more than 50 new flats, with parking, were built in 1995 (today from c. £350,000 to £680,000 at penthouse level).

Sutherland Avenue is classic Maida Vale, wide, tree-lined parking down the centre, its vista stopped to the E by the '60s Stuart Tower. At the western end (W of **Shirland Rd**), stand ornate stucco houses, with wrought-iron balustrades at the first floor. Then come slightly smaller models, then enormous Victorian red-bricks. Note 'The Sutherlands' – cream Italianate villa by the circus at the E end: now 10 flats, one with a first floor conservatory, plus a house. Shirland Rd marks a price, as well as a physical, divide: W of it, **Sutherland Avenue** runs down to the **Harrow Rd**; a 2-bed flat that would cost £215,000 here would rise to £345,000 if located 30 yards away across Shirland on the eastern stretch that runs up to **Maida Vale** (the road). **Lauderdale Rd**, running from the E end of **Sutherland Rd** W to **Elgin Rd** has more mansion flats, with large gardens behind those of the S side.

Elgin Avenue starts in the E at Maida Vale tube, runs W to cross **Shirland Rd** and on into western Maida Vale (see below). Compared with **Sutherland Avenue** it is busier and more anonymous, lined with comfortable red-brick mansion blocks. Elgin Mansions is a big flats block with access to communal gardens. On the corner of **Elgin Avenue** and **Morshead Rd**, a traditional-style red-brick block of 2- and 3-bed flats (£160–190,000) was built in 1995. **Elgin Mews, North** and **South**, are tucked behind the shops around Maida Vale tube. **Mews North** has been rebuilt: smart town-houses. **Mews South** is original: pretty, painted brick homes.

Grantully Rd runs beside Paddington Recreation Ground: hardly scenic, but at least green and open. Facing it are mansion flats; Leith Mansions then Ashworth Mansions – a quiet corner. **Ashworth Rd**, which crosses **Elgin Avenue**, has mansion flats at the N end. A surprise here: **Ashworth Rd**, S of **Elgin**, suddenly becomes Surrey: low-built between-the-wars pairs of houses joined by garages – the nearest semis to Marble Arch? Low eaves, deep porches, stockbroker-Tudor and £850–900,000. . .

Morshead Rd, **Wymering Rd** and **Widley Rd**, plus **Essendine Rd**, are red-brick mansions. Wymering Mansions has undergone £4.5 million in refurbishments over the last few years: 2-bed flats are around £235,000 with 3-bed around £270,000. Views from the **Morshead** ones (Nos 25 onwards) are across the recreation ground.

Randolph Avenue and **Lanark Rd** run parallel to Maida Vale, with large houses (mostly recent flat conversions). The smart new villa-style blocks of flats in **Lanark** were built by Westminster Council in '83 as starter homes. These now appear on the open market. Other **Randolph Avenue** homes are flats carved out of some very large Victorian semi-detached stock-brick and stucco houses, though a few do remain as single homes – with £2 million-plus price tags. The S end of **Randolph Avenue** runs down to the canal and enters Little Venice. There are big stucco terraces here. The red-brick electricity sub-station in **Randolph Mews** was transformed into a house in 1988 – complete with a conservatory bathroom (one-way glass!). As far back as 1996 this sold for £1.6 million. At the N end, Nos 171 onwards overlook the recreation ground. The N end of **Lanark** is a council estate with tower blocks.

Maida Vale, a major road, bounds the district. To the E is St John's Wood. At the far N end, almost in Kilburn (or St John's Wood borders if you're being kind) is Regent's Plaza, a big and smart hotel/flats complex. Flats can be had here on long leases from £250–350,000 plus for 2- and 3-beds. The W side of **Maida Vale** starts (from the N) with a Council estate; then past **Elgin Avenue's** '30s mansions, then more council, then Y-shaped Stuart Tower: private 1-bed flats, enjoying fine views from upper floors. South of **Sutherland Avenue** are big 1890s mansion blocks such as Blomfield Court and Sandringham Court. On the E side of the road are more of the same: these are still in W9. Look here for spacious flats, but without the garden access of those in the communal-gardens roads. Four-bed flats in these blocks can now reach £495,000.

In a major development by Galliard, the old Clarendon Hotel is being rebuilt behind its facade: ranging from studios to 3-bed penthouses, the brand-new flats go on sale in April; projected prices from c. £380–2 million or more. Going on S over the canal bridge, **Maida Vale** becomes **Edgware Rd**, a scruffy but lively shopping street.

Borders

Having converted everything in sight in Maida Vale proper, the developers moved W of the **Shirland Rd** divide into a zone which is somewhat of a no-man's-land of council estates and small terraces, many now split into flats. The S part, N of **Harrow Rd** and up towards Queen's Park station, is in Westminster's patch. The NE corner is in Brent.

The N part of the borders district is largely sprawling council estates on either side of **Carlton Vale**. South of here, the modest terraces of the **Fernhead Rd** – **Saltram Crescent** area are a good-value corner in a mixed council/private area. **Saltram** was discovered early by converters. The Westminster frontier runs from the S end of **Kilburn Park Rd** up behind **Saltram Crescent**. The streets between **Walterton Rd** and **Fernhead Rd** became a bitter battleground between Westminster Council and local tenants in the 1980s. A group of residents eventually grouped together, formed a housing association, Walterton and Elgin Community Homes, and bought their homes *en masse* from Westminster (which had been set on selling to developers). They have since been carrying out major renovations. Some homes here now appear on the market. A modern estate separates these streets from the private terraces of **Bravington Rd**,

Portnall Rd and **Ashmore Rd**: a good hunting-ground for less expensive 2-bed flats. (A 3-bed ex-council in Ashmore was £210,000 last winter.) Across the **Harrow Rd** to the S, and just in W9 and Westminster's patch, are **Hormead Rd** and **Fermoy Rd**: Victorian terraces, close to the canal. Many are flats, with 2-bed at around £170–180,000. To the W (see Kilburn, Kensal Green and Queen's Park chapter) are the council's Mozart Estate and the placid Queen's Park Estate of charming terraced council cottages.

Transport   Tubes: Maida Vale, Warwick Avenue (zone 2, Bakerloo); Oxford Circus 15 min, City 25 min (1 change), Heathrow 30 min (1 change).

Convenient for   Paddington, roads to W and N, West End. Miles from centre: 3.

Schools   Local Authority: St George's RC, North Westminster. Private: American.

SALES

Flats	S	1B	2B	3B	4B	5B
Average prices	80–200	125–300	170–400	220–800	350–950	—
Houses	2B	3B	4B	5B	6/7B	8B
Average prices	175–300	350–800	450–800	500–1 M+	1 M+	—

RENTAL

Flats	S	1B	2B	3B	4B	5B
Average prices	150+	200–325	240–400	350+	700+	—
Houses	2B	3B	4B	5B	6/7B	8B
Average prices	350–650	400–800+	750+	1000+	—	—

The properties   Gracious white stucco terraces and villas, rows of neat red-brick mansion flats, some modern mews/town-houses. Flats reign: mainly mansion or period conversions. These can be large. Small houses rare; the garden maisonette replaces, and can be lovely. Few houses: best canalside ones priced in the millions.

The market   The range of flats, rather than houses attract buyers, renters or buy-to-rent investors. Red-brick mansion flats (watch the service charges), period conversions, loads of recent luxury conversions. Large flat sizes common here, also some small mews houses. The Vale's location makes it a good long-term bet. Area's 'hidden gardens' are its best asset. Local searches: 10 working days.

Among those estate agents active in this area are:

- Greene & Co
- Fraser & Co *
- Chestertons
- Marsh & Parsons
- Foxtons *
- Cohen & Pride
- Brian Lack
- Central London Properties
- Clifton Residential
- Londonwide Estates
- Winkworth *
- Anscombe & Ringland *
- Howard Estates
- Vickers
- Pembertons
- Homeview Estates *

further details: see advertisers' index on p671

MARYLEBONE AND FITZROVIA

Map ref: p138 (5E)
Postal districts: W1, NW1, NW8
Boroughs: Westminster (Con), Camden (Lab)
Council tax: Band D Westminster £350, Camden £897
Conservation areas: Most of area
Parking: Residents/meters. Clamps

Marylebone is starting to reappear as a neighbourhood name, after half a century of obscurity as a largely commercial area. Several big-name developers have smart flats for sale here, and at last some of the decaying Georgian homes are being virtually rebuilt to provide more flats and houses. **Marylebone High St** is becoming a smart shop and restaurant centre. Nearby Paddington now has the Heathrow Express, making the area still more convenient. Baker St tube, always a useful intersection, now includes the Jubilee line to Westminster, the South Bank and Docklands, as does Bond Street station. There is an overall air of renewed prosperity – scaffolding abounds.

Marylebone is the name for most of the slice of London sandwiched between **Oxford St** and Regent's Park. It could hardly be more central – or more varied. Homes here range from the 18th century to the present day, from tiny studio apartments through mews cottages to vast family mansions: the largest came up for sale last winter – 12,000 sq ft of Great Cumberland Place freehold, including mews flat and servants' quarters – at £4.25 million. Blue plaques abound – sometimes more than one on each (very likely listed) building. Fringe neighbourhoods include the bustling Great Portland and Fitzrovia districts to the E and the rather mixed Lisson Grove/North Marylebone tract N across the roaring divide of the **Marylebone Rd**.

Marylebone's orderly 18th-century grid of streets and squares is broken by the irrepressible wiggle of **Marylebone Lane** which, with the **High St** (straight for a while, but not for long), marks the centre of the original village of Marylebone. Across to the E the grid resumes its soldierly progress to **Portland Place**, a giant boulevard more reminiscent of Paris than London, lined with many a luxurious apartment on its way up towards Regent's Park.

Parallel to the E is **Great Portland St**, and at **Cleveland St** the grid swings slightly on its axis to mark the borough boundary and the start of Fitzrovia. In the other direction, W of the still villagey **Marylebone Lane**, the orderly pattern runs across to the diagonal of the **Edgware Rd**. To the N, over the **Marylebone Rd**, W1 gives way to NW1 and **Lisson Grove**, with the **Dorset Square** neighbourhood E of Marylebone station and abutting the margins of the Park: this is the untidier but up-and-coming corner.

Despite the rediscovery of Marylebone, this is as yet not an area that springs instantly to the home-hunter's mind. Mayfair, Belgravia, Kensington – all those are, in fact, further from the hub. But this tract is a diverse one: many of its homes have been appropriated for shops or offices, its through-routes are busy. People think first of its landmarks: the BBC's Broadcasting House, the Courtauld Institute, Middlesex Hospital, the University of Westminster . . . and of course **Harley St**, heart of the medical profession.

The continuing ownership by major landlords such as the de Walden and Portman Estates means few freeholds and, frequently, short leaseholds. The Estates are at last waking up to the area's potential, with interesting opportunities for investors.

A few years back there were still real bargains, considering the location, among – particularly – the flats to be found above shops or in the less obvious of the mansion or more recent blocks. And it is still an area well worth a searching look: compare prices with more obvious but more distant places: Clapham, say, or Battersea. You have the advantage that a limited number of house-hunters even think of looking here, the disadvantage of competition from companies, or businessmen looking for pieds-à-terre. It best suits single people – no need (or parking space) for a car, the West End on your doorstep – and those unburdened with young children. Although many happy families live N of **Oxford St**, they are not typical. Proof of this is offered by estate agents in the area, many of whom say that they have never been asked by anxious parents for advice on local schools.

Recently, the competition for homes has increased, but so has the supply. For the first time in decades, it's possible to list several new homes schemes either under way or planned. And efforts to boost the attractiveness of the area are bearing fruit. Away from the bustle of Selfridges and John Lewis in **Oxford St** lie corners of surprising residential peace and tranquillity. This is an orderly and discreet part of town. Embassies signal this: Switzerland and Sweden enjoy the sober peace of the **Bryanston Square** neighbourhood.

The most common type of home here in the West End is the 3- or 4-bedroomed flat, but there is less demand for these today than for smaller apartments: more recent developments have recognized this, and produced little 1- and 2-bed flats. Only about 10 per cent of West End properties are houses; and nearly all are terraced. Despite leasehold reform, freeholds are still hard to come by. Leases, even new ones, can be short: 60 years is good. Quiz agents on leases when considering anything except a new flat – most of these have 999 years or share of freehold. Even freeholds may be subject to restrictive estate management agreements.

Differences in property prices (one flat can cost double what a seemingly similar flat costs) depend not just upon the quality and location of the property itself, but upon the length of the lease. Private landowners such as the Howard de Walden Estate (which owns 120 acres-worth of the freeholds in Marylebone, mostly around the medical area, between **Marylebone High St** and **Great Portland St**) do not often deal in long leases. Medical licences – granted by the landlords and allowing doctors to practice – inflate prices considerably. A fair amount of land is also owned by the Crown Estate (for example, parts of **Harley St** and **Park Crescent Mews West**).

Marylebone

Marylebone has always been synonymous with medical excellence, for it is here that the cream of the British medical profession is gathered, crammed into **Harley St** and its immediate environs (**Wimpole St**, for example). This district, which is bordered by the southern margins of Regent's Park, as well as **Edgware Rd** and **Great Portland St**, encompasses street-by-street variations in architecture, general character – and price.

If landlords like the De Walden Estate mean few freeholds, they also make for continuity. Thus the unchanging nature of the medical groves. They are responsible for the lovely Georgian doorways, staircases and rooflines still so much in evidence. These older buildings are supplemented by the red-brick blocks built at the turn of the century and some modern apartments that replaced wartime damage (a purpose-built block in **Wimpole St** is one of the few buildings hereabouts which can offer underground parking). Doctors must still get permission from the estate in order to mount a brass plate on the door of one of the estate houses.

There is much to choose from in Marylebone. There is the almost rustic 'olde-worlde' charm of Marylebone Village, with its pretty little shops and restaurants (and also the fashionable American College). There is the cheerfully commercialized (busy but not unpleasant) **Baker St**, home of Sherlock Holmes, sleuth of legend. **Baker St** stretches from Regent's Park at one end to the up-market Selfridges department store on Oxford St at the other; and where it bisects **Marylebone Rd** are the waxworks of Madame Tussaud's and the London Planetarium, each a focus for tourists. There is **Wigmore St**, with its world-renowned concert hall and smart shops, visited by a quite different clientele from the **Oxford St** crowds. Refurbishment of a big former store on the corner with **Welbeck St** resulted in some very smart new flats. Welbeck House, a stone block on the corner of **Wigmore St**, has vast apartments. A 2-bed flat in a portered block around here was being offered at £525,000 for an 89-year lease last winter.

Then there is **Portland Place**, the grand, wide-avenued refuge for the BBC's Broadcasting House, the Royal Institute of British Architects and a clutch of embassies. **Portland Place** homes are likely to be luxurious (discreet luxury, or dripping-gilt-and-marble luxury – but decidedly luxury) apartments in conversions or – more likely – the modern buildings that have superceded Robert Adam's original elegance. This is company, or perhaps top BBC-executive, territory. Many blocks have uniformed porters; a large and elegant one in nearby **Mansfield St** runs to maid service and its own restaurant. You can pay £1 million around here for a 4- to 5-bed flat. At the N end of **Portland Place** is a delight: instead of debouching straight onto the roaring **Marylebone Rd**, the street divides into the two curving arms of Nash's **Park Crescent**, its lovely homes sheltering behind the protective half-moon of its gardens. Most are flats: £210,000 for 1-bed. The rare family home with garage is occasionally to be had in its two mews behind.

Indeed, one of the area's special delights is the many and varied mews tucked away behind its main streets. These compact little homes – mainly modernized, but some unrefurbished – are dotted across the area, though many are concentrated in the **Harley St** environs. People pay £700,000 for 2-bed mews houses. These, of course, are often the extremely proud possessors of garages, thanks to their original function as stables – some still have rings for tethering horses. Though if you don't care for history look for the modern version to **Richardson's Mews**, just off **Warren St**, and **Weymouth Mews**, which have new houses.

There is the discreet elegance of the various squares: at the W, Marble Arch slice of Marylebone – between **Edgware Rd** and **Gloucester Place** – lie **Bryanston Square** and **Montagu Square**, with their communal gardens in the centre. These well-kept and railed patches of green are accessible only to residents and are not to be sniffed at in a district where private gardens are almost non-existent, or barely bigger than a suburban household's window box. Octagon, suppliers of mini-mansions to the Surrey golf course belt, have come into town to provide 25 new flats and three new mews houses in a clever bit of new-build, matching the old, at 16–18 **Bryanston Square**. Just one penthouse was left in December: 2-beds sold in 1999 from £225,000. The mews

E and W of the Square offer mews houses which range in price from £500,000 for 2-beds up to £1 million plus for 5-beds.

There is always a good supply of mansion flats, of every standard from down-at-heel to palatial. Century-old buildings like Bickenhall Mansions, with their high ceilings and coved fireplaces, are popular, with 4-bed long-lease flats. There are even occasional vast 9-bed flats in blocks like Orchard Court in **Portman Square**. These have been refurbished and now have, among other things, new lifts and – cunningly – 10–12 new penthouses built on top of the original block. **Harley St** is, as you might expect, another prized address, but is mostly medical consulting-rooms. A 1980s scheme in **Marylebone St**, Maybury Court, has 80 1- to 3-bed flats (from £215,000).

There are rumours that **Marylebone High St** may be pedestrianized, which will increase its attractions. Already, smart shops and restaurants – books, fashion, Conran Shop – are making this one more expensive London 'village' – to the regret of some who are nostalgic for its more local charms. A Waitrose supermarket is among the more useful newcomers. Cecil House above it will be flats, due during 2000.

New on the High St is Copperfield House, a 20-flat block: £400–595,000, plus £25,000 for a car space. In **Devonshire Place**, ten flats have been created in the conversion of two Georgian terraced houses. For those who appreciate 1960s commercial architecture and want a room with a view there is Marathon House, a converted office tower, now 107 flats, on **Marylebone Rd**. In **Old Marylebone Rd**, Galliard's Bourne House is being marketed on its proximity to Paddington and thus the rest of the world via Heathrow: £215–483,000, with penthouses from £556,000.

Great Portland St

The area E of Portland Place has a style of its own. It has been, and to a large extent still is, the centre of the London fashion trade. However quite a few warehouses and offices are being converted into homes.

Berkeley's West One House in **Wells St** has added 73 new-build homes: 1- to 3-bed flats and 3-bed town-houses. Nearby, enticingly named **Market Place** is at present just a wider bit of road, but landlords Great Portland Estates plan a piazza with shops and bars, though nothing has happened yet.

The new flats join mansion blocks around **Mortimer St**, **Riding House St** and **Foley St**. There are mews, many still commercial, and odd corners like **Booths Place**, where 2-bed flats have their own garages. **Berners St**, just N of Oxford St, has Berkeley's restoration of York House into flats: most were sold by last winter, though a 2-bed apartment was still on offer at £340,000.

Lisson Grove & Dorset Square

The area around **Lisson Grove** (NW1) remains the least fashionable part of Marylebone. The Regent's Canal runs through the area, conveying hints of

M

neighbouring Little Venice and Regent's Park. Despite these assets, and NW1 or NW8 in the address, **Lisson Grove** has yet to take off. The Lisson Green and **Church St** estates are not a plus.The Georgian façades of **Bell St**, which runs from **Edgware Rd** to **Lisson St**, have attracted attention. Europe's largest permanent, undercover antiques market on the junction of **Cosway St** and **Bell St** has given the area a boost. Barratt are building 'Prince Regent's Gate': 400 homes for sale on reclaimed railway land W of **Park Rd**: a NW1 postcode and proximity to Regent's Park should make them popular. Completing winter 2000; prices range up to £1.25m, though 1-bed flats start at £270,000. In the same scheme are 97 homes for the Acton Housing Association. Portman Gate in **Lisson Grove** is a 1980s development of 114 houses, flats and penthouses. The Wallis Building in **Penfold St** has 22 lofts in a neo-art-deco factory.

East of Marylebone station, which is faced by the superbly restored 1900 Landmark Hotel, is a quiet district of Georgian, mid-19th-century and modern houses. This is often called the Dorset Square Conservation Area – though most of Marylebone has that status. **Gloucester Place** is a roaring highway, but **Dorset Square** and **Balcombe St** and nearby roads are pleasant, low-key and mostly residential. Prices are lower than in Marylebone proper: 3-bed modern houses command from £375,000, more for period ones: a freehold 4-bed house needing work was priced at £600,000 last autumn. However, a smart Grade II-listed Georgian house was on the market last winter for £1.5m. A mews house behind Marylebone Station – one of London's quieter terminals – was £350,000 freehold late last year. **Glentworth St** has some period mansion blocks, which are well-located for the Baker Street tube and Regent's Park.

Fitzrovia

Fitzrovia is the rectangle enclosed by **Euston Rd** to the N, **Oxford St** to the S, **Great Portland St** to the W and **Tottenham Court Rd** to the E. Presiding over the northern end of the neighbourhood named after it is **Fitzroy Square**. This is a handsome, semi-pedestrianized conservation area, inhabited by offices and embassies, but also by private residents. Fitzrovia is a quiet, quirky London village with a bohemian flavour and history – William Blake lived in **Fitzroy Square** and the area as a whole has long attracted artists, writers and aesthetes. This area has gained popularity over the last decade, and is a well-known centre for advertising and TV companies, whose offices take up some of the nicest Georgian buildings. Fitzrovia divides into three sections: there is the **Charlotte St/Tottenham Court Rd** slice – a 'fun' area with pedestrian walkways. There is the grandeur of **Fitzroy Square** and its surroundings. Then there are the streets to the W between **Great Portland** and **Great Titchfield St**s, home of the wholesale fashion industry (described opposite under Great Portland St). The landmark that keeps reappearing – always, somehow, where you least expect it – is, of course, the soaring Telecom Tower.

Fitzrovia is packed with interesting period properties. Modernized blocks house hundreds of studio and 1-bedroom apartments. Old-style – and increasingly scarce – mansion blocks are being carved up to meet the demand for small, compact flats. Look for these on the west side of the neighbourhood. In **Charlotte Place**, interesting old houses have been done up by a housing association. Modern homes include a clutch of flats and mews houses in **Whitfield St** (1988) and new houses with garages in **Fitzroy Court**. The 3-bed and garage houses in **Whitfield St** date from 1990. Two-bed flats here range up from £185,000 to £300,000. In **Fitzroy Square** a smart 2-bed flat with a 2-tiered conservatory was £375,000 last December. Two new freehold houses in the Square were on the market last winter for £425,000 for 2/3 beds.

Although Fitzrovia is more up-market than Lisson Grove, there are still some relative bargains. It is popular with young couples and people who just need a 'pied-à-terre. Westminster Council is trying to ease the traffic and improve the area in general. Westminster controls the W half of Fitzrovia; Camden's patch spreads E from **Cleveland St** and includes **Fitzroy Square**. Camden hope to boost local business with a 'Business Initiative'. Some say that the area, with its unique atmosphere, proximity to Regent's Park and first-class restaurants and bars, doesn't need much improving.

Transport   Tubes, all zone 1: Baker Street (Jubilee, Circle, Hammersmith & City, Bakerloo), Oxford Circus (Bakerloo, Victoria, Central), Marylebone (Bakerloo), Marble Arch (Central). Others see map. Trains: Marylebone, Euston, Paddington (Heathrow 17 mins). From Oxford Circus: City 15 min, Heathrow 52 min (1 change).

Convienient for   West End, Regent's Park, City. Miles from centre: 1.5.

Schools   Local Authority: St Marylebone School (g). Private: Queen's College (g), Portland Place, Francis Holland (g) .

SALES

Flats	S	1B	2B	3B	4B	5B
Average prices	100–150	150–300	225–300	300–1 M+	500–1 M+	800–1 M
Houses	2B	3B	4B	5B	6/7B	8B
Average prices	350–600	450–850	600–1.2 M	800–1 M+	→1 M+	2 M+

RENTAL

Flats	S	1B	2B	3B	4B	5B
Average prices	180–250	200–500	300–500	350–1000	600–2000	800–3500+
Houses	2B	3B	4B	5B	6/7B	8B
Average prices	375–500	600–800	750–1000	–	–	–

The properties   The cry in the heart of the West End is for flats, from tiny studios to company luxury. Cheaper ones above shops, red-brick mansion blocks, conversions of the gracious period homes, now more new-build. Also mews, and a few surviving family homes. Parking atrocious, garages at a premium.

The market   Marylebone is long-established, especially the medical district. Fitzrovia is more bohemian but changing. Whole area is mixed residential/commercial, therefore cheaper than other central areas. Better value than many would expect, despite W1 postcode. Local searches: Camden 7–10 working days, Westminster 10 working days.

Among those estate agents active in this area are:
- Winkworth *
- Plaza Estates
- Chestertons
- York Estates
- Oakleys
- Hurford Salvi Carr
- Whitehouse Lewis
- Hunter & Co
- Egertons
- Alexanders
- Park Estates
- James Anthony
- Executive Homes
- Fraser & Co *
- Foxtons *
- Marylebone High St Estate Agents
- Wallsway Estates
- Central Estates
- Gibson Reed
- Elliot Son & Boyton

further details: see advertisers' index on p671

MAYFAIR AND ST JAMES'S

Map ref: p145 (1H)
Postal districts: W1, SW1
Boroughs: Westminster (Con)
Council tax: Band D £350
Conservation areas: Check with town hall
Parking: Residents/meters. Clamps

Mayfair is the place to look if you need a mansion – and not just a mansion flat. It is one of the very few places in Central London where the really rich can find a really large house, with servants' quarters and a grand suite of reception rooms and somewhere to garage the Rolls. Luckily for the rest of us, there are plenty of less opulent homes too, giving the lie to Mayfair's outdated reputation as an office and hotel district.

What Mayfair offers is street after street, square after mews, of homes of every period from 1700 to 2000. They have one thing in common: they were built for the rich, or at least their servants. Offices did indeed take over large tracts when commercial space was scarce in London following World War II bombing, but the tide of commerce has been turned back. Some lovely Georgian buildings on Park Lane once more have drawing rooms, rather than boardrooms, behind their elegant bow windows. Mayfair is reverting to type.

'Mayfair,' said a local estate agent 'has always been for the really rich'. And so you might think, if you set out to buy a whole house here. Yet this is only part of the story. Mayfair, and St James's to the S, are still surprisingly residential. This may be the centre of town, crammed with coveted shops and offices, but there are plenty of people who live here, and not all are anonymous executives or country-hopping potentates. Mayfair even has a thriving residents' association, vigilant in defence of peace and amenity. The downside is that everyone wants to live here: there were only 80 homes for sale this spring, the lowest number (recalls a local agent) for 25 years.

Top people have lived in Mayfair since early Georgian times. Never has it sunk from its position as a centre of fashionable London. Other places – Soho, Bloomsbury,

Holland Park – have had their ups and downs, but Mayfair has always been a correct address. Until within living memory it was dotted with the very grand houses (palaces really) of dukes and other noblemen. Most have gone, to be replaced by great blocks of flats and hotels – apart from 1730 Crewe House, an oasis of cream stucco amid green lawns, home to the Saudi Ambassador. Yet many of the smaller Georgian houses, and some large Victorian ones, survive, providing the slightly less ostentatious but no less luxurious London homes of today's magnates.

The less rich have a choice of flats of every degree of size and smartness up to the demi-royal, of mews cottages which range from tiny to surprisingly big, of serviced apartments, of purchases both freehold and leasehold or rentals both short and long. Buying prices start at £150,000 and go on up. And up.

Mayfair is bounded to the N by the great shopping parade of **Oxford St**, in the E by **Regent St**, to the S by **Piccadilly** – across which royal St James's slopes gracefully down to its Park – and in the W by **Park Lane**, the 8-lane highway and Red Route that separates Hyde Park from Mayfair's western rampart of hotels and car showrooms.

The NW part, about half the total, from Marble Arch down to **Berkeley Square**, belongs to the Grosvenor Estate, as does Belgravia. The rest is divided among several landlords, and until the advent of the Leasehold Reform Act, freeholds were rare.

Now this is changing, as residents exercise their right to buy. BP (British Petroleum), which owns an area of southern Mayfair, started to sell off its freeholds. Leaseholders in **Chesterfield Hill** are among those being offered the opportunity to buy their freehold. BP is keen to negotiate rather than having to go through the rigmarole of receiving tenants' notices under the enfranchisement legislation. The Grosvenor Estate, by contrast, is more reluctant to sell off freeholds without going through the legal procedures. However, it is now offering new leases of 125 years at an annual ground rent of 'one peppercorn'. The Estate maintains that its tenants are comfortable with the leasehold system and will still negotiate 20-year leases for reduced capital terms. Local agents say most freeholders and head-lease holders will work out a deal allowing tenants to extend their lease.

The other important change to this London heartland began at the end of 1990, when the 'temporary' planning permission granted for office use of many Mayfair sites – including houses – finally expired, allowing a small but significant increase in the number of people actually living here. Now around 30 per cent of the area is offices – though art galleries, restaurants, hotels, etc, account for another 40 per cent.

More than 60 office buildings have reverted to homes, about 20 of them to single houses – mansion is sometimes a better word: one in **Park St** was sold to developers in 1998 for £4.6 million, and is complete but not yet on the market. It totals 25,000 sq ft plus swimming pool. The local agents' grapevine has it that £35 million (£20 million last year) will be asked. Nor is this the largest Mayfair mansion: one is reckoned to be twice that size. Even the many-storeyed ramparts of Park Lane are yielding apartments and penthouses that gaze (across the traffic) at Hyde Park.

Mayfair

Mayfair is big, and has its quiet corners and districts of bustle. As a broad generalization, the further W, the quieter and smarter. In general, the E and S are older than the N and W. The SW corner, Shepherd Market, has an air of its own and is dealt with later in this chapter. A few controlled-rent and housing association flats apart, Mayfair is the province of the mansion block and expensively converted flat, with a slowly increasing supply of period houses – some mansion-sized – thanks to office reversions, and rather more mews cottages. No area is without homes, but in some parts (especially the E) they are hard to spot amid the shops, offices and banks. While nothing in Mayfair is cheap, the prices asked for properties can vary widely – based on the two variables of freehold/length of lease and degree of modernization/opulence.

The NE corner, around **Hanover Square**, is among the oldest parts of Mayfair – the Square dates from 1715 – but is today mostly commercial, with offices and shops spilling out from **Oxford St**. **New Bond St**, Mayfair's main shopping street (and light years away in style from **Oxford St**'s tourists and department stores), divides this area from the fashion quarter centred around pedestrianized **South Molton St**. **Davies St**, running N–S and dead straight, as so many Mayfair streets are, forms the edge of a more residential district to the W. The crowds of Oxford St are a moment away, but here is a more peaceful world of mansion blocks and converted period houses. **Gilbert St, Binney St** and **Duke St**, running parallel N–S, contain some attractive red-brick mansion blocks with gabled skylines. Many apartments sit above shops. Whole houses are rare, though the (very) occasional large one does come up. Off **Duke St** is an unusual garden, raised on a plinth over an electricity station. This once neglected square with its pavilion is happily restored. Hereabouts are some early red-brick council homes, now run by the Peabody Trust, and also mansion blocks in what Pevsner calls 'typical Northwest-Mayfair style – red-brick and pink terracotta, gables, and much smaller Renaissance detail'.

This is Grosvenor Estate country. Few realize that the northern part of Mayfair includes not only grand houses and flats but also a wide area of low-rent housing. These flats are tucked away between **Grosvenor Square** and **Oxford St** and are owned by the Grosvenor Estate and run by it in partnership with housing associations. Off **Brook St** is **Avery Row**, a narrow lane with attractive 3-storey, stucco and brown-brick terraces of flats above shops. Behind Claridges in **Brook St** is **Brook's Mews**. Its flat-fronted brick cottages face an unattractive modern development providing 5 storeys of flats. These achieve high prices as pieds-à-terre.

To the S, in a tucked-away corner above **Berkeley Square**, **Bourdon St** has Bloomfield Court, a handsome modern interpretation of the traditional red-brick mansion block built in 1989 by the Grosvenor Estate. The 1- and 2-bed flats were sold with 75-year Estate leases. Prices here tend to be c. £365,000 for a 2-bed. The block boasts no garage, but there is an NCP car park in the street. Flats in the grey concrete Grosvenor Hill Court are popular London bases. **Mount St** boasts mansion flats above some of London's premier antique shops, and is considered to be Mayfair's 'village High Street'. Here, the local bed-and-breakfast is the Connaught, and the local fish and chip shop is Scotts. A 2-bed flat in **Mount St** was on the market last winter at £845,000 for a 62-year lease. Rentals are common here. **Mount Row**, to the W of **Davies St**, has brown-brick homes with casement windows and leaded glass with mansard roofs. On the S side stand red-brick mewsy houses with shutters at their windows.

Mount St leads into **Carlos Place**, curving round into **Berkeley Square** with red-brick and terracotta Dutch-gabled blocks above galleries and restaurants. This enormous square has everything from beautiful early Georgiana, to '30s, to a modern block with stepped roof line and shops and bank below. There are handsome stucco and brick houses along the W side. No 1 Carlos Place has 10 flats, including two 3-bed maisonettes at £1.3 million, in a building newly restored by Crown Dilmun. On **Curzon St** is the Christian Science Church, behind which a courtyard of flats and offices was cunningly inserted. Expect to pay £500,000 for a small 2-bed in **Curzon St**. Smart modern blocks like Glendore House punctuate the houses of **Clarges St** and **Half Moon St**. In **Half Moon St** attractive red-brick gabled houses line the SW side. The former Naval and Military Club building runs through to Piccadilly: the club has moved to St James's Square and the old building, the famous 'In and Out' (from the signs on its gateposts) was reportedly sold in February as a private house for £50 million. Also in **Half Moon St** is the Green Park Hotel along with some attractive period properties.

Chesterfield Hill contains an attractive row of 5-storey stucco and brick period houses with handsome railings at the front, its decorative, cast-iron balconies bedecked with window boxes. This small area of **Hill St** and **Hays Mews** contains some of the most attractive mews and traditional homes, tucked away in relative peace and quiet. Approaching from **Charles St** (where grand period houses can fetch £4–8 million), you pass plaques commemorating the former residence of King William IV, the sailor king who lived there in 1826. **Hays Mews** is a wide sloping road with charming mews cottages of brick (some bare, some painted) with garages below. Curled around the top of the mews is **Red Lion Yard**, with a pretty pub giving it an 'out of London' atmosphere. Cobblestones lead to more 3-storey brick town-houses in the yard itself, and three just-done-up mews houses (see **Audley Square** below). The E end of **Hay's Mews** on the opposite side of **Chesterfield Hill** is perhaps less attractive, but has the same wide roadway, a mixture of modern houses and little 2-storey brick cottages and a 5-storey block of modern brick-built flats, Rosebery Court (main entrance **Charles St**).

Farm St has gained some new houses (real rarities in Mayfair) in the last 20 years: one 4,400 sq ft house was for sale this spring at £2.95 million freehold. Another two houses are due to make way for a single, large new mansion. Plans envisage eight bedrooms and an underground swimming pool. However, the scheme has been held up for over a year. **South St** is residential, with red-brick conversions, a primary school and a number of attractive smaller houses, for which you will nevertheless need a million or three. A Grade II-listed, 5-bed house overlooking Mount St gardens was on the market last winter for £2.7 million. A million will buy you a 4-bed flat without the garden view. **Audley Square** is a small enclave leading off **South Audley St**, off which are three mews houses in **Red Lion Yard**.

Waverton St contains Mayfair House, and the imposing brick mansion Garden House, whose name is the only clue to the hidden garden shared (by the houses only) between **South St/South Audley St/ Waverton St** and **Hill St**. Travelling up **South Audley St** there are dignified cream stucco houses and gabled red-brick and terracotta mansion flats above pleasant shops. A 50-year leasehold house was sold last year for £1.3 million. Purdey's, the famous gun shop, is on the corner of **Mount St** and **South Audley St**, with spectacular refurbished flats above. Mayfair Library, built in 1894 in a cul-de-sac alongside the Grosvenor Chapel, sits next to the Mount St Gardens, a quiet public space. The garden, with rows of benches, is overlooked by more mansion blocks. To the W is **Balfour Mews**, where the red-brick continues, sometimes relieved by stone detailing and balustrades. Balfour Cottages are a pair of pretty, painted brick homes with tub trees outside. A 2-bed maisonette was £750,000 late last year. **Reeves Mews** has brown-brick and stone flats opposite its row of mews cottages.

Culross St behind the US Embassy has terraces of traditional town-houses. They are of varying heights and materials: brick, painted brick and stucco. Some are freehold. Shutters and tiny steps up to the front doors on some homes give this road a village feel. **Green St's** tall houses, many now flats, hide another concealed garden which is shared with **Park St** and **Dunraven St**. A wide 5-bed **Green St** house, built in 1891, and expensively renovated with basement pool beneath the conservatory, was on the market last winter at £6.95 million. A 1915 5-bed neo-Georgian house backing onto the gardens sold last year for around £4 million. Another, currently split into flats, was £2.7 million this spring. **Green St** is a fertile source of flats from around £450,000 upwards.

Park St, the main spine of this NW corner of Mayfair, has some large red-brick and stone mansion blocks with colonnaded façades and balconies. It also has some splendid late-19th-century houses built as London mansions by those who had not had the luck to inherit a Park Lane palace, but who found tall, narrow Belgravia houses just too confining. Now they are returning to use as homes after 50 years as offices. Some of these buildings have become flats. New Hereford House, new in 2000 behind a Lutyens façade, has 6 penthouses (from £1.25 million) and 34 other flats from £275,000. The word 'flat' can sometimes be inadequate in Mayfair: in **North Row**, at the Marble Arch corner of Mayfair, a late '80s conversion yielded 15 house-sized apartments: the penthouses have 5 bedrooms, conservatory, roof terraces – and a summer house. One with 4 beds was on the market last winter for £1.4 million.

Certainly 'big is beautiful' is the motto (in terms of both money and square footage) in the far from aptly named **Park Lane**, with its eight roaring lines of traffic that separate Mayfair from Hyde Park. Only a handful of its grand original homes survive, having been replaced by monolithic hotels and car showrooms. This is one place where homes (or at least flats) are reappearing: the biggest recent development is Brook House, on the site of the old MEPC offices. This was sold in its entirety to an Arab group. The flats are now re-selling: the largest went for £3.95 million in December. Then there are the new penthouses on the 9th and 10th floors of Fountain House. These two floors were added specially in 1997 to create the super-apartments: 4-bedroomed, double-garaged, lofty views over Hyde Park or Mayfair . . . The largest runs to 4,400 sq ft, plus roof terrace and 45-ft living room. All have been sold at prices from £3.5–4.5 million. On a decidedly sybaritic, but domestic, scale one of the two large blocks of the Grosvenor House Hotel is in fact flats, some available to rent long-term – with the bonus of all the hotel's facilities on hand, should you so desire. Next door to the Hilton, a big commercial/homes scheme is under way on a site running back to **Curzon St**, with one listed house being kept and other buildings to be demolished. Completion date is 2002.

Grosvenor Square, the largest square in the district at 6 acres, is best known as the site of the enormous American Embassy. The other sides have some smart flats, reckoned the most luxurious cache in Mayfair. Mostly owned, these days, by overseas buyers or companies, the majority are on short leases. The odd longer lease is appearing, for example a huge unmodernised flat here was on the market this spring at £3 million for 80 years and a smaller 2-bed flat with a 56-year lease was £1.25 million. **Upper Brook St**, which runs W from the Square towards Hyde Park, has some very large and expensive houses: one sold in 1998 with a 50-ft drawing room, a swimming pool and an adjoining mews house with parking for four cars.

The SE corner of Mayfair, towards **Piccadilly Circus**, has fewer homes. **Albany**, the famous warren of prestige 'chambers' off **Piccadilly**, is very exclusive and inhabited by the great, the good and the long-term rich. There are flats above shops, a few mews, and some blocks in streets such as **Hay Hill**: a mansion flat here was £1.75 million in at the end of 1999.

Shepherd Market

Shepherd Market is an unexpected village of narrow Georgian streets and small-scale buildings, incongruous amid Mayfair's grandeur. Once it was frowned upon as being seedy and the haunt of prostitutes. Today the area's image has greatly changed; more streets have been pedestrianized and it is seen as Mayfair's restaurant quarter. The pretty cottages to be found there are now being gradually done-up and are much sought-after. Nevertheless, there is a variety of property in the area ranging from modern luxury apartments through period mansion blocks to tiny town-houses and mews cottages.

Approaching from **Hertford St**, there are mansion flats in brick and stucco blocks and some handsome old houses. A massive 7-storey block, Carrington House, occupies the corner site of **Hertford St**, **Shepherd St** and **Carrington St**, where 1- and 2-bed flats come up for sale (£365,000 for 2-beds). Until recently the flats were rented on short lets and had a high turnover of residents. Turning into **Shepherd St** there are some attractive old cream-painted little 2-storey cottages. The brick and painted-brick homes over shops are now much in demand. On the other side of the street is a modern red-brick block, May Fayre House, whose flats are available to rent.

The Shepherds Tavern sports bow windows and a jaunty, flower-hung exterior which sets the tone for the pretty village that scatters down **Shepherd St** and round into **Shepherd Market**. On the left of **Shepherd St** is a terrace of flat-roofed homes over shops. In **Shepherd Place** are more small, 2-bedroomed houses. Larger 3-storey brick and stucco buildings line the continuation of **Hertford St**; cobblestones lead you on towards 3-storey mewsy houses.

St James's

The best homes in St James's are palaces, and are unlikely to be for sale. Non-royals have to hunt hard for a flat, harder for a house. **Cleveland Row**, next-door to St James's Palace, is mostly offices though there is at least one house. **Little St James's St** has some old houses in mixed use, and there are some exclusive flats in **St James's Place** – the best with wonderful views over Green Park. This is the plushest address in St James's. This area is much favoured by English buyers (and increasingly by Italians), but spurned by some of the more serious shopping nations (notably the Middle East) because it's too far from the shops. More flats are found along the park itself, reached from **Arlington St**, which itself is a source of flats: the 1936-built Arlington House has some vast ambassadorial-sized ones.

Despite the scarcity of St James's homes, people buying here are choosy . . . One otherwise impeccable penthouse famously suffered a 6-figure reduction: the block's entrance was cramped, and there was no private lift.

St James's St itself has a mere handful of homes. Some flats are in a corner block next to **Little St James's St**. Further E is **St James's Square**, which was once a dignified assembly of town-houses, but by 1990 had only one residential building. However, Berkeley Homes have converted a house on the corner with **King St**: this adds 10 2- and 3-bed flats to the stock at prices starting at £1.25 million. **Bury St** has some flats in tall buildings, often above shops and offices, as does **Duke of York St. Duke St** and **Ryder St** both have some mansion blocks. A plush 3-bed flat with a 100-year-plus lease in St James's Chambers was £945,000 this year. The best source of flats is **Jermyn St**, where Nos 76 and 25 were both redeveloped to provide 23 and 35 flats respectively. Long leases are now selling for £365,000 for 1-bed and £515–575,000 for 2-beds.

Carlton Gardens has a new development of six flats including two penthouses in a modern (Sir James Sterling-designed) building which are on the market for £3.1–£3.65 million in February for 125-year Crown Estate leases.

Transport   Tubes, all zone 1: Marble Arch, Bond St (Central); Oxford Circus (Victoria, Bakerloo, Central); Piccadilly Circus (Bakerloo, Piccadilly); Green Park (Victoria, Piccadilly, Jubilee). From Green Park: Oxford Circus 2 min, City 10 min (1 change), Heathrow 1 hr.

Convenient for   West End, City, Hyde Park, Canary Wharf. Miles from centre: 1.

Schools   Local Authority: Westminster City C of E.

SALES

Flats	S	1B	2B	3B	4B	5B
Average prices	120–200	150–500+	275–1 M	600–1.5 M	800–2.5 M+	1.5–3.5 M+

Houses	2B	3B	4B	5B	6/7B	8B
Average prices	600–750++	750–1 M+	950–2 M+	1.3–2 M+	2.5–5 M+	4.5–12 M+

RENTAL

Flats	S	1B	2B	3B	4B	5B
Average prices	250–300	325–600	450–1400	550–2000	1000–3000+	2000+

Houses	2B	3B	4B	5B	6/7B	8B
Average prices	550–1200	575–1500+	1400–3000+	2000–13000	–	–

The properties   Mostly flats and mostly grand ones, in mansion blocks or conversions of period homes – and now also of office blocks. Some mews cottages and a small but increasing number of lovely Georgian and Victorian houses. Degree of luxury ranges from the ordinary mansion flat to the super-opulent. St James's has fewer homes, but some with lovely park views.

The market   Very little on the market, what there is ranges from £150,000 all the way to £9 million. Freeholds slowly becoming more common. Flat prices vary wildly, with length of lease and degree of opulence key price factors. Check service charges in big blocks. Inhabitants are highly international plus old-established or very rich British. Mayfair is enjoying something of a renaissance: more US families and other high-finance types now the Jubilee Line goes straight to Canary Wharf, and younger renters, who find it better value than Notting Hill (yes, really). Local searches: 10 working days.

Among those estate agents active in this area are:

- Wetherell
- Strutt & Parker *
- Keith Cardale Groves
- DTZ Debenham Thorpe
- Beauchamp Estates
- Knight Frank
- Egerton
- FPDSavills
- Chestertons
- W A Ellis *
- Mercer Pasqua
- Foxtons *
- John C Vaughan
- Blenheim Bishop
- Cluttons
- Goldenberg
- Park Lane Apartments
- Properties of Mayfair*

further details: see advertisers' index on p671

MORDEN, MITCHAM AND COLLIERS WOOD

Map ref: p121 (3K)
Postal districts: SW19
Boroughs: Merton (Lab)
Council tax: Band D £866
Conservation areas: Several – check with town hall
Parking: New scheme for Morden likely this year; those for Colliers Wood and Mitcham met strong local opposition

This is where Victorian London's southward sprawl came to a reluctant halt among the villages, fields and woodlands of Surrey. Here the ubiquitous London terrace dies out, to be succeeded by leafy suburban streets. Urban expansion last received a boost in 1926, when the Northern line made it to Morden; now the area – tubeless Mitcham in particular – could face something of a renaissance as the effects of the new Tramlink, direct to Wimbledon's mainline train/District tube station, are felt.

The borough of Merton, which takes in all this area, shelters a wide spread of suburbia of every 20th-century vintage (wartime bombs made room for more) lapping around the remnants of the past. Wimbledon, on its hill, commands the W of the borough. To the SE is Croydon. The area between centres around the valley of the Wandle, which flows north from here through to the Thames at Wandsworth. Merton itself is ancient, but little survives except the parish church and a stretch of road called **Merton High St**. Merton Priory, which for some reason the borough decided to elevate to an abbey (it wasn't), was the medieval focus for the villages of Mordern, Mitcham and especially next-door Colliers Wood. Much of Merton has been annexed by South Wimbledon – the name of the tube station. Marooned across the rail tracks on that west side is the interesting turn-of-the-century enclave that still carries Merton's name, Merton Park (see Wimbledon, Raynes Park and Merton Park chapter).

Morden also clings onto what's left of the rural charm: there is a church dating from 1636, and behind the church a pub with 16th-century foundations. Morden Hall Park belongs to the National Trust; through it wanders the Wandle river, dividing and rejoining to form lake and islands – but its Georgian buildings such as the Hall itself and a 'gentleman's villa' have found interesting new occupations (pub/restaurant, council offices . . .). The snuff mill and stables are craft shops; there's a garden centre and (free) city farm. Mitcham is an old place too, with a few survivals of its rural days – and one of the largest caches of recently built homes in South London. Of Colliers Wood the only notable landmark is the underground station – or was, until the advent, at the Merton end, of the vast flanks of the Sainsbury's Savacentre, more or less where Merton Priory once stood and the young Thomas à Becket was educated.

The **Merantun Way** relief road and the Savacentre improved **Merton High St**. The Savacentre is not quite the 'Crystal Palace lookalike the size of Brent Cross, with leisure complex, pubs and restaurants alongside the shops' we expected. 'More like a huge warehouse but nicer', a local commented, kindly. It does, though, include travel agent, post office, playcentre, shoemender, etc, to supplement the super-Sainsbury's, plus café, petrol, fast food and masses of free parking. It forms part of the river Wandle development area, alongside **Christchurch Rd** behind **Merton High St**. Then came the Tandem Centre, by the **Merantun Way/Christchurch Rd** roundabout (large Boots, Holiday Hypermarket, Next, Comet . . .); now, between this and the Savacentre, comes 'The Priory' (PC World, Currys . . .) after months of major traffic disruption.

Across **Merantun Way** lies something altogether more attractive, however: the Merton Abbey Mills complex, which has successfully revived some old Wandle-side buildings into a pleasant corner of craft shops, bookshops, pubs, restaurants and museum. Here Liberty's used to print their famous silks, and William Morris had his workshops: clothworking and dyeing had in fact been carried out on this spot since the Huguenots arrived in the reign of the first Elizabeth.

Mitcham and Morden mushroomed in the 1920s and '30s, after the extension of the Northern line tube speeded commuting into the City. The result was wide areas of neat, semi-detached homes. Mock-Tudor detailing was popular – this is quite a restrained example. The tile-roofed porch-cum-bay is also typical. After a period of disdain, these houses are now fashionable.

This Morden/Mitcham/Colliers Wood corner appeals strongly to those who need to get at a tube station yet prefer the charms of suburbia to more cramped living further in. Homes for all here: a wide range of styles and prices, from ex-council to modern new-build (1-bed starter homes are a freehold alternative to flats); from city terraces to semi-detached suburbs.

The Northern line takes a good half-hour to get into West End or City, and the many railways offer faster progress. Yet the Morden tube does, in a definite way, tie the area into London. Now the Tramlink – actually a light rail line like Docklands' – at last improves the area's E–W links, until now restricted to the clogged S London roads. Between Wimbledon and Mitcham Junction there are tram stops at Dundonald Road, Merton Park, Morden Rd, Phipps Bridge, Belgrave Walk and Mitcham; it runs to Croydon and beyond – and you can change at East Croydon for Gatwick Airport.

Morden

Morden, until the mid-1920s, was a small agricultural community. The landscape was dramatically changed by a high-concentration council housebuilding programme and today can be described as '1930s-semi suburbia'.

Morden is at the southern extremity of the Northern line tube. Atop the terminus is a large modern office complex, with Civic Centre and library. From here the tube reaches Waterloo in 30 min, the City in 40. A 20–25 min drive away, the Reigate/ Leatherhead M25 intersection gives access to both Heathrow and Gatwick Airports.

Generally, Morden is a green, leafy, residential area and includes three large open spaces: Morden Hall Park (more than 50 acres of National Trust parkland, with craft centre, city farm etc), Morden Park (swimming baths, playing-fields) and, to the W, Cannon Hill Common. Houses facing, or with views of, park areas are naturally the great favourites. Premier roads include the leafy **Lower Morden Lane**, and **Hillcross Avenue** and streets off it (mainly 1930s 3-bed solid semis, with front and rear gardens and garages). Flats and bungalows are scarce and so is building land, though Croudace Homes did manage to find room for 75 1- and 2-bed flats, some with bay windows, in landscaped gardens in **Bordesley Rd**.

The St Helier Estate, built by the LCC in the 1920s and '30s and considered advanced for its time, is a large area of wide, well-planned roads (**Blanchland Rd** is typical) of 2/3-bed red-brick terraces with gardens fore and aft. These pre-war council-built houses are of high quality and popular with first-time buyers – they account for 25 per cent of all sales in the district. Many new owners have added imaginative (and sometimes misplaced) exterior features to their homes.

St Helier has its own train station; just to the S, a few streets across the border into Sutton, new homes replace the old school site off **Hexham Rd/Glastonbury Rd**.

Mitcham

Mitcham, once renowned for its lavender fields and watercress beds, is an odd blend of bustling town, light industry and country village. Though it, like Morden, has a Surrey postal address, it comes under Merton Council.

Determined to retain its rural atmosphere, Mitcham resisted efforts to link it to London's underground. Consequently, it now presents commuters with a goodish walk or a bus ride to the nearest tube stations (Colliers Wood or Tooting Broadway). Mitcham Junction station (a mile from the centre of Mitcham) serves Victoria (18 min), and is also an interchange with the new E–W Tramlink. There is good access to the M23 (Gatwick) and M25 (Heathrow), but the centre of town is busy and often congested with through traffic. A new road and pedestrianization from the bottom of **London Rd** to **Upper Green West** helped.

Georgian cottages, manor houses, 18th-century houses and Eagle House (a superb example of Queen Anne architecture) are reminders of Mitcham's rural past. **Commonside East**, looking out over Common and pond, has a row of pretty 2-bed Victorian terraced cottages. These, like homes facing Fair Green and Mitcham Park, are the streets people aspire to – a waiting list has been known to develop for the homes of the **Cricket Green** conservation area, for example. (The game in question is reputed to have been played there for over 300 years.) Other desirable streets include **Gorringe Park Avenue** and **The Close**.

The 1980s saw quite a few new schemes in Mitcham but the early '90s slump, and the lack of land, saw the pipeline dry up. The Swan pub and adjacent old houses have been demolished to make way for new homes: watch this space. Meanwhile buyers can expect plenty of choice from resales of the last rash of building. Examples are the 1- and 2-bed flats and houses and 4-bed semis off **London Rd**; in **Church Rd**, Cannons Place has 2/3/4-bedroomed houses with private gardens and garages/parking. At

Lower Green West, Mitcham Village Studios is a converted Georgian school house, now studios and apartments. **Chestnut Grove** has 20 Victorian-copy 1- and 2-bed flats and 2/3-bed houses. More new homes, too, have appeared in **Crossways Rd** on the edge of Streatham Park.

New developments also sprouted in the **Western Rd** area, influenced no doubt by the new Savacentre near its Merton end. Laing's were busy here, building every size from studio flats to 3-bedroom houses. The biggest site by far for new homes is the old King's College playing-fields behind **Lavender Avenue**. A thousand homes have appeared here, as the street map (with its squiggly closes and little squares) clearly shows. This is a good source of 2- and 3-bed houses and 1- to 3-bed flats. For other new homes developments, look in the **Mount Rd/Lewis Rd** area, across **Western Rd.**

A point to watch here is that since new streets these days are usually blocked to through traffic from the outset, pinch-points occur when the deluge of residents try to leave for work. One such is the right-turn from **Lavender Avenue** into **Western Rd**.

Mitcham, like most of the capital's satellites, divides into the good, the bad and the definitely ugly – but strenuous efforts have been taking place to reduce the latter. This has included the removal of some hardly scenic tower blocks by **Phipps Bridge** and their replacement with attractive low-level housing, and much improvement to other such council-built estates. Privatized ex-council homes allow for a low start to the wide range of prices, and can provide a great deal of space for your money.

Colliers Wood

Colliers Wood is sandwiched between **Merton** and **Tooting High Sts**. Somewhat overshadowed by a large grey tower of offices, it was dismissed for years as a 'depressed' area. It perked up in the late '80s, and is showing signs of doing so again now that the neighbours are going up in the world. A good hunting-ground, especially for first-time home-owners, but still not a name to entice buyers. As a result, some bits get 'moved' to South Wimbledon or even Tooting by estate agents and developers. By way of revenge, Colliers Wood has annexed the eastern part of Merton, so counts the vast Savacentre and the Merton Abbey Mills as part of its patch. The car boot sale at the latter is its Saturday entertainment.

Nearby Wandle Park (part-owned by the National Trust) provides some welcome green space. With direct access to Central London from Colliers Wood tube station (Northern line: 25 min Waterloo, 35 the City), it's good commuter territory. Homes here are a pleasant mix of 1880s, 1930s and 1960s houses with pretty stucco/stock-brick Edwardian villas, many Victorian terraces (some with bay windows) and some conversion flats. Bargain-hunters search out the pockets of Victorian terraces which survived the last wave of improvers undisturbed.

Few houses have off-street parking, but most have the bonus of long back gardens. The better roads are bordered by **Cavendish Rd** and include **Marlborough Rd**, **Clive Rd** and **Warren Rd**, **Daniel** and **Defoe Close**s, **Norfolk** and **Harewood Rds**. Some have bollards, preventing noisy through traffic.

The other side of **Colliers Wood High St**, the streets around **Boundary** and **Acre Rds** are very popular with those who work at St George's Hospital Tooting, just across the tracks, which can be reached by a footbridge at the end of **Boundary Rd**. Since patients have discovered this too, a residents' parking scheme is under consultation.

Mead Park, Wimpey's big development in the Wandle Valley NW of the **High St**, has provided this corner with 160 new homes, from studios to town houses on ex-sewage-works land; a short walk away from both the tube and Haydons Rd Thameslink station.

Merton

(See introduction.) The Merton Park Estate is described in the Wimbledon chapter.

Transport   Tubes: Colliers Wood, S Wimbledon, Morden (zone 3, Northern).
From Morden: Oxford Circus 35 min (1 change), City 40 min,
Heathrow 90 min (2 changes). Trains: Mitcham Junction to
Victoria, London Bridge. Tramlink to Wimbledon (for District line),
East Croydon (for Gatwick).

Convenient for   Tubes to Central London, routes South, Wimbledon.

Schools   Merton Education Authority. High Schools: Eastfields High (b),
Raynes Park, Rutlish (b), Rickards Lodge (g), Rowan (g),
Tamworth Manor, Ursuline Convent (g), Watermeads, Wimbledon
College (b). Private: see Wimbledon chapter.

SALES

Flats	S	1B	2B	3B	4B	5B
Average prices	50–60	60–80	70–90	80–100	120+	–
Houses	2B	3B	4B	5B	6/7B	8B
Average prices	95–115	100–180	175–200	200+	–	–

RENTAL

Flats	S	1B	2B	3B	4B	5B
Average prices	80–100	115–125	138–160	175–185	210+	–
Houses	2B	3B	4B	5B	6/7B	8B
Average prices	150–160	175–250	200–275	230–275+	–	–

The properties   Victoriana peters out after Colliers Wood, replaced by semis.
Behind the busy main roads, all three areas have large estates
of 1930s terraces. These generally provide the most common
source of converted flats or 2/3-bed homes: larger, 4+ bed are
scarce. The top houses are found alongside Mitcham's parks.
New homes are plentiful – including 1-bed 'starter homes': the
freehold alternative to flats. Inexpensive ex-council homes now
widely available. Three-bed flats are rare: generally ex-council or
above shops.

M

The market   First-time buyers find good-size, good-value homes here.
Mitcham prices, held back by lack of a tube except for the best
family homes (see above), could now be boosted by Tramlink.
Local searches: 10 working days, but can fast-track urgent cases.

Among those estate agents active in this area are:

- Goodfellows
- Tarrant & Co
- Andrews
- Barnard Marcus
- Singletons

- Christopher St James
- Ellisons
- Drury & Cole
- Bairstow Eves
- Greenes

MUSWELL HILL

Map ref: p29 (3F)
Postal districts: N2, N10, N11, N13, N22
Boroughs: Barnet (Lib Dem/Lab
  Coalition), Haringey (Lab), Enfield (Lab)
Council tax: Band D Barnet £760,
  Haringey £898, Enfield £732
Conservation areas: Highgate Wood,
  Alexandra Palace
Parking: Free

The hilltop suburb of Muswell Hill is a place of pilgrimage once more, though St Mary's Well, with its miraculous healing waters, has long since disappeared beneath **Muswell Rd.** Today's pilgrims are drawn by schools, or by economics as prices in neighbouring Hampstead and Highgate move beyond the reach of mere mortals' pockets. It is re-established as a place in its own right – a prosperous, middle-class family area, where the pilgrimage vehicle of choice is a four-wheel drive.

Lottery money has been conjured up to 're-Edwardianize' the centre, with new old-style street lamps to mark the turn of the Millennium. This further adds to the distinctive and dignified character of this pleasantly hilly residential neighbourhood. it is not anonymous: a community, if not (as some would have it) a 'village'.

The eccentric architecture of Muswell Hill sails red-bricked above the more polluted air of lower domains. The little town, with the **Broadway** as its high street, is set in a splendid position on one of the highest hills in North London, giving long, long views over the City and West End: both St Paul's and Canary Wharf can be seen on clear days. Indeed, the air is purer (and some say colder) than that of its lower neighbours, not only thanks to height, but surely because of the Highgate Wood and Queen's Wood at the end of **Muswell Hill Rd** and the extensive parkland surrounding Alexandra Palace. There are, indeed, many other smaller pockets of parkland, complete with bowling greens and tennis courts, which invoke the leisurely Edwardian era of the suburb's flowering. There is that sense of being a place apart, a slight but definite distancing from the main thrust of London.

The wider area is defined to the N and E by a loop of the **North Circular Rd,** taking in the more industrial/commercial end of **Colney Hatch Lane** and **Bounds Green** plus its tube, across to **Wood Green**. To the S, it meets Hornsey/Crouch End at the southern tip of Alexandra Park, and reaches down to Highgate tube on the A1/**Archway Rd**.

Although the actual Muswell, with its early monastic links, dates back to medieval times, little was built here at all except the odd elegant country retreat until the mid-Victorian period. Most of the building was started in the early 1900s, however, and went on apace until the onset of World War I, in large estates of varying-sized houses, as well as many-storeyed mansion blocks of bachelor apartments (big by today's standards) on the **Broadway** itself, and those purpose-built flats above the shops.

Shopping in the **Broadway** is small and friendly, with everything you need for immediate purposes; delicatessens abound, there are several useful small, late-opening supermarkets and a Marks & Spencer food hall. There has been a flowering of cafés, art shops, coffee houses and other independent shops and restaurants. The necessary chain- and departmental-store shopping is supplied by the nearby Brent Cross shopping centre and the more humdrum centre at Wood Green. Closer to home, there's a 24hr Tesco superstore on the **North Circular** (junction with **Colney Hatch Lane**). There's a cinema and swimming pool in the area, as well as the golf course and Alexandra Palace, restored for arts, leisure and other uses, but chronically under-funded and in debt. Interestingly, as the main estates were built on Methodist Church land there are few original pubs; this, however, has been rectified of late with several newcomers, plus bars and restaurants, on the **Broadway** drag. Muswell Hill night life has a distinctly youthful air, if not as rock'n'roll as Crouch End.

The greatest drawback (or blessing, according to some) is the lack of a nearby tube. Highgate and Bounds Green are a 10-min bus ride away, and Finsbury Park's a good 15. There are several bus routes to the West End and to the City, which is also served by train from Alexandra Palace to Moorgate, and by an express bus in weekday rush hour.

Nevertheless, this is a car driver's area and many households have two. Streets tend to be wide and parking is not the nightmare it is in denser-packed suburbs, though double-parking makes some journeys rather like a slalom. The number of people using their cars to get to work or schools is reflected at the frustrating bottleneck of the main Muswell Hill roundabout and junction of **Archway Rd**.

So, on the whole, the sort of people buying and living in this area are families: middle-class, dual-income ones, many in the media-type industries or smart, *Guardian*-reading, high-income professionals who holiday in Bordeaux or Tuscany. ('In fact, typical New Labour – dream champagne socialists' was one summing up.) There is a very high density of au pair girls in Muswell Hill. Stemming from this, most local schools have a good reputation as they are well-supported by aware parent groups, who donate not only money but a great deal of time and energy to their children's education. There is thus an obvious requirement for houses/flats in the 'right' catchment area. Stress levels, and prices for strategically placed homes, can be high.

Muswell Hill

Muswell Hill has always had a genteel air. Its homes are mostly ranged in grandiose Edwardian terraces or set in wide leafy roads (which have escaped parking restrictions so far – except for the weekend of the spectacular Guy Fawkes fireworks). They boast almost bizarre architectural features including spires and balconies, heavily ornamented gables, pillastered bays. About 25 years back, many houses were divided into flats or maisonettes. Restoration, not conversion, is the watchword these days, with the demand for family homes making it more cost-effective to keep the big houses intact – or to restore them to splendid family homes of up to 6 bedrooms. Those without enough bedrooms follow the nanny-loft option to magic the 5th out of the attic – though as agents point out, the magic often won't work as far as enhanced values are concerned if the house is left with more bedrooms than the living space allows.

There are three covetable enclaves that ring **Muswell Hill Broadway**: one to the E of the Broadway across to **The Avenue**, above the park; another, the grid of streets at the W end of the Broadway between **Fortis Green Rd**, **Grand Avenue** and **Midhurst Avenue**; a third in the angle of Highgate Wood and Queen's Wood, to the E of **Muswell Hill Rd**.

This last enclave holds some of Muswell Hill's choicest homes. These select streets to the S, in the angle of **Cranley Gardens** and **Wood Vale**, also lie nearest to Highgate tube. Prestigious **Onslow Gardens**, **Woodland Rise**, **Woodlands Gardens**, **Connaught Gardens**, **Wood Vale**, as well as the main **Muswell Hill Rd**, are lined with very large houses, sometimes with balconies and basement areas which are definite assets. Often set further back, or higher up, from the road, these houses command high prices for the most luxurious – anything from £450–650,000-plus (the odd £700,000-plus one). A large 6-bed house in **Church Crescent**, close to the Broadway, went last autumn for £770,000 – and it needed £100,000 spending on it. Some up-market retirement flats in the same road add to the generation mix.

The popular Fortis Green conservation area has a grid of similar roads, more convenient for East Finchley tube, spreading out from the top of **Muswell Hill Rd** westwards to **Midhurst Rd**. **Grand Avenue** matches its name: one of the prime streets, it also has no through traffic – and prices start at £500,000 for single-fronted houses, at £700,000 for double-fronted ones. **Collingwood Avenue**, **Leaside Avenue**, **Fortismere Avenue** and **Birchwood Avenue** are popular – but expensive. Half-a-million-plus houses again, though some 1920s 3-beds go for c. £300,000.

Modern '80s developments here include the 4-bed town-houses of **Alexandra Mews**, and the 3-bed flats of 'The Copse', a refurbishment of ex-police flats – both on **Fortis Green**, both very nice. Cheaper but not so large and grand are the streets off nearby **East Finchley High Rd** itself – smaller-scale versions intermingled with 1930s semis; much more everyday roads, but highly convenient for the tube and only an extra 5 min tube journey (above ground at this point) to town. Look for the 'county' roads: pleasant, grey-brick Victorian terraces with names like **Lincoln Rd**, **Leicester Rd**, etc; with luck, a small 3-bed house in one of these can be found for £225–250,000, though the best can approach £350,000. To the S across this end of **Fortis Green**, the streets down to Cherry Tree Wood get dearer again (and closer to East Finchley tube).

The third coveted enclave lies off **Dukes Avenue** behind **The Broadway**, stretching north-eastwards across to encircling **Alexandra Park Rd**. The peaceful streets are tree-lined and wide enough to take four cars abreast (no parking restrictions as yet). The houses are mostly large – anything from 3- to 6-bed, some double-fronted – with longish gardens and festoons of the 'original features' so beloved of estate agents.

There are other, somewhat plainer Edwardian estates stretching from the far side of **Alexandra Park Rd**: the 'lake' roads – **Windermere Rd**, **Grasmere Rd** (very popular, close to the golf course: c. £375,000) – across to **Sutton Rd**, **Wilton Rd** and **Greenham Rd** off the W side of **Colney Hatch Lane**: popular, but here the houses do not have quite the same dignified air. However, they still command £320,000-plus, plenty of space, are close to Coldfall Wood and still not far away from the main shopping area. Some developments have been squeezed into the area: **Kendalmere Close**, **Audley Close**, **Louis Mews** have appeared, and in 1997 St Saviour's Court, well-planned, spacious houses and flats backing onto the deer park off **Alexandra Park Rd**.

Less sought-after areas, commensurately cheaper in price, lie to the N up towards the **North Circular Rd**. Between **Colney Hatch Lane**, the **North Circular**, **Alexandra** and **Wetherill Rds** the tenor gets decidedly more commercial (small industrial outcrops, **Hampden Rd** bus terminus and even a tattoo shop are to be found here), but this corner, though mixed, is improving: prices, and new developments, have risen in recent years. Edwardian homes jostle with smaller Victoriana, '20s and '50s blocks with '80s and '90s schemes: detached modern 4-bed houses in **Pembroke Mews**,

Cambridge Gardens, a cul-de-sac of new homes; retirement flats in **Wetherill Rd**.

Houses off **Coppetts Rd** to the W, although in leafy streets, are generally less popular, thanks to a '60s block of flats and a fairly large council estate of indifferent architectural value. Here, however, new flats and houses are appearing, both housing association and private, on land sold off by Coppetts Wood (tropical diseases) Hospital. Rialto and Laing are active here, with homes from £200,000 up. Laing's clutch starts at £215,000 for 3-beds with 4-beds from £280,000. South of the hospital is a group of roads in green surroundings: **Hill Rd** and **Steedes Rd** are rated among the best streets.

Look E of **Colney Hatch Lane** for the area's most affordable homes: the houses are smaller, and there are ex-council 3-bed flats at £100-115,000. The Lane crosses the North Circular to the old lunatic asylum, now a major new homes site (see Totteridge chapter).

Newer parts of Muswell Hill regarded favourably are the 1920s Collins-built private estate off the main Hill (the road that runs up to the **Broadway** from the S tip of Alexandra Park) itself. The Rookfield Estate (or 'Garden Village') has neat houses set in private roads – with five barriers to bar through traffic: £350–500,000 for 3- and 4-bed houses here. A decade later the 1930s bay-fronted houses of **Creighton Avenue** and **Pages Lane**, as well as those lining **Alexandra Park Rd**, made a broad sweep across the area. The area N of here up towards the golf course has seen big prices rises in the last year: the £330,000 paid for a 1930s semi with no garage was reckoned 'extraordinary'.

To the E, where **Park** and **Priory Rds** meet is dubbed 'Park Village' by hopeful agents. This corner, including the pleasant streets round Priory Park, is disputed with Crouch End.

Bounds Green and Wood Green

If you are not willing or able to invest the larger sum required for Muswell Hill proper, the surrounding areas may be the answer. Bounds Green to the E, perhaps the best investment now, has the same sort of good-quality, solid houses – not such elegant roads, but close to the tube (Piccadilly line: a straight run to West End and Heathrow). Start thinking about £230,000-plus for a 3-bed semi. More neat semis with garages, set back from quiet, more suburban roads, lie to the W between Muswell Hill golf course. **Bounds Green Rd** and **Durnsford Rd**.

Some smaller Victorian 'artisan dwellings' around Bowes Park are still affordable: agents tip this corner, with its villagey atmosphere, close to tube and with own rail station, as a good starting point for first-time buyers. This also goes for the small, quiet roads near Alexandra Palace station, which hold purpose-built maisonettes as well as houses.

Back on the Muswell Hill side of the tracks, but N22, not N10, the triangle between **Durnsford/Albert Rds**, **Victoria Rd** and the rail line is leafy and popular: it is likely to figure in estate agents' details as 'Alexandra Park'. **Clifton Rd** and **Clyde Rd** are the best streets, and the W, Muswell Hill, end of **Victoria Rd**. More flats here, and solid houses: 3-bed Edwardian terraces, with original features,

c. £280,000. E sides of **Crescent Rise** and **Dagmar Rd** back onto the tracks, making homes cheaper: a 2-bed house, c. £185,000.

Over this line to Wood Green, desirability lessens, but **Truro** and **Nightingale Rds** are good value for first-time buyers. However, the small pocket between **Park Avenue–Station Rd**, N of Wood Green Common, has little 2-bed, 2-storey Victorian cottages (c. £140–150,000) in leafy streets. These are no-through-roads, thus peaceful despite the rail line nearby: popular with City commuters. To the N lies a little cache of pretty railway cottages, between **Bridge Rd** and the station. Further afield, towards **White Hart Lane**, are busy rows of red-brick Edwardian houses, mostly flats and maisonettes. Wood Green has its Shopping City, but is less select – with a very much more urban, bustling, multicultural atmosphere – than the tranquil climes of Muswell Hill. However, Shopping City and **High Rd** are smartening: Hollywood Green (cinema, bars, cafes) opens soon.

Transport	Tubes: Bounds Green, Wood Green (zone 3, Piccadilly – direct to Heathrow); East Finchley, Highgate (zone 3, Northern). From Highgate: Oxford Circus 20 min (1 change), City 25 min, Heathrow 1 hr 15 min (1 change). Trains: Alexandra Palace to City 12 min.
Convenient for	Brent Cross shopping centre, Ikea, Wood Green Shopping City. North Circular Rd, A1/M1. Miles from centre: 6.
Schools	Barnet, Haringey and Enfield Education Authorities: Fortismere School. Private: Channing (g), Highgate School (b), Norfolk House.

S A L E S

Flats	S	1B	2B	3B	4B	5B
Average prices	80–100	90–125	100–250	160–300	–	–
Houses	2B	3B	4B	5B	6/7B	8B
Average prices	120–160	155–300+	300–500	350–700	700+	–

R E N T A L

Flats	S	1B	2B	3B	4B	5B
Average prices	90–130	115–175	150–210	185–300	–	–
Houses	2B	3B	4B	5B	6/7B	8B
Average prices	–	200–350	300–500	500–600	–	–

The properties	Solid, superior Edwardian houses, some very large, providing roomy conversions as well as excellent family homes. Also some mansion flats. Smaller houses '20s/'30s, but smallest are modern or little Victorian terraces in fringe areas.
The market	Spacious houses attract families – many of media/professional/ liberal persuasion – who find value in this green, well-schooled area. Big jump in quality (and prices) from 3- to 4-bed homes. Local searches: Barnet 5 days, Haringey 2 weeks, Enfield 10 days.

Among those estate agents active in this area are:

- Sturt & Tivendale
- Keats
- Delemere
- Kinleigh Folkard & Hayward
- Prickett & Ellis
- Winkworth *
- Anscombe & Ringland
- Bairstow Eves
- Barnard Marcus
- Martyn Gerrard
- JHK
- Tatlers
- Holden Matthews

* further details: see advertisers' index on p671

NEW CROSS AND DEPTFORD

Map ref: p80 (6A)
Postal districts: SE14, SE8
Boroughs: Lewisham (Lab)
Council tax: Band D £727
Conservation areas: include
Telegraph Hill, Albury St
Parking: Free

Back in Tudor times Deptford was to London what Heathrow is now: the launching pad for trade and adventure, a place full of bustle, business (and thieving) and well-paid work. Here the East India Company's ships were built. Drake, Frobisher and Raleigh set out from here – and it was at Deptford that Queen Elizabeth knighted Drake on his return from his voyage around the world. Times change . . . Henry VIII's Royal Naval Yard finally closed in 1961, and the Victualling Yard, which Pepys knew, was all but razed in the 1960s to make way for a council estate. The end of the nearby Surrey Docks in the '70s destroyed the rest of Deptford's economy.

At last the trend is upwards after half a century of decline. Improving transport, a more enlightened approach to the surviving bits of local history, and the spillover from Docklands and Millennium-obsessed Greenwich are all playing their part. The more residential areas of New Cross and New Cross Gate, to the S and SW of Deptford, have been regaining some of the favour they found in Victorian times.

Transport is the real key: The East London line to New Cross, for so long SE London's only tube line, now has an interchange with the Jubilee line Extension at the smart new Canada Water station: at last Waterloo and Central London are a single change away. Deptford, meanwhile, now has a station on the southwards-extended DLR (Docklands Light Railway): direct to Canary Wharf and the City. There are even future plans to extend the East London line: yet more cross-town links. And there's rail: New Cross's terraces were built to house City clerks who got to work via trains which ran, and still run, into London Bridge. New Cross station also has a useful link to Gatwick. All the stations are in zone 2 – which means commuting is relatively cheap.

In response to these changes home-buyers have been moving in: agents cannot quite believe their good fortune. The 10,000 students of Goldsmith's College underpin rental values, boosting buyers' confidence. Prices in the area went up in 1998 when other areas were stagnating and went on rising in 1999. Although Deptford has still got one of London's few High Streets free of estate agent's offices, the big chains are discovering New Cross with its tube station, and the DLR's arrival in Deptford should spark more interest there too.

Many of Deptford's homes are council-built and (still) owned, but its stock of private houses still includes inexpensive, unmessed-about, unmodernized ones. New developments are appearing, including a big scheme at the mouth of Deptford Creek. Resales on these residential developments offer plenty of choice.

The larger, once-grand terraces of New Cross make for good flat conversions. The Telegraph Hill area at the southern end is a pleasant and surprising corner (long discovered by property writers). It is one of several conservation areas: prices in these can be a good jump higher than elsewhere. A knowledgeable local agent reckons that a 2-bed flat in a conservation area costs the same as a 3-bed elsewhere.

These areas are among the few in London offering a decent choice of homes below £85,000. Ex-council homes, 1980s 'starter' homes (including that oddity the 1-bed house) and conversions of Victorian houses into flats offer plenty of choice. A decent-sized 3-bed Victorian house on Telegraph Hill might reach £200,000.

Deptford

'Deptford,' said an inhabitant, 'is *local*'. This was the closest she could get to explaining why this untidy, unkempt corner of town, cheerfully grimy in some parts, plain grim in others, nevertheless feels like a proper place – unlike many a politer but more faceless tract of South London. Deptford lies on the river, between Greenwich and the Surrey Docks. Deptford Strand was the scene of historic events as disparate as Peter the Great's apprenticeship in shipbuilding and the murder of Christopher Marlowe in a riverside tavern. Deptford Creek suffered in the general decline, but is being cleaned up and is the focus for housing and other schemes.

Deptford's industrial and sea-faring past is still in evidence, with streets such as **Mechanics Path, Shipwrights Rd, Frigate Mews** and **Bronze St**, not to mention the statues of famous admirals which adorn the Town Hall. The **High St** was long a byword for scruffiness. In 1550 it was 'so noisome and full of filth that the King's Majesty might not pass to and fro to see the building of His Majesty's ships'. The Navy paid for it to be re-paved, and Whitehall money has again financed a tidy-up in the last few years. Over on **Griffin St/Deptford Church St** is the new Wavelength Leisure Centre, which includes a swimming pool and library. St Paul's Church, another pointer to Deptford's past status, lies between the **High St** and **Church St**. This magnificent Baroque building was erected for the people of Deptford in the 1720s, after their request for a 'grand church' – they got it. Deptford market is useful (and very cheap), the best days being Wednesday and Saturday, when the **High St** is closed to traffic.

A scheme by Fairview is bringing flats and houses to the mouth of Deptford Creek off **Creek Rd**. The development, called with awful inevitability 'Millenium Quay', should be finished by 2001: homes available last winter included 3-bed houses from £190–217,000 and 4-bed town houses at £280,000. A new fitness suite is among the development's attractions. At the head of the Creek, Mumford's Mill, a Grade II-listed flour mill, is flats and business units. New flats have appeared on the **High St** near the station, and other houses have been added in **Mary Ann Gardens**. Look for **Albury St,** a cobbled Georgian street that escaped the bombing – but not years of decline while waiting for the GLC, which had emptied the houses, to restore them. However, its 18th-century terraces (some virtually untouched) have at last been renovated to English Heritage standards.

Around the back of **Albury St**, facing onto **Creek Rd**, are some new houses and flats.

Heading up towards Surrey Docks along **Evelyn St**, you pass large houses, many with semi-basements. These are nice when restored, but suffer from main-road noise. There are small Victorian terraces in **Gosterwood St** and **Etta St**, and 3-bed ones in **Alloa Rd, Trundleys Rd** – and in **Scawen Rd**, where the houses can look out over Deptford Park. At the other end of **Trundleys Rd**, near the one-way system leading to Surrey Docks, is 1990-vintage 'Chester Circus': 30 handsome homes ranging from studios to 3-bed houses. Opposite here, on the corner of **Evelyn St** and **Sayes Court**, is Sayes Hall Court: 55 flats and houses built in 1989 around a courtyard.

Between **Evelyn St** and the river lies the Pepys Estate, a '60s council scheme: multi-storey concrete towers and low-rise blocks built on the site of bombed Georgian merchants' terraces . . . but look in your A–Z map book for **Deptford Strand** and, at right angles to it, The Terrace, along **Longshore**. Here are the remains of that Georgian heritage: houses in The Terrace, and what were waterside warehouses now converted into flats – some private, some council. The Pepys was a model estate in the '60s (it won a clutch of design awards) and is now recovering from its former dangerous reputation. Aragon Tower, the largest, has stunning views, as estate agents would say, over the river and Central London (there being nothing very high in the Surrey Docks to get in the way). Inside, the Pepys blocks have split-level flats with the sort of layout that costs serious money in the private sector. With the new fashion for tower-block living (see Trellick Tower in North Kensington), these flats are in demand.

The same cannot be said of the grimmer blocks of Milton Court, another council estate, which runs between **Milton Court Rd** and **Sanford St**, in the angle between two railway lines. This is not the place for your evening stroll. Between **Sanford St** and the railway line is a 1980s Wimpey estate of houses built for sale: **Southern Gate Way** and **Sterling Gardens**. The area to the NW, on the borders with Rotherhithe and the Surrey Docks, is also fast improving due to the spillover effect from Docklands. Surrey Quays tube is on the same line as New Cross and New Cross Gate, and one stop away from the Canada Water interchange. There are vast areas of new housing in Surrey Docks (see Docklands chapter).

New Cross

New Cross, apparently, used to be a pretty village until it started being used as a coaching stop to avoid taking tired horses over Blackheath – then a notorious haunt of highwaymen on the Dover Rd. This proved to be its eventual downfall, as its high street evolved into the main road which effectively sliced the place in half. New Cross thus has once-grand early (some very early) Victorian terraces (whose potential depends on distance from the road) which are extremely convenient for trains, tube and buses – but feels somewhat transient, compared to Deptford's far more villagey feel. However, from time to time a new restaurant or a new, smarter shop appears: a general tidy-up seems to have begun. Previously seedy old pubs are being reinvented as 'nicer' theme bars. A major boost to the area was the arrival of a large Sainsbury's foodstore at the bottom of Telegraph Hill which opened in 1995. Much recent development is squeezed in close to busy rail lines, and Barratt are about to start work on a big scheme here.

Central New Cross is unlovely, but look around the evocatively named **Friendly St**, with its artisan cottages, and among the turn-of-the-century houses around **St John's Vale** and the mid-19th-century ones in **Florence Rd**. Houses get grander as they reach the tops of these roads and that bit closer to Brockley. Many of the tall houses along **Lewisham Way** and **New Cross Rd** have been converted into flats; these 5-storey houses near Goldsmith's College are set comparatively far back from the road. There are also some 3-bed flats – mostly over shops. The college has been making big investments in new student housing, but flats to rent are still in demand.

A surplus Lewisham College building nearby has been converted into 66 homes. Just to the N of the main road, near New Cross station, **Glenville Grove** has a newish small estate of flats surrounded by older council-built homes, many of which are now privately owned. The new flats change hands at upwards of £65,000 for a 1-bed. To the W, near New Cross Gate tube, **New Cross Rd** has plenty of large terraced houses, either split into flats or being converted.

Go S from the two stations, past the '30s terraces and the 4-bed purpose-built Victorian mansion flats on **New Cross Rd**, and you come to a neighbourhood with an identity all its own. These are the pleasant boulevards, lined by trees and flanked by roomy (and some huge) Victorian homes, which run up and around Telegraph Hill and its park. The telegraph station which gave the hill its name passed the news of Waterloo. This corner was developed by the Haberdashers' Company, a pleasant, quiet area that has become increasingly popular: the houses yield nice flat conversions or make good-size family homes. **Pepys Rd, Kitto Rd** and **Vesta Rd** also have magnificent, panoramic views over Central London. Lower down the hill, **Musgrove Rd** has 3-storey Victorian houses that convert well into flats. **Waller Rd** has 5-bed houses. Some of the houses at the lower ends of the streets have suffered from subsidence, and may need underpinning: watch your survey. S of the park, **Drakefell Rd** has Victorian terraces, some flats. A good 3-bed Telegraph Hill flat might command £155,000; though there is a range from just under £100,000 for a 1-bed.

Almost directly N of Telegraph Hill, across **New Cross Rd**, is the Hatcham Park conservation area. There are still houses in need of refurbishment, though many have been tidied up. Streets include **Brocklehurst St** (3-bed cottages), **Billington Rd** (4/5-bed Victorian terraces with gardens), **Camplin St** (2-bed terraces), **Hundson Rd**, **Hatcham Park Rd** (3-bed, 3-storey houses around £145,000) and **Hatcham Park Mews**. Many homes here were sold to tenants of the Haberdashers' estate. There is a good, well-regarded school in **Hundson Rd**. Off **Avonley Rd** is a Barratt-built estate of 1990 studios, flats and houses. All have garaging or parking-space.

Transport	Tubes: New Cross, New Cross Gate (zone 2; East London Line); Oxford Circus 25 min (2 changes), City 20 min (2 changes), Heathrow 70 min (2 changes). Trains: New Cross, New Cross Gate, Deptford (London Br, Charing X, Cannon St). DLR from Deptford Creek.
Convenient for	Docklands, City, Greenwich. Miles from centre: 4.5.
Schools	Local Authority: Haberdashers' Aske's, Hatcham, South East London Secondary School.

SALES

Flats	S	1B	2B	3B	4B	5B
Average prices	40–60	55–95	65–140	110–160	—	—

Houses	2B	3B	4B	5B	6/7B	8B
Average prices	80–130	115–250	150–400	250–500	250+	—

RENTAL

Flats	S	1B	2B	3B	4B	5B
Average prices	75–120	90–200	130–250	185–250	—	—

Houses	2B	3B	4B	5B	6/7B	8B
Average prices	150–250	150–350	250–500	400–600	—	—

The properties   Deptford's stock of homes for sale (much housing is council) include some unmodernized 3-bed Victorian and older terraces. New developments appearing. New Cross is full of 19th-century terraces, many converted into flats; they are stately in Telegraph Hill (flats or 4/5-bed houses), run-down on the main roads, cottagey in conservation areas.

The market   Cheap, convenient (only tubes for miles) homes attract first-time buyers unable to aspire to nearby Surrey Docks or Greenwich. Many relative bargains to be had: some with river views. Families head for the enclave of Telegraph Hill. The DLR extension links Deptford to Docklands. Local searches: 3 weeks.

Among those estate agents active in this area are:

- Burnet, Ware & Graves
- Oak Estates *
- Seigo Homes
- Trafalgar Property Services
- Quest Residential

- Wilson Rogers
- Halifax Property Services
- Meridian Estates
- Winkworth*

further details: see advertisers' index on p671

N

NEWHAM

Map ref: p49 (K7)
Postal districts: E6, E7, E12, E13, E15, E16
Boroughs: Newham (Lab)
Council tax: Band D £768
Conservation areas: include Woodgrange, Three Mills
Parking: Controlled parking zones in East Ham and Stratford – and more planned

Newham boasts the biggest building site in Europe – after Berlin. The wide and watery landscape of the Royal Docks is changing so fast that a year away will leave a returning visitor baffled. Where did that new university spring from? Who dug that gleaming modernist tube line? A giant exhibition centre on the one hand, new schools on the other – and hundreds of new, and desirable, homes.

The Royals are just a slice of the big borough of Newham. Boosted by the Royals' success, new transport links and lavish government spending, the rest of the area is on the up too. From the perspective of most other places, its homes look cheap.

It took the new Jubilee line to convince the rest of London that Newham was worth a second look. The sophisticated steel and glass stations at Canning Town, West Ham and Stratford do just what the architects hoped: they raise the morale of the whole area. Houses in Silvertown, recently rated the most benighted corner of a depressed borough, sold for £35,000 in 1998. Since Canning Town tube opened they've leaped to £65,000. The swooping canopy over the Stratford interchange makes a crucial contribution to the revival of the town centre – London Transport's architect cruelly but aptly called pre-Jubilee line Stratford 'an abandoned city'.

Newham takes in what might be called the outer East End. The old boroughs of East Ham and West Ham, themselves successors to a dozen medieval hamlets, mushroomed in the second half of the 19th century. In 1965 they merged to become Newham (why not New Ham?). The '70s and '80s saw the final closure, and the start of redevelopment, of the giant Royal Docks which take up the southern swathe of the borough and were once its biggest employer. For long years they stood windswept and empty. Now the great sheets of water sport, around their margins, a successful and expanding airport, a new university, a technology park, several thousand homes and some prestige offices. An enormous exhibition centre is being built.

Stratford International station, on the London–Paris rail line, will bring an international interchange to Newham by 2007 – if it gets built. There is an uneasy suspicion that this end of the Channel Tunnel Rail Link , the route into St Pancras, may never happen, though the main bit, through Kent, is under way. (See Transport chapter.)

Another long-running infrastructure project did get finished: the link road which takes traffic out to the M11 and M25. There's talk of new Thames bridges (note the plural) though no concrete plans yet exist. London City Airport, in the docks, is doing well, with over one million passengers a year and flights to 23 cities in the UK and Europe, the latest being . . . Sheffield. Access to the airport is faster now Canning Town station has opened: this serves the new Jubilee line, the DLR and the Silverlink service round North London to Richmond. There's a shuttle bus to the terminal every 5 minutes.

Among ongoing projects for the Royals is an 90,000 sq m exhibition centre on the N side of Royal Victoria Dock that will be the biggest in London. It's due to open in mid-2000. The University of East London campus alongside Royal Albert Dock is now open: it's linked to a new technology park, the Thames Gateway Technology Centre, with 'business incubation units' for new hi-tech companies. Three new schools, including the just-opened Royal Docks Community School, have been built; another is planned.

Over a quarter of Newham's houses were destroyed in the Blitz. This, plus the borough's legacy of poor housing, led to a programme of slum clearance and regeneration: the result was 115 tower blocks (reduced now to less than 100 after the most notorious were blown up), post-war terraces, recent gentrification of the few remaining Victorian villas, and a general '70s cladded tattiness. But the 1980s saw a renewal of private new-build, with the stress on low-rise developments. This continued through the 1990s, with the last couple of years seeing a rash of new schemes around the Royals. Newham still has drab, seedy districts. Equally, most parts are affordable, though prices are not as bargain-basement as they were.

The Jubilee line Extention has received the limelight, but Newham has always had reasonable tube and rail links into the City and West End, and has historically been a dormitory area for London's armies of clerks and shop-workers.

Stratford is the nerve centre, dominating the N of Newham. After the Royals, it's the area which has seen the biggest changes. Already a good transport interchange, it's improving and could be a key point in the whole of London. The new Jubilee station has interchanges with the Central line, the DLR, Silverlink Metro (North London line) and trains into Liverpool Street. The international station could add Paris, Brussels and Berlin to the options, making Stratford an interchange between the Continent and all points N of London. Stratford's status as a major shopping and entertainment centre has been enhanced by new developments (see later in this chapter).

Newham takes in a dozen other distinct neighbourhoods, each with their history. The fields and hamlets are far in the past: it can take nearly an hour to creep from Canning Town on the western tip of Newham to East Ham on a No 15 bus at rush hour, even though the upgraded A13 has off-loaded much of the City-bound traffic.

South of the A13 are the Royal Docks, with names like Canning Town, Custom House, Silvertown and that bizarre former enclave of Kent, North Woolwich. Follow Newham's eastern frontier, the River Roding, northwards and you eventually hit Little Ilford, sitting to the W of its larger namesake and perched on Newham's NE edge. The **Romford Rd** takes you back to town through cosmopolitan Manor Park and the respectable Victorian villas of Forest Gate back to Stratford. To the SW lies West Ham – industrial, terraced and cheap. The map shows the differences between the two Hams: East is newer, with regular grids of terraced houses dating from 1880–1914;

West Ham is older, less rigidly laid out, with a mix of homes, some very basic, and prices to match. Flat conversions are generally rare in Newham because the council does not allow properties under 1,184 sq ft to be converted – and most Newham homes are smaller than this.

Stratford

The Jubilee line has made Stratford easier to get to, and the M11 link has alleviated a little of its horrendous traffic. The Safeway superstore in The Grove opened last Christmas, and Tesco are building a store on former railway land behind the station. The Grove development includes a new parade of shops, a library, hotel and parking for 300 cars. In **Salway Rd**, next to the existing shopping centre, a performing arts centre to complement the recently-renovated Theatre Royal opens this autumn. The road now also boasts a 4-screen multiplex cinema, Stratford Picture House, that specializes in first-run and art house movies. On **Great Eastern Rd** Barratt is about to start work on turning an office block into 140 1- and 2-bed flats.

Stratford's good transport and young and optimistic atmosphere attract home-buyers who work in the City or Docklands yet who need cheap housing. A studio flat in south Stratford will now cost £45,000 – £10,000 up on a year ago, while £85,000 (up from £70,000) gets you a 2-bed house in a decent road.

Maryland Point was a bustling agricultural village in the 17th century; today it marks Stratford's northern tip, on the outskirts of Leytonstone: the name survives in Maryland Station (trains to Liverpool St). This is where you'll find the real **Albert Square**: an anticlimax of a road that doesn't resemble a square or 'The Square'. Neatly anonymous terraced houses line this street – and, indeed, most of the area bounded by **Forest Lane** to the S and Forest Gate to the E. But don't knock it until you've had a look: new flats are to be found there and they are modestly priced. On the other (W) side of **Leytonstone Rd** you can pick up a newish 2-bedroomed terrace for about £85,000 – a word of warning though: it's pretty isolated here. No tubes or shops. Closer to Stratford centre, **Windmill Lane** and **Carolina Close** are popular for their purpose-built flats. These and nearby roads could be well-placed for the Stratford International station and associated developments on the goods yard to the W.

Move further S and the picture brightens – follow **West Ham Lane** past Queen Mary's Square, an enclave of 1980s 1- and 2-bedroomed flats. This countryside development is part privately owned and part rented to East London Housing Association tenants. Prices were pocket-money, and flats were instantly snapped up when new because it's so convenient (and next to the police station). Nearby **Aldworth Rd** is popular: its 2-bed houses will set you back around £95,000.

The **Portway** is a pleasure, and opposite the surprisingly verdant West Ham Park. Don't stick to the road itself – slip down one of the side-streets. **Church St North** is definitely mewsy; walk through here and you'll catch a glimpse of what Stratford could be all about. Recently built town-houses stand elegant in the privacy of this quiet off-shoot. Just N of West Ham Park, **Mathews Park Avenue** is in the perhaps optimistically named 'Little Hampstead of Stratford'; bigger houses are situated here (3-bed, £120,000-plus – up £30,000 in a year), the location is excellent: 12 min walk from the station and close to the park. No restaurants, but the local pubs are good. This area is tipped as the best place to buy in Stratford – leafy **Ham Park Rd**, which skirts the park, especially: here the properties are large, Victorian and have lots of original features. A 5-bed house could set you back £200,000-plus.

Plashet

Plashet is a rather ill-defined neighbourhood E of Stratford and N of Upton Park. There has been some investment in the area's largest shopping centre, **Green St**, with the old Ace cinema demolished to make way for much-needed car parking. The grubby parade of shops by the cinema may be replaced by new shop units and also some housing – when a developer comes forward. Plashet has some of Newham's more desirable homes and a highly regarded girls' school. Look in **Stopford Rd** for family homes: 3-bed and large 1930s houses at £90–110,000. The neighbourhood extends E along **Plashet Rd** beyond **Green St** as far as **High St North**, East Ham. The cluster of streets to the N of **Plashet Rd** is known as Upton: slightly smarter than Upton Park, and with the use of the latter's tube station.

Further N, Huge Edwardian mansions line the **Romford Rd**, heading towards Forest Gate: many have been converted into B & Bs, others remain run-down – definitely room for tidying-up and conversion here. But you'd better consider double glazing and a bus pass, for the houses are set nearer the road, traffic charges through day and night, and double yellow lines extend to Ilford. For the more up-market (or un-handy) buyer, East Ham and parts of Forest Gate are a better starting point.

Forest Gate

'Up-and-coming' are the enthusiastic words which spring to estate agents' lips when they mention Forest Gate. The neighbourhood has long been considered the jewel of Newham's crown, with larger Victorian houses still very much sought-after by agents. Indeed, it could be said to have arrived. Not all of Forest Gate is smart, though with £23 million of Government money due to be spent, plus £70 million from elsewhere, it could get a lot smarter very soon.

Capel Rd overlooks Wanstead Flats, the southernmost outpost of Epping Forest (hence 'Forest Gate'). Don't be surprised to see cows wandering off the Flats onto this speed-humped and very popular street. A clutch of 5 new 4- and 5-bed houses is being built in the road: prices around £225,000 are predicted. Although it has an E7 postcode, Capel Rd's £160,000 family-sized terraces face even more desirable homes across the park in the neighbouring borough of Redbridge.

'Woodgrange Village' isn't really a village, but an estate agent's term for the gentrified area bordering less-fashionable Manor Park. Great for home-buyers who prefer more salubrious surroundings and don't mind travelling by train. The conservation area of the Woodgrange estate instantly 'ups' the price of houses in this part of Forest Gate, and even the nearby run-down council blocks have undergone a face-lift, so buying here could be a shrewd move. Council policy is to permit no more building here to preserve the area's character. Prices for a 2-bedroomed terrace are around the £90,000 mark near the pretty little station (trains to either Barking or Gospel Oak, so it's more ornament than use). The Woodgrange estate itself boasts handsome 1880s villas in orderly, leafy streets to the E of **Woodgrange Rd**. Wander down **Richmond Rd**, **Hampton Rd** or **Windsor Rd** to view these regal residences, which might cost anything from £150–200,000 – though a 5/6-bed house in Windsor Rd went for a quarter of a million last year. Some have front drives and distinctive, original glass porches extending across the width of the house, fringed with decorative wooden 'teeth'.

Manor Park

Manor Park is largely devoted to resting places. Lacquer-black horse-and-carriage Cockney funerals regularly plod to the huge City of London Cemetery and Manor Park's own smaller graveyard. But the area itself is far from dead; it's brash, bustling and cosmopolitan, especially in the area around the **Romford Rd** – indeed, one of the most important developments planned here (but a long time in coming) is a block of around 100 homes on part of the site of the present Woodgrange Cemetery. **Romford Rd** lies just to the S of the railway track, a useful natural boundary. The A406 forms the E boundary, **High St North** the W, and East Ham's tube line cuts across to the S.

The neighbourhood of Little Ilford, on the E side, provides a quiet backwater, and the parks and playing-fields in the W of Manor Park form a welcome break from the row upon row of terraced housing. The heart of Manor Park is a comparatively sleepy area centring around poetic-sounding streets – **Browning Road, Coleridge Avenue, Shakespeare Crescent** and **Shelley Avenue** reside here. Three-bed terraces in these ever-popular streets fetch £110,000 (for a large one) while £80–85,000 is a reasonable price to pay for a 2-bed Victorian terrace. Flat conversions abound: £60–65,000 buys a large 2-bed flat and £55–59,000 is the going rate for a 1-bed period conversion. Popular homes for first-time buyers are 1-bed flats above shops in **Romford Rd**, which go for around £55,000 (£38,000 12 months back). Woodgrange Park House on Romford Rd was being redeveloped over the winter into 60 new flats. Yes, compared to the rest of London it's dirt cheap, but entertainment-wise there's not much to recommend it, unless you fancy a trip to nearby Ilford for a taste of night clubbing. But it is near East Ham tube station, Woodgrange Park and Manor Park stations, and the area boasts some marvellous Indian restaurants.

Capel Manor is the jewel in Manor Park's crown. A Grade II-listed manor house was carefully converted 10 years ago into luxury flats, with town-houses neatly attached to its flanks. Resale prices: flats range from £85,000 and houses cost £150–200,000.

Plaistow and West Ham

Plaistow is deceptively large, running from the station along the **High St**, down **Greengate St** and **Prince Regent Lane** to the A13. To the E it extends to the Abbey Arms pub on the **Barking Rd**, continuing to **Green St** which marks the Boleyn neighbourhood of Upton Park. This is another neighbourhood to gain Government cash: up to £50 million aimed at refurbishing housing and improving amenities. Scattered between the stock-brick terraces are new purpose-built flats. A Wimpey development of such flats lies tucked away behind the Memorial Recreation Ground (the birthplace of West Ham Football Club). Rowan Court in the **Broadway** and flats in **Plaistow Park Rd** offer a similar style. For something slightly cheaper, larger and older look in **Balaam St** (pronounced Bale-am).

Plaistow allegedly means a place where people gather to play, and if you are sports-mad a house near the roaring **Newham Way** (A13) could be ideal – a fantastic new leisure centre, the Newham Centre, has been built here. To the N of the road lies a spacious neighbourhood. Houses in **Holborn Rd, Botha Rd** and **Denmark St** have more breathing space – but they are treacherously near the busy A13. And you are a fair walk from the tube station here.

One Plaistow neighbourhood has become very popular over the last few years: the New City estate , a triangular grid of around 15 roads of terraced 20th-century houses centring on **New City Rd**, with **Boundary Rd** marking the E edge, **Barking Rd** (the A124) the N and **Tunmarsh Lane** to the S. This district abuts the well-regarded Central Park estate in East Ham.

West Ham station has been upgraded as part of the Jubilee line extention and now connects the Fenchurch to Tilbury line, the Jubilee line and the District line. West Ham is still the cheapest end of the borough to live and, in proximity to the City, it is the innermost. Much of West Ham's housing is owned by Newham Council: the rest is small and terraced: a typical 2-bed house can be had for £80,000. West Ham can seem like an industrial wasteland to the uninitiated. Don't be fooled by the A–Z map – West Ham, to locals, is considered to be the area around the tube station, nowhere near West Ham Park, Stratford (see above). This confusion arises from the days before Newham when the borough existed as East Ham and West Ham. West Ham Town Hall, for example, is in the middle of Stratford.

West Ham itself is a small area roughly consisting of the terraced streets off **Manor Rd**. In the late 1980s Barratt beautifully modernized the old council estate – now retitled Woodlands, the flats are huge and very smart. To the W of **Manor Rd**, Gainsborough Park is a big, 1990-vintage development between West Ham and Canning Town.

Silvertown, Canning Town & North Woolwich

These neighbourhoods are attracting the smart money in Newham. Until a year or three back, the only money spent here was on policing and cleaning up the graffiti, but the Docklands boom and the Jubilee Line are attracting private homebuyers.

Canning Town was built in the 1850s and rated a slum as early as 1855. That and the devastation caused by bombing in World War II gave the opportunity for the building of enormous tracts of municipal housing, including the Kier Hardy Estate. But then the Docks closed, and the sprawling estates lost their economic mainspring. Five or six years ago cautious people from West Ham would avoid Canning Town after nightfall: today things are improving. Canning Town and Custom House very nearly died with the docks: the flood of '53 almost assured them a watery grave. The Thames Barrier takes away that risk, and the community soldiers on in mainly council-built tower blocks and terraces. These now change hands for virtually twice their 1997/8 prices: 2-bed houses are typically £65,000.

The renaissance is due in some part to a £20-million-plus rehab scheme by Newham Council, but the biggest factor is the transport links. City Airport and Canary Wharf are 5 minutes away, the West End, by Jubilee line, just 20.

Silvertown is a sliver of land between the enormous Royal Victoria Dock and the Thames. Some 19th-century terraces survive, but most homes here are new, a product of the Docklands building boom. Britannia Urban Village is a big Wimpey scheme on the S shore of the Dock, with a total of 1,300 homes, 300 being released each year. Prices start at £140,000 for 2-bed flats, with 3-bed town houses at £230,000. Barrier Point, on **Silvertown Way** overlooking the River and the Thames barrier, is Barratt's big contribution, with flats in a tower and stepped blocks, most gaining splendid views along the river and across the adjoining new park. Early buyers did well: flats that sold for £96,000 in 1998 were changing hands last winter for £145,000.

North Woolwich has London's only vehicle ferry, linking the North and South Circular Roads (or so the maps would have you believe). A few older and 1980s homes cluster around the terminal, but the news is further E at Gallions Reach, where Fairview are building 900 homes on riverside land.

Upton Park and East Ham

Upton Park is a fairly small neighbourhood, stretching from the tube station in **Green St** down to the Boleyn pub on the **Barking Rd** and extending eastward to **Katherine Rd**. **Green St** continues to prosper as a speciality Asian shopping centre, and with further Government regeneration money in the pipeline more improvments are planned to add to the leisure complex in the transformed East Ham baths next to the Town Hall off **Barking Rd**. Purpose-built flats and new terraces are scattered in the streets around the football ground. West Ham Football Club's Upton Park ground has undergone a huge rebuilding programme. There are plans to rebuild the West and East Stands, taking the capacity from its present 26,000 to 40,000. **Inniskilling Rd** typifies the older-style streets crammed with 2-bed terraces which go for around £86,000. East Ham is better for shopping, and Upton Park's Queens Market has recently had a council-financed facelift.

East Ham is considered to be one of the best parts of Newham. House prices reflect this. Central Park is a popular inter-war terraced estate. **Cotswold Gardens** contains the only line of semis on the estate, which sell for up to £110,000. **Lonsdale Rd, Henniker Gardens, Haldane Rd** and most of the other streets contain 2-bed '30s terraces selling for around £85,000 – some with ground-floor bathrooms. All have neat gardens at the rear which are secluded and much cherished. **Central Park Rd** and its off-shoots contain larger, often pebbledashed, versions. Houses in this area boast 3 double bedrooms and go on the market for up to £120,000. For convenience, investigate the streets on the E side of **High St North**. Streets like **Lathom Rd, Caulfield Rd, Clements Rd** and **Skeffington Rd** are within easy reach of the tube and close to the shops. Apart from the usual high street stores East Ham has a famous and colourful covered market.

Burges Rd, Leigh Rd and Watson Rd are a quiet backwater despite being close to the A406. But don't worry, these rat-runs have now been blocked off, leaving a quiet, respectable neighbourhood to clock up the house prices, which reach £105–110,000 for a 3-bedroomed house hereabouts. Pockets of select 4-bedroomed dwellings can also be found in this corner of East Ham.

But there's a big difference between East Ham's **High St South** and **High St North**: look to the E of **High St South** and you'll see suburbs mirroring those in Central Park but a fraction cheaper. The huge minareted town hall divides the 'posher' south and the less-well-favoured north of East Ham.

Beckton and Custom House

Since the Royals returned to the Newham Council fold after the Docklands years (when the LDDC, not the Town hall, ran things), the old names are being used more: Silvertown and Canning Town (see above); Custom House and Beckton. The Docklands boom has at least meant this part is no longer cut off: the DLR rail link, the Jubilee line and sundry new roads have joined these districts onto London.

Beckton saw some early, and successful, Docklands-inspired housing. The new estates were Docklands' first concentration of cheap new homes – with 700 for rent and thousands to buy – and a runaway success. Beckton is now well-established with a brisk resale market in its modern homes (none over 15 years old), but less new-build. These are traditional homes with gardens and room to park the car – none of your Docklands warehouses here, thank you. Local agents produce special Beckton property lists: 1-bed flats start below £60,000, while houses start at £95,000: £125,000 buys you a 3-bed one with a garage and a good garden. Just to encourage you, all these prices have leapt 25 per cent in the year since December 1998.

Transport	Tubes: Stratford, West Ham (Central & Jubilee); Plaistow, East Ham (District – and Hammersmith & City during peak hours), Canning Town (Jubilee). From Stratford: Oxford Circus 30 min, City 12 min, Heathrow 90 min (1 change). DLR: Stratford and Royals Docks to Tower, Isle of Dogs. Trains: Stratford (Liverpool St 8 min), others see map.
Convenient for	City, Docklands, City Airport; Epping Forest, M11; A12, A13 for M25. Miles from centre: 7.
Schools	Local Authority: Brampton Manor, Cumberland, Eastlea, Forest Gate, Langdon, Lister, Little Ilford, Plashet, Rokeby, Sarah Bonnell, Stratford, Trinity, Royal Docks Community School, St Angela's RC, St Bonaventures RC, St John's RC. Private: Grangewood.

SALES

Flats	S	1B	2B	3B	4B	5B
Average prices	35–55	50–65	55–85	65–90	–	–

Houses	2B	3B	4B	5B	6/7B	8B
Average prices	70–95	85–140	110–250	180–250+	–	–

RENTAL

Flats	S	1B	2B	3B	4B	5B
Average prices	90–120	100–1350	130–155	135–220	180–230	–

Houses	2B	3B	4B	5B	6/7B	8B
Average prices	130–165	170–220	180–250	220–300	–	–

The properties Largely 1900s terraces of 2/3-bed homes and p/b flats. Woodgrange Park boasts larger period houses, as do a few other pockets. East Ham's Central Park estate has mainly inter-war family homes. Custom House and Beckton have wide tracts of new homes, as do Royal Docks.

The market Prime hunting-ground for first-rung-of-the-ladder home-buyers with some very affordable homes. At the other end of the scale the handsome Woodgrange estate conservation area houses cost up to £250,000, and new-build family homes are to be had at all prices. Local searches: 10 working days.

Among those estate agents active in this area are:
- Douglas Allen Spiro
- Bairstow Eves
- Guardian Estates
- Halifax
- Adam Kennedy
- Taylors
- Abbotts
- Taylor Simpson
- Spicer McColl
- J Webb
- A J Scott
- McDowalls
- Bryants
- Collins
- Harrt Suttons

N

NOTTING HILL AND NORTH KENSINGTON

Map ref: p59 (7H)
Postal districts: W11, W2, W10
Boroughs: Kensington &
  Chelsea (Con)
Council tax: Band D £534
Conservation areas:
  Oxford Gardens, Norland,
  Ladbroke, Pembridge,
  Avondale Park Gardens
Parking: Controlled parking
  zone: residents/meters,
  clamping

Notting Hill has, alone among London's residential areas, become a star in its own right: no-one yet has made a movie called Fulham. In a generation, the area has cast off its seedy, even dangerous, image yet retained its arty, bohemian air. To this the 1990s added a solid note of respectability. North Kensington, ever the poorer relation, has made real gains in status. Now, Notting Hill is a key part of fashionable London: cosmopolitan, raffish, a bit daring – the antithesis of Fulham. However, it is still an area of striking contrast, with £1 million-plus houses in the same street as council blocks.

To generalize, the wealthy and respectable live on top of the hill in their big family houses backing on to acres of delightful communal gardens, and the poor and the unconventional at the bottom. The big houses have, in many cases, seen a revival in their status: until the 1970s the area was a warren of bed-sits and dilapidation.

Notting Hill the area is N of **Notting Hill Gate**, bounded on the E by the border between Kensington borough and the City of Westminster, and on the W by Holland Park neighbourhood (see Holland Park chapter). The N border with North Ken is by some reckoned to be the M40 motorway, the **Westway**; by others to be further S, at the foot of the slope on which Notting Hill sits. The corner to the NW, in the angle of the M40 and the M41, is not Notting Hill. Once called Notting Dale, a notorious slum, it is now quieter, more respectable Avondale. All of Notting Hill is in W11, but not all W11 is Notting Hill.

All of W10 lying S of the **Harrow Rd** is North Kensington: a small part of W10 forms the Queen's Park neighbourhood of Kilburn and Kensal (see Kilburn, Kensal Green and Queen's Park chapter).

Over the years, the less well-off have been pushed further N by gentrification. This accounts for the high proportion of council and housing trust developments in the relatively deprived N of the borough, particularly in Golborne and Kensal Town. The mix of social classes and the multi-racial nature of the area, with its large West Indian, Moroccan and Filipino communities, make Notting Hill/North Kensington a cosmopolitan and lively place to live. The streets are busy at midnight, and there is a distinct inner-city feel to the place. This character in recent years has attracted first art galleries then cafés, bars and restaurants to the area, which now rivals Soho. Now, film-loving tourists tramp the streets in search of familar front doors.

Whereas property prices in the rest of Kensington and Chelsea are beyond the means of all but the well-off, people on moderate incomes are still able to get a foothold on the property ladder in this area. This is partly thanks to the council's Right to Buy scheme which encouraged tenants to become leaseholders. Local housing associations also operate shared-ownership schemes which allow the tenant to part-own their home – the Rootes site development and the major Peabody scheme on British Gas land, both in North Kensington, are the latest examples.

It used to be possible to point to Notting Hill and North Kensington homes as better value than those other parts of Kensington and Chelsea. This is now only true in W10, and even there a fairly ordinary 3-bed house will top £400,000. The point is that Notting Hill has plenty of choice, especially in flats, mews houses and grander houses, and North Kensington offers yet more flats plus (to the suprise of those who only know the grittier bits) family homes with gardens.

Other assets include the (sometimes hidden) communal gardens of Notting Hill, and the direct underground links to the West End and City. The area gains too from its position on the 'right' side of London for Heathrow, a big plus for relocating foreigners.

There is plenty of property to rent here: investors have been active for some time and there are lots of flats and a good sprinkling of houses. Flats to rent are especially plentiful in the SE corner of the area, towards **Notting Hill Gate** and **Queensway**, and around **Ladbroke Grove**, which has been boosted by the new BBC complex in nearby White City.

One unusual feature of the housing scene here is the domination by housing trusts and associations. These own very large amounts of property – usually homes they have bought up and converted, though some are new-build. For instance, the Kensington Housing Trust owns over 500 homes in the Golborne ward alone, which it rents out at about 20% of the market rate. Unlike council properties, many of the trusts' homes are dotted around in otherwise owner-occupied streets. And once in housing association hands they stay that way, never being resold. This 'freezes' whole sections of streets and reduces the number of homes on the open market.

Two major street events also shape the character of the area – the internationally famous **Portobello Rd** market (Saturdays) and the annual Notting Hill Carnival, Europe's biggest street festival. It draws more than 2 million people to the area every August Bank Holiday weekend. The festivities are usually concentrated in the Colville/Tavistock and Golborne neighbourhoods. For two days, the streets are alive with pulsating rhythms and superbly colourful floats. Residents either love it or hate it. Carnival is notably more peaceful than in years gone by, and is more organized, with sound systems now having to be registered and illegal systems banned. Despite this, many locals leave town for the Bank Holiday weekend: there are even plans to organize evacuation of groups of locals. A new event is the Portobello Festival which brings a week of music, literature and arts to the area.

Portobello Rd has had a market since the 1860s when it was known as The Lane. Antiques, bric-a-brac, fruit-and-vegetable and clothing stalls spread for two-thirds of a mile along the road from **Simon Close** to **Golborne Rd**, with the antiques concentrated at the S end. The market is a major tourist attraction, drawing thousands of visitors to the street every Saturday. Council proposals to tidy it up brought a flurry of protests from locals, who like it the way it is: scruffy and lively. Controlled parking has come to North Kensington to the dismay of some stall holders, who find it restricts their access to the market.

The social N–S divide in the area is accentuated by the physical barrier of the **Westway** elevated motorway. Built in the mid-'60s, it runs S of **Cambridge Gardens**. The space under the **Westway** has been put to good use by the North Kensington Amenity Trust. Small community groups, community transport groups, a fitness centre, centre for the elderly and an information point can be found in the archways. The large new restaurant close to Ladbroke Grove tube has just been joined by an internet café. Long-term (and seemingly permanent) residents include the group of travellers whose caravans have been parked below the **Westway** near Shepherd's Bush since the early 1970s.

Ladbroke Grove is the area's main traffic artery, stretching from the desirable leafy S boundary of the neighbourhood to the scruffy N border. The main shopping centre for the area is **Notting Hill Gate** to the S, the eastward continuation of **Holland Park Avenue**. **Notting Hill Gate** also boasts two cinemas (at the moment) and a number of popular restaurants and pubs. The Electric Cinema in **Portobello Rd** is being done up and should re-open soon.

Shopping – fashion, interiors, antiques, anything designer from handbags to herbs – is excellent, though the more bohemian locals complain that chain stores and identikit coffee bars are driving out more characterful stores. On a more prosaic level Sainsbury's store at the N end of **Ladbroke Grove** has brought superstore shopping to the area.

Rising property prices and general prosperity have led residents to spend money on their homes, and there has been a rash of painting, decorating and modernizing. Few of the truly picturesque, peeling-stucco slums survive, at least S of the Westway. However, the council's planners are tightening controls, making it harder to extend homes upwards (loss of light is feared) and downwards.

Notting Hill

This is the smarter half of the area, but even here the contrasts can be great: serene mansions to the south, stimulating street-life to the north.

Pembridge

Pembridge stretches N from Notting Hill Gate as far as **Westbourne Grove**, bounded by the W by **Kensington Park Rd** and on the E by **Chepstow Place** and **Ossington St**. The eastern part of the neighbourhood is in W2. **Pembridge Rd**, the S half of the main route between the Gate and **Westbourne Grove**, leads into the heart of this sedate and leafy neighbourhood. To the E lies **Pembridge Square**, the only one in the borough lined by large detached villas. The 4-storey ornamental stucco houses overlook a narrow private central garden. Some remain as family homes but many have been converted, some into spacious flats (£950,000 for a 5-bed), a few into hotels and schools: scaffolding is a feature of the area as the tall buildings are painted and tidied. The E side of the square is across the borough boundary in Westminster.

South of the square, a short walk from bustling **Notting Hill Gate**, are the cul-de-sacs of **Linden** and **Clanricarde Gardens**. In **Linden Gardens** is The Limes, a 6-storey modern development with private parking. There is also the private, gated **Linden Mews** with its quaint brick houses and **Garden Mews** where four new houses can be found. Tall ornate stucco terraces characterize both streets. In **Clanricarde Gardens**, the large houses of bed-sits have mostly now been converted into smart flats: a 2-bed would be in the region of £275,000. The scale changes in **Ossington St** on the E edge of the neighbourhood. Here terraces of smaller stucco houses face the backs of buildings fronting **Palace Court**. At the end of the street is little **Victoria Grove Mews**. More large houses are found N of **Pembridge Square** in leafy **Pembridge Place** and **Dawson Place**. Both are lined by paired stucco villas with front gardens. **Dawson Place** also has detached villas, some with the same decorative cast-iron and glass entrance canopies as the imposing Victorian mansions in Holland Park. Prices are not dissimilar: to around £4 million. Groups and pairs of substantial, £825,000, houses curve around **Pembridge Villas**, the N half of the main route through the neighbourhood. A three-bed flat commanded £585,000 last November. Leading off to the NW, **Pembridge Crescent** has more groups and pairs of stucco villas. These contrast with the 2-storey painted cottages in **Pembridge Mews**.

Chepstow Crescent, which has mainly 3/4-storey brick and stucco terraces with wrought-iron balconies and a couple of hideous post-war flats blocks, leads into tree-lined **Chepstow Villas**, considered the most prestigious address in the neighbourhood. About half of the elegant paired stucco or brick-and-stucco villas remain as family houses. Leading N from here into the Colville/Tavistock neighbourhood is **Ledbury Rd**, a pleasant and smart street of 3-storey stucco houses with antique and designer clothes shops, galleries and bars. (Only 28 years ago an architectural author warned his readers not to walk down this street alone.) A new addition is the 2-storey **Ledbury Mews East** development. Behind the much-improved Walmer Castle pub is a clutch of workshops, and Westbourne Grove Church hides tiny **St John's Mews** with more. **Denbigh Rd** has a mix of properties ranging from Longlands Court council estate to low-rise modern brick homes and painted stucco houses. **West Hill Court** is a new mews of 2/3-bed flats reached via an archway opposite the council estate. A winged stucco arch halfway along the E side leads through to **Pencombe Mews**, a group of 3-storey town-houses.

The W side of the neighbourhood is dominated by **Portobello Rd**, although only part of the famous market falls within its boundaries. S of **Chepstow Villas** stands a row of charming gaily painted 2-storey stucco cottages with front gardens. Street trees add to the leafy look. These face the backs of the big red-brick and stone 1890s flats blocks fronting **Kensington Park Rd**. Lying at the rear of the cottages is **Simon Close**, a small cul-de-sac of modern 2-storey town-houses.

Although this stretch of **Portobello Rd** is quiet during the week, on Saturdays it is invaded by thousands of tourists from all over the world heading for the market. Antique stalls spread along both sides of the street, spilling around into **Denbigh Close**, a pleasant cobbled cul-de-sac of mews cottages,

Stucco is the trademark of the Ladbroke area. The pillared porch, the rusticated stucco around the ground-floor window, the steps, the railings, the balcony, all are typical of these large houses. Some are now flats, which benefit from the lofty rooms. Many of the houses back onto communal gardens: the area was planned as one estate, though built over quite a long period.

some with roof terraces. **Denbigh Terrace**, one street away, has an attractive pastel-shaded stucco terrace of 2/3-storey and basement family houses on the southern side, looking across to Longlands Court council estate.

The Crescents/Ladbroke

This is the most prosperous and elegant part of the area, set on the highest ground at the top of the hill, and benefiting from an expansive street-plan of crescents and gardens. The area dates from the mid-Victorian age and many large houses survive undivided. It is here that people apply for planning permission for underground swimming pools beneath a conservatory in their back garden and double car lifts in place of the front one.

Clarendon Rd on the W edge of the neighbourhood sets the tone of this highly desirable area. The best stretch, between **Lansdowne Walk** and the smart Clarendon Cross shops, has big paired brick and stucco villas with front gardens. South of here are terraces of 3-storey and basement Victorian houses, modern town-houses and flats. North of the junction with **Elgin Crescent**, the street becomes more mixed and less attractive with the appearance of council blocks and a parade of shops. However, a terrace of 4-storey pastel houses on the E side has the advantage of backing on to the beautiful communal gardens between **Elgin Crescent** and **Blenheim Crescent**.

Terraces of 3-storey together with semi-basement houses line both sides of tree-lined **Blenheim Crescent**. Properties on the S side back on to the communal gardens. **Blenheim Crescent** is like a different street to the E across **Ladbroke Grove**, combining a mix of private (S), council and housing trust properties (N), which merge with the shops, pubs and cafés in the stretch between **Kensington Park Rd** and **Portobello Rd**. Tucked away here is **Codrington Mews**.

Leafy **Elgin Crescent**, more salubrious and sought-after than Blenheim, has terraces of mainly 3-storey painted stucco houses with basements and attic windows. Huge communal gardens lie at the rear on both sides of the street. As with **Blenheim Crescent**, many houses have been converted to flats.

South of **Elgin Crescent**, the streets climb uphill. **Arundel Gardens** has mainly 4-storey brick and stucco terraces with small ornate iron balconies on the first floor. **Ladbroke Gardens** is lined by ornate stucco terraces with attic windows. This street leads into **Stanley Crescent** with its huge 6-storey brick and stucco paired villas at the bottom of the hill, and a terrace of 4- and 5-storey ornate painted stucco houses at the top. Interesting gaps and intriguing arches between the houses give glimpses of the sky, trees and gardens at the rear. The houses overlook communal gardens between the Crescent and **Kensington Park Gardens**.

The summit of the hill was developed in the form of an oval cut in two by **Ladbroke Grove**. **Stanley Crescent** forms one half of the oval, and across the Grove to the W is the complementary **Lansdowne Crescent**. An elegant white 'iced wedding cake' terrace curves halfway round the semi-circle to the N. The richly decorated houses have distinctive rounded façades, Corinthian-columned entrance porches and £3-million-plus price tags. Big paired brick and stucco villas, stone-gabled houses and some modern brick town-houses spread around the rest of the crescent.

More extensive communal gardens lie behind **Lansdowne Crescent** and **Lansdowne Rd**, another choice residential street, lined with trees taller than the buildings. Terraces of 3-storey and basement stucco painted houses, some gabled, wind around the hill, merging with pairs of villas where the street drops down again to **Holland Park Avenue**. South along **Lansdowne Rd**, at the junction of **St John's Gardens**, the road becomes 'No Entry'. You are now entering a complex series of one-way streets aimed at reducing traffic speed and flow: it can be very confusing. **Lansdowne Walk** has groups of handsome stucco and brick-and-stucco houses. On the NE corner of the street, set back from **Ladbroke Grove**, is Bartok House, considered one of the best blocks of flats in the Notting Hill area. The modern brown-brick development with its own communal gardens joins up with a terrace of brick and stucco houses (split into flats) and another modern flats block. These flats face **Ladbroke Grove** but are separated from the road by a private driveway and a screen of trees and lawns. Tall trees in the gardens surrounding St John's Church on the hilltop add to the leafy outlook. The church spire can be seen from miles around rising above the treetops. This stretch of **Ladbroke Grove** and the leg between **Ladbroke Square** and **Ladbroke Rd** (attractive 4-storey wide-fronted painted stucco houses) are the best sections of this long road.

Lying between the houses in **Kensington Park Gardens** and **Ladbroke Square** are the largest private gardens in the borough – indeed, at 7 acres, one of the largest in London. Despite its name **Ladbroke Square** is made up of a long terrace of 4- and 5-storey brick and stucco houses on one side of the street, facing the gardens. Most are divided into flats. A sumptuous penthouse atop one of the Kensington Park Gardens houses was £2.5 million for 3,500 sq ft last autumn. The gardens are enclosed by tall trees and hedges, and street trees stretch along adjoining roads as far as the eye can see.

Ladbroke Rd, a relatively busy but pleasant local road, has a mix of smaller terraces: Bonham House, a 4-storey block of flats, big detached houses and a 5-storey 1900s flats block. Traffic has been slowed by a new roundabout at the junction with **Ladbroke Terrace**. Notting Hill police station stands on the corner with **Ladbroke Grove** and the Kensington Temple at the E junction with **Pembridge Rd**. Leading off here are a series of small streets and cobbled mews including **Wilby Mews**. The mews, tucked in behind the flower-bedecked Ladbroke Arms pub, has a mix of little 2- and 3-storey cottages and five new houses set around a wide inner courtyard. More low, painted Victorian cottages are found in **Horbury Mews**. **Horbury Crescent** has curving terraces of larger brick and stucco properties. Hidden away behind the houses at the SE end of **Ladbroke Rd** and the shops in **Pembridge Rd** and **Notting Hill Gate** is **Bulmer Mews**, a development of 2-storey brown-brick houses with garages (1987).

Forming the E border of the neighbourhood is **Kensington Park Rd**, a busy bus route. Terraces of 3-storey brick and stucco buildings with shops, restaurants and wine bars on the lower floors line the N end of the street. They give way to terraces on the W side, broken up by stretches of the area's splendid communal gardens and Kelvin Court, a 5-storey block of flats. Really grand houses in this road have sold for well into the millions; some famous names have homes here. You might scrape in at around £1 million, though raise the budget to £1.2 million if you need 5 beds.

N

Avondale

Newly created private squares and mews stand amid large council estates and housing association developments in this very mixed, rather confusingly laid out but increasingly fashionable neighbourhood in the W of the area. It is on the border with Hammersmith borough, and is cut off to the W and N by motorways.

The W end of **Lancaster Rd**, a short walk from Ladbroke Grove station and the shops clustered around it, combines residential, education, health and light industrial uses. A terrace of 3-storey and basement brick and stucco houses, many split into flats, lines the NE arm of the street. Opposite stands the Royalty Studios, a complex of studios/workshops. Next door is the London Lighthouse HIV/AIDS hospice and support centre. Standing alongside is the City of Westminster College annex, empty while its future is debated. Thomas Jones Primary School is due to close.

Notting Hill's new Holmes Place health club – complete with stainless steel pool – opened in late 1999 in **Lancaster Rd**.

Ruston Mews, in the shadow of the **Westway**, is a recent development of mews houses. **St Mark's Rd** leads under the **Westway** into **St Quintin Avenue**, a busy bus route. **Bartle Rd** runs between **Lancaster Rd** and the **Westway**. Off it are **St Andrew's Square** and **Wesley Square** with their modern 3-storey brick houses with off-street parking and pleasant communal gardens. Properties are shielded from **Lancaster Rd** by a high brick wall, adding to the sense of enclosure and privacy. Opposite is part of the large Lancaster West estate.

Beyond Notting Hill Methodist Church, **Lancaster Rd** becomes **Silchester Rd** and you cross into W10. Where the road ends with the junction of **Bramley Rd**, Arthurs Court has been built, a 3-storey development. Opposite is the new 4-storey Goodrich Court, sited on **Bramley Rd** at the junction of **Darfield Way**, a dead-end road which leads onto the Silchester West Estate and **Waynflete Square** and **Shalfleet Drive**. Eleven new flats make up **Charlotte Mews**. The estate with its tower blocks spreads through **Verity Close** where it becomes a cul-de-sac of modern 2/3-storey red-brick terraced houses with small gardens. Some of these council-built houses are now appearing on the market: prices are keen, with £225,000 being asked for a 2-bed house last autumn. The remainder of the estate stretches along the N side of **Cornwall Crescent**, where it joins up with more council flats. A Victorian terrace stands on the S side.

More Victorian terraces are found to the N in **Ladbroke Crescent** – 3-storey, basement and attic, painted stucco houses converted into flats. At the NW end of **Walmer Rd** is Kensington Sports Centre with swimming and many other sports. More brick council blocks extend S along the street, leading to the smart **Hippodrome Mews** development. Here 3-storey brown-brick town-houses line two private mews overlooking Avondale Park. Terraces of modern brick low-rise housing association properties are found in **Wilsham St** and **Kenley Walk** S of the park and **Runcorn Place** and **Hesketh Place** to the N. Beside **Kenley Walk** and at the top of **Wilsham St** lies a new development of 2/3-storey town-houses. There is no way through for cars but pedestrians can walk to **Walmer Rd**.

Private residential property in the SW corner of the neighbourhood is concentrated in **Avondale Park Rd**, **Mary Place**, **Sirdar Rd**, **Stoneleigh Place** and **Stoneleigh St**, **Treadgold St** and **Grenfell Rd**. **Avondale Park Rd** has been cut off to form a cul-de-sac. Many of the 2/3-storey terraced houses found here are split into flats. Tucked away in the middle of this group is **Avondale Park Gardens**, a pleasant square of 2-storey brick artisan cottages with walled front gardens set around a small central green with trees. Avondale Park Primary School is also found here. The cottages, which were built by the former LCC after the World War I, passed on to the council, which gradually sold them off. Bordering this chunk of private property is the big Henry Dickens council estate, fronting **St Ann's Villas**.

Boundary changes in 1996 extended the Borough of Kensington and Chelsea in this area, removing an anomaly so that both W11 postcode and borough border now follow the physical barrier of the M41 highway. A clutch of streets W of Henry Dickens Court on **Bramley Rd** that used to be in Hammersmith and Fulham are now in the Royal Borough. **Rifle Place** leading into **St Katherine's Walk** is a new square of 3-storey flats in light brown-brick set around gardens. This development continues along **Bramley Rd** until the junction with **Freston Rd**. **Mortimer Square** with its low stucco and brick homes is another new addition. The Designers Guild building in **Olaf St** houses a collection of media companies: five new houses have just been built in front of it. This is an area rich in media-related companies and small business units and the Royal Borough is encouraging more to locate here. At the top end are residential blocks and other small business units. Just off the square, near the junction is a cul-de-sac with a collection of motor workshops and offices.

This neighbourhood will be close to the proposed, enormous White City development just W of the motorway (see Shepherd's Bush chapter).

Colville/Tavistock

This is the heart of the 'other' Notting Hill, down the slope and a world away from the snowy crescents of Ladbroke. Even here, things are changing fast. **Westbourne Grove** with its proliferation of increasingly smart antique shops, galleries and other ways of spending money is a main W–E route between Notting Hill and Bayswater. Where **Westbourne Grove** meets **Denbigh Rd** is a little group of shops, graced by a modernist public loo and flower stall, on an island in the road, which has won architectural prizes. On Saturdays antique and bric-a-brac stalls spill around the corner into the NW arm of the street from the famous **Portobello Rd** market. Stucco/brick terraces line this end of **Westbourne Grove**, many of which have shops on the ground floor. **Lambton Mews**, with its health club and business premises, is tucked away to the S. Around the corner on the E side of **Kensington Park Rd** is an attractive terrace of 3-storey and basement painted houses with front gardens. More antique shops are found at the S end of **Ledbury Rd**, beneath the 3/4-storey brick and stucco properties which stretch along the W side. The E side is in Westminster.

Off to the W is tree-lined **Lonsdale Rd**, probably the nicest street in the neighbourhood together with the S end of **Colville Rd**. Hidden between the two are **Colville Mews** and **Lonsdale Mews**, with businesses and homes, including 5 very modern new houses (from £900,000, due this summer) in Colville Mews. Attractive terraces of 3-storey painted houses stand in **Lonsdale Rd**, E of the brown-brick Portobello Court council estate, which spreads back to **Westbourne Grove**. Taller stucco terraces line the E side of **Colville Rd** and 4-storey semi-detached villas the W. **Colville Terrace** has 4/5-storey stucco houses, mostly converted into flats. This neighbourhood is showing the fruits of a long programme of council improvements.

Powis Square to the N has a mix of private 4-storey stucco terraced houses to the W and a long modern terrace of 4-storey brick council flats to the E. They lie on either side of a public garden with a children's playground in the middle. Standing at the N end of the square is the Tabernacle Community Centre, recently revamped with lottery money and now boasting a community café.

Another public garden and playground lies to the W in **Colville Square**. Backing on to the E side of the garden is the 5-storey and basement Pinehurst Court flats block (painted stucco – and recently cheered up using City Challenge cash), which actually fronts **Colville Gardens**. It is set back off the road behind railings, lawn and trees, and the buildings are newly painted in cream and yellow. Overlooking the W side of **Colville Square** are more 4-storey and basement terraces. Lining the W side of the square in **Talbot Rd** are a series of tall modern red-brick housing trust flats blocks.

Westbourne Park Rd, another busy W–E road, contains mainly brick and stucco terraces with clusters of shops on the ground floor. The council's Covent Gardens Estate and a modern housing trust development take up the S side of the street from **Ladbroke Grove** to **Kensington Park Rd**. Off to the N is **All Saint's Rd**, once notorious only for drug dealing and street robberies, but now home to fashionable restaurants and smart shops at rents higher than in Ledbury Rd. In 1997 the council, in partnership with the police and City Challenge, introduced closed-circuit television (CCTV) into **All Saint's Rd** and surrounding areas. This has improved the streets but some displacement is being felt by residents who live in **Clydesdale Rd** and **Westbourne Park Rd**. There are some homes here in flats above the shops.

All Saint's Rd also lies in the heart of Carnival territory. The two-day Notting Hill Carnival is concentrated in the streets around here (see area profile). Crossing **All Saint's Rd** and running parallel to **Westbourne Park Rd** is **St Luke's Mews**, with one end housing an interesting blue building with small offices and some new mews houses. On the opposite side of **All Saint's Rd**, the Mews continues with older more characteristic homes.

N

McGregor Rd off the E side of **All Saint's Rd** is lined by 3-storey and basement Victorian terraces. It is a designated play street from 8am to sunset. Traffic is banned during these hours except for access.

Long stepped terraces of modern yellow-brick housing trust co-ownership flats stretch along **Tavistock Crescent**. It runs into **Tavistock Rd** (3-storey brick and stucco terraces), which is pedestrianized at its W junctions with **Portobello Rd**. **Basing St**, where cars are allowed, has 2-storey stucco and brick houses. This stretch of **Portobello Rd** takes in the heart of the market. Antique and bric-a-brac stalls line the section between **Westbourne Grove** and **Elgin Crescent** (Saturdays only). Fruit-and-veg stalls (Monday–Saturday) take over between here and the covered market under **Westway** – bric-a-brac, new and second-hand clothing (Fridays and Saturdays). From **Acklam Rd** to **Golborne Rd** there is a junk market on Friday morning and Saturday.

Several small mews off the E side of **Portobello Rd** are used by market traders to store their barrows and stock. But **Alba Place**, a short cul-de-sac between **Lancaster** and **Westbourne Park Rds**, also has gaily painted 2/3-storey cottages, some with roofs terraces, at its E end: one was for sale at £400,000 last autumn. Opposite is **Hayden's Place**, a cobbled road with no homes but the Portobello Studios at the end. An up-market development of new red-brick cottages stands in **Dunworth Mews** between **Westbourne Park Rd** and **Talbot Rd**.

Lancaster Rd, which leads W to **Ladbroke Grove**, has mainly 3-storey terraces and paired villas in varying states of repair, divided into flats. The Serbian Orthodox Church and community centre stands on the S side near the junction with the Grove across the road from the Lancaster Youth Club. The council library stands on the corner of **Ladbroke Grove** and **Lancaster Rd**. Next door to St Saviour's Church is the Campden Technical Institute (built and owned by Campden charities).

North Kensington

From here on we are N of the motorway, and into North Kensington and the W10 postcode. North Kensington has a fair amount of poverty, quite a lot of sub-standard housing and higher than average unemployment. As a result a lot of council and government money has been spent here over the past decade.

North Ken (as it's commonly known) has its gritty streets but it also has surprises: family homes amid greenery, near-suburban in atmosphere yet a stroll from the bright lights of W11.

Golborne

Golborne is tucked into the NE corner of the area, bounded by the railway line to the N and E and the **Westway** to the S. Most of the Golborne area is dominated by council and housing trust/association developments, mainly low-rise look-alike modern brick dwellings. They are concentrated in **Bevington Rd, Swinbrook Rd, Acklam Rd, Wornington Rd** and **St Ervan's Rd**. The early-1960s Wornington Green estate, owned by Kensington Housing Trust, is typical: there are 539 homes, and the estate has been much improved by a 'greening the estate' scheme and by anti-crime measures.

Portobello Rd, Golborne Rd and **Ladbroke Grove** have some conversion flats, often above shops. These are the cheapest homes in the area – except for ex-local authority flats. The latter can start at £90,000 for a 1-bed flat, while a conversion will be £30–40,000 more. This stretch of **Portobello Rd** N of the Westway fly-over is on the fringe of the famous market. It is given over to stalls selling mainly second-hand clothing and household goods. More stalls spread along **Golborne Rd**, a bustling local shopping centre in its own right. A sign of the times: in **Southern Row** the old Albion pub has become a home, with office/living space and a 900 sq ft reception room.

Kensal Town

In the far N of the area, and about as far in atmosphere from the lush Kensington heartlands, is Kensal Town. Crossing **Golborne Rd** railway bridge into Kensal Town is like entering another world. Grim concrete council blocks scar the landscape on the E side of this socially deprived neighbourhood, lying between the railway line in the S and the Grand Union Canal in the N.

Dominating the skyline at the gateway to Kensal Town is 30-storey Trellick Tower. This grey concrete 1970s council block is regularly singled out in opinion polls as one of the capital's biggest eyesores – but residents enjoy spacious flats and stunning views, and modernist architects revere it: it was listed Grade II last year. Some flats are for sale: a 2-bed, as seen on a TV makeover programme, was on the market last winter at £170,000. Agents say these flats sell fast: you either love them or hate them. However, most are still owned by the council or housing trusts.

The rest of Kensal is taken up by trading estates, workshops and industrial uses, mainly concentrated in **Kensal Rd**, with only a handful of private homes scattered about the neighbourhood. But this corner is home to two splendid community gardens: Meanwhile Gardens complete with wildlife section; and Emslie Horniman's Pleasance, a park with sports area which was smartened up with lottery cash in 1998.

On the W side of **Ladbroke Grove** alongside the railway line is the 1930s Kensal House complex. A big Sainsbury's supermarket stands immediately to the N. Behind the supermarket site, between the railway line and the canal, is the 10-acre gasworks site, which stood vacant for 20 years until 1998. The Peabody Trust plans 288 homes (a mix of affordable housing and private homes), 35 live/work units and industrial units to a master plan by star architect Piers Gough. A restored canal basin will allow waterbus services to connect through to Little Venice.

On the other side of the canal in the NW corner of the neighbourhood is Kensal Green Cemetery, a favourite haunt of wildlife enthusiasts – and an official conservation area. A canal-side activity centre offers canoeing etc to young people.

St Quintin Estate/Oxford Gardens

This neighbourhood, cut off to the S by the **Westway**, is as distinct in its way as Golborne to the E. Immediately N of the motorway lies the main concentration of family homes. Hundreds of 2-storey, red-brick terraced houses, built between 1890 and 1925, dominate the SW corner, in **Oxford Gardens, Highlever Rd, Balliol Rd, Finstock Rd, Kingsbridge Rd, Kelfield Gardens, St Helen's Gardens, Wallingford Avenue** and the W end of **Barlby Rd**. Most have reasonably sized front and rear gardens and many of the streets are lined with trees. A mix of 3- and 4-bed houses, they are still cheap in Kensington terms: you might pay £425–475,000 for a 4-bed house. Properties are cheaper towards the less accessible north and at the W end of **Oxford Gardens**, where they back onto the fly-over.

Cutting through this enclave is **St Quintin Avenue**, a pleasant tree-lined street, popular despite being a main through-route between **Scrubs Lane** and **Ladbroke Grove**. Pairs of semi-detached brick and pebbledash and red-brick and stucco houses stretch along the avenue from the local shopping centre in **North Pole Rd**. Halfway along on the N side is St Quintin Health Centre and Princess Louise Hospital for the Elderly. Behind the hospital lies Kensington Memorial Park, 5 acres of public open space. **Oakworth Rd, Hill Farm Rd** and **Methwold Rd** N of the park are given over to inter-war council dwellings comprising 2-storey brick houses and flats.

Late-Victorian 3-storey and basement brick and stucco terraces, and 2-storey brick and painted pebbledash houses with timber porches, appear in the N end of tree-lined **Highlever Rd**. More 2-storey pebbledash houses stretch along the W end of **Barlby Rd** into **Dalgarno Gardens** and **Pangbourne Avenue**. At this junction is the new

Blakes Close development of affordable homes with car parking. A small parade of local shops lies at the junction of **Dalgarno Gardens** and **Barlby Rd**. On the W edge of the area, close to the motorway, **Bracewell Rd** has 4-bed houses. An 11-acre former industrial site on the N side of **Barlby Rd** has just been transformed into a massive council and housing association estate with hundreds of people living in shared-ownership and rented 2/3-storey flats and houses. Near where **Barlby Rd** meets **Ladbroke Grove** is the Pall Mall depositary building which is offices. The Shaftesbury Centre and Barlby Hall, two recent additions, house community projects.

The NW corner of the neighbourhood is dominated by the Peabody Trust flat blocks in **Dalgarno Way** and Sutton Dwellings in **Sutton Way**. The latter – the latest part of the borough to have CCTV – flanks Little Wormwood Scrubs, a 22-acre recreation ground just over the borough border in Hammersmith. Also along the N boundary are warehouses/industrial uses and Barlby Rd railway sidings. At the NE end of **Barlby Rd** is **Barlby Gardens**, a small enclave of 2-storey brick and pebbledash houses set back off the road around a tiny green. On the S side of the road is Barlby Primary School. South of the school, between **Ladbroke Grove** and **Exmoor St**, are the council's Treverton and Balfour/Burleigh Estates, built to house returning servicemen from World War II. The estate is one of the most popular in North Kensington with a long-standing, close-knit community. **Exmoor St** and **Hewer St**, between the two estates, have 2-storey late-Victorian houses, mainly 3-bedroom. They go more cheaply because of the warehousing in the area and their proximity to St Charles Hospital, Kensington's general hospital.

The main entrance to the hospital is in **St Charles Square**, which is half made up of private homes and half housing association: 3-storey and basement brick and stucco semi-detached houses converted into flats. Clustered around the square is a Carmelite Monastery, the RC Sion-Manning Girls' School and St Charles 6th-form College plus St Pius X Church.

The most sought-after properties in the neighbourhood lie S of the square in **Chesterton Rd** W, **Bassett Rd** and **Oxford Gardens** (between **St Helen's Gardens** and **Ladbroke Grove**). These were designed for the first railway commuters when the Metropolitan Railway from the Hammersmith and City line opened up North Kensington in the 1860s, linking it to the City.

Both sides of **Chesterton Rd** are linked by 4-storey Victorian terraced houses. The more expensive, leafier **Bassett Rd** has big 4-storey paired and detached brick and stucco houses with front gardens. Many have been split into flats, some large: one, very modern in contrast to the Victorian exterior, was £600,000 last winter for 3 beds. More large semi-detached houses, mostly split into flats and bed-sits, are found in **Oxford Gardens** and **Cambridge Gardens**. Properties here have front gardens and cherry trees line the former, bursting into a cascade of white blossom between April and May. This is the best stretch of **Oxford Gardens**, with big flats and whole houses on offer. The E arms of both streets across **Ladbroke Grove** are more mixed, with a number of council and housing trust properties. Off **Cambridge Gardens** is **Trinity Mews**, a 1988 development of live/work studios.

A handful of streets across to the E of **Ladbroke Grove** link architecturally with the neighbourhood but have little garden space. **Bonchurch St** and **St Michael's Gardens** S are both lined by 3-storey and basement brick and stucco houses converted into flats. The Romanesque-style St Michael of All Angels Church stretches along the N side of the latter, fronting **Ladbroke Grove**. **St Lawrence Terrace** features high Victorian rows, notably 3-storey and basement brick houses with bands of stucco to give a striped effect. Some properties are still unconverted.

Transport   Tubes, all zone 2: Notting Hill Gate (Central, District, Circle); Holland Park (Central); Latimer Road, Ladbroke Grove, Westbourne Park (Hammersmith & City). From Notting Hill Gate: Oxford Circus 10 min, City 20 min, Heathrow 42 min (1 change). Trains: Kensal Green to Liverpool St 30 min. Heathrow Express from Paddington 16 min.

Convenient for   Kensington Gardens, West End, City, A40 to West, Bayswater, Paddington Station (Heathrow Express). BBC Television Centre. Miles from centre: 3.5.

Schools   Local Authority: Sion Manning RC (g). Grant maintained: St Charles 6th-form College (b) (g).

SALES

Flats	S	1B	2B	3B	4B	5B
Average prices	100–150+	130–300	175–500	220–700	250–900	–
Houses	2B	3B	4B	5B	6/7B	8B
Average prices	200–400	280–500+	400–1 M	600–1.5 M	→1.5–3 M	→3 M+

RENTAL

Flats	S	1B	2B	3B	4B	5B
Average prices	200–275	200–350	280–500	350–500+	500–700+	–
Houses	2B	3B	4B	5B	6/7B	8B
Average prices	400–900	450–1200	→700–1600	1000+	2000+	–

The properties   Handsome Victorian terraces and paired villas characterize the area, from the grand white crescents and rows at the Hill's top, smaller brick/stucco streets, to the newly fashionable (and occasionally undone-up) roads down the Hill and in North Kensington, punctuated by council blocks.

The market   Inhabitants are as mixed as the area: young people (rich and not-so-rich) buying the profusion of small flats; Far East investors, media millionaires, the more raffish kind of banker. Flats, mainly converted, are the market staple, though affluent families are moving in to W11 (and politer bits of W10). Cheapest homes at the North Kensington end. Local searches: 10 working days.

Among those estate agents active in this area are:

- John Wilcox
- Marsh & Parsons
- John D Wood
- Foxtons *
- Winkworth *
- Chestertons
- Anscombe & Ringland *
- Jackson-Stops & Staff
- F W Gapp
- Property Fair

- FPDSavills
- Leslie Marsh & Co
- Townends
- Faron Sutaria
- Knight Frank
- Granvilles
- De Groot Collis
- Bushells
- Barnard Marcus

* further details: see advertisers' index on p671

PECKHAM

Map ref: p95 (2H)
Postal districts: SE15, SE22
Boroughs: Southwark (Lab)
Council tax: Band D £809
Conservation areas:
  Several, check with
  town hall
Parking: Residents/
vouchers

You can throw away your street map for large parts of North Peckham: the streets, or rather the decks and alleys of the benighted council estates, have gone. So have the estates – or large chunks of them. In their place are mixed developments of brand-new houses and flats in a recreated 'traditional street pattern'.

Meanwhile, Peckham Rye, the southern half of the area, leapt in price in 1999. It's surprisingly pretty and spacious houses in green surroundings – it has more green spaces than many a more well-thought-of area of London – are increasingly sought out by refugees from pricier tracts further west.

Like next-door Dulwich, Peckham pins its transport hopes on the extension of the East London line. Queen's Road and Peckham Rye stations would gain tube links – if the scheme goes ahead, and not until 2005 (see Transport chapter). Until then, people travel by the (useful and frequent) trains and the (friendly, if slower) buses: the No 12, which wends its way right through the heart of the West End, is a favourite.

The grimy and congested east-west main road – **Peckham Rd/High St/Queen's Rd** – links Camberwell in the W with New Cross in the E and divides the area into its two very different neighbourhoods. One of the original London suburbs for rail-commuting clerical workers, the area was carpeted by many small streets of late-Georgian and Victorian terraces, with grander houses round the green sweep of the Rye's common. Not any more. Much of the north of Peckham was rebuilt following war damage and slum clearance. This is at the root of the sharp contrast between the north and south of Peckham: the southern bit, Peckham Rye, survived. The north was rebuilt.

Sadly, North Peckham's 20th-century reincarnation was an expensive mistake. Ambitious and architecturally daring, boasting all the fashionable clichés of their various dates (between 1955 and 1976) the estates were a social disaster. By 1994, Southwark council had had enough: unemployment and crime were rife, the homes were falling into disrepair when they were inhabited at all. Government money – £60 million – released another £250 million, including private sector cash. North Peckham's rejuvenation under the umbrella of The Peckham Partnership is the largest urban renewal project in the UK. No cosmetic makeover here: they've knocked down 3,000 flats, replacing them with 2,050 traditional houses and flats in good, old-fashioned London streets. Back to where we came in. Two years or so into the scheme, the new streets are graffiti-free and sport neat, flowery front gardens. The last couple of tower blocks are staying: their makeover has won a Royal Institute of British Architects award. They include some of the 1,500 homes being totally refurbished.

Next, turn southwards: by contrast Peckham Rye, across the **High St** and S of the railway, is a surprise. A mature Victorian suburb opens up, sloping away round either side of a pleasant and picturesque common and park. Respectable streets of solid homes have more in common with Dulwich and Forest Hill, their neighbours to the W and SE, than they ever do with Peckham proper on the other side of the tracks.

Much of North Peckham was – until the Partnership got to work – council-owned. Indeed, Southwark at one point had 50,000 council homes, Peckham boasting the biggest concentration. Right to Buy made no progress on these notorious estates. A few Victorian terraces survived amid the concrete, but there was little to rent, except from the council, and less to buy. The Partnership's plans are good news for those who lived in the five benighted estates and have been re-housed, and for newcomers: there are 600 good-value new homes to buy – and more for shared ownership. Those few Victorian streets that escaped the planners have seen their surroundings improve, and their position – just down the road from City and Docklands – reinforced.

Down in Peckham Rye there are plenty of Victorian, and a few Georgian, homes plus a scattering of perfectly habitable council (many now ex-council) homes. Nunhead has a similar mix. Renting from private landlords is on the increase right across the area: good-value prices have seen an influx of investors in the last two years, and tenants like the cheap commuting.

Peckham

The traffic grumbles along **Peckham High St** in a vain attempt to reach the Dover Rd (laughing at bemused foreign drivers is a local sport). On either side, the North Peckham area extends to the **Old Kent Rd** to the NE, the old canal to the N, **Pomeroy St** to the E and **Southampton Way** to the W. The railway line bridging **Rye Lane** forms the most widely accepted frontier with Peckham Rye to the S.

The N part of the neighbourhood ends with the unexpected amenity of Burgess Park, a large green space, complete with lake, carved out of the slum streets by Southwark council over the last quarter of a century. More new parks are emerging in the areas cleared of the giant estates. Near one such park is 'Peckham Village', site of some of the new flats and houses for sale: Laing and Copthorne are among the developers; prices in the current releases start at just over £100,000 for 2-bed homes.

Some parts of North Peckham escaped both the Blitz and the post-war clearance: N of **Queen's Rd** are streets of small terraces such as **Asylum Rd**, which runs from the **Old Kent Rd** to the Queen's Rd station. This also includes some old almshouses, built for retired licensed victuallers (almshouses, especially with alcoholic connections, are a feature of Peckham). Very rarely, one appears for sale: tiny, 1-bed houses. A 1-bed flat in this road was £75,000 last autumn. The streets between **Asylum Rd** and **Meeting House Lane** are similar, with houses and converted flats. **Kings Grove** has some roomy 3-storey flat-fronted houses. Further W, **Friary Rd** boasts some surviving late-Georgian town-houses and to the N **Glengall Rd** too has handsome stucco flat-fronted, raised ground floor houses. Terraced homes to the S of the **Old Kent Rd** can be very good value: a 3-bed Victorian house in **Elcot Avenue** was £120,000 last winter.

The E borders of Peckham, beyond Queen's Rd station, have some quiet if unexciting streets of Victorian terraces such as **Dayton Grove** and **Astbury Rd**. Useful properties, good-value (houses from around £85,000) in a convenient and improving corner. The first developers are discovering this end of Peckham, too: in **Woods Rd**, off **Queen's Rd** to the S and close to Queen's Rd station, Fairclough's Maple Court, a pleasing scheme of 1- and 2-bed flats aimed at first-time buyers, is now priced at £80–110,000. To the E of the station, in **York Grove**, 'The Assembly' is a conversion of a late-Victorian school into 41 1- and 2-bed flats (1-beds £80–112,000).

Peckham High St, at its junction with **Rye Lane**, holds the local shops. There's a mall, the Aylsham Centre, which includes a Safeway (with petrol station) and car park. Partnership money has been lavished on the shopping centre, too. The brand-new 'Peckham Pulse' is just across the high street in **Melon Rd**: two swimming pools, a leisure/fitness centre with gym, hydrospa and café. Alongside, the smart new library in **Peckham Hill St** has just opened.

Back S of the high street and W of **Rye Lane**, a maze of central Peckham streets makes up the most interesting residential corner in this district. There are Victorian terraces and some large detached houses in the conservation areas of **Holly Grove**, **Elm Grove**, **Highshore Rd**, **Bellenden Rd** (handsome flat-fronted cottages) and **Lyndhurst Way** and **Chadwick Rd**, just S of the tracks. **Holly Grove** has some fascinating Georgian houses: 3 beds for £320,000, while **Elm Grove** offers 5-bed double-fronted early-Victorian semis at around £350,000. St James's Gate in **Highshore Rd** is a gated mews with nine new 3-bed houses from £170,000. **Lyndhurst Square** is an interesting 1840s cul-de-sac of gabled, large-gardened houses on the Camberwell borders. **Denman Rd**, to the W, shares the same leafy environment but has later-Victorian purpose-built maisonettes. As well as the nearby park, common green spaces include Warwick Gardens, behind **Lyndhurst Grove**, the gardens in **Holly Grove** and **Elm Grove**.

Peckham Rye

South of the station you are in Peckham Rye. **Choumert Square**, tucked away W of **Rye Lane**, contains some of the smallest, but most desirable, houses in the neighbourhood: tiny 2-beds which sell for £110,000. The immaculately tended trellised rose gardens have won best-kept square awards, and the proud locals open their patios to the public. Nearby **Choumert Rd** has yet more almshouses, an extremely vibrant street market at the E end and some handsome mid-Victorian terraced houses which can fetch £185,000. **Blenheim Grove** – conveniently, if noisily, close to the station – has some recently converted 1-bed flats. Look, too, at the charming little 2-bed early Victorian cottages at this end of neighbouring **Chadwick Rd**.

West of **Peckham Rye** and N of **East Dulwich Rd** is a district of small terraced houses with streets including **Nutbrook St**, **Maxted Rd** and **Bellenden Rd**, **Amott St** and **Ady's Rd**. Some houses in the latter are bigger than they look, having 5 bedrooms, and can be good value. The houses in **Fenwick Rd** are larger still, 3-storey early-Victorian with big bays. Many are flats, thiough one which survives as a 6-bed single home was on the market last winter for £310,000. At the other end of the scale, **Linwood Close** has recent 1- and 2-bed houses. To the W this district shades into East Dulwich (the cheaper end of that select suburb: see the Dulwich chapter).

The clutch of streets round **Nigel Rd** (**Nigel**, **Relf** and **Anstey Rds**) have benefited from a clear-sighted Southwark council scheme to replace roofs and windows, garden walls and fascia detailing – and pay at least 75 per cent of the bill. The result: a smart Victorian street-scape instead of scruffy, ill-maintained houses that the owners could not afford to repair. These roads have some mid-20th century terraces too: £110,000 buys a neat 2-bed version. In contrast, the site of an old pub at the junction of **Peckham Rye** and **East Dulwich Grove** has sprouted 'The Rye Apartments': a dozen smart, modern 1- and 2-bed flats from £85,000–150,000.

Going S, **Rye Lane** suddenly widens and there, for all the world like some small market town, is a little green surrounded by a cluster of shops. Across the **East Dulwich Rd**, Peckham Rye Common and Park open out in a sweep uphill to the S. There is an attractive new development here: 1-, 2- and 3-bed houses and flats with private parking facing the green. Three-bed houses command about £145,000. Opposite, on the other side of the green, there is another pleasant recent development, again 1- and 2-bed flats.

Peckham Rye (the road) divides to run down either side of the common; the E side has some of the area's very few 1930s purpose-built flats (these can start from £70,000 for ex-local authority ones). Here, too, a little Georgiana has survived intact – with 100-ft gardens to supplement the sweeping expanse of common they overlook. These fetch in the region of £350,000. Adjoining the common to the S is Peckham Rye Park, which includes a water garden, rockeries, a beautiful trellised rose garden, a bowling green and duck pond.

Southwards again from the park is the Park Estate: big houses, most Victorian, some 1920/30s. **Colyton Rd** faces N over the park: a road of impeccable suburban style. To the S, wonderfully-named streets like **Mundania Rd**, **Therapia Rd** and **Marmora Rd** boast Victorian semis, and a few detached, with up to 7 bedrooms and prices from £325,000 to half a million. The inhabitants cite their SE22 post code and say they are in Dulwich, really . . .

East of the common and park there are neat flat-fronted terraced houses in streets such as **Somerton Rd** and **Waveney Avenue**. Prices here are lower than on the W side of the common, which is closer to Dulwich: £215,000 for a 4-bed Victorian terraced house. Nearby **Carden Rd** and **Tresco Rd** offer early 19th-century 5-bed semis at around £230,000. Further N and further from the common – but closer to the station – **Consort Rd** has 3-bed ones for £155,000. The **Rye Hill Estate**, originally council, is much privatised: deals range up from 1960s studio flats in leafy grounds at £55,000, and there are larger flats. Streets include **Torridge Gardens** and adjoining **Limes Walk** with their low-rise houses: these are roomy and well-designed, with large bedrooms. The Nunhead Estate of council flats (1930s brick blocks) also overlooks the common.

Nunhead

To the E of Peckham Rye is a neighbourhood of little 2- and 3-bed Victorian houses that run southwards off **Nunhead Lane** and **Evelina Rd**, the latter providing the busy main shopping streets. It's a quiet, tucked-away corner that spreads around the hilly slopes of the romantic, overgrown Nunhead Cemetery and the adjacent park. In the last year Nunhead has attracted attention as buyers appreciate its value and peace.

As with Dulwich and Peckham, there is no tube; however Nunhead too has its own rail station. There is free parking off the main roads, and the main streets have all the shops necessary for day-to-day living – good baker and famous fish-shop included.

The better properties are found S of **Evelina Rd**, on the Rye borders (see above). **St Mary's Rd** has early-Victorian 3-bedroom houses on one side and larger Victoriana on the other. **Machell Rd** has tidy, flat-fronted, 19th-century cottages which fetch some £130,000. Some sheltered homes are appearing here as part of the Peckham Partnership, as is a new mews by Pavilion Developments with town houses for sale. A former college building, listed though 1950s, is to become 'The Pioneer Building': a gallimore scheme of flats and town houses with a fitness centre.

Nunhead also has a fair turnover of ex-council houses, as many former tenants have found it worth their while to buy. **Seldon Rd**, for instance, has unpretentious '60s terraced houses with the benefit of a parking space: 3-beds for £85,000. Ex-council 2-bed houses in **Daniels Rd** have views across to Westminster from the front, across the leafy cemetery behind: £105,000 in November – up £25,000 since May. Like its neighbour Peckham, Nunhead has very few purpose-built flats. However, most of the larger period houses have been made into flats. An old hostel – formerly the Camberwell Workhouse – off **Gordon Rd** was converted into flats in 1996.

The cemetery and the allotments blanket the slopes of a considerable little hill. The triangle E from **Stuart Rd** towards Brockley has several peaceful streets. Agents report that this corner saw dramatic price rises in 1999. **Limesford Rd** and **Harlescott Rd** are late-Victorian cottages which command around £190,000. **Lanbury Rd** has '30s cottage-style council homes: £145,000. The **Ivydale Rd/Kelvington Rd** corner has more of these. Here, too, are waterworks and a golf course. **Brenchley Gardens** bounds the area, from One Tree Hill up towards Brockley with more council homes in a green setting. In a leafy corner at the end of **Brockley Way** behind Camberwell New Cemetery, and well above the railway, are 1998 mews houses by Whelan Homes.

Transport   Trains: Queen's Rd (Peckham), Peckham Rye to London Bridge, Blackfriars, Victoria; Nunhead to Blackfriars, Victoria.

Convenient for   Dulwich, Docklands, South Circular Rd and Elephant & Castle. Tubes at Kennington, Oval, Brixton, New Cross and Elephant & Castle. Miles from centre: 3.

Schools   Local Authority: Warwick Park, St Thomas the Apostle RC (b), Waverley (g), Private: Alleyn's (see also Dulwich chapter).

SALES

Flats	S	1B	2B	3B	4B	5B
Average prices	45–65	65–100	85–150	90–165	125+	—
Houses	2B	3B	4B	5B	6/7B	8B
Average prices	125–175	150–260	180–300	200–400	275+	—

RENTAL

Flats	S	1B	2B	3B	4B	5B
Average prices	100–150	125–175	140–200	160–230	200–275	—
Houses	2B	3B	4B	5B	6/7B	8B
Average prices	100–150	185–275	210–345	230–370	275+	—

The properties   Peckham Rye has pleasant Victorian/Edwardian (a few earlier) terraces and larger family homes, some Georgian, focused on the little green and the common. Flats are mainly conversions. North Peckham is more mixed: large council estates mostly replaced with new houses for sale and to let; some older terraces.

The market   Peckham, in common with other areas in London's SE sprawl, has surprising, nice corners of good homes at some of London's most reasonable – though fast-increasing – prices. These include some pretty terraces. Local searches: 15 working days.

Among those estate agents active in this area are:
- Roy Brooks
- Burnet Ware & Graves
- Kinleigh Folkard & Hayward
- Winkworth *
- Charterhouse
- Acorn
- Ludlow Thompson
- Andrews & Robertson

further details: see advertisers' index on p671

PIMLICO AND WESTMINSTER

Map ref: p77 (5G)
Postal districts: SW1
Boroughs: Westminster (Con)
Council tax: Band D £350
Conservation areas: Several, check with town hall
Parking: Residents/meters

There has been more buzz on the homes scene in Westminster over the past couple of years than at any time in the last century. The last time so many new homes were on the market was during the Edwardian mansion flats boom. Westminster is still known far more for its grand buildings than its homes, although the Georgian front door of its most famous residence, 10 Downing Street, gets more TV coverage than most. It is possible to live in Westminster without being Prime Minister, as many MPs and officials – and City workers – have discovered however, and new developments and cunning conversions are appearing at a brisk pace.

Pimlico, which shares the SW1 postcode, is already almost entirely residential; its long white terraces a hunting-ground for wonderfully central flats and pieds-à-terre either to rent or buy – though family-sized homes are scarce.

Both areas have their own individual presence and charm. While being very much at the centre of things (a main line terminus and major tourist attractions bring their own problems), they have the river and the Royal Parks to bring air and perspective into the city streets. And outside working hours the residential corners can be surprisingly peaceful. Both areas fall within the City of Westminster and are run from City Hall in **Victoria St** – or Oil St, as rude residents called it after the ranks of looming tower blocks, home to oil-company HQs and glass-fronted government offices. During the week **Victoria St** is a canyon of bustling commerce, yet but a few hundred yards away is the quiet of **Vincent Square**, with period houses overlooking a public school's cricket pitch. And a few streets away from Victoria station are the stucco terraces and squares of Pimlico, almost as handsome as Belgravia and a lot less expensive.

Pimlico

Bordered by plush Belgravia and august Westminster, Pimlico, tucked into a bend in the river, remained for a long time remarkably unknown. The social mix of the community changed as, throughout the 1980s, a tenanted and rather run-down district became a place of converted flats and the first smart developments.

This is MP land, full of politicians' pieds-à-terres or main homes within the division bell boundary – the zone close enough to the House for them to rush from dinner, or whatever, to be counted through the lobbies. If you live in one of the streets known for a high political population, watch out for the regular stampede when there's a vote. **Cambridge St** is a typical 'little Westminster': at one count, 25 MPs had homes there. They are joined by City people who love the central location and good transport links.

Pimlico used to be part of the Grosvenor Estate, like Belgravia. Thomas Cubitt, the Estate's architect and builder, laid out the straight streets and regular squares. The land was open, marshy and used for market gardens and pasture. In order to raise the level above the Thames floods, Cubitt with typical ingenuity brought thousands of tons of gravel and earth up by barge from St Katharine's Dock, which he happened to be excavating at the same time. If your Pimlico cellar is damp, remember that it's sitting at original marsh level.

Pimlico may look superficially like Belgravia – lots of snowy Regency stucco, classical detailing and regularity – but it was never quite as smart. During most of the 20th century its tall terraces were the province of the small hotel, the house clumsily divided into bed-sits, the shared bathroom. The Grosvenor Estate sold off the whole area in the 1950s, preferring to concentrate on Belgravia and Mayfair. It was only in the 1972/3 property boom, which coincided with the opening of Pimlico's Victoria line tube station, that Pimlico began to be 'discovered'. The big old homes were converted into smarter flats, the MPs and busy people of all sorts found out how close it is to everything, and Pimlico started to change. The process was helped (though some would claim hindered) by the council's pioneering scheme to ban through traffic. The place is a maze of one-way streets, blocked-off cul-de-sacs and residents' parking bays, and thus remains remarkably peaceful, a place apart, despite being so central.

An average Pimlico property today is a big Cubitt town-house split into flats of varying sizes and sophistication, but usefully including some small, pied-à-terre sized ones. Family houses exist, but this is primarily apartment-land. The network of streets at the heart of Pimlico ('The Grid') are predominantly Cubitt terraces: **Clarendon**, **Cambridge**, **Alderney** and **Sutherland Sts** for example, and **Gloucester**, **Winchester**, **Sussex**, the **Moretons** and the **Westmorelands**; here you can pay £360,000 for a 2-bed maisonette, £750–800,000 for a 4/5-bed house. But even here there are gaps in the stucco and brick, often caused by wartime bombing, which have been at various times filled by small and often ugly blocks of flats. These are less admired ('quite unpleasant' remarked one local agent) than the period conversions.

Other exceptions are the mews cottages both behind the squares and terraces and, occasionally, on the main roads: **Clarendon St** has a few such. Look for the cobbled, sloping charm of **Warwick Square Mews**; **St George's Square** also has its mews, and **Moreton Terrace** boasts two: **North** and **South**. Modern mews houses in **Charlotte Place**, off **Wilton Rd**, go for around £450–500,000. Some houses survived the mania for conversion to flats: try **Cambridge** and **Alderney Sts** and **Westmoreland Terrace**. For new-build, turn to **Buckingham Palace Rd**, 'only 600 metres from Sloane Square' (but also the multi-lane highway from Victoria Station which bounds the area to the N), where Berkeley have added a block of 93 1- to 3-bed flats – plus gym, business centre and parking, which accounts for prices from £320,000.

Pimlico is short of open space, though there's Ranelagh Gardens over on the Chelsea side and the splendid (if rather more public) St James's Park on the other. So the three large garden squares have long been its most desirable addresses – apart from the riverside flats. The big houses in the squares convert readily into spacious flats. **St George's Square** has some interesting recent conversions, and lots of tiny flats and maisonettes; prices vary widely. A 2-bed maisonette in a Grade II house here went for £510,00 last winter; round the corner in **Aylesford St,** which backs onto **St George's Square Mews**, small 2-bed flats start at around £230,000.

The elegant stucco terraces surrounding the gardens make **Eccleston Square**, **Warwick Square** and **St George's Square** hugely attractive – in that order. With an eye to the lack of parks, while the first two have private gardens, those of St George's and **Bessborough Gardens** are both open to the public.

The only new London square to be created since the war, **Bessborough Gardens** is part of the Crown's Millbank Estate. The gardens (locked at night) have a fountain in honour of the Queen Mother's 80th birthday. The L-shaped terrace surrounding the garden on two sides is classic Cubitt: the smooth stucco finish, decorative iron-work balconies, the mouldings of windows and pillared doorways . . . or so you might think: but these rows didn't exist until the late '80s! The Wimpey-built replacements of war- and flood-damaged terraces for the Crown Estate have provided a cache of new flats and penthouses, from studio to 3-bedroomed. The detailing inside matches the exterior, and on occasion the sales team had trouble convincing buyers that the apartments really were new (recent price for a 2-bed, 2-bath example, £400,000). Much more development has followed on the Crown Estate: next door to **Bessborough Gardens** and sharing its entrance in **Drummond Gate**, is **Lindsay Square** which has 29 new town-houses. In **Balvaird Place**, just opposite Pimlico tube station, there are 40 2- to 4-bed town-houses with garages.

The main road along the riverside is **Grosvenor Rd**; it does not hug the embankment, however, and wherever it bends slightly inland a waterside development has been squeezed in. The most successful of these is Crown Reach, which lies just W of Vauxhall Bridge, past a former office block (see below) and an undistinguished earlier flats block. Its jutting, staggered riverside gives the maximum light, privacy and unimpeded views to its apartments and their balconies, while the landward side's sweeping gull's-wing roofs have become a landmark. The 22-storey office tower at the corner by the bridge has become 'The Panoramic', which is accurate enough as a name. It has 88 flats which range in size (from studios) and price (from c. £225,000) up to a glorious 2-floor penthouse. Other plush and pricey waterfront blocks include River Lodge, parked on a narrow site almost in front of **Dolphin Square**, and St George's Wharf, which appeared in 1990. These have been joined by the Belvederes, with 43 apartments and penthouses (2-beds, c. £270,000-plus). The list goes on: another 40, plus a house, to come over the next year at Eagle Wharf.

P

Lupus St runs E–W, a wide busy road paralleling **Warwick Way**, the other main cross-route to the N. At the W end of Lupus St is the Churchill Gardens Estate, a tidy, modern square of blocks (many with splendid river views) owned by Westminster City Council. Here, too, are local shops (and estate agents). At the E end, the splendidly uncompromising modern lines of Pimlico School are reticent in one thing only: the mass of the 'glass school', as it is generally known, stands, amid its playground, considerably below the level of the surrounding streets. Unfortunately, equally uncompromising repair costs have led to the council's desire to tear it down and build a new school, plus 170 luxury flats to pay for it. The unholy row over this goes on.

Beyond the school rises the riverside, red-brick mass of **Dolphin Square**. A huge '30s flats development, it was at the time of its building the biggest in Europe. Its 1,200 flats surrounding a private courtyard are half rented, half privately owned (on fairly short leases). It is large enough to form a complete community, with its own shops, garage, pub and restaurant: the latter, open to non-residents, overlooks the indoor pool.

To the E along **Vauxhall Bridge Rd** are the low-built red-brick steps of Lillington and Longmore Gardens, with their roof gardens, third-storey trees and terraces: council built, and better-looking than many a private development. Many tenants both here and at Churchill Gardens bought their homes, which appear on the resale market far cheaper than other Pimlico properties (studio flat, Longmore Gardens, c. £90,000). On **Peabody Avenue** and the wonderfully named **Turpentine Lane**, and further E towards **Vauxhall Bridge Rd**, are two estates of red-brick rented flats run by the Peabody charitable trust.

Behind Lillington Gardens the irregular meander taken by **Tachbrook St**, contrasting with Cubitt's orderly grid, betrays its earlier origins. This is Pimlico's village high street, complete with not only shops but a thriving, much-prized street market. To the N it joins **Warwick Way** (once a track through the marshes), and to its W lies **Belgrave Rd**: largely unreconstructed Pimlico, this. It is a main through-route to Victoria and is still full of cheap hotels, although recent years have seen a quickening of the pace of change in **Belgrave Rd** as more of these are converted into flats. Residents are lobbying hard for the road, which is a busy route that parallels **Vauxhall Bridge Rd** (now to be red-routed), to have traffic-calming measures; those living on or near **Vauxhall Bridge Rd** feel equally strongly that **Belgrave Rd** should be red-routed too, and take its share of the traffic: watch this space.

Westminster

Westminster is once more climbing the scale of visibility as a place to own a home. Some big blocks have been done up, and new developments have added smart flats. Indeed SW1, with more than 500 new homes completed during 1999, is one of the busiest central post codes. That said, it is still true that homes are a secondary matter here: Westminster is first and foremost the home of Parliament and the Civil Service. The nearest shopping facilities are either over in **Tachbrook St**, or in **Victoria St**, which boasts the Army and Navy store and Sainsbury's. Westminster shopping does have one saving grace, however: the excellent morning street market in **Strutton Ground**.

Tucked away in side roads there are homes that can be peaceful, considering their centre-hub position; the most plentiful are the mansion blocks whose brickwork echoes the Roman Catholic Cathedral. But there are also, by contrast, modern flats, a few neat terraced homes and a little cache of unsuspected Georgiana. The last couple of years have seen Vincent Square re-emerge as a residential neighbourhood.

Westminster the place – as opposed to the borough – starts across the **Vauxhall Bridge Rd** from Pimlico, and runs up to St James's Park in the N. The stretch between the park and the river is home mainly to the Ministries of this or that along Whitehall. **Downing St** boasts only temporary accommodation: sheltering, strictly for their terms of office, the Prime Minister and the Chancellor of the Exchequer. The riverside holds the only other exception: the fantastical turrets of **Whitehall Court**, where you can pay a small fortune for a very short lease: views of the river and the Changing of the Guard. Some of the flats are enormous – up to 5 bedrooms.

Mansion flats are the staple form of the homes that lie between the main through-road, **Victoria St**, and St James's Park. Vandon Court in **Petty France**, for example, offers a range from studios upwards. This corner has hidden delights, though: glorious **Queen Anne's Gate**, where the stately houses date from the reign of that monarch and are nearly all wasted as offices (even if one is the National Trust HQ). Near Victoria station lies tiny, hidden **Victoria Square**: its homes date from 1838. And a stone's throw from the Palace, off **Buckingham Gate**, a small 1796 house in **Strafford Place** was £1.1 million last year. (A 1-bed mansion flat in the same street cost £217,000.)

But the bulk of Westminster's homes lie S of **Victoria St**. Again at the end nearest the station, Edwardian mansion flats are the norm. The first ultra-smart '80s block was built in **Artillery Row**. **Morpeth Terrace** and **Carlisle Place** are typical of this corner, both lined with similar red-brick blocks. Inside, the flats are impressive: large rooms, high ceilings; entrance halls with shining wood panelling and crusty uniformed porters. Nearby is a cache of new homes with that most covetable asset, garaging: the Crown Estate has developed adjoining sites in **Old Pye St** and **Abbey Orchard St** – 1- and 2-bed flats and penthouses. In **Ashley Gardens**, near the station, 32 flats in one mansion block were refurbished and sold to 'traditional British buyers' – perhaps the great-grandsons of the Empire types who bought these flats to be near 'The Stores' and their West End clubs. Across in **Marsham St** , Marsham Court is one of the best-known of the 1930s blocks: a short walk from the Houses of Parliament, MPs queue for these convenient mansion flats (2-bed, 3rd floor: £247,000. A similar sized modern flat in the 1993 Octavia House: £279,000).

The area's largest current development has appeared on the old Westminster Hospital site around **St John's Gardens** in the angle of **Marsham St** and **Horseferry Rd**. This has 186 luxury flats; a 1-bed last winter, £200,000. In nearby **Page St** is the chequerboard frontage of the listed, Luytens-designed Grosvenor Estate flats, built as affordable housing between the wars: homes here are still more modestly priced (2-bed, £155,000).

Albeit tree-lined, street succeeds street until, crossing **Rochester Row**, the vast green rectangle of **Vincent Square** surprisingly opens up. Some houses are lucky enough to overlook this open space – larger than **Belgrave Square** – used as a playing-field by the boys of Westminster School. Watching the summer cricket is an increased population of Square-dwellers: three big developments have been added here. At No 87, Berkeley's 24 1- to 3-bed flats, duplexes and penthouses: Vincent House, a refurbished 'NY-style period building' with 39 flats and town-houses (the latter £535,000): The Atrium, a 6-storey building, locally controversial for its height, priced from £400,000 (2-bed, no view) to a £700,000 penthouse.

It is towards Westminster Abbey that the oldest buildings are found. These include the Georgian gems of **Smith Square, Lord North St** and surrounding streets. Some have been lost, some serve other purposes (such as the Conservative Central Office), but some are still enviable homes: a 1722 gem in **Cowley St** (with a garage) was £950,000 last autumn. In **Rochester Row**, 24 new 1- to 3-bed flats and duplexes were added in 1998. Between **Vincent Square** and **Horseferry Rd** is **Maunsel St**, a pretty terrace of brick cottages with gardens. Rowan House and Stockton Court are two recent blocks of 2-bed flats in **Greycoat St**. A new development called Greycoat House added 30 more 2- and 3-bed flats.

Some of the Edwardian blocks in Westminster are being refurbished, and other blocks have moved from rental to sale. Gladstone Court in **Regency St** is four red-brick blocks surrounding a central inner courtyard. Regalian's 1988 conversion resulted in 52 luxury apartments sharing a fitness complex. Alice House in **Douglas St** was another block to get the 5-star treatment in 1987. Back in **Regency St**, Regency Court is a modern 6-storey block with basement parking (2-bed balcony flat, £270,000); close by are three new mews houses in a courtyard, plus an office building with three penthouse flats. In the same street is a new courtyard with 10 flats and a single house. Artillery Mansions, on **Victoria St**, has been extensively done up last year to create 174 flats – studios to 3-bed – around two courtyards with fountains. A site between **Marsham St** and **Tufton St** has been redeveloped as Millicent Court, with 36 flats and three houses around a communal garden and with underground parking.

The other source of Westminster homes can be found in the southernmost corner, towards Vauxhall Bridge. En route, in **John Islip St**, is Millbank Court convenient '60s flats: high ones get river views. The far end of **John Islip St**, and the streets surrounding it in the angle of the river and **Vauxhall Bridge Rd**, form the Westminster side of the Crown's Millbank Estate. There are neat terraced houses in **Ponsonby Place** (a 4-bed, period stucco-fronted house, £695,000) and **Ponsonby Terrace**, and beautiful converted apartments in the river-facing white stucco **Millbank** terraces (the stretch culminating in the Paolozzi leaping dancer statue was painstakingly restored and converted by Rosehaugh). The Crown's houses are a mixture of fair-rent homes and others available, when they come up, on long leases.

Transport	Tubes, all zone 1: Pimlico (Victoria); Victoria (Victoria, District, Circle); Westminster, St James's Park (Circle, District). From Victoria: Oxford Circus (5 min), City 20 min, Heathrow 1 hr (1 change).
Convenient for	West End and City; airports. Miles from centre: 1.5.
Schools	Local Authority: Pimlico School, Grey Coat Hospital C of E (g). Private: Francis Holland (g), Westminster School (b), The American International School.

SALES

Flats	S	1B	2B	3B	4B	5B
Average prices	95–200	140–350	180–500	220–750	400–2 M+	—
Houses	2B	3B	4B	5B	6/7B	8B
Average prices	300–625	400–800	500–950	600–1.5 M	700–2 M	—

RENTAL

Flats	S	1B	2B	3B	4B	5B
Average prices	150–300	200–400	250–700	300–850	350–1000	—
Houses	2B	3B	4B	5B	6/7B	8B
Average prices	—	500–900	600–1000	700–2000	—	—

The properties	Regency stucco terraces, now mainly flats; mews cottages; p/b flats in Dolphin Square; ultra-mod or repro schemes (the best repro indistinguishable from the outside), and council blocks. Westminster has mainly mansion flats (some very large), plus a few 19th-century and Georgian houses: look here for new schemes and conversions since Westminster, long overlooked as a place to live, is once more in the spotlight.
The market	Young professionals can buy or rent here; also MPs and pied-à-terre seekers; they find some imaginative conversions of Pimlico's stucco houses into flats. Quality, though, varies widely depending on vintage: Pimlico's rise from down-at-heel bed-sit land to high fashion began in the '70s. Local searches: 10 working days.

Among those estate agents active in this area are:

- Tuckerman
- Dauntons
- Knight Frank
- Bensons
- Barnard Marcus
- Winkworth *
- Hamptons
- Chestertons
- FPDSavills
- Jackson Stops & Staff
- Cluttons
- DTZ Debenham Thorpe
- Best Gapp & Cassells

* further details: see advertisers' index on p671

POPLAR

Map ref: p64 (6D)
Postal districts: E14
Boroughs: Tower Hamlets (Lab)
Council tax: Band D £674
Conservation areas: Include
  York Square, Naval Row
Parking: Restricted

The Docklands revolution changed more than the economy and population of London's East End. It changed the names, too. Poplar, once a little village, grew in 1817 into a parish and took in the Isle of Dogs and Blackwall. The docks came, and with them tens of thousands of workers. From 1900 to 1964 Poplar blossomed as a proud if prickly borough, although World War II and its savage bombings had left but half the population and few indeed of the buildings. Its town hall ruled Bow – until Tower Hamlets subsumed them both.

Then came the 1980s, London Docklands Development Corporation and the Isle of Dogs Enterprise Zone. Much of Poplar's territory was lost: its name became little used as the incoming residents of the mushrooming new Docklands developments (for these, see the Docklands chapter) said that they lived 'on the Isle of Dogs' or 'at Limehouse'. The West India Docks, which once formed a boundary to the S, have been replaced by the new highway of **Aspen Way**, which funnels traffic in and out from the City via the Limehouse Tunnel.

As Docklands becomes an historical chapter rather than a place, the old neighbourhoods re-emerge – and Poplar is a place once more, back to its roots as a village around its inland **High St**. Although the greater proportion of homes in traditional Poplar and Limehouse were built by the council at a less-than-lovely point in architectural history, now the place is a-buzz with construction – and this time it's not smart schemes for City whiz-kids. The refurbishment of the many blocks of flats is slowly spreading through the area, under the HARCA Estate Renewal Challenge Fund: it makes quite a difference to the feel of the place, especially in areas like **Selsey St** and **Thomas Rd** (see below). Quite a few flats have been bought by their tenants in the last decade, and these now appear on the market, offering bargain alternatives to the astronomical world to the S. (The ultra-smart dock and riverside developments that have sprung up since the '80s are dealt with fully in the Docklands chapter.)

Poplar and Limehouse are within two miles of the City of London. With no tube station in the vicinity – Bromley-by-Bow and Mile End are the nearest – the opening of the Docklands Light Railway (DLR) gave the area a much-needed boost. Limehouse, Westferry, Poplar and All Saints stations provide a regular service to Stratford (interchanges with trains and tube), Bank and Tower Gateway, and the Royal Docks for the City Airport to the E. And now the DLR also connects, at Canary Wharf, with the Jubilee line, opened just about in time for the Millennium.

Poplar and Limehouse are bordered by the Isle of Dogs to the S, Bow to the N and Stepney to the W. To the E of Poplar is the Blackwall Tunnel Northern Approach motorway. **East India Dock Rd** is the area's main thoroughfare. The enormous (and expensive) road-building programme linked to the Docklands regeneration has given the area several new roads: make sure your street map is an up-to-date one. The main highway is the E–W dual carriageway from the City via Limehouse Tunnel, on across the S edge of Poplar, then over a new bridge across the River Lea to the Royal Docks; N–S is the **Blackwall Tunnel Approach Rd,** and a fast link out of town via the M11. This lot has eased the chaos on the **East India Dock Rd.**

The docks were the main source of employment, Poplar's *raison d' etre*, until the '60s, and a large part of the fascinating history of Poplar and Limehouse. The area includes six conservation areas – **York Square** close to the border with Stepney, St Anne's Church, St Matthias Church, All Saints Church, **Naval Row** and **Narrow St.** One of Poplar's attractions is lively **Chrisp St** market, which is part of the Lansbury Estate, named after Labour Party stalwart George Lansbury. It is one of the more appealing parts of Poplar, with a true small-town atmosphere. Sadly the restaurants of Chinatown are now for the most part a distant memory.

Poplar

The Lansbury Estate, which includes **Chrisp St** market, is one of Poplar's more attractive parts. The Estate, built in the early '50s, comprises much of the district to the N of the busy **East India Dock Rd.** Apart from the market and shopping area, there's a good health centre and the Every Theatre. **Duff St, Grundy St, Susannah St** and **Ida St** have much-improved terraced ex-council houses. Houses in **Bygrove St,** N of **Grundy St,** are split into maisonettes and flats with roof gardens. Some of the newer town-houses and terraced houses in **Brabazon St, Carmen St** and at the N end of **Chrisp St** have been purchased from the council by their owners and tastefully improved. So, too, have smart terraced houses with very attractive small gardens in **Giraud St,** and flats and maisonettes in **Hobday St** and **Cordelia St,** which has Poplar Boys Club on its corner next to the Young Prince pub and Susan Lawrence Primary School halfway down.

Quite a lot is happening on the Lansbury Estate: 38 houses and flats in **Broomfield St,** plus 24 more flats for rent, have been refurbished here; and Bellway Homes have added six large houses and a dozen 3-bed flats. Busbridge House in **Brabazon St** is being modernized: phase I is due to be finished this March.

To the W of the Lansbury Estate, the towering St Mary's and St Michael's Roman Catholic Church, opposite Mayflower Primary School, is flanked by more terraced ex-council houses in **Canton St** and **Pekin Close** which take their names from the nearby area once known as Chinatown. North of **Canton St,** with its neat gardens, is St Philip Howard Roman Catholic Mixed Comprehensive School and then Bartlett Park, a rare stretch of greenery.

Down at the S end of **Chrisp St**, on the S side of **East India Dock Rd**, is the DLR's All Saints station. The station sits between the two conservation areas of All Saints Church and St Matthias Church. The grounds of All Saints Church are overlooked by some of Poplar's most desirable private homes: imposing 3- and 4-storey Victorian terraced houses in **Newby Place** and **Mountague Place**. Similar houses can be found to the W in **Woodstock Terrace** facing the very well-tended, and well-used, Poplar recreation ground, which houses Poplar Bowls Club's green, and the entrance to St Matthias Church. In Hale St, overlooking the recreation ground, the 1890s Mission to Seamen – a splendid piece of neo-Jacobean red-brick – has become 'York House': 12 flats, of which the five remaining last Autumn were priced at £175–240,000.

South of **Woodstock Terrace** and **Newby Place** lies **Poplar High St**, with council flats on each side. The area along Poplar High St has gained from the road-building to the S. It is now quiet, and an increasingly desirable place to live. The refurbished council flats of the Will Crooks Estate and the new Tower Hamlets College (very high standards) are among local successes. Next to the college a sports centre, the Workhouse Leisure Centre, was opened last year. The Church Housing Association owns much of the S side of the street, but there are 24 new flats in Stoneyard Lane, very convenient for Poplar DLR station. Several ongoing developments of flats and business units are taking place in **Poplar High St**.

On eastwards, beyond the Blackwall Tunnel highway in its cutting, is **Naval Row**, another conservation area. Pre-war flats here have been modernized: new leases on the 2-bed flats were marketed after conversion. The old Poplar power station has gone to make way for part of **Aspen Way**, the new E–W highway. Near the Blackwall Tunnel entrance, Copthorne Homes have added some flats and houses, and other schemes are afoot.

The Blackwall Tunnel N–S motorway is flanked to the W by the still-run-down Teviot Estate: some of the blocks that were derelict and abandoned last year – such as Mount Everest, in the corner of **Everest Place** and **Zetland St** – have been demolished. However, **Daniel Bolt Close**, with its '60s-built 3-storey terraced houses, is popular with buyers.

Bright St, **Byron St**, **Burcham St** and **Hay Currie St** are dominated by Langdon Park School and a sports centre and social club. **Byron St** also includes The Germans pub (it used to be called the Duke of Wellington).

A redundant church in **St Leonard's Rd** has become St Michael's Court, a clutch of 34 smart flats – including a very desirable one in the church tower. Opposite, on the edge of Langdon Park, are a dozen new houses. Further up **St Leonard's Rd** a pub has become six flats. These, together with the former church conversion, form a pleasant group – though the shops facing the church stand empty at present.

East of the motorway are some of Poplar's worst properties. The area is still rather out-of-the-way and run-down. The flats in Oban House, **Oban St**, have been refurbished, and there's a development of 14 1-, 2- and 3-bed flats for shared ownership in **Blair St**. Both streets also have terraced houses. Canning Town Bridge over Bow Creek provides Poplar's eastern boundary with Newham.

In the N of the area, **St Paul's Way** marks the boundary with Bow. The steady work on local council-built homes continues on the Burdett Estate, which stretches S to Limehouse Cut through **Wallwood St**, **Burgess St**, **Selsey St** and **Thomas Rd** where small industrial units can be found on the S side. The Poplar HARCA scheme is refurbishing 186 flats for completion this summer.

Limehouse

Limehouse, to the W of the area, is the corner that has seen the greatest renaissance as the Limehouse Basin became part of 'Docklands', and was surrounded by enviable new waterside homes – and as the road tunnel beneath it was at last completed. Limehouse has not only kept hold of its romantic name (though nowadays London's Chinatown is to be found at Leicester Square), but is indeed expanding somewhat. The Limehouse Cut, the canal which runs from Limehouse up between Poplar and Bow to the River Lea, has seen several smart waterside developments following the Docklands example. Although these are thought of as Limehouse, the original area lies largely to the W of **Burdett Rd/West India Dock Rd**.

The N end of **West India Dock Rd** is flanked by Barley Mow council estate, and there is a stark contrast as the Estate sweeps down to very expensive, fashionable **Narrow St**, whose riverside houses were among the first to be 'discovered' by West End artists and politicians. Now the Limehouse Link tunnel entrance affects the W end of the street. This is a conservation area and is covered in greater detail in the Docklands chapter. W leads to **The Highway** and Tower of London.

West India Dock Rd continues to the N across **East India Dock Rd** into **Burdett Rd**, where some of the larger properties on either side have been converted into split-level flats. W of **Burdett Rd** are the council homes of **Turners Rd**, **Clemence St**, **Dora St** and **Norbiton Rd** which all lead into **Salmon Lane** – where some delightful Victorian houses can be found on either side at the W end (Mercers Estate).

This corner, too, is seeing a lot of redevelopment. The top of **Turners Rd** is closed due to a large housing scheme in progress, and there are more houses under construction between **Turners Rd** and **Clemence St**. **Dora St** has eight flats and seven houses under way, completing this summer. Twenty-three large flats were added to **Salmon Lane** last year. Attractive Victorian properties are found S of **Salmon Lane** in **Barnes St** and **York Square**, a conservation area, as well as **Flamborough St** which includes the Queens Head pub. The Grade II-listed houses in **Barnes St** command premium prices. In **Wakeling St** 11 new houses have appeared. This is a favoured corner, with real character.

The southern end of **Barnes St** leads into busy **Commercial Rd**, almost opposite the Limehouse DLR station. Further E along **Commercial Rd** is St Anne's Church which is another conservation area. **Aston St** is Limehouse's western boundary with Stepney while the northern boundary with Bow is **Rhodeswell Rd**, which includes East London Stadium with its football pitch and athletics track and open-air concerts.

Where Limehouse Cut canal passes under **Burdett Rd** is Limehouse Court, a new canalside development (built in 1990) in **Dod St** with 50 homes and 50 commercial units. Further along the canal, Enterprise Works in **Hawgood St** uses the Limehouse name despite being in E3. The courtyard development consists of work-homes, ranging from 4-storey houses to 1-bedroom flats. And further E at the **Morris Rd** bridge, 'The Limehouse Cut', a big 4-phase conversion of warehouses into work-homes, sold in shell finish, proved successful in the late '80s.

Further S, there is lots happening around the Westferry DLR station on the edge of the Isle of Dogs. **Grenade St** has the Compass Point development, with flats to rent, and Compass Point West with 1- and 2-bed flats by Furlong Homes. In **West India Dock Rd** is a new Peabody Trust development; and in the same corner the old Limehouse Church Hall is now flats to let by the Quality Street Company. The Peabody Trust are working on 1- and 2-bed flats for rent on **West India Dock Rd/Gill St**.

Transport	Docklands Light Railway: Limehouse, Westferry, Poplar, All Saints. Trains: Limehouse.
Convenient for	Docklands, City, rail interchange at Stratford, Fenchurch St. Routes East. Blackwall Tunnel to South. Miles from centre: 4.5.

Schools   Local Authority: Langton Park, St Paul's Way, St Philip Howard RC.

SALES

Flats	S	1B	2B	3B	4B	5B
Average prices	55–70	65–80	75–90	85–100	–	–
Houses	2B	3B	4B	5B	6/7B	8B
Average prices	100–130	120–150	150–200+	175–250	–	–

RENTAL

Flats	S	1B	2B	3B	4B	5B
Average prices	95–180	100–180	145–250	160–300	–	–
Houses	2B	3B	4B	5B	6/7B	8B
Average prices	150–300	190–450	250–450	–	–	–

The properties   Warehouse conversions and work-homes plus new flats schemes: prices below Docklands, but well above existing local homes, which are largely 2/3-bed flats and maisonettes, many of them ex-council. Studios and big houses are scarce.

The market   The lower end of the flats price scale represents ex-council sales; exceptions at top end are the new canalside schemes, and the occasional listed home around Salmon St. Riverside Narrow St, annexed by Docklands (see Docklands chapter), is not included here. Local searches: 2–4 weeks.

Among those estate agents active in this area are:

- Alex Neil
- W J Meade
- FPDSavills
- McDowalls
- Keatons *

further details: see advertisers' index on p671

P

PUTNEY AND ROEHAMPTON

Map ref: p91 (4G)
Postal districts: SW15
Boroughs: Wandsworth (Con)
Council tax: Band D £369
Conservation areas: Include Dover House Estate, Putney Embankment, Parkfields
Parking: Residents/meters

With the River Thames, Putney Heath, Putney and Wimbledon Commons and Richmond Park bordering the area, Putney offers much to the dog- and child-owning classes. Younger flat-dwellers find plenty of homes for sale and (increasingly) to rent, and find the **High St** useful for shopping and entertainment. Tubes take you to Fulham, and on to Sloane Square for the shops and the West End. There's a train line to Waterloo, which is handy for the City. Most Putneyites, however, struggle around by car.

The majority of Putney houses are substantial late-Victorian and Edwardian properties built for the middle classes and those who aspired to that status. The social mix has not changed much. Good schools and plenty of parks make this a natural next step for Fulham and Battersea flat-dwellers setting up their family home.

The huge number of flat conversions in East and central Putney, plus the many mansion blocks and a sprinkling of new developments, attract the younger buyers; families look further south and west within the area. Five- and six-bedroom houses are, if not the norm, certainly not unusual – particularly in West Putney, which has one of the biggest concentrations in London. Wandsworth Council was a pioneer of the selling off of council homes, and the large areas they once owned are now widely private. These ex-council homes, many near Putney Heath, offer a cheaper buy for newcomers to the area. You don't have to be someone in the City to afford a SW15 postcode. Indeed, the postcode takes in Roehampton, whose enormous blocks of council-built flats gazing out over Richmond Park are now partly private.

Putney people are sworn enemies of property developers and people who cut down trees or build unsuitable extensions to their homes. As a result, the machinations of those trying to get onto committees of the astonishingly active Putney Society, an 'illegal' tree-felling, or the council's latest bid to solve the area's traffic problems are major topics of conversation. The problem of getting a daughter into Putney High School also provides a fruitful source of local debate. Most Putney residents pay a Commons Rate (seldom more than £10–15 a year) towards the maintenance of Putney Common, Putney Heath and Wimbledon Common. Each of these commons has its own special character. Putney Heath is wild and much is heavily wooded, while Putney Lower Common is old meadow-land with a few spinneys and hosts a fair in May and the annual 'country' Putney Show each summer. Richmond Park, which marks the borough boundary, is glorious for walking, cycling and horse-riding with livery and riding stables at Roehampton Gate and Robin Hood Gate.

At the heart of Putney is the traffic-choked **High St**, which boasts some surprisingly good shopping, including multiples like Sainsbury's, BHS and Marks & Spencer. The Putney Exchange mall has Waitrose and several more chain stores. There is a cinema (ABC) at the junction of the **High St** and **Putney Bridge Rd**. An ever-increasing number of bars and restaurants line the **High St**, which is noticeably busy in the evenings.

The **High St** sweeps down the hill to Putney Bridge, with its handsome lamp-posts and the riverside parish church. St Mary's is sadly dwarfed by towering, slab-sided office blocks – but St George are hoping for permission for a scheme that would ameliorate the 16 floors of the ICL tower with a rounded, galleried extension: this would add almost 100 flats and a restaurant to this bleak waste of waterfront. Over a year of wrangling has yet to produce a plan locals and the council will accept. West of the bridge on this corner of **Lower Richmond Rd** and the **Embankment**, a boat-shaped modernist restaurant (very non-Putney) gets spectacular river views.

Every area in London has it own special problem. In Putney, that problem is the motor car. **Putney Bridge** and **Upper Richmond Rd** act as a magnet for commuters from across the whole of South and West London (anything to avoid the Wandsworth one-way system) and the result is monumental traffic jams during rush hours. The three-year closure of Hammersmith Bridge did not help. Traffic jams mean rat-running: 'traffic calming' measures, one-way streets and parking restrictions proliferate. Hammersmith Bridge is now open again, but a bitter row has developed about whether buses should have priority. Wandsworth Council, attentive to the anguished cries from traffic-choked Putney, wants it fully open to cars. The councils at either end of the bridge, keen to cut car commuting, want buses to have the whip hand.

Rail commuters are well catered for with the District line tube via Putney Bridge on the Fulham side of the river, or East Putney (**Upper Richmond Rd**); and rail into Waterloo from Putney (High St) or Barnes.

Anybody considering buying a house in Putney — especially in West Putney or Thamesfield — should perhaps first read Jilly Cooper's *The Common Years*. The book caused severe offence to a number of Putney notables (not to mention those who walked their dogs with Mrs Cooper) but it remains a remarkably accurate reflection on aspects of life in Putney . . . a sort of conservative Hampstead.

Thamesfield

This little wedge-shaped area lies between the river and the **Lower Richmond Rd** to the W of **Putney Bridge**, running W to Putney Hospital and the common. Generally, prices here are slightly lower than in West Putney, with smaller, cottage-style, late-Victorian terraces predominant. There are also pockets of older Regency and early Victorian houses — and a few exceptionally large houses around Putney Common.

Lower Richmond Rd runs from **Putney High St** along the length of Thamesfield to Putney Common, where it meets **Queens Ride**. There are small parades of shops sufficient for day-to-day needs strung along it, as well as a leavening of smart restaurants, bars and antique shops. Estate agents cluster thickly here, avid for gossip no doubt. The road carries through-traffic from Richmond and Barnes, but does not suffer as severely as **Upper Richmond Rd** — which forms part of the South Circular. One-way streets and other such barriers curb rat-running. There are mainly terraced houses on **Lower Richmond Rd**, although there are some Victorian detached and semi-detached villas set well back: notably attractive are Nos 139–144.

West from **Putney High St** are three large Victorian mansion blocks — Star and Garter Mansions, Kenilworth Court and University Mansions. Most but not all of the flats have river views, although you may need to crane your neck. Some flats in Star and Garter Mansions and Kenilworth Court may suffer noise from the nearby pubs. Expect to pay £320,000 for a 3-bed flat in Kenilworth Court (up £50,000 in a year). Among the mansion blocks are some council-built flats, such as those in **The Platt**: some come onto the market and offer a good location at reasonable prices.

The roads leading off **Lower Richmond Rd** towards the river tend, in the main, to be smaller mid- and late-Victorian terraced cottages, some purpose-built maisonettes and flats. **Ruvigny Gardens**, which forms a loop off **Lower Richmond Rd**, features larger 3-storey Victorian terraced houses; some now converted to flats, some backing on to the **Embankment**, with gates at the end of the garden for launching your boat. Don't skimp on surveys close to the river: problems with settlement have been reported among properties in Putney which stand very near the Thames.

Festing Rd is one of the most popular streets in this area, with 4-bed houses at about £450,000. Some of its homes are purpose-built Victorian flats and maisonettes. It runs down to **Putney Embankment** and its boathouses. By the junction is Leader's Gardens, a small, attractive park with tennis courts and play area. Popular **Ashlone Rd**, a street of mid-Victorian terraces, also leads down to Leader's Gardens. Adjoining **Ashlone Rd** is **Stockhurst Close**, a small council development of flats, some with river views. **Pentlow St** features attractive Victorian houses, mainly 3-bed houses, some semi-detached. A 4-bed house in this street would make £400,000 or thereabouts. A 2-bed reached £350,000 – but it was very special inside and had starred in a glossy magazine. **Sefton St** offers small Victorian terraces leading to **Horne Way**, inter-war blocks of council-built flats backing onto sports grounds. **Commondale**, overlooking Putney Hospital and Common, is a row of 2-bed cottages, some flat-fronted. The prettiest ones were built in the 1870s to house the 'deserving poor' with money provided by Putney Pest House and wealthy benefactors. In **Danemere St** an infill development, Waters Place, has added a dozen 3- and 4-bed town-houses, now selling at up to £430,000; while the Victorian ones command about £380,000.

There are plenty of flats above shops on **Lower Richmond Rd**. **Putney Embankment** has few homes available — they are generally tied to the boathouses and rowing clubs which line the river. Ruvigny Mansions, a small Victorian block, has spacious flats, most with river views. It is inadvisable to leave cars parked on the Embankment owing to the tide's unfortunate habit of rising above road level. This is, however, popular with local garages called upon to repair the damage.

Lower Richmond Rd to Upper Richmond Rd

On the other (S) side of **Lower Richmond Rd** from **Commondale** is **Putney Common**, a tiny no-through-road used as a turn-around point for the No 22 bus, which terminates here. Past the pub on the corner of **Lower Richmond Rd** are three cottages, then late '60s flats (Commonview) backed by a builders' merchant's yard, then All Saints' primary school and church. A path leads through into **Egliston Mews** and **Egliston Rd**.

Lower Common South is a road of huge detached houses, mainly 1870s–80s, mainly red-brick and wonderfully ornate, set well back from the road and overlooking Putney Common — this is one of the very rare 'common' views not to be spoiled by heavy traffic. Residents should stay away one weekend a year — during the Putney Show. These homes are very, very rarely for sale – when they do prices are around £1.5 million. **Chester Close** and **Sherwood Court**, off **Lower Common South**, have small, attractive, late-'70s 'traditional' 3-bed town-houses.

Egliston Rd (Jilly Cooperland) has vast mid- and late-Victorian detached houses with a handful of almost-as-large semi-detached early Edwardian homes; virtually all have substantial off-street parking and very large gardens. **Egliston Mews**, at the junction of **Egliston Rd** and **Lower Common South**, is a smart development of flat-fronted 4-bed, 2-bath town-houses, in 'developers Georgian' style. Red-brick Dryburgh Mansions occupies a larger corner site between **Dryburgh Rd** and **Egliston Rd**. Unfortunately, the lovely big roomy flats have short leases. A huge late-Victorian mansion, Dryburgh Court, is split into five flats. The main part of **Dryburgh Rd** runs parallel to the Barnes–Putney railway line and has late- Victorian/early Edwardian houses, mainly semi-

Elaborate Edwardian is the hallmark of suburban Putney. These homes, solid and spacious, are eclectic in style. This one has copious 'Tudor' detailing In the heavy gable, the stuck-on 'timbers' and the tall chimneys. Other styles to be found frequently in the same house are Queen Anne and Gothic. However mongrel their architecture, they find favour with families.

detached, some detached. Odd numbers back onto the railway but have reasonable-sized gardens as barriers. Hidden at the end of the road is tiny **Beauchamp Terrace** with Victorian cottages. The low numbers are nearer the railway.

Erpingham Rd runs between **Dryburgh Rd** and **Lower Richmond Rd**, with 3-storey early Edwardian semi-detached and terraced houses, and there are some unusually large conversion flats. Rat-running is still a problem although **Dryburgh Rd** is closed to traffic at the **Upper Richmond Rd** junction during the morning rush hour. **Felsham Rd**, with its late-Victorian terraced houses, and a few early Victorian and larger ones, runs from **Erpingham Rd** through to **Putney High St** – but not for cars. The same is true for **Hotham Rd**. Roads running off are generally unexceptional South London late-Victorian/Edwardian terraces.

Stanbridge Rd, which crosses **Felsham Rd**, has some pleasant semi-basement flat-fronted mid-Victorian houses, while **Westhorpe Rd** attracts such exalted residents as MPs and the like. Houses in **Roskell Rd** are slightly larger 2- and 3-storey Victoriana, some semi-detached. By the mid-100s **Felsham Rd** houses are larger, mainly 3-storeys. In **Henry Jackson Rd** is a council-built infill development of low-rise homes. Thereafter more small council-built blocks and St Mary's Church of England Primary School with Putney St Mary's Youth Club (which has a good local reputation) opposite. **Bemish Rd** includes some flat-fronted Victorian cottages and larger Edwardian houses and is now closed to through traffic.

Charlwood Rd provides a welcome release from red-brick Edwardiana with pairs of Georgian/Regency flat-fronted cottages and larger detached houses set well back from the lane running from **Felsham Rd** across **Hotham Rd** to **Clarendon Drive**. Perhaps the prettiest houses are between **Felsham Rd** and **Hotham Rd**: this is rightly a conservation area. **Redgrave Rd** also has pretty, smart mid-Victorian homes.

The E end of **Lacy Rd** is dominated by the Putney Exchange shopping centre. Putney Exchange includes some flats, up to 3 bedrooms, which are popular to rent as they have 24hr security and parking. Otherwise **Lacy Rd** includes 2- and 3-storey Victorian terraces, some small Victorian cottages, a pub, some shops and some council infill development. **Modder Place** has nice plain flat-fronted 2-bed cottages and looks directly onto unprepossessing '60s council-built flats, Crown Court Estate, which is why they can be less expensive than neighbouring roads — not because the estate agent made a mistake with the valuation. A group of cul-de-sacs — pedestrian-only **Quill Lane**, **Lifford St** and **Stratford Grove** — lie between the red-brick walls of the shopping centre and the 1960s estate. For all that, the flat-fronted 2-storey cottages retain their charm. West from **Lacy Rd**, **Hotham Rd** is mainly Edwardian 2- and 3-storey houses, most semi-detached (just) with an adult education centre and Hotham Primary School at the junction with **Charlwood Rd**. Most houses here have four or more bedrooms.

Clarendon Drive features more 2- and 3-storey late-Edwardian and '20s semi-detached houses. Houses on the S side of the road back onto the railway line but have gardens of up to 100 ft to keep it at bay. This road also has Our Lady of Victories Catholic Primary School and the RSPCA animal hospital (as seen on TV). From Clarendon Drive there's a road barrier blocking access to **Norroy Rd** which, along with parallel **Chelverton Rd** with its good-sized late-Victorian family houses, is convenient for Putney rail station. **Spencer Walk**, to the W off **Charlwood Rd**, has pretty, early Victorian, flat-fronted 3-storey houses with semi-basements and some modern infill town-houses. Some train noise is possible here, as is noise from the popular Quill pub, but few crime problems: it is the 'local' for detectives and senior officers from Putney police station in **Upper Richmond Rd** (soon to close, though).

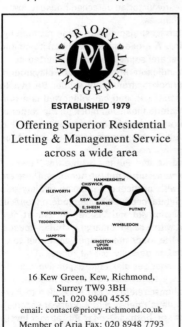

Upper Richmond Rd is a major trunk road (the South Circular A205) and is busy at all times. However, the majority of houses on the road are set well back. From the junction with **Putney Hill** it becomes increasingly commercial. Thereafter growing numbers of '30s and more modern mansion blocks appear as the road heads E towards Wandsworth. Off-street parking is essential. Where **Upper Richmond Rd** meets **West Hill** there is a development of 14 flats and 26 houses with an indoor swimming pool. The W section of the road features many blocks of flats ranging from early '20s to fairly new. Maintenance charges on the older blocks are off-putting to some buyers. Brittany House (corner of **Balmuir Gardens**) gained new penthouses in a total refurbishment about 12 years back. Among the best-known blocks close to **Putney High St** are old-style Ormonde Court and '30s-built Belvedere Court at the junction with **Dryburgh Rd**, overlooking Putney Leisure Centre and convenient for early morning

P

swims. All properties on this side of **Upper Richmond Rd** back onto railway lines although most have long gardens to cut noise levels. Harwood Court (opposite **Colinette Rd**) is another '30s-style block while **Isis Close** is a modern '60s-built development. Wellwood Court is next, then **Breasley Close** a council-built infill of flats and houses; **Fairdale Gardens** is a small town-house development. Northumberland Row in **Dyers Lane** (a no-through road) is a small terrace of mid-Victorian cottages, some flat-fronted, overlooking modern council homes.

Probably the best-known houses in **Upper Richmond Rd** are the 'Nelson Houses', a row of half a dozen lovely late-Georgian/early Victorian detached houses supposedly built for Nelson's sea captains. Set well back from the road, they boast gravel sweeps and Regency iron-work canopies. A house here, in need of doing up, was on the market last winter for £850,000.

East Putney

Popular with people moving into the area who cannot yet afford to live in Thamesfield or West Putney, choose not to live in Wandsworth or Earlsfield, and are determined to have SW15 on their headed writing paper. Prices for the late-Victorian/early Edwardian terraced houses are generally below those in Thamesfield and West Putney, even though transport and shopping facilities are better, with the rail station on **Putney High St**, East Putney District line tube on **Upper Richmond Rd** and Putney Bridge tube just over the river.

Putney Bridge Rd runs parallel to the river from **Putney High St** to Wandsworth, meaning very heavy traffic at times. Wandsworth Park runs most of the length of **Putney Bridge Rd**, so many of the late-Victorian terraces of 2- and 3-storey houses and purpose-built flats have views across the greenery to the river and the Hurlingham Club beyond. Few of the houses are very special, with the exception of Park Lodge at the junction with **Atney Rd**: an early Victorian detached house followed by the single-storey Sir Abraham Dawes Almshouses.

Fawe Park Rd, with its early Edwardian terraces, also suffers some rat-running, and even numbers back onto the railway line. A 4-bed house here can command £375,000, trains notwithstanding, and there are some sizeable converted flats. Terraced houses in **Skelgill Rd** overlook Brandlehow Primary School playground, while the 3-bed houses in **Brandlehow Rd** overlook the front of the school. **Bective Rd** is a popular mix of flat-fronted mid-Victorian cottages and bay-windowed late-19th century terraces. Disraeli Gardens is a large Victorian mansion block on the corner of **Bective Rd** and **Fawe Park Rd. Wadham Rd** has a very popular mix of small, pretty, flat-fronted, late-Victorian cottages, many 2-bed, 2-storey, some 3-storey. But the tube line runs at roof level behind.

Oxford Rd runs between **Upper Richmond Rd** and **Putney Bridge Rd**. 'Sleeping Policemen' have reduced the speed of the rat-runners, but not the numbers. There are some large detached mid-Victorian houses with porticoed entrances (mainly odd numbers). The remainder are Edwardian semi-detached with some modern (council) infill. **Montserrat Rd, Werter Rd** (with its Sainsbury's) and **Disraeli Rd** (smart new library) run from **Oxford Rd** to **Putney High St** with a range of large Victorian houses, most of which are now converted into flats. The roads are all one-way, either to or from **Putney High St**, and suffer from frustrated, hopelessly lost rat-runners.

Deodar Rd, off **Putney Bridge Rd,** is the most popular (and expensive – up to £1,000,000) street in East Putney. It has large 3-storey semi-detached houses: odd numbers overlook the river and are the last houses before Central London to have private moorings at the end of their big gardens (although actual boats are scarce). There are drawbacks of course — the District line bisects **Deodar Rd** (at roof level). The Blades development gets river views and has three stucco-fronted houses and

3-bed flats, backed by a commercial development of workshops with studio accommodation above.

Oakhill Rd links **Upper Richmond Rd** (and the rat-runners) to **Putney Bridge Rd**. The street is first Victorian and more recent mansion flats, then detached double-fronted mid-Victorian, then smaller red-brick terraces. Streets running between **Oakhill Rd** and **West Hill** — Schubert **Rd, Galveston Rd, Mexfield Rd, Cromford Rd, Santos Rd** — are generally substantial Edwardian terraces, with an increasing number converted to flats, causing some parking problems, but all convenient for East Putney tube. Off **Upper Richmond Rd** is **Wood Close**, a modern development of small town-houses complete with garages.

For the new flats across in SW18, E of Wandsworth Park, see the Wandsworth chapter. They are not in Putney whatever the brochures say.

Putney Heath and Putney Heights

Putney Heath is wild and heavily wooded, and walkers can get to the neighbouring Wimbledon Common by an underpass under the A3. A small neighbourhood at the junction of **Telegraph Rd** and **Portsmouth Rd** is isolated in the midst of the heath. It is approached via **Wildcroft Rd** and includes the Telegraph pub and the unusual 1930s Wildcroft Manor mansion flats, built in mock-Tudor style with exposed beams: large 3- and 4-bed flats here. Many go to overseas buyers who are unworried by hefty service charges. Then comes Highlands Heath, also '30s mansion flats with slightly smaller homes, lower service charges and tennis and squash courts. Both blocks back onto the heath. Prices start at around £160,000 for 1-bed, rising to £280,000 for a 4-bed). **Heathview Gardens** and **Bristol Gardens** have among the most popular — and pricey — houses in this enclave and indeed in the area: vast 6-, 7- and 8-bedroom Edwardian detached houses in quiet tree-lined roads with large gardens, some running onto the heath. Virtually all remain in single occupation. **Bensbury Close** has small flat-fronted mews cottages, 2- to 4-bed houses. **Portsmouth Rd**: small (in comparison with **Heathview Gardens**) detached houses overlooking the heath, include Bowling Green Cottage, a flat-fronted, white-washed country cottage thought to date back to the early 18th century. **Bowling Green Close** is a private development of extraordinary large 1930s Art Deco detached houses, very rarely on the market. Lynden Gate is 1980s Developers' Regency: 3-storey semi-basement stuccoed town-houses, 2- and 3-bed in a high-security development surrounded on three sides by the heath and woodland.

Putney Heath (the road) runs from Roehampton to **Putney Hill** and suffers from serious rat-running at rush hours with traffic out to beat the **Roehampton Lane**/A3 junction lights. It's mainly council-built developments (increasingly owner-occupied) along the heath, then Exeter House, a large 1930s mansion block development in its own large grounds. Many, but not all, the flats have magnificent views over the heath. Prices vary a lot: 2-bed ex-council flats can be about £100,000, with smarter ones of the same size twice that. **Manorfields** is a huge 1930s mansion flat development of 9-plus acres on the corner site between **Putney Heath** and **Westleigh Avenue**. Prices for these flats are higher than at Highlands Heath (see above) because public transport is closer. Newnham House, rebuilt in the 1980s after a gas blast levelled it, has superb 2-, 3- and 4-bed flats, all with good views of beautifully kept landscaped grounds with specimen trees and ponds. The service charges are high but full-time gardeners and porterage explain why.

The triangle bordered by **Putney Hill, West Hill** and **Upper Richmond Rd** offers the largest choice of modern purpose-built flats in Putney, although there is also a wide selection of older Victorian and Edwardian houses. **Putney Hill** is a busy through-road, but flats in the blocks on either side of the road remain popular. Properties include some substantial double-fronted mid-Victorian houses still in single occupation and some popular, mainly '30s and '50s, blocks of flats, while Fairhaven is a Victorian detached mansion now converted to flats. Putney High School for Girls (fee-paying) and its prep branch Lytton House front onto **Putney Hill** between **Carlton Drive** and **Lytton Grove**. **Radcliffe Square**, between **Lytton Grove** and **Kersfield Rd**, is a '70s flats development. At the top of Putney Hill is a no-through-road spur of **Putney Heath Lane** with two mansion blocks including Ross Court, which is popular for its large flats with big rooms.

St John's Avenue is probably the best road for (well-heeled) flat buyers in Putney, with some of the top modern blocks in the area — Downside, Claremont, Marlin House, all well-maintained with indoor swimming pools and 5-minute walk to East Putney tube. **Carlton Drive** is also lined with modern '60s blocks of flats, but is slightly less popular. There's a 1990s version at no 38: 2-bed flats at £330,000, with a big (and secure – current buzz-word) garden. Despite the classy names, however, neither road is the prettiest in Putney. **Rayner's Rd**, between the two, has a fine mix of rather scruffy flats and huge 6-bed detached houses.

Lytton Grove is a mixture of good-sized late-Victorian detached and semi-detached houses with some '30s and modern infill. Some of the houses are now converted to (fairly spacious) flats. The road suffers from bad rat-running, especially in peak hours. Houses on the N side of the road between the junctions with **Holmbush Rd** and **Rusholme Rd** back onto the tube line, but sidings between rails and gardens cut some of the noise.

Kersfield Estate by the junction with **Putney Hill** is '60s council-built flats and houses. **Tintern Close** and **Arlesey Close** feature quite small modern town-houses, then a mix of late-Victorian/Edwardian detached and semi-detached. **Chepstow Close**, a good modern town-house development (flat-fronted, 3-storey with garages), backs onto tube lines. Clock House Place is a red-brick cluster of Victorian-style homes.

Kersfield Rd is mainly modern early '60s blocks of flats with some late-'30s flats (private), although **Littleton Close** is council-built. Blocks include Heath Royal, Garden Royal, Heath Rise, a series of modern-style blocks close to **Putney Hill** with well-kept gardens. Flats range from 1- to 4-bed. Council blocks in the area are of reasonable quality, built during the same period and in similar style to many of the private blocks — spot the difference.

Putney Heath Lane has a mix of good-sized 2- and 3-storey early Edwardian semi-detached and terraced houses interspersed with modern mansion flat developments. Some houses are detached (just). **Van Dyke Close** is town-houses and flats. Behind is **Lavington Stables** — a tiny mews too small to find in the A–Z. **Rusholme Rd** has flats at the junction with **Putney Heath Lane**, thereafter late-Victorian red-brick detached and semi-detached houses, an increasing number now conversion flats. Modern flats at the junction with **Holmbush Rd** overlook a triangle of grass.

Keswick Rd runs between **Upper Richmond Rd** and **West Hill** and – like **Lytton Grove** – suffers badly from rat-running. Some potential buyers may also be put off by the (above ground) tube line running behind, but gardens and large grassy sidings cut noise levels. There are also some exceptional, large early Victorian houses, typically 5-bed, 3-reception, with large gardens. There is an eclectic mix here: big mock-Tudor mansions, hideous blocks and imitation cottages. Developers wait for the elderly inhabitants of the monster houses to sell up or die so they can create yet more flats. The service station on the **Upper Richmond Rd** is to go, to be replaced by 40 flats, offices and shops.

Cavalry Gardens is a recent, sybaritic complex of houses and flats, both new and converted, with its own pool and sauna, off **Upper Richmond Rd**. **Portinscale Rd** off

Keswick Rd features some large detached Victorian houses and '20s and '30s infill of Tudor-style herringbone brick. The road suffers some rat-running. By the junction with **West Hill** is Burntwood School and Portinscale Estate (modern houses/low-rise flats). Opposite are large '70s flats.

West Hill — a continuation of the A3 — is exceptionally busy at all times. The safest time to cross is during rush hour when the traffic is generally stationary. Close to **Tibbett's Corner** underpass is **Colebrook Close**, off **West Hill**, an extraordinary 'Spanish Hacienda' style development of houses and maisonettes built in the '30s by a film company for stars and starlets visiting Britain for filming.

Thereafter are large, mainly late-Victorian houses: most, fortunately, set well back from the road with off-street parking and for the most part converted to spacious flats. At the eastern end, close to Wandsworth, further conversions are under way. Barratt have successfully converted an old college into 'Crown Mansions': flats and duplexes up to £455,000. Most are now sold.

West Putney

This is where you live when you have made it in life and have chosen not to commute into London each day from Berkshire or Hampshire. There are some small houses, flats, even council estates – but the vast, detached late-Victorian houses in wide tree-lined avenues are the Putney properties of popular imagination. They house three-car families with daughters at Putney High or St Pauls, sons at a good boarding school and a husband with a secure seat on the Board and a useful handful of non-executive directorships. Demand for family homes in this area is so great that '60s/'70s conversions into flats are being bought for restoration into single units.

West Putney is bordered by **Upper Richmond Rd** to the N, **Putney Heath** to the S, **Putney Park Lane** and **Putney Hill**. It is a wholly residential area save for the shops and offices of the **Upper Richmond Rd** and is a conservation area.

The area is laid out on a grid pattern with four roads — **Westleigh Avenue, Chartfield Avenue, Hazlewell Rd** and **Howard's Lane** — running parallel to the **Upper Richmond Rd**. Cutting between and across are roads such as **Larpent Avenue, Castello Avenue** and **St Simon's Avenue**, which run parallel to **Putney Hill**. Major building started in the 1870s, and houses range from huge detached Victorian and early Edwardian through to mid-'20s architect-designed flights of fancy, with some '50s and early '60s infill. The area is exceptional in the number of large detached or generous semi-detached houses on offer.

Westleigh Avenue running W from **Putney Hill** starts with low-rise council homes; then there is a mix of Victorian, Edwardian and newer detached houses all set well back from the road. From the junction with **Pullman Gardens**, council houses and small blocks of flats back onto a '50s and '60s council-built estate (the mainly low-rise flats, houses and maisonettes of **Cortis Rd, Pullman Rd** and **Heyward Gardens**). Houses on the S side of **Westleigh Avenue** between **Cotman Close** and **Pullman Gardens** back onto Elliot Comprehensive School in **Pullman Gardens**. By the junction with **Granard Avenue** is Granard Primary School, then small council houses. Leading off **Westleigh Avenue, Genoa Avenue** is mainly late- Victorian 3-storey semi-detached with some big detached, 1920s houses and small council infill. **Solna Avenue** has small modern council houses, most now owner-occupied. At the junction with **Westleigh Avenue, Granard Avenue** is small neat council houses then substantial detached — many '20s, '30s and '50s double-fronted with fine views.

Chartfield Avenue is a mixture of late-Victorian/Edwardian detached houses set back from the road with some substantial inter-war stockbroker-Tudor homes. As with **Westleigh Avenue** there are substantial amounts of council property, with the Ashburton Estate between **Putney Hill** and **Genoa Avenue**. Some of the largest

Victorian detached double-fronted houses are now converted to vast flats; 3-bedroom, garden, 2-reception roomed ones are not unusual. Roads leading off **Chartfield Avenue** from **Putney Hill** include **Chartfield Square** and **Cherryfield Drive**, which are undistinguished modern town-houses, the former overlooked by an ugly '60s office block on **Putney Hill**. Late-'60s council flats (not high-rise) and houses opposite in **Winchelsea Close**.

Gwendolen Avenue has popular large 1880s detached and semi-detached houses: one sold recently for £1.9 million. The 1980s added some large 5-bed Victorian-style semi-detached houses; **St Simons Avenue** features more very large detached houses and a church at the junction with **Hazlewell Rd**. **Genoa Avenue** and **Castello Avenue** are smaller (but large by any other standards) 2/3-storey semi-detached and detached red-brick houses. **Larpent Avenue** has some modern infill, but generally substantial late-Victorian detached and semi-detached 2- and 3-storey houses. Some houses (the low even numbers) have extraordinary domes on the front elevations — Turkish architect perhaps? **Luttrell Avenue** has late-Victorian/early Edwardian semi-and detached houses.

Hazlewell Rd is mainly 2- and 3-storey late-Victorian and early Edwardian detached and semi-detached houses, some with 6 bedrooms. There are some smaller modern infill houses (also detached). The road suffers occasional rat-running. **St John's Avenue** runs between **Hazlewell Rd** and **Putney Hill** with very large 1880s 3-storey semi-detached and detached homes. **Ravenna Rd** and **Burston Rd**, large semi-detached and detached, are also convenient for Putney station. **Tideswell Rd** has 3-storey Edwardian semi-detacheds (one has doubled in price – to £1 million – over the past three years); **Holroyd Rd** is Edwardian 2- and 3-storey semis. Prices in this road have gone from c. £350,000 in 1990 to £850,000 today. **Coalecroft Rd** (a conservation area): even numbers are very pretty flat-fronted early Victorian cottages, mainly 3-bedrooms; odd numbers are good-sized Edwardian semi-detached. Rather alarmingly, the police station on **Upper Richmond Rd** is to be replaced by new homes.

Howard's Lane is a wonderfully esoteric blend of house styles ranging from vast mid- and late-Victorian and early Edwardian to stunning early '20s architect-designed — with a few Victorian and modern terraces thrown in for good measure. The road includes one of the most desirable houses in Putney at 115 **Howard's Lane**: a detached Art Deco flight of fancy with a vast red dragon weather vane. Howard's Lane houses start off in the E as small (for West Putney) terraced and semi-detached mainly 4-bed houses. Nos 50–60 Howard's Lane is a nice-looking town-house development with integral garages, then mainly larger late-Victorian detached and semi-detached houses. **Kingslawn Close** at the junction with **Woodborough Rd** is an attractive town-house and flat development with communal gardens including tennis courts.

(P)

Leading off Howard's Lane to the N are **Carmalt Gardens** and **Balmuir Gardens**, turn-of-the-century, 4-bed semi-detached (just) houses. **Tideswell Rd** and **Enmore Rd** are similar but slightly larger. An attractive new cul-de-sac, **Fairfax Mews**, has been squeezed in off **Upper Richmond Rd** by St George: 14 new houses. **Parkfields** is a narrow, hidden one-way lane concealing enchanting Georgian and early Victorian cottages and some larger Georgian houses. It is a conservation area with restored original lamp-posts in the road. Convenient for a small parade of similar period shops in **Upper Richmond Rd**. **Dealtry Rd**, **Colinette Rd** and **Campion Rd** all have 3-storey Edwardian terraced and semi-detached homes and some 1960s town houses. **Pettiward Close** is a modern cul-de-sac with 3/4-bed houses.

The area between **Woodborough Rd**, **Malbrook Rd** and **Upper Richmond Rd** boasts some of the biggest and most popular houses in Putney. Two- and 3-storey ornate mid- and late-Victorian detached houses with 4, 5 or 6 beds, plus drives and huge gardens. There is a small council infill block halfway up **Woodborough Rd**.

At the junction of **Woodborough Rd** and **Upper Richmond Rd** are private flats: The Briars, Somerset Lodge and also modern flats at the junction with **Briar Walk** – a road which in late 1998 saw the first £2 million house sale in Putney. Pear Tree Court, which is similar, is at the junction of **Malbrook Rd** with **Upper Richmond Rd**.

West of here is considered to be Roehampton, though the transformation is subtle. The boundary is **Putney Park Lane**, not a road but rather a woodland track marooned in suburbia, running N–S between the houses and past the bottoms of gardens.

Roehampton

Drive up the A3 **Kingston Vale** towards Putney and to your left you will see what anywhere else would be a series of luxury blocks of flats overlooking the green acres of Richmond Park. They are, in fact, the 'point' blocks of the vast Alton Estate built in the '50s and early '60s by the GLC, now owned and managed by Wandsworth Council. The views from them must be terrific — and the views of them, when seen across the park, gives an inkling of what was in the minds of tower block architects. A swing in architectural fashion has made the estate a talking point once again: parts are listed.

Roehampton is bordered by Richmond Park and Richmond Golf Course to the S and W, **Upper Richmond Rd** to the N and by enchanting rural **Putney Park Lane** to the E. It is an area of contrasts — it is just a 5-minute walk from the modern towers of the Alton Estate to the small Victorian terraces of **Medfield St** or to the top-of-the-range houses of **Roedean Crescent**.

The area bordered by Richmond Park, **Clarence Lane**, **Roehampton Lane** and the A3/**Kingston Rd** is mainly council-built properties known under the generic name of Alton but is in fact a number of different estates. Low-rise blocks and houses are increasingly owner-occupied, and tower flats with views over the park are becoming popular. On the corner of **Roehampton Lane** and **Alton Lane** a block of 25 flats is being built. **Laverstoke Gardens** and **Holybourne Avenue** back onto listed Manresa House, now the Roehampton outpost of the University of Greenwich. As usual with these big estates the planners forgot about the transport and shopping needs of inhabitants: the only shops of note are a tatty parade in **Danebury Avenue**. Heading out of Roehampton along the A3, however, there is the ASDA hypermarket.

Roehampton Village, just across **Roehampton Lane**, could not be more different. **Roehampton High St** has pretty early and mid-Victorian houses and small, bay-windowed 'village' shops. There is a 'Village Café', a 'Village Hairdresser' and an ironmonger 'established 1885'. St George have just finished 'Hanover Mews', a dozen 2-, 3- and 4-bed houses off **Roehampton High St**. Most, but not all, of **Medfield St** overlooks Putney Heath and comprises 2- and 3-bed mid-Victorian terraced cottages (one sold in 1999 for £230,000) and a row of larger red-brick terraced houses (late-Victorian) with tall chimneys, some semi-basements. The road is a bus route and suffers congested traffic during rush hours. **Ponsonby Rd**, running S off **Medfield St** back to **Roehampton Lane**, has small flat-fronted pairs of Georgian cottages overlooking the heath, then beautiful Roehampton Church and Roehampton Church School (primary). Part of Queen Mary's Hospital has closed, and it's rumoured the rest will follow – to be replaced, of course, by housing.

On the other side of **Roehampton High St**, **Nepean St**, **Akehurst St** and **Umbria St** form a quiet enclave of semi-detached and detached houses ranging from 6-bed Edwardian semis through to early 1930s (some modern infill), many now flat conversions. They have large gardens and are generally very quiet, tree-lined roads. **Rodway Rd** however suffers occasional traffic rat-running.

From Putney Heath, **Dover House Rd** leads down to the **Upper Richmond Rd** and passes through the Dover House estate, built in the 1920s by the LCC – like the Magdalen Park estate in Earlsfield (see Southfields and Earlsfield chapter) – as a 'cottage' estate. Its borders run from **Crestway** down **Dover Park Rd** to **Upper Richmond Rd**, with **Huntingfield Rd** and **Swinburne Rd** the borders to the W, and peaceful **Putney Park Lane** to the E. The houses are a mix of inter-war chalet style semi-detached and terraced with steeply inclined roofs and dormer windows, and pretty flat-fronted terraces and semis. The estate is now a conservation area – too late for some houses, where new owners have pebbledashed, rendered or fake-stone-clad. The area is now well-known to postal-zone-conscious buyers without the cash for Putney proper. The estate is quiet (with the exception of **Dover House Rd**, which suffers some through traffic), with 'village' greens and open spaces. Among those most in demand are houses backing onto **Putney Park Lane**, an unmade-up tree-lined lane running between Putney Heath and **Upper Richmond Rd**.

Roads leading down to the estate from Putney Heath such as **Dover Park Drive** and **Longwood Drive** feature large, mainly detached, family houses, most built in traditional styles in the '30s and '50s. **Coppice Drive** backs onto playing-fields behind Queen Mary's Hospital. Off **Upper Richmond Rd** are mainly late-Edwardian and early '20s homes with some modern private developments. **Putney Park Avenue** is again a private, unmade-up, tree-lined road which features ferocious speed humps and a mix of Edwardian and newer houses with a small modern flat development at the top of the avenue: a very quiet road. **Marrick Close** has a small development of modern town-houses. **Dungarvan Avenue** and **Langside Avenue**, with their substantial '20s semi-detached houses, could suffer rat-running. Cornerways is modern flats on the corner of **Daylesford Avenue** and **Upper Richmond Rd**. A useful small parade of shops stands on either side of the **Dover House Rd** junction.

Roehampton Lane (A306) is at all hours of the day an exceptionally busy road, used as a route by traffic from Richmond and the South Circular to the A3 and Kingston. The best houses are set back from the road behind high walls or in private closes: some are exceptionally large. **Roehampton Close** has '20s and '30s mansion blocks set in large private grounds well away from **Roehampton Lane**, with easy access to Barnes station and the A3. **Eliot Gardens**, modern 3-storey town-houses with garages, is set back off **Roehampton Lane**. Upper numbers of **Roehampton Lane** towards Roehampton proper are mainly '30s terraced and semi-detached homes set rather close to the road and with views of the Alton Estate.

On the edge of Richmond Park and bordered by playing-fields and Roehampton Golf Course, **Roedean Crescent** features large detached double-fronted houses, mainly '30s and '50s, built in traditional styles with vast gardens – most with in-and-out drives as well. Neighbouring **Roehampton Gate** is also quiet and has smaller, detached pre-war houses: also popular, but fetching lower prices. Prices of the big 1930s detached houses in **Priory Lane** by **Roehampton Gate** also tend to be lower due to traffic – if you consider around £1 million low. At the northern (Barnes Common) end of **Priory Lane** is the 1970s brick-and-concrete Lennox council estate to the W, usually with some properties for sale, and Rosslyn Park rugby football club to the E.

Transport   Tubes: East Putney (zones 2/3, District), Putney Bridge (zone 2, District). To Oxford Circus 25 min (1 change), City 25 min, Heathrow 50 min (1 change). Trains: Putney, Barnes to Waterloo.

Convenient for Putney Common and Heath, Richmond Park, the Thames. Routes to the SW and W. Miles from centre: 5.

Schools   Local Authority: Burntwood (g), Elliott. Private: Ibstock Place, Putney High (g), Putney Park (g), Hurlingham, Prospect House.

SALES

Flats	S	1B	2B	3B	4B	5B
Average prices	80–120	110–190	150–230	170–350	300–500	350–500+

Houses	2B	3B	4B	5B	6/7B	8B
Average prices	220–300	230–450	350–550+	500–1 M	700–1 M	1.5 M+

RENTAL

Flats	S	1B	2B	3B	4B	5B
Average prices	100–170	180–250	200–500	300–600	400–870	—

Houses	2B	3B	4B	5B	6/7B	8B
Average prices	250–380	300–600	500–800	600–1000	800–2000	—

The properties Family houses, some vast. Enormous range of flats: p/b , mansion flats and conversions, and new mews squeezed into the corners. Riverside, heath and common locations attract prices in millions. Smaller Victorian cottages near centre and river. Putney Hill is E–W divide: W is best.

The Market   East Putney is slightly cheaper: flats, small terraces. Then in price order come smarter cottages W of the High St, smart inter-war and modern flats on Putney Hill and spacious family homes near the Heath. Mansions with grounds, rather than mere gardens, range up to £2 million. Families tend to stay put: schools are good and gardens large. Local searches: 3–4 weeks.

Among those estate agents active in this area are:

- Allan Fuller
- Barnard Marcus
- Kinleigh Folkard & Hayward
- Haart
- Andrews
- Townends
- Scotts
- Winkworth *
- Douglas & Gordon
- Bairstow Eves
- Bradford & Bingley
- Allan Briegel
- Hugh Henry
- Geoffrey Jardine
- Foxtons *
- Warren
- FPD Savills
- Chesterton
- James Anderton
- Featherstone Leigh

further details: see advertisers' index on p671

P

REGENT'S PARK

Map ref: p60 (2E)
Postal districts: NW1
Boroughs: Westminster
  (Con), Camden (Lab)
Council tax: Band D
  Westminster £350,
  Camden £897
Conservation areas: All
  Crown Estate
Parking: Restricted in park

London, on the whole, is not a planned city. Centuries of piecemeal expansion and a strong sense of the sanctity of individuals' property have left it without the grand boulevards and squares of Continental cities. The one exception is Regent's Park. As its name implies, the graceful terraces and handful of glorious villas were planned during the Regency. Nash, with the backing of the Prince Regent, conceived the startling scheme in 1811, making each terrace of houses appear a single, Classical palace, set in a sylvan landscape – the gleaming white façades accentuating the difference between London's town streets and this idealized countryside.

Regent's Park still forms part of the Crown Estate, and benefits from its careful management and long-term planning, which has led to the restoration of all the great terraces since 1945. (It survived proposals to demolish half the terraces in the brave new world of the 1950s.) A common policy has been to sell individual houses in the terraces on relatively long leases – 60 years is typical – on the condition that the leaseholder completely restores the house. The Estate stipulates the architect, has a veto over the plans and retains control over the exterior. When a lease on one of the splendid individual villas with which the park is studded came up for sale, the Estate told would-be buyers that it, the Crown, would also choose the interior decorator and the landscape designer. All the buyer had to do, of course, was to pay their fees.

The grand sweep of **Portland Place** leads triumphantly up to the park from Oxford Circus, dividing at the end into the graceful double curve of **Park Crescent** (see Marylebone chapter). The six-lane **Marylebone Rd** is decently shielded from view by the curve of its garden. North of the main road is more greenery, **Park Square**, with its two facing rows of Nash houses forming an entrance to the park. Here a number of the listed houses of **Park Square East**, together with half a dozen flats around the corner in Albany Terrace, which fronts onto **Marylebone Rd**, were sold in the early

1990s with new Crown leases following renovation. These surround the old Diorama – a Victorian precursor to the cinema, nowadays an arts centre.

Clockwise around the **Outer Circle**, terrace succeeds snow-white terrace, each with a distinguishing feature within the overall Classical style. The short **Ulster Terrace** has pairs of bow-fronted windows at either end; then come the gardens of **York Terrace East** and **West**, flanking **York Gate**: these houses face onto their own private roads, while their backs look N over the park. The East stretch is original, and is offices and apartments: it is considered the more exclusive of the two. The West terrace was rebuilt behind the façade and has good, popular flats, complete with underground garage and security.

Most of the terraces have mews, some of which are still linked to the grand houses so you can buy one of each. Or you can choose a mews house on its own – perhaps in **Park Square Mews**, tucked into the corner behind **Ulster Terrace** and **Park Square West**.

Continuing the clockwise progress, **Cornwall Terrace** is the earliest of the park terraces, dating from 1820 and designed by Decimus Burton. Some of the 19 houses are offices. Again, there are bow windows at either end and three great, full-height porticoes with Classical columns. **Clarence Gate** leads out to the top of **Baker St**. Small, elegant **Clarence Terrace**, with 2- to 4-bed flats, and studios in the basement, is next in line, backing onto busy **Park Rd**. Those buying in these Classical rows are not keen on basements: a 2-bed 'lower ground floor' example was £275,000 recently, but similar square footage, more elevated in position and treated luxuriously, can reach £800,000-plus.

Next comes **Sussex Place**, curving round behind its own garden and served by a private road. Its astonishing row of five pairs of Saracen's-helmet-shaped cupolas give it a unique, exotic air. The graceful façade is original, but behind it is a modern re-building carried out for the London Business School – whose principal has a particularly enviable private residence. The next building along, **Hanover Terrace**, is set back behind a garden, its insubstantial-looking statues still adorning its blue-painted portico. This sweep has been completely restored following the Crown's sale of 20 refurbishment leases. These enviable homes have private, west-facing gardens with their own mews houses behind.

The astonishing London Central Mosque with its gold dome stands on the western edge of the park: a splendid building whose outlines somehow marry well with Nash's Classical façades. From here on, the canal curves around the northern edge of the park. Between it and the **Outer Circle** is Hanover Lodge, the fourth of the splendid park 'villas' to revert from an institution to a privately owned home. Five new detached villas by architect Quinlan Terry have been built in the grounds. Opposite, within the park, is vast Winfield House, the American ambassadorial residence. London Zoo takes up the N corner of the park, its muted roars and trumpetings carried on the summer nights' breezes.

On the E side the terraces take up the tale once more: seven of **Gloucester Gate's** houses underwent no-expense-spared refurbishment in 1989: at that time the smallest went for a modest £1.4 million, the beautiful show house seemed cheap at £2.65 million; the largest (two houses made one) sold for £5 million. All seven boast mews houses with garages. There are also flats in the terrace: today you can pay well over a million for a balconied apartment – outstanding and interior-designed, but still a flat). You do get a 95-year lease and a garage. Next in the sequence comes **St Katherine's Precinct**, with 4-storey houses, which leads to the Danish Church.

Cumberland Terrace was rebuilt behind its splendid, pedimented façade after World War II as houses and flats. The leases here can range from around 23 to 47 years, with correspondingly varying prices – but a Grade I-listed slice of this grandeur, a whole 6-bed, 4-bath mansion with attendant mews house behind, was £3.55 million last autumn. **Cumberland Place** boasts a lovely, large Classical villa, bow-windowed at either end. The rest of the row 'suitable for re-instatement into 3 houses' was offered last year on 150-year Crown leases. **Chester Terrace** is a long row of 42 more normal-sized houses which remain as individual homes. They were completely rebuilt behind the façade 35 years ago, so allied to their Regency proportions are such modern facilities as lifts and integral garages. The self-contained wings set forward at either end are linked to the main terrace behind them by flying buttress-like archways. Expect prices of £2–2.5 million for these lovely homes. The mews behind, **Chester Close North**, was rebuilt at the same time – but in mid-'60s style.

Cambridge Terrace, with its Georgian curved-top windows, nowadays contains flats (a 3-bed last winter, £895,000), maisonettes and houses plus 30,000 sq ft of offices after a 1980s programme of modernization. Behind, **Cambridge Terrace Mews** is a development of modern houses (leasehold), which share a communal garden: a 4-bed, 3-bath one, with own patio as well, was £875,000 last winter.

The next block, **Cambridge Gate**, was built half a century later than its Regency neighbours in sandy stone, and has an ornate and overdecorated air beside their white stucco. Nos 1–9 **Cambridge Gate** are the latest Regent's Park houses to have been modernized and converted: No 1, among the largest homes in Regent's Park, was on the market last year for £9 million: for this you get 16,500 sq ft of space that includes six bedroom/bathroom/dressing-room suites, vast reception rooms that include a library, a lofty top-floor studio and roof terraces (no garden then – but there's always the park. . .), and a mews house to hold the garaging, the staff and the 8-metre swimming-pool/ballroom.

On past the uncompromising modern lines of the Royal College of Physicians, and the little Regency cul-de-sac of **St Andrew's Place**, you return to **Park Square**, overlooking its private square gardens, having completed the circuit.

Within the park, around the **Inner Circle**, are the enchanted Open Air Theatre and a handful of scattered 'villas'. Most had dwindled into institutional use, but now some, like Hanover Lodge, are becoming homes again. These glorious original mansions, where the lucky owner can easily imagine himself to be in a country house, are among London's finest. New Crown leases have been sold in the last 15 years on The Holme, Nuffield Lodge and St John's Lodge, with stringent clauses about renovation and upkeep. The Holme was the first, in a splendid position beside the lake: it has its own section of water, out to the island, roped off.

Albany St runs parallel with the E edge of the park. Handsome terraced Georgiana here yields a 3-bed home with self-contained studio flat, £895,000, at the S end of the road; a smaller one at the N, Camden, end with a decent (99-year) lease but in need of attention: £350,000. At the S end, **Prince Regent's Terrace**, a row of flat-fronted brick houses, was remodelled into enviable duplexes in 1988: they could be bought singly or as pairs to make a house. At the same time five mews houses were added to **Peto Place** behind. Further N, several rows of mews belonging to the park terraces open off **Albany Rd**. There is also some recent housing in brick and stucco style. On the E side is the **Cumberland Market** estate, a complex of serviceable brick buildings let by the Crown Estate as fair rent housing. The 500 flats were all renovated a decade ago. In **Redhill St** 1999 saw a new courtyard of 2- and 3-bed houses partially rebuilt behind a period façade. Four were left last autumn at £325–395,000 freehold.

Park Village West is an oddity, a curving lane off **Albany Rd** where the Regency style reappears laced with Gothic in a surprising collection of little Nash 'country cottages'. **Park Village East**, which lies behind, suffered when the houses on the E side were demolished to widen the Euston railway – and note that this is being upgraded with new overhead power cables – disturbing the locals' peace here and at the extreme E end of **Prince Albert Rd**.

Houses in this mock-village rarely come up for sale, but last winter saw two in

Park Village West: a 4-bed, 2-bathroom one at £1.2 million, and another, needing renovation but with a new 99-year lease, for £650,000.

Prince Albert Rd runs in a sweep along the N bank of the canal, its grand parade of flats, from turn-of-the-century to modern luxurious, attracting top prices with their splendid park views. It was here, in the early 1980s, that London first acquired a stock of international-standard flats – for jet-set buyers for whom 'Georgian' meant merely 'second-hand'. At the E end, by the canal, are some surviving pairs of 1850s villas. Nos 6–15, which are in pairs, were expensively reconstructed in 1989: these are vast, 6-bedroomed homes, some with swimming pools, with 99-year leases: long for the Crown Estate; what is more, the normal sub-letting prohibition does not apply. (A recent sale netted £1.85 million).

St Mark's Square has mid-19th-century houses and links with the Primrose Hill neighbourhood (see Camden Town chapter). The green sweep of the Hill rises up to the right, then the blocks of mansion flats for which **Prince Albert Rd** is famous begin. Prince Albert Court is dark purply-grey brick, St James's Close is red-brick 1930s. Park St James, set back on **St James's Terrace**, was the first new block for some 15 years when built in 1984. Stockleigh Hall is 1920s, stucco and red-brick: a 3-bed flat here needing modernization was a mere £380,000 for a 76-year lease in December: service charge is over £4,000, however. Viceroy Court is also '20s with inset balconies and curving ends. **Bentinck Close** is more '30s; then comes 1920s Oslo Court. These blocks are a good hunting-ground for a decent-sized 3/4-bed flat. Large 3-bed flats here can be had for around £550,000, with a 5-bed flat in **Bentinck Close** commanding £1 million despite being 'in need of updating'.

Avenue Rd runs down to meet **Prince Albert Rd** from the heart of St John's Wood. On the corner, luxurious 2 **Avenue Rd** has large projecting balconies; facing it is a white stone balconied block, Imperial Court. The pair are well-established modern blocks, 20–25 years old, and flats here command premium prices. A 4-bed, 3-bath flat in Imperial Court, with a large terrace overlooking the park, was £1.3 million in January for a 990-year lease – plus service charges of £8,500 a year. Then comes Edwardian splendour: the red and white mansion blocks of Northgate which stand on the corner of **Prince Albert Rd** and **St John's Wood High St**. These are elegant, well-proportioned, well-thought-of flats. A 5-bed, 3-bath 'family apartment' was £875,000 for a 129-year lease in December. Service charges, mind you, are £6,500 a year.

Park Rd runs along the western edge of the park, a fertile ground for ever more flats schemes. Except at the extreme N end, blocks in this road lack the park views – penthouses may be an exception. The 12-year-old Beverly House is a U-shaped building on a rather cramped site, with windows eyeball to eyeball across a courtyard. The places to live here are the truly vast penthouses: 6,000 sq ft over two floors.

Crown Court (1980s) has just 23 flats of from 1 to 5 bedrooms in its seven floors. The entrance is via an enormous foyer behind an arched brick colonnade, guarded by uniformed porters. The flats each have balconies or roof gardens, reached through more arches. Abbey Lodge, '20s mansion blocks, is on the W side of the road and backs onto the **Nash Terraces**, which resume with **Kent Terrace**. This, being tucked behind **Hanover Terrace**, is one of the few not to overlook the park. At the S end of **Park Rd** are some pretty early 19th-century houses, not part of the Nash ensemble.

There is scant space for new developments surrounding the park, but Barratt have discovered a plot in the old goods yard behind Marylebone Station which is 'only 250 yards' from the park. Here, off **Park** and **Rossmore Rds** and within the NW1 postcode, 'Prince Regent's Gate' is a 400-flat complex with swimming pool and fitness suite, underground parking, electronic gates, 24hr uniformed concierge – the whole NW1 lifestyle. The layout of the stepped-roof crescent that forms the main block allows terraces for many of the 1- to 3-bedroomed flats and penthouses. By last July, 80 had been sold before building began, including a million-pound penthouse. Prices start at £235,000; the first people should be able to move in this autumn, with completion in 2002. The scheme also includes plans for 100 flats for the Acton Housing Association.

Transport　　Tubes: Regent's Park (Bakerloo), Baker Street (Metropolitan, Bakerloo, Circle, Jubilee). From Regent's Park: Oxford Circus 3 min, City 20 min (1 change), Heathrow 55 min (1 change).

Convenient for　　West End, City, Euston, King's Cross and St Pancras Stations. Roads to West and North. Miles from centre: 1.5.

Schools　　Local Authority: Haverstock School, Maria Fidelis Convent RC, St Marylebone C of E. Private: Cavendish School (g), Francis Holland School (g).

SALES

Flats	S	1B	2B	3B	4B	5B
Average prices	125–300	175–400+	250–800	375+	500–1.2 M	—
Houses	2B	3B	4B	5B	6/7B	8B
Average prices	450–750	700–1 M	800–2 M	1 M+	2 M+	→20M

RENTAL

Flats	S	1B	2B	3B	4B	5B
Average prices	200–350	250–450	350–700	450–1500	600–2000	—
Houses	2B	3B	4B	5B	6/7B	8B
Average prices	600–900	1100–2000	1500+	4000+	—	—

The properties　　Charmed circle of top-quality homes gaze out over the park: the lovely, snowy Regency terraces hold houses and apartments, many of them no-expense-spared redevelopments behind the dignified facades. Also a handful of London's finest mansions: villas for millionaires scattered within the park. Luxury 20th-century flats on Prince Albert and Park Rds, and mews cottages behind the terraces.

The market　　Crown Estate leases are typically 40 years (but more recently some 99); strict conditions on upkeep and use: no sub-letting. Always demand from foreign and British buyers for some of London's smartest homes. Local searches: Westminster 10 working days, Camden 7–10 working days.

R

Among those estate agents active in this area are:

- Aston Chase
- Ancombe & Ringland *
- John D Wood
- FPDSavills
- Keith Cardale Groves
- Regents Residential
- Knight Frank
- Cluttons
- Hamptons
- Oakleys
- Regent's Park Property Services
- Winkworth *
- Kay & Co
- Goldschmidt & Howland
- Foxtons *
- Chestertons

further details: see advertisers' index on p671

RICHMOND AND KEW

Map ref: p88 (5D)
Postal districts: TW9, TW10
Boroughs: Richmond upon
  Thames (Lib Dem)
Council tax: Band D: £908
Conservation areas: Include
  Richmond town, riverside
  and Green, Kew Green
Parking: Residents/meters
  in centre

Richmond is a town. It is in no real sense a suburb of London, cut off as it is by its enormous park. The Thames and the tube link Richmond, just, to London, but the people who live here see themselves, perhaps more than any other inhabitants of areas in this book, as citizens of Richmond, Surrey rather than the wider city. And who can blame them for keeping the place to themselves? It has a river front, 2,500 acres of primeval English landscape – oaks and deer-dotted rolling grassland – in its park, and beautiful buildings. Vulgar commerce may take Richmond people by train or tube into Town, and they vehemently claim that the West End theatres are just as accessible as their own, but their heart remains in the borough.

Increasingly, people from elsewhere come to Richmond to be entertained, to eat out, to visit the pubs and bars, to stroll by the river. In the affluent reaches of South West London and Surrey, it's Kingston for shopping and Richmond for leisure.

Politically, Richmond takes in Twickenham, Kew, Petersham, Ham and a wide swathe to the W down to Hampton Court. The Thames, meandering beneath Richmond Hill and past Kew Gardens, links all these places. Here we cover Richmond and Kew; Twickenham has its own chapter. Within its boundaries Richmond has palaces, wide parks, miles of river bank and no less than 40 conservation areas. It is 9 miles SW of Central London.

Originally it was called Shene, meaning (it's alleged) 'bright and shining place'. Henry VII renamed the town after his earldom in Richmond, Yorkshire. He built a palace S of Richmond Green (the remains of which can be seen as Palace Gate), making the town a fashionable royal resort until Charles II moved to Windsor and Shene Palace fell into disrepair. Richmond continued to attract noble visitors (as is evident from the villas along **Petersham Rd**), artists and writers. The Old Deer Park (N), Richmond Park (E) and Thames-side walks still draw families and frazzled commuters who can shake off the city dust (Waterloo 20 min by express train). There is a wealth of good prep schools and church schools. The German School at Ham attracts diplomats and City people. Australian/American expatriates like the quintessential Englishness; the Japanese come for the golf courses (Old Deer Park/Fulwell/Sudbrook Park) and the reasonable proximity to the Japanese School in Acton. They all like being a fast drive away from Heathrow – and no-one seems to mind that the planes trundle over the Green so low you can count the rivets. Richmond will have to wait until next year for a decision on the Terminal 5 plans at Heathrow.

Prices are high, and stayed high when other areas slumped: this is a very popular area. It is *par excellence* a place for families. Once they get established, they stay put – to the despair of agents who are short of homes to sell. Agent after agent reports that the market is made up of local people. Sometimes they trade down, more often they (try to) trade up. Last winter, agents were complaining once more of a shortage of good property to sell.

After a brief pause, the start of 1999 saw the market brisk again, as it has been since 1996. Rises of 25% were seen for the top areas in 1999. The best family homes, on Richmond Hill and in Petersham/Ham, now command prices around £1.2 million. City people and foreign businessmen drive this market. Those seeking more affordable, but still spacious, family homes look to Kew and across the river to St Margarets. Demand is fuelled by Richmond Borough's schools, which at primary level regularly top the league tables.

There is a fair supply of 1-bed flats but in prime areas near the river, hill and green, they can cost £160,000-plus. A 2-bed flat may be around £260,000 if it has good views and a roof terrace. Most 3-bed flats are found in mansion blocks.

Richmond and its satellites have a wealth of wonderful period houses. These range from Queen Anne through all stages of Georgian to the most opulent of Victorian. When they come up for sale, which is rarely, they can cost anything up to £3 million – more for the mansions of Ham. Even quite staid-looking homes top £1 million here.

Richmond Town

Richmond is squeezed between the river, its park, the Old Deer Park and the open fields of Petersham. Most of it was built up in or before Victorian times: there is very little modern housing. The fact that Richmond town is a conservation area means that there are few unpleasant parts. A busy railway line passing behind **Pembroke Villas** and **Old Palace Yard** will make no difference to the price of property because the substantial houses and early 19th-century cottages have such lovely outlooks onto the green. Indeed, demand is high. Shopping is pleasant S of the green around **George St**, the town's high street. There's a full-blown department store (Dickins & Jones) and all the more tasteful high street chains, plus a Tesco Metro and Marks & Spencer. The smart shops extend S along **Hill St** towards the bridge, taking up the E side of the riverside complex (see below). Restaurants and bars are plentiful, though most were of the mid-level chain or theme sort until Canyon got the smart set to walk along the riverside path. Alleyways lead off **George St**, with delicatessens, coffee shops, restaurants, bookshops and craft shops. **Church Walk**, one of these alleyways, opens onto Richmond Parish Church.

Richmond Green is surrounded by homes, ranging from 17th to 20th century. Most of the beautiful 18th-century houses on the SE side, where the street is called **The Green**, are offices. In the SW corner is **Old Palace Terrace**, seven houses built in 1692. One was on the market last winter at £895,000. On round to the SW is **Little Green**, where a 4-bed 1728 house was £975,000 in October. On the NW side are some splendid large Victorian villas; on the NE side some handsome 1970s houses.

Behind **Old Palace Yard** and **The Wardrobe**, where three surviving houses are the remains of Richmond Palace, is **Maids of Honour Row** (1724) which was built for the maids of George II's queen. Off **Old Palace Yard** is Trumpeters House, a perfect piece of riverside Georgian, now four flats. The two lodge houses (3-bed) share its acre of gardens, and the lodge on the market last winter has an acre of its own, too: £1.25 million for a 50-year Crown lease. Think in terms of £2 million. . . . Next is the Old Court House, Wentworth House, and then **Garrick Close**, which holds a collection of neo-Georgian town-houses. **Friars Lane** (where a 1-bed flat pushes £200,000, and a 3-bed house £955,000) runs close to **Maids of Honour Row**; it curves down to the river where it joins **Cholmondeley Walk** past Queensbury House, with its neat '30s flats, and a row of pretty Georgian houses. The restored Palladian villa, Asgill House, is at the N end of the riverside **Cholmondeley Walk**. Commanding spectacular views of the bridge and river is the early 19th-century **St Helena's Terrace**, a handsome row of houses built above their own boathouses. A clutch of smart houses is tucked behind, off narrow, picturesque **Water Lane**. A local sport here is watching strangers park by the river and then return to find a car full of river water: tides rise swiftly.

Further S, beside the river walkway which leads to Richmond Bridge, is the million Riverside complex of offices, flats and shops. Designed by Quinlan Terry, and developed in the 1980s by Haslemere Estates, the scheme was one of the most argued-over pieces of architecture of recent years, pitting neo-Classicists against Modernists in a bitter professional row. Terry used a variety of Classical genres to produce neo-Classical façades which hide offices, shops, restaurants and a car park. Unrivalled views of the river are a plus for the studios, 1- and 2-bed flats, maisonettes and a penthouse. Expect to pay £180–190,000 for a 1-bed flat here.

On the other side of the town, past the station, a church in **Kew Rd** has been split into 15 flats, ranging from studios to 3-bed. A 2-bed split-level flat was £550,000 last winter, another (less spacious) £400,000. Both had parking. Just across the road, a dozen new flats sold quickly. The roads between **Kew Rd** and the Old Deer Park are pretty if congested. Difficult parking is reflected, say agents, in prices like £210,000 for 2-bed houses in **Rosendale Rd**. A pair of work/home studios have been squeezed in on **Kew Foot Rd**.

R

Richmond Hill

The main residential area of central Richmond is on the slopes of Richmond Hill, which rises S and SE of the town towards Richmond Park.

The oldest homes are nearest the town: **Ormond Rd** has some Queen Anne houses, some of **The Vineyard is Georgian or** Regency, but further up towards the Park most homes are Victorian. There are some favourite roads, but all Hill locations are desirable. For 5-bed Victorian houses places to look are **Mount Ararat Rd, Grosvenor Rd, Montague Rd** and **Dynevor Rd.** All lie E of **Richmond Hill**, the street which begins with a clutch of antique shops (Georgian houses behind them) and rises to the terrace gardens on one side and a row of expensive homes, with wonderful open views, on the other. **Church Rd** has big houses, some flats, but has quite a lot of traffic. **The Vineyard**, which crosses **Mount Ararat Rd**, is one of the prettiest streets of Richmond Hill. It comprises houses from late-17th to early 19th centuries, including almshouses, all clustered around St Elizabeth of Portugal RC Church. A 3/4-bed Regency villa was priced at £1.1 million last autumn. **Onslow Avenue** has Edwardian 5-bed houses.

Further E between **Albert Rd** and **Princes Rd** is an area of tiny cottages known as **The Alberts**. These have been popular for years and they have nearly all been tidied up. Prices for 2-beds begin at c. £230,000; 3-beds might be up to £350,000.

The top of **Richmond Hill** is lined with a mixture of prized 18th- and 19th-century houses (some split into flats) which enjoy a wonderful distant view of the Thames painted by J M Turner and Reynolds. These views are not cheap: a 3-bed flat was £500,000 in December, while one in **Montague Rd**, without the views, was £300,000.

Turn E into **Queen's Rd**, which hugs Richmond Park, go past the American University buildings and on the left is a range of enormous houses, many split into flats. These command about £900,000 as whole houses. On the right-hand side are houses and flats of the 1970s, '80s and '90s and some side-roads which lead towards the park. **Cambrian Rd** leads to a gate into the park. West of **Queen's Rd** there are some pretty roads, such as **Park Rd**, offering a blend of early Victorian 3-storey houses and 2-bed cottages. **Marchmont Rd** and **Denbigh Gardens** have Edwardian and 1920s/'30s detached houses. **King's Rd,** with some large Victorian Gothic detached houses (one was £2.1 million last year) and a terrace of 1850s 4/5-storey ones, runs up to the prominent church at the junction with **Friars Stile Rd**, which has a clutch of smart shops and also some 5-bed period houses. Plans to build flats on a site in King's Rd were fought off by locals last winter. Laing now propose four houses instead.

North of **Sheen Rd** in **Dunstable Rd, Sheen Park, Townshend Terrace** and **St Mary's Grove** there are a mix of Edwardian, Victorian and Regency cottages and large 3-storey houses, some of which have been converted into flats. Houses here may be cheaper than those on Richmond Hill, but the disadvantage is that some back onto the railway line. The Victorian 3-bed houses in **Townshend Terrace** were £380,000 last winter.

Between **Sheen Rd** and **Lower Mortlake Rd** is a grid of roads with 2/3-bed period cottages. Recently renovated, they fetch around £180,000. The old council depot site in **Cedar Terrace, Lower Mortlake Rd,** now boasts 90 new homes: 2-bed maisonettes and 2-bed terraced houses. **Sheendale Rd** has beautiful (if cramped, and gardenless) Regency cottages. **St George's Rd, Bardolph Rd** and **Trinity Cottages** are pretty but they face a small industrial development and will be close to the Sainsbury's supermarket due to be built by the end of 2000. Disgruntlement about this development – councillors and locals fear traffic chaos – is not shared by estate agents, who say house prices will go up.

Either side of the **Lower Richmond Rd** are Victorian terraced cottages which overlook a very busy road. East of **Manor Rd**, which joins **Sheen Rd** and **Lower Richmond Rd** via a constantly busy railway level crossing, there are council-built houses on **Kings Farm Avenue** and **Carrington Rd**. Roads between **Sheen Court Rd,**

Tangier Rd and Warren Rd offer '30s-built 3/4-bed houses, which can fetch £250–290,000. South of Upper Richmond Rd post-war houses are to be found, particularly on Berwyn Rd, Orchard Rise and Sheen Common Drive. Proximity to park and common raises prices here to around half a million. Courtlands is a large 1930s complex of mansion flats: big blocks in well-kept grounds with 'private' signs.

Petersham and Ham Common

These villages on the borders of Richmond offer rural living to people who cannot bear to be more than half an hour by car from Hyde Park Corner. They have served this function for 300 years, as the dignified Georgian homes testify. The fast journey may only be possible at two o'clock in the morning, but Richmond does well as a substitute for the West End for most purposes, and Kingston's shopping centre is just down the road.

Petersham is surrounded on nearly every side by green spaces: deer-grazed Richmond Park to the E, the cattle-dotted water meadows by the Thames to the N, the dignified Ham House grounds to the W. Its only snag is the snarling traffic that creeps past the high brick walls that shut off the grand houses. Houses do occasionally come up for sale, but for a taste of fine living try the flats in one of the grandest mansions. The old vicarage, a Victorian 9-bed pile with 2.8 acres of garden adjoining the Park, was £3.8 million last winter. Its 1907 church, also redundant, is being converted into one enormous home. There are some smaller houses in Petersham, including a few 20th-century ones in a more suburban setting over towards Ham, but most are at least a century old. The German School – and the excellent local primary school – attract families. Sandy Lane has some Surrey-style detached houses at £500,000-plus.

Ham Common is a splendid, large triangle of manicured rural England, with the gates to ducal Ham House to add class. There are grand Georgian homes here on the Petersham scale, and a few smaller cottages. A Georgian 3-bed cottage on the Green was £395,000 last autumn. A new mansion has been built on the S side in impeccable neo-Georgian. Much of Ham is suburbia, including a big (mostly ex-) council estate over towards the Thames and the well-regarded '60s Parkleys estate. Towards Richmond Park, Church Rd has 20th-century houses, mostly big and grand. A dozen new ones sold fast in 1998 despite being next door to the (very polite) Latchmere House prison.

Kew

Kew has a village feel, with a green complete with cricket pitch – though the constant South Circular traffic, coupled with the Heathrow planes, dispels any rural illusions. It also has a village property market, with one agent finding that 75 per cent of this business is with locals moving around the area. The new estate of 400-plus homes planned on the old sewage works to the E of the area should bring in some new blood, however (see below). Kew prices vary over quite a big bracket, with ex-council 1930s cottages at one end, priced from £175,000; and 5-bed detached Victorian houses at the other, topping £1.2 million. There is a sprinkling of modern homes, some of which offer coveted parking or garages. A 3-bed town-house wil go for £250,000 with parking, £225,000 without.

Kew is a peninsula bounded by the Thames. To the N and E, across the river, are Brentford and Chiswick, with Richmond to the S and Mortlake to the SE. The world-famous botanical gardens at Kew, together with the Old Deer Park, take up to 50 per cent of the area. Despite the green space, Kew is surrounded by main roads. Busy **Kew Rd** bears traffic SW from Kew Bridge and the M4/North Circular junction at Chiswick roundabout. From the green, **Mortlake Rd**, part of the South Circular, forks SE. Between these roads is the bulk of the area's housing. The roads on the Kew Gardens side of **Sandycombe Rd** and the railway line are most sought-after, with the eastern side (sometimes called North Sheen) increasing in desirability.

The area has firmly shrugged off its fuddy-duddy image. It was considered an old peoples' area, but the ever-growing pressure for spacious houses near open space and good schools has seen an influx of young families. Agents report that half their customers are newcomers to the area, half locals trading up. Richmond Borough's schools, which are excellent up to age 11, plus several in-demand private ones, reinforce the attraction. Such is the demand that the council are planning to expand Darell Primary School, and a new school may form part of the sewage-works scheme.

Kew Green and Gardens

The most prestigious property is found around **Kew Green**, where the best of the gracious Georgian houses and cottages, surrounded by mature trees, decked with wisteria and backing onto the river and/or facing the green can top £1 million. Few ever change hands, to the frustration of local agents. To the E of the green, in an enclave bounded by river, green and railway, **Bushwood Rd**, **Priory Rd**, and **Maze Rd** are leafy Victorian/Edwardian 3-bed terraces which can command prices of up to £550,000, with £600,000 for a 4/5-bed semi. Close to the bridge, **Thetis Terrace** and **Cambridge Cottages** and **Watcombe Cottages** have 2-bed cottages. Some overlook the Thames and Strand-on-the-Green.

The enormous modern Public Record Office, on the riverside E of the rail bridge, is a Kew landmark. A piece of land between it and the river is destined for 207 flats if developers St George get their way: this is the fifth such scheme, four public enquiries having refused successive plans for this site since 1989. Just down river, the 24-acre sewage works is to being decommissioned and replaced with 400 more homes in a joint venture between Thames Water and Berkeley Homes (St George's parent company). This scheme proposes quite a bit of open land, a new path to the riverside, and low-built blocks along the present open riverside. There will be some very large houses, and the usual mix of flats and town-houses. Rows continue over the details as Chiswickites across the river complain of ruined views and Kew worries about traffic: access will be off the South Circular and along **Townmead Rd**.

South into **Kew Rd** from the green, there is a clutch of interesting houses on the left-hand side, facing Kew Gardens, ranging from **Hanover Place** (early 18th century) to later styles with Regency bow windows. These give way to large Victorian villas interspersed with modern blocks of mansion flats: if high enough they can have views over Kew Gardens. A few 20th-century houses offer lower prices: a 3-bed 1930s house was £395,000 last winter, with upstairs views of Kew Gardens. Past Newens (the traditional English tea shop serving Maid of Honour tarts), **Kew Gardens Rd** dog-legs around towards **Station Approach**. Large 3-storey Victorian houses dominate; some flats, some spacious family homes.

Station Approach and Station Parade join at Kew Gardens station (District line and North London line). Shops, restaurants and cafés cater for visitors to the gardens – a steady stream in summer – and the locals. The only other shopping area is **Sandycombe Rd** which has an odd mish-mash of useful shops, and the little shops dotted around the green. Thirlstone (Berkeley Homes again) have built 35 homes (flats from £150,000, 4-bed houses £495,000) at 'Layton Place' on land N of **Station Approach**. Lindlay Place, close by, is 12 flats for shared ownership for the elderly.

Popular **Lichfield Rd** and **Ennerdale Rd** join **Kew Rd** and **Sandycombe Rd**. Here the large Victorian family houses with 5 beds (some converted into desirable flats) push £1 million, especially if double-fronted. In **Sandycombe Rd** prices vary with the side of the road: the E side (odd numbers) back onto the tube line. **Ennerdale Rd** (transversed by **The Avenue**) stretches S down to the T-shaped **Lion Gate Gardens**, (whose large Victorian houses make for roomy flat conversions) and on to **Stanmore Gardens** where the Victorian houses are interspersed with solid '30s styles. Turning E into **Gainsborough Rd** there is a recent development of neo-Georgian houses on the site of a school; opposite some little council houses. On **Kew Rd**, between **Lichfield Rd** and **Hatherley Rd**, are some recent blocks of studio and 1- and 2-bed flats.

To the W of **Sandycombe Rd** there are **Victoria Cottages** and **Elizabeth Cottages**, which fetch a little more because they do not back onto the railway. **Alexandra Rd** and **Windsor Rd** have terraced 2-bed cottages. East of the railway and **Sandycombe Rd**, towards **Mortlake Rd**, are **Atwood Avenue, Marksbury Avenue** and **Chelwood Gardens** where large '30s houses have been renovated to provide solid family homes. Gardens on this side of Kew are more spacious. For cheaper 3-bed houses (Victorian/Edwardian) look towards **Dancer Rd, Darell Rd** and **Raleigh Rds**, although these roads do run down to a busy stretch of the **Lower Richmond Rd**, otherwise the A316, the direct link to the M3. This corner will be affected by the **Manor Rd** Sainsbury's. This end of Kew is within walking distance of North Sheen station, with direct trains to Waterloo.

Transport	Tubes: Kew Gardens, Richmond (zone 4, District). To Oxford Circus 35 min (1 change), City 40 min, Heathrow 45 min (1 change). M25. Trains: Richmond, North Sheen to Waterloo 20-plus min; also N London line/Silverlink from Richmond and Kew Gardens.
Convenient for	Heathrow, M3/M4 for South and West, River Thames, Richmond Park, Kew Gardens. Miles from centre: 8.
Schools	Richmond Education Authority: Christ's School, Grey Court, Shene School. Private: St Catherine's Convent School (g), St James's (b), German School (Petersham). See also Twickenham.

R

SALES

Flats	S	1B	2B	3B	4B	5B
Average prices	100–140	130–250	150–350+	200–500+	–	–
Houses	2B	3B	4B	5B	6/7B	8B
Average prices	210–425	250–590+	300–750+	400–800+	690–1M+	–

RENTAL

Flats	S	1B	2B	3B	4B	5B
Average prices	140–190	150–300	200–350+	250–400	–	–
Houses	2B	3B	4B	5B	6/7B	8B
Average prices	260–390	300–400	310–600+	550–1500	900–2,000	–

The properties   Wide range of desirable houses from early Georgian through mid-Victorian (the majority) to modern, plus mansion flats and conversions. River and parkside locations among the most charming in London. Two-bed flats are most popular; family homes always scarce. Kew offers family homes and flats at (by comparison) better-value prices.

The market   Demand brisk, especially for family homes. Rentals increasingly popular, with movers from Chiswick, Hammersmith and Fulham. Big premiums paid for best locations on riverside and Richmond Hill. English (especially City-working) and foreign (German, Scandinavian, American) families find area gives happy mix of London and country. Local searches: 7 working days.

Among those estate agents active in this area are:

- Victor Lown
- Nightingale Chancellors
- Dixon Porter
- Barnard Marcus
- Mann & Co
- Jardine & Co
- Chancellors
- Gascoigne Pees
- Phillip Hodges
- FPDSavills
- Hamptons
- Halifax
- Priory Management *
- GA Property

further details: see advertisers' index on p.671

R

SHEPHERD'S BUSH

Map ref: p58 (7D)
Postal districts: W12
Boroughs: Hammersmith &
Fulham (Lab)
Council tax: Band D £827
Conservation areas:
Ingersoll Rd, Arminger,
Ethelden Rds
Parking: Meters or permits

The biggest – and, due to changes in planning, perhaps the last – major new shopping complex inside the M25 is about to be built next door to Shepherd's Bush Green. The Bush, a still rather dowdy part of West London, is crying out for a bit of sparkle and decent shops, but how the inevitable increase in traffic will be handled remains to be seen: the area is already famous for its bottlenecks.

However, the plus side of the White City scheme, as it is called, is that more than £100 million is to be spent on upgrading public transport – and work has already started on the link road into the M41 **West Cross Route**. Shopaholics will, though, have to contain themselves a little longer: the building of the stores, restaurants and 20-screen cinema complex will not start until next year, and is likely to take four years.

The site is the old tube depot to the W of the M41/railway corridor, across to **Wood Lane** and S of **Ariel Way** – handy for the area's other claim to fame, the huge BBC HQ. A few streets of homes divide it from the green, but there will be access to the new mall from the E corner of the green, by the Central Line station. Next to the tube, a new train station will serve the West London Line, with some trains going via Clapham Junction direct to Gatwick Airport. Also, with luck, an interchange between the Central Line and the Hammersmith & City Line (at present there's a separate tube station for each line, both called Shepherd's Bush, fully half a mile apart). Bus routes will be improved, too.

Two department stores are planned, of which one should be a giant Marks & Spencers. The other end of the site will have a supermarket (Sainsburys has been mentioned) opening onto Wood Lane. In between the two, more shops and a fabric-roofed 'winter garden' with cafés and restaurants. Below the whole thing will be 4,500 parking spaces – which brings us back to traffic . . . .

Until the end of the 18th century Shepherd's Bush was just another area of countryside around London. But buildings shot up during the 19th century as the capital expanded rapidly and Shepherd's Bush, well-placed on a main route from the W, soon became a centre. Its triangular green became a focus for travelling traders on their way to market. The origins of the quirky name remain a mystery, although various theories have emerged over the years. Some say the area was named after a famous landowner. Others insist that the body of a murdered shepherd was found in bushes on the green several centuries ago. But by far the most popular explanation springs from its position on a major droving route. It is likely that shepherds rested their flocks on the green before the final hike up to Smithfield Market. The only sheep there today are the ones that decorate the Central Line tube station.

Most houses here are of the solid 2- or 3-storey workaday terraced variety, built in the late 19th century, and Shepherd's Bush changed very little until the second half of the 20th century when council blocks, motorways and shopping precincts arrived.

Apart from the major traffic roundabout near the green, which links with the M41, the character of Shepherd's Bush has survived relatively unscathed and much of the dominant Victorian and Edwardian architecture is still intact after a century.

Much of the personality of today's Bush is derived from the heavy presence of the BBC. Its vast HQ up **Wood Lane** now shelters nearly all the programme-making staff, with only a few bosses and accountants still enjoying the West End ambience of Broadcasting House. This has changed the area's restaurant profile. While it is certainly no Notting Hill or Soho, the area has gained a rash of up-market 'dining pubs' and other interesting eateries that are certainly kept going by the media people. The BBC tribe joins the cheerful cosmopolitan mix of Asians, Irish, West Indians, Poles, Africans and representatives of most other ethnic groups.

Traditionally a good first-time buyer's hunting-ground, the Bush is now also being scouted by those priced out of surrounding areas. Brook Green, Hammersmith and Fulham lie to the S; Holland Park, then deeply trendy Notting Hill, across the roundabout to the E. Shepherd's Bush is also extremely well situated for public transport and for the major routes in and out of London. It is midway between the A40 **Oxford Rd** in the N and the M4 – gateway to Heathrow and the West. The Nos 12 and 94 buses take shoppers direct to the West End.

Like many other central parts of London (and despite its name), Shepherd's Bush lacks open spaces and there is a shortage of trees and greenery – also of family houses with large gardens. Shopping is humdrum and will remain so until the White City mall emerges. There is, though, a colourful market off the **Uxbridge Rd** under the railway bridge. The Bush Theatre on the green is a well-respected fringe venue.

Many of the taller Victorian terraces were converted into 1- and 2-bedroom flats during the 1980s, but this practice

An essentially Victorian area, Shepherd's Bush shows every variation of the Victorian pattern-book builder's craft. Builders took house plans and details 'off the shelf', resulting in ornamentation like this bay, with its sash windows, stone, or perhaps stucco, parapet and decoration around the tops of the pillars. The house is built of London stock-brick, which when clean contrasts well with the stucco.

was checked by local planning policy; now some of the bigger houses are being turned back into family homes. There is still a lot of rented property, and some streets remain relatively undeveloped. The boom in flats conversions brought parking problems to many a street; residents pay for permits, and towaway trucks prowl.

Good big family houses, still in the minority, are most common near **Goldhawk Rd**, which marks the boundary with Hammersmith: look W of **Askew Rd**, around **Rylett Rd** and **Ashchurch Park Villas** (the latter is probably the lordliest road in Shepherd's Bush) and Wendell Park; prices here reflect those across the border round Ravenscourt Park.

Shepherd's Bush does not have enclaves as recognizably self-contained as Bedford Park or Brook Green, but properties of a similar type do tend to form neighbourhoods. The most sought-after areas lie between the **Uxbridge** and **Goldhawk Rds**. Newer 1914–1930s-style houses can be found near Wendell Park, and the district N of **Cobbold Rd**, really East Acton (see that chapter), is a mix of purpose-built Edwardian maisonettes and Victorian terraces. Moving E, Cathnor Park has a village atmosphere that disappears at **Boscombe Rd** – known for its 4-storey Victorian terraces, largely converted into flats.

North of the **Uxbridge Rd**, homes are generally smaller, although tall houses are found between **Wood Lane** and **Loftus Rd**. West, to **Wormholt Rd**, is a mix of purpose-built Edwardian maisonettes and rows of solid 2-storey Victorian terraces. Streets of larger 1930s semis border the Cleverley and Flower estates, which lie to the E of **Old Oak Rd**. North of **Sawley Rd** council-built property is the norm although much of the stock W of **Bloemfontein Rd** is now privately-owned. Out E towards **Wood Lane** lies the sprawling White City estate: far fewer owner-occupied flats here: it is not an aesthetic gem. Council-built homes, in the form of the Old Oak Estate, continue N of the **Westway** near East Acton tube station. These, by contrast, are pleasant cottage-style homes and are a conservation area. They often now appear for sale.

Two small but very distinct neighbourhoods complete the picture. The first, just N of the **Westway**, offers a mix of Edwardian terraces and purpose-built maisonettes. The second is 'Caxton Village', off the green; a quaint network of Victorian terraces.

S

Wendell Park

This is the farthest W and most sylvan bit of W12. Beyond **Emlyn Rd**, across the borough border, lies Bedford Park, and the 1914 terraced homes that overlook Wendell Park also have an Arts-and-Crafts air. These tree-lined streets also hold 3- or 4-bed late-Victorian family homes. The delightful little park and nearby tennis courts give this quiet, prosperous area a sense of space.

Rylett Rd, Rylett Crescent and **Ashchurch Park Villas** and **Ashchurch Grove** to the E contain some of the most expensive properties in Shepherd's Bush. Many of the large family houses are still intact despite the '80s conversion blitz. Some are double-fronted, well-proportioned homes, others 3- or 4-storey Victorian terraces; they ooze Classic style with their ornate pillars and regal front steps. Note, too, **Balmoral Mews** and **Cosmer Close** off **Rylett Crescent**. Some houses have garages, gardens can be huge and residents spend a lot on their upkeep. (They may also prefer to call this corner 'Ravenscourt Park': the welcome green space of the large park lies across on the Hammersmith side of the busy Goldhawk Rd.) Stamford Brook tube is a walkable distance away.

Roads in this district, including **Binden Rd** and **Bassein Park Rd**, are wide with plenty of trees and ornate shrubs. A 3-bed house and garden in **Bassein Park Rd** was £395,000 last winter; **Ashchurch Grove** had larger, 4/5-bedroomed homes for £550,000 and £625,000; a 6-bed one in **Binden Rd** £520,000. A grand home in **Hartswood Rd**, which runs down from Wendell Park, was £850,000.

The section of **Goldhawk Rd** that runs E–W rather than N–S is more desirable. Very pleasant 3-storey Victorian houses have attractive raised ground entrances. Going N, purpose-built Edwardian maisonettes can be found W of **Askew Rd** towards the **Uxbridge Rd**. The attractive red-brick Victorian houses are particularly plentiful in **Cobbold Rd**: smaller homes in this speed-humped road, where a 2-bed house was £260,000. Further N in **St Elmo Rd** Victorian terraces dominate. Many have been converted into flats – a 1/2-bed garden flat, £175,000 – but it is still possible to buy a whole house in this popular area.

Over to the W, just across the borough boundary and in the W3 postcode, is a group of streets around **Valetta Rd** that agents are trying to name 'Little Malta' (they just can't resist it, can they?); again, a good source of flats in the £120–180,000 bracket. This district abuts the Wendell Park area, and homes are similar.

Cathnor Park

Similar style continues E of **Askew Rd**. Most homes are 2-storey although elegant 3-storey versions have been converted successfully in **Westville Rd**. Wedged between two bustling districts is little Cathnor Park. **Melina Rd**, a particularly pretty corner of this village area, has some of the rare cottage-style houses in Shepherd's Bush (a 3-bed, double-fronted example, £275,000). Others in the road are 3-storey terraces with basements and front doorsteps. Check the **Percy Rd** area for other pleasant cottage-style homes, as well as 2- and 3-storey houses. **Greenside Rd** has a well-recommended primary school.

Central Shepherd's Bush

Moving E beyond **Coningham Rd** the houses are taller and mostly divided: this is the heart of flat-land. The seven or so roads W of the green are among the most popular in Shepherd's Bush. They are ideally situated for two Hammersmith & City Line tube stations as well as regular buses on **Goldhawk** and **Uxbridge Rd**s.

Coningham Rd is busy, though the constant stream has been slowed by traffic calming. For a quieter life try **Hetley Rd, St Stephens Avenue** or **Godolphin Rd**, where 1-bed flats can sell for £130,000, a 2-bed with garden, £195,000; a whole house in **Hetley Rd**, £379,000 for 4 beds and patio garden. Many of the streets are one-way – others are closed in the middle to block off rat-running between **Uxbridge Rd** and **Goldhawk Rd**. The flats have classic elegance, sash windows and high ceilings. Outside the roads are relatively wide, light and tree-lined.

Moving N of the **Uxbridge Rd** divide, properties are generally smaller and the neighbourhood generally less well-regarded. Exceptions, though, lie W of **Wood Lane**, where **Frithville Gardens** and **Stanlake Rd** have very pleasant 5-bed houses: thanks to the demand for such good-sized family homes – and to the presence of Hammersmith park and the BBC headquarters at the top of the road, the tube at the bottom, typical house prices are £450,000; £550,000 at best; a 3-bed flat £225,000. However, nearby **Tunis Rd** has a completely different character. Its Victorian terraces have attracted many conversions, and the gardens here are tiny. Hammersmith Park is all that is left of the Franco-British Exhibition of 1908, an oasis of ornamental gardens, pavilions and pools.

Loftus Rd – an attractive tree-lined street and conservation area – has one major drawback: the stadium which is home to Queen's Park Rangers football club and Wasps rugby club. This normally quiet road turns into a sea of fans at match weekends. Long-term, QPR want to move, but for the moment they remain. This area has a mixture of flats and houses, and a strong residents' committee looks after the neighbours' interests with respect to the presence of QPR.

West of **Loftus Rd** lies an area of Victorian terraces and purpose-built Edwardian maisonettes. **Bloemfontein Rd** (where 3-bed maisonettes, c. £220,000, can be found) runs straight through the neighbourhood and can be busy. Drivers are inclined to use it as a cut-through from the **Westway** in the N to the **Uxbridge Rd**. More peaceful streets to the W; **Oaklands Grove** is considered something of a gem. This corner has its park, too: Wormholt Park, with, on the **Bloemfontein Rd** side, the popular Janet Adegoke Leisure Centre.

West of **Wormholt Rd**, across to **Old Oak Rd** and the borough boundary, the houses are newer – 1930s mostly. The neighbourhood is pleasant; it borders the Cleverley and the cottage 'Flower' estates to the N.

This model village, again originally council-built and officially called the Wormholt Estate, is universally known as the 'Flower Estate' since street names include Daffodil, Clematis, Lilac – and Hemlock: pleasant and varied in style.

Much of the stock is privately owned and the neighbourhood is very well tended. **Sawley Rd** is particularly attractive: flat-fronted grey-brick homes with arched doors. Although ex-council properties are not to everyone's taste, the 2- and 3-bed houses in the Flower estate are, say agents, highly saleable. Average prices for 3-beds at c. £180–200,000. The estate's cosy village atmosphere changes dramatically E of **Bloemfontein Rd**.

The White City estate, five roads arranged in a criss-cross pattern, houses council tenants in huge blocks of oppressive red-brick. **South Africa Rd** to the S runs alongside to Queen's Park Rangers FC and can be used as a cut-through to **Wood Lane** and the BBC stronghold.

North of the **Westway** is also council-built housing. Busy **Du Cane Rd** runs between **Scrubs Lane** and **Old Oak Lane** in Acton past Hammersmith Hospital and Wormwood Scrubs Prison. The area is dominated by the huge prison compound which looks out over the common towards Willesden Junction and Brent in the distance.

Old Oak

This no-man's-land area, often referred to as East Acton, is depressing and lacks identity. But a little farther down **Du Cane Rd** towards East Acton tube station is the Old Oak estate, with a strong community atmosphere. The estate is isolated from the rest of the area by the railway line. To the NE is the open space of Wormwood Scrubs, to the E the eponymous prison. West of the railway is similar estate housing, bounded to the S by the busy six lane **Western Avenue**. **Braybrook St** on the edge of Old Oak Common has attractive flat-fronted terrace brick houses with sash windows. It is surprisingly 'countrified'; sadly though the village feel is marred by the view of the imposing prison walls, bright floodlights and watch-towers.

Caxton Village

'Caxton Village', possibly the most convenient spot in the whole of Shepherd's Bush, will get more useful still when the giant White City mall is built behind it. Off the **Uxbridge Rd**, N, side of the green, this select neighbourhood of little Victorian terraces is in walking distance from three tube stations, two on the Hammersmith & City Line and Shepherd's Bush on the Central (a 2-bed house in Caxton Rd itself, £275,000 last winter). The plan for the shopping complex buries the car parks that previously loomed over these streets.

Borders

Just N of the **Westway** is a quaint collection of roads on the Kensington and Chelsea border. The streets running off **Eynham Rd** are a mixture of purpose-built Edwardian maisonettes and tall terraces converted into flats. The roads are surprisingly quiet considering their close proximity to the Westway junction with the M41.

Transport	Tubes, all zone 2: Shepherd's Bush (Central, Hammersmith & City); White City, East Acton (Central); Goldhawk Rd (Hammersmith & City). From Shepherd's Bush: Oxford Circus 15 min, City 25 min, Heathrow 1 hr.
Convenient for	BBC Centre, West End, Notting Hill, Heathrow, M4/M40 to West. Miles from centre: 4.5.

Schools   Local Authority: Sacred Heart (g); London Oratory (b); Lady Margaret (g). Private: Latymer (b) (g); Godolphin (g).

SALES

Flats

S	1B	2B	3B	4B	5B
Average prices					
90–110	130–160	175–220	190–270	230–300	—

Houses

2B	3B	4B	5B	6/7B	8B
Average prices					
240–280	260–330	350–450	400–600	500–700	—

RENTAL

Flats

S	1B	2B	3B	4B	5B
Average prices					
130–180	180–220	220–300	260–350	350–500	450–550

Houses

2B	3B	4B	5B	6/7B	8B
Average prices					
250–300	280–380	350–500	450–600	500–600	600–700

The properties   Victorian terraces are the staple: smaller 2-storey ones as single homes, taller ones often converted to satisfy demand for 1/2-bed flats. Some larger family homes, mainly near Hammersmith borders, now command large sums. Also pockets of Edwardian p/b maisonettes; some roomier inter-war houses. Cheaper: ex-council; cottages, eg 'Flower' Estate, especially popular.

The market   BBC land: the gleaming new White City headquarters set the seal on the Bush's renaissance. Young buyers find the Bush convenient, with good transport to town for those who don't work for the Beeb. Those who do pay big sums for the small stock of big family houses. For the rest, singles in studios become couples in flats, but children usually presage move to more family area. Local searches: 10 working days.

Among those estate agents active in this area are:

- Barnard Marcus
- Willmotts
- Sturges
- Collingwoods
- Barber & Co
- Finlay Brewer *

- Northfields *
- Winkworth *
- Foxtons *
- Scotts *
- Townends
- Robertson Smith & Kempson *

* further details: see advertisers' index on p671

S

SOHO AND COVENT GARDEN

Map ref: p140 (8A)
Postal districts: W1, WC2
Boroughs: Westminster (Con), Camden (Lab)
Council tax: Band D Westminster £350,
   Camden £897
Conservation areas: Whole area
Parking: Residents/meters, clamps, tow-trucks

Soho and Covent Garden are in the very heart of London. Their streets are shaped by their Georgian past, though they are, these days, largely business and entertainment centres, attracting tourists and Londoners alike to their theatres, clubs and restaurants. They are also sought-after places to work, congenial places to employ designers from graphic to fashion, editors from film to book, creators of cartoons, web-sites and concepts of every sort. Quite a few of these creative types would like to live here too, but they face stiff competition from shops, restaurants and offices (not just their own). And from the burgeoning Chinese community based around **Gerrard St**.

In the past year, Soho has faced competition as a fashionable work location from areas like Clerkenwell, Shoreditch and the South Bank. This has done nothing to lessen the pressure on space, be it for homes (prices up by 15–30% depending on which agent you talk to), for office space, or for a place at the bar or a table in a restaurant. The re-opening of the Opera House has given Covent Garden a boost. Here there are more new homes to buy – in theory, for they sell out fast – and agents report that two out of three would-be buyers prefer Covent Garden to Soho. Not that anyone can afford to be choosy: property is scarce in both.

The two areas are very different. Covent Garden's the more public: a meeting-place, alive with the excitement of theatre and opera, and with the equal showmanship of the market-place – one of the best places in Central London to walk and talk, to see and be seen. Soho has long been London's 'foreign' quarter, the place where daring Englishmen ventured for a little Continental naughtiness and a good meal. It's still true, though the food may be Chinese or Indonesian.

Today, Soho is perhaps the younger, and certainly the more daring, of the two, more prone to inner-city pleasures and vices of every sort. Homelessness and drugs have placed heavy burdens on both districts: they attract every lost teenager in Britain, and quite a few from further afield.

Both areas are zealously conserved, with many historic buildings under preservation orders. Consequently the pressure on space is intense. Everyone wants their office, shop, market stall or restaurant here. And both areas have been well and truly rediscovered as a place to live. Stories of cheap Soho flats above shops, or old banana warehouses in Covent Garden, are now as much wistful legends as the tales of affordable Docklands warehouses.

What homes there are in Soho and Covent Garden are not immediately apparent, often being tucked away behind the scenes in odd corners off commercial streets, or above the ground-floor shops and first-floor offices. Studios and flats dominate the lists. There are probably only a dozen houses in the whole area. The supply is growing, though (as price rises show) it is still not up with demand.

New developments aside, the most common sort of home is the upper floors of a shop or restaurant forming a 2/3-bedroom maisonette. There are no gardens; balconies and patios, occasionally found in new properties, add greatly to prices. They are rare in conversions. Only a handful of flats are available at any one time with brisk demand reported, even in quiet times. Many properties are purchased as pieds-à-terre by business people and can be easily let if not required all year round.

Prices vary dramatically with the size and character of the properties. This is true of sales and of lettings, which are by far the most common way to find a home here.

The obvious advantage of the area is location. It is within easy strolling distance of West End shops and theatres. The City is a 10 min tube ride away. The main demand for homes seems to come from bankers and brokers who work in the City and from people with businesses in the West End – the bachelors of both species. In Soho one finds prosperous young single people who enjoy the night life and may work in the advertising or film or computer-based industries. In Covent Garden, people with a country home who want a pied-à-terre in town. Quite a few homes are owned by companies for the use of their top people. Others are held as investments and rented out to companies and visiting foreigners.

Before these folk discovered the area, people lived here. And they still do. The original population is more mixed, made up of elderly people and families who work in the traditional local industries – theatre, crafts such as leatherwork and tailoring, shops and restaurants – and who live mainly in rented homes.

Both areas are entirely jumbled: shops, offices, theatres, restaurants, bars and homes often occur in the same street. These amenities provide the plus side to living here but also cause the disadvantage of congestion, both traffic and pedestrian, noise and extreme difficulty in parking. A less tangible benefit is atmosphere.

Old-timers say Covent Garden is past its best – Peter York's 'theme park' tag is uncomfortably accurate – but Soho is if anything on the up and still manages to preserve a raffish, villagy feel. It's a great place to live and to work, but a wonderful one to live in if you don't have to work. Or sleep. Nowhere in London is idleness more fun.

S

Soho

Soho is the area S of **Oxford St**, N of **Leicester Square** and E of **Regent St**. **Charing Cross Rd** divides it from Covent Garden to the E.

In the 16th century Soho was a Royal Park where hunting took place – 'So-ho!', an ancient cry, being the presumed origin of the name. It was developed with grand houses in the 17th century and later settled by the Huguenots, giving the area its abiding Continental character. By 1711 there were 600 French householders in Soho, and 3,000 foreign lodgers, mostly French. The population increased rapidly in overcrowded houses until a serious outbreak of cholera in 1854 after which aristocratic residents moved out and prostitutes and other dubious characters moved in. At the start of the 20th century new theatres were built along **Shaftesbury Avenue** and **Charing Cross Rd**. Restaurants, invariably started by foreigners, gave the area a gastronomic reputation. One famous French restaurant was started by a French family in answer to desperate pleas by visiting compatriots for something decent to eat.

After World War II strip clubs and clip joints increased in this area and the residential population declined rapidly. This exodus of residents has now stopped and, thanks to a massive clean-up campaign mounted by Westminster City Council after pressure from the Soho Society, the number of sex clubs has been reduced from more than 100 to a couple of dozen. Westminster proudly announced 12 shut-downs of illegal sex shops during 1999. The area is now famous for its restaurants, bars, clubs and cafés, specialist shops, designer workshops and smart offices. Sadly, the French connection, three centuries old, is now broken. The last truly French grocer, Roche, closed in the early '80s.

Soho is still a maze of narrow streets and alleys, and forms a conservation area. Many 18th-century and early 19th-century buildings remain, interspersed with later infill developments of varying styles. Residential Soho has seen a renaissance in recent years. Lovely old houses have been restored, new flats squeezed in, redundant commercial blocks converted. The most sought-after home is the 1-bed flat. The loft apartment has made its appearance, though there are few 'true' lofts as the old buildings with high ceilings do not exist. Soho 'lofts' are often more like open-plan flats. Other homes are flats above shops or more modern, purpose-built infill developments, again usually over commercial property at ground- and possibly first-floor level.

South of **Shaftesbury Avenue**, **Wardour St**, **Gerrard St** (pedestrianized) and **Lisle St** form the core of Chinatown, a tightly-knit neighbourhood that is characterized by the many excellent restaurants, supermarkets and bakeries. Property here is largely owned by the Chinese community and the stock of homes is under great pressure: the 1997 Hong Kong handover increased the arrival rate considerably.

North of **Shaftesbury Avenue**, the area where **Brewer St**, **Berwick St**, **Wardour St** and **Old Compton St** meet is the scruffier part of Soho. But such is demand, prices here are only relatively cheaper. These streets still house the largest share of the sex industry (including **Great Windmill St**, **Archer St**, **Tisbury Court** and **Walkers Court**) and there are a few flats, mainly above shops in **Brewer St**. Typical prices start around £140,000 for a studio. In nearby **Rupert**

Behind the shopfronts and the neon, much of Soho is old. It was a fashionable suburb in the 17th and 18th centuries, and some houses still survive from these periods. These, in Meard St, were restored after years in disrepair. Door, elaborate doorcase and railings are all perfect examples of their period.

S

St, Consolidated Properties created shops and 20 flats out of four houses in 1997. Consolidated are major freeholders in the Soho and Covent Garden areas.

Several renowned Italian delis and cafés are also found in these streets, and further along **Old Compton St**, now much improved due to the council clean-up, there are one or two small infill developments. **Golden Square** and the surrounding roads, **Upper** and **Lower St James St**, **John St** and **Great Pulteney St** are much more 'respectable' and quieter, but again few homes are available as this is more of a business district. However the former Ear, Nose & Throat Hospital in **Golden Square** itself recently became 14 flats. **Golden Square** is a desirable place to live – Soho's only green oasis now that **Soho Square** has become somewhat notorious (especially after dark). Prices for the few **Golden Square** flats can exceed £500,000.

On the W fringe of Soho, towards **Regent St, Kingly St**, the famous **Carnaby St** and **Fouberts Place** are largely shopping areas – rather self-conciously calling themselves 'West Soho' – and the occasional flat may come on to the market. However, close by in **Marshall St** is Marshall House, a 1989 block of 12 1-bedroom and nine 2-bedroom flats. At the other end of the street, Stirling Court is a 1970s 10-floor flat block. **Newburgh** and **Marshall Sts** have recently been recobbled, **Fouberts Place** has been repaved as well. A whole house in Marshall St, split into bedsits, was £750,000 last autumn. Sandringham Court in **Dufours Place** is a popular development, completed by Barratt in 1987; resales do come up occasionally, and the block is also popular for lettings. Flats may occasionally be had in the Georgian terraced houses of **Lexington St**.

Great Marlborough St, Noel St and N of here is unlikely to be fruitful for homes, being more of a business/office area. **Poland St, Broadwick St** with its Georgian terraces and **D'Arblay St** are more popular and more expensive. A triplex with its own pation in D'Arblay St was £499,000 last winter. Sandringham Court off Broadwick St is popular: 1-bed flats are c. £230,000. **Poland St** has a modern mixed block of offices and flats. There are popular developments at 15 **Hollen St** and 68 **Broadwick St**: watch for the rare resales. A small block of eight flats on the corner of **Poland St/Broadwick St** produces the occasional resale. Spacious newly converted studios in **D'Arbley St** proved popular in the late '80s. They now command around £275,000 (1989: £110,000). **Berwick St**, S of **Broadwick St**, houses the well-known fruit-and-vegetable market and is therefore very noisy and delightfully messy during the day.

Meard St is unique, having a splendid terrace of early 18th-century houses (Grade II listed): a few are still in single occupation, most have been split into flats. Tenanted until 1987, the estate was then auctioned and split up. Resales are appearing. Prices tend to be high to reflect the scarcity of this kind of period house: one 4-bed house has that Soho rarity, a garden. This is a pedestrian through-way – but beware of cycle couriers.

The next street along, **Bourchier St**, has 17 recent flats with parking spaces in a Wates-built scheme. The streets leading N from **Shaftesbury Avenue** to **Soho Square** are grander. **Dean St, Frith St** and **Greek St** are prestige addresses (though the hostel in **St Anne's Court**, off **Dean St** has lowered the tone somewhat). Flats in these streets will be pricey and in the square itself, the most expensive of all. Agents say that Greek St prices are 40% above those of those around Great Windmill St. There are several fine restaurants and famous clubs. At the northern end of these streets one or two Georgian houses may remain intact. There are some houses in **Frith St**, for instance: one has become an hotel, another has been expensively restored as a home or office. Kings House, a modern block in the NE corner of **Soho Square**, houses 10 flats within it. Townsend House in **Dean St** is a 1950s block. The big Mezzo restaurant nearby has some flats above it in 'Soho Lofts', a Manhattan Lofts development. These are accessed via **Richmond Mews**: £425–450,000. A £795,000 flat round in **Dean St** offered 1 bed and a box room – though 2 baths and a terrace – in October.

Busy **Wardour St** is famous for the film industry but there is little scope for accommodation. On the edge of Soho is Centrepoint House, an 8-storey block next to the famous office tower on **St Giles High St**. The 36 2-bed maisonettes were refurbished in 1990 and are now c. £185,000 for a 24-year lease on a 2-bed duplex.

Covent Garden

The area S of **High Holborn**, E of **Kingsway** and N of **The Strand** takes its name from the development, in the early 17th century, of a former convent garden to form an Italian-style piazza laid to an Inigo Jones design. The original fashionable residents soon moved further W and by the middle of the century a fruit-and-vegetable market had started and grew rapidly. In the 18th century it became an area of seedy lodging houses and brothels. By the early 19th century the neighbourhood had been transformed by the market which had expanded and been taken over by traders in all manner of goods.

In 1830, the Duke of Bedford organized the construction of the market building in an attempt to restore order. The market remained, in greater or lesser degrees of picturesque confusion, until 1974. Londoners grew to love the fruit, vegetable and flower stalls, the ribaldry of the market traders – and the pubs which opened at four in the morning to cater for them. Covent Garden became a unique mixture of market traders and actors, banana wholesalers and ballet dancers.

When the market finally moved out, an epic row began about the area's fate. A giant scheme to knock most of it down was thwarted by an energetic local campaign and the GLC converted the central market building into a specialist shopping centre which has become a hugely successful tourist attraction. This started the transformation of the area around the market which originally comprised many fruit-and-vegetable warehouses, hardware stores and workshops of various kinds. Warehouses have been converted into flats, many small shops stayed and more have opened, and many courts and alleys have been pedestrianized.

Houses are very scarce, a few remaining around **Mercer St** and **Shorts Gardens**. Agents reckon there are only six freehold houses in Covent Garden. Most available accommodation is flats above shops and restaurants or in a selection of enviable, purpose-built developments, mainly recent, and again usually with commercial uses at ground-floor level. The eastern side of the neighbourhood has some blocks of flats belonging to housing associations and charities such as the Peabody Estate. These add to the number of residents, but not to the market for homes. A new Marks & Spencer store in **Long Acre**, plus the existing Tesco Metro in **Garrick St**, mean that shopping is getting useful as well as pleasurable.

The borough boundary between Camden and Westminster runs along **Shelton St**. To the N lies Seven Dials, where **Monmouth St**, **Upper St Martin's Lane**, **Shorts Gardens**, **Earlham St** and **Mercer St** converge. 1990 saw the Seven Dials monument restored to its position at the meeting-point. The slender column of this faithful copy, adorned with its six sundials, forms the seventh itself. Seven Dials is a very popular place to live, together with **Neal St** and **Neal's Yard**, now both pedestrianized – the latter packed with wholefood cafés and organic farm produce. One particularly coveted development is **Seven Dials Court**, built around an attractive landscaped courtyard at first-floor level and approached from **Shorts Gardens** leading through to **Neal's Yard**.

Matthews Yard off **Shorts Gardens** is a 1989 development of three houses, three 1/2-bed flats and three 4-bed maisonettes. Georgian conversions in **Monmouth St** are popular, while 15 recent flats, Fielding Court, date from 1990. A former warehouse in **Tower St** was converted into loft-style apartments in 1997. At 19 **Mercer St** is the Terry

S

Farrell-designed development in the Comyn Ching triangle. There are seven luxury flats with balconies or roof terraces and a rare house, dating from the 17th century. Moving over to **Endell St** (still in Camden), you will find a noisier, so somewhat cheaper, corner. Only relatively, though: the smart new flats around a courtyard in the Ventana development are £400–900,000 for 2-bed and 3-bed penthouse flats. Conversions can be found in **Betterton St. Drury Lane** is again a rather busy street – especially around theatre-time – but a number of developments have been appearing. 'Garden Court', on the corner of **Drury Lane** and **Broad Court**, has 12 1-bed flats, four 2-bed and a 4th-floor penthouse with three terraces. No 145 Drury Lane is Taylor Woodrow's smart new block of 51 flats with a Japanese garden, no less – and parking spaces at £35,000 on top of prices from £390,000 (2-beds) to £795,000. There were two penthouses left at Christmas. Off the S end of Drury Lane Bruce House is a Grade II listed building owned by Westminster Council; a men's hostel has been rebuilt behind the façade as a purpose-built home for about 60 people. Over in **Macklin St**, N towards Holborn, a Victorian building has been split into six flats. Barratt's new block in **Newton St**, completed in 1999, has 2- and 3-bed flats.

On the corner of **Upper St Martin's Lane** and **West St** a re-clad office tower has 12 flats in a low-rise section, Meridian Place. Very smart Art Deco style. Garrick House in **St Martin's Lane** is new this year: 24 flats with a handful left last winter, priced from £340,000 for a 2-bed up to £1 million for a penthouse. Otherwise, theatres, clubs, restaurants and offices occupy this street. **Long Acre** is largely shops and offices but the quieter **Floral St** has a couple of extremely popular mid-1980s developments – about 20 flats at Nos 16 and 30, where resales have proved infrequent.

All streets close to the Piazza are very much coveted, although most of the buildings which actually overlook the market – and the buskers performing in front of the portico of St Paul's Church – are in commercial use. There are some superb flats in St Paul's Court, overlooking the churchyard. They were converted from a commercial building in 1974: one 2-bed was £795,000 in December. Period conversions may be available occasionally in **King St, Henrietta St, Maiden Lane** and **New Row**. A 5-floor building in **Bull Inn Court**, off Maiden Lane, with office/residential permission was £475,000 last October. There is at least one 3-bed triplex flat in **James St**. Off **Bedford St**, behind the Coliseum in **Bedford Court**, is a development of 10 flats with private balconies. **Hanover Place** has some converted warehouse buildings. Period conversions occasionally appear in **Russell St, Tavistock** and **Wellington Sts**.

Some council flat resales are becoming available in Covent Garden. In some blocks, virtually all the flats are privately-owned. The walk-up 5-storey blocks around **Tavistock St** and further N off **Drury Lane** yield 1-bed flats for the young and fit at £165–170,000. Those in **Martlett Court** are popular: Sheridan, Beaumont and Fletcher Buildings. Ex-council flats are likely to be up to 30 per cent cheaper than equivalent private homes.

Strand

Just beyond Covent Garden, between **The Strand** and **Embankment**, houses in **Craven St** have been refurbished as part of the Charing Cross Redevelopment Scheme. One or two houses survive in this unexpectedly peaceful corner: a 1730 5-storey, 7-bed one in **Craven St** was to let at £2,500 pw in December, and York Buildings has some flats for sale at around £315,000 for 2-beds. **Trafalgar Square** must be the best-known address in London: now you can live there, with 12 flats carved out of a bank by Natwest Properties last year. Natwest have done the same with another building in nearby **St Martin's Place**. A block in **King William IV St** has some very smart flats.

South of **The Strand** in **Buckingham St**, a handsome Georgian house has been modernized to provide six flats on the third and fourth floors. Most of this pleasant area S of **The Strand** is commercial, but other flats may be found above offices. Last year saw 66 flats converted from an office building, Little Adelphi, in **John Adam St**. These are mostly let. Sale prices are typically £270,000 for a 1-bed, £325,000 for 2-bed. And of course there are the splendid serviced apartments next to the Savoy Hotel. If you have to ask the price – you can't afford it.

Transport
Tubes, all zone 1: Leicester Square (Piccadilly, Northern), Covent Garden (Piccadilly), Oxford Circus (Victoria, Central, Piccadilly), Tottenham Court Road (Central, Northern). From Leicester Square: Oxford Circus 10 min (1 change), City 15 min (1 change), Heathrow 1 hr. Trains: Charing Cross.

Convenient for
Everywhere: West End entertainment and shopping. City.

Schools
Local Authority: Westminster City C of E (b), Grey Coat Hospital C of E (g).

SALES

Flats	S	1B	2B	3B	4B	5B
Average prices	145+	190–425	185–500	400–650	600–1M	—
Houses	2B	3B	4B	5B	6/7B	8B
Average prices	—	→1.4M	→	—	—	—

RENTAL

Flats	S	1B	2B	3B	4B	5B
Average prices	200–600	230–600	400–600	500–1000	—	—
Houses	2B	3B	4B	5B	6/7B	8B
Average prices	400–1000	800–2500	→	—	—	—

The properties
Pressure from commercial uses means very few buildings are homes. But these include rare, lovely pre-Victorian houses, flats above shops, conversions of warehouses, etc, and some stylish new-build aimed at company and foreign-investor markets. An exciting, historic (if noisy) place to live.

The market
Restricted supply and growing demand as area was cleaned up raised prices in late '80s. Demand held up well through the early-'90s recession and prices held steady in late 1998 when other areas, like Clerkenwell, saw falls. Prices have doubled since 1990 — at least. Local searches: Westminster 10 days, Camden 7–10 days.

S

Among those estate agents active in this area are:

- Chestertons
- Knight Frank
- Barnard Marcus
- Copping Joyce
- LDG
- Hurford Salvi Carr
- Winkworth *
- E A Shaw
- De Groot Collis
- Foxtons *
- Frank Harris *

further details: see advertisers' index on p671

THE SOUTH BANK

Map ref: p78 (2C)
Postal districts: SE1, SE17, SE16
Boroughs: Lambeth (Lab),
  Southwark (Lab)
Council tax: Band D Lambeth
  £750, Southwark £809
Conservation areas: Many, check
  with town halls
Parking: Varies but always scarce

Right now, this is perhaps London's most exciting quarter. Call it the South
Bank, or Bankside, or Southwark, or even (heaven forbid) South Central: no one name
is quite right, but a unit it certainly is. It takes in a great sweep of London on the south
bank of the Thames from Waterloo to Rotherhithe, opposite the West End and the City.
Wander its gritty back streets, stroll the superb waterfront promenade (do you know
it's there?) and you will see more life, more innovation, more money being spent (and
with more flair) than anywhere else in town.

   The Jubilee Line Extension has given this area a big boost, as a place to vist and
to live. From Waterloo the new line runs E to Southwark, London Bridge, Rotherhithe,
Surrey Docks and on to Canary Wharf. In the other direction it offers a fast link to
Westminster and the West End. Suddenly, the South Bank is accessible.

   Suddenly, too, it is the cultural heart of London. The new Tate Modern in the
massive old Bankside power station, the new/old Globe Theatre and its museum, the
National Theatre – and signs that at last the South Bank culture centre around the
Festival Hall will get a radical makeover. And, of course, the Wheel, raising spirits
right along the Thames as it comes into view at unexpected places, and the equally
beautiful new Millennium Bridge like a spear straight into the City.

   But what about living here? More and more people do. The big excitement, in
terms of new homes supply and price rises, took place in 1995–97. Things went quiet
for a while, but it's reckoned that around 1,000 new homes for sale will appear here
by 2003. Add in ex-council re-sales and there are now homes to choose from, and
with transport and environment still improving it is still a good place to look.

S

The map above covers perhaps a dozen neighbourhoods, each very different. The riverside strip from County Hall downstream to Tower Bridge has a certain unity, a string of monuments tied together by the Queen's Walk, but stray a block S and you are in Waterloo, Bankside, Borough, Bermondsey. Some are ancient names: Borough High Street saw the Romans pass and it has relics of every age since. To the E, the Shad Thames docks and warehouses of Bermondsey are a new neighbourhood: Tower Bridge, some call it. Butler's Wharf is here. The Docklands chapter describes it. Go further S to find Lambeth (the old parish, not the modern borough), the N edge of Kennington, the Elephant and Castle, Walworth and the Old Kent Rd.

This is a very mixed area: it contains public and commercial buildings of every kind. There are theatres and railway stations, office blocks and hospitals. There is also quite a lot of council-built housing in tall and often grim blocks. A few years ago, it was hard to find anything to buy or rent in this part of London. Now, the choice is much greater. A rash of conversions of old schools, offices and factories; resale of council-built homes, new-builds in odd inland corners, riverside warehouse flats – all of a sudden there is a homes market, for both buyers and renters.

High-level rail lines and busy roads, plus the concentration of commerce and industry, have until very recently forced homes into small pockets. The area has traditionally been one of poverty and overcrowding, and some of the present-day council estates are little or no improvement on their slum predecessors. But with commercial buildings becoming homes, neighbourhoods are changing fast. Even the big estates are looking up as private buyers pick up cheap flats, and council and housing association improvements take effect.

The catalysts for change have been the City, with its earning power and need for easy access; the river; the new Jubilee Line tube and the Millennium. The riverside strip is startling to anyone who has not seen it for a few years. Restaurants, shops, bars, designer workshops, cafés jostle the cultural showplaces. The only way to judge the South Bank is to go and look. Preferably on foot, or by bike. To use a local saying: 'cor, oo'd 'ave thought it!'

Waterloo, South Bank, Bankside and The Borough

County Hall, once the giant riverside home of the old Greater London Council, is now a hotel, health club, an aquarium – and flats (see below). The South Bank cultural complex lines the river from County Hall round past Waterloo Bridge to the National Theatre, and the land to the S and E is mostly taken up by Waterloo station. Waterloo has grown to include the Eurostar terminal, Waterloo International and has gained the vital Jubilee tube. The area round it may bear watching, as it is rumoured it will become a 'Transport Development Zone' under new planning rules, which could mean more and taller office buildings (presumably to replace those turned into flats in the last recession).

North of the station, **Theed St**, **Whittesley St** and **Roupell St** are quiet roads of little terraced early-19th-century houses on a human scale which are popular buys: 2-beds perhaps £375,000. Off **Theed St** is the 'Royal Millenium Village' development (never use one buzzword when three will do seems to be the developer's motto) with 2-bed, 2-bath flats and mews houses. South of Waterloo East station are some '30s council flats in **Wootton St**.

S

Coin St to the N was the centre of a big and controversial redevelopment scheme, the row in essence pitching commercial interests against community activists supported by Lambeth Council. The activists won, and the area consequently includes rented homes for 1,300. Some of the homes are in restored 1829 terraces. **Duchy St** and **Aquinas St** are part of the Duchy of Cornwall Estate (see Kennington). **Aquinas St** has 1911 cottages. Some are being sold freehold as they come vacant.

Behind Waterloo station, **Lower Marsh** is showing signs of improvement. Some smart flats in a concierged block in nearby **Westminster Bridge Rd** have resale prices of around £140,000 for 1-bed, with 2-beds at £250,000. Developers Barratt insisted on calling the neighbourhood 'South Westminster'. **Lower Marsh** is a bustling shopping street, with a market. Some flats over shops. Cobbled **Launcelot St**, off **Lower Marsh**, has a handful of cottages. East of **Baylis Rd** is a large council-built estate with some attractive homes. Resales here include 1-bed flats from £80–125,000. Further S, **Mead Row** has some flats run as a housing cooperative. **Hercules Rd** has a mix of small 19th-century cottages, some 3-storey houses (£300,000 plus) and council blocks. **Lambeth Rd** is on the fringe of Kennington and has some similar early 19th-century houses.

A new source of flats is the conversion of offices. County Hall's inland blocks, just across the street from Waterloo International, have become flats. They have been steadily appearing since 1995, and 2000's batch includes the North & South Squares: 2- and 3-beds, £330–500,000. Earlier batches sold briskly, and on the resale market a river-view 2-bed would approach £300,000 this spring. The old Shell building, the downstream block next to Waterloo Bridge, became 'The White House' in 1996 amid much hype. Developer Galliard is now marketing penthouses from £600,000 and 'staterooms' at £500,000. Next to it, the dramatic drum of the Imax cinema now takes up the former seedy 'bullring' at the S end of Waterloo Bridge.

To the E the borough of Southwark (not to be confused with The Borough) begins. The Oxo Tower, with its high-profile restaurant, has done a lot to smarten up the riverside. There are some housing association flats lower down the building. On the riverside, there is little housing E of the LWT tower except some council homes and expensive flats (River Court) in **Upper Ground** and some smart riverside flats in part of the King's Reach development. A converted office block in **Broadwell** off **Stamford St** has yielded 16 flats.

East of Blackfriars Bridge, the enormous brick-built Bankside Power Station is now the new Tate Modern. Nearby, a commercial building has become loft apartments called 'The Gallery'. Close to the bridge are some riverside Southwark Council flats. **Bankside** has one of London's most desirable houses, Cardinal's Wharf. The house was already old when Christopher Wren lived there while building St Paul's. Alongside it, the late Sam Wanamaker's reconstruction of Shakespeare's Globe Theatre is a triumphant success: a magnet for the whole neighbourhood.

On **Bankside** Berkeley's Benbow House, 71 flats around £400,000, sold out in hours last year. The penthouses can still be had for approaching £2 million. Inland, past the sites of the rediscovered Elizabethan theatres, the Rose and the Globe, some new homes have enviable positions. On **Southwark Bridge Rd**, a handsome Georgian terrace, Anchor Terrace, has been restored as 29 flats. It is on the site of the original Globe Theatre: the new one is a street away. A few of the 2-bed homes were still being marketed late last year between £180–300,000 with 1-bed flats from £195,000. The block at the corner of **Great Suffolk St** and **Southwark St** was an address known to thousands as a big Inland Revenue office. No longer, to hearty cheers its about to become homes and offices. A block away on **Great Guildford St** Peabody has just built 17 rental homes and 4 shops.

One of the new Jubilee line underground stations is on **Blackfriars Rd** just where it meets **The Cut**. The latter street is the focus of a council re-hab scheme. There are plenty of council-built properties here. **Nelson Square** and nearby streets have council flats, both low-rise and in towers. This continues down towards the S, though **Blackfriars Rd**, like all the main streets in the area, has a few surviving earlier houses, some Georgian. Most of these have, however, become offices, though the tide is on the turn with one or two becoming homes again. Off **Blackfriars Rd** there are modern houses in **Scoresby St** and a 1980s development, Bridge House Court, with 28 mews-style houses and flats built around a garden and over a car park. **Southwark Bridge Rd** has some Victorian houses, now flats: £90,000 buys a 1-bed example. The residential streets S of **St George's Circus** are described in the Kennington chapter.

West of London Bridge, renovated St Mary Overie Dock, which contains a replica of Sir Francis Drake's 'Golden Hind', is the centrepiece of a new range of riverside offices and flats. This successful development sweeps back to form a precinct round glorious Southwark Cathedral. Another reminder of past glories, the end wall and rose window of Winchester Palace, still stands, lending its name to **Winchester Square**.

Borough High St meanders S from London Bridge and is the centre of the oldest part of South London. Just S of the Cathedral is Borough Market, an atmospheric survival of Victorian London much used as a film set. Progress is about to overtake it: a big railway viaduct, part of Thameslink 2000, may go through at high level: a public inquiry is under way. And the market itself is destined to be 'London's Larder': a centre for fine foods. With the Vinopolis wine exhibition in **Tooley St,** and a rash of new restaurants, this will make The Borough a gourmet's paradise.

On the other side of the **High St**, **St Thomas St**, behind London Bridge station, has some Georgian houses. **Snowfields**, behind Guys Hospital, has some good old houses, nearly all split into flats, and is a popular location: the doctors provide a ready public for these convenient homes. Local agents say they very rarely come onto the market. **Union St** has some working-men's cottages built late in the 19th century. To the S, as far as **Lant St**, here is a little neighbourhood of mostly 19th-century housing, all built by various philanthropists and public bodies. As such, they are rarely for sale. **Union St** has a converted hop warehouse, now flats: the Maidstone Building.

The district between **Borough High St** and **Southwark Bridge Rd** has some warehouse conversions. Examples are the nine lofts in **Redcross Way** sold in 1999; there are more in **Lant Street, Marshalsea Rd** and adjoining streets. In **Swan St**, E of the High St and near Borough tube, some of Bellway's 100 flats in Berwick Court were still on the market last winter at £200,000-plus. On the High St itself Town Hall Chambers, an island site which English Heritage had on its 'at risk' register, has been rescued by developers Silverstreet and is now 10 flats (all sold in 1999, £170–550,000).

Turn down **Trinity St** to discover a surprising residential enclave: the Trinity estate, on land owned by Trinity House. **Trinity St** and **Trinity Church Square** have early 19th-century houses belonging to the Seamens' Widows' Housing Trust. **Merrick Square** (1850s) and **Cole St** are similar. Some houses and flats are now being sold, others are available at very cheap rents. New 'loft-style' houses here were on the market in 1997 in a scheme called 'The Courtyard'. Builders are adding further new homes here: Fairclough's Trinity Court round in **Harper St** has 2-bed flats from £265,000 and 4-bed houses from £385,000. Bellway's Chadwick Square is adding flats (from £146,000). **Bath Terrace** has some Victorian flats in a large block. Studio flats are c. £60,000.

Walworth and The Elephant

There are big plans for the regeneration of The Elephant and Castle, a 1960s traffic interchange-cum-shopping centre which even the local council agree is one of London's biggest eyesores. £25 million of government money has allowed Southwark Council to start reclaiming the area for sanity, but real hopes rest on a £600 million scheme to 'transform the area from a place to avoid to a place to be'. Three consortia, involving respected names, have put in plans. One consortium will be chosen this year to devise a master plan. Ideas include putting all the traffic underground, and creating a piazza on top. A plan for a tram-line up to Waterloo and on across the river, and S to Peckham, would boost public transport. A key building here is the former Alexander Fleming House, once HQ of the government's social security department and designed in suitably alienating concrete by Erno Goldfinger. This architect's status as a guru of

Modernism led to the block being listed, despite its legendary unpleasantness as a place to work. Now it is 'Metro Central', a block of 413 flats successfully marketed by St George as being 'at the centre of London'. A 2-bed was £185,000 last winter.

From the Elephant the **Walworth Rd** runs S towards Camberwell. Once it, like other such streets, was lined with handsome houses, but few survive. **Albany Rd** runs off to the E, forming the boundary between the new Burgess Park, with its boating lake and adventure playground, to the S and the enormous Aylesbury Estate, built to house more than 8,000 people on 64 acres. The Aylesbury is now a 'New Deal for Communities' project with £188 million of government cash being spent on improving the homes. The triangle between **Walworth Rd**, the Elephant and the **New Kent Rd** has equally little to recommend it, though a few corners of 19th-century housing survive amid the council slabs. Some such houses occur in and around **Brandon St** and **Chatham St**. Many have been converted into flats. However, if it is a low price you seek, ex-council flats can be bought here for a tenth of what is asked a mile to the N.

Surrey Square boasts some 1790s houses, which sell for £300,000-plus, and some 1970s ones which are cheaper. **East St** is another place to look, although the area is busy on days when the street market is held. Six new flats have recently been completed in **Fremantle St**, a sign of change in the area. Some purpose-built Edwardian maisonettes can be found in **Aylesbury Rd** and **Wooler St**. A few ex-council flats are beginning to come onto the market, even on these unprepossessing estates. Victorian 3-bed houses (£220,000) in nearby **Searles Rd** have been joined by a school conversion: lofts at £300,000. Down off the **Old Kent Rd** and close to Burgess Park, the five new houses in gated, secure **Pepler Mews** are around £300,000. Across the main road Galliard are 'recreating' **Marcia St**, which means they are building Victorian-style 4-bed houses where the originals once stood.

Bermondsey

The Docklands chapter covers the exciting Butler's Wharf/Shad Thames quarter between **Tooley St** and the river. Inland, the Docklands effect has been encouraging interest in the pockets of housing between the river strip and the **Old Kent Rd**. This district has a surprising number of homes, including some of the oldest in London. The Bricklayers Arms site, once a railway yard, became a vast estate of new homes as just about every big builder descended on it around 1989. Sadly, many of the homes were repossessed in the ensuing recession. Housing associations now own about half the 600 homes. A new road, **Mandela Way**, leads through the site. Nearby, the Abbey development has some pleasant cottage-style 1/3-bed properties built a dozen years ago. To the E, the district S of **Southwark Park Rd** has some pleasant streets of Victorian terraced cottages. **Lynton Rd**, **Simms Rd**, **Esmerelda Rd** and **Strathnairn Rd** have flat-fronted cottages which are mostly well-kept and attractive. Further S, **Avondale Square** has 3-storey mid-Victorian terraced houses. To the N, **Yalding Rd** has some pretty flat-fronted houses.

Bermondsey Square is in truth only a corner of handsome houses overlooking the antiques market and busy road to Tower Bridge. East of here is **Grange Rd**, the centre of some activity in recent years as houses have been renovated and buildings converted for homes. Three houses in **Grange Walk** have medieval origins, being the last survivors of the great Bermondsey Abbey. There are some Victorian houses, too. A school in the street has been cleverly converted into characterful flats and galleried studio houses; further conversions and new-build are appearing in this corner. The 165-home Grange Park scheme, between **Grange Rd** and **Rouel Rd**, was completed by Laing in 1988. There are 2- and 3-bed houses and 1- and 2-bed flats. The 1860s industrial Alaska Building's 1- and 2-bed flats were converted a couple of years ago and 2-beds now go for £240,000. **Leroy St** has some Victorian flats in a 4-storey terrace. **Neckinger Cottages** has neat 2-bed houses. **Bermondsey St**, which leads back up to London Bridge station, is the old village centre and has some surviving old houses and smart modern businesses. **Pages Walk** has three new 2-bed cottages. **Long Lane** has some modern council-built houses, and a new Metropolis scheme with 39 flats from £150,000. Off **Tower Bridge Rd, Leathermarket S**t has a big block of 1994-built flats around a courtyard. In **Tanner St**, opposite a little park, is another converted Victorian print works and five new-build houses from £305,000.

Transport	Tubes: Waterloo, Elephant & Castle (zones 1/2, Northern, Bakerloo); London Bridge, Borough (zone 1, Northern, Jubilee); Lambeth North (zone 1, Bakerloo), Southwark (zone 1, Jubilee). From Elephant & Castle: Oxford Circus 22 min (1 change), City 7 min, Heathrow 1 hr (2 changes). Trains: Waterloo, London Bridge.
Convenient for	City, West End, Docklands. Miles from centre: 1.5.
Schools	Local Authority: London Nautical (b), Bacon's School C of E, Notre Dame High RC (g).

SALES

Flats	S	1B	2B	3B	4B	5B
Average prices	59–200	65–310	80–500	90–500+	100–500+	—
Houses	2B	3B	4B	5B	6/7B	8B
Average prices	195–400+	200–500+	300–600+	—	—	—

RENTAL

Flats	S	1B	2B	3B	4B	5B
Average prices	120–170	150–300	170–450	350–450	400+	—
Houses	2B	3B	4B	5B	6/7B	8B
Average prices	250–350	300–400	—	—	—	—

The properties	Big changes as warehouse and office conversions, plus new-build, join ex-council homes to widen property choice. Houses scarce, flats of all sizes plentiful. Locations vary from riverside smart to very inner-city.
The market	Once a place for bargains, now becoming mainstream. Ex-council homes and resales on big developments offer lower prices. Lofts and conversions, some very smart, attract international buyers. New tube and Millennium-led schemes have raised area's profile. Local searches: Lambeth 10 days, Southwark 15 days.

Among those estate agents active in this area are:

- Alex Neil
- Cluttons Daniel Smith
- Kinleigh Folkard & Hayward
- Barnard Marcus
- Halifax
- Cityscope
- Burnet Ware & Graves

- Winkworth *
- Olivier Jacques
- Duncan Allen
- Edwards
- Williams Lynch *
- Daniel Cobb

further details: see advertisers' index on p671

SOUTH KENSINGTON, EARL'S COURT AND WEST BROMPTON

KNIGHTSBRIDGE

SW7

ROAD

CROMWELL

Gloucester
Road

South
Kensington

EARLS
COURT

SW5

Earls
Court

OLD BROMPTON

ROAD

SOUTH
KENSINGTON

CHELSEA

FULHAM

West
Brompton

WEST
BROMPTON

ROAD

SW10

FULHAM

N

Map ref: p76 (4B)
Postal districts: SW3, SW7,
  SW5, SW10
Boroughs: Kensington & Chelsea
  (Con)
Council tax: Band D £534
Conservation areas: Most of
  area
Parking: Residents/meters.
  Clamps

A steady revival over the past 10 years has returned these three areas to the state of bourgeois respectability intended by their 19th-century developers. The three diverse districts form a largely residential triangle between Chelsea and Kensington proper. They date from the second half of the 19th century, when there was growing demand for large family homes close to the West End.

The enormous dignified terraced houses typical of the area had a short run of luck. The demise of domestic servants made them unviable and most spent the middle half of the 20th century as hotels or cheap, if seedy, rented flats and bed-sits. But no longer. The area is still dotted with hotels, be they smart South Kensington establishments or Earl's Court B&Bs; but the rocketing values of the 1980s finally made it viable to expend care and attention on the tall decaying houses. Skips, scaffolding and interior decorators moved in en masse as the classier developers set to work. Clever – indeed, state-of-the-art – conversions transformed **Evelyn Gardens**, the **Onslows**, the **Cranleys**, the **Courtfields**. Then the '90s saw conversions mop up most of the lingering South Ken hotels and spread into Earl's Court.

The area as a whole lies between **West Cromwell Rd**, **Cromwell Rd**, and **Imperial Institute Rd** to the N, **Fulham Rd** to the S, the West London railway line in the W and **Brompton Rd** and The Oratory church in the E. It contains some of the most expensive houses in London – the handsome £8-million-plus villas in **The Boltons** – and a seemingly endless supply of converted and purpose-built flats.

Two major factors influenced the development of the area, previously covered with market and nursery gardens. The first was the Great Exhibition of 1851 in Hyde

S

Park, profits from which were used to build the major museums complex on the border with Knightsbridge and the two main routes along which they stand, **Cromwell Rd** and **Exhibition Rd**. The second and most important influence was the arrival of the Metropolitan and District railways during the 1860s, which allowed speedy access to Central London. Ease of access remains one of the biggest attractions of the area.

Every neighbourhood except West Brompton has tube stations within walking distance. West Brompton Station on the District Line is W of the Brompton Cemetery and is convenient for a few streets in Earl's Court. Its usefulness has increased since a connecting station has been added to the West London Line, which has useful trains to Clapham Junction and Willesden Junctin and some long-distance services.

The Piccadilly Line calls at all three of the other local tube stations and runs direct to Heathrow Airport: a big plus for this international area. **Cromwell Rd** also links directly with the M4 to Heathrow, drawing tourists to the hotels in the area and the transitory population which characterizes Earl's Court in particular.

The area is probably the most cosmopolitan in the already various Royal Borough. Earl's Court, once known as the Polish Corridor then Kangaroo Valley after successive waves of settlers, is now home to an increasingly affluent mini-United Nations and is also a favourite haunt of London's gay community. Some Middle Eastern families still remain in South Ken but it is no longer the 'Saudi Ken' of the 1970s. The French have colonized the area around the Lycée Français near the tube.

One thing all the neighbourhoods have in common is garden squares, although there is only one public garden – in **Redcliffe Square**, West Brompton – unless you count Brompton Cemetery, adopted as a de facto park by the locals.

The most densely populated part of the area lies to the N of **Old Brompton Rd**, where red-brick mansion blocks abound and the majority of houses have been converted to flats. The most desirable chunk lies between here and the **Fulham Rd**. Many of the terraces of big brick and stucco houses have been converted into flats but there are still enclaves of single-family houses in small-scale villagy streets, charming cobbled mews and peaceful cul-de-sacs. Shops are generally clustered around tube stations and restricted to the main roads bounding the neighbourhoods.

Old Brompton Rd, running E–W, a busy boulevard, cuts through the middle of the area. Here the shops, pubs and big brick mansion blocks tend to congregate in groups, the shops near main junctions such as **Earl's Court Rd** and around South Ken station. A string of smart shops, restaurants, bars and antique shops stretch along most of **Fulham Rd** with a concentration of fashion stores at Brompton Cross (the junction with **Sloane Avenue**). **Cromwell Rd**, a wide noisy 6-lane highway leading to the M4, has hotels standing side-by-side with tall terraced houses divided into flats.

Wellcome Trust and Thurloe Estates

This strip between **Old Brompton Rd** to the N and **Fulham Rd** to the S, extending W to **Drayton Gardens**, is the heart of residential South Kensington. Until 1995 most of this district was owned by the Henry Smith's Charity, landowners since the 17th century. Smith's Charity sold its estate to the Wellcome Trust in 1995 in a controversial deal which hit the headlines when angry leaseholders argued they had not been given first refusal to buy the freeholds of their homes. A number of leaseholders have bought their freeholds, but they are still a minority. More people have extended their leases to 105 years. However, short leases are still common, and the time-consuming efforts of leaseholders to extend leases keeps homes off the market leading to shortages of homes to sell.

All householders, including freeholders, are still subject to strict controls on how they maintain their properties under an estate management scheme imposed by Wellcome: no pink front doors here, please. The Trust's holding is concentrated around **Onslow Gardens, Cranley Gardens, Evelyn Gardens** and the **Pelhams**. A freehold, or in the case of a flat a share of one, can boost prices. A degree of estate control also applies to the Thurloe Estate (lying between **Pelham St** S, **Thurloe Place** N and **Brompton Rd** E). The Thurloe Estate has sold off the freehold of a number of properties, but here too, all residents are subject to an estate management scheme.

One of the gems of the Wellcome Estate is **Pelham Crescent**. Elegant white stucco terraced houses sweep in a semi-circle around leafy private gardens, which screen the Victorian crescent from the Brompton Cross end of **Fulham Rd**. Stretches of black iron railings, columned porches and green Victorian street lamps complete the scene. Most of the houses are still in single-family occupation: expect to pay £1.7–2.5 million. The white stucco continues into **Pelham Place**, which curves across · **Pelham St**, a feeder road between South Kensington, Knightsbridge and the **Fulham Rd**. **Pelham Place** leads to **Thurloe Square**, one of the area's most exclusive garden squares. Here 4-storey and basement brick and stucco houses (mainly split into flats) stand on three sides of an elongated private garden. Residents in the SE corner of the square enjoy an exceptional view of the entrance to the Victoria & Albert Museum at the top of **Thurloe Place** with its imposing crown-shaped stone tower.

To the E of the square lies a group of Georgian terraced houses in **Alexander Square** and neighbouring streets. Despite its name, **Alexander Square** is a single street of early 19th-century 3/4-storey brick and stucco houses, overlooking small private gardens. The gardens act as a barrier between the houses and **Brompton Rd** as it winds from Knightsbridge to **Fulham Rd**. Just beyond here, **Brompton Rd** merges with **Fulham Rd** at fashionable Brompton Cross, with its cluster of ultra-smart shops and restaurants and the Art Nouveau Michelin Building. **Sydney Place** combines with the S leg of **Onslow Square** E to form the main through-route from South Kensington to Chelsea.

Onslow Square proper lies to the W of the main road. Immaculate terraces of 4-storey 1846 houses with columned porches overlook award-winning gardens in this choice square. The houses were split into flats during a major conversion programme in the 1960s. Buyers pay £495,000 or so for a 2-bed flat. White stucco and brick-and-stucco terraces of varying sizes, with the same columned porches, are the dominant style in **Onslow Gardens** (tree-lined communal gardens), **Sumner Place, Cranley Place** and the N arms of **Cranley Gardens**. Most of these have already been converted into flats, many at top-of-the-market levels. Leasehold prices typically range from £200,000 for a 1-bed flat; from £335,000 for a 2-bed. Values shoot up for share of freehold: £1.25 million was being asked for a 3-bed garden flat in Cranley Gardens last winter. More properties round here are being refurbished as single houses. The spacious, 1980s-done-up houses in **Sumner Place** have leases of around 50

S

Stucco and the term cottage do not often go together but they co-exist happily in this house in Elvaston Place, called a cottage despite its Classical rusticated stucco and elegant door surround. Trees hide the lower pair of windows: there are six, set symmetrically in the façade. The six-panel door echoes the windows. These features recur on the larger homes.

years. In nearby **Neville Terrace** a new-build freehold house sold in 1997 for £5.5 million, including a staff cottage. **Neville St**, next along, has 4-bed houses which go for £2.2 million. In **Onslow Mews East**, what looks like a row of cottages is in fact two handsome 3-bed 1980s-built houses. Parallel to the W side of Cranley Gardens is **Cranley Mews**, where pretty, typical mews houses sell for prices around £575,000 – though with a big range of sizes and prices. At the S end of **Cranley Gardens** and **Evelyn Gardens**, stucco gives way to Victorian red-brick flat blocks. The most attractive examples are the newly refurbished Dutch-style buildings with unusual brick and white stucco porches which line the S arm of **Evelyn Gardens**. It is a rare building round here that has not been converted and smartened up over the last 15 years.

In contrast to this densely populated area is a network of small streets just off **Fulham Rd**, N of **Elm Place**. They lie outside the Wellcome Estate. **Elm Place** itself (2-storey vine-clad late-Georgian cottages with tiny front gardens) and **Selwood Place** (fine Georgian terrace on the N side) are charming, leafy streets. **Selwood Place** is blocked off at its W end by the back of St Peter's Armenian Church in **Cranley Gardens**.

The northern part of the Brompton Hospital, on the corner of **Foulis Terrace** and **Fulham Rd**, is now a complex of 73 1- to 5-bed flats known as The Bromptons: all sold at prices (in 1999) from £450,000 for a 1-bed flat to £3.7 million for a 5-bed family apartment. A current sample price is £1.1 million for a 3-bed flat. Pool, gym and underground parking are provided. A boundary quirk gives it an SW3 post code.

An arched brick entrance and steps on the E side of **Elm Place** leads up to **Regency Terrace**, a group of 3-storey brick and stucco terraced maisonettes above the rear of shops fronting **Fulham Rd**. As the name suggests, the houses line a Regency-style terrace at first-floor level, complete with black iron railings and street lamps. They look down on **Lecky Street**, a quiet little private cul-de-sac of white 2-storey houses with columned porches. A number of mews streets are spread throughout the area, by far the most picturesque being **Roland Way**, tucked away off **Roland Gardens**. Pretty painted cottages decorated with hanging baskets and colourful window boxes give this cobbled private street its charm. A row of 27 luxury 3/4-bedroom freehold terraced houses appeared in the late '80s in the newly named **Eagle Place** and in **Roland Way** itself. These are much in demand, with barriers at either end of the road for improved security. Prices from £775,000.

The S end of **Roland Way** leads into **Thistle Grove**, a shady pedestrian walkway lined with green Victorian lanterns and trees overhanging the rear walls of **Evelyn Gardens**. Small houses and cottages of varying styles merge with tall brick and stone mansion blocks. **Drayton Gardens**, which forms the W boundary of the area, combines a mix of styles from brick and stucco terraced houses with front gardens (NW) to Dutch-style brick and stone mansion blocks and modern flats. The most recent development here is a Fairbriar scheme for 13 2- and 3-bed flats: these were all sold to one buyer before they were complete, though some were on the market again last winter from £400,000. At the S junction with **Fulham Rd** stands the cinema and the former South Kensington Squash Club. The squash club has been sold with permission for redevelopment as flats, but work has not yet started.

The **Fulham Rd** from here back E to Brompton Cross has many expensive shops and restaurants, belying the scruffy reputation the street held a decade or two ago. It is now far smarter (and a bit quieter) than the **King's Rd**. The **Fulham Rd** is sometimes considered to be in Chelsea, but in this stretch forms a clear boundary between the two districts. The postal district boundary puts a few homes N of the **Fulham Rd** into SW3. The traffic – and parking – in this road is especially problematic.

Museum/Lycée Area

As its name suggests, the area is dominated by the major museums standing along **Exhibition/Cromwell Rds**. The Science, Natural History, Geological and Victoria & Albert Museums were built following the Great Exhibition of 1851. The museum developments and improved transport links attracted wealthy residents to the area. Nowadays, the neighbourhood is particularly popular with the French, who have established their own colony near the Lycée Français. The school, together with the French Institute, covers a whole block stretching from **Cromwell Rd** through to **Harrington Rd**.

South Kensington underground station and a number of busy main roads have attracted a mix of shops, hotels and other uses, ranging from the College of Psychic Studies to the British Association of Cancer Research, both in **Queensberry Place**. The Aga Khan's gleaming cultural centre for Ismaili Muslims stands in **Thurloe Place** opposite the V&A Museum. Amid all the hustle and bustle, **Bute St**, with its cluster of small shops, manages to retain a delightfully village-type atmosphere. The busy junction by the tube station is dominated by the red-brick inter-war Melrose Court flats block on the S side. The council has given planning permission for complete redevelopment of the station with houses, shops and offices being built on a concrete deck over the platforms. This scheme was scuppered by the early '90s recession, and last winter its revival seemed in doubt once more. A plan for a big health club with swimming pool in **Pelham St** was being considered at the time of going to press.

Many of the houses around **Queen's Gate** and on E are enormous, and they have nearly all been divided into flats at various periods and to various levels of quality. The latest example is the conversion of a house in **Elvaston Place**:

prices from £235,000 to £1.3 million. In **Queen's Gate Terrace** Prince Albert House has become 32 flats (£365,000 to £3 million) behind the stucco facades. The only exceptions can be found in **Reece Mews**, a pleasant little cobbled street running N–S between **Harrington Rd** and **Old Brompton Rd**. An attractive development of new 2-storey brick mews houses fits in well with the older 3-storey painted cottages.

The NW corner of the mews lies empty, forming part of the Iranian Embassy site. The Iranian government planned to build an embassy on the site, which fronts **Queen's Gate**, in the 1970s but the idea was abandoned after the Ayatollah Khomenei's revolution. Planning consent has now expired and the site is now a car park. Standing next to the empty plot is St Augustine's Church. On the other side of the church, **Manson Place** is a wide cul-de-sac of tall brick and stucco terraces, much improved in recent years.

Courtfield

Between **Cromwell Rd** in the N and **Old Brompton Rd** in the S is a varied district which looks to Gloucester Rd rather than South Kensington tube as its transport centre. **Queen's Gate**, running N–S is a wide tree-lined boulevard – wide enough for central parking – flanked by tall brick and stucco apartment buildings and hotels (see also Kensington). Flats range in price between £160–200,000 for a studio and £1.3 million. To the W lies **Stanhope Gardens** with its companion mews to the W, E and S, where a number of small-scale development schemes and quality conversions have taken place. **Stanhope Gardens** itself is one of a series of garden squares in the neighbourhood. Four-storey brick and stucco terrace houses line the private gardens, the E arm forming the most attractive stretch. Developers LCR has transformed the W side of **Stanhope Gardens** into flats behind the original Victorian stucco façade. These are in two blocks known as Stanhope Court and Charlesworth House which have 83 1- to 3-bed flats. A 2-bed flat with underground parking sold recently for £485,000 but prices range from £300,000 up to over £1 million. The mews behind contains 2/3-storey brick/painted cottages, some with roof terraces and most with their own garages.

Clareville St to the S branches off busy **Gloucester Rd**. Painted houses and cottages stand alongside a handful of offices, the Chanticleer Theatre and the Webber Douglas Academy of Dramatic Art. The street becomes a lane as it runs S past Our Lady of Victories RC School (Fulham and South Kensington adult education institute) and wends its way towards **Old Brompton Rd**. Parallel is tree-lined **Clareville Grove**, a peaceful oasis within walking distance of both Gloucester Rd and South Ken tube stations. It is easily the most highly regarded street in the neighbourhood with its variety of attractive period houses, front gardens and hedges. The street becomes more mixed to the S with Clareville Court, a modern brick flats block near the junction with **Old Brompton Rd**. Across **Gloucester Rd**, **Hereford Square** is one of the best preserved garden squares in Kensington, its three symmetrical terraces of 3/4-storey white stucco houses built in 1848 remain unaltered, except where some parts were rebuilt following war damage. Prices for houses here are upwards of £1.5 million.

Between the square and **Bolton Gardens** to the W, the streets are dominated by concentrations of red-brick Victorian mansion flats. In **Gledhow Gardens** and **Bina Gardens** they overlook private gardens. **Wetherby Gardens**, a popular street, has a mix of styles ranging from brick and stucco paired villas to late-19th-century Dutch-style red-brick buildings. A 3-bed flat in **Wetherby Gardens** might be over £500,000. Exceptional examples of this 'South Ken Dutch' look, with its steep gables, riot of terracotta decoration and tall chimneys, are found in **Harrington Gardens** and **Collingham Gardens**. Gilbert of the Gilbert and Sullivan opera partnership lived in **Harrington Gardens**. The houses have since been converted into smaller units or for other purposes. They have rear communal gardens and properties on the E arm of the square also pleasantly overlook private gardens behind houses in **Wetherby Gardens**. Nos 48/50 **Harrington Gardens** have been converted into 19 flats.

To the N lies **Courtfield Gardens**, another garden square lined with tall Victorian brick and stucco terraces of varying quality. This square is being transformed by the conversion of hotels into smart flats: from taking up a majority of the tall houses, hotels are now down to a handful. As a result, values have risen: local agents reckon that the price of flats has gone up 10–20 per cent due to this alone. The latest scheme will see 33 flats carved out of five adjoining houses. There are still hotels in the streets between here and **Cromwell Rd**, with big hotels clustering around Gloucester Rd tube station to the E. A 12-storey block of mainly 1- and 2-bed short-let flats has been built on what was a vacant site behind the station. Dotted among the tall terraces and mansion blocks is a series of mews, mostly residential, such as **Laverton Mews** – a tiny cobbled cul-de-sac – and **Gaspar Mews** with its white-painted cottages.

Earl's Court

When Earl's Court was developed, in the second half of the 19th century, it was intended to be, and was regarded as, a select suburb. The well-to-do moved into the substantial Victorian terraced houses which sprang up alongside the original Georgian gardeners' village. The surviving gardeners, and the service workers, lived alongside in modest little cottages. Ironically, by the latter third of the 20th century the situation had reversed: the workers set up home in the run-down big houses, divided into flats and bed-sits, and the prosperous payed high prices to live in the remaining cottages.

As the new century dawns there are clear signs of a reversion to plan here: hotels, bed-sits and hostels are retreating in the face of smart flat conversions. Backpackers still throng Earl's Court station, but their choice of cheapish hotels and hostels is diminishing as grants from the council have allowed hotels to upgrade.

The quaint colour-washed cottages lie tucked away in a triangle of streets behind busy **Cromwell Rd** and **Earl's Court Rd**, known as Kenway Village or Earl's Court Village. Although only a few minutes' walk from the hubbub of **Earl's Court Rd**, this pocket of freehold family dwellings retains its villagy character, in sharp contrast to the rest of the area. Properties here are among the most sought-after in Earl's Court. The enclave formed the heart of the original village, the earliest homes in **Kenway Rd** dating back to the 1820s. Tree-lined **Wallgrave Rd** is the quietest and most popular street, pleasant and leafy with 2-storey and basement brick cottages fronted by black wrought-iron railings. There is a small communal garden here owned by local residents.

Child's Place and **Child's St** are cul-de-sacs running parallel to each other but noisier because they lie directly off **Earl's Court Rd**. The former has mainly 3-storey brick houses and the latter 2-storey cottages (c. £350–400,000) with small flowery front gardens. A black wrought-iron gate in **Child's St** leads into **Child's Walk**, a charming private passageway of 2-storey cottages lying no more than 10 ft apart. Tubs of flowers, window boxes and benches (complete with large snoozing cat) line the short alleyway, giving the impression of a single patio garden. A larger house here was on the market last year for £495,000. **Kenway Rd** itself is a mix of 2- and 3-storey cottages and houses, rubbing shoulders with shops and restaurants. Houses here go for £450–625,000; a 1-bed flat can cost £200,000. At the top of the road, a traffic-free corner holds the entrance to 171 Cromwell Rd, a handsome, recent block of 12 flats with garaging.

North of the village, at the busy junction of **Cromwell Rd** with **Earl's Court Rd**, are two 1980s apartment blocks. The flats have not worn well. Across **Cromwell Rd**, the

Edwardian Moscow Mansions, now reburbished and much sought-after, has house-sized penthouses selling for up to £600,000. South of the village, **Hogarth Rd** marks the N boundary of the area's hotel land. With **Earl's Court Gardens** (family-sized houses with 70-ft gardens fetching £725–950,000), it forms a buffer of Victorian terraced buildings between Kenway village and the red-brick gabled mansion blocks which dominate the rest of the area off **Earl's Court Rd**. **Barkston Gardens**, a fashionable group of red-brick buildings, overlooks a large tree-lined private garden enclosed by hedges and iron railings. Most of the N side is hotels but the rest 2/3-bed flats, with the best ones fetching up to £700,000. The **Bramham Gardens** blocks are also built around a tree-lined garden square.

Earl's Court Rd itself is dirty, noisy and battered by heavy traffic. It forms the southbound leg of the Earl's Court one-way system, nicknamed 'Juggernaut Alley'. Several attempts to devise relief road schemes – the latest in 1989 – have all come to nothing, but a Red Route is now in place taking in **Warwick Rd** and **Earl's Court Rd**.

In the recent past the character of **Earl's Court Rd** was determined largely by the transitory and tourist population which gravitated towards the area because of its central location. Now the street is smartening up: a leaven of coffee shops and restaurants is Fast-food shops, restaurants, late-night supermarkets, travel agents and newsagents predominate, spreading along both sides of the road from the underground station. West of **Earl's Court Rd**, the streets of terraces lying between **Warwick Rd** W and **Penywern Rd** S make up the main chunk of hotel land. **Nevern Square** with its red- and brown-brick buildings fronting private gardens is primarily residential, however, with only a single, new interior-designed hotel. One block S at the junction of **Trebovir Rd** and **Warwick Rd** sits Kensington Mansions, a 5-storey and basement 1880s block: flats here go for £350–600,000.

Earl's Court Square is the neighbourhood's main square, lined on three sides by 4/5-storey ornate stucco-fronted houses, mostly divided into flats. The buildings look on to mature gardens surrounded by tall trees. The old Chelsea Hotel is being converted into 43 flats (£235–900,000). The S arm of the square comprises 3-storey plus basement red-brick and stone gabled buildings. These set the tone for the taller red-brick gabled Wetherby Mansions on both sides of the SE arm of the square. **Warwick Rd** is lined with late-Victorian mansion blocks and undistinguished terraces.

Lying to the W is a series of crescents – **Philbeach Gardens**, **Eardley Crescent** and **Kempsford Gardens**. The condition of properties varies widely but the area is improving, as evidenced by the number of 'luxury' conversion schemes. Many developments have taken place recently, for example the conversion of an **Eardley Crescent** house into 10 flats priced from £295,000.

Tree-lined **Philbeach Gardens** enjoys the advantage of 2½ acres of exceptional landscaped gardens, forming a huge rear communal garden for the homes which sweep around the E curve of the crescent. Styles vary considerably from the heavy brown- and red-brick buildings at the N entrance of the crescent to the more desirable brick and stucco houses, with columned porches, at its mid-point.

Eardley Crescent and **Kempsford Gardens**, dubbed Brompton Village by one estate agent, have mainly 4-storey brick and stucco properties, like **Philbeach Gardens**, divided into flats. All three streets suffer from traffic from the Earl's Court Exhibition Centre immediately behind, and the council has imposed a special residents' parking scheme which runs until mid-evening during exhibitions. Properties at the mid-point of the W curve of **Philbeach Gardens** also back onto the railway line: this can lower flat prices by £100,000.

West Brompton

Brompton is one of those London villages which has effectively ceased to exist. Few people, nowadays, would describe themselves as living in Brompton, and this part of SW10, bounded by **Old Brompton Rd** to the N, **Fulham Rd** to the S, and running W from **Drayton Gardens**, is known either as Chelsea or Kensington, depending on your predelictions. Or, indeed, as straightforward 'Fulham Road' – though straight may be the wrong word for the clutch of bars, restaurants and clubs between **Hollywood Rd** and **Drayton Gardens**.

West Brompton gained improved transport links this year when a station opened on the West London Line, which links Clapham Junction with Olympia and points North. This is next to the District Line tube station.

The residential, as opposed to recreational, focal point of the neighbourhood is **The Boltons,** where handsome white stucco villas are set around an eye-shaped oval garden – unique in London. The enormous semi-detached freehold houses with their columned porches and rich ornamentation were built in the 1850–60s to attract the wealthy to the area. They still do. They were originally sold for £1,350 each. Now they fetch around £8 million. Some have staff accommodation in the grounds or are still linked to the mews houses at the rear. One – sans staff accomm – was £3.75 million last winter. In the middle of the central gardens is St Mary's Church, with its angel-bedecked spire rising high above the treetops.

The Boltons also gives its name to a network of similarly salubrious streets of big stucco-fronted houses with the same 'villas-in-gardens' character. A big house in **Bolton Gardens** was split into seven flats last winter, priced at £340,000 rising to £1 million. Leafy **Gilston Rd** has some fine examples with high-walled front gardens. **Milbourne Grove** and **Harley Gardens** are desirable small streets with a mix of paired stucco villas and brick and stucco 3/4-storey terraced houses. Houses on the E side of **Harley Gardens** overlook the walled back gardens of properties in **Gilston Rd**, as do the pastel-painted stucco terraced houses in **Priory Walk**.

Large paired brick and stucco villas predominate in **Tregunter Rd**, where properties have the advantage of forecourt parking – a feature of **The Boltons**. One in 'tired' condition sold to a showbiz person for £4 million last year. **The Little Boltons**, forming the W boundary of the neighbourhood, has more brick and stucco semi-detached houses but on a less grand scale. Caught up in this sea of stucco is cobbled **Cresswell Place**, a charming backwater of 2/3-storey brick cottages. It comes as an unexpected surprise as one turns the corner from **Cresswell Gardens**. No wonder that mistress of the unexpected, Dame Agatha Christie, lived here – her charming, tile-hung, dormered former home is surmounted by her 'writing room' built into the eaves. To the S lies **Cavaye Place**, a pleasant cul-de-sac of colourful cottages.

Redcliffe Rd a short distance away off **Fulham Rd** is a popular street for rented accommodation. Lined with cherry trees, it is ablaze with blossom in the spring. One street away is **Seymour Walk** – one of the earliest streets in the area, which retains its attractive period character. The oldest terrace in this exclusive cul-de-sac of 2/3-storey houses dates back to 1797. A kink in the road at the S end of the street hides it from **Fulham Rd** and a tree-lined terrace seals off its N end, creating a sense of peaceful seclusion.

Hollywood Rd to the W introduces a commercial note into this predominantly residential area. Smart restaurants, galleries, antique shops and bars creep around the corner from **Fulham Rd** into the S end of the street. A new gated mews of 18 town-houses and eight flats appeared at the start of the '90s on the W side of the street on the site of the former Unigate depot. Further N on the opposite side of the street is **Hollywood Mews**, entered through an arch. Modern 2-storey white painted cottages sit around a tiny courtyard with trees in the middle. **Hollywood Rd**, with its mix of brick and stucco homes and red-brick flats, merges with **Harcourt Terrace**, a pleasant street of terraced houses divided into flats.

A surprise lies in store in **Redcliffe Mews**, lying at right angles to **Harcourt Terrace**. The mews was rebuilt in 1987 in traditional style featuring attractive 2-storey brick cottages with gaily coloured garages and entrances. Despite its proximity to noisy **Redcliffe Gardens**, the mews is surprisingly quiet thanks to a barrier of big houses separating the two. A short walk away lies **Redcliffe Square**, divided in half by the southbound stretch of the one-way traffic system running between Earl's Court and Chelsea. The square is lined by tall ornate brick and stucco terraced houses with French Renaissance-style dormers and polished marble porch columns. Properties on the W side of the square overlook tree-lined gardens occupied by St Luke's Church and those on the E side face the only public gardens in West Brompton. The houses have been converted into flats, as have those in **Redcliffe Gardens**, where £250,000 buys a 1-bed flat; £320,000-plus a 2-bed, £400,000 upwards a 3-bed.

Cathcart Rd, **Fawcett St**, **Redcliffe Place**, **Redcliffe St**, **Westgate Terrace** and **Ifield Rd** form another network of streets dominated by 3/4-storey and basement brick and stucco terraced houses split into flats. Cutting a swathe through the area is **Finborough Rd**, the northbound leg of the one-way system. A short distance from the noise and fumes of the main road lies the tranquil haven of Brompton Cemetery, which doubles as a local park. The cemetery provides a leafy backdrop for the enclave of pretty artisan cottages in The Billings, just off **Fulham Rd**. **Billing Place**, **Billing St** and **Billing Rd** form a series of three private cul-de-sacs containing 2-storey and basement terraced cottages.

Transport   Tubes: South Kensington, Gloucester Rd (zone 1, District, Circle, Piccadilly); Earl's Court (zone 1, District, Piccadilly); West Brompton (zone 2, District). Trains: new West Brompton station links to Clapham Junction/Willesden line. From South Kensington: Oxford Circus 12 min (1 change), City 21 min (1 change), Heathrow 41 min.

Convenient for West End. Heathrow by tube or M4. Miles from centre: 2.

Schools Local Authority: St Thomas More, Holland Park School. Private: Lycée Français, Falkner House (g), St James Independent Schools.

SALES

Flats	S	1B	2B	3B	4B	5B
Average prices	90–180	150–400	200–500	240–750	400–1M+	500–2M+

Houses	2B	3B	4B	5B	6/7B	8B
Average prices	300–550	400–750+	500–2M+	600+	900+	1M+

RENTAL

Flats	S	1B	2B	3B	4B	5B
Average prices	200–300+	250–450+	300–600+	425–1M	550–1M+	600–1M+

Houses	2B	3B	4B	5B	6/7B	8B
Average prices	400–600	500–1000+	650–1800	860+	1M+	1M+–

The properties The peaceful, leafy streets and squares hold large brick and stucco terraces, target of much redevelopment into luxury flats. Flats, converted or p/b, reign, but there are enclaves of mewsy cottages, artists' studios and large villas.

The market South Kensington, once a down-at-heel district, now gleams with fresh paint after 15 years of hectic refurbishment. Now the luxurious flats sell to European, American and local buyers. The huge villas of The Boltons account for the £8 million figure above. Earl's Court is fast catching up to its more salubrious neighbours. Local searches: 10 days.

Among those estate agents active in this area are:

- Tylden-Lofts & Calvert
- Farrar & Co
- Farley & Co *
- Cluttons Daniel Smith
- Hobart Slater
- W A Ellis *
- Russell Simpson
- Hamptons
- Druce
- Blenheim Bishop
- Douglas & Gordon
- Friend & Falcke *
- Barnard Marcus
- Scotts *
- Hogarth Estates
- Plaza
- Winkworth *
- Marsh & Parsons
- Lane Fox
- Jackson-Stops & Staff
- Beaney Pearce *
- Humberts
- Foxtons *
- De Groot Collis
- Aylesford
- Faron Sutaria
- Anscombe & Ringland *

further details: see advertisers' index on p671

SOUTHFIELDS AND EARLSFIELD

Map ref: p108 (1A)
Postal districts: SW18, SW19
Boroughs: Wandsworth (Con)
Council tax: Band D £370
Conservation areas: Numerous,
    particularly towards
    Wimbledon Common
Parking: Free off main roads

The quiet streets of sober, steady houses in Earlsfield and Southfields slumbered until recently, neglected by all but very local buyers. Neighbouring Putney, Wimbledon and Wandsworth Common have more obvious charms. But since the end of the home market's long sleep from 1990–96, 'young professionals' have been thronging the offices of both sales and letting agents here: with prices rocketing in those surrounding areas, it was inevitable that this corner should be rediscovered.

Incomers find plenty of terraced houses and flats in quiet streets, and semis (some quite large) in leafy ones. A rash of ex-council homes – some on lovely, green hillsides – and even the odd warehouse conversion have boosted the range of homes. Last year saw ex-council – especially those with garages – shoot up in price.

South from Wandsworth, the River Wandle must once have run through water meadows and woods. That was some centuries ago, for the river was discovered as a source of power by medieval millers, and later turned the wheels of some of the first factories in London, which were linked in 1803 by the world's first railway company. Now the Wandle and its flat valley is best known as a barrier to E–W traffic. The valley has parks and playing-fields, depots and factories – but only two bridges linking the Victorian suburb of Earlsfield, to the E, with its slightly younger (and today politer) neighbour Southfields to the W. With the busy A3 and the notorious Wandsworth one-way bottleneck to the N, public transport is the key to this area: Southfields has the District Line tube, while Earlsfield has trains to Clapham Junction and Waterloo.

Southfields

Southfields is a wholly residential area which blends – with surprising success – classic 1930s suburbia with older Edwardian properties. Between the District line railway and **Merton Rd** the houses are mainly Edwardian; from **Wimbledon Park Rd** W and N to **West Hill** (the A3) and Wimbledon Common come classic 1930s semi-detached and detached houses, with some older Edwardian/Victorian ones. From **Beaumont Rd** W to **Wimbledon Parkside** are many large '60s/early '70s council-built estates. The smaller blocks and houses here are largely owner-occupied: Wandsworth Council was a pioneer of Right to Buy.

The area has always been popular with families wanting good-sized houses in generally quiet roads. Newer arrivals to the area (notably to 'The Grid' – see below) are young couples, especially second-time buyers planning to start families, and families priced out of other areas.

Replingham Rd, near the tube station, is a pleasant street that provides the only shops of any note in Southfields, and a couple of new-style pubs and cafes; otherwise the nearest major shopping centres are in Wimbledon, Putney or Wandsworth. You'll find the occasional corner shop, but there are virtually no pubs in the 'Grid' area because of covenant restrictions laid down when the land was sold for building. The area suffers somewhat from hordes of tennis fans during Wimbledon Fortnight, but enterprising locals can let their homes out for considerable sums.

Central Southfields and The Grid

The Southfields Grid, bordered by **Astonville St**, **Elsenham Rd**, **Revelstoke Rd** and **Replingham Rd**, takes its nickname from the orderly layout of the streets (these run N–S) and roads (E–W). The Grid was begun with the opening of Southfields station in 1889, but was not completed until 1905. Properties are mainly spacious 3- and 4-bed Edwardian houses, although a few have been converted into flats. Typical prices for the Grid are around £270–340,000 for a 3- or 4-bed house (with a 3-storey, 5-bedroom house in **Heythorpe St** last winter at £375,000); £170–200,000 for a 2-bed conversion. A number of the houses in **Trentham St**, **Replingham Rd** and **Revelstoke Rd** are actually purpose-built maisonettes; the supply of newly converted flats on the Grid dried up some years back after Wandsworth Council banned any more conversions. Houses closest to Southfields station suffer some parking problems. There are some small council infill blocks in **Elsenham St** and even-numbered houses back onto the District line to Wimbledon – but have long gardens as compensation. Between **Merton Rd** and **Astonville St** there are some recent 2/3-bed houses in **Handford Close**. By Southfields station, **Crowthorne Close** is one of the few modern non-council developments in the area, with 2- and 3-storey blocks of flats, some backing onto the tracks.

The triangle bordered by **Granville Rd, Pulborough Rd** and **Merton Rd** features generally Edwardian houses in tree-lined roads slightly narrower than in the Grid. Odd-numbered houses in **Pulborough Rd** back onto the tube line but benefit from exceptionally long gardens and the large railway landholding as a buffer. From around £275,000 (3-bed terrace). The streets between **Pirbright Rd** and **Smeaton Rd** are mainly late-Victorian/ Edwardian terraces, while **Longfield St** and **Smeaton Rd** itself are smaller Victorian versions (2-bedroom), which sell for around £210–240,000. But in **Standen Rd** is a new departure for the area: a fashionable warehouse-style conversion, which yielded flats at prices that made the locals blink: from around £195,000 for 1-bed flats, 2-beds at £275,000 up to 2/3-bed penthouses for £450,000. Those braving the name to live here may be amused to know that 'Tiffany Heights' is an old pea-canning factory.

West of the tube line, the land rises quite steeply up towards Wimbledon Common and Putney Heath. **Gartmoor Gardens** has attractive large Edwardian houses with ornate metalwork balconies on the first floor, some now converted to flats. Proximity to Southfields station compensates for some noise from trains. Houses on the S side of **Southdean Gardens** back onto Wimbledon Park: very popular but rarely on the market. Prices last winter were around £360,000 for good 4-bed, 2-bath houses, though ones backing onto the park may fetch quite a bit more.

Sutherland Grove, running N from the W side of Southfields station to **West Hill**, features 1930s semis (mainly 3-bed) with off-street parking. About £240,000 buys you one with a decent garden. Also a few vast (6-bed plus) Edwardian houses, not all of which have been converted into popular flats.

The tube line (District) is above ground here and runs E of **Sutherland Grove**, crossing **Granville Rd** and then going into a tunnel by the junction with **Melrose Rd** and **Cromer Villas**. **Gressenhall Rd** has Edwardian-style houses and a mosque. The roads leading off **Sutherland Grove**, notably **Skeena Hill, Cromer Villas** and **Girdwood Rd**, are larger '30s, the majority Tudor-style, with integral garages. Internally, the houses vary enormously. Most, notably in **Coombemartin Rd**, are set well back from the road. From the junction of **Skeena Hill** and **Coombemartin Rd** there are small modern blocks of council-built flats, and the W side of **Coombemartin Rd** back onto a (low-rise) estate.

Parkside

The area bordered by **Beaumont Rd** in the E, Wimbledon Common to the W, **Queensmere Rd** (the border with Wimbledon) to the S and **West Hill** is a complex mixture of council-built estates (high- and low-rise flats, some houses) and private detached houses – some very large which fetch equally large prices. The area is quite hilly, with some splendid views eastwards towards Central London, and there are plenty of trees. Don't let the council-built housing deter you from a good look around this interesting corner.

The heaviest concentrations of council estates are between **Wimbledon Park Rd** and **Albert Drive, Augustus Rd** and **Whitlock Drive**. The area between **Beaumont Rd** and **Princes Way** from **Augustus Rd** to **West Hill** is almost exclusively council-built. But all the estates are well-landscaped. A lot of the flats are now owner-occupied, and there are a few small housing association schemes. Resales of council-built properties offer the cheaper homes of the area: 1-bed flats are from £65-70,000, but 3-bed houses with garage have leaped to around £230-280,000.

Beaumont Rd, running between **West Hill** and **Wimbledon Park Rd**, has modern council-built properties on either side and a small parade of shops by **Keevil Drive**. **Albert Drive** runs between **Augustus Rd** and **Victoria Drive**. Again there is a mix of council and private blocks and good-sized private houses (mainly detached). Between

Albert Drive and **Wimbledon Park Rd** are mid- and late-'60s council-built blocks. On the other side of the road are some modern infill red-brick detached houses, set well back from the road, then larger detached stockbroker Tudor red-brick homes. Midway down **Albert Drive** former police flats in a 1950s block have been redeveloped as 'Southfields Village' with 2-bed flats. The same developer also undertook another similar scheme: Augustus Court off **Augustus Rd.**

Augustus Rd runs W up the hill from Southfields station to **Inner Park Rd**, and has a mix of '30s houses and older, large detached houses. The occasional late-Georgian house with 6 beds very occasionally appears on the market. A number of private flat developments are grouped close to the junction with **Inner Park Rd**, including The Acorns (red-brick modern) and Dorada Court. There are also modern houses and flat developments, brick-built, mainly '60s and early '70s. Increasingly, from the junction with **Albert Drive**, large detached houses appear, mainly stockbroker Tudor but also older houses including the late-Georgian-style 'White House'. Some '50s infill, but all set well back from the road with large front gardens and off-street parking.

Princes Way runs roughly N–S between **West Hill** and **Wimbledon Park Rd.** From the junction with **Augustus Rd** towards **Wimbledon Park Rd** is Linden Lodge School for the Blind, set in large grounds, then private flats and an attractive town-house development, **King Charles Walk. Weydown Close** is modern low-rise council-built.

Off **Augustus Rd** is John Paul II Catholic Boys' Secondary School. The school buildings are followed by more mainly council-built property on either side of the road. Off **Princes Way** at the N end is the private **Fleur Gate** development of attractive brick-built Victorian-style terraced town-houses. Opposite the junction with **Castlecombe Drive** (council housing) is a small row of detached Tudor-style '30s houses.

Tree-lined **Victoria Drive** runs N–S parallel to **Princes Way** between **West Hill** and **Wimbledon Park Rd.** In character it is similar to **Princes Way** with a mix of (mainly) council-built and private property. Pines Court, a modern private block, has a selection of studio flats. **Oak Park Gardens** is a small and attractive development of town-houses followed by larger Tudor-style 1930s houses.

Inner Park Rd runs in a half-circle from Wimbledon Parkside to meet **Augustus Rd** and then back to Wimbledon Common, featuring a similar mix to the rest of **Parkside.** Close to the junction with **Parkside** stands a modern block of 16 red-brick 1- and 2-bed flats. Opposite are low-rise council flats (Windlesham Grove); thereafter private blocks of flats in older style. 'Marlborough' has some studio flats. **Pilsdon Close**, with small town-houses and flats, is set back; then comes **Holly Tree Close**, with private flats. Some exceptionally large older Victorian detached houses have mainly now been converted into flats.

Opposite the junction with **Augustus Rd** is the Argyll Estate, a mix of high- and low-rise flats. Three tall council blocks here were demolished a decade ago to be replaced with flats and houses. **Limpsfield Avenue**, with 1930s-style houses, detached and semi-detached, some mock-Tudor, backs onto a council estate. **Kingsmere Rd** has detached mainly '30s houses. A spur of **Inner Park Rd** (easy to miss), close to **Parkside** marks the entrance to **Roundacres**, a small early '60s curved, terraced house-and-flat development in communal gardens. Large, traditional-style red-brick '50s-style houses stand at the entrance.

S

Queensmere Rd marks the border with Merton and is very much Wimbledon rather than Southfields in feel and prices. The fairly steep tree-lined road has mainly large modern detached houses set well back from the road. **Queensmere Close** is a bungalow development. The vast former college site on the corner with **Parkside** is being developed by Laing with an extensive (and expensive) collection of new houses and flats. (See Wimbledon chapter.)

Wimbledon Park Rd suffers traffic at rush hour, though calming measures have helped. North from the junction of **Bathgate Rd** come blocks of flats, modern council-built and older-style private. Lakeview Court flats are very comfortable and well-run, looking over Wimbledon Park and its lake. Thereafter large detached '30s- and '50s-style houses are set well back off the road up towards Southfields station, where Edwardian semi-detached and then terraced houses take over.

West Hill

The little triangle between the **West Hill** junction with **Sutherland Grove, West Hill Rd** and **Granville Rd** likes to considers itself West Hill (Putney) not West Hill (Southfields) and has good access to East Putney tube. It is a mix of large Edwardian semi-detached houses and 1930s semis with some modern infill and some early and mid-Victorian detached houses on **West Hill Rd**. Among the most popular roads is the 1930s **Sispara Gardens** (large semi-detached houses with integral garages) while **Cromer Villas** has a mix of '30s and Edwardian semis. **Coldstream Gardens** has '60s-style town-houses and flats, **Valonia Gardens** is neat 1930s semis with some '50s infill built '30s-style. **Melrose Rd**, as it meets **West Hill Rd**, has big terraced and semi-detached Edwardian homes. **West Hill** itself, though, is stationary much of the time: it leads to the dreaded Wandsworth One-Way System.

    Merton Rd to the E is a very busy through-road carrying traffic between Wimbledon and Wandsworth and is also a commuter cut-through from the A24 to the Wandsworth one-way system. Large detached and semi-detached houses (some stuccoed) appear between **West Hill Rd** and **Wimbledon Park Rd**. Thereafter, going S, the houses are semi-detached 3/4-bed late-Victorian, set well back from the road. A primary school stands at the junction with **Standen Rd**. Southfields Secondary School lies between **Burr Rd** and **Bodmin St**, with a modern town-house development opposite. Then come late-Edwardian mansion flats, originally council, now owner-occupied. At the junction of **Burr Rd** and **Kimber Rd** is Coleman Mansions, an early '30s-style block of flats with views over Kings George's Park, but industry and heavy traffic restricts prices. **Kimber Rd** is one of the few to cross the Wandle Valley and thus attracts considerable traffic. Speed humps have helped reduce rat-running.

Wandle Valley

Between **Merton Rd** and **Garratt Lane** lie a handful of early Edwardian terraces bordered by King George's Park and **Ravensbury Rd**, which are the no-man's-land between Earlsfield and Southfields. Estate agents are unable to agree on where these roads are: Wimbledon Park (bit optimistic, this), Southfields or Earlsfield.

    Penwith Rd, being one of the few roads to cross the Wandle, suffers exceptionally heavy traffic which keeps prices for mainly purpose-built late-Victorian 2-bed flats lower than the rest of the area at £95–115,000 – little changed in the last year. **Acuba Rd** (Edwardian) and **Bodmin St** are quieter as is **Strathville Rd** despite a small industrial development. **Dounsforth Gardens**, a small modern town-house development off **Strathville Rd**, backs onto the River Wandle. Acuba House, an Edwardian block of flats, was council; now it's mainly owner-occupied. It borders on King George's Park playing-fields, which have a new health and fitness centre. Upper floors of **Bodmin St** have an open outlook over the park and playing-fields. The playing-fields N of **Bodmin St** have in part been replaced with homes.

Earlsfield

Earlsfield is bordered by **Allfarthing Lane, Garratt Lane** and **Burntwood Lane** and runs E up the hill from the Wandle Valley towards Wandsworth Common. Earlsfield, like Battersea, is trying to expand, as it becomes more fashionable, to take in areas that have been Tooting or Wandsworth since they were built. Popularity first rose in the heady days of the late '80s, but the area didn't quite make it into respectability (unlike Southfields) before the 1990 recession. Now once again an increasing number of buyers are finding themselves outpriced in Battersea, Clapham and Wandsworth Common and are heading down **Earlsfield Rd**. They seek streets close to the station and parks, and prefer private to council-built homes – though the gap is closing.

The area between **Garratt Lane** and Wandsworth Common is essentially residential, but note the land on either side of River Wandle, between **Garratt Lane** and **Merton Rd**, is still mainly industrial. There are parks and a playing-field, and a few streets of houses, but warehouses and light industry dominate.

Between **Magdalen Rd** and **Burntwood Lane** is a large, pleasant, council-built 'cottage' estate running from **Tilehurst Rd** in the E to **Swaby Rd** in the W. The homes are a mixture of simple '20s and '30s-style terraced and semi-detached houses, most with gardens much larger than average (50–80 ft is not unusual). A double front door reveals houses that were built as two separate flats, rather than converted. This estate is now nearly totally owner-occupied. The far-sighted bought 3-bed estate houses (freehold) for the price of a 3-bed Victorian flat – and within easy reach of Earlsfield station in **Magdalen Rd**. Traffic has been a perennial problem, but road humps etc have calmed things down.

Open View and **Field View** overlook playing-fields; **Tilehurst Rd**, marking the E end of the estate, suffers some rat-running; and **Magdalen Rd** and **Burntwood Lane** suffer serious traffic at peak hours. Some buyers are prepared to put up with the traffic to live near the junction with **Garratt Lane** for closeness to the station. The majority of the mainly '30s semis in **Burntwood Lane** have open views over the school, golf course and the grounds of Springfield University Hospital.

Swaby Rd, running N towards the station, has generally late-Victorian small terraced houses and some purpose-built Edwardian maisonettes. Running between **Tranmere Rd** (late-Victorian terraces, some maisonettes) and **Garratt Lane** are the well-regarded trio **Quinton St**, **Isis St** and **Littleton St**. There are spacious (for Earlsfield) 3-bed turn-of-century terraces increasing in popularity, especially **Littleton St** (Earlsfield third bedrooms elsewhere tend to be very small). A large Victorian primary school stands at the junction of **Tranmere Rd** and **Waynflete St**. Some houses in **Quinton St** and **Isis St** have been converted to flats. W of **Garratt Lane**, a gated development of 2- and 3-bed houses is due in **Weybourne St**. **Garratt Lane** itself has some flats, cheaper than their neighbours due to the busy road: £60,000 might buy a 1-bed.

To the N of the railway that slices diagonally through Earlsfield, properties between **Allfarthing Lane**, the N limit of the area, and **Earlsfield Rd** are generally small late-Victorian and early Edwardian terraces with some small council-built infill blocks. Traffic calming measures have improved congestion in **Earlsfield Rd**, which runs between **Garratt Lane** and **Trinity Rd**. High numbers (**Garratt Lane** end) are small late-Victorian houses set close to the road (no off-street parking and noise nuisance). Then comes modern council infill at the junction with **Inman St**. From the junction with **Dingwall St** houses are increasingly set back from the road (important given the volume of traffic) and grow from 2- to 3-storey, many now converted to flats with off-street parking.

Odd numbers of **Earlsfield Rd** back onto the railway line but generally have large gardens and the fact that the railway line is set well below garden level means noise is reduced. Houses near the **Heathfield Rd** junction enjoy a view across the railway line of Wandsworth Prison (you could always pretend it's a castle . . .). Here are some larger, 5-bed semi-detached late-Edwardian 3-storey houses to be found. **Bassingham Rd**, **Bucharest Rd** and **Brocklebank Rd**, leading off **Earlsfield Rd** to **Swaffield Rd**, are early Edwardian/late-Victorian terraced houses, with ornate door surrounds and windows. They are mainly 3-bedroom houses, some converted into flats. At the junction of **St Ann's Hill** and **Garratt Lane** is a converted school house (early Victorian), now flats. **Swaffield Rd** and **St Ann's Hill** suffer rat-running.

Aslett St, Treport St, Delia St and **Daphne St** are all late-Victorian terraces – some maisonettes – and popular with first-time buyers. Where conversions have taken place the second bedroom tends to be fairly small. There is a development of 1-bed flats in **Aslett St**, which has a school at the **St Ann's Hill** end, and a handful of new town-houses. 'Spencer Walk' in **Aslett St** is a new clutch of 3- and 4-bed houses. This part of Earlsfield is very convenient for the shopping facilities of Wandsworth and a Sainsbury's superstore on **Garratt Lane**. **Barmouth Rd, Swanage Rd** and **Cader Rd** E of **St Ann's Hill** are more Wandsworth Common than Earlsfield; 3- and 4-bed late-Victorian/early Edwardian terraces with higher prices than the Earlsfield average.

Transport	Tubes: Southfields (zone 3, District). To Oxford Circus 30 min (1 change), City 30 min, Heathrow 55 min (1 change). Trains: Earlsfield to Clapham Junction and Waterloo.
Convenient for	Wimbledon Common and tennis. Tube to town via Fulham and Sloane Square, trains to Waterloo. Miles from centre: 5.
Schools	Local Authority: Southfields Community, Ernest Bevin (b), Burntwood School (g), John Paul II RC. Private: Emanuel

SALES

Flats	S	1B	2B	3B	4B	5B
Average prices	65–95	100–160	125–220	150–300	–	–
Houses	2B	3B	4B	5B	6/7B	8B
Average prices	175–240	240–300	300–400	350–500	–	–

RENTAL

Flats	S	1B	2B	3B	4B	5B
Average prices	125–150	150–250	185–550	275–575	370+	–
Houses	2B	3B	4B	5B	6/7B	8B
Average prices	230–460	275–575	370–800	500+	–	–

The properties	Mainly Edwardian terraced homes, including many p/b and some converted flats, plus some larger houses towards Putney. Also (being in Wandsworth) ex-council from '20s cottages to '70s tower flats.
The market	Southfields, with its tube, is more expensive, especially for flats: 2-bed flats popular with young sharers. Earlsfield is buzzing with economic refugees from pricier areas. Cheaper buys in ex-council cottage estates and flat blocks: though the town-houses particularly have leapt in price, can still be well below averages above. Local searches: 3–4 weeks.

S

Among those estate agents active in this area are:
- Douglas & Gordon
- Kinleigh Folkard & Hayward
- Hamptons
- Bells
- Winkworth *
- FPDSavills
- Haart
- McKenzie
- Barnard Marcus
- Foxtons *
- Hooper & Jackson
- Craigie & Co
- Tower

further details: see advertisers' index on p671

SOUTHGATE AND PALMERS GREEN

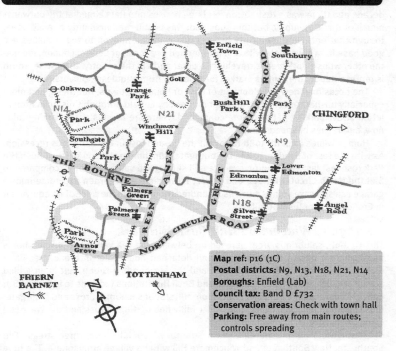

Map ref: p16 (1C)
Postal districts: N9, N13, N18, N21, N14
Boroughs: Enfield (Lab)
Council tax: Band D £732
Conservation areas: Check with town hall
Parking: Free away from main routes;
controls spreading

That part of the North Circular Rd which runs between the Lea Valley in the E and
Arnos Grove tube in the W separates two remarkably different areas. Below this
dividing line, the northern parts of Tottenham and Wood Green have petered out into
a rather colourless hinterland, but head N and as soon as you cross the **North Circular**,
the atmosphere immediately begins to change.

The large suburban tract beyond the **North Circular Rd**, which comprises
Southgate (N14), Palmers Green (N13), Winchmore Hill (N21), and Upper (N18) and
Lower (N9) Edmonton, lies far enough from the centre of London to lead a life
independent of City and West End business, but still suits the commuter – inwards or
outwards. While the train journey to Moorgate in the City takes around 20 min from
stations like Palmers Green, Lower Edmonton and Winchmore Hill, the M25, M1, M11
motorways and the A10 (**Great Cambridge Rd**) are all within reach – if more often than
not congested. Live here, and you can work anywhere N of London.

Edmonton, and the parts of Palmers Green lying closest to the **North Circular Rd**,
are at first similar in style to N Tottenham and Wood Green, with fairly similar
shopping facilities serving similar inter-war properties; but already the *feel* of the
place is different. Down the wind comes the first whiff of the Alpine North – or, at
least, the fresh air from the Green Belt, blowing via a thousand Alpine-planted rock
gardens. Indeed, this area changes quite dramatically the further N one travels into
it, becoming more and more green, leafy, suburban and also prosperous: with golf
clubs, parks, tree-lined streets, huge modern detached houses as well as a
proliferation of 1980s and '90s developments.

The area is populated to a large extent by prosperous, middle-class families and retired (early if possible) couples who moved into the region 20–30 years ago. There is also a large Greek Cypriot community, and a smaller Asian one in Palmers Green. A decade ago there was a rush to convert large houses into flats aimed at the outwards march of the '80s yuppy, but this subsided: this is still predominantly a family area, though that encircling motorway bracket just over the horizon to the N makes it a good base for a household with one partner tied to a local, or Central London, job and the other whose work means travelling to other parts of the country. Otherwise, youth is represented by the rentals market for students from Middlesex University.

The occasional new development of flats or houses appears, but these, and more especially further conversions, are kept in check by Enfield Borough's disinclination to let on-street parking get any more congested. There are much stricter parking rules now, and rashes of speed humps.

Homes values took till 1988 to regain the ground lost in the early '90s recession. As with the rest of London, prices in Southgate, Winchmore Hill and parts of Bush Hill Park rose fast last year, but on average still show good value for money compared to S of the **North Circular Rd**. A 4-bed house, Edwardian, with garden and sometimes a garage can still save you as much as a hundred thousand on the price of its equivalent in Crouch End or Muswell Hill.

Southgate, Winchmore Hill, Bush Hill Park

This well-off, salubrious area, perched up between the Lea Valley and Barnet, holds in the main a wealth of large semis and detached houses set in broad, tree-lined streets. The proximity to Enfield Town and the surrounding Green Belt is an added advantage. It's served by Enfield Town and Bush Hill stations (30 mins to Liverpool St); Enfield Chase, Grange Park and Winchmore Hill stations to King's Cross and Moorgate; plus Oakwood and Southgate tubes (Piccadilly line to King's Cross and the West End – and on, of course, to Heathrow).

Southgate is a prosperous, leafy suburb which falls into three areas: Old Southgate, New Southgate and Winchmore Hill with its village atmosphere. The tube station is Southgate's most surprising landmark: a spirited bit of '30s design, the circular building looks like a spaceship heading for Mars rather than the underground; it is in fact a listed building. It stands on **Southgate Circus**, near to a 1990 flats development of 1- and 2-bed flats whose convenience makes for price tags in the region of £90-100,000 for the 1-beds, £115-145,000 for the 2-beds. Right on the Circus, too, is **Bourneside Crescent**, where a 3-bed penthouse was £270,000 last winter. Central Southgate may revolve (literally) around the hub of the Circus, but close by are playing fields, tennis courts, cricket club and parks – in particucular Grovelands Park, with its large boating lake, in the grounds of which stands a sports centre and Grovelands Priory Hospital. The hot news of the neighbourhood is the arrival of Marks & Spencers, coming to **Winchmore Hill Rd**.

The road leading S from Southgate Circus (**High St**/**Cannon Hill**) is bordered by a college and a variety of attractive properties, including little mewsy cottages. The Southgate and District Reform Synagogue now stands on the site of the house that once belonged to the poet Leigh Hunt.

Southgate's most favoured homes are the Minchenden estate: a semi-circle of closes and conifered gardens, enclosed by **Morton Way, Powys Lane/Cannon Hill** and **Waterfall Rd**. Other favoured corners include **Meadway**, in the angle between the **High St** and **Bourne Hill**. Tucked away behind a high wall in the old part of Southgate off **Cannon Hill**, the Legal & General building, once the manor house, has been converted into exclusive, original-featured 2/3-bed apartments.

Among the neat, untroubled streets of comfortable inter-war houses, new things are appearing – carefully. One development off **Fox Lane** is an interesting conversion of an old school house into flats, and reflects the policy of preserving the original atmosphere of the area: 2-bed flats in Corrib Court go for around £240,000. Churchill Court, which provides a cache of 1- and 2-bedroom retirement apartments and lies to the W of the A10 on **Church St**, is another example of the many modern developments in the area, a peaceful alternative to similar schemes closer to the centre of London. These include houses, as well as flats; for instance the large homes in **Crothall Close**.

Going N along **Village Rd** towards Bush Hill Park, the roads become increasingly wider and more tree-lined, with solid 3- and 4-bedroom semis. Through the centre of the area marches **Wellington Rd**, the streets off which hold surprisingly large family houses with big gardens, and small 'courts' of neo-Georgian homes. Just off **Park Avenue**, Croft Mews' modern 2-bedroom flats and houses are positioned right next to an up-market tennis club.

Agents refer to the streets E across the tracks between the Bush Hill Park–Enfield Town railway line, **Southbury Rd** and the **Great Cambridge Rd** as 'the Triangle'. These streets, which contain the Bush Hill Park recreation ground, they reckon more desirable than comparably priced ones in Edmonton, and a good corner for home-hunters.

The large homes bordering Bush Hill Park Golf Course continue to be impressively suburban, but it is the village atmosphere of Winchmore Hill to the S, with its neat streets, quaint houses, tidy gardens and attractive pubs, that suggests the prosperity of the area. Older houses cluster picturesquely round the village green (delightful – and extremely neat); last year saw the addition of a small group of town-houses in Georgian style to the SW corner. **Broad Walk**, which leads off **The Green** with its antique shops, is the Beverly Hills of Southgate/Winchmore Hill. Rock stars and celebrities crop up in these vast, recently built properties which have equally vast cars parked in their driveways. £700,000 for a house in this road is around the norm: they have been known to reach the £1.2 million mark. Around **The Green** itself, and thus close to Winchmore Hill Station, 2-bed flats go for around £200,000. **Broad Walk** leads into **The Bourne**, which borders the pleasant Grovelands Park. **Seaforth Gardens** and **Queen Elizabeth's Drive** both border the park, and some houses have gates leading directly into it. **Church Hill** leads from Winchmore Hill station to leafy **Eversley Park Rd**. **Abbey Rd** is counted among the nicest streets, while **Eversley Crescent** is the prettiest.

Eversley Park Rd leads northwards to the Highland Village development, with its cul-de-sacs of new homes handy for Grange Park Primary, set in the park itself. The redevelopment of the old hospital here yields interesting flats: a top-floor one, at £170,000, has its own belfry.

Palmers Green

To the south lies Palmers Green, a quiet (away from main roads) family suburb. In its heyday it was a bastion of Edwardian respectability, whose numerous turn-of-the-century 3- and 4-bedroom houses, replete with original features, were set along leafy roads. Many of these were converted into flats – particularly in the **Ulleswater Rd**, **Derwent Rd**, **Lakeside Rd**, **Grovelands Rd** and **Old Park Rd** ladder – but the trend has now been reversed. The best side of Palmers Green is the Southgate side. This is still a good place to look for larger homes at reasonable prices: a 5-bed Victorian house can still be under £300,000. In the Old Lakes estate, off **Grovelands Rd**, large Victorian houses boast original features and stained-glass windows. This, along with the Monkfrith and Minchenden estates, is counted among the area's best corners.

Pedestrianization of part of the high street, and more parking restrictions, are promised, but still awaited: the aim is to make the main roads once more people-friendly. There are good shopping facilities off **Green Lanes** with a number of shops that are open late (and both Sainsbury's and Safeway have big stores in the area) but, an increase in restaurants notwithstanding, not much in the way of night life. During the day, however, and at weekends, residents relax in Broomfield Park, which adds numerous sports and leisure facilities to its tranquil lakes. Agents – and developers – look fondly on the area around the park, bounded by **Aldermans Hill** to the N, **Green Lanes** to the E, **Bowes Rd** to the S and **Wilmer Way** to the W. As well as the green open space, this hilly corner gets some lovely views. Last year Stanley House Garden, a new development of 2-bed flats, appeared on a smallish site looking out over the park from **Aldermans Hill**.

Housebuilders Fairview have been steadily adding to the local stock: Harper's Close is an electronically gated courtyard scheme; another, Chequers Green in **Chequers Way**, S of the North Circular, has added over 30 houses and 100 flats. The latest is Westminster Gardens, **Westminster Drive** – again, one street back from the North Circular: 3-bed, 2-bath plus garage houses here were £182,000 last winter.

Transport in the area has happily improved. Nearest tube stations are Arnos Grove or Bounds Green though the train service into King's Cross and Moorgate is not all it could be outside of peak hours. However, there are now more buses, including the night bus from Trafalgar Square which runs up **Green Lanes**, and a good bus service into Wood Green and Enfield. Near the station there is a modern development of studios, 1- and 2-bed flats – some are galleried. A few streets away, **Windsor Rd** and **Park Avenue** sport large Edwardian houses which yield popular flat conversions. There are recent Barratt flats and houses in **Arnos Rd**, convenient for Arnos Grove tube.

The widening of the **North Circular Rd**, affecting the stretch E from **Green Lanes** through Palmers Green to Edmonton – a scheme which included the building of two fly-overs/underpasses – has much improved the flow through to the M11 and Essex. Surrounding areas, especially Edmonton, should now see the benefits.

Edmonton

Upper Edmonton/Lower Edmonton is bounded by the A10 to the W, the William Girling Reservoir to the E and the **North Circular** to the S. The area is served by Silver St and Lower Edmonton rail stations and possesses one of the largest leisure centres in the South-East of England, Picketts Lock. There is also sailing on the reservoir.

Edmonton is perhaps the least 'desirable', in estate agents' terms, of the four areas – marked by a crop of huge, unsightly high-rise council blocks and a concrete shopping centre which, remarked a local, bears a marked resemblance to a wartime bunker. Of the two, Upper Edmonton is more 'inner city' in style, with very little green.

Small, flat-fronted 2- to 3-bed terraced houses (Victorian/Edwardian) can go for as little as £80,000. These and inter-war semis – some of which have been converted into flats – are standard in this area, although styles are certainly varied and stone cladding ubiquitous. Typical price for a 1930s terraced house in reasonable order is around £120,000. Homes are mixed with post-war council-build and tower blocks, and with commercial or industrial corners, but also broken up by recreation grounds or the odd football pitch; some homes, too, get green, open views out towards Essex. The Huxley, Galliard, Midland, Latymer and Westerham estates offer good-value properties, with 3-bed homes starting for as little as £85,000. The area's nicer roads are **Charlton Rd**, which includes a late-'80s flats development, **Nightingale Rd** and **Oxford Rd**, leafy and neat. A new homes development in **Scotland Green Rd**, grouped round communal gardens, has sizes and prices that range from 1-bed flats around £55,000, to 3-bed houses for £100,000.

Near the North Circular lies Pymmes Park, complete with lake, tennis courts and bowling green. More trees generally here, in streets like **Sweet Briar Walk** which skirts the park, and around **Silver St**. South of the North Circular and W of the **Great**

Cambridge Rd, the Empire Estate (**Canada Avenue, Tasmania Terrace**, etc) on the borders with Wood Green, is sought after. A new development in Cherry Blossom Close has 2-bed flats starting at £99,000.

Just off **Church St** in **Lion Rd**, there is a development of 1- and 2-bed flats (around £55-60,000) conveniently placed for Lower Edmonton station. Moving W along **Church St** (inter-war semis) the area becomes increasingly attractive with many playing-fields and sportsgrounds providing pleasant backdrops to the houses. Here the A10, bustling importantly off towards Cambridge, runs for a while with allotments bordering both sides of the road.

Transport	Tubes: Southgate, Arnos Grove, Oakwood (zone 3, Piccadilly). From Southgate: Oxford Circus 35 min (1 change), City 30 min (1 change), Heathrow 1 hr 15 min. Trains: Palmers Green, Winchmore Hill to Moorgate, King's Cross; Bush Hill Park, Lower Edmonton to Liverpool St.
Convenient for	North Circular, M25, M1, M11, A10. Parks and sports/leisure. Milesfrom centre: 8.
Schools	Enfield Education Authority: Latymer, Alyward, Winchmore, Southgate, Edmonton County, Enfield Grammar (b), Enfield County (g), Broomfield St Anne's RC (g). Private: Palmers Green High (g).

SALES

Flats	S	1B	2B	3B	4B	5B
Average prices	60–80	75–95	100–150	175–275	—	—

Houses	2B	3B	4B	5B	6/7B	8B
Average prices	150–200	180–350	225–450	325–500	500–600	—

RENTAL

Flats	S	1B	2B	3B	4B	5B
Average prices	125–130	150–170	165–200	200–250	—	—

Houses	2B	3B	4B	5B	6/7B	8B
Average prices	200–230	250–350	300–450	450–550	—	—

The properties	Leafy, suburban homes with gardens in Southgate and Winchmore Hill including some large expensive ones. Lots of modern houses and flats. Palmers Green has Edwardian 3/4-bed houses, some now flats, Edmonton has smaller terraces and inter-war homes.
The market	Commuter country, with trains to City and good access to motorways to attract executives. Junior ranks buy converted flats and terraces in cheaper areas; some expensive new-build. High rental demand from students. Local searches: 10 days.

Among those estate agents active in this area are:
- Meadway Estates
- Bairstow Eves
- Castles
- Chester Stevens
- Winkworths*
- Adam Kennedy
- Barnard Cook Wood & Loach
- The Property Bureau
- Select Agencies
- A & E Estates
- Bennett-Walden

* further details: see advertisers' index on p671

ST JOHN'S WOOD

Map ref: p60 (2B)
Postal districts: NW8
Boroughs: Westminster (Con)
Council tax: Band D £350
Conservation areas: Most of the area – check with city hall
Parking: Meters and residents. Clamps

London's 'first suburb' – both in the sense of being just about the foremost and just about the closest-in – has now become even better connected. Geographically it is set in the angle of the green, open tracts of Regent's Park and Primrose Hill, yet just across that park lies the West End. And now in terms of communications, the area has got it made. The opening of the final link in the Jubilee Line means that Canary Wharf can be reached direct in 20 minutes, and it's one change – at Waterloo, now a mere 10 minutes away – to Paris. The 15-minute Paddington–Heathrow Express, opened in 1998, is handy for the rest of the world.

Despite thus being pretty well the centre of the universe, and despite the many modern apartment blocks which have replaced earlier mansions, the pace and the style of these select streets are still set, it seems, by the lazy, summer sound of wood on willow that drifts across the high, enclosing walls of Lord's Cricket Ground. Away from the busy artery of **Wellington Rd** and the hustle and bustle of the **High St,** The Wood's life is conducted at strolling pace – and a very pleasant place to stroll it is. Other reasons for the area's appeal include shopping, with the High St boutiques supplemented by the good range along the **Finchley Rd**; religion – the London Central Mosque in Regent's Park, a number of synagogues, Lord's Cricket Ground – and (always cited by agents as paramount) the American School in **Loudoun Rd**.

The international set that St John's Wood attracts means a high number of renters (especially the Americans) as well as buyers – which in turn makes it a blue-chip corner for investors. But there is a very settled backbone, and a sense of belonging appears to develop quickly, wherever one's starting-point. An active residents' association defends the place against vulgarity, though they can do little to curb the traffic. That settled feel is one of wealth; this is no place for violent change. It took Lord's until 1998 to admit women.

Until Regency times this was indeed still largely a wood – albeit a royal one. Hayfields abounded. The development which took place here in the early 19th century, as London spread westward, was aimed at the 'carriage people' and was brilliantly successful. Instead of the more economical terraces that had spread across the centre of town, large and elegant Regency villas with gardens and coach houses, standing alone or in pairs, were built – and remain the hallmark of St John's Wood.

These fine houses set the tone and attracted the 'right' people – a state of affairs which has largely persisted. Its inhabitants are well-established men and women who see a home in St John's Wood as fair reward for their hard work; globe-trotting business people; diplomatic staff. Ambassadors find the area sympathetic. First-time buyers are apt to be at least in their 30s, and equipped with trust fund or undiminished City bonus.

During the 1990s overseas investment, particularly from Singapore and other parts of the Far East, drove the market up. New schemes were bought off-plan – The Pavilion Apartments in **St John's Wood Rd**, which overlooks Lord's, entirely so: see below. Older mansion blocks saw active investment buying. Last year saw prices rocketing once more. The ratio of rent:buy, which had been running at about 50:50, swung back in favour of buying, with one agent's figures showing that the price of 3-bed houses here rose at about three times the rate of Islington's.

As various as the St John's Wood dwellers are the St John's Wood homes. Every size, from pied-à-terre flatlets to vast and splendid mansions; every period, from those Regency villas (and a few rare Regency Gothic cottages) via stock-brick terraces, high Victoriana, artists' studio houses, substantial between-the-wars mansion blocks, bomb-damage infill, '60s town-houses (garages!), small outbreaks of excellent recent houses – and flats, flats and more flats up to the super-luxury '90s models which come with share of porter and pool at the cost of the average West Country manor.

The earlier history of the area still has a bearing on buying homes here today. After the Priors of St John lost the land at the Reformation it was split up; a long, narrow strip (lying along the **Edgware Rd**) became, eventually, part of the Harrow School Estate. A larger section belonged to the Crown: Charles II used some of it to settle a debt. In 1720, 200 acres of this was bought (for £20,000) by Henry Eyre, a prosperous merchant, whose estate remains largely intact today and is remembered in the name of Eyre Court, a popular block on the corner of the **Finchley Rd** and **Grove End Rd**. Thus many freeholds in the area are owned by Harrow School (a typical lease is around 64 years), the Eyre Estate (shorter leases, around 50 years) and (a few) Eton College, and most property is leasehold. Paradoxically, some of the best houses are on these short leases. There are roads where one side has, say, 47-year leases, the other 70; which explains strange price discrepancies. The short leases also explain why these prestige houses can cost no more than those in Hampstead, further out. The Leasehold Reform Acts have changed some of the financial equations: see Buying and Selling chapter.

It's a neat area: its wide and leafy roads lie mainly in Westminster (which stops at the aptly named **Boundary Rd**, though a more tangible frontier is the railway line that separates this area from South Hampstead to the N), and encompass most of NW8. Pencil-straight **Maida Vale** (the road) rules it off to the W, with Regent's Park and Primrose Hill lapping round the eastern periphery. Its internal geography is split – neatly, of course – by the main through-route of **Wellington Rd/Finchley Rd** into two distinct halves: the Lord's side and the Park side.

The Lord's side

The Lord's side refers, of course, to St John's Wood's most sacred shrine – the cricket ground. On this, western, side of the **Wellington Rd/Finchley Rd** divide lie most of the area's other religious institutions: churches, synagogues, etc.

The area's southernmost boundary is **St John's Wood Rd**, which busy road divides Lord's and St John's Wood from Lisson Grove and Marylebone. Across the cricket ground, **Cavendish Avenue** holds some of the largest houses and gardens, attracting celebrity buyers. A splendid, galleried studio house boasted almost 4,000 sq ft of space and almost £2 million on the price tag last winter. This is, too, a good corner for hypochondriacs: at one end of the avenue is **Wellington Place**, at the end of which stands one of London's most expensive private hospitals, Humana's Wellington Hospital (South). At the other end is **Circus Rd** (whose name reflects an early, thwarted, plan to develop St John's Wood around a large circus with streets and squares containing pairs of houses) across which is the back of the Catholic St John and St Elizabeth Hospital.

The other source of grand mansions is **Hamilton Terrace**, which runs the length of the area: this is the Wood's premier boulevard. Wide, tree-lined, prestigious, it stretches about three- quarters of a mile. Begun in 1820, its variety of homes include semi- and detached mansions so large that they now provide the best hunting-ground for conversions (at a premium because of the preponderance of purpose-built flats); many, though, are only on short leases. When intact, however, houses here range from modest to ambassador-class (the one in our drawing boasts 10 bedrooms, 5 receptions, drive, garage, swimming pool . . .). Its 86-year lease was £3.5 million in late '98; by late last year, a freehold house with a mere 6 beds (albeit all en-suite) cost £4 million. Three-bed flats – sorry, apartments – in the road were to be had for £695,000 on the E side, £575,000 on the W.

Flats (or apartments, maisonettes, duplexes, penthouses: terms escalate along with the size and price) can have great views out over greenery – the most coveted being the 22-yard strip with the Test Match being played on it. The Pavilion Apartments, a landmark block on nine floors in **St John's Wood Rd**, launched in spring '99 with prices then running from £160,000 (1-bed) to £1,950,000 (3-bed penthouse), all with parking, 24hr porterage; some with terrace and, yes, view of Lord's. The marketing suite closed five months early with nothing left to sell. It completes this spring, and resales are already showing a 20 per cent hike. This year, the interest is switching to **Hall Rd**, where the old telephone exchange is being converted by Yoo – John 'Manhatten Lofts' Hitchcox and design guru Philippe Starck. Choose a lifestyle conforming to one of four concepts: 'classic', 'minimal', 'nature', 'culture'. Sizes range fron 800 sq ft to 2,889 (excluding terrace), prices from £450,000 to £2.8 million: ready early 2001. In the surrounding streets, a jumble of ages and styles provide flats for all requirements: pre-war ones are in evidence in **Scott Ellis Gardens** and **Hall Rd**, while **Abbey Rd** and **Abercorn Place** have good examples of flats built just after the war. On the corner of the two, 38 **Abercorn Place** is a 1988-built block of eight smart apartments. Under its raised roof, a penthouse enjoys the entire top floor. Next door to it is a delight: a Regency artists' studio house designed by Decimus Burton.

 Grove End Rd, which runs N from **St John's Wood Rd**, is a pleasant street with a mixture of flats, in blocks from mansion to modern, and large houses. Among the latter is Tadema Lodge, a magnificent house with features that include a swimming pool complex and ballroom, designed by the artist James Tissot and later owned by Sir Lawrence Alma-Tadema. The St John and St Elizabeth Hospital, founded by colleagues of Florence Nightingale, stands opposite St John's Wood United Synagogue, one of the three well-known synagogues in the area. It joins **Wellington Rd** just opposite **Acacia Rd**, on the corner of which is the St John's Wood tube station.

 Running N from **Grove End Rd** is **Loudoun Rd,** where you'll find the famous American School – a magnet for US families – and, opposite it, the boys' prep school Arnold House. The street's consequent traffic problems were much improved by sleeping policemen. Parallel to **Loudoun Rd** is **Abbey Rd**, made famous by the Beatles, who cut their records here (today, spot those Spice Girls at the Studios). It, too, has sprouted stylish new developments: the 1990 complex of eight houses and 100 apartments at No 20 was among the first to be marketed extensively in Hong Kong, helped by Beatles-linked promotion: a key gimmick was a pedestrian crossing mock-up on which prospective buyers were photographed in a re-creation of the famous album cover. A new phase of this scheme is completing this spring; a 1-bed flat now costs c. £230–270,000; naturally there's parking/pool/porterage. Another new development is appearing at the old garage site on the corner with **Abercorn Place**: at time of writing preliminary work has started, and the agents report serious interest in 17 of the planned 24 apartments. With so many flats **Abbey Rd**, busy but wide and leafy, is also very popular on the rentals market.

Off **Abbey Rd** lies one of the prettiest corners of St John's Wood. Roads like **Blenheim Terrace, Nugent Terrace** and **Boundary Rd** have a smaller-scale, village-like atmosphere. There you'll find little rows of shops and little parks like the one in **Violet Hill**. Houses round pretty **Alma Square** have access to its gardens. These 4-floor, 5/6-bedroomed terraced homes, which date from the 1850s, break the million-pound barrier. Some have been converted. A small new flats development appeared in the square two years back.

On **Finchley Rd** the 1930s Apsley House was crowned in 1990 with six luxurious new penthouse flats. This became a popular trend for blocks in the area – Clive Court on **Maida Vale** is another example – popular except, of course, with the erstwhile top-floor dwellers, whose penthouses are now merely penultimate.

The Park side

East of the **Wellington Rd/Finchley Rd** divide – which connects St John's Wood with Swiss Cottage – the Park side of St John's Wood boasts not only the Hill and the Park, but the **High St**, and some peaceful corners to live. **Queen's Grove**, with its terraced houses boasting large Ionic and Corinthian columns, is a quiet, leafy road leading to Primrose Hill. **Norfolk Rd** and **Acacia Rd** are both pretty streets with stuccoed and brick houses, sought-after – even fought-over – by those who prefer older-style houses. Lilly Langtry, Edward VII's actress mistress, dwelt in **Acacia Rd**; recent prices included £1.65 million for a Georgian home here, £2,500,000 for a big Victorian 5-bedroomed one.

Woronzow Rd, where learner drivers practise their three-point turns, contains the (comparatively) less expensive terraced houses (eg 4-bed terraced, £895,000). The Woronzow in question was a Russian count who left £500 to build almshouses: they were erected in **St John's Wood Terrace** in 1827, but were rebuilt in the 1960s.

Newer houses in St John's Wood can be seen further towards Swiss Cottage. **Queensmead** is an estate of 17 town-houses and three blocks of flats owned by the Eyre Estate, built in the late '60s. They were let until 1990, when some were refurbished and sold: £895,000 can get you a 6-bed town-house here. **The Marlowes** is another sought-after clutch of town-houses: they look, comments a local, like flats tipped on their sides, but are desirable because of their location. **St John's Wood Park** also contains other modern homes. 'The Rosetti' in **Ordnance Hill** is a 1995 scheme where 1-bed flats currently fetch £300,000. **Ordnance Hill** houses the King's Troop Royal Horse Artillery – a splendid sight to see in the early morning when the horses are exercised: this can involve 60 horses with gun carriages.

Running between **Circus Rd** and **Prince Albert Rd** is **St John's Wood High St** with its boutiques, bistros, wine merchants and chemists. Round the corner is Panzers, St John's Wood's most up-market grocer, and the post office. Council-built flats (select ones, to match the area) lie behind the **High St**. Some in **Barrow Hill, Allitsen Rd** and **Townshend Rd** now appear for sale, having been bought by their tenants.

At the end of the **High St** is the roundabout presided over by St John's Wood Church, a large elegant building. **Prince Albert Rd** curves around the N side of the park (see Regent's Park). The Pavilions at 24–26 **Avenue Rd**, a luxurious development of six flats, a sumptuous penthouse and swimming pool, was built in 1988. **Avenue Rd** is a grand thoroughfare, highly desirable to the international set: ambassadors from all nations make their homes in the large mansions with landscaped gardens, overseas business people buy flats. Here, too, is a 7-bed, 6-reception modern mansion with dramatic atrium within but carefully Regency-styled exterior, which seems to indicate that St John's Wood pockets, although long, have their limits: no one appears to have rushed to pay £7.5 million for the freehold.

Eastern Borders

Across **Avenue Rd**, a small clutch of streets run E to Primrose Hill. Look for flats, and modern town-houses, in streets such as **St Edmund's Terrace**, **Ormonde Terrace**. For villagy Primrose Hill proper, across the 200-ft-high hill, see the Camden chapter.

To the N of Primrose Hill lies a group of roads with huge, handsome Edwardian red-brick villas. Look for them in **Harley Rd**, **Wadham Gardens** and **Elsworthy Rd**. To the S, the giant modern blocks along **Prince Albert Rd** are covered in the Regent's Park chapter.

Transport	Tubes: St John's Wood, Swiss Cottage (zone 2, Jubilee); Maida Vale (zone 2, Bakerloo). From St John's Wood: Oxford Circus 15 min (1 change), City 30 min (1 change), Heathrow 30 min (1 change). Trains: South Hampstead (direct to Euston).
Convenient for	West End, Regent's Park, Lord's Cricket Ground. Routes to North and West. Paris, Canary Wharf thanks to Jubilee Line Extension, Heathrow thanks to Paddington Express. Miles from centre: 3.5.
Schools	Local Authority: Quintin Kynaston, Jewish Free School. Private: The American School, Francis Holland (g), International Community School. See also: Hampstead, Kentish Town.

SALES

Flats	S	1B	2B	3B	4B	5B
Average prices	100–140	140–250+	250–450	350+	500+	→

Houses	2B	3B	4B	5B	6/7B	8B
Average prices	350–600+	500–1M	750–2M	1M+	1.5M+	2.5M+

RENTAL

Flats	S	1B	2B	3B	4B	5B
Average prices	200–250	250–350	300–600	400–1000	800+	—

Houses	2B	3B	4B	5B	6/7B	8B
Average prices	500+	600–1500	800+	1500+	—	—

The properties	Smart suburb with big, early 19th-century villas, and outstanding range of homes: virtually every size and style of house and flat from late-Georgian terraces to state-of-the-art modern represented somewhere here. Abundant mansion and modern flats blocks. These become stratospheric (height and price) towards Regent's Park (which chapter see) and Lord's: London's highest concentration of penthouses.
The market	Cosmopolitan: diplomats, business folk, celebrities, all buy here for big family houses, and international-class apartments that can cost as much and more than whole houses.) Much overseas investment/bolt-hole buying. Local searches: 10 days.

Among those estate agents active in this area are:

- Anscombe & Ringland *
- Knight Frank
- Bargets
- Winkworth *
- The Estate Office
- Behr & Butchoff
- Goldschmidt & Howland
- John D Wood
- Arlington Residential
- Brian Lack
- Foxtons *
- Cluttons Daniel Smith
- Keith Cardale Groves
- Hamptons
- FPDSavills

further details: see advertisers' index on p671

S

STEPNEY AND WHITECHAPEL

Map ref: p63 (4K)
Postal districts: E1
Boroughs: Tower Hamlets (Lab)
Council tax: Band D £674
Conservation areas: Numerous – check
   with town hall
Parking: Meters/yellow lines towards City

Stepney, Whitechapel and Wapping, an area defined quite precisely by the E1 postal district, is the heart of the old East End. Lying directly alongside the City of London, war and slum clearance brought great changes, leaving it a curious mixture of some of London's best and worst housing. Now the ferment in its neighbouring areas brings more. The City's expansion has crossed the border into Stepney, while the Docklands building boom has brought wealth to riverside Wapping (see Docklands chapter). Some squalor remains – little more than a stone's throw from the thriving City – but this is changing fast.

The most fundamental difference is the vogue for living in and around the City, which until five years ago had a nocturnal population consisting of more cats than humans. The W edge of this area is Spitalfields and Aldgate, both of which are seeing enormous changes that involve homes as well as offices. A linked trend is the 'loft' movement: the City fringes and the wider area are rich in redundant buildings that, like the old Docklands warehouses, can make spacious homes: see also the City chapter. The property market (a new phrase to this part of town) woke up as those priced out of Islington, Clerkenwell and Docklands took a look at Stepney. The stigma attached to the East End was fading – and, most important and best of all, the regeneration of the East End doesn't just mean 'outsiders' moving in, but is strongly local-based: the grim worst-period council towers are tumbling, estates are being renovated or entirely rebuilt, new homes earmarked for affordable housing for locals are appearing under the aegis of urban regeneration schemes.

That said, Stepney is as convenient for the City as Docklands, if not so chic, and buyers are finding it attractive. Unlike most of modern Docklands, Stepney's neighbourhoods have been around for a long time . . . the sense of history, of real life in an existing community, and of course the prices of the homes, are all more congenial to some buyers, particularly the young.

The Stepney and Whitechapel area has three main roads running E–W: **The Highway, Commercial Rd** and **Whitechapel Rd** which is a continuation of **Mile End Rd**. All three lead to the City and are, therefore, perpetually busy. The Liverpool St main line cuts Stepney off from Bethnal Green to the N, while the canal divides it from Poplar to the E. Wapping and the river underlines it to the S, and the City lies to the W. The old centre of Stepney was a thriving village in medieval times. All that is left is Stepney Churchyard, surrounding St Dunstan's Church, **Stepney High St**: one of Stepney's most picturesque corners. The church, too, is being renovated, with the help of lottery cash. Although the Victorians re-faced the exterior, the foundation is so old that it is not only named after the saint but was *rebuilt* by him, in the 10th century. Nearby, in **Stepney Way**, is Stepping Stones Farm – an unusual sight in such a highly populated area.

This part of London drips with history, a fact reflected by no fewer than a dozen conservation areas. The Tower of London falls within Stepney's boundary while Jack the Ripper once stalked the streets of Whitechapel in search of victims. Whitechapel (which, by the way, is named after Stepney's second church, a chapel added in the 13th century) is dominated by the world-famous London Hospital, directly opposite Whitechapel tube station and **Whitechapel Rd** market (known locally as 'The Waste'). Cultural attractions include the Whitechapel Gallery, the first and most famous of several art galleries. According to the Whitechapel, there are 7,000 artists living and working in the wider East End.

The area used to be in parts strongly Jewish, but now a Muslim flavour predominates, especially around **Brick Lane** and the mosque in **Whitechapel High St**. This corner has over the centuries always been a haven for incoming communities: in 1900 Jewish, Irish, German, Scandinavian and Chinese peoples lived here.

Apart from the explosion of new housing developments in Wapping (described in the Docklands chapter), some of Stepney's most coveted homes are to be found in the **Albert Gardens/Arbour Square** conservation area, which includes Arbour Square police station. Parking here is not such a problem as nearer the City and around the London Hospital. The least desirable housing is on either side of the W end of **Commercial Rd**. These areas are dominated by the East End 'rag trade' and scores of clothing manufacturers and wholesalers operate here. Many of these small businesses are run by Asians. Vehicles loading and unloading in the cramped streets make driving in this area a particular problem.

Spitalfields is on the way up, with new City-linked developments in train. It includes three conservation areas – **Elder St**, **Fournier St** and **Artillery Passage** which still hold some beautiful, intact homes left by even earlier immigrants, the Huguenot silk merchants: these date from very early Georgian days. For details, see the City chapter.

Watney Market, S of **Commercial Rd**, is another far from attractive area but it has the asset of the DLR's Shadwell station. The famous Petticoat Lane market is in **Middlesex St** on Sunday mornings, and there is also a market throughout the week in nearby **Wentworth St**.

Stepney

At the eastern end of the neighbourhood, conveniently close to Stepney Green tube, an enclave of streets is hidden in the angle between **Globe** and **Mile End Rds**. **Portelet Rd**, **Carlton Square**, **Holton St**, **Grantley St**, **Massingham St** and **Tollet St** are well-placed near the Mile End annexe of the London Hospital. These delightful 2-storey Victorian terraced houses, some with semi-basements and steps up to the front door, are also near Tower Hamlets Central Library in **Bancroft Rd** and various Queen Mary and Westfield College buildings. **Bancroft Rd**'s amenities also include a music rehearsal space in the old railway arches. Residents in **Grand Walk**, at the E end of **Mile End Rd**, have new terraced houses made magic by the Grand Union Canal, which also facilitates the occasional houseboat and anglers. Across the canal, **Canal Rd** has disappeared in the massive, ongoing development of Mile End Park. In **Copperfield Rd**, also by the park, Bellway converted a canalside building into 40 flats last year. Here, too, is the Falcon Works: 20 new affordable-housing 1- and 2-bed flats for locals.

Across to the S of **Mile End Rd**, down to **Ben Jonson Rd**, is the sprawling, hitherto run-down Ocean council estate, which takes in **Beaumont Square**, **White Horse Lane**, **Matlock St**, **Commodore St**, **Solebay St**, **Emmott St**, **Shandy St**, **Duckett St** and **Harford St**. Now, though, this is being extensively rebuilt – especially between Harford and Duckett Sts N of Ben Jonson Rd – with new access roads and hundreds of new houses. Housing associations and the Central Stepney Regeneration Project are active here, building and renovating: again for renting to locals at affordable rates; Laing are adding 41 such new homes in a large new estate opposite the gasworks on **Harford St**.

White Horse Lane has 2-storey terraced houses with distinctive open porches and to the E the green of **Beaumont Square**, which faces the London Independent private hospital (currently getting a face-lift). **Maria Terrace**, off **Beaumont Square**, has a row of 10 3-storey Victorian houses. Close by in **Louisa St**, nine 3-bedroomed houses have been built. And in **Rectory Square**, behind **Stepney Green**, developers have converted a synagogue into flats and houses: one sold for £199,750 last winter.

Stepney Green – not the open, featureless expanse between **Stepney Way/Redman's Rd**, but the street of the same name just to the N – is an unexpected gem. Behind the narrow strip of green, enclosed by railings, stand a row of Queen Anne/early 18th-century houses, in what is reputed to be the only blue-cobbled street left in South East England. They are supplemented by some faithful modern copies. One of these is Trinity Mews, on **Redman's Rd**, a mixed development of homes and commercial premises which includes town-houses with studio workspace. In **White Horse Lane** is 'The Rosery', an old rectory now divided into nine smart flats.

Opposite are the ivy-fronted red-brick Cressy House and Dunstan House, and another area of transformation, what was the Stifford Estate (council). This included **Tinsley Rd**, **Cressy Place**, **Redmans Rd**, **Jamaica St**, **Stepney Way** and **Smithy St**. Last year we reported that in **Jamaica St** three boarded-up tower blocks loomed over the Stifford – one with the painted message 'FOR SALE, £4.99 O.N.O. ONE CARELESS OWNER

HA! HA!'. The hint was taken: now on the site of some of the blocks 106 homes – flats and houses, to rent, for sale, or shared ownership – are appearing courtesy of the Stifford Regeneration Project, another public/private partnership that includes Lovell Homes and the Paddington Churches Housing Association.

Back to the **Mile End Rd** where, in the stretch between **Globe Rd** and **Cambridge Heath Rd**, **Cephas Avenue** has attractive 2- and 3-storey Victorian terraced houses, many with steps and railings and some with flat roofs, always in high demand. Now 18 houses and a retail park are being built between Cephas Avenue and **Nicholas Rd**. In **Cephas St** a church conversion yielded 37 flats last year, and Durkan Homes are now converting no. 95 next door. Nearby **Cooper's Close** has neat 4-storey modern flats. **Cleveland Way** has smart new housing association flats and Cleveland Place, a 1998 development of 10 flats; a further enclave shelters behind electronic gates.

Close to Whitechapel tube and in stark contrast to its busy surroundings in **Mile End Rd** is Trinity Green, a small 1961 Civic Trust Award development with beautiful gardens surrounded by railings and wall. And just before the **Mile End Rd** becomes **Whitechapel Rd**, Copthorne Homes is starting a development of 2-bed flats, 2/3-bed maisonettes and 3-bed town-houses on the corner with **Cambridge Heath Rd**.

Commercial Rd to the S, towards Wapping, lives up to its name with heavy traffic – this is also the A13, the main road out east from the City's Aldgate – and is dotted on either side with council estates such as Pitsea, Watney Market, Exmouth and Mountmorres. The garden square of **Albert Gardens** is a peaceful haven from the noise of the through-route. These desirable 4-storey Victorian terraced houses are part of a conservation area which also includes **Havering St**, where 3-storey Victorian houses with railings lead down to a railway arch; a 2/3-bed house here was £248,995 last winter. Viewed from the rear, the roofs of Havering St give an unusual wave effect. To the W, St Mary and St Michael's Roman Catholic Church and Primary School are next to the Watney Market council estate which includes **Deancross St**, **Sidney St**, **Hainton Path**, **Hungerford St**, **Tarling St**, **Watney St**, **Dunch St**, **Timberland Rd**, **Bigland St** and **Burwell Close**. Across from Tarling St, in **Sutton St**, the Samuel Lewis Housing Trust are adding fair-rent homes: 1-bed flats, 2- and 4-bed houses and a 6-bed one.

The Exmouth Estate, N of **Commercial Rd**, includes **Clark St**, **Musbury St**, **Cornwood Drive**, **Jubilee St**, **Exmouth St**, **Summercourt Rd**, **Jamaica St**, **Aylward St**, **Clovelly Way** and **Clearbrook Way**. A new development for this corner, too, to replace Tower Hamlets College buildings between **Clark** and **Jubilee Sts**. To the E of the Estate is the **Arbour Square** conservation area, where Arbour House council flats are situated alongside 3-storey Victorian terraced houses, some with front steps, facing a garden square. Houses on the S side of the square have a drawback as they back onto far less attractive 4-storey terraced houses in **Commercial Rd**.

Further E along **Commercial Rd** is Bromley St, where railings surround delightful 2-storey Victorian terraced houses, refurbished in 1986, leading to the British Prince pub on the corner and adjoining the Mountmorres council estate. Similar homes are to be found in **Belgrave St**, as are 74 homes added last year by a housing trust on a rent or shared-ownership basis. A new road is being built between the two streets for a homes scheme to be called Lighterman Mews. **Belgrave St** leads back up to **Stepney High St** and picturesque St Dunstan's Church at the heart of old Stepney (see introduction, above), much favoured for local weddings. The church is surrounded by Stepney Churchyard, and facing the churchyard is **Mercers Cottages**, four beautiful terraced homes with a communal front garden.

The **York Square** conservation area, to the SE of the green, is half in Stepney and half in Limehouse. The Stepney half includes **White Horse Rd** and **Barnes St**. Run-down 3- and 4-storey terraced houses in **White Horse Rd** face attractive 3-storey Victorian terraced properties with railings and hanging baskets of flowers. Similarly attractive 2-

storey Victorian terraces in **Barnes St**, on the opposite side of **Commercial Rd** to Limehouse rail and DLR stations. On **Cable St** Sceptre Court (1998) has underground parking; Cable St has an excellent cycle path that runs from the City to the Limehouse Link tunnel entrance. For Limehouse and Wapping, see under Docklands.

Whitechapel

The world-famous London Hospital dominates the centre of Whitechapel. The front entrance of the hospital stands in **Whitechapel Rd**, directly opposite Whitechapel tube station and **Whitechapel Rd** market. Some of the Victorian terraced houses at the back of the hospital are owned by the hospital itself, for example in **Philpott St**, and used for research. Other hospital buildings are to be found in **Newark St**, part of the **Sidney Square** conservation area. The conservation area also includes part of **Cavell St**, **Halcrow St**, **Ford Square**, **Ashfield St**, **Sidney Square** and the E end of **Varden St**.

Sidney Square is attractive with 3-storey Victorian terraced houses that have tiny wrought-iron balconies on the second floor; but parking is a big problem in this area. City Walk is a large, luxury-level flats scheme by Furlong Homes in **Raven Row**, to the W of the hospital. At the junction of **Cavell St**, named after Nurse Edith Cavell, and **Varden St** is a new development of 20 luxury apartments. More 3- and 4-storey Victorian terraced houses, some converted into flats, are found in **Ford Square**. Many of these houses are now occupied by the local student population. The area's cramped streets also include many Asian-run garment manufacturers and wholesalers: vans loading and unloading sometimes make access difficult.

The renowned Whitechapel Bell Foundry, established in 1570, is at the junction of **Fieldgate St** and **Plumber's Row**; this street, too is sprouting new homes: Mulberry Court's 'spacious City apartments' were from £99,995 last autumn. The Whitechapel Gallery in the **High St**, just refurbished, is a world-famous art venue which balances the cultural with the practical: it's also a well-known local place to eat. The East London Mosque, on **Whitechapel Rd,** is a focal point for the Muslim community. To the N of **Whitechapel Rd**, the new Sainsbury's improved the area's shopping. Nearby in **Durward St** is 'Cityside', a conversion of an old school. Also situated on **Whitechapel Rd** is Albion Yard, the converted old Albion brewery.

From **New Rd** westwards, the nearer the City, the greater the concentration of developers' boards. Between **Whitechapel Rd, Commercial Rd** and **New Rd**, a vast development is trying to reinvent the area as the 'Aldgate Triangle'; 235 flats, in the first of three buildings designed by architects CZWG launched last October, ranged from £125–260,000 for 1- to 3-beds, complete with 2-storey gym and Renaissance-style gardens, we are told. The developers are Ballymore, who were already at work last year on a big site off **Gower's Walk**, S of **Commercial Rd**: among the homes there are smart warehouse conversions. St George's 'Skyline Plaza' flats on **Commercial Rd** has 130 flats sharing a roof garden with splendid views.

Streets from **Leman St**, which includes a police station, across to **Mansell St** are now generally accepted as part of the City itself and are strict no-parking zones (the Citys boundary actually runs down Mansell St). **Prescot St** has already seen the conversion of a 1930s office building into flats, and now Berkeley Homes is adding 'Londinium Tower': 84 1-, 2- and 3-bed flats with parking below.

For Spitalfields and Brick Lane, see the City chapter.

Transport   Tubes: Stepney Green, Whitechapel, Aldgate East (Hammersmith & City, District); Wapping (East London); Aldgate (Metropolitan, Circle); Tower Hill (Circle, District); Shadwell (East London). DLR (Docklands Light Railway). Trains: Limehouse. From Stepney

Green: Oxford Circus 15 min (1 change), City 10 min (1 change), Heathrow 60 min (1 change).

Convenient for   Docklands, City. Miles from centre: 3.5.

Schools   Local Authority: Bishop Challoner RC (g), Bow (b), Central Foundation (g), Mulberry (g), Sir John Cass, Stepney Green (b), Swanlea School.

SALES

Flats	S	1B	2B	3B	4B	5B
Average prices	60–115	80–150	90–180	100–200	–	–

Houses	2B	3B	4B	5B	6/7B	8B
Average prices	90–250	100–280	175–300 ›	–	–	–

RENTAL

Flats	S	1B	2B	3B	4B	5B
Average prices	140–240	210–300	240–350	–	–	–

Houses	2B	3B	4B	5B	6/7B	8B
Average prices	70–150	80–150	120–250	180–380+	–	–

The properties   Loft conversions and new-build flats appearing as City workers discover the area. Homes here range from ex-council to Grade II listed, from flats to new mews schemes, from Edwardian red-brick to Georgiana on Stepney Green.

The market   Prices reflect range, and closeness of City and Wapping. Small, everyday rows rub shoulders with large listed houses. A few 7-bed Edwardian homes: occasionally to be found undone-up. For Wapping riverside and Spitalfields see Docklands and City. Local searches: 2–4 weeks.

Among those estate agents active in this area are:

- Prevost
- Baker Allen
- Ludlow Thompson
- Alex Neil
- Look
- Medowalls
- Keatons *
- W J Meade
- Tower
- Land & Co
- Alan Selby

further details: see advertisers' index on p671

S

STOKE NEWINGTON

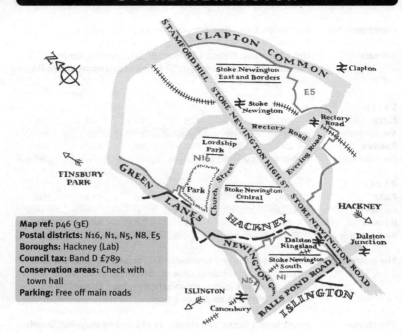

Map ref: p46 (3E)
Postal districts: N16, N1, N5, N8, E5
Boroughs: Hackney (Lab)
Council tax: Band D £789
Conservation areas: Check with
   town hall
Parking: Free off main roads

Go due north from London Bridge: through the City, up the Roman-straight A10. An exodus of younger (ie, poorer) media types, City workers and young families did so in the last decade, and made a home in Stoke Newington. On the fault line between east and west (Highbury end of Islington to W, Hackney to E), new residents mingled with those three generations in. The newer arrivals find they've joined a community; people know each other and get together to protect their area, support their local schools or just to hold street parties: there is a very popular midsummer festival in **Church St**.

Exciting additions are appearing – typified, perhaps, by the most visible: Stoke Newington last year gained a new landmark building, on the corner of **Albion Rd** at the head of the Green. The distinctive rounded, balconied tower of Holland House is, as you might expect, yet another clutch of luxurious flats and penthouses such as are springing up all over town – if rather more distinguished than most. The gated parking, the stripped-wood floors, the state-of-the-art kitchens, even cable TV points . . . and a stipulation that buy-to-let purchasers need not apply. For this is a development by the Peabody Trust, the charitable foundation that has been providing quality homes for the poor since before the days of council housing, and this scheme will fund yet more affordable homes for local people. Indeed, 24 of the Holland House flats are sold on a shared-ownership basis, to give those who couldn't otherwise get onto the housing ladder a start.

Millennium year sees the opening of the new £13 million pound Clissold Leisure Centre (this includes two 25-metre pools plus another with easy access for those less mobile or disabled), also a Millennium Peace Garden in **Boleyn Rd**; the lottery has played fairy godmother to a major new watersports centre – there's even talk of a theatre, no less. But the thing that would really set the seal on this corner is a tube station. At last even that holy grail has come closer, with plans now on the table to extend the East London Line: this currently ends at Shoreditch, but the proposed northern extension would add the underground to this area's two train stations, Canonbury and Dalston. Don't, though, hold your breath until they announce that funding is in place. For now, trains to the City are good, and the trusty 73 bus goes all the way to Victoria via King's Cross, Euston and Oxford St.

Largely in N16, Stoke Newington lies N of **Balls Pond Rd**, E of **Green Lanes**, S of **Allerton Rd**, **Fairholt Rd** and **Dunsmure Rd**, and W of **Clapton Common**, with **Brooke Rd**, **Evering Rd**, **Rectory Rd** and **Shacklewell Lane** completing the circle. It is an amalgam of the ancient villages of Shacklewell and Stoke Newington itself, the northern points of Kingsland and the southern reaches of Stamford Hill. The villages are Domesday-ancient; the area was popular as a place to retreat in the 17th century, thrived in Georgian times, became built-up in Victoria's reign. Here in the 1830s Thomas Cubitt was sharpening his skills before moving on to create Belgravia and Pimlico. The area prospered until the early 20th century, when the more well-to-do moved further out. Many homes became tenanted; wartime bombs hastened their demise.

Post-war redevelopment brought ugly low-rise council-built blocks, latterly 'improved' by surface treatments such as bright paint and the landscaping of open areas. Much has been done to restore and renovate streets to a modern version of Victorian splendour – work carried out by the council, locals and the numbers of young middle-class families who have found homes here. It is an ongoing task.

Conservation areas now abound, local shopping is well-served, and restaurants – both fast-food and conventional – are numerous. Pubs have been joined by smart wine bars; arts and crafts shops and bookshops supplement the high-street basics. There's a popular jazz club here, The Vortex. All help to make the distance from Stoke Newington to the West End seem increasingly irrelevant. The Rio Cinema, with its imaginative programming, is now open once more after a lottery-aided refit.

Outdoors, spacious Clissold Park boasts a truly eccentric 'zoo', bowling green, tennis courts, bandstand for summer sonatas, and now the aforementioned brand-new leisure centre nearby, while Abney Park Cemetery is the resting place for many eminent Victorians, beneath wonderful Gothic tombs.

The two main thoroughfares are the A10, which in its northwards charge changes its name from **Kingsland High St** via **Stoke Newington Rd** to **Stoke Newington High St**, and the E–W **Stoke Newington Church St**. Although most of the length of the High St remains cheerfully scruffy, the area between the **Church St** and **Northwold Rd** intersections is becoming smarter. New restaurants are opening, and other long-empty premises are being renovated. There is even an example here of the fashion to turn redundant Victorian schools into lofty 1-, 2- and 3-bed flats, which sold fast last year. This scheme also has some houses: the remaining few were £365–395,000.

Church St – the high street of the original village – still boasts many buildings of 18th-century origins, and it is still the centre of Stoke Newington. The area's great mix of classes and cultures is reflected in its shops and eateries, lately joined by a rash of health-food shops, delis, exclusive second-hand book dealers and (even more tellingly) a welter of estate agents. On the Dalston borders to the S, **Ridley Rd** market sells all manner of goods at knock-down prices – and has a 24hr bagel shop.

Lordship Park

The most northerly of Stoke Newington's four neighbourhoods is Lordship Park – not a park but a road, though both Clissold Park and Abney Park Cemetery are in this leafy corner that runs N from **Stoke Newington Church St** to the reservoirs. **Lordship Park/Manor Rd**, the main thoroughfare, is an E–W bus and general traffic route. At the W end are monumental 4-storey houses, set back from the road, making them quieter than might be assumed. These give way to smaller 2-storey bay-fronted houses towards the E.

North of **Lordship Park** is **Allerton Rd**, a great choice if you want to take up outdoor pursuits. One end of it is overshadowed by a bizarre Gothic water tower – now home to Britain's premier indoor climbing centre (a flats scheme next to it – up to c. £160,000 – are graced with the name 'Castle View'). And homes on the N side of of the street have gardens backing onto the reservoirs. No longer needed, one has re-emerged as the Stoke Newington West Reservoir Centre, whose splendid new facilities include dinghy sailing, fishing, windsurfing, sub-aqua training and dragon-boat racing, while the East Reservoir is now a developing wildlife reserve. On the W side of **Green Lanes**, the former filter beds hold a mix of housing association and open-market homes; at the junction with Portland Rise, a new cache of 2- and 3-bed flats, and 4-bed town-houses, from £150,000.

Allerton Rd leads into **Queen Elizabeth's Walk**: here you can pay up to half a million for a 4-bed house at the S end, where the houses overlook Clissold Park. The back gardens of these are in turn overlooked by council-built low-rise. Look out for the lovely double-fronted terraces in the Walk – rare beauties. Tree-lined **Fairholt Rd** and shop-studded **Dunsmure Rd** complete Stoke's northern reaches. Both contain generous bay-fronted family houses, some flats, some council. Look here and round about for large houses at (comparatively) lower prices. In **St Andrew's Mews** 53 flats appeared, set around a landscaped courtyard. Last winter only 2-beds at £117,000 were left.

Running S, houses tend to be less tidied, and the occasional unrenovated one is to be found. **Bethune Rd**, **Heathland Rd**, **St Andrews Grove** and busy **Lordship Rd** are all edged by large, often renovated and split up, Victorian bay-fronted houses. The E–W streets – **Paget Rd**, **St Kilda's Rd** and **Grangecourt Rd** – are smaller with mainly 2-storey terraces; some very pretty, notably the S side of **Grangecourt Rd** and **St Kilda's Rd** between **Bethune Rd** and **Heathland Rd**. The area has a strong Hasidic Jewish community, and homes often do not appear on the open market.

South of **Manor Rd** the streets are noticeably smarter. Most of the renovation work here has already been done, though the odd patch of less-tended Victorian terrace still peeks out from between the glistening paintwork and new planting. Here **Bouverie Rd** matches **Queen Elizabeth's Walk** in desirability. Homes with even numbers back onto the cemetery and there is light industrial at the S end. Odd-numbered houses are either large, 4-storey and flat-fronted or charming 2-storey terraces. Low odd numbers have small gardens. This street, though, is used as a traffic short-cut; more peaceful are the pleasant homes in **Yoakley Rd**, **Grayling Rd** and **Grazebrook Rd**. **Yoakley Rd** has a charming Victorian terrace in the E side, broken now and then by small eccentric detached villas. Again houses here rarely come on the market – and are snapped up if they do. Much of the W side is boring council low-rise. Running E–W, **Grayling Rd** has lovely 2-storey bay-fronted houses and **Grazebrook Rd** has 3-storey terrace on the W side overlooking the edge of a largish, modern council estate. **Fleetwood St** runs N off **Church St**, a short, one-sided, Victorian terrace running up to the cemetery and local fire station: 3-bedroom houses here are c. £200–260,000. Running parallel, **Summerhouse Rd** also has some beautiful Victorian homes. And in **Wilmer Place** a new development by Furlong Homes will include commercial properties as well as homes. There are 10 flats – 1-beds for £110–115,000, 2-beds £150,000 – plus 14 town-houses, priced from £235,000 to £345,000.

Stoke Newington Central

Stoke Newington central – the old village of Shacklewell – lies S of **Church St**, W of the **High St**, and has as its southern border a stretch of **Green Lanes**, **Matthias Rd** and **Barrett's Grove**. It is this central area, with its mix of 2-storey terraces interspersed with streets of bigger buildings, which saw the first ungentlemanly price leaps in the late '80s, although the large houses to the NE of this area made the biggest jumps this time around.

The area is split in two by **Albion Rd**, a bus route and general N–S thoroughfare. Here

3-storey terraces give way to large renovated Victorian blocks. Further S, **Albion Rd** narrows and is lined by 3-storey, bay-fronted Victorian houses, converted to 1- to 3-bed flats by a housing association and only very occasionally up for sale. At No 147, however, a new private development includes the conversion of a Grade II-listed house into two 2-bed flats and two 3-beds, with four houses being built in the grounds. Next door, No 149 is yielding a dozen 2-bed shared-ownership flats for Tower Housing Association.

To the W of **Albion Rd**, running up to Clissold Park, lies that section which hopeful estate agents some years back began to dub the 'North Islington Overspill Quadrant', no less. Despite the hyperbole this patch is well worth a look. **Winston Rd** has small 2-storey houses, and off **Winston Rd** look out for **Reedholm Villas** – a wee gem of a cul-de-sac. **Springdale Rd** and **Aden Grove** have bigger homes; **Burma Rd's** are 3- and 4-storey ones. **Clissold Crescent** and **Carysfort Rd** also have larger houses, many sporting original features such as decorative porch tiles or glasswork. Most gardens are tiny, however.

Clissold Crescent also boasts two exciting new developments. On the E side of the road, replacing the old swimming baths, is the £13 million hi-tech building of the brand-new Clissold Leisure Centre, with its swimming and diving pools, dance hall, fitness hall, health suite. Opposite there are plans for a new public theatre to be built in the grounds of Stoke Newington School. At the southern end of the crescent is a recent development of housing-association and private flats, part of which overlooks a car breaker's yard. In **Carysfort Rd** is a factory conversion which has live/work units that sell from c. £125,000.

An example of another deeply fashionable development trend, the shell-finish warehouse flat, is emerging on **Church St** close to Clissold Park. Two of six flats in Albion House, both 1,000 sq ft, are being marketed this way: one with roof terrace, £220,000; without, £190,000. A third, finished and with terrace, is £285,000. And nearby, in Hawksley Rd, another redundant Victorian school building is becoming 1-, 2- and 3-bed flats . . . .

To the E of **Albion Rd**, N of **Barbauld Rd** and **Dynevor Rd** is a maze of charming little streets, lined mainly with 2- and 3-bedroomed houses. Though occasionally turned into tiny flats, for the most part these streets remain relatively unspoilt. Some houses are bigger, having a semi-basement floor as in the N side of **Dumont Rd**; light industry behind. S of **Barbauld Rd** and the kink in **Nevill Rd** the area changes. The well-designed low-rise estate on the E side of **Nevill Rd** faces shops with flats above. From here the horizontal ladder of roads – **Beatty Rd** down to **Barrett's Grove** – hold some larger 3- and 4-storey houses. **Beatty Rd**, **Walford Rd** and **Brighton Rd** have houses with large gardens on their N sides. These streets hold many flat conversions, but watch for subsidence problems in some houses.

The further S you go, the untidier the streets become. **Palatine Rd** has smaller 2-storey houses, but the western end of the street finishes with a strange ziggurat configuration of buildings, recently renovated. **Prince George Rd** enjoys an open space halfway down, with tennis courts. **Belgrade** and **Princess May Rds** and **Barrett's Grove** are a mix of 2- and 3-storey houses.

North of **Allen Rd**, **Milton Grove** and **Shakspeare Walk** are 4-storey terraces, now frequently flats – narrowish streets considering the heights of the buildings but some houses have superb-sized gardens at back. **Shakspeare Walk's** (yes that *is* how it's spelt) mix of houses and flats are particularly popular. **Londesborough Rd**, **Osterley Rd** and **Clonbrook Rd** have 3-storey houses and many council flats.

South of **Allen Rd** the area gives way to a bleak '50s estate, which the council improved a great deal with bright paint, trees and turf. The streets surrounding this area hold friendly local shops with a wide and interesting range of goods.

Stoke Newington South

This area lies S of **Green Lanes**, **Matthias Rd** and **Barrett's Grove**, and N of the **Balls Pond Rd**. To the W it is bordered by **Wallace Rd** and **Petherton Rd**, and to the E by **Kingsland High St** and the S end of **Stoke Newington Rd**. At the end of **Green Lanes** lies **Newington Green**, its 'green' now a small public garden enclosed by railings and, in effect, a roundabout. Its earlier days are recalled by a small group of Georgian houses and four even earlier which, amazingly, have survived from the 1650s. At this end of **Green Lanes**, at the junction with Albion Rd, the charitable Peabody Trust has added Holland House, its landmark tower of 20 leasehold (1- and 2-beds; £125–190,000) and 24 shared-ownership flats, plus restaurant and medical centre: see introduction, above.

Starting in the NW corner of the neighbourhood, **Leconfield Rd** snakes southwards and is edged with 2-storey bay-fronted Victorian houses, with semi-basements. The light industry at the N end is the downside, while large gardens are the upside. **Poet's Rd**, similar in size to the **Leconfield Rd** end, is the first in a ladder of streets: **Ferntower Rd**, **Pyrland Rd**, **Beresford Rd** and the E end of **Grosvenor Avenue**. All have large 3- and 4-storey buildings, with good-sized gardens, but the S side of **Grosvenor Avenue** backs on to the railway, as does N side of **Northampton Grove**, where pretty 2-storey cottages are uncomfortably hemmed in by light industry. **Northampton Park** curves S to join the **Balls Pond Rd** and is a wide tree-lined street of handsome Victorian villas interspersed with one agreeable low-rise development, and one laughable modern attempt at Victorian proportions.

Crowning this area is wide **St Paul's Place**, where the 4-storey, flat-fronted unspoilt terrace has gracious curved windows, and stucco-finished first storey painted uniformly grey. This street has an air of calm superiority unlike anything nearby. Discreet **Bingham St** is lined with lovely double-fronted but modest-sized houses. It joins **Newington Green Rd**, an extension of **Albion Rd**, which runs N–S and takes buses and through traffic. Lined with shops, pubs and restaurants, it is the place for live music and holds most of the immediate area's amenities. Some flats are available above shops, and well-maintained council-built terraces lead into a medium-sized high-rise estate, entered by **Mildmay St** and **Mildmay Avenue**. This introduces the 'Mildmay' area, where prices are high – sometimes deservedly, sometimes not. Running E–W through the middle of this corner is **Mildmay Grove**, eccentrically not one but two streets, separated along their length by the railway line. The houses stand behind front gardens, and gaze at each other across the walls which separate the grand terraces from the trains. Large gardens at the rear help to hold prices. Busy **Mildmay Park** runs N–S. It is scruffy at the S end, bordered by 4-storey flat-fronted buildings, mostly flats, and some light industry. Now Notting Hill Housing Trust are building sheltered housing in the road, and there's a mixed residential/ commercial scheme on the corner with Balls Bond Road.

Mildmay Rd runs E–W. There are some charming 3- and 4-storey buildings, a featureless '60s block, and homes at the E end overlook another bleak council high-rise. In between, wide **Wolsey Rd** and **Queen Margaret's Grove** are well worth a look, but there is a lot of council-build in the latter. **King Henry's Walk** zigzags N–S and is a hotchpotch of mostly well-kept council-build to the N, and Victorian shops sandwiched between less arresting structures. Continuing the Tudor theme, **Boleyn Rd** runs N–S with a grim wasteland and run-down buildings at the N end. **Pellerin Rd** runs E, and has pretty 2-storey Victorian houses on one side. Down towards Dalston the southern end of **Boleyn Rd** and the streets off it have been desolate for years; a place where houses once stood and others, boarded up, patiently waited for the renewal which has taken place further north. **Bradbury St** saw the start of renovations in this area. Now at last two new developments, one Peabody and one Housing Corporation, are under way, and in another example of community-spirited Stoke Newington, tenants and residents have transformed a disused playground in Boleyn Rd into a 'Millennium peace garden'.

Stoke Newington East and Borders

This neighbourhood is E of **Stoke Newington Rd**, **High St** and **Stamford Hill** and bordered to the N and E by the busy **Clapton Rd**. The SE border follows **Brooke Rd**, then S again down **Rectory Rd** and **Shacklewell Lane**. The S edge is marked by E–W running **Sandringham Rd**. The further N the larger the houses, interspersed by the large Stamford Hill and Broad Common estates. This big area is split by main E–W through roads: **Cazenove Rd**, **Northwold Rd**, **Evering Rd** and **Manse Rd**.

At the northernmost, Stamford Hill end, **Leweston Place** has Victorian terraces on one side of the road and '30s semis on the even side. **Darenth Rd** has large Victorian bay-fronted houses, some with basements. At its S end **Lynemouth Rd** and **Lampard Grove**, blighted by an unlovely MFI store. Moving eastwards, **Alkham Rd**, **Kyverdale Rd**, **Osbaldeston Rd**, **Forburg Rd** and charming **Chardmore Rd** have similar Victorian houses (also a stylish conversion of a church to flats in **Alkham Rd**). These are quiet, tree-lined streets – skip-lined, too: the houses are now much in demand Their size (big basements) makes them popular with young families. (This is something of a baby-boom area.)

South of **Cazenove Rd** many houses have been converted into flats and, although streets seem narrow for the size of buildings, large gardens compensate in some. E of **Fountaine Rd**, the streets become smaller again, with 2-storey and basement Victorian terraces, bordering the Northwold council estate. **Northwold Rd** has the local shops, and southwards **Alconbury Rd**, **Geldeston Rd**, **Narford Rd** and **Reighton Rd** have mostly well-maintained medium-sized Victorian houses. From the street these houses look smaller than those further N, but they often go back a long way and contain a generous number of rooms. In the better parts of **Reighton Rd** a 5-bed unrenovated house might sell for £180,000; a renovated one c. £2.5 million.

Moving W, **Norcott Rd**, **Maury Rd**, **Benthal Rd** and **Jenner Rd** are now quiet due to an eccentric traffic system. These houses enjoy generous gardens, and the potential of an 'end of terrace' property is exploited by the conservatories built over the porches of two at the junctions of **Norcott** and **Brooke Rds**. Odd-numbered houses in **Jenner Rd** back onto the railway, but generally these are desirable streets.

Between the **High St** and **Rectory Rd**, N of **Brooke Rd**, is the Brooke Rd Estate; this improves towards the E, and is bordered on that side by a beautiful 4-storey flat-fronted terrace facing the remains of Stoke Newington Common. Running S **Darville Rd**, **Bayston Rd** (the better pair), **Leswin Rd** and (E–W) **Tyssen Rd** have smaller 2-storey houses, some with basements (from c. £215,000). **Tyssen Rd** is remarkably peaceful, despite the proximity of the **High St**.

South of **Evering Rd**, curving **Amhurst Rd** returns the homeseeker to larger houses, 3-storey with semi-basements. **Foulden St** and **Sydner Rd** are narrower and have smaller houses; again closer to the **High St** commercial buildings impinge. The S side of **Farleigh Rd** (which has some big houses) backs onto the Somerford Estate, and the E end is overlooked by The Beckers, a bleak '60s eyesore estate. This is the least expensive part of Stoke Newington. Further S, the Somerford Estate is bordered by areas of light industry. What housing there is is sandwiched between ugly factories and a '30s council block making this section less appealing than anywhere further N.

Stoke Newington's N–S spine, **Stoke Newington Rd** which becomes first the **High St** and then **Stamford Hill**, is itself a source of homes above its lining of shops. The flats are mostly tenanted, though some do come up for sale. The road, it has to be said, is busy all day and most of the night. However, you can't find a location more convenient, and since some of the buildings are quite large, flats can often be light and spacious. On the old bus depot site, opposite MFI on **Stamford Hill**, a mixed retail/homes scheme is planned.

Transport	Trains: Stoke Newington, Rectory Rd to Liverpool St. See also map.
Convenient for	City. Buses to tube at Highbury & Islington (Victoria line direct to West End). Miles from centre: 4.5.
Schools	Local Authority: Clapton (g), Kingsland, Hackney 6th-form Centre, Our Lady's Convent RC, Skinners Senior (g), Stoke Newington.

SALES

Flats	S	1B	2B	3B	4B	5B
Average prices	60–80	75–150	110–220	150–250	180–250+	—

Houses	2B	3B	4B	5B	6/7B	8B
Average prices	160–230	190–300	250–430	300–500	500–700	—

RENTAL

Flats	S	1B	2B	3B	4B	5B
Average prices	100–130	130–170	160–240	250–350	—	—

Houses	2B	3B	4B	5B	6/7B	8B
Average prices	180–280	230–320	290–350	450–500	—	—

The properties	Mid- to late-Victorian terraces, rapidly being done up, plus a few Georgian ones around Newington Green. Better houses and gardens generally to E of High St. Some p/b flats in Victorian and '30s blocks, plus council-built houses and flats. More new developments, conversion of old schools or churches, live/work schemes, etc, appearing ...
The market	Professionals/media people/Islington refugees move here. Council now insist on one family (ie 3-bed) unit per conversion. 1/2-bed flats thus in shorter supply; 3-bed houses most plentiful. The area S of Church St is the most popular — and highly priced. Local searches: 10 working days.

S

Among those estate agents active in this area are:
- Philip Phillips
- Holden Matthews
- Michael Naik *
- Brooks
- Next Move
- Patrick Joseph
- Oakwood *
- Winkworth *
- Foxtons *

further details: see advertisers' index on p671

STREATHAM

Map ref: p109 (5J)
Postal districts: SW16, SW2
Boroughs: Lambeth (Lab), Wandsworth (Con)
Council tax: Band D Lambeth £750, Wandsworth £370
Conservation areas: Several incl Streatham Village, Ullathorne/ Abbotsleigh Rds
Parking: Residents/Free

Streatham's return to respectability continues. It spent much of the early and mid-'90s in the doldrums: Wandsworth and Clapham soaked up all the demand in those depressed years. The buyers returned when prices in these neighbouring areas, and more recently in Tooting, climbed out of reach. Two groups formed the vanguard: first-time buyers who found Streatham affordable on an average income, and the well-heeled buying a big family house on the proceeds of a cramped Clapham terrace. Now the whole market is busy, with buyers competing for the smarter family homes, and equal pressure on the more affordable corners such as Streatham Vale. In general, here you get more for your money: flat conversions are spacious, and there is a good selection of family houses (some very large) with gardens.

Rising house prices may be underpinned by the arrival of a tube service. Don't hold your breath: 2005 is the earliest date for a southward extension of the East London Line, via New Cross and East Dulwich, which would give access to Docklands. This would be in addition to the Thameslink train service to London Bridge, which will benefit from the planned big investment in extra track capacity: at the moment, the trains are very crowded. Meanwhile, Streatham relies on three rail stations (Streatham, Streatham Hill, Streatham Common) and some good, reliable buses. **Streatham High Rd** is rated London's second-busiest bus route.

Streatham is blighted by the relentlessly busy A23, one of the main routes out of London, which does uneasy double duty as the area's main street. It used to be a proper shopping centre, with a branch of John Lewis. But the traffic (and the old Lambeth council) managed to kill off most of the commerce. 'New Lambeth' has hired a town centre manager to boost the **High Rd's** economy, with CCTV cameras, trees

S

and new railings, and improving safety for pedestrians. While the emphasis is still on quick-turnover leisure – a bowling alley, a skating rink, a swimming pool, two cinemas, a bingo hall and a night club – some new shops have opened in the last 12 months. There's also been a welcome rash of new pubs, cafés, wine bars and restaurants. A Sainsbury's close to Streatham Common has added to local amenities.

Streatham goes back a long way: the former village first became popular as a spa in the late 17th century, and growth was assured by its location on the main road to Croydon and Brighton. City merchants built magnificent estates here in the early 19th century, especially on the N side of Streatham Common. Streatham Hill station was opened in 1856 and in the 1870s–80s farmland was sold to property developers eager to capitalize on the success of the railways; as a result many estates were broken up. However, modern Streatham is divided into several neighbourhoods based to a large extent on these same estates. Homes are a mix of Victorian/Edwardian of all sizes and smaller 1930s, the grand original villas mostly having been demolished. A fair number of large period properties have been converted into flats over the years.

Furzedown

Furzedown covers the area N of the Tooting–Streatham railway, W of **Mitcham Lane** and **Thrale Rd** and E of **Rectory Lane**. Two-thirds is considered part of Streatham – roughly the roads N of **Southcroft Rd** and E of **Freshwater Rd**. The rest is counted as Tooting. The whole neighbourhood is in Wandsworth Borough, not Lambeth. Furzedown is a popular family area with comfortably-sized 2-, 3- and 4-bed houses – and some larger ones. It consists mainly of Edwardian terraces, the best examples being in **Clairview Rd**, off **Thrale Rd**, lovingly looked-after large 6-bed properties. The rest of Furzedown has pockets of Victorian and '30s terraced houses. Catching the 'overspill' from Tooting – which has a tube – prices are relatively high: **Ribblesdale Rd**, **Nimrod Rd** and **Pretoria Rd** have 3- and 4-bed houses: in Pretoria a 3-bed will be around £225,000; £250,000 for a 4-bed. Prices are cheaper to the E of **Mitcham Lane** as the transport is less good. **Rural Way**, off **Streatham Rd**, has a modern development of smart 3/4-bed houses.

Streatham Park

Streatham Park is bordered by **Tooting Bec Rd**, **Mitcham Lane**, **Thrale Rd** and the railway line to the E. This was once the 18th-century Thrale family's estate. Visits by their close friend Dr Samuel Johnson are documented in the road names: **Thrale Rd** and **Dr Johnson Avenue** (across Tooting Bec Common). The Thrale mansion was demolished in 1863 and the area now holds smart, well-maintained council blocks – notably the GLC-built Fayland Estate – mostly now privately owned. A few stately period villas from Streatham's 18th-century heyday overlook Tooting Bec Common: pricey, if a little noisy with the main road opposite, interspersed with modern infill (flats and houses). S of the council blocks, properties are small Edwardian, grand Victorian (with some conversions) and quaint '30s whimsy. The whole area is leafy, quiet and very attractive – and enjoys Wandsworth Borough's favourable council tax.

The small neighbourhood to the E of the railway, towards the parish church, is possibly the oldest part of Streatham. **Pinkerton Place**, off **Tooting Bec Gardens**, has comfortable early '80s purpose-built flats; small rooms, but well-designed. Surrounding properties are mainly stately Victorian; road names relating to the Lake District (**Thirlmere Rd**, **Rydal Rd**, etc) have large 6/7-bed period houses, mostly flats. Tree-lined **Riggindale Rd** has some beautiful conversions of semi-detached Victoriana (typical 2-bed flats around £100,000). In **Thrale Rd** 1-bed flats can be found at about £75-80,000. The parish church, St Leonards, is on the corner of **Tooting Bec Gardens**, overlooking an awesome traffic blackspot where all the main roads converge.

Central Streatham

Central Streatham comprises roads running E from **Garrad's Rd** to **Streatham High Rd**. It contains some truly splendid houses. Well-placed for shops in the **High Rd** and the rail stations of Streatham and Streatham Hill, its leafy roads are popular. Homes here are mainly attractive '20s and '30s detached and semi-detached houses in a variety of styles – stucco and bay windows/tile-hung gables/mock-Tudor. There are large, impressive turn-of-the-century 6-bed houses in **Steep Hill, Becmead Avenue, Prentis Rd** and **Woodbourne Avenue**. Fewer houses in this area have been converted into flats, though developers are keen to contribute new ones whenever possible. Meanwhile, **Woodbourne Avenue** has some 5-bed mock-Tudor houses; in **Kingscourt Rd** the Victorian 4-bed houses command £245-260,000. Emsworth Court in **Ockley Rd** is flats with squash club adjoining; and **Tarrington Close** has '70s houses. One noticeable feature of 'Central' is the epidemic of doctors' and dentists' name-plates on the walls; a good plus is that most houses have off-street parking – which is needed, due to the nearby **High Rd**. The roads to the N, running up to Streatham Hill station, contain period properties in varying states of repair. A number of these large houses have been converted – particularly on the eastern side of the area near the **High Rd**. There are some spacious '30s houses in **Broadlands Avenue**.

New homes are appearing on the corner of **Woodbourne Avenue** and **Garrad's Rd**: Try Homes' 'Park Gate' has 22 3- and 4-bed houses, and 18 flats in a converted Victorian building. Prices range from £130-160,000 for the flats, £330-365,000 for the houses. Interesting that the developer is convinced the site is in Tooting – or would like buyers to think it is (it abuts Tooting Bec Common). Not many years back, Streatham would have been the preferred name.

Streatham Hill

Streatham Hill lies N of the station and **Leigham Court Rd**, E of **Rastell Avenue** and **New Park Rd**, S of **Christchurch Rd** and W of **Hillside Rd/Leigham Vale**. This increasingly popular area is in the SW2 postcode, which no longer has a stigma now Brixton is so fashionable. It's well-placed for transport: Brixton's Victoria line tube is a bus-ride away and Streatham Hill station is on the corner of **Sternhold Avenue**. The side W of Streatham Hill is mainly attractive period property, with purpose-built flats and some flat conversions, maisonettes and houses. **Killieser Avenue, Criffel Avenue** and **Kirkstall Rd** are particularly popular, with charming terraces and some larger houses. **Criffel Avenue** also has some particularly nice maisonettes. There's a cache of respectable '30s houses in the area.

The Telford Park estate N of **Sternhold Avenue** is well-regarded: these 4-, 5- and even 6-bed late-Victorian and Edwardian homes attract overspill from Balham and Brixton, say agents. Prices have exceeded half a million for the monster ones, while a 5-bed semi in **Thornton Rd** was on the market last winter for £380,000. **Telford Avenue, Killieser Avenue** and **Montrell Rd** also have some good converted flats, while a 1980s development in **Telford Avenue** yielded six 1/2-bedroom flats, some with gardens.

The corner between the **South Circular** and **Streatham Hill** holds many conversions; Lambeth's planners eventually stepped in to curb these in streets such as **Tierney** and **Montrell Rds**, although these hold some splendid examples already. **Palace Rd**, which is closed off at its junction with the South Circular, has a few surviving large 19th-century houses and an ex-GLC estate with an attractive grassy setting. **Leigham Vale** has some big (5-bed) Victorian terraces.

Nearer the station are the popular 'ABCD' streets (**Amesbury, Barcombe, Cricklade** and **Downton Avenues**) which feature late-Victorian red-brick terraced cottages and maisonettes, built by the philanthropic Artisans & General Dwellings Company in

1889–94 on the site of the old Leigham Court estate: these were the forerunners of local authority housing. There are a few conversions (flats:houses ratio is about 1:4), and attractive later terraces also in **Cricklade** and **Downton**. Look for the original stained glass in **Cricklade**, the largest gardens in popular **Downton**. (In all four, gardens get smaller towards the **High Rd**.) Beneath the 'ABCDs' are largely '20s and stately red-brick, eg the leafy **Mount Nod Rd**, but also note **Hitherfield** – its Victorian cottage terraces lining a steep hill are reminiscent of a Hovis advertisement.

The mansion flats along **Streatham Hill**, like those along **Streatham High Rd**, vary as to popularity: some are good first-time buys, some have high service charges. The Uttings estate, also known as Culverhouse, lies just beneath the Hill E of the **High Rd** and W of the railway line: a quietly respectable area, popular with local residents. It has a mix of late-Victorian and smart chalet-style '20s/'30s houses. **Pendennis** and **Pinfold Rds** have '30s semis; the former has 60-ft gardens, the latter large 5/6-bed houses. Demand exceeds supply, especially for the attractive 1930s houses.

Streatham Village

Streatham Village – a name to make the hearts of local historians beat faster – isn't as old as it sounds. The original nucleii of Streatham, around St Leonards Church and Streatham Common, date back to medieval times, whereas the 'Village' was only started in the 19th century. Houses are now very mixed in style, but rather appealing, especially the charming and much-in-demand 2/3-bed Victorian cottages in **Sunnyhill** and **Wellfield Rds**. Well-located for transport between Streatham and Streatham Hill stations, and near to the main shopping street, it is a designated conservation area. Some newly-built 'cottages' priced around £175,000 compete with the originals. There are also larger Victorian villas in red brick, and some skillful conversions are to be found: a 2-bed maisonette might be £140,000.

Older cottages, '30s houses and more modern 2/3-bed units will be found in **Sunnyhill Rd**. **Angles Rd** houses Peregrine Court – a courtyard development of 25 flats and houses. The streets lying to the S, between **Gleneldon Rd, Valley Rd, Streatham Common North** and the **High Rd**, contain a real mix of properties from Victorian through to early 20th century and council housing, including 30 new 1/2-bed flats and houses in increasingly desirable **Valley Rd**, where maisonettes range from £125-140,000. In the same street 1930s 3-bed houses command £160-170,000 The 1980s purpose-built block on the corner of **Valley** and **Leigham Court Rds** is popular. Impressive red-brick homes are found in **Gleneldon Rd**. The nearby **High Rd** has flats, both above shops and in purpose-built 20th-century blocks.

Leigham Court

Leigham Court, on its steep hill, lies between **Leigham Court Rd, Valley Rd** and **Streatham Common North Side.** Basically council-built (though now mostly privately owned) to the N, and largeish smart '30s 4-bed semis and smaller, older houses to the S. New developments keep springing up here. **Leigham Court Rd** itself was once lined with large detached Victorian mansions, standing in their own grounds – most have been turned into sought-after flats and commercial uses. The council has ambitious plans for the already pleasant Leigham Court Estate, now a conservation area.

Streatham Common

One of the original nucleii of the town was centred here, the site of the first spring that became a spa. This area, very popular with the professional classes, is filled with handsome Victorian and Edwardian houses with large gardens on the E side of the **High Rd** – pricey, highly desirable being near to the Common, with quiet leafy roads – and cheaper, if smaller and less well-maintained, houses to the W of the **High Rd**. The

Hopton Rd/Polworth Rd corner is close to the **High Rd**, the Common and the station: 2-bed flats go for £135,000; 6-bed houses have reached £700,000 – though this is exceptional, with £280-300,000 nearer the norm for 5-beds. **Streatham Common North** has good Victorian 4- and 5-bed houses priced from £320-380,000. E of the Common, 'much-requested' **Ryecroft Rd** loops round, with detached 3- and 4-bed houses boasting large gardens. **Crown Lane** had some modern 4-bed town-houses. **Ferrers** and **Natal Rds** have smaller cottages, some of which have been converted into flats and are relatively cheap. Popular roads are **Heybridge Avenue, Fontaine Rd, Copley Park** and **Braxted Park** (E of the **High Rd**).

A big old convent in two acres of land beside the common is scheduled for redevelopment as housing, though no details are yet available.

Green Lane, on the very southern edge of the neighbourhood, has 4-bed detached homes. Traffic has increased in the area since the opening in 1997 of a large Sainsbury's/Homebase on Streatham High Rd, opposite the S side of the common. To the W of the area, **Lewin** and **Barrow Rds** have many popular conversions. There are more flats in **Gleneagle Rd** – just to the N of the tracks, and cheaper. **Conyer's Rd** houses a 1980s 22-home development of 1/2-bed flats and 1/3-bed houses, and seven new 4-bed town-houses. Towards W Norwood, in SE27, Canterbury Mews is a handsome new addition to **Canterbury Grove**.

Streatham Vale

The cheapest part of Streatham, offering good value for money, the Vale is attracting a lot of interest as buyers get priced out of other neighbourhoods. Its borders run along the railway lines to the N and W, and along **Greyhound Terrace** and **Hassocks Rd**. It's an area of very intensive housing with roads packed tightly together – more like Tooting than Streatham. Most of the area was built by Wates in the '20s and '30s and consists of row upon row of 2-storey terraced and semi-detached houses. In a typical road a 3-bed house with a small garden might be £125,000. There are also a few flat conversions dotted around.

Transport	Trains: Streatham Common (Victoria, London Bridge), Streatham (London Bridge 21 min, Blackfriars 23 min); Streatham Hill (Victoria 15 min).
Convenient for	Routes to Gatwick Airport and South Coast. Miles from centre: 5.
Schools	Local Authority: Dunraven School (mixed), Bishop Thomas Grant (mixed, RC), La Retraite RC (Girls). Private: Streatham Hill & Clapham High (girls).

SALES

Flats	S	1B	2B	3B	4B	5B
Average prices	40–55	65–85	80–120+	135 →	–	–
Houses	2B	3B	4B	5B	6/7B	8B
Average prices	120–160	130–220	150–350	250–600	–	–

RENTAL

Flats	S	1B	2B	3B	4B	5B
Average prices	100–115	150+	200+	–	–	–
Houses	2B	3B	4B	5B	6/7B	8B
Average prices	200–250	250–500	250–600	400–600	–	–

S

The properties   Some new developments now joining roomy terraced Victorian/ Edwardian homes and '20s/'30s semis, plus large blocks of 1900–1940 mansion flats. Some (much) larger houses; Victorian and inter-war. Those overlooking the leafy common particularly pleasant. Selling of homes by Lambeth Council has boosted supply of converted and purpose-built flats and 20th-century houses on the market.

The market   Price differentials between Streatham and its neighbours are fast eroding – though here you get more space and leafier surroundings for your money. However, there's still no tube (though trains, buses plentiful) which means comparitively lower prices in the more humdrum corners: a boon to first-time buyers. Old-established families plus newcomers seeking larger homes with gardens and good-value flats. Rents have been static over the last year, prices continued to rise. Local searches: Lambeth 10 days, Wandsworth 3–4 weeks.

Among those estate agents active in this area are:

- Halifax Property
- Townends
- Hooper & Jackson
- Westburys
- Winkworth *
- Haart
- Kinleigh Folkard & Hayward

further details: see advertisers' index on p671

S

TOTTENHAM AND FINSBURY PARK

Map ref: p31 (4F)
Postal districts: N22, N18, N17, N15, N4
Boroughs: Haringey (Lab), Islington (Lab/Lib Dem), Hackney (Lab)
Council tax: Band D Haringey £898, Islington £912, Hackney £789
Conservation areas: Check with town hall
Parking: Free

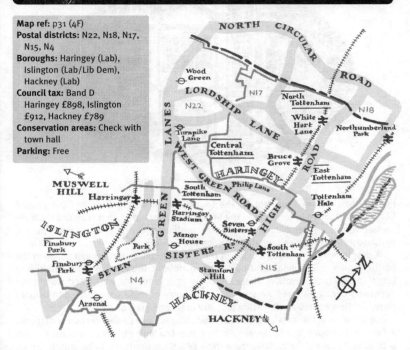

More and more 'outside' people are coming to Tottenham to buy, altering what was an entirely local market. And a good number of the area's rented homes, which were often of low standard, are either being smartened up or sold as values rise. It is a good hunting-ground for first-time buyers, and these are increasingly foot-soldiers in London's army of 'young professionals'. 'A good area for teachers.' commented one observer.

Here, shell-shocked buyers from further south and west will still find the £100,000 terraced house, the £60,000 2-bed flat. The streets may not be smart, the homes less so, but the area has better transport links than other parts of North East London and is starting to establish itself as an affordable, identifiable place to live.

Agents report that the market for flats has been very brisk since the end of 1998. Transport links, especially the Victoria Line, attract these buyers. Buy-to-let investors are taking advantage of the area's low prices, and are achieving gross yields of 9 or 10 per cent.

Tottenham is a fairly clear square on the map, bounded to the N by the A406 (**North Circular Rd**), to the S by the **Seven Sisters Rd** and the Haringey/Hackney border, to the E by the Lea Valley reservoir complex and to the W by the Great Eastern Railway and the northern part of **Green Lanes (High Rd)**.

Until the last quarter of the 19th century, Tottenham was a small village, boasting several fine houses. Today only one or two of these remain, saved by conversion into public buildings – such as Bruce Castle, which now houses the local history museum. With the advent of the railways, and especially cheap workmens' fares, street after street of small terraced houses were built. The population trebled to over 46,000 in the 20 years before 1861. Not all the terraces survived the Blitz and the council bulldozers – though in some cases the brave new tower blocks that replaced them are themselves being demolished. Expansion continued during the inter-war period, particularly in the Dowsett estate region on the E side.

A programme of council housing in the '60s resulted in further expansion in the northern area of Tottenham, including the monolithic Broadwater Farm Estate E of Lordship Recreation Ground. There are some light industrial works and warehouse depots bordering Hackney Marshes, although some of these have tended to fall into disrepair. New homes are replacing industry in several places.

Optimism is in the air with several big spending schemes either certain or planned. A £102 million operation to rejuvenate the upper Lea Valley is about to start: the aim is to attract new business. **Tottenham High Rd**'s shop-fronts are to be smartened up at a cost of £4 million. An ambitious plan for a 12.5-acre arts and conference complex close to White Hart Lane stadium on the High Rd would bring 7 cinemas, 3 theatres, a conference centre, a public square with bars and restaurants . . . we shall see.

The area is predominantly residential, composed mainly of 2- and 3-bed terraced houses built 1890–1920 and flat conversions. Even modernized, many of these houses have downstairs bathrooms (due to their layout), but estate agents in the area agree that around 30 per cent retain original features, such as fireplaces and cornicing and sash windows – and that these are the easiest to sell. Of course, original features are much rarer in conversions, though standards have improved greatly since the council brought in stricter controls. Most houses are small and rather ordinary: compared to areas like Crouch End, Tottenham lacks distinctive, family-sized homes.

Tottenham has excellent transport links, with quick access by rail and tube to the West End and the City, and by road to the North Circular, M25, M1 and M11. Such links are a major advantage of living in Tottenham. Buses are frequent, and particularly good for local travel. Transport, especially proximity to tubes, is what decides prices here. The area is truly cosmopolitan, with a corresponding diversity in the shops and cultural activities available to residents. Shopping is good around Wood Green and Finsbury Park, and new bars and restaurants are appearing all the time.

T

South Tottenham (N15)

The area lies S of **West Green Rd** and **Philip Lane**, N of **Seven Sisters Rd** and **Amhurst Park**, W of the **High Rd** and E of **Green Lanes**. Homes with an N15 postcode tend to be more expensive than equivalent properties in N17, because of their proximity to

Stamford Hill, Stoke Newington and Turnpike Lane; the short distance from Seven Sisters tube also helps. Most homes in this neighbourhood are 2- and 3-bedroomed terraced houses, built during the later 19th and early 20th centuries. Many of the larger houses have been, or are being, converted into flats.

There are good shopping facilities on **West Green Rd**, **Philip Lane** and **Seven Sisters Rd**, including Sainsbury's on **Green Lanes**, Tesco at Seven Sisters and Safeway at Stamford Hill. There are abundant local grocers, butchers and ethnic food shops.

The W side of the **High Rd** from Seven Sisters tube to **Philip Lane** – an area that includes several small garment factories – includes (working up from the S) a row of 3-storey terraced houses, built in the 1880s, which have either been converted into flats or much modernized. On **Pelham Rd** and **Portland Rd** is an attractive, modern Barratt development, with small terraces of 2-bed properties and good parking space here for residents.

Continuing northwards, the former Jewish Home and Hospital has been converted into 80 flats to rent by the Circle 33 Housing Trust. Next come the Tottenham College of Technology, the town hall (opposite **Tottenham Green**) and, off **Town Hall Rd**, the Tottenham Green Leisure Centre, with library, squash courts and swimming pool.

The triangular area bounded by **Philip Lane**, **West Green Rd** and the railway comprises a series of roughly parallel streets of 2- and 3-bed terraced houses, dating from the 1900s, broken by the popular **Clyde Circus** and **Clyde Rd**. (There are, though, larger 5/7-bedroom homes on **Bedford Rd**, some of which have escaped conversion to flats.) The E side of this area is popular as it is closest to the tube. Similar terraces exist S of **West Green Rd** in the rectangle formed with **Green Lanes**, **St Ann's Rd** and the **High Rd**, with **Seaford Rd**, **Roslyn Rd** and **Greenfield Rd** particularly good. Houses in this corner become increasingly expensive towards **Green Lanes** and **Turnpike Lane**, with **Cranleigh Rd** and **Conway Rd** typical examples of the higher price range of 2- and 3-bed properties.

The region S of **St Ann's Rd** and **Seven Sisters Rd** is bisected by **Hermitage Rd** and includes the block of neat Victorian streets made up of **Kimberley Gardens**, **Chesterfield Gardens** and **Roseberry Gardens**, which link up to **Warwick Gardens**. These streets serve motorists as short cuts between busy **St Ann's Rd** and **Grand Parade**. St Ann's General Hospital lies behind **Warwick Gardens**, with the railway running to the S of it. The Harringay Green Lanes station has trains to Gospel Oak one way and Leyton and Barking the other – and no useful tube connections in between.

On the other side of the tracks, this district includes a major development area, with Harringay Stadium now replaced by a large Sainsbury's. Next door, McAlpine's 1998–9 new homes scheme has provided 221 homes, ranging from 1-bed flats to 4-bed houses in streets such as **Wiltshire Gardens** and **Surrey Gardens**. Prices here are comparable with the surrounding Victorian terraces in **Vale Rd**, **Eade Rd** and **Finsbury Park Avenue**, though the latter are larger.

Central Tottenham (N17)

Lying N of **West Green Rd** and **Philip Lane**, S of **Lordship Lane**, W of the **High Rd** and E of **Westbury Avenue**, this region is served by Bruce Grove rail station (trains to the City in 20 min) and (in the W) by Turnpike Lane (Piccadilly Line tube). Here there are mainly 2- and 3-bed terraces and the big Broadwater Farm council estate.

Characteristic mid-range early 20th-century 2- and 3-bed terraces (some are now flats) cluster in the eastern part of the area – **Napier Rd**, **Steele Rd**, **Chester Rd** and **Morrison Avenue**. In particular, **Mount Pleasant Rd** saw extensive development in the '80s, again with houses being converted into flats. Until recently a notorious rat-run, it is now controlled by width restrictions. The constant stream of traffic might now affect neighbouring **Downhills Park Rd** and **Dongola Rd**. The streets off **Broadwater**

Rd (not to be confused with the Farm estate) are sought after, with 4-bed houses commanding £160–170,000.

Green spaces come in the form of Lordship and Belmont recreation grounds and Downhills Park – house prices rise around these open spaces. Look here for larger houses in leafy roads: **Keston Rd** is one such. This neighbourhood has a quiet, settled air, and is well thought of despite being remote from a tube. To the E, roads off **Philip Lane** are also popular. The Broadwater Farm council estate still casts a shadow over nearby streets (**Higham Rd**, **The Avenue**, northern end of **Mount Pleasant Rd**), though happily some of the worst blocks are being demolished.

North Tottenham (N17)

Tottenham's northern reaches stop at a point some half-mile below the **North Circular Rd**, where N17 becomes N18 and the borough boundary also runs. The area is bounded to the S by **Lordship Lane**, on the W by the A10, and on the E by the **High Rd**. There are some inter-war semis around **Lordship Lane**. Pleasant post-war council houses lie N of **Lordship Lane** and **The Roundway**.

Interesting areas include the dense grid of little streets in the Tower Gardens conservation area, enclosed by **Lordship Lane** and **The Roundway** and bisected by **Risley Avenue**. These Arts & Crafts-style brick, tile and pebble-dash cottages date from 1903-1914 and the area is, say the town hall proudly, 'increasingly recognised as one of the mpost important council estates in the country.' It was one of the first garden suburbs in the world. The houses are well-built and the layout is spacious, and they make popular buys (some are rented by housing associations, others privately-owned). But don't think about changing the paint on your windows or doors without permission.

Eastwards **Church Lane** has very pleasant mews-type houses near the popular Antwerp Arms, and borders Bruce Castle Park (with the Elizabethan Bruce Castle which houses the Museum of Local History). This corner has most of Tottenham's Georgian buildings. It also has a clutch of attractive late-19th-century cottages in the **Kings Rd**/**Church Rd** corner. Developers Rialto have built Somerset Gardens here, between **Creighton Rd** and **White Hart Lane**: this has added 356 studio, 1- and 2-bed flats to the area's housing stock. They sell at good-value prices: 1-bed flats £65,000.

Further N is Tottenham Cemetery, White Hart Lane rail station (and football stadium – see below) and the **Great Cambridge Rd**, with purpose-built council houses leading up to the **North Circular**. The North Circular has been widened, despite local opposition. Shopping has been improved by the Sainsbury's midway up the **High Rd**.

East Tottenham (N15 and N17)

This area lies between **High Rd** to the W and Hackney Marshes to the E, bounded on the N by the **North Circular** and to the S by **Clapton Common Rd**. **Ferry Lane**, running W–E beneath Tottenham Hale tube station, marks the dividing line between N17 and N15. Part of the industry zone to the E has been redeveloped as a shopping centre.

The northerly area is characterized by the Northumberland Park estate, a development area with generally cheaper house prices because of the proximity to White Hart Lane, Tottenham Hotspur's football stadium. **Park Lane**, in particular, fails to live up to its name. Mainly 2-bed terraced houses here, and some conversions into flats. Off Hampden Rd builders Croudace have squeezed in Hampden Mews: 19 2- and 3-bed houses and some flats. One-bed flats are £75,000; town-houses £150,000. S of **Lansdowne Rd** is the popular Dowsett Rd estate, with **Sherringham Avenue**, **Seymour Avenue** and **Thackeray Avenue** popular as they are within striking distance of the tube/rail station at Tottenham Hale.

Tottenham Hale station has just had nearly £6 million spent to improve the interchange between tube, rail and bus and to install 56 CCTV cameras. Tottenham

Hale (Victoria Line tube, and trains) provides a useful alternative to Seven Sisters tube. The Stanstead Express airport service stops here.

The area enclosed by the **High Rd** and the one-way system (**Chestnut Rd/Broad Lane**) has a strange combination of older, gentrified properties and rather shabby houses. **Tynemouth Rd** is still a good first-time buyers' street, with **Talbot Rd** a slightly more up-market version. South of this area the property tends to decline, but there is room for improvement in this region. The first stage of a retail development is complete, with a series of 'shed' stores – carpets, furniture etc.

Fairview built 250 homes on **Bream Close**, S of **Ferry Lane**, in 1995. This patch of land has arms of the River Lea on two sides, justifying its name: Heron Wharf. There are light, airy river views. Studios now sell for £55,000; 1-beds £65–70,000. To the E a nature reserve has just been created in the Lea Valley.

South of **Broad Lane** and the railway, towards Stamford Hill, is the area known as 'Tottenham Village' by residents and local estate agents. Centring on **Wargrave Avenue** and **Grovelands Rd**, prices are higher here. **Wakefield Rd**, just N of the railway, is worth a look for its larger houses.

Border Areas

To the S (in Stamford Hill) and to the W (in Harringay and Wood Green) are good home hunting-grounds, although these are also more costly. Three-bedroomed terraced houses, for example, in the section known as the Harringay Ladders (the series of parallel streets stretching from **Umfreville Rd** up to **Turnpike Lane** on the W side of **Green Lanes**) are popular, particularly in the central section (**Allison Rd, Seymour Rd**). A fair number of the Ladder's houses have been converted into 1- and 2-bed flats in streets such as **Frobisher Rd** and **Hewitt Rd**. **Green Lanes** and **Wightman Rd** – the Ladder 'uprights' – are busy traffic through-routes. Traffic calming has, however, eased problems in the Ladder's 'rungs' between the two.

Finsbury Park

Southwards the Haringey borough boundary dips down to take in the green acres of Finsbury Park and some of its surrounding streets – **Stroud Green Rd** marks the border with Islington Borough, Seven Sisters with Hackney.

The most significant difference between Finsbury Park and the rest of the Tottenham area is in the size and quality of the houses – there is a much greater number of large, attractive 3- and 4-storey houses. There is also more variety in the style of housing, with more double-fronted, semi-detached properties.

As a result, many of the streets are more aesthetically pleasing than the streets of smaller, 2-storey terraced houses in the main Tottenham area. The larger houses – originally 5- and 6-bed – are ideal for conversion into flats, something which developers have exploited to the full. There are still houses available which remain as single properties, though these tend to be run-down and bought by developers.

People are moving into Finsbury Park from Crouch End and Islington, attracted by the large houses and cheaper prices. Once here, they deny any connection with Haringey borough, feeling more kinship with Islington to the S. Indeed, some streets are in Islington, others in Hackney. It's worth checking which, as council taxes vary.

The Finsbury Park area is characterized, naturally, by the huge park, which is bordered by **Green Lanes, Seven Sisters Rd, Endymion Rd** and the railway line running from Harringay station to Finsbury Park station. Facilities within the park include boating lake, a pleasant café, tennis, cricket, gardens and an area set aside for concerts, festivals, fairs and other special events. In a region otherwise largely bereft of greenery, the park represents an important leisure area to the community. Other facilities in the area include the Michael Sobel Sports Centre on **Tollington Rd**. Ten acres of old railway land here has recently been transformed into 218 new houses and a garden centre. Rented homes 'at affordable prices' have been built here.

Finsbury Park is difficult to categorize because it lies in three boroughs. House prices and local services vary considerably within the neighbourhood. Its main advantage is its excellent transport. The area is served by Finsbury Park tube (Piccadilly and Victoria Lines) and rail station (quick access to the West End and the City), by Manor House and Arsenal tubes (Piccadilly), and a very good bus service.

The centre of Finsbury Park is marked by the X-shaped road junction formed by **Stroud Green Rd, Blackstock Rd** and **Seven Sisters Rd. Seven Sisters Rd** leading down from Manor House is bordered on its W side by the park and on the E by a series of hotels, most of which serve as DHSS/temporary accommodation. Behind the hotels, in the triangle formed by **Portland Rise, Gloucester Drive** and **Seven Sisters Rd**, are some very attractive homes, including detached 2-storey double-fronted houses, which convert into roomy flats. Further SW **Finsbury Park Rd** and **Queen's Drive** are among the best roads, in stark contrast to **Blackstock Rd** which they adjoin.

The central area of Finsbury Park is built around the tube/rail stations, which have been made part of a shopping complex. There are plans for a big upgrade to the station with links to the park. The one-way traffic system here can be confusing if you're new to the area, and it is famous for its jams. Parking is a problem everywhere.

The rectangle formed by **Seven Sisters Rd, Queens Drive, Blackstock Rd** and **Brownswood Rd** (incorporating **Wilberforce Rd**) was a red-light district in the '40s, but the roads have been blocked off to prevent kerb-crawling, giving rise to relatively quiet, tree-lined streets – the properties are good here, fetching higher prices. **Finsbury Park Rd** is perhaps the best street: its Victorian houses have handsome porches and big windows. One-bed flats go for £110–120,000; houses needing work up to £300,000; smart ones up to £400,000. King's Crescent Estate on the S side of **Brownswood Rd** is being demolished. A large tract of new homes has been built on the old filter beds behind **Queens Drive**. The triangle formed by **Blackstock Rd, St Thomas's Rd** and **Gillespie Rd** houses large, attractive properties, many of which have again been converted into flats. The problem here is traffic and crowds when Arsenal Football Club are at home. Parking is restricted on match days over a wide area. The upside is 5-bed houses for around £300,000 – and the N5 (Highbury) postcode. (They were £100,000 cheaper a year ago . . .) Some incomers are gambling on the football club moving, as has been mooted. Some new homes are appearing in hidden corners off the W side of **Blackstock Rd**.

The area to the SW of **Stroud Green Rd** and N of **Seven Sisters Rd** is made up of attractive streets such as **Charteris Rd, Fonthill Rd** and **Moray Rd** with many 4-storey houses converted into flats, and also includes the Finsbury Park Trading Estate. **Alexander Grove** has larger houses. Further S is a large council estate in the rectangle formed by **Durham Rd, Seven Sisters Rd, Birnham Rd/Moray Rd** and **Hornsey Rd**. SE of here is the Sobell Sports Centre, an excellent modern leisure centre. Check out the properties in the **Corbyn St** area just off **Hornsey Rd**: they were badly bombed during the war and there have been some subsidence problems.

North of **Stroud Green Rd,** some streets of Victorian 3-storey houses offer close proximity to the tube. Most are flats but a few houses survive. Examples are **Woodstock Rd, Perth Rd, Woods Rd, Ennis Rd**. Opinions differ about this quarter: some agents cite rat-run traffic, others praise the solid 3- and 4-bed Victorian houses and point to the amenity of a good 'local' in **Perth Rd**. Just to the N, on the Stroud Green borders, Bellway's 'Regents Quarter' in **Tollington Way** offers new flats and town-houses.

Back up in the Tottenham direction, some spacious, green streets close to Manor House tube are uneasily split between the **Woodberry Down** council-built estate and a surviving clutch of large single-occupant houses.

Finsbury Park properties in the Borough of Islington will continue to carry a slight cachet: the owner can say 'I live in Islington' rather than 'in Finsbury Park'. Nowadays, Finsbury Park's changing status is marked by the new wine bars, restaurants and refurbished pubs. But better-off drivers mean more cars: the area's hitherto unrestricted parking is going, and traffic wardens have been making forays into the area.

Transport Tubes: Finsbury Park (zone 2, Piccadilly, Victoria); Arsenal, Manor House, Turnpike Lane, Wood Green (zones 2/3, Piccadilly); Tottenham Hale, Seven Sisters (zone 3, Victoria). From Seven Sisters: Oxford Circus 20 min, City 25 min (1 change), Heathrow 1 hr (1 change). Rail: 16 min to Liverpool St. Good buses.

Convenient for North Circular, A10 to Cambridge, Wood Green Shopping City, Alexandra Park.

Schools Local Authority: The Drayton, Gladesmore Community School, High Cross, Northumberland Park.

SALES

Flats	S	1B	2B	3B	4B	5B
Average prices	50–90	65–130	75–180	90–220	—	—
Houses	2B	3B	4B	5B	6/7B	8B
Average prices	100–250	130–350	200–375	–	–	–

RENTAL

Flats	S	1B	2B	3B	4B	5B
Average prices	70–150	110–190	135–220	170–250	–	–
Houses	2B	3B	4B	5B	6/7B	8B
Average prices	200–300	225–350	250–450	375–500	–	–

The properties Terraced houses (2/3-beds) built 1890–1920 are most common. Fair number of inter-war houses. Flat conversions and council resales mean more small houses and 1/2-bed flats.

The market Affordable prices for first-time buyers of flats and original-features terraced houses. Finsbury Park rates highest; N17 least expensive: far from tube, close to council estates and football. Local searches: Haringey 10 working days, Islington 10 working days, Hackney 10 working days.

Among those estate agents active in this area are:

- Winkworth *
- Adam Kennedy
- Christopher Charles
- Bairstow Eves
- Paul Simon
- Davies & Davies
- Network
- Michael Naik *

further details: see advertisers' index on p671

TOTTERIDGE AND WHETSTONE

Map ref: p14 (1C)
Postal districts: N20, N11
Boroughs: Barnet (Lib
  Dem/Lab coalition)
Council tax: Band D £760
Conservation areas:
  Totteridge, Friern Barnet
Parking: Free

Take Hampstead Garden Suburb's Bishops Avenue, move its mansions to the
northern fringes of London and dot them along a meandering country lane, add
ponies and paddocks – there you have Totteridge.

This foretaste of open countryside and its attendant areas of Whetstone, with its
busy shopping parade and the Northern line tube, and Friern Barnet, are still London
– just. To the N lies Barnet proper, out of the London postal area and suddenly,
indefinably, Hertfordshire. Southwards lies Finchley, and the metropolis. A sign that
these areas have joined London proper is the enhanced interest in them over the last
decade by West End estate agents, as people looked further out for almost-country
homes. Friern Barnet is also the scene of an explosion of luxury flats and town-
houses on the land freed by the closure of the famous Colney Hatch lunatic asylum.

Totteridge

Though it has a London postcode (N20), Totteridge is to all intents and purposes a
country village – albeit one largely consisting of grand mansions. To the N of **Totteridge
Common/Village/Lane** and the roads around lie the golf course and wide open spaces,
with the village itself as a pretty focal point. Totteridge is not a big place and while the
mini-palaces see a regular ebb and flow of well-known faces (half of N London's
premiership footballers, currently), at the 4/5-bed, family-home level, people know
each other: their children attend the village school, or they are active in the local
residents' association or perhaps through one of the local sports clubs. Not, probably,
over the garden fence, though: houses in the area tend to be set in large, secluded plots
of land. On Sundays Totteridge folk can drop in to the Orange Tree pub for a drink, then

take the dogs for a walk and head down to Laurel Farm to feed the ducks. Its denizens tend to be professionals or media/show-biz people who relish the privacy that a Totteridge home affords. This is not Hampstead (positively ostentatious by comparison) where people go to be seen; here remarkable faces go by relatively unremarked-upon.

There are few, if any, small houses in Totteridge – which is known for its 4- or 5-, or indeed 6- or 7- or 8-bedroomed, homes complete with tennis court, sauna and good security systems. **Totteridge Lane** and any of the roads that run off it are prime locations: many of the roads are private and have views over the golf course or acres of Green Belt land. Think in millions for houses in the best roads, which include, as well as **Totteridge Lane**, **Village** and **Common**, **Pine Grove**, **Grange Avenue** and properties in and around **The Green**. Another is **Northcliffe Drive** which, along with **Harmsworth Way**, recalls the great press barons who lived here.

Interestingly, £1.8million is a popular price this year, buying you, for example, a 5-bed detached Tudor-style property completed with heated outdoor pool, or on **Totteridge Green**, a split-level 5-bed bungalow. Naturally both come with substantial garden. Then there's Terenure House and York House, newly built on adjacent plots behind remote-control wrought-iron gates on **Totteridge Lane**. These newly-built palaces were £1.85 and £1.8 million respectively this spring. £5 million is asked for one Edwardian manor-house copy (but then, it does boast 85 acres), and the music-industry mogul's pad thought to be the top home here is now estimated to be worth c. £15 million. Not a few properties in the estate agents' windows in this N20 region bear a polite note to would-be residents: 'price available on application': if you need to ask, as the saying goes, you can't afford it . . . .

If you do not have a newspaper empire, 3-bed semis and flats in roads like **Southway** and **Lynton Mead** can be had for less than £300,000; towards the tube station, in **Coppice Walk** and **Greenway**, 1930s 3-bed detached houses reach £300,000-plus. By the time your budget has sailed past £750,000 – via, say, a 4-bed property on **Totteridge Lane** for £475,000 – heated swimming pools and electronic gates start to figure in the details . . . . Some half-million-pound apartments appeared in **The Grange** a while back, and a 2-bed in the conversion of the listed Totteridge House (in the village) recently fetched £345,000, but generally speaking Totteridge is not the place to look for flats. Agents suggest Friern Barnet (see next page) or Woodside Park (see Finchley chapter) for luxury purpose-built blocks and new developments.

Totteridge lies in the borough of Barnet, which has one of the best local authority education records in the country – but most of Totteridge's residents prefer to send their offspring to the many private and public schools in the surrounding areas. For communications, the M1 and M25 are not far. However, for those without a chauffeur transport is more difficult: there's a poor bus service, though the Northern line does come out to Totteridge and Whetstone. There are no shops to speak of, but The Spires, Barnet's shopping centre, adds major stores to the **Whetstone High Rd** selection, and a hopper bus goes to Brent Cross shopping centre. **Totteridge Lane** is a long, winding and wooded road: a daunting walk from the tube on dark evenings. Most Totteridge householders seem, however, to have enough cars to make walking a sport rather than a necessity. Expect to pay around (you've guessed it) £1.8 million for your private, gated residence, though two newly-built houses were priced at £2,250,000 apiece over a year ago. Prices unlikely to fall until somebody torpedoes the entertainment industry.

Whetstone

Totteridge becomes Whetstone when **Totteridge Lane** reaches the tube station, where the area becomes Whestone just in time for the **High Road** (A1000). Housing becomes more affordable by the average family at this point: a 3-bed semi on **Birley Road** – with

Naylor Rd, a quiet and particularly popular corner almost opposite the tube station – recently sold for a fraction under £210,000. The workaday Whetstone High Road gives the area a more downmarket appearance than the surrounding roads and properties (some 6-bedroomed) really deserve. Though there are plenty of modern purpose-built blocks along the High Road itself, to the E there are some wonderful character-filled semis and detached houses, such as those on the elegant-sounding **Athenaeum Road** and **Chandos Avenue.** Many of these houses have their own garages – something rarely seen in nearby Finchley. **Church Gate** is a 1980s cul-de-sac of 5-bedroomed houses behind electronic gates off **Church Crescent.** There are plenty of 1- and 2-bed maisonettes to be found in Whetstone: a 2-bed recently fetched £120,000 on **Marlborough Gardens.**

Heading S along the **High Rd** past the parade of shops is the elegant corner of Oakleigh Park, with its own station. **Oakleigh Park Gardens** has terraced older houses and family-style semis, while **Oakleigh Park North** and **Oakleigh Park South** are quiet, leafy and well-located, as are the surrounding streets: large houses, a mixture of mainly semi-detached homes with good gardens (in **Oakleigh Avenue** a 4-bed detached and garaged house was £337,000 last winter). **Oakleigh Park North** (especially favoured) has some big individual detached homes; and, nearer the High Road, fine purpose-built blocks. **Oakleigh Rd North/Oakleigh Rd South,** similar in name, but not in stature to the 'Parks', form the main road from Whetstone to Southgate. A new development of 4- and 5-bed luxury houses appeared in 1998, but generally it's a mixture of small houses and shops, and prices hereabouts tend to be cheaper than elsewhere in Whetstone.

Friern Barnet

Running off **Whetstone High Rd, Friern Barnet Lane** leads past the North Middlesex Golf Course and lovely Friary Park, a green and leafy start to the northernmost edges of Friern Barnet proper. The rest of the area is similar in feel to next-door Finchley with its mix of 1930s semis, smart purpose-built flats and maisonettes, but is less popular than either of its nearest neighbours as it lacks the Northern line link into town. Prices are generally cheaper than for equivalent properties in surrounding areas, partly because of the transport problem, and partly because of the ex-council status of large areas of housing, such as the roads between **Woodhouse Rd** and **Summers Way.** A 2/3-bed detached house on **Short Way,** for example, was recently on the market for £110,000.

The great landmark of Friern Barnet is the (listed) former psychiatric hospital in **Friern Barnet Rd.** The asylum building itself is now 'Princess Park Manor', a luxury block of 260 1-, 2-, 3- and 4-bed flats by Comer Homes, complete with fitness centre – and shuttle bus to the tube. The first phase in the renovation was completed in late 1997 and the rest finishes this year. The 37-acre hospital grounds have been split between myriad new homes developments, all in their final stages. The developers have all focused on 2-, 3- and 4-bedroom modern houses and town-houses (a euphemism for terraced), with a couple of additional luxury flats blocks. Examples include Halliwick Park (Barratt), with 200 houses in total; Princes Gate (Bellway Homes), which adds another 280; and Alexandra Mews (Martin Grant Homes).

Alexandra Mews, as the name suggests, is a smaller scheme of 39 town-houses in a more secluded corner, with the 3- and 4-bed houses fetching £250–300,000, and 2-beds from £163,000. The 280-house Princes Gate estate will be completed with a block of 39 luxury 2- and 3-bed flats and penthouses, from around £160,000. Release prices for the 3- and 4-bed town-houses are from £229,995.

The Friern Barnet area already offers a wide range of homes: there's a mix of small terraces, purpose-built flats, and plenty of Victorian and Edwardian conversions. Then there are the fine large semi- and detached houses in and around **Friern Barnet Lane,** probably the prime street; its location near Friary Park makes it doubly popular. **Friern Barnet Rd,** running towards New Southgate, has much cheaper properties, with many solid houses built in the Victorian and Edwardian era. Nearby in **Woodhouse Rd**, which joins Friern Barnet to Finchley, are 1930s semis and terraces, and ex-council. Close to the **North Circular** and with a rail line into King's Cross, Friern Barnet is a good hunting-ground and something of a contrast to well-established Whetstone and Totteridge. Look here for less expensive, smaller homes that attract first-time buyers.

Transport	Tubes: Totteridge & Whetstone (zone 4, Northern). To Oxford Circus 45 min (1 change), City 45 min, Heathrow 1 hr 30 min (1 change).
Convenient for	North Circular, M1/M25, Brent Cross. Miles from centre: 9.
Schools	Barnet Education Authority: Ravenscroft School, Friern Barnet County School, Queen Elizabeth's (b), Queen Elizabeth High (g), Dame Alice Owen, Copthall (g). Private: Friern Barnet Grammar, Mill Hill, Haberdashers' Aske's.

SALES

Flats	S	1B	2B	3B	4B	5B
Average prices	65–70	80–115	95–350	130–350+	–	–
Houses	2B	3B	4B	5B	6/7B	8B
Average prices	150–160	130–350+	250–2M	375–2.5M	1–2M	–

RENTAL

Flats	S	1B	2B	3B	4B	5B
Average prices	100–130	130–180	150–280	→325	–	–
Houses	2B	3B	4B	5B	6/7B	8B
Average prices	160–200+	220–450	280–500+	400–500	–	–

The properties	Totteridge has grand 5/8-plus bedroom houses set in near-countryside. Whetstone also has luxury houses, though slightly smaller, and smart p/b flats. Friern Barnet has a range from ex-council and smaller terraced homes to large detacheds.
The market	People in Totteridge have arrived: show-biz, sports celebs, smart professionals, with children and attendant ponies and pets. Amenities here can be anything from a swimming pool to a sunken recording studio. Whetstone has a bigger range of people and properties; Friern Barnet is more urban, with scope for less prosperous buyers. Young couples, single professionals and retired couples are all eager buyers at the old asylum site. Local searches: 5 working days.

Among those estate agents active in this area are:
- Anscombe & Ringland *
- Statons
- Ferrier Tomlin
- Henry Charles
- Barnard Marcus
- Spicer McColl
- Blade
- Jeremy Leaf
- Martyn Gerrard
- Joe Raymond
- Bairstow Eves

further details: see advertisers' index on p671

TWICKENHAM AND TEDDINGTON

Map ref: p104 (1A)
Postal districts: TW1, TW7
Borough: Richmond
    upon Thames (Lib Dem)
Council tax: Band D £908
Conservation areas: Many,
    including Twickenham
    Riverside, St Margarets
Parking: Mostly unrestricted
    except retail centres

From open fields through retreats for the rich to endless suburbia: so much of West London has the same history. Thames-side Twickenham and Teddington succumbed like the rest but managed to keep the grand houses, and the riverside offers a sort of national gallery of the covetable homes of the 18th and 19th centuries. Marble Hill, Orleans House, York House, Strawberry Hill stand stately on or close to the river, and amid them on a lesser (and still lived-in) scale are Montpelier Row and a hundred other lovely Georgian houses. Now the area's character ranges from this semi-rural riverside grandeur to small '30s semis overlooking a dual carriageway.

Essentially these are suburbs of family homes, from cottages to mansions. Purpose-built flats make their appearance along the river and in the town centres, and there are flats converted from Victorian houses. The surviving Georgiana is much in demand – as indeed are any large family homes: once happily ensconced here, families tend to stick.

Twickenham lacks the sophisticated charm of Richmond, a bridge-span away – though local people feel as though they have the best of both worlds. Homes until now have cost substantially less than on the other side of the river, but residents can still enjoy Richmond's amenities – and parking is easier. Kingston, with its big shopping centre, is close by, Heathrow is not far; there are pleasant Thames-side walks with views of Richmond and Petersham Meadows. Now, however, the price gap is being eroded; any shop that closes on **Richmond Rd**, which leads to the bridge, or in **Crown Rd**, which joins it, quickly re-opens now as a stylish restaurant, or something chi-chi in the lifestyle/gifts/interiors line. More practically, Marks & Spencers, already in Richmond, is opening a branch here too.

Twickenham is under 10 miles from the West End, and travel in is almost as quick as from Richmond. Its western boundary is the very busy A316, which leads to Central London in the E and the M3 in the W; the eastern is the Thames. Within this tract are hardly any undesirable corners. A good range of state schools (Orleans Park and Waldegrave Girls' Comprehensives and St Catherine's Girls' RC School) attracts families, as do St Paul's Girls' and St Paul's Boys' public schools in Barnes and Hammersmith, and Hampton School (boys) and Lady Eleanor Holles (girls) in nearby Hampton.

The rugby stadium at Whitton (it's called Twickenham) is just across the A316: it can attract enormous crowds and the traffic jams are epic. Controversy has surrounded the increasing use of the massive stadium, and the tide seems to have turned: locals succeeded in getting a Pavarotti concert cancelled last year.

Teddington, S of Twickenham, shares the river and schools though it lacks the architecture. Prices (naturally) rise towards Richmond, the river and stations, and fall towards the A316; and while its more everyday homes offer somewhat cheaper prices to compensate for longer commuting times, don't expect that to weigh in the cost of the smart new riverside developments. Apart from the river, there are the wide open spaces of Bushy Park to the S to wander; beyond that is Hampton Court.

The area's wide range of homes takes in quite a selection of good family houses around £270–400,000 in pleasant locations. Two-bed cottages, which are dotted throughout Twickenham, can cost £150,000-plus. Flats abound in the St Margarets area (small purpose-built, small conversions and renovated mansions) and depending on the location a 1-bed flat can cost from £90–150,000. Bargain-hunters should look to the **Chertsey Rd/Staines Rd** area with its 3-bed '30s semis. Lower prices are also to be found in Whitton to the N of the A316. Renting is well-established, though students find it tough: families and professional people dominate the market.

East Twickenham/St Margarets

St Margarets, tucked into a bend of the river opposite Richmond and with its own station, used to be a good hunting ground for value-for-money homes. It is now well established, though still cheaper than Richmond. Last year saw builders' skips proliferate, especially around 3- or 4-bed Edwardiana. Buyers are young professional first-time buyers and families, who start small and graduate to bigger local homes.

South of Richmond Bridge, **Richmond Rd** is flanked by red-brick mansion flats which overlook gardens leading down to the Thames, and by small shops which are open late and have flats above them. Turn S again off **Richmond Rd** into the triangle between it, the river and Marble Hill Park, with the cool cream symmetry of the Palladian Marble Hill House. Here **Cresswell Rd** has semi-detached Victorian houses with huge bay windows which pass the half-million mark (a 4-bed example was £575,000 last winter). Neighbouring **Morley Rd** and **Denton Rd** carry on the style on a smaller scale: say £430,000 for a 3-bed house with garden. **Cambridge Park**, curving around Marble Hill Park, has large double-fronted mansions (mostly flats) mixed with small modern developments set back from the road behind mature trees. Conversions can yield good-sized flats: 3-beds, c £300,000. Behind it, **Cambridge Park Court** has a row of 3-storey semi-detached Victorian houses (also mostly flats) that back onto the greenery.

On the river-bank itself, 'Richmond Bridge', a big complex of flats and town-houses, has replaced the much-loved Richmond Ice Rink. Phase II of this development, which added two more apartment blocks behind the first three, plus more town-houses, had sold out by the close of '99 bar the odd penthouse. Expect to pay around £340,000 for a 2-bed flat, rising to a million or more for 3 bedrooms and river views.

Richmond Rd swings on SW towards the heart of Twickenham. Across it, **Crown Rd** has an eclectic mix of shops at its N end, near St Margarets station, including smart interiors, bric-a-brac and nice cafés. **Crown Rd** and **Sandycombe Rd** stretch N to **St Margarets Rd** and offer a mix of 2-bed cottages and pleasant 3/4-bed red-brick family houses. Sandycombe Lodge, designed by J W Turner as his country retreat, is still a house. **Marble Hill Close,** situated close to the park, has neat 3-bed '30s semis priced around £270,000. A 3-bed house in nearby **Napoleon Rd** went last winter for £340,000. A year earlier it cost £289,950.

The Barons, on the opposite side of the **Crown Rd/St Margarets Rd** junction, curves down past Twickenham Film Studios into a semi-circle. Here large 3-storey houses with pillared porticoes cluster around what may once have been a private communal garden but where there is now a block of flats. To the E is **Rosslyn Rd,** with enormous double-fronted Victorian houses, now mostly flats or offices.

North of **Rosslyn Rd** is **Riverdale Rd** where the 1870 Gothic mansions, shaded by trees, give a touch of the Sir Walter Scotts. This is a fine example of a Victorian suburb, although the great houses are now splendid flats (2 beds, around £200,000). Further N is **Ravensbourne Rd** with its half-timbered post-war houses and, swinging left into **Park House Gardens,** fine white-washed Art Deco semi-detached houses run down to the river. Here is **Duck's Walk,** where homes with moorings face the river. Six town-houses built two years ago as 'Richmond Bridge Moorings' sold when new for £650–750,000. Agents estimate current prices at £850,000 to over a million.

The northernmost corner of St Margarets lies across **The Avenue** , which leads to Twickenham Bridge. Look here at a cache of five roads – **St Margarets Drive, Ranelagh Drive, St Peters Rd, St Georges Rd** and **Ailsa Rd** (the latter three form an exclusive area known as 'The Trust Grounds'). Mansions either face grandly onto the road or are hidden by high walls. They all back onto secret private parkland, where owners' children play contentedly and summer barbecues are held. The price of membership is high, starting around £600,000 for smaller properties, though a house in **St Peters Rd** sold in 1997 for £1.5 million.

Winchester Rd runs S from (but does not join) the roundabout at the junction of **The Avenue/Chertsey Rd/St Margarets Rd**; it has Victorian/Edwardian flat-fronted houses and 2-bed maisonettes. Between **Winchester Rd** and the open space of Moor Mead Ground is a grid of popular streets handy for St Margarets station: maisonettes (c £165,000) and terraced houses. The exception is **Sydney Rd,** where (despite the parking problems) people pay up to £190,000 for the 2/3-bed maisonettes in this prettier, tree-lined street. **St Margarets Grove** and

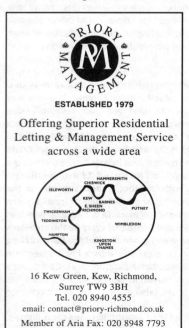
T

Brook Rd have pretty 2-bed cottages; homes here fetches around £180–250,000 (**Brook Rd** is cheaper). Some cottages in this road have gardens that back onto the River Crane.

Cole Park Rd twists up the E side of Cole Park and is lined with detached double-fronted Edwardian, '30s and modern houses. Across the tracks **Amyand Park Rd** hugs the railway from close to Twickenham station up to **St Margarets Rd**. A mixed bag of 3-storey houses with basements (now mostly flats) is to be found, though some face the rather busy railway. A 2-bed flat with garden might cost £180,000. The terraced cottages in **St Margarets Grove** are popular, though some have downstairs bathrooms.

Riverside and Marble Hill

The prestige homes of Twickenham can be found S of **Richmond Rd**. **Montpelier Row** (1724) skirts the W side of Marble Hill Park: a fine example of a Georgian terrace. **Chapel Rd** with its cottages leads through to equally cottagy **Orleans Rd** where the road, shaded by huge horse chestnuts, swings around Orleans House Gallery into the pretty **Riverside** winding up to The White Swan past some spectacular late-18th-century white and pastel-washed houses. These Thames-side delights almost never come onto the market; one did, however, last winter: 5 bedrooms, £695,000. N of **Riverside** is **Lebanon Park,** where you can expect to pay handsomely for the 3/4-bed, red-brick Edwardian family houses. Parallel to this runs **Sion Rd**, with a terrace of 12 houses running down to the river. Cross a footbridge (when it's not being mended, the only dry access) and Eel Pie Island has some modern houses with moorings for those who reckon boats are more important than cars.

Central Twickenham

South of **Heath Rd** is a network of roads (including **Pope's Grove, Upper Grotto Rd, Cross Deep Gardens**) which are a mix of Victorian houses with basements, harsh red-brick cottages and pleasant Edwardian family houses. Prices in the £220–350,000 range (a 4-bedroomed **Pope's Avenue** town-house last winter: £324,000). **Cross Deep Gardens** also has houses with lawns which lead down to the river and penthouse flats; these push house prices up above half a million. Here, too, is Addison Court, a 1980s development of 21 flats. On **Cross Deep** itself, which follows the river, a derelict pub between **Pope's Grove** and **Holmes Rd** is being redeveloped into a 27-bed hotel with, of course, river views, this spring.

King St is the main street of Twickenham, where the buses stop and where most of the shops are. However Twickenham is crying out for more chain stores: a Marks & Spencer, long top of the wish-list, is at last to appear in the site of the Volvo garage on **Heath Rd**. However, things have gone quiet over last year's plans to redevelop the old swimming pool site on the **Embankment** into flats, a cinema and more: watch this space . . . . Rumours that the District Line will be extended from Richmond 'within two or three years' depend upon the outcome of the tube privatisation plans: see Transport chapter.

Further W, **Heath Rd** feeds into **The Green**, a tree-lined triangle with large white 18th-century cottages to the S which give way to modern flat developments. There are pretty 18th-century cottages to the W. To the N, **May Rd, Knowle Rd** and **Colne Rd** have a mix of doll-sized cottages and modern houses. More young people are moving in here. W towards Fulwell prices drop, to rise again at Hampton Hill.

Strawberry Hill and Teddington

Horace Walpole's 18th-century Gothic mansion of Strawberry Hill is now a college, and its grounds are streets of suburban houses. This neighbourhood forms the S edge of Twickenham. Tree-lined streets like **Waldegrave Park** are lined with big detached

Victorian villas, some split into flats, and batches of '50s–'70s infill: town-houses, mostly, including some of the Span ones that excite architects. There is a lot of inter-war housing around here: smart semis ranging down the scale to rather tired-looking 1920s terraces. Two large new 6-bed semis appeared in **Waldegrave Park** for £750,000 apiece in 1998; a more typical 4-bed home in **Waldegrave Gardens** reached £650,000 last winter. Berkeley's pair of semis in **Elmfield Avenue** were £395,000.

Teddington itself has a station and a somewhat humdrum **High St** (with a few lovely Georgian homes). The best residential roads lie to the E – towards the river. Here, **Kingston Rd** runs N-S towards Hampton Wick and Kingston Bridge. Closer to the river, **Lower Teddington Rd** forms the spine of a district of moderately smart homes set in plenty of greenery – but a longish way from shops or transport. Riverside complexes of flats and town-houses line the E side, many in private estates. The most interesting houses are late-19th-century and 1930s ones in **Melbourne Rd** and **Trowlock Avenue** (4-beds c £425,000 here) which lead down to the river and share a private riverside green. Beyond is a true oddity: Trowlock Island, a long thin strip packed with bungalows. Most started as shacks, many are now very smart; all (when and if they appear on the open market) are expensive – this is true off-shore living, mooring included, and you'll pay for the privilege. The only access is by a chain ferry with a handle you have to wind.

Broom Water and **Broom Water West** have some of Teddington's smartest houses: big, with gardens down to a private creek. To the W of **Broom Rd** and **Lower Teddington Rd** are some 1991 flats in **Trematon Place**, plus streets, such as **Munster Rd** and **King Edward's Grove**, of tall, gabled 1890–1910 semis and 1960s town-houses.

On **Kingston Rd** is the site of the Normansfield Hospital: Laing Homes plan homes here by 2002. Across **Kingston Rd** to the W, popular roads include **Langham Rd**, **Kingston Lane** and **Udney Park Rd**: three parallel streets running N-S from **Teddington High St**. These quiet, residential roads have a mix of 4- to 7-bedroomed Edwardian semis and detacheds; a 5-bed example in **Langham Rd** sold for £285,000 in late 1996, was back on the market three years later for half a million. The 7-bed ones fetch around £825,000.

On the Thames the Lensbury Club, an enviable corporate sports and leisure complex, sits on an even more enviable riverside site. Plans for some redevelopment fell through, however: planners are not keen on losing playing fields. Then, beside the weir, there are the studios of Thames TV, lined with plaques remembering famous comedians. On the inland side is **Rivermead Close**, a big estate of '70s dark-brick houses and flats. **Ferry Rd** leads down to the footbridge over the lock, and a pair of popular pubs. It has a few Victorian homes – cottages and converted houses – and the entrance to one of the many flats blocks set beside the Teddington riverside.

Further on down, Berkeley Homes built The Moorings (not the only homes of this name along this stretch): 1- and 2-bed flats priced, in 1998, around £170–240,000. Last year a 2-bed example, originally £170,000, sold for £260,000. Teddington Wharf, a St George's development on the old Tough's Boat Yard site, is 1- to 3-bed flats and penthouses: the roofline features striking glass conservatories. These too saw price jumps last year; a 3-bed riverside one was £350,000. Older flats blocks along the river include '60s Fairwater House. Modern river-view 2-bed flats are priced from about £180,000, with moorings; £240,000 for 3-bed. The rest of the Teddington riverside, running along a road that changes its name from (N–S) **Strawberry Vale** to **Twickenham Rd** to **Manor Rd**, is a mix of blocks of flats from the '30s to today, Victorian and earlier villas, and inter-war suburban detached. Many have their own moorings, and all have fine views of the wooded, open Ham Lands and beyond to Richmond Park.

Going inland, there's a big tract of mixed 1880–1910 and 1930s housing, with everything from handsome Arts and Crafts detached to little terraced cottages, smartened-up council-built houses, and '70s town-houses. Similar housing appears W of the railway line, which runs behind the W side of **Waldegrave Rd**. The handsome double-fronted (though semi-detached) Victorian houses in **Cambridge Rd** can fetch up to £650,000 for a 5-bed one. Cheaper homes are further W: ex-council houses, Victorian cottages. If you can find a 3-bed house for under £150-160,000 you've got a good deal.

Transport	Trains: Twickenham, St Margarets, Teddington, to Waterloo via Richmond or Kingston. Twickenham to Waterloo 25 min.
Convenient for	Heathrow, River Thames, roads to West. Miles from centre: 9–10.
Schools	Richmond Education Authority: Rectory School, Teddington School, Waldegrave Girls' School, Whitton School, Orleans Park School. St Catherine's Catholic School (girls) Private: Hampton School (b), Lady Eleanor Holles (g), St James (b); see also Barnes & Hammersmith.

SALES

Flats	S	1B	2B	3B	4B	5B
Average prices	60–110	90–160	120–250	140–450+	–	–
Houses	2B	3B	4B	5B	6/7B	8B
Average prices	150–250	160–350+	200–550+	300–800+	700–1.5M	850→

RENTAL

Flats	S	1B	2B	3B	4B	5B
Average prices	115–160	138–210	160–460	210–460+	275–800	325–925
Houses	2B	3B	4B	5B	6/7B	8B
Average prices	200–345	220–575	275–690	345–925	460→	460→

The properties	From riverside splendour – 18th-century and newer houses plus a clutch of new flats – to railway cottages, with plenty of suburbia of most sizes and vintages in between, and an increasing number of converted and new-built flats.
The market	Big premiums are paid for best riverside locations, while mainstream family homes are cheaper than neighbouring Richmond. Good schools attract families. Local searches: 7 days.

Among those estate agents active in this area are:
- Bells
- Barton & Wyatt
- Camerons Residential
- Milestone & Collis
- Mann & Co
- Jardine & Co
- Chancellors
- Churchills
- Priory Management *

- Featherstone Leigh
- Dexters
- Chase Buchanan
- Hamptons
- G A Property
- Bradford & Bingley/Gascoigne-Pees
- Phillip Hodges
- Townends

* further details: see advertisers' index on p671

WANDSWORTH

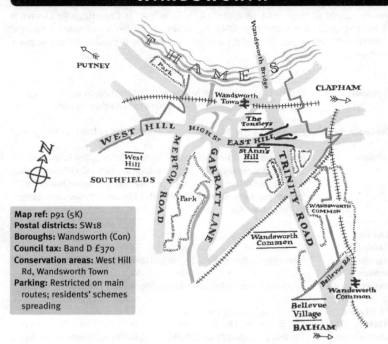

Map ref: p91 (5K)
Postal districts: SW18
Boroughs: Wandsworth (Con)
Council tax: Band D £370
Conservation areas: West Hill
  Rd, Wandsworth Town
Parking: Restricted on main
  routes; residents' schemes
  spreading

Those who say they live in Wandsworth rarely mean it. They mean the
borough of Wandsworth, which takes in a wide swathe of south-west London from
Putney to Streatham and which is confused with, and has in many ways replaced, the
tightly-knit former village where the River Wandle meets the Thames. This tribute to
the town hall's persuasive powers stems from the low (even non-existent) poll tax
levied a decade back. The current council tax is lower than most, protecting the
investment of the junior execs of both sexes who flocked to the rather ordinary late-
Victorian suburbs of Balham, Southfields, Tooting and the rest (see separate
chapters) and made them, in a decade, into one of London's middle-class hot-spots.

Here we're concerned with actual Wandsworth, real existing Wandsworth, the
neighbourhoods around the old village and (more important by far) its Common. The
centre is best-known today for its one-way system, in the midst of which lies the
monumental town hall, protected from all but the bravest council-tax payer by the
A3/South Circular traffic.

The Wandsworth Common tract is at first sight uninspiring: a prison looms on the
horizon, a pointless 6-lane road funnels traffic up from the gigantic intersection at the
S end of Wandsworth Bridge, the green space is bisected by a railway line. But there
are plenty of family-sized Victorian/Edwardian homes, plus trains into Waterloo from
nearby Clapham Junction and into Victoria from the Common's own station. The
Common streets share a plethora of prep schools and designer shops with the
neighbouring 'twixt the commons' bit of Battersea.

Back in Wandsworth proper, the focus now is on the riverside, where former
industrial land is rapidly being recycled as blocks of flats, which stare glumly across

the Thames at their mirror-images on the Fulham shore. The 1980s saw considerable tidying-up around Wandsworth, including a much-needed facelift for Wandsworth Town station and, best of all, extensive work on council estates. This means that ex-council homes are now a serious option: cheaper (but not that much cheaper) than the twiddly late-19th-century terraces that predominate. Other more recent homes include some solid 1920s/30s suburbia W of the Common, on the Earlsfield borders.

The busy Wandsworth town centre offers the soon to be done-up Arndale shopping centre (Tesco, Boots, Woolworths etc) with high-rise council flats above. There is a large Sainsbury's in **Garratt Lane**. A landmark in the centre is the Victorian Ram Brewery (Young's). However the new inhabitants look for money-spending opportunities to **Bellevue Rd**, a chi-chi strip of shops and bars beside the Common, to similar **Northcote Rd** in Battersea, to Putney – or across the bridge to Fulham.

Central and riverside

The riverside, between Wandsworth centre and the Thames, was industrial but is now the scene of much of the development action in the area. It is changing fast as developers seize on the Thames-side sites, made more interesting by the Wandle mouth. Some industry remains, such as the council depots at the end of otherwise pretty **Frogmore**, but every inch is under seige from developers. St George's rather stolid riverside blocks at 'Riverside West' in **Smugglers Way** are onto Phase Three with prices starting at £230,000 and 3-bed flats around £430,000. The developer's site map identifies as a neighbour the Ship Inn to the E of the site (known to every Henry in SW London for its Thames-side BBQs), but fails to mark the Solid Waste Transfer Station upwind to the W. Just across the road to the S, the old gasworks site next to B&Q is to be a 184-bed Holiday Inn hotel. A new amenity here is a footbridge over the creek, linking **The Causeway** with **Enterprise Way**.

Further W, beyond the rubbish depot and the mouth of the Wandle, is the former Shell site accessed via **Point Pleasant** and **Osiers Rd**. A big 450-flat scheme with a 17-storey office tower was thrown out by the Minister back in 1998, and further plans are awaited. The next site upstream, towards Putney, is nowadays Prospect Quay: two new riverside flats blocks, an office/leisure block and a restaurant. A quay, houseboats and a 'drinks pontoon' add to the amenities. Inland, the 52-flats Parkland Square block was under way last winter: prices from £195-695,000.

Downstream, the giant site next to Wandsworth Bridge, once the Guinness-owned distillery and now known (appropriately, to judge by the plans) as 'Gargoyle Wharf', lies empty after another big planning row in 1998/9 led to Rialto withdrawing a 20-storey scheme. A new plan, envisaging 16-storey towers with 658 flats, an hotel, a nursing home, shops/offices and a police station, was being considered in January.

Property in central Wandsworth is mainly commercial with some small industrial premises. Exceptionally beautiful early Georgian houses (now commerce and industry) are to be found in **Wandsworth Plain**. Thereafter are privatized blocks of modernized '30s council flats that are set well back from the road. Behind is **Frogmore** with its flat-fronted cottages and a modern, private development. **Sudlow Rd** joins **Frogmore** to **North Passage** and has mid-Victorian cottages.

The Tonsleys

Bordered by **Old York Rd**, **Trinity Rd**, **East Hill** and **Fairfield St**, this is a quiet enclave of attractive small Victorian cottages (mainly 2- and 3-bed), with some large 4- and 5-bed houses, running up and across the hill which rises out of the Wandle basin.

The Tonsleys is near Wandsworth Town station (12 min to Waterloo via Clapham Junction), and was discovered by '80s yuppies. The area is popular with Fulham price refugees (easy access to parents in Parson's Green via Wandsworth Bridge) and

W

constantly echoes with the sound of building work as the cottages are further tidied.

The building of the **Swandon Way** relief road has turned **Old York Rd** from a busy, scruffy through-route into a bijou backwater, with no through traffic and new planting and paving. Mexican restaurants, a Pizza Express, bars and amusing shops burgeon. Some new flats are due here this year. South of **Old York Rd** is **Alma Rd** with large 3-storey Victorian houses and a pub at the junction with **Fullerton Rd**. Three new buildings – likely to be flats – are under construction in **Alma Rd**. In **Ebner St** (running parallel with **Alma Rd**) a church and C of E primary school have been rebuilt. The development includes an adult education centre. Especially pretty roads are **Dalby Rd** and **Bramford Rd** which run down the fairly steep hill from **Dighton Rd** to **Old York Rd**. **Tonsley Place** and **Tonsley Rd** have modernized 2- and 3-bed cottages. Two-bed modernized ones can command £280,000-plus. Mixed blocks of '30s council and private flats (Fairfield Court) front **Fairfield St** (very heavy traffic: it's part of the one-way system) along with four large, semi-detached mid-Victorian houses.

There are larger, 3-storey 4/5-bed houses in **Dempster Rd**, **Fullerton Rd** and **Birdhurst Rd**, N of **East Hill**. **Birdhurst Rd** overlooks busy **Trinity Rd**, which is in a cutting at this point, so traffic noise is no great problem. A 1990 homes development (including a shopping parade) on **East Hill** backs into **Fullerton Rd**. The 64 flats and six houses are known as 'Tonsley Heights' and are grouped round a new street called **Bloomsbury Way**. Rialto were the developers of this Victorian pastiche. A new flats complex, Almand House, has just been finished further down **East Hill**. Across **Trinity Rd**, close to **York Rd**, the old school site in **Eltringham St** now has offices and homes.

St Ann's Hill

South of **East Hill**, between **St Ann's Hill**, **Allfarthing Lane** and **Wandsworth Common Westside**, homes are mainly well-sized, late-Victorian and Edwardian with some modern infill developments. (These include low-rise council-built flats, most of which are now privately owned.) Property prices rise approaching the Common.

Popular roads include **Geraldine Rd**, **Melody Rd** and **Cicada Rd** (Geraldine's rat-running traffic is now slowed by speed humps). The architectural styles are mixed but most of the houses are large, late-Victorian 2- and 3-storey buildings. Some houses in **Geraldine Rd** top £600,000 for a 4-bed, though others – smaller or less well done-up – command closer to £400,000. The area is a prime hunting-ground for any remaining unmodernized houses. Four such homes on the corner of **Rosehill Rd** have been virtually rebuilt behind their Victorian brick facades, with splendid double-height extensions at the back to maximize space. They were on the market last winter from £755-885,000. The 3-bed/2-bath town-houses of The Washhouse are in **St Ann's Crescent**, partly overlooking the unusual, late-Georgian 'pepper pot' church. Wycombe Place is a new townhouse development here: 3-bed, 2-bath, garage for £395,000.

Although **St Ann's Hill** acts as the main through road from **East Hill** to **Allfarthing Lane** and **Earlsfield Rd**, it has speed humps and does not suffer too badly. Houses on and surrounding **St Ann's Hill** are mainly early Edwardian 3-bed terraces, but there are some '30s-built semi-detached houses on **St Ann's Hill**. Between **St Ann's Hill** and **Garratt Lane** there is a good supply of purpose-built late-Victorian maisonettes and flats. A council estate running along the lower end of **Allfarthing Lane** (**Iron Mill Rd**, **Vermont Rd**) and up to the Wandsworth end of **St Ann's Hill** makes for price differentials. Allfarthing School and St Anne's C of E school are popular primaries.

Huguenot Place is at the junction of **East Hill**, **Wandsworth Common Northside** and **Westside**. The heavy traffic maroons the attractive 18th-century church, Book House and the Huguenot cemetery. There are some flats and houses, including Huguenot Mansions, which all suffer road noise.

West Hill

This neighbourhood is SW of Wandsworth town centre and is bounded in the N by the endlessly busy **West Hill,** which funnels traffic from the A3 into the maw of the Wandsworth one-way system. **Merton Rd** joins **West Hill** at the junction with **Wandsworth High St** and **Putney Bridge Rd,** and features some good mid- and late-Victorian semi-detached and terraced houses. Many of the houses are set well back from the road with off-street parking, so are not worried by the heavy traffic. **Wimbledon Park Rd** leads down through the neighbourhood to Southfields tube station, lined with a mix of Victorian houses and low-rise council-built flats. **West Hill Rd,** leading from **Merton Rd** to **West Hill** (A3), has prices on a par with Putney. The houses vary in style: there are early, mid- and late-Victorian and some 1930s and '50s homes. Many of the properties are detached or semi-detached. Houses in **Sispara Gardens** and **Viewfield Rd** are set well back and have off-street parking. **Lebanon Rd, Amerland Rd** and **Ringford Rd** all lead off **West Hill,** and are more East Putney than Wandsworth. There is a small council-built infill in **Lebanon Gardens** whose now privately-owned 4-bedroomed houses occasionally come up for sale.

Further E, at the junction with **Broomhill Rd** and **Merton Rd,** is an attractive, simple development of mews-style town-houses, some with balconies and garages. Older and larger 2- and 3-storey late-Victorian houses follow from this more peaceful point on **Merton Rd** to the junction with **Buckhold Rd.**

A small council cottage-style estate off **Buckhold Rd** has mainly flat-fronted traditional-style houses. Most were bought by tenants under 'Right to Buy', and these homes now appear on the market. The large gardens of those on the eastern side of **Longstaff Crescent** back on to King George's Park.

Wandsworth Common

The Common is quite a long way from Wandsworth Town. This adds to the name confusion mentioned above: Wandsworth Common station is in SW12, and the nearby Bellevue Village neighbourhood is SW17, so they are really in Balham and Tooting if one is strict, but it would not be wise to say so locally. **Wandsworth Common Westside** (the street) is at the NW corner, on the E edge of the St Ann's Hill neighbourhood. It is protected from the traffic of **Trinity Rd,** (dual-carriageway at this point) by a slice of the Common, wide at the junction with **Earlsfield Rd** and narrowing to the junction with **East Hill.** **Westside** offers large 4- and 5-bed mid-Victorian houses; especially attractive is the row of ornate Gothic-style houses between **Quarry Rd** and **Heathfield Rd.** Further along **Heathfield Rd** just before the junction with **Earlsfield Rd** is **Heathfield Gardens,** a secret row of enchanting Regency cottages of varying sizes overlooking the common. Across **Earlsfield Rd** and further along **Heathfield Rd** is another Wandsworth landmark: Wandsworth Prison. Just opposite is Heathfields, a 'mews' development of flats and houses, with 2/4-bed houses. Across the road, **Wilde Place** has 29 well-built 2- to 4-bed town-houses. Past the prison lies the pretty early Victorian flat-fronted cottages of **Alma Terrace** facing open land: they achieve £300,000-plus. Beyond are 1920s and '30s blocks of flats.

Spencer Park, overlooking the Common from the N side, is the area's gem: it has a stunning range of large, detached and semi-detached houses built in a variety of styles as show houses for the Great Exhibition in 1851. Some have now been converted into flats or are used by institutions, but a number remain as large family homes: prices of over £2 million have been mooted. Their secret is that they back onto a large and private communal garden. Spencer Court on **Windmill Rd** is a 1930s block of flats overlooking the railway lines and the Victorian Emanuel School beyond.

Wandsworth Common Northside forms part of the traffic-plagued South Circular. Many houses have been converted into flats and those on the S side of the road are

W

popular for their views over Wandsworth Common. Behind lie **Elsynge Rd** and **Spencer Rd**, where there is a mixture of exceptionally large, fine Victorian houses with enormous gardens, many remaining in single occupation, and smaller late-Victorian houses and double-fronted 'cottages'. Prices for the better houses have shot past a million: £1.3 million was being asked last winter for a 5-storey one in **Elsynge Rd** – and the best in **Spencer Rd** are even more. On **Northside** itself, Fairview have taken six 5-floor Victorian houses back to their roots: 5-beds, an au pair flat and a garage.

Approached from an easy-to-miss turning off **Trinity Rd** is Wandsworth's most spectacular building: the splendidly Gothic Royal Victoria Patriotic Building. Built to care for orphan daughters of servicemen killed in the Crimean War, it now houses a theatre school, restaurant, design studios and individualistic flats (some in towers and turrets) which are popular with artistic and media types. It is set rather unfortunately between a major railway and an estate of council towers and is perhaps more fun to look at than out of. Not many come up for sale; when they do, people pay around £500,000. A new bridge over the railway off **Windmill Rd** gives access to **John Archer Way** and 'Windmill Green', a Fairview development of 200 flats and 65 houses set just N of the Royal Victoria Patriotic Building. Security is a feature: railway cuttings on two sides and the Emanuel School grounds on the third. The last handful of houses were on sale last winter: 4-beds at £365,000.

The more traditional charms of 'The Toastrack', a grid of streets surrounded on three sides by the Common, have been attracting family buyers since the 1980s. This group lies off **Trinity Rd** and takes in **Dorlcote Rd, Nicosia Rd, Baskerville Rd, Henderson Rd** and **Patten Rd**. Here are large, detached or semi-detached 5/6-bed late-Victorian houses, some with exceptionally large gardens. Houses on **Dorlcote Rd** overlook the Common from the front, whilst the gardens of houses in **Routh Rd** and **Baskerville** back onto the Common: seven-figure prices here. There are some flats in Greenview Court on **Baskerville Rd.**

West of **Trinity Rd** from the Toastrack are some unusually large, often double-fronted houses with good-sized gardens, which can fetch very surprising prices for exceptional properties. These are to be found in the roads adjoining **Lyford Rd**, most notably **Herondale Avenue, Loxley Rd, Frewin Rd** and **Westover Rd. Lyford Rd** is a no-through road running N-S between **Magdalen Rd** and **Burntwood Lane**. Houses that lie between **Routh Rd** and **Lyford Rd** back onto a wild and overgrown extension of Wandsworth Common, adding to the rural illusion beloved of many of the inhabitants. Another recent development in the **Trinity Rd** area has appeared close to **Magdalen Rd**: Trinity Grange has five 3- and 4-bedroom houses and nine flats.

Between **Routh Rd** (where Lloyd George lived) and **Burntwood Lane** are large 3-storey Edwardian and late-Edwardian houses (some semi-detached) overlooking the Common. The distinctive White House by the junction with **Frewin Rd** was designed by Voysey.

Bellevue Village

The area bordered by **Trinity Rd, St James's Drive** and Wandsworth Common offers pretty mid-Victorian cottages, some flat-fronted and larger than they look. The cottages were once inhabited by the working classes but are now occupied by interior designers, junior merchant bankers and divorcees whose alimony payments don't stretch to Fulham. Inhabitants tend to be seriously short-tempered owing to the fact that there is no available parking space and each house appears to have three cars. **Bellevue Rd** is lined with art galleries, chi-chi delicatessens, wine bars and restaurants which all add to the chaotic parking. At last there are plans for a residents' parking zone. None of this existed 15 years ago: Bellevue was a quiet suburban parade of butchers, bakers and junk shops.

St James's Drive has larger mid-Victorian terraced houses, some semi-basement and stuccoed, all suffering road noise. The former St James's Hospital site is now housing association homes. SW of Bellevue, almost in Tooting, **Brodrick Rd**, **Wandle Rd** and **Hendham Rd** have large late-Victorian mainly 3-storey terraced and (just) semi-detached houses. **Brodrick** and **Wandle Rd** are popular with families, offering easy access to Tooting Bec tube, but is really Tooting (see chapter) not Wandsworth. One advantage is Wandsworth Common station, which has a good service into Victoria.

Transport   Trains: Wandsworth Town (Waterloo 12 min), Wandsworth Common, Clapham Junction.

Convenient for   Wandsworth and Clapham Commons, Clapham Junction. Fulham Miles from centre: 4.

Schools   Local Authority: Burntwood (g), ADT College (b), Southfields College. Private: Emanuel (b & g). Many prep schools.

SALES

Flats	S	1B	2B	3B	4B	5B
Average prices	80–140	135–180	160–300+	175–375	—	—
Houses	2B	3B	4B	5B	6/7B	8B
Average prices	300–350	300–500	300–700	420–850+	600–850+	600–950+

RENTAL

Flats	S	1B	2B	3B	4B	5B
Average prices	120–190	150–200	200–320	250–320	250–360	330–600
Houses	2B	3B	4B	5B	6/7B	8B
Average prices	220–350	300–400	400–600	500–800	—	—

The properties   Wide range, but main type is Victorian terraced in a range of locations, with cottage-style in the Tonsleys and Bellevue and grander ones near the Common, stratospheric in Spencer Park. Some '30s and '50s suburban houses in SW of area. New homes by the river and Common. Watch for resales of good ex-council flats and houses.

The market   While the town centre stays forever Wandsworth, the enclaves of fashionable homes – Tonsleys, Bellevue, 'Toastrack' (all close to stations) – are now well and truly established, and the riverside is on its way. Watch out for agents and builders selling Balham, Southfields etc as Wandsworth. Local searches: 3–4 weeks.

Among those estate agents active in this area are:
- Bells
- Realm Estates
- Barnard Marcus
- Raymond Bushell
- FPDSavills
- Friend & Falcke *
- John D Wood
- Halifax Property
- Hamptons
- Douglas & Gordon
- Edwin Evans
- Robert Trindle & Co
- Vanstons
- Sullivan Thomas
- Kinleigh Folkard & Hayward
- Courtenay *
- Foxtons *
- Craigie & Co

* further details: see advertisers' index on p671

W

WEST HAMPSTEAD

Map ref: p43 (6K)
Postal districts: NW6, NW2
Boroughs: Camden (Lab)
Council tax: Band D £897
Conservation areas: Check
  with town hall
Parking: Free off main
  roads, but congested

West Hampstead has now got a commercial heart to go with its excellent travel links and ample supply of converted and mansion flats. The O2 complex, which opened in 1998, brings giant Sainsbury's and Homebase stores, multi-screen cinema, 10 restaurants and bars, chi private gym and large branch of Books Etc – and epic traffic jams – to this quintessential flat-land area. This, plus the equally long-awaited Jubilee Line Extension which greatly enhances the communications, sent property prices up 15 per cent in 1998 and another 20 per cent in 1999.

Now that the O2 centre is complete, all eyes have turned to Railtrack's proposal to develop land it owns in **West End Lane**, near the tube station. Apart from creating a major new transport interchange, linking local bus services with the tube network as well as Silverlink and Thameslink overground services, Railtrack would also dearly like to build some houses, shops and offices to help finance the scheme.

Its first proposal, for a modernistic glass and steel block and some 115 houses behind, generated huge opposition (backed by Oscar-winning actress Emma Thompson, who lives around the corner), was thrown out. Railtrack is now busy consulting residents, and a new plan is being drawn up by consultants Ove Arup.

Victorian West Hampstead is not nearly as old, and certainly nothing like as grand, as its illustrious big sister up the hill to the E; but it has a style and location that attracts young professionals who live there until they can afford the inflated prices of Hampstead proper. The development of the area took place after the middle of the last century, much of it on the large tracts of land owned by the Maryon Wilson and Eyre estates which to this day hold the freehold of large areas of leasehold property.

A few of the streets (on the E, or Hampstead side) were built with the relatively well-heeled middle classes in mind, but the bulk of the area was designed to cater for the needs of the Victorian age's growing lower-middle class. The result was large numbers of 2-storey, 2- and 3-bed terraced houses and semis. The area was also among the first to see the erection of those large blocks of purpose-built flats called mansion blocks, the word 'mansion' possibly designed to salve the blighted aspirations of those who could not afford houses. Paradoxically these flats, with their many, spacious and elegant rooms, are among the most popular properties today.

The change in the area over the last 30 years has been dramatic. Steeply rising prices and the spillover effect from Hampstead have proved an irresistible temptation to the traditional inhabitants. From the 1960s on, properties were converted into flats at a brisk rate – perhaps as few as 10 per cent of the original houses remain in single occupation. That estimate maybe a bit low but nevertheless the rarest beast in West Hampstead is a 4-bedroom family house.

West Hampstead is very much a young person's area, conveniently located between the **Finchley Rd** and **Kilburn High Rd**, both good routes N and S. **West End Lane**, which runs through the centre of West Hampstead, has plenty of restaurants and bars, and the sort of shops that cater for the single and the transient – late-night grocers, futons, stripped-pine furniture. As well as the mobile young, a settled tranche of people with interesting jobs (the media, the stage, etc) give a more stable, community feel. Both groups agree that an old-fashioned, non-'theme' pub would enhance the area.

The spine of the area is **West End Lane**, which leads S into **Abbey Rd** and **St John's Wood Rd**; it has the tube and two train stations. Transport links from West Hampstead are excellent, especially now that the Jubilee Line is fully open. In addition to these three stations, there are tube stations at Finchley Rd and Kilburn, and train stations at Finchley Rd, Frognal and Brondesbury nearby. Trains offer the North London Line, direct services to King's Cross, and (it's hoped) a fast link to Heathrow in 2003. There are scores of bus routes, too. Despite excellent public transport services, West Hampstead residents like to have a car. With houses converted into three or four flats (estate agents' boards abound) that means a lot of vehicles and parking in the streets is a nightmare. Being in Camden Borough, these car users face persecution: residents' parking permits are a certainty, and a clamp-down on school runs and commuting by car is threatened. The O2 centre, with its huge car park, has attracted yet more traffic, though the jams have eased now the initial excitement is over.

W

Fortune Green and 'West End'

West Hampstead is bisected diagonally by **West End Lane** leading, at the N end, into **Fortune Green Rd** which gives access to a whole group of roads rather marooned from the rest of the suburb by the Midland rail line. These include some quiet and peaceful enclaves compared with the bustle and congestion of the rest of the area.

Behind the pleasant open space of Fortune Green itself is the Hampstead Cemetery, which casts a protective shadow over streets like **Gondar Gardens** and **Hillfield Rd**, one of the few corners in the area where the Victorian builders produced family houses of any size. Many have now been converted, but occasional 4- or 5-bedroom houses do still come onto the market.

Also interesting is the group of streets known as 'The Greeks' – not surprisingly since they include **Agamemnon Rd, Ajax Rd, Ulysses Rd** and **Achilles Rd**. These are still well supplied with modestly sized family houses, and is perhaps the best preserved corner of the entire suburb. Agents cite this as the 'best' part of West Hampstead.

Closer to **Finchley Rd** is the area once known as the West End (of Hampstead, presumably), now dominated by the large mansion blocks in **West End Lane, Mill Lane, Lyncroft Gardens, Cannon Hill** and **Honeybourne Rd**, including Buckingham Mansions, Marlborough Mansions, Cholmley Gardens, Yale Court and Harvard Court. Formerly rented, they are all now owner-occupied, and the large flats are very popular. Leases vary, but for a long lease you might pay £335,000 for a 2-bed flats, £400–500,000 for a 4-bed. **Cannon Hill** also has some well-regarded Edwardian blocks.

The smartest streets in West Hampstead are E of **West End Lane: Alvanley Gardens** with its large detached houses grandly overlooking the grounds of Hampstead Cricket Club in **Lymington Rd**, and the attractive semis of **Crediton Hill**. A 3-storey Victorian house in **Kylemore Rd** was recently on the market for £420,000, while a 5-bed house in **Alvanley Gardens** was £995,000.

South of **Mill Lane** (whose bars, antique shops and the like reflect to some extent the inhabitants of the area) are residential streets such as **Sumatra Rd, Broomsleigh St, Solent Rd, Narcissus Rd** and **Pandora Rd** – all typical of the 2- and 3-storey terraces which West Hampstead has to offer. Most of these houses have been split into flats: it is here that first-time buyers can gain a foothold in the area with 1-bed flats starting at around £165,000 and 2-beds from £180,000.

The surviving houses can command £415,000 for a 4-bed, £550–600,000 for a 5/6-bed. There is also an interesting enclave of streets, including **Menelik Rd, Somali Rd** and **Asmara Rd**, in the NW2 corner of the area, which are close to the open spaces of Fortune Green.

Iverson and Kingsgate

This is the triangle between the Midland railway line to the N, **West End Lane** and **Kilburn High Rd**. Towards the N, busy **Iverson Rd** leads past light industrial areas and large new council estates to the slightly less smart area of **Maygrove Rd,** **Loveridge Rd** and **Fordwych Rd,** where the large number of builders' skips which appear there regularly show that here, too, things are constantly on the move.

Further S, **Sherriff Rd** and **Hemstal Rd** lead from **West End Lane** to the densely packed streets around **Kingsgate Rd.** These are mainly 2-storey small terraced houses, and if there is a less expensive part of the area, this is it. Here the population is less affluent than elsewhere, with a number of council estates. There are, however, pleasant corners and bargains to be found, both in terms of flats and small houses, and **Lowfield, Kylemore, Gladys** and **Hilltop Rds** are well worth looking at. Two-bed flats range between £210,000 and £275,000. Homes in this corner have the advantage of useful shopping on **Kilburn High Rd.**

Roads further S such as **Messina Avenue, Gascony Avenue** and **Mazenood Avenue** have 3-storey Victorian houses at around £525,000, and 1-bed flats converted from similar houses at £160–180,000. There are also blocks of purpose-built flats.

Cross the **Kilburn High Rd** to the W and you are still in NW6, but not in West Hampstead: see the Kilburn chapter. Up the High Rd is Kilburn tube, which is in the Jubilee Line (like West Hampstead).

The southernmost strip of the area, between a railway line and **Boundary Rd,** is almost completely dominated by very large council blocks, including the Abbey Estate and the extraordinary 1,000-ft long concrete sweep of Camden's Alexandra Rd Estate in **Rowley Way.**

The Maryon Wilson estate/South Hampstead

The area bounded by **Broadhurst Gardens, Finchley Rd, Belsize Rd** and **Priory Rd** was built between 1874 and the late-1890s, and contains some of the most attractive, most popular and most expensive properties in West Hampstead (sometimes, however, this patch is called South Hampstead). A 5-bed house in **Priory Rd** was £895,000 this spring. They are close not only to the transport and considerable shopping facilities of **West End Lane** but also to the major shopping centre in **Finchley Rd** – with a large Waitrose supermarket and the Habitat furniture and household goods store.

Particularly attractive, in streets such as **Canfield Gardens, Compayne Gardens** and **Fairfield Gardens,** are the red-brick mansion blocks, often with endearing turrets on the corner properties, and large communal gardens. Some of the best of these properties are owned by the pioneering Fairhazel Housing Cooperative (the first of its kind) and are not available on the open market. Those that are on sale might cost £375,000 for a 3-bed.

But there are other elegant roads, including **Broadhurst Gardens, Greencroft Gardens, Aberdare Gardens, Cleve Road** and **Goldhurst Terrace,** where there is a brisk trade in both purpose-built and converted flats, including some luxurious recent conversions. Here and there you might even find the odd large house in single occupation for sale – but you would have to move very fast (and have a capacious chequebook) in order to beat would-be developers to the purchase. Here, too, you will find modern 3-bed houses for around £475,000. There has been talk for a few years of making this tract a conservation area, but still no decision.

Transport	Tubes: West Hampstead, Kilburn (zone 2, Jubilee); Finchley Rd (zone 2, Jubilee, Metropolitan). From West Hampstead: Oxford Circus 15 min (1 change), City 30 min (1 change), Heathrow 60 min (1 change). Trains: West Hampstead (King's Cross 10 min, Thameslink and North London Line/Silverlink).
Convenient for	Hampstead Heath, West End, M1/A1 to the North. Miles from centre: 4.
Schools	Local Authority: St George's RC, Hampstead Comprehensive, Quintin Kynaston Comprehensive.

SALES

Flats	S	1B	2B	3B	4B	5B
Average prices	65–110	120–200	140–270	175–400	270–400	350–500
Houses	2B	3B	4B	5B	6/7B	8B
Average prices	200–350	280–450	350–550	450–700	550–1M	600–1M

RENTAL

Flats	S	1B	2B	3B	4B	5B
Average prices	120–250	175–350	210–550	280–600	425–750	550–900
Houses	2B	3B	4B	5B	6/7B	8B
Average prices	275–330	325–650	400–1000	410–1100	820–1200	—

The properties	Victorian terraced homes, most of which now converted to flats. A few surviving family houses. Lots of big mansion flats, some almost St John's Wood-smart, some almost Kilburn-scruffy.
The market	Rapid turnover of flat-buyers, who use the area as a staging-post before moving on to family homes. Conversions vary in quality. Mansion flats can be a better bet, but check service charges and leases. Local searches: 7–10 days.

Among those estate agents active in this area are:
- Kinleigh Folkard & Hayward
- Greene & Co
- Brian Lack & Co
- Bairstow Eves
- Cedar Estates
- Anscombe & Ringland *
- Harris & Co
- Parkheath Estates
- Paramount
- Foxtons *
- Goldschmidt & Howland
- Felicity J Lord *

further details: see advertisers' index on p671

W

WEST NORWOOD,NORBURY AND GIPSY HILL

Map ref: p110 (4C)
Postal districts: SE19, SE27
Boroughs: Croydon (Lab),
    Lambeth (Lab), Southwark
    (Lab)
Council tax: BAND D CROYDON
    £758, Lambeth £750,
    Southwark £809
Conservation areas: Several,
    check with town hall
Parking: Free

The South London suburbs of Norwood and Gipsy Hill lie on the slopes to the W of Crystal Palace. Clues to the area's past are found in its names: Norwood is the old North Wood, which covered the hills S of the Thames basin. Tracts survive to this day, most notably the Lawns woodland area and Sydenham Hill woods. Gypsies, who gave Gipsy Hill its name, considered the woods their own until forced out by the 19th-century enclosure acts. A glance at the map shows the unusually large amount of green pockets, parks and playing-fields in this corner, even without the vast Crystal Palace Park that crowns the heights.

Ambitious plans in the early 19th century to establish a Regency-style spa town around a mineral-water spring on Beulah Hill never materialized. The spa itself quickly failed thanks to a change in fashion, with the promotion of sea water as the latest remedy. Later, the arrival of the illustrious Crystal Palace gave the area a taste of prosperity. It was short-lived: 80 years on the towering edifice burnt to the ground, and locals still vividly recall the spectacle of that 1936 night. Today the impressive facilities of the National Sports Centre are the star local attraction, and a review aimed at maintaining it as a national centre for excellence and as a local amenity is under way. Plans for the palace itself – today an empty concrete plinth – to rise again as hotel and multi-cinema complex have been given the go-head after a lengthy

W

battle with the local community – and eco-warriors – and the developers. More details are in the Crystal Palace chapter.

The area has plenty of attractions for home-buyers, with a wide range of flats and houses, and fast rail links to Central London. House-hunters spill over from pricier Dulwich and Streatham; first-time buyers are attracted by the many flat conversions in large Victorian houses. Agents say that people rent here, get to like the area, and then buy. When looking for homes, it is worth bearing in mind that, along with the choice of roads and types of property comes the choice of boroughs – Lambeth to the N or Croydon to the S, while Bromley covers a corner.

The high land affords some spectacular views of London and outlying areas – most rewarding at sunrise and dusk. Larger homes are usually found on the higher ground, the legacy of the affluent Victorian suburb that the Crystal Palace brought into being, but there are also some sensitive council-built developments, chiefly on **Central Hill**.

The northernmost, and most inner-London, neighbourhood is West Norwood, with a shopping street running N towards Tulse Hill, a rail station and the unusual combination of church and cemetery at its urban centre. Its outer reaches, W towards neighbouring Streatham and E towards Dulwich, are more popular.

Gipsy Hill, on the W side of the commanding Crystal Palace heights, has some attractive Georgian homes – building began in 1806 – and startling views of the City. Its centre, near the **South Croxted Rd** and Dulwich Wood Park roundabout, has an attractive character largely untypical of the area. It too has a rail station. The SE19 area as a whole is particularly suitable for families, with some good state schools and reasonably priced 3-bed houses.

Upper Norwood is in Croydon Borough: as high as its name implies. The houses slope on S and W towards Norbury, which is a southern outlier of Streatham, and Thornton Heath, like Norbury with a station, borders on Croydon.

Upper Norwood

Church Rd is the local high street: it has declined in the last few years, and in an attempt to revive it landlords are being encouraged (nay, bribed) by the council to rent or sell empty shops. There are grants to smarten up shop-fronts, and talk of a one-way system at the 'triangle' at the S end of the road to improve life for shoppers. The scheme is part of the bigger Crystal Palace Partnership, a consortium made up of the local boroughs which uses government money to boost the area. The partnership has also bid for Home Office funding to install CCTV in the town centre – a decision is expected this year. In the longer term, there are hopes that the Croydon Tramlink may be persuaded to climb the hill from South Norwood.

The N end of **Beulah Hill** starts modestly with a 1930s parade of shops, then a large church and St Joseph's College. Victorian semis occupy the left side, '60s town-houses the right. As the road ascends to leafier heights, these give way to large 1930s semis and detached homes, some in mock-Tudor style. Interesting buildings make an appearance, like No 17, an 1860 villa, and there's opportunity for sweeping views. St Valery is an impressive Victorian mansion with full-height bay windows. Set away from the road are walled-off groups of 1960s town-houses on sites of demolished Victorian mansions: the maps show these developments as closes and crescents. On the right, Beulah Spa pub. More large, detached '30s Tudor-timber style and Victorian properties complete the road. Some homes here (and in Woodfield Close) can command high prices. On **Beulah Hill** itself, Dickens Wood, eight new detached houses luxuriating in a 2.4-acre site, sold in 1999 at prices up to £550,000.

Spa Hill, running S from **Beulah Hill**, fringes The Lawns, a park and surviving pocket of woodland, site of the ill-fated spa. A cottage-style lodge by Decimus Burton also survives. Detached inter-war houses with garages climb **Spa Hill**.

Early 19th-century All Saints, with rural churchyard, stands on the corner of **Beulah Hill** and **Church Rd**. By night the spire, which before the advent of the nearby TV masts dominated the skyline, is illuminated. Opposite, a big old house & outbuildings on 1.6 acres in the shadow of the TV mast, called Beaulieu Heights and 226 **South Norwood Hill**, is for sale by Croydon Council with 'potential for a range of uses.' **Church Rd** has some 1930s semis, council blocks, Victorian red-brick mansions and a school. Again, closes and curvy roads lead to 20th century replacements for the Victorian villas. The latest is a new development of 4-bed houses in Turkey Oak Close. Homes in this quiet cul-de-sac fetch £275,000 plus. **Old Vicarage Gardens**, a luxury-level enclave of 1- and 2-bed retirement apartments in garden setting, is off Church Rd on the right. Despite all the in-filling, some of the houses date from the early 19th century. The stucco of the 19th-century Queen's Hotel, which was visited by all the notables of the Victorian age, has gained a modern annexe. The road continues on past the Westow Hill 'Triangle' as far as Crystal Palace (see chapter for more details).

Roads off to the N of **Beulah Hill** are mainly 1930s residential. (There's an absence of shops that go to make a community.) **Hermitage Rd** has 1930s semis and council houses. Larger '30s semis in **Eversley Rd** front a pleasant green. **Ryefield Rd** has recent town-houses. **Harold Rd** gives its name to a conservation area that includes many fine late-19th-century houses. This takes in **Bedwardine Rd**, part of **Central Hill**, **Gatestone Rd**, **South Vale** – whose 1860s houses are about the area's oldest – **Vermont Rd** and the recreation ground. The council (in this case Croydon) has issued guidelines for home-owners and would-be developers here: demolition of period buildings, or hiving off large gardens, will not meet with approval.

Central Hill has Norwood Park and the imposing Gothic-style Fidelis convent. Further up the hill there's a post-war council estate as well as recent terraced town-houses. Also large Victorian houses – some in multiple occupancy. Roads to the S such as **Essex Grove** and **Gatestone Rd** slope down attractively with Victorian semis. Victorian detached and semis overlook the vast, but carefully crafted, hillside Central Hill Estate to the N. Next to the council estate is Gipsy Hill police station.

Gipsy Hill

Proximity to the **Westow Hill** 'Triangle' with its shops and amenities (see Crystal Palace) is a bonus for **Gipsy Hill**, a popular neighbourhood that tumbles attractively down the slopes from the road of the same name. Some Georgiana survives here, and even humdrum homes are made special if they share the wonderfully long views. It borders West Dulwich to the N, and usefully it is in fare zone 3. It is not peppered with new developments: developers have a hard time competing with the room sizes and lower service charges that period conversions offer. Large single homes are hunted out by professional couples, often wanting space either to work from home or to keep a nanny if they commute in to town.

There's a magnificent view of London, with City skyscrapers prominent, from **Gipsy Hill**, the road. Highlights of this busy road are the white stuccoed buildings and red-brick Victorian mansions. Roads leading off such as **Camden Hill Rd** and **Highland Rd** have period houses. Several homes in Camden Hill Rd were being smartened up last winter. In **Highland Rd** is Highland Court, several blocks of 1930s flats with private parking. This private estate in a wooded setting has a new block with balconies facing **Gipsy Hill Rd**. Christ Church has been happily restored in the past few years. Past the station is a small green.

The Paxton pub, shops, restaurants and a wine bar make an attractive start to **Gipsy Rd**. Renovation characterizes this gently rising road of varied Victorian properties, which ends with council-built estates. Near Kingswood Primary School is **Salters Hill** – a road of council homes with occasional Victoriana, which overlooks

W

Norwood Park. The large-scale Victorian villas to be found in Gipsy Hill yield some serious-sized flats: the wide-eaved, 3-storey houses in (aptly) **Victoria Crescent**, for example. Here, too, there's a late-20th-century option: New Green Place with its 3-storey blocks of flats behind iron entrance gates.

West Norwood

Between Streatham and West Dulwich, West Norwood has good bus as well as train links to Brixton (with its Victoria Line tube) and the West End.

On the West Dulwich border, tree-lined **South Croxted Rd** has Victorian semis, 1960s town-houses and some council estates. There's a shopping area on the junction with **Park Hall Rd**. This neighbourhood saw much change in the 1980s as developers and new residents moved into the area.

At the centre of the neighbourhood, **Norwood Rd**, also called **The Broadway**, is Victorian red-brick. The road forks by St Luke's Church with its Corinthian six-column portico. There's a modern library next to the 39-acre West Norwood Cemetery of 1836. A recent change in the road layout, to improve traffic flow, means the triangle of **Norwood High St**, **Ernest Avenue** and **Knights Hill** now makes up a large roundabout.

In the cosmopolitan streets around West Norwood station (Victoria 18 min) good-quality Victorian houses can be found at reasonable prices. The E fork off **Norwood Rd** becomes **Norwood High St** which has few shops and is low-rise. **Dunelm Grove** is an attractive, modern cottage-style council estate. **Elder Rd,** the continuation of the **High St,** starts off with ugly grey council blocks but improves. There are 1930s semis with nicely tended gardens. **Eylewood Rd** and **Norwood Park Rd** have '30s terraces and semis respectively. There's a concentration of high-rise council blocks up by **Bentons Rise** and **Aubyn Hill**. Facing Norwood Park (tennis courts) in **Elder Rd**, what was the House of Industry for the Infant Poor is now flats. Behind this splendid piece of Georgiana Portland Homes have also added mewsy flats and houses in **Elderwood Place.** Next door is Norwood School. **Knights Hill**, which runs S from West Norwood station, is Victorian and untidy. Promisingly-named Rothschild Avenue is at present an unprepossessing mix of industry and derelict land. However builders Fairview have bulldozed Lambeth College and are planning flats and 3-/4-bed town-houses.

Popular **Lancaster Avenue**, off **Norwood Rd**, has family-owned Victorian houses with pleasant front gardens. Rosemead Mixed Preparatory School is at the West Dulwich end. **Hawkley Gardens** has town-house terraces. **Lavengrove** and **Tulsmere Rds** have turn-of-the-century bay-fronted terraces. **Chatsworth Way** is mainly Victorian and has a modern church with a needle-like spire. A housing association has just finished building 2-bed flats and houses at the High St end. **Idmiston Rd** has Victorian houses with fancy wrought-iron balconies. The turreted red-brick Barston Towers graces the corner with **Barston Rd.** The road ends modestly with Victorian terraces. **Chancellor Grove** is similar. **Rosendale Rd**, with large Victorian bay-fronted semis, is broad and tree-lined S of **Thurlow Park Rd** – the South Circular. A parade of shops and an unattractive council block are other features. Continuing after **Park Hall Rd** are tall bay-fronted balconied Victorian properties, some flat conversions.

Tritton Rd has Victorian semis. On the corner with **Martell Rd** is Lambeth Industrial Enterprises. Also in **Martell Rd** is the ugly '30s white Park Hall Rd Trading Estate building. The larger Victorian semis offer flats. The high wall and cast-iron railings of the cemetery occupy the S of **Robson Rd** to West Norwood, but the cottagy Victorian terraces on the N side are, say agents, popular. The lack of land means new homes can spring up on the smallest of sites. A good example is the development of flats in **Bloom Grove** which fit neatly between a row of Victorian mansions.

West of **Norwood Rd**, council houses and blocks start **York Hill**. Knollys Rd, 1930s terraces, Victorian and recent blocks, has been the scene of much renovation.

Pyrmont Grove and Royal Circus have quite pleasant Victorian terraces. The entrance to a recent new development is in Lansdowne Hill. Broxholm Rd and Glennie Rd are terraced – Edwardian and '30s. There's a bustling weekday market at the bottom of Lansdowne Hill. Larger properties are found at the higher points of these hill roads. Canterbury Grove has large Victorian and turn-of-century semis; also council, 1930s, Victorian and recent terraces, including 1960s Yeoman Close. Thirties semis are found in Uffington Rd and Rockhampton Rd. Thurlestone Rd and Wolfington Rd are Victorian/turn-of-the-century. St Julian's Farm Rd goes from 1930s semis and Victorian/turn-of-the-century to smaller properties lower down – a very popular street, due in part to its proximity to a good primary school. A striking modern block of 10 flats on Casewick Rd is built in white brick with a lighthouse-style turret.

Quiet pre-war suburbia includes Lamberhurst Rd (bay-fronted semis), Cheviot Rd and Greenhurst Rd (terraces), and Roxburgh Rd (semis). Near the Knights Hill end, Lakeview Rd and Truslove Rd have large areas of council homes, with a lot of upgrading going on.

Leigham Court Rd on the Streatham borders has 1930s mansion blocks and private blocks of flats – built high for the views, also '30s semis. Groveside Homes was responsible for the sympathetic studio, 1-bed flats, and 2-bed town-houses in Fawcett Rd. St Julian's Primary School features, too. Victorian detached houses and imposing red-brick mansions precede Fern Lodge council estate, just improved, and a weathered '30s block before ending at Streatham Common N.

Norbury

The rise in prices in this neighbourhood which began in 1997 has continued. More families are moving into Norbury, particularly from areas like Streatham and Tooting. Norbury is seen as more up-market than Thornton Heath. Ex-council property, mainly houses, has become increasingly available around here.

London Rd's dull aspect is emphasized by the Victoriana. Shopping is unexciting, but provides most things necessary for day-to-day living. Large offices, including the headquarters of Wates, signal the approach to Croydon. Most of the area was developed between the wars, and roads such as Ardfern Avenue, Melrose Avenue, Ederline Avenue and Dunbar Avenue set the tone. Property to the E of London Rd is more sought-after than that in the streets towards the Mitcham border. Gibsons Hill, Norbury Hill and Virginia Rd are of the same period. That they look to the wooded areas of Beulah Hill helps to relieve the monotony. Kensington Avenue also has a post-war council estate. To the W of London Rd, the Pollards Hill area is attractive suburbia – neat greens and trimmed hedges. Detached 1930s houses encircle the small common at the summit. 1997 saw the conversion of the area's gem: Norwood Grove Mansion stands amid parkland off Gibsons Hill on the site of a Charles II hunting box. Its hilltop views are now shared by three new flats.

Croydon Borders: Thornton Heath

In this area W of South Norwood, first-time buyers find affordable purpose-built and conversion flats; families find a range of late-Victorian and Edwardian terraces and inter-war semis. This area has yet, however, to attract much attention from outsiders.

Suburban Thornton Heath is very much a 19th-century creation spurred on by the arrival of the railway. Good rail links to town and proximity to Croydon continue as chief attractions. The more expensive homes are found in the upper reaches towards Norbury – in roads such as Florida, Maryland, Georgia and Carolina.

Popular, too, are the 3-bed houses in and around quiet Winterbourne Rd – 1930s bay-fronted terraces. Closeness to local schools and shopping facilities in London Rd are advantages here. Larger and older homes are found in Warwick Rd. Flat-hunters

W

should concentrate on **Mersham, Moffat, Hythe, St Paul's** and **Liverpool Rds** – mostly 1- or 2-beds – while families may have better luck in the area towards Mitcham. Busy **London Rd** and **Brigstock Rd** are worth investigation – especially for conversions. The Mayday Hospital dominates the lower half of **London Rd**. The less popular roads S of the **High St (Ecclesbourne Rd, Kynaston Avenue, Bensham Lane)** comprise former council houses and also older-style terraces.

Roads around the Crystal Palace Football Ground in **Whitehorse Lane** are best avoided – although, more usefully, there's a large Sainsbury's superstore here too. The influx of football fans has an influence on house prices nearby. St Cuthberts, between **Whitehorse Lane** and **Ross Rd**, is a 1988/89 clutch of flats and town-houses.

Transport	Trains: West Norwood, Gipsy Hill and Norbury to Victoria; West Norwood and Gipsy Hill to London Bridge.
Convenient for	Crystal Palace Park, National Sports Centre. Routes to the South. Miles from centre: 5.5.
Schools	Local Authority: Harris City Technical College, Stanley Tech, Selhurst High (b), Westwood Girls High. Grant-maintained: St Joseph's College RC (b), Norbury Manor (g), Virgo Fidelis RC (g).

SALES

Flats	S	1B	2B	3B	4B	5B
Average prices	45–60	55–80	90–120	130–160	–	–
Houses	2B	3B	4B	5B	6/7B	8B
Average prices	110–130	130–190	210–300	250–400	280+	300+→

RENTAL

Flats	S	1B	2B	3B	4B	5B
Average prices	95–122	115–150	138–230	175–250	275–575	–
Houses	2B	3B	4B	5B	6/7B	8B
Average prices	138–200	200–300	200–325	220–415	275–415	415+

The properties	Popular Victorian/Edwardian homes are the staple. Larger Victorian houses have become flats, and there are plenty of family homes with good gardens: Victorian, semis, '60s town-houses, '30s Tudor. On Gipsy Hill, mansion and p/b flats. Upper Norwood has mainly flats, while Thornton Heath/S Norwood is good hunting-ground for smaller houses at bargain prices.
The market	First-time buyers find relatively inexpensive flats, good rail links to town, while families come in search of more home for their money. Searches: Croydon 27 working days, Lambeth 10 working days, Southwark 15 working days.

Among those estate agents active in this area are:

- Galloways
- Nicholas Ashley
- Winkworth *
- Harvey & Wheeler
- Norwood Accom.
- Volker & Volker
- Lynx
- Stapleton Long
- Wates
- K & O Properties
- Kinleigh Folkard & Hayward

further details: see advertisers' index on p671

W

WILLESDEN AND BRONDESBURY PARK

Map ref: p42 (6E)
Postal districts: NW6,
 NW10, NW2
Boroughs: Brent (Lab)
Council tax: Band D £678
Conservation areas:
 Mapesbury estate,
 Willesden and Harlesden
 town centres
Parking: Free off main roads

Willesden is the old lady of NW London suburbs, a faded beauty who is still recovering from the indignity suffered in 1965 when she was amalgamated with Wembley to form the Borough of Brent — notorious in the 1980s for its 'loony-left' council, now in somewhat calmer waters under 'New' Labour.

However, her bone structure is good, and her horizons are broadening: the nearest major station is Paddington – from whence Heathrow is now reached in 15 min – and she's on the Jubilee Line: already a good route, it now wafts her inhabitants direct to Westminster, Canary Wharf and even The Dome. Some of the neighbours are nice, too; she's a stone's throw from West Hampstead.

Pockets of tree-lined Willesden are still elegant, and neighbouring Brondesbury Park is a *very* acceptable address. Willesden and Brondesbury Park cover three postal districts. In order of desirability, NW6 is the most prestigious and covers Brondesbury Park; then comes NW2 and the part of Willesden towards Cricklewood and Dollis Hill; and finally NW10 where the area merges with less-classy Harlesden and Neasden. A number of railway lines carve up the area; prices can differ considerably from one end of a road to the other, from one side to the other. Grand houses stand in close contrast to council blocks; most properties are Edwardian or 1930s. The Mapesbury estate and Brondesbury Park in particular attract buyers who would until recently have tried for better-established areas close by, such as West Hampstead and Maida Vale.

When it comes to amenities Willesden has plenty to offer. A huge library complex with public halls, cinema, a café-bar and a bookshop was opened in 1989 on the corner of **Willesden High Rd** and **Grange Rd**; there is even talk of squeezing in the

W

borough's local history museum. Willesden Sports Centre, fronting **All Souls Avenue**, has swimming pools, an impressive sportsground, well-maintained children's play-area and open space to wander in.

The shops, centred around **Willesden High Rd**, are good; they tend to be local, rather than of the big-name variety (though there is a Somerfield supermarket) but most of them are small and specialized, where shopkeepers remember a regular face, and in many cases open late in the evening. Amid the hardware and grocers' shops are a number of restaurants catering for the younger inhabitants who dwell in the many flat conversions around Willesden Green – among them a trendy tapas bar and one of the country's first vegetarian Indian restaurants, popular with minor celebrities, the odd Hollywood star and the area's MP: will Willesden supply London's first mayor? Ken Livingstone certainly hopes so.

Willesden

Willesden was given to the Dean and Chapter of St Paul's Cathedral by King Athelstan in 938 – hence names like **Chapter Rd**. A visit to the local archive, in **Olive Rd**, will furnish more details. The area is more compact than sprawling Willesden Green; Church End is to the W; **Robson Avenue**, falling between Roundwood Park and Willesden Sports Centre, marks the E divide with Willesden Green, and the Jubilee line is at the top. Much is green, open space: Roundwood Park, schools/sports fields – and the expanse of the New and Jewish Cemeteries. The part of **Willesden High Rd** in the Willesden area is rather shabbier than the section towards Willesden Green, but the small shops are varied. Homes include the occasional small development such as the mid-'90s 1-bed flats in **Beaconsfield Rd** which sell for around £75,000.

Willesden Green and Mapesbury

Willesden Green used to be a place where well-established Jewish families lived until they moved to leafy suburbs such as Wembley and Stanmore. In recent years the ethnic and religious make-up has broadened, and parts became conversion territory in the 1980s, with houses sub-divided into flats. Houses tend to be larger in Willesden Green than in Willesden, and prices have increased steadily here according to the estate agents whose boards make Willesden red, yellow and pink as well as Green. The general rule of thumb is that the closer you are to Willesden Green station (Jubilee Line), the better – although the best area, the Mapesbury estate which boasts large, half a million pound-plus houses, breaks this rule.

The Mapesbury estate consists of the roads in the triangle formed by **Chichele Rd/Walm Lane**, the A5 (known at this point as **Shoot Up Hill**) and **Willesden Lane** (though note that the conservation area is slightly smaller – from **Anson Rd** to the tube line – while the active residents' association counts in roads across **Walm Lane** as far as **Riffel Rd**). This is the West Hampstead overspill, and residents would love Kilburn tube re-named – at least as North Kilburn, if not Mapesbury. **Mapesbury Rd**, **Dartmouth Rd**, **Teignmouth Rd** and **Chatsworth Rd** are names to look out for if you want a well-located conversion in a stylish Victorian property. Or, indeed, a 4-bed house (expect to pay £400,000). There are less conventional flats, too: the old Baptist Church on the corner of **Anson Rd** and **Sneyd Rd** is now 14 homes 'with lots of odd-shaped rooms': 1-beds from £150,000 and 2-beds from £210,000.

The 1980s mania for splitting houses into flats fell out of favour with planners; the fashionable '90s equivalent, the conversion of redundant commercial or industrial buildings, is evidenced by Jubilee Heights, on **Shoot Up Hill**, at the SE border of the Mapesbury estate. Here Dari Construction in 1988 converted Telephone House into 77 flats with all the luxurious accessories: swimming pool, gym, Jacuzzi and 24hr porterage. These now change hands for £120,000 for a 1-bed, £200,000 for a 2-bed.

W

Behind Jubilee Heights in **Exeter Rd**, another new development added 30 new homes to the neighbourhood's stock in 1999: Cedar Lodge's 2-bed, 2-bath town-houses are now valued at £220–240,000. On the southern borders, in **Cavendish Rd**, Wilcon Homes have just finished another scheme: four blocks of nine flats; the 1- and 2-bed flats of Chatsworth Court are re-selling for up to £135,000. Cavendish runs by the tracks, but has the advantage of Brondesbury train station at the far end.

Out of the estate, on the other side of **Walm Lane, St Paul's Avenue** and **Blenheim Gardens** are also popular with flat-hunters thanks to adjacent Willesden Green tube. On **Walm Lane**, Rutland Park Mansions – once known as the biggest squat in London – was refurbished in 1996 by Paddington Churches Housing Association as flats. On the corner of **Walm** and **Willesden Lanes**, Rialto have built Mapes Hill Place, a development of flats and town-houses which resell for up to £95,000 for the 1- and 2-bed flats, and up to £120,000 for the 2-bed town-houses.

Other prestige roads in Willesden Green are found S of **Willesden High Rd** in the Dobree estate, built in the 1930s: **Dobree Avenue, Bryan Avenue, Rowdon Avenue, Alexander Avenue** and **Peter Avenue**. The estate did not, alas, prove lucky for its builders: two brothers went bankrupt and were forced to sell off the commodious homes they had created as a job lot. It is still possible to buy undone-up homes here, and prices vary with the condition.

The 'royal roads', which lie N of **Willesden High Rd**, are also popular and should satisfy a tighter budget; roads like **Sandringham Rd, Balmoral Rd** and **Windsor Rd** fall between Dollis Hill and Willesden Green tube stations. You might have to find £250,000 for a smartened-up 3-bed terraced house, with less tidy ones from £200,000. A 1-bed flat might be £115,000. Prices vary a good deal hereabouts. A 2-bed flat could cost twice as much on the Mapesbury estate as on the 'wrong side' – ie, backing onto the tracks – in **Chapter Rd**. To the N, Willesden Green becomes Cricklewood, and prices go down again.

All Souls Avenue (the Oxford college was a major landowner in the area) runs N–S through Willesden Green and has small semi-detached houses. At the N end lies Clarendon Court, a big '30s block on the corner of **Chamberlayne Rd** and **Sidmouth Rd**. **Sidmouth Rd** itself is a busy road, home of the South Hampstead bowls and tennis club.

Spreading down towards Kensal Rise, the triangular grid of peaceful, orderly roads that fans out between **All Souls Avenue** and **Chamberlayne Rd** is disturbed by **Chelmsford Square**, a charming oval of semi-detached homes around tennis courts. More modest, pretty streets are to be found in this direction.

Willesden Lane, a main thoroughfare connecting Willesden and Kilburn, has a wide variety of purpose-built blocks, among them Marlow, Belvedere, Beechworth, Bramerton and Hadleigh Courts – the last consisting of eight flats built in 1987. Again agents warn of high service charges in some blocks – but the enticement of secure parking is irresistible to many. A new block of flats, with 20 1-beds, 8 2-beds and 2 penthouses, will be on the market this June at prices yet to be set. Down towards the **Willesden High Rd** end, Paddington Churches Housing Association have contributed Sheil Court, an attractive development of flats. The Willesdenites are spiritual people: a Hindu temple and a Jewish school are to be found on the Lane, while **Walm Lane** has a church, a synagogue and a mosque, and **Chichele Rd** an Islamic youth centre. The Willesden Registry Office is also in **Willesden Lane**: it sees a great variety of marriages.

Brondesbury Park

Brondesbury Park is more exclusive than Willesden Green. Like Willesden Green, the district used to be very Jewish; both areas have witnessed a move away. The population is now far more mixed. Houses date from the 1930s or later; the roads are wide and tree-lined, and parking is not as problematic as in West Hampstead and Swiss Cottage. Communications are good, the A5 and Kilburn tube (Jubilee line) providing access to the West End.

Manor House Drive, off **Brondesbury Park**, is a beautiful crescent, the best road in the area. Many of its detached houses are double-fronted, all have front and back gardens, many with security gates. Six-bed properties complete with swimming pools along **Christchurch Avenue** and **The Avenue** can now expect to sell for at least £750,000, and a 4-bed unmodernized Christchurch house sold for £600,000 at auction last August. Agents claim that these are mostly owned by foreign governments and are used by diplomats from areas as far-flung as China and Nigeria. **Christchurch Avenue, Cavendish Rd** and **The Avenue** also have very attractive conversions in large Victorian houses. **Aylestone Avenue** is a wide tree-lined street with both detached and semi-detached family houses. Christ Church itself became flats (and a small chapel) in the 1980s in an imaginative conversion.

Brondesbury Park (the road) has seen changes; some of the large detached houses here have been converted into flats and purpose-built blocks have been built. Also in **Brondesbury Park** is one of the most substantial developments in the area: the Honeyman Close scheme of 40-odd town-houses and a leisure complex. The 4-bed, 2-bath houses are decorated in the spirit of the Arts and Crafts designer Charles Rennie Mackintosh. At the end of the road towards **Willesden High Rd** the Heathfield Squash Club, next to a synagogue, was recently redeveloped as 1- and 2-bed housing association retirement homes. On the corner of **Brondesbury Park** and **Coverdale Rd**, Wates has put up Kingsbridge and Westwood Courts, two blocks of 2-bed flats. A third was completed in 1998.

Parts of Brondesbury Park are very expensive, but a house with a garden may still be bought for the sort of money that buys a flat in Maida Vale.

Harlesden

Harlesden was once avoided and the Craven Park estate feared as a blight on resell. But things are gradually changing for the better. Harlesden has some lovely houses, Edwardian and Victorian, most with their original features intact. With an improved Bakerloo Line service, and despite some spectacular crime stories in the papers, the area's potential is becoming evident. The town centre has been improved with funds supplied by a government regeneration fund and new people are moving in. These include young City workers and people taking advantage of housing association 'affordable rents' and shared-ownership deals.

The better Harlesden roads are **Springwell Avenue, Harlesden Gardens, Ancona Rd** and **Cholmondeley Avenue**, and parts are described by agents as 'Kensal Rise Borders' to entice Ladbrook Grove trendies. Harlesden prices are the lowest in this area, but have risen steadily. A 3-bed Victorian terraced house in Crownhill Rd was £165,000 last winter. A Fairview scheme of studio and 1-bed flats in **Trenmar Gardens** has proved popular. Affordable-rent 1- and 2-bed flats have been converted from an old pub on the corner of **Harlesden High Road** and **Scrubs Lane**.

Brent Council hopes to attract more City workers and commuters to the area with a £2 million revamp of the run-down Willesden Junction train station, in partnership with Railtrack and Silverlink. Work has started, and rubbish cleared up after a local newspaper campaign. The work will also improve access to the bus terminal. The council's more ambitious dreams envisage the Junction becoming a major staging-post on an outer-London rail service that would see many more trains on the route down through Olympia to Clapham Junction, and could be extended round to East London. This would be helped by a proposed new station to serve the major West

London shopping centre planned near the BBC's White City HQ at Shepherd's Bush, the one just opened at West Brompton, and a third promised on the Chelsea-Fulham border at Chelsea Harbour. Indeed, this West London Line could go from nowhere to somewhere. . . Watch this space.

Transport Tubes: Willesden Green, Kilburn, Dollis Hill (zones 2/3, Jubilee). From Willesden Green: Oxford Circus 25 min (1 change), City 35 min (1 change), Heathrow 1 hr 10 min (1 change). Trains: Brondesbury, Brondesbury Park, Kensal Rise (N London Line/Silverlink & West London Line).

Convenient for North Circular and Edgware Rds. Miles from centre: 5.

Schools Brent Education Authority: Willesden High, Cardinal Hinsley RC (b), Convent of Jesus & Mary Language College (g), Private: N W London Jewish.

SALES

Flats

	S	1B	2B	3B	4B	5B
Average prices	80–100	80–140	95–200	120–300	240–500	350+

Houses

	2B	3B	4B	5B	6/7B	8B
Average prices	120–140	125–260	250–350	350+	500+	550+

RENTAL

Flats

	S	1B	2B	3B	4B	5B
Average prices	100–720	150–210	180–250	225–330	300–400	350–450

Houses

	2B	3B	4B	5B	6/7B	8B
Average prices	180–260	300–360	350–370	500+	600+	1000+

The properties Large blocks of flats, late-Victorian villas, plus many streets of terraced homes and later semis. Some larger 20th-century homes. Brondesbury Park has some big, imposing late-Victorian houses.

The market Willesden Green's fast tube attracts young flat-buyers. Elsewhere still a family neighbourhood – not to mention a celebrity one: £800,000-plus mansions in best roads. Developers turn redundant Telecom offices into marbled and mahoganied flats. Local searches: Brent 5–10 days.

Among those estate agents active in this area are:
- Dunlop & Co
- Ellis & Co
- Haart
- Simon Lewis & Co
- Gladstones
- Chattin Estates
- Camerons Stiff
- Bairstow Eves
- Rainbow Reid
- Beavers
- Camerons
- Empire Estates

W

WIMBLEDON, RAYNES PARK AND MERTON PARK

Map ref: p107 (6H)
Postal districts: SW19,
   SW20
Boroughs: Merton (Lab)
Council tax: Band D
   £866
Conservation areas:
   Include common,
   village, Ridgway,
   Merton Park,
   W Wimbledon
Parking: Meters in centre
   and several residents'
   parking schemes

For 11 months of the year peaceful, leafy Wimbledon is a self-possessed, splendid, south-west London suburb, enjoying the illusion of being a country town manqué with its charming old village centre, the vast common and the busy bustle of **The Broadway** end with its high-street shops and station, both main line and underground – plus, from this spring, trams. In the twelfth month, there's tennis.

It lasts for a mere fortnight, but for the duration of the international tennis tournament, Wimbledon's fame reaches global proportions. The press, royalty and the sport's superstars arrive, police re-direct the traffic, residents as far away as neighbouring Southfields find no-parking cones outside their houses or – if in unrestricted streets – that people have parked across their entrance drives. A general state somewhere between carnival and seige prevails. But, almost as soon as the last cries of 'Henman' have died away, the town – despite the film and theatre folk who have found year-round homes here – resumes its sedate, well-heeled, well-ordered SW19 life, a place with considerably more to offer than sport.

This London suburb is only 9 miles from Charing Cross, but maintains a rural charm with its 1,100-acre common which stretches to Putney Vale. It was much loved by William Wilberforce and by William Pitt, who said it saved his sanity. For centuries the common was used for cattle grazing, duelling, archery and rifle practice. Today it is patrolled by rangers and is a haven for joggers, horse riders, ramblers, golfers, dog walkers, cyclists and nature lovers – the trees and scrub harbour more than 60 species of birds as well as squirrels, badgers, rabbits, foxes, weasels and natterjack toads. One of its noted attractions is the restored Windmill, now a museum. Not surprisingly, houses bordering this semi-wooded expanse (mainly mansions built by Victorian merchants) and luxurious modern flats with views across the common, command the area's highest – indeed, astronomical – prices. Competing with the loyal, long-time locals (the place hops with local societies and residents' associations) are international families who look here for good-sized homes a fast train-ride from town.

Town Centre/South Wimbledon

There is still a great divide in property prices between 'up the hill' (common, Parkside and the original village) and 'down the hill' (**The Broadway**), which takes in the main shopping centre and station serving up both trains and the District Line tube. But this 'lower' area, which also includes the Wimbledon Theatre (Victorian) and the famous Polka Children's Theatre, a hotel and several restaurants, has become increasingly fashionable and far from cheap.

This 'New' Wimbledon grew up around the railway in the 1850s, when housing was built for those working for carriage-folk up the hill. Today, this part of Wimbledon is home to commuters keen to be within walking distance of the station with its fast trains to Waterloo. Its heart has been largely redeveloped as a shopping/offices centre, with everything a small town needs. The smart (and just revamped) shopping mall – called, naturally, Centre Court – runs alongside the station. This houses a variety of shops and Tesco Metro are planning to develop the Old Town Hall area of the shopping centre. Across the road, which has been narrowed to enhance the pedestrians' environment (or improve their chances) there's a new record store and a bookshop/cafe, and a new Safeway is imminent. Furture plans include a cinema and bowling alley – and a town square. W of the station is Wimbledon's own department store, Ely's, a Sainsbury's and sundry car parks; across **Worple Rd** is a 1998 development of 1-bed (c. £180,000) and 2-bed (c. £265,000) flats and a health club.

East of the town centre, **Queens Rd** has mainly solid older-type semis, 3/4-bed, with large gardens, and joins **Haydons Rd** to South Wimbledon. Running parallel, **King's Rd** contains 4-bed double-fronted Edwardian houses, some facing South Park Gardens. (This corner is referred to as South Park.) At the junction of **Trinity Rd** and **South Park Rd**, Nairn Court is 23 flats with parking spaces in secluded courtyard. Meade Park off **Haydons Rd** offers 1- and 2-bed flats and a few houses.

The streets in this corner between **The Broadway** and **Haydons Rd** – including **Evelyn Rd** and **Ashley Rd**, which are typical – have 2- and 3-bed terraced homes with small gardens. A 2-bed house within reach of the station might be £275,000. Roads S of the busy **Broadway** are quiet, residential and handy for the station. This used to be bargain corner for first-time buyers, but no more: 4-bed houses in **Pelham Rd** are now £500,000. A red-brick school building in this street was converted into 28 flats and two penthouses, with 64 new flats on the old playground. In a quiet cul-de-sac off **Hartfield Rd** is Hartfield Court, with two large modern 5/6-bed, 2-bath houses with garage and garden. New homes here are more likely to be flats: just opposite the station at the N end of **Hartfield Rd** there are 2-bed flats from £265,000 and 3-beds at £310,000. Round in **Hartfield Crescent**, 'Cascades' sold at similar prices.

Across the tracks, going up **Wimbledon Hill Rd** ('The Hill') from the station, five 1990s 3-bed, 2-bath houses with integral garages and gardens appeared in a quiet cul-de-sac in **St George's Rd**. The road is lined with mansion flats – some '30s, some brand-new but in retro style: The Hollies has 2-bed, 2-bath flats which fetch £280,000; Aspen Lodge has 2-beds at £260–310,000.

Alwynne Rd and **Compton Rd**, close to the library in the town centre, hold solid '30s semis with gardens. Wimbledon Girls' High School is on the left, and to the right are terraced town-houses. Higher left is **Draxmont Approach** (luxury balconied flats); right, **Belvedere Drive**, with large houses and the 'Bluegates' estate.

Wimbledon Village

The **High St** begins at the top of the hill and runs through the village, still Georgian in feel. Smart (they used to be quaint) shops on either side sell high fashion, luxury gifts and interior-designer services. There are restaurants, bars and two historic pubs – the Rose & Crown, where the poet Swinburne drank, and the Dog & Fox; the village riding school is at the rear. Many charming artisan cottages – lovingly renovated, expensive, no room to park – lie off **Church Rd**, **Belvedere Square** and **Lancaster Place**. Opposite, tucked behind new shops, is **Haygarth Place** (24 red-brick, 4-bed terraced town-houses, underground car park; plus four original cottages, modernized, with car space). At the approach to the village, off **Belvedere Grove**, are three new 3-bed mews town-houses in a former car park backing onto the National Westminster Bank.

Every inch of the village has been utilized: the last major site, behind historic Eagle House (1613), provided 14 luxury private houses – three of which front onto **Marryat Rd**. The Malt House and the cottage/coach house were also converted.

The Common

At the War Memorial a left turn takes you towards **Southside Common**: here pretty Victorian villas face out over the greenery in the first of a clutch of streets that run out into this corner of the common. **West Side Common** strikes out across the grass towards the furthest-flung, **North View**, past Chester House (Georgian), some 1930s houses and a cul-de-sac of council-built homes (about half, unsurprisingly, owner-occupied: they sell for £250,000). Stately Cannizaro House is now a luxury hotel; its magnificent gardens are open to the public, with an open-air theatre in the old herb garden. Two 18th-century mansions, The Keir and Stamford House – split into flats – both gaze out across the common. **North View**, **Camp View** and **West Place** form a square of tall red-brick Victorian houses surrounded by common and golf course. Along **Camp Rd**, popular **Eversley Park** (Octagon Developments) is set in a landscaped garden; nearby a charming cottage, once the dairy for Camp Farm, sold for £650,000 in 1998 and is now reckoned to be £750–800,000.

From **Southside Common** long tree-lined roads run down to **The Ridgway**: homes in **Lingfield Rd**, **The Grange**, **Murray Rd**, **Lauriston Rd** and **Clifton Rd** are a mixture of styles, mostly Victorian; many reverse conversions here, with houses which had been poorly split into flats from the '50s onwards reverting to single-family homes. On the other hand, No 11 **The Grange** has been converted into eight prestige apartments with rear parking and mature garden. In **Lingfield Rd**, which runs parallel to the **High St**, Michael Shanly homes mirrored the Victorian style with Brackenbury Lodge, a double-fronted gabled house that contains six flats. At **Woodhayes Rd** is **Peregrine Way**, a modern development of detached Colonial-style 4-bed houses among mature trees.

This corner also provides some exceptionally large mansions: in the millions, if they come up for sale. Eight new ones are being added, in questionable if grand taste, in Kinsella Gardens next to the golf course: £1.5 million. All the coveted houses and flats here are within walking distance of King's College Boys' School. Opposite, across little **Crooked Billet** green, stand the delightful old Crooked Billet and Hand in Hand pubs, surrounded by tiny, former farm labourers' cottages which change hands for £250,000. Just behind the pubs are some 3-/4-bed houses which go for half a million.

Parkside

Return to **Parkside**, which runs along the E side of the common and leads, eventually, to Putney. With the common on your left, on the right is the enclave of premier roads

(**Marryat Rd, Peek Crescent, Parkside Avenue, Parkside Gardens, Calonne Rd, Somerset Rd, Bathgate Rd** and **Burghley Rd**). These are lined with solid houses of every period over the last 100 years, varying widely in their size and state of luxury. The largest and most opulent top £3 million. There have been several instances of clumsy flat conversions being removed, and the houses returning to single-family occupation. A Parkside house 'with potential for 8 beds' was on the market last winter at £1.95m.

On the corner of **Somerset Rd** and **Parkside**, an enclave of late-'80s flats boast balconies, underground car park, electronic gates. To the E of this favoured group of roads, down the hill, is the All England Tennis Club. Parkside Hospital (private) and the residence of the Apostolic Nuncio (the Papal ambassador's official London home) are also to be found along **Parkside**. Near the Village end is an elegant conversion of a mansion into five flats, with electronic gates and video-screened entrance. **Alfreton Close** is an attractive cul-de-sac of Scandinavian-style family houses in mature woodland. Opposite, in **Windmill Rd** on the site of the Clock House are 12 ultra-luxurious flats with underground parking and resident porter. Nearby **Clockhouse Close**, built on common land, has six luxury detached family houses.

The Putney/Wimbledon border, leafy but dominated by council flats (see the Southfields chapter), is the scene of the largest development in the area. 'Wimbledon Parkside', by Laing, which has been transforming the vast, pleasantly hilly site of the old Southlands College at the junction of **Parkside** and **Queensmere Rd**. This has already resulted in **Southlands Drive**, a rather cramped enclave of Victorian-style houses behind smart railings; a woodland path has been laid out to one side, an unfortunate water feature graces the entrance road. Things then got better: a large, good-looking flats block emerged on the hillside behind these, with its grounds running up to the council houses that run along the leafy ridge; a refurbished listed building now provides flats . . . .. The main part of the site has 2-bed, 2-bath and 3-bed, 2-bath flats in the central, 6-storey apartment blocks, with living rooms in the octagonal corner turrets, all sold. A clutch of town-houses were from £465,000 a year ago: there's a rumour of one on the market at £600,000.

Off **Somerset Rd** is a modern development, Oakfield Estate; Cedar Court is high-density town-houses and flats; Burghley House and Somerset House – tower blocks, some flats with views of the Centre Court – have lift, porterage and underground car park. All these roads suffer an annual invasion (30,000 visitors daily) during the Tennis Fortnight. Oaklands Park in **Bathgate Rd** is a recent clutch of 13 £1.2 million 5-bed houses. **Church Rd** and **Burghley Rd** cross a neighbourhood of more large houses, some of them older than the Parkside ones. Off **Burghley Rd** is St Mary's Parish Church (mentioned in the Domesday Book) leading into **Church Rd** and **Welford Place**, an exclusive private development of terraced town-houses with children's play-area, indoor swimming complex and sauna.

West Wimbledon

The Village is linked to West Wimbledon by **The Ridgway**, Wimbledon's oldest road, running parallel to **Worple Rd** (down the Hill). **Sunnyside**, to the left, has a row of delightful 2-bed cottages with long front gardens but no parking. Then **Ridgway Place**, with a group of houses on both sides built by the Haberdashers' Company in 1860. Further along is a 'villagy' area comprising **Denmark Rd, Thornton Rd** and **Hillside**. There is a row of small shops, two pubs and livery stables here. A 2-bed cottage was £395,000 last winter. **Berkeley Place** and **Ridgway Gardens** are cul-de-sacs with large conversion flats. **Edge Hill**, with its many flats, is popular with Catholics because of nearby Wimbledon College RC Boys' School and Sacred Heart Church. Fourteen flats and two penthouses appeared on the site of the old chapel.

W

The Downs has purpose-built 1930s flats either side. Lower left is **Gordon Court**, 2-bed, 2-bath, balconied apartments. Marian Lodge is a 1997 scheme of 31 flats with underground parking and gym. On the site of St Teresa's Hospital, **South Ridge** is an enclave of 4-bed town-houses. The Ursuline Convent School for Girls and Hazlehurst Girls' School are neighbours. On the corner of **The Downs** and **Worple Rd** is the smartly detailed Lantern Court: 23 flats (garage, video entryphone, 2-bath, open fireplaces in sitting rooms). **Lansdowne Rd**, a cul-de-sac with purpose-built and conversion flats, leads to **Cumberland Close** and **Lansdowne Close**; family town-houses, some with roof terraces with spectacular views. In the last few years a group of town-houses has been added opposite the new hospice. **Arterberry Rd** has the Norwegian school and older-type family houses with spacious gardens. Chimneys Court, on the corner of **Ridgway**, has 10 2-bed, 2-bath flats and a 3-bed penthouse, all with underground parking. These sell for £290,000 upwards. The house next to it sold for £1.6 million.

The line of **Ridgway** now continues as **Copse Hill**. The lodge to the area's 18th-century Big House (all that remains of Prospect Place) is now two houses behind remote-controlled gates. On the common side, **Ernle Rd**, **Wool Rd** and **Dunstall Rd** have 4- and 5-bed detached houses with big gardens, some backing on to the golf course or woodland. Also off **Copse Hill** to the right is **Rokeby Place**, detached 4/5-bed family houses. On the left are two recently converted Victorian mansions, Birch Lodge (10 flats) and Possil House (four maisonettes). **Cedarland Terrace** consists of five Georgian-style town-houses with wide sweeping drives. Facing the Atkinson Morley Hospital is **Thurstan Rd**, off which is **Grange Park Place**, with detached 5-bed, 5-bath houses backing on to the golf course, built on the site of the old Cottage Hospital. These sell for £1.3–1.7 million. On **Ridgway** are two newly-renovated Georgian semi-detached cottages which sold last autumn for £650,000 each. **Drax Avenue** is a leafy private road of Sussex farmhouse-style and mock-Tudor 5-bed detached houses, some with galleried reception halls and oak staircases. Leading down to **Coombe Lane**, both sides of **Copse Hill** have solid 1930s 3/4-bed semis with garages, front and rear gardens. A small scheme of 3-bed 2-bath semis with red pavers is in **Cottenham Park Rd**. From here, turn left for Raynes Park.

Raynes Park

Raynes Park lies at the bottom of the hill from Wimbledon Common; it is split in half by the railway line. Once, this was little more than an undervalued backwater of Edwardian cottages, and purpose-built flats and maisonettes in wide, well-planned tree-lined streets. Today, it still retains a small-town atmosphere and is ripe for improvement. (Note the infallible signs: estate agents now refer to the northern side of the railway as 'West Wimbledon'.)

Worple Rd, a busy main thoroughfare with blocks of new flats and small hotels, leads back to Wimbledon town centre. Agents detect signs of improvement along this convenient road: a 5-bed semi sold last winter for £525,000. Elinor Court, **Worple Rd**, has four architect-designed flats and a penthouse. Roads off to the right have good small semis with prices dictated by the closeness of the railway: in **Southdown Rd**, the side backing on to the elevated railway is considerably cheaper than the other side. On the left are very desirable family houses in roads such as **Thornton Hill**, **Denmark Avenue** and **Spencer Hill**. These climb the hill to **Ridgway** (by which time they have joined Wimbledon Village); the higher up, the better the views.

Hollymount School (primary, mixed) is in leafy **Cambridge Rd**, together with 3/4-bed family houses. **Amity Grove** has mainly 3-bed Edwardian bay-window cottages. South of the line, off **Kingston Rd**, are 'the apostles': 12 long parallel cul-de-sacs running down to **Bushey Rd**; an inexpensive mix of 2-bed Edwardian terraced and semi-detached, some 1930s; street parking, tiny front gardens – the glimpse of the open green space of Prince George's playing-fields at the end of each cul-de-sac adds appeal. They are never on estate agents' books for long. The 'apostles' begin at **Gore Rd** and end at **Bronson Rd**, Wimbledon Chase. Bisecting **Bushey Rd**, **Grand Drive** has inter-war 3/4-bed semi- and detached family houses, many with views over playing-fields. To the E of the fields is a big sports and leisure centre. **Cannon Close**, one of several cul-de-sacs off **Grand Drive**, has 3-bed '30s semis with access to the common.

Merton Park

Merton's main claim to residential fame is the Merton Park Estate, one of the first garden suburbs, developed in the last three decades of the 19th century. John Innes, a millionaire property developer and horticulturalist (you've used the compost), laid out the estate. The area's green appearance survives.

The earliest streets to be built, in the 1870s, were **Dorset Rd**, **Mostyn Rd** and **Kingswood Rd**. Later in the century, larger houses of the Arts and Crafts and other styles were added. The details are reminiscent of Bedford Park, but the styles are more mixed. So, too is the scale: Innes decreed that cottages as well as solid villas be built. Development continued into Edwardian times, as the houses in **Melrose Rd** and **Watery Rd** show. Building went on until the '30s, with the opening of the tube at Morden providing a renewed spur. A little developing has gone on since: off **Dorset/Erridge Rds**, in a quiet cul-de-sac, are the 14 3/4-bed detached houses and a bungalow of Hamilton Gate. Lynwood Place, four town-houses, c. £250,000, are off **Henfield Rd**. This year **Dorset Rd** will find itself backing not onto railway tracks but the new tram line: will this be more peaceful?

Wimbledon Park

The rolling, leafy roads of Wimbledon Park contain some extremely large, discreet and enviable houses, in a corner that centres on the eponymous park. This, however, boasts putting, cricket, bowling and large lake, with fishing and water sports – and, of course, tennis. The All England Club is here, but except for That Fortnight the splendidly hilly roads that spread out S of the park are a peaceful and select neighbourhood. On a map the street pattern betrays the spacious layout of roads like **Home Park Rd**, **Arthur Rd**, **Leopold Rd**, and the large gardens. In this corner stood Wimbledon's original manor house and its successors – hence the park, whose layout is attributed to Capability Brown. It was indeed, as the road name betrays, the home park.

To the E of the railway line, between **Durnsford Rd** and the tracks, the roads N of Wimbledon Park station (District Line) such as **Melrose Avenue**, **Braemar Avenue**, **Normanton Avenue** and **Ashen Grove** are a continuation of the Southfields 'grid' to the N (see chapter) over the borough and postcode boundaries. These are mainly long terraces of neat, solid 2/3-bed late-Victorian/Edwardian houses, with rear gardens and street parking; they are snapped up because they are relatively cheap (bordering Wandsworth), convenient (the tube) and close to the park and schools. Cheap is indeed relative here: agents in Wimbledon enthuse over the 'great value' of 5-bed houses in **Melrose Avenue** at £550–600,000. You can drop the price by £100,000 for each fewer bedroom, they say. By the tube station is a varied and useful row of shops.

Arthur Rd winds uphill all the way from **Durnsford Rd** via the station to Wimbledon Village, becoming more and more tree-lined, with large, detached houses in secluded grounds (one might have thought the town hall could have resisted the naming of **Camelot Close**, on the left; the more so since its 4/5-bed double-fronted detacheds are in Georgian style).

Curving N from **Arthur Rd**, **Home Park Rd** houses gaze out over Wimbledon Park and the Tennis Club. In the angle of **Leopold Rd/Lake Rd** is a clutch of schools: Ricards Lodge (girls' high), and two good state schools, Park House middle school

W

and Bishop Gilpin primary, which has a good record for its girls going on to the local high schools. **Vineyard Hill Rd, Dora Rd** and **Kenilworth Avenue** have terraces of 3/4-bedroomed family houses.

Transport	Tubes: Wimbledon, Wimbledon Park (zone 3, District); South Wimbledon (zone 3, Northern). Oxford Circus 35 min (1 change), City 35 min, Heathrow 1 hr (1 change). Trains: to Waterloo 12 min. Tram from Wimbledon via Merton Park to Croydon.
Convenient for	Common, Heathrow and Gatwick Airports. Miles from centre: 7.
Schools	Merton Education Authority: Wimbledon College RC (b), Ursuline Convent School (g), Rutlish School (b). Private: Norwegian School, Wimbledon High (g), Hazelhurst School (g), Ricards Lodge (g), King's College School (b).

SALES

Flats	S	1B	2B	3B	4B	5B
Average prices	70–110	120–200+	145–400+	200–500+	275–700	—
Houses	2B	3B	4B	5B	6/7B	8B
Average prices	215–350	250–600+	300–800+	400–800+	700–2.5M	→2.5M

RENTAL

Flats	S	1B	2B	3B	4B	5B
Average prices	105–170	150–230	175–450	210–550	530–700	—
Houses	2B	3B	4B	5B	6/7B	8B
Average prices	200–375	210–600	370–1000	400–1200	—	—

The properties	Homes (and prices) range from 3-bed terraces and modern flats near town centre ('down the Hill') via the cottages of the village to the swimming-pooled mansions near the common ('up the Hill'). Also flat conversions, Edwardian villas, '30s semis, new town-houses, flats and more flats. Further Victorian/Edwardian charm in Raynes and Merton Parks.
The market	Something for everyone – at a price. Fast trains for commuters, good schools for families. Locals stay loyal and move within area: competition, therefore, for big family homes. Overseas buyers favour Wimbledon – as do investors, especially in the village and West Wimbledon. Once here, you're hooked, whether heading up to a large family house or trading down to a smart flat. Local searches: 10 working days.

Among those estate agents active in this area are:

- Ellisons
- Hawes & Co
- Kinleigh Folkard & Hayward
- Lauristons
- Bairstow Eves
- Chestertons
- G A Property Services
- Hamptons
- John D Wood & Co
- Knight Frank
- Ludlow Thompson
- Robert Holmes & Co
- Haart
- Foxtons*

further details: see advertisers' index on p671

W

Index of streets and areas

Advertisers' Index